TORT LAW

Text, Cases, and Materials

Jenny Steele

Professor of Law, University of Southampton

OXFORD
UNIVERSITY PRESS

OXFORD
UNIVERSITY PRESS

Great Clarendon Street, Oxford OX2 6DP

Oxford University Press is a department of the University of Oxford.
It furthers the University's objective of excellence in research, scholarship,
and education by publishing worldwide in

Oxford New York

Auckland Cape Town Dar es Salaam Hong Kong Karachi
Kuala Lumpur Madrid Melbourne Mexico City Nairobi
New Delhi Shanghai Taipei Toronto

With offices in

Argentina Austria Brazil Chile Czech Republic France Greece
Guatemala Hungary Italy Japan Poland Portugal Singapore
South Korea Switzerland Thailand Turkey Ukraine Vietnam

Oxford is a registered trade mark of Oxford University Press
in the UK and in certain other countries

Published in the United States
by Oxford University Press Inc., New York

© Jenny Steele, 2007

British Library Cataloguing in Publication Data

Data available

Library of Congress Cataloging in Publication Data

Data available

Typeset by Newgen Imaging Systems (P) Ltd., Chennai, India
Printed in Great Britain
on acid-free paper by
CPI Bath

ISBN 978–0–19–924885–8

1 3 5 7 9 10 8 6 4 2

This book is dedicated to the memory of Thomas Steele

PREFACE

Law is by no means a merely dry and technical subject, but students often find their early experiences of the subject frustrating. In particular, the really interesting issues are often glimpsed dimly through a fog of detail. With this in mind, the first concern of this book is to guide students through the subject. The second concern is to explore the interesting uncertainties and disagreements that remain. The book uses its combination of text and materials to provide a comprehensible account of the law, starting with basic propositions but not avoiding the most challenging and interesting issues. The aim is to combine some of the best features of a textbook and a Cases and Materials book in one volume, with a greater emphasis on explanation than is usually found in either, and its combination of text and extracts is designed to be read as a whole.

In selecting the materials, the key focus is on English case law, although there are very important areas where statutory materials are of equal importance. Academic work is most often extracted where it helps to explain the legal materials, and (as is sometimes the case) where it is so influential that it is virtually a part of the primary materials. Cases from other jurisdictions have generally been included where they have influenced English law, but not on the whole (and with one or two exceptions) simply for the purposes of comparison. This is partly for reasons of space, but also signifies respect for the discipline of comparative law, which is not to be dabbled in lightly. Where there has not been space to extract academic material showing the full diversity of points of view about issues raised, then footnotes and the listed 'Further Reading' will guide interested students to other valuable sources. Lecturers will no doubt disagree with some of the arguments pressed in the text and this too may provoke students to develop their own view. Though no two courses in Tort Law are alike, every effort has been made to produce a clearly structured text so that students and lecturers can easily identify the most relevant chapters and sections for their own present purposes.

I am extremely grateful to Rachael Willis and Sarah Hyland at Oxford University Press, and to the whole team who have worked on this book, for their support and encouragement in bringing it to completion. I have benefited enormously not only from their expertise, but also from the comments of a number of anonymous readers whose responses to draft chapters have been extremely generous, honest and constructive. I would like to take the opportunity of thanking those reviewers. I hope to have used their comments to produce a book that supports the way the subject is currently taught in a wide range of law schools, while still remaining provocative in some respects.

I am also grateful to a large number of colleagues and former colleagues for their comments on various parts of the text. Particular thanks are due to Kit Barker with whom I shared the teaching of tort law for some years at Southampton. I am bound to have used a few of his ideas without noticing and apart from reading some of the chapters, he was the originator of the chart of torts which has been extended and adapted for use in Chapter 1. Thanks also to Nick Hopkins, Rob Merkin, Nick Wikeley, Andrew Halpin, Ed Bates, Sarah Nield, Caroline Jones, Mike Newark, Natalie Lee, Jon Montgomery, Emma Laurie, and Mark Telford for help and comments on various chapters. Finally many thanks (and apologies) to Adrian and to our two children, Joseph and Theo, who have had to do without me on quite a few occasions in the last year. Hopefully the book will earn some nicer epithets now that it can be used, than have attached to it at home during its gestation.

I have done my best to set out the law as it stood at the start of November 2006, although one or two additions have been possible.

Jenny Steele
Southampton
December 2006

ACKNOWLEDGEMENTS

Grateful acknowledgement is made to all the authors and publishers of copyright material which appears in this book, and particularly to the following for permission to reprint material from the sources indicated.

AMERICAN LAW INSTITUTE: extracts from Restatement (2nd) Torts sections 8A (including comments and illustrations), 519 and 522; Restatement (3rd) Torts: Liability for Physical Harm (Proposed Final Draft No 1) section 1 (including comment). Copyright by the American Law Institute, reprinted with permission. All rights reserved.

BLACKWELL PUBLISHING: extracts from *Modern Law Review*: David Howarth, 'Against *Lumley v Gye*' (2005) 68 *MLR* 195–232; K. W. Wedderburn, 'Intimidation and the Right to Strike' (1964) *MLR* 257–281.

CAMBRIDGE UNIVERSITY PRESS: extracts from C. Hodges, 'Approaches to Product Liability in the Member States' in D. Fairgrieve (ed.), *Product Liability in Comparative Perspective* (Cambridge University Press, 2005); S. Waddams, *Dimensions of Private Law: Categories and Concepts in Anglo-American Legal Reasoning* (Cambridge University Press, 2003).

EDINBURGH UNIVERSITY PRESS: extract from Stephen Guest, *Ronald Dworkin* (Edinburgh University Press, 1997).

HART PUBLISHING: extract from P. Cane, *The Anatomy of Tort Law* (Hart, 1997).

HARVARD LAW REVIEW ASSOCIATION: extracts from Dean Thayer, 'Liability Without Fault' (1916) 29 *Harvard Law Review* 801–815; Warren and Brandeis, 'The Right to Privacy' (1890) 4 Harvard Law Review 193.

A. J. E. JAFFEY: extract from A. J. E. Jaffey, 'Volenti non fit injuria' (1985) 44 *Cambridge Law Journal* 87.

OXFORD UNIVERSITY PRESS: extracts from E. Barendt, L. Lustgarten, K. Norrie, and H. Stephenson, *Libel and the Media: the Chilling Effect* (Oxford University Press, 1997); D. Feldman, *Civil Liberties in England and Wales* (Oxford University Press, 2nd edn, 2002); D. Ibbetson, *A Historical Introduction to the Law of Obligations* (Oxford University Press, 1999); A.W.B. Simpson, *Leading Cases in the Common Law* (Oxford University Press, 1995).

REED ELSEVIER (UK) LTD, trading as LEXISNEXIS BUTTERWORTHS: extracts from M. Millner, *Negligence in Modern Law* (Butterworths, 1967).

A. W. B. SIMPSON: extract from *Leading Cases in the Common Law* (Oxford University Press, 1995).

SWEET & MAXWELL LTD: extracts from P. Kennedy, 'Is this the way we want to go?' (2005) *Journal of Personal Injury Law* 117–128; C. Witting, 'The Three Stage Test Abandoned in Australia—Or Not?' (2002) 118 *Law Quarterly Review* 214.

Every effort has been made to trace and contact copyright holders but this has not been possible in every case. If notified, the publisher will undertake to rectify any errors or omissions at the earliest opportunity.

OUTLINE TABLE OF CONTENTS

DETAILED CONTENTS

PART III THE TORT OF NEGLIGENCE

TABLE OF CASES

TABLE OF STATUTES

TABLE OF EUROPEAN MATERIALS

PART I

INTRODUCTORY

1

INTRODUCTION: THE SHAPE OF TORT LAW TODAY

CENTRAL ISSUES

i) Tort law consists of a wide array of civil wrongs for which law provides a remedy. In this introduction, we map out the diverse torts which will be considered in this text, and identify in broad terms the nature of the 'wrongs' with which they are concerned.

ii) Although this mapping exercise sets out the building blocks of various torts, it should not be thought that tort law is *uniquely* concerned with the relative positions of two parties. Tort law has significant social and economic impact. Over many years, legislation

has improved the ability of tort law to compensate for accidental harm and to spread the risks of such harm. Currently, there is a new political concern with over-extensive liability, particularly where such liability may affect the provision of public amenities.

iii) At the same time, some expansion of liability in tort is a real possibility given the important influence of the Human Rights Act 1998. At the end of this chapter, we introduce the ways in which this statute may affect, and has affected, the law of tort.

1. TORTS AS WRONGS, AND THE MAP OF TORT LAW

Torts are 'wrongs'. To be slightly more precise, torts are civil wrongs for which law will provide a remedy. This remedy will be enforceable against one party, to the benefit of the other, and it will reflect (and perhaps correct) the wrong committed. There are other civil wrongs which are not torts, notably breaches of contract and of equitable obligation. Torts make up the most diverse bunch of civil wrongs in English law, protecting a wide range of interests against different types of invasion.

Unfortunately, we cannot go much further than this in defining the law of tort. There is no widely accepted definition of a 'tort' which would distinguish clearly between torts, and all other civil wrongs (although the word 'tort' is considered clear enough in its meaning to be used in a statute).[1] Equally, there are a number of liabilities introduced by statute which resemble tort very closely. The key focus of this book is the common law of tort. We introduce a few instances of statutory liability where the statute significantly amends existing common law duties, or (in the case of the Protection from Harassment Act 1997) partially fills a gap long argued to exist in common law (although this statute does a lot else besides). But we do not attempt to set out the range of 'tort-like' liabilities that exist in statutory form.[2]

Peter Cane, *The Anatomy of Tort Law* (Oxford: Hart Publishing, 1997), 11–13

The law of tort is part of a larger body of civil (as opposed to criminal) law sometimes called 'the law of obligations'. Other parts of the law of obligations are the law of contract, the law of restitution and the law of trusts. The law of obligations may be contrasted with the law of property. The law of property consists of rules (which we might call 'constitutive rules') which establish (proprietary) rights and interests which the law of obligations protects by what might be called 'protective rules'. For example, tort law protects real property through the tort of trespass: to enter someone's land without their permission and without legal justification is to commit the tort of trespass to land. Property law defines who owns what land, and tort law protects the rights of the owner against unwanted intruders.

Although contract law and the law of trusts may be treated as part of the law of obligations, in fact these bodies of law contain both constitutive and protective rules. The law of contract not only establishes an obligation to keep contracts, but also lays down rules about how contracts are formed or, in other words, about what constitutes a binding contractual undertaking which there is a legal obligation to fulfil. . . . By contrast, tort law and the law of restitution are purely protective—they establish obligations designed to protect interests created by constitutive rules of the law of property, trusts or contracts or which arise in some other way.

Both the law of obligations and the law of property are part of what we call 'civil law' as opposed to criminal law. Civil law is a social institution by which we organize and interpret human conduct in a particular way. A central feature of civil (or, as it is sometimes called, 'private') law is 'bilateralness' or (more euphoniously) 'correlativity'.[3] What this means in simple terms is that civil law organizes relationships between individuals on a one to one basis. In the law of obligations, for instance, one person's obligation corresponds ('is correlative') to another person's right. . . .

The idea of correlativity provides the framework within which I will analyze the law of tort. Every cause of action in tort and, therefore, every principle of tort liability, has two basic (sets of) elements, one concerned with the position of one party to a bilateral human interaction (the 'victim' of the tortious conduct) and the other concerned with the position of the other party to that interaction (the perpetrator of the tortious conduct, or the 'injurer'). . . .

The aim of this 'correlative analysis' is to understand and explain the law of tort as a system of ethical principles of personal responsibility or, in other words, a system of precepts about how people may, ought and ought not to behave in their dealings with others.

---

[1] Private International Law (Miscellaneous Provisions) Act 1995: see *Douglas v Hello! (No 3)* [2006] QB 125, Chapter 14.

[2] For a full discussion see K. Stanton, P. Skidmore, M. Harris, and J. Wright, *Statutory Torts* (Sweet & Maxwell, 2003). We will of course consider a range of statutory interventions into the operation of the common law of torts (see for example Chapter 7 below).

[3] We have omitted a lengthy footnote here which contrasts Cane's analysis of correlativity *between the parties* with a different and more challenging idea—expounded by Ernest Weinrib in *The Idea of Private Law*

The view of tort law above makes a valuable starting point for our present project. Torts are wrongs, and the wrongs in question are defined by reference to the relationship between the parties. But caution is needed in interpreting the very last point made in the extract above: that tort expresses precepts about 'how people may, ought or ought not to behave in their dealings with others'.

There are two reasons for caution here. One is that the *absence* of a liability in tort does not imply that people 'may' behave in the way the defendant has behaved. It just means that there is no available cause of action in tort in respect of the behaviour, for one (or more) of many potential reasons. For example, there may be applicable sanctions or remedies independent of tort law.[4] Although torts are 'wrongs', not all actions to which tort liabilities fail to attach are acceptable or 'right'.

Secondly, the existence of a liability in tort does not always mean that the defendant ought *not* to have behaved as he or she did. Admittedly it *will* mean this on many occasions. For example, one should not be negligent if one can help it, and one certainly should not engage in deliberate acts of deceit. But sometimes, there is liability even though it cannot be said that the defendant should have behaved differently. For example, the negligent party may be a learner driver who could not be expected to drive better; or the defendant may have carefully accumulated a dangerous thing, which has escaped, and it is thought the risk of escape should not fall on the claimant; or the defendant may have honestly believed that the umbrella they took home was their own, and not the claimant's. In all of these examples, there may be liability in tort, despite the perfectly proper behaviour of the defendant.[5] Wrongs may be states of affairs that need a remedy, irrespective of whether anyone was at fault.

Parties

Since we have said that the relationship between the parties is essential to understanding the defining features of any tort, we should at this point introduce the parties and explain the applicable terminology.

Since 1999, the wronged party or 'victim' of the tort who brings an action has been referred to in England and Wales as the **claimant**. Previously, this party would have been referred to as the **plaintiff**, and that is the term still used in other common law jurisdictions. Since this book reproduces extracts from cases, statutes, and academic commentary many of which predate this change, the reader will (unfortunately) need to get used to both sets of terminology. We will keep the historically appropriate language of 'plaintiff' and defendant when discussing older material, in order to avoid inconsistency between the extracts and the text.

Fortunately, there has been no change in terminology affecting the other parties involved. The alleged wrongdoer (the party who is said to have committed a tort) is referred to as the **tortfeasor**. The tortfeasor is not necessarily a party to the action, and the word 'tortfeasor' is not a litigation term. The appropriate term for the person who is on the receiving end of the claim in tort (who is generally *but not always* the tortfeasor) is **defendant**.

We have just mentioned that the defendant will not always be the tortfeasor (the person who actually committed the tort). This is an important feature of the law of tort. The defendant will not be the tortfeasor where the action is brought on the basis of **vicarious liability** for

(Harvard University Press, 1995)—to the effect that rights and obligations are *themselves* 'correlative' (an obligation is inherent in the existence of the right).

[4] There may be a criminal sanction which suffices; there may be no precedent on which liability may be based; or it may be thought undesirable as a matter of policy to impose liability.

[5] The torts in question are negligence, the action in *Rylands v Fletcher*, and conversion (respectively).

the torts of employees and agents (Chapter 9), or against an insurer pursuant to the Third Parties (Rights Against Insurers) Act 1930 (below). In each case, it must be established that the *tortfeasor* (and not the defendant) has committed a tort. In a much larger group of claims, the named defendant *is* the tortfeasor, but the defence is paid for, conducted, and where appropriate settled by the defendant's **liability insurer**,[6] who will also be paying for any damages that may be awarded.

Torts

Nobody is quite sure how many torts there are. Some years ago, Bernard Rudden argued that (at the time of counting) there were 70 identifiable torts.[7] In fact, the boundaries are fluid and it is not impossible for new torts to be recognised, or old ones to be revived. For example, the action for misfeasance in a public office (Chapter 2, Section 8.2) has undergone a significant revival in recent years. From time to time, wholly new torts have been urged. Recent (unsuccessful) examples include a proposed tort of 'unlawful exile' (*Chagos Islanders v Attorney General* [2003] EWHC 2222), and of unlawful interference with body parts (*In re Organ Retention Litigation* [2005] QB 506). Recently, a new tort of publishing private information or images seems to have emerged, influenced by close analysis of the Human Rights Act 1998 (explained below). (The Court of Appeal has said that the action is *not* a tort; while some members of the House of Lords have clearly referred to it as a tort. So the position is not quite clear.) The terrain of tort law is apt to change.

The Nature of Torts: Defining the 'Wrongs'

In *The Anatomy of Tort Law* (extracted above), Peter Cane argues that the ethical nature of the law of tort, which he considers to be based upon responsibility, will be best understood by breaking down the various torts into certain components. These components are **protected interests** on the part of the claimant; **sanctioned conduct** on the part of the tortfeasor; and **remedies** for the wrong. Between them, these three components strike a balance, in each case, between the claimant and the tortfeasor. They express the nature of tort law as concerned with what Cane calls 'correlativity' (the relationship between the parties). Cane argues that this approach is better than a more traditional exposition, which simply adopts and applies the existing requirements of recognized torts as 'legal formulae', without reflection on the ethical underpinnings of the wrongs concerned. On that approach, the structure of the law of tort is presented, uncritically, as though it was largely the product of historical accident.

Cane's exercise in unpacking or 'dismantling' the law of tort into the three components mentioned above is very useful. Spelling out the various elements of different torts in this way can help us to map the diverse ways in which conduct of one party may interfere with interests of another party, so as to amount to an actionable wrong. In other words, this is a way of expressing the diversity of the terrain that is covered by tort law.

Cane goes on to argue against too much adherence to legal categories such as distinct causes of action in the form of different torts, or even 'tort' and 'contract'. He suggests that different causes of action with different criteria should not be available on the same facts, and that the

---

[6] A *liability insurer* is simply someone who agrees to indemnify the insured party for civil liability that they may incur to others. A *first party insurer* agrees to indemnify the insured party for losses they suffer directly, not through liability to others.

[7] B. Rudden, 'Torticles' (1991–2) 6/7 *Tulane Civil Law Forum* 105.

ethical principles of personal responsibility discovered by unpacking the various torts in this way will be better applied without excessive reference to these categories.[8] Again, there are reasons to hesitate about this prescription. For one thing, if the various torts describe different ways in which an interaction may be 'wrong', why and indeed how should we decide that a single way of approaching the facts is valid? *Which* way should those facts be approached? This sort of thinking has contributed to the near demise of strict liability under the rule in *Rylands v Fletcher*, for example (Chapter 11). It has also led to the baffling classification of trespass to the person as an 'intentional' tort (explained further in Chapter 2: see especially the comment of J.A. Jolowicz extracted there, in respect of *Letang v Cooper*).

For another thing, it is fine to point out that the various torts are 'wrongs' that can be understood in terms of the relationship between two parties. But it is dangerous to assume from this that questions about the two parties are the *only* questions that are needed in order to resolve a question of tort. There are many reasons why courts may be cautious in defining the boundaries of a given cause of action. Not all of these are 'formulaic' reasons, or derived from history. It may be very difficult to decide, when concluding that a given defendant is liable to a specific claimant, in what other future circumstances such liability will appear equally appropriate. It may also be difficult to determine what the wider policy considerations affecting future cases are likely to be. For both of these reasons, there may be sound reasons to confine the identified 'wrong' to cases closely analogous to the facts in hand. This is not an argument against moral notions in law, or against the recognition of general principles. But general principles will not always suffice, and one moral blueprint will not fit all facts. The different definitions of 'wrongs' in the law of tort and the persistence of untidy distinctions between them reflects the diversity of relevant *reasons* in law.

In the following extract, Stephen Waddams warns against striving for total and single-minded consistency in legal principle. His argument also cautions against 'mapping' legal concepts in too restrictive a way.

Stephen Waddams, *Dimensions of Private Law: Categories and Concepts in Anglo-American Legal Reasoning* (Cambridge: CUP, 2003), 231–2

A single-minded search for precision in private law tends to be self-defeating as new terminology is devised, and concepts and sub-concepts are multiplied and then further refined, in an attempt to accommodate awkward cases. It has . . . encountered judicial resistance, and has led to warnings that 'a preoccupation with conceptualistic reasoning' may lead to 'absurd' conclusions.[9] Such warnings do not indicate a rejection of concepts, or of reason, or of classification; they signal a recognition that in law, as elsewhere, strict adherence to principle (admirable in itself) may, 'if relentlessly pursued' in a single dimension of a complex question, ultimately impede, rather than assist, sound judgment.

. . .

The failure of any scheme to explain the actual decisions of the courts led, in the twentieth century, to scepticism of formal explanations and to the emergence of alternative accounts

---

[8] It is sometimes said that the argument on the basis of different torts should no longer happen since we have done away with the 'forms of action'. But rather the reverse is true: since claimants no longer have to choose the right procedure ('form'), they are free to argue the substantive merits in alternative ways ('cause').

[9] *Lister v Hesley Hall* [2002] 1 AC 215, at 224 (Lord Steyn). (This case is extracted in Chapter 9.)

which, in their extreme forms, tended to reduce law to considerations of policy or utility. These views led in turn to counter-reaction and to a reassertion of formal principle. These approaches have sometimes seemed so radically opposed to each other as to open unbridgeable chasms. . . . From the present perspective it can be seen that though consideration of principle, utility, and policy have each played an important part, none, considered alone, supplies a full explanation of the past. It is not so much that various *alternative* approaches are *permissible* (as though in some spirit of agnostic toleration) as that various *complementary* approaches are *necessary* (to the understanding of a complex phenomenon).

The examination of the issues considered in this study has shown that several concepts, including property, contract, wrongdoing, and unjust enrichment, though distinct, and each of fundamental importance, have, in relation to many legal issues, interacted with each other and with public policy. It may justly be said that the law has accommodated a considerable degree of complexity and imprecision, but the use of such stronger and pejorative words as 'incoherent', 'chaotic', 'dysfunctional', or a 'mess' might be taken to imply that greater order and precision were attainable without sacrifice of other values, a proposition by no means self-evident. The lack of a single or simple explanation of private law has not excluded reasoned argument or, in practice, a considerable measure of coherence, predictability, and stability. The result has not been perfect order. But it does not follow that it has been chaos.

Waddams' eclectic view of private law has been criticized in terms which illustrate the depth of feelings involved in questions of classification in private law (though this depth of feeling may be baffling to beginners).[10] But it is suggested that Waddams is quite right to point out that there is a tension between many different factors in legal decision-making. The sort of principled approach that would look only at one dimension of a series of complex problems should not be allowed to dominate. What is not likely to emerge, if this is correct, is a tidy picture. But equally, we should not be too hasty in criticizing the law purely on the basis of untidiness.

The Structure of Our Map of Tort

The following table sets out key components of a number of torts. The dimensions of our map are similar to the first two of Cane's categories, namely protected interests, and relevant conduct. We also include a column specifying whether the tort requires 'actual damage', since this criterion provides a very important division between different torts. In torts which do not require damage, the invasion of the claimant's interest is 'actionable *per se*' (without more). There is no column relating to Cane's third element, remedies. This is not to downgrade the importance of remedies. The reason is simply that it would be hard to 'map' remedies in an interesting and informative way in this kind of tabular form. There is even an argument that broadly the same remedies are available for all torts, in appropriate circumstances, so that we would simply end up with a dull and repetitive list.[11] These are not the sorts of issues that can be captured in this general table. Interesting issues about remedies are therefore left for later chapters.

---

[10] A. Beever and C. Rickett, 'Interpretive Legal Theory and the Academic Lawyer' (2005) 68 MLR 320–37.

[11] For example it is not clear whether there may be an injunction in a negligence case where there is a continuing failure to take care, but this is quite possible. See N. McBride, 'Duties of Care—Do They Really Exist?' (2004) 24 OJLS 417–41.

Table 1.1 An introductory map

Tort(s)[12]	Protected Interests	Need to show 'damage'? ('DAMAGE-BASED'?)	Relevant 'wrongdoing': what must the tortfeasor do? (STANDARD OF LIABILITY)[13]
1. Trespass to the person: a. Battery b. Assault c. False imprisonment	Bodily integrity/ right of self-determination	No	Battery: unlawful interference with bodily integrity Assault: immediate threat which deliberately puts C in fear of a battery False imprisonment: total unlawful restraint of claimant's liberty *Contact, threat* or *restraint* must be intended. Unlawfulness or harm need *not* be either intended, or careless. INTENTIONAL AND STRICT ELEMENTS
2. 'The action in *Wilkinson v Downton*'	Freedom from mental harm	Yes	Intention to inflict mental harm; intention may be imputed where likelihood of such harm is obvious. INTENTION TO HARM; BUT INTENT MAY BE IMPUTED; NEED NOT BE ACTUAL
3. Action for harassment under Protection from Harassment Act 1997	Freedom from harassment	No	Course of conduct amounting to harassment; constructive knowledge that this conduct would amount to harassment. CONSTRUCTIVE KNOWLEDGE OF HARASSMENT

---

[12] This table does not chart the full range of torts, because there are too many: see the text above.

[13] This table does not specify available defences. In practice, defences may have a large impact on the strictness, or otherwise, of the relevant action. This is exemplified by our discussion of the action in *Rylands v Fletcher* in Chapter 11, and of liability under the Consumer Protection Act 1987 in Chapter 15.

Table 1.1 (*cont.*)

Tort(s)	Protected Interests	Need to show 'damage'? ('DAMAGE-BASED'?)	Relevant 'wrongdoing': what must the tortfeasor do? (STANDARD OF LIABILITY)
4. 'Unlawful means' economic torts and simple conspiracy	Economic interests	Yes	Intention to harm the claimant's interests; generally (and apart from simple conspiracy), **unlawful means** INTENTION TO HARM IN STRONG SENSE
5. Inducing breach of contract	Contractual interests	Yes	Intention to procure the breach of contract INTENTION IN A STRONG SENSE
6. Deceit	Economic interests (and perhaps others)	Yes	Giving a false statement with: Intention that C should rely; and Knowledge of (or recklessness as to) the falsity of the statement INTENTION IN TWO SENSES
7. Malicious falsehood	Reputation and economic interests	Yes, except where defined by statute as actionable *per se*[14]	Malicious publication of *falsehoods*: 'malice' comprises *either* Intent to harm; *or* Lack of belief in truth of statement INTENT TO HARM *OR* LACK OF BELIEF (BAD FAITH)
8. Malicious prosecution and analogous torts[15]	Freedom from prosecution/intrusion through criminal process; imprisonment?	Yes	Initiating prosecution/obtaining search warrant (etc) with: subjective malice, criminal process and lack of reasonable cause BAD FAITH AND UNREASONABLENESS

---

[14] Defamation Act 1952, s 3.
[15] An example of an analogous tort is 'malicious procurement of a search warrant'.

Table 1.1 (*cont.*)

Tort(s)	Protected Interests	Need to show 'damage'? ('DAMAGE-BASED'?)	Relevant 'wrongdoing': what must the tortfeasor do? (STANDARD OF LIABILITY)
9. Misfeasance in a public office	Economic/personal?	Yes	Exercise of power by a public official with targeted malice (intent to harm the claimant); *or* Intentional or reckless *abuse* of power INTENT TO HARM, *OR* RECKLESSNESS
10. Negligence	Personal, property, or economic interests (from damage)	Yes	Careless conduct, but only if this amounts to breach of a duty to take care, owed to the claimant NEGLIGENCE
11. Private nuisance	Relevant interests in land (Use and enjoyment; easements)	No	Unreasonable interference with relevant interests. Careless conduct not required in most cases UNREASONABLE INTERFERENCE; MAY BE STRICT IN TERMS OF CONDUCT
12. Public nuisance	Personal and property interests	Yes	Interference with comfort or convenience of a class of Her Majesty's subjects UNREASONABLENESS; STRICT AS TO CONDUCT
13. The action in *Rylands v Fletcher*	Interests in land	Yes	Accumulation of a dangerous thing; non-natural user of land STRICT; SUBJECT TO NON-NATURAL USER
14. Occupiers' liability	Personal and (for visitors) property	Yes	Breach of occupancy duty: failing to ensure that premises are 'reasonably safe' REASONABLENESS—NEGLIGENCE?

Table 1.1 (*cont.*)

Tort(s)	Protected Interests	Need to show 'damage'? ('DAMAGE-BASED'?)	Relevant 'wrongdoing': what must the tortfeasor do? (STANDARD OF LIABILITY)

15. Defamation:
  a. Libel
  b. Slander
	Reputation	No (libel); Yes (most forms of slander)	Publication of a defamatory statement referring to the claimant. (No need for intention or carelessness)
			STRICT

16. Publication of private information and images	Privacy in respect of information and images	No	Publication of information or images where there is a reasonable expectation of privacy STRICT
17. Product liability under the Consumer Protection Act 1987	Personal and property interests (against damage)	Yes	Manufacture or first supply of a product containing a defect STRICT
18. Breach of statutory duty	Various: as the statute prescribes	Yes/no depending on what is protected by the statute	Breach of the statutory duty: may be strict or fault-based VARIABLE: MAY BE STRICT
19. Trespass to land	Possession of land	No	Interference with right to possession. Entering land must not be 'involuntary', but trespass may be entirely inadvertent STRICT
20. Conversion	Possession of goods	No	Action inconsistent with the rights of the claimant. Intent to assert dominion over the goods. Bona fide acts (without knowledge of C's rights) may amount to conversion STRICT

Conduct and the Special Case of Negligence

It will be noticed that there are many torts of strict liability and several torts requiring intention, but only one general tort which truly depends on 'negligence'.[16] This invites a number of comments.

First, most undergraduate courses in the law of tort are substantially concerned with the tort of *negligence*. This is understandable given the practical importance of negligence and the sheer volume of case law in that tort,[17] but it means that courses in tort law are not generally particularly representative of the whole subject. Second, 'negligence'—in the sense of the careless infliction of harm—has been broadened into a very general principle, while other 'wrongs' have remained relatively confined in their scope. Indeed, we will see that 'fault-based' thinking has tended to affect the interpretation of other torts also. This feature of the law of tort—the generalization of a negligence principle—may reflect the fact that liability on the basis of fault is considered to express a suitable approach to the relationship between the parties; alternatively, it may reflect the fact that such liability is thought to pursue a relevant and appropriate objective.

On the other hand, the progress of the tort of negligence can also be used to illustrate the *dangers* of a general approach (as well as its attractions). A great deal of difficult case law is generated by the need to set limits to the tort of negligence. One of the most abstract ideas in the law of tort is the 'duty of care in negligence'. The ambit of negligence is confined by considering whether it is appropriate for such a duty to be imposed.[18]

Protected Interests

Protected interests could be defined in very broad terms (dignitary interests, interests in the person, economic interests, property interests). But this would give us little detailed information concerning the precise ambit of some of the torts above, and may actually be misleading.

'Property interests' provide a good illustration of the detailed differences between protected interests. Property interests *of different sorts* are protected *against invasion of different types* by various torts. So **negligence** protects against **damage** to property; **private nuisance** overlaps with negligence but more broadly protects against **interference with use and enjoyment** of land; **trespass to land** protects against **interference with possession** of land, and need not involve any diminution in value at all; and **conversion** protects interests in possession of chattels against actions which are actually *inconsistent with* those interests (most particularly, where the defendant *treats the chattel as their own*). When comparing these four actions, one must bear in mind the different property interests protected *and* the difference this variation may make to the remedies awarded.

The Structure of this Book

There are different ways of structuring the law of tort. This text follows a broad and general progression from the torts which require a degree of intention; through those which require carelessness or other unreasonableness; to those which are broadly strict (requiring no fault at all). There is also some essential material common to all torts.[19] It is not claimed that this

---

[16] Occupiers' liability may be described as a special case of negligence where the duty relates specifically to *keeping premises reasonably safe*, rather than (more generally) acting in a reasonable way.

[17] The part of this book dealing with negligence is also the longest.

[18] See Chapter 6, which is entirely concerned with application of the 'duty of care' idea.

[19] This material is included in Chapters 7, 8, and 9.

direction is entirely without anomalies or controversies.[20] But it offers the best chance of understanding the broad spectrum of the wrongs involved.

An obvious alternative is to group torts according to protected interests (though if done consistently, this would require certain torts to be broken down into different pieces). A 'protected interests' approach is particularly valuable if the goal is to set out the remedies available through tort law alongside other potential sources of remedies, protection, or compensation (industrial injuries schemes, social security benefits, insurance schemes, and so on). For some years, that functional approach was in the ascendancy. There now appears to be a new interest in the contours of private law as a whole. Although this text does not adopt a 'protected interests' approach, it is still important that some of the insights of such an approach should be retained. In particular, it should not be assumed that the *only* goal of tort law is to remedy wrongs perceived in terms of the relationship between two parties.

2. THE FORWARD-THINKING ELEMENT IN TORT LAW

There is one particular misconception which may be created by explaining torts in terms of 'wrongs'. That is, it may appear from this that tort law should be understood entirely or almost entirely by thinking about situations in which a tort has already happened (or started happening, in the case of a continuing nuisance for example). That is not the case. Through the actions of the legislature and to some extent the courts, damage-based torts including negligence in particular (and, where appropriate, the action for breach of statutory duty) have been developed as a response not only to harm, but also to the *risk* of harm.[21]

Ideally, remedies for negligently inflicted harm would have the effect of eradicating negligence without eradicating the beneficial activities which give rise to a risk of negligence. But this is not altogether possible. Therefore, there is a tension within the tort of negligence between correcting a 'wrong' (such as culpably caused harm), and distributing a risk that wrongs will occur.[22] Since negligently inflicted harm cannot be eradicated or totally avoided, and since all of us are open to behaving carelessly from time to time, the question becomes, *what should be done about the risk?*

The idea that tort law might have a 'function' outside remedying of wrongs is perhaps less fashionable at present than it once was. But the evidence is overwhelming that in some instances the law of tort is used in order to distribute losses and compensate injuries. It does this primarily in combination with liability insurance.

Peter Cane, *Atiyah's Accidents, Compensation and the Law*
(6th edn, Cambridge: CUP, 2004), 27–8.

> . . . there have been many legal developments in the last 75 years or so which have been designed to facilitate the operation of the fault-based tort system of accident compensation. These include the system of compulsory third party insurance for road traffic victims and of

---

[20] Trespass to the person is particularly awkward to classify. These torts are generally described as 'intentional' but they have much in common with strict liability. This is explained in Chapter 2.

[21] Discussion of distribution of risks of harm is explicit in the discussion of product liability in Chapter 15, and of the action under *Rylands v Fletcher* in Chapter 11. It is particularly important to the discussion of vicarious liability, which is common to all torts, in Chapter 9.

[22] See in particular the case of the negligent learner driver, *Nettleship v Weston* [1971] 2 QB 691 (Chapter 3).

compulsory insurance by employers for liability to their employees. There is also a body called the Motor Insurers' Bureau which is designed to fill the gap in the compulsory motor insurance system caused by those who fail to insure in accordance with the legal requirements; in addition, the MIB accepts liability in some hit-and-run cases and in cases where the party at fault was insured but the insurer has become insolvent.

Much other legislation has been passed which has improved the operation of the law of torts as a compensation mechanism: the Law Reform (Miscellaneous Provisions) Act 1934 allows actions to be brought against the estate of a negligent person; the Law Reform (Contributory Negligence) Act 1945 changed the law to allow plaintiffs to recover some damages despite having contributed by their own negligence to the injuries suffered; the Law Reform (Personal Injuries) Act 1948 abolished the doctrine of common employment and enabled employees to sue their employers where they suffered injury as result of the negligence of a fellow-employee; and the Occupiers' Liability Acts of 1957 and 1984, among other things, simplified the law by making the occupier of premises liable for negligence.

Legislation has often aimed to provide a route to compensation through liability insurance.[23] In the case of road traffic accidents and work injuries (which make up the largest categories of personal injury), liability insurance is compulsory. And by the Third Parties (Rights Against Insurers) Act 1930, the victim of a tort may sue a liability insurer directly, if the insured tortfeasor is insolvent. Even so, accident compensation through tort law remains largely dependent on the 'fault' principle.[24] Seen from the point of view of insurance against mishaps, the fault principle is a cause of under-compensation. But this is not the point of view that has most political currency today, as we will explain.

3. TWO CURRENT CHALLENGES

Here we consider two current challenges to the law of tort. The impact of these will be developed further in later chapters of this book.

3.1 'COMPENSATION CULTURE'

Tort law has recently been the subject of renewed political debate. Part of this debate surrounds the supposed creation of a 'compensation culture'. We explore this alleged phenomenon[25] in Chapter 8, and to some extent in Chapter 12. Critics of the (supposed) 'compensation culture' suggest that there is an unhealthy preoccupation with seeking compensation for any loss, insult or disappointment that is suffered; and that this is tending to sap the moral fibre of the nation, to disrupt the provision of public services, and to deny individuals and the economy the benefit of healthy risk-taking. Some of these factors have in the past been summed up in the idea of a 'blame culture'.

Some have argued that the antidote to the 'compensation culture' is enhanced 'personal responsibility'.[26] It is emphasized that victims of accidents have responsibility for their own

---

[23] The common law doctrine of vicarious liability may also has this effect, which is probably one among many reasons for the doctrine: see Chapter 9.

[24] Apart from the statutory form of liability under the Consumer Protection Act 1987 and the action in *Rylands v Fletcher*, the majority of damage-based torts are dependent on fault or intention: see the table above.

[25] Most studies suggest that the real phenomenon is actually the emergence of *debate about* compensation culture. See Chapter 8.

[26] See for example Jonathan Morgan, 'Tort, Insurance and Incoherence' (2004) 67 MLR 384.

safety. In the UK, this generally means that individual victims of accidents should take responsibility for accidents which were their own fault.[27] Taking responsibility is an alternative to the 'nanny state' (represented, in this instance, by tort law). In Australia, responsibility is broadened to take into account the possibilities for self-insurance.[28] 'Protecting oneself' includes both *avoiding* risks, and *insuring* risks. This is connected to the particular Australian experience of a liability insurance 'crisis' in recent years. We will suggest that the political preoccupations involved in this debate are too complex to be summarized solely in terms of personal responsibility, and that it is unrealistic to think that this idea can provide the solutions. Personal responsibility is after all what underlies the perception that liability for wrongs is justified at all, and is often the reason why *more* liability is urged.[29]

Emerging doubts about the law of tort (expressed through the medium of 'compensation culture') offer some support to the point made by Patrick Atiyah, that in a political system in which welfare provision is increasingly supplied through insurance and personal planning, it will eventually come to be accepted that the law of tort is not the solution to the problem of accidental harm.[30] Not many commentators have been willing to accept Atiyah's solution, and it does indeed have troubling distributive implications; but to the extent that he suggested such a change would be an inevitable consequence of contemporary politics, the current direction of debate suggests that he may have been right.

The change in political attitudes is nicely summarized in the following extract.

The Hon JJ Spigelman AC (Chief Justice of New South Wales), 'Tort Law Reform: An Overview' (2006) 14 Tort L Rev 5–15

Until about the middle of the 20th century judges were regarded, so far as I am aware universally in all common law jurisdictions, as mean, conservative and too defendant oriented. This led parliaments to extend liability: Lord Campbell's Act; the abolition of the doctrine of common employment; the abolition of the immunity of the Crown; the creation of worker's compensation and compulsory third party motor vehicle schemes; and provision for apportionment in the case of contributory negligence.

In Australia, about 20 to 25 years ago, the process of legislative intervention changed its character. It proceeded on the basis that the judiciary had become too plaintiff-oriented. There may very well be an iron law which dooms judges to always be a decade behind the times. That is probably a good thing. Fluctuations in intellectual fashion and transient crises or enthusiasms make it difficult to discern a permanent change.

. . .

Contemporary judges generally reached maturity at about the time that the welfare state was a widely accepted conventional wisdom. The 'progressive' project for the law of that era was

---

[27] See the discussion of *Tomlinson v Congleton* [2004] 1 AC 46, in Chapter 12.

[28] The possibility of taking steps to avoid loss (or cover risk) is part of the consideration of 'vulnerability' of the plaintiff, which is a key concept in Australian case law relating to the duty of care in negligence (at least in economic loss cases).

[29] Unless based on a very formalistic approach bound by precedent, an approach to negligence which did not take into account policy considerations would be inclined to produce much more extensive liability than we have today: see the discussion in Chapter 6.

[30] Atiyah suggests that *personal insurance* (rather than liability insurance) will be the solution: *The Damages Lottery* (Hart Publishing, 1997).

to expand the circumstances in which a person had a 'right' to sue. We are now more conscious of limits—social, economic, ecological, and those of human nature. . . . For several decades now economic and social limits on the efficacy of governmental intervention have received greater recognition. The law cannot remain isolated from such general trends in social philosophy.

In particular there has been a significant change in expectations within Australian society, as elsewhere, about persons accepting responsibility for their own actions. The previously dominant idea that any personal failing is not your fault, that everyone can be categorised as a victim, has receded. The task is to restore an appropriate balance between personal responsibility for one's own conduct and social expectations of proper compensation and care.

What is being described here is not the introduction of 'responsibility' for the first time, but a *change* in the idea of responsibility. Rather than responsibility to take care for others (and not to harm them), the emerging political philosophy recognizes personal responsibility to deal with risks. Sometimes this means acting with due regard for one's own interests, and not expecting others to accept the blame for failing to help us out. This might be called 'victim responsibility', and that seems to be what most people have in mind when they propose that tort law needs to be limited. Alternatively, it may mean taking responsibility for insuring and planning risks. This is a more forward-looking question.

In the UK, changes have (so far) been more moderate. Scepticism about the justice and acceptability of tort liability underlies the introduction of a new statutory regime relating to medical accidents. The NHS Redress Act 2006 outlines a 'no-fault' process for investigating medical accidents. The aims of this scheme are informed by the perceived shortcomings of tort law, but it does not replace the right to sue in tort. Its primary goals are to speed up the process of enquiry into medical accidents; to discourage NHS staff from covering their tracks in order to avoid 'blame'; and to foster the provision of modest and timely redress in contrast to the perceived culture of secrecy and blame which a civil action may encourage.

Part I of the Compensation Act 2006 both states some restrictions on the operation of negligence liability,[31] and (at the same time) makes it possible for certain personal injury claimants to recover in full for their injury, where they would obtain only partial compensation at common law.[32]

3.2 HUMAN RIGHTS ACT 1998

The Human Rights Act 1998 has significantly changed the contours of English law. Its impact on private law (including tort) is still emerging and the possibilities need some spelling out.

---

[31] S 1, discussed in Chapter 3 below. It would appear that the section is intended to *reinforce* the approach already taken to establishing breach of duty.

[32] S 3, designed specifically to reverse the effect of *Barker v Corus* [2006] UKHL 20; [2006] 2 WLR 1027 in mesothelioma claims: see Chapter 4.

Human Rights Act 1998 (1998, c. 42)

The Convention Rights

1. (1) In this Act the Convention rights means the rights and fundamental freedoms set out in

    (a) Articles 2 to 12 and 14 of the Convention,

    (b) Articles 1 to 3 of the First Protocol, and

    (c) Articles 1 and 2 of the Sixth Protocol,

as read with Articles 16 to 18 of the Convention.

(2) Those Articles are to have effect for the purposes of this Act subject to any designated derogation or reservation (as to which see sections 14 and 15).

(3) The Articles are set out in Schedule 1. . . .

Interpretation of Convention Rights

2. (1) A court or tribunal determining a question which has arisen in connection with a Convention right must take into account any

    (a) judgment, decision, declaration or advisory opinion of the European Court of Human Rights,

    (b) opinion of the Commission given in a report adopted under Article 31 of the Convention,

    (c) decision of the Commission in connection with Article 26 or 27(2) of the Convention, or

    (d) decision of the Committee of Ministers taken under Article 46 of the Convention,

whenever made or given, so far as, in the opinion of the court or tribunal, it is relevant to the proceedings in which that question has arisen.

. . .

Public authorities

Acts of Public Authorities

6. (1) It is unlawful for a public authority to act in a way which is incompatible with a Convention right.

(2) Subsection (1) does not apply to an act if

    (a) as the result of one or more provisions of primary legislation, the authority could not have acted differently or

    (b) in the case of one or more provisions of, or made under, primary legislation which cannot be read or given effect in a way which is compatible with the Convention rights, the authority was acting so as to give effect to or enforce those provisions.

(3) In this section public authority includes

    (a) a court or tribunal, and

    (b) any person certain of whose functions are functions of a public nature,

but does not include either House of Parliament or a person exercising functions in connection with proceedings in Parliament.

(4) In subsection (3) Parliament does not include the House of Lords in its judicial capacity.

(5) In relation to a particular act, a person is not a public authority by virtue only of subsection (3)(b) if the nature of the act is private.

Proceedings

7. (1) A person who claims that a public authority has acted (or proposes to act) in a way which is made unlawful by section 6(1) may—

   (a) bring proceedings against the authority under this Act in the appropriate court or tribunal, or

   (b) rely on the Convention right or rights concerned in any legal proceedings,

but only if he is (or would be) a victim of the unlawful act.

(2) In subsection (1)(a) "appropriate court or tribunal" means such court or tribunal as may be determined in accordance with rules; and proceedings against an authority include a counter-claim or similar proceeding.

. . .

(5) Proceedings under subsection (1)(a) must be brought before the end of—

   (a) the period of one year beginning with the date on which the act complained of took place; or

   (b) such longer period as the court or tribunal considers equitable having regard to all the circumstances,

but that is subject to any rule imposing a stricter time limit in relation to the procedure in question.

(6) In subsection (1)(b) "legal proceedings" includes—

   (a) proceedings brought by or at the instigation of a public authority; and

   (b) an appeal against the decision of a court or tribunal.

(7) For the purposes of this section, a person is a victim of an unlawful act only if he would be a victim for the purposes of Article 34 of the Convention if proceedings were brought in the European Court of Human Rights in respect of that act.

Judicial remedies

8. (1) In relation to any act (or proposed act) of a public authority which the court finds is (or would be) unlawful, it may grant such relief or remedy, or make such order, within its powers as it considers just and appropriate.

(2) But damages may be awarded only by a court which has power to award damages, or to order the payment of compensation, in civil proceedings.

(3) No award of damages is to be made unless, taking account of all the circumstances of the case, including—

   (a) any other relief or remedy granted, or order made, in relation to the act in question (by that or any other court), and

   (b) the consequences of any decision (of that or any other court) in respect of that act, the court is satisfied that the award is necessary to afford just satisfaction to the person in whose favour it is made.

(4) In determining—

(a) whether to award damages, or

(b) the amount of an award,

the court must take into account the principles applied by the European Court of Human Rights in relation to the award of compensation under Article 41 of the Convention.

(5) A public authority against which damages are awarded is to be treated—

(a) in Scotland, for the purposes of section 3 of the Law Reform (Miscellaneous Provisions) (Scotland) Act 1940 as if the award were made in an action of damages in which the authority has been found liable in respect of loss or damage to the person to whom the award is made;

(b) for the purposes of the Civil Liability (Contribution) Act 1978 as liable in respect of damage suffered by the person to whom the award is made.

(6) In this section—

"court" includes a tribunal;

"damages" means damages for an unlawful act of a public authority; and

"unlawful" means unlawful under section 6(1).

. . .

Freedom of expression

12. (1) This section applies if a court is considering whether to grant any relief which, if granted, might affect the exercise of the Convention right to freedom of expression.

(2) If the person against whom the application for relief is made ("the respondent") is neither present nor represented, no such relief is to be granted unless the court is satisfied—

(a) that the applicant has taken all practicable steps to notify the respondent; or

(b) that there are compelling reasons why the respondent should not be notified.

(3) No such relief is to be granted so as to restrain publication before trial unless the court is satisfied that the applicant is likely to establish that publication should not be allowed.

(4) The court must have particular regard to the importance of the Convention right to freedom of expression and, where the proceedings relate to material which the respondent claims, or which appears to the court, to be journalistic, literary or artistic material (or to conduct connected with such material), to—

(a) the extent to which—

(i) the material has, or is about to, become available to the public; or

(ii) it is, or would be, in the public interest for the material to be published;

(b) any relevant privacy code.

(5) In this section—

"court" includes a tribunal; and

"relief" includes any remedy or order (other than in criminal proceedings).

We have not extracted the relevant Convention rights here, although Article 10 is reproduced and briefly discussed below. Relevant Convention rights are extracted in later chapters as and when they are appropriate to particular issues.

The Influence on Tort Law

Horizontal effect

When the statute was enacted, the chief controversy among private lawyers was whether it would have 'horizontal effect'. Clearly, the statute is intended to have 'vertical effect', creating new actions, remedies, and court powers in respect of acts of 'public authorities' (section 6) and Parliament in its legislative function (to a limited extent, set out in section 4). But is it intended to affect private law, particularly in cases where the defendant is not a 'public authority'?

One potential trigger for horizontal effect is section 6. Section 6 specifies that 'it is unlawful for a public authority to act in a way which is inconsistent with a Convention right'. By section 6(3), 'public authority' *includes* 'a court or tribunal'. Therefore, it is unlawful for a court or tribunal to act inconsistently with a Convention right. There has been considerable discussion of what this should be taken to mean for the future development of private law.

Widely divergent views were initially expressed as to whether section 6 would give 'horizontal effect' to Convention rights. Notably, Sir William Wade argued that the Convention rights would have *direct* horizontal effect after the Human Rights Act, becoming applicable even in disputes between private parties ('Horizons of Horizontality' (2000) 116 LQR 217, supported by J. Morgan, 'Questioning the 'True Effect' of the Human Rights Act' (2002) 22 LS 259). Others denied that the rights would be directly applicable in this way, but conceded that the Convention rights would have 'indirect' horizontal effect.

A 'weak' interpretation of indirect horizontal effect would mean that courts would be in some way influenced by the Convention rights in their interpretation of the law. (See for example H. Beale and N. Pittam, 'The Impact of the Human Rights Act 1998 on English Tort and Contract Law', in Friedmann and Barak-Erez, *Human Rights in Private Law* (Hart Publishing, 2001).) A stronger interpretation of indirect horizontal effect holds that courts will consider themselves under a duty to interpret, apply, and develop the common law in such a way as to ensure that the Convention rights are protected. This 'strong' interpretation of indirect horizontal effect would suggest that existing common law doctrines will come to be transformed, and has been supported for example by Murray Hunt. In the following extract, he summarizes a 'strong direct' position.

Murray Hunt, 'The Effect on the Law of Obligations', in B. Markesinis (ed.), *The Impact of the Human Rights Bill on English Law* (Oxford: Clarendon Press, 1998), 180

The case law of the Convention, the text of the Bill, the purpose disclosed by the White Paper and in the Parliamentary debates, together with the current practice of our courts all point irresistibly towards the Convention being horizontally applicable when the Human Rights Act comes into effect, save that it will not give rise to an independent cause of action for breach of Convention rights. This does not necessarily mean to say that the Human Rights Act will immediately confer new causes of action against private parties where none previously existed. But it does mean that the private law of obligations will be developed by courts so as to be compatible with Convention rights, and that is likely to mean, over time, the metamorphosis of existing causes of action so as to fulfil the State's international obligation to secure the rights contained in the Convention and fulfil the clear intention of both Government and Parliament that enactment of the Human Rights Act will ensure that nobody will any longer be without a remedy in domestic law for breach of their Convention rights.

Six years after the Act entered into force, does experience suggest that the Convention rights are having horizontal effect in tort law in particular?

In Chapter 14, we will explain that the House of Lords has denied (as Hunt predicts above) that *new causes of action will be recognized* as a result of the Human Rights Act (*Campbell v MGN* [2004] 2 AC 457). But we will also note that in that case, the rules of an existing cause of action were (following the Court of Appeal in *Douglas v Hello!* [2001] QB 967) amended to protect 'privacy' in its own right. This was certainly influenced by the requirements of Article 8 ECHR, but it was not achieved through interpretation of section 6. Instead, it was section 12 (included in the extract above) which was used to add some elements of 'privacy' to the range of interests protected through the law of tort. At first sight it will appear strange that a section concerned with having *particular regard to the Convention right to freedom of expression* should be the means by which 'privacy interests' became recognized as protected interests in the law of tort. As we will explain, the reasoning process applied was to understand 'the Convention right to freedom of expression' in terms of all aspects of Article 10 ECHR, which both expresses the right (in Article 10(1)), and states the ways in which it may be limited.

Article 10, European Convention on Human Rights and Fundamental Freedoms

Freedom of expression

1

Everyone has the right to freedom of expression. This right shall include freedom to hold opinions and to receive and impart information and ideas without interference by public authority and regardless of frontiers. This Article shall not prevent States from requiring the licensing of broadcasting, television or cinema enterprises.

2

The exercise of these freedoms, since it carries with it duties and responsibilities, may be subject to such formalities, conditions, restrictions or penalties as are prescribed by law and are necessary in a democratic society, in the interests of national security, territorial integrity or public safety, for the prevention of disorder or crime, for the protection of health or morals, for the protection of the reputation or rights of others, for preventing the disclosure of information received in confidence, or for maintaining the authority and impartiality of the judiciary.

In *Douglas v Hello!*, the acceptable limitations expressed in Article 10(2) were regarded as an inherent aspect of the right stated in Article 10(1). One of these limitations is 'the protection of the reputation or rights of others'. This was taken to mean that the right to freedom of expression is inherently qualified by the need to protect other Convention rights. Other legitimate restrictions—aimed more at collective goals such as protection of public safety and disorder—were *also* considered to be inherent in the definition of the right itself. It is important to note this because the interpretation of Convention rights adopted by the UK courts is not that those rights are aimed exclusively at protection of the interests of individuals; nor that individual interests protected by the Convention rights necessarily 'trump' more collective interests (see further Chapter 13).

Actions under Sections 7 and 8

The Human Rights Act also creates free-standing rights of action in cases where a Convention right has been violated *by a public authority* (section 7).[33] A civil remedy may be available in such an action, under section 8. An action under section 7 is not an action in tort. There is a shorter limitation period, of one year,[34] although this may be extended if the court thinks it equitable to do so.

The availability of an action under the Human Rights Act has on a number of occasions influenced the development of tort law. A particularly plain example is *JD v East Berkshire NHS Trust* [2004] 2 WLR 58, where the Court of Appeal decided not to follow an earlier decision of the House of Lords (*X v Bedfordshire* [1995] 2 AC 633). Since an action would lie in future under section 7 of the Human Rights Act 1998, it was considered better to reconsider the policy issues which had led the House of Lords to decide that no duty of care was owed *in tort* in respect of the claim. Thus, the existence of a remedy under the Human Rights Act influenced the treatment of policy reasons in the tort of negligence.

It should be underlined that this is *not* to say that policy factors are *irrelevant* to an action under the Human Rights Act. Protection of the Convention rights must be proportionate and in the case of nearly all the Convention rights (as for example Article 10), the rights may be limited in order to protect countervailing interests and objectives.

We will look in more detail at the influence of the Human Rights Act in the chapters that follow. One of the real tests ahead for the law of tort is the need to consider whether protected interests, and circumstances of protection, should be realigned to reflect Convention rights.

FURTHER READING

Atiyah, P., *The Damages Lottery* (Oxford: Hart Publishing, 1997).

Cane, P., *The Anatomy of Tort Law* (Oxford: Hart Publishing, 1997).

Clarke, M., *Policies and Perceptions of Insurance Law in the Twenty-First Century* (Oxford: Oxford University Press, 2005), Chapter 8.

Gearty, C., *Principles of Human Rights Adjudication* (Oxford: Oxford University Press, 2004), Chapter 8.

Spigelman, J.J., 'Negligence: The Last Outpost of the Welfare State' (2002) 76 ALJ, 432.

Steele, J., *Risks and Legal Theory* (Oxford: Hart Publishing, 2004), Chapters 2 and 3.

Weir, T., *Tort Law* (2nd edn, Oxford: Oxford University Press, 2006), Chapter 1.

Williams, G., 'The Aims of the Law of Tort' (1951) 4 CLP, 137.

---

[33] Some guidance on the meaning of 'public authority' is set out in section 6 itself. It is a much analysed expression. For a recent discussion see H. Quane, 'The Strasbourg Jurisprudence and the Meaning of a "Public Authority" under the Human Rights Act' (2006) PL 103–23.

[34] The limitation periods applicable in tort claims are explored

PART II

INTENTIONAL INTERFERENCES

2

TORTS OF INTENTION

CENTRAL ISSUES

i) In English tort law, considerable emphasis is placed on careless conduct inflicting harm. Perhaps curiously, torts involving *intentional* conduct receive much less attention. This chapter explains the reasons (some of them more satisfactory than others) for the limited impact of the 'intentional torts'.

ii) We will begin by exploring intention itself, to the extent that this idea is used in tort law. We will note considerable variation within the intentional torts. This variation affects both the required **target** of intention (*what* must be intended?), and the required **level** of intention (what does it mean to *intend* something?).

iii) We then break down the 'intentional torts' into a number of groups. The first of these, **trespass to the person**, comprises three torts: battery, assault, and false imprisonment. Trespass to the person has been confined in modern law to acts which are in some sense 'intentional' (*Letang v Cooper*). Even so, trespass torts do *not* depend on showing intentional infliction of harm. Rather, they concern acts whose *intended consequences* (for example, physical contact, or physical restraint) are judged to be unlawful. Modern case law has significantly restricted the role of trespass to the person, but trespass torts remain significant in situations where the 'lawfulness' of physical intervention or restraint is in issue.

iv) The action in *Wilkinson v Downton* is a damage-based tort of intention. A remedy may lie for physical and psychiatric harm which is 'intentionally' caused by a false statement, and not through any physical impact. The level of intention required in this action is relatively undemanding. It is not required that harm was the actual *purpose of* the defendant, so long as it was virtually certain to result. In England, courts have resisted academic argument that *Wilkinson v Downton* should be developed in order to provide remedies for injury falling short of psychiatric or physical illness, particularly in the form of 'anxiety and distress'. The Protection from Harassment Act 1997 now provides civil remedies (as well as setting out criminal offences) in respect of a course of conduct that amounts to harassment. The available remedies include injunctions (to restrain the harassment) and damages which may compensate for 'anxiety and distress'.

v) The **intentional economic torts** require a higher level of intention than *Wilkinson v Downton*, and it is now clear that in most of them, harm to the claimant's interests must be an *intended target of* the defendant's action. Even so, in virtually all of the economic torts, intentional harm is not enough. Something additionally 'unlawful' or otherwise 'wrongful' about the defendant's acts is required. This requirement has been criticized as inhibiting generalization of English tort law as a whole; but we will see that a number of academic commentators have more recently agreed (though writing from different perspectives) that restrictions of this sort may be necessary.

vi) Finally, we turn to torts concerning intentional abuse of process (**malicious prosecution**) and of power (**misfeasance in a public office**). Misfeasance in a public office may be committed with a lower level of intention than is required in the economic torts ('recklessness'). This further variation has been explained by the courts as turning on the different nature of the 'wrong' defined by this tort. The 'gist' of this tort is injurious *abuse of power*. Power exercised recklessly is power abused.

1. 'INTENTION'

There is considerable diversity in the meaning of 'intention' in the torts considered in this chapter. Intention has two dimensions:

1. The **target** of intention

Here we ask, *what* must be intended? For example, in trespass to the person (assault, battery, and false imprisonment), neither harm nor unlawfulness needs to be intended. In battery, the target of intention is simply physical contact. In *Wilkinson v Downton* by contrast, the target of intention is harm: it must be shown that the tortfeasor 'intended' (though in a rather weak sense) to cause harm to the claimant.

2. The **level** of intention required

Once we have answered the first question (what must be intended?) we still have to ask, *what is the relevant state of mind?* What do we mean by 'intending' something? This is a more difficult question to answer. For example, must the outcome be a (or the) *goal* of the defendant's action? Or is it enough that it is almost certain to follow? Again the answer varies. In *Wilkinson v Downton*, a strong degree of likelihood is sufficient for intention to be 'imputed by law'. In the economic torts by contrast, harm to the claimant must generally be a *goal* or *purpose* of the action, or at least a necessary means to the intended goal. Being 'foreseeable' or even 'virtually certain' will not suffice.

Is a General Definition of Intention Possible—or Desirable?

It follows from the above examples that no general definition of intention is shared by the English torts of intention. We will have to spell out the relevant meaning of intention in respect of each tort. By contrast, the American Law Institute has set out the following general statement of the meaning of intention in American tort law as a whole:

American Law Institute, Restatement of the Law, Second, Torts

Section 8A   Intent

The word "intent" is used throughout the Restatement of this Subject to denote that the actor desires to cause consequences of his act, or that he believes that the consequences are substantially certain to result from it.

Comment:

a. "Intent," as it is used throughout the Restatement of Torts, has reference to the consequences of an act rather than the act itself. When an actor fires a gun in the midst of the Mojave Desert, he intends to pull the trigger; but when the bullet hits a person who is present in the desert without the actor's knowledge, he does not intend that result. "Intent" is limited, wherever it is used, to the consequences of the act.

b. All consequences which the actor desires to bring about are intended, as the word is used in this Restatement. Intent is not, however, limited to consequences which are desired. If the actor knows that the consequences are certain, or substantially certain, to result from his act, and still goes ahead, he is treated by the law as if he had in fact desired to produce the result. As the probability that the consequences will follow decreases, and becomes less than substantial certainty, the actor's conduct loses the character of intent, and becomes mere recklessness, as defined in Section 500. As the probability decreases further, and amounts only to a risk that the result will follow, it becomes ordinary negligence, as defined in Section 282. All three have their important place in the law of torts, but the liability attached to them will differ.

Illustrations:

1. A throws a bomb into B's office for the purpose of killing B. A knows that C, B's stenographer, is in the office. A has no desire to injure C, but knows that his act is substantially certain to do so. C is injured by the explosion. A is subject to liability to C for an intentional tort.

2. On a curve in a narrow highway A, without any desire to injure B, or belief that he is substantially certain to do so, recklessly drives his automobile in an attempt to pass B's car. As a result of this recklessness, A crashes into B's car, injuring B. A is subject to liability to B for his reckless conduct, but is not liable to B for any intentional tort.

How does this statement compare with the various forms of intention required in English tort law? The first thing to notice is that so far as *the target of intention* is concerned, the definition requires only that the *consequences* of the act should be intended. It does *not* state that *injury* or *harm* must be intended. In the case of shooting, for example, it is clear that if there is intent to have physical contact (to shoot the claimant), this amounts to 'an intent in respect of the consequences', whether or not *harm* is intended (this is illustrated by comment 'a' in the extract above). This is consistent with the key English case of *Letang v Cooper* [1965] 1 QB 232, extracted below.

In respect of the *level* of intention (our second question of intention, above), the US Restatement seems to be broader and less demanding than a substantial number of English torts. It includes some results which are merely the side-effects of action (though they must be 'substantially certain' to result) and not the *purpose* of the action. On the other hand, the definition excludes recklessness, which *is* sufficient to amount to intention in the English tort of misfeasance in a public office and (in respect of some of their elements) in deceit and malicious falsehood.

Philosophical Criticism of the Restatement Definition

Commenting on the Restatement, John Finnis has criticized the treatment of 'substantially certain' consequences as equivalent to 'intended' consequences. Finnis suggests that only those outcomes which are *desired* by the actor should count as intended consequences.

John Finnis, 'Intention in Tort Law', in D. Owen (ed.), *Philosophical Foundations of Tort Law* (Oxford: Clarendon Press, 1995), 229–47, at 243

The assimilation of what even Holmes called 'actual intention' with a merely deemed, fictitious intention has been repudiated with increasing force and clarity in English, if not American, criminal law. But it is installed . . . at the heart of American tort doctrine by the *Restatement (Second) of Torts'* definition of intent . . . [Finnis quotes from section 8 of the Restatement, as above]. Thus the golfer whose only hope of winning at the last hole is to take a very long drive across water 'intends'—according to the Restatement—to miss the green and lose the ball in the pond.

In a footnote (fn 64 at p. 243), Finnis adds a critical comment in respect of the Restatement position (see comment 'b' in the extract above), that with declining probability 'the actor's conduct loses the character of intent'. 'Degrees of intent', he argues, are not recognized in 'common sense and philosophy'.

A new Restatement of US tort law—or rather, of the aspects of US tort law relating to *physical harm*—is currently being drafted. In the current Final Draft,[1] the American Law Institute proposes to retain the dual meaning of 'intent'.

Restatement (Third) of Torts: Liability for Physical Harm
(Proposed Final Draft No 1)

Section 1   Intent

A person acts with intent to produce a consequence if:

  (a) the person acts with the purpose of producing that consequence; or

  (b) the person acts knowing that the consequence is substantially certain to result.

Comment

a. The dual definition

. . . There are obvious differences between the actor who acts with the desire to cause harm and the actor who engages in conduct knowing that harm is substantially certain to happen. There is a clear element of wrongfulness in conduct whose very purpose is to cause harm. While there are circumstances in which acting in such a way is appropriate, tort law can

---

[1] The version extracted is current as at April 2006.

fashion affirmative defenses (such as necessity and defense of self and of property) that takes those circumstances into account. Whether the objective of tort law is fairness or deterrence or some combination of the two, liability for purposeful harms is generally easy to justify.

When the actor chooses to engage in conduct with knowledge that harm is certain to follow, this choice, with its known consequence, provides a distinctive argument in favor of liability. Nevertheless, there are complications . . . Not only does the actor not desire to produce the harmful result, but the actor may be engaging in a generally proper activity for generally proper reasons . . . This can provide an element of justification or reasonableness that is lacking for purposeful harms. . . .

This Section, while accepting the combined definition of intent incorporated into Section 8A of the Restatement Second of Torts, differs from Section 8A in unblending the definition and setting forth separate subsections dealing with purpose and knowledge. The reason for this is to accommodate courts that in particular contexts might want to distinguish between intent in the sense of purpose and intent in the sense of knowledge. . . .

In comment 'a' above, the American Law Institute expresses the view that in the case of actions whose *purpose* is to cause harm, liability 'is easy to justify'. Some aspects of English tort law do not reflect such a view: see in particular the economic torts in Section 7 of this chapter. Here, there needs also to be an extra element, normally in the form of 'unlawful means'. Intention to cause harm is not enough.

This leads us to an important point. Apart from the fact that the definition in the US Restatement does not happen to fit all of the English torts of intention, there might be dangers in accepting that the existence of intention could justify liability in and of itself. In English tort law, intentional harm is not often regarded as a *sufficient* 'wrong-making factor'.[2] A key case to this effect is *Allen v Flood* [1898] AC 1,[3] in which the House of Lords decided that bad motive did not suffice to render an otherwise lawful act 'unlawful'. American courts rejected *Allen v Flood* and the law took a different path still reflected in the Restatement: *Tuttle v Buck* 119 NW 946 (Minn 1909).

Summary: The Limited Role of 'Intention' in English Intentional Torts

Although the intentional torts collected here are very important, intentional infliction of harm is rarely a sufficient basis for liability in the English law of tort. Intention does not have the same significance in English tort law as it does in American tort law.[4]

FURTHER READING

Atiyah, P., 'American Tort Law in Crisis' (1987) 7 OJLS 279.

Finnis, J., 'Intention in Tort Law', in D. Owen (ed.), *Philosophical Foundations of Tort Law* (Oxford: Clarendon Press, 1995).

---

[2] The term 'wrong-making factor' is used by Finnis, above, who supports generalization of liability for truly 'intended' harms.

[3] This case is discussed in Section 7 of the present chapter.

[4] The legacy of *Allen v Flood* is not the only reason for this. A review of the ways in which torts of intention, negligence, and strict liability (particularly trespass, negligence, and defamation respectively) were treated by early American and English textbook writers can be found in James Gordley, *Foundations of Private Law: Property, Tort, Contract, Unjust Enrichment* (OUP, 2006), 173–80.

2. TRESPASS TO THE PERSON

2.1 THE RELEVANT TORTS AND THEIR GENERAL FEATURES

There are three torts which together make up 'trespass to the person'. These are **battery**, **assault**, and **false imprisonment**.

Battery

Battery requires an act of the defendant which directly and intentionally brings about contact with the body of the claimant, where the contact exceeds what is lawful. Battery is actionable without proof of damage. There need not be an intent to harm; nor even an intent to act unlawfully. The necessary intention is to bring about the physical contact.

It has been argued that battery does not *need* to be intentional and that it may be committed recklessly or even carelessly.[5] Historically this is correct. But we will see that the impact of *Letang v Cooper* and the presumption in the important recent cases explored below is that the contact must be intentional. A major change would be needed to resurrect 'negligent trespass to the person' in English law.

Directness

The idea that the contact must be **direct** is a legacy of history. As Hale LJ put it in *Wong v Parkside* [2003] 3 All ER 932:

> **7**   As every law student knows, the common law distinguished between an action in trespass and an action on the case. Trespass to the person consisted in the direct infliction of harm (or the threat of the immediate infliction of such harm) upon the claimant. But the law recognised that physical harm might be inflicted indirectly. If intentional, this was the tort recognised by the High Court in *Wilkinson v Downton* [1897] 2 QB 57 . . . . If negligent, it was eventually recognised as the tort of negligence in *Donoghue v Stevenson* [1932] AC 562.

Like all good historical summaries, this compresses a long period of development into a short space. M. J. Prichard, 'Trespass, Case and the Rule in *Williams v Holland*' (1964) CLJ 234–53, places the origins of the tort of negligence (liability for carelessly caused harm outside a particular relationship) at a much earlier date than *Donoghue v Stevenson*, with the case of *Mitchil v Alestree* (1676). Prichard too particularly notes that trespass was limited by the need for directness or 'immediacy'. *Mitchil v Alestree* involved the dangers created by breaking unruly horses in Lincoln's Inn fields: when the horses bolted, they were no longer controlled by the defendant, and the damage was not directly or 'immediately' caused by the defendant's act.

---

5 F. A. Trindade, 'Intentional Torts: Some Thoughts on Assault and Battery' (1982) 2 OJLS 211–37, explains that this used to be the case but that these days battery is confined to cases of intentional contact.

The following extract from a major review of assault and battery in the Commonwealth jurisdictions particularly emphasizes the requirement of 'intention':

F. A. Trindade, 'Intentional Torts: Some Thoughts on Assault and Battery' (1982) 2 OJLS 211, at 216–17

The first ingredient of the tort of battery is that whatever has to be done to the plaintiff by the defendant to make the activity actionable as a battery must be done *directly*. It is an ingredient which is common to all three torts of trespass to the person, assault, battery and false imprisonment but it is not sufficiently emphasised in the textbooks. . . .

The example given by Fortescue CJ in *Reynolds v Clarke*[6] of tumbling over a log left unlawfully on the highway (consequential) and being hit by a log being thrown unlawfully onto the highway (direct) emphasised the element of immediate contact with which 'direct' acts came to be associated. But it was not only hits by something thrown at you which were regarded as 'direct'. An act which set in motion an unbroken series of continuing consequences, the last of which ultimately caused contact with the plaintiff was still regarded as sufficiently 'direct' for the purposes of trespass. So when the defendant rode his motorcycle into B who collided with the plaintiff who was thrown to the ground, it was held that the facts constituted a 'direct' act for an action in trespass.[7]

A consequence of the 'directness' requirement is that although the tort of battery might justify an action against a party who is generally 'blameless' (for example, a surgeon who carries out surgery having been falsely informed that a patient has consented), it does not tend to allow actions against 'peripheral parties' (for example, a local authority which does not spot that a builder has not complied with the approved plans; or a mother who fails to report criminal acts of abuse on the part of her husband). In particular, it does not appear to allow a claim for 'nonfeasance' (or failure to act).

Intention

As we noted above, the target of intention in the tort of battery is *physical contact*.

F. A. Trindade, 'Intentional Torts: Some Thoughts on Assault and Battery' (1982) 2 OJLS 211, at 220

. . . In battery what is required is intentional contact not an intention to do harm—and it is not correct to say that trespass can be brought 'only for the direct physical infliction of *harm*'. As Talbot J said in *Williams v Humphrey* [*The Times* 13 February 1975; p. 20 (transcript)]: 'it was argued that for the act to be a battery, there must be an intent to *injure*. I do not accept this contention. The intention goes to the commission of an act of force. This seems to be the principle in many cases of trespass to the person'.

On the other hand, it has recently been accepted that a doctrine called **transferred intent** can apply in the tort of battery. That is to say, a person who intends to have physical contact with one person can commit battery against another, if the aim goes awry, or if both are hit.

---

[6] (1725) 1 Stra 634, 636.
[7] *Hillier v Leitch* [1936] SASR 490.

This was the case in *Bici and Bici v Ministry of Defence* [2004] EWHC 786, a first instance decision of Elias J.[8] Here the Ministry of Defence was held to be vicariously liable in both negligence and battery when soldiers acting as peace-keepers in Kosovo shot at a car, killing one civilian and injuring another.[9] The soldiers had intended to shoot an individual on top of the car who was wielding a rifle, and the intent to hit him was treated as 'transferred' so that they also committed a battery against the passenger inside the car. We will have cause to return to *Bici v Ministry of Defence* below since it raised many difficult and important questions in respect of available defences,[10] and the interaction of negligence and trespass.

Assault

Assault requires no physical contact but is a direct threat by the defendant which intentionally places the claimant in reasonable apprehension of an imminent battery.

Assault is, therefore, a 'secondary' tort, which is defined in terms of apprehension of battery.

The target of intention in assault is not entirely clear. In *Read v Coker* the requirement is said to be intent to commit a battery. In *Bici v Ministry of Defence* it is intent to put in fear of violence. The latter is more consistent with *R v Ireland* [1998] AC 147 (below).

In *Stephens v Myers* (1830) 4 C & P 349, 172 ER 735, a member of the audience at a parish meeting threatened to hit the chairman. No assault was established because the defendant was at some distance from the plaintiff and surrounded by others, and was considered to have no 'present means' of executing his threat. By contrast, in *Read v Coker* (1853) 13 CB 850, 138 ER 1437, the plaintiff was threatened by a group of workmen who said they would break his neck if he did not leave the premises. An assault *was* established since they had the means of carrying out their threat.

The threat may of course take the form of words. But what of silence? In *R v Ireland* [1998] AC 147, a case of criminal assault occasioning psychiatric harm, the House of Lords held that a menacing *silence* could amount to an assault, provided it put the victim in reasonable fear of immediate violence. This is not inconsistent with the requirement for a positive act: a series of phone calls, consisting of silence, is what provided the occasion with its menace.

In *Bici v Ministry of Defence* (the facts of which were outlined above), Elias J maintained that the defendant must *intend* to put the claimant in fear of imminent violence. In this particular case, although there was an intention to commit a battery, which was then transferred to the unintended victim, there was *no* intention to put anyone *in fear of violence*. As such, a claim in assault failed.

False imprisonment

False imprisonment is unlawful and total bodily restraint of the claimant, by the defendant.

False imprisonment is rather different in its requirements from the torts above, and it is considered separately below (Section 4). The target of intention in false imprisonment is bodily restraint of the claimant.

---

[8] Unfortunately, Elias J used the expression 'transferred malice'. Nothing in the nature of 'malice' or 'ill-will' is required in the tort of battery, and the better expression is 'transferred intent'. In criminal law, the preferred expression is now 'transferred *mens rea*'.

[9] For the idea of vicarious liability, see Chapter 9.

[10] Elias J explained that if the soldiers would have had a valid defence in respect of the intended victim, for example that they were acting in reasonable self-defence, this defence would also have been 'transferred' and would operate as a defence to an action brought by the unintended victim.

actionable per se.

All trespass torts are actionable without proof of damage. 'Consent' is a vital defence to each of them but is of particular practical importance to battery. It has been contended that consent is *more than* a defence to battery, lack of consent amounting to an element of the tort. For convenience, we deal with that argument under 'Defences'. There is a range of available remedies reflecting the fact that trespass is not centrally concerned with compensation, although it will compensate if harm results from the trespass. The available remedies include compensatory damages; punitive damages in appropriate circumstances (particularly if the tort is committed by a public official);[11] or a declaration that the contact, threat or restraint is *unlawful*.[12] In some circumstances, courts may issue a declaration that a planned intervention is lawful.[13]

Ashley v CC Sussex

The breadth of recoverable damages in trespass is not truly settled. Logically, recovery of 'all' harm flowing from a trespass could be extreme and one would expect some sort of remoteness rule to be applied, the question being which one? In *Smith New Court Securities v Citibank* [1997] AC 254, the 'foreseeability' test for recoverable damage, which applies in the tort of negligence, was not applied to another tort of intention, namely an action in deceit. We explain why not in Section 7.5 below. The reasons for applying the more generous 'directness' rule in a case of deceit do not translate especially easily to trespass to the person, where there needs to be an 'unlawful' act but need not be any bad motive nor intentional harm. On the other hand, the fact that the interference is judged unlawful may itself be a good enough reason why all the *direct* consequences of the act should be attributed to the defendant.

The main purpose of trespass torts is not to compensate for injury, but to defend against actions which transgress the acceptable boundaries of physical interference.

Tony Weir, *A Casebook on Tort* (10th edn, London: Sweet & Maxwell, 2004), 322–3

The law of tort does not have one function only: few things do. It is true that most tort claimants want compensation for harm caused to them by someone else and that in this sense (and in this sense only) the main function of tort law is to ordain such compensation. It has another function, however, which, though traditional, has rarely been more important than now, namely to vindicate constitutional rights. Not every infraction of a right causes damage. That is precisely why the law of trespass does not insist on damage. But if jurists believe that damage is of the essence of a tort claim, they will regard trespass as anomalous, deride it as antiquated, ignore the values it enshrines and proceed to diminish the protection it affords to the rights of the citizen. When constitutional rights are in issue what matters is whether they have been infringed, not whether the defendant can really be blamed for infringing them. But if jurists think of negligence as the paradigm tort (and they do so for no better reason than that a great many people are mangled on the highway) they will regard it as the overriding principle of the law of tort that you do not have to pay if you were not at fault (and, equally, that you always have to pay if you were at fault) . . . . If a defendant can say that he acted reasonably, a negligence lawyer will let him off, without bothering to distinguish the reasonable but erroneous belief that the projected behaviour was *authorised* from the reasonable but erroneous belief that it was *safe*.

---

[11] Chapter 8.
[12] *Ashley v Chief Constable of Sussex Police* [2006] EWCA Civ 1085, below.
[13] Declarations of lawfulness are often used in medical cases although the basis for this is not straightforward: see *In re F* [1990] 2 AC 1 (below).

Weir's analysis explains why the focus of the trespass torts is not 'damage'; *and also* why these torts are not (despite their 'intentional' label) centrally concerned with the quality of the defendant's ⟨conduct⟩

2.2 TRESPASS IN HISTORY AND MODERN LAW: FORMS OF ACTION AND CAUSES OF ACTION

During the medieval period, trespass *was* the law of (what would now be called) 'tort'. 'Trespass' meant little more specific than 'wrong'.

S. F. C. Milsom, *Historical Foundations of the Common Law*
(2nd edn, Oxford: OUP, 1981), at 305

> Had some lawyer in the late fourteenth century undertaken to write a book about what we should call tort, about actions brought by the victims of wrongs, he would have called his book 'Trespass'.[]

The *substantive* requirements of the law at this stage are shrouded in mystery, largely because the majority of issues, other than procedural issues, were treated as matters of fact to be determined by the jury. Also obscuring the nature of trespass is the habit of claiming that harm had been occasioned *vi et armis* (with force and arms), even if it clearly had not.[14] Whatever the reason for this (and it may have been perceived to be a necessary feature of a claim in trespass in the royal courts), trespass became associated with *forcible* wrongs.[15]

The more directly relevant period of history for our purposes was to follow. A new form of action, 'the action on the case', began to develop, outside the jurisdiction of the royal courts. There were two forms of trespass, denoting different *forms of action*, and the two could not be mixed. The one was simply 'trespass'; the other was 'trespass on the case'. It was the action on the case which flourished, and from which the tort of negligence evolved.

Initially, the main distinctions between the forms of action called trespass and case were procedural. The drafting of writs was the principal skill of English civil lawyers. But actions 'on the case' also became distinct from trespass in substantive terms. On the one hand they required 'damage' to be shown (not a necessary feature of trespass then or now); on the other hand they allowed remedies for *indirect* or *consequential* harm, rather than purely for *direct* and *forcible* interference, as in trespass. The distinction between the action in trespass, and the action 'on the case', seems to have focused upon these principles of directness and force.

The following extract outlines the situation which was reached by the eighteenth century, and which still leaves its mark today.

---

[14] Ibbetson, *A Historical Introduction to the Common Law*, at 44, gives the example of *Rattlesdene v Grunestone* (1317). Here it was claimed that the defendant, having sold the plaintiff a barrel of wine but before delivery, removed the cap 'by force of arms, with swords bows and arrows etc', and replaced some of the wine with salt water. As Ibbetson says, 'It is hard not to suspect that the true basis of the claim was a shipping accident'.

[15] This is not because the only 'wrongs' understood in medieval times were 'forcible'. Ibbetson points out that defamation (harm to reputation) was recognized at an early stage but was hived off to the ecclesiastical courts. Likewise, an action in 'covenant' was developed which broadly concerned contractual wrongs, leaving 'trespass' to deal (primarily at least) with forcible interventions.

S. F. C. Milsom, *Historical Foundations of the Common Law*
(2nd edn, Oxford: OUP, 1981), 283–4

By the eighteenth century almost all litigation at common law was being conducted in *ostensurus quare* actions of trespass and case. Trespass was now a term of art referring to *ostensurus quare* writs alleging a breach of the king's peace, which had become common during the thirteenth century. Although these writs covered various harms to persons, goods and land, they were understood as representing a single entity: the essence of trespass was direct forcible injury. . . .

Actions on the case by the eighteenth century covered the remainder of our law of torts and almost the whole of our law of contract; and by contrast with the direct forcible injury of trespass they were identified with consequential harm. They were begun by *ostensurus quare* writs which did not allege a breach of the king's peace, but did describe the factual background more fully in a preamble . . . . Their full name 'trespass on the case' seemed to show that they were a development from trespass, a conscious reaching out from the central idea of direct forcible injury. . . .

The procedural implications of the different 'forms of action' were eventually abolished by the Judicature Acts of 1873 and 1875. It is often said that courts should now be free to respond to *the merits of the case*. This does not mean however that it should make no difference which tort is argued. Torts are not forms of action (a procedural idea); but they do have different substantive principles. If this had not been misunderstood in the case of *Letang v Cooper* [1965] 1 QB 232 (extracted and discussed below), the modern history of the trespass torts might have been quite different.

The potential for overlapping torts is illustrated by the following case.

✳ *Ashley v CC Sussex Police* [2006] EWCA Civ 1085 (CA)

The claimants were relatives of an individual (J) who had been fatally shot by the police during an armed raid. In a criminal prosecution, the police constable who had fired the shot was acquitted of J's murder. The claimants turned to civil law, suing the police commissioner (S) in a number of torts: false imprisonment (during the raid); negligence in the planning and execution of the raid; misfeasance in a public office for conduct after the event; assault and battery in respect of the shooting.[16] S admitted liability in negligence and in false imprisonment, but defended the other claims. Because S had admitted liability in negligence, success in the claim for assault and battery could not increase the damages payable to the claimants. They would not stand to be compensated twice merely because more than one cause of action was applicable to the loss.

The Court of Appeal reversed a decision of Dobbs J giving summary judgment for S in relation to the claims in misfeasance and assault and battery. The majority of the Court of Appeal took the view that it was appropriate for the assault and battery claim to proceed to trial, even though there was no prospect of damages being awarded under this head. The claimants could proceed on the basis that they sought a *declaration* that S had been unlawfully killed, in view of the acquittal of the officer and the absence of an inquest or official inquiry into the killing.

---

[16] Some of these claims relate to wrongdoing on the part of the police authorities; others propose that the commissioner is liable 'vicariously' for a tort on the part of the police constable (see Chapter 9). The specific claims against S in assault and battery are claims for *vicarious* liability.

Auld LJ (dissenting) thought that to seek such a declaration was an *abuse of process*, as it amounted to using the civil courts for a *collateral purpose*. (That is, not the purpose for which the tort exists; and therefore an *inappropriate* purpose.)

The argument of the majority underlines what we have said here about the distinctive nature of the actions in trespass to the person. Seeking a declaration as to unlawful killing could only be regarded as a 'collateral' purpose if the *main point* of the action in battery is understood in terms of compensation for harm. This as we have said is not its main point. Trespass is centrally concerned with the boundaries of legitimate physical interference with the person; and a declaration of unlawfulness would fulfil this purpose appropriately.

Sir Anthony Clarke MR, *Ashley v Chief Constable of Sussex Police*
[2006] EWCA Civ 1085

96   The role of the civil courts is not solely to provide compensation. As I see it, the civil justice system exists to adjudicate on the merits of individual claims by application of the law to the facts. The role of a civil court is to determine the parties' legal rights and liabilities. Such a determination can result in different types of relief, including compensation by way of damages, an injunction or declaration. The pursuit of a declaration that the respondent is liable in the tort of battery for the shooting of the deceased by PC Sherwood is a remedy available to the court. While it does of course remain within the court's discretion whether declaratory relief should be granted, it seems to me, without wishing to prejudice the matter if it arises before the trial judge, that the court may well think it appropriate to grant such a declaration if the respondent fails to show that PC Sherwood used reasonable force in necessary self-defence. . . . I agree with Auld LJ that it is a matter for the discretion of the court whether justice as between the parties requires a declaration to be made.

The Master of the Rolls went on to point out that it is not unknown for matters previously before criminal courts to be brought to civil trial. In the present case:

98   On the facts here it is true that PC Sherwood was acquitted of murder on the direction of the trial judge. However at that trial both the standard and burden of proof and the ingredients of the alleged offence were different from the standard and burden of proof and the ingredients of the tort of battery.

2.3 THE LIMITED ROLE OF TRESPASS IN ACTIONS FOR PERSONAL INJURY

The following three modern cases (each of them based on flawed logic) have progressively limited the role of trespass *in personal injury law*.

Fowler v Lanning [1959] 1 QB 426

The plaintiff's statement of claim, which was expressed in terms of trespass to the person, asserted simply that 'the defendant shot the plaintiff'. No particulars of negligence (nor of intention) were set out. The defendant argued that this statement of claim 'disclosed no cause of action'; and that the plaintiff must at least allege negligence, setting out facts which would support a finding of negligence.

Diplock J interpreted the issue at stake in terms of burden of proof. In a trespass action, was the burden on the defendant to show that the injury was caused by 'inevitable accident'? This would treat 'due care' as (in effect) a *defence* to the action. Alternatively, was the burden on the plaintiff to show that the shooting was either intentional, or negligent? Diplock J decided the latter was the case, and the burden of alleging and showing carelessness was on the plaintiff.

Trespass had to be either intentional, or negligent, and the plaintiff had to establish that this was so. (It is important to note that *Letang v Cooper*, below, went a step further, and said that battery was an *intentional* tort.)

Fowler v Lanning, **Diplock J**, at 439

I think that what appears to have been the practice of the profession during the present century is sound in law. I can summarise the law as I understand it from my examination of the cases as follows:

(1) Trespass to the person does not lie if the injury to the plaintiff, although the direct consequence of the act of the defendant, was caused unintentionally and without negligence on the defendant's part.

(2) Trespass to the person on the highway does not differ in this respect from trespass to the person committed in any other place.

(3) If it were right to say with Blackburn J. in 1866 that negligence is a necessary ingredient of unintentional trespass only where the circumstances are such as to show that the plaintiff had taken upon himself the risk of inevitable injury (i.e., injury which is the result of neither intention nor carelessness on the part of the defendant), the plaintiff must today in this crowded world be considered as taking upon himself the risk of inevitable injury from any acts of his neighbour which, in the absence of damage to the plaintiff, would not in themselves be unlawful—of which discharging a gun at a shooting party in 1957 or a trained band exercise in 1617 are obvious examples. . . .

(4) The onus of proving negligence, where the trespass is not intentional, lies upon the plaintiff, whether the action be framed in trespass or in negligence. . . .

Glanville Williams, noting this case at [1959] CLJ 33, wondered why this should not be an appropriate case for invoking the maxim *res ipsa loquitur* which applies in the tort of negligence (Chapter 3.1.4): given the known hazards of carrying a fire arm, an injury of this nature would not generally occur *without* negligence. It might be argued that the mere fact of being shot by the defendant *does* disclose a cause of action, unless the defendant brings some evidence supporting an innocent explanation.[17]

Diplock J seemed to suggest that in trespass, the relevant *intention* or *carelessness* (if it exists) is intention or carelessness *as to the injury*. He argues that trespass does not lie 'if the *injury* to the plaintiff . . . was caused unintentionally and without negligence on the plaintiff's part' (emphasis added). We have proposed that the relevant intention relates only to *contact*.

It is suggested that not too much should be read into Diplock J's words in this respect, since the issue was not crucial to *Fowler v Lanning*. The case involved a shooting incident, and in such a case intention to injure or carelessness as to injury are ordinarily identical with the

---

[17] *Res ipsa loquitur* probably does not reverse the burden of proof, but places on the defendant the task of showing *some* evidence weighing against an inference of negligence.

intention to have physical contact (ie, to shoot). If there is intention to shoot then there typically is intention to injure;[18] if there is carelessness as to shooting, then there is surely carelessness in respect of injury. The same goes for accidents on the highway. In these 'accident' cases, trespass and negligence might have overlapped very strongly but for the next case extracted, which effectively removed trespass from the law of 'accidents'.

Letang v Cooper [1965] 1 QB 232

It may be wondered why anyone would frame their action in terms of trespass, if the facts could also be said to support a claim in negligence. One reason is that the claimant may not have any knowledge at all about the incident and why it happened, so that they cannot prove lack of care. This probably explains the claim in *Fowler v Lanning* (above), but since Diplock J's decision in that case trespass torts will be unable to assist a claimant in these circumstances (although if the claim is brought in negligence, the maxim *res ipsa loquitur* may do so). Another, more technical reason explains our next case although, as we will go on to explain, the incentive to prefer trespass for this reason no longer exists. In fact, a claimant would now have reason to prefer negligence.

In *Letang v Cooper*, the plaintiff alleged that she was sunbathing in the grounds of a Cornish hotel when the defendant drove his car over her legs, causing her personal injury. She brought her action in trespass to the person, rather than negligence, for the simple reason that she had run out of time to bring the negligence action. The claim was 'time barred'. To understand this case, we must therefore say something about 'limitation of actions'.

Limitation of actions: the problem in Letang v Cooper

In general, tort actions must be brought within a period of six years from the time that the action 'accrues' (in this case, the time of the impact and consequent injury).[19] However, according to the legislation in place at the time of this incident, the available time was reduced to a period of three years 'in the case of actions for damages for negligence, nuisance or breach of duty . . . where the damages claimed by the plaintiff . . . consist of or include damages in respect of personal injuries to any person'.[20]

A period of over three years had elapsed, so an action in negligence was plainly out of time, but what of an action in trespass to the person? This sort of action was not mentioned by name in the relevant statutory provision quoted above, and the first instance judge held that the action in trespass attracted the general six year limitation period. The Court of Appeal reversed this decision.

Lord Denning MR, *Letang v Cooper,* at 238–40

The argument, as it was developed before us, became a direct invitation to this court to go back to the old forms of action and to decide this case by reference to them. The statute bars an action on the case, it is said, after three years, whereas trespass to the person is not barred for six years. The argument was supported by reference to text-writers, such as Salmond on Torts, 13th ed. (1961), p. 790. I must say that if we are, at this distance of time, to revive the

---

[18] Though not, admittedly, in relatively rare cases where there is an intention to disarm, for example.
[19] The rules of 'limitation' and their rationale are explained in Chapter 7.
[20] Law Reform (Limitation of Actions, etc) Act 1954, s 2(1).

distinction between trespass and case, we should get into the most utter confusion. The old common lawyers tied themselves in knots over it, and we should do the same. . . .

. . . These forms of action have served their day. They did at one time form a guide to substantive rights; but they do so no longer. Lord Atkin, in *United Australia Ltd. v. Barclays Bank Ltd.* [[1941] AC 1, 29] told us what to do about them: "When these ghosts of the past stand in the path of justice clanking their mediaeval chains the proper course for the judge is to pass through them undeterred."

The truth is that the distinction between trespass and case is obsolete. We have a different sub-division altogether. Instead of dividing actions for personal injuries into trespass (direct damage) or case (consequential damage), we divide the causes of action now according as the defendant did the injury intentionally or unintentionally. If one man intentionally applies force directly to another, the plaintiff has a cause of action in assault and battery, or, if you so please to describe it, in trespass to the person. "The least touching of another in anger is a battery," *per* Holt C.J. in *Cole v. Turner.* [(1704) 6 Mod. 149] If he does not inflict injury intentionally, but only unintentionally, the plaintiff has no cause of action today in trespass. His only cause of action is in negligence, and then only on proof of want of reasonable care. If the plaintiff cannot prove want of reasonable care, he may have no cause of action at all. Thus, it is not enough nowadays for the plaintiff to plead that "the defendant shot the plaintiff." He must also allege that he did it intentionally or negligently. If intentional, it is the tort of assault and battery. If negligent and causing damage, it is the tort of negligence.

The modern law on this subject was well expounded by Diplock J. in *Fowler v. Lanning*, with which I fully agree. But I would go this one step further: when the injury is not inflicted intentionally, but negligently, I would say that the only cause of action is negligence and not trespass. If it were trespass, it would be actionable without proof of damage; and that is not the law today.

In my judgment, therefore, the only cause of action in the present case, where the injury was unintentional, is negligence and is barred by reason of the express provision of the statute.

It is plain that Lord Denning sought to make trespass to the person depend upon 'intention'. This being the case, it is unfortunate that he slips here between references to 'inflicting injury intentionally', and 'intentionally applying force directly to another'. These two approaches specify different 'targets of intention'. The correct approach was clarified by a later Court of Appeal, in *Wilson v Pringle* (extracted further below):[21]

Croom-Johnson LJ, *Wilson v Pringle* [1987] QB 237, at 249–50

The judgment of Lord Denning M.R. [in *Letang v Cooper*] was widely phrased, but it was delivered in an action where the only contact between the plaintiff and the defendant was unintentional. . . . In our view, . . . [I]t is the act and not the injury which must be intentional. An intention to injure is not essential to an action for trespass to the person. It is the mere trespass by itself which is the offence.

[21] This aspect of the judgment in *Wilson v Pringle* is not called into doubt by the developments in cases such as *In Re F* [1990] 2 AC 1, also extracted below.

To return to *Letang v Cooper*, Lord Denning turned next to the statutory wording. As we will see, this part of his reasoning was subsequently disapproved by the House of Lords in *Stubbings v Webb* (below).

Lord Denning MR, *Letang v Cooper* at 241–2

So we come back to construe the words of the statute with reference to the law of this century and not of past centuries. So construed, they are perfectly intelligible. The tort of negligence is firmly established. So is the tort of nuisance. These are given by the legislature as sign-posts. Then these are followed by words of the most comprehensive description: "Actions for . . . breach of duty (whether the duty exists by virtue of a contract or of a provision made by or under a statute or independently of any contract or any such provision)." Those words seem to me to cover not only a breach of a contractual duty, or a statutory duty, but also a breach of any duty under the law of tort. Our whole law of tort today proceeds on the footing that there is a duty owed by every man not to injure his neighbour in a way forbidden by law. Negligence is a breach of such a duty. So is nuisance. So is trespass to the person. So is false imprisonment, malicious prosecution or defamation of character. Professor Winfield indeed defined "tortious liability" by saying that it "arises from the breach of a duty primarily fixed by the law: this duty is towards persons generally and its breach is redressible by an action for unliquidated damages": See Winfield on Tort, 7th ed. (1963), p. 5.

In my judgment, therefore, the words "breach of duty" are wide enough to comprehend the cause of action for trespass to the person as well as negligence. In support of this view, I would refer to the decision of this court in *Billings v. Reed*, [[1945] KB 11] where Lord Greene M.R. gave the phrase "breach of duty" a similar wide construction. I would also refer to the valuable judgment in Australia of Adam J. in *Kruber v. Grzesiak* [[1963] 2 VR 621]. The Victorian Act is in the self-same words as ours; and I would, with gratitude, adopt his interpretation of it.

I come, therefore, to the clear conclusion that the plaintiff's cause of action here is barred by the Statute of Limitations. Her only cause of action here, in my judgment, where the damage was unintentional, was negligence and not trespass to the person. It is therefore barred by the word "negligence" in the statute. But even if it was trespass to the person, it was an action for "breach of duty" and is barred on that ground also.

Diplock LJ took a different (but equally dubious) route to the conclusion that trespass and negligence were mutually exclusive.

Diplock LJ, at 244–5

The factual situation upon which the plaintiff's action was founded is set out in the statement of claim. It was that the defendant, by failing to exercise reasonable care, of which failure particulars were given, drove his motor car over the plaintiff's legs and so inflicted upon her direct personal injuries in respect of which the plaintiff claimed damages. That factual situation was the plaintiff's cause of action. It was the cause of action for which the plaintiff claimed damages in respect of the personal injuries which she sustained. That cause of action or factual situation falls within the description of the tort of negligence and an action founded on it, that is, brought to obtain the remedy to which the existence of that factual situation entitles the plaintiff, falls within the description of an action for negligence. The description "negligence" was in fact used by the plaintiff's pleader; but this cannot be decisive for we are concerned not with the description applied by the pleader to the factual situation and the action founded on it, but with the description applied to it by Parliament in the enactment to be construed. It is true that that factual situation also falls within the description of the tort of trespass to the person. But that, as I have endeavoured to show, does not mean that there are two causes of action. It merely means that there are two apt descriptions of the same cause of action. It does not cease to be the tort of negligence because it can also be called by another name. An action founded upon it is nonetheless an action for negligence because it can also be called an action for trespass to the person.

It is not, I think, necessary to consider whether there is today any respect in which a cause of action for unintentional as distinct from intentional trespass to the person is not equally aptly described as a cause of action for negligence. The difference stressed by Elwes J. that actual damage caused by failure to exercise reasonable care forms an essential element in the cause of action for negligence, but does not in the cause of action in trespass to the person, is, I think, more apparent than real when the trespass is unintentional; for, since the duty of care, whether in negligence or in unintentional trespass to the person, is to take reasonable care to avoid causing actual damage to one's neighbour, there is no breach of the duty unless actual damage is caused. Actual damage is thus a necessary ingredient in unintentional as distinct from intentional trespass to the person. But whether this be so or not, the subsection which falls to be construed is concerned only with actions in which actual damage in the form of personal injuries has in fact been sustained by the plaintiff. Where this factor is present, every factual situation which falls within the description "trespass to the person" is, where the trespass is unintentional, equally aptly described as negligence. I am therefore of opinion that the facts pleaded in the present action make it an action "for negligence . . . where the damages claimed by the plaintiff for the negligence . . . consist of or include damages in respect of personal injuries to" the plaintiff, within the meaning of the subsection, and that the limitation period was three years.

As we saw, Lord Denning proposed that 'trespass' is only an apt description where the act in question is 'intentional'. Diplock LJ (a little more obscurely) said that the facts should only be *described* in one way. If the contact was careless rather than deliberate, the facts should be described in terms of negligence, even if they could also be said to disclose a trespass; and the rules of negligence should apply. There should be no overlap between different torts with different reasoning. (He did not explain why it was the *negligence* reasoning that should prevail.)

The Diplock approach was pertinently criticized by J. A. Jolowicz in the following note. Jolowicz pointed out that the abolition of the 'forms of action' was meant only to banish *procedural* consequences. Indeed, the abolition of 'forms of action' was meant to have precisely the opposite of the effect proposed by Diplock LJ. It should now be possible to argue alternative torts *with different substantive rules* alongside one another, instead of choosing a single *procedure* and being restricted accordingly.

J. A. Jolowicz, 'Forms of Action—Causes of Action—Trespass and Negligence' [1964] CLJ 200, at 202

It is . . . true, or should be true, that no *procedural* consequences flow from the pleader's choice of description for his cause of action. It is not true, however, that no consequences flow from the fact that more than one description is appropriate for a given factual situation. If the *substantive* rules appropriate to one description entitle the plaintiff to succeed it is no answer for the defendant to say that according to the rules appropriate to a different but equally apt description the plaintiff's action fails. If for example I say that X, a trader, is selling goods which he knows to have been stolen, my words may be described as 'slander of title' (or 'injurious falsehood'), a tort in which actual malice is required. But they are also aptly described as slander actionable *per se* and therefore, if the words are in fact untrue, it is no defence for me to prove that I honestly believed what I said. This, indeed, is the principal consequence of the so-called abolition of the forms of action. It is not necessarily true that only one description of the factual situation is apt. And if the court proceeds to confine itself to one set of rules only where more than one apply, it is, in effect, restoring to the forms of action—these "ghosts of the past"—much of their former prominence, not passing through them undeterred.

A host of recent cases could be cited to prove Jolowicz's point. They allow a number of substantive torts to be argued on the same set of facts, leading to success in one despite inevitable failure in others. For example, it is clear that a claimant may succeed in negligence or malicious falsehood while failing, or being otherwise unable to proceed, in libel: *Spring v Guardian Assurance* [1985] 2 AC 296 (Chapter 6); *Kaye v Robertson* [1991] FSR 92 (Chapter 14); *Joyce v Sengupta* [1993] 1 WLR 337. *Ashley v Chief Constable of Sussex* (extracted earlier in this section) is another clear illustration.

The judgment of Diplock J in *Letang v Cooper* might appear to state that negligence and trespass are mutually exclusive: the facts should give rise to a claim in negligence, or in trespass, but not both. This, however, is not the case. This is further illustrated by *Bici*.

In *Bici v Ministry of Defence* [2004] EWHC 786 (the facts of which we outlined earlier), Elias J recognized that shooting could involve *both* a breach of a duty of care towards the person shot (negligence), *and* the intentional tort of trespass towards that person. As we saw above (Section 2.1), the soldiers were held liable in trespass to a person who was shot accidentally, when they had intended to hit someone else. The basis for this was the doctrine of 'transferred intent'. Elias J dealt explicitly with an argument that this was inconsistent with *Letang v Cooper*:

70   [Counsel] contends that this principle [transferred malice or intent] is inconsistent with the well-known case of *Letang v Cooper* . . . where the Court of Appeal held that a negligent trespass to the person could only be pursued in negligence and not in trespass. The identical argument was run and rejected in *Livingstone*.[22] As Hutton J pointed out, the observations of the Court in *Letang* do not preclude a court finding liability in trespass where there is intention to apply force to someone; the claimant as the injured party sues because of the intentionally wrongful act.

Unfortunately, a possible confusion is introduced by the reference in the last few words of this extract to an 'intentionally wrongful act'. We have seen that trespass does not need to be *intentionally wrongful*; and indeed the soldiers in *Bici* were thought to have had no intention to act wrongfully. They intended to shoot someone who (they believed) posed an immediate threat to their safety. They were liable not because they intended to act wrongfully, but because they misjudged the situation and their action therefore fell outside the protection of 'self-defence'.[23]

Bici shows that whether an intentional contact will also be actionable in *negligence* depends on whether a duty of care was owed to the person harmed, and whether that duty was breached. In principle, if there is such a duty (as there is between peace-keeping forces and

---

[22] *Livingstone v Ministry of Defence* [1984] NILR 356.
[23] A defence to trespass torts: see below.

local civilians—although not of course between hostile armies engaged in war), then it is possible to breach it through intentional action, as well as through careless action. Negligence and trespass can, in such circumstances, coexist.

It is important to note that this coexistence is not confined to cases of 'transferred intent', like *Bici*. In *Ashley v CC West Sussex* (above), the police officer fully intended to shoot the deceased, but claimed that he did so 'lawfully' (in reasonable self-defence). Again, the claim was arguable both in negligence, and in trespass.

Summary: trespass and negligence in personal injury cases

In the case of direct and *intentional* contact, both trespass and negligence can apply to the same facts, provided that (for the negligence action) a 'duty of care' was owed and breached. The same will be true in the special case of 'transferred intent', where there was an intention to have physical contact with someone, but this was not the claimant. In the case of merely *negligent* contact however, the effect of *Letang v Cooper* is that any action will be governed by the rules of negligence. In effect, only the negligence action may be pursued.

Stubbings v Webb [1993] AC 498

We have seen that in *Letang v Cooper*, Lord Denning argued that trespass involves a 'breach of duty' so that, in a case involving personal injury, it could not attract a more generous limitation period than negligence.

In *Stubbings v Webb* the House of Lords had to decide which limitation period applied to a case of alleged sexual abuse occasioning lasting psychiatric harm. The relevant acts, if proven, would clearly amount to trespass to the person as the physical contact was 'intentional'.

The limitation problem in Stubbings v Webb

The applicable limitation period in *Stubbings v Webb* was determined by the Limitation Act 1980.[24] Section 11(1) of this Act used the same wording as the earlier statutory provision considered in *Letang v Cooper* to define the actions which must be brought within three years. Now however, it would be beneficial to the claimant to argue that trespass should be treated in the *same* way as negligence (the conclusion reached by Lord Denning, but not by Diplock LJ,[25] in *Letang v Cooper*).

Limitation Act 1980

Special time limit for actions in respect of personal injuries

11.—(1) This section applies to any action for damages for negligence, nuisance or breach of duty (whether the duty exists by virtue of a contract or of provision made by or under a statute or independently of any contract or any such provision) where the damages claimed by the plaintiff for the negligence, nuisance or breach of duty consist of or include damages in respect of personal injuries to the plaintiff or any other person.

. . .

---

[24] See Chapter 7 where a general account of this statute will be found.
[25] Diplock LJ, it will be recalled, did not say that trespass was within the wording of the section; he said instead that where trespass is careless, it 'is' negligence. This should have no impact on a case of 'deliberate' trespass, like *Stubbings v Webb*.

(4) . . . the period applicable is three years from—

(a) the date on which the cause of action accrued; or

(b) the date of knowledge (if later) of the person injured.

14.—(1) In sections 11 and 12 of this Act references to a person's date of knowledge are references to the date on which he first had knowledge of the following facts—

(a) that the injury in question was significant; and

(b) that the injury was attributable in whole or in part to the act or omission which is alleged to constitute negligence, nuisance or breach of duty; and

. . .

In addition, section 33 of the Limitation Act 1980 gives the court discretion to allow a claim to be brought *outside* the existing time limit, *but only in those cases which fall within section 11.* Claims which do not come within the wording of section 11 cannot benefit from this extended limitation period.

Application in Stubbings v Webb

The plaintiff in *Stubbings v Webb* argued that the requirements of section 141(b) had not been satisfied in her case until some years after the acts of abuse themselves, which took place during childhood.

The House of Lords held however that trespass to the person in the form of rape and sexual abuse did *not* fall within section 11. Therefore, section 14 was also not applicable. Trespass was subject to a non-extendable limitation period of six years, which would begin to run when the victim reached adulthood; whereas a negligence claim would have been extended *at least* until three years from the plaintiff's date of knowledge. The claim was out of time.

Lord Griffiths was inappropriately sceptical that an individual who had been subjected to serious sexual abuse and rape in childhood could be 'unaware' that their subsequent mental problems flowed from these acts:

Lord Griffiths, at 506

The plaintiff's case was that although she knew she had been raped by one defendant and had been persistently sexually abused by the other she did not realise she had suffered sufficiently serious injury to justify starting proceedings for damages until she realised that there might be a causal link between psychiatric problems she had suffered in adult life and her sexual abuse as a child. The Court of Appeal after considerable hesitation accepted this argument on behalf of the plaintiff. If it was necessary to decide the point I should not have found it easy to agree with the Court of Appeal. Personal injury is defined in section 38 of the Act of 1980 as including "any impairment of a person's physical or mental condition" and I have the greatest difficulty in accepting that a woman who knows that she has been raped does not know that she has suffered a significant injury.

It is now more clearly recognized that acts of abuse in childhood may cause lasting psychiatric harm and that the victims of abuse often require counselling before they can understand the causal link to later problems.[26] The nature of such cases was more sensitively handled both

---

[26] See J. Conaghan, 'Tort Litigation in the Context of Intra-Familial Abuse' (1998) 61 MLR 132.

by the Court of Appeal in *Stubbings v Webb* itself and by a later Court of Appeal in the following case. Since the passage from Lord Griffiths' judgment above was simply a 'dictum' (and not the reason for his decision), the Court of Appeal was able to decide not to follow its logic.

In *KR v Bryn Alyn*, 14 claimants alleged that they had been sexually abused while in care at residential homes run by the defendant. Their claims were in negligence.

Auld LJ, *KR v Bryn Alyn Community (Holdings) Ltd* [2003] 1 QB 1441

42   However artificial it may seem to pose the question in this context, section 14 requires the court, on a case by case basis, to ask whether such an already damaged child would reasonably turn his mind to litigation as a solution to his problems? . . . it might only be after the intervention of a psychiatrist that a claimant realises that there could have been a causal link between the childhood abuse and the psychiatric problems suffered as an adult, an argument accepted by the Court of Appeal, but which Lord Griffiths found difficult to accept, in *Stubbings v Webb*.

43   The posing of such questions may have become less artificial in recent years. As a result of the publicity given to inquiries of the sort conducted by Sir Ronald Waterhouse in 1997 and 1998 and the disturbing increase in the number of criminal prosecutions and civil suits for child abuse, some of it a very long time ago. The momentum of increase in public awareness of such conduct, of which Bingham LJ spoke in 1992 in *Stubbings v Webb* [1992] QB 197 is likely to have begun to usher in a generation more sensitive to its seriousness and "significance" in a section 14(2) sense.

This statement about the likely state of mind of the victim of sexual abuse remains persuasive. But its relevance to interpretation of section 14(2) has recently been doubted: *Catholic Care (Diocese of Leeds) v Young* [2006] EWCA Civ 1534 (Court of Appeal). This more recent case will have significant adverse effect on claimants suing in negligence in respect of childhood sexual abuse. Issues relating to section 14 are further discussed in Chapter 7.

On the other hand, it is true to say that such claims also display precisely the characteristics which require the adoption of limitation rules as a matter of policy and justice. Defendants may be faced with claims many years after the alleged events, causing considerable problems with the gathering of evidence and creating genuine uncertainty and anxiety.[27]

In any event, the interpretation of section 14 was not the basis of the decision in *Stubbings v Webb*. Instead, Lord Griffiths accepted an argument which had been rejected by Lord Denning in *Letang v Cooper*.[28] By reference to the recommendations of the Tucker Committee,[29] Lord Griffiths argued that the 'date of knowledge' qualifications applicable from 1954 onwards

---

[27] In *Stubbings v UK* [1996] ECHR 44; [1997] 1 FLR 105, an argument that the English law on limitation as interpreted in *Stubbings v Webb* was in violation of Article 6 ECHR was rejected by the European Court of Human Rights. The limitation in time within which an action could be brought was not disproportionate to the policy and justice goals of limitation. The available period was, indeed, longer than the period allowed for in many international treaties.

[28] He did so on the basis that courts were now free, following the decision in *Pepper v Hart* [1993] AC 593, to consult the record of Parliamentary debates through *Hansard*, in order to construe the intentions of the proposer of a statute. This is a supplement to interpretation of the words of the statute themselves, and was not an accepted technique at the time of *Letang*.

[29] Report of the Committee on the Limitation of Actions 1949 (Cmd. 7740).

were *intended* (by their drafters) only to cover what he called 'accident cases', not *intentional* assaults. He also considered that Lord Denning had been wrong to say that 'trespass to the person' involves a 'breach of duty':

Lord Griffiths, *Stubbings v Webb*, at 508

Even without reference to Hansard I should not myself have construed breach of duty as including a deliberate assault. The phrase lying in juxtaposition with negligence and nuisance carries with it the implication of a breach of duty of care not to cause personal injury, rather than an obligation not to infringe any legal right of another person. If I invite a lady to my house one would naturally think of a duty to take care that the house is safe but would one really be thinking of a duty not to rape her? But, however this may be, the terms in which this Bill was introduced to my mind make it clear beyond peradventure that the intention was to give effect to the Tucker recommendation that the limitation period in respect of trespass to the person was not to be reduced to three years but should remain at six years. The language of section 2(1) of the Act of 1954 is in my view apt to give effect to that intention, and cases of deliberate assault such as we are concerned with in this case are not actions for breach of duty within the meaning of section 2(1) of the Act of 1954.

Stubbings v Webb further limits the reach of trespass in cases of *actual personal injury*. It is all very well to argue that in an accident case such as *Letang* the job will be done instead by the tort of negligence, but this argument does not help in the case of deliberate sexual assaults. In a case of sexual abuse, it is unlikely that a court would accept that the defendant has acted 'negligently'. [30] The problem is illustrated by cases where there is also a claim in negligence against a third party who *fails to prevent* abuse. A claim against such a person may benefit from an extended limitation period, thanks to sections 14 and 33.

This was illustrated in *S v W* [1995] 1 FLR 862. The plaintiff had been abused by her father (the first defendant) during childhood. Her father had been convicted on several charges of incest. The claimant brought civil actions both against her father (in trespass), and against her mother, the second defendant, for failing to protect her or to report the acts of abuse. The Court of Appeal held that the action against the mother was an action in negligence and was not out of time. The action against the father was statute-barred on the authority of *Stubbings v Webb*. Millett LJ criticized the reasoning in *Stubbings v Webb* but the Court of Appeal could not, of course, depart from a House of Lords decision.

The anomaly has not so far been removed, but as mentioned above the interpretation of section 14 in negligence cases is itself becoming more restrictive. (There is further discussion of the impact of *Stubbings v Webb* and the choice of tort in claims of abuse in Chapters 7 and 9.)

Summary

While *Letang v Cooper* effectively removed trespass from the law of accidents, *Stubbings v Webb* has impaired the ability of trespass to provide remedies for certain 'non-accidental'

[30] In fact there is no definitive reason to think that the tort of negligence *only* applies to unintended harms, as *Bici* and *Ashley* (above) both illustrate. The question in negligence is whether a duty of care is owed, and was breached. For example, a person who deliberately drives into another vehicle would surely be in breach of the duty of care owed to other road users. A similar point is made by Tan Feng Keng, 'Failure of Medical Advice: Trespass or Negligence' (1987) LS 149, at note 53: negligence 'is a legal liability relationship where a duty is determined to exist and there is a breach of this negligently or intentionally . . .'.

personal injuries. Where sexual abuse is concerned, this creates a serious anomaly in the civil law since the tort of negligence is generally thought (rightly or wrongly) not to apply to the primary wrongdoer. If so, then in a range of very important circumstances it is easier to proceed against a secondary party (who has not prevented or reported the injury, or not supervised the abuser, for example), than against the primary wrongdoer.

Important Note: 'Intention' and Sexual Battery

Stubbings v Webb and *S v W* draw our attention back to the meaning of 'intention'. Naturally enough, it tends to be assumed that acts of sexual abuse are a distinctively 'intentional' instance of trespass to the person, unlike shooting people or running them over which may quite typically be done carelessly, and (in the latter case) only exceptionally deliberately. But a moment's reflection will show that even here, the idea of 'intention' does not turn on intention to cause harm—nor even on intention to *do wrong.*

Some sexual abusers no doubt *intend to do harm*; others intend to act without consent and in this sense *intend to override the will of another person* or to *do what is prohibited*; others do not intend any of these and believe they are doing no harm, or wrong, at all. The latter are still guilty of **criminal offences**. Under the Sexual Offences Act 2003 the required state of mind for the offences is defined in terms of intended physical contact of a 'sexual' nature, in circumstances where there is no reasonable belief in having acquired a valid consent.[31] Special offences relating to sexual conduct with children do not allow for consent to be relevant at all, presumably because children are deemed to be incapable of consent.[32] The definition of the state of mind required for rape—absence of reasonable belief in consent—in no way requires that the defendant *intended* intercourse to be non-consensual.

For sexual offences then, the touching by the defendant of the victim must be 'intentional', but the actual wrong (between adults, the non-consensual nature of the touching) need not. Therefore, criminal law defining sexual offences exhibits a very similar idea of 'wrongdoing' to the one we have identified in trespass to the person. In both criminal and civil law relating to unlawful *sexual* contact, the 'wrong' is supplied by inappropriateness or unlawfulness together with (or incorporating) lack of valid consent. It is not primarily supplied by intention.

2.4 BATTERY: THE NATURE OF THE REQUIRED CONTACT

So far, we have said that intentional and direct touching of the claimant amounts to a battery. We will see below (Defences) that valid consent, necessity, or self-defence will render lawful what would otherwise be a battery. But even so, this definition is very broad. How have the courts limited the scope of the tort?

---

[31] Generally, even the sexual nature of the contact is defined by law, not by reference to the intention of the defendant. On the other hand, a defendant may be able to argue that there was no sexual intention in the case of ambiguous contact, such as kissing: s 78(b). For analysis see J. Temkin and A. Ashworth, 'The Sexual Offences Act 2003: Rape, Sexual Assaults and the Problems of Consent' [2004] *Crim L Rev* 328–46; E. Finch and V. Munro, 'Breaking Boundaries: Sexual Consent in the Jury Room' (2006) 26 LS 303–320.

[32] This incapacity was spelt out in previous legislation, but is not now: J. R. Spencer, 'The Sexual Offences Act 2003: Child and Family Offences' [2004] *Crim L Rev* 347–60.

Collins v Wilcock [1984] 1 WLR 1172

The plaintiff police officer had cautioned the defendant prostitute. When the defendant walked away, the officer took hold of her arm. The defendant scratched the officer's restraining arm. In the Court of Appeal, the *defendant* argued that the police officer had committed a battery in holding her. The Court of Appeal accepted the defendant's argument. There was no implied power upon the officer to detain the defendant for the purpose of the caution. The touching went beyond conduct which is generally accepted. It was a trespass, so that the officer could not be said to have been acting in the course of her duty. The conviction was quashed.

Robert Goff LJ analysed the older case law and presented it in an updated and clarified form. His formulation is adapted to define the limits of appropriate intervention by public officials such as police officers.

Robert Goff LJ, at 1177

We are here concerned primarily with battery. The fundamental principle, plain and incontestable, is that every person's body is inviolate. It has long been established that any touching of another person, however slight, may amount to a battery. So Holt C.J. held in *Cole v. Turner* (1704) 6 Mod. 149 that "the least touching of another is anger is a battery." The breadth of the principle reflects the fundamental nature of the interest so protected. As Blackstone wrote in his *Commentaries*, 17th ed. (1830), vol. 3, p. 120:

> "the law cannot draw the line between different degrees of violence, and therefore totally prohibits the first and lowest stage of it; every man's person being sacred, and no other having a right to meddle with it, in any the slightest manner."

The effect is that everybody is protected not only against physical injury but against any from of physical molestation.

But so widely drawn a principle must inevitably be subject to exceptions. For example, children may be subject to reasonable punishment; people may be subjected to the lawful exercise of the power of arrest; and reasonable force may be used in self-defence or for the prevention of crime. But, apart from these special instances where the control or constraint is lawful, a broader exception has been created to allow for the exigencies of everyday life. Generally speaking consent is a defence to battery; and most of the physical contacts of ordinary life are not actionable because they are impliedly consented to by all who move in society and so expose themselves to the risk of bodily contact. So nobody can complain of the jostling which is inevitable from his presence in, for example, a supermarket, an underground station or a busy street; nor can a person who attends a party complain if his hand is seized in friendship, or even if his back is, within reason, slapped: see *Tuberville v. Savage* (1669) 1 Mod. 3. Although such cases are regarded as examples of implied consent, it is more common nowadays to treat them as falling within a general exception embracing all physical contact which is generally acceptable in the ordinary conduct of daily life. We observe that, although in the past it has sometimes been stated that a battery is only committed where the action is "angry revengeful, rude, or insolent" (see *Hawkins, Pleas of the Crown*, 8th ed. (1824), vol. 1, c. 15, section 2), we think that nowadays it is more realistic, and indeed more accurate, to state the broad underlying principle, subject to the broad exception. . . .

'Wrongful' touching, amounting to a battery, is here defined as touching which goes beyond that which is generally acceptable. It does not need to be hostile or (certainly) to be aimed at

transferred malice

injuring the claimant. In *Wilson v Pringle* [1987] QB 237, a case of physical injury sustained in horseplay between schoolboys, a differently constituted Court of Appeal thought the above formulation too wide and impractical in application.

Croom-Johnson LJ, *Wilson v Pringle* at 252–3 (giving the judgment of the court)

. . . Robert Goff L.J.'s judgment [in *Collins v Wilcock*] is illustrative of the considerations which underlie such an action, but it is not practicable to define a battery as "physical contact which is not generally acceptable in the ordinary conduct of daily life."

In our view, the authorities lead one to the conclusion that in a battery there must be an intentional touching or contact in one form or another of the plaintiff by the defendant. That touching must be proved to be a hostile touching. That still leaves unanswered the question "when is a touching to be called hostile?" Hostility cannot be equated with ill-will or malevolence. It cannot be governed by the obvious intention shown in acts like punching, stabbing or shooting. It cannot be solely governed by an expressed intention, although that may be strong evidence. But the element of hostility, in the sense in which it is now to be considered, must be a question of fact for the tribunal of fact. It may be imported from the circumstances. Take the example of the police officer in *Collins v. Wilcock*. . . . She touched the woman deliberately, but without an intention to do more than restrain her temporarily. Nevertheless, she was acting unlawfully and in that way was acting with hostility. She was acting contrary to the woman's legal right not to be physically restrained. We see no more difficulty in establishing what she intended by means of question and answer, or by inference from the surrounding circumstances, than there is in establishing whether an apparently playful blow was struck in anger. The rules of law governing the legality of arrest may require strict application to the facts of appropriate cases, but in the ordinary give and take of everyday life the tribunal of fact should find no difficulty in answering the question "was this, or was it not, a battery?" Where the immediate act of touching does not itself demonstrate hostility, the plaintiff should plead the facts which are said to do so.

Although we are all entitled to protection from physical molestation we live in a crowded world in which people must be considered as taking on themselves some risk of injury (where it occurs) from the acts of others which are not in themselves unlawful. If negligence cannot be proved, it may be that an injured plaintiff who is also unable to prove a battery, will be without redress.

Croom-Johnson LJ reasons here that because the police officer's actions involved questions of *legality*, it should be easier to establish the necessary *extra* element, which is 'hostility', in such a case.

However, the very fact that the Court of Appeal was willing to describe the police officer's unauthorized act in *Collins v Wilcock* as 'hostile' shows how artificial that idea really is. In the next case extracted, Lord Goff (now in the House of Lords) restored the authority of the views he had set out in *Collins*. This case has been central to the development of medical law and to the modern law of trespass to the person.

In Re F (Mental Patient: Sterilization) [1990] 2 AC 1

The patient, who had the mental age of a small child, had formed a sexual relationship with a male patient. It was thought undesirable to prevent the relationship from being conducted, but it was also thought that the patient would be unable to cope with pregnancy or childbirth should she conceive. Sterilization was judged to be in her best interests, but since she was unable to comprehend the procedure or its purpose (and therefore could not validly consent) could the proposed operation be carried out without committing a trespass?

In the following passage, Lord Goff explains the relationship between *the definition of contact sufficient to amount to a trespass*; and *the defence of consent* (further considered in section 3.1).

Lord Goff, at 72–3

I start with the fundamental principle, now long established, that every person's body is inviolate. As to this, I do not wish to depart from what I myself said in the judgment of the Divisional Court in *Collins v. Wilcock* . . . , and in particular from the statement, at p. 1177, that the effect of this principle is that everybody is protected not only against physical injury but against any form of physical molestation.

Of course, as a general rule physical interference with another person's body is lawful if he consents to it; though in certain limited circumstances the public interest may require that his consent is not capable of rendering the act lawful. There are also specific cases where physical interference without consent may not be unlawful—chastisement of children, lawful arrest, self-defence, the prevention of crime, and so on. As I pointed out in *Collins v. Wilcock* [1984] 1 W.L.R. 1172, 1177, a broader exception has been created to allow for the exigencies of everyday life—jostling in a street or some other crowded place, social contact at parties, and such like. This exception has been said to be founded on implied consent, since those who go about in public places, or go to parties, may be taken to have impliedly consented to bodily contact of this kind. Today this rationalisation can be regarded as artificial; and in particular, it is difficult to impute consent to those who, by reason of their youth or mental disorder, are unable to give their consent. For this reason, I consider it more appropriate to regard such cases as falling within a general exception embracing all physical contact which is generally acceptable in the ordinary conduct of everyday life.

In the old days it used to be said that, for a touching of another's person to amount to a battery, it had to be a touching "in anger" (see *Cole v. Turner* (1794) 6 Mod. 149, *per* Holt C.J.); and it has recently been said that the touching must be "hostile" to have that effect (see *Wilson v. Pringle* [1987] Q.B. 237, 253). I respectfully doubt whether that is correct. A prank that gets out of hand; an over-friendly slap on the back; surgical treatment by a surgeon who mistakenly thinks that the patient has consented to it—all these things may transcend the bounds of lawfulness, without being characterised as hostile. Indeed the suggested qualification is difficult to reconcile with the principle that any touching of another's body is, in the absence of lawful excuse, capable of amounting to a battery and a trespass. Furthermore, in the case of medical treatment, we have to bear well in mind the libertarian principle of self-determination which, to adopt the words of Cardozo J. (in *Schloendorff v. Society of New York Hospital* (1914) 105 N.E. 92, 93) recognises that:

> "Every human being of adult years and sound mind has a right to determine what shall be done with his own body; and a surgeon who performs an operation without his patient's consent commits an assault . . . "

. . .

It is against this background that I turn to consider the question whether, and if so when, medical treatment or care of a mentally disordered person who is, by reason of his incapacity, incapable of giving his consent, can be regarded as lawful. As is recognised in Cardozo J.'s statement of principle, and elsewhere (see e.g. *Sidaway v. Board of Governors of the Bethlem*

Royal Hospital and the Maudsley Hospital [1985] A.C. 871, 882, *per* Lord Scarman), some relaxation of the law is required to accommodate persons of unsound mind. In *Wilson v. Pringle* [1987] Q.B. 237, the Court of Appeal considered that treatment or care of such persons may be regarded as lawful, as falling within the exception relating to physical contact which is generally acceptable in the ordinary conduct of everyday life. Again, I am with respect unable to agree. That exception is concerned with the ordinary events of everyday life—jostling in public places and such like—and affects all persons, whether or not they are capable of giving their consent. Medical treatment—even treatment for minor ailments—does not fall within that category of events. The general rule is that consent is necessary to render such treatment lawful. If such treatment administered without consent is not to be unlawful, it has to be justified on some other principle.

The case raised a fundamental question for medical law. Given that valid consent could not be obtained, was there an *alternative justification* for treatment, which would render it *not unlawful*?

One possible alternative was that treatment could be performed on the basis of 'necessity' (a recognized defence to trespass). But necessity is not a sufficiently generous principle: it would only justify a narrow range of emergency treatment. This might be adequate for those suffering a *temporary* lack of consciousness. Indeed, in such an instance it would be beneficial if surgeons did *not* feel entitled to carry out other work which they thought would on balance be for the best. But what of those suffering long-term or permanent lack of capacity? Lord Bridge pointed out a significant problem that might arise if only necessary treatment could lawfully be carried out:

Lord Bridge, *In re F*, at 52

It seems to me to be axiomatic that treatment which is necessary to preserve the life, health or well being of the patient may lawfully be given without consent. But if a rigid criterion of necessity were to be applied to determine what is and what is not lawful in the treatment of the unconscious and the incompetent, many of those unfortunate enough to be deprived of the capacity to make or communicate rational decisions by accident, illness or unsoundness of mind might be deprived of treatment which it would be entirely beneficial for them to receive.

Moreover, it seems to me of first importance that the common law should be readily intelligible to and applicable by all those who undertake the care of persons lacking the capacity to consent to treatment. It would be intolerable for members of the medical, nursing and other professions devoted to the care of the sick that, in caring for those lacking the capacity to consent to treatment they should be put in the dilemma that, if they administer the treatment which they believe to be in the patient's best interests, acting with due skill and care, they run the risk of being held guilty of trespass to the person, but if they withhold that treatment, they may be in breach of a duty of care owed to the patient. If those who undertake responsibility for the care of incompetent or unconscious patients administer curative or prophylactic treatment which they believe to be appropriate to the patient's existing condition of disease, injury or bodily malfunction or susceptibility to such a condition in the future, the lawfulness of that treatment should be judged by one standard, not two. It follows that if the professionals in question have acted with due skill and care, judged by the well known test laid down in *Bolam v. Friern Hospital Management Committee* [1957] 1 W.L.R. 582, they should be immune from liability in trespass, just as they are immune from liability in negligence.

The only solution was to say that all treatment which was *in the best interests of the patient* would be lawful. This approach will be codified by the Mental Capacity Act 2005, when the relevant sections come into force.[33]

In re F is also significant because of the order made by the court. The House of Lords found that where incompetent *adults* were concerned, the court had no jurisdiction to 'consent to' or 'approve' a particular operation as being in the patient's best interests.[34] However, the House of Lords decided that under the inherent jurisdiction of the High Court, it could make a **declaration** to the effect that the operation *was lawful*. Declarations of lawfulness have subsequently been widely used. By section 4(9) of the Mental Capacity Act 2005, a 'reasonable belief' that the decision made is in the patient's best interest will suffice to avoid civil liability (other than in negligence: section 5(3)).

3. DEFENCES TO ASSAULT AND BATTERY

3.1 CONSENT

It will be clear from *In re F* (above) that consent is a defence of the first importance in trespass to the person. Indeed, battery could potentially be defined as a direct, intended and non-consensual physical invasion. This difference would be of some practical importance, because it is generally for a *defendant* to show that a defence is made out, while a claimant must establish the main elements of a tort. To treat 'lack of consent' as part of the definition of trespass would therefore shift the burden of proof regarding consent from defendant, to claimant. Surprisingly perhaps, there is limited English authority on this important point.

In *Freeman v Home Office (No 2)* [1984] QB 524, McCowan J (at first instance) ruled (at 539–40) that the burden is on the *claimant* to establish his or her own *lack* of consent. His ruling seemed to contradict the various authorities he cited on the point (gleaned both from Commonwealth case law[35] and English textbooks). He was persuaded by an attractive argument put by counsel for the Home Office, to the effect that these authorities were principally concerned not with consent in the context of trespass, but with the rather different defence of *volenti* which can also be called 'willing acceptance of risk' (and which is certainly a defence to *negligence*: Chapter 5). It is true that 'consent' and *volenti* are separate defences, but this does not justify the conclusion that lack of consent is therefore not a defence at all. As such, we could accept the first three sentences of the following extract, while doubting the last four (in italics).

McCowan J, *Freeman v Home Office (No 2)*, at 539–40

Mr. Laws submits that volenti is consent to the risk of injury and is accordingly a defence most apt to a claim in negligence. What a plaintiff consents to in a case of alleged battery is not risk but a specific intrusion on his body. Therefore, consent to a surgical operation is not properly

---

[33] By section 1(5), an act done or decision made on behalf of a person who lacks capacity must be done (or made) in that person's 'best interest'. 'Best interests' are further defined in section 4. The first commencement order under the Mental Capacity Act (SI 2006/2814) brings into force only ss 35–41. Full commencement is expected in spring 2007.

[34] For the position with children (minors) who are incompetent to consent, see the discussion of *Re A (Conjoined Twin)*, below. Powers under the Mental Capacity Act 2005 will not apply where the person who lackes capacity is under the age of sixteen (section 2(5)).

[35] Particularly *Reibl v Hughes* (1980) 114 DLR (3d) 1.

an example of volenti. *[The action fails not because of volenti but because there is no tort. Volenti, he submits, does not arise at all unless the tort of battery, which he defines as "the unconsented to intrusion of another's bodily integrity" is made out. That definition, he says, meets the vice at which the tort is aimed. I accept Mr. Laws' submission and rule that the burden of providing absence of consent is on the plaintiff.]*

If the definition of trespass accepted by McCowan J was right, there would be no obvious reason why other issues which go to lawfulness—including self-defence—should not also be a part of the definition of trespass. In *Ashley v CC Sussex* [2006] EWCA Civ 1985, the Court of Appeal noted this controversy (at para [31]). The court declined to say whether it regarded *Freeman* as correct on this point. However, the court held—after prolonged analysis of civil and criminal authorities—that *self-defence* was for the *defendant* to establish. Consent was not directly in issue.

This particular point in McCowan J's judgment did not fall for decision on appeal, since it was no longer relevant. It was treated as clear that the plaintiff *had indeed consented to* the administration of drugs.[36] However, Lord Donaldson helpfully pointed out that consent and *volenti* may both arise in a trespass action:

Freeman v Home Office (No 2) [1984] QB 524, at 557

The maxim "volenti non fit injuria" can be roughly translated as "You cannot claim damages if you have asked for it," and "it" is something which is and remains a tort. The maxim, where it applies, provides a bar to enforcing a cause of action. It does not negative the cause of action itself. This is a wholly different concept from consent which, in this context, deprives the act of its tortious character. "Volenti" would be a defence in the unlikely scenario of a patient being held not to have in fact consented to treatment, but having by his conduct caused the doctor to believe that he had consented.

Consent to Medical Treatment: Two Types of Problem Case

Consent to medical treatment has been a significant issue in two very different types of case. The first type of case concerns the lawfulness of treatment in the absence of consent. In fact this category is further divided into cases where treatment is *refused*; and other cases where valid consent simply cannot be obtained. The second type of case concerns treatment where consent is given, but that consent is not based on sufficient knowledge about the treatment or its likely consequences.

Type 1: Treatment without Consent

Refusal

Where a competent adult refuses treatment, it is unlawful (amounting to the tort of battery and also potentially to a criminal offence against the person) to inflict that treatment upon him or her. This is the case even if the likely or inevitable result of refusal is the patient's death. The patient does not need to have any rational grounds for refusal, nor any grounds for refusal

---

[36] The decision in *Sidaway v Bethlem Royal Hospital* [1984] QB 493 had meanwhile made it clear that only broad knowledge of the treatment is required for consent to be valid and effective.

at all. In other words, the *right of self-determination* (which is underpinned by the value of autonomy) is a trump card, which overrides the patient's best interests. Even sanctity of life does not outweigh the patient's right to self-determination. At least, that is the principle.

The role of autonomy as a trump card has been stated many times by English courts.

Lord Donaldson MR, *In re T (Adult: Refusal of Treatment)* [1993] Fam 95, at 112

The conflict of principle

This situation gives rise to a conflict between two interests, that of the patient and that of the society in which he lives. The patient's interest consists of his right to self-determination—his right to live his own life how he wishes, even if it will damage his health or lead to his premature death. Society's interest is in upholding the concept that all human life is sacred and that it should be preserved if at all possible. It is well established that in the ultimate the right of the individual is paramount. But this merely shifts the problem where the conflict occurs and calls for a very careful examination of whether, and if so the way in which, the individual is exercising that right. In case of doubt, that doubt falls to be resolved in favour of the preservation of life for if the individual is to override the public interest, he must do so in clear terms.

Butler-Sloss LJ, *Re MB* [1997] 2 FCR 541

A competent woman who has the capacity to decide may, for religious reasons, other reasons, for rational or irrational reasons or no reasons at all, choose not to have medical intervention, even though . . . the consequence may be death or serious handicap of the child she bears, or her own death.

Lord Phillips MR, *R v GMC* [2005] EWCA Civ 1003

30 . . . treating a patient in the manner that doctors consider in his best interests may be at odds with his wishes. . . . Where a competent patient makes it clear that he does not wish to receive treatment which is, objectively, in his best interests, it is unlawful for doctors to administer that treatment. Personal autonomy or the right to self-determination prevails.

If an adult patient is competent and withholds consent, nobody may say what is in his or her best interests, nor even what is 'necessary'. As we saw above in our discussion of the House of Lords' decision in *In re F*, if the patient is judged *not competent to consent*, then not only is it lawful to administer 'necessary' treatment, but also (where incompetence is likely to be long-term, rather than transient), to care for the patient according to his or her best interests. Indeed there is a duty to do so, enforced by the tort of negligence.

On the other hand, despite these clear statements, in none of the cases from which we have just quoted was there held to be a valid refusal to consent to treatment. *R v GMC* was not a refusal of treatment case at all, but quite the reverse: the terminally ill applicant sought a declaration that doctors should not *be able to withdraw* artificial feeding if, in future, they judged cessation of treatment to be in his best interests. *In re MB* and *In re T* on the other hand were refusal of treatment cases. Their outcomes illustrate that despite the weight of judicial statements supporting the right to refuse life-saving treatment, courts may often find a way of ruling that on the facts, the *refusal* of treatment is invalid.

In Re T (Adult: Refusal of Treatment) [1993] Fam 95

The patient had been raised as a Jehovah's witness, although the level of her commitment to the faith was doubtful. She consented to undergo an emergency caesarean section but, probably under the influence of her mother, made it known that she did not wish to receive a blood transfusion. She signed a refusal form.[37] Her condition deteriorated and it was judged that a transfusion was vital to her well-being. The hospital applied to the court for a declaration that the transfusion would be lawful, notwithstanding the general *refusal* of consent.

It was found that the refusal of consent *was not effective*, since the patient had been strongly influenced by the wishes of her mother, had been wrongly advised as to alternatives, and had probably not anticipated the grave situation which had developed. The transfusion could be administered on the basis of **necessity**.

In Re MB [1997] 2 FCR 541

The pregnant patient needed a caesarean in order to save the life of her unborn child. She consented to the operation itself, but suffered from needle-phobia and on each occasion that the anaesthetic was offered, she refused it. The Court of Appeal held that her refusal was instilled by panic. At the critical moment, the needle dominated her thinking and she was incapable of making a decision. Her 'true' wishes were represented by consent to the operation; refusal of the anaesthetic was not valid since the patient was temporarily incompetent.

St George's Healthcare NHS Trust v S [1999] Fam 26

In this case, it was determined that it *is* a trespass to impose treatment (in this case, a caesarean section) not only in order to save the life of a competent mother who refuses treatment, but also to save her unborn child. The interests of the foetus do not weigh against the competent mother's autonomy. In this case, the caesarean had already been carried out, and the mother sought an order that this was unlawful. There was no longer an emergency. Where there is an emergency, it is suggested that the temptation to deny the validity of refusal will remain very great.

No possibility of consent or refusal: 'best interests' vs sanctity of life?

In the 'refusal' cases, sanctity of life *and* best interests of the patient are in principle trumped by autonomy or self-determination. What of the case where there is *neither consent nor refusal*, because the patient is permanently unable to give or withhold consent? Here, the trump card of 'autonomy' cannot come into play.[38] In the next case extracted the House of Lords held that in such a case, given that the best interests of the patient prevail, even life-saving or life-sustaining treatment need not be offered or maintained if it is judged not to be in the best

---

[37] The design of these forms was strongly criticized by the Court of Appeal, as aimed chiefly at avoiding legal liability. Given that they were hard to understand, they were unlikely to be effective for this purpose.

[38] Difficult questions surround the status of *advance* expressions of a patient's wishes (to have treatment at all costs, or to have treatment withdrawn in specified circumstances). These questions were inconclusively discussed by the Court of Appeal in *R v GMC, ex p. Burke* [2004] 3 FCR 579. The Court of Appeal was unwilling to be drawn into extensive analysis of this question, which did not arise on the facts. Sections 24–26 of the Mental Capacity Act 2005, when in force, will govern the validity and effect of advance decisions to *refuse* particular treatment. These sections allow (amongst other things) for declarations as to the validity and effect of such refusal.

interests of the patient to receive it. It is important to note that this is an application of *In re F*: if the patient is not competent to decide, then the treatment must be determined by the patient's best interests.

 Airedale NHS Trust v Bland [1993] AC 789

The patient had been in a 'persistent vegetative state' for three years. He was judged to have no prospect of recovery. A declaration was sought that it would be lawful to withdraw the artificial feeding which was maintaining his life. Without such a declaration, the medical team which withdrew treatment might be open to civil proceedings for trespass and criminal prosecution for murder.[39]

The House of Lords held that the 'best interests of the patient' required that treatment to prolong his life should be discontinued. The patient had not expressed any advance wishes as to what should happen if he should be in such a state, so that there was **no consent to the treatment.** (Equally, of course, there was no *refusal* of treatment.) Applying the reasoning in *In re F*, the lack of consent to treatment could make the treatment a trespass, if it was not judged to be *in the patient's best interests*. This is the only sense in which *Bland* is a case about trespass. The medical team sought a declaration that they could *cease* to treat, and Lord Goff explained that non-treatment (even if it involves some physical steps) is essentially an omission; and an omission cannot amount to a battery. Larger concerns in respect of withdrawal of treatment were raised concerning the criminal law, but these are beyond the scope of this book. The following passage is particularly germane to the role of consent.

> **Lord Goff,** at 864
>
> First, it is established that the principle of self-determination requires that respect must be given to the wishes of the patient, so that if an adult patient of sound mind refuses, however unreasonably, to consent to treatment or care by which his life would or might be prolonged, the doctors responsible for his care must give effect to his wishes, even though they do not consider it to be in his best interests to do so: see *Schloendorff v. Society of New York Hospital* (1914) 105 N.E. 92, 93, *per* Cardozo J.; *S. v. McC. (orse S.) and M. (D.S. Intervener); W. v. W.* [1972] A.C. 24, 43, *per* Lord Reid; and *Sidaway v. Board of Governors of the Bethlem Royal Hospital and the Maudsley Hospital* [1985] A.C. 871, 882, *per* Lord Scarman. To this extent, the principle of the sanctity of human life must yield to the principle of self-determination (see *ante*, pp. 826H-827A, *per* Hoffmann L.J.), and, for present purposes perhaps more important, the doctor's duty to act in the best interests of his patient must likewise be qualified. On this basis, it has been held that a patient of sound mind may, if properly informed, require that life support should be discontinued: see *Nancy B. v. Hôtel-Dieu de Québec* (1992) 86 D.L.R. (4th) 385. Moreover the same principle applies where the patient's refusal to give his consent has been expressed at an earlier date, before he became unconscious or otherwise incapable of communicating it; though in such circumstances especial care may be necessary to ensure that the prior refusal of consent is still properly to be regarded as applicable in the circumstances which have subsequently occurred: see, e.g., *In re T. (Adult: Refusal of Treatment)* [1993] Fam. 95. I wish to add that, in cases of this kind, there is no question of the patient having committed suicide, nor therefore of the doctor having aided or abetted him in doing so. It is simply that the patient has, as he is entitled to do, declined to consent to treatment which

---

[39] In fact, a declaration does not in theory preclude a future criminal prosecution: *Airedale NHS Trust v Bland* [1993] AC 789, at 862.

might or would have the effect of prolonging his life, and the doctor has, in accordance with his duty, complied with his patient's wishes.

But in many cases not only may the patient be in no condition to be able to say whether or not he consents to the relevant treatment or care, but also he may have given no prior indication of his wishes with regard to it. In the case of a child who is a ward of court, the court itself will decide whether medical treatment should be provided in the child's best interests, taking into account medical opinion. But the court cannot give its consent on behalf of an adult patient who is incapable of himself deciding whether or not to consent to treatment. I am of the opinion that there is nevertheless no absolute obligation upon the doctor who has the patient in his care to prolong his life, regardless of the circumstances. Indeed, it would be most startling, and could lead to the most adverse and cruel effects upon the patient, if any such absolute rule were held to exist. It is scarcely consistent with the primacy given to the principle of self-determination in those cases in which the patient of sound mind has declined to give his consent, that the law should provide no means of enabling treatment to be withheld in appropriate circumstances where the patient is in no condition to indicate, if that was his wish, that he did not consent to it.

Several members of the House of Lords appeared to say in *Bland* that the best interests of the patient outweigh the sanctity of life itself. It is important to note that this has been doubted. John Keown, 'Restoring Moral and Intellectual Shape to the Law After *Bland*' (1997) 113 LQR, 482–503, argued that the sanctity of life should *not* be regarded as 'giving way' to best interests in such a case. On the other hand, sanctity of life does not on his view require the continuation of life at all costs (this would be a doctrine which Keown calls 'vitalism'). On this account, life-saving treatment can indeed be withheld *while respecting the sanctity of life*, provided that attention focuses on *whether the treatment is of any therapeutic benefit*, rather than on the question of *whether the patient's life is no longer of value*. In other words, treatment may be judged futile, but no person's *life* should ever be judged futile.

Keown's analysis has prompted a very large literature.[40] It was adopted by Ward LJ in the next case considered.

 In Re A (Children) (Conjoined Twins: Surgical Separation) [2001] Fam 147

In deciding whether to approve treatment of an incompetent minor, a court must be guided by 'the best interests of the child': section 1(1) of the Children Act 1989. Therefore, the wishes of *parents* may clearly be overridden. Indeed, there is no question of starting with the parents' wishes and determining whether they are 'reasonable': the welfare of the child is paramount.

In Re A was a case of conjoined twins. It posed an acute problem for a 'best interests' approach because surgery to separate the twins would result inevitably in the death of one of them, Mary. On the other hand, not to proceed with surgery would inevitably lead to the death of both twins. Jodie, the twin who would be expected to survive surgery, was sustaining Mary's life and could not do so for very long. The parents withheld their consent, but their refusal was overridden by the court.

---

[40]   D. Price, 'Fairly Bland: an Alternative View of a Supposed New 'Death Ethic' and the BMA Guidelines' (2001) 21 LS 618; A. McGee, 'Finding a Way Through the Legal and Ethical Maze: Withdrawal of Treatment and Euthanasia' (2005) 13 *Med LR* 357; J. Keown, 'Restoring the Sanctity of Life and Replacing the Caricature: A Reply to David Price' (2006) 26 LS 109. Similarly—and controversially—section 4(5) of the Mental Capacity Act 2005 provides that decisions as to life-sustaining treatment *must not* be motivated by a desire to bring about

Much of the crucial argumentation in *Re A* concerned criminal law. The Court of Appeal held that the separation would not amount to murder because it could be said to be 'necessary'.[41] But on what basis could the court validly approve the operation on the basis of *civil* law, given the ruling principle that they must give effect to the best interests of the child?

Ward LJ and Brooke LJ conceded that they could not apply the thinking in *Bland* directly to this case. The operation could not be considered as being *in the best interests of Mary*:[42]

Ward LJ, at 190

The question is whether this proposed operation is in Mary's best interests. It cannot be. It will bring her life to an end before it has run its natural span. It denies her inherent right to life. There is no countervailing advantage to her at all. It is contrary to her best interests. Looking at her position in isolation and ignoring, therefore, the benefit to Jodie, the court should not sanction the operation on her.

On the other hand, the court could not, consistently with its duty to act in the best interests of the child, simply refuse consent for the operation. This would lead to the death of Jodie, as well as Mary. Instead, Ward LJ explained that the court must act *in the best interests of both twins*. This meant engaging in a balancing act but, applying Keown's analysis of 'sanctity of life', this would not mean weighing the *value* of the two lives against one another, as all lives are of equal value; rather it would depend on the *worthwhileness of the treatment* (or withholding the treatment) to each of the twins. Since in Jodie's case the treatment was expected to lead to a reasonably fulfilling life in future, and in Mary's case withholding treatment could only delay death for a short time, this approach led to the conclusion that *in the best interests of the twins* (taken together and balanced in this way), consent to the operation should be granted.

Type 2: 'Uninformed Consent'

The doctrine of 'informed consent' originated in the United States. This doctrine holds that consent to medical treatment is real and valid only if it is based on sufficient information about the risks involved. Generally speaking, sufficiency of information would be judged, for the purposes of this doctrine, according to the requirements of a 'prudent patient'.

The doctrine of informed consent was rejected by the House of Lords in *Sidaway v Bethlem Royal Hospital* [1985] AC 871, holding that questions of *information* and *advice as to risks* should be addressed solely through the tort of negligence, not through trespass to the person.

In the tort of negligence, the question is what information *the reasonable doctor would have given*, and this test is inconsistent with informed consent. Informed consent is therefore not accepted in English law, although the recent negligence case of *Chester v Afshar* surprisingly seems to revive it in effect.

A major issue concerns the choice of tort where a medical practitioner obtains consent for surgery, without giving full information about the attendant risks. In English law the issue was

death. For discussion see J. Coggon, 'Ignoring the Moral and Intellectual Shape of the Law After *Bland*' (2007) 27 LS 110–25.

[41] The court therefore distinguished the case of a cabin boy killed to maintain the life of fellow shipwrecked crew members, who were duly convicted of murder: *R v Dudley and Stevens* (1884–85) 14 QBD 273.

[42] Robert Walker LJ disagreed on this point.

more or less settled in *Chatterton v Gerson* [1981] QB 432: so long as consent was 'real'—which required that the patient knew the general 'nature of the operation'—it would operate as a defence to an action in trespass.

Bristow J, *Chatterton v Gerson* [1981] QB 432

In my judgment what the court has to do in each case is to look at all the circumstances and say "Was there a real consent?" I think justice requires that in order to vitiate the reality of consent there must be a greater failure of communication between doctor and patient than that involved in a breach of duty if the claim is based on negligence. *When the claim is based on negligence the plaintiff must prove not only the breach of duty to inform, but that had the duty not been broken she would not have chosen to have the operation. Where the claim is based on trespass to the person, once it is shown that the consent is unreal, then what the plaintiff would have decided if she had been given the information which would have prevented vitiation of the reality of her consent is irrelevant.*

In my judgment once the patient is informed in broad terms of the nature of the procedure which is intended, and gives her consent, that consent is real, and the cause of the action on which to base a claim for failure to go into risks and implications is negligence, not trespass. Of course if information is withheld in bad faith, the consent will be vitiated by fraud. Of course if by some accident, as in a case in the 1940's in the Salford Hundred Court where a boy was admitted to hospital for tonsilectomy and due to administrative error was circumcised instead, trespass would be the appropriate cause of action against the doctor, though he was as much the victim of the error as the boy. But in my judgment it would be very much against the interests of justice if actions which are really based on a failure by the doctor to perform his duty adequately to inform were pleaded in trespass.

In this case in my judgment even taking the plaintiff's evidence at its face value she was under no illusion as to the general nature of what an intrathecal injection of phenol solution nerve block would be, and in the case of each injection her consent was not unreal. I should add that getting the patient to sign a pro forma expressing consent to undergo the operation "the effect and nature of which have been explained to me," as was done here in each case, should be a valuable reminder to everyone of the need for explanation and consent. But it would be no defence to an action based on trespass to the person if no explanation had in fact been given. The consent would have been expressed in form only, not in reality.

(Emphasis added)

The italicized section of the first paragraph above draws attention to an important difference in respect of causation between the torts of negligence, and battery. We will return to this below.

The rejection of a claim in battery in *Chatterton v Gerson* may well have been influenced by the decision in *Letang v Cooper* which (as we have seen) made negligence and trespass seem mutually exclusive, while also obscuring the nature of the relevant intention in trespass. Since *Collins v Wilcock* and (most importantly) *In re F* (extracted above), it is no longer the case that battery is 'quite inappropriate' to an action in which no hostility is involved.

Shortly after *Sidaway*, Tan Keng Feng criticized the exclusion of trespass from the aspects of medical law relating to advice, and explored the interface between the torts by reference to their general conception of what makes an actionable wrong:

Tan Keng Feng, 'Failure of Medical Advice: Trespass or Negligence?'
(1987) 7 LS 149–68, at 167–8

There are two aspects to the patient's participation in medical decision-making: one pertaining to the patient's exclusive non-clinical right to self-determination, and the other pertaining to the patient's right, shared with the doctor, to participate in clinical matters in the medical treatment process. Trespass protects the first aspect and negligence protects the second. The difference lies in the degree of failure of medical advice and not in the type of medical advice that is not communicated.

Two problems limit the effectiveness of negligence analysis in this context. We do not try to deal with these problems in full in this chapter, since negligence is given extended treatment in the next part of the book. But we will outline what the problems are.

The 'Standard of Care' Problem

In *Sidaway v Bethlem Royal Hospital* [1985] AC 871, the House of Lords concluded that the trespass route was closed and that *adequacy of advice* could only be addressed as an element of the tort of negligence. Lord Scarman, who was alone in thinking that the proper content of advice as to risks of treatment should be approached as a matter of law for the courts, not of professional practice, nevertheless said briefly that he agreed with Hirst J in *Hills v Potter* [1984] 1 WLR 641: 'it would be deplorable to base the law in medical cases of this kind on the torts of assault and battery' (at 883).

One implication of arguing such cases in terms of *negligence* is that a special test of relevance to a professional exercising special skill—the *Bolam* test—will apply when determining whether appropriate steps have been taken. This test and its controversies are discussed in Chapter 3.1, but it largely places the decision as to 'reasonableness' in the hands of the profession, not of the court. Apart from Lord Scarman, the House of Lords in *Sidaway* held that there was no room to adjust the *Bolam* test to absorb an idea of 'informed consent'. The appropriate test for the content of the duty of care in negligence is supplied (in such a case) by considering *the steps the reasonable medical practitioner should take*. 'Informed consent' would require definition of *what the prudent patient would have required to know*. The two are generally incompatible.[43]

The Causation Problem

The problem of causation referred to in *Chatterton v Gerson* arose for consideration by the House of Lords in *Chester v Afshar* [2005] 1 AC 134, a case in negligence.

The claimant had undergone surgery on the advice of a consultant. It was accepted that he ought to have warned her of a small risk (about 1 per cent) that the operation would lead to paralysis. Had he warned her, she would probably have undergone the same surgery, but not so soon. In all likelihood therefore, there would have been no injury, since this was a rare piece

---

[43] Lord Bridge suggested however that the reasonable doctor should respond honestly to questions asked by an inquisitive patient. Failure to do so might be a breach of duty.

of bad luck which would have been most unlikely to occur on that hypothetical later occasion. This sort of causation point would almost inevitably arise in due course if negligence is used for dealing with lack of information as to risks, as the discussion of Bristow J in *Chatterton v Gerson* (above) made clear. The likely reason why it was not considered sooner is the protective nature of the *Bolam* test. In *Chester*, the duty to advise of a small risk appears to have been almost conceded by the defendant, though perhaps inadvertently.[44] This meant that the issue of causation of harm had to be dealt with.

We will explain in Chapter 4, 'Particular Causation Problems', *exactly* why the problem of causation was so difficult. *Chester v Afshar* will be extracted there. Certainly the injury would most likely not have occurred if the patient had been properly advised; but on the other hand she would still have undergone the surgery and the surgeon therefore did not expose the claimant to any greater risk. *He did not, judged at the time of the breach, fail in a duty to keep her safe or give her the opportunity to be safe.* In essence the problem is caused by approaching the duty to advise solely through the tort of negligence, which is primarily concerned with *keeping reasonably safe*, not through the tort of battery, which is concerned with *protecting rights of self-determination.*

At the same time, we should concede some potential problems with treating such a case within trespass. One is that there needs to be some clear way of expressing the *limits* to the necessity to inform. 'Reasonableness' is more at home in negligence that it is in trespass. On the other hand, as we saw in connection with *Collins v Wilcock*, there is room for a flexible standard in trespass to the person. This standard would more naturally lead to a focus on the 'prudent patient' rather than the 'reasonable doctor'.[45] Ultimately, there is a judgment to be made. Bearing in mind the nature of the doctor–patient relationship, which is the more appropriate way to settle the appropriate giving of information? A second problem concerns the extent of damages that may be recoverable. But this worry is no longer well founded, since the House of Lords in *Chester v Afshar* awarded compensation *in the tort of negligence* for the full extent of the damage, *whether or not* this flowed from the breach of duty.[46] A third problem is that trespass is confined to 'direct' contact, and its application to advice in respect of self-administered medication, for example, is doubtful.

To summarize, *Chester v Afshar* is poised awkwardly between the torts of battery, and negligence, because the *wrong* is denial of self-determination, rather than exposure to risk; but the *harm* is personal injury 'by accident'.

Chester v Afshar is extracted in Chapter 4.

3.2 NECESSITY

It is a defence to battery that the defendant applied only such force as a reasonable person would consider 'necessary' in the circumstances. Similar defences apply in assault (threatening a battery in order to achieve an appropriate goal, such as the safety of others) and false imprisonment (imprisoning someone to protect them, or others).

[44] The defendant did not argue that it was reasonable not to inform of the relevant risk. He argued instead that he *had* warned of the risk. The claimant's evidence was preferred.
[45] See for example Harvey Teff, 'Consent to Medical Procedures, Paternalism, Self-Determination or Therapeutic Alliance' (1985) 101 LQR 432; Margaret Brazier, 'Patient Autonomy and Consent to Treatment: The Role of the Law?' (1987) 7 LS 169–93.
[46] The same result has also been reached in Australia, and this undoubtedly influenced the House of Lords: *Chappel v Hart* (1998) 195 CLR 232.

Evidently, the relevant circumstances must create a genuine *need* for the trespass. Through the standard of the 'reasonable person', the defence of 'necessity' introduces a 'reasonableness' element into the trespass torts.[47]

We have seen that in a medical case where the patient is suffering a transient inability to consent, the defence of necessity will be vitally important. It is an important defence in cases of emergency and in cases, such as *Re A*, where a choice must be made between the interests of two or more people. But as *Re F* made clear, necessity is not a sufficient guiding principle in cases of long-term incompetence to consent. Necessity is also overridden by a *refusal* of consent to be treated (or, presumably, rescued) more generally.

3.3 SELF-DEFENCE

In *Bici v MOD* [2004] EWHC 786, Elias J pointed out some crucial differences between self-defence in relation to a *criminal* charge of battery, and in relation to battery in tort.

Elias J

42 . . . As far as the criminal law is concerned, it is a defence if [the soldiers] had an honest belief that they were going to be attacked and reacted with proportionate force . . . In civil law however, the belief must be both honest and reasonable. . . . In trespass, any unlawful interference with the bodily integrity of the claimant will not be unlawful if it is justified, and it will be justified if the defendant apprehended that he would be imminently attacked and used reasonable force to protect himself. In this case the claimants properly concede that if the soldiers did reasonably believe that Fahri Bici was about to shoot at them, then they were entitled to shoot first; such a response would be reasonable and proportionate.

More protection is given to the honest defendant in *criminal* proceedings, than in the law of tort. The defendant to criminal proceedings needs to hold an honest belief that he or she is about to be attacked; the belief held by the tort defendant must be both honest *and reasonable*. The passage above was approved by the Court of Appeal in *Ashley v Chief Constable of Sussex Police*, where a criminal prosecution had already failed. In *Ashley*, the Master of the Rolls went on to consider the status of an act of self-defence that rests on a mistaken belief.

Sir Anthony Clarke MR, *Ashley v Chief Constable West Sussex Police*
[2006] EWCA Civ 1085

82 . . . [M]y conclusions may be summarised as follows:

  i) In criminal proceedings the burden of negativing self-defence is on the prosecution. By contrast, in civil proceedings the burden is on the defendant to establish self-defence.

  ii) In criminal proceedings a defendant who mistakenly but honestly believes that it is necessary to act in self-defence is entitled to be judged on the basis that his mistaken belief is true. By contrast, in civil proceedings, his belief must be both honestly and reasonably held.

---

[47] Note however that in the special circumstances set out in Criminal Justice Act 2003, s 329 an honest belief suffices: see Chapter 5.

iii) In both civil and criminal proceedings, action taken in self-defence must be reasonable but, in judging what is reasonable, the court must have regard to all the circumstances of the case, including the fact that the action may have to be taken in the heat of the moment.

3.4 CONTRIBUTORY NEGLIGENCE

Under the Law Reform (Contributory Negligence) Act 1945, damages are reduced by the court to reflect the relative 'responsibility' of claimant and defendant. The defence is fully explored in relation to negligence in Chapter 5. It is not altogether clear whether the partial defence of contributory negligence is available in a claim for trespass.

It has been *suggested* by one member of the House of Lords that the defence of contributory negligence would not apply to any case where *harm* is intentionally caused (Lord Rodger, *Standard Chartered Bank v Pakistan Shipping* [2003] 1 AC 959).[48] The reason is clear: contributory negligence has the effect of *reducing* damages where both parties share responsibility for the harm suffered. In a case where that harm was *intended*, the defendant's intention is likely to overwhelm any contributory fault on the part of the claimant.

Trespass however does not depend on intentional *harm*. Only the contact, threat, or imprisonment needs to be intended. As such, do these logical reasons apply in the same way?

In *Bici* (above), Elias J referred to a decision of the High Court of Northern Ireland, in which Hutton J had reduced the claimant's damages in trespass by one half on grounds of contributory negligence. The defendant had been participating in a riot, and had been hit by a plastic baton round: *Wasson v Chief Constable of Northern Ireland* [1987] NI 420. This is also consistent with observations of Lord Denning MR in *Murphy v Culhane* [1977] QB 94, to the effect that damages might be reduced where the deceased had been involved in a violent affray.[49]

However, Elias J argued that it would at least be *very unusual* for a plea of contributory negligence to succeed in a case of trespass to the person if the *claimant's* 'fault' consisted of mere carelessness, and the defendant's is intentional:

111 . . . it would in my view be a very rare case where damages should be reduced in circumstances where the defendant's conduct is intentional and unjustified and the claimant's is merely negligent. Moreover, in my view this feature should in most cases at least defeat a claim to contributory negligence, whether the cause of action is framed in trespass or negligence. . . .

As things stand, the availability of the defence of contributory negligence in trespass seems to depend upon all the circumstances of the case and particularly on categorization of the claimant's and defendant's fault in terms of intention or carelessness. This would be rather inconvenient given the complexity of the idea of intention, as outlined in the introduction to this chapter.

---

[48] This was a case in deceit. It was unanimously held by the House of Lords that the defence of contributory negligence is not available in deceit: see Section 7 below.

[49] Alternatively, there may be no damages in such a case, on grounds of illegality: see Chapter 5.

4. FALSE IMPRISONMENT

False imprisonment, as we explained in our general section above, consists of unlawful and total physical restraint of the liberty of the claimant, brought about by the defendant. Like the other trespass torts, false imprisonment is actionable *per se*. The gist of the action is the unlawful interference with the right to liberty. Thus in *Murray v Ministry of Defence* [1988] 2 All ER 521 (a decision of the House of Lords), it was said that false imprisonment would be actionable even if the claimant is unaware of the restraint on his or her freedom and suffers no harm from it (though nominal damages may then be awarded).

Any individual may falsely imprison another by trapping them in a room or a car or in some other way entirely impeding their freedom of movement. But in *Bird v Jones* (1845) 7 QB 742, a plaintiff who was prevented by an obstruction from crossing Hammersmith Bridge was *not* 'falsely imprisoned', because he was free to turn back. Equally, it seems that a 'reasonable condition' may be placed on exit from a place which the claimant has voluntarily entered—at least if they have done so in pursuance of a contract and the 'contractual route out' is still open. In *Robinson v Balmain New Ferry* [1910] AC 295, the plaintiff had paid to gain entry to a wharf in order to catch a boat but had changed his mind and sought to make his way out through the turnstile through which he had come in. It was considered reasonable for the defendant to charge a penny for him to leave the wharf.

In contemporary law, the tort of false imprisonment is most used where police officers are said to have exceeded their powers or where detention in prison exceeds lawful limits. The relationship between trespass to the person and 'unlawfulness' is particularly clear in such cases, and this tort has a strong 'constitutional' element. Two elements to the constitutional role of false imprisonment should be noted:

1. The definition of 'lawfulness' of detention will frequently depend upon analysis of powers of arrest and/or detention;

2. Where the defendant is a 'public authority' within the terms of the Human Rights Act 1998, the tort of false imprisonment may coexist with an action for damages in respect of a violation of the Convention right to liberty (Article 5 ECHR): HRA 1998, sections 7 and 8.

The Elements of the Tort

It is generally accepted that, since *Letang v Cooper*, this form of trespass to the person like the others must be confined to intentional conduct on the part of the defendant.[50] But equally, we have made it clear that the target of intention in trespass to the person is neither unlawfulness, nor harm. The next case powerfully illustrates this.

 ### *R v Governor of Brockhill Prison, ex p. Evans* [2001] 2 AC 19

Ms Evans had been sentenced to two years' imprisonment. The governor of Brockhill Prison calculated her release date in a manner which was clearly consistent with judicial decisions interpreting relevant statutory provisions. Doubt was then cast on the judicial rulings, and

---

[50] F. A. Trindade, 'The Modern Tort of False Imprisonment', in N. J. Mullaney (ed.), *Torts in the Nineties* (LBC, 1997), contrasts English with Australian and New Zealand law in this respect.

Ms Evans applied for an order for her release. A subsequent judicial ruling confirmed that the doubts were correct, and an order was made. By this time, the claimant had spent 59 days too long in captivity. The House of Lords held that the prison governor was liable in damages for false imprisonment. The gist of the tort is unlawfulness, *not* inappropriate conduct. Detention for those additional days was now known to have been unlawful, even if the governor could not have been aware of that at the time.

Peter Cane, 'The Temporal Element in Law' (2001) 117 LQR 5–10

The theoretical reason why fault is irrelevant to liability for false imprisonment is that the focus of the tort is the plaintiff's right, not the defendant's conduct. . . . [The Crown] was forced to make the difficult argument that her continued detention was . . . justified. This approach rests on a misunderstanding of the tort of false imprisonment. As an element of this tort, 'justification' goes to the legally protected scope of personal liberty, not to the quality of the conduct that constitutes the deprivation of liberty. Once it was conceded that Evans was entitled to be released on September 17, there was no basis for arguing that her continued detention after that date was 'justified'. There are suggestions in the judgments that this is because false imprisonment is a strict liability tort. However, strict liability is merely a corollary of the fact that false imprisonment is constituted by deprivation of liberty without legal authorisation.

Cane argues that the problem in *Ex p. Evans* is not its interpretation of false imprisonment (which is correct), but its assumption that the law was *retrospectively* changed by the new judicial decision, so that the claimant's detention was to be regarded as unlawful at the time. He argues that it would have been better to accept that the detention *was* lawful, only *becoming* unlawful prospectively, when the judicial interpretation changed.[51] Seen in this way, the prison governor should not have been liable in tort (although Cane argues that it would be right for the government to compensate the claimant). This is not because the governor was 'careful', since Cane agrees that this is correctly said to be no defence to an action in false imprisonment. It is because the detention was lawful at the time; and if detention is lawful, there is no false imprisonment.

Ex p. Evans was distinguished by the Court of Appeal in the case of *Quinland v Governor of Swaleside Prison and Others* [2003] QB 306, applying the (pre-*Evans*) case of *Olutu v Home Office* [1997] 1 WLR 103. In each of these cases, a prison governor detained a prisoner pursuant to a court order requiring detention. By these orders, the governor was not permitted to release the prisoner until the stated date. In *Ex p. Evans* by contrast, the governor himself had calculated the release date. In *Quinland* and *Olutu*, the existence of the court order was found to 'justify' the continued detention of the prisoner, by the governor. He did not commit a tort.

The status of unlawfulness and justification

The above cases turn on lawfulness of detention, and justification for detention. But what exactly is the status of these considerations?

---

[51] Cane is here rejecting the 'declaratory' theory of law. This holds that the role of the court is not to change the law when it disapproves or overrules a previous decision, but only to 'declare' what the law was all along.

vans, Lord Hope said (at 32):

> lse imprisonment is a tort of strict liability. But the strict theory of civil liability is
> ent with the idea that in certain circumstances the harm complained of may have
> ...ed justifiably. This is because it is of the essence of the tort of false imprisonment
> ...at the imprisonment is without lawful justification.

Lord Hope describes lack of 'lawful justification' as being 'of the essence of the tort'. This recalls our discussion of consent in respect of the tort of battery, where we noted that in *Freeman v Home Office (No 2)*, it was held that lack of consent, being central to the definition of the tort of battery, was for the claimant to establish. Is the same true, therefore, of lack of 'lawful justification' in false imprisonment? Must the *claimant* show that the imprisonment was unjustified?

In *Austin and Saxby v Commissioner of Police of the Metropolis* [2005] EWHC 480, a case of detention without arrest by police officers, Tugendhat J suggested otherwise:

> 157 In a claim for false imprisonment the burden of proof clearly rests upon the claimant to prove the imprisonment, and (subject to one point) upon the defendant to prove the justification for it. . . .

Justification is, therefore, to be treated as a defence.

The 'one point' which qualifies this arose, in this particular case, where the police officer 'detained' the claimants without arresting them, on the basis of a reasonable suspicion of a threat which might justify that detention. The burden of proof would then appear to be on the claimant to show that this *exercise of discretion* is *unreasonable*.[52]

Reasonableness in arrest and detention—an aspect of 'unlawfulness'

Cases concerned with police powers of arrest and detention typically include discussion of the *reasonableness* of the beliefs held by the arresting (or detaining) officer. But this does not mean that we have to resile from our general point, that trespass to the person is concerned with unlawfulness, not with unreasonable conduct. The question of reasonableness arises only because the *lawfulness of arrest* is defined in relevant statutes *by reference to the holding of 'reasonable suspicion'* on the part of the arresting officer. Reasonableness of belief is thus an aspect of unlawfulness. The following case may serve as an example:

Chief Constable of Thames Valley Police v Earl Gideon Foster Hepburn [2002] EWCA Civ 1841

The claimant H was struck with a baton, handcuffed, and strip-searched during a raid on a public house in High Wycombe. A warrant permitted a search of the premises for drugs and related paraphernalia, but did not permit any individuals to be stopped and searched. H sought damages.

---

[52] On this point, Tugendhat J followed *Al Fayed v Metropolitan Police Commissioner* [2004] EWCA Civ 1579.

Sedley LJ

... Nobody is required in this country to satisfy a police officer that he or she is not committing an offence. The power to detain and search arises only where conditions prescribed by law, typically a reasonably founded suspicion, can be shown to exist; and it is conceded here that PC Hargreaves at the initial stage entertained no such suspicion as would have allowed him to hold and search Mr Hepburn under s 23(2)(a) of the Misuse of Drugs Act 1971.

Certain comments of Sedley LJ in *Hepburn* have been doubted and the decision itself was distinguished in *Connor v Chief Constable of Merseyside* [2006] EWCA Civ 1549; officers had the power to take reasonable steps to detain the occupants of a house when executing a search warrant. But it remains clear that the question of 'reasonableness' is relevant to the question of *lawfulness* of detention.

Limits to false imprisonment

False imprisonment also has its equivalent of *Sidaway*. As we have seen, *Sidaway* confirmed the view that consent based on broad understanding of the nature of medical treatment was sufficient to exclude a claim in battery. In *Hague v Deputy Governor of Parkhurst Prison and Others* [1992] 1 AC 58, the House of Lords held that a lawful detention did not become unlawful when the *conditions* of detention were in breach of applicable Prison Rules.[53] In effect, this means that false imprisonment is not the proper route to take in order to gain compensation where conditions of detention are unacceptable. It does not mean that there is no source of compensation in such a case. There may be an action for breach of statutory duty; in negligence; for misfeasance in a public office; or under the Human Rights Act. For example in *Karagozlu v Commissioner of Police for the Metropolis* [2006] EWCA Civ 1691, loss of 'residual' liberty was held to be actionable damage for the tort of misfeasance in a public office (here the claimant was transferred from open to closed prison).

FURTHER READING

Brazier, M., 'Patient Autonomy and Consent to Treatment: the Role of the Law?' (1987) 7 LS 169.

Ibbetson, D., *A Historical Introduction to the Law of Obligations* (Oxford: OUP, 1999), Chapter 3.

Keown, J., 'Restoring Moral and Intellectual Shape to the Law After *Bland*' (1997) 113 LQR, 482–503.

Tan Keng Feng, 'Failure of Medical Advice: Trespass or Negligence?' (1987) 7 LS 149–68.

Trindade, F., 'Intentional Torts: Some Thoughts on Assault and Battery' (1982) 2 OJLS 211–37.

Trindade, F., 'The Modern Tort of False Imprisonment', in N J Mullaney (ed.), *Torts in the Nineties* (Sydney: LBC Information Services, 1997).

---

[53] See also *Cullen v Chief Constable of RUC* [2003] 1 WLR 1763: detention lawful at its inception would not become unlawful through breach of codes of conduct.

5. INTENTIONAL INFLICTION OF PHYSICAL OR MENTAL HARM

Wright J, *Wilkinson v Downton* [1897] 2 QB 57

In this case the defendant, in the execution of what he seems to have regarded as a practical joke, represented to the plaintiff that he was charged by her husband with a message to her to the effect that her husband was smashed up in an accident, and was lying at The Elms at Leytonstone with both legs broken, and that she was to go at once in a cab with two pillows to fetch him home. All this was false. The effect of the statement on the plaintiff was a violent shock to her nervous system, producing vomiting and other more serious and permanent physical consequences at one time threatening her reason, and entailing weeks of suffering and incapacity to her as well as expense to her husband for medical attendance. These consequences were not in any way the result of previous ill-health or weakness of constitution; nor was there any evidence of predisposition to nervous shock or any other idiosyncrasy.

. . . The defendant has, as I assume for the moment, wilfully done an act calculated to cause physical harm to the plaintiff—that is to say, to infringe her legal right to personal safety, and has in fact thereby caused physical harm to her. That proposition without more appears to me to state a good cause of action, there being no justification alleged for the act. This wilful injuria is in law malicious, although no malicious purpose to cause the harm which was caused nor any motive of spite is imputed to the defendant.

It remains to consider whether the assumptions involved in the proposition are made out. One question is whether the defendant's act was so plainly calculated to produce some effect of the kind which was produced that an intention to produce it ought to be imputed to the defendant, regard being had to the fact that the effect was produced on a person proved to be in an ordinary state of health and mind. I think that it was. It is difficult to imagine that such a statement, made suddenly and with apparent seriousness, could fail to produce grave effects under the circumstances upon any but an exceptionally indifferent person, and therefore an intention to produce such an effect must be imputed, and it is no answer in law to say that more harm was done than was anticipated, for that is commonly the case with all wrongs. The other question is whether the effect was, to use the ordinary phrase, too remote to be in law regarded as a consequence for which the defendant is answerable. Apart from authority, I should give the same answer and on the same ground as the last question, and say that it was not too remote. . . .

Wilkinson v Downton is our first example of an action which depends on showing *intentionally caused harm*. The target of intention in *Wilkinson v Downton* is harm to the claimant. In fact, it is a tort both of *intention*, and of *damage*. So too are (most of) the 'economic torts' (Section 7. below). That comparison was clearly in the mind of Wright J, since the claimant attempted to argue the case in 'deceit' (one of the economic torts). Deceit requires that the defendant made *a false statement, with the intention that the claimant should rely upon that statement to her detriment.* There was a false statement in this case, and the plaintiff was able to claim in deceit for her bus fare to the scene of the supposed accident. But the basis of liability in deceit is that *a person who makes a false statement intended to be acted on must make good the damage naturally resulting from its being acted on.* The plaintiff's physical injury flowed from *believing* the statement, but *not* from acting upon it.

If the claim did not fall within the action for deceit, then the main obstacle to its success was the restrictive decision in *Victorian Railways Commissioners v Coultas* (1888) 13 App Cas 222. This decision had treated psychiatric harm suffered as a result of a railway accident as unrecoverable for being 'too remote'. That case, Wright J reasoned, could be distinguished because it did not concern a *'wilful'* act. In fact, change soon followed.[54]

But the need to distinguish *Coultas* at the time of *Wilkinson v Downton* probably explains why Wright J described the damage as 'wilful'. Paying attention to the highlighted passages in the above extract, it is clear that Wright J did not claim that the defendant actually *desired* the plaintiff to suffer harm. The law here *imputes* intention to the defendant. *Wilkinson v Downton* fits the *second* form of intention mentioned in the US Restatement on Torts (extracted in Section 1 above), by which a party is held to intend consequences which are substantially 'certain' to follow from his or her actions. It makes no claim that this is *the same thing as* desiring the result. Indeed, Wright J may even be read as saying that in the absence of any other motive, the virtual certainty of the result is *evidence* that the outcome was desired.

The existence of this cause of action was confirmed by the Court of Appeal some years later in *Janvier v Sweeney* [1919] 2 KB 316. The defendant's agent Barker purported to be a detective inspector from Scotland Yard, and represented that the plaintiff was wanted for corresponding with a German spy. This pretence or falsehood was possibly even more likely to cause harm to the plaintiff. On the other hand, the *purpose* of the defendant (to get hold of some letters that were suspected to be forgeries) is surely *not* an intention to cause harm. In *Janvier*, the 'imputed' intention is clearly inconsistent with the actual motive of the defendant.

Wilkinson v Downton has very rarely been applied successfully in England. It was, however, argued with partial success in the case of *C v D* [2006] EWHC 166. Here, the claimant was sexually abused in childhood whilst boarding at an abbey school. It is likely that, here, it was assumed that negligence would not offer the appropriate analysis, since the abuse was (in the particular sense we discussed in respect of *Stubbings v Webb*, above) 'intentional'. The action in *Wilkinson v Downton* could only offer a remedy where actual personal injury (in the form of a recognized psychiatric illness) could be shown to have followed from the relevant act.

As we have said, Wright J had to place heavy emphasis on 'wilfulness' because of the need to distinguish *Coultas*. Given that *Coultas* no longer rules out the availability of damages in negligence for the result of a mere shock (without physical contact), *Wilkinson* is generally thought to have lost its purpose. It might rediscover its purpose if it ceased to be a tort concerned with *actual personal injury in the form of physical or mental harm*, and began to compensate for the less tangible consequences of wilful acts of the defendant, which do not amount to sufficient 'damage' for an action in negligence.

There has been considerable academic support for a development of *Wilkinson v Downton* to cover less tangible injuries, such as distress or anxiety.[55] In the United States, *Wilkinson* has indeed developed into an action in respect of the consequences of 'harassing and outrageous acts', provided the product of such acts amounts to 'severe emotional distress'. It is important to note that what follows is only the broad general principle stated in section 46, and that it is

---

[54] *Bell v Great Northen Railway Company of Ireland* (1890) 26 LR Ir 428, mentioned by Wright J, had already declined to follow *Coultas* in Ireland; within a few years, a barmaid put in fear for her safety was able to claim for the consequences in English law: *Dulieu v White* [1901] 2 KB 669 (see further Section 6.1).

[55] See J. Bridgeman and M. Jones, 'Harassing Conduct and Outrageous Acts: A Cause of Action for Intentionally Inflicted Mental Distress?' (1994) 14 LS 180. Generally, this form of damage is not sufficient to ground an action in negligence *per se*, but may be recoverable sometimes as a head of consequential loss: P. Giliker, 'A "new" head of damages: damages for mental distress in the English law of torts' (2000) 20 LS 19–41.

subject to qualification and explanation:

American Law Institute, Restatement of the Law, Second, Torts

Section 46   Outrageous Conduct Causing Severe Emotional Distress

(1) One who by extreme and outrageous conduct intentionally or recklessly causes severe emotional distress to another is subject to liability for such emotional distress, and if bodily harm to the other results from it, for such bodily harm.

In *Wong v Parkside Health NHS Trust* [2003] 3 All ER 932, the Court of Appeal rejected an argument that *Wilkinson v Downton* had been similarly extended in English law. This was a case of bullying at work which would, if the events occurred now, give rise to claims under the Protection from Harassment Act 1997.[56] In the following extract, Hale LJ considers the scope of *Wilkinson v Downton*.

Hale LJ, *Wong v Parkside NHS Trust* [2003] 3 All ER 932

11   Professor Fleming states in The Law of Torts (9th edn, 1998) p 38:

'Cases will be rare where nervous shock involving physical injury was fully intended (desired). More frequently, the defendant's aim would have been merely to frighten, terrify or alarm his victim. But this is quite sufficient, provided his conduct was of a kind reasonably capable of terrifying a normal person, or was known or ought to have been known to the defendant to be likely to terrify the plaintiff for reasons special to him. Such conduct could be described as reckless.'

This might be read to mean that the tort is committed if there is deliberate conduct which will foreseeably lead to alarm or distress falling short of the recognised psychiatric illness which is now considered the equivalent of physical harm, provided that such harm is actually suffered. We do not consider that English law has gone so far.

12   For the tort to be committed, as with any other action on the case, there has to be actual damage. The damage is physical harm or recognised psychiatric illness. The defendant must have intended to violate the claimant's interest in his freedom from such harm. The conduct complained of has to be such that that degree of harm is sufficiently likely to result that the defendant cannot be heard to say that he did not 'mean' it to do so. He is taken to have meant it to do so by the combination of the likelihood of such harm being suffered as the result of his behaviour and his deliberately engaging in that behaviour. This view is consistent with that taken by Dillon LJ in *Khorasandjian v Bush* . . . [1993] QB 727 at 735–736:

' . . . false words or verbal threats calculated to cause, and uttered with the knowledge that they are likely to cause and actually causing physical injury to the person to whom they are uttered are actionable: see the judgment of Wright J in *Wilkinson v Downton* . . . cited by Bankes LJ in *Janvier v Sweeney* [1919] 2 KB 316 at 321–322. . . . There was a wilful false statement, or unfounded threat, which was in law malicious, and which was likely to cause and did in fact cause physical injury, viz illness of the nature of nervous shock.'

---

[56]   The events predated the Act. Although the claimant had been physically assaulted by one of the defendants, a claim in battery on the basis of this attack was ruled out. By statute, battery cannot be the subject both of a successful private prosecution (as was the case here) *and* of a further civil claim.

Having also outlined the reasons why the claim in battery could not succeed, Hale LJ turned to a further serious aspect of the harassment in this case, namely *a threat of violence* against the claimant.

> **17** The threat is different. It is the most serious of the other allegations made against the second defendant. But the claimant herself conceded to the judge that it had not caused her illness. The trigger had been the earlier incidents which had led to her two-day absence in January. Without it, all that is left is a catalogue of rudeness and unfriendliness, behaviour not to be expected of grown-up colleagues in the workplace, but not behaviour so calculated 'to infringe her legal right to personal safety' (see Wilkinson v Downton . . .) that an intention to do so should be imputed to the second defendant.

Hale LJ went on to conclude that English common law had not developed an action for harassment before the Protection From Harassment Act 1997. The centrepiece of a claim that it had done so was the case of *Khorasandjian v Bush* [1993] QB 727. *Khorasandjian* is now of limited authority. Its interpretation of the action in *private nuisance* (used by the Court of Appeal in order to allow an injunction in respect of behaviour that did not threaten any physical harm, but which interfered with 'use and enjoyment' of the home) was later disapproved by the House of Lords in *Hunter v Canary Wharf* [1997] AC 655. But *Khorasandjian* is otherwise still good authority that an injunction may be issued to restrain harassing behaviour that threatens to cause actual personal injury to the claimant.

In *Hunter v Canary Wharf*, Lord Hoffmann made a passing remark which offered some hope of extending remedies in tort for intentional infliction of harm:

Lord Hoffmann, *Hunter v Canary Wharf* [1997] AC 655, at 707

. . . I see no reason why a tort of intention should be subject to the rule which excludes compensation for mere distress, inconvenience or discomfort in actions based on negligence . . . The policy considerations are quite different.

This possibility was pursued (unsuccessfully) by the claimants in *Wainwright v Home Office* [2004] 2 AC 406.

The claimants sought compensation where they had been subjected to an unjustifiably intrusive strip search, which was not conducted in accordance with prison rules. The House of Lords rejected a claim based on *Wilkinson v Downton*.[57] Again, Lord Hoffmann did not entirely rule out a remedy for intentionally caused anxiety and distress in its own right. But he emphasized that if such a claim were to be recognized, it would depend on much stronger 'intention' than the sort of intention referred to by Wright J. No such strong intention was present in this case.

---

[57] In Chapter 14, we deal with a separate aspect of the House of Lords' judgment in *Wainwright*, relating to the claimants' argument that English law now recognizes a general tort of privacy. That argument also failed.

Lord Hoffmann, *Wainwright v Home Office* [2004] 2 AC 406

44 I do not resile from the proposition that the policy considerations which limit the heads of recoverable damage in negligence do not apply equally to torts of intention. If someone actually intends to cause harm by a wrongful act and does so, there is ordinarily no reason why he should not have to pay compensation.[58] But I think that if you adopt such a principle, you have to be very careful about what you mean by intend. In *Wilkinson v Downton* Wright J wanted to water down the concept of intention as much as possible. He clearly thought, as the Court of Appeal did afterwards in *Janvier v Sweeney*, that the plaintiff should succeed whether the conduct of the defendant was intentional or negligent. But the *Victorian Railway Comrs* case prevented him from saying so. So he devised a concept of imputed intention which sailed as close to negligence as he felt he could go.

45 If, on the other hand, one is going to draw a principled distinction which justifies abandoning the rule that damages for mere distress are not recoverable, imputed intention will not do. The defendant must actually have acted in a way which he knew to be unjustifiable and either intended to cause harm or at least acted without caring whether he caused harm or not. Lord Woolf CJ, as I read his judgment [2002] QB 1334, 1350, paras 50–51, might have been inclined to accept such a principle. But the facts did not support a claim on this basis. The judge made no finding that the prison officers intended to cause distress or realised that they were acting without justification in asking the Wainwrights to strip. He said, at paragraph 83, that they had acted in good faith and, at paragraph 121, that: "The deviations from the procedure laid down for strip-searches were, in my judgment, not intended to increase the humiliation necessarily involved but merely sloppiness."

46 Even on the basis of a genuine intention to cause distress, I would wish, as in *Hunter's* case, to reserve my opinion on whether compensation should be recoverable. In institutions and workplaces all over the country, people constantly do and say things with the intention of causing distress and humiliation to others. This shows lack of consideration and appalling manners but I am not sure that the right way to deal with it is always by litigation. The Protection from Harassment Act 1997 defines harassment in section 1(1) as a "course of conduct" amounting to harassment and provides by section 7(3) that a course of conduct must involve conduct on at least two occasions. If these requirements are satisfied, the claimant may pursue a civil remedy for damages for anxiety: section 3(2). The requirement of a course of conduct shows that Parliament was conscious that it might not be in the public interest to allow the law to be set in motion for one boorish incident. It may be that any development of the common law should show similar caution.

47 In my opinion, therefore, the claimants can build nothing on *Wilkinson v Downton*. It does not provide a remedy for distress which does not amount to recognised psychiatric injury and so far as there may be a tort of intention under which such damage is recoverable, the necessary intention was not established. I am also in complete agreement with Buxton LJ [2002] QB 1334, 1355–1356, paras 67–72, that *Wilkinson v Downton* has nothing to do with trespass to the person.

Lord Hoffmann here makes the point that even if 'genuine' intention is required, the development of an intentional tort which remedies anxiety and distress alone will go further than the civil actions (and criminal offences) outlined in the Protection from Harassment Act 1997 (below), for this requires a 'course of conduct'. We will see in respect of the economic torts

---

[58] It is doubtful whether this comment fits with the economic torts, considered in Section 7 below.

(Section 7) that common law has been reticent about the creation of causes of action based *purely* on intentional infliction of harm—even if that intention is quite strong.

6. STATUTORY ACTION FOR HARASSMENT

Protection from Harassment Act 1997[59]

1 Prohibition of harassment

(1) A person must not pursue a course of conduct—

    (a) which amounts to harassment of another, and

    (b) which he knows or ought to know amounts to harassment of the other.

    . . .

(3) Subsection (1) does not apply to a course of conduct if the person who pursued it shows—

    (a) that it was pursued for the purpose of preventing or detecting crime,

    (b) that it was pursued under any enactment or rule of law or to comply with any condition or requirement imposed by any person under any enactment, or

    (c) that in the particular circumstances the pursuit of the course of conduct was reasonable.

3 Civil remedy

(1) An actual or apprehended breach of [section 1(1)] may be the subject of a claim in civil proceedings by the person who is or may be the victim of the course of conduct in question.

(2) On such a claim, damages may be awarded for (among other things) any anxiety caused by the harassment and any financial loss resulting from the harassment.

    . . .

7 Interpretation of this group of sections

(1) This section applies for the interpretation of sections 1 to 5.

(2) References to harassing a person include alarming the person or causing the person distress.

[(3) A "course of conduct" must involve—

    (a) in the case of conduct in relation to a single person (see section 1(1)), conduct on at least two occasions in relation to that person . . .]

    . . .

(4) "Conduct" includes speech.

[(5) References to a person, in the context of the harassment of a person, are references to a person who is an individual.]

---

[59] As amended most recently by the Serious Organised Crime and Police Act 2005. Some of the additions are concerned with harassment aimed at procuring criminal or other wrongful acts and we omit them for reasons of space.

Liability under the 1997 Act is based on actual or constructive knowledge that conduct is likely to amount to harassment. This requirement may be fulfilled without any actual realization on the part of the defendant that he or she is 'harassing' the claimant. There is certainly no need for the defendant to *wish* to have the effect of making the claimant feel 'harassed', or to suffer anxiety.

There must however be a 'course of conduct', and a single incident will therefore not suffice, no matter how serious. The primary remedy is an injunction, but damages are also available. The Act also creates criminal offences of harassment.

It is difficult to fit the 'protected right or interest' of the claimant under this statute into the general scheme of tort liability. Clearly, by section 3(1) and (2), the available remedies include compensation for harm suffered, and this harm may include 'anxiety and distress'. However, this form of harm is not a *requirement* of the civil action under the Act which, quite simply, protects *against harassment*.

The statute can therefore be interpreted as protecting against *intrusion* and in some recent cases, violation of a right to privacy has been identified as the relevant wrong. We explore these cases in Chapter 14, where we see that a balance may have to be struck in some such cases between 'privacy', and freedom of expression. In fact the relationship between statutory harassment, and freedom of expression, extends beyond the privacy cases since it has been held that 'harassment' under the Act may consist of publication of newspaper articles which victimize the claimant (*Thomas v News Group Newspapers* [2001] EWCA Civ 1233); or demonstrations aimed at preventing contractors and others from going about their business (*Daiichi UK Ltd and Ors v Stop Huntingdon Animal Cruelty and Ors* [2004] 1 WLR 503).[60] These cases indicate that although the statute was introduced to deal with a particular problem, known as 'stalking' (which was also the sort of activity involved in *Khorasandjian v Bush*), its reach is much broader.

In Chapter 9, we will see that the House of Lords has recently accepted that an employer may be *vicariously liable* for harassment under the Act (*Majrowski v Guy's and St Thomas's NHS Trust* [2006] UKHL 34). The claimant in *Wong v Parkside* would now be able not only to proceed against the individual workplace bullies, but to claim compensation against the employer *even if that employer had not been negligent in its own right in failing to prevent the bullying*.[61] On the other hand, in *Daniels v Commissioner of Metropolitan Police* [2006] EWHC 1622, it was made clear that an employer will not be vicariously liable under the Act for a series of individual acts of bullying where the employees concerned are acting independently. For the employer to be vicariously liable for the statutory torts of their employees under this Act, the acts of the employees must amount to a *course of conduct*, with a common purpose.

FURTHER READING

Bridgeman, J., and Jones, M., 'Harassing and Outrageous Acts' (1994) 14 LS 180.

Conaghan, J., 'Harassment and the Law of Tort: *Khorasandjian v Bush*' (1993) Fem LS 189.

---

[60] The 'persons' protected by the Act (s 1; s 7) are individuals and a corporation is not protected under the Act. However, individual contractors were able to bring an action for harassment. The protestors in this case were considered to be intimidating and aggressive.

[61] In *Wong v Parkside* itself, there was an unsuccessful claim that the employer had not done enough to prevent the behaviour of the co-workers.

Conaghan, J., 'Gendered Harms and the Law of Tort: Remedying (Sexual) Harassment' (1996) 16 OJLS 407.

Handford, P., '*Wilkinson v Downton* and Acts Calculated to Cause Physical Harm' (1985) 16 UWAL Rev 31.

Trindade, F., 'The Intentional Infliction of Purely Mental Distress' (1986) 6 OJLS 219.

Witting, C., 'Tort Liability for Intended Mental Harm' (1998) 21 UNSWLJ 55.

7. INTENTIONAL INTERFERENCE WITH ECONOMIC INTERESTS

Most undergraduate law courses omit coverage of the important torts collected here. Therefore, this part of the chapter is relatively concise. It is designed to operate both as an introduction for inquisitive readers who are not expected to study the economic torts, and as a useful outline with supporting material for those whose are.

These torts require genuine intention to cause damage. The kind of intention they require is stronger than the form of intention we saw in *Wilkinson v Downton*. Yet at the same time, in (nearly) all the economic torts, this strong form of intention *is not enough*. Something more is needed before there is said to be an actionable wrong. The 'abstentionist' approach to liability to be seen in the economic torts is an important element in the general understanding of tort law.

The economic torts have for a long time defied any simple framework. Luckily, the job of identifying and classifying the torts has been made a lot easier by the recent efforts of academic commentators even if they disagree with one another on certain important points.[62] The Court of Appeal has also provided a very helpful panoramic view of part of the field (especially intention itself) in *Douglas v Hello! (No 3)* [2006] QB 125.[63]

We will group the economic torts into two categories:

(a) Group A economic torts, involving actions or threats;

(b) Group B economic torts, involving misrepresentation.

With one exception, the economic torts selected here[64] require *intentional causation of economic harm*. They are genuinely intentional torts of damage. The one exception—inducing breach of contract—still requires intention, but intention to induce breach (rather than cause harm) is the central concern.

Equally, in all or nearly all of these torts, *intention is not enough*. Otherwise, there would simply be a tort of 'intentionally causing economic loss'. Such a tort would be very awkward in a competitive market economy (even more so in a society which still recognises the legitimacy of trade union activity). Generally speaking (and with exceptions), the torts in Group A also require some 'unlawful means', while the torts in Group B require false representations.

---

[62] The Court of Appeal in *Douglas v Hello! (No 3)* particularly expressed their appreciation of Hazel Carty, *An Analysis of the Economic Torts* and P. Sales and D. Stilitz, 'Intentional Infliction of Harm by Unlawful Means' (1999) 115 LQR 411.

[63] At the time of writing, this case is under appeal to the House of Lords.

[64] We do not include passing off in this chapter. It primarily protects against damage to goodwill, not against economic losses, and is not dependent on intention.

7.1 THE STARTING POINT: INTENTIONALLY CAUSING LOSS IS NOT A SUFFICIENT BASIS FOR LIABILITY

All of our economic torts require intention. But our starting point is that intentionally causing economic harm is not in itself sufficient to justify liability. This is very important when comparing these torts with the tort of negligence. In negligence, there has been some temptation to say that *carelessly causing foreseeable harm* is sufficient to justify liability, unless there is some sufficient reason why not.[65] This broad approach (in terms of general principles of foreseeability, carelessness, and causation) is now not generally adopted, and has been resisted particularly strongly in the case of *economic* losses.[66]

The economic torts help to illustrate why the search for such reasons is important. Most of the cases we will consider in this chapter involve damage inflicted *between competitors* or (if this is genuinely different) *between trade unions and their targets*. There is no general duty to avoid harming one another's interests intentionally, and (therefore) certainly no duty to avoid doing so carelessly. No general obligation (moral or legal) to 'keep safe from economic harm' exists between parties who are in a competitive or antagonistic relationship.

The following judicial statement begins to explain *both* the starting point just noticed ('intention is not enough'), *and* the complexity of the economic torts: if intention is generally not enough, and if 'something more' is required, then it is not so surprising that the 'something more' can come in different forms.

Bowen LJ, *Mogul Steamship v McGregor, Gow and Co* (1889) 23 QBD 598

No man, whether trader or not, can . . . justify damaging another in his commercial business by fraud or misrepresentation.[67] Intimidation, obstruction and molestation are forbidden;[68] so is the intentional procurement of a violation of individual rights, contractual or other,[69] assuming always that there is no just cause for it. . . .[70] But the defendants have been guilty of none of these acts. **They have done nothing more against the plaintiffs than pursue to the bitter end a war of competition waged in the context of their own trade.** To the argument that a competition so pursued ceases to have a just cause or excuse when there is ill-will or a personal intention to harm, it is sufficient to reply (as I have already pointed out) that **there was here no personal intention to do any other or greater harm to the plaintiffs than such as was necessarily involved in the desire to attract to the defendants' ships the entire tea freights of the ports** . . .

At the start of this quotation, Bowen LJ lists some ways in which intentionally causing economic harm to others is considered 'unjustified'. He goes on to explain that if no transgression of the sort listed is present, then it is generally legitimate to further one's own interests even though someone else will thereby suffer economic loss. Finally, he leaves open the question

---

[65] This was broadly the *Anns v Merton* test for the duty of care, since superseded by the more detailed *Caparo* approach: Section 3.2.

[66] We explore some of the reasons for this in Section 6.2.

[67] See the torts in Group B, below.

[68] See the Group A tort of intimidation.

[69] See the Group A tort(s) of 'inducing breach of contract' and perhaps 'causing harm by unlawful means'.

[70] Note: this draws attention to a defence of 'justification', below.

whether an extremely strong form of intention—possibly captured in the expression 'ill-will'—is sufficient in itself to justify liability for the intended harm. In the case he had to decide, there was no ill-will of the relevant sort.

Notably, the strong sort of intention he mentions here would require that the defendant intended, *as his or her primary purpose*, to cause harm to the claimant—and not simply to protect or advance his or her own interests. In the House of Lords, Lord Watson amplified these remarks about intention:

Lord Watson, *Mogul Steamship v McGregor, Gow and Co* [1892] AC 25, at 42

There is nothing in the evidence to suggest that the parties to the agreement had any other object in view than that of defending their carrying-trade during the tea season against the encroachments of the appellants and other competitors, and of attracting to themselves custom which might otherwise have been carried off by these competitors. That is an object which is strenuously pursued by merchants great and small in every branch of commerce; and it is, in the eye of the law, perfectly legitimate. If the respondents' combination had been formed, not with a single view to the extension of their business and the increase of its profits, but with the main or ulterior design of effecting an unlawful object; a very different question would have arisen for the consideration of your Lordships. But no such case is presented by the facts disclosed in this appeal.

The 'very different question' referred to by Lord Watson soon fell to be considered by the House of Lords in *Allen v Flood*. Where action was not in itself 'unlawful' but was motivated by a dominant motive to *harm* (called, rather imprecisely, 'malice'),[71] could this motive in itself make the harm actionable? Or was it necessary to show *both* unlawful means, *and* ulterior purpose? A specially constituted panel of nine judges was assembled to decide this question, indicating how important it was perceived to be. The answer, given by a 6–3 majority, was that economic harm was not actionable, no matter what the intention of the defendant, unless some independent unlawfulness was present.

Allen v Flood [1898] AC 1

The plaintiffs (respondents) were shipwrights employed on repairs to the woodwork of a ship. The association of which they were members allowed them to work on both wood and iron. The boilermakers association (whose members worked with iron alone) took exception to this arrangement. They felt that shipwrights should be confined to working with wood. Ironworkers on the ship discovered that the respondent shipwrights had previously worked on the ironwork of another ship.

The ironworkers called for their delegate (Allen, the defendant), and told him they planned to walk out. He spoke to the employers and secured the dismissal of the shipwrights. The shipwrights sued Allen for maliciously causing them economic loss. Crucially, the employers were within their rights to dismiss the shipwrights and did so with no breach of any contractual term; equally, the ironworkers were not contractually obliged to continue their work. As a

---

[71] We will not hesitate too long over the meaning of this word. More recently, the different levels of intention have been set out by the Court of Appeal in *Douglas v Hello!*, without reference to 'malice'. The Court of Appeal's approach is explained below.

result, no breach of contract was either threatened, or procured. Had Allen *procured* a breach of the employer's contract, then the shipwrights would have been able to sue the employer for breach; and would also have had an action against Allen on the authority of *Lumley v Gye* (1853) 2 E & B 216.

Allen v Flood has been criticized *both* for an unduly restrictive approach to recovery of intentional harm,[72] *and* for a lack of clarity in the idea of 'malice'.[73] Whether the first criticism is well placed is a matter for debate. The second criticism however is not unfair. It is not at all clear that Allen's motive really *ought* to be described as malicious, or as really different from the motive of the competitor out to win the entire market (and thereby to put his rivals out of business) in *Mogul Steamship*. He was trying to protect the interests of his trade association at the expense of another; and the reason for doing this was not predominantly to cause harm to shipwrights, even if this was a necessary corollary. It was to benefit boilermakers. Indeed this point was (briefly) made explicit by Lord Herschell at 132:

> The object which the defendant, and those he represented, had in view throughout was what they believed to be the interest of the class to which they belonged; the step taken was a means to that end.

But Finnis has suggested that in general, the handling of 'malice' and 'intention' in *Allen v Flood* was far too loose.

J. Finnis, 'Intention in Tort Law', in Owen (ed.), Philosophical Foundations of Tort Law, 239–40

Inept handling of the concept of intention (under whatever name) marks most of the judgments in *Allen v Flood*, most notably in their failure to identify the equivocation in the conception of 'malice' with which the legal sources and professional discourse then current, and the trial judge's direction to the jury, confronted them. On that conception, malice includes having a purpose 'to benefit oneself at the expense of one's neighbour'. But 'at the expense of' extends equivocally to two very different cases: (1) where loss to the neighbour is the ultimate *or intermediate* object/ purpose/ intent (and benefit to oneself is not more than a welcome side-effect), and (2) where benefit to self is the object (and loss to the neighbour is only a foreseen, perhaps even a welcome, side-effect). To be sure, the House of Lords rejected the conception of malice which involves this confusion; the judges discerned its incompatibility with the lawfulness of any winner-takes-all commercial competition. Yet they did not identify the confusion's source: failure to distinguish the intention to secure all the available trade (and in this sense 'win') from the certain side-effect of such trading success—causing loss to the loser.

Perhaps it is unwise to scour the judgments in *Allen v Flood* too closely for analysis of the motives involved. The essence of the majority decision was that Allen's motive did not matter. No form of malice or ill-will (if present) would have sufficed to make his actions into an

[72] Heydon, *The Economic Torts* (2nd edn, Sweet & Maxwell, 1978). Sir John Salmond was also a noted critic of *Allen v Flood*.
[73] Finnis, 'Intention in Tort Law', further extracted below.

actionable wrong. The headnote to *Allen v Flood* clearly states:

> An act lawful in itself is not converted by a bad motive into an unlawful act so as to make the doer of the act liable to a civil action. . . .
>
> . . . the appellant had violated no legal right of the respondents, done no unlawful act, and used no unlawful means, in procuring the respondents' dismissal; . . . his conduct was therefore not actionable however malicious or bad his motive might be . . .

The main question for those who take a philosophical approach to intention is not so much whether *Allen v Flood* was clear enough about the nature of 'malice' (it would almost certainly fail that test), but whether it took intention seriously enough as a 'wrong-making factor'.

Finnis, 'Intention in Tort Law' (above), 238

> . . . One's conduct will be right only if *both* one's means *and* one's ends are right; therefore, *one* wrong-making factor will make one's choice and action wrong, and *all* the aspects of one's act must be rightful for the act to be right. The acting person's intentions must be right all the way down (or up).

But the question to be addressed was not whether Allen's actions were *right*. It was whether they were wrong in such a way as to attract legal liability. Finnis concedes that intentional harm will not *always* justify legal liability; but, following J. B. Ames ('How Far an Act May be a Tort Because of the Wrongful Motive of the Actor' (1905)18 Harv L Rev 411), he contends that a defendant may *escape* liability for intentional harm only for particular reasons such as legal privilege, or because the defendant only compels the claimant to do what he has a duty to do, or because the defendant's malevolence only extended to an omission or non-feasance (where there was no positive duty to act). This implies that intentionally caused harm *ought always* to attract a remedy. This is at odds with the 'abstentionist' approach (to use the word applied by Hazel Carty)[74] that operates in respect of the economic torts generally. This approach is to be contrasted with the position in the US Restatement (extracted at the start of this chapter). In his Clarendon lectures on the economic torts (*Economic Torts*, Clarendon Press, 1997), Tony Weir implied that this abstentionist approach had (at the time of writing) little support:

> The centenary of *Allen v Flood* falls just before Christmas 1997, and I shall be celebrating it, apparently on my own.

That would not be the case today. Ten years later, *Allen v Flood* has won many more friends and admirers. Possibly, it is growing disenchantment with the expanding tort of negligence (covering the whole of Part III of this book) that has made this sort of 'judicial abstentionism' a much more appealing option.[75]

---

[74] H. Carty, *An Analysis of the Economic Torts*, at 6.
[75] Note also the discussion in Chapter 1 of growing resistance to over-extensive liability.

Tony Weir has proposed a single framework for the economic torts which takes the clear negative line established in *Allen v Flood* as the starting point for a positive proposition, namely:

> It is tortious intentionally to damage another by an act which the actor was not at liberty to commit.[76]

This organizes the economic torts as a whole around two ideas: intentional harm; and unlawful means. This is an attractive proposition because it combines simplicity with abstentionism.

There are however some significant difficulties in attempting to unify the economic torts in this way.[77] In what follows, we will point out some of these difficulties. The two problem torts (which are most resistant to unification) are the torts of simple conspiracy, and of inducing breach of contract.

7.2 GROUP A: ECONOMIC TORTS INVOLVING ACTIONS OR THREATS

The following torts make up this group.

1. Conspiracy to injure.

There are two conspiracy torts:

- simple conspiracy, and
- 'unlawful means' conspiracy.

2. Interfering with contractual relations.

There are at least two torts fitting this description. The second of them could perhaps be split into a series of smaller torts, although this may be unnecessary:

- inducing breach of contract, and
- preventing performance.

3. Intimidation.

4. 'Unlawful interference with trade'/intentional infliction of harm by unlawful means.

This is sometimes known as 'the genus tort', implying that the others are mere species of it. As already noted, there are one or two anomalous economic torts which do not fit into the genus tort—or might not, depending on their interpretation.

7.3 INTENTION AND MEANS IN THE GROUP A ECONOMIC TORTS

In this section, we will briefly explore each of the torts above according to the nature of the intention required (what does it mean to cause loss intentionally in this context?), and the relevant unlawful means (or equivalent).

---

[76] 'Chaos or Cosmos? *Rookes, Stratford* and the Economic Torts' [1964] CLJ 225, 226.
[77] See generally R. Bagshaw, 'Can the Economic Torts be Unified?' (1998) 18 OJLS 729–39 (reviewing Weir, *The Economic Torts*).

Where *intention* is concerned, an excellent starting point is provided by the following judicial statement of five possible meanings of 'intention'. The statement refers explicitly to 'unlawful interference' (the 'genus tort'), but was also applied to the two conspiracy torts in *Douglas* itself and to interference with contract in *Mainstream Properties v Young and Others*. In effect then, this approach is applicable to all the Group A economic torts, since the others seem at least compatible with (perhaps a part of) the 'genus'.

One of the strengths of the following analysis is that it does not depend upon any vague ideas about relevant 'states of mind', such as 'ill-will' or 'malice'.

Intention in the Economic Torts: Five Possible Meanings

Lord Phillips MR, *Douglas v Hello! (No 3)* [2006] QB 125 (giving the judgment of the court)[78]

159 There are a number of contenders for the test of the state of mind that amounts to an "intention to injure" in the context of the tort that we have described as "unlawful interference". These include the following:

(a) an intention to cause economic harm to the claimant as an end in itself;

(b) an intention to cause economic harm to the claimant because it is a necessary means of achieving some ulterior motive;

(c) knowledge that the course of conduct undertaken will have the inevitable consequence of causing the claimant economic harm;

(d) knowledge that the course of conduct will probably cause the claimant economic harm;

(e) knowledge that the course of conduct undertaken may cause the claimant economic harm coupled with reckless indifference as to whether it does or not.

A course of conduct undertaken with an intention that satisfies test (a) or (b) can be said to be "aimed", "directed", or "targeted" at the claimant. Causing the claimant economic harm will be a specific object of the conduct in question. A course of conduct which only satisfies test (c) cannot of itself be said to be so aimed, directed or targeted, because the economic harm, although inevitable, will be no more than an incidental consequence, at least from the defendant's perspective. None the less, the fact that the economic harm is inevitable (or even probable) may well be evidence to support a contention that test (b), or even test (a), is satisfied.

Nothing less than intention of forms (a) or (b)—both described by Lord Phillips as 'aimed', 'directed', or 'targeted' at the claimant—would be sufficient for any of the economic torts considered by the Court of Appeal in this case. The stronger of these forms of intention—category (a)—was required for the tort of simple conspiracy. Category (a) would probably fit the definition of 'targeted malice' in *Mogul Steamship* (above), but the term 'malice' has been wisely set aside. This decision means, in effect, that in no Group A economic tort[79] is it sufficient to say that the defendant intended to use unlawful means and that he or she *knew that* or *foresaw* or *was reckless as to whether* this would cause harm to the claimant.

In the light of this, we now address the individual economic torts.

[78] At the time of going to press, judgment of the House of Lords is awaited in respect of an appeal from this decision.

[79] We are not categorizing 'misfeasance in a public office' with the economic torts. Recklessness as to the consequences can be sufficient in this tort.

Conspiracy Torts

Unlawful means conspiracy requires that two or more persons combine together to use unlawful means in order to harm the claimant. There must be a common design aimed at the claimant; and *action* in concert (not just agreement). On the other hand, only one of the conspirators needs to have used unlawful means. Actual loss by the claimant must be shown.

In this tort, the relevant unlawful means will generally be the commission of another tort. There is some doubt whether a breach of contract is sufficient 'unlawful means' for this form of conspiracy, but it seems that it is.[80] In *Douglas v Hello! (No 3)*, the Court of Appeal held that a breach of an equitable duty of confidence does constitute sufficient unlawful means for this form of conspiracy (see further Chapter 14).

Simple conspiracy requires two or more persons to act in combination for the predominant purpose of causing injury to the claimant. There is no need for the acts performed to be unlawful in themselves.

Simple conspiracy is an exception to the clear principle in *Allen v Flood*, that intentional harm, without unlawful means, is not actionable in itself. The only explanation for this tort (though the explanation is almost universally recognized as rather weak) is that the *fact of combination* is so wrong or so threatening in itself that it stands in for the use of unlawful means. This tort was recognized in *Quinn v Leatham* [1901] AC 495, where Lord Shand chose to distinguish *Allen v Flood* on the basis that *Allen* was not after all a case of malicious harm, whereas *Quinn* was. We have already said (above) that this interpretation of *Allen* may be correct; but even so the House of Lords in *Allen v Flood* clearly thought that malice *would not suffice* in the absence of unlawful means.

The idea behind simple conspiracy seems to be that individual self-interest is fine, provided one stops short of unlawful means, but that collective self-interest and combination are bad in themselves. In *Lonrho v Shell Petroleum (No 2)* [1982] AC 173, Lord Diplock identified the flaws in this reasoning:

Lord Diplock, *Lonrho v Shell Petroleum (No 2)* [1982] AC 173

. . . Why should an act which causes economic loss to A but is not actionable at his suit if done by B alone become actionable because B did it pursuant to an agreement between B and C? An explanation given at the close of the 19th century by Bowen L.J. in the *Mogul* case when it was before the Court of Appeal (1889) 23 Q.B.D. 598, 616, was:

> "The distinction is based on sound reason, for a combination may make oppressive or dangerous that which if it proceeded only from a single person would be otherwise."

But to suggest today that acts done by one street-corner grocer in concert with a second are more oppressive and dangerous to a competitor than the same acts done by a string of supermarkets under a single ownership or that a multinational conglomerate such as Lonrho or oil company such as Shell or B.P. does not exercise greater economic power than any combination of small businesses, is to shut one's eyes to what has been happening in the business and industrial world since the turn of the century and, in particular, since the end of World War II. . . .

---

[80] *Kuwait Oil Tanker v Al Bader (No 3)* [2000] 2 All ER (Comm) 271.

Lord Diplock went on to say that the tort is too well-established to ignore. The only solution was to confine its ambit through a particularly demanding intention requirement.

Lord Diplock, *Lonrho v Shell Petroleum (No 2)*, at 189

This House, in my view, has an unfettered choice whether to confine the civil action of conspiracy to the narrow field to which alone it has an established claim or whether to extend this already anomalous tort beyond those narrow limits that are all that common sense and the application of the legal logic of the decided cases require. My Lords, my choice is unhesitatingly the same as that of Parker J and all three members of the Court of Appeal. I am against extending the scope of the civil tort of conspiracy beyond acts done in execution of an agreement entered into by two or more persons for the purpose not of protecting their own interests but of injuring the interests of the plaintiff.

This explains why, in *Douglas v Hello! (No 3)*, the Court of Appeal stated that category (a) intention is required in the tort of simple conspiracy.

Interference with Contractual Relations

In the tort of **inducing breach of contract**, the defendant must have deliberately and with knowledge of the contract persuaded, procured, or induced a contracting party to breach a contract with the claimant. *Breach of contract* and *harm to the claimant* must both result.

This tort has inspired a considerable amount of academic comment for two reasons. One is that it appears difficult to fit within the general schema of economic torts suggested by *Allen v Flood*. The other is that the effect of this tort is to extend the impact of contractual rights and duties *to third parties*. It uses *tort* in order to protect *contractual* interests against all comers.

Lumley v Gye [1853] 2 E & B 216

Johanna Wagner was an opera star. The plaintiff was manager of Her Majesty's Theatre and the defendant had a rival opera house at Covent Garden. Johanna Wagner had contracted to sing exclusively at the plaintiff's theatre. The defendant persuaded Johanna Wagner to breach her contract, and to sing for him instead. The court agreed that there was a case to be argued at trial—it was not a claim doomed to fail for not disclosing a cause of action.[81]

The weight of opinion now appears to be that the tort initiated in *Lumley v Gye* is the most difficult to fit within the Group A 'genus' tort.[82] Most but not all commentators also argue that an extended form of *Lumley v Gye*, *preventing* performance (below), actually is consistent with the genus tort.

Problem 1: 'unlawful means'

'Inducing breach of contract' seems to most commentators not to require 'unlawful means', since there is nothing independently unlawful about offering someone a better deal. Weir on the other hand argues that the relevant 'unlawful means' is the breach of contract which is induced.

---

[81] In fact, the claim did ultimately fail at trial.
[82] See the works by Carty, Simester and Chan, Bagshaw, and Howarth that are cited and extracted in this section.

In *Allen v Flood* itself, the House of Lords emphasized the 'unlawfulness' involved in *Lumley v Gye* in order to distinguish it from the facts in *Allen* itself. This can only have referred to the breach of contract. For example, the House of Lords expressly disapproved the decision in *Temperton v Russell* [1893] QB 715, which had extended liability under *Lumley v Gye* to a case where the defendant had maliciously *prevented someone from entering into a contract*:

Lord Herschell, *Allen v Flood*, at 121–3

It seems to have been regarded as only a small step from the one decision (*Lumley v Gye*) to the other [*Temperton v Russell*], and it was said that there seemed to be no good reason why, if an action lay for maliciously inducing a breach of contract, it should not equally lie for maliciously inducing a person not to enter into a contract. So far from thinking it a small step from the one decision to the other, I think there is a chasm between them. The reason for a distinction between the two cases appears to me to be this: that in the one case the act procured was the violation of a legal right, for which the person doing the act which injured the plaintiff could be sued as well as the person who procured it; whilst in the other case no legal right was violated by the person who did the act from which the plaintiff suffered: he would not be liable to be sued in respect of the act done, whilst the person who induced him to do the act would be liable to an action.

(At 123)

. . . Upon a review, then, of the judgment in *Lumley v Gye*, I am satisfied that the procuring what was described as an unlawful act—namely a breach of contract, was regarded as the gist of the action.

In *Lumley v Gye* itself, Wightman J argued as follows:

. . . It was undoubtedly prima facie an unlawful act on the part of Miss Wagner to break her contract, and therefore a tortious act of the defendant maliciously to procure her to do so . . .

Even so, none of these statements quite pinpoints the use of unlawful *means*. To *procure* something unlawful is not the same as *using unlawful means to procure it*.

Why can we not simply accept that the breach of contract is sufficient 'unlawfulness'? A particular problem is possible inconsistency between the torts of *inducing breach* and *preventing performance* (below). The action for preventing performance requires independent unlawful means, *besides* the breach of contract induced. Furthermore, an action for preventing performance may be available *even if the failure to perform is no breach at all* (provided that there are independently unlawful means).[83] It would seem odd to treat breach as unlawful means in one tort, but not in the other.

Commentators have proposed the following possible explanations of the 'unlawfulness' involved when breach of contract is induced.

1. Contractual rights are themselves closely analogous to a form of property, and as such they are to be strongly protected not only between the parties to the contract, but also

---

[83] For example, failure to perform may not amount to a breach in circumstances where the contract only requires 'reasonable efforts' to be undertaken.

against all the world. This is described by Roderick Bagshaw, drawing on Anson, *Principles of the English Law of Contract*, as the 'orthodox' interpretation ('Can the Economic Torts be Unified?' (1998) 18 OJLS 729, at 735).[84] This approach is far-reaching in its potential effects unless we explain exactly how the analogy is to be limited.

2. Inducement causes a contracting party to *decide* to breach the contract and in this way it constitutes a direct attack on a truly contractual right. *Prevention of performance* on the other hand does not protect a contractual right as such (the contracting party does not decide to breach the contract, and may not breach it at all), but only the economic interest in having it performed. This is broadly the argument of the article next extracted.

Simester and Chan, 'Inducing Breach of Contract: One Tort or Two?'
[2004] CLJ 132–65, at 151

We conclude that neither Weir's nor Bagshaw's accounts are capable of explaining fully what is wrong with inducing breach of contract. The underlying reason for this, we think, is that both accounts disregard an important, contract-related, wrong that is involved in persuading C to breach. This wrong reflects a second moral right that P acquires when she enters into a contract with C, over and above the obvious moral and legal right to performance. Assuming, as we do, that the foundation of contract law is agreement by means of promises, let us consider the nature of promising. As Raz puts it, the principles that best explain the activity of promising:[85]

> Present promises as creating a relationship between the promisor and promisee—which is taken out of the general competition of conflicting reasons. It creates a special bond, binding the promisor to be, in the matter of the promise, partial to the promisee. It obliges the promisor to regard the claim of the promisee as not just one of the many claims that every person has for his respect and help but as having peremptory force.

A promise changes the relationship between promisor and promisee : the promise, once given, *creates* a reason that did not previously exist, obliging the promisor to treat the promisee as special.

On either analysis, inducing breach is not an intentional tort of *damage* like the other economic torts, but a tort aimed directly (and intentionally) at a *contractual right*.

Problem 2: intention

There is a very considerable distinction between the target of intention in this tort, and the target of intention in the other economic torts. Here, the intention is directed at *bringing about the breach of contract*.[86] Elsewhere, it was *harm* that needed to be intended. But is the 'level' of intention required any different?

---

[84] For further development see R. Bagshaw, 'Inducing Breach of Contract', in Horder (ed.), *Oxford Essays in Jurisprudence,* Fourth Series (OUP, 2000).

[85] J. Raz, 'Promises and Obligations', in P. M. S. Hacker and J. Raz (eds), *Law, Morality and Society* (Clarendon Press, 1977) 210, 227–8.

[86] This casts doubt on the Court of Appeal's clear statement in *Douglas v Hello! (No 3)* that 'the gist of all the economic torts is the intentional infliction of economic harm' ([221]).

H. Carty, *An Analysis of the Economic Torts,* at 51

. . . a desire to injure is not required. Rather, the claimant must show that his contract right was intentionally attacked—for whatever reason the defendant intended to procure the breach of the claimant's contract. The best way to avoid misunderstandings of the intention requirement in the tort is to focus on the notion of intended *breach* rather than intended *injury*. . . . the claimant must show he was targeted by the defendant: but with this tort the target specifically must be the claimant's contract. . . . In this sense the claimant is 'aimed at'—the contract must be breached to secure the defendant's intended goal. So an intention to procure the breach must be shown . . .

The *level of intention* is therefore no different in this particular tort. The only difference is in the *target* of that intention.

This interpretation is consistent with *Lumley v Gye* (above), but potentially inconsistent with the later case of *Miller v Bassey* [1994] EMLR 44, which has been strongly criticized.[87] Now, in *Douglas v Hello! (No 3)* (above) and *Mainstream Properties v Young and Others* [2005] EWCA Civ 861, the Court of Appeal has preferred the minority opinion of Peter Gibson LJ in *Miller v Bassey,* to the majority opinion of Beldam LJ,[88] and therefore (for the time being)[89] vindicated the analysis of both Carty and Weir.

In *Miller v Bassey,* the defendant (singer Shirley Bassey) was sued for inducing breach of contract when *she* decided not to perform. The plaintiffs were musicians who would have been paid for performing at the recording studio, had she not been in breach; the recording studio seems to have been forced to breach its contract with them, when she withdrew her services. Beldam LJ thought it arguable that the singer should be liable for inducing breach of their contracts, despite the fact that she would not have had their contracts at the forefront of her mind (if indeed she was aware of them).

Peter Gibson LJ dissented:

Peter Gibson LJ, *Miller v Bassey* (dissenting)

The conduct of the defendant [must] be aimed directly at the plaintiff, the contracting party who suffers the damage, in the sense that the defendant intends that the plaintiff's contract should be broken [and it is not] sufficient that the conduct should have the natural and probable consequence that the plaintiff's contract should be broken.

This dissenting approach has now been accepted as correct by the Court of Appeal both in *Douglas v Hello! (No 3)* (where it was not strictly in issue) and in *Mainstream Properties* (where it was). Turning back to our introductory remarks about intention at the start of this chapter, the problem with the majority approach in *Miller v Bassey could* be explained as a simple confusion over the idea of 'intention', independent of the particular complexities of the tort of

---

[87] Particularly by T. Weir, *Economic Torts.*

[88] It is slightly hard to say whether Beldam LJ stated a majority opinion, or not. This was a 'striking out' action, considering only whether the claimant had an arguable claim which deserved to go to a full trial. Ralph Gibson LJ expressed agreement in principle with the view of Peter Gibson LJ, but thought that the issue was not sufficiently well settled by the authorities to merit striking out without full argument.

[89] *Mainstream Properties,* like *Douglas v Hello! (No 3),* is under appeal to the House of Lords at the time of writing.

inducing breach of contract. But the reasoning in *Mainstream* also supports the abstentionist approach, and Arden LJ offered *policy* reasons for preferring a strong form of intention for this tort as in the other economic torts:[90]

Arden LJ

31 Mr Lomas [counsel for the defendants] emphasises that the tort of inducing breach of contract is unique. It entails liability because of interference with a contract to which the defendant is not a party, and in respect of an act which is not unlawful. The only unlawfulness is the actual interference. **This makes defendants to such claims the guardians of their competitors' interests**. Therefore, the imposition of a requirement for intention is soundly based in policy.

Previously, it had been argued by some commentators that strong intention (of a category (b) form: targeted at the claimant) was not required for this particular tort. Roderick Bagshaw for example noted that:

R. Bagshaw, 'Can the Economic Torts be Unified?', at 737

. . . the authorities tend to refer to 'knowingly and intentionally' procuring the breach rather than insisting on an intention to cause any consequential harm. Moreover, the authorities tend to concentrate on the defendant's knowledge, and to define 'intention' in a broad way.

As we have just seen, although this remains correct in terms of the 'target' of intention, the 'level' of intention has been narrowly interpreted for the time being.

It is time then to give some more attention to abstentionism in respect of inducing breach of contract, as the most problematic of the economic torts.

Abstentionism, Policy Argument, and *Lumley v Gye*

Recent discussions of *Lumley v Gye* take us into some deeper disagreements which are not restricted to the law of tort, but concern the purpose of the law of contract.

It is possible to argue that contract law exists to fulfil important moral or ethical goals such as the protection of promises. Such an approach might explain the tort of inducing breach of contract as a natural off-shoot of contract itself, giving *extra* protection to something which inherently deserves protection. On the other side of the divide is an approach to contract which is typically associated with economic analysis (but need not be) and which holds that contractual remedies exist because the institution of contracting *serves a public interest goal*. (We will come to a possible intermediate position, below).

The difference between these outlooks can lead their holders to propose very different solutions to problems that arise. Those who think that contract remedies exist to fulfil moral or ethical goals will tend to accept and encourage the idea that additional remedies should be available to deter breach. By contrast, those who think that the state takes the trouble to protect contractual interests *in order to serve a collective interest or public purpose* (typically, wealth creation or economic advancement) might argue, by contrast, that breach can be

---

[90] It should be noted that Sedley LJ in the same case expressed reservations about the policy judgment made here, though he hesitantly agreed with Arden LJ.

'efficient' (productive).[91] They might suggest that it is not always right to make available extra remedies which will make the breach more 'expensive' to the relevant party. *Lumley v Gye* provides such an additional remedy and removes the incentive to *bring about* breach through persuasion. Another very important example of such an additional remedy, which Howarth pertinently compares with *Lumley v Gye*, is the 'account of profits' remedy which was recognized in *AG v Blake* [2001] 1 AC 168, as being available for breach of contract.

It is possible to hold a view which is somewhere in between these two extremes. For example, it may be accepted that contract and the legal protection of contract *serve collective goals*, while at the same time proposing that the worth of contracting *in this sense* will be undermined if contracts are too easily breached. This argument might hold that certainty needs to be maintained, and proceeding against the person who does the persuading is therefore beneficial. But once an instrumental justification of contract is adopted, this admits all manner of further questions about whether certainty is *always* to be preferred. In other words, might abstentionism not serve the relevant public goals more successfully?

David Howarth has recently presented a range of arguments, derived not only from economic efficiency but also from the potential for *morally justified* breach, to argue that the general rule in *Lumley v Gye* is suspect and should be confined to narrow limits. He particularly draws attention to the context in which the *Lumley v Gye* tort has operated—employment contracts, and especially trade union activity.

David Howarth, 'Against *Lumley v Gye*' (2005) 68 MLR 195–232, 231–2

Summary and Conclusions

Lumley should be seen primarily in its industrial relations context, as the foundation of the law on strikes. Although it is important in other commercial contexts, none of them compare in historical importance with strike law. If *Lumley* is unsatisfactory in its industrial relations context, as it appears to be, we should consider reforming it. But reform that merely exempted industrial relations cases from the scope of *Lumley* is itself unsatisfactory because it gives rise to the false appearance that trade unions would be obtaining 'special' treatment. We need to look for a wider reform of *Lumley* that takes its non-industrial relations uses into account, but which gives priority, if necessary, to its industrial relations uses.

One objection to the radical reform of *Lumley* is that one can infer from *Lumley* liability from the very existence of contract law. But, as we have seen, justifying *Lumley* involves imposing contract law on parties, such as trade unions, who are unwilling participants in state contract law. The justifications for imposing contract law on the unwilling do not reach *Lumley* as it applies to strikes, and possibly not as it applies in other circumstances as well.

Another objection to radical reform is the argument that *Lumley* liability is justified because it adds to our certainty that contracts will be performed. The main problem with that argument is that it assumes that it is always worthwhile to add to certainty, a position that ignores the costs of producing such extra certainty. Although we cannot be sure that we have reached the point at which the costs of extra certainty outweigh its benefits, we have reasons, particularly in industrial relations cases, to be sceptical about whether, if the parties had to construct their own law by agreement, they would opt for a *Lumley* rule, at least in its present form.

[91] See for example D. Campbell and D. Harris, 'In Defence of Breach' (2002) 22 LS 208. Support for 'efficient breach' is not an *inevitable* consequence of taking an efficiency-based approach to the law of contract. But it is a possibility.

The argument from certainty also ignores the point, inherent in efficient breach analysis, that additional certainty that a bad deal will be fulfilled should be counted as a bad thing, not a good thing. That point, of course, raises the status of efficient breach analysis, but those who criticise efficient breach analysis on moral grounds miss the point that it is also immoral for one party to a contract to insist on performance where the contract would not have been agreed had the parties known at the time what they know now.

The possibility of immoral insistence on contractual performance, and its confluence with efficient breach analysis, suggests that there should be a wider defence to *Lumley* that would allow the court to take such moral and economic points into account. . . .

The introduction of normative economic and moral arguments at the 'justification' stage (as Howarth proposes) could lead to some very complex and politically charged reasoning. Arguably, the effect would be almost the reverse of the 'abstentionist' approach in *Allen v Flood*. For example, is it really appropriate for courts to be asked to judge the *moral and political merits* of any given strike action? In practical terms then, there are reasons to think that Howarth's proposals may not be feasible. But this is not to detract from the strength of his attack on *Lumley* itself.

The next extract considers whether the outcome in *Lumley v Gye* has been unnecessarily, and unwisely, elevated into a general principle.

Stephen Waddams, 'Johanna Wagner and the Rival Opera Houses' (2001) 117 LQR 431, 452–3[92]

. . . The wide proposition that deliberate inducement of a breach of contract always amounts to a tort has led to much difficulty and (I would suggest) ought not to be accepted in so wide a form. The hypothetical case of a father advising his daughter to break an engagement of marriage is one where there is a strong public and private interest in freedom of action on the part of both. No injunction has in any such a case been issued against the daughter or against the father, nor has an action in tort succeeded against the father. Again, generally speaking, an ordinary employee has been free in modern times to change employment, even without giving proper notice to a former employer, subject to the obligation to pay damages. It has been perceived as an undue restriction on that freedom either to restrain the employee by injunction, or to hold the second employer, even with knowledge of the inadequate notice, liable in tort. In the light of an appreciation of the background facts, *Lumley v Gye* can be distinguished from such a case just because it was not a case of an ordinary employee. Johanna Wagner was a 'hot property', and it was precisely for this reason that the injunction was granted. The case therefore was a very special one, and hardly need stand for the general proposition that inducement of all breaches of contract is always tortious. It could equally be explained by postulating a much narrower rule, for example that inducing breach of contract is wrongful where it infringes something analogous to a proprietary interest, where it causes an unjust enrichment, and where the public policy favouring freedom of action is outweighed by strong countervailing considerations. In practice, . . . the courts have not always attached all the usual consequences of torts to inducing breach of contract.

Waddams goes on to discuss the case of *Warren v Mendy* [1989] 1 WLR 853. Here a boxer was unhappy with his manager and sought a new one. The existing manager sought an injunction

92 A version of this article is also included in Waddams, *Dimensions of Private Law* (CUP, 2003).

against the new manager on the basis that he was seeking to induce a breach of contract. The injunction was refused by the Court of Appeal on the basis that it was an undue restriction of the boxer's freedom.

Prevention of Performance Torts

These torts are emanations of *Lumley v Gye* and were said to exist in the case of *Thomson v Deakin* [1952] Ch 646, where several variations were listed. Carty argues that it is quite misleading however to see them as variations of the same tort as 'inducing breach of contract'. Whereas inducing breach of contract focuses on the protection of the claimant's existing contractual rights, these torts focus on *harm* done to the claimant *by unlawful means*. The focus is not on the breach by a contracting party (the defendant being a third party to the contract), but on the *unlawful steps taken by the defendant to stop the contract from being performed, or to make it less valuable to the claimant*. As such, she argues that 'prevention' torts should be subsumed within 'the genus tort' (below). Consistently with this interpretation, breach of contract is immaterial, and it is the economic interests of the claimant (not the contractual right) that are protected.

As a result, these torts will have the following requirements:

The defendant must have *used independently unlawful means* in order to prevent performance of a contract, with the intention of causing loss to the claimant.

Since they are compatible with, or part of, the 'genus', we can assume that the relevant intention will be of type (b).

Intimidation

In the tort of **intimidation**, the defendant deliberately threatens a third party in order to compel that third party to harm the claimant. The threat itself must be unlawful, so this tort is consistent with the requirement of 'unlawful means' in *Allen v Flood*.

Lord Wright, *Crofter v Veitch* [1942] AC 435, at 467

There is nothing unlawful in giving a warning or intimation that if the party addressed pursues a certain line of conduct, others may act in a manner which he will not like and which will be prejudicial to his interests, so long as nothing unlawful is threatened or done.

In *Rookes v Barnard* [1964] AC 1129, the plaintiff brought an action against members of a union from which he had resigned. The union threatened to withdraw labour unless the plaintiff was removed from his job. The defendants were individuals who spoke in favour of this action at a union meeting. Agreements between BOAC (the employer) and the union provided that there would be 100 per cent union membership, and no strikes. It was conceded by the defendants' counsel (perhaps unwisely) that the threatened strike would therefore be in breach of an implied term of the employment contracts.

The House of Lords decided that a threat to breach contract could amount to a tort, despite the absence of any threat of force or violence.

In the article next extracted, Lord Wedderburn explains the historical interplay between courts and legislature where the liabilities of trade unions were concerned. This is further illustration of the importance of the context in which legal principles will operate.

K. W. Wedderburn, 'Intimidation and the Right to Strike'
(1964) 27 MLR 257–81, at 257–8

Professor Jenks, commenting on the cases that culminated in *Quinn v Leatham* and *Taff Vale Ry v ASRS*, wrote: "The House of Lords had first invented a new civil offence ('civil conspiracy') and had then created a new kind of defendant against whom it could be alleged." [*Short History of English Law*, p. 337 (1934 ed. First published 1912]. In 1964, in *Rookes v Barnard*, the House of Lords has invented a new extension of civil liability, and then reduced to insignificance the protections of the Trade Disputes Act 1906, which should have been a defence against it.

The story has often been told how judges in the nineteenth century extended old and created new liabilities in criminal and civil law to the disadvantage of a growing trade union movement. The unions increasingly pressed Parliament for statutory protection only to find that the judges had moved onto some new liability. The manipulation of such vague crimes as 'obstruction', 'molestation', 'threats' and 'intimidation' was (after defective attempts in 1859 and 1871) impeded eventually by the definitions of 1875. The vague crime of 'conspiracy' to which the judges had particularly turned after 1871 was excluded from the realm of trade disputes in the same year. Up to that time 'there never had been any attempt to make out any civil liability' for conspiracy; but 'then came the new world and the new ideas'; and the judges devised a civil responsibility for conspiracy which became 'very serious'. [Lord Chancellor Loreburn (1906) 166 Parl.Deb., col. 693, speaking on the Trade Disputes Bill] Together with the liability for inducing breach of contract, invented in 1853, and (some thought) perhaps a residual tort of 'malicious interference' with business, the judges had by 1901 reacquired in civil law the capability to repress strikes which statute had denied them in the criminal law. The torts in question had indeed 'arisen out of the circumstances of modern industrial relations' [Lord Everhsed, *Rookes v Barnard*, p 293]; but no modern observer can fail to notice that they arose from judges who reflected the attitudes of the middle class towards the labour movement. The Trade Disputes Act, 1906, was passed to protect trade unionists against these liabilities, and to allow for the confrontation of conflicting industrial interests without constant recourse to the courts.

The House of Lords in *Rookes v Barnard*, has now extended such tort liability once again in a trade dispute. Briefly, their lordships decided, for the first time, that threats to break a contract can be tortious 'intimidation', on a par with threats of violence; and that the 1906 Act does not protect such 'intimidation'. An element of what might justly be called mystification could be thought to lie in placing this kind of threat into a category where it can be at once equated with such things as threats of violence. As 'intimidation', the contractual characteristics can . . . be more easily forgotten.

Intentionally Causing Loss through Unlawful Means/Unlawful Interference with Trade/the 'Genus' Tort

In *Merkur Island Shipping v Laughton* [1983] 2 AC 570, Lord Diplock referred to this action as the 'genus' tort. But it does not, as he implies, encompass all of the Group A torts. It does incorporate intimidation and the 'peripheral' versions of interference with contract, which do not involve 'inducing breach'.

Unlawful interference with trade requires that the defendant should use unlawful means with the intention of causing harm to the claimant. Actual harm to the claimant must flow from the defendant's acts.

'Unlawful means' include torts (including the other economic torts!), breach of contract, criminal acts, and (probably) breaches of statutory provisions. The Court of Appeal decision in *Douglas v Hello! (No 3)* settles (for the time being) that the *intention* required must be of either category (a) or (b), and therefore 'targeted at' the claimant.

7.4 GROUP B: FALSE STATEMENTS

Deceit requires that the defendant should knowingly make a false representation to the claimant, with the intention that the claimant should rely upon it. The claimant must rely upon the representation, to his or her detriment.

Unlike the Group A torts, *and* unlike malicious falsehood (below), deceit typically applies in a 'two-party' situation. The person *relying upon the statement* is the claimant.

In *Pasley v Freeman* (1789) 3 Term Rep 51, the defendant falsely represented that a third party was credit-worthy. The plaintiff sold goods to the third party in question and suffered loss through reliance on the misrepresentation. The defendant was liable, despite not making any gain. In *Derry v Peek* (1889) 14 App Cas 337, the House of Lords strictly limited the ambit of deceit by holding that misrepresentations giving rise to harm were not actionable except in the presence of 'fraud' or contractual breach. 'Fraud' generally means that the defendant *knows* that the statement is false, or is *reckless* as to its truth or falsity. 'Recklessness' involves *neither knowing nor caring* whether the statement is true, or false.

It is important to note that there are two 'targets' for intention in deceit:

- It must be intended that C should rely. This seems to mean that it is D's *purpose* (or perhaps a *necessary means* to D's primary goal) that C should rely; *and*

- D must either know the statement to be false, or be reckless as to its truth or falsity.

The second of these provides the element of 'fraud' required by *Derry v Peek*. 'Recklessness' only suffices for this second element.

An exception to the fraud requirement was carved out for cases of 'fiduciary relationship' (or relationships close to this) in *Nocton v Lord Ashburton* [1914] 2 AC 932. Much later, in *Hedley Byrne v Heller* [1964] AC 465, this exception was developed to allow claims *in the tort of negligence* for merely negligent misrepresentation, in defined circumstances. A large body of case law now exists in respect of liability under *Hedley Byrne*: see Chapter 6. Not only does the action in negligence require no fraud, it also requires no *intention* that C should rely. (On the other hand, knowledge of the purpose for which C will use the information or advice given does appear to be essential.) Despite the growth of negligence liability, deceit is distinctive because it allows for recovery of a broader range of loss than negligence; and the defence of contributory negligence is not available: see *Smith New Court v Citibank*, and *Standard Chartered Bank v Pakistan Shipping*, below.

Malicious falsehood requires that the defendant should maliciously publish falsehoods concerning the claimant or his or her property. Except where statutory exceptions apply, there must also be 'special damage'.

Bowen LJ, *Ratcliffe v Evans* [1892] 2 QB 524

. . . an action will lie for written or oral falsehoods, not actionable *per se*, or even defamatory, where they are maliciously published, where they are calculated in the ordinary course of things to produce and where they do produce, actual damage.

Damage

At common law, the action in malicious falsehood required that the claimant should show *actual damage* caused by the falsehood. In other words, malicious falsehood is centrally a tort of damage, rather than (like libel and the torts of trespass to the person) a tort actionable '*per se*'. In fact, in many instances malicious falsehood is now actionable without proof of damage.

Defamation Act 1952

3.—(1) In an action for slander of title, slander of goods or other malicious falsehood, it shall not be necessary to allege or prove special damage—

   (a) if the words upon which the action is founded are calculated to cause pecuniary damage to the plaintiff and are published in writing or other permanent form; or

   (b) if the said words are calculated to cause pecuniary damage to the plaintiff in respect of any office, profession, calling, trade or business held or carried on by him at the time of the publication.

Malicious falsehood is nevertheless distinctly different from defamation (Chapter 13) because of its 'malice' requirement.

'Malice' in malicious falsehood

Hazel Carty, *An Analysis of the Economic Torts* (Oxford: OUP, 2001), 161–2

. . . it is clear now that 'malice' is a key feature of the tort and must be proved by the claimant in all cases of malicious falsehood. . . .

The real issue has become to pinpoint the definition of malice applied by the courts. A review of case law reveals that malice can be proved in various ways, summarized by Heydon [*The Economic Torts*, p. 83] as either personal spite, or an intention to injure the plaintiff without just cause or excuse or knowledge of the falsity of the statement. However, it is difficult to separate personal spite from the related concepts of improper motive and intention to injure without lawful excuse. . . . It is simpler and consistent with leading modern case law to define malice as either 'motive' malice (*mala fides* means that an honest belief will not negative liability) or 'deceit' malice (lies where indifference as to the effect on the claimant will not negate liability). The absence of good faith is, therefore, due to either the knowledge of falsity or the malicious intention. So, 'if you publish a defamatory statement about a man's goods which is injurious to him, honestly believing that it is true, your object being your own advantage and no detriment to him, you obviously are not liable' [Stable J in *Wilts United Dairies v Robinson* 57 RPC 220, p. 237].

Either 'deceit malice' or 'motive malice' will suffice:

- If there is intent to harm (motive malice), honest belief in truth will not assist the defendant.
- If there is no belief in truth (deceit malice), lack of intent to harm will not assist the defendant.

In recent years, malicious falsehood has been allowed to fill certain gaps left by the law of defamation (Chapter 13). In *Joyce v Sengupta* [1993] 1 WLR 337, it was no bar to an action in malicious falsehood that the harm to the claimant could have been described in terms of damage to *reputation* (which is protected by defamation)—provided, of course, that actual damage (as well as malice as explained above) could be established. The reason for choosing an action in malicious falsehood in that case was that legal aid was unavailable for an action in defamation. This particular *reason* for preferring malicious falsehood is now a matter of history, since actions in defamation can be funded through 'conditional fee agreements' (Chapter 8). However, it remains important that malicious falsehood can apply in areas which would more naturally be thought of as concerned with reputation. In *Kaye v Robertson* [1991] FSR 62 , an injunction was issued to prevent publication of a potential malicious falsehood, in circumstances where such an injunction was *not* available in defamation. Because of the need to show malice and (sometimes) damage, the action in malicious falsehood is taken to pose a minimal threat to freedom of expression, and interim (pre-trial) injunctions are more freely available than in defamation.

7.5 MEASURE OF DAMAGES IN THE ECONOMIC TORTS

The available remedies ought to fit the rationale of any given tort. The majority of economic torts ought therefore to allow for recovery of *damage* caused by the relevant 'wrong'. The wrong is generally intentionally caused harm brought about through unlawful means (category A), or harm brought about by intentional falsehood (category B).

The House of Lords has ruled that damages for **deceit** in particular are not confined to damage that is *foreseeable* (which is the case in a claim for negligence). Rather, all those losses that were the *direct consequence* of reliance on the false representation are recoverable. Furthermore, damages in respect of a *negligent* misstatement are limited to those damages which are regarded as 'within the scope' of the particular duty of care that was owed. Thus if the duty is only one to give information, and not to 'advise' in a general way, then only damage that can be fairly attributed to the incorrectness of the information can be recovered in negligence. In deceit however, because there is an intention that the claimant should rely *and* fraud in respect of the statement, *all* direct consequences of the statement (subject to a duty to mitigate) can be recovered.

Lord Steyn, *Smith New Court Securities v Citibank NA* [1997] AC 254, at 283

The context is the rule that in an action for deceit the plaintiff is entitled to recover all his loss directly flowing from the fraudulently induced *transaction*. In the case of a negligent misrepresentation the rule is narrower: the recoverable loss does not extend beyond the consequences flowing from the negligent *misrepresentation*: see *Banque Bruxelles Lambert SA v Eagle Star Insurance Co Ltd* [1997] AC 191.

'Directness' is clearly intended to be distinct from 'foreseeability' (see the extract below), but it is not an entirely straightforward idea. An illustration is drawn from the case of *Twycross v Grant* (1877) 2 CPD 469: Cockburn CJ explained in this case that if a fraudulently misdescribed horse subsequently catches a disease and dies, the buyer could not recover the whole value of the horse.[93] It could be explained, roughly, that the disease amounts to a 'new cause'.

---

[93] This example is given by Lord Steyn at 281.

Should the *Smith New Court* approach be applicable to all those torts where harm to the claimant is actually intended? Arguably, it should. But Lord Steyn places considerable emphasis in the extract below on the element of 'fraud' in an action for deceit. This particular element is not present in the other economic torts; although most of the others require 'unlawful means'.

The Reasons for Denying the Defendant the 'Benefit' of a Reasonable Foreseeability Measure

---

Lord Steyn, *Smith New Court v Citibank,* at 279–80

The justification for distinguishing between deceit and negligence

That brings me to the question of policy whether there is a justification for differentiating between the extent of liability for civil wrongs depending on where in the sliding scale from strict liability to intentional wrongdoing the particular civil wrong fits in. It may be said that logical symmetry and a policy of not punishing intentional wrongdoers by civil remedies favour a uniform rule. On the other hand, it is a rational and defensible strategy to impose wider liability on an intentional wrongdoer. As *Hart and Honoré, Causation in the Law*, 2nd ed. (1985), p. 304 observed, an innocent plaintiff may, not without reason, call on a morally reprehensible defendant to pay the whole of the loss he caused. The exclusion of heads of loss in the law of negligence, which reflects considerations of legal policy, does not necessarily avail the intentional wrongdoer. Such a policy of imposing more stringent remedies on an intentional wrongdoer serves two purposes. First it serves a deterrent purpose in discouraging fraud. Counsel for Citibank argued that the sole purpose of the law of tort generally, and the tort of deceit in particular, should be to compensate the victims of civil wrongs. That is far too narrow a view. Professor Glanville Williams identified four possible purposes of an action for damages in tort: appeasement, justice, deterrence and compensation: see "The Aims of the Law of Tort" (1951) 4 C.L.P. 137. He concluded, at p. 172:

> "Where possible the law seems to like to ride two or three horses at once; but occasionally a situation occurs where one must be selected. The tendency is then to choose the deterrent purpose for tort of intention, the compensatory purpose for other torts."

And in the battle against fraud civil remedies can play a useful and beneficial role. Secondly, as between the fraudster and the innocent party, moral considerations militate in favour of requiring the fraudster to bear the risk of misfortunes directly caused by his fraud. I make no apology for referring to moral considerations. The law and morality are inextricably interwoven. To a large extent the law is simply formulated and declared morality. And, as *Oliver Wendell Holmes, The Common Law* (ed. M. De W. Howe), p. 106, observed, the very notion of deceit with its overtones of wickedness is drawn from the moral world.

7.6 DEFENCES

Justification

The tort of inducing breach of contract is clearly qualified by a defence of 'justification' (indeed this defence is mentioned in the extract from the judgment of Bowen LJ in *Mogul Steamship*, above). It seems that the defence requires some 'compelling reason' for inducing the breach. In those torts which, unlike inducing breach of contract, require some independently unlawful means, it has been wondered whether these unlawful means could ever be 'justified'. In respect of the 'genus' tort, Carty argues that any such defence (if it exists) would be 'very residual'.[94] Arguably, because the tort of intimidation has been developed to include a threatened breach of contract (*Rookes v Barnard*), intimidation like inducing breach of contract should benefit from a justification defence. It seems less likely that there could be 'justification' for a fraud or malicious falsehood (Group B), but this is not out of the question.

It is clear that 'due care' or 'lack of malice' *cannot* amount to 'justification' in the economic torts, since presence of a relevant state of mind is part of the definition of each of them.

Contributory Negligence

In *Standard Chartered Bank v Pakistan National Shipping Corpn* [2003] 1 AC 959, the House of Lords clearly decided that fault on the part of the claimant did *not* give rise to a defence of contributory negligence in the tort of deceit. This defence requires the court to reduce damages to reflect fault on the part of both parties and is fully explored in relation to negligence in Chapter 5. The essential reason why it was held not to apply in deceit is that no such defence to deceit was recognized before 1945. The Law Reform (Contributory Negligence) Act 1945 did not *introduce* a defence of contributory negligence, it only converted it from a total defence (no damages at all) to a partial one (damages reduced).

Lord Rodger added some further comments. He argued that in no tort of intentional damage should the defence be available. (The other members of the House did not comment on this.)

Lord Rodger of Earlsferry, *Standard Chartered Bank v Pakistan Shipping Corpn* [2003] 1 AC 959

42   .... In agreement with Mummery J in *Alliance & Leicester Building Society v Edgestop Ltd* [1993] 1 WLR 1462, Lord Hoffmann has concluded that there is no common law defence of contributory negligence in the case of fraudulent misrepresentation. I respectfully regard that conclusion as compelling. As Mummery J pointed out, if the negligence of the plaintiff had been a defence to an action of deceit at common law, this would have meant that it would have been a complete defence, absolving the fraudulent defendant of all liability. Such an extreme doctrine could hardly have passed through the law without leaving its mark in the cases. But there is no trace of it. **Indeed, the signs are that before 1945 the defence of contributory negligence was thought not to apply where the defendant intended to cause the plaintiff harm**. I do not repeat the citations given by Mummery J but draw attention to two further indications of the way that the law was generally understood.

43   In 1882 Sir Frederick Pollock drafted a Civil Wrongs Bill for the Government of India, the aim being to set out a codified, if slightly simplified, version of English tort law. To Pollock's lasting disappointment the Bill was never enacted. Pollock dealt with contributory negligence in clause 64 which, significantly, was drafted in such a way that it would operate as a defence only in the case of negligence by the defendant or someone for whose negligence he was answerable. Similarly, five years later in his *Law of Torts* (1887) Pollock treated contributory negligence in the chapter on negligence and indicated that the defence would not apply in the

---

94 Carty, *An Analysis of the Economic Torts*, 121–2.

case of an intentional harm (Appendix D, p 484). He remained of this view more than 40 years later in the last edition to come from his pen: *Law of Torts* 13th ed (1929), pp 615 and 675–676.

44 Similarly, in an authoritative essay on "Contributory Negligence" in American law, written in 1908 and reprinted in his *Studies in the Law of Torts* (1926), pp 528–529, Bohlen stated:

> "If the defendant's wrong be intentional, only consent, express or necessarily implied from the circumstances, will bar recovery . . . the unanimous current of decision is that when the defendant's wrong is something more than mere negligence—when it involves an intent to cause harm—contributory negligence is no defense."

45 In *Murphy v Culhane* [1977] QB 94, an interlocutory decision, Lord Denning MR said that a widow's claim for damages for the death of her husband might fall to be reduced under the 1945 Act because it had resulted from a criminal affray in which he had participated. That would appear to conflict with the view that contributory negligence had never been a defence open to a defendant who had intended to harm the plaintiff. There were other arguments available to the defendant, however, and *Murphy v Culhane* is distinguishable from the present case. I should wish to reserve my opinion as to whether this particular observation of Lord Denning MR should be regarded as sound.

There are good reasons to suggest that in torts which are actionable only where the defendant intended harm to the claimant, there is no room for a defence of contributory negligence. This justification only applies where, as Lord Rodger puts it, *the defendant intended to cause the [claimant] harm*. As we have seen throughout this chapter, we have to be very careful in our categorization of 'intentional torts', because it is not always the case that what is intended is the harm. Indeed, even in deceit, it is reliance on a falsehood, rather than harm, that must be intended.

We addressed the implications of this in respect of trespass to the person, above. But similarly, if inducing breach of contract is not an action based on intentional harm, the question of contributory negligence in this tort may need separate consideration.

FURTHER READING

Bagshaw, R., 'Can the Economic Torts be Unified?' (1998) 18 OJLS 729–39.

Bagshaw, R., 'Inducing Breach of Contract', in J. Horder (ed), *Oxford Essays in Jurisprudence*, Fourth Series (Oxford: OUP, 2000).

Carty, H., *An Analysis of the Economic Torts* (Oxford: OUP, 2001).

Howarth, D., 'Against *Lumley v Gye*' (2005) 68 MLR 195–232.

Sales, P., and Stilitz, D., 'Intentional Infliction of Harm by Unlawful Means' (1999) 115 LQR 411.

Simester, A., and Chan, W., 'Inducing Breach of Contract: One Tort or Two?' [2004] CLJ 132–65.

Waddams, S., 'Johanna Wagner and the Rival Opera Houses' (2001) 117 LQR 431.

Weir, T., *Economic Torts* (Oxford: Clarendon Press, 1997).

8. INTENTIONAL ABUSE OF POWER AND PROCESS

8.1 MALICIOUS PROSECUTION AND ANALOGOUS TORTS

The tort of malicious prosecution is committed where the defendant has maliciously and without reasonable or probable cause 'prosecuted' the claimant for a criminal offence, and where the prosecution has ultimately ended in the claimant's favour.

Although this tort is clearly of use to an individual who is the subject of malicious and improper prosecution by relevant authorities, the defendant need not be a public 'prosecutor'. 'Prosecuting' for the purposes of this tort is broad enough to incorporate the role of the Crown Prosecution Service *and* of police officers who are responsible for charging the claimant and assembling evidence. It will also include a private individual who instigates a prosecution and offers to give evidence. At least, this will be the case where the individual in question brings evidence and they alone can attest to the truth of the charge: see *Martin v Watson* [1996] AC 74. Here the defendant went to the police and said that the plaintiff had exposed himself to her. An individual who instigates a *private prosecution* will also be treated as having 'prosecuted' the claimant.

'Lack of reasonable and probable cause' and 'malice' are two separate requirements for this tort, which is committed only when there is a subjective type of 'malice', combined with an *objective* lack of reasonable or probable cause. The subjective form of malice involved may refer to any sort of 'improper motive'.

The tort only extends to *criminal* prosecutions. In *Gregory v Portsmouth City Council* [2000] 1 AC 419, the House of Lords decided that initiation of *disciplinary proceedings* did not fall within the tort. The House also confirmed that malicious initiation of *civil* proceedings does not give rise to liability under this or an analogous tort. At the same time, there *is* a claim in tort for malicious initiation of bankruptcy proceedings (or, in the case of a company, winding up proceedings).

Torts Analogous to Malicious Prosecution

The following torts are variations on the theme of malicious prosecution. They relate to initiation of a criminal process which falls short of prosecution.

Malicious procurement of an arrest warrant

In *Roy v Prior* [1971] AC 470, the defendant was a solicitor acting for a man accused of a criminal offence. The defendant sought to serve the plaintiff with a witness summons. When the plaintiff did not appear at trial, the defendant secured a warrant for his arrest, and he was kept in custody for several hours. The House of Lords held that these facts might disclose a cause of action, provided the plaintiff could show *both* malice, *and* lack of reasonable and probable cause.

Malicious procurement of a search warrant

Malicious procurement of a search warrant may be actionable on the same principles: *Gibbs v Rea* [1998] AC 786. The harm against which this tort protects appears slightly different from the harm in the last two torts, in that the procurement of the warrant will lead primarily to disruption, anxiety and invasion of privacy (and consequential harm) rather than loss of liberty or the threat of it.

The right to respect for one's private life and for one's home is protected by Article 8 ECHR (extracted and discussed in Chapter 14). In the recent case of *Keegan v UK* (18 July 2006), the European Court of Human Rights decided that the rights of the applicants under Article 8, and under Article 13 (requiring compensation for violation of Convention rights) had not been appropriately protected by domestic law. A search warrant had been obtained without reasonable cause and the door of the applicants' home was violently forced open at 7 am, causing considerable fear, anxiety and distress. A claim in tort failed for lack of evidence of malice, in the sense of lack of honest belief in probable cause.[95] Kennedy LJ dismissed the claim with some reluctance and pointed out that in future, an action may lie under the Human Rights Act 1998 for this sort of intrusion:

Kennedy LJ, *Keegan and Others v Chief Constable of Merseyside*
[2003] EWCA Civ 936

33 That an Englishman's home is said to be his castle reveals an important public interest, but there is another important public interest in the detection of crime and bringing to justice of those who commit it. These interests are in conflict in a case like this and on the law as it stood when these events occurred, which is before the coming into force of the Human Rights Act 1998, which may be said to have elevated the right to respect for one's home, a finding of malice on the part of the police is the proper balancing safeguard.

The European Court of Human Rights concluded that the available action in tort, as it applies to actions taking place before the commencement of the Human Rights Act 1998,[96] does not allow proper regard to be had to the proportionality and reasonableness of the police action. The 'balance' struck is not the appropriate one.

European Court of Human Rights, *Keegan v UK*, 18 July 2006, App No 28867/03

44 . . . The Court observes that the courts held that it was in effect irrelevant that there were no reasonable grounds for the police action as damages only lay where malice could be proved, and negligence of this kind did not qualify. The courts were unable to examine issues of proportionality or reasonableness and, as various judges in the domestic proceedings noted, the balance was set in favour of protection of the police in some cases. In these circumstances, the Court finds that the applicants did not have available to them a means of obtaining redress for the interference with their rights under Article 8 of the Convention.

On one view, this calls into question the existence of a malice requirement when the interests protected by tort law have similar content to the Convention rights. It suggests that a test based on reasonableness is more appropriate for protection of such interests, and possibly that the contents of such torts should change. On another view, it is better for such issues to be pursued through actions under the Human Rights Act 1998 where this is applicable.[97] Otherwise, there will be inconsistency in the principles of applicable torts, depending on

---

[95] A claim based in trespass to land also failed, because the intrusion to the premises was lawful on the face of it.

[96] October 2000.

[97] Actions under the Human Rights Act 1998 are only available against *public authority* defendants.

whether a Convention right is engaged in a particular case. This illustrates the emerging challenge to tort law from the new status of Convention rights that we discussed in Chapter 1.[98]

8.2 MISFEASANCE IN A PUBLIC OFFICE

The tort of misfeasance in a public office is committed when a public officer exercising his or her power *either*:

(a) does so with the intention of injuring the claimant *or*

(b) acts (or decides not to act)[99] in the knowledge of, or with reckless indifference to, the illegality of his or her act or failure to act and in the knowledge of, or with reckless indifference to, the probability of causing injury to the claimant or to persons of a class of which the claimant was a member.

The claimant must suffer damage as a consequence.

The existence of the two very different forms of this tort captured as (a) and (b) above was accepted by the House of Lords (except Lord Millett, who argued that they really come down to the same thing) in *Three Rivers District Council v Bank of England (No 3)* [2003] 2 AC 1. This litigation arose from the collapse of BCCI (a bank). The claimants were depositors who lost money when the bank collapsed; they claimed that the Bank of England either wrongly (with the requisite mental element) granted a licence to the bank; or wrongly (with the requisite mental element) failed to revoke the licence when it was clear that BCCI was likely to collapse.[100]

The tort encompasses acts *and* failures to act, but not *all* failures to act will suffice. According to Lord Hobhouse (at [230]), in the case of an omission (such as the failure to *revoke* licences in *Three Rivers* itself), there must be an actual *decision* not to act, rather than a mere failure to consider whether or not to do so. If there is a mere failure to think about it, then the only cause of action is negligence. Lord Hope would go one step further, to include 'wilful or deliberate failure' to take a decision whether to act. In what follows, we will refer to 'acts' to include the relevant sort of 'intended' omission.

The Mental Element

Variation (a)—targeted malice

In variation (a), there is no need to show that, apart from the intention to harm the claimant, the act of the official was 'unlawful'. Exercise of public power with intent to harm *is in itself unlawful*. The intent to harm provides the abuse of power.

In *Three Rivers* itself, it was accepted that the acts and omissions of the Bank of England could not be said to have been performed with 'targeted malice'. The only possibility was that variation (b) might be established.

Variation (b)—intentional or reckless abuse of power

The second variation requires knowledge or 'reckless indifference' in respect of two different things.

---

[98] See also the discussion of *Watkins v Home Office*, below.

[99] Or perhaps, according to Lord Hope, wilfully fails to decide whether to act.

[100] The expensively litigated claim eventually collapsed in its turn. So also did the claim for misfeasance brought by shareholders in Railtrack, *Weir v Secretary of State for Transport* [2005] EWHC 2192.

First, the official must either know, or be reckless whether, his or her act is illegal (in excess of the power conferred). Second, the official must *also* know, or be reckless whether, injury would be caused to the claimant as a result of the illegal act. Since the concept of 'recklessness' has caused significant difficulties in *criminal* law, there was some discussion of what 'recklessness' might mean in this context. In particular, is it a *subjective* state of mind, by which is meant that the official considered the matter and genuinely did not care whether the action was in excess of power, and would cause the claimant harm (the *Cunningham* test)?[101] Or, is it sufficient that there was an obvious risk, which the official failed to consider in terms of the likely impact on the claimant (the *Caldwell* test)?[102] According to Lord Steyn, whatever the position in criminal law, in this tort recklessness is to be judged subjectively, in terms of what the official actually *thought*.

Lord Steyn, at 193

Counsel argued for the adoption of the *Caldwell* test in the context of the tort of misfeasance in public office. The difficulty with this argument was that it could not be squared with a meaningful requirement of bad faith in the exercise of public powers which is the raison d'être of the tort. But, understandably, the argument became more refined during the oral hearing and counsel for the plaintiffs accepted that only reckless indifference in a subjective sense will be sufficient. This concession was rightly made. The plaintiff must prove that the public officer acted with a state of mind of reckless indifference to the illegality of his act: *Rawlinson v Rice* [1997] 2 NZLR 651.

As we have seen, reckless indifference does not suffice for the economic torts, which clearly require *targeted intent*. The difference in mental element between the torts is explained by their different focus. The 'gist' of misfeasance is abuse of power.[103]

The Damage Requirement

When we mapped torts in Chapter 1, we specified that misfeasance in a public office is actionable only where there is damage to the claimant. Unlike the trespass torts, it is not a tort 'actionable *per se*'. This was recently confirmed by the House of Lords in *Watkins v Secretary of State for the Home Department and Others* [2006] UKHL 17; [2006] 2 AC 395, a case where prison officers had unlawfully interfered with a prisoner's mail. Importantly, the House of Lords rejected an argument that the action in misfeasance should also be available, in the absence of actual damage, where a 'fundamental right' or 'constitutional right' was interfered with. Lord Bingham offered a number of reasons why the tort should not be modified to protect such a right in the absence of damage.

Lord Bingham, *Watkins v Secretary of State for the Home Department*
[2006] UKHL 17

26 . . . the respondent contends that the importance of the right in question requires or justifies the modification of a rule, if there be such, that material damage must be proved to

---

[101] *R v Cunningham* [1957] 2 QB 396.
[102] *R v Caldwell* [1982] AC 341.
[103] Lord Phillips MR commented specifically on this point in *Douglas v Hello! (No 3)*, at [222].

establish a cause of action. I do not, however, think that the House should take or endorse this novel step, for a number of reasons. The first is that it would open the door to argument whether other rights less obviously fundamental, basic or constitutional than the right to vote and the right to preserve the confidentiality of legal correspondence, were sufficiently close to or analogous with those rights to be treated, for damage purposes, in the same way. Since, in the absence of a codified constitution, these terms are incapable of precise definition, the outcome of such argument in other than clear cases would necessarily be uncertain. My second reason, already touched on, is the undesirability of introducing by judicial decision, without consultation, a solution which the consultation and research conducted by the Law Commission may show to be an unsatisfactory solution to what is in truth a small part of a wider problem. Thirdly, the lack of a remedy in tort for someone in the position of the respondent, who has suffered a legal wrong but no material damage, does not leave him without a legal remedy. Prison officers who breach the rules (even in the absence of bad faith), and the governors of both prisons, would be amenable to judicial review. Errant officers would be susceptible to disciplinary sanctions, and failure to initiate such proceedings could also, on appropriate evidence, be challenged by judicial review. The officers might well be indictable for the common law offence of misconduct in public office: see Attorney General's Reference (No 3 of 2003) [2005] QB 73. Breach of a fundamental human or constitutional right would also, in all probability, found a claim under section 7 of the Human Rights Act 1998, as it would in this case where the violation occurred after the Act came into force. I have myself questioned, albeit in a lone dissent, whether development of the law of tort should be stunted, leaving very important problems to be swept up by the European Convention (D v East Berkshire Community Health NHS Trust [2005] 2 AC 373, para 50), but the observation was made in a case where, in my opinion, the application of familiar principles supported recognition of a remedy in tort, not a case like the present where the application of settled principle points strongly against one. A fourth reason for not adopting the rule for which the respondent contends is to be found in enactment of the 1998 Act: it may reasonably be inferred that Parliament intended infringements of the core human (and constitutional) rights protected by the Act to be remedied under it and not by development of parallel remedies. . . .

Lord Bingham argues here that if the right in question is not protected in relevant circumstances by the law of tort, then the claimant should have recourse to an action under section 7 of the Human Rights Act 1998, and should not seek to rewrite the fundamental principles of an action in tort to accommodate their claim. Established torts themselves express a balance between claimants, defendants, and other interests, and core features of this balance should not be cast aside in response to arguments based on Convention rights. These rights may be appropriately protected in other ways.[104]

Recently, in *Karagozlu v Commissioner of Police of the Metropolis* [2006] EWCA Civ 1691, the Court of Appeal has held that loss of liberty is itself capable of amounting to 'material or special damage' in the sense required by the House of Lords' decision in *Watkins*. The category of material damage is therefore broader than 'financial loss or physical or mental injury' (the terminology used by Lord Bingham in *Watkins* at para [1])—or, perhaps, loss of liberty is closely analogous to physical injury. The Court of Appeal reasoned to this conclusion partly by reference to the tort of malicious prosecution. Lord Steyn clearly said in *Gregory v Portsmouth City*

---

[104] The position in *D v East Berkshire*, a case mentioned by Lord Bingham in the passage above, is quite different. The argument there concerned policy considerations affecting the application of the tort of negligence. There was no question of fundamentally altering the nature of the tort.

Council [2000] 1 AC 419, 426 (a case argued in malicious prosecution) that '[d]amage is a necessary ingredient of the tort'; and it is plain that loss of liberty is considered sufficient 'damage' for the purposes of that tort. The Court of Appeal also argued that there was nothing in the House of Lords' judgment in *Watkins* to contradict the idea that loss of liberty was damage.

The court of Appeal also argued that the decision in *R v Deputy Governor of Parkhurst Prison, ex p. Hague* [1992] 1 AC 58 was no impediment to their conclusion. In *Ex p. Hague* the House of Lords ruled that change in the conditions in which a prisoner is kept did not render the imprisonment—which was generally lawful —unlawful for the purposes of an action in false imprisonment. We have already said that false imprisonment is primarily concerned with unlawfulness not with wrongful damage. Since the claimant in *Karagozlu* argued that he had been wrongly transferred from open prison to more confined conditions in a closed prison, it appears that loss of 'residual liberty' constitutes damage for the purposes of an action in misfeasance, but will not suffice to render imprisonment unlawful for an action in false imprisonment. This illustrates the importance of the distinction between torts of damage, and torts actionable *per se*.

Recoverable Damage/Remoteness

In *Three Rivers*' Lord Steyn also considered the **extent of recoverable damage** in the tort of misfeasance in a public office. We have already noted that in the case of deceit, all *directly* caused damage can be recovered. The defendant does not gain 'the benefit' of the foreseeability test which, in the tort of negligence and in private nuisance, limits the recoverable damages to those of a type which the defendant could have foreseen. Lord Steyn concluded that even the foreseeability test was too generous to the claimant in this particular tort, even though it is an intentional tort. Only the damage *actually foreseen* by the defendant as likely or probable should be recoverable (Lord Steyn at 195–6).

In support of this view, it can be argued that misfeasance in a public office is different from the intentional economic torts discussed above, as they in turn are different from the torts of trespass to the person and the action in *Wilkinson v Downton*. There is no reason to say that all torts of intention, given their considerable and often justified variations, should be subject to the same remoteness rule; and the solution reached was deliberately aimed at achieving balance in protection of different interests and policy goals. On the other hand, against Lord Steyn's solution is the practical difficulty that proving what damage a *recklessly indifferent* official *actually had in mind* may prove to be far from straightforward.

Although misfeasance in a public office is in a sense a resurgent tort, it is hedged in by significant restrictions relating to state of mind; damage; and the extent of recoverable damage.

PART III

THE TORT OF
NEGLIGENCE

3

ESSENTIALS OF NEGLIGENCE:
ESTABLISHING LIABILITY

CENTRAL ISSUES

i) Negligence dominates the modern law of tort. One of the reasons for this is the broad appeal of the fault principle on which it is based. Liability under the fault principle depends on showing that the defendant's conduct has **fallen short of an objective standard**.

ii) The fault principle or negligence standard has a positive and a negative implication. The **negative** implication is that there is 'no liability without fault'. This as we will see in Section 1 (Standard of Care) is partly misleading, because the objective standard does not vary in order to fit the particular abilities of defendants. The negligence standard does not require personal fault in the fullest sense.

iii) The **positive** implication of the fault principle is that where there is faulty conduct which foreseeably causes damage, the defendant *ought* to make good the damage caused. But this aspect of the negligence standard, together with the range of damage which it will compensate, raises the spectre of virtually limitless liability. There may be reasons of fairness and of policy why some parties who have carelessly caused foreseeable harm

ought not to be subject to negligence liability. The Duty of Care plays a key role in limiting the reach of the tort of negligence. There will be liability only if the tortfeasor **breached a duty of care owed to the claimant**.

iv) In Section 3, we track the development of the duty of care. In *Donoghue v Stevenson* [1932] AC 562, Lord Atkin recognized that the existing examples of duties to take care could be seen as aspects of a single tort. Through the 'neighbour principle', he sought to state what these 'duty situations' had in common. In *Anns v Merton* [1978] AC 728, Lord Wilberforce went further and stated a single, universal test for the duty of care in negligence. A duty would arise on the basis of 'neighbourhood', unless there was some distinct reason to deny a duty. More recently, this generalizing trend has been reversed. Since *Caparo v Dickman* [1990] 2 AC 605, a tortfeasor will be subject to a duty of care only if there are *positive reasons* for holding the defendant responsible for the claimant's loss. Under *Caparo*, the duty of care does not so much play a unifying role, as provide a mechanism for distinguishing between those defendants who should and should not take responsibility for avoiding the harm.

v) **Negligent omissions** raise distinct issues in respect of duty, but also of breach, causation, and remoteness. We consider such issues at the end of the section on duty of care, and identify particular categories of case law where the omissions issue will be found to be relevant.

vi) Breach of a duty of care is not sufficient basis for an action in negligence. Negligence is a damage-based tort, and the claimant must also show that appropriate damage was caused by the defendant's breach of duty. Traditionally, there have been two distinct questions of causation. The first is known as 'cause in fact'. On the face of it, this states a simple factual test. But as we will begin to discover in Section 3, this impression is not accurate. Questions of cause in fact are so

complex that we defer some of them to Chapter 4.

vii) There is also a second question about the relationship between the breach of duty, and the damage. Controversy persists over whether this question (traditionally called 'cause in law' or 'remoteness') is really a question of causation at all. In *The Wagon Mound* (1961), the Privy Council attempted to establish that there was only one causal question ('cause in fact'), and that the remaining question of remoteness was best expressed in terms of foreseeability. That attempt was never wholly successful, and elements of causal language persisted. A more recent interpretation of remoteness questions is to ask whether the damage is 'within the scope of the duty' owed by the defendant to the claimant. 'Scope of duty' analysis, like the *Wagon Mound* foreseeability test, has also not wholly succeeded in distinguishing itself from causal questions.

1. STANDARD OF CARE: WHAT IS NEGLIGENCE?

In order to succeed in a claim in negligence, the claimant must show that the following criteria are met:

1. The defendant owes the claimant a duty to take care.
2. That duty has been breached.
3. The defendant's breach of duty has caused the claimant to suffer loss or damage of a relevant sort. This is a question of 'cause in fact'.
4. That damage is caused in law by the defendant's negligence/is not too remote/is within the scope of the duty.

It is easy to see why the majority of texts begin with the first question, whether a duty of care is owed. It appears to be the logically prior question. And yet, 'duty of care' is a relatively abstract and difficult notion, which does not have an exact parallel in any other tort, and whose purpose is open to argument. By contrast, the standard of care is more easily grasped, and it is of equal importance. The standard of care defines what conduct will count in law as negligence or lack of care, and in this sense it defines the 'content' of the tort.

Historically too, lack of care (together with damage) could be said to be the prime mover in the development of the tort. According to David Ibbetson, a series of 'innominate' (unnamed) tort actions involving loss to the claimant were redefined during the nineteenth century as components of a tort of negligence. What they had in common was the nature of the defendant's conduct, and thus 'carelessness' was the key feature of the emerging tort:

David Ibbetson, *A Historical Introduction to the Law of Obligations*
(Oxford: OUP, 1999), 169

The law of torts at the beginning of the nineteenth century was still recognizably medieval. It was characterized by a division between the action of trespass and the action on the case, the latter of which was subdivided into a number of nominate forms and a large residual group linked together by nothing stronger than that the defendant was alleged to have caused loss to the plaintiff. In the nineteenth century a substantial part of this residual group coalesced as the tort of negligence. This brought about a wholesale realignment of the law of torts, as this tort, defined by reference to the quality of the defendant's conduct, cut across the previously existing categorisation of torts.

While some other torts (for example the actions in defamation) are defined according to the interest they protect, the tort of negligence was and is defined primarily according to the 'quality of the defendant's conduct'. In this text, we will therefore begin our exploration of negligence with the standard of care, but readers may of course use sections of this chapter in whichever order suits them.

'Mapping' Torts and the Negligence Standard

In Chapter 1, we discussed the way that torts may be 'mapped' according to their essential elements. These elements included the nature of the protected interests, and the nature of the defendant's 'wrong'. We noted that in some torts, such as libel, there is no required element of fault on the part of the defendant. If the conduct of the defendant affects the claimant's interests in a relevant way, then remedies may be awarded. In the case of negligence however, there clearly is a requirement that the defendant's conduct should be defective (and that damage must be caused). Negligence is not the only tort in which conduct must be defective if the claimant is to succeed. But the distinctive feature of negligence is that conduct is judged according to whether it falls short of a relevant objective standard.

This distinctive negligence standard has tended to infiltrate other torts, sometimes displacing existing and different standards of liability: see for example Chapter 11 on *Rylands v Fletcher*. This may be because the idea of liability based on fault has intuitive appeal. But on the other hand, the 'objective' standard, which we introduce in the section that follows, is quite adaptable, and its exact link with personal fault is open to question.

The relevant standard peculiar to negligence is that of the 'reasonable person'. In general, we must judge the defendant by the standards of a reasonable person who is undertaking the task or activity in the course of which the negligence is said to arise.[1] The 'reasonable person' test is generally an objective one, which is not adjusted to fit the particular qualities of the defendant.

---

[1] As will be seen from the extracts below, most cases until very recently referred not to reasonable 'persons' but to reasonable 'men'. We will assume that this terminology makes no substantive difference, and that the 'reasonable man' is no different from the 'reasonable woman'. Some writers have doubted this. See generally Mayo Moran, *Rethinking the Reasonable Person* (OUP, 2003).

As such, although negligence is concerned with 'falling short' of a relevant standard, it does not necessarily involve actions for which we would 'blame' an individual defendant. Sometimes, even senior judges seem to forget this, and suggest that because negligence is not a tort of strict liability, it must depend on personal fault (see for example the judgment of Sir Nicolas Browne-Wilkinson V-C in *Wilsher v Essex AHA* [1987] QB 730, discussed below). In the sense that it sets standards which are sometimes not reasonably attainable for particular defendants, negligence does indeed involve an element of 'strict' liability of a certain sort. This is inherent in the 'objective' standard, as we will see.

1.1 THE OBJECTIVE STANDARD

Nettleship v Weston [1971] 2 QB 691

In *Nettleship v Weston*, the defendant was a learner driver. She was given driving lessons by the plaintiff, a family friend. She 'froze' at the wheel, so that her car mounted the pavement and struck a lamp-post. This caused injury to the plaintiff instructor. The plaintiff and defendant were in joint control of the car, since the instructor was operating the gear stick and handbrake while the defendant was steering.

The Court of Appeal held that the defendant's conduct fell below the required standard of care, which was the same objective standard owed by every driver. One of the judges, Salmon LJ, dissented on this point. There was a reduction of damages on account of the instructor's own fault in respect of the accident.

In Chapter 5, we will consider this case again in respect of defences, in particular the failed defence of *volenti non fit injuria* (acceptance of risk). For the time being, we concentrate on those elements of the case that relate to the standard of care.

Lord Denning MR

The Responsibility of the Learner Driver in Criminal Law

Mrs. Weston was rightly convicted of driving without due care and attention. In the criminal law it is no defence for a driver to say: "I was a learner driver under instruction. I was doing my best and could not help it." Such a plea may go to mitigation of sentence, but it does not go in exculpation of guilt. The criminal law insists that every person driving a car must attain an objective standard measured by the standard of a skilled, experienced and careful driver . . .

The Responsibility of the Learner Driver Towards Persons on or near the Highway

Mrs. Weston is clearly liable for the damage to the lamp post. In the civil law if a driver goes off the road on to the pavement and injures a pedestrian, or damages property, he is prima facie liable. Likewise if he goes on to the wrong side of the road. It is no answer for him to say: "I was a learner driver under instruction. I was doing my best and could not help it." The civil law permits no such excuse. It requires of him the same standard of care as of any other driver. "It eliminates the personal equation and is independent of the idiosyncrasies of the particular person whose conduct is in question": see *Glasgow Corporation v. Muir* [1943] A.C. 448, 457 by Lord Macmillan. The learner driver may be doing his best, but his incompetent best is not good enough. He must drive in as good a manner as a driver of skill, experience and care, who is sound in wind and limb, who makes no errors of judgment, has good eyesight and hearing, and is free from any infirmity . . .

The high standard thus imposed by the judges is, I believe, largely the result of the policy of the Road Traffic Acts. Parliament requires every driver to be insured against third party risks. The reason is so that a person injured by a motor car should not be left to bear the loss on his own, but should be compensated out of the insurance fund. The fund is better able to bear it than he can. But the injured person is only able to recover if the driver is liable in law. So the judges see to it that he is liable, unless he can prove care and skill of a high standard: see *The Merchant Prince* [1892] P. 179 and *Henderson v. Henry E. Jenkins & Sons* [1970] A.C. 282. Thus we are, in this branch of the law, moving away from the concept: "No liability without fault." We are beginning to apply the test: "On whom should the risk fall?" Morally the learner driver is not at fault; but legally she is liable to be because she is insured and the risk should fall on her.

The Responsibility of the Learner Driver towards Passengers in the Car

. . . The driver owes a duty of care to every passenger in the car, just as he does to every pedestrian on the road: and he must attain the same standard of care in respect of each. If the driver were to be excused according to the knowledge of the passenger, it would result in end-less confusion and injustice. One of the passengers may know that the learner driver is a mere novice. Another passenger may believe him to be entirely competent. One of the passengers may believe the driver to have had only two drinks. Another passenger may know that he has had a dozen. Is the one passenger to recover and the other not? Rather than embark on such inquiries, the law holds that the driver must attain the same standard of care for passengers as for pedestrians. The knowledge of the passenger may go to show that he was guilty of con-tributory negligence in ever accepting the lift—and thus reduce his damages—but it does not take away the duty of care, nor does it diminish the standard of care which the law requires of the driver: see *Dann v. Hamilton* [1939] 1 K.B. 509 and *Slater v. Clay Cross Co. Ltd.* [1956] 2 Q.B. 264, 270 . . .

Comments

Lord Denning MR had three reasons for holding the learner driver to the same standard as an experienced driver. First, she had already been convicted of driving without due care and attention, illustrating that the criminal law did not excuse the learner driver who was doing her 'incompetent best'. It would be strange if tort law, which in these circumstances has as its consequence the payment of compensation from an insurance fund, should *more* readily accept excuses than does the criminal law, whose sanctions here are generally punitive.

Lord Denning's second reason is practicality, and this reason is echoed by Megaw LJ. It would be inappropriate, and confusing, for the driver of a car to owe different duties to different passengers in the car, and to different individuals outside the car, depending on what they knew or did not know about the driver's competence.

Lord Denning's third reason concerns insurance. We should consider this reason with care. Lord Denning states very clearly that the law in this area (those events governed by the Road Traffic Acts) is less concerned that there should be 'no liability without fault', and more con-cerned with the distributive question, 'on whom should the risk fall?' This statement very effectively flags up a continuing dispute within the tort of negligence, concerning the purpose and nature of the tort as a whole. It is clear that negligence liability shifts a loss from a person whose conduct is defective, to someone who has suffered injury as a consequence. It is less clear why it does so, particularly where there is compulsory insurance. Is the shifting of losses justified by the faulty conduct of individual defendants? If so, why do we require them to insure, since this will make sure that they do not bear the loss themselves? Alternatively, is the shifting of loss justified through more distributive questions concerning the most effective or fairest means of spreading loss, ensuring (as Lord Denning put it) that no individual has to bear the loss alone?

These sorts of questions must be addressed and will be developed through a number of chapters of this book. But it would be wrong to assume that the background insurance position has only one effect on the case law, namely that judges will 'see to it' (in Lord Denning's blunt expression) that those who carry liability insurance will be liable for losses they cause. This is by no means always the case. English courts have on many occasions been eager to prevent claimants from pursuing those with deep pockets (including insurance companies) simply in order to transfer losses from themselves. A clear example is *Transco v Stockport MBC* [2003] UKHL 61; [2004] 2 AC 1, a case concerning the limits of strict liability for escapes, which is considered in Chapter 11 below.

In *Tomlinson v Congleton* [2003] UKHL 47; [2004] 1 AC 46, a case regarding the duties of occupiers to those on their premises, it was made clear by the House of Lords that individual claimants retain personal responsibility for their own safety. Despite the 'deeper pockets' of the defendant occupier (in this case, a local authority), there would be liability only if the defendant failed to take reasonable steps to make the claimant safe. In this case, a momentary act of carelessness (diving into water that was too shallow) led the claimant, a teenager, to break his neck. He was rendered tetraplegic. In the paragraph below, Lord Hoffmann makes clear that the law of tort does not operate simply to compensate people for such tragedies. There is liability only if there has been a breach of duty by the defendant:

Lord Hoffmann, *Tomlinson v Congleton*

4.   It is a terrible tragedy to suffer such dreadful injury in consequence of a relatively minor act of carelessness. . . . John Tomlinson's mind must often recur to that hot day which irretrievably changed his life. He may feel, not unreasonably, that fate has dealt with him unfairly. And so in these proceedings he seeks financial compensation: for loss of his earning capacity, for the expense of the care he will need, for the loss of the ability to lead an ordinary life. But the law does not provide such compensation simply on the basis that the injury was disproportionately severe in relation to one's own fault or even not one's fault at all. Perhaps it should, but society might not be able to afford to compensate everyone on that principle, certainly at the level at which such compensation is now paid. The law provides compensation only when the injury was someone else's fault. In order to succeed in his claim, that is what Mr Tomlinson has to prove.

This was a case under the Occupiers' Liability Act 1984, but that statute embodies a duty which is close in type to negligence (see Chapter 12).

It remains true that the question stated by Lord Denning, 'on whom should the risk fall?', is a pertinent consideration in many key negligence cases, and it is as well to get it out in the open now. It is relevant to issues of duty, causation, and remoteness; and it is certainly relevant to the way in which the standard of care is set. But the question when asked plainly may yield some answers which are very different from the answer given by Lord Denning in *Nettleship v Weston*. The very clear statement by Lord Hoffmann above illustrates that, despite the objectivity of the standard of care, there must be shown to have been a falling short of this standard, before there can be liability on the basis of negligence.

Mansfield v Weetabix [1998] 1 WLR 1263

A contrast to *Nettleship v Weston* is provided by the difficult case of *Mansfield v Weetabix* [1998] 1 WLR 1263. Here, the Court of Appeal held that the driver of a lorry had not been negligent. The evidence was that he had entered a 'hypoglycaemic state': the brain was starved of glucose so that it was unable to function properly. The condition was gradual rather than sudden, but the court found that the defendant would have been unaware of the mounting effect on his driving. No blame attached to his continuing to drive despite two other incidents (one requiring police attention at the scene) shortly before his vehicle ploughed into the claimants' shop causing extensive damage. In the absence of blame, there could be no liability:

> **Leggatt LJ,** at 1268
>
> In my judgment, the standard of care that [the driver] was obliged to show in these circumstances was that which is to be expected of a reasonably competent driver unaware that he is or may be suffering from a condition that impairs his ability to drive. To apply an objective standard in a way that did not take account of [his] condition would be to impose strict liability. . . .

The Court of Appeal did not clearly explain why this case could be distinguished from *Nettleship v Weston*, except to say that the latter authority 'does not refer to cases in which a driver is unaware that he is subject to a disability'. Whilst it would of course be negligent to continue to drive when aware of a significant impairment, it has never been suggested that it is negligent for a learner to take driving lessons because of their lack of skill. Therefore, this factor does not help to distinguish the cases. On the contrary, it underlines a similarity between them, which is that neither defendant was to blame for their failure to drive in a careful manner.

The medical condition in this case was such that it did not deprive the defendant of all control over his actions. It would not amount to 'automatism', which according to *Roberts v Ramsbottom* [1980] 1 WLR 823 is required if a defendant is to escape *criminal* liability. Thus the consistency between criminal and tortious liability which we noted in respect of *Nettleship v Weston* has been disrupted by *Mansfield v Weetabix* with the very result that we thought would be hard to justify: in terms of criminal liability, which may be said to be broadly concerned either with culpability or with community expectations concerning acceptable behaviour, there is a stricter standard than there is in tort law, which is concerned with the allocation of a loss between two parties, and in which a greater range of balancing considerations would normally be thought to be permissible.

The Court of Appeal in *Mansfield v Weetabix* may also have misused the authority of *Snelling v Whitehead* (The Times, 31 July 1975 (HL), subsequently reported as *(Note)* [1998] RTR 385). In *Snelling v Whitehead*, the House of Lords underlined that negligence law requires fault in some sense. Thus, there was no liability in that case when a cyclist suffered serious injuries after a collision with a car. The car driver, though insured, could not be said to be at fault. Certainly this is a reminder that Lord Denning's broader statements in *Nettleship v Weston* should not be taken at face value. Courts will not 'see to it' that insured drivers are liable if there is no failure to achieve the objective standard. But this does not really help us with the scenario in *Mansfield v Weetabix*. The defendant in *Snelling v Whitehead* could not be said to have fallen below the objective standard. When the House of Lords in that case stated that negligence does not operate on the basis of strict liability, it was reasserting the objective standard of care. In *Mansfield v Weetabix* by contrast, the objective standard of care was set aside for someone who could not fulfil it. This is a very different matter. To say that the objective standard would amount to strict liability as against such a person is true in a sense, but this element of strict liability is, in fact, a generally accepted aspect of the tort of negligence, and is inherent in the objective standard.

On one view, this means that negligence cannot be entirely justified on the basis of moral considerations, because it does not demand 'fault' in a full sense. But there is another view, which is that objective standards are themselves justifiable on moral grounds, because they concern 'responsibility', even if they do not match typical ideas about 'fault'. See in particular T. Honoré, 'Responsibility and Luck: The Moral Basis of Strict Liability' (1988) 104 LQR 14–39.

Variations of the Objective Standard

Children

Where children are concerned, the applicable standard of care will be determined according to age. This is not intended to be an exception to the objective standard. A child will not be judged according to his or her particular level of maturity or ability. Rather, the approach is an application of the objective standard, adjusted to the case in hand. Children will be held to the standard of the 'typical' child of their own age.

Mullin v Richards 1998 1 WLR 1304 (CA)

The plaintiff suffered an injury to her eye when a plastic ruler broke during a mock sword-fight at school. The plaintiff's claim against the education authority (based on alleged failures of supervision) was unsuccessful, but the judge awarded damages against her fellow pupil, subject to a reduction of 50 per cent for contributory negligence.[2] The Court of Appeal reversed the decision to award damages. Both schoolgirls were 15 years of age, and the extract below deals with the question of whether the injury could be said to have been foreseeable. In answering this, age was a relevant factor.

> **Hutchison LJ,** at 1308–9
>
> The argument centres on foreseeability. The test of foreseeability is an objective one; but the fact that the first defendant was at the time a 15-year-old schoolgirl is not irrelevant. The question for the judge is not whether the actions of the defendant were such as an ordinarily prudent and reasonable adult in the defendant's situation would have realised gave rise to a risk of injury, it is whether an ordinarily prudent and reasonable 15-year-old schoolgirl in the defendant's situation would have realised as much. In that connection both counsel referred us to, and relied upon, the Australian decision in *McHale v. Watson* (1966) 115 C.L.R. 199 and, in particular, the passage in the judgment of Kitto J., at pp. 213–214. I cite a portion of the passage . . .
>
> > "The standard of care being objective, it is no answer for him, [that is a child] any more than it is for an adult, to say that the harm he caused was due to his being abnormally slow-witted, quick-tempered, absent-minded or inexperienced. But it does not follow that he cannot rely in his

2 See Chapter 5.

defence upon a limitation upon the capacity for foresight or prudence, not as being personal to himself, but as being characteristic of humanity at his stage of development and in that sense normal. By doing so he appeals to a standard of ordinariness, to an objective and not a subjective standard."

Mr. Stephens also cited to us a passage in the judgment of Owen J., at p. 234: "the standard by which his conduct is to be measured is not that to be expected of a reasonable adult but that reasonably to be expected of a child of the same age, intelligence and experience." I venture to question the word "intelligence" in that sentence, but I understand Owen J. to be making the same point essentially as was made by Kitto J. It is perhaps also material to have in mind the words of Salmon L.J. in *Gough v. Thorne*

> "The question as to whether the plaintiff can be said to have been guilty of contributory negligence depends on whether any ordinary child of 131/2 can be expected to have done any more than this child did. I say 'any ordinary child.' I do not mean a paragon of prudence; nor do I mean a scatter-brained child; but the ordinary girl of 131/2."

Sporting events

In certain circumstances, decisions have to be made and actions taken when time is short. The law continues to require that the defendant must exercise reasonable care, but it is accepted that 'reasonable care' may be different in these circumstances.

Wooldridge v Sumner [1963] 2 QB 43

The plaintiff, a photographer, was seriously injured when the defendant, a participant in a horse show, rode his horse too fast around a corner and veered into the area where the photographer was standing.

Diplock LJ, at 67–8

The matter has to be looked at from the point of view of the reasonable spectator as well as the reasonable participant; not because of the maxim volenti non fit injuria, but because what a reasonable spectator would expect a participant to do without regarding it as blameworthy is as relevant to what is reasonable care as what a reasonable participant would think was blameworthy conduct in himself. The same idea was expressed by Scrutton L.J. in *Hall v. Brooklands* [[1933] 1 K.B. 205, 214]: "What is reasonable care would depend upon the perils which might be reasonably expected to occur, *and the extent to which the ordinary spectator might be expected to appreciate and take the risk of such perils.*"

A reasonable spectator attending voluntarily to witness any game or competition knows and presumably desires that a reasonable participant will concentrate his attention upon winning, and if the game or competition is a fast-moving one, will have to exercise his judgment and attempt to exert his skill in what, in the analogous context of contributory negligence, is sometimes called "the agony of the moment." If the participant does so concentrate his attention and consequently does exercise his judgment and attempt to exert his skill in circumstances of this kind which are inherent in the game or competition in which he is taking part, the question whether any mistake he makes amounts to a breach of duty to take reasonable care must take account of those circumstances.

The law of negligence has always recognised that the standard of care which a reasonable man will exercise depends upon the conditions under which the decision to avoid the act or omission relied upon as negligence has to be taken. The case of the workman engaged on repetitive work in the noise and bustle of the factory is a familiar example. . . . a participant in a game or competition gets into the circumstances in which he has no time or very little time to think by his decision to take part in the game or competition at all. It cannot be suggested that the participant, at any rate if he has some modicum of skill, is, by the mere act of participating, in breach of his duty of care to a spectator who is present for the very purpose of watching him do so. If, therefore, in the course of the game or competition, at a moment when he really has not time to think, a participant by mistake takes a wrong measure, he is not, in my view, to be held guilty of any negligence.

Furthermore, the duty which he owes is a duty of care, not a duty of skill. Save where a consensual relationship exists between a plaintiff and a defendant by which the defendant impliedly warrants his skill, a man owes no duty to his neighbour to exercise any special skill beyond that which an ordinary reasonable man would acquire before indulging in the activity in which he is engaged at the relevant time. It may well be that a participant in a game or competition would be guilty of negligence to a spectator if he took part in it when he knew or ought to have known that his lack of skill was such that even if he exerted it to the utmost he was likely to cause injury to a spectator watching him. No question of this arises in the present case. It was common ground that Mr. Holladay was an exceptionally skilful and experienced horseman.

The practical result of this analysis of the application of the common law of negligence to participant and spectator would, I think, be expressed by the common man in some such terms as these: "A person attending a game or competition takes the risk of any damage caused to him by any act of a participant done in the course of and for the purposes of the game or competition notwithstanding that such act may involve an error of judgment or a lapse of skill, unless the participant's conduct is such as to evince a reckless disregard of the spectator's safety."

It could be argued that Diplock LJ was over-elaborate in his argument here. Why should we need to introduce the idea of 'consent' on the part of the spectator, when we could simply say that the standard of care varies with the circumstances, reflecting the fact that even the reasonable person will be less able to take precautions in those circumstances? (At times, Diplock LJ uses the Latin phrase 'Volenti non fit injuria'. He is referring to a defence which we will consider in Chapter 5, and which he found to be inapplicable on the facts.) In fact, Diplock LJ makes two separate points about the standard of reasonable care:

1. in the heat of the moment, a reasonable person may be unable to avoid causing injury; and

2. reasonable care varies with the expectation of a person in the position of the claimant.

Although Diplock LJ's judgment refers specifically to duties owed to spectators, it is clear that duties may also be owed to fellow-participants and the standard of care owed will be similarly judged. In *Condon v Basi* [1985] 1 WLR, a local league footballer broke the leg of the plaintiff, an opposing player, with a tackle. The Court of Appeal accepted the authority of *Rootes v Shelton* [1968] ALR 33, a decision of the High Court of Australia. In *Condon v Basi*, Sir John Donaldson MR pointed out that there were two different approaches to the standard of care in the case of *Rootes v Shelton*. One of these (the approach taken by Barwick CJ) takes up the second point derived from *Wooldridge v Sumner* because it refers to the level of risk that has been accepted by fellow participants. The other, the judgment of Kitto J, was more straightforward, concentrating simply upon reasonableness 'in relation to the special circumstances of the conduct': this is the first point from *Wooldridge v Sumner* above. Non-compliance with the rules of the game would be one consideration, but would not be conclusive of negligence. Sir John Donaldson MR said that he would prefer the more straightforward approach of Kitto J, but that it did not matter on the facts of *Condon v Basi* itself, where the defendant through his foul play showed 'reckless disregard' of his opponent's safety.

The second point about standard of care derived from *Wooldridge v Sumner* is that the standard of care would vary with the expectations of a reasonable person in the situation of the claimant. In *Wooldridge* this meant a reasonable *spectator*, but in other cases it would mean a reasonable *participant*. For example in *Caldwell v Maguire* [2002] PIQR 6, a professional jockey suffered career-ending injuries through the aggressive (and careless) riding of fellow jockeys. There was no doubt that their actions were in breach of the applicable rules. This however would not suffice: the threshold of liability was high, to take account of the circumstances in which the breaches of the rules came about.

In *Blake v Galloway* [2004] EWCA Civ 814; [2004] 1 WLR 2844, the Court of Appeal reviewed the sporting authorities in order to determine the right approach to an injury suffered in the course not of sport but of simple 'horseplay'. Five teenagers were throwing bark and twigs at one another for amusement when one of them suffered an eye injury. The Court of Appeal concluded that there had been no breach of duty. Participation in the game was thought to make its tacit 'rules' consensual. Applying the case law on sporting injuries, this meant that the test for breach of duty would require something more than a simple 'error of judgment or lack of skill' (Dyson LJ at [17] quoting Diplock LJ in *Wooldridge*).

Dyson LJ, *Blake v Galloway*

14   The offending blow was caused by a piece of bark which was thrown in accordance with the tacit understandings or conventions of the game in which the claimant participated. It was thrown in the general direction of the claimant, with no intention of causing harm, and in the same high-spirited good nature as all the other objects had been thrown.

15   I recognise that the participants in the horseplay owed each other a duty to take reasonable care not to cause injury. What does that mean in the context of play of this kind? . . . . I consider there is a sufficiently close analogy between organised and regulated sport or games and the horseplay in which these youths were engaged for the guidance given by the authorities to which I have referred to be of value in the resolution of this case. The only real difference is that there were no formal rules for the horseplay. But I do not consider that this is a significant distinction. The common features between horseplay of this kind and formal sport involving vigorous physical activity are that both involved consensual participation in an activity (i) which involves physical contact or at least the risk of it, (ii) in which decisions are usually expected to be made quickly and often as an instinctive response to the acts of other participants, so that (iii) the very nature of the activity makes it difficult to avoid the risk of physical harm.

16   I would, therefore, apply the guidance given by Diplock LJ in *Wooldridge*, although in a slightly expanded form, and hold that in a case such as the present there is a breach of the duty of care owed by participant A to participant B only where A's conduct amounts to recklessness or a very high degree of carelessness.

The decision in *Blake v Galloway* makes clear that the different approach to breach in sporting cases is not simply a question of what expectation is reasonable 'in the heat of the moment', since the pressure and speed referred to in the sporting cases did not exist. In this particular case, the less demanding standard imposed on the defendant is justified purely by the consensual nature of the game.

The ordinary skilled person professing to have a special skill

Just as the applicable standard of care is lowered in the case of children, and adjusted for actions taken 'in the heat of the moment', so also it will be higher if the defendant is performing actions which require special skill. In the leading case of *Bolam v Friern Hospital Management Company* [1957] 1 WLR 582, McNair J advised the jury that the question of 'negligence' in a medical procedure should be approached as follows:

> In the ordinary case which does not involve any special skill, negligence in law means a failure to do some act which a reasonable man in the circumstances would do, or the doing of some act which a reasonable man in the circumstances would not do; and if that failure or the doing of that act results in injury, then there is a cause of action. How do you test whether this act or failure is negligent? In an ordinary case it is generally said you judge it by the action of the man in the street. He is the ordinary man. In one case it has been said you judge it by the conduct of the man on the top of a Clapham omnibus. He is the ordinary man. But where you get a situation which involves the use of some special skill or competence, then the test as to whether there has been negligence or not is not the test of the man on the top of a Clapham omnibus, because he has not got this special skill. The test is the standard of the ordinary skilled man exercising and professing to have that special skill. A man need not possess the highest expert skill; it is well established law that it is sufficient if he exercises the ordinary skill of an ordinary competent man exercising that particular art.

McNair J went on to discuss how the law should approach differences of opinion among medical practitioners, and we return to this element of his judgment below.

Wilsher v Essex Area Health Authority [1987] QB 730 (CA)

Mustill and Glidewell LJJ explained that there would be no exception to the 'objective' standard of care where an inexperienced or newly qualified medical professional was concerned. Rather, the applicable standard would be set according to the post that is filled by the defendant. Where the plaintiff was cared for in a specialist unit, in this case a neonatal unit, the applicable standard of care was a high one. This standard would be variable according to the post held within the team providing care for the plaintiff, but it would not be variable according to the level of experience held by the particular individual member of staff. (There was an appeal to the House of Lords from this case on the issue of causation, but the House of Lords did not reconsider the issue of standard of care.)

Mustill LJ, at 750–1

> The second proposition, advanced on behalf of the defendants, directs attention to the personal position of the individual member of the staff about whom the complaint is made. What is expected of him is as much as, but no more than, can reasonably be required of a person having his formal qualifications and practical experience. If correct, this proposition entails that the standard of care which the patient is entitled to demand will vary according to the chance of recruitment and rostering. The patient's right to complain of faulty treatment will be more

limited if he has been entrusted to the care of a doctor who is a complete novice in the particular field (unless perhaps he can point to some fault of supervision in a person further up the hierarchy) than if he has been in the hands of a doctor who has already spent months on the same ward: and his prospects of holding the health authority vicariously liable for the consequences of any mistreatment will be correspondingly reduced.

To my mind, this notion of a duty tailored to the actor, rather than to the act which he elects to perform, has no place in the law of tort. Indeed, the defendants did not contend that it could be justified by any reported authority on the general law of tort. Instead, it was suggested that the medical profession is a special case. Public hospital medicine has always been organised so that young doctors and nurses learn on the job. If the hospitals abstained from using inexperienced people, they could not staff their wards and theatres, and the junior staff could never learn. The longer-term interests of patients as a whole are best served by maintaining the present system, even if this may diminish the legal rights of the individual patient: for, after all, medicine is about curing, not litigation.

I acknowledge the appeal of this argument, and recognise that a young hospital doctor, who must get on to the wards in order to qualify without necessarily being able to decide what kind of patient he is going to meet, is not in the same position as another professional man who has a real choice whether or not to practise in a particular field. Nevertheless, I cannot accept that there should be a special rule for doctors in public hospitals—I emphasise *public*, since presumably those employed in private hospitals would be in a different category. Doctors are not the only people who gain their experience, not only from lectures or from watching others perform, but from tackling live clients or customers, and no case was cited to us which suggested that any such variable duty of care was imposed on others in a similar position. To my mind, it would be a false step to subordinate the legitimate expectation of the patient that he will receive from each person concerned with his care a degree of skill appropriate to the task which he undertakes, to an understandable wish to minimise the psychological and financial pressures on hard-pressed young doctors.

For my part, I prefer the third of the propositions which have been canvassed. This relates the duty of care not to the individual, but to the post which he occupies. I would differentiate "post" from "rank" or "status." In a case such as the present, the standard is not just that of the averagely competent and well-informed junior houseman (or whatever the position of the doctor) but of such a person who fills a post in a unit offering a highly specialised service. But, even so, it must be recognised that different posts make different demands. If it is borne in mind that the structure of hospital medicine envisages that the lower ranks will be occupied by those of whom it would be wrong to expect too much, the risk of abuse by litigious patients can be mitigated, if not entirely eliminated.

Sir Nicolas Browne-Wilkinson V-C had a different view of the matter, suggesting that there could be negligence on the part of the individual only if that individual was *actually* at fault, and that this would depend on whether he could fairly be held to a higher standard in the light of his qualifications. (He suggested, instead, that a hospital may be liable for breach of its primary duties, if it fails to provide a sufficiently qualified team of staff for specialized work. This, however, would leave less scope for successful claims, since it is in many cases reasonable to allow staff to gain experience through carrying out work with patients.) The general view of Mustill LJ expressed above more accurately encapsulates the *objective* nature of the standard of care in negligence, since it is not personal to individuals. Indeed there is controversy over whether he allowed *too much* variation in the standard of care applicable (Jones, *Textbook on*

Tort, 8th edn, 209). Glidewell LJ in the same case stated a more uncompromising version of the objective test, applicable to all those who undertook a relevant task.

The standard of care to be applied in any given case will depend upon the activity being performed by the defendant. In support of Mustill LJ's 'mixed' approach, it is clear that the relevant standard will in some cases also depend on the kind of skill that the defendant professes to have (as opposed to their level of experience, which should be irrelevant).

In *Phillips v William Whiteley* [1938] 1 All ER 566, a jeweller who pierced ears was held to the standards of care and hygiene to be expected of a reasonable jeweller, not to the standards of a qualified medical practitioner performing the same procedure. In *Luxmoore-May v Messenger May Baverstock* [1990] 1 WLR 1009, provincial auctioneers and valuers were on analogy with medical cases subjected to a standard of care appropriate to a 'general practitioner', which was lower than the standard applied to 'one of the leading auction houses' (at 1020). But there are limits to this relativism. In *Shakoor v Situ* (2000) 1 WLR 410, the defendant was a practitioner of Chinese traditional medicine. A patient died of liver failure after a course of treatment which was aimed at curing a skin complaint. Within Chinese traditional medicine, this course of treatment was considered to be both effective and safe. It would appear that the only basis on which to doubt the safety of the treatment was a series of letters and articles published in *The Lancet*, an orthodox medical journal. Bernard Livesey QC, sitting in the Queen's Bench Division, considered that a practitioner of Chinese traditional medicine in England, when prescribing medicines, has a duty to ensure that these are reasonably safe. Furthermore, when judging whether they are reasonably safe, the applicable standard is that of the ordinary careful general practitioner of *orthodox* medicine. The practitioner had chosen to operate 'alongside' orthodox medicine. Perhaps a clearer reason is that those seeking any form of medical treatment are entitled to expect that reasonable care will be taken as to its safety: if evidence comes to light concerning the safety of any treatment, it is reasonable to expect all practitioners to take into account that evidence, no matter what their background.

In the event however, the practitioner was not held to have been negligent. The ordinary, careful *general practitioner* (the applicable standard) would not be aware of the papers in *The Lancet*. These were in any case too equivocal to put such a practitioner on notice that the treatment was unsafe, even if he or she had read them.

Assessing Professional Skill and Care: Practice and Opinion

Earlier, we extracted a statement by McNair J, in the case of *Bolam v Friern Hospital Management Committee* [1957] 1 WLR 583, concerning the correct approach to the standard of care in respect of activities which require special skill. Another important aspect of his summary of the law concerned *differences of opinion* among practitioners. How should the law approach a case of alleged negligence against a professional person where that person's conduct is supported by some, but perhaps not all, fellow professionals? Should the court be free to choose which opinion to prefer? Indeed, should the existence of settled professional practice be decisive at all? The words used by McNair J on this point have become known as 'the *Bolam* test'. This test has been applied on numerous occasions, and has been explicitly approved by the House of Lords: see *Maynard v West Midlands RHA* [1984] 1 WLR 634; *Sidaway v Bethlem Royal Hospital Governors* [1985] 1 All ER 643.

McNair J, at 587

. . . he is not guilty of negligence if he has acted in accordance with a practice accepted as proper by a responsible body of medical men skilled in that particular art. . . . Putting it the other way round, a man is not negligent, if he is acting in accordance with such a practice, merely because there is a body of opinion who would take a contrary view.

This approach could remove the final judgment on carelessness from the court, in cases where a defendant adheres to a recognized professional practice. In an article published soon after *Bolam*, JL Montrose pointed out that there is no reason to take issue with the second sentence in the statement by McNair J reproduced above: certainly a 'man' is not to be held negligent *merely* because there is a body of opinion against his practice. It is the first sentence which, according to Montrose, appears to make due care synonymous not with what *should* be done, but with what is generally done—or at least with what is defended by a responsible body of appropriately skilled professionals. Montrose gives some powerful reasons why courts should not defer to those with expertise too readily:

J.L. Montrose, 'Is Negligence an Ethical or a Sociological Concept?'
(1958) 21 MLR 259, at 263

It is surely negligent not to provide against risks which ought to have been known. The fact that it was not appreciated by men experienced in the particular province is, of course, strong evidence that it could not reasonably have been guarded against, but not conclusive evidence. Experts may blind themselves by expertise. The courts should guard the citizen against risks which professional men and others may ignore.

Bolam in the Medical Context

The application of the *Bolam* test within the medical context has led to accusations of a protectionist stance towards doctors. Two broad problems have been identified with the courts' interpretation of the *Bolam* test in such cases, at least up until the decision in *Bolitho* (below).

First, *Bolam* has been applied in these cases in such a way that the court's judgment is replaced with the judgment of the defendant's medical expert, as long as the expert is found to be honest and respectable. Brazier and Miola explain this effect, while also proposing that this is particular to medical cases:

Brazier and Miola, 'Bye-Bye Bolam: A Medical Litigation Revolution?'
(2000) 8 *Med L Rev* 85–114

What distinguishes medical litigation from other areas of professional liability is in part that a series of judgments (or maybe a gloss on those judgments) have given rise to a perception that all *Bolam* requires is that the defendant fields experts from his or her medical specialty prepared to testify that they would have followed the same course of management of the patient-plaintiff as did the defendant. If such experts can be identified, are patently honest and stand by their testimony vigorously, neither they nor the defendant will be asked to justify their practice . . . Yet in other professional negligence claims, time after time, judges have made it clear that expert opinion must be demonstrably responsible and reasonable.

Second, it has been suggested that many aspects of medical negligence litigation have been inappropriately 'Bolamized'.[3] In other words, wherever a tricky issue arises concerning the standard of care in a medical context, the habitual response of the courts has been to reach for the *Bolam* test, and to resist making their own judgments. Brazier and Miola, in the article quoted above, suggest in particular that three aspects of medical ethics have been treated in this way: informed consent (particularly through the judgment of Lord Diplock in *Sidaway v Royal Bethlem Hospital* [1985] 1 All ER 643); the treatment of medically incapacitated patients; and (they contend) the treatment of mature minors as considered in *Gillick v West Norfolk Area Health Authority* [1985] 3 All ER 402. Against this background, the judgment of the House of Lords in the following case is highly significant.

Bolitho v City of Hackney Health Authority [1998] AC 232

In principle, this case clarifies that the *final* judgment on breach of duty lies with the court, not with medical practitioners. Certain of Lord Browne-Wilkinson's comments, including his approval of dicta in *Hucks v Cole* (a case from 1968 reported at [1993] 4 *Med LR* 393), show the importance of this clarification of the *Bolam* test.

In *Bolitho*, a two-year-old boy suffered brain damage, and later died, as a result of cardiac arrest following respiratory failure. He was in the care of hospital staff and had suffered two severe episodes of respiratory difficulties before the final attack. On both occasions the nurses caring for the little boy called for a doctor to attend, but on neither occasion did a doctor attend. It was the plaintiff's case that the doctor should have attended the little boy; that he should have been intubated following the first two episodes; and that if this had been done then this would have prevented the respiratory failure and cardiac arrest. It was the doctor's case that even if she had attended, she would not have intubated the child, so that her failure to attend had not, she argued, caused the injury.

Arguably, it is unacceptable that the doctor's own evidence that she would not have intubated, even if she had attended, could be decisive as to causation, although of course that evidence will be scrutinized by the court for persuasiveness. Causation issues are discussed in Section 3 of this chapter. The following extract deals with the standard of care of a medical professional. In particular, the question arose of whether it would have been negligent of the doctor not to intubate the child, had she attended him after the two initial attacks. If this course of inaction would have been negligent, then her defence to the negligence claim would fail.

Lord Browne-Wilkinson, at 238–9

As to the second of the judge's questions (i.e. whether any competent doctor should have intubated if he had attended Patrick at any time after 2 p.m.), the judge had evidence from no less than eight medical experts, all of them distinguished. Five of them were called on behalf of Patrick and were all of the view that, at least after the second episode, any competent doctor would have intubated. Of these five, the judge was most impressed by Dr. Heaf, a consultant paediatrician in respiratory medicine at the Royal Liverpool Children's Hospital, which is the largest children's hospital in the United Kingdom. On the other side, the defendants called three experts all of whom said that, on the symptoms presented by Patrick as recounted by Sister Sallabank and Nurse Newbold, intubation would not have been appropriate. Of the

---

[3] M. Davies, 'The "New *Bolam*" Another False Dawn for Medical Negligence?' (1996) 12 PN 10.

defendants' experts, the judge found Dr. Dinwiddie, a consultant paediatrician in respiratory diseases at the Hospital for Sick Children, Great Ormond Street, most impressive.

The views of the plaintiffs' experts were largely based on the premise that over the last two hours before the catastrophe Patrick was in a state of respiratory distress progressing inexorably to hypoxia and respiratory failure. The defendants' experts, on the other hand, considered the facts as recounted by Sister Sallabank indicated that Patrick was quite well apart from the two quite sudden acute episodes at 12.40 p.m. and 2 p.m. The judge held that the evidence of Sister Sallabank and Nurse Newbold as to Patrick's behaviour (which he accepted) was inconsistent with a child passing through the stages of progressive hypoxia.

Having made his findings of fact, the judge directed himself as to the law by reference to the speech of Lord Scarman in *Maynard v. West Midlands Regional Health Authority* [1984] 1 W.L.R. 634, 639:

> " . . . I have to say that a judge's 'preference' for one body of distinguished professional opinion to another also professionally distinguished is not sufficient to establish negligence in a practitioner whose actions have received the seal of approval of those whose opinions, truthfully expressed, honestly held, were not preferred. If this was the real reason for the judge's finding, he erred in law even though elsewhere in his judgment he stated the law correctly. For in the realm of diagnosis and treatment negligence is not established by preferring one *respectable* body of professional opinion to another. Failure to exercise the ordinary skill of a doctor (in the appropriate speciality, if he be a specialist) is necessary." (Emphasis added.)

The judge held that the views of Dr. Heaf and Dr. Dinwiddie, though diametrically opposed, both represented a responsible body of professional opinion espoused by distinguished and truthful experts. Therefore, he held, Dr. Horn, if she had attended and not intubated, would have come up to a proper level of skill and competence, i.e. the standard represented by Dr. Dinwiddie's views. Accordingly he held that it had not been proved that the admitted breach of duty by the defendants had caused the catastrophe which occurred to Patrick. . . .

At 241–3

The *Bolam* test—should the judge have accepted Dr. Dinwiddie's evidence?

As I have said, the judge took a very favourable view of Dr. Dinwiddie as an expert. . . .

However, the judge also expressed these doubts:

> "Mr. Brennan also advanced a powerful argument—which I have to say, as a layman, appealed to me—to the effect that the views of the defendant's experts simply were not logical or sensible. Given the recent and the more remote history of Patrick's illness, culminating in these two episodes, surely it was unreasonable and illogical not to anticipate the recurrence of a life-threatening event and take the step which it was acknowledged would probably have saved Patrick from harm? This was the safe option, whatever was suspected as the cause, or even if the cause was thought to be a mystery. The difficulty of this approach, as in the end I think Mr. Brennan acknowledged, was that in effect it invited me to substitute my own views for those of the medical experts."

Mr. Brennan renewed that submission both before the Court of Appeal (who unanimously rejected it) and before your Lordships. He submitted that the judge had wrongly treated the *Bolam* test as requiring him to accept the views of one truthful body of expert professional advice even though he was unpersuaded of its logical force. He submitted that the judge was wrong in law in adopting that approach and that ultimately it was for the court, not for medical opinion, to decide what was the standard of care required of a professional in the circumstances of each particular case.

My Lords, I agree with these submissions to the extent that, in my view, the court is not bound to hold that a defendant doctor escapes liability for negligent treatment or diagnosis just because he leads evidence from a number of medical experts who are genuinely of opinion that the defendant's treatment or diagnosis accorded with sound medical practice. In the *Bolam* case itself, McNair J. [1957] 1 W.L.R. 583, 587 stated that the defendant had to have acted in accordance with the practice accepted as proper by a "*responsible* body of medical men." Later, at p. 588, he referred to "a standard of practice recognised as proper by a competent *reasonable* body of opinion." Again, in the passage which I have cited from *Maynard's* case [1984] 1 W.L.R. 634, 639, Lord Scarman refers to a "respectable" body of professional opinion. The use of these adjectives—responsible, reasonable and respectable—all show that the court has to be satisfied that the exponents of the body of opinion relied upon can demonstrate that such opinion has a logical basis. In particular in cases involving, as they so often do, the weighing of risks against benefits, the judge before accepting a body of opinion as being responsible, reasonable or respectable, will need to be satisfied that, in forming their views, the experts have directed their minds to the question of comparative risks and benefits and have reached a defensible conclusion on the matter.

There are decisions which demonstrate that the judge is entitled to approach expert professional opinion on this basis. For example, in *Hucks v. Cole* [1993] 4 Med.L.R. 393 (a case from 1968), a doctor failed to treat with penicillin a patient who was suffering from septic spots on her skin though he knew them to contain organisms capable of leading to puerperal fever. A number of distinguished doctors gave evidence that they would not, in the circumstances, have treated with penicillin. The Court of Appeal found the defendant to have been negligent. Sachs L.J. said, at p. 397:

> "When the evidence shows that a lacuna in professional practice exists by which risks of grave danger are knowingly taken, then, however small the risk, the court must anxiously examine that lacuna—particularly if the risk can be easily and inexpensively avoided. If the court finds, on an analysis of the reasons given for not taking those precautions that, in the light of current professional knowledge, there is no proper basis for the lacuna, and that it is definitely not reasonable that those risks should have been taken, its function is to state that fact and where necessary to state that it constitutes negligence. In such a case the practice will no doubt thereafter be altered to the benefit of patients. On such occasions the fact that other practitioners would have done the same thing as the defendant practitioner is a very weighty matter to be put on the scales on his behalf; but it is not, as Mr. Webster readily conceded, conclusive. The court must be vigilant to see whether the reasons given for putting a patient at risk are valid in the light of any well-known advance in medical knowledge, or whether they stem from a residual adherence to out-of-date ideas."

Again, in *Edward Wong Finance Co. Ltd. v. Johnson Stokes & Master* [1984] A.C. 296, the defendant's solicitors had conducted the completion of a mortgage transaction in "Hong Kong style" rather than in the old fashioned English style. Completion in Hong Kong style provides for money to be paid over against an undertaking by the solicitors for the borrowers subsequently to hand over the executed documents. This practice opened the gateway through which a dishonest solicitor for the borrower absconded with the loan money without providing the security documents for such loan. The Privy Council held that even though completion in Hong Kong style was almost universally adopted in Hong Kong and was therefore in accordance with a body of professional opinion there, the defendant's solicitors were liable for negligence because there was an obvious risk which could have been guarded against. Thus, the body of professional opinion, though almost universally held, was not reasonable or responsible.

These decisions demonstrate that in cases of diagnosis and treatment there are cases where, despite a body of professional opinion sanctioning the defendant's conduct, the defendant can properly be held liable for negligence (I am not here considering questions of disclosure of risk). In my judgment that is because, in some cases, it cannot be demonstrated to the judge's satisfaction that the body of opinion relied upon is reasonable or responsible. In the vast majority of cases the fact that distinguished experts in the field are of a particular opinion will demonstrate the reasonableness of that opinion. In particular, where there are questions of assessment of the relative risks and benefits of adopting a particular medical practice, a reasonable view necessarily presupposes that the relative risks and benefits have been weighed by the experts in forming their opinions. But if, in a rare case, it can be demonstrated that the professional opinion is not capable of withstanding logical analysis, the judge is entitled to hold that the body of opinion is not reasonable or responsible.

I emphasise that in my view it will very seldom be right for a judge to reach the conclusion that views genuinely held by a competent medical expert are unreasonable. The assessment of medical risks and benefits is a matter of clinical judgment which a judge would not normally be able to make without expert evidence. As the quotation from Lord Scarman makes clear, it would be wrong to allow such assessment to deteriorate into seeking to persuade the judge to prefer one of two views both of which are capable of being logically supported. It is only where a judge can be satisfied that the body of expert opinion cannot be logically supported at all that such opinion will not provide the benchmark by reference to which the defendant's conduct falls to be assessed. . . .

Lord Browne-Wilkinson went on to explain that this was not 'one of those rare cases' where there were grounds to dismiss the body of expert opinion as illogical. In particular, he was mindful of the nature of intubation:

Intubation is not a routine, risk-free process. Dr. Roberton, a consultant paediatrician at Addenbrooke's Hospital, Cambridge, described it as "a major undertaking—an invasive procedure with mortality and morbidity attached—it was an assault." It involves anaesthetising and ventilating the child. A young child does not tolerate a tube easily "at any rate for a day or two" and the child unless sedated tends to remove it.

In the end, the crucial determinant whether the *Bolitho* restatement of the *Bolam* test will make any difference will be judicial attitudes. There are some signs of a greater judicial willingness to question the practices of the medical profession, evidenced not only by *Bolitho* (which in its holding on causation is weak evidence in any event), but also by the more recent case of *Chester v Afshar* [2004] UKHL 1; [2005] 1 AC 134 (Chapter 4 below). The latter case appears to represent a substantial change in judicial attitude on the subject of medical duties to warn or informed consent. Writing before the decision in *Chester v Afshar*, Brazier and Miola (extracted above) also pointed to a range of circumstances affecting general public confidence in the medical profession, and most particularly the idea that the profession should have control over internal review. They cite the serious revelations concerning the Bristol Royal Infirmary, and the failure of fellow professionals to raise questions concerning Doctor Harold Shipman, as influencing public opinion in a powerful way. Certainly, it would seem unlikely that the medical profession will escape the much more general trend towards external, rather than purely internal, review of standards, complaints, and professional practice.

Associated with this trend, more opaque guidelines on accepted practice are increasingly available, and this too will make it more difficult for medical practitioners to hide behind the *Bolam* test.

Penney and Others v East Kent Health Authority [2000] Lloyd's Medical Law Reports 41 (CA)

The claimants had all developed cervical cancer after being told that their cervical smear tests were negative, showing no abnormalities. They claimed that the individuals responsible for screening had been negligent in failing to identify abnormalities in their samples, and/or in failing to categorize the cases as outside the normal range. The Court of Appeal upheld the judge's decision as to liability.

As a first step, it had been concluded by the trial judge that the *Bolam* test has no application to a finding of fact as opposed to a decision as to what course to take. In this instance, the judge was therefore entitled to choose between the different experts on the question of what was actually shown on the slides, in other words whether they did show an abnormality. This was entirely approved by the Court of Appeal: '. . . the Bolam test has no application where what the judge is required to do is to make findings of fact' (para 27). It should be pointed out that the distinction between fact and opinion is not one that is always clearcut, so that even this preliminary statement may be an instance of 'deBolamization'. If courts are ready to categorize events as 'facts' to be determined to the satisfaction of the court, there will be less scope for the *Bolam* test to apply.

The further question was whether a reasonably competent screener could have treated the slides as negative. The experts were divided on this second issue, which relates to breach of duty. However, all the experts agreed that a negative result should be attached to a slide only if there could be 'absolute confidence' that there were no problems with it. If it fell into a 'grey area', then the screener must not designate it as negative. Applying the *Bolitho* test, the judge concluded that the view of the defendants' expert, that a reasonably competent cytoscreener could designate the screen as negative, was illogical in the light of this agreed standard for the conduct of such procedures. The expert's views were internally inconsistent. The Court of Appeal held that, in these circumstances, the judge was entitled to reach his conclusion:

Lord Woolf MR

67   The judge was not rejecting the general approach of the Authority's experts . . . . He was finding that because of the observable abnormalities on the slides the slides should not have been labelled negative in order to comply with the approach (the absolute confidence approach) that those experts supported.

Although the Court of Appeal did not clearly spell out in this case whether the *Bolitho* case made a substantial difference to their conclusions, the non-application of *Bolam* to findings of fact and the willingness to point out inconsistency in expert opinion suggest a greater freedom for courts to make their own judgments, rather than to accept the views of experts.

The same approach was applied to a case of 'wrongful birth' in *Cheryl Ann Conway v Cardiff and Vale NHS Trust* [2004] EWHC 1841 (QB). The claimant had undergone amniocentesis during pregnancy, and this test failed to identify a congenital abnormality in the foetus. It was accepted that the pregnancy would have been terminated, had the abnormality been identified. Experts for the parties did not agree whether a competent cytogeneticist could have missed the abnormality without fault. The judge decided *first* that, *as a matter of fact*, the abnormality would have been visible on the slides. He then decided *second*, since the abnormality was visible, a reasonably competent cytogeneticist could not have missed it. This bears out the point made in respect of *Penney* above, that this approach removes some matters from the reach of the *Bolam* test, by describing them as issues of 'fact'. They thus become questions of evidence to be considered, as usual, on the balance of probabilities.[4]

Bolam Outside the Medical Context

Issues concerning the *scope* of *Bolam* arose in *Adams v Rhymney Valley DC* (2001) PNLR 4. Here, the majority of the Court of Appeal was prepared to accept that a local council benefited from the *Bolam* test in respect of the design of window locks for a domestic property, even though nobody within the council had put their minds to the question of risks and benefits associated with particular locks—in particular, nobody had weighed the risk of fatality in the case of fire (inherent in windows with a removable key) as against the risk that children might be able to unlock the windows and thus fall from the first floor (in windows with a catch and *not* a removable key). There is much to commend the following dissenting view of the applicability of *Bolam*:

> **Sedley LJ** (dissenting)
>
> **16.** The reason why the *Bolam* test has no relevance to a case such as this is that its purpose is to enable the court to determine whether a person professing and purporting to exercise a particular skill has exercised it with sufficient competence to escape a charge of negligence. In the present case the problem is that nobody in the council purported to exercise the relevant design skill. Had they done so, the judge's conclusion that 'the Council exercised the skill of a reasonable designer of windows' might, in the light of the expert evidence which he accepted, have been conclusive. But a defendant which has failed altogether to set about exercising a professional skill cannot expect to be judged as if it had exercised it: the court cannot proceed as if an educated choice was made when it knows that it was not. . . .

Sedley LJ concluded that on balance, if the council had put its mind to the matter in a competent manner, it would have decided that windows without removable keys were the safer option on the upper storey of the house. Thus the council could not benefit from the judge's finding, that a competent designer of windows could have chosen the design that was actually installed, and which contributed to the death of the claimants' young children when trapped by a fire. Whichever view one prefers about the applicability of *Bolam*, this difference of approach clearly illustrates what the effect of the *Bolam* test is. Once Sedley LJ had decided that it did not apply, he was free to come to his own conclusion as to the likely outcome of careful deliberation. It is precisely this process that is ruled out by the *Bolam* test.

1.2 ESTABLISHING BREACH: WHEN DOES THE REASONABLE PERSON TAKE RISKS?

If a risk is held to have been not reasonably foreseeable, then clearly it is not negligent to have run that risk. But there are some circumstances in which the reasonable person would choose

---

4 In respect of 'the balance of probabilities', see our discussions of *res ipsa loquitur*, and of cause in fact, below.

to run a risk which they *do* foresee. No liability will attach to a defendant who acts reasonably in this sense.

The treatment of reasonable risk-taking clearly differentiates negligence liability, from strict liability. The negligence position is that only unreasonable behaviour gives rise to liability. This appears on the face of it to be fair. On the other hand, this means that defendants may therefore create risks to others for their own benefit, without accepting any legal consequences. This allows defendants to profit (in the loosest possible sense) at the expense of those who are put at risk. In some situations then, there is an argument of fairness *against* the negligence standard, and in favour of stricter liability.[5]

Overseas Tankship (UK) Ltd v The Miller Steamship Co ('The Wagon Mound No 2') [1967] 1 AC 617[6]

This was an appeal to the Privy Council from the Supreme Court of New South Wales. The respondents had two ships at Sheerlegs Wharf in Sydney Harbour, undergoing repairs. The appellant was charterer of another ship, *The Wagon Mound*, which was taking on oil from the nearby Caltex Wharf. Because of the carelessness of *The Wagon Mound*'s engineers, a large quantity of oil overflowed onto the surface of the water and drifted towards Sheerlegs Wharf where it accumulated around the respondents' vessels. That oil was set alight, causing extensive damage to the two vessels.

There were two *Wagon Mound* cases arising from this incident. The difference between them turns on a question of fact.

In *Overseas Tankship v Morts Dock & Engineering Co Ltd* (*The Wagon Mound No 1*) [1961] AC 688, an action was brought by the owners of Sheerlegs Wharf (whose welding activities had probably led to the ignition of the oil) for damage to their wharf. This action was unsuccessful because the ignition of the oil while it was on the surface of the water was found to have been unforeseeable. *The Wagon Mound (No 1)* is a leading authority on remoteness of damage, and is extracted in the relevant section below.

In the present case (*The Wagon Mound No 2*), the owners of the two damaged ships brought an action against the charterer of *The Wagon Mound*. This subsequent action was successful. This is what sometimes causes confusion. How can this claim have succeeded, if it was concluded in the first case that the ignition of the oil was unforeseeable? The answer is that in this case, there was a different finding of fact by the first instance court. This was an entirely separate action brought by different plaintiffs in respect of different damage. The finding of fact in the first Wagon Mound case was irrelevant. No doubt also the argument of the plaintiffs in this second case was more robustly advanced because the shipowners had played no role in causing the fire. In *The Wagon Mound No 1*, the wharf owners were in a difficult position. If they argued that the ignition of the oil was foreseeable, they might themselves be considered negligent in continuing their welding activities.

In this second case, it was concluded that the ignition of the oil though unlikely was nevertheless foreseeable. The question was whether it was justifiable (not negligent) to create this particular risk by spilling the oil, given that the risk was so low.

---

[5] This can be described as an 'enterprise risk' justification. See Chapters 9, 11, and 15.

[6] Note the discussion in the extract below of *Bolton v Stone* [1951] AC 850, which we have not extracted separately.

The Privy Council held that the spillage of oil was negligent. The reasonable person will sometimes take foreseeable risks where this is worthwhile. But here, there was no benefit to be derived from spreading the oil on the water.

Lord Reid (delivering the judgment of the Board)

Bolton v. Stone posed a new problem. There a member of a visiting team drove a cricket ball out of the ground onto an unfrequented adjacent public road and it struck and severely injured a lady who happened to be standing in the road. That it might happen that a ball would be driven onto this road could not have been said to be a fantastic or far-fetched possibility: according to the evidence it had happened about six times in 28 years. And it could not have been said to be a far-fetched or fantastic possibility that such a ball would strike someone in the road: people did pass along the road from time to time. So it could not have been said that, on any ordinary meaning of the words, the fact that a ball might strike a person in the road was not foreseeable or reasonably foreseeable—it was plainly foreseeable. But the chance of its happening in the foreseeable future was infinitesimal. A mathematician given the data could have worked out that it was only likely to happen once in so many thousand years. The House of Lords held that the risk was so small that in the circumstances a reasonable man would have been justified in disregarding it and taking no steps to eliminate it.

But it does not follow that, no matter what the circumstances may be, it is justifiable to neglect a risk of such a small magnitude. A reasonable man would only neglect such a risk if he had some valid reason for doing so, e.g., that it would involve considerable expense to eliminate the risk. He would weigh the risk against the difficulty of eliminating it. If the activity which caused the injury to Miss Stone had been an unlawful activity, there can be little doubt but that *Bolton v. Stone* would have been decided differently. In their Lordships' judgment *Bolton v. Stone* did not alter the general principle that a person must be regarded as negligent if he does not take steps to eliminate a risk which he knows or ought to know is a real risk and not a mere possibility which would never influence the mind of a reasonable man. What that decision did was to recognise and give effect to the qualification that it is justifiable not to take steps to eliminate a real risk if it is small and if the circumstances are such that a reasonable man, careful of the safety of his neighbour, would think it right to neglect it.

In the present case there was no justification whatever for discharging the oil into Sydney Harbour. Not only was it an offence to do so, but it involved considerable loss financially. If the ship's engineer had thought about the matter, there could have been no question of balancing the advantages and disadvantages. From every point of view it was both his duty and his interest to stop the discharge immediately. . . .

In their Lordships' view a properly qualified and alert chief engineer would have realised there was a real risk here and they do not understand Walsh J. to deny that. But he appears to have held that if a real risk can properly be described as remote it must then be held to be not reasonably foreseeable. That is a possible interpretation of some of the authorities. But this is still an open question and on principle their Lordships cannot accept this view. If a real risk is one which would occur to the mind of a reasonable man in the position of the defendant's servant and which he would not brush aside as far-fetched, and if the criterion is to be what that reasonable man would have done in the circumstances, then surely he would not neglect such a risk if action to eliminate it presented no difficulty, involved no disadvantage, and required no expense.

Some risks, though foreseeable, are very low in probability. The fact that a risk is small (in probability terms) does not justify us in ignoring it. There must, as Lord Reid says, be some valid reason for neglecting it. For example, the cost of precautions may be very high. In *The Wagon Mound* itself, there was no justification for releasing oil into the harbour, so that even if the risk of ignition was tiny, there was no good reason for having disregarded it.

The mention made in the extract above of 'weighing' the risk against the difficulty of avoiding it supports the view that English negligence law adopts something along the lines of the 'Learned Hand' test. This test is derived from the approach of the American judge Learned Hand in the case of *US v Carroll Towing Co* (1947) 159 F 2d 169, 173. The approach represents the test for whether a duty was breached in terms of a formula:

> if the probability be called P; the injury, L, and the burden [ie, of precautions or avoidance], B; liability depends on whether B is less than L multiplied by P; ie whether B < PL

The Learned Hand test is itself interpreted by some commentators as enshrining an economic approach to negligence law in which the optimum, which is to say most economically productive, level of risk and precautions will be encouraged.

Although all the elements mentioned in the Learned Hand test are important in English cases on breach of duty, there is no evidence that the question of breach is interpreted in a mathematical or purely economic fashion by English courts. The overriding question is not a mathematical one (which has the lower value, B or PL?). Rather, it is an evaluative one. The question is, as Lord Reid put it in the extract above, whether 'a reasonable man, careful of the safety of his neighbour, would think it right to neglect [the risk]'. Issues of probability and cost are merely elements in this judgment. Since the reasonable man is, in Lord Reid's statement, 'careful of the safety of his neighbour', the test that he states is probably weighted towards safety, whereas a literal interpretation of the Learned Hand test is not. In addition, English courts have been more openly evaluative of the activities of defendants. In *Watt v Hertfordshire CC* [1954] 1 WLR 835, for example, it was thought that greater risks with safety may reasonably be taken if the risk is in the interests of saving life or limb, particularly in an emergency. According to Lord Denning in that case, fewer risks would be justified in a commercial context, for example in trying to maximize productivity. Similarly, where the risk-taking activity has no justification, then there is no question of weighing it against the risk of damage—this was the case in the *Wagon Mound* itself. In a strongly economic application of the Learned Hand test, social utility would (by contrast) be determined *purely* by the relative profit and cost elements of the test.

1.3 COMPENSATION ACT 2006, SECTION 1: RISKS AND 'DESIRABLE ACTIVITIES'?

The following rather peculiar legislative provision *appears* to be directed at the question of reasonable risk-taking, though the terms in which it is expressed do not relate particularly closely to established questions at common law.

Compensation Act 2006

1 Deterrent effect of potential liability

A court considering a claim in negligence or breach of statutory duty may, in determining whether the defendant should have taken particular steps to meet a standard of care (whether by taking precautions against a risk or otherwise), have regard to whether a requirement to take those steps might—

(a) prevent a desirable activity from being undertaken at all, to a particular extent or in a particular way, or

(b) discourage persons from undertaking functions in connection with a desirable activity.

Few commentators think that this section will have any beneficial effect. This is partly because it might actually increase litigation, as people seek to clarify what is meant by a 'desirable activity'.[7] But equally, courts already take into account issues surrounding the nature of the defendant's activity in the context of a claim in negligence (and, probably, breach of statutory duty). Indeed, the Explanatory Notes to the Compensation Act 2006 include the following statement concerning section 1:

Explanatory Notes to Compensation Act 2006

10. This provision is intended to contribute to improving awareness of this aspect of the law; providing reassurance to the people and organisations who are concerned about possible litigation; and to ensuring that normal activities are not prevented because of the fear of litigation and excessively adverse behaviour.

11. This provision is not concerned with and does not alter the standard of care, nor the circumstances in which a duty to take that care will be owed. . . .

The government has admitted that section 1 is really intended to 'send out a message' that good risks should go ahead. It was not intended to change the law.[8] This is (to say the least) an unusual goal for legislation, and quite a dangerous one given that legislation is inclined to have an effect whether intended or not.[9]

In truth, the target of governmental anxiety is not that courts have been too ready to impose crushing liability against those undertaking beneficial activities. There is little evidence of any such phenomenon. Rather, the concern is that too many people will *believe* that crushing liability will follow any damaging error that is made, and this belief will have adverse effects on public amenity and productive economic activity. We return to these themes in Chapter 8.

The impact of section 1 remains to be seen. If it has any impact on the law itself (as opposed to its desired impact on *perceptions* of law), it appears that this will have been accidental.

---

[7] The Constitutional Affairs Committee in its Report on Compensation Culture (3rd Report Session 2005–6) expressed the view that such 'satellite' litigation would be an inevitable result of s 1.

[8] See K. Williams, 'Legislating in the Echo Chamber' (2005) 155 NLJ 1938.

[9] TUC evidence to the Constitutional Affairs Committee, for example, queried whether those injured while working in 'desirable' industries might find that their claims are met with arguments under s 1.

1.4 *RES IPSA LOQUITUR* AND ABSENCE OF EVIDENCE OF FAULT

Generally speaking, it is for the claimant to establish that all elements of a cause of action are present.[10] In tort, the relevant standard of proof is the civil standard, 'balance of probabilities'. To establish breach, it must be shown that it is *more likely than not* that the defendant was careless. The claimant must also show, on balance, that the negligence caused the harm.

It is tempting to think that the maxim *res ipsa loquitur* ('the thing speaks for itself') reverses this burden of proof, placing the burden of showing *lack* of negligence on the defendant. But it does not. The maxim does not change the burden of proof at all. But it does mean that sometimes, the circumstances themselves may be treated as evidence of carelessness.

If a claim in negligence is to disclose a good cause of action, evidence of carelessness must be pleaded. If no evidence of carelessness is provided, a defendant may apply for summary judgment (the claim will fail without further argument). This initial hurdle has nothing to do with the balance of probabilities.

Sometimes, it is very difficult for a claimant to get past this first 'evidentiary' stage, because all information about the defendant's *conduct* is simply outside their knowledge. The claimant may know nothing about the manufacturing processes of the defendant, knowing only that the goods they consumed were defective and led to illness. Or the claimant may know nothing about the way in which the defendant discharged his or her gun, knowing only that the end result was that they were shot.[11] On some such occasions, a court may decide that the circumstances 'speak for themselves'. The mere facts of the injury as recounted by the claimant *suggest* negligence.

The classic statement of this 'doctrine' is as follows.[12] Bags of sugar being loaded by the defendant's crane fell and struck the plaintiff:

Erle CJ, *Scott v The London and St Katherine Docks Company* [1865] 3 H & C 596

But where the thing is shown to be under the management of the defendant or his servants, and the accident is such as in the ordinary course of things does not happen if those who have the management use proper care, it affords reasonable evidence, in the absence of explanation by the defendants, that the accident arose from want of care.

Where this is the case, the effect is that some evidence of *lack* of carelessness must be brought by the defendant. The burden of proving negligence lies on the claimant in the usual way, and must be discharged to the usual standard, namely on the balance of probabilities. If the circumstances *strongly* suggest negligence, then the claimant may have little else to do than state the facts. This is why it may *appear as though* the burden has shifted to the defendant.

---

[10] It is for the *defendant* on the other hand to establish that a relevant *defence* is made out (see further Chapter 5).

[11] In *Fowler v Lanning* [1959] 1 QB 426, the maxim *res ipsa* was not invoked in such circumstances. Perhaps it should have been: see Chapter 2.

[12] In fact, *res ipsa* is probably not a doctrine so much as a complex name for a common sense inference from the facts.

These distinctions are well illustrated by the following case. The plaintiffs (and in one case the deceased relative of a plaintiff) were passengers in a light bus. They were injured (or killed) when the defendants' coach left its side of the road and ploughed across a central reservation into oncoming traffic. These basic facts were confirmed by a police report.

Lord Griffiths (giving the judgment of the Court), *Ng Chun Pui v Lee Chuen Tat*
(Privy Council, on Appeal from the Court of Appeal of Hong Kong) [1988] RTR 298

The plaintiffs called no oral evidence and relied upon the fact of the accident as evidence of negligence or, as the judge put it, the doctrine of *res ipsa loquitur*. There can be no doubt that the plaintiffs were justified in taking this course. In ordinary circumstances if a well-maintained coach is being properly driven it will not cross the central reservation of a dual carriageway and collide with on-coming traffic in the other carriageway. In the absence of any explanation of the behaviour of the coach the proper inference to draw is that it was not being driven with the standard of care required by the law and that the driver was therefore negligent. If the defendants had called no evidence the plaintiffs would undoubtedly have been entitled to judgment.

The defendants however did call evidence and gave an explanation of the circumstances . . .

(The explanation offered was that a car in front of the coach had performed a dangerous manoeuvre. The driver was not negligent in his response.)

The judge however was of the view that . . . because the plaintiffs had originally relied upon the doctrine of *res ipsa loquitur*, the burden of disproving negligence remained upon the defendants and they had failed to discharge it. In their Lordships' opinion this shows a misunderstanding of the so-called doctrine of *res ipsa loquitur*, which is no more than the use of a latin maxim to describe a state of evidence from which it is proper to infer negligence. Although it has been said in a number of cases it is misleading to talk of the burden of proof shifting to the defendant in a *res ipsa loquitur* situation. . . .

. . . in an appropriate case the plaintiff establishes a *prima facie* case by relying upon the fact of the accident. If the defendant adduces no evidence there is nothing to rebut the inference of negligence and the plaintiff will have proved his case. But if the defendant does adduce evidence that evidence must be evaluated to see if it is still reasonable to draw the inference of negligence from the mere fact of the accident. Loosely speaking this may be referred to as a burden on the defendant to show he was not negligent, but that only means that faced with a *prima facie* case of negligence the defendant will be found negligent unless he produces evidence that is capable of rebutting the *prima facie* case. . . . In so far as resort is had to the burden of proof the burden remains at the end of the case as it was at the beginning upon the plaintiff to prove that his injury was caused by the negligence of the defendants.

No breach of duty could be established in this particular case. The defendant's account of the facts was accepted, and in the light of this he was judged according to the standard of a reasonable person placed in a position of peril. It should be noted that the maxim *res ipsa loquitur* was applicable in this case—the facts suggested negligence, so that the defendant had to give an explanation consistent with proper care having been taken. But the defendant successfully offered such an explanation. The burden of proof remained with the plaintiff throughout.

FURTHER READING

Brazier, M., and Miola, J., 'Bye-Bye Bolam: A Medical Litigation Revolution?' (2000) 8 *Med L Rev* 85–114.

Charlish, P., 'Sports: Ordinary Negligence in the Final Furlong' (2005) JPIL 308–19.

Grubb, A., 'Causation and the *Bolam* Test' (1993) 1 *Med L Rev* 241.

Kidner, R., 'The Variable Standard of Care, Contributory Negligence and *Volenti*' (1991) 11 LS 1.

Norrie, K., 'Medical Negligence: Who Sets the Standard?' (1985) 11 JME 135.

Teff, H., 'The Standard of Care in Medical Negligence: Moving on from *Bolam*?' (1998) 18 OJLS 473–84.

Witting, C., 'National Health Service Rationing: Implications for the Standard of Care in Negligence' (2001) 21 OJLS 443.

---

2. DUTY OF CARE: AN INTRODUCTION

This section provides a general introduction to the 'duty of care', and particularly to the way in which this concept has evolved. There will be detailed consideration of its applications in Chapter 6. We return to general questions about the duty of care, and an appraisal, at the end of that chapter.

It will not be enough to show that the defendant was careless in the sense discussed above. In addition, it must be established that the defendant owed to the claimant a duty to take care, so that carelessness amounts to a breach of that duty. Furthermore, the breach of duty must be shown to have caused recoverable damage (Section 4 below), which is within the scope of the duty and/or not too remote a consequence of the lack of care (Section 5 below).

In the present section, we will:

1. consider the origins of the general duty of care in *Donoghue v Stevenson*, and its subsequent evolution through the defining cases of *Anns v Merton* and *Caparo v Dickman*; and

2. reflect briefly on the nature of the duty concept and the part it plays in the tort of negligence.

3. THE EVOLUTION AND CONTENT OF THE DUTY CONCEPT: *DONOGHUE* TO *CAPARO*

NERAL TORT OF NEGLIGENCE: *DONOGHUE V* *?ON*

? Donoghue) v Stevenson [1932] AC 562

:laimed damages for personal injuries from the respondent, a manufacturer of e alleged that a bottle of ginger beer manufactured by the defendants was by a friend in a café in Paisley, the bottle being made of dark opaque glass so that she could not see its contents. She further alleged that the café proprietor had poured some of the ginger beer into a glass, and she had drunk some of it, before her friend proceeded to pour out the remainder. At this point a decomposing snail floated out of the bottle. As a result of the nauseating sight of the snail, and in consequence of the impurities in the ginger beer that she had drunk, she claimed to have suffered shock, and gastro-enteritis. The respondents argued that these alleged facts disclosed no valid action, and the House of Lords dealt with this purely legal question on the basis of assumed facts.[13] The best-known passage in English and Scottish tort law[14] appears in the judgment of Lord Atkin, and is highlighted below. But a real flavour of the importance of this case will only be gained by comparing Lord Atkin's approach with the dissent of Lord Buckmaster.

Lord Buckmaster (dissenting)

At 568

The case of *Winterbottom v. Wright* (10 M & W 109) is . . . an authority that is closely applicable. Owing to negligence in the construction of a carriage it broke down, and a stranger to the manufacture and sale sought to recover damages for injuries which he alleged were due to negligence in the work, and it was held that he had no cause of action either in tort or arising out of contract. This case seems to me to show that the manufacturer of any article is not liable to a third party injured by negligent construction, for there can be nothing in the character of a coach to place it in a special category. It may be noted, also, that in this case Alderson B. said (10 M & W 115): "The only safe rule is to confine the right to recover to those who enter into the contract; if we go one step beyond that, there is no reason why we should not go fifty.". . .

At 578

In *Mullen v. Barr & Co.*[1929 S.C. 461, 479], a case indistinguishable from the present excepting upon the ground that a mouse is not a snail, and necessarily adopted by the Second Division in their judgment, Lord Anderson says this: "In a case like the present, where the goods of the defenders are widely distributed throughout Scotland, it would seem little short of outrageous to make them responsible to members of the public for the condition of the contents of every bottle which issues from their works. It is obvious that, if such responsibility attached to the defenders, they might be called on to meet claims of damages which they could not possibly investigate or answer."

In agreeing, as I do, with the judgment of Lord Anderson, I desire to add that I find it hard to dissent from the emphatic nature of the language with which his judgment is clothed. I am of opinion that this appeal should be dismissed, and I beg to move your Lordships accordingly.

Lord Atkin, at 578–83

My Lords, the sole question for determination in this case is legal: Do the averments made by the pursuer in her pleading, if true, disclose a cause of action? I need not restate the particular facts. The question is whether the manufacturer of an article of drink sold by him to a distributor, in circumstances which prevent the distributor or the ultimate purchaser or consumer from discovering by inspection any defect, is under any legal duty to the ultimate purchaser or

---

13 To this day, it is not known whether there was a decaying snail in the bottle of ginger beer.
14 Although in Scotland the subject is not tort but 'delict'.

consumer to take reasonable care that the article is free from defect likely to cause injury to health. I do not think a more important problem has occupied your Lordships in your judicial capacity: important both because of its bearing on public health and because of the practical test which it applies to the system under which it arises. The case has to be determined in accordance with Scots law; but it has been a matter of agreement between the experienced counsel who argued this case, and it appears to be the basis of the judgments of the learned judges of the Court of Session, that for the purposes of determining this problem the laws of Scotland and of England are the same. . . . The law of both countries appears to be that in order to support an action for damages for negligence the complainant has to show that he has been injured by the breach of a duty owed to him in the circumstances by the defendant to take reasonable care to avoid such injury. . . . We are solely concerned with the question whether, as a matter of law in the circumstances alleged, the defender owed any duty to the pursuer to take care.

It is remarkable how difficult it is to find in the English authorities statements of general application defining the relations between parties that give rise to the duty. The Courts are concerned with the particular relations which come before them in actual litigation, and it is sufficient to say whether the duty exists in those circumstances. The result is that the Courts have been engaged upon an elaborate classification of duties as they exist in respect of property, whether real or personal, with further divisions as to ownership, occupation or control, and distinctions based on the particular relations of the one side or the other, whether manufacturer, salesman or landlord, customer, tenant, stranger, and so on. In this way it can be ascertained at any time whether the law recognizes a duty, but only where the case can be referred to some particular species which has been examined and classified. And yet the duty which is common to all the cases where liability is established must logically be based upon some element common to the cases where it is found to exist. To seek a complete logical definition of the general principle is probably to go beyond the function of the judge, for the more general the definition the more likely it is to omit essentials or to introduce non-essentials. The attempt was made by Brett M.R. in *Heaven v. Pender* (11 QBD 503, 509), in a definition to which I will later refer. As framed, it was demonstrably too wide, though it appears to me, if properly limited, to be capable of affording a valuable practical guide.

At present I content myself with pointing out that in English law there must be, and is, some general conception of relations giving rise to a duty of care, of which the particular cases found in the books are but instances. The liability for negligence, whether you style it such or treat it as in other systems as a species of "culpa," is no doubt based upon a general public sentiment of moral wrongdoing for which the offender must pay. But acts or omissions which any moral code would censure cannot in a practical world be treated so as to give a right to every person injured by them to demand relief. In this way rules of law arise which limit the range of complainants and the extent of their remedy. The rule that you are to love your neighbour becomes in law, you must not injure your neighbour; and the lawyer's question, Who is my neighbour? receives a restricted reply. You must take reasonable care to avoid acts or omissions which you can reasonably foresee would be likely to injure your neighbour. Who, then, in law is my neighbour? The answer seems to be—persons who are so closely and directly affected by my act that I ought reasonably to have them in contemplation as being so affected when I am directing my mind to the acts or omissions which are called in question. This appears to me to be the doctrine of *Heaven v. Pender* (11 QBD 503, 509), as laid down by Lord Esher (then Brett M.R.) when it is limited by the notion of proximity introduced by Lord Esher himself and A. L. Smith L.J. in *Le Lievre v. Gould*. ([1893] 1 QB 491, 497, 504) Lord Esher says: "That case established that, under certain circumstances, one man may owe a duty to another, even though there is no contract between them. If one man is near to another, or is near to the property of another, a duty lies upon him not to do that which may cause a personal injury to that other, or may injure his property." So A. L. Smith L.J.: "The decision of *Heaven v. Pender* (11 QBD 503) was founded upon the principle, that a duty to take due care did arise when the person or property of one was in such proximity to the person or property of another that, if due care was not taken, damage might be done by the one to the other." I think that this sufficiently states the truth if proximity be not confined to mere physical proximity, but be used, as I think it was intended, to extend to such close and direct relations that the act complained of directly affects a person whom the person alleged to be bound to take care would know would be directly affected by his careless act. That this is the sense in which nearness of "proximity" was intended by Lord Esher is obvious from his own illustration in *Heaven v. Pender* of the application of his doctrine to the sale of goods. "This" (i.e., the rule he has just formulated) "includes the case of goods, etc., supplied to be used immediately by a particular person or persons, or one of a class of persons, where it would be obvious to the person supplying, if he thought, that the goods would in all probability be used at once by such persons before a reasonable opportunity for discovering any defect which might exist, and where the thing supplied would be of such a nature that a neglect of ordinary care or skill as to its condition or the manner of supplying it would probably cause danger to the person or property of the person for whose use it was supplied, and who was about to use it. It would exclude a case in which the goods are supplied under circumstances in which it would be a chance by whom they would be used or whether they would be used or not, or whether they would be used before there would probably be means of observing any defect, or where the goods would be of such a nature that a want of care or skill as to their condition or the manner of supplying them would not probably produce danger of injury to person or property." I draw particular attention to the fact that Lord Esher emphasizes the necessity of goods having to be "used immediately" and "used at once before a reasonable opportunity of inspection." This is obviously to exclude the possibility of goods having their condition altered by lapse of time, and to call attention to the proximate relationship, which may be too remote where inspection even of the person using, certainly of an intermediate person, may reasonably be interposed. With this necessary qualification of proximate relationship as explained in *Le Lievre v. Gould*, I think the judgment of Lord Esher expresses the law of England; without the qualification, I think the majority of the Court in *Heaven v. Pender* were justified in thinking the principle was expressed in too general terms. There will no doubt arise cases where it will be difficult to determine whether the contemplated relationship is so close that the duty arises. But in the class of case now before the Court I cannot conceive any difficulty to arise.

Lord Macmillan, at 609–11

It humbly appears to me that the diversity of view which is exhibited in such cases as *George v. Skivington* on the one hand and *Blacker v. Lake & Elliot, Ld.*, on the other hand—to take two extreme instances—is explained by the fact that in the discussion of the topic which now engages your Lordships' attention two rival principles of the law find a meeting place where each has contended for supremacy. On the one hand, there is the well established principle that no one other than a party to a contract can complain of a breach of that contract. On the other hand, there is the equally well established doctrine that negligence apart from contract gives a right of action to the party injured by that negligence—and here I use the term negligence, of course, in its technical legal sense, implying a duty owed and neglected. The fact that there is a contractual relationship between the parties which may give rise to an action for breach of contract, does not exclude the co-existence of a right of action founded on negligence as between the same parties, independently of the contract, though arising out of the relationship in fact brought about by the contract. Of this the best illustration is the right of the injured railway passenger to sue the railway company either for breach of the contract of safe carriage or for negligence in carrying him. And there is no reason why the same set of facts should not give one person a right of action in contract and another person a right of action in tort. . . .

Where, as in cases like the present, so much depends upon the avenue of approach to the question, it is very easy to take the wrong turning. If you begin with the sale by the manufacturer to the retail dealer, then the consumer who purchases from the retailer is at once seen to be a stranger to the contract between the retailer and the manufacturer and so disentitled to sue upon it. There is no contractual relation between the manufacturer and the consumer; and thus the plaintiff, if he is to succeed, is driven to try to bring himself within one or other of the exceptional cases where the strictness of the rule that none but a party to a contract can found on a breach of that contract has been mitigated in the public interest, as it has been in the case of a person who issues a chattel which is inherently dangerous or which he knows to be in a dangerous condition. If, on the other hand, you disregard the fact that the circumstances of the case at one stage include the existence of a contract of sale between the manufacturer and the retailer, and approach the question by asking whether there is evidence of carelessness on the part of the manufacturer, and whether he owed a duty to be careful in a question with the party who has been injured in consequence of his want of care, the circumstance that the injured party was not a party to the incidental contract of sale becomes irrelevant, and his title to sue the manufacturer is unaffected by that circumstance. The appellant in the present instance asks that her case be approached as a case of delict, not as a case of breach of contract. She does not require to invoke the exceptional cases in which a person not a party to a contract has been held to be entitled to complain of some defect in the subject-matter of the contract which has caused him harm. The exceptional case of things dangerous in themselves, or known to be in a dangerous condition, has been regarded as constituting a peculiar category outside the ordinary law both of contract and of tort.

At 618–19

The law takes no cognizance of carelessness in the abstract. It concerns itself with carelessness only where there is a duty to take care and where failure in that duty has caused damage. In such circumstances carelessness assumes the legal quality of negligence and entails consequences in law of negligence. What, then, are the circumstances which give rise to this duty to take care? In the daily contacts of social and business life human beings are thrown into, or place themselves in, an infinite variety of relations with their fellows; and the law can refer only to the standards of the reasonable man in order to determine whether any particular relation gives rise to a duty to take care as between those who stand in that relation to each other. The grounds of action may be as various and manifold as human errancy; and the conception of legal responsibility may develop in adaptation to altering social conditions and standards. The criterion of judgment must adjust and adapt itself to the changing circumstances of life. The categories of negligence are never closed. The cardinal principle of liability is that the party complained of should owe to the party complaining a duty to take care, and that the party complaining should be able to prove that he has suffered damage in consequence of a breach of that duty. Where there is room for diversity of view, it is in determining what circumstances will establish such a relationship between the parties as to give rise, on the one side, to a duty to take care, and on the other side to a right to have care taken.

There are two dimensions to the significance of this case.

1. It secured the independence of tort from contract. The judgment of Lord Macmillan was particularly important in this regard.

2. Through the judgment of Lord Atkin in particular, it recognized a *general* tort of negligence, not confined to specific duty situations.

Tort and Contract in *Donoghue*

Donoghue recognized that a remedy may be available through the tort of negligence, where 'privity of contract' would prevent the consumer from having any contractual claim. The doctrine of 'privity' restricts contractual remedies to those who are parties to the contract:

E. McKendrick, *Contract Law: Text, Cases and Materials*
(2nd edn, Oxford: OUP, 2005), at 1168

. . . The general rule which English law has adopted is that the contract creates rights and imposes obligations only between the parties to the contract: the third party thus neither acquires rights under the contract nor is he subject to liabilities. This general rule is known as the doctrine of privity of contract.

Since the consumer in this case had not entered into a contract with the defendant manufacturer of the goods (nor, indeed, with the retailer, who sold the ginger beer to her friend), she had no contractual remedy. Even today under the Contracts (Rights of Third Parties) Act 1999, a non-contracting consumer in the position of Mrs Donoghue would not have a contractual remedy, as no rights of action are conferred upon her by the contracting parties. *Donoghue* is the key case establishing that the cause of action in tort for negligence is independent of contract, and is not bound by the rules of privity which restrict contractual remedies. Duties to take care are imposed quite independently of contractual duties, so that they may be owed to parties who are strangers to the contract.

The relationship between tort and contract dominated Lord Macmillan's judgment. He analysed tort and contract as providing two ways of looking at the same set of facts, so that tort duties may coexist with contractual duties without the need to have identical content.

The same step had already been taken in the United States in *MacPherson v Buick Motor Co* (1916) 217 NY 382 (a decision of the New York Court of Appeals which was adopted by most state jurisdictions). *MacPherson v Buick* is referred to in the majority judgments of both Lord Atkin and Lord Macmillan, although it appears that its authority was not pressed by counsel for Mrs Donoghue (see further A. Rodger, 'Lord Macmillan's Speech in *Donoghue v Stevenson*' (1992) 108 LQR 236). The extracts from Lord Buckmaster's dissenting judgment above, and especially the strength of his criticism, indicate how significant this aspect of *Donoghue v Stevenson* was felt to be, at the time of the judgment. Lord Buckmaster was primarily concerned to prevent the traditional rules of contract law, particularly privity, from being undermined by a developing law of negligence. The complex relationship between tort and contract has evolved further in recent years, and it is important to the discussion in Chapter 6 below.

The Duty of Care in *Donoghue*

Progressively over the succeeding years, attention began to focus on Lord Atkin's analysis of the duty concept. It is clear that the terminology of 'duty' existed in the case law prior to *Donoghue v Stevenson*. Then, as now, there could only be liability on the basis of negligence if the defendant owed a legal duty to the injured party to take care for his or her safety. The distinction marked by the duty concept was and is the distinction between carelessly inflicted damage which involves the breach of a duty of care, and carelessly inflicted damage in respect of which there is no duty and therefore can be no liability. But the law prior to *Donoghue v Stevenson* consisted of a series of isolated instances where a 'duty to take care' was recognized, and these were not united by any general theory. Many of the situations were contractual or perceived to be similar to contract (for example, the position of carriers in respect of their passengers), and this may have been the source of the 'privity of tort fallacy'—the doctrine that tort duties could not exist in the presence of contract between parties who were not contractually related.

Lord Atkin was not the first judge to set out a general theory which sought to explain the particular instances of negligence liability. Brett MR (later Lord Esher) had propounded a broad test based on foreseeability in the case of *Heaven v Pender* ((1883) 11 QBD 503, 509):

> Whenever one person is by circumstances placed in such a position with regard to another that every one of ordinary sense who did think would at once recognise that if he did not use ordinary care and skill in his own conduct with regard to those circumstances he would cause danger of injury to the person or property of the other, a duty arises to use ordinary care and skill to avoid such danger.

He did not gain the agreement of his fellow judges in that case, and Lord Atkin agrees that the above statement is 'demonstrably too wide'. Lord Macmillan on the other hand thought that, with appropriate qualification, it could provide a useful practical guide, although not a formal definition. Later, in statements approved of and adopted by Lord Atkin, Lord Esher and A.L. Smith LJ added the important qualification of 'closeness', 'directness', or 'proximity' (*Le Lievre v Gould* [1893] 1 QB 491, 497, 504).

Lord Atkin agreed that proximity was the necessary *additional* component which would restrict the circumstances in which a duty to take care could be said to arise. Equally importantly, he understood proximity to have a special meaning. This meaning would not be restricted to *physical* closeness, but could reflect a variety of aspects of the relationship between the parties in terms of closeness (see the second highlighted passage in his judgment, above). In the particular case in hand, it was the fact that the goods were expected to reach the eventual consumer without intermediate tampering and without inspection, that supplied the necessary closeness and 'directness'.

Foreseeability and **proximity** continue to be core elements in the test for the duty of care today.

Donoghue v Stevenson and the Unified Tort of Negligence

In 1957, looking back at the influence of *Donoghue v Stevenson*, R. V. F. Heuston argued that the neighbour principle had been over-emphasized. It was never intended by Lord Atkin to amount to a universal test for the existence of a duty of care in negligence, and had 'been called upon to bear a weight . . . manifestly greater than it could support': Heuston, '*Donoghue v*

Stevenson in Retrospect' (1957) 20 MLR 1, 23. Heuston may well have been right in a narrow but important sense. Lord Atkin prefaced his broader remarks with a warning: to seek a 'complete logical definition is probably to go beyond the function of the judge'.[15]

However, to deny the validity of the neighbour principle as a *test* is perhaps to miss the historical contribution of *Donoghue v Stevenson*—though it is a point that Heuston would surely have wished to make more forcefully in the light of *Anns v Merton*, which is extracted and discussed below. Looking historically at the law of negligence, the issue of the day at the time of *Donoghue* was one of generalization. Could there be said to be a general tort of negligence, or was there just a 'wilderness of single instances' (Ibbetson, *A Historical Introduction to the Law of Obligations*, 179) where a duty could be said to arise? Lord Atkin's explanation of the duty of care was significant because it treated those isolated single instances as aspects of a broad and integrated tort of negligence. It may not have occurred to him to worry whether his explanation could be used as a precise test. Historically, the important question was simply whether there was such a thing as a single tort of negligence. The alternative was that the law only recognized a series of distinct and separate duty situations, in which the defendant would be liable for losses caused should he or she act negligently in breach of the duty.

Donoghue v Stevenson is generally recognized as beginning the process through which a general tort of negligence emerged. This process had been encouraged by many of the tort scholars of the day (among them Winfield, 'The History of Negligence in the Law of Torts' (1926) 42 *LQR*, 184; Pollock, *Torts* (13th edn, 1929)). In the next extract, Ibbetson traces this broader historical development up to about 1970, a few years before *Anns v Merton*. Subsequently, we will turn to the attempt to set out a universal 'test' for the duty of care in *Anns*.

David Ibbetson, *A Historical Introduction to the Law of Obligations*, 190–3

The turning point came with the well-known decision in *Donoghue v Stevenson* . . . In point of detail, this [decision] amounted to a reversal of the line of cases stemming from *Winterbottom v Wright*; it was never afterwards doubted that the person injured by a defectively manufactured product might in principle have an action against the negligent manufacturer.

There were three possible routes to this conclusion. Most minimally, it could simply have been said that the cases following *Winterbottom v Wright* had been overruled, and that a duty of care was in fact owed by the manufacturer to the ultimate consumer. This would have been sufficient to explain the decision in the case. It would not, however, have involved any qualification of the traditional analysis in terms of a multiplicity of duties of care; nor would it have involved any qualification of the traditionally conservative 'incremental' approach to liability whereby the plaintiff was expected to demonstrate the existence of a duty of care by showing that the case fell within an already recognised duty situation or was very closely analogous to one. Such a minimalist approach was consistent with the speeches of Lord Thankerton and Lord Macmillan, and was the favoured interpretation of the case by contemporary commentators . . .

Secondly, *Donoghue v Stevenson* could have been treated as accepting an approach based upon a multiplicity of duty situations, but without any requirement that new duty situations

---

[15] This warning against reliance on overly general statements were particularly noted by Lord Devlin in the key case of *Hedley Byrne v Heller* [1964] AC 465, and quoted again by Lord Oliver in *Caparo v Dickman* (below).

could be recognized only by very close analogy to duty situations that had previously been recognised. This was implicit in Lord Macmillan's speech, and his central conclusion that 'the categories of negligence are never closed' . . . Such an approach inevitably involved some element of generalization, though Lord Macmillan himself was diffident about laying down any such principle.. [*[1932] AC 562, 619* . . .].

Finally, and most generally, *Donoghue v Stevenson* might have involved the wholesale rejection of the analysis dependent upon a multiplicity of duties of care in favour of a single requirement of taking reasonable care. This was, famously, the approach of Lord Atkin . . . .

In practice there was not a great deal of difference between the approaches of Lord Macmillan and Lord Atkin, for both of them allowed the law considerable flexibility to adapt to new situations. At a rhetorical level Lord Atkin's approach was particularly valuable, for it provided ready support for any conclusion that a judge wished to reach, and it provided a useful starting point for academic analysis. As a matter of reality, though, it was Lord Macmillan's more careful approach that was followed. . . . Text-book writers, while paying lip service to Lord Atkin's statement, still dealt with the law in terms of more or less discrete categories of duty situation, albeit that they were couched at a more general level . . . Judges, too, although less hidebound by previous precedents, did not expand the law into a whole range of new situations simply on the grounds that the defendant had carelessly caused foreseeable harm to the plaintiff. Two types of case in particular stood in the way of the wholesale recognition of a general duty of care of the sort formulated by Lord Atkin: cases where a trespasser had been injured, and cases where financial loss had been suffered by reliance upon a negligent representation. . . .[16]

After a brief flirtation in the late nineteenth century, the Common law had turned its face against allowing actions for negligent statements (as opposed to negligent acts or omissions) . . . .. The wider view of *Donoghue v Stevenson*, though, contained no such limitation, and by the early 1950s it was being argued (unsuccessfully) that liability should be imposed [*Candler v Crane Christmas & Co [1951] 2 KB 164. But see the dissenting judgment of Denning L.J. based on the nineteenth century cases in the Court of Chancery* . . .]. As in the case of trespassers, this was at first rejected, but in 1963 the House of Lords laid down that there was no relevant difference between causing loss by negligent statement and causing loss in some other way [*Hedley Byrne & Co v Heller & Partners Ltd [1964] AC 465*]. Thus an action was held to lie in principle (though not on the facts of the case) against a bank that had negligently represented to the plaintiff that its customer was a good credit risk, as a result of which the plaintiff had allowed the customer's order to continue in place and had hence suffered loss.

Hedley Byrne v Heller and *Herrington v British Railways Board* [a case on trespassers] removed the two largest obstacles to the acceptance of Lord Atkin's broad approach. By around 1970 the law of negligence was beginning to be conceptualized in terms of an ocean of liability for carelessly caused foreseeable harm, dotted with islands of non-liability, . . . rather than as a crowded archipelago of individual duty situations . . . .'

Ibbetson's account is valuable for its analysis of the trend toward general principle, particularly taken together with his account of the historical origins of negligence law in a series of isolated instances. However, we should be careful to note that he perhaps overstates, in this particular passage, the generality both of the neighbour principle *and* of the *Hedley Byrne*

---

[16] Ibbetson here considers duties to trespassers, which we will debate in Chapter 12.

decision. We have already noted the important role of proximity or directness in the neighbour principle. Although *Hedley Byrne v Heller* contributed greatly to the emergence of a general 'tort of negligence' and the recognition of novel categories of duty, it did so with attention to the special requirements of a particular relationship.

We will explore *Hedley Byrne* in Chapter 6.2. For now, we will consider the 'ocean of liability' to which Ibbetson refers.

3.2 THE 'OCEAN OF LIABILITY': THE *ANNS* TEST AND THE *PRIMA FACIE* DUTY OF CARE

The historical trend toward generalization in the tort of negligence reached its peak with the case of *Anns v Merton LBC* [1978] AC 728, and a number of cases decided under its influence.[17] Here, we are not chiefly concerned with the facts of *Anns*, though they are briefly set out below. The decision was overruled by the House of Lords in *Murphy v Brentwood District Council* [1991] 1 AC 398 (Chapter 6.2). For now, we are more interested in the attempt made by Lord Wilberforce to express a universal test which would determine whether a duty of care is owed. His approach was optimistic in more than one sense. Not only was it optimistic for its belief that a single, simple statement could define the circumstances in which a duty of care could be said to arise. It also exhibited a faith in principled legal development, which is becoming harder to maintain in the light of later cases. Ultimately, we will need to consider the extent to which principled development continues to be exhibited in the current law. We will continue that exercise in Chapter 6.

Lord Wilberforce's 'two-stage test' elevated the neighbour principle in *Donoghue v Stevenson* into a universal test. As will be explained below, many features of the two-stage test proved to be controversial, and this has prompted the emergence of a more complex approach (*Caparo v Dickman*, extracted and discussed below). It would be easy to identify *Caparo* with a return to the pre-*Donoghue* days of isolated duty instances. But that interpretation of *Caparo* is, as we will see, exaggerated. The truth is that the current approach to the duty of care exhibits a real tension between the recognition that negligence is a single unified tort, and the need to determine more specific criteria which will guide decisions in different classes of case. A truly universal tort of negligence would have almost boundless potential to throw up new duty situations, and foreseeability is not a sufficient criterion to control this potential. Understanding the problems with *Anns v Merton* will be a useful step in helping us to appreciate the subtleties and the frustrations of the current law.

It is also important to note that in principle, the rejection of *Anns* has not been universal. In Canada, *Anns* remains the leading authority on the duty of care. Nevertheless, the version of *Anns* applied in Canada has been considerably amended (*Cooper v Hobart* 2001 SCC 79; see J. Neyers, 'Distilling Duty: The Supreme Court of Canada Amends *Anns*' (2002) 118 LQR 221), at least when compared with the understanding of *Anns v Merton* which developed in this jurisdiction in the years preceding *Caparo v Dickman*.

Anns v Merton LBC [1978] AC 728

The plaintiffs were lessees of flats in a two-storey block. The block began to suffer cracked walls and sloping floors, and the plaintiffs alleged that this was because the foundations of the

---

[17] See for example *Ross v Caunters* [1980] Ch 297; *Junior Books v Veitchi* [1983] 1 AC 520; *Lawton v BOC Transhield* [1987] ICR 7.

block were too shallow. Statutory powers under the Public Health Act 1936 allowed the defendant local authority to approve plans, and to inspect foundations before they were covered up. Plans had duly been approved, specifying foundations to a depth of 3 feet or more. The eventual foundations were of a depth of only 2′6″.

For the purposes of the House of Lords' decision, it was not determined whether any inspection of the foundations had been made. Thus the case proceeded on the basis of the two alternative claims that either (a) the local authority had negligently failed to inspect the foundations, or (b) the local authority had been responsible for negligently inspecting the foundations. In the course of his judgment, Lord Wilberforce made the following general remarks about the duty of care in negligence.

Lord Wilberforce, at 751–2

Through the trilogy of cases in this House—*Donoghue v. Stevenson* [1932] A.C. 562, *Hedley Byrne & Co. Ltd. v. Heller & Partners Ltd.*[1964] A.C. 465, and *Dorset Yacht Co. Ltd. v. Home Office* [1970] A.C. 1004, the position has now been reached that in order to establish that a duty of care arises in a particular situation, it is not necessary to bring the facts of that situation within those of previous situations in which a duty of care has been held to exist. Rather the question has to be approached in two stages. First one has to ask whether, as between the alleged wrongdoer and the person who has suffered damage there is a sufficient relationship of proximity or neighbourhood such that, in the reasonable contemplation of the former, carelessness on his part may be likely to cause damage to the latter—in which case a prima facie duty of care arises. Secondly, if the first question is answered affirmatively, it is necessary to consider whether there are any considerations which ought to negative, or to reduce or limit the scope of the duty or the class of person to whom it is owed or the damages to which a breach of it may give rise: see *Dorset Yacht* case [1970] A.C. 1004, *per* Lord Reid at p. 1027. Examples of this are *Hedley Byrne's* case [1964] A.C. 465 where the class of potential plaintiffs was reduced to those shown to have relied upon the correctness of statements made, and *Weller & Co. v. Foot and Mouth Disease Research Institute* [1966] 1 Q.B. 569; and (I cite these merely as illustrations, without discussion) cases about "economic loss" where, a duty having been held to exist, the nature of the recoverable damages was limited: see *S.C.M. (United Kingdom) Ltd. v. W. J. Whittall & Son Ltd.* [1971] 1 Q.B. 337 and *Spartan Steel & Alloys Ltd. v. Martin & Co. (Contractors) Ltd.* [1973] Q.B. 27.

Problems with the '*Anns* Test'

Problem 1: the disappearance of 'proximity' as an independent criterion

Clearly, Lord Wilberforce considered himself to be encapsulating Lord Atkin's 'neighbour principle' as the first stage of his two-stage test. Yet there is a problem with the way in which he expressed the neighbour principle. He gave the impression that 'proximity or neighbourhood' is a *function of* foreseeability: '*a sufficient relationship of neighbourhood or proximity such that, in the reasonable contemplation of the former, carelessness on his part may be likely to cause damage to the latter . . .*'. In fact, in *Donoghue v Stevenson* as we have explained, proximity of relationship was deliberately added as a way of qualifying the foreseeability test, and was clearly intended to add extra *limits* to a test based on foreseeability. It was not simply another way of establishing foreseeability, which seems to have become its role in *Anns*.

This aspect of the *Anns* test was particularly criticized by Richard Kidner, 'Resiling from the *Anns* Principle: The Variable Nature of Proximity in Negligence' (1987) 7 LS, 319. Writing before the decision in *Caparo v Dickman* (below), but in an article which largely anticipated that decision and specifically its rejection of *Anns*, Kidner suggested that to neglect proximity in this way was a significant error. It might lead courts to overlook some very significant policy (and other) reasons which had been decisive in the pre-*Anns* case law, including *Donoghue* itself, since such reasoning was often conducted under the heading of 'proximity'. Proximity had acquired a 'coded meaning' in these pre-*Anns* cases, and varied as between different categories of case.

Kidner, 'Resiling from the Anus Principle' (1987) 7 LS 319, at 323–4

. . . as a yardstick for the extension of old duties or the establishment of new duties the *Anns* principle does not advance the law very far, for outside the area of foreseeable physical damage the degree of proximity necessary to bring about a duty of care will and always has been an issue. *Anns* tends to obscure that fact by giving the impression that foresight is the dominant criterion . . . , obscuring the need to apply historical and policy considerations to the question of other levels of proximity.

It is not entirely clear whether the disappearance of proximity as an independent criterion was deliberate. In *Anns* itself, Lord Wilberforce mentioned proximity, but it seems he thought the proximity question was adequately resolved by the following passage:

Lord Wilberforce, *Anns v Merton*, 753–4

. . . One of the particular matters within the area of local authority supervision is the foundations of buildings—clearly a matter of vital importance, particularly because this part of the building comes to be covered up as building proceeds. Thus any weakness or inadequacy will create a hidden defect which whoever acquires the building has no means of discovering: in legal parlance there is no opportunity for intermediate inspection. So, by the byelaws, a definite standard is set for foundation work (see byelaw 18 (1) (*b*) referred to above): the builder is under a statutory (sc. byelaw) duty to notify the local authority before covering up the foundations: the local authority has at this stage the right to inspect and to insist on any correction necessary to bring the work into conformity with the byelaws. It must be in the reasonable contemplation not only of the builder but also of the local authority that failure to comply with the byelaws' requirement as to foundations may give rise to a hidden defect which in the future may cause damage to the building affecting the safety and health of owners and occupiers. And as the building is intended to last, the class of owners and occupiers likely to be affected cannot be limited to those who go in immediately after construction.

. . . as I have suggested, a situation of "proximity" existed between the council and owners and occupiers of the houses . . . [Lord Wilberforce went on to consider the nature of the statutory context and its influence on common law duties of care].

This passage draws upon Lord Atkin's discussion in *Donoghue v Stevenson* of proximity in the sense of absence of opportunity for intermediate inspection of goods. Lord Wilberforce makes the comparison directly: in *Donoghue*, the bottle was opaque and not likely to be opened before it reached the consumer; in *Anns* the foundations were bound to be covered and so were likely to lead to a hidden defect. It is also apparent that Lord Wilberforce has here run together the notions of proximity and foreseeability: it must be in the reasonable contemplation of the builder and of the local authority that failure to comply with the bye-laws would affect the health and safety of occupiers in the future, and thus the requirement that there should be 'proximity or neighbourhood' is satisfied. Lord Wilberforce did not consider, under the heading of 'proximity', issues concerning the nature of the relationship between local authority and subsequent purchasers. He did not consider the role of the local authority as a 'peripheral party'.[18] Nor did he explore in terms of proximity the difference between a *manufacturer* of dangerously defective goods (as in *Donoghue* itself), and a local authority which is accused of failing to ensure that the goods—in this case premises—are safely constructed. A more extensive range of issues, independent of foreseeability, would today be likely to be considered under this heading.

The impact of *Anns*, in some of the cases that followed, was indeed that 'proximity' was run together with foreseeability. In *Ross v Caunters* [1980] Ch 297, an intended beneficiary brought an action in negligence against solicitors for their role in an invalid will. Sir Robert Megarry V-C approached the question of proximity as if it was determined through foreseeability:

Sir Robert Megarry V-C, at 308

First, there is the close degree of proximity of the plaintiff to the defendants. There is no question of whether the defendants could fairly have been expected to contemplate the plaintiff as a person likely to be affected by any lack of care on their part, or whether they ought to have done so: there is no "ought" about the case. This is not a case where the only nexus between the plaintiff and the defendants is that the plaintiff was the ultimate recipient of a dangerous chattel or negligent mis-statement which the defendants had put into circulation. The plaintiff was named and identified in the will that the defendants drafted for the testator. Their contemplation of the plaintiff was actual, nominate and direct. It was contemplation by contract, though of course the contract was with a third party, the testator.

It was the fact that the beneficiaries were known, hence more than foreseeable, that made them proximate. Indeed, Sir Robert Megarry V-C felt able to justify a *prima facie* duty of care on the basis of 'obviousness' (a very strong version of 'foreseeability'), thanks to the decision in *Anns*:

Sir Robert Megarry V-C, at 310

If one approaches the present case in the manner indicated by Lord Wilberforce, I can see only one answer to the question that has to be asked at the first stage. Prima facie a duty of care was owed by the defendants to the plaintiff [the intended beneficiary] because it was obvious that carelessness on their part would be likely to cause damage to her.

The complex case law on recovery for economic losses was regarded as relevant only at the second stage, where it had to be considered whether there were any factors to negative the duty. This was consistent with the treatment of the economic loss cases in Lord Wilberforce's dictum, extracted above. In the later case of *White v Jones* [1995] 2 AC 207, it was observed by the House of Lords that the simple approach in *Ross v Caunters* could not withstand the change marked by *Caparo v Dickman* (below). In particular, the absence of a direct

---

[18] See the important article by Jane Stapleton, 'Duty of Care: Peripheral Parties and Alternative Opportunities for Deterrence' (1995) 111 LQR 301.

relationship between the defendant solicitor, and the intended beneficiary, was perceived to give rise to problems of proximity, which is once again understood as a criterion independent of foreseeability. The decision in *White v Jones*, and the current approach to cases of negligence in respect of wills, are further considered in Chapter 6. *Ross v Caunters*, like *Anns v Merton* in this jurisdiction,[19] is now a part of legal history.

Problem 2: the universal test and prima facie duty of care

So far, we have been chiefly concerned with the content of the test. But the structure and scope of the test caused further problems.

It is clear that Lord Wilberforce expected his approach to apply to all cases where the court had to decide whether to recognize a duty of care in negligence. For a period of time, courts were ready to accept that this represented the correct way forward for negligence law. However, problems began to be noted in two directions. First, negligence law was likely to expand into unpredictable areas. The range of situations in which one's negligence is foreseeably likely to cause harm is very broad indeed. The 'ocean of liability' referred to by Ibbetson was a real possibility. Second, courts were tempted to reconsider established areas under the influence of *Anns*, questioning existing restrictions. Reasoning which had been applied to restrict liability in previously decided cases was prone to be swept aside or addressed only at the second stage.

By the time this second stage was reached, a *prima facie* duty was already said to have arisen. Thus considerations at this stage appeared (literally) secondary when compared to the idea of 'neighbourhood' in the first stage. '*Prima facie* duty' would be a simple matter of foreseeability, checked by the weak concept of proximity or directness referred to above, rather than requiring detailed justification in each case. 'No duty' or 'no liability' cases would begin to require exceptional justification. In a number of cases, courts even used the language of 'immunity' to describe the denial of a duty of care at the second stage: see for example *Hill v Chief Constable of South Yorkshire Police* [1989] 1 AC 53. As we will see in Chapter 6.3, this has led to difficulties of compatibility with the European Convention on Human Rights, and particularly Article 6 (right of access to a court or tribunal). Adoption of the more nuanced approach under *Caparo*, which incorporates policy considerations on equal terms with foreseeability, has helped to resolve this problem.

All of this raises the very difficult question of the relationship between the two stages of the two-stage test.

Anns v Merton and Legal Principle

The general or universal test in the first stage of *Anns* can be interpreted as being based on legal principle. Many judicial statements in recent tort cases make reference to the need to be 'principled' in developing the law. 'Principled' distinctions are contrasted with 'arbitrary' distinctions. An example can be found in Lord Nicholls' judgment in *Fairchild v Glenhaven Funeral Services* [2003] 1 AC 32:

> To be acceptable our law must be coherent. It must be principled. The basis on which one case, or one type of case, is distinguished from another should be transparent and capable of identification.

---

[19] The last aspect of *Anns* to fall was its analysis of negligence in the context of statutory powers. But that too has gone, with *Gorringe v Calderdale* [2004] 1 WLR 1057 (Chapter 6.3).

There has also recently been some judicial comment contrasting 'principle' with 'policy'. Certain judges have sought to explain that the type of 'policy' that is relevant to the determination of whether the defendant owes a duty of care is primarily 'legal' policy. In this section, we briefly outline the characteristics of principle and policy, and identify their relative roles in the cases of *Anns v Merton* and *Caparo v Dickman*.

According to Ronald Dworkin,[20] 'principles' have two characteristic features. First, principles can be generalized. Principles which have been employed in answering one question can be used to generate solutions to a different question, provided that question is similar in a relevant way. Decisions which are based on principled statements might be thought to exert 'gravitational force'—as Dworkin puts it—beyond the area in which they are formally binding, because they are capable of being generalized. *Donoghue v Stevenson* and *Anns v Merton* appear to be excellent examples of this. However, we will see that the later history of negligence displays a retreat back to analysis of specific facts. At the very least, 'principled' decisions should be reconcilable with one another when viewed with hindsight. Yet in some areas of negligence, even the search for consistency (with hindsight) has been abandoned.[21]

'Foreseeability', as a criterion, is easily generalized through the idea of the reasonable person. In any given situation, what would a reasonable person in the position of the defendant have foreseen? To promote foreseeability appears to promote simplicity, coherence, and fairness. Indeed the emergence of foreseeability as the key criterion both in duty of care analysis, and in other elements of the tort of negligence, is linked to a trend towards universal tests. Proximity on the other hand has traditionally been more sensitive to factual variations. The existence of a proximity test of this sort would not prevent the law from being *consistent*. But it means consistency must be sought at a very detailed level.

What is the other dimension of 'legal principle'? Dworkin argues that 'principles', as opposed to 'policies', have particular content. Their content must reflect the rights of the parties, and not broader policy goals. This is well summarized and explained in the following extract.

Stephen Guest, *Ronald Dworkin* (2nd edn, Edinburgh: EUP, 1997), 50–1

Principles and Policies

Dworkin's well-known distinction between principle and policies serves several purposes. It is intended to capture distinctions which lawyers frequently use in describing what judges should or should not do. I think it succeeds descriptively in that. . . .

'Principle' and 'policy' are terms of art for [Dworkin] and he provides formal definitions in chapters 2 and 4 of *Taking Rights Seriously*. . . . Roughly, principles describe rights, and policies describe goals.

A 'principle' [is] a standard that is to be observed, not because it will advance or secure an economic, political or social situation deemed desirable, but because it is a requirement of justice or fairness or some other dimension of morality.

---

[20] See particularly *Taking Rights Seriously*, Chapters 2 and 4.
[21] *White v Chief Constable of South Yorkshire Police* [1999] 2 AC 455; *McFarlane v Tayside* [2000] 2 AC 59.

Principles describe rights which aim at establishing an *individuated* state of affairs. So, he says:

> A political right is an individuated political aim. An individual has right to some opportunity or resource or liberty if it counts in favor of a political decision that the decision is likely to advance or protect the state of affairs in which he enjoys the right, even when no other political aim is served and some political aim is disserved thereby, and counts against that decision that it will retard or endanger that state of affairs, even when some other political aim is thereby served.

Policies, on the other hand, describe goals which aim at establishing an *unindividuated* political state of affairs:

> A 'policy' [is] that kind of standard that sets out a goal to be reached, generally an improvement in some economic, political, or social feature of the community.

We speak of making something a 'matter of principle' and mean that we should act whatever the consequences are because fairness, or justice, or some other matter of morality is involved. Lawyers have no difficulty at all in speaking in this way about legal rights nor, indeed, do most people. . . .

'Policy' is a more ambiguous term and is, at times, used very loosely, sometimes to mean just that the judge has run out of clear arguments and is striking out on his own . . . More often, though, it is used in the way Dworkin says it is, that is, it is a reference to the consequences that would follow from deciding in favour of one of the parties. The usual example is where the judge decides one way because to decide otherwise would 'open the floodgates of litigation'. All law students are familiar with that sort of reasoning.

As Guest says, one of the hallmarks of 'principle' is supposed by Dworkin to be that it gives 'individuated' reasons for decisions. A principle does not aim at a state of affairs that will be of general benefit, but concentrates on the rights and responsibilities of the particular parties affected.

We can see that foreseeability fits the 'content' requirement for principles, just as it fitted the form of principle by being easily generalizable. It is based on reasons that relate to the *individual defendant*, and not to broader social policy goals. Proximity, as it has subsequently been developed, is a very different matter.

In *Law's Empire* (Fontana, 1986), Dworkin theorizes that law 'works itself pure', gradually casting aside detailed issues based on particular facts and aiming at a more universal respect for principle and right. The recent history of negligence suggests rather the reverse. Both in terms of substance and of form, negligence is becoming less 'principled' in both of Dworkin's senses. Recent cases as we will see in Chapter 6 show greater attention to the impact on social goals such as economic welfare, and greater attention to the specific facts of individual situations. We will also note the emergence of multiple judicial theories and of sometimes arbitrary control devices. And yet, there is a continuing search for coherence in negligence law, albeit with greater tolerance of variation according to the specific context of a given case. What seems untrue, in the case of negligence law at least, is that principle defined according to *content* is in any sense dominant over policy. Analysis of policy factors has become a dominant feature of duty of care questions.

The contrast between two aspects of the 'duty of care' enquiry—factors relating to foreseeability, and factors relating to policy—are conveniently summarized in the following extract. Here, Millner suggests that the duty of care concept is essentially policy-based. Were it not for policy questions, the duty of care would be 'dispensable'.

Millner, *Negligence in Modern Law* (London: Butterworths, 1967), 230

The duty concept in negligence operates at two levels. At one level it is fact-based, at another it is policy-based. The fact-based duty of care forms a part of the enquiry whether the defendant's behaviour was negligent in the circumstances. The whole enquiry is governed by the foreseeability test, and 'duty of care' in this sense is a convenient but dispensable concept.

On the other hand, the policy-based or notional duty of care is an organic part of the tort; it is basic to the development and growth of negligence and determines its scope, that is to say, the range of relationships and interests protected by it. Here is a concept entirely divorced from foreseeability and governed by the policy of the law. 'Duty' in this sense is logically antecedent to 'duty' in the fact-determined sense. Until the law acknowledges that a particular interest or relationship is capable in principle of supporting a negligence claim, enquiries as to what was reasonably foreseeable are premature. The syntheses achieved in *Donoghue v Stevenson* and the *Hedley Byrne* case were concerned with duty of care in this sense and show the duty concept as an antenna with which to probe delicately the novel categories of relationship and classes of injury which come before the courts for recognition. The dynamics of the duty of care are largely outside the conceptual framework of negligence. The social forces which favour stability and those which promote change interact in a profoundly complex and subtle manner to yield normative solutions in law and morals. For this reason, there is no simple explanation of the subtle shifts in the scope and character of the duty of care or the precise timing of such movements. No analysis is worth its salt which is not based upon a concrete and detailed study of the society in which the changes are generated.

Summary

It is one thing to say that there is a single unified tort of negligence. Lord Atkin in *Donoghue v Stevenson* did this, and when he did so he answered an important question which was widely asked at the time: did negligence exist as an independent tort? To say that there is a single test for establishing a duty of care in negligence is quite a different matter. Lord Wilberforce in the *Anns* case thought the time had come to attempt the latter, but with hindsight he was wrong. In Canada, where the *Anns* test is still approved, it seems not to operate as a universal test in this way.

The single universal test based primarily on foreseeability was unsuccessful for a number of reasons. It paid insufficient attention to the detailed reasons for decided cases in specific areas; it paid insufficient attention to the analysis of the relationship between the parties in those cases; and it did not give priority to questions of practical impact. Furthermore, it appeared to provide a 'hierarchy' of reasons, in which principle was more important than pragmatic reasons, and in which a *prima facie* duty arose on the basis of principle alone. As we have seen, commentators such as Millner (before *Anns*) and Kidner (some years after *Anns*) objected that policy is inherent to the recognition of a duty of care. It should not be relegated to a role where it merely 'negatives' such duties on specific occasions. Although there may be a general tort of negligence, that does not mean there is a general test for a duty of care, based on foreseeability of damage. On the other hand, at the most basic level, legal decision-making should be 'principled' in the sense that the distinction between cases is based on sound reasoning. This essential feature applies just as strongly to 'policy' decisions as to any other.

3.3 AN 'IRRESISTIBLE FORCE'? *CAPARO*, THREE FACTORS, AND INCREMENTAL DEVELOPMENT

In the period of development surrounding *Donoghue v Stevenson* and the decades leading up to *Anns v Merton*, it might have seemed that generalization was the main force at work in the tort of negligence. But, as we discussed in Chapter 1, tort as a whole has proved resistant to generalization. In *Caparo v Dickman* [1990] 2 AC 605, the 'irresistible force' described by Christian Witting later in this section is one that works *against* generalization and universality.

The incremental approach, which recommends the consideration of 'duty questions' through close scrutiny of 'established categories', was advocated in a number of cases prior to *Caparo v Dickman*. These cases are referred to in the first paragraph of the extract from Lord Bridge's judgment, below. But it was in the case of *Caparo* that the House of Lords made its decisive move, authoritatively stating that the *Anns* approach could no longer be supported as appropriate, and attempting to outline most fully what the new approach would be.

Caparo Industries plc v Dickman and Others [1990] 2 AC 605 (HL)

Defendant auditors had prepared an annual report in respect of a company, F plc. This they were obliged to do by virtue of sections 236 and 237 of the Companies Act 1985. The claimants had purchased shares in F plc both before and after the publication to shareholders of the audited accounts. The claimants argued that they had relied on the published accounts in deciding to purchase sufficient shares to take over the company. They alleged that the auditors had been negligent in their preparation of the accounts, and that they owed a duty of care to the claimants. It was foreseeable both that F plc would be susceptible to a take-over bid; and that any investor seeking to make such a bid would rely upon the accuracy of the accounts. The Court of Appeal decided that a duty of care was owed by the auditors to the claimants, not in their role as investors, but in their capacity as existing shareholders in F plc.

The House of Lords allowed the auditors' appeal. In preparing the annual accounts, no duty of care was owed to the claimants either as investors, or as shareholders. Foreseeability would not be sufficient to form the basis of such a duty. Since this was a case of economic loss caused by allegedly negligent statements, it would be essential to show that there was a 'special relationship' between the parties, as explained in the leading case of *Hedley Byrne v Heller and Partners Ltd* [1964] AC 465.

The extracts below concern the general approach to establishing whether a duty of care was owed.

Lord Bridge of Harwich, 617–18

But since the *Anns* case a series of decisions of the Privy Council and of your Lordships' House, notably in judgments and speeches delivered by Lord Keith of Kinkel, have emphasised the inability of any single general principle to provide a practical test which can be applied to every situation to determine whether a duty of care is owed and, if so, what is its scope: see *Governors of Peabody Donation Fund v. Sir Lindsay Parkinson & Co. Ltd.* [1985] A.C. 210, 239f–241c; *Yuen Kun Yeu v. Attorney-General of Hong Kong* [1988] A.C. 175, 190e–194f; *Rowling v. Takaro Properties Ltd.* [1988] A.C. 473, 501d–g; *Hill v. Chief Constable of West Yorkshire* [1989] A.C. 53, 60b–d. What emerges is that, in addition to the foreseeability of damage, necessary ingredients in any situation giving rise to a duty of care are that there should exist between the party owing the duty and the party to whom it is owed a relationship characterised by the law as one of "proximity" or "neighbourhood" and that the situation should be one in which the court considers it fair, just and reasonable that the law should impose a duty of a given scope upon the one party for the benefit of the other. But it is implicit in the passages referred to that the concepts of proximity and fairness embodied in these additional ingredients are not susceptible of any such precise definition as would be necessary to give them utility as practical tests, but amount in effect to little more than convenient labels to attach to the features of different specific situations which, on a detailed examination of all the circumstances, the law recognises pragmatically as giving rise to a duty of care of a given scope. Whilst recognising, of course, the importance of the underlying general principles common to the whole field of negligence, I think the law has now moved in the direction of attaching greater significance to the more traditional categorisation of distinct and recognisable situations as guides to the existence, the scope and the limits of the varied duties of care which the law imposes. We must now, I think, recognise the wisdom of the words of Brennan J. in the High Court of Australia in *Sutherland Shire Council v. Heyman* (1985) 60 A.L.R. 1, 43–44, where he said:

> "It is preferable, in my view, that the law should develop novel categories of negligence incrementally and by analogy with established categories, rather than by a massive extension of a prima facie duty of care restrained only by indefinable 'considerations which ought to negative, or to reduce or limit the scope of the duty or the class of person to whom it is owed.' "

One of the most important distinctions always to be observed lies in the law's essentially different approach to the different kinds of damage which one party may have suffered in consequence of the acts or omissions of another. It is one thing to owe a duty of care to avoid causing injury to the person or property of others. It is quite another to avoid causing others to suffer purely economic loss.

Lord Roskill, at 628

I agree with your Lordships that it has now to be accepted that there is no simple formula or touchstone to which recourse can be had in order to provide in every case a ready answer to the questions whether, given certain facts, the law will or will not impose liability for negligence or in cases where such liability can be shown to exist, determine the extent of that liability. Phrases such as "foreseeability," "proximity," "neighbourhood," "just and reasonable," "fairness," "voluntary acceptance of risk," or "voluntary assumption of responsibility" will be found used from time to time in the different cases. But, as your Lordships have said, such phrases are not precise definitions. At best they are but labels or phrases descriptive of the very different factual situations which can exist in particular cases and which must be carefully examined in each case before it can be pragmatically determined whether a duty of care exists and, if so, what is the scope and extent of that duty. If this conclusion involves a return to the traditional categorisation of cases as pointing to the existence and scope of any duty of care, as my noble and learned friend Lord Bridge of Harwich, suggests, I think this is infinitely preferable to recourse to somewhat wide generalisations which leave their practical application matters of difficulty and uncertainty.

Lord Oliver of Aylmerton, at 632–3

. . . it is now clear from a series of decisions in this House that, at least so far as concerns the law of the United Kingdom, the duty of care in tort depends not solely upon the existence of the essential ingredient of the foreseeability of damage to the plaintiff but upon its coincidence with a further ingredient to which has been attached the label "proximity" and which was described by Lord Atkin in the course of his speech in *Donoghue v. Stevenson*[1932] A.C. 562, 581 as:

> "such close and direct relations that the act complained of directly affects a person whom the person alleged to be bound to take care would know would be directly affected by his careless act."

It must be remembered, however, that Lord Atkin was using these words in the context of loss caused by physical damage where the existence of the nexus between the careless defendant and the injured plaintiff can rarely give rise to any difficulty. To adopt the words of Bingham L.J. in the instant case [1989] Q.B. 653, 686:

> "It is enough that the plaintiff chances to be (out of the whole world) the person with whom the defendant collided or who purchased the offending ginger beer."

The extension of the concept of negligence since the decision of this House in *Hedley Byrne & Co. Ltd. v. Heller & Partners Ltd.* [1964] A.C. 465 to cover cases of pure economic loss not resulting from physical damage has given rise to a considerable and as yet unsolved difficulty of definition. The opportunities for the infliction of pecuniary loss from the imperfect performance of everyday tasks upon the proper performance of which people rely for regulating their affairs are illimitable and the effects are far reaching. A defective bottle of ginger beer may injure a single consumer but the damage stops there. A single statement may be repeated endlessly with or without the permission of its author and may be relied upon in a different way by many different people. Thus the postulate of a simple duty to avoid any harm that is, with hindsight, reasonably capable of being foreseen becomes untenable without the imposition of some intelligible limits to keep the law of negligence within the bounds of common sense and practicality. Those limits have been found by the requirement of what has been called a "relationship of proximity" between plaintiff and defendant and by the imposition of a further requirement that the attachment of liability for harm which has occurred be "just and reasonable." But although the cases in which the courts have imposed or withheld liability are capable of an approximate categorisation, one looks in vain for some common denominator by which the existence of the essential relationship can be tested. Indeed it is difficult to resist a conclusion that what have been treated as three separate requirements are, at least in most cases, in fact merely facets of the same thing, for in some cases the degree of foreseeability is such that it is from that alone that the requisite proximity can be deduced, whilst in others the absence of that essential relationship can most rationally be attributed simply to the court's view that it would not be fair and reasonable to hold the defendant responsible. "Proximity" is, no doubt, a convenient expression so long as it is realised that it is no more than a label which embraces not a definable concept but merely a description of circumstances from which, pragmatically, the courts conclude that a duty of care exists.

There are, of course, cases where, in any ordinary meaning of the words, a relationship of proximity (in the literal sense of "closeness") exists but where the law, whilst recognising the fact of the relationship, nevertheless denies a remedy to the injured party on the ground of public policy. *Rondel v. Worsley* [1969] 1 A.C. 191 was such a case, as was *Hill v. Chief Constable of West Yorkshire* [1989] A.C. 53, so far as concerns the alternative ground of that decision. But such cases do nothing to assist in the identification of those features from which the law will deduce the essential relationship on which liability depends and, for my part, I think that it has to be recognised that to search for any single formula which will serve as a general test of liability is to pursue a will-o'-the wisp. The fact is that once one discards, as it is now clear that one must, the concept of foreseeability of harm as the single exclusive test—even a prima facie test—of the existence of the duty of care, the attempt to state some general principle which will determine liability in an infinite variety of circumstances serves not to clarify the law but merely to bedevil its development in a way which corresponds with practicality and common sense.

Lord Oliver quoted from Brennan J in *Sutherland Shire Counties* and Lord Devlin in *Hedley Byrne* before continuing—

At 635

Perhaps, therefore, the most that can be attempted is a broad categorisation of the decided cases according to the type of situation in which liability has been established in the past in order to found an argument by analogy. Thus, for instance, cases can be classified according to whether what is complained of is the failure to prevent the infliction of damage by the act of the third party (such as *Dorset Yacht Co. Ltd. v. Home Office* [1970] A.C. 1004, *P. Perl (Exporters) Ltd. v. Camden London Borough Council* [1984] Q.B. 342, *Smith v. Littlewoods Organisation Ltd.* [1987] A.C. 241 and, indeed, *Anns v. Merton London Borough Council* [1978] A.C. 728 itself), in failure to perform properly a statutory duty claimed to have been imposed for the protection of the plaintiff either as a member of a class or as a member of the public (such as the *Anns* case, *Ministry of Housing and Local Government v. Sharp* [1970] 2 Q.B. 223, *Yuen Kun Yeu v. Attorney-General of Hong Kong* [1988] A.C. 175) or in the making by the defendant of some statement or advice which has been communicated, directly or indirectly, to the plaintiff and upon which he has relied. Such categories are not, of course, exhaustive. Sometimes they overlap as in the *Anns* case, and there are cases which do not readily fit into easily definable categories (such as *Ross v. Caunters* [1980] Ch. 297). Nevertheless, it is, I think, permissible to regard negligent statements or advice as a separate category displaying common features from which it is possible to find at least guidelines by which a test for the existence of the relationship which is essential to ground liability can be deduced.

Commentary

The necessary ingredients of the duty of care

It is clear from each of the judgments extracted that foreseeability of harm will not suffice, even in order to establish a '*prima facie*' duty of care. The approach in *Anns v Merton* is rejected. Equally, all of the extracts specify that the following 'ingredients' are necessary:

1. harm to the plaintiff/claimant must be foreseeable;

2. the situation must be one of proximity or neighbourhood;

3. the situation must be one in which it is 'fair, just and reasonable' to impose a duty of care.

Clearly, 'proximity' has re-emerged as a distinct element in the analysis of the situation, separate from foreseeability. Equally importantly, each of the factors above is given equal status in determining whether a duty of care is owed. Since it is acknowledged that these factors include considerations of 'practical' reasons (which we might broadly categorize as 'policy'), policy is no longer restricted to a merely subsidiary role.

Although it is common to refer to *Caparo* as establishing a 'three-stage test', it does not operate in terms of distinct stages in the same way that the *Anns* test did. No single factor takes priority. A duty of care will only arise if, in all the circumstances and taking into account the factors above, it seems appropriate that it should do so. Policy is part of the positive process of establishing a duty of care, rather than a merely limiting factor.

Ingredients not tests

To refer to a 'three-stage test' may be misleading in another sense, too. For it suggests that *Caparo* does in fact set out a 'test'. In stating the three 'ingredients' of the duty of care enquiry, Lords Bridge and Oliver both explain that these will not operate as 'tests' as such. Instead, words such as 'proximity' are only 'convenient labels', which summarize the reasons why the court has decided that the relationship is one that ought to give rise to a duty of care. The description of a particular relationship as 'proximate' is therefore a conclusion. It marks the court's judgment that the situation in question displays the hallmarks of 'proximity'. What this does not tell us is what the hallmarks of proximity actually are.

In what sense can a 'pragmatic' approach based on a court's judgment in all the circumstances, 'guided' only by concepts that turn out to be mere labels, be expected to steer future courts to coherent and predictable decision-making? The existence of important concepts which nevertheless appear not to operate as 'tests' has been a major source of frustration in recent tort cases.

Categories and incrementalism

In theory, help should be at hand in the 'categories' of decided cases which are to be given attention under the *Caparo* approach. Guidance on what sort of considerations will be relevant for the determination of a novel case can, under *Caparo*, be gleaned from previously decided cases in similar categories. Of particular importance in *Caparo v Dickman* itself was that the damage caused was purely economic, involving no physical damage to property or the person; equally, that the damage was allegedly caused by negligent statements rather than acts. For both of these reasons, the simple version of 'proximity' to be found in *Donoghue v Stevenson* would not suffice. In theory, this idea of categories ought to aid the predictability of decision-making, because it ought to be relatively clear which sorts of reasons will be decisive in the novel case before the court.

Also associated with the role of categories is the idea of 'incremental development'. Simply, duties of care should be recognized more easily in situations which are similar to previously recognized 'duty situations'. Negligence should develop step by step, allowing proper consideration of the practical impact of the extended duties, rather than allowing huge leaps into unknown territory.

Before we evaluate the use of categories and of incremental development, we should dispose of one misguided question. Does the emphasis on 'categories', together with the idea of 'incrementalism', return us to the 'wilderness of single instances', or separate duty situations, obtaining before the decision in *Donoghue*? It does not. It is true that Lord Oliver's remarks in some respects appear to reverse the effect of *Donoghue*. In particular, he observes that 'one looks in vain for some common denominator by which the existence of the essential relationship can be tested'. This directly, probably deliberately, contrasts with Lord Atkin's famous dictum, 'there must be, and is, some general conception of relations giving rise to the duty of care, of which the particular cases found in the books are but instances'. Even so, it is now recognized that all instances in which a duty of care is held to exist are aspects of a single tort.

In *Donoghue*, Lord Macmillan famously stated that the 'categories of negligence are never closed'. The current position is that the categories of negligence are also not entirely separate.

The recent case law on duty of care shows considerable generalization from one category to another. For example, the concept referred to as 'voluntary assumption of responsibility' has been relied upon in diverse situations such as negligent misstatement (*Hedley Byrne v Heller* [1964] AC 465), negligent professional services (*Henderson v Merrett* [1995] 2 AC 145), negligent failure to diagnose dyslexia (*Phelps v Hillingdon* [2001] 2 AC 619), and police failure to safeguard the interests of informants (*Swinney v Chief Constable of Northumbria* [1997] QB 464). Does this cross-fertilization suggest the return of principle in a more cautious, more sophisticated, more pragmatic form? It all depends whether the concepts applied have at least some reasonably stable and identifiable meaning. The challenge is that if they do not, then the use of previous cases can only be of limited assistance, and 'cross-fertilization' will only be a matter of labels, rather than principles.

Evaluation

It will be apparent that where *Caparo* applies to a truly novel case, the decision as to whether a duty of care arises will be highly unpredictable. Since all of the component factors we listed above will enter into a decision which is finally made by a court on pragmatic grounds, it will be very hard to predict whether a duty of care will be said to arise, or not.

We will have to address such issues through examination of the case law in Chapter 6. For the time being, we will address some arguments that have been put both for, and against the *Caparo* approach. First, we will return to Millner for a very perceptive but possibly idealized statement of the nature of the duty of care enquiry as initiated by *Hedley Byrne v Heller* [1964] AC 465. Although this extract is taken from a work which is 40 years old, given our analysis of *Caparo v Dickman* (above) it can be argued that the *Anns* case simply took a wrong turning from *Hedley Byrne*. It is interesting to note that Millner's pre-*Anns* statement accords to a large extent with the aspirations of the *Caparo* approach.

M. Millner, *Negligence in Modern Law* (London: Butterworths, 1967), 236–7

... the controlled extension of negligence liability into novel fields demands solutions of great delicacy. How far and upon what conditions shall the law afford a remedy for careless invasions of interests which are as yet protected not at all, or not beyond deliberate or reckless infringement? At first glance, the abstraction achieved in *Donoghue v Stevenson* offers solutions of beguiling simplicity. But there is no such royal road. Outside the broad context of that case, the 'neighbour principle' falters. It yields not an answer but a point of departure for further and more particular enquiry. This phase in the evolution of negligence is specialised and sophisticated, and the crux of it is the formulation—in the *Hedley Byrne* manner—of *supplementary criteria* of a refined type. Thus the negligence principle works powerfully to rationalise the law, giving it a more coherent pattern of liability as diversified as befits the complex modern society which it serves.

Clearly, Millner's approach in this extract endorses diversity in approach, of a sort which the *Anns* test discouraged. It suggests that the appropriate response is to develop 'supplementary criteria'. But it also assumes that more diversified criteria can be more 'sophisticated', and that the courts' social antennae (to borrow a metaphor from our previous extract from the same book) can guide them to appropriate rules.

Recent case law suggests that the last point is very much in doubt. For example, the law on psychiatric harm has given rise to a number of artificial and unprincipled restrictions whose connection to exact policy goals is obscure and which have been described at the highest judicial level as 'disfiguring' the law in this area (Lord Hoffmann, *Gregg v Scott* [2005] UKHL 2, para 87) (Chapter 4.4 below). The case law on economic loss is permeated by deep divisions over the appropriate 'test' or even 'label' to apply in problematic cases, with battle-lines particularly being drawn up over the meaning and applicability of the concept of 'voluntary assumption of responsibility' and whether it is part of, or in competition with, the three-stage 'test' (Chapter 6.2). In cases of 'wrongful conception', a chaos of judicial theories including some based primarily on judicial 'intuition' and a vaguely defined notion of 'distributive justice' has failed to result in a clear and coherent approach (Chapter 6.5 below). Referring to these last cases, Laura Hoyano has argued as follows:

Laura Hoyano, 'Misconceptions About Wrongful Conception'
(2002) 65 MLR 883, 905–6

Unfortunately distributive justice has proved to be just as empty a label as 'proximity'; not only does it not tell us *how* to make decisions, but it fails to *explain* or *justify* those decisions. A principled approach can enhance the flexibility which gives the common law its vitality, if the courts directly confront policy factors, both intrinsic and extrinsic to the relationship of the particular parties [Cooper v Hobart [2001] SCC 79, at para 30], and generate reasoned decisions supported by empirical evidence . . . '.

Hoyano suggests that the problem for the *Caparo* approach lies, certainly not with its incorporation of policy concerns, but with the use of 'labels' in legal decision-making. The problem, as she explains it, goes deeper than 'predictability'. Even after decisions are made, it is hard to understand what the justification for the decision actually was. In Chapter 6, we will address the argument that these labels have distracted from the real process of legal decision-making in such cases.

However, at this stage we should not accept too readily that the main problem here lies with the 'labels' adopted, nor that if we could clear these labels away from the duty of care enquiry then decision-making would be either fairer or more effective. The next extract defends the *Caparo* approach against criticism by the Australian High Court in *Sullivan v Moody* (2001) 75 JLR 1570, and particularly defends the benefits of labels such as 'proximity'.

C. Witting, 'The Three-Stage Test Abandoned in Australia—or Not?'
(2002) 118 LQR 214, 217–19

Following the High Court's decision in *Sullivan v Moody*, it appears that duty questions in Australia will now be determined according to a multi-factoral approach. Courts will search for "salient features", which point to a duty, and will make their determinations in light of previous authoritative decisions . . . This approach appears to have the advantage of ensuring that decisions are not hidden behind potentially inscrutable catch-phrases such as "proximity". At least, that is the theory. But is the abandonment of the concept of proximity likely to prove so advantageous? One problem likely to arise is a level of indeterminacy in the weighing of "salient features". This is because the search for features such as physical closeness, knowledge, control and vulnerability need not "add up" to anything. Courts will ostensibly be required to make their decisions based upon mere intuition about the overall weightiness of the factors found to be present. But surely it helps to be *looking for something* in isolating the salient features of a case—something which gives those features their "salience"? As adumbrated, part of the problem with the use of the term "proximity" has been the failure to specify the reason for its importance. The real question is whether the concept of proximity has a determinate function in the formulation of the duty of care.

It is submitted that *each* element within the *Caparo Industries* three-stage test has a coherent function to play in determining whether a duty of care ought to be found to exist. The test for foreseeability is "agent-general" in that it examines the ability to foresee an accident from the point of view of *any* reasonable person in the position of the defendant. . . . Foreseeability thus acts in a negative way by excluding from liability those persons who had no such minimal capacity to take action in order to avoid damage.

Proximity is the more difficult concept to explain. But explanation is assisted by keeping in mind the point that proximity is a concept which, ultimately, requires an evaluation of facts. . . . The essential function of the test for proximity is . . . to *identify* those persons (if any) who were most appropriately placed to take care in the avoidance of damage.

At 220–21

If the observations in this note are correct—it being possible to outline the essential functions played by each of the elements of the *Caparo Industries* three-stage test for duty—it would appear that the High Court of Australia has acted without due care in abandoning that test. It is difficult to conceive how duty issues can properly be analysed without resort to each of the three elements of the test. It is clear that courts must look for factors which indicate a minimum ability to avoid the causation of damage and for factors which identify particular persons as being appropriately placed to take care so as to avoid such damage. Foreseeability and proximity, respectively, serve these functions. But the decision whether or not to impose a duty will be, ultimately, a normative one—a question of legal policy, if you like. For this reason, *Caparo Industries* is likely to remain an irresistible force in the law of negligence. The High Court of Australia, in disapproving that case, is indeed, with respect, in error.

Witting's defence of *Caparo* is at a general level. For example, he does not set out to examine specific applications of 'proximity' in decided economic loss cases, to determine whether the theory has led to sound decision-making. But he makes the point that in considering and evaluating the facts of the case, it helps to be guided by the notion of proximity because it helps to be '*looking for something*'. In this respect, we are left with an important question. Do notions such as 'proximity' give any real guidance as to what we are 'looking for' when we evaluate the particular relationship in question? With the development of the 'categories' of case law, and of 'supplementary criteria' such as 'voluntary assumption of responsibility', is the duty of care enquiry under *Caparo* becoming more 'sophisticated' (to refer to Millner's aspiration in 1967), or more 'vacuous' (Hoyano, 2002)? This is what we must consider, along with the case law itself, in Chapter 6.

FURTHER READING

Buckland, W., 'The Duty to Take Care' (1935) 51 LQR 637.

Heuston, R., '*Donoghue v Stevenson* in Retrospect' (1957) 20 MLR 1.

McBride, N., 'Duties of Care in Negligence—Do They Really Exist?' (2004) 3 OJLS 417–41.

Rodger, A., 'Lord Macmillan's Speech in *Donoghue v Stevenson*' (1992) 108 LQR 236.

Stapleton, J., 'In Restraint of Tort', in Birks, P. (ed.), *The Frontiers of Liability*, Vol 2 (Oxford: OUP, 1994), 83–102.

Stapleton, J., 'Duty of Care Factors: A Selection from the Judicial Menus', in Cane P., and Stapleton, J. (eds), *The Law of Obligations: Essays in Honour of John Fleming* (Oxford: OUP, 1998), 59–95.

Weir, T., 'The Staggering March of Negligence' in Cane P., and Stapleton, J. (eds), *The Law of Obligations: Essays in Honour of John Fleming* (Oxford: OUP, 1988), 97–140.

Winfield, P.H., 'Duty in Tortious Negligence' (1934) 34 Col LR 41.

4. HOW NEGLIGENCE DEALS WITH OMISSIONS

Sometimes, the defendant's alleged negligence consists in *not* doing something. In some such cases, the court places emphasis on the fact that the defendant's conduct is in the nature of an omission, rather than an act: see for example *Perl v Camden*, *Dorset Yacht v Home Office* (Section 7 below). In others, the 'omission' factor is not treated as particularly relevant: see, for example, *Anns v Merton* (above). Although *Anns v Merton* now seems isolated in this respect (*Gorringe v Calderdale* [2004] UKHL 15, discussed below), the status of omissions in negligence law is still uncertain, and there are few authoritative statements on how to approach them. In this section we will provide a short explanation of what the issues are (and dismiss some other issues as irrelevant). We will then briefly outline some categories of omission case that are encountered in different parts of this chapter and will be encountered in later chapters.

4.1 DISTINGUISHING ACTS FROM OMISSIONS

There is ambiguity in the very distinction between acts, and omissions. A 'mere' omission or 'pure' omission can be said to involve doing nothing at all (an expression used by Lord Hoffmann in the case of *Gorringe v Calderdale* [2004] UKHL 15, where a highway authority had not chosen to renew road markings advising motorists to slow down approaching the brow of a hill). We can certainly contrast this sort of case with omissions that occur *in the course of acting*. A clear example of an omission in the course of acting is where a driver fails to put his foot on the brake. Negligence law would have no difficulty in treating this as equivalent to an act. It is a case of driving inappropriately. At the other end of the scale, the 'classic' example of a pure omission attracting no liability is the failure to warn a stranger. If I see somebody about to walk over a cliff and fail to shout a warning I am generally under no duty to act. On the other hand, we will see below that this outcome depends on who that person is and whether I have any pre-existing relationship with or duty in connection with that person. Alternatively, it may depend on whether I have any special role in connection with the danger itself, for example if it arises on land that I occupy.

4.2 CONTENTIONS AGAINST LIABILITY FOR OMISSIONS

It cannot be said that omissions in general are outside the tort of negligence. Salmond and Heuston offer the following general statement:

Salmond and Heuston (20th edn, p. 224)

In the absence of some existing duty the general principle is that there is no liability for a mere omission to act. There is a basic distinction between causing something and failing to prevent it happening.

There is surprisingly little authority for this statement. The editor of *Salmond and Heuston* cites the judgment of Lord Diplock in *Dorset Yacht v Home Office* [1970] AC 1004:

Lord Diplock, at 1060

The branch of English law which deals with civil wrongs abounds with instances of acts and, more particularly, of omissions which give rise to no legal liability in the doer or omitter for loss or damage sustained by others as a consequence of the act or omission, however reasonably or probably that loss or damage might have been anticipated. The very parable of the good *Samaritan (Luke 10, v. 30)* which was evoked by Lord Atkin in *Donoghue v. Stevenson* illustrates, in the conduct of the priest and of the Levite who passed by on the other side, an omission which was likely to have as its reasonable and probable consequence damage to the health of the victim of the thieves, but for which the priest and Levite would have incurred no civil liability in English law. Examples could be multiplied. You may cause loss to a tradesman by withdrawing your custom though the goods which he supplies are entirely satisfactory; you may damage your neighbour's land by intercepting the flow of percolating water to it even though the interception is of no advantage to yourself; you need not warn him of a risk of physical danger to which he is about to expose himself unless there is some special relationship between the two of you such as that of occupier of land and visitor; you may watch your neighbour's goods being ruined by a thunderstorm though the slightest effort on your part could protect them from the rain and you may do so with impunity unless there is some special relationship between you such as that of bailor and bailee.

Lord Reid, at 1027

. . . when a person has done nothing to put himself in any relationship with another person in distress or with his property mere accidental propinquity does not require him to go to that person's assistance. There may be a moral duty to do so, but it is not practicable to make it a legal duty.

But none of this implies that there is *never* a positive duty to act in negligence law. Lord Diplock's statement only gives examples of cases where there is no positive duty. Lord Reid only says that no duty arises on the basis of 'accidental propinquity'. As with our example of the stranger about to walk over the cliff, having the *opportunity* to avoid the harm is not sufficient to give rise to a duty of care. As Lord Diplock went on to say by way of parallel with

Lord Atkin's question 'who is my neighbour?' in *Donoghue v Stevenson*:

Lord Diplock, at 1061

This appeal, therefore, also raises the lawyer's question: "Am I my brother's keeper?" A question which may also receive a restricted reply.

The question receives a restricted reply. It does not receive a *wholly negative* reply.

The following statement was made by Lord Goff in *Smith v Littlewoods* [1987] AC 241, in which the defendants took insufficient precautions to prevent vandals from entering a disused cinema. It perhaps goes further than the statements above.

Lord Goff

Why does the law not recognise a general duty of care to prevent others from suffering loss or damage caused by the deliberate wrongdoing of third parties? The fundamental reason is that the common law does not impose responsibility for what are called pure omissions.

The other members of the House of Lords made no such remarks, and appeared to treat the case as one where there was no *breach* of duty. Seen in its context, Lord Goff's statement is consistent with our conclusion above, that in cases where the defendant has merely done nothing to prevent harm, there will need to be some positive reason (beyond foreseeability of harm and opportunity to avoid it) for holding that the defendant ought to have acted. In the case of strangers and in the absence of special circumstances, no positive duty to warn or to rescue is recognized in English law. In *Smith v Littlewoods*, Lord Goff made clear that in his view, 'literal' neighbourhood in the sense of occupation of land, even if coupled with foreseeability, was not sufficient to compel a duty to *make premises secure*. This is in contrast with the duty not to *create* a danger on one's premises that may be exploited by a third party, and also in contrast with the duty to keep people on one's premises reasonably safe while they are there (Chapter 12.1).

Set out below are three possible reasons for suggesting that omissions are outside the reach of the tort of negligence. Let us consider each contention in turn. We will see that the first contention has some validity if it is appropriately limited. The others however are likely to mislead.

'There is No Positive Duty to Act in Negligence'

As a first step, this statement needs to be limited to 'pure' omissions. In *Donoghue v Stevenson* Lord Atkin's remarks clearly referred to 'acts or omissions which . . . would be likely to injure your neighbour'. But even if we do limit the statement to 'pure' omissions, it is still too broad. There are occasions where there is liability for negligently failing to act. Salmond and Heuston (above) stated that the general principle against liability exists 'in the absence of some existing duty'. They may have in mind a particular relationship between the parties, or a particular function, a special reason for saying that the positive duty arises. For example, if the person who fails to shout a warning is a parent of the endangered person, or is employed in order to ensure the safety of the particular individual, then there will be positive duties (*Lewis v Carmarthenshire County Council*, below).

A point we will later make in respect of third party acts (Section 6.3 below) is equally valid for omissions generally. It is easier to accommodate the sort of duty analysis required for cases of omission through the *Caparo* test than it was through *Donoghue* as interpreted by *Anns v Merton*. The *Caparo* test requires that there must be positive reasons why the particular defendant should be responsible for avoiding the damage. 'Duty of care' is no longer guided by the broad criterion of foreseeability. In the move to more distinct duty-situations, the method applied to omissions cases is broadly similar to all others. The court must seek positive reasons for singling out the defendant as the person to bear responsibility for the harm. Opportunity to avoid foreseeable (or even obvious) harm will not be sufficient in the case of pure omissions.

'Omissions are Either not Culpable, or Less Culpable than Acts'

This view is implicit in the following statement (which may also question whether omissions are causally equivalent to acts (see below)).

J.C. Smith and P. Burns, 'Donoghue v Stevenson—The Not So Golden Anniversary'
[1983] 46 MLR 147, 154

> There is a basic difference between doing something and merely letting something happen. If a person has £100, and knows that if he donates it to UNESCO the life of an African child, who would otherwise die, would be saved, and if he does not donate the sum, it cannot be said that that he killed the child. It can only be said that he let the child die. The difference is fundamental when it comes to issues of culpability and responsibility.

It is true that the difference between killing and not saving is fundamental, but it does not follow that a failure to save is always non-culpable. As Tony Honoré has persuasively argued,[22] the very expression 'omission' itself implies a particular form of 'not doing'. An 'omission' is a not-doing where there was a reason to *expect* that someone would act. An omission may indeed be culpable, depending on the reasons for expecting the positive action. For example, not feeding a child in one's care is a highly culpable omission. Not giving aid to assist those in need may become culpable, in certain circumstances. The question is not whether the omission is less culpable than an act with the same consequences, it is whether the omission is 'unreasonable' according to the ordinary test for breach of the duty of care. As we have already seen in respect of the standard of care (Section 1 of this chapter), negligence does not generally distinguish between different degrees of culpability.

'Mere Inaction only 'Fails to Prevent'. It does not 'Cause' Anything'

The idea that inaction does not 'cause' anything is supported by Richard Epstein, 'A Theory of Strict Liability' 1972 *Journal of Legal Studies* 151–204. It is, however, misguided. It is true that omissions cannot be the sole cause of harm: they can only fail to prevent a chain of events. As such, there is scope for sophisticated argument over whether acts and omissions are 'causally equivalent'. Fortunately, none of this matters for the purposes of law. As we will see in

---

[22] Honoré, 'Are Omissions Less Culpable?', in Cane and Stapleton (eds), *Essays for Patrick Atiyah* (1992).

the following sections, a breach of duty only needs to be 'a' cause of harm. The breach does not need to be 'the' cause of harm. Omissions can clearly pass the 'but-for' test set out below. We simply amend that test in order to ask, 'what would have happened if the defendant *had acted*?' Then, there are further questions of remoteness or attribution (Section 6 below). Omissions are clearly capable of satisfying these further tests. For example, where there is a distinct legal duty to *prevent* a particular type of event, and this duty is breached, there is no logical difficulty at all in describing the breach as a cause in fact and it is clear that it may also be a cause in law (*Stansbie v Troman*, *Reeves v Commr of Police for the Metropolis*, both extracted in Section 6 below).

In ordinary usage, it is quite normal to attribute causal effects to omissions under some circumstances. For example, an omission to train one's staff in safety procedures may be described as 'causing' fatalities, even if those fatalities have other more immediate causes too. In *Environment Agency v Empress Car Co (Abertillary) Ltd* [1999] 2 AC 22, a trespasser entered the defendants' land and released pollutants into a stream. There was a criminal prosecution under section 85(1) of the Water Resources Act 1991. That section provided for alternatives. There was liability where the defendant *either* 'caused' pollution, *or* 'knowingly permitted' the pollution to occur:

> 85(1) A person contravenes this section if he causes or knowingly permits any poisonous, noxious or polluting matter or any solid waste matter to enter controlled waters.

As a matter of statutory interpretation, the difference in terminology between 'causing' and 'knowingly permitting' must be significant. Otherwise, why would these two alternatives be used? Lord Hoffmann pointed out that the expression 'knowingly permitting' *presupposes* a causal link between default of the defendant, and the outcome. The very existence of such a provision shows that in ordinary language, an omission can be a cause. As Lord Hoffmann said (at 32):

> . . . the fact that a deliberate act of a third party caused the pollution does not itself mean that the defendant's creation of a situation in which the third party could so act did not also cause the pollution for the purposes of section 85(1).

Whether or not we determine that an omission amounts to a 'cause' will depend on whether the person who is now alleged to have failed to act *should* have acted in these circumstances in order to prevent the damage, and if so whether it is appropriate to attribute the damage to their failure to act. The question of cause therefore leads us back to the questions of breach (was there anything wrong with not acting?) and of duty (is there a positive reason to designate the defendant as a person who is responsible for avoiding this particular harm?). There are also relevant questions of remoteness. In *Empress Car*, the question was whether the act of the trespasser had broken the chain of causation. Since the trespasser's action was neither abnormal nor extraordinary, the court of first instance had been entitled to find that the defendants had 'knowingly permitted' the pollution.

None of the three objections provides the basis for a general rule against liability for omissions. However 'duty' and 'remoteness', rather than breach of duty or 'but-for' causation, are likely to provide the most appropriate conceptual analysis. Was there a positive duty to prevent the kind of damage that occurred? Was the eventual injury within the scope of the defendant's positive duty?

4.3 CASE LAW: IN WHICH SITUATIONS ARE OMISSIONS IMPORTANT?

Most of the cases we will mention here are discussed and where appropriate extracted in other parts of this book. Therefore, for present purposes we will simply explain some of the categories in which omissions have been particularly relevant in the case law.

Failure to Control Third Parties or Prevent Third Party Acts

In *Home Office v Dorset Yacht* [1970] AC 1004, a duty was owed by Borstal Officers, to take reasonable care to control particular third parties. Those third parties were young offenders in their care, and the damage suffered by the plaintiffs (vandalism to property nearby) was 'the very kind of thing' that could be expected to follow if care was not taken. We explore the role of *Dorset Yacht* in respect of remoteness below. Another illustration of a duty to control third parties is *Carmarthenshire CC v Lewis* [1955] AC 549, but here the third party did not commit any deliberate act of wrongdoing. The plaintiff was injured in a road accident caused when a small child ran out onto the road. The child should have been at school under supervision of the defendants, but had been allowed to wander off. It was held that the school owed a duty to road users to ensure that the child was not able to stray onto the highway. As in *Dorset Yacht*, there was clearly a special relationship between the defendant and the third party whose actions caused damage.

In Section 6, we will also address cases of alleged failure to prevent strangers from causing harm. These cases have generally not led to liability: see, for example, *Lamb v Camden* [1981] QB 625, *Smith v Littlewoods* [1987] AC 241. Similarly, it has been held that the police owe no duty of care to the public as a whole, nor to a general at-risk group, to exercise due care in the 'investigation or suppression of crime' (*Hill v Chief Constable of West Yorkshire* [1989] AC 53; no duty to young women in a particular geographical area to apprehend a serial murderer). In *Brooks v Commissioner of the Police for the Metropolis* [2005] UKHL 24, the *Hill* approach was also held to rule out an action brought by an eyewitness to and victim of crime in respect of the treatment of him by the police (Chapter 6 below). The dismissal of this action was based primarily on the nature of the duties contended for by the claimant, which it was held would conflict with police functions in respect of the investigation and suppression of crime.

It is clear that if there is a special reason for recognizing a duty that requires steps to be taken precisely in order to avoid harm from the actions of strangers (such as in *Stansbie v Troman* [1948] 2 KB 48, Section 6 below), then the damage done will not be too remote if it is within the risk that provides the reason for this duty.

Failure to Exercise Statutory Powers

The status of 'pure omissions' has been particularly important in recent cases where the defendants would, if they acted, be doing so under a statutory power. It is now determined that the existence of a power, which merely permits action, rather than in any sense compelling action, cannot be the basis of a positive duty to act for the purposes of the tort of negligence: *Stovin v Wise* [1996] AC 923 and *Gorringe v Calderdale* [2004] UKHL 15. In *Anns v Merton*, the opposite result was adopted. These cases are considered in Chapter 6.

Failure of Emergency Services to Act in Order to Prevent Harm: No Duty to Rescue?

In a series of cases, the Court of Appeal has confirmed that emergency services such as the police (*Alexandrou v Oxford* [1993] 4 All ER 328), the fire service (*Capital and Counties Bank v Hampshire* [1997] QB 1004), and the coastguard (*OLL v Secretary of State for Transport* [1997] 3 All ER 897) owe no common law duty to attend an emergency where, for example, a burglar alarm has alerted them to an incident, or an emergency call has been made. The latter two cases were influenced by the decision in *Stovin v Wise*. Furthermore, their liability when they do arrive has been restricted to damage flowing from any *positive* careless acts which *add to the damage that would have been suffered* in the absence of their actions (*East Suffolk Rivers Catchment Board v Kent* [1941] AC 74, discussed in Chapter 6 below). Therefore, a fire service would not be liable for attending the scene of a fire and standing idly by without fighting it. It has not added to the damage. However, the service would be liable for acting in such a way that the damage was made worse. We explain in Chapter 6 that acceptance of this element of the *East Suffolk* case is hard to justify in a reasoned fashion.

In *Kent v Griffiths* [2001] QB 36, the Court of Appeal attempted to distinguish the position of the ambulance service from the line of cases above, suggesting that the ambulance service should be treated as owing a duty by analogy with the duty of care of other medical professionals. The approach in this case may have been influenced by the decision of the European Court of Human Rights in *Osman v UK* [1999] 1 FLR 193, implying that 'immunities' against negligence liability on policy grounds would be incompatible with Article 6 of the European Convention on Human Rights. We will consider the question of immunities in Chapter 6 below.

Duties to Warn

There is no general duty to warn a stranger of an impending danger. There are, however, distinct duties to warn. One such duty is the duty to advise of risks associated with a medical procedure (*Chester v Afshar*, considered in Chapter 4 below).

4.4 POSITIVE DUTIES TO TAKE CARE IN TORT MORE GENERALLY

Outside the tort of negligence, it is clear that in specific circumstances, tort law recognizes positive duties to take reasonable steps to avoid harm to others. The sources of positive duty include the Occupiers' Liability Acts 1957 and 1984 (Chapter 12 below). Those statutes impose duties to make visitors and others reasonably safe from dangers arising from the state of premises, and this will include duties to *warn* of dangers where appropriate. In nuisance (Chapter 10 below), there are limited duties to take steps to remove the source of a nuisance arising on one's premises, whether created by a third party or by a force of nature. These duties, however, are subjective in the sense that they take into account the resources of the defendant, and as such they are distinct from the general approach taken within the tort of negligence (*Goldman v Hargrave* [1967] 1 AC 645; *Leakey v National Trust* [1980] QB 485).

While positive duties to take action will generally be more onerous that negative duties to avoid causing harm through one's actions, it is chiefly in the tort of negligence, with its potential for broad and unpredictable liability to a wide variety of parties, that the question of liability for omissions has caused controversy.

FURTHER READING

Epstein, R., 'A Theory of Strict Liability' (1972) Journal of Legal Studies 151–204.

Honoré, T., 'Are Omissions Less Culpable?', in Cane, P. and Stapleton, J. (eds), *Essays for Patrick Atiyah* (Oxford: OUP, 1992).

Smith, J.C. and Burns, P., '*Donoghue v Stevenson*—The Not So Golden Anniversary' (1983) 46 MLR 147.

5. CAUSATION AND ATTRIBUTION OF DAMAGE

5.1 INTRODUCTION: HOW MANY 'CAUSATION' QUESTIONS ARE THERE?

We have already seen that liability in negligence depends on showing that a duty of care has been breached.

Negligence is a tort of 'damage', and the claimant must also establish that the defendant's breach caused the damage in respect of which a remedy is claimed.

The traditional analysis of causation in the law of tort holds that there are two distinct questions of causation involved in the tort of negligence and in those other torts that require damage. Here we set out the two generally recognized questions, cause in fact, and cause in law or remoteness. We will then explain the general problems of categorization and terminology which plague this aspect of the law of tort. Some say that there is only one causation question, though their description of the second question below varies; others that there are more than two questions of causation.

The Traditional Division: Two Questions

On a traditional approach, there are two basic questions of causation:

1. Was the defendant's breach of duty or other tortious intervention a **factual cause** of the damage? This is the question addressed in Section 5.2.

2. Is the damage **attributable to** the defendant's breach of duty (or other tortious conduct)? This is the more elusive question addressed in Section 6.

The first question is apparently rather simple. It seems to ask about facts. As we will see, it is not as simple as it looks. However, there is at least a recognized starting point for such questions, which is whether the breach of duty was a 'but for' cause of the harm. In other words, would the harm have come about 'but for' the tort? This test is sometimes not sufficient because too many factors pass this initial test. On other occasions it is not necessary because factors which clearly are causes are unable to pass the test. So it is set aside. On other occasions still, there are difficulties of *proving* that it is satisfied. Even so, it states a recognized test with a recognized purpose—to show whether the harm is historically linked as a matter of cause and effect with the damage.

The second question cannot be so easily identified. Is this second question concerned with 'causation' at all?

A Single Causal Question?

There are those who argue that the only question of causation in the law of tort is the first, relating to factual causation. Other questions of attribution are not about cause. Of these approaches, we can pick out two variations:

1. Some have argued that the second question of attribution is a purely legal question about 'the foreseeability of the harm; the scope of the duty', or 'the scope of the risk against which the defendant had a duty to guard'. All these approaches try to align the question of attribution with the question of duty.

2. Others have argued that the second question is best expressed quite honestly and openly in terms of 'the scope of liability for consequences'.

The second of these two approaches is championed by Jane Stapleton, 'Cause in Fact and the Scope of Liability for Consequences' (2003) 119 LQR 388. It has the merit of being simple to state. There are two tests: one concerns factual causation, the other asks whether the harm is within the scope of the consequences for which there should be liability. But it has the disadvantage that it is a very open enquiry and many factors could, in principle, be relevant at the second stage.

Variations of the first of the two approaches above, aligning attribution with duty, will be encountered in the case law extracted in Section 6. In particular, the foreseeability approach was adopted in *The Wagon Mound (No 1)* [1961] AC 388; while the 'scope of duty' approach has been adopted by Lord Hoffmann, in particular, in important cases such as *Reeves v Commissioner of Police for the Metropolis* [2000] 1 AC 360, and *South Australia Asset Management Corporation v York Montagu* [1997] AC 191.

Multiple Causal Questions

Not everyone agrees that the only question of causation encountered in the law is the question of factual causation. Hart and Honoré, in a highly influential work, argued that the test for 'but for' causation does not establish, as a matter of ordinary language, whether the factor in question is to be called a 'cause'.[23] Too many factors will satisfy the test. Even if the 'but for' test identifies those factors which pass a threshold of 'historical involvement', not all such factors deserve to be identified as 'causes'. Equally, Hart and Honoré argued that the remoteness test in law involves genuinely 'causal' elements. It was not simply a matter of defining liability by reference to the content of the duty owed.

Jane Stapleton has been critical of the Hart and Honoré approach, though that approach has clearly influenced some of our most senior judges.[24]

---

[23] H. L. A. Hart and T. Honoré, *Causation in the Law* (2nd edn, Oxford: OUP, 1985).
[24] Lord Hoffmann, 'Causation' (2005) 121 LQR 592.

J. Stapleton, 'Occam's Razor Reveals an Orthodox Basis for Chester v Afshar' (2006) 122 LQR 426, 426[25]

Lawyers across the common law world often find "causation" problematic. This is because we do not actually agree on what we mean by that and other causal terms. Sometimes by "causation" lawyers mean just the objective question of historical "fact": whether the defendant's breach of obligation had anything at all to do with the production of the claimant's injury. Other times lawyers use causal terminology not merely for this idea of historical involvement but for a separate notion of "causal connection" which, together with a third notion of "remoteness", concerns the normative evaluation of whether this particular consequence of the defendant's breach is one for which he should be held legally responsible. The most well known version of this three-step approach was that championed by Hart and Honoré.

For them, even where a factor is historically involved in the production of an outcome, or to use their terms, even when it is "a causally relevant factor" in relation to that outcome, it will not be a "cause" of it where there is no "causal connection" between the factor and outcome. Yet it is not at all clear what they mean by a "causal connection", what therefore beyond historical involvement they mean by a "cause", and where the line between "causal connection" and "remoteness" lies.

The three-step Hart and Honoré approach is both inconvenient and obfuscatory. Clarity in legal reasoning will not be improved in this area until it is abandoned in favour of a two-step analysis consisting of the factual issue of historical involvement and the normative question of whether a particular consequence of breach should be judged to be within the scope of liability for the breach.

It is true that the Hart and Honoré approach is inconvenient and subtle. Then again, they were seeking to describe a multi-faceted phenomenon. Given the influence of their work, we should spend a little space identifying some of its key features. We should then be better placed to consider, particularly in Section 6 of this chapter, to what extent ideas of 'cause' still make themselves felt in the second question of attribution ('remoteness', 'scope of liability for consequences', or whatever else it may be called) identified above.

Causation and Ordinary Language

Lord Hoffmann, *Environment Agency v Empress Car Co (Abertillary) Ltd* [1999] 2 AC at 29

The courts have repeatedly said that the notion of causing is one of 'common sense'. So in *Alphacell v Woodward* [1972] AC 824, 847 Lord Salmon said:

'what or who has caused an event to occur is essentially a practical question of fact which can best be answered by ordinary common sense rather than abstract metaphysical theory.'

Hart and Honoré, *Causation in the Law* (2nd edn, 1985) p1

... the assertion often made by the courts, especially in England, that it is the plain man's notions of causation (and not the philosopher's or the scientist's) with which the law is concerned, seems to us to be true.

[25] Footnotes omitted.

The quotations above reinforce a common theme of English law in respect of causal enquiries. Law does not depend upon either science or philosophy for its notions of causation. Rather, it employs 'common sense' notions which are inherent in the way that ordinary people talk about cause.

At first sight, this position appears naive. It would seem to deny the many problems associated with causation, taking refuge in a fictional 'shared understanding'. Common sense is, notoriously, not something on which people can commonly agree, so what hope is there for using this concept to arrive at solutions to difficult questions of causation?

According to Hart and Honoré, law's 'common sense' approach does not involve a denial of the complexities of causal statements, but is actually based on an appreciation of such complexities. Equally, and to the extent that it rejects scientific approaches, the law's approach does not do so through lack of understanding. Rather, according to Hart and Honoré, law relies on 'common sense' primarily because the concerns of the law in discussing cause are often similar to the concerns of everyday language, and different from the concerns of science or philosophy. As John Gardner has put it:

'Common sense [in Hart's work] does not have its popular Forrest Gump overtones. It has a technical oppositional meaning specific to philosophers . . .' (Book review of Lacey, *A Life of HLA Hart* in [2005] 121 *LQR* 329, 331)

A distinction between the concerns of science and the concerns of law is made in the following extract. Here, Hart and Honoré are concerned to distinguish some common scientific questions about cause from some 'everyday' attempts to *explain* particular events in terms of what caused them.

Hart and Honoré, *Causation in the Law,* pp. 33–5

Abnormal and normal conditions

In the sciences causes are often sought to explain not *particular* occurrences but *types* of occurrence which usually or normally happen: the processes of continuous growth, the tides, planetary motions, senile decay. In ordinary life, by contrast, the particular causal question is most often inspired by the wish for an explanation of a *particular* contingency the occurrence of which is puzzling because it is a departure from the normal, ordinary, or reasonably expected cause of events: some accident, catastrophe, disaster, or other deviation from the normal cause of events. . . .

(p. 35) . . . What is normal and what is abnormal is, however, relative to the context of any given inquiry . . . If a fire breaks out in a laboratory or in a factory, where special precautions are taken to exclude oxygen during the manufacturing process, since the success of this depends on safety from fire, there would be no absurdity at all in *such* a case in saying that the presence of the oxygen was the cause of the fire. The exclusion of oxygen in such a case and not its presence is part of the normal functioning of the laboratory or the factory, and hence a mere condition . . .

. . . the distinction between cause and conditions may be drawn in different ways. The cause of a great famine in India may be identified by the Indian peasant as the drought, but the World Food authority may identify the Indian government's failure to build up reserves as the cause and the drought as a mere condition . . .

We can particularly highlight two implications of the above extract:

1. The answer to any question of causation in respect of the law will depend upon the reason for asking the question.

2. In isolating the factor or factors which we consider to deserve the title of 'cause', there is generally more attention paid, in everyday language as in law, to 'abnormal' events.

The influence of Hart and Honoré's work is clearly to be seen in the following extract. The case from which this passage is drawn concerned *criminal* liability under a particular statutory provision, but Lord Hoffmann's judgment has since been referred to in a number of crucial cases on causation in the tort of negligence:

Lord Hoffmann, *Environment Agency v Empress Car Co (Abertillery) Ltd* [1999] 2 AC 22, at 29

The first point to emphasise is that common sense answers to questions of causation will differ according to the purpose for which the question is asked. Questions of causation often arise for the purpose of attributing responsibility to someone, for example, so as to blame him for something which has happened or to make him guilty of an offence or liable in damages. In such cases, the answer will depend upon the rule by which responsibility is being attributed. Take, for example, the case of the man who forgets to take the radio out of his car and during the night someone breaks the quarterlight, enters the car and steals it. What caused the damage? If the thief is on trial, so that the question is whether he is criminally responsible, then obviously the answer is that he caused the damage. It is no answer for him to say that it was caused by the owner carelessly leaving the radio inside. On the other hand, the owner's wife, irritated at the third such occurrence in a year, might well say that it was his fault. In the context of an inquiry into the owner's blameworthiness under a non-legal, common sense duty to take reasonable care of one's own possessions, one would say that his carelessness caused the loss of the radio.

In everyday *explanations* as to what 'caused' a particular event, some events and states of affairs are reduced to the level of 'mere conditions' of the occurrences in question. Out of the many conditions which form the necessary history of an adverse event, we tend to select one (sometimes more than one) as 'causes'. As Hart and Honoré point out, this will generally be an 'abnormal' condition, although what is counted as abnormal will vary with the context. Human intervention will often be selected as a cause, particularly so if it is in some way 'faulty'. But as Lord Hoffmann explains, this depends on the reason for asking. If we want to know whether a car owner should have taken more precautions, even a deliberate criminal act on the part of another may become part of the general 'context' of the event, amounting perhaps even to a 'normal condition'. So one can, by an omission, 'cause' loss of a car radio, even though it is taken by someone else—at least if there is a positive duty to act.[26]

This last point shows that for the purposes of 'cause in fact', we do not need to ask whether the defendant's breach of duty was *the* cause of accidental damage. Rather, the breach needs to be *a* cause of that damage. Lord Hoffmann also pointed out, in the *Empress Car* case, that an

---

[26] Criminal lawyers have generally not been quick to accept this proposition. For an exception, see the discussion by T. H. Jones, 'Causation, Homicide and the Supply of Drugs' (2006) 26 LS 139–40.

event may have *more than one cause*. However, 'mere conditions'—factors which we would most naturally treat as being essential to the history of the event, but which we would not select as a relevant 'cause' of the event—will *also* pass the 'but for' test. For Hart and Honoré, 'mere conditions' are *not* to be called 'causes', even though they pass the 'but for' test.[27]

In summary, the idea of 'but-for causation' is treated by Hart and Honoré as no more than a useful way of asking whether the defendant's breach of duty was effective in the history of events which led to the claimant's loss, while avoiding 'abstract metaphysics'. 'But for' causation is an important element in our common understanding of the nature of 'cause', particularly when causal questions are asked for the purposes of attribution of responsibility. 'But for' causation will, however, not always provide the tools that we need.

Hart and Honoré treat causation as a multi-layered concept best understood through close analysis of the way in which we use language in everyday life and in law. The purpose of the enquiry into causation will help to determine the meaning of causation in a given case. There are many important 'causation' questions in law.

An alternative embraced by many commentators is to regard the second 'causal' question with which we started, 'remoteness', as a question entirely of law.

It will be plain that the first causal question to be addressed, 'cause in fact', is the simpler to understand, if not always simple to apply.

5.2 'BUT FOR' CAUSATION

It should be especially underlined that for the purposes of causation in the tort of negligence, it is not enough to show that the defendant's *conduct* has been the cause of the damage suffered by the claimant. Rather, it is the *breach of the duty of care* that must have caused the relevant damage.

In determining questions of factual causation, the starting point is 'but for' causation: would the claimant's injury have occurred 'but for' the defendant's negligence? If the same injury would have occurred even without the defendant's negligence, then that negligence is not a 'necessary cause' of the damage or loss to the claimant. The idea of necessary cause is also referred to in the Latin version as *causa sine qua non*.

Since tort is a civil action, the claimant must establish that the breach of duty is a 'but for' cause of his or her injury or loss *on the balance of probabilities*. That is to say, the claimant must convince the court that it is more likely than not that the injury would *not* have occurred *without* the negligence (or other tortious intervention) of the defendant. The following case provides a classic illustration of the 'but for' test.

Barnett v Chelsea and Kensington Hospital Management Committee [1969] 1 QB 428

Three night-watchmen presented themselves at a casualty department provided and run by the defendants, complaining to the nurse that they had been vomiting for three hours after drinking tea. The nurse reported their complaints by telephone to the duty medical officer, who instructed her to tell the men to go home to bed and call in their own doctors. This,

---

[27] This is why Tony Honoré does not regard the harm suffered by the claimant in *Chester v Afshar* (or analogous cases) as *caused by* the failure to advise of risks. We explore this further in Chapter 4.

reportedly, is what the duty medical officer said:

> Well, I am vomiting myself and I have not been drinking. Tell them to go home and go to bed and call in their own doctors, except Whittal, who should stay because he is due for an X-ray later this morning (at 431).

All of the men left. About five hours later, one of them died from poisoning by arsenic, which had been introduced into the tea. Nield J concluded that he would have died from the poisoning even if he had been admitted to the hospital and treated with all due care five hours earlier.

Nield J, at 433–4

My conclusions are: that the plaintiff, Mrs Bessie Irene Barnett, has failed to establish, on the balance of probabilities, that the death of the deceased, William Patrick Barnett, resulted from the negligence of the defendants, the Chelsea and Kensington Hospital Management Committee, my view being that had all care been taken, still the deceased must have died. But my further conclusions are that the defendant's casualty officer was negligent in failing to see and examine the deceased, and that, had he done so, his duty would have been to admit the deceased to the ward and to have treated him or caused him to be treated.

This case illustrates just how important the causation requirement is. It will no doubt have appeared to the plaintiff that the 'but for' test was an obstruction to justice in this case. There had been a proven breach of a duty of care in that there was a failure to diagnose and treat, and a man had died as a consequence of the condition for which he should have been treated. But causation is not a merely technical requirement. It is itself linked to questions of fairness and justice, primarily through the idea of responsibility. In this instance, where the arsenic was introduced to the tea with criminal intent, the defendants should not be held liable for consequences that they *could not have prevented*. Questions of causation rest to some extent upon reasons of responsibility.

Further Illustrations of the 'But for' Test

Hypothetical Acts of the Claimant: *McWilliams v Sir William Arroll Co Ltd* [1962] 1 WLR 295 (HL, Scotland)

The appellant was the widow of a steel erector, who had been working at a height of seventy feet when he fell and was fatally injured. No safety belt had been provided. The appellant claimed damages both for breach of common law duties of care, and for breach of the duty contained in the following statutory provision:

Section 26(2), Factories Act 1937

Where any person is to work at a place from which he is liable to fall a distance of more than ten feet, then . . . means shall be provided, so far as is reasonably practicable, by fencing or otherwise for ensuring his safety.

The facts are amplified in the extract below. The respondents argued successfully that because the deceased would not have worn a belt, even if it had been provided, their breaches of duty had not caused his death.

Viscount Simonds, at 301–2

The deceased was a steel erector of many years' experience and was employed by the first respondents in erecting a steel tower for a crane for the use of the second respondents in their shipbuilding yard at Port Glasgow. Whilst so employed he fell from a height of about 70 feet and was fatally injured. I need not describe in detail the nature of his work. It was dangerous work, as all such work must appear to a layman, but it was not specially dangerous work. It was the work he had been accustomed to do for many years. On the day of the accident he was not wearing a safety belt. It was proved that a safety belt was not on that day available for his use if he had wanted to use it. A belt had been available until two or three days before the accident but then had been removed, together with the but in which it had been stored, to another site. It is a matter of conjecture whether the deceased knew that it had been removed.

In these circumstances, the simple case was made that the respondents were in breach of their duty to provide a safety belt for the use of the deceased; he was not wearing one when he fell to his death; if he had been wearing one, he would not, or at least might not, have so fallen: therefore the respondents are liable.

To this simple case the respondents make answer. Let it be assumed that they were in breach of their duty in not providing a safety belt on the day of his accident and, further, that if he had then been wearing one, the accident would not have occurred. Yet there is a missing link: for it was not proved that the deceased was not wearing a belt because it was not provided; and alternatively, if any question of onus of proof arises, it was proved that if one had been provided, the deceased would not have worn it.

. . . The evidence showed conclusively that the deceased himself on this and similar jobs had except on two special occasions (about which the evidence was doubted by the Lord Ordinary) persistently abstained from wearing a safety belt and that other steel erectors had adopted a similar attitude. Nor was their attitude irrational or foolhardy. They regarded belts as cumbersome and even dangerous and gave good reason for thinking so. It was, however, urged that on this single occasion the deceased might have changed his mind and that the respondents did not and could not prove that he had not done so.

My Lords, I would agree that, just as a claim against a dead man's estate must always be jealously scrutinised, so also an inference unfavourable to him should not be drawn except upon a strong balance of probability. But there is justice to the living as well as to the dead, and it would be a denial of justice if the court thought itself bound to decide in favour of the deceased because he might, if living, have told a tale so improbable that it could convince nobody. That, my Lords, is this case and in my opinion the courts below were amply justified in receiving the evidence given (not only by the respondents' witnesses) as to the attitude adopted by the deceased and other steelworkers to the wearing of belts and acting upon it.

Concurring judgments were delivered by Viscount Muir LC, and by Lords Reid, Morris, and Devlin.

This case offers another illustration of the potency of 'but for' causation. Viscount Simonds' judgment is dominated by the perceived 'injustice' to the defendants if they should be held to be liable in negligence for damage that their actions, if careful, would probably not have prevented. Causation is, again, related to responsibility. The only 'responsibility' in question is responsibility for *consequences*. If no consequences flow from the breach of duty, then I am not responsible in tort for that breach. If there is an injury, but I could not have prevented that injury through proper conduct, then again I am not responsible, even if my behaviour is culpable. Even a clear breach of a statutory duty will give rise to no liability in tort if it is not shown to have caused the eventual damage.[28]

Hypothetical Acts of the Defendant

Matters become more complex if the defendant's negligence has removed an opportunity for the *defendant* which might prevent the loss to the claimant. In assessing whether this negligence has 'caused' the claimant's injury, the court must try to determine what the defendant *would* have done, 'but for' his or her own original negligence. It seems obvious that the defendant will argue that he or she would not have acted so as to save the defendant from harm, even if the opportunity had arisen to do so. In accordance with the general approach to causation, the court must then assess this evidence for persuasiveness. On balance, what does the court think that the defendant would have done? This is illustrated by the *Bolitho* case, which we extracted in Section 1 of this chapter. The facts of *Bolitho* are set out there.

In the following extract from the same case, Lord Browne-Wilkinson confirms the way that the causation requirement operates in such a case. However, he also confirms that if the defendant's hypothetical failure to save the claimant from harm *would in itself be negligent*, then this will be treated differently. The defendant can rely on a hypothetical future act or omission of his or her own, but *not* if that act or omission would itself be negligent. In this instance, whether the hypothetical act or omission would be *negligent* must be answered by application of the *Bolam* test.

Bolitho v City and Hackney Health Authority [1998] AC 232

Lord Browne-Wilkinson, at 239–41

Where, as in the present case, a breach of a duty of care is proved or admitted, the burden still lies on the plaintiff to prove that such breach caused the injury suffered: *Bonnington Castings Ltd. v. Wardlaw* [1956] A.C. 613; *Wilsher v. Essex Area Health Authority* [1988] A.C. 1074. In all cases the primary question is one of fact: did the wrongful act cause the injury? But in cases where the breach of duty consists of an omission to do an act which ought to be done (e.g. the failure by a doctor to attend) that factual inquiry is, by definition, in the realms of hypothesis. The question is what would have happened if an event which by definition did not occur had occurred. In a case of non-attendance by a doctor, there may be cases in which there is a doubt as to which doctor would have attended if the duty had been fulfilled. But in this case there was no doubt: if the duty had been carried out it would have either been Dr. Horn or Dr. Rodger, the only two doctors at St. Bartholomew's who had responsibility for Patrick and were on duty. Therefore in the present case, the first relevant question is "What would Dr. Horn or Dr. Rodger have done if they had attended?" As to Dr. Horn, the judge accepted her evidence that she would not have intubated. By inference, although not expressly, the judge must have

---

[28] Note, however, the case law taking a more relaxed approach to *proof* of causation in respect of work-related injuries and (particularly) diseases: Chapter 4 below.

accepted that Dr. Rodger also would not have intubated: as a senior house officer she would not have intubated without the approval of her senior registrar, Dr. Horn.

Therefore the *Bolam* test had no part to play in determining the first question, viz. what would have happened? Nor can I see any circumstances in which the *Bolam* test could be relevant to such a question.

However in the present case the answer to the question "What would have happened?" is not determinative of the issue of causation. At the trial the defendants accepted that if the professional standard of care required any doctor who attended to intubate Patrick, Patrick's claim must succeed. Dr. Horn could not escape liability by proving that she would have failed to take the course which any competent doctor would have adopted. A defendant cannot escape liability by saying that the damage would have occurred in any event because he would have committed some other breach of duty thereafter. I have no doubt that this concession was rightly made by the defendants. But there is some difficulty in analysing why it was correct. I adopt the analysis of Hobhouse L.J. in *Joyce v. Merton, Sutton and Wandsworth Health Authority* [1996] 7 Med.L.R. 1. In commenting on the decision of the Court of Appeal in the present case, he said, at p. 20:

> "Thus a plaintiff can discharge the burden of proof on causation by satisfying the court *either* that the relevant person would in fact have taken the requisite action (although she would not have been at fault if she had not) *or* that the proper discharge of the relevant person's duty towards the plaintiff required that she take that action. The former alternative calls for no explanation since it is simply the factual proof of the causative effect of the original fault. The latter is slightly more sophisticated: it involves the factual situation that the original fault did not itself cause the injury but that this was because there would have been some further fault on the part of the defendants; the plaintiff proves his case by proving that his injuries would have been avoided if proper care had continued to be taken. In the *Bolitho* case the plaintiff had to prove that the continuing exercise of proper care would have resulted in his being intubated."

There were, therefore, two questions for the judge to decide on causation. (1) What would Dr. Horn have done, or authorised to be done, if she had attended Patrick? And (2) if she would not have intubated, would that have been negligent? The *Bolam* test has no relevance to the first of those questions but is central to the second.

There can be no doubt that, as the majority of the Court of Appeal held, the judge directed himself correctly in accordance with that approach. The passages from his judgment which I have quoted (and in particular those that I have emphasised) demonstrate this. The dissenting judgment of Simon Brown L.J. in the Court of Appeal is based on a misreading of the judge's judgment. He treats the judge as having only asked himself one question, namely, the second question. To the extent that the Lord Justice noticed the first question—would Dr. Horn have intubated—he said that the judge was wrong to accept Dr. Horn's evidence that she would not have intubated. In my judgment it was for the judge to assess the truth of her evidence on this issue.

Accordingly the judge asked himself the right questions and answered them on the right basis.

This is clearly an application of the 'but for' test for causation, adjusted to the circumstances. However, it raises particular issues because the defendant's evidence as to his or her own likely actions will be crucial. That evidence will be scrutinized for persuasiveness, and it will also be measured against the relevant standard of care. But still, the defendant's own carelessness in such a case will give that defendant the opportunity to present a hypothetical course of action and claim it to be the most likely. As we saw previously in this chapter, above, the claimant's problems are compounded because the *Bolam* test will apply to the hypothetical events. If the claimant cannot show that the defendant would have acted so as to avoid the harm (and here the defendant controls much of the evidence), then she or he will in effect have to show that *no competent doctor* would have acted so as to prevent the damage.

Multiple Causes

Particular problems arise where multiple events contribute to the injury suffered by the claimant, most particularly where there are multiple torts. In this section, we only introduce one aspect of such cases. Other aspects of 'multiple cause' are considered in respect of 'intervening acts' (p. 194 below), in respect of proof of causation (Chapter 4), and in respect of contribution between tortfeasors (Chapter 7). However, we will indicate where appropriate how these other issues link with the causal question considered here.

Indivisible damage and concurrent torts

A first (and frequently difficult) question is whether the claimant's damage should be treated as 'divisible' or 'indivisible'. If it is indivisible, the general principle is that each tortfeasor who can be said to have contributed to the damage is held fully responsible for that damage, subject to any deduction for contributory negligence on the part of the claimant (Chapter 5, Defences): *Dingle v Associated Newspapers* [1961] 2 QB 162. A number of torts contributing to *the same damage* are referred to as **concurrent torts**. In a case of concurrent torts, the claimant is not compelled to pursue all those defendants who have contributed to the harm, and does not take the risk that one of the defendants will be insolvent. A defendant who is held liable for causing injury may pursue contribution proceedings in order to recover a proportion of damages from a fellow tortfeasor. The treatment of indivisible harm for these purposes is fully considered in Chapter 7. It should be noted that this sort of case—where all have *contributed to* an indivisible injury—is different in principle from the case where all have breached a duty, and it is not clear which defendant has caused the (indivisible) harm: see the discussion of *Fairchild v Glenhaven* [2003] 1 AC 32 in Chapter 4.

Divisible damage and consecutive torts

Where damage is considered to be *divisible*, the claimant in an action against any specific defendant will be awarded damages only for that part of the injury that is caused by the specific defendant's breach. It is not always obvious whether the injury is 'divisible'. In *Thompson v Smith's Ship Repairers* [1984] QB 405, loss of hearing through occupational exposure was held to be 'divisible' damage. It got progressively worse with each exposure. Only some periods of exposure to noise were tortious, so the damages payable were confined to the *additional* hearing loss suffered through that tortious exposure.[29]

In the following cases, damage caused by the original tort seemed to have been swallowed up by the effects of the later event. What, if anything, is the continuing responsibility of the original tortfeasor?

---

[29] This case and the contrast with indivisible damage are discussed in Chapter 7; see also *Holtby v Brigham and Cowan (Hull) Ltd* [2000] 3 All ER 423 (Chapter 4).

Baker v Willoughby [1970] AC 467

The plaintiff suffered injury to his leg in a road traffic accident through the tort of the defendant. Shortly before his tort action was heard, he was shot in the same leg during an armed robbery and the leg had to be amputated. This was a case of consecutive torts, although there was no prospect of proceeding against the second tortfeasor. Equally, there was no question of holding the first tortfeasor liable for the loss of the leg itself—there was no meaningful causal link between the first and the second torts.[30] The first tortfeasor had not put the plaintiff in danger, for example.

The House of Lords held that the first tortfeasor should pay for the damage he had 'caused' notwithstanding the intervention of the second incident. This makes perfect sense because, if the second tortfeasor had been available to be sued, he would have had to pay only for the *additional* pain, suffering, loss of amenity and loss of earnings that he had caused.

Lord Pearson, *Baker v Willoughby*, at 496

I think a solution of the theoretical problem can be found in cases such as this by taking a comprehensive and unitary view of the damage caused by the original accident. . . . The original accident caused what may be called a "devaluation" of the plaintiff, in the sense that it produced a general reduction of his capacity to do things, to earn money and to enjoy life. For that devaluation the original tortfeasor should be and remain responsible to the full extent, unless before the assessment of the damages something has happened which either diminishes the devaluation (e.g. if there is an unexpected recovery from some of the adverse effects of the accident) or by shortening the expectation of life diminishes the period over which the plaintiff will suffer from the devaluation. If the supervening event is a tort, the second tortfeasor should be responsible for the additional devaluation caused by him.

Jobling v Associated Dairies [1982] AC 794

Here the plaintiff suffered a back injury at work through the tort of the defendant. He later developed a disease to which he had a predisposition. The House of Lords held that the disease had to be taken into account in assessing damages. The award for lost earnings must be reduced to reflect the fact that such earnings would have stopped at a certain date in any event. From the point of view of the law of damages, this too makes perfect sense, because reductions will be made if there is a known *risk* of future incapacity independent of the tort, to avoid compensating for injuries that are not caused by a tort (they would have happened anyway). But there is an ugly clash with the *Baker* decision. Could they *both* be correct? Why should a second tort be different from a supervening *illness*? There really is no good answer to this and the House of Lords in *Jobling* expressed doubts about the solution reached in *Baker v Willoughby*.

These clashing authorities were considered by the Court of Appeal in the next extract.

Rahman v Arearose [2001] QB 351

The claimant had been assaulted at work causing injury to his right eye. It was found that his employers (the first defendants) were partly to blame for this injury through breaches of duty

---

[30] Does this in itself suggest that there is more to causation than 'but for' cause?

in respect of his safety. He required a bone graft, which was negligently performed at the second defendants' hospital. His optic nerve was severed and he lost all sight in the eye. (As a consequence of these events, he also suffered psychiatric damage. This aspect of the case is discussed in Chapter 7 in respect of contribution.)

The Court of Appeal effectively followed *Baker*, holding that the first defendant remained responsible for the effects of the initial injury, even after the apparently 'supervening' cause. As in *Baker* this appears correct, since the second defendant (who in this instance *is* available) should only be liable for the *additional* damage caused. They had deprived him of sight in an *already* damaged eye and added to *existing* distress, all of which would affect damages. Laws LJ attempted to leap free of the conflict between the two House of Lords' decisions above by describing them both as to do with 'responsibility'.

Laws LJ, *Rahman v Arearose* [2001] QB 351

31 The problem at the heart of this case rests in the law's attempts to contain the kaleido-scopic nature of the concept of causation within a decent and rational system for the compensation of innocent persons who suffer injury by reason of other people's wrongdoings. The common law has on the whole achieved just results, but the approach has been heavily pragmatic. . . .

32 Although the reasoning in *Jobling's* case involved the raising of some judicial eyebrows as to the approach taken by the House in *Baker's* case, with great respect I see no inconsistency whatever between the two cases. Once it is recognised that the first principle is that every tortfeasor should compensate the injured claimant in respect of that loss and damage for which he should justly be held responsible, the metaphysics of causation can be kept in their proper place: of themselves they offered in any event no hope of a solution of the problems which confront the courts in this and other areas. . . .

33 So in all these cases the real question is, what is the damage for which the defendant under consideration should be held *responsible*. The nature of his duty (here, the common law duty of care) is relevant; causation, certainly, will be relevant—but it will fall to be viewed, and in truth can only be understood, in light of the answer to the question: from what kind of harm was it the defendant's duty to guard the claimant? That, if I may say so, is I think the insight of Lord Hoffmann's lecture to the Chancery Bar Association on 15 June 1999 on "Common Sense and Causing Loss". Novus actus interveniens, the eggshell skull, and (in the case of multiple torts) the concept of concurrent tortfeasors are all no more and no less than tools or mechanisms which the law has developed to articulate in practice the extent of any liable defendant's responsibility for the loss and damage which the claimant has suffered.

This is interesting, because it interprets questions of cause in fact as really concerned with responsibility, and not as mere 'factual' matters at all. (It also relates questions of 'liability for consequences' to issues of cause in fact, as well as cause in law, showing quite how 'kaleido-scopic' the issues of causation really are.) This neatly illustrates that 'cause in fact' though more accessible superficially than remoteness (or cause in law) is nevertheless not all to do with factual questions.

Mason CJ, *March v Stramare* (1991) 171 CLR 506 (High Court of Australia)

22. . . . The cases demonstrate the lesson of experience, namely, that the [but for] test, applied as an exclusive criterion of causation, yields unacceptable results and that the results which it yields must be tempered by the making of value judgments and the infusion of policy considerations. That in itself is something of an irony because the proponents of the "but for" test have seen it as a criterion which would exclude the making of value judgments and evaluative considerations from causation analysis: see Weinrib, "A Step Forward in Factual Causation" (1975) 38 Modern Law Review 518, at p 530.

We will leave 'cause in fact' for now, but return in Chapter 4. There we will particularly consider cases where *proof* of causation has been problematic; and the very difficult issue of 'lost chances'. What sort of 'damage' must be 'caused'?

6. CAUSATION: 'CAUSE-IN-LAW'/REMOTENESS/SCOPE OF LIABILITY

6.1 INTRODUCTION: THREE VERSIONS OF THE REMOTENESS QUESTION

At the start of Section 5, we pointed out that there have been different interpretations of the 'remoteness' question, some more compatible than others with the idea that this is a question about 'causation'.

Imagine that the remoteness question is stated in the following three very different ways. This exercise will help us to understand diverging currents in the case law.

1. Is the full extent of the damage fairly attributable to the defendant's breach of duty or other tortious intervention?

This was the question adopted by the Privy Council in *The Wagon Mound (No 1)*, the leading authority on remoteness of damage, which is extracted below. Fairness of attribution was interpreted in terms of 'foreseeability'. In cases of negligence, this aligns remoteness with duty of care and breach. Of our three interpretations of remoteness, this is the least like a 'causal' test. This has been the authoritative test since 1961, and as we will see below it was supposed to sweep away the problems associated with more 'causal' language. But it has failed to resolve all of the difficulties, and 'causal' language persists in certain areas of the case law. At the end of this section, we will address the possibility that duty and remoteness questions are better aligned through analysis of the 'scope of the duty'.

2. Is the damage a *direct* consequence of the defendant's breach, or has the chain of causation been broken?

This was the approach endorsed by the Court of Appeal in *Re Polemis and Furness Withy & Co* [1921] 3 KB 560. It appears to pose a factual question, but since the 'chain of causation' is not a real entity, it was never anything more than a metaphor. It was disapproved by the Privy Council in *The Wagon Mound*, yet vestiges of this approach tend to survive. In particular, some issues are framed in terms of 'new cause' or '*nova causa interveniens*' (or, in the case of human interventions, '*novus actus interveniens*'), even if analysis in terms of 'directness' is no longer expected to provide the answers.

3. Even if the defendant's breach is a condition of the damage suffered, so that it satisfies the 'but for' test, is it a 'cause' of that damage?

This formulation opens up a range of possibilities, based on common sense, ordinary language and intuition. It is more like question 2 than question 1. Unlike the *Wagon Mound* variant of 1, it does not address questions of what the *defendant* might have been able to foresee, in order to establish what is 'fair'. Instead, it looks with hindsight at what has occurred in order to identify whether a particular condition can be treated as 'causing' the damage. However, it is broader than 2, because 'a break in the chain of causation' is not the only reason why a condition may not be considered a cause; and it does not seek a solution in logical or pseudo-scientific analysis of events. An example is the broad 'common sense causal approach' of Hart and Honoré.

The above possibilities can be used to explain some continuing inconsistencies in the case law, to which we now turn.

6.2 FORESEEABILITY OF THE TYPE OF HARM: *THE WAGON MOUND (NO 1)*

The Issue: *Re Polemis* and 'Direct Consequences'

In *The Wagon Mound (No 1)* (below), the Privy Council considered the correctness of a previous Court of Appeal decision, *Re Polemis and Furness Withy & Co* [1921] 3 KB 560 (generally known as *Re Polemis*). *Re Polemis* held that a defendant who is shown to have been at fault is liable for all *direct* consequences of that fault, even if the resulting damage is unforeseeable.

Re Polemis and Furness Withy & Co [1921] 3 KB 560

Through the negligence of stevedores employed by the defendant charterers, a board fell into the hold of a ship where tins of benzene and/or petrol were being shifted. The fall of the plank was followed by a rush of flames and the total destruction of the ship. On a claim against the charterers for the full value of the ship, arbitrators found that the fire which destroyed the ship was caused by a spark igniting vapour in the hold; that the spark was caused by the fall of the plank into the hold; and that the causing of the spark (and therefore the fire) could not reasonably have been anticipated from the falling of the board, though some mechanical damage to the ship might reasonably have been anticipated. The Court of Appeal held that the charterers were liable for all the direct consequences of the negligence of their servants, even though those consequences could not reasonably have been anticipated:

Warrington LJ, at 574

The presence or absence of reasonable anticipation of damage determines the legal quality of the act as negligent or innocent. If it be thus determined to be negligent, then the question whether particular damages are recoverable depends only on the answer to the question whether they are the direct consequence of the act.

Martin Davies, 'The Road From Morocco: Polemis Through Donoghue to No-Fault'
(1982) 45 MLR 534–55, 534

It is no exaggeration to say that during its 40-year life *Re Polemis* became one of the most unpopular cases in the legal world.

Davies argues that *Polemis* was, initially, a perfectly acceptable decision, popular in the shipping world and not at the time criticized for creating over-expansive liability to defendants. Although he is critical of the later *Wagon Mound* decision, Davies does not seek to defend the general approach in *Re Polemis* as providing a better interpretation of causal questions. Rather, he argues that developments in the tort of negligence had, by the time of his article in 1982, created problems for both remoteness tests, and he simply points out that *Polemis* itself should be judged in terms of its effect at the time of the decision. In particular, having established that the successful claim was one in tort and not in contract,[31] Davies adds that the relevant *duty* which was breached by the negligence of the stevedores was necessarily a specific one, since the case predated the recognition of a generalized duty of care in *Donoghue v Stevenson*. The specific duty in question was owed by the charterer of the ship, hired (chartered) from the shipowner.

Why is it so important to establish the source of the defendants' duty of care in *Re Polemis*? It is important because that duty was, like all pre-Donoghue duties of care, a particularised relational one. It was owed by the defendants to the plaintiffs alone, and it arose from the nature of the special relationship between the parties. To forget this is to misunderstand why the *Re Polemis* rule took the form it did. The true original intention behind the *Re Polemis* remoteness rule can only be recognised by seeing it in the context of a pre-1932 duty of care. A wide remoteness rule was unexceptionable when duty was narrowly conceived. Extensive liability of defendants is not a problem when those defendants can only be liable to a limited class of plaintiffs, or even a single plaintiff only. . . .

We should notice that Davies here only mentions one reason why the *Polemis* rule was unpopular. He does not mention that Viscount Simonds also took exception to the very idea that such cases should be dealt with in terms of causation. In the extract below, Viscount Simonds refers to the 'never-ending and insoluble problems of causation'. Elsewhere in his judgment, he was more scathing, suggesting that courts 'were at times in grave danger of being led astray by scholastic theories of causation and their ugly and barely intelligible jargon' (at 419). Martin Davies suggests that the *Polemis* rule was 'self-applying', but in fact it threw up considerable difficulty. Having said that, the Privy Council was mistaken if it thought that the move to foreseeability would result in a single and easily applicable test.

Overseas Tankship (UK) Ltd v Morts Dock and Engineering Co Ltd (The Wagon Mound (No 1)) [1961] AC 388

The facts of this case are set out in Section 1 of this chapter.

---

[31] A. D. McNair, 'This Polemis Business' (1931) 4 CLJ 125.

Viscount Simonds (delivering the judgment of the Board, at 422–6)

Enough has been said to show that the authority of *Polemis* has been severely shaken though lip-service has from time to time been paid to it. In their Lordships' opinion it should no longer be regarded as good law. It is not probable that many cases will for that reason have a different result, though it is hoped that the law will be thereby simplified, and that in some cases, at least, palpable injustice will be avoided. For it does not seem consonant with current ideas of justice or morality that for an act of negligence, however slight or venial, which results in some trivial foreseeable damage the actor should be liable for all consequences however unforeseeable and however grave, so long as they can be said to be "direct." It is a principle of civil liability, subject only to qualifications which have no present relevance, that a man must be considered to be responsible for the probable consequences of his act. To demand more of him is too harsh a rule, to demand less is to ignore that civilised order requires the observance of a minimum standard of behaviour.

This concept applied to the slowly developing law of negligence has led to a great variety of expressions which can, as it appears to their Lordships, be harmonised with little difficulty with the single exception of the so-called rule in *Polemis*. For, if it is asked why a man should be responsible for the natural or necessary or probable consequences of his act (or any other similar description of them) the answer is that it is not because they are natural or necessary or probable, but because, since they have this quality, it is judged by the standard of the reasonable man that he ought to have foreseen them. Thus it is that over and over again it has happened that in different judgments in the same case, and sometimes in a single judgment, liability for a consequence has been imposed on the ground that it was reasonably foreseeable or, alternatively, on the ground that it was natural or necessary or probable. The two grounds have been treated as coterminous, and so they largely are. But, where they are not, the question arises to which the wrong answer was given in *Polemis*. For, if some limitation must be imposed upon the consequences for which the negligent actor is to be held responsible—and all are agreed that some limitation there must be—why should that test (reasonable foreseeability) be rejected which, since he is judged by what the reasonable man ought to foresee, corresponds with the common conscience of mankind, and a test (the "direct" consequence) be substituted which leads to no-where but the never-ending and insoluble problems of causation. "The lawyer," said Sir Frederick Pollock, "cannot afford to adventure himself with philosophers in the logical and metaphysical controversies that beset the idea of cause." Yet this is just what he has most unfortunately done and must continue to do if the rule in *Polemis* is to prevail. A conspicuous example occurs when the actor seeks to escape liability on the ground that the "chain of causation" is broken by a "nova causa" or "novus actus interveniens." . . .

At an early stage in this judgment their Lordships intimated that they would deal with the proposition which can best be stated by reference to the well-known dictum of Lord Sumner: "This however goes to culpability not to compensation." It is with the greatest respect to that very learned judge and to those who have echoed his words, that their Lordships find themselves bound to state their view that this proposition is fundamentally false.

Their Lordships conclude this part of the case with some general observations. They have been concerned primarily to displace the proposition that unforeseeability is irrelevant if damage is "direct." In doing so they have inevitably insisted that the essential factor in determining liability is whether the damage is of such a kind as the reasonable man should have foreseen. This accords with the general view thus stated by Lord Atkin in *Donoghue v. Stevenson*: 'The liability for negligence, whether you style it such or treat it as in other systems as a species of 'culpa', is no doubt based upon a general public sentiment of moral wrongdoing for which the offender must pay.' It is a departure from this sovereign principle if liability is made to depend solely on the damage being the "direct" or "natural" consequence of the precedent act. Who knows or can be assumed to know all the processes of nature? But if it would be wrong that a man should be held liable for damage unpredictable by a reasonable man because it was "direct" or "natural," equally it would be wrong that he should escape liability, however "indirect" the damage, if he foresaw or could reasonably foresee the intervening events which led to its being done: cf. *Woods v. Duncan*. Thus foreseeability becomes the effective test. In reasserting this principle their Lordships conceive that they do not depart from, but follow and develop, the law of negligence as laid down by Baron Alderson in *Blyth v. Birmingham Waterworks Co.* [(1856)11 Ex. 781]

Commentary

The Privy Council dismissed as an 'error' Lord Sumner's dictum in *Weld-Blundell v Stephens* [1920] AC 956, 999, that foreseeability 'goes to culpability, not to compensation'. On the face of it, *The Wagon Mound (No 1)* determines that there should no longer be different tests for the breach of duty, and the extent of the damage which is recoverable. This decision is not based on analysis of causation. In fact, the judgment shows a strong distaste for causal language, and in principle it ought to leave 'cause in fact' as the only remaining question of causation in tort law. This was precisely the interpretation of *The Wagon Mound* adopted by Glanville Williams, a strong supporter of a foreseeability-based approach, who saw *The Wagon Mound* as decisive.

G. Williams, 'The Risk Principle' [1961] 77 LQR 179–212, 179

. . . If *The Wagon Mound* is accepted by the English courts, as surely it must be . . . [w]e shall be spared most of what the Board called "the never-ending and insoluble problems of causation," together with the subtleties of *novus actus interveniens*, and shall be left with a comparatively simple rule the application of which involves merely an adjudication of fact. In future, broadly speaking, there will not be two questions in the tort of negligence, a question of initial responsibility and one of "proximity," [by which Williams means 'proximate cause' or remoteness] but only one question—was the defendant negligent as regards this damage? He will not be liable to the "unforeseeable plaintiff," nor even to the foreseeable plaintiff in respect of unforeseeable damage. This amounts to a complete acceptance of what is conveniently called the risk principle, namely, that negligence is to be considered not in the abstract but only in relation to a particular risk.

The ambition was to replace two tests (duty and remoteness) with one (foreseeability). But it swiftly became clear that this was over-ambitious in both respects.

Although the change in the law effected by *The Wagon Mound* had wide academic support, there were large ambiguities in the decision itself. It is clear that Viscount Simonds expected his approach to appeal to the sense of fairness. It is argued to be *unfair* to make a defendant liable for very extensive damage which was unforeseeable, simply because some trivial damage *was* foreseeable. But what exactly did the *Wagon Mound* decide would be the relevant rule? Attention to the detail of the judgment shows that the Privy Council distinguished between foreseeable and unforeseeable *types* of damage: 'the essential factor in determining liability is whether the damage is of such a kind as the reasonable man should have foreseen' (final paragraph extracted above). If this is taken literally, then if the damage is unforeseeable in extent, but foreseeable in *type*, then all of the damage will in fact be recoverable. This was the understanding of the case which immediately followed (see for example Dias, 'Trouble on Oiled Waters' [1967] CLJ 62, 72), and indeed it is the way that the rule in *The Wagon Mound* has generally been interpreted (see the discussions of *Smith v Leech Brain* and *Hughes v Lord Advocate*, as well as more recent case law, below). But importantly, this means that the rule as expressed is not fully consistent with the idea that only foreseeable harm is fairly recoverable. Some harm which was not foreseeable will be recoverable, if it is of the appropriate type. This in turn is not consistent with the rhetoric of 'fairness' at the start of the extract.

There is a further ambiguity. The Privy Council held that damage by fouling was foreseeable in this case, but that damage by fire was not. Is this consistent with the distinction mentioned above in terms of different *kinds* of damage, or does it suggest a different distinction, in terms of damage done by a different *process*? The interpretation of *The Wagon Mound* in later cases such as *Hughes v Lord Advocate* has approached foreseeability in terms of type of damage and *not* in terms of the process by which it comes about.

How to Judge Foreseeability

According to the Privy Council, the view taken by the courts below that the damage was direct and therefore recoverable, depended upon hindsight. This, the court argued, was unfair to the defendant, since '[a]fter the event even a fool is wise. But it is not the hindsight of a fool; it is only the foresight of a reasonable man which alone can determine responsibility'. Instead, the Privy Council adopted a test of reasonable foresight (not hindsight) judged from the point of view of a reasonable person *in the position of the defendant at the time of the breach*.

This form of foreseeability is referred to by Hart and Honoré as 'foreseeability in a practical sense'. According to Hart and Honoré, normal *causal* statements are not like this. They are generally retrospective and are to do with attribution rather than fault.

6.3 REMAINING PROBLEMS

Pre-existing Vulnerability: *Smith v Leech Brain and Co Ltd* [1962] 2 QB 405

The plaintiff was the widow of a steel galvanizer employed by the defendants. Part of his job involved lowering articles by means of an overhead crane into molten metal. He was afforded inadequate protection against splashing by molten metal and suffered a burn on his lower lip. The burn promoted cancer, from which he died three years later. In this first instance decision, Lord Parker CJ considered whether he was permitted by the Privy Council decision in *The Wagon Mound* to depart from the directness rule in *Re Polemis*. *Re Polemis* was a Court of Appeal decision and in principle binding upon the lower court; the Privy Council decision had only persuasive authority.

He held that the *Wagon Mound* made no difference to a case such as this. The initial injury (the burn) was of a readily foreseeable type, and the subsequent cancer was treated as merely extending the amount of harm suffered.

Lord Parker CJ, at 413–15

. . . I find that the burn was the promoting agency of cancer in tissues which already had a pre-malignant condition. In those circumstances, it is clear that the plaintiff's husband, but for the burn, would not necessarily ever have developed cancer. On the other hand, having regard to the number of matters which can be promoting agencies, there was a strong likelihood that at some stage in his life he would develop cancer. But that the burn did contribute to, or cause in part, at any rate, the cancer and the death, I have no doubt.

The third question is damages. Here I am confronted with the recent decision of the Privy Council in *Overseas Tankship (U.K.) Limited v. Morts Dock and Engineering Co. Ltd. (The Wagon Mound)*. But for that case, it seems to me perfectly clear that, assuming negligence proved, and assuming that the burn caused in whole or in part the cancer and the death, the plaintiff would be entitled to recover. It is said on the one side by Mr. May that although I am not strictly bound by the *Wagon Mound* since it is a decision of the Privy Council, I should treat myself as free, using the arguments to be derived from that case, to say that other cases in these courts—other cases in the Court of Appeal—have been wrongly decided, and particularly that *In re Polemis and Furness Withy & Co.* was wrongly decided, and that a further ground for taking that course is to be found in the various criticisms that have from time to time in the past been made by members of the House of Lords in regard to the *Polemis* case.

. . .

For my part, I am quite satisfied that the Judicial Committee in the *Wagon Mound* case did not have what I may call, loosely, the thin skull cases in mind. It has always been the law of this country that a tortfeasor takes his victim as he finds him. It is unnecessary to do more than refer to the short passage in the decision of Kennedy J. in *Dulieu v. White & Sons [[1901] 2 KB 669]*, where he said [679]: "If a man is negligently run over or otherwise negligently injured in his body, it is no answer to the sufferer's claim for damages that he would have suffered less injury, or no injury at all, if he had not had an unusually thin skull or an unusually weak heart." . . .

The Judicial Committee were, I think, disagreeing with the decision in the *Polemis* case that a man is no longer liable for the type of damage which he could not reasonably anticipate. The Judicial Committee were not, I think, saying that a man is only liable for the extent of damage which he could anticipate, always assuming the type of injury could have been anticipated. I think that view is really supported by the way in which cases of this sort have been dealt with in Scotland. Scotland has never, so far as I know, adopted the principle laid down in *Polemis*, and yet I am quite satisfied that they have throughout proceeded on the basis that the tortfeasor takes the victim as he finds him.

In those circumstances, it seems to me that this is plainly a case which comes within the old principle. The test is not whether these employers could reasonably have foreseen that a burn would cause cancer and that he would die. The question is whether these employers could reasonably foresee the type of injury he suffered, namely, the burn. What, in the particular case, is the amount of damage which he suffers as a result of that burn, depends upon the characteristics and constitution of the victim.

Lord Parker argued that the *Wagon Mound* decision did not alter the existing rule that the defendant must 'take his victim as he finds him'. He sought to make this rule compatible with *The Wagon Mound* by suggesting that the 'thin skull' or 'egg-shell skull' rule only operates so as to allow the defendant to be liable for *more extensive damage* than he might have foreseen. It does not allow defendants to be liable if, without the vulnerability, no damage (or no damage of the same type) would be foreseeable at all. This is not completely compatible with the dictum from *Dulieu v White* on which Lord Parker relies, since this includes a reference to situations where 'no injury at all' would have been suffered by someone without the vulnerability. Of course, acceptance of his approach also depends on accepting that the *Wagon*

Mound does not require the *extent* of the damage to be foreseeable. It can now be accepted that this is an appropriate interpretation of that case.

Hart and Honoré argue that this attempt to reconcile the 'egg-shell skull' cases with the *Wagon Mound* is 'mere window dressing': 'the truth is that this aspect of common sense causal discourse has survived the *Wagon Mound*' (*Causation in the Law*, p. 274). However, the decision in *Smith v Leech Brain* itself can be reconciled with the *Wagon Mound* if we accept Lord Parker's approach of treating the eventual damage suffered as the same in type as the damage that was foreseeable. Lord Parker argued that once the burn was foreseeable, the cancer only raised the issue of how extensive *damages* should be. Is cancer the same 'type' of damage as a burn? We argued above that the interpretation of 'types' of damage holds the key to distinguishing the *Wagon Mound* from *Re Polemis* in many cases. If cancer is the same type of damage as a burn, then it seems that personal physical injury is very generously treated for the purposes of this test. If it is not the same type of damage, then the 'egg-shell skull' rule is a decisive departure from the *Wagon Mound*.

Glanville Williams, from whose important article we extracted above, also supported the retention of the egg-shell skull rule both for physical injury and for mental harm. He supported the rule on grounds of policy, justice, and fairness, and did not seek to make it compatible with the 'risk principle'. But this may be because he thought that *The Wagon Mound* would limit recovery to those damages that were foreseeable in *extent*.

Williams, 'The Risk Principle' [1961] 77 LQR 179, 196

It seems to me that, balancing one consideration with another, and expressing the opinion with considerable doubt, the thin skull rule is on the whole a justifiable exception to the risk principle. In a situation where our sympathy for the plaintiff conflicts with our sense of justice towards the defendant, the risk principle normally requires us to concentrate our attention upon justice to the defendant, acquitting him of consequences in respect of which he was not at fault. However, where the plaintiff has suffered bodily injury, it is difficult to maintain the cold logical analysis of the situation. Human bodies are too fragile, and life too precarious, to permit a defendant nicely to calculate how much injury he may inflict without causing more serious injury.

It is clear from subsequent cases that the egg-shell skull rule has been retained. Examples include *Robinson v Post Office* [1974] 1 WLR 1176 (allergic reaction leading to very extensive injuries, further discussed under 'third party interventions', later in this chapter) and *Malcolm v Broadhurst* [1970] 3 All ER 508 (exacerbation of a long-standing nervous condition by a car accident: 'there is no difference in principle between an egg-shell skull and an egg-shell personality', per Geoffrey Lane J), applied in *Page v Smith* (below). *Malcolm v Broadhurst* applied the pre-*Wagon Mound* authority of *Love v Port of London Authority* [1959] 2 Lloyd's Rep 541, illustrating that the Privy Council case had less immediate impact than might have been expected.

Two recent House of Lords decisions further enhance the status of the egg-shell skull rule, but do not fully resolve the question of compatibility with *The Wagon Mound*.

Page v Smith [1996] AC 155

The plaintiff's car was involved in a collision with a car driven by the defendant. The plaintiff suffered no immediate physical injury in the impact but three hours later felt exhausted and the exhaustion continued. Before the accident, he had suffered from chronic fatigue syndrome (otherwise known as myalgic encephalomyelitis or 'ME') over a period of 20 years, with varying degrees of severity. The plaintiff brought an action claiming damages for personal injury on the basis that the condition had now become chronic and permanent, so that he was unlikely to take full-time employment again. At first instance, Otton J found for the plaintiff. The Court of Appeal allowed an appeal on the basis that the injury was not reasonably foreseeable. On further appeal to the House of Lords, a majority found for the plaintiff on the issue of remoteness, but the case was remitted to the Court of Appeal for further consideration of the issue of factual causation: had the damage 'in fact' been caused by the accident?

A key feature of the case was the difficulty in categorizing the plaintiff's injury as either 'physical' or 'psychiatric'. If it was psychiatric, then would the *Wagon Mound* test preclude the claim on the basis that the 'type' of harm was unforeseeable? The majority rejected this conclusion, appealing directly to the egg-shell skull rule (Lord Lloyd said at p. 193 that where the plaintiff is within the range of foreseeable physical injury the defendant 'must take his victim as he finds him').

We consider this case further in Chapter 6. Its chief controversy is that it did not apply the usual restrictive test for foreseeability *in cases of psychiatric harm* to a plaintiff who was within the area of foreseeable *personal* injury.

Lack of Funds: The Demise of *The Leisbosch Dredger*

In *The Leisbosch Dredger* [1933] AC 449, the plaintiffs' ship sank as the result of the defendant's negligence. The dredger was engaged in work under contract and a contractual penalty would be paid if the work was not completed on time. Because the plaintiffs were short of funds, they were unable to buy another dredger and had to hire one at great expense in order to avoid the contractual penalty. They claimed for the whole of their financial loss, but the House of Lords held that nothing attributable to the plaintiffs' own lack of funds or 'impecuniosity' could be recovered. This decision was approved by the Privy Council in *The Wagon Mound (No 1)*, presumably because it did not allow for 'all direct consequences' to be recovered. It did, however, employ causal language in expressing the view that the cost of the hire of a dredger was not an 'immediate physical consequence' of the defendant's negligence. In the words of Donaldson LJ in *Dodd Properties v Canterbury City Council* [1980] 1 WLR 433, 458, Lord Wright 'took the view that, in so far as the plaintiffs had in fact suffered more than the loss assessed on a market basis, the excess flowed directly from their lack of means and not from the tortious act'. This is a judgment as to cause.

The Leisbosch Dredger has been taken to establish that the 'egg-shell skull rule' does not apply to financial vulnerability. The case was distinguished in a number of cases with strong disapproval (for example *Alcoa Minerals v Broderick* [2002] 1 AC 371, a decision of the Privy Council; *Dodd Properties v Canterbury City Council* [1980] 1 WLR 433). *The Leisbosch Dredger* was finally departed from by the House of Lords in the case of *Lagden v O'Connor* [2004] 1 AC 1067. This amounts to an overruling of the older decision.

Lagden v O'Connor [2004] 1 AC 1067

The claimant was unemployed and in poor health. His 10-year-old car was damaged through the negligence of the defendant. Because of his financial situation, the claimant was unable to pay for the hire of a car while his was off the road. He therefore took advantage of a credit hire agreement which would advance the cost of hiring a vehicle for a period of 26 weeks.

This would of course involve greater cost than the typical 'spot hire' rate, since it included some credit. It also included an insurance element. The House of Lords determined that the cost of this package was recoverable against the negligent defendant.

Lord Hope

61 . . . The wrongdoer must take his victim as he finds him . . . This rule applies to the economic state of the victim in the same way as it applies to his physical and mental vulnerability. It requires the wrongdoer to bear the consequences if it was reasonably foreseeable that the injured party would have to borrow money or incur some other expenditure to mitigate his damages.

In this case, the court was prepared to find that the greater expense to which the claimant was put was at least broadly foreseeable. Arguably then, despite its approval in *The Wagon Mound*, *The Leisbosch Dredger* worked against the foreseeability approach, and has been departed from for that reason. It is one of the peculiarities of the egg-shell skull rule that it has been accepted and now extended to financial vulnerability without a clear determination of whether it is an application of the foreseeability principle, or an exception to it.

Causal Sequence and Type of Damage: *Hughes v Lord Advocate* [1963] AC 837

A manhole in a city street was left open and unguarded. It was covered with a tent and surrounded by warning paraffin lamps. An eight-year-old boy entered the tent and somehow knocked one of the lamps into the hole (or perhaps lowered it in). An explosion occurred causing him to fall in to the hole and be severely burned. On appeal to the House of Lords, it was held that the workmen breached a duty of care owed to the boy, and that the damage was reasonably foreseeable.

Lord Reid, at 845

It was argued that the appellant cannot recover because the damage which he suffered was of a kind which was not foreseeable. That was not the ground of judgment of the First Division or of the Lord Ordinary and the facts proved do not, in my judgment, support that argument. The appellant's injuries were mainly caused by burns, and it cannot be said that injuries from burns were unforeseeable. As a warning to traffic the workmen had set lighted red lamps round the tent which covered the manhole, and if boys did enter the dark tent it was very likely that they would take one of these lamps with them. If the lamp fell and broke it was not at all unlikely that the boy would be burned and the burns might well be serious. No doubt it was not to be expected that the injuries would be as serious as those which the appellant in fact sustained. But a defender is liable, although the damage may be a good deal greater in extent than was foreseeable. He can only escape liability if the damage can be regarded as differing in kind from what was foreseeable.

So we have (first) a duty owed by the workmen, (secondly) the fact that if they had done as they ought to have done there would have been no accident, and (thirdly) the fact that the injuries suffered by the appellant, though perhaps different in degree, did not differ in kind from injuries which might have resulted from an accident of a foreseeable nature. The ground on which this case has been decided against the appellant is that the accident was of an unforeseeable type. Of course, the pursuer has to prove that the defender's fault caused the accident, and there could be a case where the intrusion of a new and unexpected factor could be regarded as the cause of the accident rather than the fault of the defender. But that is not this case. The cause of this accident was a known source of danger, the lamp, but it behaved in an unpredictable way.

The decision to allow recovery in this case, in which a known source of danger behaves in an unforeseeable way and thereby creates damage which is more extensive than might have been expected, decisively qualifies the claim that *The Wagon Mound* limits liability to foreseeable damage. In lower courts, the case law has not been consistent. For example, in *Doughty v Turner* [1964] 1 QB 518, the Court of Appeal drew a distinction between burning caused by a splash of hot liquid (foreseeable) and burning caused by an explosion (unforeseeable). In *Tremain v Pike* [1969] 1 WLR 1556, a first instance decision, it was suggested that illness contracted through contact with rat's urine (which was thought to be unforeseeable) was different in type from illness suffered through a rat bite (which was foreseeable). However, the principal reason for the decision in *Tremain* was that because the risk of infection from rat's urine was not foreseeable, there was no reason why the employer in that case should have taken the additional precautions necessary to protect against infection by rat's urine. Thus there was no breach of duty and the judge's remarks about remoteness were *obiter dicta*. Crucially, the steps necessary to protect against the *unforeseeable* infection would have been different from those needed to protect against the known danger associated with rat bites. In the other cases we have examined here (including *Page v Smith*, *Hughes v Lord Advocate*, and *The Wagon Mound* itself), there is only one set of steps required to remove the risk however broadly or narrowly it is defined.

The authority of *Hughes v Lord Advocate* has been reinforced through the following case.

Jolley v Sutton LBC [2000] 1 WLR 1082

A boat was left abandoned for about two years on land owned by the defendants. The council made plans to remove the boat, but these plans were not implemented. Two boys, the plaintiff and a friend, aged 13 and 14, used a car jack to prop up the boat and to repair it. The boat fell off the prop and crushed the plaintiff, who suffered serious spinal injuries leading to paraplegia. He brought an action against the council for negligence and breach of duty under the Occupiers Liability Act 1957, section 2(2)(3).[32] At first instance, judgment was given for the plaintiff subject to a reduction in damages of 25 per cent for contributory negligence (see Chapter 5 below, Defences). The judge found that the presence of the boat would foreseeably attract children and that the type of accident and injury was reasonably foreseeable. The House of Lords agreed.

The judgment of Lord Steyn was chiefly concerned with examination of the facts of the case. He said that 'very little needs to be said about the law'. However, he defended the compatibility of *Hughes v Lord Advocate* (above) with *The Wagon Mound (No 1)*:

(At 1090) . . . The speech of Lord Reid in *Hughes v. Lord Advocate*[1963] A.C. 837 is . . . not in conflict with *The Wagon Mound No. 1*. The scope of the two modifiers—the precise manner in which the injury came about and its extent—is not definitively answered by either *The Wagon Mound No. 1* or *Hughes v. Lord Advocate*. It requires determination in the context of an intense focus on the circumstances of each case . . ..

---

[32] Chapter 12.

The judgment of Lord Hoffmann is far more concerned with the question of which approach to take as a matter of law:

It is . . . agreed that the plaintiff must show that the injury which he suffered fell within the scope of the council's duty and that in cases of physical injury, the scope of the duty is determined by whether or not the injury fell within a description which could be said to have been reasonably foreseeable. *Donoghue v. Stevenson* [1932] A.C. 562 of course established the general principle that reasonable foreseeability of physical injury to another generates a duty of care. The further proposition that reasonable foreseeability also governs the question of whether the injury comes within the scope of that duty had to wait until *Overseas Tankship (U.K.) Ltd. v. Morts Dock and Engineering Co. Ltd. (The Wagon Mound)* [1961] A.C. 388 (*"The Wagon Mound No. 1"*) for authoritative recognition. Until then, there was a view that the determination of liability involved a two-stage process. The existence of a duty depended upon whether injury of some kind was foreseeable. Once such a duty had been established, the defendant was liable for any injury which had been "directly caused" by an act in breach of that duty, whether such injury was reasonably foreseeable or not. But the present law is that unless the injury is of a description which was reasonably foreseeable, it is (according to taste) "outside the scope of the duty" or "too remote."

It is also agreed that what must have been foreseen is not the precise injury which occurred but injury of a given description. The foreseeability is not as to the particulars but the genus. And the description is formulated by reference to the nature of the risk which ought to have been foreseen. So, in *Hughes v. Lord Advocate* [1963] A.C. 837 the foreseeable risk was that a child would be injured by falling in the hole or being burned by a lamp or by a combination of both. The House of Lords decided that the injury which actually materialised fell within this description, notwithstanding that it involved an unanticipated explosion of the lamp and consequent injuries of unexpected severity. Like my noble and learned friend, Lord Steyn, I can see no inconsistency between anything said in *The Wagon Mound No. 1* and the speech of Lord Reid in *Hughes v. Lord Advocate*. The two cases were dealing with altogether different questions. In the former, it was agreed that damage by burning was not damage of a description which could reasonably be said to have been foreseeable. The plaintiffs argued that they were nevertheless entitled to recover by the two-stage process I have described. It was this argument which was rejected. *Hughes v. Lord Advocate* starts from the principle accepted in *The Wagon Mound No. 1* and is concerned with whether the injury which happened was of a description which was reasonably foreseeable.

The short point in the present appeal is therefore whether the judge [1998] 1 Lloyd's Rep. 433, 439 was right in saying in general terms that the risk was that children would "meddle with the boat at the risk of some physical injury" or whether the Court of Appeal were right in saying that the only foreseeable risk was of "children who were drawn to the boat climbing upon it and being injured by the rotten planking giving way beneath them:" *per* Roch L.J. [1998] 1 W.L.R. 1546, 1555. Was the wider risk, which would include within its description the accident which actually happened, reasonably foreseeable?

My Lords, although this is in end the question of fact, the courts are not without guidance. "Reasonably foreseeable" is not a fixed point on the scale of probability. As Lord Reid explained in *Overseas Tankship (U.K.) Ltd. v. Miller Steamship Co. Pty. (The Wagon Mound No. 2)* [1967] 1 A.C. 617, 642 other factors have to be considered in deciding whether a given probability of injury generates a duty to take steps to eliminate the risk. In that case, the matters which the Privy Council took into account were whether avoiding the risk would have involved the defendant in undue cost or required him to abstain from some otherwise reasonable activity. In *Bolton v. Stone* [1951] A.C. 850 there was a foreseeable risk that someone might one day be hit by a cricket ball but avoiding this risk would have required the club to incur very large expense or stop playing cricket. The House of Lords decided that the risk was not such that a reasonable man should have taken either of these steps to eliminate it. On the other hand, in *The Wagon Mound No. 2*, the risk was caused by the fact that the defendant's ship had, without any need or excuse, discharged oil into Sydney Harbour. The risk of the oil catching fire would have been regarded as extremely small. But, said Lord Reid, at p. 642:

> "it does not follow that, no matter what the circumstances may be, it is justifiable to neglect a risk of such a small magnitude. A reasonable man would only neglect such a risk if he had some valid reason for doing so, e.g., that it would involve considerable expense to eliminate the risk. He would weigh the risk against the difficulty of eliminating it."

. . . The council admit that they should have removed the boat. True, they make this concession solely on the ground that there was a risk that children would suffer minor injuries if the rotten planking gave way beneath them. But the concession shows that if there were a wider risk, the council would have had to incur no additional expense to eliminate it. They would only have had to do what they admit they should have done anyway. On the principle as stated by Lord Reid, the wider risk would also fall within the scope of the council's duty unless it was different in kind from that which should have been foreseen (like the fire and pollution risks in *The Wagon Mound No. 1*) and either wholly unforeseeable (as the fire risk was assumed to be in *The Wagon Mound No. 1*) or so remote that it could be "brushed aside as far-fetched:" see Lord Reid in *The Wagon Mound No. 2* [1969] 2 A.C. 617.

I agree with my noble and learned friend, Lord Steyn, and the judge that one cannot so describe the risk that children coming upon an abandoned boat and trailer would suffer injury in some way other than by falling through the planks. . . .

. . . In the present case, the rotten condition of the boat had a significance beyond the particular danger it created. It proclaimed the boat and its trailer as abandoned, res nullius, there for the taking, to make of them whatever use the rich fantasy life of children might suggest.

In the Court of Appeal, Lord Woolf M.R. observed, at p. 1553, that there seemed to be no case of which counsel were aware "where want of care on the part of a defendant was established but a plaintiff, who was a child, had failed to succeed because the circumstances of the accident were not foreseeable." I would suggest that this is for a combination of three reasons: first, because a finding or admission of want of care on the part of the defendant establishes that it would have cost the defendant no more trouble to avoid the injury which happened than he should in any case have taken; secondly, because in such circumstances the defendants will be liable for the materialisation of even relatively small risks of a different kind, and thirdly, because it has been repeatedly said in cases about children that their ingenuity in finding unexpected ways of doing mischief to themselves and others should never be underestimated. For these reasons, I think that the judge's broad description of the risk as being that children would "meddle with the boat at the risk of some physical injury" was the correct one to adopt on the facts of this case. The actual injury fell within that description and I would therefore allow the appeal.

We should notice two important features of the discussion by Lord Hoffmann above. First, at the beginning of the extract, Lord Hoffmann adopts terminology that was not present in *The Wagon Mound* but which he treats as compatible with that decision: was the damage within the scope of the duty owed by the defendants? Alternatively, was it 'within the risk' against which the defendant should protect the claimant? The language of 'within the risk' is familiar from Williams' article on 'The Risk Principle' (above). But the language of 'scope of duty' is a relatively new development. It was employed by Lord Hoffmann not only in this case, but also in the cases of *Reeves v Commissioner of Police for the Metropolis* [2000] 1 AC 360 and *South Australia Asset Management Co v York Montague Ltd* [1997] AC 191, both extracted in this chapter. Arguably, this development would allow us to interpret *The Wagon Mound*'s emphasis on foreseeability as just one aspect of a broader question, namely whether the damage suffered was within the scope of the duty. This as we will see may pave the way for *The Wagon Mound* to be updated.

Second, and much less helpfully, Lord Hoffmann then merged the question of remoteness with the question of breach. Since the defendants should in any event have removed the boat in order to avoid the admittedly foreseeable danger of injury, he argues that there is no reason to suggest that the defendants were free to leave the boat in place because there was only a small possibility that the sort of events in question might happen. The truth is that such an approach, if applied without the 'kind of damage' limitation, would effectively do away with any separate question of remoteness based on foreseeability or scope of duty, and would simply ask whether avoidance of the damage would have required any other precautions than those already required by the need to avoid the *foreseeable* injury. For example, it would lead to reversal of the decision in *The Wagon Mound (No 1)* itself, on the basis that avoidance of the serious risk of damage by fire (unforeseeable) required no further precautions than avoidance of the trivial risk associated with fouling (foreseeable). The oil should not have been released. Since there is no obvious intention to depart from *The Wagon Mound* in this case, the idea that the avoidance of the wider risk would cost no greater precautions than avoidance of the lesser and more foreseeable risk should only operate *together with* the requirement that the damage suffered should be of a 'foreseeable type'. In this case the foreseeable risk posed by the rotten boat was held to be that children 'would meddle with the boat at the risk of some physical injury'. The risk is very broadly defined. Lord Hoffmann in his closing remarks invites the conclusion that this is a special approach adapted to known sources of hazard to children, since in such a case all manner of accidents are to be expected.

Intervening Acts: What is a *Novus Actus Interveniens*?

Cases involving a human act which intervenes between the defendant's breach of duty, and the claimant's loss, have traditionally been addressed through the expression '*novus actus interveniens*' ('new intervening act'). Included in this section will be some instances where no damage would have occurred at all but for the intervening act (for example *Home Office v Dorset Yacht*, *Reeves v Commr of Police*); but there are also certain other cases where the intervention of a third party (or of the claimant) *adds to* the damage suffered, where there was some initial harm (*Knightley v Johns*; *Robinson v Post Office*; *McKew v Holland & Hannen & Cubbitts*). In some cases in both categories, the defendant is released from liability to the extent that the damage flows from the intervening act. In other cases, the defendant is held liable for the full extent of the damage.

Traditionally, the question in such cases has been whether the intervening act is to be held to amount to a 'new cause', 'breaking the chain of causation'. Clearly, this is a 'causal' idea, and it is the origin of the expressions *novus actus interveniens*, and *nova causa interveniens*. These expressions were singled out in *The Wagon Mound* as providing a 'conspicuous example' of the problems caused by the *Polemis* approach, leading (in words borrowed from Pollock) to the 'logical and metaphysical controversies that beset the idea of cause'. But here *The Wagon Mound* has singularly failed to replace the causal approach with any success. In these cases, the language of *novus actus* continues to be employed more often than the language of foreseeability. Can these cases be decided *without* recourse to the 'logical and metaphysical controversies' associated with causation?

Let us start by identifying how *The Wagon Mound* approach ought in principle to proceed if applied to such cases. As it has been interpreted in later cases such as *Hughes v Lord Advocate*, *The Wagon Mound* approach ought to hold that provided the type of damage suffered was in a practical sense foreseeable to the defendant at the time of the negligence, the causal sequence (including intervention by a third party) makes no difference. But it is clear that the intervention of a third party does make a difference to the analysis adopted. Foreseeability of the type of harm is not a guide to the result in such cases.

On several occasions, an attempt has been made to resolve cases in this area by reference to foreseeability. However, foreseeability in these cases was never used in the true *Wagon Mound* sense, where it was applied to the type of damage. Rather, it was asked whether *the chain of events* was foreseeable. Could the intervention of the third party have been foreseen? Also, 'foreseeability' no longer, in such cases, referred to the question of whether the *defendant* could have foreseen the intervention of the third party. This was the 'practical' sense of foreseeability that we mentioned above in our commentary on *The Wagon Mound*. Instead, foreseeability was judged with hindsight. But even with this change, the 'foreseeability' approach has not proved successful and it is suggested below that it has now been abandoned.

What other possibilities are there? It is possible that the broader causal approach of Hart and Honoré can provide assistance. As we saw, this approach retains a focus on causal language, while denying that this might lead to highly technical or 'metaphysical' solutions. On this approach, the relevant distinction to be drawn would be between 'normal' and 'abnormal' interventions. This would not necessarily tally with the distinction between interventions that are foreseeable and unforeseeable, nor between those that are negligent and non-negligent, nor between those that are deliberate and accidental. All such factors may be relevant, but none decisive. As such, this would leave much to the opinion of the deciding tribunal. This, however, appears to be an inevitable aspect of this category of case.

In some more recent cases, as well as a few older ones, a direct appeal to the purpose and extent of the relevant duty has been employed to resolve the issues. In some important respects, this emerging approach based on distinct duties and their scope is better suited to the more purposive and nuanced approach to establishing the duty of care to be found in current English law.

For convenience, we will break down our examination of 'intervening acts' into acts of third parties, and acts of the claimant.

Intervening Acts of Third Parties

In some of the cases discussed here, such as *Knightley v Johns* or *Lamb v Camden*, the initial negligence of the defendant provides the conditions for another party to cause more extensive damage. The question is whether these further effects are recoverable against the original defendant. In other cases, such as *Dorset Yacht v Home Office*, the defendant's negligence may consist in doing nothing to *prevent* a third party from causing harm. In the latter type of case, there will be a question concerning the nature of any *positive duty to act*.

Intervening Deliberate Acts: *Dorset Yacht v Home Office* [1970] AC 1004

In this case, a number of trainees (young offenders) were sent, under the control of three officers, to Brownsea Island on a training exercise. The officers were under instruction to keep the trainees in custody. However, the officers simply went to bed, leaving the trainees to their own devices. During the night, the trainees attempted to escape from the island and in the course of doing so they damaged the respondents' yacht. The claim in negligence was for property damage (to the yacht) caused by breach of the duty to maintain control over the trainees, all of whom had offending records and several of whom had a record of attempting escape.

Lord Reid, at 1027

. . . it is said that the respondents must fail because there is a general principle that no person can be responsible for the acts of another who is not his servant or acting on his behalf. But here the ground of liability is not responsibility for the acts of the escaping trainees; it is liability for damage caused by the carelessness of these officers in the knowledge that their carelessness would probably result in the trainees causing damage of this kind. So the question is really one of remoteness of damage. And I must consider to what extent the law regards the acts of another person as breaking the chain of causation between the defendant's carelessness and the damage to the plaintiff.

There is an obvious difference between a case where all the links between the carelessness and the damage are inanimate so that, looking back after the event, it can be seen that the damage was in fact the inevitable result of the careless act or omission and a case where one of the links is some human action. In the former case the damage was in fact caused by the careless conduct, however unforeseeable it might have been at the time that anything like that would happen. At one time the law was that unforeseeability was no defence: *In re Polemis and Furness, Withy & Co. Ltd.* [1921] 3 K.B. 560. But the law now is that there is no liability unless the damage was of a kind which was foreseeable: *Overseas Tankship (U.K.) Ltd. v. Morts Dock and Engineering Co. Ltd. (The Wagon Mound) (No. 1)* [1961] A.C. 388.

On the other hand, if human action (other than an instinctive reaction) is one of the links in the chain it cannot be said that, looking back, the damage was the inevitable result of the careless conduct. No one in practice accepts the possible philosophic view that everything that happens was predetermined. Yet it has never been the law that the intervention of human action always prevents the ultimate damage from being regarded as having been caused by the original carelessness. The convenient phrase novus actus interveniens denotes those cases where such action is regarded as breaking the chain and preventing the damage from being held to be caused by the careless conduct. But every day there are many cases where, although one of the connecting links is deliberate human action, the law has no difficulty in holding that the defendant's conduct caused the plaintiff loss.

> "There are some propositions which are beyond question in connection with this class of case. One is that human action does not per se sever the connected sequence of acts. The mere fact that human action intervenes does not prevent the sufferer from saying that injury which is due to that human action as one of the elements in the sequence is recoverable from the original wrongdoer" (*per* Lord Wright in *The Oropesa* [1943] P. 32, 37).

What, then, is the dividing line? Is it foreseeability or is it such a degree of probability as warrants the conclusion that the intervening human conduct was the natural and probable result of what preceded it? There is a world of difference between the two. If I buy a ticket in a lottery or enter a football pool it is foreseeable that I may win a very large prize—some competitor must win it. But, whatever hopes gamblers may entertain, no one could say that winning such a prize was a natural and probable result of entering such a competition.

Lord Reid considered the case law and continued (at 1030):

These cases show that, where human action forms one of the links between the original wrongdoing of the defendant and the loss suffered by the plaintiff, that action must at least have been something very likely to happen if it is not to be regarded as novus actus interveniens breaking the chain of causation. I do not think that a mere foreseeable possibility is or should be sufficient, for then the intervening human action can more properly be regarded as a new cause than as a consequence of the original wrongdoing. But if the intervening action was likely to happen I do not think that it can matter whether that action was innocent or tortious or criminal. Unfortunately, tortious or criminal action by a third party is often the "very kind of thing" which is likely to happen as a result of the wrongful or careless act of the defendant. And in the present case, on the facts which we must assume at this stage, I think that the taking of a boat by the escaping trainees and their unskilful navigation leading to damage to another vessel were the very kind of thing that these Borstal officers ought to have seen to be likely.

The officers were under a duty to keep the trainees under their control. But if that duty was breached, for what damage could the Home Office be held liable as employers of the officers? This was the remoteness question dealt with by Lord Reid in the extract above. Lord Reid's judgment (particularly the last paragraph above) is peppered by references to different ways of judging either foreseeability, or likelihood. A 'mere foreseeable likelihood' is dismissed as insufficient. Rather, the act of the third party 'must at least be very likely' to happen. Here, the attempted escape and consequent damage are treated as the 'very kind of thing' that the officers 'ought to have seen to be likely'.

This approach is ambiguous. It mentions not only foreseeability but also probability ('likelihood'). Alternatively, the expression 'the very kind of thing' that would be likely to happen could be taken to refer to the *reason* for imposing a positive duty of care to keep the trainees in custody. This would amount to a particular version of 'the risk principle'. The duty here is a particular and positive duty, to exercise control over a third party where the defendants had a specific responsibility in connection with that third party.

That the role of the expression 'the very kind of thing' might be better explained in terms of the purpose and scope of the duty, rather than in terms of degrees of foreseeability or likelihood, is reinforced by reference to the well-known case of *Stansbie v Troman* [1948] 2 KB 48. This case was decided well before *The Wagon Mound* but is generally accepted to be correct. A contractor carrying out decorations in the plaintiff's house was left alone and entrusted with a key; on going out, he left the door unsecured and burglars entered, stealing property. The case was one of breach of contract through negligent conduct, but the following explanation is of general importance to tort law:

Tucker LJ, at 51–2

[Counsel] referred to *Weld-Blundell v. Stephens* and, in particular, to the following passage in the speech of Lord Sumner: "In general (apart from special contracts and relations and the maxim respondeat superior), even though A. is in fault, he is not responsible for injury to C. which B., a stranger to him, deliberately chooses to do. Though A. may have given the occasion for B.'s mischievous activity, B. then becomes a new and independent cause." I do not think that Lord Sumner would have intended that very general statement to apply to the facts of a case such as the present where, as the judge points out, the act of negligence itself consisted in the failure to take reasonable care to guard against the very thing that in fact happened.

Perhaps the influence of *The Wagon Mound* led Lord Reid to superimpose onto this duty-oriented approach the confusing language of foreseeability and likelihood. In a sense, *Stansbie v Troman* vindicates a 'risk principle', but not a risk principle based on foreseeability. The purpose of the duty imposed is to prevent damage being done by a third party; therefore, such damage cannot be outside the risk for which the defendant is responsible.

The following case is rather different from *Dorset Yacht* because the defendants did not have control over the third party. It was not a case where it was suggested that they ought to have taken positive steps to control the third party (see the extract from Lord Denning's judgment, below). Rather, it was argued that they ought not to have provided the third party with the *opportunity* to cause foreseeable damage. And unlike the case of *Stansbie v Troman*, there was no contractual duty between plaintiff and defendant.

Lamb v Camden LBC [1981] QB 625

The defendants were alleged to have been negligent in causing the bursting of a water main which led to the flooding of the plaintiff's house together with physical damage. Because of the need for repairs, the house remained empty for some time. It was eventually invaded by squatters who caused considerable damage. The plaintiff sought to recover damages from the council for the damage caused by the squatters. At first instance, the official referee held that the damage by squatters was foreseeable to the council's servants when they damaged the water main, but that the damage was not recoverable because their actions were not 'likely'. This seems to be an attempt to apply certain of Lord Reid's dicta, above, but this would not seem to be a case where the damage is 'the very kind of thing' that would follow from the breach of duty. The judges in the Court of Appeal were agreed that the appeal by the owners of the house should be dismissed, but gave varying reasons as is illustrated by the extracts from two of the judgments below. In the first extract, Oliver LJ attempts to apply a test of reasonable foreseeability to the case of third party acts. In his view, instead of holding that the damage was 'foreseeable but not likely', the official referee should have held that the damage was 'not reasonably foreseeable' at all.

> **Oliver LJ,** at 642
>
> It cannot be said that you cannot foresee the possibility that people will do stupid or criminal acts, because people are constantly doing stupid or criminal acts. But the question is not what is foreseeable merely as a possibility but what would the reasonable man actually foresee if he thought about it, and all that Lord Reid seems to me to be saying [in the case of *Home Office v Dorset Yacht*] is that the hypothetical reasonable man in the position of the tortfeasor cannot be said to foresee the behaviour of another person unless that behaviour is such as would, viewed objectively, be very likely to occur. Thus, for instance, if by my negligent driving I damage another motorist's car, I suppose that theoretically I *could* foresee that, whilst he leaves it by the roadside to go and telephone his garage, some ill-intentioned passer-by may jack it up and remove the wheels. But I cannot think that it could be said that, merely because I have created the circumstances in which a theft might become possible, I ought reasonably to foresee that it would happen.

It seems obvious that Oliver LJ here proposes a *special* test—that the behaviour would be 'very likely to occur'—for use in determining the 'reasonable' foreseeability of a third party intervention. There is no such requirement for foreseeability to be based on something 'very likely' in the general run of negligence cases. As exemplified by *Bolton v Stone* and *The Wagon Mound (No 2)*, some low probability events are nevertheless treated as foreseeable. Oliver LJ's approach may therefore turn on a highly disputable assumption, that the effects of third party interventions are in some respect less 'reasonably' foreseeable than other events, despite the fact (as he notes) that 'people are constantly doing stupid or criminal acts'.

Alternatively, the reason for requiring a special test may be nothing to do with either foreseeability, or likelihood. As we suggested in respect of *Dorset Yacht* above, foreseeability may be a distraction. Can Lord Denning's judgment in the same case offer us an improved approach?

Lord Denning, at 636–8

The truth

The truth is that all these three—duty, remoteness and causation—are all devices by which the courts limit the range of liability for negligence or nuisance. As I said recently, in *Compania Financiera "Soleada" S.A. v. Hamoor Tanker Corporation Inc.* [1981] 1 W.L.R. 274, 281E–F. " . . . it is not every consequence of a wrongful act which is the subject of compensation. The law has to draw a line somewhere." Sometimes it is done by limiting the range of the persons to whom duty is owed. Sometimes it is done by saying that there is a break in the chain of causation. At other times it is done by saying that the consequence is too remote to be a head of damage. All these devices are useful in their way. But ultimately it is a question of policy for the judges to decide . . .

A question of policy

Return to the present case

Looking at the question as one of policy, I ask myself: whose job was it to do something to keep out the squatters? And, if they got in, to evict them? To my mind the answer is clear. It was the job of the owner of the house, Mrs. Lamb, through her agents. That is how everyone in the case regarded it. It has never been suggested in the pleadings or elsewhere that it was the job of the council. No one ever wrote to the council asking them to do it. The council were not in occupation of the house. They had no right to enter it. All they had done was to break the water main outside and cause the subsidence.

. . . On broader grounds of policy, I would add this: the criminal acts here—malicious damage and theft—are usually covered by insurance. By this means the risk of loss is spread throughout the community. It does not fall too heavily on one pair of shoulders alone. The insurers take the premium to cover just this sort of risk and should not be allowed, by subrogation, to pass it on to others.

In the final paragraph above, Lord Denning suggests that the 'remoteness' analysis in such cases is really a mechanism for addressing the policy issues associated with liability for third party actions. Policy is of course a matter of judgment and opinion and it will vary from case to case. So in a sense, this insight provides relatively little guidance to the likely outcome in future cases. On the other hand, the penultimate paragraph above could be seen as concerned, not with open-ended and general 'policy', but with duty analysis wholly consistent with the modern approach to be found in *Caparo v Dickman*. As we saw, *Caparo* asks for positive reasons to hold the defendant responsible for the damage done, precisely including questions concerning the appropriateness of identifying the defendant as the person who ought to take precautions.

A duty-based approach to the question of third party interventions in the form of criminal acts is also encapsulated in the following extract.

Perl (Exporters) Ltd v Camden LBC [1984] 1 QB 342

The defendants left their premises unsecured because of a broken lock. Burglars gained access to the defendants' premises and by knocking a hole in the wall made their way into the adjoining premises. These premises were let by the defendants to the plaintiffs, who were retailers of knitwear. Garments were stolen. The judgment of Goff LJ makes a break with remoteness analysis based on 'foreseeability', and perceives the issues instead in terms of whether a *duty* is owed.

Robert Goff LJ, at 358–60

There may well be cases in which it can be said that the occupier of property can reasonably foresee that, if he leaves his property unprotected thieves may enter and thereby gain access to neighbouring property. For example, it may be notorious that burglars are operating in a certain part of a town; and an occupier of premises may reasonably foresee that, if he goes away for a weekend and leaves his house unprotected—perhaps if it is empty or, to take an example considered in argument, if he always leaves a window open for his cat—a burglar may enter and thereby work unmolested over the weekend to gain access to the house next door where there is a valuable collection of pictures. Even so, in my judgment, there are considerations in such circumstances which ought to negative the broad duty of care for which the plaintiffs' counsel contended.

The vital feature in the type of case under consideration is, as I see it, that the plaintiffs are seeking to render the defendants liable in negligence for the wrongdoing of a third party. Now there may indeed be circumstances where a person may be liable for a third party's wrongdoing. He may of course be liable in contract (see *Stansbie v. Troman* [1948] 2 K.B. 48); he may be liable under the Occupiers' Liability Act 1957 . . . ; he may be liable in nuisance, if he causes or permits persons to gather on his land, and they impair his neighbour's enjoyment of his land . . . ; and he may be vicariously liable for the third party's wrongdoing. He may even be liable in negligence, when the wrongdoer is a person who, by virtue of a special relationship, is under his control: see *Home Office v. Dorset Yacht Co. Ltd.* [1970] A.C. 1004. Speaking for myself, I do not rule out the possibility that there are other circumstances in which a person may be liable in negligence for the wrongdoing of a third party . . . . I have in mind certain cases where the defendant presents the wrongdoer with the means to commit the wrong . . . But such cases are very different from the present case, where the allegation is that the defendants failed to exercise reasonable care to prevent a third party from causing damage to the plaintiffs. In *Smith v. Leurs*, 70 C.L.R. 256, in a passage which was cited with approval in *Home Office v. Dorset Yacht Co. Ltd.* [1970] A.C. 1004, 1038, 1055, 1063, Dixon J. said, at p. 262:

> "The general rule is that one man is under no duty of controlling another man to prevent his doing damage to a third. There are, however, special relations which are the source of a duty of this nature."

It is of course true that in the present case the plaintiffs do not allege that the defendants should have controlled the thieves who broke into their storeroom. But they do allege that the defendants should have exercised reasonable care to prevent them from gaining access through their own premises; and in my judgment the statement of principle by Dixon J. is equally apposite in such a case. I know of no case where it has been held, in the absence of a special relationship, that the defendant was liable in negligence for having failed to prevent a third party from wrongfully causing damage to the plaintiff. . . . Indeed, the consequences of accepting the plaintiffs' submission in the present case are so startling, that I have no hesitation in rejecting the suggestion that there is a duty of care upon occupiers of property to prevent persons from entering their property who might thereby obtain access to neighbouring property. Is every occupier of a terraced house under a duty to his neighbours to shut his windows or lock his door when he goes out, or to keep access to his cellars secure, or even to remove his fire escape, at the risk of being held liable in damages if thieves thereby obtain access to his own house and thence to his neighbour's house? I cannot think that the law imposes any such duty.

Goff LJ leaves open the possibility that, in respect of risks that are 'obvious' or 'very likely', there will be liability for carelessly providing an opportunity for others to do harm. But it is an attractive feature of Goff LJ's approach that it does not suggest that any degree of foreseeability will generally justify liability for the deliberate acts of a third party. Rather, there is generally no duty to prevent their actions. I owe no duty to my neighbour that would prevent me from leaving a window open for my cat, even if it is 'foreseeable'—and perhaps 'reasonably foreseeable'—that someone will gain access through the window to my property and thus to my neighbour's. The approaches of Lord Reid in *Dorset Yacht*, and of Oliver LJ in *Lamb v Camden*, are perhaps a reflection of negligence law's experiment with foreseeability as a generalizing guide to liability in the period surrounding *The Wagon Mound* and, later, *Anns v Merton*. As such, they probably belong in the past.

no duty,
↓
rather than
remoteness
issue

A similar approach was adopted by Lord Goff in *Smith v Littlewoods* [1987] AC 241.

Lord Goff

It is very tempting to try to solve all problems of negligence by reference to an all-embracing criterion of foreseeability, thereby effectively reducing all decisions in this field to questions of fact. But this comfortable solution is, alas, not open to us. The law has to accommodate all the untidy complexity of life; and there are circumstances where considerations of practical justice impel us to reject a general imposition of liability for foreseeable damage. An example of this phenomenon is to be found in cases of pure economic loss, where the so-called "floodgates" argument . . . compels us to recognise that to impose a general liability based on a simple criterion of foreseeability would impose an intolerable burden upon defendants. . . . As the present case shows, another example of this phenomenon is to be found in cases where the plaintiff has suffered damage through the deliberate wrongdoing of a third party; and it is not surprising that once again we should find the courts seeking to identify specific situations in which liability can properly be imposed. Problems such as these are solved in Scotland, as in England, by means of the mechanism of the duty of care; though we have nowadays to appreciate that the broad general principle of liability for foreseeable damage is so widely applicable that the function of the duty of care is not so much to identify cases where liability is imposed as to identify those where it is not. . . .

Attempted Rescues

A number of cases have arisen where third parties have attempted to ease a situation created by the negligence of the defendant, thereby inadvertently causing further damage either to themselves, or to others. These can be categorized as 'rescue' cases. In general, an attempted rescue will not amount to a *novus actus*, since it is in many cases both a foreseeable and a 'natural and probable' result of the negligently created situation. Even where the rescuer has behaved in a manner that could ordinarily be described as careless, the law will generally be reluctant to release a negligent party from his obligation to compensate a rescuer who is injured: see for example *Videan v BTC* [1963] 2 QB 650. But there are limits to the law's protective stance. In *Cutler v United Dairies* [1933] 2 KB 297, the Court of Appeal found that the plaintiff's attempt to hold the head of an agitated horse amounted to a *novus actus interveniens*, and that he assumed the risk of injury, even though the driver of the horse had called for help. Soon after, however, in *Haynes v Harwood* [1935] 1 KB 146, a police officer's effort to hold a horse in a crowded street was held not to be a *novus actus*, so that he could recover from the defendants for his injuries.

Haynes v Harwood is more in tune with the general law on rescuers. In general, rescuers are treated as foreseeable; it is accepted that they are often acting in the heat of the moment so that the standard of care applied to them must take this into account; and it is recognized that they are often put in the position of deciding whether to attempt a rescue by the circumstances that confront them.

In *The Oropesa* ([1943] P 32; [1943] 1 All ER 211), arising from an attempt to salvage a negligently damaged ship after a collision at sea, it was found that there was nothing unreasonable about the decision to attempt salvage, even though it resulted in the death of one of the ship's crew. The salvage attempt did not break the chain of causation. In the course of his judgment, Lord Wright attempted to express a general principle in the following terms. This paragraph has a good claim to deserve the deeply critical remarks of Lord Simonds in *The Wagon Mound* when he rejected the language of causation as 'ugly and barely intelligible':

Lord Wright, at 39

If the master and the deceased in the present case had done something which was outside the exigencies of the emergency, whether from miscalculation or from error, the plaintiffs would be debarred from saying that a new cause had not intervened. The question is not whether there was new negligence, but whether there was a new cause. . . . To break the chain of causation it must be shown that there is something which I will call ultroneous, something unwarrantable, a new cause which disturbs the sequence of events, something which can be described as either unreasonable or extraneous or extrinsic. I doubt whether the law can be stated more precisely than that.

This shows the hallmarks of the *Re Polemis* approach. It takes refuge in unfamiliar language in order to describe what will constitute a break in the chain of causation, while offering no precise tools for deciding whether the acts in question fit their description. But has *The Wagon Mound* test of 'foreseeability' made the task any easier in respect of attempted rescues?

In *The Oropesa*, although the salvage attempt may have been 'mistaken', it was not 'unreasonable'. The next, more recent case involves a situation where the attempted rescue *was* (in the method of its execution) unreasonable.

Knightley v Johns [1982] 1 WR 349

In this 'unusual and unlucky accident', as Stephenson LJ described it (at 353), a car driven negligently by the first defendant overturned in a tunnel. The fourth defendant, a police inspector attending the scene after the accident, apparently forgot to abide by a standing order which would require him to close the tunnel to traffic immediately. He therefore sent two police constables on motor cycles to ride back through the tunnel against the traffic in order to close it. The plaintiff, one of the two police motorcyclists, was hit head-on by the second defendant's car, which was travelling at around 35–40 mph through the tunnel. Did the carelessness of the police inspector (the fourth defendant) operate to break the chain of causation?

Stephenson LJ, at 366–7

. . . The question to be asked is accordingly whether that whole sequence of events is a natural and probable consequence of the first defendant's negligence and a reasonably foreseeable result of it. In answering the question it is helpful but not decisive to consider which of these events were deliberate choices to do positive acts and which were mere omissions or failures to act; which acts and omissions were innocent mistakes or miscalculations and which were negligent having regard to the pressures and the gravity of the emergency and the need to act quickly. Negligent conduct is more likely to break the chain of causation than conduct which is not; positive acts will more easily constitute new causes than inaction. Mistakes and mischances are to be expected when human beings, however well trained, have to cope with a crisis; what exactly they will be cannot be predicted, but if those which occur are natural the wrongdoer cannot, I think, escape responsibility for them and their consequences simply by calling them improbable or unforeseeable. He must accept the risk of some unexpected mischances: see *Baker v. T. E. Hopkins & Son Ltd.* [1959] 1 W.L.R. 966, 984 *per* Willmer L.J. and *Chadwick's* case [1967] 1 W.L.R. 912, 921 *per* Waller J. But what mischances?

The answer to this difficult question must be dictated by common sense rather than logic on the facts and circumstances of each case. In this case it must be answered in the light of the true view to be taken of the events leading up to Inspector Sommerville's acts—or rather his act and omission—and the plaintiff's—and Police Constable Easthope's—acts. I have expressed my view of all these links in the chain leading from the first defendant's negligence to the plaintiff's collision with the second defendant. I have decided, respectfully disagreeing with the deputy judge, that the inspector was negligent in failing to close the tunnel and, respectfully agreeing with the deputy judge, that the plaintiff was not negligent in riding the wrong way after being ordered to do so by the inspector or in deciding on the spur of the moment to ride his motorcycle close to the wall in lane 1.

I am also of the opinion that the inspector's negligence was not a concurrent cause running with the first defendant's negligence, but a new cause disturbing the sequence of events leading from the first defendant's overturning of his car to the plaintiff's accident and interrupting the effect of it. This would, I think, have been so had the inspector's negligence stood alone. Coming as it did on top of the muddle and misunderstanding of Mr. Williams's telephone call and followed by the inspector's order to remedy his own negligence by a dangerous manoeuvre, it was the real cause of the plaintiff's injury and made that injury too remote from the first defendant's wrongdoing to be a consequence of it.

In the long run the question is, as Lord Reid said in the *Dorset Yacht Co.* case [1970] A.C. 1004, one of remoteness of damage, to be answered as has so often been stated, not by the logic of philosophers but by the common sense of plain men . . . In my judgment, too much happened here, too much went wrong, the chapter of accidents and mistakes was too long and varied, to impose on the first defendant liability for what happened to the plaintiff in discharging his duty as a police officer, although it would not have happened had not the first defendant negligently overturned his car. The ordinary course of things took an extraordinary course. The length and the irregularities of the line leading from the first accident to the second have no parallel in the reported rescue cases, in all of which the plaintiff succeeded in establishing the original wrongdoer's liability. It was natural, it was probable, it was foreseeable, it was indeed certain, that the police would come to the overturned car and control the tunnel traffic. It was also natural and probable and foreseeable that some steps would be taken in controlling the traffic and clearing the tunnel and some things be done that might be more courageous than sensible. The reasonable hypothetical observer would anticipate some human errors, some forms of what might be called folly, perhaps even from trained police officers, and some unusual and unexpected accidents in the course of their rescue duties. But would he anticipate such a result as this from so many errors as these, so many departures from the common sense procedure prescribed by the standing order for just such an emergency as this? I can see that it is a question on which the opinions of plain men and women in the jury-box and judges who have now to perform their function may reasonably differ. I can only say that in my opinion, the deputy judge's decision carries the first defendant's responsibility too far . . .

This extract shows again that *The Wagon Mound* cannot be regarded as having eased the situation in respect of intervening acts. Stephenson LJ employs a wide variety of language in order to seek to explain his conclusion that the chain of causation was broken. Among these is the language of foreseeability, but also of that which is 'natural and probable'—language that is equally associated with *Re Polemis* and which was supposed to be superseded by foreseeability as a result of *The Wagon Mound*. Also prominently featured is the language of 'chains of events'; and the negligence of the fourth defendant is referred to as 'the real cause' of the accident. Clearly, this is 'causal' language. We can glean from this case that a very unusual sequence of events involving the carelessness of a third party rescuer (especially but not only if this involves an extended sequence of links) may be sufficient to make the damage too remote a consequence of the defendant's initial negligence; we can also be clear that it will not be sufficient simply to show some fault, carelessness, error or perhaps even 'folly' on the part of third parties after the event, so simple negligence will not do. And it is also clear that the defendant must accept the risk of *some* 'expected mischances'. A complex series of unexpected events of this nature *may* however be sufficient to break the causal chain. As to when that will be the case, Stephenson LJ suggests that this will be a matter of opinion.

This messy solution in the case of *Knightley* is consistent with the prediction of Glanville Williams. In 'The Risk Principle', to which we have referred from time to time in this chapter, Williams described cases like this one (where the initial harm of the defendant's negligence is added to in rather unexpected ways involving the acts of a third party) as cases of 'ulterior harm'. In respect of these cases, he conceded that the foreseeability approach is in effect seeking to replicate a more 'causal' approach. He also accepted that (just like the causal approach) foreseeability would not give a tidy answer:

(P. 200) In respect of ulterior harms . . . I think that Hart and Honoré are right in saying that the test of foreseeability is a way of distinguishing between normal and abnormal consequences . . . The question is whether the harm is within ordinary experience. I would add, however, that the distinction is governed to some extent not only by statistical considerations but by notions of policy. That this is an imprecise rule is shown by the divergent results obtained by different courts at different times. It is here that we reach the limits of predictability in determining the consequences for which a tortfeasor will be held liable.

Williams also predicted an important element of the approach in *Knightley v Johns*, which is that negligence or even 'folly' on the part of a third party will not *necessarily* lead to a break in the chain of causation. He suggested, in particular, that where it was foreseeable that the plaintiff would require medical treatment as a result of the defendant's negligence, even *negligent* medical treatment might sometimes be within the general risk and would not necessarily break the chain of causation (p. 200, n. 49).

In *Robinson v Post Office* [1974] 1 WLR 1176, the plaintiff slipped on an oily ladder, and suffered a grazed shin. This injury was treated as being caused through the defendant employer's breach of duty. A doctor administered an anti-tetanus injection which, due to a pre-existing susceptibility on the part of the plaintiff, resulted in encephalitis and permanent disability. It was found that although there was some negligence on the part of the doctor, that negligence was not an operating cause of the plaintiff's injuries because it did not pass the 'but-for' test: even if the doctor had followed approved procedures, these would still not have indicated that the plaintiff's particular reaction was likely. This in turn was taken to be significant in holding that the employers were fully liable in that the chain of causation was not broken; the actions of the doctor in administering the injection were not a '*novus actus*'. However, it seems from the approach in *Knightley v Johns*, supported by the views of Glanville Williams, that even if medical negligence were to be established, this need not necessarily amount to a *novus actus*.

Intervening Act of the Claimant: *McKew v Holland & Hannen & Cubitts (Scotland) Ltd* [1969] 3 All ER 1621

The appellant sustained injury in the course of his employment for which the defendants were liable. The injuries were mild although his leg was inclined to 'give way' from time to time. He would have recovered within two weeks or so but for a subsequent accident which left him with permanent injuries. The appellant decided to attempt to descend a steep staircase without a handrail and without assistance. His leg gave way, he attempted to leap down the stairs, and in this way he suffered extensive injuries. In Lord Reid's judgment, the decision to attempt such a manoeuvre (rather than the manner in which he did it) meant that the appellant's own act amounted to a *novus actus interveniens*.

Lord Reid

In my view the law is clear. If a man is injured in such a way that his leg may give way at any moment he must act reasonably and carefully. It is quite possible that in spite of all reasonable care his leg may give way in circumstances such that as a result he sustains further injury. Then that second injury was caused by his disability which in turn was caused by the defender's fault. But if the injured man acts unreasonably he cannot hold the defender liable for injury caused by his own unreasonable conduct. His unreasonable conduct is novus actus interveniens. The chain of causation has been broken and what follows must be regarded as caused by his own conduct and not by the defender's fault or the disability caused by it. Or one may say that unreasonable conduct of the pursuer and what follows from it is not the natural and probable result of the original fault of the defender or of the ensuing disability. I do not think that foreseeability comes into this. A defender is not liable for a consequence of a kind which is not foreseeable. But it does not follow that he is liable for every consequence which a reasonable man could foresee. What can be foreseen depends almost entirely on the facts of the case, and it is often easy to foresee unreasonable conduct or some other novus actus interveniens as being quite likely. But that does not mean that the defender must pay for damage caused by the novus actus. It only leads to trouble that if one tries to graft on to the concept of foreseeability some rule of law to the effect that a wrongdoer is not bound to foresee something which in fact he could readily foresee as quite likely to happen. For it is not at all unlikely or unforeseeable that an active man who has suffered such a disability will take some quite unreasonable risk. But if he does he cannot hold the defender liable for the consequences.

This extract makes clear that the issue of the claimant's own intervening acts does not turn on foreseeability. The claimant must act reasonably, even if unreasonable behaviour is foreseeable. The decision seems harsh, and it also seems inconsistent with the availability of a partial defence in the form of contributory negligence (Law Reform (Contributory Negligence) Act 1945). The difficult relationship between contributory negligence, and causation issues, is discussed in Chapter 5.

Next we extract a very significant decision of the House of Lords. This confirms that there is no general rule to the effect that the claimant's acts will break the chain of causation if they are not reasonable. But the precise solution adopted here will apply to a limited range of cases.

Reeves v Commissioner of Police for the Metropolis [2000] 1 AC 360

The deceased was held in custody in a police cell. Police officers had been warned that he might commit suicide, although when attended by a doctor he was found not to be showing signs of clinical depression or other psychiatric disorder. He could be regarded as being at risk, but of sound mind. The deceased took advantage of the fact that the flap of his cell door had been left open, and hanged himself. The House of Lords held that his suicide did not constitute a *novus actus interveniens*, and that his death was caused by the officers' breach of their duty to protect him. Damages were reduced on account of his contributory negligence, which can only be the case if there is considered to be 'fault' on both sides (Law Reform (Contributory Negligence) Act 1945, s 1(1), Chapter 5).

Lord Hoffmann, at 367–9

The commissioner [of police] appeals to your Lordships' House. Mr. Pannick argued two points on his behalf. The first was the question of causation: was the breach of duty by the police a cause of Mr. Lynch's death? The way he put the answer was to say that the deliberate act of suicide, while of sound mind, was a novus actus interveniens which negatived the casual connection between the breach of duty and the death. He said at first that he was going to argue the application of the maxim volenti non fit injuria as a separate point. But when it came down to it, he accepted that if the breach of duty was a cause of the death, he could not succeed on volenti non fit injuria. I think that is right. In the present case, volenti non fit injuria can only mean that Mr. Lynch voluntarily caused his own death to the exclusion of any causal effect on the part of what was done by the police. So I think it all comes to the same thing: was the breach of duty by the police a cause of the death?

On the first question, Mr. Pannick relied upon the general principle stated in *Hart and Honoré, Causation in the Law*, 2nd ed. (1985), p. 136: "the free, deliberate and informed act or omission of a human being, intended to exploit the situation created by a defendant, negatives casual connection." However, as *Hart and Honoré* also point out, at pp. 194–204, there is an exception to this undoubted rule in the case in which the law imposes a duty to guard against loss caused by the free, deliberate and informed act of a human being. It would make non-sense of the existence of such a duty if the law were to hold that the occurrence of the very act which ought to have been prevented negatived causal connection between the breach of duty and the loss. This principle has been recently considered by your Lordships' House in *Environment Agency (formerly National Rivers Authority) v. Empress Car Co. (Abertillery) Ltd.* [1998] 2 W.L.R. 350. In that case, examples are given of cases in which liability has been imposed for causing events which were the immediate consequence of the deliberate acts of third parties but which the defendant had a duty to prevent or take reasonable care to prevent.

Mr. Pannick accepted this principle when the deliberate act was that of a third party. But he said that it was different when it was the act of the plaintiff himself. Deliberately inflicting damage on oneself had to be an act which negatived causal connection with anything which had gone before.

This argument is based upon the sound intuition that there is a difference between protecting people against harm caused to them by third parties and protecting them against harm which they inflict upon themselves. It reflects the individualist philosophy of the common law. People of full age and sound understanding must look after themselves and take responsibility for their actions. This philosophy expresses itself in the fact that duties to safeguard from harm deliberately caused by others are unusual and a duty to protect a person of full understanding from causing harm to himself is very rare indeed. But, once it is admitted that this is the rare case in which such a duty is owed, it seems to me self-contradictory to say that the breach could not have been a cause of the harm because the victim caused it to himself.

Morritt L.J. drew a distinction between a prisoner who was of sound mind and one who was not. He said, at p. 190, that when a prisoner was of sound mind, "I find it hard to see how there is any material increase in the risk in any causative sense." In *Kirkham v. Chief Constable of the Greater Manchester Police* [1990] 2 Q.B. 283, 289–290 Lloyd L.J. said much the same. It seems to me, however, they were really saying that the police should not owe a person of sound mind a duty to take reasonable care to prevent him from committing suicide. If he wants to take his life, that is his business. He is a responsible human being and should accept the intended consequences of his acts without blaming anyone else. Volenti non fit injuria. The police might owe a general moral duty not to provide any prisoner with the means of committing suicide, whether he is sound mind or not. Such a duty might even be enforceable by disciplinary measures. But the police did not owe Mr. Lynch, a person of sound mind, a duty of care so as to enable him or his widow to bring an action in damages for its breach.

My Lords, I can understand this argument, although I do not agree with it. It is not, however, the position taken by the commissioner. He accepts that he owed a duty of care to Mr. Lynch to take reasonable care to prevent him from committing suicide. Mr. Lynch could not rely on a duty owed to some other hypothetical prisoner who was of unsound mind. The commissioner does not seek to withdraw this concession on the ground that Mr. Lynch has been found to have been of sound mind. For my part, I think that the commissioner is right not to make this distinction. The difference between being of sound and unsound mind, while appealing to lawyers who like clear-cut rules, seems to me inadequate to deal with the complexities of human psychology in the context of the stresses caused by imprisonment. The duty, as I have said, is a very unusual one, arising from the complete control which the police or prison authorities have over the prisoner, combined with the special danger of people in prison taking their own lives.

Mr. Pannick also suggested that the principle of human autonomy might be infringed by holding the commissioner liable. Autonomy means that every individual is sovereign over himself and cannot be denied the right to certain kinds of behaviour, even if intended to cause his own death. On this principle, if Mr. Lynch had decided to go on hunger strike, the police would not have been entitled to administer forcible feeding. But autonomy does not mean that he would have been entitled to demand to be given poison, or that the police would not have been entitled to control his environment in non-invasive ways calculated to make suicide more difficult. If this would not infringe the principle of autonomy, it cannot be infringed by the police being under a duty to take such steps. In any case, this argument really goes to the existence of the duty which the commissioner admits rather than to the question of causation.

The most important feature of the approach taken here is that it prioritizes the particular duty in question, which was conceded by the police commissioner to be owed to the deceased. If a prisoner at risk who commits suicide is held solely responsible for the consequences of his actions in these circumstances, then the well-recognized duty to protect prisoners who are at risk of suicide would be entirely empty of content. The actions of the deceased were readily foreseeable, but this is not the reason given by Lord Hoffmann in the extract above, just as Lord Reid rejected foreseeability as sufficient to extend the defendant's liability in cases of first party intervening acts, in the *McKew* case. Rather, this is a case where the purpose of the duty is to protect the recipient of the duty against harm done to himself. (See further discussion in Chapter 5.)

Conclusion: Intervening Acts

Foreseeability does not provide a sufficient criterion for determining whether there is a *novus actus*. In fact, foreseeability misses the point that needs to be resolved in such cases, which appears to be one of attribution. 'Common sense' causal principles along the lines suggested by Hart and Honoré may provide a part of the answer by focusing our attention on 'normal' or 'abnormal' events, rather than the culpability or otherwise of those who intervene. As Glanville Williams concedes, this judgment will be a personal one on the facts of the case and in respect of these cases, 'the limits of predictability' have been reached. An alternative is to approach the question of *novus actus* in the light of an analysis of the purpose and scope of the duty of care. The language used by Lord Reid in *Dorset Yacht*, where he described the incident as 'the very kind of thing' that would be foreseen, could be taken to reflect such an approach, as can the case of *Stansbie v Troman*. In *Dorset Yacht*, the approach was only obscured by the language of foreseeability and probability employed. Duty analysis is also apparent in the cases of *Perl Exporters* (Goff LJ) and *Reeves v Commissioner of Police for the Metropolis* (Lord Hoffmann). Analysis of such cases cannot proceed on the basis of foreseeability, but is more in tune with the *Caparo* approach since it is dependent on consideration of the nature, scope, and purpose of the duty owed by the defendant. This brings us conveniently to a compatible development in respect of a different category of remoteness case.

6.4 'SCOPE OF DUTY' ANALYSIS

In his article 'The Road From Morocco', extracted above, Davies contended that if there was any injustice created by the remoteness test in *Re Polemis*, it stemmed from the development of over-extensive and non-specific duties of care. *The Wagon Mound* could be said to be a response to this development; perhaps also it shared the general optimism of the period which led to a ground-swell of support for generalization in the law of tort and in the tort of negligence in particular. In more recent years, the concept of 'duty' has become more specific to particular circumstances. Perhaps it is time to update *The Wagon Mound*, to reflect this change in the approach to duty.

The following decision, like the cases of *Jolley* and *Reeves*, gives priority to analysis of the 'scope of the duty'. Unlike those cases, it marks a departure from traditional approaches in order to resolve a new problem. That problem is partly created by the evolution of duty analysis in the field of economic losses. For example, where information is relied upon, the duty is owed only in respect of reliance for certain defined purposes (see *Caparo v Dickman*, above). The solution reached could be seen as a version of the 'risk principle', amended to take account of change in the nature of the duty of care.

South Australia Asset Management Corporation v York Montague Ltd ('SAAMCO') [1997] AC 191; on Appeal from *Banque Bruxelles Lambert SA v Eagle Star Insurance Co Ltd*

This decision, which dealt with three appeals, raised questions of wide applicability concerning losses of value in the UK property market during the early 1990s. In each of the cases, it was found at first instance that the defendants had negligently over-valued certain properties and that the plaintiffs in reliance on these valuations had advanced loans secured upon the properties. Subsequently, the borrowers defaulted and the lenders' security proved to be worth less than the sums advanced. A general fall in the market value of property had enhanced the losses suffered. Would the valuers be liable for the full extent of the losses suffered, or only for some portion of those losses?

Lord Hoffmann, at 210–13

My Lords, the three appeals before the House raise a common question of principle. What is the extent of the liability of a valuer who has provided a lender with a negligent overvaluation of the property offered as security for the loan? The facts have two common features. The first is that if the lender had known the true value of the property, he would not have lent. The second is that a fall in the property market after the date of the valuation greatly increased the loss which the lender eventually suffered.

The Court of Appeal (*Banque Bruxelles Lambert S.A. v. Eagle Star Insurance Co. Ltd.* [1995] Q.B. 375) decided that in a case in which the lender would not otherwise have lent (which they called a "no-transaction" case), he is entitled to recover the difference between the sum which he lent, together with a reasonable rate of interest, and the net sum which he actually got back. The valuer bears the whole risk of a transaction which, but for his negligence, would not have happened. He is therefore liable for all the loss attributable to a fall in the market. They distinguished what they called a "successful transaction" case, in which the evidence shows that if the lender had been correctly advised, he would still have lent a lesser sum on the same security. In such a case, the lender can recover only the difference between what he has actually lost and what he would have lost if he had lent the lesser amount. Since the fall in the property market is a common element in both the actual and the hypothetical calculations, it does not increase the valuer's liability.

The valuers appeal. They say that a valuer provides an estimate of the value of the property at the date of the valuation. He does not undertake the role of a prophet. It is unfair that merely because for one reason or other the lender would not otherwise have lent, the valuer should be saddled with the whole risk of the transaction, including a subsequent fall in the value of the property.

Much of the discussion, both in the judgment of the Court of Appeal and in argument at the Bar, has assumed that the case is about the correct measure of damages for the loss which the lender has suffered . . .

I think that this was the wrong place to begin. Before one can consider the principle on which one should calculate the damages to which a plaintiff is entitled as compensation for loss, it is necessary to decide for what kind of loss he is entitled to compensation. A correct description of the loss for which the valuer is liable must precede any consideration of the measure of damages. For this purpose it is better to begin at the beginning and consider the lender's cause of action.

The lender sues on a contract under which the valuer, in return for a fee, undertakes to provide him with certain information. Precisely what information he has to provide depends of course upon the terms of the individual contract. There is some dispute on this point in respect of two of the appeals, to which I shall have to return. But there is one common element which everyone accepts. In each case the valuer was required to provide an estimate of the price which the property might reasonably be expected to fetch if sold in the open market at the date of the valuation.

There is again agreement on the purpose for which the information was provided. It was to form part of the material on which the lender was to decide whether, and if so how much, he would lend. The valuation tells the lender how much, at current values, he is likely to recover if he has to resort to his security. This enables him to decide what margin, if any, an advance of a given amount will allow for a fall in the market, reasonably foreseeable variance from the figure put forward by the valuer (a valuation is an estimate of the most probable figure which the property will fetch, not a prediction that it will fetch precisely that figure), accidental damage to the property and any other of the contingencies which may happen. The valuer will know that if he overestimates the value of the property, the lender's margin for all these purposes will be correspondingly less.

On the other hand, the valuer will not ordinarily be privy to the other considerations which the lender may take into account, such as how much money he has available, how much the borrower needs to borrow, the strength of his covenant, the attraction of the rate of interest or the other personal or commercial considerations which may induce the lender to lend.

Because the valuer will appreciate that his valuation, though not the only consideration which would influence the lender, is likely to be a very important one, the law implies into the contract a term that the valuer will exercise reasonable care and skill. The relationship between the parties also gives rise to a concurrent duty in tort: see *Henderson v. Merrett Syndicates Ltd.* [1995] 2 A.C. 145. But the scope of the duty in tort is the same as in contract.

A duty of care such as the valuer owes does not however exist in the abstract. A plaintiff who sues for breach of a duty imposed by the law (whether in contract or tort or under statute) must do more than prove that the defendant has failed to comply. He must show that the duty was owed to him and that it was a duty in respect of the kind of loss which he has suffered. Both of these requirements are illustrated by *Caparo Industries Plc. v. Dickman* [1990] 2 A.C. 605. The auditors' failure to use reasonable care in auditing the company's statutory accounts was a breach of their duty of care. But they were not liable to an outside take-over bidder because the duty was not owed to him. Nor were they liable to shareholders who had bought more shares in reliance on the accounts because, although they were owed a duty of care, it was in their capacity as members of the company and not in the capacity (which they shared with everyone else) of potential buyers of its shares. Accordingly, the duty which they were owed was not in respect of loss which they might suffer by buying its shares . . . .

In the present case, there is no dispute that the duty was owed to the lenders. The real question in this case is the kind of loss in respect of which the duty was owed.

How is the scope of the duty determined? In the case of a statutory duty, the question is answered by deducing the purpose of the duty from the language and context of the statute: *Gorris v. Scott* (1874) L.R. 9 Ex. 125. In the case of tort, it will similarly depend upon the purpose of the rule imposing the duty. Most of the judgments in the *Caparo* case are occupied in examining the Companies Act 1985 to ascertain the purpose of the auditor's duty to take care that the statutory accounts comply with the Act. In the case of an implied contractual duty, the nature and extent of the liability is defined by the term which the law implies. As in the case of any implied term, the process is one of construction of the agreement as a whole in its commercial setting. The contractual duty to provide a valuation and the known purpose of that valuation compel the conclusion that the contract includes a duty of care. The scope of the duty, in the sense of the consequences for which the valuer is responsible, is that which the law regards as best giving effect to the express obligations assumed by the valuer: neither cutting them down so that the lender obtains less than he was reasonably entitled to expect, nor extending them so as to impose on the valuer a liability greater than he could reasonably have thought he was undertaking.

What therefore should be the extent of the valuer's liability? The Court of Appeal said that he should be liable for the loss which would not have occurred if he had given the correct advice. The lender having, in reliance on the valuation, embarked upon a transaction which he would not otherwise have undertaken, the valuer should bear all the risks of that transaction, subject only to the limitation that the damage should have been within the reasonable contemplation of the parties.

There is no reason in principle why the law should not penalise wrongful conduct by shifting on to the wrongdoer the whole risk of consequences which would not have happened but for the wrongful act. Hart and Honoré, in *Causation in the Law*, 2nd ed. (1985), p. 120, say that it would, for example, be perfectly intelligible to have a rule by which an unlicensed driver was responsible for all the consequences of his having driven, even if they were unconnected with his not having a licence. One might adopt such a rule in the interests of deterring unlicensed driving. But that is not the normal rule . . . .

Rules which make the wrongdoer liable for all the consequences of his wrongful conduct are exceptional and need to be justified by some special policy. Normally the law limits liability to those consequences which are attributable to that which made the act wrongful. In the case of liability in negligence for providing inaccurate information, this would mean liability for the consequences of the information being inaccurate.

I can illustrate the difference between the ordinary principle and that adopted by the Court of Appeal by an example. A mountaineer about to undertake a difficult climb is concerned about the fitness of his knee. He goes to a doctor who negligently makes a superficial examination and pronounces the knee fit. The climber goes on the expedition, which he would not have undertaken if the doctor had told him the true state of his knee. He suffers an injury which is an entirely foreseeable consequence of mountaineering but has nothing to do with his knee.

On the Court of Appeal's principle, the doctor is responsible for the injury suffered by the mountaineer because it is damage which would not have occurred if he had been given correct information about his knee. He would not have gone on the expedition and would have suffered no injury. On what I have suggested is the more usual principle, the doctor is not liable. The injury has not been caused by the doctor's bad advice because it would have occurred even if the advice had been correct.

Applying the approach set out in the above extract, Lord Hoffmann reasoned that in the first of the appeals, *SAAMCO v York Montague* itself, the plaintiffs could recover the entire loss caused by the fall in market value, subject to a deduction for contributory negligence (for an explanation of this defence, see generally Chapter 5 below). The property had been valued at £15 million, and the true value was £5 million, £11 million had been advanced. After the market fall, the property was sold for just under £2.5 million, a loss of just over £9.5 million. The plaintiffs were entitled to recover their full loss (subject to deduction for contributory negligence) because:

> **(At 222)** The consequence of the valuation being wrong was that the plaintiffs had £10 million less security than they thought. If they had had this margin, they would have suffered no loss. The whole loss was therefore within the scope of the defendants' duty.

In reaching this solution, the active question in Lord Hoffmann's analysis is what would have been the case if the valuation which *was* given had turned out to be correct? The plaintiffs would have had an extra £10 million security. Their loss was just over £9.5 million, which was within this bracket, so they were entitled, *prima facie*, to recover that amount. As Lord Hoffmann put it, if the information had been correct, there would have been no loss.

His language tends to obscure the novelty of the solution. Asking what was the 'consequence of the valuation being wrong' is not in this instance the same as asking what would have happened if the defendant had given a correct valuation. The latter is a question of 'but for' causation and it was the one asked by the Court of Appeal. The answer given was that the plaintiffs would not have entered into the transaction and so they would have suffered no loss on that property. The difference is made clear by the result of applying the approach to the other appeals.

In the other appeals, the valuations were less grossly inaccurate. The plaintiffs would still have suffered some loss if the valuation given had turned out to be correct, so they were awarded less than the full amount. For example, in the case of *Bank of Kuwait v Prudential Property Services Ltd* the lenders advanced £1.75 million on the security of a property valued at £2.5 million. The correct value was between £1.8 million and £1.85 million. After the market fall, it was sold for £950,000. According to Lord Hoffmann:

> **(At 222)** In my view the damages should have been limited to the consequences of the valuation being wrong, which were that the lenders had £700,000 or £650,000 less security than they thought. . . .
>
> I would therefore allow the appeal and reduce the damages to the difference between the valuation and the correct value.

Stapleton argues ([1997] 113 LQR 1) that in each case the effect is to place a 'cap' on damages so that they should not exceed the difference between the valuation given (which she calls V) and an accurate valuation at the time (V'). The damages may of course be less than this amount, if the plaintiff's loss is lower than the misevaluation. This was the case in the *SAAMCO* appeal itself as explained above. But we should be careful to note that although this is the *effect* of the decision in these cases, the *method* is not to place a cap. Lord Hoffmann made this clear in *SAAMCO* at 219–20:

> An alternative theory was that the lender should be entitled to recover the whole of his loss, subject to a "cap" limiting his recovery to the amount of the overvaluation. This theory will ordinarily produce the same result as the requirement that loss should be a consequence of the valuation being wrong, because the usual such consequence is that the lender makes an advance which he thinks is secured to a correspondingly greater extent. But I would not wish to exclude the possibility that other kinds of loss may flow from the valuation being wrong and in any case, as Mr. Sumption said on behalf of the defendants York Montague Ltd., it seems odd to start by choosing the wrong measure of damages (the whole loss) and then correct the error by imposing a cap. The appearance of a cap is actually the result of the plaintiff having to satisfy two separate requirements: first, to prove that he has suffered loss, and, secondly, to establish that the loss fell within the scope of the duty he was owed.

The point is reinforced in the subsequent decision of *Nykredit v Edward Erdman Ltd (No 2)* [1997] 1 WLR 1627 (concerning calculation of interest).

Lord Hoffmann, at 1638–9

> . . . in order to establish a cause of action in negligence [the plaintiff] must show that his loss is attributable to the overvaluation, that is, that he is worse off than he would have been if it had been correct.

> It is important to emphasise that this is a consequence of the limited way in which the House defined the valuer's duty of care and has nothing to do with questions of causation or any limit or "cap" imposed upon damages which would otherwise be recoverable. It was accepted that the whole loss suffered by reason of the fall in the property market was, as a matter of causation, properly attributable to the lender having entered into the transaction and that, but for the negligent valuation, he would not have done so. It was not suggested that the possibility of a fall in the market was unforeseeable or that there was any other factor which negatived the causal connection between lending and losing the money. There was, for example, no evidence that if the lender had not made the advance in question he would have lost his money in some other way. Nor, if one started from the proposition that the valuer was responsible for the consequences of the loan being made, could there be any logical basis for limiting the recoverable damages to the amount of the overvaluation. The essence of the decision was that this is not where one starts and that the valuer is responsible only for the consequences of the lender having too little security.

> Proof of loss attributable to a breach of the relevant duty of care is an essential element in a cause of action for the tort of negligence. Given that there has been negligence, the cause of action will therefore arise *when the plaintiff has suffered loss in respect of which the duty was owed*. . . . [Emphasis added]

Like Viscount Simonds in *The Wagon Mound*, Lord Hoffmann denies that his solution is related to causation. But it certainly depends on identifying which effects were 'the consequence' of the breach of duty, and it is hard to imagine discussion of consequences without any reference to causation. However, this is not an exercise in *factual* causation. In terms of factual causation, it can be accepted that the breach was, as the Court of Appeal said, a cause of the loss. But that is not sufficient to establish that the loss is recoverable.

The reasoning is subtle, and the case has been hugely influential, so we will outline the ways in which it is controversial and distinctive.

The Reasoning

Scope of duty

It will be apparent from the extracts above that Lord Hoffmann's reasoning turns on identifying 'the scope of the duty'. This is the first of two steps in his reasoning. At this first stage, Lord Hoffmann determined that the scope of the duty was to offer a correct valuation.

In relation to the 'scope of duty' analysis, Lord Hoffmann offers the analogy of a mountaineer who approaches a doctor for advice on the condition of his knee. If the doctor says that the knee is sound and this particular information is incorrect, it might lead the mountaineer to undertake an expedition when otherwise he would have stayed at home. If he then suffers a fall which is unrelated to the condition of the knee, then the doctor's misinformation will pass the 'but for' test: it will be a 'condition precedent' of the accident. Nevertheless, it would be wrong to attribute the injury to the incorrect information. The doctor's role was only in respect of the condition of the knee. In the course of criticizing the approach in *SAAMCO*, Jane Stapleton nevertheless accepts that this example illustrates effectively that issues of 'but for' causation do not provide all the answers in cases of this sort ((1997) 113 LQR 1, 2). She further suggests, however, that Lord Hoffmann is mistaken when he treats the nature of the 'wrong' in such cases as failure to give *accurate information*, rather than failure to give a *careful valuation* (at 5). But Lord Hoffmann gives clear reasons for suggesting that where a defendant is called upon only to give particular and specific *information* in relation to a transaction or other course of action, the only duty is to take care to give that information accurately. In other cases, there may be a broader duty to offer advice. In the latter sort of case, there may, for example, be a duty to advise on the possibility of a general market fall and loss of security. We can agree that there is room to differ in this interpretation of the scope of the duty. 'Scope of duty' analysis will be subjective at both stages. But for the same reason it seems too simplistic to describe it as mistaken. The greater controversy exists, it is suggested, at the next stage.

Identifying the 'consequences'

At the next stage, Lord Hoffmann applied an unprecedented kind of 'but for' test. He asked what would have happened if the defendant's valuation (which is to say the valuation *actually given* by the defendants) had been correct. As we have already seen, this is not the same as asking what would have happened if the defendant had provided a correct valuation. That would have been a question of factual causation, and this is not. It is designed specifically to establish which losses will be treated as *attributable to* the breach of duty. Lord Hoffmann's approach can be regarded as a question of remoteness in the sense that it determines attribution. It does not, however, employ the language of foreseeability, which would also give too broad an answer. It identifies the scope and purpose of the duty with some precision (a subjective exercise) and then asks which aspects of the damage suffered are attributable to breach of the duty so understood. To express this second stage in terms of 'but for' causation is to use familiar language in an unfamiliar way.

Appraisal

The solution reached in *SAAMCO* though subjective at both stages appears to represent an appropriate compromise on the facts while also setting out a general method for future cases.

The *fairness* of the decision may be tested by considering the following question: if the defendants had not been negligent and the plaintiffs had not entered into these transactions, would they have entered into other transactions (since this was their business), thereby suffering some losses on the falling market? If so, then in this sense, as well as in terms of intuitive ideas about 'cause', we can accept that it would be unfair to attribute the entire loss to the defendant's breach of duty.

In the later case of *Platform Home Loans v Oyston Shipways* [1999] 2 WLR 518, a differently constituted House of Lords had difficulty applying the *SAAMCO* reasoning. The issue in that case involved the relationship between the method of addressing the consequence of the breach in *SAAMCO* and the provisions of the Law Reform (Contributory Negligence) Act 1945. We will address these issues in Chapter 5 below when we address the defence of contributory negligence. David Howarth has compared the simple, yet subtle approach in *SAAMCO* and its reception in *Platform Home Loans* with the fate met by *The Wagon Mound* in the case law that followed:

David Howarth, 'Complexity Strikes Back—Valuation in the House of Lords'
(2000) 8 *Tort L Rev* 85, 89

Platform Homes stands in relation to *SAAMCO* as *Hughes v Lord Advocate* [1963] AC 837, *Smith v Leech Brain & Co Ltd* [1962] 2 QB 405 and *Knightley v Johns* [1982] 1 All ER 851 stand to *The Wagon Mound (No 1)* [1961] AC 388. *Wagon Mound* and *SAAMCO* attempt ambitious simultaneous solutions to complex problems. The subsequent cases, dazzled by the elegance of these solutions, do not challenge them directly but decline to follow them into undermining other valuable doctrines.

It is suggested that the comparison between *The Wagon Mound* and *SAAMCO* is an appropriate one on many levels. Both cases seek to deny the importance of causal language and instead assert the primacy of duty analysis. Both are relatively rare examples where the Privy Council and House of Lords respectively put aside disagreements and provided a single agreed judgment, perhaps in the interests of clarity, perhaps in an attempt to enhance the value of the decision as a future precedent. The complexities of remoteness of damage have, however, survived *The Wagon Mound* as we have seen, and *SAAMCO* has not been as decisive as planned. Importantly though, it must be conceded that the alignment of duty and remoteness of damage does need further consideration in the light of the *Caparo* approach to the duty of care. This is precisely what the House in *SAAMCO* attempted to do, and this broad aspect of the approach has been very influential (see for example the case of *Chester v Afshar* [2004] UKHL 41 discussed in Chapter 4 below).

General Conclusions

It cannot be argued that the problems of remoteness have been satisfactorily resolved, either by *The Wagon Mound* or subsequently. Although remoteness issues have typically received less attention than issues of duty, the case law on remoteness still presents an unsatisfactory mosaic of different approaches and apparent 'rules' depending on the type of case in hand. We have identified that 'foreseeability' has never wholly succeeded in displacing causal language, and we have also identified the emergence of a new emphasis on the scope and purpose of the duty of care. This new approach could be regarded as an updated interpretation of 'the risk principle', which holds that the defendant is liable only for those consequences falling within the scope of the risk created by his or her breach of duty. Because duty of care under *Caparo* is no longer addressed primarily in terms of foreseeability, so the identification of which consequences fall within the relevant risk will also need to be adjusted. *SAAMCO* shows an attempt to do just this, in circumstances where the problem of attribution was, in terms of justice and fairness as well as policy, one that needed to be addressed.

FURTHER READING: CAUSATION AND ATTRIBUTION OR 'REMOTENESS'

Hart, H.L.A., and Honoré, T., *Causation in the Law* (2nd edn, Oxford: OUP, 1985).

Hoffmann, Lord, 'Causation' (2005) 121 LQR 59.

Howarth, D., 'Complexity Strikes Back—Valuation in the House of Lords' (2000) 8 *Tort L Rev* 85.

Stapleton, J., 'The Gist of Negligence: Part II' (1988) 104 LQR 389.

Stapleton, J., 'Cause in Fact and the Scope of Liability for Consequences' (2003) 119 LQR 388.

Stauch, M., 'Risk and Remoteness of Damage in Negligence' (2001) 64 MLR 191.

Williams, G., 'The Risk Principle' (1961) 77 LQR 179.

4

PARTICULAR CAUSATION PROBLEMS

CENTRAL ISSUES

i) This chapter considers three separate problems of causation. All three of these problems have required the recent attention of the House of Lords. The second has provoked a legislative response in section 3 of the Compensation Act 2006.

ii) The first of the three problems concerns failure to advise of risks inherent in a medical procedure. In *Chester v Afshar* [2004] UKHL 41; [2005] 1 AC 134, as in the earlier Australian case of *Chappel v Hart* (1998) 195 CLR 232, the claimant was not advised of a small but significant inherent risk. Surgery was carefully carried out, but the inherent risk materialized. The House of Lords, like the Australian High Court, decided that the claimant should be compensated for the full consequences of the risk. The chief difficulty lies in identifying the relevant question of causation in this case. Were the problems related to 'cause in fact', or 'cause in law'? Should these be seen as problem cases at all? We will say it is right to see these as problem cases, and argue that the cases shed light on fundamental issues relating to the nature of the tort of negligence.

iii) The second problem to address is concerned with proof of causation. But its implications for 'causation of damage' in the tort of negligence are fundamental. In *Fairchild v Glenhaven Funeral Services Ltd* [2002] UKHL 22; [2003] 1 AC 32, the House of Lords accepted that in certain circumstances, it will be sufficient proof of causation to show that a given breach has materially contributed to the *risk* of injury. Subsequently in *Barker v Corus* [2006] UKHL 20; [2006] 2 WLR 1027, the House of Lords decided that such a defendant should be liable only for a *proportion* of the injury suffered. This proportionate approach to an indivisible injury (fatal cancer) was a fundamental departure. For the specific case of *mesothelioma* (the kind of cancer concerned in *Fairchild* and *Barker v Corus*), the result was swiftly reversed by legislative action: section 3 of the Compensation Act 2006. The broader implications of the House of Lords judgment are as yet unknown.

iv) One area which could in theory be affected by the decision in *Barker* makes up our third problem, loss of chance. Between *Fairchild* and *Barker*, in *Gregg v Scott* [2005] UKHL 2; [2005] 2 AC 176, the House of Lords refused to recognize increase in risk (or loss of opportunity) as damage in its own right. Traditional causal principles were applied. A doctor negligently failed to refer a patient for investigation. The patient proved to be suffering from a malignant cancer, and claimed that the breach had caused him to lose *a better chance of surviving the cancer*. Rejection of this claim appeared compatible with *Fairchild*, but is hard to reconcile with *Barker v Corus*. It also appears to leave another anomaly in the law, since there are clearly cases where loss of the chance of *financial gain* will be compensated.

1. INTRODUCTION: SETTING ASIDE CAUSAL PRINCIPLES

Should normal principles of causation be set aside for reasons of justice and fairness? All of the cases considered in this chapter could be interpreted as raising this question. In this regard, we should remind ourselves that causal principles are themselves often justified by reference to justice and fairness, and most particularly by reference to ideas of responsibility.[1] Indeed, causation of harm is inherent to the idea of a 'wrong' defined by the tort of negligence. This has been forcefully expressed by Tony Honoré in a comment on *Chappel v Hart*:

A. Honoré, 'Medical non-disclosure, Causation and Risk: *Chappel v Hart*' (1999) 7 TLJ, 1, 2–3

. . . causal principles are not without good reason to be swept aside on grounds of legal policy in favour of imposing the risk of harm on a party who has not caused it. Otherwise judges and litigants run the risk of dispensing or receiving palm tree justice. That we are responsible for the harm we cause by our wrongful conduct is not some ancient shibboleth that the law has outgrown. In actions for tort or breach of contract, as Lord Hoffmann has emphasised in a different context [Honoré here refers to the *SAAMCO* case, extracted in chapter 3 above], defendants are normally liable only for the harm caused by their wrongful act or omission. It is only exceptionally that the law transfers to a defendant the whole risk of the loss, whatever its cause, that would not have occurred but for the defendant's conduct.

In this particular instance, Honoré (unlike most commentators and indeed most judges) thought that the harm had *not* been 'caused' by the breach of duty in question. The reason for this is implied in the last sentence extracted: the 'but for' test *does not establish causation*.[2] Nevertheless, Honoré thought it *was* appropriate to set aside normal causal principles in this case, as we will see.

---

[1] See our discussion of *Rahman v Arearose* [2001] QB 351, Chapter 3.5 above.

[2] It only identifies 'conditions precedent', with historical involvement. These are not necessarily 'causes'. This approach to 'but for' in Honoré's earlier work with H. L. A. Hart is explained in Chapter 3.5 above.

2. DISCLOSURE OF MEDICAL RISKS

Chappel v Hart (1998) 195 CLR 232 and *Chester v Afshar* [2004] UKHL 41; [2005] 1 AC 134

These are very similar cases, the first Australian, the other English. The outcome in these cases was the same, but the reasons were varied.

It seems that widespread academic approval of the outcome in *Chappel v Hart* influenced the decision of the House of Lords in *Chester v Afshar*. It is however a notable feature of these cases that even among those judges and academics who are agreed on the outcome, there is disagreement over the reasons why that answer is correct. We will briefly outline the Australian decision and then extract the English case more fully. Our chief focus is on causation; although we will necessarily say something about the nature of the 'duty' in *Chester v Afshar*.

Chappel v Hart (1998) 195 CLR 232

The plaintiff suffered from a progressive throat condition which required surgery. There was a very slight risk that the surgery would lead to paralysis of the vocal chords and leave the patient with a weak and gravely voice. The plaintiff was a school teacher, so it was particularly important to her to have a strong voice. Dr Chappel did not warn the plaintiff of the risk in question. She underwent the surgery, with precisely the result that her voice was left weak and gravely. The majority of the High Court of Australia held that a doctor may be held liable for injury about which he had a duty to inform the patient, but not for injury the risk of which fell outside the duty to warn. As such, the majority judges appear to have concluded that normal causal principles, appropriately adapted to the case, had been fulfilled.

Unfortunately, the clarity of the decision is blurred because the majority judges also accepted that Dr Chappel was not the most experienced of surgeons, and treated this as causally relevant:

Gaudron J, para 19

Once it is accepted, as in my view it must be, that the risk of injury would have been less if, as Mrs Hart deposed, she had retained the services of the most experienced surgeon in the field, the argument that, at best, Mrs Hart was entitled to nominal damages must be rejected. Rather, Mrs Hart is entitled to damages for the injury suffered.

On the other hand, Gaudron and Gummow JJ also went on to argue that the inherent risk in having the operation on another day was so small that it should not be taken into account in assessing damages. As Peter Cane has pointed out, this seems inconsistent with the part of the judgment quoted above:

Peter Cane, 'A Warning About Causation' (1999) 115 LQR 21–7

If the inherent risk was too small to take into account in assessing damages, perhaps the potential reduction in risk available at the hands of the most skilled and experienced surgeon was too small to support the weight it bore in the causation argument.

Perhaps the reference to a potential reduction in risk was an effort to convert *Chappel v Hart* into an easier case than it actually was, in which a warning would have significantly altered the likelihood of harm coming about. But alternatively, the possibility of finding a more experienced surgeon may give added weight and purpose to the recognized duty to inform a patient of the risks of surgery.

The minority in *Chappel v Hart* accepted that the damage satisfied the 'but for' test, but suggested that the failure to warn **was not the legal cause of the injury**. The outcome was of course 'foreseeable' (within *The Wagon Mound*): it was a known risk. As we said in connection with *The Wagon Mound* in Chapter 3, a small risk can nevertheless be foreseeable. Indeed it was a risk of which the doctor was well aware. But in the view of the minority, that outcome could not be *attributed to* the breach of duty. Since advising of the risk would not lead the plaintiff to avoid the risk (she would undergo surgery anyway), the resulting damage was **merely coincidental to the failure to warn**.

It is difficult to fit this conclusion—that the breach of duty did not *cause* the harm—into the two traditional questions of causation identified in Chapter 3. Such a conclusion could be justified on the basis of Hart and Honoré's analysis of causation in terms of ordinary language, explained in Chapter 3 above. Although this injury passed the 'but for' test (it would in all probability *not have occurred* on another occasion), it might not be appropriate to refer to it as a 'cause'. The injury resulted from careful surgery which sooner or later would have to be undergone. It might be regarded as 'just one of those things'.

Notably, Tony Honoré approved of the majority's *conclusion* in *Chappel v Hart*, but not of its reasoning. He agreed with the minority that the doctor's failure to warn was not a *cause* of the injury. But it was appropriate for causal principles to be set aside in this case. On this occasion the defendant was responsible, on moral grounds, for the claimant's injury, even though his breach of duty had not caused that injury. This element of Honoré's argument was relied upon by Lord Steyn in *Chester v Afshar*, and the relevant passage from his case note is quoted by Lord Steyn at [22]. It seems reasonable to conclude that Honoré's analysis affected not only the conclusion reached by the majority in *Chester v Afshar*, but also the view of Lord Steyn (which might otherwise appear mysterious) that the breach did not cause the injury, despire being a 'but for' condition. In effect, though not explicitly, he is applying the Hart and Honoré approach to causation.

Chester v Afshar [2004] UKHL 41; [2005] 1 AC 134

The defendant neurosurgeon advised the claimant to undergo a surgical procedure on her spine. Even if carefully performed, there was a slight risk (placed at 1–2 per cent) that the claimant would suffer serious neurological damage as a result of this surgery. This risk, which was clearly recognized by practitioners of neurosurgery, was not drawn to the claimant's attention. The claimant had a fear of surgery generally, and the evidence was that she would not have agreed to undergo the surgery right away if she had been advised of the risk. However, she admitted that she would most probably have agreed to the surgery in the fullness of time, as it would be the only realistic means of improving her condition.

Since it seems that the development of serious neurological damage was 'random' (existing despite the skill of the defendant and not related to the physical characteristics of the claimant), on the balance of probability it was clearly much more likely than not that surgery performed at another time would *not* have led to the same unfortunate result. The 'but for' test is therefore satisfied. But on the other hand, the surgery had not been performed carelessly. The surgeon had not increased the risk, nor had he led the claimant to run the risk, because she would have run the same risk anyway, albeit on another day.

On the balance of probability, but for the breach of duty the claimant would have run the same risk, but with a different outcome.

The Court of Appeal [2002] EWCA Civ 724; [2003] QB 356, thought the case could be resolved by applying normal causal principles. The court identified, correctly, that the 'but for' test was satisfied. The court also accepted that the damage fell within the scope of the duty that was breached, so that the breach could be said to have caused the damage. It was the kind of damage about which the defendant ought to have warned the claimant. The Court of Appeal proposed that this case raised the question of 'attribution' or remoteness, not in the form of foreseeability, but in the form explained by Lord Hoffmann in *Banque Bruxelles v Eagle Star Insurance* ('*SAAMCO*') (see Chapter 3.6 above):

Sir Denis Henry (delivering the judgment of the Court)

43 . . . We accept that the "but for" test is necessary but not always sufficient to establish causation in law. Even if the claimant would not have been on the operating table that day if the defendant had given her a proper warning, the defendant is not liable for coincidences which have nothing to do with him, such as the anaesthetic failure referred to by Gummow J [in *Chappel v Hart*] or lightning striking the operating theatre. The classic example of this point was given by Lord Hoffmann in *Banque Bruxelles Lambert SA v Eagle Star Insurance Co Ltd* [1997] AC 191, 213:

> "A mountaineer about to undertake a difficult climb is concerned about the fitness of his knee. He goes to a doctor who negligently makes a superficial examination and pronounces the knee fit. The climber goes on the expedition, which he would not have undertaken if the doctor had told him the true state of his knee. He suffers an injury which is an entirely foreseeable consequence of mountaineering but has nothing to do with his knee."

44 In cases such as the present, however, it simply cannot be said that the injury suffered had nothing to do with the problem which had taken the claimant to the doctor. It was a consequence of that very problem and the doctor's attempt to put it right. Furthermore it was a consequence about which the claimant had expressed her concern to the doctor and been wrongly reassured. The closer analogy is with the mountaineer who consults his doctor because he is afraid that his knee will give way under the strain of mountain climbing, is wrongly reassured that it will not, and who is injured because his knee does give way. The doctor was not to blame for the knee giving way, any more than the doctor (if the first operation was not negligently performed) was to blame for the cauda equina syndrome in this case, but he was to blame for the mountaineer being on the mountain at all.

The reasoning in the extract above is logical, coherent, and in accordance with precedent. The only possible problem with the Court of Appeal approach lies with an issue that it does not address. Although the damage satisfies both the 'but for' test, and the 'scope of duty' test, the claimant was almost certain to run a similar risk in the future, so that the defendant has not increased the risk of harm. The Court of Appeal (at [4]) raised this issue, only to treat it as a matter of quantification: the defendant should at least be liable for having caused the harm sooner than would otherwise have been the case.

Sir Denis Henry

45 What if the mountaineer would not have taken the risk immediately but cannot rule out the possibility that his love of mountaineering was such that he would have been prepared to run it at some later date? Logic would again suggest that this should only make a difference if

it was more likely than not that he would do so: the mere possibility that his feelings would eventually get the better of him does not break the chain. Furthermore, by causing him to go up the mountain when he would not have done so the doctor had caused him to suffer the injury earlier than he would otherwise have done. He has therefore lived for longer with the consequences of a broken leg (or whatever) than he would otherwise have done. The question then becomes one of quantification rather than causation, as the judge held in this case.

This example seems not to hit the target. In the example, the mountaineer's knee will give way when he eventually goes up a mountain. The doctor has caused him to suffer this injury sooner, rather than later. In *Chester v Afshar*, the claimant would be almost certain *not* to suffer the harm if she had the operation later. Therefore, the whole loss is in issue, not just an acceleration of a likely future loss.

Chester v Afshar, House of Lords [2004] UKHL 41; [2005] 1 AC 134

In the House of Lords, the issues were treated as much more problematic from the point of view of causal principles. The fact that the defendant had not increased the risk of suffering the injury was accepted to raise a problem of causation.

In dissent, Lord Bingham seems to have thought that the claimant's damage did not satisfy the 'but for' test.

Lord Bingham (dissenting)

8   It is now, I think, generally accepted that the "but for" test does not provide a comprehensive or exclusive test of causation in the law of tort. Sometimes, if rarely, it yields too restrictive an answer, as in *Fairchild v Glenhaven Funeral Services Ltd* [2003] 1 AC 32. More often, applied simply and mechanically, it gives too expansive an answer: "But for your negligent misdelivery of my luggage, I should not have had to defer my passage to New York and embark on *SS Titanic*." But, in the ordinary run of cases, satisfying the "but for" test is a necessary if not a sufficient condition of establishing causation. Here, in my opinion, it is not satisfied. Miss Chester has not established that but for the failure to warn she would not have undergone surgery. She has shown that but for the failure to warn she would not have consented to surgery on Monday, 21 November 1994. But the timing of the operation is irrelevant to the injury she suffered, for which she claims to be compensated. That injury would have been as liable to occur whenever the surgery was performed and whoever performed it.

Unfortunately, Lord Bingham incorrectly suggests that the 'but for' test is not satisfied. We have already said that the damage does pass the 'but for' test, and the point is also explained clearly by Lord Steyn, at [19] below. On the other hand, in the final sentence of this paragraph, Lord Bingham does specify the issue which *does* create a potential problem of causation: the injury would have been at least as likely to occur **whenever** the surgery was performed and **whoever** performed it. This, as we will see below, led Lord Steyn to acknowledge that usual causal principles were not satisfied in this case. But it has nothing to do with 'but for' causation.

Lord Hoffmann joined Lord Bingham in dissent, and we will address his judgment below. It will be especially useful to compare his judgment with the majority judgment of Lord Steyn.

Lord Steyn's judgment is likely to be the most often referred to in future litigation, because of the strength of his endorsement of patient autonomy.

Lord Steyn

16 A surgeon owes a legal duty to a patient to warn him or her in general terms of possible serious risks involved in the procedure. The only qualification is that there may be wholly exceptional cases where objectively in the best interests of the patient the surgeon may be excused from giving a warning. This is, however, irrelevant in the present case. In modern law medical paternalism no longer rules and a patient has a prima facie right to be informed by a surgeon of a small, but well established, risk of serious injury as a result of surgery.

17 Secondly, not all rights are equally important. But a patient's right to an appropriate warning from a surgeon when faced with surgery ought normatively to be regarded as an important right which must be given effective protection whenever possible.

18 Thirdly, in the context of attributing legal responsibility, it is necessary to identify precisely the protected legal interests at stake. A rule requiring a doctor to abstain from performing an operation without the informed consent of a patient serves two purposes. It tends to avoid the occurrence of the particular physical injury the risk of which a patient is not prepared to accept. It also ensures that due respect is given to the autonomy and dignity of each patient. Professor Ronald Dworkin (*Life's Dominion: An Argument about Abortion, Euthanasia and Individual Freedom* (1993)) explained these concepts at p 224:

> "The most plausible [account] emphasises the integrity rather than the welfare of the choosing agent; the value of autonomy, on this view, derives from the capacity it protects: the capacity to express one's own character—values, commitments, convictions, and critical as well as experiential interests—in the life one leads. Recognising an individual right of autonomy makes self-creation possible. It allows each of us to be responsible for shaping our lives according to our own coherent or incoherent—but, in any case, distinctive—personality. It allows us to lead our lives rather than be led along them, so that each of us can be, to the extent a scheme of rights can make this possible, what we have made of ourselves. We allow someone to choose death over radical amputation or a blood transfusion, if that is his informed wish, because we acknowledge his right to a life structured by his own values."

19 Fourthly, it is a distinctive feature of the present case that but for the surgeon's negligent failure to warn the claimant of the small risk of serious injury the actual injury would not have occurred when it did and the chance of it occurring on a subsequent occasion was very small. It could therefore be said that the breach of the surgeon resulted in the very injury about which the claimant was entitled to be warned.

20 These factors must be considered in combination. But they must also be weighed against the undesirability of departing from established principles of causation, except for good reasons. The collision of competing ideas poses a difficult question of law.

21 That such problems do not necessarily have a single right answer is illustrated by the judgment of the Australian High Court in *Chappel v Hart* (1998) 195 CLR 232. . . . this Australian case reveals two fundamentally different approaches, the one favouring firm adherence to traditionalist causation techniques and the other a greater emphasis on policy and corrective justice.

22 The House was referred to a valuable body of academic literature which discusses problems such as arose in *Chappel v Hart* 195 CLR 232, and in the present case, in some detail. Not surprisingly, the authors approach the matter from slightly different angles. It is, however, fair to say that there is general support for the majority decision in *Chappel v Hart*, and for the view which prevailed in the Court of Appeal in the present case . . . The case note by the co-author of the seminal treatise on causation is particularly interesting [Honoré, 'Medical Non-Disclosure, Causation and Risk: *Chappel v Hart*' (1999) 7 TLJ 1]. Professor Honoré said, at p 8:

> "does it follow that Mrs Hart should not recover ? Or is this a case where courts are entitled to see to it that justice is done despite the absence of causal connection? I think it is the latter and for the following reason. The duty of a surgeon to warn of the dangers inherent in an operation is intended to help minimise the risk to the patient. But it is also intended to enable the patient to make an informed choice whether to undergo the treatment recommended and, if so, at whose hands and when. Dr Chappel violated Mrs Hart's right to choose for herself, even if he did not increase the risk to her. Judges should vindicate rights that have been violated if they can do so consistently with the authority of statutes and decided cases. In this case the High Court did just this, in effect by making Dr Chappel, when he operated on Mrs Hart, strictly liable for any injury he might cause of the type against which he should have warned her. For Dr Chappel *did* cause the harm that Mrs Hart suffered, though not by the advice he failed to give her. He did so by operating on her and, though he operated with due care, he slit open her oesophagus with disastrous consequences. Morally he was responsible for the outcome of what he did . . . All the High Court has therefore done is to give legal sanction to an underlying moral responsibility for causing injury of the very sort against the risk of which the defendant should have warned her. Do the courts have power in certain cases to override causal considerations in order to vindicate a plaintiff's rights? I believe they do though the right must be exercised with great caution."

In my view Professor Honoré was right to face up to the fact that *Chappel v Hart*—and therefore the present case—cannot neatly be accommodated within conventional causation principles. But he was also right to say that policy and corrective justice pull powerfully in favour of vindicating the patient's right to know.

23   It is true that there is no direct English authority permitting a modification of the approach to the proof of causation in a case such as the present. On the other hand, there is the analogy of *Fairchild v Glenhaven Funeral Services Ltd* [2003] 1 AC 32 which reveals a principled approach to such a problem. . . . The *Fairchild* case is, of course, very different from the facts of the present case. A modification of causation principles as was made in the *Fairchild* case will always be exceptional. But it cannot be restricted to the particular facts of the *Fairchild* case. Lord Bingham of Cornhill observed in the *Fairchild* case that "It would be unrealistic to suppose that the principle here affirmed will not over time be the subject of incremental and analogical development": p 68, para 34. At the very least the *Fairchild* case shows that where justice and policy *demand* it a modification of causation principles is not beyond the wit of a modern court.

24   Standing back from the detailed arguments, I have come to the conclusion that, as a result of the surgeon's failure to warn the patient, she cannot be said to have given informed consent to the surgery in the full legal sense. Her right of autonomy and dignity can and ought to be vindicated by a narrow and modest departure from traditional causation principles.

25   On a broader basis I am glad to have arrived at the conclusion that the claimant is entitled in law to succeed. This result is in accord with one of the most basic aspirations of the law, namely to right wrongs. Moreover, the decision announced by the House today reflects the reasonable expectations of the public in contemporary society.

26 The result ought to come as no surprise to the medical profession which has to its credit subscribed to the fundamental importance of a surgeon's duty to warn a patient in general terms of significant risks: *Royal College of Surgeons, Good Surgical Practice* (2002), ch 4, guidelines on consent.

Lord Steyn accepts that the 'but for' test is satisfied, but he says that the wider causal principles of the tort of negligence are not satisfied. He does not, as such, say why, but he refers with approval to Honoré's analysis of *Chappel v Hart*. The probable reason then is that the defendant has not increased the risk of harm. In the note on *Chappel v Hart* discussed with approval by Lord Steyn, Tony Honoré comments as follows:

A. Honoré, 'Medical Non-disclosure, Causation and Risk: *Chappel v Hart*'
(1999) 7 TLJ 1, 7

Dr Chappel's advice related to a risk which Mrs Hart was bound, sooner or later, to run. On the assumption that the risk to her would have been the same whenever she had the operation, Dr Chappel neither exposed her to a risk that she need never have run nor increased the risk she was bound to run in any case. . . . So his failure to warn was not, on that assumption, a cause of the injury that Mrs Hart suffered, though it was certainly a but-for condition . . .

But Lord Steyn's decision to set aside causal principles relating to increase in risk, and find in favour of the claimant, is not based on the same reasoning adopted by Honoré. Earlier, we said that Honoré's analysis is based in *responsibility* on the part of the surgeon. In the passage quoted by Lord Steyn, Honoré places heavy emphasis on the fact that the surgeon *did* cause the injury, through his acts, although he did not cause that injury through his *breach of duty*. Lord Steyn's reasoning, by contrast, is dominated by the importance of patient autonomy, which he concludes is the chief purpose of the recognized duty to warn.

In para [18] above, Lord Steyn points out two purposes of the duty to obtain informed consent:

1. It tends to avoid the occurrence of the particular physical injury the risk of which a patient is not prepared to accept.

2. It also ensures that due respect is given to the autonomy and dignity of each patient.

The first purpose would be easily recognizable as falling within a duty to take care in negligence. The difficulty is that *on this occasion, the duty to advise of risks does not have the goal of avoiding injury or making safe. This is because it is admitted that the same risk will be run in any event, in due course.*

Therefore, it is only the second purpose—protection of autonomy and dignity—that justifies suspension of causal principles.

This ringing endorsement of patient autonomy is more surprising than one might think. It has been broadly welcomed by most commentators,[3] but it represents a new direction in English law. In *Sidaway v Bethlem Royal Hospital* [1985] AC 871, as we explained in Chapter 3, the House of Lords clearly determined that the doctrine of informed consent played no part in

---

[3] See for example A. Grubb, 'Consent to Treatment: the Competent Patient', in A. Grubb and J. Laing (eds), *Principles of Medical Law* (2nd edn, OUP, 2004). There are some dissenters, who point out that the doctor–patient relationship may become fraught with worrying statistics as a result of this decision.

English law. In that case, there was no breach of duty when a doctor did not inform a patient of a small risk—as in *Chester*, a risk of around 1–2 per cent—inherent in treatment. The *Bolam* test was applied, and the duty to advise was judged according to the standard of the 'reasonable doctor', *not* 'the prudent patient'. On that standard, withholding information was 'reasonable'.

One possibility is that this change in direction came about by accident. The existence of a duty to warn of the small risk in *Chester v Afshar* appears not challenged. Rather, the surgeon claimed that he *had* warned of the risk, but the claimant's evidence was preferred. But there are reasons for thinking that the change in direction is not accidental. Lord Hope, among the majority judges, particularly referred to academic criticism of the failure to develop a doctrine of 'informed consent';[4] and when Lord Steyn used the term, he surely cannot have been unaware that *Sidaway* had denied that such a thing existed in English law. Lord Walker, also in the majority, said in terms that:

92 . . . in the twenty years which have elapsed since *Sidaway*, the importance of personal autonomy has been more and more widely recognised.

In conclusion, special considerations affect the outcome of surgery conducted without informed consent, even if carefully carried out. According to Lord Steyn, the need to protect the autonomy of the patient is sufficient reason to justify full damages to be awarded against the surgeon who fails to warn of the risk. Through failing to give appropriate information, he becomes, in effect, strictly liable for those risks about which he ought to have warned the claimant. Lord Hoffmann, in his dissenting judgment, disagreed.

We should note a problem. Lord Steyn explains his decision by arguing that one of law's most basic aspirations is 'to right wrongs' (at [25]). The trouble is, as we said in Chapter 1 and have repeated from time to time, we have to take care to specify what 'wrong' we are concerned with. The 'wrong' with which Lord Steyn is concerned appears to be violation of patient autonomy. He refers only once to the other potential 'wrong' of carelessly caused harm, mentioned above as the first of two reasons for the duty to warn. This is for the simple reason that the warning in this case could not in any sense affect whether the patient would run the risk. It could not make her any safer; although in this instance as it turned out the lack of warning did have the consequence (in a 'but for' sense) that she suffered harm. The duty to give a warning in order to make sense is judged with foresight; causation of harm is judged with hindsight.

As explained in Chapter 2, protection of autonomy in respect of personal physical integrity is an interest protected by the torts of trespass to the person. Breach of the duty specified by Lord Steyn—a duty to advise with the objective of protecting patient autonomy, whether it makes the patient any safer or not—does not fit comfortably into the 'wrong' defined by the tort of negligence. It fits extremely comfortably within trespass to the person. Furthermore, if the case was argued in trespass there would be no problem of causation. Injury clearly flowed from a physical application of force without consent, and there is no need in trespass to show that the harm flows from a *breach of duty* (the problem in this case).[5] We said in Chapter 2 that a problem of causation was bound to follow from arguing such claims in negligence, rather

---

[4] Lord Hope at [57], referring to M. Jones, 'Informed Consent and Other Fairy Stories' (1999) 7 Med L Rev 103.

[5] It is not altogether clear whether damages in trespass are limited by a 'foreseeability' test. But that does not matter in this case, where the damage is a foreseeable (though rare) consequence of surgery.

than trespass, if ever *Sidaway* was evaded and a duty to warn recognized.[6] That is what happened in *Chester v Afshar*.

Lord Hoffmann's dissenting judgment is particularly interesting in light of these comments about the relevant duties.

Lord Hoffmann (dissenting)

28   My Lords, the purpose of a duty to warn someone against the risk involved in what he proposes to do, or allow to be done to him, is to give him the opportunity to avoid or reduce that risk. If he would have been unable or unwilling to take that opportunity and the risk eventuates, the failure to warn has not caused the damage. It would have happened anyway.

29   The burden is on a claimant to prove that the defendant's breach of duty caused him damage. Where the breach of duty is a failure to warn of a risk, he must prove that he would have taken the opportunity to avoid or reduce that risk. In the context of the present case, that means proving that she would not have had the operation.

30   The judge made no finding that she would not have had the operation. He was not invited by the claimant to make such a finding. The claimant argued that as a matter of law it was sufficient that she would not have had the operation at that time or by that surgeon, even though the evidence was that the risk could have been precisely the same if she had it at another time or by another surgeon. A similar argument has been advanced before this House.

31   In my opinion this argument is about as logical as saying that if one had been told, on entering a casino, that the odds on the number 7 coming up at roulette were only 1 in 37, one would have gone away and come back next week or gone to a different casino. The question is whether one would have taken the opportunity to avoid or reduce the risk, not whether one would have changed the scenario in some irrelevant detail. The judge found as a fact that the risk would have been precisely the same whether it was done then or later or by that competent surgeon or by another.

32   It follows that the claimant failed to prove that the defendant's breach of duty caused her loss. On ordinary principles of tort law, the defendant is not liable. The remaining question is whether a special rule should be created by which doctors who fail to warn patients of risks should be made insurers against those risks.

33   The argument for such a rule is that it vindicates the patient's right to choose for herself. Even though the failure to warn did not cause the patient any damage, it was an affront to her personality and leaves her feeling aggrieved.

34   I can see that there might be a case for a modest solatium in such cases. But the risks which may eventuate will vary greatly in severity and I think there would be great difficulty in fixing a suitable figure. In any case, the cost of litigation over such cases would make the law of torts an unsuitable vehicle for distributing the modest compensation which might be payable.

35   Nor do I agree with Professor Honoré's moral argument for making the doctor an insurer, namely that his act caused the damage. That argument seems to me to prove both too much and too little. Too much, because it is an argument for making a doctor the insurer of any

---

[6] We also explained that this problem of causation was mentioned in passing by Bristow J in *Chatterton v Gerson* [1981] QB 432, the forerunner of *Sidaway*.

damage which he causes, whether the patient knew of the risk or not. Too little, because it would excuse the doctor in a case in which he had a duty to warn but the actual operation was perfectly properly performed by someone else, for example, by his registrar.

Comments

1. Lord Hoffmann makes this appear to be a far easier case than it actually is. He suggests (at [28]) that this is a case where the *damage* 'would have happened anyway'. The fact is that this is a case where the damage would almost certainly not have happened anyway. This is not because the risk was increased by the surgeon, but precisely because it was such a small risk in the first place. For the same reason, the example of the roulette wheel is not wholly convincing. That is an example where the gambler would almost certainly have lost whenever he took his chance. The 'but for' test would not be satisfied. Our case is the reverse of this.

2. A direct comparison can be made between Lord Hoffmann's treatment of the duty to warn, and Lord Steyn's treatment of the same duty. Lord Hoffmann adopts the idea (mentioned only once by Lord Steyn) that the purpose of a duty to warn of risks is to allow the patient to avoid the risk (at [28]). That is not the whole story. The purpose of the duty recognized by Lord Steyn (which we have said does not fit easily within the tort of negligence) is primarily to *allow the patient to decide whether to run the risk*.

Because of the stance taken in respect of points 1 and 2, Lord Hoffmann did not directly deal with the issue of whether a 'but for condition' which does not increase a risk is nevertheless a cause. But perhaps we can glean that he thinks it is not, from his treatment of 'autonomy duties':

3. In paras [33]–[34], Lord Hoffmann admits that the failure to warn may be an 'affront to the personality' of the claimant. But he regards this as capable only of giving rise to a 'modest solatium'. As we have already said, in trespass to the person liability for consequences flows from unlawful denial of the right to physical self-determination. Lord Hoffmann says in para [32] that liability for consequences would in this case be 'strict' because the failure to warn did not cause any damage (for all the reasons discussed above). In trespass to the person, liability is strict, provided there is an act done with the relevant intention (to have physical contact). On trespass analysis, the contact would be tortious *because of the lack of informed consent*. It would not be tortious because of the 'failure to warn'. As such, there is no difficulty in saying that the loss flows from the trespass, and a trespass analysis would allow recovery of the full loss. If it were not for *Chatterton v Gerson* and *Sidaway v Bethlem Royal Hospital*, which declined to approach such questions through the trespass route, established legal principle would provide full compensation for invasion of precisely the right referred to by Lord Hoffmann as possibly justifying a 'modest solatium'.

We have suggested above that the causal problems would not arise if the case was regarded as one of trespass. That is because the failure to advise fits neatly with the notion of a wrong expressed by the trespass torts. It does not easily fit the idea of a wrong embodied in the tort of negligence, which is concerned with protection from harm (not, typically, with protection of autonomy).[7] However, in case we are now truly about to develop a doctrine of informed consent in English law, let us admit a major problem with trying to approach such a case via trespass.

Lord Hoffmann cogently rejects (at [35]) Tony Honoré's reasons for liability in such a case (quoted by Lord Steyn at [22]). Honoré suggested that an exception to causal principles

---

[7] See also the trouble encountered in *Rees v Darlington* [2004] 1 AC 309, Chapter 6.5.

should exist where the surgeon fails to give the required warning and obtain consent, and then goes on to cause the injury by his own hand. Lord Hoffmann suggests that this would give rise to absurd results, since it would excuse the doctor where someone else goes on to perform the operation. The same would be true of trespass. It is the unlawful application of force which gives rise to liability in trespass, not the failure to warn. This was the strength of the trespass analysis, because it avoids the causal problem. But it is also a weakness, because it would only permit liability on the part of the surgeon.[8]

FURTHER READING

Amirthalingam, K., 'Medical Non-Disclosure, Causation and Autonomy' (2002) 118 LQR 540.

Cane, P., 'A Warning About Causation' (1999) 115 LQR 21.

Hoffmann, The Rt Hon Lord, 'Causation' (2005) 121 LQR 592.

Jones, M., '"But for" causation in actions for non-disclosure of risk' (2002) PN 192–204.

Jones, M., 'A Risky Business' (2004) *Tort Law Journal* 192–204.

Skegg, P.D.G., 'English Medical Law and "Informed Consent": An Antipodean Assessment and Alternative' (1999) 7 Med L Rev 135.

Stapleton, J., 'Occam's Razor Reveals an Orthodox Basis for Chester v Afshar' (2006) 122 LQR 426.

---

3. PROBLEMS OF PROOF: CONTRIBUTION TO RISK

Fairchild v Glenhaven Funeral Services Ltd [2002] UKHL 22; [2003] 1 AC 32

Three widows brought actions against former employers of their husbands. All three of the deceased employees had developed mesothelioma, an incurable form of cancer whose only known cause is exposure to asbestos dust. Mesothelioma is not a 'progressive' disease. That is to say, it is not made worse by prolonged exposure.

On any view, mesothelioma is an 'indivisible' injury. Any given tortfeasor, *provided causation could be established*, should be liable in full, subject to contribution from other tortfeasors. Establishing causation was, however, the problem. There was (and could be) no physical evidence to show *which* tortfeasor (which period of exposure) had caused the harm. Available scientific opinion suggests that mesothelioma can be caused by exposure to a small number of asbestos fibres, and perhaps even by inhalation of a single fibre.

Although the claimants in *Fairchild* could not prove on the balance of probabilities that any specific employer had through their breach caused the disease to develop, they could show that all of their previous employers had breached relevant duties, and that their injuries flowed from such a breach. Equally, although further exposure does not worsen the disease,

---

[8] In Chapter 2, we also admitted some other limitations to protection of patient autonomy through trespass. But we also outlined a number of cases where trespass is used in medical decisions. *Sidaway* predated the evolution of these cases.

it was accepted that exposure to more fibres does increase the risk that a mesothelioma will develop. The House of Lords decided that on the particular facts, the claimants need not prove on the balance of probabilities that the defendants' breaches of duty had caused their loss. It would suffice for a claimant to show that a given defendant's breach of duty had contributed to the risk of harm. This amounted to a suspension of established principles of *proof* of 'but for' causation.

This case could be said to be symptomatic of the present era of personal injury litigation. The authors of the next extract suggest that the current developmental stage in tort law is different from the *Donoghue* era because tort law faces a different set of problems:

A. Porat and A. Stein, *Tort Liability Under Uncertainty* (Oxford: OUP, 2001), 8

The most important of these problems is that of untraceable and indivisible damage. Untraceable damage is damage that the fact-finder cannot causally attribute to any particular wrongdoer even when she can identify the wrongdoers who externalised the risks that might have materialized into damage. The difference between risks that did (or did not) materialize, on the one hand, and risks that might have materialized, on the other, is evidential in nature. If the fact-finder were to have enough evidence, he or she could identify the origin/s of the damage; however, evidence that could facilitate this identification is unavailable. Indivisible damage is damage that the fact-finder cannot apportion between the relevant parties by causally attributing its fractions to their respective causes. In an indivisible-damage case, the causes of the aggregate damage are known, but its fractions are without any identifiable causal traces. The indivisible-damage problem is, therefore, a variant of the more general problem of untraceable damage. . . . we refer to this general problem as the problem of indeterminate causation.

The Legal Context of *Fairchild*: Previous Case Law

Which of them caused the damage?

As noted above, a key problem for the claimants in *Fairchild* was that it was impossible to establish which employer's breach of duty had caused their damage. As such, the case raised very similar problems to the Californian case of *Summers v Tice* (1948) 119 P 2d 1 and the Canadian case of *Cook v Lewis* [1951] SCR 830. In each of these cases, the plaintiff was shot by one member or another of a shooting party. In each case, the plaintiff could not establish which member of the shooting party had caused his injuries. The solution was to hold that any member of the party who could be shown to have acted in breach of duty could be held liable for the damage caused, *unless* that defendant could show that his actions had not caused the plaintiff's injury. The burden of proof is reversed. This approach was incorporated to the American Law Institute, Restatement of the Law, Torts, Second (1965), section 433(3):

> Where the conduct of two or more actors is tortious, and it is proved that harm has been caused to the plaintiff by only one of them, but there is uncertainty as to which one has caused it, the burden is upon each such actor to prove that he has not caused the harm.

A similar problem arose in a very different context in the Californian case of *Sindell v Abbott Laboratories* (1980) 26 Cal 3d 588. This was a class action for personal injuries arising from exposure to the anti-miscarriage drug 'DES'. The drug had been manufactured by a very large number of companies, and since the plaintiffs' case concerned allegations of failure in the pre-market testing of the drug all of these were potentially in breach. This case was very different from the 'hunting' cases in that any of around 200 companies may have manufactured the injury-producing drugs. The Californian court held that in these circumstances, the fair response was to impose liability according to the 'market share' of any given company. This would relieve the company of the need to exonerate itself from blame, or to proceed against other manufacturers for compensation, whilst ensuring that it was practically possible to bring a successful action. However, a claimant would not achieve full compensation unless all manufacturers of the drug could be joined as parties. This contrasts with the general legal approach, which is to allow the claimant to bring an action against any one of a number of tortfeasors and recover damages in full. The general approach is clearly designed for the convenience of claimants, but it is an 'all or nothing' approach and that means that in some circumstances the claimant will gain nothing.

The English authorities: was it the breach that caused the damage?

The following cases were regarded as directly in point by the House of Lords in *Fairchild*.

Progressive Diseases and Contribution to the Harm: *Bonnington Castings v Wardlaw* [1956] AC 613

A steel dresser was exposed to silica dust at work, and as a result contracted pneumoconiosis. Part of his exposure (from use of swing grinders) was in breach of his employers' statutory duty under the Grinding of Metals (Miscellaneous Industries) Regulations 1925, because dust guards used with the grinders were not kept clear from obstruction. However, some of his exposure (caused by use of a pneumatic hammer) was treated as 'innocent' because no practicable precautions could have been taken to reduce the exposure.

Lord Reid, at 621–2

The medical evidence was that pneumoconiosis is caused by a gradual accumulation in the lungs of minute particles of silica inhaled over a period of years. That means, I think, that the disease is caused by the whole of the noxious material inhaled and, if that material comes from two sources, it cannot be wholly attributed to material from one source or the other. I am in agreement with much of the Lord President's opinion in this case, but I cannot agree that the question is: which was the most probable source of the respondent's disease, the dust from the pneumatic hammers or the dust from the swing grinders? It appears to me that the source of his disease was the dust from both sources, and the real question is whether the dust from the swing grinders materially contributed to the disease. What is a material contribution must be a question of degree. A contribution which comes within the exception de minimis non curat lex is not material, but I think that any contribution which does not fall within that exception must be material. . . .

(At 622)

I think that the position can be shortly stated in this way. It may be that, of the noxious dust in the general atmosphere of the shop, more came from the pneumatic hammers than from the swing grinders, but I think it is sufficiently proved that the dust from the grinders made a substantial contribution. The respondent, however, did not only inhale the general atmosphere of the shop: when he was working his hammer his face was directly over it and it must often have happened that dust from his hammer substantially increased the concentration of noxious dust in the air which he inhaled. It is therefore probable that much the greater proportion of the noxious dust which he inhaled over the whole period came from the hammers. But, on the other hand, some certainly came from the swing grinders, and I cannot avoid the conclusion that the proportion which came from the swing grinders was not negligible. He was inhaling the general atmosphere all the time, and there is no evidence to show that his hammer gave off noxious dust so frequently or that the concentration of noxious dust above it when it was producing dust was so much greater than the concentration in the general atmosphere, that that special concentration of dust could be said to be substantially the sole cause of his disease.

Questions of quantification of damage did not arise in the House of Lords' decision, and no comment was made by the House on that issue.

Pneumoconiosis is a progressive disease: it is worsened with further exposure. Therefore, Lord Reid was able to conclude that showing material contribution to the dust in the atmosphere was sufficient to show a contribution *to the disease itself*—not just to the *risk* of the disease. This is, therefore, a very different case from *Fairchild*. However, to the great advantage of claimants, the House of Lords also held that there was no need to show that the contribution of the defendant's breach to the dust inhaled exceeded or even approached 50 per cent. It only had to make a 'material' contribution. In this case, it was recognized that more of the dust in the atmosphere came from the 'innocent' source, than from the breach of duty, but the defendants were still liable for the disease.

Some careless judicial language in subsequent case law implied that contribution to the *risk* of disease was analytically the same as contribution to *the disease itself*. For example, in another case involving pneumoconiosis, *Nicholson v Atlas Steel Foundry Ltd* [1957] 1 WLR 613, the defendants had not provided proper ventilation. Even with good ventilation, there would have been some dust exposure, but the breach of duty increased the exposure. Lord Cohen said this:

Lord Cohen, at 622

Pneumoconiosis is a progressive disease. The longer a workman is exposed to an intense cloud the graver must be the risk of infection. . . . The respondents are admittedly not to blame for the generation of this cloud, but any failure to provide proper ventilation must, I think, lengthen the period during which the cloud remains intense. It seems to me to follow that the respondents' failure to provide adequate ventilation must increase the risk to which the workmen are exposed. Reading the evidence as a whole, I think it establishes (to use the language of Lord Reid in *Wardlaw*'s case) 'on a balance of probabilities the breach of duty caused or materially contributed to the injury'.

At the start of the paragraph above, Lord Cohen misstates the nature of a progressive disease. It is only because greater exposure worsens the *disease*, not just the risk of the disease, that the inference drawn in *Bonnington Castings* (and in *Nicholson*) is legitimate. This would be extremely important in the case of *McGhee v National Coal Board*.

Non-progressive Diseases and Contribution to Risk of Harm:
McGhee v National Coal Board [1973] 1 WLR 1

The plaintiff was employed emptying brick kilns in hot and dusty conditions, and developed dermatitis. He alleged that this was caused by the defendants' breach of duty in that he should have been provided with washing facilities, including showers. The plaintiff had been forced to cycle home caked in dust and sweat. The difficulty faced by the plaintiff was one of evidence. In the course of his judgment in *Fairchild v Glenhaven* (at [17]), Lord Bingham offers an extract from the first instance decision in *McGhee* on the part of the Lord Ordinary (Lord Kissen), which is reported at 1973 SC (HL) 37. It very effectively analyses the problem of evidence in *McGhee*.

Lord Kissen

As I have maintained earlier, the pursuer, in order to succeed, must also establish, on a balance of probabilities, that this fault on the part of the defenders 'caused or materially contributed to his injury', that is to his contracting dermatitis. Dr Hannay's evidence was that he could not say that the provision of showers would probably have prevented the disease. He said that it would have reduced the risk materially but he would not go further than that. Dr Ferguson said that washing reduces the risk. Pursuer's counsel maintained that a material increase in the risk of contracting a disease was the same as a material contribution to contracting the disease and that Dr Hannay established this by his evidence. I think that defenders' counsel was correct when he said that the distinction drawn by Dr Hannay was correct and that an increase in risk did not necessarily mean a material contribution to the contracting of the disease. The two concepts are entirely different. . . .

In the House of Lords, Mr McGhee's appeal was allowed. But what exactly was the reason for that decision? Lord Reid appears to have decided to reject the very clear (and correct) distinction referred to by Lord Killett (above). Lord Wilberforce on the other hand may have accepted that distinction, but decided that the particular facts of this case required that 'contribution to risk' was to be *treated* the same as contribution to injury. Lord Simon seems to have blurred the distinction altogether.

Lord Reid, at 4–5

It has always been the law that a pursuer succeeds if he can show that fault of the defender caused or materially contributed to his injury. There may have been two separate causes but it is enough if one of the causes arose from fault of the defender. The pursuer does not have to prove that this cause would of itself have been enough to cause him injury. That is well illustrated by the decision of this House in *Bonnington Castings Ltd. v. Wardlaw* [1956] A.C. 613 . . . .

In the present case the evidence does not show—perhaps no one knows—just how dermatitis of this type begins. It suggests to me that there are two possible ways. It may be that an accumulation of minor abrasions of the horny layer of the skin is a necessary precondition for the onset of the disease. Or it may be that the disease starts at one particular abrasion and then spreads, so that multiplication of abrasions merely increases the number of places where the disease can start and in that way increases the risk of its occurrence.

I am inclined to think that the evidence points to the former view. But in a field where so little appears to be known with certainty I could not say that that is proved. If it were, then this case would be indistinguishable from *Wardlaw's* case. But I think that in cases like this we must take a broader view of causation. The medical evidence is to the effect that the fact that the man had to cycle home caked with grime and sweat added materially to the risk that this disease might develop. It does not and could not explain just why that is so. But experience shows that it is so. Plainly that must be because what happens while the man remains unwashed can have a causative effect, though just how the cause operates is uncertain. I cannot accept the view expressed in the Inner House that once the man left the brick kiln he left behind the causes which made him liable to develop dermatitis . . . . Nor can I accept the distinction drawn by the Lord Ordinary between materially increasing the risk that the disease will occur and making a material contribution to its occurrence.

Lord Wilberforce, at 5–6

. . . it was not enough for the appellant to establish a duty or a breach of it. To succeed in his claim he had to satisfy the court that a causal connection existed between the default and the disease complained of, i.e., according to the formula normally used, that the breach of duty caused or materially contributed ta the injury. Here two difficulties arose. In the first place, little is known as to the exact causes of dermatitis. The experts could say that it tends to be caused by a breakdown of the layer of heavy skin covering the nerve ends provoked by friction caused by dust, but had to admit that they knew little of the quantity of dust or the time of exposure necessary to cause a critical change. Secondly, there could be little doubt that the appellant's dermatitis resulted from a combination, or accumulation, of two causes: exposure to dust while working in hot conditions in the kiln and the subsequent omission to wash thoroughly before leaving the place of work; the second of these, but not the first, was, on the findings, attributable to the fault of the respondents. The appellant's expert was unable to attribute the injury to the second of these causes for he could not say that if the appellant had been able to wash off the dust by showers he would not have contracted the disease. He could not do more than say that the failure to provide showers materially increased the chance, or risk, that dermatitis might set in. . . .

But the question remains whether a pursuer must necessarily fail if, after he has shown a breach of duty, involving an increase of risk of disease, he cannot positively prove that this increase of risk caused or materially contributed to the disease while his employers cannot positively prove the contrary. In this intermediate case there is an appearance of logic in the view that the pursuer, on whom the onus lies, should fail—a logic which dictated the judgments below. The question is whether we should be satisfied, in factual situations like the present, with this logical approach. In my opinion, there are further considerations of importance. First, it is a sound principle that where a person has, by breach of a duty of care, created a risk, and injury occurs within the area of that risk, the loss should be borne by him unless he shows that it had some other cause. Secondly, from the evidential point of view, one may ask, why should a man who is able to show that his employer should have taken certain precautions, because without them there is a risk, or an added risk, of injury or disease, and who in fact sustains exactly that injury or disease, have to assume the burden of proving more: namely, that it was the addition to the risk, caused by the breach of duty, which caused or materially contributed to the injury? In many cases, of which the present is typical, this is impossible to prove, just because honest medical opinion cannot segregate the causes of an illness between compound causes. And if one asks which of the parties, the workman or the employers, should suffer from this inherent evidential difficulty, the answer as a matter of policy or justice should be that it is the creator of the risk who, ex hypothesi must be taken to have foreseen the possibility of damage, who should bear its consequences.

Lord Simon of Glaisdale, at 8

. . . In my view, a failure to take steps which would bring about a material reduction of the risk involves, in this type of case, a substantial contribution to the injury . . . .

Wilsher v Essex Area Health Authority [1988] AC 1078

A prematurely born baby suffered a condition known as RLF, which led to blindness. This condition may have been caused by the defendants' breach of duty in exposing the baby to excess oxygen. However, there were a number of other possible causes which were not related to the defendants' actions but were the natural consequence of premature birth. The House of Lords rejected an argument (accepted by the Court of Appeal) that *McGhee* should apply to assist the plaintiff, in that the defendants materially contributed to the risk that the baby would suffer RLF and could therefore be treated as materially contributing to the injury. The House of Lords endorsed the dissenting opinion of Sir Nicolas Browne-Wilkinson V-C in the Court of Appeal, where he had argued as follows:

Sir Nicolas Browne-Wilkinson V-C [1987] QB 730, 771–2

There are a number of different agents which could have caused the RLF. Excess oxygen was one of them. The defendants failed to take reasonable precautions to prevent one of the possible causative agents (e g excess oxygen) from causing RLF. But no one can tell in this case whether excess oxygen did or did not cause or contribute to the RLF suffered by the plaintiff. The plaintiff's RLF may have been caused by some completely different agent or agents, e g hypercarbia, intraventicular haemorrhage, apnoea or patent ductus arteriosus. In addition to oxygen, each of those conditions has been implicated as a possible cause of RLF. This baby suffered from each of those conditions at various times in the first two months of his life. There is no satisfactory evidence that excess oxygen is more likely than any of those other four candidates to have caused RLF in this baby. To my mind, the occurrence of RLF following a failure to take a necessary precaution to prevent excess oxygen causing RLF provides no evidence and raises no presumption that it was excess oxygen rather than one or more of the four other possible agents which caused or contributed to RLF in this case. The position, to my mind, is wholly different from that in the *McGhee* case [1973] 1 WLR 1, where there was only one candidate (brick dust) which could have caused the dermatitis, and the failure to take a precaution against brick dust causing dermatitis was followed by dermatitis caused by brick dust. In such a case, I can see the common sense, if not the logic, of holding that, in the absence of any other evidence, the failure to take the precaution caused or contributed to the dermatitis. . . . A failure to take preventative measures against one out of five possible causes is no evidence as to which of those five caused the injury.

The House of Lords agreed with these comments and declined to extend *McGhee* to a case in which there were several possible causes for the injury other than exposure to the same substance or agent (on this occasion, excess oxygen) that is present through the breach of the defendant. This distinction is hard to justify. Indeed, no reason is given for supporting it. But it would preserve the authority of *McGhee* in single agent cases, and it was endorsed by a later House of Lords in both *Fairchild* and *Barker v Corus* (below).

In *Wilsher* however, the House also cast doubt on the general authority of *McGhee*.

Lord Bridge suggested (at 1090) that *McGhee* 'laid down no new principle of law whatever', and that the majority decision was based not on an adaptation of legal principle but on an 'inference of fact'. Thus considerable doubt surrounded the status of *McGhee*, until the case of *Fairchild* was heard in the House of Lords. To a large extent, that authority was restored—though only in 'single agent' cases.

Fairchild v Glenhaven Funeral Services Ltd
[2002] UKHL 22; [2003] 1 AC 32

As we noted above, these appeals related to employees who had been exposed to asbestos dust during periods of employment with more than one employer. It was common ground that the mechanism initiating the genetic process which culminated in mesothelioma was unknown, and that the trigger might be a single, a few, or many fibres. It was also accepted that once caused the injury was not aggravated by further exposure but that the greater the quantity of fibres inhaled the greater the risk of developing the disease. The Court of Appeal, applying *Wilsher* rather than *McGhee*, concluded that the claimants had not established on the balance of probabilities which employer had caused their injury. The claimants therefore could not succeed in their actions. The House of Lords allowed appeals by the claimants.

Each of the five judges in *Fairchild* presented their views at substantial length. We will therefore need to be selective. Our focus will be on the various ways in which their Lordships interpreted *McGhee*, and the ways in which they stated the limits within which the special approach to proof of causation derived from *McGhee* would be applied.

Lord Bingham of Cornhill

2   The essential question underlying the appeals may be accurately expressed in this way. If (1) C was employed at different times and for differing periods by both A and B, and (2) A and B were both subject to a duty to take reasonable care or to take all practicable measures to prevent C inhaling asbestos dust because of the known risk that asbestos dust (if inhaled) might cause a mesothelioma, and (3) both A and B were in breach of that duty in relation to C during the periods of C's employment by each of them with the result that during both periods C inhaled excessive quantities of asbestos dust, and (4) C is found to be suffering from a mesothelioma, and (5) any cause of C's mesothelioma other than the inhalation of asbestos dust at work can be effectively discounted, but (6) C cannot (because of the current limits of human science) prove, on the balance of probabilities, that his mesothelioma was the result of his inhaling asbestos dust during his employment by A or during his employment by B or during his employment by A and B taken together, is C entitled to recover damages against either A or B or against both A and B? To this question (not formulated in these terms) the Court of Appeal . . . gave a negative answer. It did so because, applying the conventional "but for" test of tortious liability, it could not be held that C had proved against A that his mesothelioma would probably not have occurred but for the breach of duty by A, nor against B that his mesothelioma would probably not have occurred but for the breach of duty by B, nor against A and B that his mesothelioma would probably not have occurred but for the breach of duty by both A and B together. So C failed against both A and B. The crucial issue on appeal is whether, in the special circumstances of such a case, principle, authority or policy requires or justifies a modified approach to proof of causation. . . .

Lord Bingham set out the facts of the case and analysed the relevant English case law on causation including *Bonnington* and *McGhee* (above) before continuing:

21 This detailed review of *McGhee* permits certain conclusions to be drawn. First, the House was deciding a question of law. Lord Reid expressly said so, at p 3. The other opinions, save perhaps that of Lord Kilbrandon, cannot be read as decisions of fact or as orthodox applications of settled law. Secondly, the question of law was whether, on the facts of the case as found, a pursuer who could not show that the defender's breach had probably caused the damage of which he complained could none the less succeed. Thirdly, it was not open to the House to draw a factual inference that the breach probably had caused the damage: such an inference was expressly contradicted by the medical experts on both sides; and once that evidence had been given the crux of the argument before the Lord Ordinary and the First Division and the House was whether, since the pursuer could not prove that the breach had probably made a material contribution to his contracting dermatitis, it was enough to show that the breach had increased the risk of his contracting it. Fourthly, it was expressly held by three members of the House (Lord Reid at p 5, Lord Simon at p 8 and Lord Salmon at pp 12–13) that in the circum-stances no distinction was to be drawn between making a material contribution to causing the disease and materially increasing the risk of the pursuer contracting it. Thus the proposition expressly rejected by the Lord Ordinary, the Lord President and Lord Migdale was expressly accepted by a majority of the House and must be taken to represent the ratio of the decision, closely tied though it was to the special facts on which it was based. Fifthly, recognising that the pursuer faced an insuperable problem of proof if the orthodox test of causation was applied, but regarding the case as one in which justice demanded a remedy for the pursuer, a majority of the House adapted the orthodox test to meet the particular case. The authority is of obvious importance in the present appeal since the medical evidence left open the possibility, as Lord Reid pointed out at p 4, that the pursuer's dermatitis could have begun with a single abrasion, which might have been caused when he was cycling home, but might equally have been caused when he was working in the brick kiln; in the latter event, the failure to pro-vide showers would have made no difference. In *McGhee*, however, unlike the present appeals, the case was not complicated by the existence of additional or alternative wrongdoers.

Lord Bingham further outlined the facts and decision in *Wilsher v Essex Area Health Authority* (above) before continuing:

22 . . . It is plain, in my respectful opinion, that the House was right to allow the defendants' appeal in *Wilsher*, for the reasons which the Vice-Chancellor had given and which the House approved. It is one thing to treat an increase of risk as equivalent to the making of a material contribution where a single noxious agent is involved, but quite another where any one of a number of noxious agents may equally probably have caused the damage. The decision of the Court of Appeal did indeed involve an extension of the *McGhee* principle, as Mustill LJ recog-nised: [1987] QB 730, 771–772. . . . But much difficulty is caused by the following passage in Lord Bridge's opinion in which, having cited the opinions of all members of the House in *McGhee*, he said, at p 1090:

"The conclusion I draw from these passages is that *McGhee v National Coal Board* [1973] 1 WLR 1 laid down no new principle of law whatever. On the contrary, it affirmed the principle that the onus of proving causation lies on the pursuer or plaintiff. Adopting a robust and pragmatic approach to the undisputed primary facts of the case, the majority concluded that it was a legit-imate inference of fact that the defenders' negligence had materially contributed to the pursuer's injury. The decision, in my opinion, is of no greater significance than that and to attempt to extract from it some esoteric principle which in some way modifies, as a matter of law, the nature of the burden of proof of causation which a plaintiff or pursuer must discharge once he has established a relevant breach of duty is a fruitless one."

This is a passage to which the Court of Appeal very properly gave weight [2002] 1 WLR 1052, 1080, para 103, and in argument on these appeals counsel for the respondents strongly relied on it as authority for their major contention that a claimant can only succeed if he proves on the balance of probabilities that the default of the particular defendant had caused the damage of which he complains. As is apparent from the conclusions expressed in paragraph 21 above, I cannot for my part accept this passage in Lord Bridge's opinion as accurately reflecting the effect of what the House, or a majority of the House, decided in *McGhee*, which remains sound authority. I am bound to conclude that this passage should no longer be treated as authoritative.

Lord Bingham then turned to 'the wider jurisprudence', considering case law from around the world on similar issues, concluding:

32 This survey shows, as would be expected, that though the problem underlying cases such as the present is universal the response to it is not. Hence the plethora of decisions given in different factual contexts. . . . In some jurisdictions, it appears, the plaintiff would fail altogether on causation grounds, as the Court of Appeal held that the present appellants did. Italy, South Africa and Switzerland may be examples. . . . But it appears that in most of the jurisdictions considered the problem of attribution would not, on facts such as those of the present cases, be a fatal objection to a plaintiff's claim. Whether by treating an increase in risk as equivalent to a material contribution, or by putting a burden on the defendant, or by enlarging the ordinary approach to acting in concert, or on more general grounds influenced by policy considerations, most jurisdictions would, it seems, afford a remedy to the plaintiff. Development of the law in this country cannot of course depend on a head-count of decisions and codes adopted in other countries around the world, often against a background of different rules and traditions. The law must be developed coherently, in accordance with principle, so as to serve, even-handedly, the ends of justice. If, however, a decision is given in this country which offends one's basic sense of justice, and if consideration of international sources suggests that a different and more acceptable decision would be given in most other jurisdictions, whatever their legal tradition, this must prompt anxious review of the decision in question. In a shrinking world (in which the employees of asbestos companies may work for those companies in any one or more of several countries) there must be some virtue in uniformity of outcome whatever the diversity of approach in reaching that outcome.

Policy

33 The present appeals raise an obvious and inescapable clash of policy considerations. On the one hand are the considerations powerfully put by the Court of Appeal [2002] 1 WLR 1052, 1080, para 103 which considered the claimants' argument to be not only illogical but

"also susceptible of unjust results. It may impose liability for the whole of an insidious disease on an employer with whom the claimant was employed for quite a short time in a long working life, when the claimant is wholly unable to prove on the balance of probabilities that that period of employment had any causative relationship with the inception of the disease. This is far too weighty an edifice to build on the slender foundations of *McGhee v National Coal Board* [1973]

1 WLR 1, and Lord Bridge has told us in *Wilsher v Essex Area Health Authority* [1988] AC 1074 that *McGhee* established no new principle of law at all. If we were to accede to the claimants' arguments, we would be distorting the law to accommodate the exigencies of a very hard case. We would be yielding to a contention that all those who have suffered injury after being exposed to a risk of that injury from which someone else should have protected them should be able to recover compensation even when they are quite unable to prove who was the culprit. . . ."

The Court of Appeal had in mind that in each of the cases discussed in paragraphs 14–21 above (*Wardlaw*, *Nicholson*, *Gardiner*, *McGhee*) there was only one employer involved. Thus there was a risk that the defendant might be held liable for acts for which he should not be held legally liable but no risk that he would be held liable for damage which (whether legally liable or not) he had not caused. The crux of cases such as the present, if the appellants' argument is upheld, is that an employer may be held liable for damage he has not caused. The risk is the greater where all the employers potentially liable are not before the court. . . . It can properly be said to be unjust to impose liability on a party who has not been shown, even on a balance of probabilities, to have caused the damage complained of. On the other hand, there is a strong policy argument in favour of compensating those who have suffered grave harm, at the expense of their employers who owed them a duty to protect them against that very harm and failed to do so, when the harm can only have been caused by breach of that duty and when science does not permit the victim accurately to attribute, as between several employers, the precise responsibility for the harm he has suffered. I am of opinion that such injustice as may be involved in imposing liability on a duty-breaking employer in these circumstances is heavily outweighed by the injustice of denying redress to a victim. Were the law otherwise, an employer exposing his employee to asbestos dust could obtain complete immunity against mesothelioma (but not asbestosis) claims by employing only those who had previously been exposed to excessive quantities of asbestos dust. Such a result would reflect no credit on the law. It seems to me, as it did to Lord Wilberforce in *McGhee* [1973] 1 WLR 1, 7 that:

> "the employers should be liable for an injury, squarely within the risk which they created and that they, not the pursuer, should suffer the consequence of the impossibility, foreseeably inherent in the nature of his injury, of segregating the precise consequence of their default."

Conclusion

34 To the question posed in paragraph 2 of this opinion I would answer that where conditions (1)–(6) are satisfied C is entitled to recover against both A and B. That conclusion is in my opinion consistent with principle, and also with authority (properly understood). Where those conditions are satisfied, it seems to me just and in accordance with common sense to treat the conduct of A and B in exposing C to a risk to which he should not have been exposed as making a material contribution to the contracting by C of a condition against which it was the duty of A and B to protect him. I consider that this conclusion is fortified by the wider jurisprudence reviewed above. Policy considerations weigh in favour of such a conclusion. It is a conclusion which follows even if either A or B is not before the court. It was not suggested in argument that C's entitlement against either A or B should be for any sum less than the full compensation to which C is entitled, although A and B could of course seek contribution against each other or any other employer liable in respect of the same damage in the ordinary way. No argument on apportionment was addressed to the House. I would in conclusion emphasise that my opinion is directed to cases in which each of the conditions specified in (1)-(6) of paragraph 2 above is satisfied and to no other case. It would be unrealistic to suppose that the principle here affirmed will not over time be the subject of incremental and analogical development. Cases seeking to develop the principle must be decided when and as they arise. For the present, I think it unwise to decide more than is necessary to resolve these three appeals which, for all the foregoing reasons, I concluded should be allowed.

35   For reasons given above, I cannot accept the view (considered in the opinion of my noble and learned friend, Lord Hutton) that the decision in *McGhee* [1973] 1 WLR 1 was based on the drawing of a factual inference. Nor, in my opinion, was the decision based on the drawing of a legal inference. Whether, in certain limited and specific circumstances, a legal inference is drawn or a different legal approach is taken to the proof of causation, may not make very much practical difference. But Lord Wilberforce, in one of the passages of his opinion in *McGhee* quoted in paragraph 20 above, wisely deprecated resort to fictions and it seems to me preferable, in the interests of transparency, that the courts' response to the special problem presented by cases such as these should be stated explicitly. I prefer to recognise that the ordinary approach to proof of causation is varied than to resort to the drawing of legal inferences inconsistent with the proven facts.

Lord Hoffmann

61   What are the significant features of the present case? First, we are dealing with a duty specifically intended to protect employees against being unnecessarily exposed to the risk of (among other things) a particular disease. Secondly, the duty is one intended to create a civil right to compensation for injury relevantly connected with its breach. Thirdly, it is established that the greater the exposure to asbestos, the greater the risk of contracting that disease. Fourthly, except in the case in which there has been only one significant exposure to asbestos, medical science cannot prove whose asbestos is more likely than not to have produced the cell mutation which caused the disease. Fifthly, the employee has contracted the disease against which he should have been protected.

62   In these circumstances, a rule requiring proof of a link between the defendant's asbestos and the claimant's disease would, with the arbitrary exception of single-employer cases, empty the duty of content. . . .

63   So the question of principle is this: in cases which exhibit the five features I have mentioned, which rule would be more in accordance with justice and the policy of common law and statute to protect employees against the risk of contracting asbestos-related diseases? One which makes an employer in breach of his duty liable for the employee's injury because he created a significant risk to his health, despite the fact that the physical cause of the injury *may* have been created by someone else? Or a rule which means that unless he was subjected to risk by the breach of duty of a single employer, the employee can never have a remedy? My Lords, as between the employer in breach of duty and the employee who has lost his life in consequence of a period of exposure to risk to which that employer has contributed, I think it would be both inconsistent with the policy of the law imposing the duty and morally wrong for your Lordships to impose causal requirements which exclude liability. . . .

73   The question is how narrowly the principle developed in *McGhee's* case and applied in this case should be confined. In my opinion, caution is advisable. *Wilsher's* case shows the dangers of over-generalisation. In *Rutherford v Owens-Illinois Inc* (1997) 67 Cal Rptr 2d 16 the Supreme Court of California, in a valuable and lucid judgment, said that in cases of asbestos-related cancer, the causal requirements of the tort were satisfied by proving that exposure to a particular product was a substantial factor contributing to the "plaintiff's or decedent's risk of developing cancer": see p 32. That is precisely the rule your Lordships are being invited to apply in this case. The Californian Supreme Court stated the principle specifically in relation to asbestos-related cancer cases. No doubt it could also apply in other cases which were thought to have sufficient common features, but that was left for decision on a case-by-case basis. Likewise I would suggest that the rule now laid down by the House should be limited to cases which have the five features I have described.

74   That does not mean that the principle is not capable of development and application in new situations. As my noble and learned friend, Lord Rodger of Earlsferry has demonstrated, problems of uncertainty as to which of a number of possible agents caused an injury have required special treatment of one kind or another since the time of the Romans. But the problems differ quite widely and the fair and just answer will not always be the same. For example, in the famous case of *Sindell v Abbott Laboratories* (1980) 607 P 2d 924 the plaintiff had suffered pre-natal injuries from exposure to a drug which had been manufactured by any one of a potentially large number of defendants. The case bears some resemblance to the present but the problem is not the same. For one thing, the existence of the additional manufacturers did not materially increase the risk of injury. The risk from consuming a drug bought in one shop is not increased by the fact that it can also be bought in another shop. So the case would not fall within the *McGhee* principle. But the Supreme Court of California laid down the imaginative rule that each manufacturer should be liable in proportion to his market share. Cases like this are not before the House and should in my view be left for consideration when they arise. For present purposes, the *McGhee* principle is sufficient. I would therefore allow the appeals.

Lord Rodger of Earlsferry

168   . . . Following the approach in *McGhee* I accordingly hold that, by proving that the defendants individually materially increased the risk that the men would develop mesothelioma due to inhaling asbestos fibres, the claimants are taken in law to have proved that the defendants materially contributed to their illness.

Lord Nicholls of Birkenhead delivered a concurring judgment, also rejecting the idea that *McGhee* was based on a factual inference. Lord Hutton concurred in the result but thought *McGhee* was based on a factual inference.

Fairchild accepts that in certain circumstances, the claim is not defeated by the impossibility of proving that the breach of duty caused the injury suffered. In the course of reaching this conclusion, most members of the House of Lords (with the clear exception of Lord Hutton) accepted that the *McGhee* case laid down a principle of law, and did not rest purely on a 'robust' inference of fact. In fact as we saw above the judgments in *McGhee* and successor cases such as *Nicholson* were very ambiguous. Lord Hope (who was Junior Counsel for the Coal Board in *McGhee*) has expressed the view that Lord Bingham in particular (at [21], extracted above) correctly interprets that case:

Lord Hope of Craighead, 'James McGhee—A Second Mrs Donoghue?' [2003] 62 CLJ 587–604, 599

. . . Lord Bingham grasped the point of Lord Reid's judgment precisely when he said that, recognising that the pursuer faced an insuperable problem of proof if the orthodox test of causation was applied, but regarding the case as one in which justice demanded a remedy for the pursuer, a majority of the House adapted the orthodox test to meet the particular case. As Lord Rodger explained [para 142], what Lord Reid has done is to accept that the pursuer must prove that the defender's conduct materially contributed to the onset of the condition and then to hold, as a matter of law, that the proof that the defender's conduct materially increased the risk was sufficient for this onus to be discharged.

The House of Lords in *Fairchild* has clearly accepted that proof of material contribution to a *risk* of injury is not the same as proof of material contribution to the injury itself, particularly in the case of a non-progressive disease. This is the distinction that was blurred in *McGhee*, and which was perhaps not fully recognized by any member of the House of Lords in that case apart from Lord Wilberforce. (Lord Hope, in the article above, recounts that the House clearly saw no merit in the defendants' arguments from the start.) But the House has accepted that *as a matter of law*, in certain circumstances proof of contribution to the risk will be sufficient evidence of causation. It is necessary for the defendant to have increased the risk. According to Lord Hoffmann, this would mean that a case such as *Sindell v Abbott Laboratories* (above) would not fall within the *Fairchild* approach, because the existence of one more manufacturer does not 'increase the risk' associated with sale of the product.

When will Proof of Contribution to Risk Suffice?

At the very least, it is necessary to show that the state of scientific knowledge is such that proof of causation of damage is *impossible*. In addition, some of their Lordships emphasized that the duty which is breached would be substantially 'drained of content' if the rule on proof of causation is not relaxed. On the other hand, it is clear that the *McGhee–Fairchild* approach will not be applied to a case like *Wilsher*, in which the claimant is exposed to a variety of different risks. It will apply only where the claimant's injury was caused by exposure to the same type of risk (or the same 'noxious substance') to which the defendant exposed him or her.

'Innocent' Periods of Employment

Lord Rodger specifically reserved his judgment on one particular issue.

> 170 . . . the principle applies where the other possible source of the claimant's injury is a similar wrongful act or omission of another person, but it can also apply where, as in *McGhee*, the other possible source of the injury is a similar, but lawful, act or omission of the same defendant. I reserve my opinion as to whether the other possible source of the injury is a similar but lawful act or omission of someone else or a natural occurrence.

This issue was not resolved in any of the judgments. In practical terms, this is important. It suggests that if there is a case where one former employer who exposed the claimant to asbestos dust can be shown to have been *not negligent* (for example because they took proper precautions, or because their exposure of the claimant took place before the date on which such exposure could be said to give rise to foreseeable harm), then the solution reached in *Fairchild* may not apply. This is in part a consequence of admitting that the *McGhee* principle is a matter of law, and not a mere inference from the facts. The question is where the rule applies. This is one of the issues that arose in *Barker v Corus* (below).

An Issue Not Addressed: Apportionment

In neither *Bonnington*, *McGhee*, nor *Fairchild* was the House of Lords invited to address the issue of apportionment. This is specifically pointed out in the judgment of Lord Bingham, above. But why should Lord Bingham have mentioned apportionment at all? As we have explained, mesothelioma (unlike asbestosis for example, or progressive deafness caused by occupational exposure)[9] is an indivisible disease. It cannot be argued that more than one defendant contributed to the disease. It is simply that we do not know *which* defendant actually caused it.

The controversy that would attach to apportionment in such a case is encapsulated in the following extract, which followed the Court of Appeal judgment in *Barker v Corus*, but predates the House of Lords' judgment (extracted below). The author responds to paragraph 34 of Lord Bingham's judgment in *Fairchild*, which states that 'no argument was addressed to the House that . . . there should be an apportionment of damages because the breaches of duty of a number of employers had contributed to cause the disease . . .' (the full paragraph is extracted above). This extract states the orthodox view which was later disturbed by *Barker*.

C. McCaul, 'Holtby and the End Game' (2006) JPIL 6–11, 7

It is impossible to understand this observation [of Lord Bingham] in the light of legal principles as they currently stand. Apportionment of damage does not arise because there has been a breach of duty by a number of different defendants. To adopt such an approach is to look at the problem from the wrong end of the telescope. It is necessary to look at the damage, not the breach, in order to see whether apportionment is appropriate. If the damage is indivisible, then it matters not how many defendants' breaches of duty have caused it.

Nevertheless, their Lordships' invitation was accepted by the defendants in *Barker v Saint Gobain Piplines plc*.[10] The defendant's argument ran principally along the lines that, if it required a legal fiction to enable a mesothelioma sufferer to win on liability, then the Courts should be prepared to depart from the well-established script relating to indivisible injury when it came to assessing damages. In other words, that an indivisible injury should be divided up. Neither Moses J at first instance nor the Court of Appeal was impressed and ruled that the indivisibility of mesothelioma prevented apportionment.

The House of Lords however *was* impressed by the argument encapsulated in this extract. On the face of it, *Barker v Corus* seems to be the first UK case to apportion an indivisible injury.[11] In a moment we will analyse the reasoning which led to this conclusion; and then consider the swift legislative rejection of what the House of Lords had done (section 3 of the Compensation Act 2006). First, we should consider a few important issues concerning apportionment.

---

[9] *Holtby v Brigham and Cowan* [2000] 3 All ER 423; *Thompson v Smith Ship Repairers* [1984] QB 405, respectively.

[10] On appeal to the House of Lords (below), this case is referred to as *Barker v Corus* (a number of appeals were joined).

[11] In Chapter 7, we will note that in *Rahman v Arearose* [2001] QB 351, the Court of Appeal accepted that a psychiatric disorder was, on the facts, divisible damage. Though controversial, this is quite different. The Court of Appeal was persuaded that the various personality disorders from which the claimant suffered could be separated and attributed to different causes. Not so with mesothelioma.

Apportionment before *Barker*

Until *Barker*, courts were resolute in refusing to apportion indivisible damage. This is illustrated by *Sylvia Phillips v Syndicate 992 Gunner* [2003] EWHC 1084 (Eady J).

This case draws attention to the role of liability insurers in compensation for asbestos-related disease. We should not forget that mesothelioma claims, while not individually particularly large,[12] are likely to be numerous. Exposure to large liability, together with the lapse of time between exposure and onset of disease, means that many employers are insolvent by the time of the claim. This makes the issue of apportionment particularly pressing, because only if there is joint and several liability is the risk of insolvency passed to the employers and their insurers. Otherwise, it rests with claimants and there may be significant under-compensation. Equally, in many cases the only course of redress for the claimant is against the employer's insurer under the Third Parties (Rights Against Insurers) Act 1930. If the insurers are able to claim that their liabilities are proportionate, then the claimant will suffer the same vulnerability to under-compensation that joint and several liability is designed to avoid.

Sylvia Phillips was a claim under the Third Parties (Rights Against Insurers) Act 1930. The defendant insurer argued that its liability should be proportionate to its period of cover. The insurer had been on cover during a period when its insured (Kinkia Limited, now insolvent) exposed the deceased husband of the claimant to asbestos dust. This exposure had 'materially contributed to' the risk of developing mesothelioma. The defendant insurer sought a reduction in the sums payable by them to the claimant on the basis that they had been on cover for only a part of the period of exposure. Eady J refused to apportion the period of exposure in this way, partly because the *Fairchild* principle required only that there should be a material contribution to the risk of injury in order to establish joint and several liability.[13] The principle of full liability was maintained in an action against the insurers.

Damage and risk

We have noted several times that existing legal principle distinguishes sharply between divisible and indivisible damage. A number of academics have urged that proportionate damages should be more readily available. In the context of loss of chance in a medical setting (addressed in the next section), this argument generally aims to secure some compensation for claimants who would otherwise fail (although logically, it should mean that others who can prove causation on established principle should then enjoy lower damages awards). In the context of *Fairchild*, the courts already apply the principles in *Bonnington Castings* and *McGhee* to compensate claimants who cannot show a causal link on balance of probabilities, at least in 'single agent' cases. So in this context, the argument would tend to lead to reduced compensation for people suffering disabling industrial diseases.

Before *Barker v Corus*, it was suggested by Ariel Porat and Alex Stein, 'Indeterminate Causation and Apportionment of Damages: An Essay on Holtby, Allen and Fairchild' (2003) 23 OJLS 667–702 that the House of Lords in *Fairchild* ought to have adopted an apportionment approach similar to the one adopted in two Court of Appeal cases, *Holtby v Brigham & Cowan (Hull) Ltd* [2000] 3 All ER 423 and *Allen v British Rail Engineering Ltd* [2001] EWCA Civ 242. Contrary to the accepted legal position, Porat and Stein suggest that the current all or

[12] See Chapter 8, on assessment of damages. Since mesothelioma is fatal, and occurs after the lapse of many years, damages for lost earnings and care costs will be relatively modest.

[13] See R. Merkin, 'Insurance Claims and Fairchild' (2004) 120 LQR 233.

nothing approach may lead to 'excessive deterrence' and allow claimants to 'receive compensation in amounts that they clearly do not deserve' (p. 675).[14]

The *Holtby* case does mark a potentially important development in respect of asbestos-related disease but it is important to note that it does not deal with the same issue as *Fairchild*.

Holtby v Brigham & Cowan (Hull) Ltd [2000] 3 All ER 423

The claimant was exposed to asbestos dust for several years in his work as a marine fitter. For about half of the relevant period, he worked for the defendant. He developed asbestosis. Asbestosis, unlike mesothelioma, is a progressive disease. It is made worse by each exposure. At first instance, Judge Altman held that the defendant was liable only for the extent that he had contributed to the disability. Rejecting a simple mathematical approach, he reduced the general damages by 25 per cent.

The Court of Appeal upheld the decision of Judge Altman. In terms of legal authority, the court referred to the judgment of Mustill J in *Thompson v Smiths Shiprepairers* [1984] QB 405 (extracted in Chapter 7). Here, there had been exposure over a number of years to dangerous noise levels leading to deafness. Since a substantial part of the *damage* could be shown to have been done before the time that the defendants were in breach of duty, Mustill J suggested that the right approach was to attempt an apportionment of damage accordingly. In that case, the apportionment was difficult because of the medical evidence available. It was not clear what part might be played by the early years of exposure as compared with the later years, which were at a higher frequency. *Holtby* by contrast was a relatively easy case:

Stuart-Smith LJ

22 . . . There is no such problem here since the progression is linear depending on the amount of dust inhaled. All dust contributes to the final disability.[15]

An apportionment could therefore be attempted. The judge had been right to err on the side of the claimant in making the apportionment, so that a reduction of 25 per cent could not be criticized. Clarke LJ dissented, on the basis that this placed too great a burden on the claimant. He pointed out, correctly, that if this was the appropriate approach it was odd that it had not been mentioned by any of the judges in the cases of *Bonnington* or *Nicholson* quoted above (at [34]).

Although it is hard to see how the *Holtby* decision can be reconciled with *Bonnington Castings*, it does not deal with precisely the same issue as *Fairchild*. It was a case concerning a progressive disease, where the court felt that it could attempt to quantify the contribution of the breach to the disease suffered on the basis of the scientific evidence. It is *not* a case of liability for exposure to risk *per se*. It is a case where the physical damage itself is said to worsen along with the exposure to risk.

---

[14] Why do people who cannot trace some of the employers who exposed them to the risk of industrial injury or disease not 'deserve' to be compensated in full? It is easy to see that the last remaining employer (or even insurer) might not 'deserve' to pay the damages in full, but that is not the same thing. And why is incentive to abide by industrial safety duties to be called *excessive deterrence*?

[15] On the other hand, as mentioned in *Barker v Corus*, a simple division on a time basis may not be adequate. Intensity of exposure and type of asbestos are also relevant. See further N. Wikeley, *Compensation for Industrial Disease* (Dartmouth, 1993).

All of this should indicate why the decision of the House of Lords in *Barker v Corus* to apportion damages for indivisible injury is even more controversial than *Fairchild* itself.

Barker v Corus [2006] UKHL 20; [2006] 2 WLR 1027

These appeals raised both of the two outstanding issues referred to in respect of *Fairchild* above. Like *Fairchild*, in the appeals heard here, the claimants (or their husbands) had contracted mesothelioma through occupational exposure to asbestos dust over a number of years. Unlike *Fairchild*, in addition to periods of exposure on the part of employers including the defendant, in one case the deceased had also been self-employed for a period of time, and had been exposed to asbestos dust during this period of self-employment. Thus the question arose whether the *Fairchild* approach to proof of causation could apply where the disease had not necessarily been caused by a breach of duty, and where it might have been caused by the actions of the claimant himself. At first instance, Moses J had determined that this possibility was adequately dealt with by reducing damages on the basis of contributory negligence. He applied a reduction of 20 per cent.

The second issue to be resolved was the issue of apportionment. The defendant argued that the damages awarded should have been reduced to reflect the limited extent to which the defendant could be proven to be responsible for the damage suffered. The trial judge, Moses J, held that there should be no apportionment of damages. The Court of Appeal upheld his decision on both issues.

Issue 1: Self-exposure

The House of Lords had no difficulty in agreeing with the Court of Appeal on this point. Where there was a period of self-employment, this did not defeat the *Fairchild* principle, since that was in any case based on *McGhee* where there was a potential non-tortious cause. In developing this point, the House also explicitly endorsed the 'single agent' rule in *McGhee*, as a way of limiting the operation of the *Fairchild* principle. In single agent cases, there is no need to show that all of the exposures were tortious.

Issue 2: Apportionment

This was the far more difficult issue. Most of the majority judges (though not Baroness Hale who agreed in the outcome purely on grounds of fairness and policy) adopted a view of *Fairchild* which would make it possible to distinguish the existing case law on divisible damage. That is, they said that in *Fairchild*, the House of Lords had *not* held that 'material contribution to risk' was treated as equivalent, within the exception, to 'material contribution to damage'. Lord Rodger, in dissent, argued persuasively that this is precisely what had been said in *Fairchild* and that this must be so, because their Lordships had all applied *McGhee*, which proceeded on this basis.

We extract selectively from their Lordships' judgments, in respect of apportionment. It will be seen that Lord Hoffmann and Lord Scott took a novel approach to liability under *Fairchild*. They suggested that *exposure to risk* is itself the harm which is caused by the defendants' breach of duty. This was expressly *not* argued for by defendants' counsel. This was (explicitly) in case such an argument should open the door to claims where no physical injury is suffered at all. Counsel will have had in mind the ongoing 'pleural plaques' litigation, explained at the end of this chapter.[16] How far does Lord Hoffmann succeed in explaining why this should not be of concern?

Lord Hoffmann, *Barker v Corus*

[31] My Lords, the reasoning of Moses J and the Court of Appeal would be unanswerable if the House of Lords in Fairchild v Glenhaven Funeral Services Ltd had proceeded upon the fiction that a defendant who had created a material risk of mesothelioma was deemed to have caused or materially contributed to the contraction of the disease. The disease is undoubtedly an indivisible injury and the reasoning of Devlin LJ in Dingle v Associated Newspapers Ltd would have been applicable. But only Lord Hutton and Lord Rodger adopted this approach. The other members of the House made it clear that the creation of a material risk of mesothelioma was sufficient for liability. . . .

Creating a risk as damage

[35] Consistency of approach would suggest that if the basis of liability is the wrongful creation of a risk or chance of causing the disease, the damage which the defendant should be regarded as having caused is the creation of such a risk or chance. If that is the right way to characterize the damage, then it does not matter that the disease as such would be indivisible damage. Chances are infinitely divisible and different people can be separately responsible to a greater or lesser degree for the chances of an event happening, in the way that a person who buys a whole book of tickets in a raffle has a separate and larger chance of winning the prize than a person who has bought a single ticket. . . .

Fairness

[40] So far I have been concerned to demonstrate that characterising the damage as the risk of contracting mesothelioma would be in accordance with the basis upon which liability is imposed and would not be inconsistent with the concept of damage in the law of torts. In the end, however, the important question is whether such a characterisation would be fair. The Fairchild exception was created because the alternative of leaving the claimant with no remedy was thought to be unfair. But does fairness require that he should recover in full from any defendant liable under the exception? . . .

[43] In my opinion, the attribution of liability according to the relative degree of contribution to the chance of the disease being contracted would smooth the roughness of the justice which a rule of joint and several liability creates. The defendant was a wrongdoer, it is true, and should not be allowed to escape liability altogether, but he should not be liable for more than the damage which he caused and, since this is a case in which science can deal only in probabilities, the law should accept that position and attribute liability according to probabilities. The justification for the joint and several liability rule is that if you caused harm, there is no reason why your liability should be reduced because someone else also caused the same harm. But when liability is exceptionally imposed because you may have caused harm, the same considerations do not apply and fairness suggests that if more than one person may have been responsible, liability should be divided according to the probability that one or other caused the harm.

---

[16] *In re Pleural Plaques*; *Grieves v Everard*. The Court of Appeal judgment [2006] EWCA Civ 27 is extracted below; an appeal before the House of Lords is expected to be heard in June 2007.

Quantification

[48]   Although the Fairchild exception treats the risk of contracting mesothelioma as the damage, it applies only when the disease has actually been contracted. Mr Stuart-Smith, who appeared for Corus, was reluctant to characterise the claim as being for causing a risk of the disease because he did not want to suggest that someone could sue for being exposed to a risk which had not materialised. But in cases which fall within the Fairchild exception, that possibility is precluded by the terms of the exception. It applies only when the claimant has contracted the disease against which he should have been protected. And in cases outside the exception, as in *Gregg v Scott*, a risk of damage or loss of a chance is not damage upon which an action can be founded. But when the damage is apportioned among the persons responsible for the exposures to asbestos which created the risk, it is known that those exposures were together sufficient to cause the disease. The damages which would have been awarded against a defendant who had actually caused the disease must be apportioned to the defendants according to their contributions to the risk. It may be that the most practical method of apportionment will be according to the time of exposure for which each defendant is responsible, but allowance may have to be made for the intensity of exposure and the type of asbestos. These questions are not before the House and it is to be hoped that the parties, their insurers and advisers will devise practical and economical criteria for dealing with them.

Lord Scott also considered the damage caused by the defendants in this case to be increase in the risk of mesothelioma.

Lord Rodger (dissenting)

[80]   Lord Hoffmann suggests that in *Fairchild v Glenhaven Funeral Services Ltd* the majority did not proceed on the basis that a defendant who had created a material risk of mesothelioma was deemed to have caused or materially contributed to the contraction of the disease. That may well be true of his own speech, given the interpretation which he had sought to place on the speeches in *McGhee v National Coal Board*. In my view, however, it is not true of the speech of Lord Bingham of Cornhill who referred to six conditions and said ([2002] 3 All ER 305 at [34], [2003] 1 AC 32):

> '. . . Where those conditions are satisfied, it seems to me just and in accordance with common sense to treat the conduct of A and B in exposing C to a risk to which he should not have been exposed as making a material contribution to the contracting by C of a condition against which it was the duty of A and B to protect him . . . '

That is an exact transposition of the reasoning of Lord Reid to the circumstances of *Fairchild v Glenhaven Funeral Services Ltd*. And Lord Bingham is indeed saying that in these circumstances someone who exposes the victim to a risk to which he should not have been exposed is to be treated as making a material contribution to the victim's contraction of the condition against which it was his duty to protect him. It was on this basis that Lord Bingham concluded that the appeals should be allowed-because the plaintiffs had proved that the defendants had caused the men's death or injury. This is scarcely surprising since the plaintiffs' appeals were argued on exactly that basis.

[89]   As Mr Gore QC rightly emphasised on behalf of Mr Patterson, the real reason why the defendants want to get rid of liability in solidum is that quite a number of the potential defendants and their insurers in the field of mesothelioma claims are insolvent. So, if held liable in solidum, solvent defendants or, more particularly, their insurers will often find that they have

to pay the whole of the claimant's damages without in fact being able to obtain a contribution from the other wrongdoers or their insurers, if any. So their only hope of minimising the amount they have to pay out by way of damages is to have liability to the claimant apportioned among the wrongdoers. Therefore they are asking for the introduction of apportionment because of this entirely contingent aspect of the situation regarding mesothelioma claims. If Fairchild-exception claims had first arisen in an area where the wrongdoers and their insurers were in good financial heart, matters could have been resolved satisfactorily for all concerned on the basis of liability in solidum and the use of the 1978 Act.

[90]   Of course, it may seem hard if a defendant is held liable in solidum even though all that can be shown is that he made a material contribution to the risk that the victim would develop mesothelioma. But it is also hard-and settled law-that a defendant is held liable in solidum even though all that can be shown is that he made a material, say 5%, contribution to the claimant's indivisible injury. That is a form of rough justice which the law has not hitherto sought to smooth, preferring instead, as a matter of policy, to place the risk of the insolvency of a wrong-doer or his insurer on the other wrongdoers and their insurers. Now the House is deciding that, in this particular enclave of the law, the risk of the insolvency of a wrongdoer or his insurer is to bypass the other wrongdoers and their insurers and to be shouldered entirely by the inno-cent claimant. As a result, claimants will often end up with only a small proportion of the dam-ages which would normally be payable for their loss. The desirability of the courts, rather than Parliament, throwing this lifeline to wrongdoers and their insurers at the expense of claimants is not obvious to me.

Lord Walker expressed broad agreement with Lord Hoffmann.

Baroness Hale disagreed with Lords Hoffmann, Scott, and Walker about the nature of the damage, which in her view was plainly mesothelioma. But she agreed with their conclusion on the grounds of fairness to the defendants.

Baroness Hale

[120]   My Lords, in this case, the usual courtesies are more than usually apt. It has been both a privilege and an advantage to read your Lordships' opinions in draft. To some extent, I agree with you all. Thus I agree entirely with my noble and learned friend, Lord Rodger of Earlsferry, that the damage which is the 'gist' of these actions is the mesothelioma and its physical and financial consequences. It is not the risk of contracting mesothelioma. Mr Stuart-Smith QC was indeed anxious to disclaim any such argument. He was understandably concerned to avoid the possibility that our reasoning might lead to the imposition of liability for tortiously exposing a person to the risk of harm even where that harm had not in fact been suffered.

[121]   I also agree entirely with my noble and learned friend, Lord Walker of Gestingthorpe, that while the borderline between a divisible and an indivisible injury may be debatable, mesothelioma is an indivisible injury. What makes it an indivisible injury, and thus different from asbestosis or industrial deafness or any of the other dose-related cumulative diseases, is that it may be caused by a single fibre. This much, as I understand it, is known, although the mechanism whereby that fibre causes the transformation of a normal into a malignant cell is not known.

[122]   But it does not necessarily follow from the fact that the damage is a single indivisible injury that each of the persons who may have caused that injury should be liable to pay for all of its consequences. The common law rules that lead to liability in solidum for the whole

damage have always been closely linked to the common law's approach to causation. There is no reason in principle why the former rules should not be modified as the latter approach is courageously developed to meet new situations. . . .

The approach in *Barker* was deliberately designed to apply within a narrow 'enclave' (as Lord Rodger called it). Within that enclave, its effect has now been reversed. But it might be very difficult to put the genie of 'risk as damage' back into its bottle, now that it has been released. This move seems dangerous in two ways:

1. It removes, for the purpose of this case, a fundamental distinction between risk and harm. This move might be used elsewhere to increase the amount of liability, since many people can claim that they are wrongly exposed to risk. Lord Hoffmann attempts to counter this in para [48] above by referring to the fact *that the exposures between them have caused the harm*. Will this restriction be resilient enough?

2. As Lord Rodger says, the effort to be fair to defendants has the effect of placing the very substantial risk of insolvency on the claimants who have been wrongly exposed to the risk of fatal disease, and have contracted that disease. In terms of fairness, the decision makes a choice: to under-compensate claimants, in order to protect the remaining solvent employers and available insurers. He also suggested that this was prompted not by reasons of 'corrective justice', so much as by a practical concern with preventing further insurer insolvency. Is it right for this unconventional choice to be made by the courts?

As already mentioned, the effect of this decision on claims for mesothelioma was reversed with extraordinary speed, reinstating the widely understood view that liability under *Fairchild*, like liability under *McGhee*, would be joint and several liability. Apart from this rapid reversal, the section also provides that those defendants who are thereby exposed to an inequitable burden of liability because of insolvent liability insurers may also be indemnified in a manner to be settled. The first step is to turn back the clock; but provision for greater fairness to liable parties can be made in time. This is the sort of solution which could not be achieved by a court alone.

The following is an extract from section 3.

Compensation Act 2006

3 Mesothelioma: damages

(1) This section applies where:

  (a) a person ('the responsible person') has negligently or in breach of statutory duty caused or permitted another person ('the victim') to be exposed to asbestos,

  (b) the victim has contracted mesothelioma as a result of exposure to asbestos.

  (c) because of the nature of mesothelioma and the state of medical science, it is not possible to determine with certainty whether it was the exposure mentioned in paragraph (a) or another exposure which caused the victim to become ill, and

  (d) the responsible person is liable in tort, by virtue of the exposure mentioned in paragraph (a), in connection with damage caused to the victim by the disease (whether by reason of having materially increased a risk or for any other reason).

(2) The responsible person shall be liable—

    (a) in respect of the whole damage caused to the victim by the disease (irrespective of whether the victim was also exposed to asbestos—

        (i) other than by the responsible person, whether or not in circumstances in which another person has liability in tort, or,

        (ii) by the responsible person in circumstances in which he has no liability in tort), and

    (b) jointly and severally with other liable person.

(3) Subsection (2) does not prevent—

    (a) one responsible person from claiming a contribution from another, or,

    (b) a finding of contributory negligence.

(4) In determining the extent of contributions of different responsible persons in accordance with subsection (3)(a), a court shall have regard to the relative lengths of the periods of exposure for which each was responsible; but this subsection shall not apply—

    (a) if or to the extent that responsible persons agree to apportion responsibility amongst themselves on some other basis, or

    (b) if or to the extent that the court thinks that another basis for determining contributions is more appropriate in the circumstances of a particular case.

. . .

(7) The Treasury may make regulations about the provision of compensation to a responsible person where—

    (a) he claims, or would claim, a contribution from another responsible person in accordance with subsection (3)(a), but

    (b) he is unable or likely to be unable to obtain the contribution, because an insurer of the other responsible person is unable or likely to be unable to satisfy the claim for a contribution.

A draft Regulation has been produced in respect of section 3(7), enabling a person who is liable in tort within the terms of section 3 (or their insurer) to recover a contribution from the Financial Services Compensation Scheme: Compensation Act 2006 (Contribution for Mesothelioma Claims) Regulations 2006 (Draft).

FURTHER READING

Green, S., 'Winner Takes All' (2004) 120 LQR 566.

Kramer, A., 'Smoothing the Rough Justice of the Fairchild Principle' (2006) 122 LQR 547–53.

Miller, C., 'Causation in Personal Injury: Legal or Epidemiological Common Sense?' (2006) 26 LS 544–69.

Porat, A., and Stein, A., 'Indeterminate Causation and Apportionment of Damages: An Essay on Holtby, Allen and Fairchild' (2003) 23 OJLS 667.

Stapleton, J., 'Two Causal Fictions at the Heart of US Asbestos Doctrine' (2006) 122 LQR 189–95.

Wikeley, N., *Compensation for Industrial Disease* (Aldershot: Dartmouth, 1993).

4. LOSS OF A CHANCE

The conflict between the traditional 'all or nothing' approach, and an approach based on quantification of risk, arises again in relation to this final problem. Given the judgments of the majority in *Barker*, could the tort of negligence tolerate claims for *lost chance of avoiding physical injury*? It already compensates in some circumstances for lost chance of *financial gain*. So far, the answer in respect of personal injury has been 'no'.

In cases where the claimant is unable to establish the defendant's breach as a 'but for' cause of injury, it has sometimes been argued instead that the breach has diminished the claimant's chances of a better outcome. This argument treats a chance as itself a thing of value, so that loss of or perhaps diminution in such a chance should be regarded as sufficient damage to give rise to a claim in negligence.

As mentioned above, claims for loss of chance are clearly accepted in certain cases of economic loss and of lost chance of economic gain (see for example *Kitchen v Royal Air Force Association* [1958] 1 WLR 563; *Allied Maples v Simmons and Simmons* [1995] 4 All ER 907; *Normans Bay v Coudert* [2003] EWCA Civ 215; [2004] All ER 458). In the last of these cases, members of the Court of Appeal expressed 'disquiet' about this apparent inconsistency. We will devote most space here to consideration of the House of Lords' decision in *Gregg v Scott*. A possible principled basis on which to distinguish the cases of recoverable lost chance, from those in which the traditional all or nothing approach will apply, has been outlined by Helen Reece in an article extracted below. Her article was referred to by the House of Lords in *Gregg v Scott*, and it may have influenced some of the judges, but its main point was not fully considered.

We will extract the case of *Hotson v East Berks AHA*, and outline the approach of Helen Reece in explaining that case before we consider *Gregg v Scott* itself.

Hotson v East Berkshire Area Health Authority [1987] AC 750

In *Hotson*, the plaintiff fell 12 feet out of a tree. He was taken to hospital within a few hours. Medical staff failed to notice that he had suffered an acute traumatic fracture of the left femoral epiphysis, and he was sent home. For five days he suffered severe pain. He was then taken back to the hospital, and this time the injury was correctly identified. He was treated accordingly. He suffered an avascular necrosis. This resulted from a failure of the blood supply and led to a deformity in the hip, at the head of the femur. This would almost certainly be aggravated by osteoarthritis in the future. The plaintiff sued the defendant health authority for the initial failure to diagnose the injury which led to the avascular necrosis.

The difficulty with the plaintiff's claim was that he could not establish on the balance of probabilities that, with prompt treatment, the avascular necrosis would not have developed. The trial judge (Simon Brown J) assessed the available evidence and concluded that it was more likely than not that, even with prompt treatment, the injury would still have developed. The likelihood that he would have sustained the same injury was assessed at 75 per cent. However, the trial judge allowed the plaintiff's claim, subject to a discount of 75 per cent for the likelihood that the injury would still have been sustained but for the negligence. This amounted to a successful claim for loss of a 25 per cent chance of recovery. The Court of Appeal upheld this award. The health authority appealed to the House of Lords.

In the House of Lords, the traditional 'all or nothing' approach was restored. The reasoning of the House has been criticized for not dealing with the central issues. In the extract below, Lord Bridge leaves the issue of lost chance for another day.

Lord Bridge of Harwich, at 780

I would observe at the outset that the damages referable to the plaintiff's pain during the five days by which treatment was delayed in consequence of failure to diagnose the injury correctly, although sufficient to establish the authority's liability for the tort of negligence, have no relevance to their liability in respect of the avascular necrosis. There was no causal connection between the plaintiff's physical pain and the development of the necrosis. If the injury had been painless, the plaintiff would have to establish the necessary causal link between the necrosis and the authority's breach of duty in order to succeed. It makes no difference that the five days' pain gave him a cause of action in respect of an unrelated element of damage.

(At 782–3)

. . . The plaintiff's claim was for damages for physical injury and consequential loss alleged to have been caused by the authority's breach of their duty of care. In some cases, perhaps particularly medical negligence cases, causation may be so shrouded in mystery that the court can only measure statistical chances. But that was not so here. On the evidence there was a clear conflict as to what had caused the avascular necrosis. The authority's evidence was that the sole cause was the original traumatic injury to the hip. The plaintiff's evidence, at its highest, was that the delay in treatment was a material contributory cause. This was a conflict, like any other about some relevant past event, which the judge could not avoid resolving on a balance of probabilities. Unless the plaintiff proved on a balance of probabilities that the delayed treatment was at least a material contributory cause of the avascular necrosis he failed on the issue of causation and no question of quantification could arise. But the judge's findings of fact . . . are unmistakably to the effect that on a balance of probabilities the injury caused by the plaintiff's fall left insufficient blood vessels intact to keep the epiphysis alive. This amounts to a finding of fact that the fall was the sole cause of the avascular necrosis.

The upshot is that the appeal must be allowed on the narrow ground that the plaintiff failed to establish a cause of action in respect of the avascular necrosis and its consequences. Your Lordships were invited to approach the appeal more broadly and to decide whether, in a claim for damages for personal injury, it can ever be appropriate, where the cause of the injury is unascertainable and all the plaintiff can show is a statistical chance which is less than even that, but for the defendant's breach of duty, he would not have suffered the injury, to award him a proportionate fraction of the full damages appropriate to compensate for the injury as the measure of damages for the lost chance.

There is a superficially attractive analogy between the principle applied in such cases as *Chaplin v. Hicks* [1911] 2 K.B. 786 (award of damages for breach of contract assessed by reference to the lost chance of securing valuable employment if the contract had been performed) and *Kitchen v. Royal Air Force Association* [1958] 1 W.L.R. 563 (damages for solicitors' negligence assessed by reference to the lost chance of prosecuting a successful civil action) and the principle of awarding damages for the lost chance of avoiding personal injury or, in medical negligence cases, for the lost chance of a better medical result which might have been achieved by prompt diagnosis and correct treatment. I think there are formidable difficulties in the way of accepting the analogy. But I do not see this appeal as a suitable occasion for reaching a settled conclusion as to whether the analogy can ever be applied.

As I have said, there was in this case an inescapable issue of causation first to be resolved. But if the plaintiff had proved on a balance of probabilities that the authority's negligent failure to diagnose and treat his injury promptly had materially contributed to the development of

avascular necrosis, I know of no principle of English law which would have entitled the authority to a discount from the full measure of damage to reflect the chance that, even given prompt
treatment, avascular necrosis might well still have developed. . . .

In an influential article, Helen Reece argued that there is a key distinction between 'deterministic' cases, including *Hotson*, and 'quasi-indeterministic' cases, which are appropriately dealt
with through a 'loss of chance' analysis. We will spend some time on this distinction because
it might have provided the basis for distinguishing *Hotson* in the later case of *Gregg v Scott*, had
there not been other complicating factors.

According to Reece, *deterministic* cases are appropriately dealt with on the usual all or nothing approach, where one assesses whether the damage itself was more probably than not
caused by the defendant's breach. *Quasi-indeterministic* cases on the other hand are appropriately dealt with as loss of chance cases. Reece explains the meaning of 'determinism' and 'inde-
terminism' in this context as follows:

Helen Reece, 'Losses of Chances in the Law' (1996) 59 MLR 188, 194

. . . The intuitive notion of determinism . . . , is that phenomena are deterministic when their
past uniquely determines their future and that phenomena are indeterministic when they have
a random component.

. . . An event will here be treated as indeterministic if and only if it could not have been predicted at any time in the past, it cannot be predicted in the present even given unlimited time,
resources and evidence, and we cannot imagine how it would become possible in the future,
even given the success of current research programmes. Such an event is indeterministic for
all human purposes . . . it is not humanly possible to predict the event. This type of event is
referred to as a *quasi-indeterministic* event, . . . to distinguish [it] from those processes which
scientists believe to be truly indeterministic.

Why is this distinction of relevance in deciding whether to allow a claim for loss of chance?
Because in the quasi-indeterministic case, it is not 'humanly possible' to answer the 'but for'
question. This is not a question of lack of evidence; it is a question about the limits of know-
ability. Reece argues (at 204) that the reason for adopting a rule whereby the claimant must
prove their case on the balance of probabilities is that the 'risk of non-persuasion' must fall on
the person who wishes to disturb the status quo. But this does not apply to unknowable facts:

. . . the risk which it is reasonable to expect the plaintiff to bear is the risk of uncertainty in the
evidence, not uncertainty in the world.

We should notice that despite the logical nature of the distinction outlined by Reece, this *consequence* is a matter of opinion. It returns us to the question of which risks, in terms of evidence, it is 'reasonable' to place on the claimant, or the defendant. For example, is it reasonable
that the claimant should bear the risk of lack of evidence where the defendant's breach has
removed the opportunity of obtaining that evidence? (An example is *Hotson* itself.)

Reece describes *Hotson* as a deterministic case, which could be appropriately dealt with on
the balance of probabilities.

Pp. 195–6

. . . That *Hotson* was a deterministic case becomes clear when we look at the medical facts a little more closely. Avascular necrosis develops if and only if sufficient blood cells are left intact to keep the epiphysis alive. The trial judge found that it was likely (to a degree of 75%) that insufficient blood cells were left intact after the fall, so that necrosis would have been bound to develop; but that if, on the contrary, there were enough vessels left, then the delay would have made the onset of necrosis inevitable . . .

Therefore, there was a time in the past when the cause of the necrosis could have been determined. If the blood vessels had been examined after the fall, then it would have been humanly possible to decide whether or not the plaintiff would develop necrosis even if he were treated. . . .

If this is right, then Lord Mackay captured the essential feature of the evidence when he said:

Hotson v East Berkshire Area Health Authority [1987] AC 750, at 915

It is not, in my opinion, correct to say that on arrival at the hospital he had a 25 per cent chance of recovery. If insufficient blood cells were left intact by the fall, he had no prospect of avoiding complete avascular necrosis, whereas if sufficient blood vessels were left intact. . . if he had been given immediate treatment. . . he would not have suffered the avascular necrosis.

The *Hotson* case therefore concerned a simple lack of evidence, and was not appropriately dealt with in terms of 'loss of chance'.

Gregg v Scott [2005] UKHL 2; [2005] 2 AC 176

The claimant consulted his doctor about a lump under his left arm. The doctor ought to have referred the claimant to a hospital for further investigation. Instead, he reassured the claimant that the lump was only a collection of fatty tissue. This was found by the trial judge to have been a breach of his duty of care. Had the claimant been referred for further investigation, it would have been found that a cancerous lymphoma was developing and he would have had treatment for his cancer at that stage. Because of the doctor's breach of duty, it was not until the claimant was admitted to hospital with acute chest pain some months later that the diagnosis was made and treatment commenced. Treatment was delayed by around nine months.

Defining the damage in this case is not entirely straightforward (see Lord Hope, below). But it appears that the appellant's claim was not for the pain and suffering associated with the spread of his cancer, nor for the need to undergo particular forms of treatment which might not have been necessary if the disease had been recognized promptly. The action was solely for the reduced chances of a successful recovery which resulted from the delay in treatment. As Lord Hope put it regretfully, all of the claimant's eggs were in one basket. Different interpretations of the statistical chances of recovery themselves were mentioned in the judgments. But it appears that the chance of making a full recovery (defined for these purposes as survival for 10 years) was diminished from around 42 per cent (at the time of the initial consultation), to around 25 per cent at the time of the trial. Survival was never a probability. (We should note however that the claimant's prospects of recovery were increasing at the time of the House of Lords' judgment.)

The trial judge dismissed the claim, considering himself bound to this conclusion by the authority of *Hotson* (above). The Court of Appeal by a majority dismissed the appeal. In the House of Lords, a further appeal by Mr Gregg was dismissed by a majority, Lord Nicholls and Lord Hope dissenting. Each of the judgments is very different, and we will assess each one in turn.

Lord Nicholls of Birkenhead (dissenting)

[2] This is the type of case under consideration. A patient is suffering from cancer. His prospects are uncertain. He has a 45% chance of recovery. Unfortunately his doctor negligently misdiagnoses his condition as benign. So the necessary treatment is delayed for months. As a result the patient's prospects of recovery become nil or almost nil. Has the patient a claim for damages against the doctor? No, the House was told. The patient could recover damages if his initial prospects of recovery had been more than 50%. But because they were less than 50% he can recover nothing.

[3] This surely cannot be the state of the law today. It would be irrational and indefensible. The loss of a 45% prospect of recovery is just as much a real loss for a patient as the loss of a 55% prospect of recovery. In both cases the doctor was in breach of his duty to his patient. In both cases the patient was worse off. He lost something of importance and value. But, it is said, in one case the patient has a remedy, in the other he does not.

[4] This would make no sort of sense. It would mean that in the 45% case the doctor's duty would be hollow. The duty would be empty of content. For the reasons which follow I reject this suggested distinction. The common law does not compel courts to proceed in such an unreal fashion. I would hold that a patient has a right to a remedy as much where his prospects of recovery were less than 50–50 as where they exceeded 50–50. . . .

Medical negligence

[20] . . . I turn to the primary question raised by this appeal: how should the loss suffered by a patient in Mr Gregg's position be identified? The Defendant says "loss" is confined to an outcome which is shown, on balance of probability, to be worse than it otherwise would have been. Mr Gregg must prove that, on balance of probability, his medical condition after the negligence was worse than it would have been in the absence of the negligence. Mr Gregg says his "loss" includes proved diminution in the prospects of a favourable outcome. Dr Scott's negligence deprived him of a worthwhile chance that his medical condition would not have deteriorated as it did.

[21] Of primary relevance on this important issue is an evaluation of what, in practice, a patient suffering from a progressive illness loses when the treatment he needs is delayed because of a negligent diagnosis. . . .

[23] . . . Enormous advances have been made in medical knowledge and skills in recent years, in this country and internationally. New and improved drugs and procedures make possible ever more alleviation of illnesses and injuries. But the outcome of medical treatment in any particular case remains beyond anyone's control. It is often a matter of considerable uncertainty, in some types of case more than others. Doctors cannot guarantee outcomes. Every person and his personal circumstances and history are different. The way some drugs work is not understood fully. The response of patients to treatment is not uniform, nor is it always predictable. Faced with a serious illness or injury doctors can often do no more than assess a patient's prospects of recovery. Limitations on human knowledge mean that, to greater or

lesser extent, the prognosis for a patient is inherently uncertain. Indeed, sometimes the very diagnosis itself may be problematic.

[24]   Given this uncertainty of outcome, the appropriate characterisation of a patient's loss in this type of case must surely be that it comprises the loss of the chance of a favourable outcome, rather than the loss of the outcome itself. Justice so requires, because this matches medical reality. This recognises what in practice a patient had before the doctor's negligence occurred. It recognises what in practice the patient lost by reason of that negligence. The doctor's negligence diminished the patient's prospects of recovery. And this analysis of a patient's loss accords with the purpose of the legal duty of which the doctor was in breach. In short, the purpose of the duty is to promote the patient's prospects of recovery by exercising due skill and care in diagnosing and treating the patient's condition.

[25]   This approach also achieves a basic objective of the law of tort. The common law imposes duties and seeks to provide appropriate remedies in the event of a breach of duty. If negligent diagnosis or treatment diminishes a patient's prospects of recovery, a law which does not recognise this as a wrong calling for redress would be seriously deficient today. In respect of the doctors' breach of duty the law would not have provided an appropriate remedy. Of course, losing a chance of saving a leg is not the same as losing a leg: see Tony Weir, Tort Law (2002), p 76. But that is not a reason for declining to value the chance for whose loss the doctor was directly responsible. The law would rightly be open to reproach were it to provide a remedy if what is lost by a professional adviser's negligence is a financial opportunity or chance but refuse a remedy where what is lost by a doctor's negligence is the chance of health or even life itself. Justice requires that in the latter case as much as the former the loss of a chance should constitute actionable damage.

Comment

When we extract Lord Phillips' judgment (below), we will see that he regards Lord Nicholls as having over-simplified the facts of the case. Perhaps Lord Phillips is right about this. Even so, Lord Nicholls' primary argument is a good one. Given that in a case like this a patient will only ever have a 'prospect' of recovery, which can only be defined in terms of statistical chances, the whole purpose of a doctor's duty of care is to safeguard the patient's prospects. If loss of prospects is not recoverable, then the duty serves no purpose in respect of many medical conditions. The step proposed by Lord Nicholls can therefore be presented as a necessary one, designed to reflect the limitations of medical knowledge. But the other judgments expose complications associated with this solution.

Lord Hoffmann

The quantification argument

[67]   The first argument is based upon the well-established principle that in quantifying the loss likely to have been caused by the Defendant's wrongful act, the court will take into account possibilities, even though they do not amount to probabilities: Mallett v McMonagle [1970] AC 166, 176, [1969] 2 All ER 178. A common example is the possibility that a claimant who has been injured by the defendant will suffer some complication such as arthritis in a damaged joint. This principle applies when the extent of the loss depends upon what will happen after the trial or upon what might hypothetically have happened (either before or after the trial) if the claimant had not been injured: see Doyle v Wallace [1998] PIQR Q146, in which the

loss of earnings caused by the injury would have been greater if the claimant had qualified as a drama teacher.

[68]   This principle has in my opinion no application to the present case because it applies only to damage which it is proved will be attributable to the Defendant's wrongful act. Thus in Doyle v Wallace there was no dispute that if the claimant had qualified as a drama teacher, the loss of the additional earnings would have been attributable to the injury which the defendant had caused her. Likewise, if the injured joint develops arthritis, there is usually no dispute that the arthritis will be attributable to the injury. In the present case, the question was not whether Mr Gregg was likely to survive more than 10 years (the finding was that he was not) but whether his likely premature death would be attributable to the wrongful act of the Defendant.

Lord Hoffmann considered the cases of *Hotson*, *Wilsher*, and *Fairchild*, before continuing:

[79]   What these cases show is that, as Helen Reece points out in an illuminating article ("Losses of Chances in the Law" (1996) 59 MLR 188) the law regards the world as in principle bound by laws of causality. Everything has a determinate cause, even if we do not know what it is. The blood-starved hip joint in Hotson, the blindness in Wilsher, the mesothelioma in Fairchild; each had its cause and it was for the plaintiff to prove that it was an act or omission for which the defendant was responsible. The narrow terms of the exception made to this principle in Fairchild only serves to emphasise the strength of the rule. The fact that proof is rendered difficult or impossible because no examination was made at the time, as in Hotson, or because medical science cannot provide the answer, as in Wilsher, makes no difference. There is no inherent uncertainty about what caused something to happen in the past or about whether something which happened in the past will cause something to happen in the future. Everything is determined by causality. What we lack is knowledge and the law deals with lack of knowledge by the concept of the burden of proof.

[80]   Similarly in the present case, the progress of Mr Gregg's disease had a determinate cause. It may have been inherent in his genetic make-up at the time when he saw Mr Scott, as Hotson's fate was determined by what happened to his thigh when he fell out of the tree. Or it may, as Mance LJ suggests, have been affected by subsequent events and behaviour for which Dr Scott was not responsible. Medical science does not enable us to say. But the outcome was not random; it was governed by laws of causality and, in the absence of a special rule as in Fairchild, inability to establish that delay in diagnosis caused the reduction in expectation in life cannot be remedied by treating the outcome as having been somehow indeterminate.

. . .

[82]   One striking exception to the assumption that everything is determined by impersonal laws of causality is the actions of human beings. The law treats human beings as having free will and the ability to choose between different courses of action, however strong may be the reasons for them to choose one course rather than another. This may provide part of the explanation for why in some cases damages are awarded for the loss of a chance of gaining an advantage or avoiding a disadvantage which depends upon the independent action of another person: see Allied Maples Group Ltd v Simmons & Simmons [1995] 4 All ER 907, [1995] 1 WLR 1602 and the cases there cited.

[83]   But the true basis of these cases is a good deal more complex. The fact that one cannot prove as a matter of necessary causation that someone would have done something is no

reason why one should not prove that he was more likely than not to have done it. So, for example, the law distinguishes between cases in which the outcome depends upon what the claimant himself (McWilliams v Sir William Arrol & Co [1962] 1 WLR 295) or someone for whom the defendant is responsible (Bolitho v City and Hackney Health Authority [1998] AC 232, [1997] 4 All ER 771) would have done, and cases in which it depends upon what some third party would have done. In the first class of cases the claimant must prove on a balance of probability that he or the defendant would have acted so as to produce a favourable outcome. In the latter class, he may recover for loss of the chance that the third party would have so acted. This apparently arbitrary distinction obviously rests on grounds of policy. In addition, most of the cases in which there has been recovery for loss of a chance have involved financial loss, where the chance can itself plausibly be characterised as an item of property, like a lottery ticket. It is however unnecessary to discuss these decisions because they obviously do not cover the present case. . . .

Control mechanisms

[86]   The Appellant suggests that the expansion of liability could be held in reasonable bounds by confining it to cases in which the claimant had suffered an injury. In this case, the spread of the cancer before the eventual diagnosis was something which would not have happened if it had been promptly diagnosed and amounted to an injury caused by the Defendant. It is true that this is not the injury for which the Claimant is suing. His claim is for loss of the prospect of survival for more than 10 years. And the judge's finding was that he had not established that the spread of the cancer was causally connected with the reduction in his expectation of life. But the Appellant submits that his injury can be used as what Professor Jane Stapleton called a "hook" on which to hang a claim for damage which it did not actually cause: see (2003) 119 LQR 388, 423.

[87]   An artificial limitation of this kind seems to me to be lacking in principle. It resembles the "control mechanisms" which disfigure the law of liability for psychiatric injury. And once one treats an "injury" as a condition for imposing liability for some other kind of damage, one is involved in definitional problems about what counts as an injury. Presumably the internal bleeding suffered by the boy Hotson was an injury which would have qualified him to sue for the loss of a chance of saving his hip joint. What about baby Wilsher? The doctor's negligence resulted in his having excessively oxygenated blood, which is potentially toxic: see [1987] QB 730, 764–766. Was this an injury? The boundaries of the concept would be a fertile source of litigation.

[88]   Similar comments may be made about another proposed control mechanism, which is to confine the principle to cases in which inability to prove causation is a result of lack of medical knowledge of the causal mechanism (as in Wilsher) rather than lack of knowledge of the facts (as in Hotson's case). Again, the distinction is not based upon principle or even expediency. Proof of causation was just as difficult for Hotson as it was for Wilsher. It could be said that the need to prove causation was more unfair on Hotson, since the reason why he could not prove whether he had enough blood vessels after the fall was because the hospital had negligently failed to examine him . . . .

[89]   In *Fairchild's* case [2003] 1 AC 32, 68, Lord Nicholls of Birkenhead said of new departures in the law:

"To be acceptable our law must be coherent. It must be principled. The basis on which one case, or one type of case, is distinguished from another should be transparent and capable of identification. When a decision departs from principles normally applied, the basis for doing so must be rational and justifiable if the decision is to avoid the reproach that hard cases make bad law."

[90]   I respectfully agree. And in my opinion, the various control mechanisms proposed to confine liability for loss of a chance within artificial limits do not pass this test. But a wholesale adoption of possible rather than probable causation as the criterion of liability would be so radical a change in our law as to amount to a legislative act. It would have enormous consequences for insurance companies and the National Health Service. In company with my noble and learned friends Lord Phillips of Worth Matravers and Baroness Hale of Richmond, I think that any such change should be left to Parliament.

Comment

Lord Hoffmann is concerned to maintain the traditional 'all or nothing' approach. He rejects as 'arbitrary' and unprincipled all attempts to define a small category of cases, including this one, in which 'loss of a chance' could be regarded as a loss appropriate for compensation. If no principled reason for distinguishing the cases can be found, he suggests, the introduction of claims for loss of chance will have such far-reaching implications that it ought not to be attempted by the common law, but left to Parliament. It will be noticed however that Lord Hoffmann does not entirely accurately reflect the arguments of Helen Reece whose article he cites in support of the 'all or nothing' approach (at [79]). Reece's article as we have seen proposed that there was a difference between 'deterministic' and 'quasi-indeterministic' cases, which was broadly compatible with the pattern of the case law and occasionally (as in *Hotson*, per Lord Mackay) apparent in legal reasoning. Lord Hoffmann presents her arguments as suggesting that law *always* takes a 'deterministic' approach. The only exception he mentions is the case of hypothetical acts of third parties. In *Allied Maples v Simmons and Simmons* [1995] 4 All ER 907, for example, the defendants were solicitors, whose breach had removed the opportunity of negotiating a more favourable term in a contract. But it appears from Reece's article that she would include within the 'quasi-indeterministic' category some cases which do not involve hypothetical human actions.

Lord Hope of Craighead (dissenting)

The issue of damages

[95]   The question which remains is whether the Appellant is entitled to damages. At first sight there can only be one answer to this question. A claimant who seeks damages for negligence in a case of personal injury must show on a balance of probabilities that the breach of duty caused or materially contributed to his injury. The judge held that the Appellant's condition deteriorated significantly during the period from April 1995 to January 1996. The medical experts were agreed that the lymphoma which had been developing in his left axilla spread into the pectoral muscle of the left side of his chest during this period, and that this is what precipitated the crisis in January 1996 (para 30). As both Latham and Mance LJJ said in the Court of Appeal, the delay in diagnosis caused the tumour to enlarge, invade neighbouring tissues and cause severe pain (paras 21 and 47). As Mance LJ put it, the enlarged tumour was a clear physical consequence of the doctor's negligence (para 86). On the judge's findings a conventional view of the case would be that the delay in diagnosis resulted in a physical injury which entitled the Appellant to an award of damages for the consequences of that injury.

[96]   Latham LJ developed this point more fully in para 21 of his dissenting judgment:

"It was the enlargement of the tumour which reduced the chances of successfully treating it. This aspect of the Plaintiff's claim was never addressed by the judge. Nonetheless the judge's findings amply support the submission that the Appellant had indeed suffered injury which entitled the Appellant to general damages for the pain and suffering which were the physical consequence of the spread of the tumour, an assessment of the extent to which delay resulted in more intensive therefore damaging treatment, an assessment of the increased risk of relapse and the adverse effect on prognosis, involving an assessment of the consequences to the Appellant's expectation of life."

The question whether the assessments referred to in the latter part of this quotation may result in an award of additional damages, and if so how those damages are to be quantified, is controversial. But there seems to be no reason to doubt the soundness of the propositions that it was proved on a balance of probabilities that the tumour spread because of the delay in treatment, that this was a physical injury which was caused by the doctor's negligence and that this gave him a cause of action for the pain and suffering that was caused by that injury and all its other adverse consequences.

[97]   The judge said in para 48 of his judgment that, although he had found that there was a breach of duty, he had not found the causation of loss proved. So he dismissed the claim. Your Lordships were told that the reason why the question of general damages for pain and suffering was not addressed by the trial judge is that the Appellant did not ask for damages to be awarded under this head. The claim, as presented to judge, was for damages to compensate him for the loss of, or diminution in, his expectation of life due to the doctor's negligence. The Appellant's cause of action, as Mr Maskrey QC put it, was for the reduced prospect of a complete recovery—for the loss of a chance, in other words. What he sought to show was that this reduced prospect was a consequence of the physical injury caused by the delay, and that it was itself something of value for which the Appellant was entitled to be compensated. All the Appellant's eggs were, so to speak, put in this one basket.

. . .

[119]   An analogy may be drawn with cases where it is proved that a person's employment prospects, or his prospects of promotion, have been adversely affected by a physical injury. The claimant is not required, in a case of that kind, to prove on a balance of probabilities what his employment record would have been or that he would in fact have been promoted but for his injury. It is enough for him to prove that there was a prospect immediately before he was injured which he has lost due to the wrongdoer's negligence. The claim is for the loss of prospects assessed as at that date, not for the loss of a certainty. Some evidence is, of course, needed to enable the court to assess those prospects. Without that evidence the claim would be speculative, as any decision would be based on pure guesswork. But the law does not insist on proof that events would in fact have taken the course that the prospects relied upon have indicated: see, for example, the approach which Griffiths LJ took to the claim for loss of earnings in the case of a very young child in Croke v Wiseman [1981] 3 All ER 852, [1982] 1 WLR 71, 83; see also Doyle v Wallace [1998] PIQR Q146, where there was a significant chance that the claimant would have qualified and become a drama teacher, and Langford v Hebran [2001] PIQR, Q160 where the claimant's chances of achieving fame and fortune as a kick-boxer at various stages in his career were evaluated on a scale from 80% to 20% and damages for his loss of earnings awarded accordingly. . . .

[122]   In my opinion the correct starting point for the award for the reduction in prospects is the judge's assessment of the prospects of a successful outcome if the doctor had not been

negligent. The loss which he would have suffered should be calculated in the first place on the assumption that what the Appellant lost when he was seen by the doctor was the certainty of a complete recovery. The result of that calculation will then need to be discounted to reflect the judge's findings as to the prospects of a complete recovery in view of the nature of the cancer from which the Appellant was already suffering when the doctor was negligent. For the reasons which he explained in para 51 of his judgment, the judge would have discounted the damages that he would have awarded for the loss of a certainty of a cure by 80%. I would hold that the discounting exercise which he undertook was the right approach in principle, although the figures which led the judge to his conclusion are difficult to reconcile.

[123]   For the reasons which I have given at the outset of this opinion, however, I had hoped that it was not too late for the pain and suffering which the Appellant suffered due to the tumour's enlargement and the distress caused by his awareness that his condition had been misdiagnosed to be brought into account by way of an award of general damages. Unless this is done the Appellant will be left with no remedy at all for the consequences of the doctor's negligence. Very properly, as the facts that are needed are already there in the evidence and the action remains alive until this appeal and any further proceedings which may flow from it have been disposed of, the Respondent does not suggest that it would be either incompetent or unfair for the Claimant to seek such an award at this stage. The majority view that the appeal must be dismissed has deprived the Appellant of that opportunity.

Comment

Although Lord Hope joined Lord Nicholls in dissent, his reasons are different. He considers that the claimant would have had a straightforward claim for the pain, suffering and other immediate consequences of the spread of the tumour, including the need for any extra treatment if such were needed as a consequence of the breach. These effects he regards as sufficient damage to be the subject of a claim. It seems difficult to argue against this view, and it appears to be accepted by Baroness Hale in the majority (below). However there is a conflict with the opinion of Lord Hoffmann. Lord Hoffmann included some difficult examples in his attempt to show that the immediate physical consequences of the breach should not be considered to give rise to a claim. For example, was the oxygenation of the blood in *Wilsher* itself an injury? But it is hard to dismiss the pain and suffering associated with the larger tumour in *Gregg* and the claimant's knowledge of his likely death. These are not invented forms of injury, and it is suggested that at least in his narrower point (this damage in itself can form the basis of a claim), Lord Hope is correct.

The remaining issue is whether the diminution in survival prospects can be included as a head of damage in such a claim. Lord Hope suggests that it may be so included, subject to a reduction to reflect the fact that recovery was never a probability. This would be to allow 'loss of chance' via assessment of damages, rather than through redefinition of the damage suffered. It is similar to an argument which was rejected in the Court of Appeal and criticized by Lord Hoffmann in this case, namely that the physical changes can be regarded as a 'hook' on which to hang a claim for loss of chance:

Jane Stapleton, 'Cause-in-Fact and Scope of Liability for Consequences'
(2003) 119 LQR 388, 423

. . . what is the minimum sufficient factor that can satisfy the orthodox form of past actionable damage in physical loss negligence claims? . . . If C can come within whatever this requirement is held to be, C may well be able to use that factor as the 'hook' on to which to hang a lost chance as consequential on the actionable injury which is then recoverable under orthodox rules.

Lord Hope derives support for his proposition from certain cases where some account of future prospects is made in assessment of damages (at [119]). But we have already seen that Lord Hoffmann distinguished these cases, suggesting that the estimated loss of prospects in such cases can be demonstrated to be the consequence of the defendant's breach (at [67]–[68]). This is precisely what remains to be proved in a case such as *Gregg v Scott*.

Lord Phillips of Worth Matravers

[125]   This appeal has raised an important issue of policy. Should this House introduce into the law of clinical negligence the right of a patient who has suffered an adverse event to recover damages for the loss of a chance of a more favourable outcome? My noble and learned friend Lord Nicholls of Birkenhead has simplified the facts in order to identify with clarity the nature of this issue. I propose to take a different approach. I intend to wrestle with the complexities raised by the facts of this case. I do so because I have found it helpful, when considering the change in our law that is proposed, to examine the practical consequences of the change. . . .

[155]   [There was a] tenuous . . . assumption that the difference between Mr Gregg's 42% chance of being a survivor (on the basis of Professor Goldstone's model) and his 25% prospect of being a survivor, as assessed at the date of trial, was attributable to the fact that, before treatment had begun, his cancer had spread to the pectoral region. Professor Goldstone's model showed that, of the 42 destined to be survivors, all but four (at the most) achieved initial complete remission. Of the 55 who achieved initial complete remission between 38 and 42 were destined to be survivors. Of the 45 who did not achieve initial complete remission, four at the most were destined to be survivors. The degree of uncertainty in these figures reflects the fact that Professor Goldstone's model gives no figure for the prospect of surviving of the small sub-category of four who achieve complete remission, not initially but after further treatment of various kinds. Mr Gregg's subsequent clinical history demonstrated that he fell into this small sub-category. It seems to me that, so far as his chances of surviving were concerned, once Mr Gregg had achieved complete remission, Professor Goldstone's model gave no reason to think that Mr Gregg was worse off than he would have been had his treatment commenced nine months earlier.

[156]   Professor Goldstone's model demonstrated, however, that what then happened to Mr Gregg placed him in a further small sub-category—the six who relapsed after remission, responded to treatment, and then relapsed again. Of these six, on Professor Goldstone's model, only one survived. This led Professor Goldstone to comment that Mr Gregg might be regarded as "possibly the one survivor". Although statistically his prospects of surviving after the second relapse were no better than one in six, by the time of the trial they had improved to 20% to 30% and were climbing daily. . . .

[169]   . . . The closer that Mr Gregg comes to being a survivor the smaller is the likelihood that the delay in commencing his treatment has had any effect on his expectation of life. At the same time, Professor Goldstone's model and his other evidence indicate that if Mr Gregg proves to be a survivor, the odds are high that he would have achieved complete and final remission if treated before his cancer had spread. On balance of probability I suspect that one is now in a position to conclude that the delay in commencing Mr Gregg's treatment has not

affected his prospect of being a survivor but has caused him all the other adverse events which I have set out above. . . .

[170]   My Lords, these reflections on the present case demonstrate, so it seems to me, that the exercise of assessing the loss of a chance in clinical negligence cases is not an easy one. Deductions cannot safely be drawn from statistics without expert assistance. I am all too well aware that I have drawn a number of deductions from the evidence in this case without expert assistance and that these are at odds with those that have been drawn by others. Even if some of my deductions can be shown to be unsound, I hope that I have demonstrated that analysis of the evidence in this case is no easy task. In contrast, the task of determining the effect of Dr Scott's negligence on a balance of probabilities was very much easier. It is always likely to be much easier to resolve issues of causation on balance of probabilities than to identify in terms of percentage the effect that clinical negligence had on the chances of a favourable outcome. This reality is a policy factor that weighs against the introduction into this area of a right to compensation for the loss of a chance. A robust test which produces rough justice may be preferable to a test that on occasion will be difficult, if not impossible, to apply with confidence in practice.

. . .

[172]   In Fairchild v Glenhaven Funeral Services Ltd [2003] 1 AC 32 this House made a change in the law of negligence in the interests of justice. The change benefits a workman who has contracted a mesothelioma after being exposed to asbestos fibres by a series of employers. An employer who has contributed 20% of that exposure and thus 20% to the employee's risk of contracting the disease will be liable in full to the employee, albeit that the chances are 5 to 1 that he is not in fact responsible for causing the disease. In this case Lord Nicholls of Birkenhead proposes a different approach in the case of a doctor whose negligence has decreased the chance that a patient will be cured of a disease. Under that proposal the doctor will be liable to the extent that his negligence has reduced the chance of a cure. My Lords, it seems to me that there is a danger, if special tests of causation are developed piecemeal to deal with perceived injustices in particular factual situations, that the coherence of our common law will be destroyed.

Comment

Lord Phillips' judgment is the most complex, since it engages with the medical evidence in order to raise considerable questions about the feasibility of Lord Nicholls' proposed solution. In respect of this particular case, the difficulty exposed is that the claimant has not, as it happens, lost his chance of survival. In fact, that chance is rising at the time of the House of Lords' judgment, although it appeared very low at the time of the trial. More generally, Lord Phillips is able to show how this feature of the present case renders more difficult the idea that loss of statistical chances can be recognized as 'damage' in medical cases.

Baroness Hale of Richmond

[223]   Until now, the gist of the action for personal injuries has been damage to the person. My negligence probably caused the loss of your leg: I pay you the full value of the loss of the leg (say £ 100,000). My negligence probably did not cause the loss of your leg. I do not pay you anything. Compare the loss of a chance approach: my negligence probably caused a reduction in the chance of your keeping that leg: I pay you the value of the loss of your leg, discounted

by the chance that it would have happened anyway. If the chance of saving the leg was very good, say 90%, the claimant still gets only 90% of his damages, say £ 90,000. But if the chance of saving the leg was comparatively poor, say 20%, the claimant still gets £ 20,000. So the claimant ends up with less than full compensation even though his chances of a more favourable outcome were good. And the defendant ends up paying substantial sums even though the outcome is one for which by definition he cannot be shown to be responsible.

[224] Almost any claim for loss of an outcome could be reformulated as a claim for loss of a chance of that outcome. The implications of retaining them both as alternatives would be substantial. That is, the claimant still has the prospect of 100% recovery if he can show that it is more likely than not that the doctor's negligence caused the adverse outcome. But if he cannot show that, he also has the prospect of lesser recovery for loss of a chance. If (for the reasons given earlier) it would in practice always be tempting to conclude that the doctor's negligence had affected his chances to some extent, the claimant would almost always get something. It would be a "heads you lose everything, tails I win something" situation. But why should the Defendant not also be able to redefine the gist of the action if it suits him better?

[225] The Appellant in this case accepts that the proportionate recovery effect must cut both ways. If the claim is characterised as loss of a chance, those with a better than evens chance would still only get a proportion of the full value of their claim. But I do not think that he accepts that the same would apply in cases where the claim is characterised as loss of an outcome. In that case there is no basis for calculating the odds. If the two are alternatives available in every case, the defendant will almost always be liable for something. He will have lost the benefit of the 50% chance that causation cannot be proved. But if the two approaches cannot sensibly live together, the claimants who currently obtain full recovery on an adverse outcome basis might in future only achieve a proportionate recovery. This would surely be a case of two steps forward, three steps back for the great majority of straightforward personal injury cases. In either event, the expert evidence would have to be far more complex than it is at present. Negotiations and trials would be a great deal more difficult. Recovery would be much less pre-dictable both for claimants and for defendants' liability insurers. There is no reason in principle why the change in approach should be limited to medical negligence. Whether or not the pol-icy choice is between retaining the present definition of personal injury in outcome terms and redefining it in loss of opportunity terms, introducing the latter would cause far more problems in the general run of personal injury claims than the policy benefits are worth. . . .

[227] . . . the Claimant would have been entitled to damages for any adverse outcomes which were caused by the doctor's negligence. But the possibilities there canvassed were not can-vassed in evidence or argument before the Judge, nor have we been invited to remit the case for further findings. With some regret, therefore, I agree that this appeal should be dismissed.

Comment

Baroness Hale's judgment is dominated by policy concerns, and in particular by the prospects that a large proportion of personal injury actions would be transformed by the 'loss of chance' analysis into actions for a lost chance of avoiding personal injury. The alternative, of allowing claimants the freedom of choosing whether to make a claim for lost chance or for physical injury, would be unfair to defendants and, presumably, too expensive. There is an unexplored question of insurance which tends to support this view: the assessment of risks by insurers would need to change radically if there was a form of 'double counting' of this type in the award of damages. Baroness Hale (at [192]) makes clear that the prospect of major upheaval is what distinguishes the medical lost chance claim from the other key recent cases we have considered in this chapter. This concern is further strengthened by the fact that in the very kind of case where the claimant most needs the lost chance analysis, where the duty is aimed at protecting prospects of recovery, it is most difficult to say whether the worst scenario will come about at all.

Concluding Remarks: *Gregg v Scott*

As Baroness Hale notes above, *Gregg v Scott* is different from previous cases where 'loss of chance' has been argued in one very significant respect. At the time of the House of Lords' judgments, it was still unclear whether the claimant was going to be a survivor. Although he had suffered significant pain, harm, and distress (none of which formed the basis of his claim), he had not lost his chance of survival. That chance had been diminished, rather than lost. In *Hotson*, the damage had been suffered, but causation was unclear. In the successful lost chance cases, such as *Allied Maples* or *Chaplin v Hicks*, it was clear that the claimant could not now be successful in negotiating a term in a contract, or in winning a beauty competition. Through the defendant's breach, the chance of success had gone. The case of *Gregg v Scott* is different because the chance is still in the future. It is a diminished chance case, rather than a lost chance case. This reason featured prominently in the majority judgments of Lord Phillips and Baroness Hale. It did not feature in the other majority judgment of Lord Hoffmann, who was more concerned to reiterate the traditional 'all or nothing' approach in general terms.

Gregg v Scott was not, then, the most suitable occasion on which to test the availability of a claim for loss of chance in cases of medical negligence. In this respect, it exposes a very real problem with compensating statistical chances.

Issues concerning the nature of the required damage in a personal injury action arise in a very different form in an appeal currently expected before the House of Lords. Here we extract the Court of Appeal judgment.

In *Re Pleural Plaques Litigation; Grieves v Everard* [2006] EWCA Civ 27

The nature of the claims, and the problem of defining 'damage', are set out by Lord Phillips at [2] below. 'Pleural plaques' are symptomless changes in the lungs, caused by exposure to asbestos. They are **not causally related** to the development of asbestos-related diseases such as lung cancer; but there is a **statistical** correlation between the development of the plaques, and the future development of such diseases. At first instance, the judge had held for the claimants. He argued that the plaques themselves did not constitute physical injury, but they were caused by the piercing of the lung by asbestos fibres. This *could* constitute injury; and the consequential losses (including the possibility of future disease) were recoverable. The Court of Appeal reversed the first instance judgment. There was no compensable physical harm in these cases.

Note: one of the claimants in this case also claimed to have suffered distinct damage in the form of 'anxiety neurosis'. This is a recognized psychiatric illness and is very different, in the eyes of the law, from pure anxiety. The parts of the judgment in this case relating to anxiety neurosis are extracted in Chapter 6.1, 'Psychiatric damage'.

Lord Phillips CJ (delivering a joint judgment with Longmore LJ)17

[2]   Five of the seven appeals in respect of liability . . . raise the issue that led to the trial of these actions as test cases. It is an important issue on which there is no direct authority at appellate level. Each of the Claimants was negligently exposed by his Defendant employer to asbestos dust. That exposure has had three foreseeable consequences. The Claimant has developed pleural plaques. The Claimant is at risk of developing one or more long-term asbestos related diseases. The Claimant has suffered anxiety at the prospect that he may suffer such disease. It is common ground, for reasons that we shall explain, that none of these consequences, if experienced on its own, would constitute damage capable of founding a cause of action in negligence. The common issue is whether, by aggregating with pleural plaques one or both of the other consequences, sufficient damage can be demonstrated to found a cause of action.

. . .

[18]   Pleural plaques undoubtedly constitute a physiological change in the body. . . . For present purposes their relevant feature is that, save in the case of about 1% which no-one has suggested has significance, they are symptomless, have no adverse effect on any bodily function and, being internal, have no effect on appearance. In short, ignoring the 1%, no one is any the worse physically for having pleural plaques.

[19]   It has always been the law in England and Wales that, negligence is not actionable per se, it is only actionable on proof of damage. While such damage need not be substantial it must be more than minimal. This is not controversial. In para 8 of his speech in *Fairchild*, Lord Bingham said:—

  'In a personal injury action based on negligence or breach of statutory duty the Claimant seeks to establish a breach by the Defendant of a duty owed to the Claimant, which has caused him damage.'

. . .

Risk Of Future Disease

[24]   Where injury caused by negligence carries with it the chance that the Claimant will suffer further physical damage in the future, the general damages recoverable by way of a final award will be increased to reflect the chance of this adverse outcome—see *Gregg v Scott*, para 67, per Lord Hoffmann. But no claim can be made in respect of the chance of contracting a future disease if this is not consequent upon some physical injury. The reason for this must once again be attributed to policy. . . .

. . .

[67]   Mr Michael Kent QC, for the Defendants, has persuaded us that there are a number of reasons of policy why it is undesirable that the development of pleural plaques should give rise to a cause of action. We can summarise these as follows. If pleural plaques give rise to a cause of action:

  i) On discovery of the existence of pleural plaques a claimant will be advised that he should bring a claim in order to protect his position, even if he would not otherwise wish to do so unless and until he developed symptomatic disease.

---

17 Lord Phillips had contributed to the House of Lords' judgment in *Gregg v Scott* (above). Here he is sitting in the Court of Appcal having become Master of the Rolls (and subseqently Lord Chief Justice).

ii) Bringing legal proceedings is stressful. It will result in the Claimant's attention being drawn to all the possible consequences of exposure to asbestos and may well create or augment the anxiety for which compensation will be claimed.

iii) There is a danger that those, such as claims managers, who make a business out of litigation, will encourage workers who have been exposed to asbestos to have CT scans in order to see whether they have pleural plaques for the sole purpose of bringing claims for compensation. Such a practice will tend to create stress and anxiety where none exists.

iv) Some Claimants will be tempted to claim a final award, thereby, in effect, gambling, to the possible prejudice of themselves and their families, that they will not contract an asbestos-related disease.

v) The costs of litigation in cases such as those before us tend to be disproportionate to the damages recoverable.

vi) It is unjust that the right to recover damages should depend upon the fortuity of whether or not the particular Claimant has developed pleural plaques.

Conclusions

[68] We have demonstrated that there is no legal precedent in this country, beyond first instance decisions, for aggregating three heads of claim which, individually, could not found a cause of action, so as to constitute sufficient damage to give rise to a legal claim. We can see no logical basis for such an approach. Nor can we see any justification for departing from logic or legal principle in the specific case of asbestos induced pleural plaques. Policy points the other way, as do decisions in Australia and the United States. For these reasons, which differ from those of the judge, we have reached the conclusion that the primary way that the Claimants put their case is unsound.

[69] Holland J held that the foundation of the Claimants' cause of action was not the pleural plaques themselves, but the penetration of the lungs by asbestos fibres that was evidenced by the existence of pleural plaques. He held that this penetration did not, of itself, give rise to a cause of action but that it did when coupled with the risk that the asbestos fibres would give rise to disease and the anxiety generated about this risk. Is this analysis a more compelling justification for holding that a cause of action has been made out? We do not believe so. Statistics indicate that a small minority of those exposed to asbestos to the extent that they develop pleural plaques will develop an asbestos related disease. In the case of any individual Claimant the odds are that the asbestos fibres in his lungs will remain innocuous. We do not consider that the presence of those fibres, as demonstrated by pleural plaques, is any more capable than the existence of the plaques themselves, of founding a cause of action.

[70] Counsel for the Claimants argued that if we hold that pleural plaques will not found a cause of action, our judgment will raise problems in relation to pleural thickening. Pleural thickening differs from pleural plaques in that its development tends to reduce lung capacity. We accept that our judgment may focus attention on the question of the stage at which pleural thickening gives rise to a cause of action, but this is an issue which will have to be considered as and when it arises.

Smith LJ dissented, arguing quite convincingly that pleural plaques, though *usually* symptomless, were a 'physical injury'.

[116]   In my judgment, such a tissue change does amount to an injury. I say so for two reasons. First, it is accepted that pleural plaques do amount to an injury in those rare cases where they are sufficiently extensive to give rise to symptoms. However, in such a case, it is not the symptoms which are the injury; it is the plaques themselves. The presence or absence of symptoms goes only to the question of how serious the injury is. One cannot say that the pleural plaques are an injury if they are sufficiently extensive to cause symptoms but not if they are limited and symptom-free. The plaques are of the same nature whether they are extensive or limited and, in my view, if extensive plaques are an injury, so are limited ones.

[117]   My second reason is related to the first. In the course of argument, it appeared to be common ground that a tissue change giving rise to a benign lesion on the surface of the body does amount to an injury, and not merely because such a lesion will usually have been caused by a cut or a burn. Even if caused by some non-traumatic mechanism such as radiation, it is accepted that it would be an injury. The Appellants argue that such a lesion is different from pleural plaques because the lesion on the skin is noticeable and causes embarrassment. It has a cosmetic effect, which sounds in damages. I accept, of course, that the damages for a lesion on the skin will take account of the cosmetic effect but it is the lesion which is the injury and the cosmetic effect merely increases the damages. I cannot accept that a visible tissue change is different in nature from a tissue change which is hidden within the body. If pleural plaques were to form on the skin instead of on the pleura, they would be an injury, not because they had a cosmetic effect but because they were a tissue change.

Even if we are persuaded that the plaques are 'injury', the difficulty is that they do not cause the later disease; therefore, that disease is not *consequential* harm for the risk of which damages fall to be assessed. If the plaques are considered as injury, but the risk of future disease is not the subject of compensation, then in principle there ought to be an award simply for the plaques. The argument against any such claim, mentioned by Lord Phillips, is one of 'disproportion', or *de minimis non curat lex*.

It should be noted that neither minority nor majority judges in this case treated 'risk' as equivalent to 'damage'.

FURTHER READING

De Saulles, D., 'The Very Seamark of my Utmost Sail: *Grieves* and the continuing asbestos wars' (2006) JPIL 119–61.

Fleming, J., 'Probabilistic Causation in Tort Law' (1989) Can Bar Rev 661.

Jansen, 'The Idea of a Lost Chance' (1999) 19 OJLS 271.

Lunney, M., 'What Price a Chance?' (1995) 15 LS 1.

Porat, A., and Stein, A., *Tort Liability Under Uncertainty* (Oxford: OUP, 2003).

Stapleton, J., 'Cause-in-Fact and the Scope of Liability for Consequences' (2003) 119 LQR 388.

Stauch, M., 'Causation, Risk and Loss of Chance in Medical Negligence' (1997) 17 OJLS 205.

5

DEFENCES TO NEGLIGENCE

CENTRAL ISSUES

i) This chapter introduces three defences to negligence. Other defences are considered in relation to specific torts, in appropriate chapters.

ii) **Contributory negligence** is the most commonly successful defence to negligence. Since 1945, if the claimant's own fault has contributed to the damage suffered then the court is required to reduce damages on the basis of relative 'responsibility'. Responsibility involves questions both of causal influence, and of fault.

iii) There are also some occasions—relatively rare and therefore narrowly defined—where the claimant's role in the injury suffered is not properly reflected by a reduction in damages. Instead, the action should fail altogether. There are two separate defences

to negligence which may achieve this outcome.

iv) The first of these is *volenti non fit injuria* or willing assumption of risk. This defence requires an agreement to waive the legal consequences of risk, or at least close and active participation in its creation. The defence is rarely successful. Broader application of the defence where there is consensual participation in (for example) sporting events has been rejected in English law.

v) The **illegality** defence (also referred to as *ex turpi causa*) exists as a matter of public policy: a claim will fail if it arises directly out of the claimant's own illegal act. Only in the last 30 years has illegality become established as a defence to tort actions, and the criteria for its application are still evolving.

1. DEFENCES TO NEGLIGENCE AND DEFENCES TO OTHER TORTS

The defences considered here are all relevant to the tort of negligence. Each of these defences is applicable to at least certain other torts. But their application is not universal. For example, contributory negligence is not a defence to an action in deceit, which depends on fraudulent misrepresentation on which it is *intended* that the claimant should rely, to his or her detriment: *Standard Chartered Bank v Pakistan National Shipping Corporation* [2002] UKHL 43;

[2003] 1 AC 959. Lord Rodger of Earlsferry put forward the view (at [42]–[44]) that in no tort of intention ('when the defendant's wrong is something more than negligence') does the defence of contributory negligence operate. At the other end of the scale, torts of strict liability such as defamation and the action in *Rylands v Fletcher* are qualified by important defences quite distinct from those in negligence. Indeed, the available defences are particularly important in understanding what amounts to tortious conduct in relation to these torts. There are many other examples of defences available to specific torts but not to negligence. For example, statutory authorization is a defence to the action in nuisance (Chapter 10), but is not applicable to an action in negligence, for the simple reason that statutes are not assumed to authorize careless actions. And the defence of 'consent', in the context of trespass, operates quite differently from '*volenti*' (sometimes also loosely referred to as consent) in the tort of negligence. Defences are closely related to the nature of the particular balance struck in particular torts between tortfeasor, claimant, and other interests. That is why we will deal with specific defences in connection with specific torts, so far as reasonably possible.

2. CONTRIBUTORY NEGLIGENCE

Since 1945, contributory negligence has been a partial defence to the majority of actions in tort, including negligence. Where the court finds that 'fault' on the part both of the claimant and of the defendant has contributed to the damage suffered, then damages will be reduced to the extent that the court thinks just and equitable.

Law Reform (Contributory Negligence) Act 1945 ('the 1945 Act')

1.—(1) Where any person suffers damage as the result partly of his own fault and partly of the fault of any other person or persons, a claim in respect of that damage shall not be defeated by reason of the fault of the person suffering the damage, but the damages recoverable in respect thereof shall be reduced to such extent as the court thinks just and equitable having regard to the claimant's share in the responsibility for the damage . . .

. . .

4.   The following expressions have the meanings hereby respectively assigned to them, that is to say—

. . .

"damage" includes loss of life and personal injury; . . .

"fault" means negligence, breach of statutory duty or other act or omission which gives rise to a liability in tort or would, apart from this Act, give rise to the defence of contributory negligence;

Until this statutory reform, fault on the part of the plaintiff operated as a complete defence if it was found that the fault contributed to the damage:

Lord Blackburn, *Cayzer, Irvine & Co v Carron Ltd* (1884) 9 App Cas 873, at 881 (HL)

The rule of law is that if there is blame causing the accident on both sides, however small that blame may be on one side, the loss lies where it falls.

This may be referred to as the 'stale-mate' rule: if both parties were to blame, the law did nothing to shift the loss. The statutory provisions mark a considerable improvement over the previous common law, not only in terms of fairness but also of simplicity, since the stale-mate rule was subject to considerable variation over the years. For example, courts in England devised a 'last opportunity' rule, whereby a plaintiff whose fault had played some part in creating a hazard could still recover damages if the defendant had the last chance to avoid the harm.[1] This rule and the many intricate variations around it need not detain us because they play no part in the current law.[2]

The move to apportionment on the basis of what the court 'thinks just and equitable' has the effect of cutting through all this. The statutory provisions impose an *obligation* on courts to give effect to fairness between the parties when considering relative responsibility for the injury: section 1(1) provides that the claim 'shall not' be defeated by reason of fault on the part of the person suffering the damage. This could be read as excluding any other defences that are justified by reference to the claimant's fault (as in illegality and in some instances *volenti*, below). This interpretation however has not been adopted.

Since fairness and justice are the guiding principles for reducing damages under section 1(1), we should note that fairness in *apportionment*, taking into account relative fault and responsibility for damage, might not produce fair *outcomes* overall. This is a particular issue in actions for personal injury, and above all in cases where there is a compulsory scheme of third party insurance in place (as is the case, for example, in respect of road traffic accidents and most injuries at work). The chances are that in these cases the claimant does not carry 'first party' personal insurance, which would cover the insured party's own loss. The portion of damages withheld because of contributory negligence frequently represents loss that the claimant must bear alone. For example, a cyclist who gets too close to a line of parked cars may well have damages reduced if a car driver carelessly opens a door into her path; and a pedestrian who does not take sufficient care in crossing the road may have damages reduced even if the car that hits her is travelling too fast. In each of these cases, since first party insurance is entirely voluntary, it is likely that there will be an element of uncompensated loss that is not covered by insurance. On the other hand, tort damages are generous and they do not represent the only means of support available to injured parties. There is an argument that the award of damages must be justified by reference to the defendant's wrong, and that it makes no sense to consider compensation without reference to wrongdoing.

Applying the Statutory Provisions: Section 1(1)

Section 1(1) of the 1945 Act specifies that damages will be reduced where damage is suffered partly as a result of the claimant's fault, and partly as a result of the fault of another party. Clearly, both parties' 'fault' (the meaning of which we consider below) must be *a cause* of the damage suffered.

It is important to be clear that it is the *damage*, not the accident (if any) that must result partly from the fault of each party. Thus, a claimant who fails to wear a seatbelt will have damages reduced if his or her injuries are rendered more severe by that failure, even though failure to wear the belt does nothing to 'cause' the accident itself.

---

[1] Illustrated by *Davies v Mann* (1842) 152 ER 588.
[2] See G. Williams, *Joint Torts and Contributory Negligence* (Stevens & Sons, 1951), Chapter 9.

Lord Denning MR, *Froom v Butcher* [1976] QB 286, at 292

The question is not what was the cause of the accident. It is rather what was the cause of the damage. In most accidents on the road the bad driving, which causes the accident, also causes the ensuing damage. But in seat belt cases the cause of the accident is one thing. The cause of the damage is another. The *accident* is caused by the bad driving. The *damage* is caused in part by the bad driving of the defendant, and in part by the failure of the plaintiff to wear a seat belt. If the plaintiff was to blame in not wearing a seat belt, the damage is in part the result of his own fault. He must bear some share in the responsibility for the damage: and his damages fall to be reduced to such extent as the court thinks just and equitable.

A particularly difficult issue has arisen concerning the definition of the 'damage' to be reduced within section 1(1) where a lender brings actions against a valuer for over-valuation of property. We will defer this issue to the end of this section, because of its complexity.

Section 1(1) refers to damage which results partly from the fault of the injured party, and partly from the fault of the defendant. The definition of 'fault' in section 4 (extracted above) is much broader than negligence or lack of care. It encompasses any act that may be tortious, or would give rise to a defence of contributory negligence at common law. We have already said that in *Standard Chartered Bank v Pakistan Shipping* contributory negligence was held not to be an available defence to deceit, which is a tort of intention. But what if the *claimant's* conduct is 'intentional'? The House of Lords has determined that in this case, the defence does apply, since intention on the part of the claimant is a stronger reason for reducing damages than mere carelessness.

Reeves v Commissioner of Police of the Metropolis [2000] 1 AC 360

The facts of *Reeves* are set out in Chapter 3. The police breached a duty of care owed to a prisoner, to keep him under watch in order to guard against a suicide attempt.

The House of Lords thought that this was a rare case where a duty is owed in order to protect a person against self-harm. As such, it would be illogical then to accept that the deceased's act in killing himself could break the chain of causation (Chapter 3.6). But could the intentional act of suicide amount to 'contributory negligence' within the meaning of the 1945 Act? The House of Lords held that it could.

Lord Hope emphasized that 'one should not be unduly inhibited by the use of the word "negligence" in the expression "contributory negligence"' (at 383). Section 1 could also apply where the claimant's fault takes the form of an intentional act.

Lord Hope, at 382–3

It has been said that this definition of "fault" comprises two limbs . . . The first limb, which is referable to the defendant's conduct, comprises various acts or omissions which give rise to a liability in tort. The second limb, which is referable to the plaintiff's conduct, deals with acts or omissions which would, but for the Act, have given rise to the defence of contributory negligence. The first is directed to the basis of the defendant's liability, while the second is concerned with his defence on the ground that the damage was the result partly of the plaintiff's own negligence . . . the question whether the deceased was at fault in this case must be considered with reference to the words used to describe the second limb.

. . . It seems to me that the definition of 'fault' in section 4 is wide enough, when examined as a whole and in its context, to extend to a plaintiff's deliberate acts as well as to his negligent acts. This reading of the word would enable the court, in an appropriate case, to reduce the amount of damages to reflect the contribution which the plaintiff's own deliberate act of self-harm made to the loss.

Lord Hoffmann, at 369

. . . I recognise, of course, that it is odd to describe Mr. Lynch (the deceased) as having been negligent. He acted intentionally and intention is a different state of mind from negligence. On the other hand, the "defence of contributory negligence" at common law was based upon the view that a plaintiff whose failure to take care for his own safety was a cause of his injury could not sue. One would therefore have thought that the defence applied a fortiori to a plaintiff who intended to injure himself. The late Professor Glanville Williams, in his book *Joint Torts and Contributory Negligence* (1951), p.199, expressed the view that "contributory *intention* should be a defence." It is not surprising that there is little authority on the point, because the plaintiff's act in deliberately causing injury to himself is almost invariably regarded as negativing causal connection between any prior breach of duty by the defendant and the damage suffered by the plaintiff. The question can arise only in the rare case, such as the present, in which someone owes a duty to prevent, or take reasonable care to prevent, the plaintiff from deliberately causing injury to himself. Logically, it seems to me that Professor Glanville Williams is right.

Children

It is clearly possible for children to be contributorily negligent in appropriate circumstances. For example, in *Young v Kent County Council* [2005] EWHC 1342, an action under the Occupiers' Liability Act 1984 (Chapter 12), a child of 12 was found to be contributorily negligent when he jumped on a skylight on the roof of a school. While the school ought to have taken more steps to keep children away from the roof, the claimant should have appreciated the risks associated with the skylight itself. Similarly, in *Honnor v Lewis* [2005] EWHC 747 (QB), damages were reduced by 20 per cent where a child of 11 stepped out into a road without checking for traffic. As we explained in our section on the standard of care, children will be judged by a standard that is relevant to their age. As such, very young children are unlikely to be found to have been contributorily negligent.

Apportionment

Apportionment of responsibility between the parties ought to be the most difficult aspect of the contributory negligence defence. According to section 1(1), this apportionment should reflect relative 'responsibility' for the damage suffered. 'Responsibility' in this context is a question partly of causal influence, and partly of degree of fault. In practice, courts arrive at a reduction in a fairly rough and ready way, without engaging in very detailed enquiries about causal impact or relative fault. This is illustrated by *Froom v Butcher*:

Lord Denning MR, *Froom v Butcher* [1976] QB 286, at 295–6

Whenever there is an accident, the negligent driver must bear by far the greater share of responsibility. It was his negligence which caused the accident. It also was a prime cause of the whole of the damage. But in so far as the damage might have been avoided or lessened by wearing a seat belt, the injured person must bear some share. But how much should this be? Is it proper to inquire whether the driver was grossly negligent or only slightly negligent? or whether the failure to wear a seat belt was entirely inexcusable or almost forgivable? If such an inquiry could easily be undertaken, it might be as well to do it. In *Davies v. Swan Motor Co. (Swansea) Ltd.* [1949] 2 K.B. 291, 326, the court said that consideration should be given not only to the causative potency of a particular factor, but also its blameworthiness. But we live in a practical world. In most of these cases the liability of the driver is admitted, the failure to wear a seat belt is admitted, the only question is: what damages should be payable? This question should not be prolonged by an expensive inquiry into the degree of blameworthiness on either side, which would be hotly disputed. Suffice it to assess a share of responsibility which will be just and equitable in the great majority of cases.

The solution in *Froom* was to adopt a 'tariff' which would apply to the large majority of seat belt cases, without having to reopen the particular question of degree of fault in each case. Where injuries would have been avoided altogether by wearing a seatbelt, there should be a reduction in damages of 25 per cent. In the more usual case, where injuries would have been less severe had a belt been worn, the reduction in damages would be 15 per cent.

In *Capps v Miller* [1989] 1 WLR 839, the plaintiff suffered severe brain damage when, through the 'atrocious driving' of the defendant, he was knocked off his moped. He was wearing a safety helmet, as was required by regulation,[3] but had not fastened it properly. Failure to wear a helmet was equated with failure to wear a seatbelt. But the Court of Appeal took the view that failure to fasten the helmet involved a lower degree of blameworthiness than failure to wear a helmet at all. As such, there should be a smaller reduction in damages than the lower figure in *Froom v Butcher*, and this was set at 10 per cent. It is worth noting that the plaintiff's helmet appears to have offered him no protection at all in this case, because it was not properly fastened. In terms of causation then, he may as well have not worn the helmet. Thus the decision to diverge from the usual tariff had nothing to do with causation. 'Degree of blameworthiness' must have been considered sufficient reason for the variation.

What happens in a more difficult case where diverse issues of causation and relative blame have to be balanced? An important example is the case of *Reeves v Chief Commissioner of the Metropolis* [2000] 1 AC 360, which we extracted above. As we saw, Lord Hoffmann explained that *intentional acts* are within the definition of 'fault' in section 4 of the 1945 Act. He continued:

Lord Hoffmann, at 372

In my view it would therefore have been right to apportion responsibility between the commissioner and Mr. Lynch in accordance with the Act of 1945. The judge and Morritt L.J. would have apportioned 100 per cent. to Mr. Lynch. But I think that this conclusion was heavily

---

[3] Motor Cycles (Protective Helmets) Regulations 1980.

influenced by their view, expressed in connection with the question of causation, that Mr. Lynch, as a person of sound mind, bore full responsibility for taking his own life. This is of course a tenable moral view . . . . But whatever views one may have about suicide in general, a 100 per cent. apportionment of responsibility to Mr. Lynch gives no weight at all to the policy of the law in imposing a duty of care upon the police. It is another different way of saying that the police should not have owed Mr. Lynch a duty of care. The law of torts is not just a matter of simple morality but contains many strands of policy, not all of them consistent with each other, which reflect the complexity of life. An apportionment of responsibility "as the court thinks just and equitable" will sometimes require a balancing of different goals. It is at this point that I think that Buxton L.J.'s reference to the cases on the Factories Acts is very pertinent. The apportionment must recognise that a purpose of the duty accepted by the commissioner in this case is to demonstrate publicly that the police do have a responsibility for taking reasonable care to prevent prisoners from committing suicide. On the other hand, respect must be paid to the finding of fact that Mr. Lynch was "of sound mind." I confess to my unease about this finding, based on a seven-minute interview with a doctor of unstated qualifications, but there was no other evidence and the judge was entitled to come to the conclusion which he did. I therefore think it would be wrong to attribute no responsibility to Mr. Lynch and compensate the plaintiff as if the police had simply killed him. In these circumstances, I think that the right answer is that which was favoured by Lord Bingham of Cornhill C.J., namely to apportion responsibility equally.

Importantly, Lord Hoffmann emphasizes here the rough and ready nature of apportionment. Causative influences cannot be accurately weighed against degrees of blameworthiness, and the policy reasons which justify a duty to prevent self-harm in this case cannot be scientifically measured against moral feelings concerning the wrongness (assuming sound mind) of self-harm. The court must seek a solution which appears to take into account all of the relevant factors.

Apportionment in Multi-party Cases

Where more than one tortfeasor has contributed to the same harm suffered by a claimant, then in general the claimant may choose to bring an action against either party, recovering damages in full.[4] It is then up to the defendant to bring separate proceedings against any other potential defendant in respect of the same damage, seeking a contribution. The aim of this two-stage process is clearly to make it easier for claimants to bring an action in respect of their full loss. The result of an order for contribution is that damages are apportioned between the two (or more) tortfeasors. In a case where more than one tortfeasor has contributed to the damage, and where there is also contributory negligence on the part of the claimant, how will the court approach the two different exercises in apportionment which are required?

In *Fitzgerald v Lane* [1989] AC 328, the plaintiff walked onto a pelican crossing on a busy street when the pedestrian lights were red. He was struck by two cars, each being driven too fast. The plaintiff suffered appalling injuries. In a fairly rough and ready analysis of the evidence, the trial judge appears to have found that all three parties—the pedestrian and the two

---

[4] Chapter 7, 'Contribution'. As we saw when we discussed causation, especially in Chapter 4, this does not apply where the defendants are considered to have caused *separate* damage to the claimant.

drivers—should be treated as having contributed equally to the damage:

> . . . I find that it is impossible to say that one of the parties is more or less to blame than the other and hold that the responsibility should be borne equally by all three.

The trial judge held that judgment should therefore be entered against each defendant for two thirds of the damage suffered. By an order for contribution, this liability would be shared between the parties. The practical effect would be that each defendant would be expected to pay one third of the total amount assessed, reflecting their equal share in the responsibility.

The House of Lords decided that this approach was wrong in law. The trial judge had run together the two separate issues of contributory negligence, and contribution between tort-feasors. According to Lord Ackner, the judge had 'misdirected himself' when he considered the responsibility of all three parties at the same time. This was an error of law: he had been asking himself the wrong question. The appropriate course in such a case is to consider the relative responsibility of the claimant first; and *only then* to consider contribution between the parties. In the absence of any reason to hold one party more to blame than the others, the result should be a reduction in damages of 50 per cent. The order against each party should be for 50 per cent of damages to be paid, subject to contribution.

Which 'Damage' Falls within Section 1(1)? *Platform Home Loans v Oyston Shipways Ltd* [2000] 2 AC 190

In Chapter 3, we examined the important case of *SAAMCO v York Montagu Ltd* [1997] AC 191, also referred to as *Banque Bruxelles v Eagle Star Insurance*.[5] There, the defendants had provided negligent valuations of certain properties, and the plaintiffs had, in reliance on those valuations, advanced loans secured on the properties. Property values generally declined. When the borrowers defaulted, the resulting losses were extensive. Although the initial valuations were negligent, the general fall in property values had enhanced the losses suffered.

As we explained in Chapter 3.6, the House of Lords held that the defendant valuers were not necessarily liable for the full losses suffered. They were liable only for those losses which were 'within the scope of their duty'. As we explained, Lord Hoffmann reasoned that the duty in such a case was a duty to take care that the valuation is accurate. As such, the only damages for which the defendants are liable are those 'attributable to' the over-valuation. Controversially, the first step in identifying those losses attributable to the over-valuation is to ask what losses would have been suffered *if the valuation given had proved to be correct*. If the valuation had been correct, the lenders would have had more security, and this would have protected them in a falling market. In effect, the extent of the over-valuation therefore sets a limit to the losses that are recoverable. But it does this through a conclusion that no other losses are regarded as attributable to the breach of duty.

In *Platform Home Loans v Oyston Shipways*, a House of Lords that did not include Lord Hoffmann had to decide how to apply the apportionment provisions of the 1945 Act to a *Banque Bruxelles* type case. The defendants had valued a property in 1990 at £1.5 million. The true value at that time was held to be £1 million. The claimants advanced a loan of £1,050,195 secured on the property. The borrower fell behind with repayments and in 1994 the plaintiffs

---

[5] The House of Lords in *Platform Home Loans* referred to this case as *Banque Bruxelles v Eagle Star*, but it is reported as *SAAMCO v York Montagu*. We will use the name *Banque Bruxelles* in this section.

sold the property for only £435,000. The sum they had lost through making the loan was £611,748. But the amount of the over-valuation was only £500,000. According to the reasoning in *Banque Bruxelles*, in the absence of contributory negligence the recoverable loss— which is to say, the loss attributable to the breach of duty—would be £500,000.

In *Platform Home Loans*, the plaintiffs had been contributorily negligent both in advancing too high a sum on the basis of the valuation received, and in omitting to ask certain vital questions before advancing the loan. However, it will be noted that the actual value of the property had also fallen, for independent reasons, between 1990 and 1994.

Given that there was found to have been contributory negligence, the key question was which loss ought to be treated as 'the damage suffered' within section 1(1). This is the loss which must be reduced to take account of the lender's contributory negligence. The majority of the House of Lords decided that 'the damage' which needed to be apportioned was (as they put it) the 'basic loss' suffered by the plaintiff. The basic loss was the full sum of £611,748. One should 'apply the reduction to the basic loss which, apart from the *Banque Bruxelles* principle would be recoverable by the lender' (Lord Hobhouse at 208). That is to say, one should calculate how much the plaintiffs had actually lost, and then reduce this amount according to their share in the responsibility for the loss. Provided the amount arrived at in this way was *within* the amount produced by the *Banque Bruxelles* principle, then there would be no further reduction in damages on account of fault. The key reason for this is that, as Lord Millett put it (at 213), the calculation required by *Banque Bruxelles* to identify the recoverable part of the loss 'has nothing to do with questions of causation'. Therefore, it is irrelevant to section 1(1), which is about loss which is 'the result' (a causal idea) of both parties' fault. Instead, the *Banque Bruxelles* calculation is 'designed to ascertain the maximum amount of loss capable of falling within the valuer's duty of care'.

In a dissenting judgment, Lord Cooke set out a very different approach. It is suggested that his approach is more consistent with the reasoning in *Banque Bruxelles*. Lord Cooke referred to section 1(2) of the Law Reform (Contributory Negligence) Act 1945, which provides:

Section 1(2)

Where damages are recoverable by any person by virtue of the foregoing subsection subject to such reduction as thereby mentioned, the court shall find and record the total damages which would have been recoverable if the claimant had not been at fault.

Lord Cooke pointed out that because of the approach adopted in *Banque Bruxelles*, the 'basic loss' of £611,748 would not have been recoverable in full in the absence of contributory negligence. As such, that full 'basic loss' could not properly be recorded as the amount that 'would have been recoverable if the claimant had not been at fault' (s 1(2)). Therefore, it could not be the sum that fell to be reduced within section 1(1). Rather:

Lord Cooke, at 198–9

. . . by English law as declared in the *Banque Bruxelles* and the *Nykredit* cases, apart from any question of contributory negligence, the valuer is not liable to the lender for the full loss of £611,748 but only for £500,000, being the difference between the negligent valuation of £1.5m. and the figure which a reasonably careful valuation would have produced, £1m. That £500,000 is the damage suffered as the result partly of the lender's fault and partly of the valuer's fault. On the recent authorities the balance of the loss, £111,748 was not suffered, even in part, as a result of the valuer's fault, because of the limited way in which this House has defined the valuer's duty of care. In other words, the balance of the loss was not "damage" within the meaning of section 1(1) of the Act of 1945 and does not fall to be apportioned . . . this is brought out very clearly when section 1(2) is considered. If the whole £611,748 were apportionable, the court would have to record that amount as the total damages which would have been recoverable if the claimant had not been at fault. But to say as much would be flatly contrary to the *Banque Bruxelles* and *Nykredit* cases.

The damages to be reduced are therefore £500,000, so the amount for which it is just and equitable that the lender should have judgment is £400,000 together with appropriate interest . . . .

. . . . In my view the 'damage' referred to four times in section 1(1) of the Act of 1945 is the damage for which, but for the Act, the claimant's action would be defeated by reason of his own fault: it does not extend to damage for which his claim would be defeated by reason of a limit on the other person's duty of care.

Arguably, the problem in *Platform Home Loans* is created by the ingenuity and subtlety of Lord Hoffmann's judgment in *Banque Bruxelles* itself. There he sought to identify the damage 'attributable to' a breach of duty while denying that this idea had anything to do with causation. In Chapter 3, we doubted whether causation can be kept wholly distinct from the idea of being 'attributable to' a breach. In *Platform Home Loans*, the majority reasoned that if the limitation on damages in *Banque Bruxelles* seriously has nothing to do with causal questions, then the amount which is to be reduced within section 1(1) must be, not the amount arrived at through the *Banque Bruxelles* principle, but the amount actually caused partly by the claimant's fault and partly by the defendant's fault, namely the entire 'basic loss'. The *Banque Bruxelles* principle was then treated by the majority as operating to establish a 'cap' on damages. Unfortunately, Lord Hoffmann also explained that setting a 'cap' was *not* the role of the principle.[6]

3. *VOLENTI NON FIT INJURIA*: WILLING ACCEPTANCE OF RISK

A defendant will escape liability for the consequences of negligence if the claimant has, expressly or impliedly, agreed to accept the legal risk associated with that negligence.

Volenti—or acceptance of risk—is of very limited application to cases of negligence today, although there have been successful cases which we must seek to explain.[7] But this has not always been the case. There was a time when courts were all too ready to find that plaintiffs had voluntarily accepted the risks in question, particularly where the plaintiff had suffered injury

---

[6] The *Banque Bruxelles* approach 'has nothing to do with questions of causation or any limit or "cap" imposed on damages which would otherwise be recoverable': Lord Hoffmann, *Nykredit v Edward Erdman Ltd (No 2)* [1997] 1 WLR 1627, 1638. The majority in *Platform Home Loans* heeded the first but not the second part of Lord Hoffmann's warning.

[7] On this occasion, we will continue to use the Latin term *volenti* as a shorthand for 'willing acceptance of risk'. Use of the simpler 'consent' would be misleading since this is *not* the same defence as 'consent' to trespass, for example.

in the course of employment. As Williams explains in the following passage, recognition of the narrow defence we have stated was a hard won battle:

G. Williams, *Joint Torts and Contributory Negligence*
(Stevens & Sons, 1951), 296–8

... In its heyday, the doctrine [of voluntary assumption of risk] was applied in almost every situation where the plaintiff knew of the risk and yet chose to undergo it rather than to give up on some enterprise on which he was engaged. At least, that was the attitude adopted in the master-and-servant cases. The extreme limit of the doctrine was represented by *Woodley v Metropolitan District Rly* [(1877) 18 QBD 685 at 696 (CA)]. The plaintiff, a workman in the employ of a contractor engaged by the defendants, had to work in a dark tunnel which he knew was rendered dangerous by passing trains. The jury found the company negligent in not stationing a person to warn the workmen of the approach of trains, and three of the five judges of the Court of Appeal (including one who was in the majority in the result reached) held that there was evidence of this. Yet three judges of the same court held that the plaintiff could not recover for his injuries, on the ground that he had voluntarily assumed the risk.

It may confidently be asserted that this appalling extension of the doctrine would not now be followed. A change in the judicial attitude took place towards the end of the last century— Beven associated it with the change of feeling represented by the passing of the Employers' Liability Act, 1880[8]—and the modern tendency has been to restrict the defence. A beginning was made in *Thomas v Quartermaine* (1887), when Bowen LJ let fall his celebrated dictum that 'the maxim is not *scienti non fit injuria* but *volenti*.'[9]

It is obvious why the broad version of the defence can be described as unjust and even, in some manifestations, 'appalling'. It rested on a wholly fictional idea of 'consent'. As Scott LJ explained in *Bowater v Rowley Regis* [1944] KB 476, 479:

> ... a man cannot be said to be truly 'willing' unless he is in a position to choose freely, and freedom of choice predicates, not only full knowledge of the circumstances on which the exercise of choice is conditioned, so that he may be able to choose wisely, but the absence from his mind of any feeling of constraint so that nothing shall interfere with the freedom of his will.

Choices in respect of employment are scarcely likely to be made in the absence of any feelings of constraint. Ultimately, the pivotal case of *Smith v Baker & Sons* [1891] AC 325 made clear that a plaintiff who continues with an activity despite knowledge of certain risks associated with it is not thereby to be treated as having accepted those risks. This major turning point left the defence with little application to cases of negligence. As Lord Pearce put it in

---

[8] This statute limited the scope of the 'doctrine of common employment'. By that doctrine, it was implied into any contract of employment that the employee consented to the risks associated with the work, including the risks posed by the negligence of fellow workers. The 1880 Act only excluded the operation of the doctrine in respect of negligence on the part of a superior worker with supervisory or managerial responsibilities. But this was a significant turning point and the remainder of the defence was abolished by the Law Reform (Personal Injuries) Act 1948, s 1. Indeed enhanced duties have long been recognized as associated with the employment relationship: Chapter 9.

[9] Knowledge (*scienti*) does not amount to consent (*volenti*).

ICI v Shatwell [1965] AC 656, 686:

> One naturally approaches [the] defence with suspicion. For in the sphere of master and ser-vant its role has been inglorious up to 1891, and, since that date, insignificant. In *Smith v Baker & Sons* it was laid down that the defence is not constituted by knowledge of the danger and acquiescence in it, but by an agreement to run the risk and to waive any rights to recompense for any injury in which that risk might result.

The Restricted Nature of the Modern *Volenti* Defence

The brief statement of the *volenti* defence in the quotation from Lord Pearce above contains all the elements set out at the start of this section. A similarly narrow view of the *volenti* defence was adopted by Lord Denning in *Nettleship v Weston* [1971] 2 QB 691.

> Knowledge of the risk of injury is not enough. Nor is a willingness to take the risk of injury. Nothing will suffice short of an agreement to waive any claim for negligence. The plaintiff must agree, expressly or impliedly, to waive any claim for any injury that may befall him due to the lack of reasonable care by the defendant.

It is important to note three limitations inherent in this statement.

Assumption of legal risk, not risk of physical consequences

There are many cases in which it is tempting to say that a claimant willingly *ran the risk of incurring harm*, but this is not sufficient for a defence of *volenti* to succeed. In the passage above, Lord Denning made clear that there is a difference between accepting *the risk of injury*, and accepting *the legal consequences of the injury*. The facts of *Nettleship v Weston* itself illustrate the contrast. The plaintiff had agreed to give driving lessons to the defendant, a neighbour. It is obvious to an instructor that a learner driver may lose control of her car *in circumstances in which a competent driver would not do so*—in other words, negligently.[10] But this is still not good enough to satisfy the narrow defence of *volenti*. This is because the instructor does not agree, merely by taking on the role of instructor in the full knowledge of the chance of negligence, to waive any right to *compensation* in the event that this should happen.

In this particular case, the plaintiff had checked that the defendant carried third party insurance, which would indemnify him in the event of injury. This was powerful specific evidence that he did not accept that the legal risk should fall on him. But Lord Denning's point was wider than this. We will address below the question of whether generally speaking, accepting a lift knowing that the driver's ability is in some way impaired may be sufficient to give rise to a successful defence of *volenti*.[11]

The *volenti* defence is now excluded from driver and passenger claims in any event:

Road Traffic Act 1988, 149   Avoidance of certain agreements as to liability towards passengers

(1) This section applies where a person uses a motor vehicle in circumstances such that under section 143 of this Act there is required to be in force in relation to his use of it such a policy of insurance or such a security in respect of third-party risks as complies with the requirements of this Part of this Act.

---

[10] This is an application of the 'objective standard of care': Chapter 3.

[11] See the discussion of *Morris v Murray* [1991] 2 QB 6 and *Dann v Hamilton* [1939] 1 KB 509 below.

(2) If any other person is carried in or upon the vehicle while the user is so using it, any antecedent agreement or understanding between them (whether intended to be legally binding or not) shall be of no effect so far as it purports or might be held—

(a) to negative or restrict any such liability of the user in respect of persons carried in or upon the vehicle as is required by section 145 of this Act to be covered by a policy of insurance, or

(b) to impose any conditions with respect to the enforcement of any such liability of the user.

(3) The fact that a person so carried has willingly accepted as his the risk of negligence on the part of the user shall not be treated as negativing any such liability of the user.

. . .

The need for an agreement

This is the most severe of the three restrictions to the defence. In the passage from *Nettleship* that we quoted above, Lord Denning stated that a *volenti* defence will only succeed where there is an *agreement* to waive any claim for injury. A clear statement of this principle is to be found in the speech of Lord Bramwell in the leading case of *Smith v Baker & Sons* [1891] AC 325.

Lord Bramwell

In the course of the argument I said that the maxim *Volenti non fit injuria* did not apply to a case of negligence; that a person never was *volens* that he should be injured by negligence—at least, unless he specially agreed to it; I think so still.

According to Glanville Williams:

Consent, in modern law, means agreement, and it would be much better if the latter word replaced the former.

Despite these authorities, *volenti* has succeeded as a defence to negligence in one or two modern cases (including *Shatwell* itself) where there is no express 'agreement'. We will consider these cases below. In each case, the claimant is closely involved in creation of the risk.

Consent to the negligence, not just the risk

Quite apart from the requirements above, any consent must be *to the negligence itself*, and not to the general risk of injury. In *Wooldridge v Sumner* [1963] 2 QB 43, Diplock LJ thought that, for this reason alone, *volenti* would generally fail as a defence to negligence. Here, a spectator was injured when a sportsman lost control of his horse.

Diplock LJ, at 68–9

The practical result of . . . the application of the common law of negligence to participant and spectator would, I think, be expressed by the common man in some such terms as these: "A person attending a game or competition takes the risk of any damage caused to him by any act of a participant done in the course of and for the purposes of the game or competition notwithstanding that such act may involve an error of judgment or a lapse of skill, unless the participant's conduct is such as to evince a reckless disregard of the spectator's safety."

The spectator takes the risk because such an act involves no breach of the duty of care owed by the participant to him. He does not take the risk by virtue of the doctrine expressed or obscured by the maxim volenti non fit injuria. . . . In my view, the maxim in the absence of expressed contract has no application to negligence simpliciter where the duty of care is based solely upon proximity or "neighbourship" in the Atkinian sense. The maxim in English law presupposes a tortious act by the defendant. The consent that is relevant is not consent to the risk of injury but consent to the lack of reasonable care that may produce that risk . . . and requires on the part of the plaintiff at the time at which he gives his consent full knowledge of the nature and extent of the risk that he ran. In *Dann v. Hamilton* [1939] 1 KB 509, 517, Asquith J. expressed doubts as to whether the maxim ever could apply to license in advance a subsequent act of negligence, for if the consent precedes the act of negligence the plaintiff cannot at that time have full knowledge of the extent as well as the nature of the risk which he will run.

In this difficult but very influential passage, Diplock LJ is making a number of separate but related points.

1. Reasonable care in specific circumstances varies not only with the activity undertaken by the defendant, but also with the expectations of a reasonable person in the position of the claimant. A reasonable spectator would expect a participant in a sporting event to take certain risks and in their context these would not amount to negligence. We dealt with this point in Chapter 3.

2. For the application of the *volenti* defence, the consent that is required is consent to the negligence itself, not to the mere physical risk of injury inherent in an activity.

3. For this reason, *volenti* will rarely succeed as a defence to a negligence action. Full and specific knowledge of the negligence involved will be required, and this is especially unlikely to be found where there is said to be consent *in advance of* the negligence in question.

While *Wooldridge v Sumner* was an action brought by a spectator against a participant, Diplock LJ's second point has been decisive in a number of cases where participants in sporting events have themselves been injured. In these cases, English courts have found it possible to dispose of *volenti* with ease. In *Smoldon v Whitworth and Nolan* (17 December 1996, Court of Appeal), an amateur rugby referee was found to have breached a duty of care owed to players (in this instance junior players or 'colts') when he failed to enforce a rule—designed for the safety of players—against collapsing scrums. Although rugby was 'a tough, highly physical game', the *volenti* defence could not succeed:

Lord Bingham of Cornhill CJ, *Smolden v Whitworth*

The plaintiff had of course consented to the ordinary incidents of a game of rugby of the kind in which he was taking part. Given, however, that the rules were framed for the protection of him and other players in the same position, he cannot possibly be said to have consented to a breach of duty on the part of the official whose duty it was to apply the rules and ensure so far as possible that they were observed.

Volenti has been found inapplicable for similar reasons in other English cases concerning sports. In *Wattleworth v Goodwood Road Racing Company Ltd and Others* [2004] EWHC 140, the deceased amateur racing driver had consented to the ordinary risks of racing cars on a circuit, but would not have consented to failures to take care in the design of safety features. There was in any event no breach of duty on the facts of the case: the design of the track's safety features was reasonable and appropriate. In *Watson v British Boxing Board of Control* [2001] QB 1134, the defendant Board—the sole organization responsible for regulating professional boxing in the UK—was (by contrast) liable in damages to the claimant, a professional boxer, who had incurred serious brain damage. The relevant breaches of duty concerned the prompt treatment of injuries and the provision of proper facilities to deal with head injuries during a fight. Although a boxer clearly consents to being hit by an opponent, it could not be said that the participant was *volenti* in respect of these particular breaches of duty.

As a result of these cases, the *volenti* defence in the context of sporting injuries has been justly described as 'otiose'.[12] On the other hand, the first of the three points drawn from the judgment of Diplock LJ in *Wooldridge v Sumner* has begun to acquire greater importance, and has been developed into an approach which limits the scope for successful negligence claims arising from careless actions in the context of sports or games, both professional and amateur.

'Consensual Participation'

In Chapter 3, we explored the variation in the standard of care where participation is 'consensual'. In Australia, the courts have gone further in this process, and threaten to evade the important limitations on the *volenti* defence which have been developed since the nineteenth century.[13] This may be part of a general trend to regard risk-taking as a matter of personal responsibility. In *Agar v Hyde* (2000) 201 CLR 552, it was found that *no duty was owed* to a participant by a sports governing body to ensure that the rules of the game achieved a reasonable standard of safety.

> ***Agar v Hyde*** (joint judgment of Gaudron, McHugh, Gummow, and Haynes JJ, at [90])
>
> The decision to participate is made freely. That freedom, or autonomy, is not to be diminished. But with autonomy comes responsibility. To hold that the appellants owed a duty of care . . . would diminish the autonomy of all who choose, for whatever reason, to engage voluntarily in this, or any other, physically dangerous pastime. It would do so because it would deter those who fulfil the kind of role played by the IRFB and the appellants in regulating that pastime from continuing to do so lest they be held liable for the consequences of the individual's free choice.

It is clear from cases such as *Smoldon*, *Wattleworth*, and *Watson*, that English courts have not gone down this path, preferring to say that participants in inherently risky sports such as rugby, motor racing, and boxing nevertheless do not consent to shortcomings in safety standards.

---

[12] D. McArdle and M. James, 'Are You Experienced? "Playing Cultures", Sporting Rules and Personal Injury Litigation after *Caldwell v Maguire*' (2005) Tort L Rev 193, 210.

[13] See especially J. Deitrich, 'The decline of contributory negligence and apportionment: choosing the black and white of all-or-nothing over many shades of grey?' (2003) TLJ 5; K. Burns, 'It's just not cricket: The High Court, sport and legislative facts' (2002) TLJ 11.

Recent Applications of the *Volenti* Defence

Although we have been careful to set out the limits to the defence of *volenti*, we have also mentioned that there are some exceptional cases where that defence can still succeed in the context of a negligence action.

Passengers, Drivers, and Pilots: *Dann v Hamilton* and *Morris v Murray*

In *Dann v Hamilton* [1939] 1 KB 509, the plaintiff had accepted a lift with the defendant. She allowed him to drive her home, though she knew that he had been drinking over the course of the evening. When the plaintiff was injured, she was held not to have consented to the risk posed by the defendant's drunkenness.[14] Subsequently, *Dann v Hamilton* was mentioned with approval by Lord Denning in *Nettleship v Weston*, and by Diplock LJ in *Wooldridge v Sumner*. But the decision was criticized in the Australian case of *Insurance Commissioner v Joyce* (1948) 77 CLR 39. As we have seen, the *volenti* defence is now excluded from road traffic actions between passenger and driver by section 149 of the Road Traffic Act 1988. Because of this, there have been few opportunities to consider whether accepting a lift from a person who is clearly incapable of driving safely could in principle be sufficient to give rise to the *volenti* defence.[15] *Morris v Murray* is in effect such a case. Since it involved a light aircraft rather than a road vehicle, it was not caught by the prohibition in the Road Traffic Act.

Morris v Murray [1991] 2 QB 6

The plaintiff and a friend (Murray) spent an afternoon drinking heavily. The two men decided to take a flight in a light aircraft, with Murray (who was found to have consumed the equivalent of 17 whiskies) at the controls. The plaintiff drove to the airfield and helped to start and refuel the aircraft. The plane crashed, killing Murray and seriously injuring the plaintiff. The *volenti* defence succeeded.

Fox LJ, at 17

. . . I would conclude . . . that the plaintiff accepted the risks and implicitly discharged Mr Murray from liability for injury in relation to the flying of the plane. . . .

. . . . It might be said that the merits could be adequately dealt with by the application of the contributory negligence rules. The judge held that the plaintiff was only 20 per cent. to blame (which seems to me to be too low) but if that were increased to 50 per cent. so that the plaintiff's damages were reduced by half, both sides would be substantially penalised for their conduct. It seems to me, however, that the wild irresponsibility of the venture is such that the law should not intervene to award damages and should leave the loss where it falls. Flying is intrinsically dangerous and flying with a drunken pilot is great folly. The situation is very different from what has arisen in motoring cases.

---

14 Writing later in (1953) LQR 317, Lord Asquith (who decided *Dann v Hamilton* as Asquith J) explained that contributory negligence, then a complete defence, had not been pleaded; he thought that if it had been pleaded, the defence would probably have been successful. This is confirmed by *Owens v Brimmell* [1977] QB 859, where the Court of Appeal reduced damages payable to a plaintiff who had accepted a lift from a drunk driver.

15 In *Pitts v Hunt* [1991] 1 QB 24, the plaintiff pillion passenger was closely involved in encouraging the wildly irresponsible driving of the deceased motorcyclist. Beldam LJ thought that the *volenti* defence would have succeeded if it had not been for s 149 of the Road Traffic Act 1988. Since the defence could not succeed, he did not give a full account of the reasons why this would be so.

The Court of Appeal in *Morris v Murray* distinguished *Dann*, and argued that the case in hand was closer on its facts to *ICI v Shatwell* (below) than to *Dann v Hamilton*. But if this is so, the difference is not down to the immediacy of the danger. The method of working used in *Shatwell* was certainly dangerous, but the method had been used many times before and (unlike *Murray*) it was far from inevitable that any injury would follow. What other reason might there be for putting *Morris v Murray* with *ICI v Shatwell* into one category, and *Dann v Hamilton* into another?

ICI v Shatwell [1965] AC 656

Two brothers were employed by the appellants as shot-firers. They chose to operate a dangerous means of testing detonators, even though they knew that this method had been forbidden by their employers on safety grounds, and prohibited by regulation for the same reason. There was an explosion, and both brothers were injured. George, who according to Lord Reid bore a greater part of the responsibility for deciding to operate the dangerous and forbidden system, brought an action in negligence and for breach of statutory duty against his employers. He accepted that his damages must be reduced for contributory negligence, but he argued that his employers were vicariously liable for the tortious conduct of his brother, who was partly to blame for his injuries.

The House of Lords held by a majority that the defence of *volenti* should succeed. Lord Reid emphasized that there had been a *deliberate decision* to disobey instructions, rather than a merely careless collaboration between the men.

> **Lord Reid,** at 672–3
>
> If we adopt the inaccurate habit of using the word "negligence" to denote a deliberate act done with full knowledge of the risk it is not surprising that we sometimes get into difficulties. I think that most people would say, without stopping to think of the reason, that there is a world of difference between two fellow-servants collaborating carelessly so that the acts of both contribute to cause injury to one of them, and two fellow-servants combining to disobey an order deliberately though they know the risk involved. It seems reasonable that the injured man should recover some compensation in the former case but not in the latter. If the law treats both as merely cases of negligence it cannot draw a distinction. But in my view the law does and should draw a distinction. In the first case only the partial defence of contributory negligence is available. In the second *volenti non fit injuria* is a complete defence if the employer is not himself at fault and is only liable vicariously for the acts of the fellow-servant. If the plaintiff invited or freely aided and abetted his fellow-servant's disobedience, then he was *volens* in the fullest sense. He cannot complain of the resulting injury either against the fellow-servant or against the master on the ground of his vicarious responsibility for his fellow-servant's conduct.

Comparing Lord Reid's analysis with the facts of *Morris v Murray*, it could be said that in the latter case, although the manner in which the deceased was piloting the plane was 'careless', the decision to engage in a glaringly dangerous activity was entirely deliberate. As such, the case may not fall within the doubts expressed by Diplock LJ in *Wooldridge v Sumner* about the application of *volenti* to 'negligence simpliciter'.

But what of the need for an agreement? This element was not mentioned by Lord Reid, but it was considered by Lord Pearce. Lord Pearce was ready to infer such an agreement from deliberate conduct on the part of the plaintiff:

Lord Pearce, at 688

In the present case it seems clear that as between George and James there was a voluntary assumption of risk. George was clearly acting without any constraint or persuasion; he was in fact inaugurating the enterprise. On the facts it was an implied term (to the benefit of which the employers are vicariously entitled) that George would not sue James for any injury that he might suffer, if an accident occurred. Had an officious bystander raised the possibility, can one doubt that George would have ridiculed it?

An explanation of *ICI v Shatwell* and *Morris v Murray* can be arrived at by combining the insights of Lords Reid and Pearce. The cases show that *volenti* may succeed in the absence of *express* agreement, provided there is deliberate collusion in the creation of the risk. On the analysis adopted by Lord Pearce, this can be seen in terms of an implied agreement: it would be obvious to both parties that the plaintiff here accepted the risk, at the time of the collaboration.[16]

4. *EX TURPI CAUSA NON ORITUR ACTIO*: 'ILLEGALITY'

Under the right circumstances, it will be a defence to a tort action to show that the claim arises directly out of illegal conduct on the part of the claimant.

This defence is sometimes described in the Latin phrase *ex turpi causa non oritur actio*: no action arises from a bad cause. Although it is usual to state this defence in such a way as to extend not only to illegal but also to *immoral* conduct, the Law Commission in its *Consultation Paper on the Illegality Defence in Tort* (Consultation Paper No 160, 2001) reported that it had found only one case (which would not be followed today) where anything less than illegality had been sufficient.[17] On the other hand, it is clear that not every taint of illegality will suffice. For example, a driver is required by law to wear a seatbelt; but we have already seen that failure to do so will lead only to reduction in damages on the basis of contributory negligence (*Froom v Butcher*, above), not to the claim being barred on grounds of illegality. In what follows, we will try to determine which sorts of illegality, and under which circumstances, will defeat a claim in tort. But first, it is important to establish the broad underlying rationale for the defence.

The Rationale for the Defence

Although it is now clear that illegality may operate as a defence throughout the law of tort, including cases of negligence, the defence is a relatively recent transplant into tort law.

---

[16] In the extract above, Lord Pearce refers to the 'officious bystander'. This is a shorthand reference to the test for implying terms into a contract, derived from the judgment of MacKinnon LJ in *Shirlaw v Southern Foundries Ltd* [1939] 2 KB 206: it is clear that both parties would have regarded the term as too obvious to merit discussion.

[17] The single exception was *Hegarty v Shine* (1877–82) 14 Cox CC 145, a decision of the Court of Appeal in Ireland. The court treated cohabitation outside marriage as sufficiently immoral to bar a claim for assault where the defendant had not revealed to the plaintiff that he was suffering from a venereal disease.

As recently as 1954, the House of Lords doubted its application to a case of personal injury (*National Coal Board v England* [1954] AC 403), and there is some continuing support for the suggestion that in personal injury actions, contributory negligence can sufficiently deal with any fault—including illegality—on the part of the claimant.[18] While contributory negligence operates on the basis of justice and fairness between the parties, illegality has an entirely different rationale.

In *Tinsley v Milligan* [1994] 1 AC 430 (discussed below), Lord Goff treated the following statement of the defence and its rationale as authoritative. This passage particularly refers to cases where there is an illegal or immoral contract, but it has been treated as applying to the illegality defence in all causes of action, including tort.

Lord Mansfield, *Holman v Johnson* (1775) 1 Cowp 341, at 343

The objection, that a contract is immoral or illegal as between plaintiff and defendant, sounds at all times very ill in the mouth of the defendant. It is not for his sake, however, that the objection is ever allowed; but it is founded in general principles of policy, which the defendant has the advantage of, contrary to the real justice, as between him and the plaintiff, by accident, if I may say so. The principle of public policy is this: *ex dolo malo non oritur actio*. No court will lend its aid to a man who founds his cause of action upon an immoral or illegal act. If, from the plaintiff's own stating or otherwise, the cause of action appears to arise *ex turpi causa*, or the transgression of a positive law of this country, there the court says he has no right to be assisted. It is upon that ground that the court goes; not for the sake of the defendant, but because they will not lend their aid to such a plaintiff. So if the plaintiff and defendant were to change sides, and the defendant was to bring his action against the plaintiff, the latter would then have the advantage of it; for where both are equally in fault, *potior est conditio defendentis*.

The frequent recourse to Latin does nothing to cloud Lord Mansfield's point. The illegality defence is not about fairness between the parties, and is certainly not applied out of 'tenderness'[19] toward a defendant who (in a case of illegal contract or joint criminal enterprise) may also have acted illegally. The illegality defence is a *rule of public policy*. The same is true in cases of contract, trust, or tort.

Even if there is a single underlying rationale for the illegality defence, it does not follow that all cases can be determined on the basis of the same or similar criteria. In its *Consultation Paper on the Illegality Defence in Tort*, the Law Commission addressed the tort cases in terms of three categories. The first two of these are adapted (not always successfully) from case law outside tort. The third is still in search of a clear rationale.

---

[18] Sedley LJ, *Vellino v Chief Constable of the Greater Manchester Police* [2002] 1 WLR 218, 232–3 (dissenting); R. Glofcheski, 'Plaintiff's Illegality as a Bar to the Recovery of Personal Injury Damages' (1999) 19 LS 6–23.

[19] Schiemann LJ, *Sacco v Chief Constable of the South Wales Constabulary*, Court of Appeal, 15 May 1998.

Law Commission, *The Illegality Defence in Tort* (Consultation Paper No 160, HMSO, 2001)

2.11 . . . the range of cases in which the defence of illegality has featured is wide. It is not easy to state the principles governing this defence in tort other than in broad terms. One possible analysis is that a claim in tort will fail on any of three grounds:

(1) where the claimant seeks, or is forced, to found the claim on his or her illegal act;

(2) where the grant of relief to the claimant would enable him or her to benefit from his or her criminal conduct (or where what is sought is compensation for loss of liberty or an indemnity for the consequences of criminal behaviour); and

(3) where, even though neither (1) nor (2) is applicable to the claim, the situation is nevertheless covered by a general residual principle that the court should not assist a claimant who has been guilty of illegal conduct of which the courts should take notice.

Category 1: The Claim is Founded on the Claimant's Illegal Act

The leading decision under this head, *Tinsley v Milligan*, shows the *limits* to the illegality defence, at least where the claim relates to the acquisition of title to property. It is not altogether clear how *Tinsley* ought to apply to tort cases. But *Tinsley* has affected the law of tort, and so it is important to grasp what was decided.

In *Tinsley v Milligan* [1994] 1 AC 340, the plaintiff and defendant contributed to the purchase price of a house. The house was vested in the sole name of the plaintiff, but on the 'understanding' that the beneficial interest in the property was jointly vested in both plaintiff and defendant. The purpose of this arrangement was an illegal one: to defraud the DSS. When the parties quarrelled and the plaintiff moved out, the plaintiff gave the defendant notice to quit and asserted sole ownership. The defendant argued that the property was held on trust for both parties. The Court of Appeal accepted the defendant's argument: there was a 'resulting trust' which was not defeated by the parties' joint illegal purpose in registering the house in the plaintiff's sole name. The 'equitable balance' in this case favoured the defendant. If the illegality defence were to succeed, it would mean that the plaintiff, relying on her own illegal purpose, could obtain not only the legal title but the beneficial title also.

In the House of Lords, the Court of Appeal's reasoning was disapproved, although the majority agreed, for different reasons, with their conclusion. Lord Goff (in dissent) would have rejected the defendant's argument on the basis that her claim to the beneficial ownership was tinged with illegality. Lord Goff drew upon the authority of *Holman v Johnson* (above) to suggest that even an undeserving party (in this case the plaintiff) could rely upon the protection of the public policy rule. As Lord Goff put it, 'a court of equity will not assist a plaintiff [20] who does not come to equity with clean hands' (at 362). This broad principle was rejected by the majority, who interpreted the defence much more narrowly.

---

[20] Or in this instance, a defendant making a counter-claim.

Lord Browne-Wilkinson explained that although a court will not *enforce* an illegal contract, this did not mean that such a contract had no effect at all in law or equity:

Lord Browne-Wilkinson, at 369

In particular it is now clearly established that at law . . . property in goods or land can pass under, or pursuant to, such a contract. If so, the rights of the owner of the legal title . . . will be enforced, provided that the plaintiff can establish such title without pleading or leading evidence of the illegality.

He went on to explain that the same applied to *equitable* interests in property, such as the beneficial ownership claimed by the defendant. On the facts of this particular case, the defendant had to bring evidence of the *arrangement* between the parties in order to make her claim. But crucially, she *did not have to depend on the **illegality** of that arrangement*. This was partly down to the 'presumption of resulting trust': the defendant only needed to show agreement to hold in equal shares, and contribution to the purchase price. A trust in her favour would then be presumed. On the contrary, it was the plaintiff who had to plead the illegality, in order to argue that *no* resulting trust should arise, since the presumption was against her.

Lord Browne-Wilkinson agreed with Lord Goff that such cases should be dealt with in a clear and predictable way, and that the outcome should not depend on the discretion of the court. In particular, he accepted that the Court of Appeal had been wrong to approach the question of illegality in terms of whether a successful claim would be an 'affront to public conscience'. This has had an indirect impact on tort cases, where precisely that test had begun to gain acceptance. It has now been abandoned.

A second way in which *Tinsley* has had an impact on tort claims is that courts have purported to 'apply' the narrow rule in *Tinsley* in order to bar tort claims on the basis of illegality (see for example *Clunis v Camden* and *Marsh v Clare* below). But it is by no means clear that the reasoning in *Tinsley* has any application to the majority of tort cases.[21]

The 'affront to public conscience' test in personal injury claims

Before *Tinsley*, 'affront to public conscience' had some claim to be recognized as the guiding criterion for the illegality defence in tort. A clear example of reliance on this idea is *Kirkham v Chief Constable of Greater Manchester Police* [1990] 2 QB 283. Here, the plaintiff's husband committed suicide while in custody. The defendants had failed to make the prison service aware that the deceased was at risk of suicide. In respect of the *ex turpi causa* defence, Lloyd LJ said (at 291):

We have to ask ourselves . . . whether to afford relief in such a case as this, arising, as it does, directly out of a man's suicide, would affront the public conscience, or, as I would prefer to say, shock the ordinary citizen. I have come to the conclusion that the answer should be in the negative.

---

[21] Cases of conversion are an exception (as indeed conversion is an exceptional tort: Chapter 17). The narrow rule adopted in *Tinsley v Milligan* was itself derived from a case of conversion: *Bowmakers v Barnett Instruments Ltd* [1945] KB 65.

The House of Lords in *Tinsley* did not disapprove *Kirkham*.[22] Since *Tinsley* though, the Court of Appeal has nevertheless abandoned the 'affront to public conscience' test on the assumption that it is no longer tenable (see *Vellino* and *Cross v Kirkby*, below). This is probably quite unnecessary, and leaves these cases without a guiding rationale.

Applying Tinsley *in tort cases*

In *Clunis v Camden & Islington Health Authority* [1998] QB 978, the Court of Appeal attempted to apply the narrow rule in *Tinsley v Milligan* to a case of negligence. The plaintiff Clunis had attacked and killed a man. He was convicted of manslaughter on grounds of diminished responsibility. He claimed damages from the defendant health authority in respect of his consequent detention, on the basis that the defendant had not managed his case properly nor provided appropriate after-care given his violent history. According to the Court of Appeal:

> In our view the plaintiff's claim does arise out of and depend upon proof of his commission of a criminal offence.

It is doubtful whether this case falls within the narrow *Tinsley* rule. Strictly, the plaintiff needed to show not that his acts were illegal, but that they had led to his lengthy detention. Besides, the plaintiff did not attack his victim in the hope of making a gain, and success in his tort claim would not result in any sense in perfecting an illegal intention. As the Law Commission noted, it would be better to deal with such a case as an example of category 2 (below).

Can a negligence claim ever fit the Tinsley rule?

Marsh v Clare [2003] EWCA Civ 284 is a very unusual case in which the *Tinsley* approach seemed to apply quite appropriately to a claim in negligence. (It was also argued as a case of misfeasance in a public office: Chapter 2.) On the other hand, because the illegality defence succeeded it was never determined whether the case was appropriately argued in negligence at all.

The claimant had entered into arrangements with a corrupt police officer H, paying H £10,000 in order to join a 'police informant witness protection programme' ('the Club') and in turn being encouraged to deal in stolen cars. Following his arrest by other officers, the claimant brought an action against the defendant Chief Constable, on the basis that she was vicariously liable for H's acts. The claimant sought to recover the sum of £10,000 paid to H and a further sum of £50,000 representing the value of stolen cars seized by police officers. Potter LJ said that the claim to recover the 'joining fee' of £10,000 fell within the Law Commission's first category. The claim for £50,000 was said, with equal force, to fall within the Law Commission's second category (explored below).

In this particular case, the claimant was indeed compelled to base his claim on the illegality of his own act (the corrupt payment). If the payment had not been illegal, there would have been no fault (negligence) nor excess of powers (misfeasance) on the part of H. We should notice though how exceptional the *result* in this case is. If a claimant wishes to compel the police to return money or chattels that have been *lawfully* seized, the scope of the illegality

---

[22] In *Reeves v Commissioner of Police for the Metropolis* [2000] 1 AC 360, which also concerned suicide by a prisoner, the illegality defence was not pursued to the House of Lords, where *Kirkham* was discussed with apparent approval.

defence is—following *Tinsley*—surprisingly narrow. In *Costello v Chief Constable of Derbyshire Constabulary* [2001] 1 WLR 1437, a claimant succeeded in an action against the police for return of a Ford Escort car seized from him on suspicion of theft. In the Court of Appeal, Lightman J rejected the proposition that no title vests in a thief.[23] Applying *Tinsley*, he also rejected the proposition that there is no obligation to return property to a thief. Only someone with a better title to the goods could defeat the claim.[24] This conclusion was reiterated by the Court of Appeal in *Gough v Chief Constable of West Midlands Police* [2004] EWCA Civ 206. It seems bizarre that it is easier to recover money or goods that have been lawfully seized (*Costello*), than to recover losses caused where payments are taken negligently or in excess of powers (*Marsh v Clare*).

Category 2: No Indemnity for Consequences of Illegal Act

In contractual cases, a 'no benefit' rule prevents enforcement of a contract where the claimant stands to gain in consequence of his or her illegal act. A true example of this rule is *Beresford v Royal Insurance Co Ltd* [1938] AC 586, decided at a time when suicide was a crime. A life insurance contract was unenforceable where the assured had committed suicide, since otherwise his representative would benefit from his crime.[25] As the Law Commission noted:

> **2.23** . . . The tort cases are not strictly speaking cases of 'benefit', at least in the sense that the claimant is seeking a profit he or she hoped to make from his or her illegal activity. They are cases in which what is sought is an indemnity for losses or liabilities he or she has incurred as a result of his or her acts.[26]

The tort cases are thus better explained in terms of a 'no indemnity rule', rather than a 'no benefit' rule. An example of the 'no indemnity rule' is *Meah v McCreamer (No 2)* [1986] 1 All ER 943. The plaintiff, who had been convicted of rape, was found liable in damages in a civil action brought by his victims. Blaming his offences on personality change brought about through the negligence of the defendant in a road traffic accident, he claimed compensation in respect of the damages payable. Woolf J held that his claim was barred on grounds of public policy. It would be inappropriate for the plaintiff to be indemnified for the consequences of his own crimes.[27]

A limited public policy bar of this type may be justified in terms of a threat to consistency or integrity within the law. The Supreme Court of Canada adopted such an argument in the

---

[23] It had been found at first instance that, on the *civil* balance ('more likely than not'), the claimant did indeed steal the car, though he was not convicted.

[24] This case, and *Webb v Chief Constable of Merseyside Police* [2000] QB 427 (successful action for return of funds seized on suspicion of drug-trafficking), are discussed with approval by Graham Battersby, 'Acquiring Title by Theft' (2002) 65 MLR 603.

[25] Suicide is no longer a crime: note the successful actions in *Kirkham* and *Reeves* (above).

[26] *Marsh v Clare* may now be a counter-example.

[27] The plaintiff had already succeeded in obtaining damages compensating him for his *conviction* for the crimes: *Meah v McCreamer* [1985] 1 All ER 367. The illegality defence was not raised in that case, whose result was doubted by the Court of Appeal in *Clunis*, above.

case of *Hall v Hebert* (1993) 101 DLR (4th) 129:

McLachlin J, at 179–80

[There] is a need in the law of tort for a principle which permits judges to deny recovery to a plaintiff on the ground that to do so would undermine the integrity of the justice system. The power is a limited one. Its use is justified where allowing the plaintiff's claim would introduce inconsistency into the fabric of the law, either by permitting the plaintiff to profit from an illegal or wrongful act, or to evade a penalty prescribed by criminal law. Its use is not justified where the plaintiff's claim is merely for compensation for personal injuries sustained as a consequence of the negligence of the defendant.

McLachlin J would not extend the no-indemnity rule to claims for personal injury (such as those arising for consideration in category 3). As the Law Commission pointed out, to deny all claims for personal injury on the part of those injured in the course of crime would imply that criminals were 'outlaws', who could be injured without legal consequence.

Category 3: 'Residual'

It is clear that there are cases in tort where the illegality defence will succeed and which do not fall within the above categories. Most personal injury actions where illegality is relevant are likely to fall into this category. An example is *Pitts v Hunt* [1991] 1 QB 24, an action in negligence brought by a pillion passenger, who had urged the deceased motorcyclist to wild exploits of dangerous and reckless driving.

In *Pitts v Hunt*, all three judges in the Court of Appeal concluded that the passenger's claim in negligence failed for illegality, but each judge gave different reasons. Dillon LJ said that 'the plaintiff's action in truth arises directly *ex turpi causa*' (at 60). The 'directness' of the relationship between illegality and injury was key. Balcombe LJ reasoned that it was impossible to determine a relevant standard of care for the illegal enterprise, so that there could be no duty (at 50). He was influenced by Australian case law.[28] Beldam LJ on the other hand reasoned that the action was barred on the grounds of public policy since the plaintiff had actively encouraged serious offences committed by the motorcyclist. The seriousness of the offences was one element to be taken into account when making a 'pragmatic' judgment about the application of the illegality defence. Both Dillon LJ (directness) and Beldam LJ (seriousness of offence) relied on the following statement:

Bingham LJ, *Saunders v Edwards* [1987] 1 WLR 1116, 1134

. . . I think that on the whole the courts have tended to adopt a pragmatic approach to these problems, seeking where possible to see that genuine wrongs are righted so long as the court does not thereby promote or countenance a nefarious object or bargain which it is bound to condemn. Where the plaintiff's action in truth arises directly ex turpi causa, he is likely to fail . . . Where the plaintiff has suffered a genuine wrong, to which allegedly unlawful conduct is incidental, he is likely to succeed.

---

[28] Particularly *Jackson v Harrison* [1978] 138 CLR 438.

This particular passage in *Saunders v Edwards* continues to be referred to in the most recent case law, even though the decision itself was disapproved by the House of Lords in *Tinsley v Milligan* (above), because the court also adopted the 'affront to public conscience' test.

The political dimension

Compensation claims for injuries sustained in the course of crime have been deeply politically controversial. As Sedley LJ pointed out in *Vellino v Chief Constable of Greater Manchester Police* [2001] EWCA Civ 1249; [2002] 1 WLR 218, the Law Commission's conclusion that criminals may sometimes be compensated for injuries suffered in the course of crime 'earned [them] the soubriquet "Enemy of the people"' (*Sunday Times*, 1 July 2001). Sedley LJ supported abandonment of the 'affront to public conscience' test, because (he thought) it implied that courts should make their decisions in the light of likely public *opinion*, 'looking over their shoulders' at what the headline writers were likely to make of the decisions.[29]

It is clear that even in a case of serious criminal intent, it is not appropriate to treat the criminal as beyond the reach of tort law, so that *anything* may be done without legal consequence. Controversy continues to flow from the decision in *Revill v Newbery* [1996] QB 567, which embraced the proposition that even the trespasser with criminal intent is not beyond the protection of the law. The plaintiff had intended to break into a shed on an allotment with a view to stealing from it. The defendant, who was sleeping in the shed with a shotgun because he planned to deter burglars, fired through a hole in the door and unintentionally injured the plaintiff. The plaintiff brought an action in negligence (and under the Occupiers' Liability Act 1984)[30] against the defendant. A defence of illegality was rejected by the Court of Appeal for reasons outlined by Evans and Millett LJJ:

Evans LJ, at 579

. . . the underlying principle is that there is a public interest which requires that the wrongdoer should not benefit from his crime or other offence. But it would mean, if it does apply in circumstances such as these, that the trespasser who was also a criminal was effectively an outlaw, who was debarred by the law from recovering compensation for any injury which he might sustain. . . .

It is abundantly clear, in my judgment, that the trespasser/ criminal is not an outlaw, and it is noteworthy that even the old common law authorities recognised the existence of some duty towards trespassers, even though the duty was limited and strictly defined . . .

Millett LJ, at 580

For centuries the common law has permitted reasonable force to be used in defence of the person or property. Violence may be returned with necessary violence. But the force used must not exceed the limits of what is reasonable in the circumstances. Changes in society and in social perceptions have meant that what might have been considered reasonable at one time would no longer be so regarded; but the principle remains the same. The assailant or

---

[29] This is very different from the reasons given by the House of Lords in *Tinsley v Milligan* for disapproving the test.

[30] Chapter 12.

intruder may be met with reasonable force but no more; the use of excessive violence against him is an actionable wrong.

It follows, in my opinion, that there is no place for the doctrine ex turpi causa non oritur actio in this context. If the doctrine applied, any claim by the assailant or trespasser would be barred no matter how excessive or unreasonable the force used against him.

Subsequently, the Court of Appeal has attempted to state a 'pragmatic' position which allows some, but not all, claims of personal injury arising out of criminal acts by the claimant to be barred on grounds of illegality. In *Cross v Kirkby* (18 February 2000), the claimant had assaulted the defendant with a baseball bat. The defendant wrestled the bat from the claimant and hit him with it, fracturing his skull. In contrast to the claimant in *Revill v Newbery*, who was offering no immediate threat to the person of the defendant, the claimant here had 'goaded the defendant into protecting himself' (Beldam LJ at [78], quoting the first instance judge). Beldam LJ explained:

[76] . . . In my view the principle [*ex turpi causa*] applies when the claimant's claim is so closely connected or inextricably bound up with his own criminal or illegal conduct that the court could not permit him to recover without appearing to condone that conduct.

The idea that the injury in this case is to be treated as 'inextricably bound up' with the illegality is quite imprecise. It should be noted that the 'proportionality' of the defendant's response should not be relevant, because as we have seen the *ex turpi causa* defence may be raised by an undeserving defendant and is not concerned with 'balance' between the parties. However, in a case of disproportionate response—such as *Revill v Newbery*—it is much less likely that the injury will be said to be inextricably bound up with the claimant's illegal conduct.

The continuing problems with the illegality defence in personal injury actions are illustrated by *Vellino v Chief Constable of the Greater Manchester Police* [2002] 1 WLR 218. The Court of Appeal delayed delivering their judgment in this case in order to have the benefit of the Law Commission Report. But this delay did not produce agreement.

The claimant Vellino had been arrested by police officers. When he attempted to escape over a balcony, he suffered very serious injuries. He brought an action in negligence, arguing that the officers should have tried harder to prevent his escape.

Of the three members of the Court of Appeal to hear *Vellino*, only Sir Murray Stuart-Smith decided the case through application of the illegality defence. We have already noted the dissenting judgment of Sedley LJ who concluded that contributory negligence could deal adequately with a case such as this. Schiemann LJ ruled that the claim failed on the different ground that no duty of care was owed to the claimant in respect of his attempted escape. As we saw in Chapter 3 above, there is generally no duty to save someone from their own carelessness. The question therefore is whether the fact of arrest should be taken to justify such a duty, and the closest comparator is not *Revill* but *Reeves v Commissioner of Police of the Metropolis* [2000] 1 AC 360. According to Schiemann LJ, this was a very different case from *Reeves*, where the duty arose from the dangers associated with detention.

16   For instance, if the officer detains the citizen then I would accept that he must take reasonable care that the citizen is not injured by lack of water. The officer might, if the roof

showed signs of collapsing, be under a duty to take or let the citizen out of the flat where he was arrested. The fact that the citizen would never have been detained had he not previously committed a crime would not prevent an action from succeeding. The reasoning behind that approach is that by the fact of detention the man is prevented from getting his own water or escaping danger. It is not the arrest which gives rise to the duty of care to the man. It is his detention. That is also why there is a duty to try and prevent known suicide risks in prison from committing suicide.

17 However, where a man breaks away from the arresting officer the position is manifestly different. By so doing the man commits a crime and he is no longer in the immediate power of the officer.

Of course there is room to doubt the specific reasons given here for distinguishing *Reeves*; but the main point is that these remarks are probably focused on the appropriate issues. In *Reeves* itself, Lord Hoffmann emphasized that the duty to prevent a claimant from harming himself was exceptional:

Reeves, at 369

The duty, as I have said, is a very unusual one, arising from the complete control which the police or prison authorities have over the prisoner, combined with the special danger of people in prison taking their own lives.

Neither of the factors mentioned by Lord Hoffmann applies in the case of *Vellino*. It is suggested that this is a case where the illegality defence is not required, because no duty to *prevent* the claimant from endangering himself is established.

Contrary to the general thrust of the Law Commission's proposals, a new statutory provision *restricts* the availability of actions in *trespass to the person*, but *not* negligence, where the trespass occurs in the course of committing an imprisonable offence. This is dependent on the claimant having been convicted of the offence. An honest belief that the trespass was necessary for one of the reasons stated in section 329(5) is sufficient to *compel* the court to refuse permission for the action to be brought, unless the defendant's acts are 'grossly disproportionate'. If permission is granted, these matters may still be raised as defences.

Criminal Justice Act 2003

329 Civil proceedings for trespass to the person brought by offender

(1) This section applies where—

(a) a person ("the claimant") claims that another person ("the defendant") did an act amounting to trespass to the claimant's person, and

(b) the claimant has been convicted in the United Kingdom of an imprisonable offence committed on the same occasion as that on which the act is alleged to have been done.

(2) Civil proceedings relating to the claim may be brought only with the permission of the court.

(3) The court may give permission for the proceedings to be brought only if there is evidence that either—

(a) the condition in subsection (5) is not met, or

(b) in all the circumstances, the defendant's act was grossly disproportionate.

(4) If the court gives permission and the proceedings are brought, it is a defence for the defendant to prove both—

(a) that the condition in subsection (5) is met, and

(b) that, in all the circumstances, his act was not grossly disproportionate.

(5) The condition referred to in subsection (3)(a) and (4)(a) is that the defendant did the act only because—

(a) he believed that the claimant—

(i) was about to commit an offence,

(ii) was in the course of committing an offence, or

(iii) had committed an offence immediately beforehand; and

(b) he believed that the act was necessary to—

(i) defend himself or another person,

(ii) protect or recover property,

(iii) prevent the commission or continuation of an offence, or

(iv) apprehend, or secure the conviction, of the claimant after he had committed an offence;

or was necessary to assist in achieving any of those things.

. . .

FURTHER READING

Battersby, G., 'Acquiring Property by Theft' (2002) 65 MLR 603.

Debattista, C., 'Ex Turpi Causa Returns to the English Law of Torts: Taking Advantage of a Wrong Way Out' (1984) 13 AALR 15.

Deitrich, J., 'The decline of contributory negligence and apportionment: choosing the black and white of all or nothing over shades of grey?' (2003) 11 TLJ 51.

Glofcheski, R., 'Plaintiff's Illegality as a Bar to the Recovery of Personal Injury Damages' (1999) 19 LS 6–23.

Halliwell, M., 'Equitable Property Rights, Discretionary Remedies and Unclean Hands' (2004) Conv 439–52.

Jaffey, A. J. E., 'Volenti non fit injuria' [1985] CLJ 87.

Law Commission, *Consultation Paper on the Illegality Defence in Tort* (Consultation Paper No 160, HMSO, 2001).

Lunney, M., 'Personal responsibility and the "new" volenti' (2005) 13 *Tort L Rev* 76–91.

Williams, G., *Joint Torts and Contributory Negligence* (Stevens & Sons, 1951).

6

DUTY OF CARE: APPLICATIONS

CENTRAL ISSUES

i) We explored the general nature of the duty of care in Chapter 3, and introduced the '*Caparo* approach' to establishing whether a duty is owed. Here, we turn our attention to particular applications of the duty concept, and consider the effectiveness of that approach.

ii) Our first set of cases relates to negligently inflicted psychiatric damage. For many years, attention in this category has focused on claims by 'secondary victims', whose psychiatric injury is caused by witnessing (or otherwise experiencing) death, personal injury, or imperilment of others. In these cases, very restrictive rules have developed and it has not been possible to justify these rules on a principled basis. On the other hand, such cases are not typical of all claims for psychiatric damage, and a significant number of 'primary victim' cases are now decided without reference to special control devices. Although the House of Lords has, unusually, declared that 'the search for principle' in this category has been called off, it seems that lower courts still seek to develop the law along principled lines.

iii) We next turn our attention to cases of 'pure economic loss'. These cases have long been recognized as posing particular difficulties. We will suggest that some order can be imposed on the case law here. There is not one general exclusionary rule applying to economic losses, but two specific exclusionary rules regarding 'relational economic losses' (where the claimant's interest in damaged property is merely contractual), and cases of mere defectiveness in a product. It is outside these categories that the difficulties arise. Particularly important, but also particularly evasive, has been the **assumption of responsibility** criterion developed from the leading case of *Hedley Byrne v Heller* [1964] AC 465. This idea has made its way into other areas of the tort of negligence (including psychiatric damage claims and claims against public authorities), so it is important to consider whether it has any substance, or is merely an empty label.

iv) The greatest volume of difficult case law surrounds the negligence liability of public authorities, which is also subject to considerable change. Restrictive rules for this area were adopted in the case of *X v Bedfordshire* [1995] 2 AC 633. These however were based on clearly articulated policy reasons and in this sense cannot be called 'arbitrary'. The influence of human rights is clear to see in recent developments, as English courts strive to avoid being seen to confer 'immunities'. This has led to expansion in liability, but there are still important 'no duty' situations. Some increased confidence in use of the *Caparo* test to deny a duty of care can be seen in the most recent case law.

v) Our final group of cases is smaller, but like the psychiatric damage cases it has caused the House of Lords to resort to unconventional reasoning. These are cases of 'wrongful birth' associated with failed sterilization operations. Like the psychiatric damage cases, the pattern of decisions in this category is hard to justify. In this instance however the problem is not one of inflexibility but of instability, as the House of Lords has reconsidered its reasons from case to case and produced conflicting decisions.

vi) Finally, we attempt an appraisal of the current state of play. We defend the use of policy reasoning in the *Caparo* approach, while also noting the existence of anomalous cases which have not been successfully explained in terms of either justice between the parties, or broader concerns.

1. PSYCHIATRIC DAMAGE

The case law in this section relates to negligently inflicted psychiatric damage. Such cases have been divided into claims by 'secondary victims', and claims by 'primary victims'. 'Secondary victims' are those who suffer psychiatric damage as a result of injury to, or death or imperilment of, another. In these cases, policy-based restrictions have applied to limit the recognized duties to take care. Not all of these restrictions apply to claims by primary victims. Indeed in some primary victim claims, none of the restrictions apply. 'Primary victims' include those who suffer psychiatric damage through stress at work, and those who are physically endangered. Other categories of primary victim claim are also emerging, for example where the defendant has assumed responsibility towards the claimant, or where there is a prior contractual relationship. Despite the restrictions applying to secondary victim claims, there seems to be expansion in the field of successful primary victim claims.

1.1 THE NATURE OF 'PSYCHIATRIC DAMAGE'

It is clear that psychiatric damage is capable of being recoverable in the tort of negligence. If a relevant form of psychiatric damage is caused by the defendant's negligence, the crucial question will be whether the defendant owed a duty to the claimant in respect of that damage.

A sharp distinction must be drawn at the outset between recognized psychiatric conditions (which may constitute 'damage'), and normal emotional distress of one sort or another.

Lord Bridge, *McLoughlin v O'Brian* [1983] 1 AC 410, at 431

The common law gives no damages for the emotional distress which any normal person experiences when someone he loves is killed or injured. Anxiety and depression are normal human emotions. Yet an anxiety neurosis or a reactive depression may be recognisable psychiatric illnesses, with or without psychosomatic symptoms. So, the first hurdle which a plaintiff claiming damages of the kind in question must surmount is to establish that he is suffering, not merely grief, distress or any other normal emotion, but a positive psychiatric illness.

In *Grieves v Everard and Others* [2006] EWCA Civ 27, a number of claimants who had been exposed to asbestos dust at work suffered physical changes to their lungs (in the form of 'pleural plaques'). The Court of Appeal decided that these changes did not amount to 'material personal injury' in themselves (Chapter 4). However, pleural plaques are associated with an increased risk of developing serious lung diseases including asbestosis and mesothelioma. The claimants suffered anxiety as a result of knowing of this risk, although the percentage chance of developing the diseases was low. The Court of Appeal held that this *anxiety* could not be the subject of compensation, in the absence of personal injury. One of the claimants however was diagnosed as suffering not from mere anxiety but from *anxiety neurosis*—a medically recognized condition triggered by the knowledge that he may contract a serious lung disease. This claimant's case was different, since his anxiety neurosis *might* be the subject of compensation—but only if a relevant duty of care was owed. In the event, the Court of Appeal held that there was no such duty.

We will return to *Grieves*, and the reasons why no duty was established, in due course.

The Distinction between Physical and Psychiatric Harm: Injury or Means of Causation?

We have said that psychiatric illness must be distinguished from 'ordinary' emotional distress. But is it possible to make a similarly clear distinction between psychiatric and *physical* disorders? Arguably, no clear distinction of this sort can be made.

Lord Wilberforce, *McLoughlin v O'Brian* [1983] 1 AC 410, at 418

Whatever is unknown about the mind-body relationship (and the area of ignorance appears to expand with that of knowledge), it is now accepted by medical science that recognisable and severe physical damage to the human body and system may be caused by the impact, through the senses, of external events on the mind.

As long ago as 1901, in the case of *Dulieu v White*, Kennedy J speculated to similar effect:

Kennedy J, *Dulieu v White & Sons* [1901] 2 KB 669, at 677

. . . For my own part, I would not like to assume it to be scientifically true that a nervous shock which causes serious bodily illness is not actually accompanied by physical injury, although it may be impossible, or at least difficult, to detect the injury at the time in the living subject. I should not be surprised if the surgeon or the physiologist told us that nervous shock is or may be in itself an injurious affection of the physical organism.

The difficulty of distinguishing between psychiatric and physical harm has long been recognized, but it is not always given the significance it deserves. The difficulty of this distinction helps to explain the reasoning in the much-criticized decision of *Page v Smith*, for example. In that case, the injury suffered by the claimant (chronic fatigue syndrome or 'ME') was genuinely difficult to categorize as physical or psychiatric. In many cases it is not the lack of any physical manifestation of harm to the claimant, but the lack of any physical mechanism of causation, which is perceived to cause the problems.[1]

1.2 CONTROL DEVICES

A number of control devices have been developed to limit recovery of psychiatric harm. The existence of these control devices gives rise to some particular difficulties.

The applicable control devices aim chiefly at avoiding over-extensive liability. The risk is that control devices of this sort will introduce distinctions between cases which, in terms of their merits, ought to be treated in a similar way. But control devices do not *inevitably* do this. Sometimes, as we will see in respect of economic losses in the next section, control devices are needed in order to protect clear policy goals. If policy reasoning is clearly explained and consistently applied, like cases can be treated alike, on policy grounds as well as on grounds of principle.

In the sphere of psychiatric harm, there are two problems with the applicable control devices. One is that the goals served by these devices have not been clear. This is important, because not identifying the real reasons for distinctions between cases will tend to lead to distortion, confusion, and unfairness. The other is that in the tragic circumstances in which many of such cases occur, the distinctions drawn can seem inhumane and even insulting. The Law Commission, when it considered the law on psychiatric harm, therefore proposed the abolition or amendment of some, but not all of these control devices (see further the final part of this section).

'Shock'

The first control device to be considered is the requirement that the injury should have been caused by shock.

Where the event that brings about the psychiatric harm is death, injury, or endangerment of another, a claimant will be owed a duty in respect of psychiatric harm *only* if the harm results from a sudden shocking event.[2] It is not altogether clear in which other cases (if any) shock is a requirement. It is possible that shock is required in cases where the claimant fears for his or her own safety (*Dulieu v White*; *Page v Smith*), though this was not the reason given for rejecting a claim based on *Page v Smith* in *Grieves v Everard* (below). But shock is clearly not required where the claimant suffers psychiatric harm through being overworked, for example.

Traditionally, lawyers referred to psychiatric injuries as 'nervous shock'. That description of the injury has now fallen into disrepute because it fails to reflect any accepted medical description of the harm. But as we have just said, the requirement that the psychiatric damage must (at least in secondary victim cases) be *caused by* sudden shock continues.

[1] In *Dulieu v White* itself there was a physiological response to shock: premature birth was brought about through shock and fear.
[2] This was clearly spelt out in *Alcock v Chief Constable of South Yorkshire Police*, below.

Brennan J, *Jaensch v Coffey* (1984) 155 CLR 549, at 566–7

The notion of psychiatric illness induced by shock is a compound, not a simple, idea. Its elements are, on the one hand, psychiatric illness and, on the other, shock which causes it. . . . I understand 'shock' in this context to mean the sudden sensory perception—that is, by seeing, hearing or touching—of a person, thing or event, which is so distressing that the perception of the phenomenon affronts or insults the plaintiff's mind and causes a recognisable psychiatric illness. A psychiatric illness induced by mere knowledge of a distressing fact is not compensable; perception by the plaintiff of the distressing phenomenon is essential.

The key purpose of the 'shock' requirement is probably to avoid claims by individuals who are considered too remote (in time and space) from the initial incident. The requirement aims to avoid opening 'the floodgates of liability'.[3] As such, it may be expected *not* to apply in cases where there is a contractual relationship, for example. The division of cases where the psychiatric effects are caused by 'shock' from those where the disorder is caused by the mere fact of death of a loved one can seem (on the facts) to be irrelevant in any principled terms. The shock requirement is patently a control device.

Reasonable Fortitude and Specific Foreseeability

There are three control devices working together in the applicable test for 'foreseeability'. According to the House of Lords in *Page v Smith*, and the Court of Appeal in *McLoughlin v Jones*, this special test applies in *secondary victim cases only*. We need to ask whether the recent decision in *Grieves v Everard* qualifies this picture.

In any case in negligence, foreseeability of harm is essential to establishing that a duty of care is owed, and that the harm is not too remote from the breach. In cases of psychiatric harm to a secondary victim, the following distinctive question applies:

Would it be foreseeable that *a person of 'ordinary fortitude'* might suffer *psychiatric injury, in the circumstances as they occurred*?

In this deceptively simple question, there are three departures from the normal approach to foreseeability.

(a) The approach in the statement above constitutes **an exception to the egg-shell skull rule** (discussed in Chapter 3.4, above). According to that rule, a defendant must generally 'take his (or her) victim as he finds him' (or her). In secondary victim cases involving psychiatric damage, it must be foreseeable that *a person of ordinary fortitude* would suffer psychiatric harm in the circumstances. If a secondary victim has a particular susceptibility to psychiatric harm (an 'eggshell personality'), they may not be owed a duty. A duty will only be owed if a person of ordinary fortitude might foreseeably suffer harm in the same circumstances.[4]

---

[3] This expression is derived from the judgment of Cardozo CJ in the American case of *Ultramares v Touche* (1931) 174 NE 441, at 444. Cardozo used the metaphor of 'opening the floodgates' to refer to prospective liability 'in an indeterminate amount for an indeterminate time to an indeterminate class'. Strictly then, 'floodgates' refers to an *uncertain* liability, rather than *too much* liability.

[4] This criterion of 'ordinary fortitude', also referred to as 'customary phlegm', provides the opportunity for deeply evaluative judgments as to what is normal. There have been suspicions of male bias in this evaluation. What degree of fortitude is expected of an ordinary pregnant woman, for example? Or is no pregnant woman regarded as 'ordinary'? The issues do not only concern gender however: consider the facts of *McFarlane v EE Caledonia*, and *Hunter v British Coal* below. What reaction to the violent deaths of one's colleagues is considered reasonable and ordinary?

(b) **Psychiatric injury** must be foreseeable, at least in secondary victim cases. As Denning LJ expressed it, again deceptively simply, 'the test for liability for shock is foreseeability of injury by shock' (*King v Phillips* [1953] 1 QB at 440).

(c) Foreseeability is also assessed in a different way. This third distinctive feature of foreseeability in secondary victim cases is not always noticed. In secondary victim cases, foreseeability of the psychiatric harm is judged with hindsight, on the basis of the events as they actually occurred. The ordinary approach in the tort of negligence is to judge foreseeability at the time of the negligent act or omission. The special kind of foreseeability which is judged with hindsight, and which applies to secondary victim claims, can be referred to as **specific foreseeability**. The ordinary kind of foreseeability has been called **foreseeability in the practical sense** (Chapter 3 above). Foreseeability in the practical sense is generally regarded as a moral notion (what harm would the reasonable person have foreseen and guarded against?).

This third distinctive feature of foreseeability in secondary victim cases is identified as a control device by Brooke LJ in the following passage. He identifies reasonable fortitude (at [24]), and the judgment of foreseeability with hindsight (at [25]), as *separate* control devices, just as we have explained above.

Brooke LJ, *McLoughlin v Jones* [2001] EWCA Civ 1743; [2002] QB 1312

24 It is now well established that English law has created special control and other mechanisms to determine the incidence of legal liability in [secondary victim cases]. One of these is that the law supposes the claimant to be a person of ordinary phlegm or fortitude. This requirement was justified by Lord Porter in *Bourhill v Young* [1943] AC 92, 117 in these terms:

> "The driver of a car or vehicle, even though careless, is entitled to assume that the ordinary frequenter of the streets has sufficient fortitude to endure such incidents as may from time to time be expected to occur in them, including the noise of a collision and the sight of illness to others, and is not to be considered negligent towards one who does not possess the customary phlegm."

25 Another, mentioned by Lord Wright in *Bourhill v Young*, at p110, is that the court asks itself in such a case what the hypothetical reasonable man, viewing the position ex post facto, would say it was proper to foresee. Lord Lloyd of Berwick rationalised this test in *Page v Smith* [1996] AC 155, 188 by saying:

> "This makes sense . . . where the plaintiff is a secondary victim. For if you do not know the outcome of the accident or event, it is impossible to say whether the defendant should have foreseen injury by shock. It is necessary to take account of what happened in order to apply the test of reasonable foreseeability at all."

26 Neither of these rules is apposite when the relationship between the parties is founded on contract, whether the breach of duty relied upon is a breach of a contractual term, or a breach of a duty of care arising out of the parties' contractual relationship which sounds in damages in tort . . . .

Brooke LJ made clear that neither foreseeability of harm to a person of reasonable fortitude, nor specific foreseeability based on hindsight, was applicable in *McLoughlin v Jones* itself, where there was a pre-existing contractual relationship between defendant and claimant, as solicitor and client (negligence on the part of the solicitor was said to have led to imprisonment of the claimant).

Further 'Control Devices': The *Alcock* Criteria

Additional control devices have been applied in secondary victim cases. These introduce particular requirements described in terms of 'proximity'. It has been stated by the House of Lords that these devices are 'arbitrary', so that they need not (and indeed cannot) be fully justified in terms of principle (*White v Chief Constable of South Yorkshire Police*, below). The existence of potentially arbitrary control devices poses the greatest challenge in this area.

We will explain the *Alcock* criteria when we deal with secondary victim cases, below.

1.3 'PRIMARY VICTIM' CASES

A great deal of attention has been devoted to secondary victim cases, not least because such cases have been frequently considered by the House of Lords. As such, it may be surprising to note that there is a wide range of cases in which the claimant may recover damages for psychiatric harm without negotiating any special control devices, on the basis that he or she is a 'primary' victim. Indeed, the present trend seems to be towards expansion of these categories, despite the restrictions imposed on recovery by secondary victims (below).

Primary Victim Cases where the Claimant is Physically Injured or Endangered

Physical injury accompanied by psychiatric harm

It is common for those suffering physical injury to recover damages not only in respect of their physical injuries but also for any mental effects (including psychiatric damage) associated with these injuries. Subject to diagnostic issues, psychiatric injuries are no less real than the physical effects and in some circumstances they may be more long-lasting. Clearly, psychiatric harm and mental illness can also contribute to the financial consequences of an injury, including loss of earnings.

Physical endangerment but the only harm is done through the psychiatric route

It is also well recognized that endangerment *without* physical impact may itself lead to mental and physical effects. Where a claimant is physically endangered, illness or injury sustained as a result of fear or 'shock' is clearly potentially recoverable.

Dulieu v White [1901] 2 KB 669

The plaintiff (who was pregnant) was behind the bar of a public house when a horse-drawn van was negligently driven into the building. There was no physical contact with the plaintiff. The Court of Appeal accepted that as a consequence of the shock, she became seriously ill and gave birth prematurely. It was held that such an injury could be compensated, but Kennedy J expressed a limitation to his decision in the following terms:

Kennedy J, *Dulieu v White,* at 675

. . . It is not, however, to be taken that in my view every nervous shock occasioned by negligence and producing physical injury to the sufferer gives a cause of action. There is, I am inclined to think, at least one limitation. The shock, where it operates through the mind, must be a shock which arises from a reasonable fear of immediate personal injury to oneself. A. has, I conceive, no legal duty not to shock B's nerves by the exhibition of negligence towards C., or towards the property of B. or C.

This is where Kennedy J drew the line in 1901. The line has been moved by later decisions, but in respect of secondary victims (Section 1.4 below) it is still accepted that a line must be drawn somewhere. Individuals who are themselves foreseeably physically endangered by the defendant's negligence are now referred to as 'primary victims'.

Page v Smith [1996] AC 155

We extracted this case in Chapter 3.6 above, where we discussed its approach to remoteness of damage. The case involved a moderate-impact road accident in which the plaintiff was mildly physically endangered but suffered no immediate physical harm. After the accident however, he suffered the exacerbation of a pre-existing condition, 'ME'. ME is very hard to categorize as either psychiatric or physical in its nature, but it had clearly been brought about 'by the psychiatric route'. By a majority, the House of Lords held that the plaintiff could in principle recover damages, subject to further consideration by the Court of Appeal of 'factual causation' (had the worsened condition truly been caused by the accident?).

The majority approach was to assess the foreseeability of *personal injury* (which included both physical and psychiatric harm) from the point of view of the defendant at the time of the negligence. In Chapter 3, we called this **foreseeability in the practical sense**. It is practical in that it focuses on what the defendant could reasonably have foreseen, at the time of the carelessness. This is the usual test applied to foreseeability in the tort of negligence; but it is not the approach applied to 'secondary' victim cases. Foreseeability in the practical sense does not require that the means by which damage actually came about should be foreseeable. This was important in *Page v Smith*, because the impact of the vehicles was not particularly forceful. Only in respect of a person with a *pre-existing disposition to illness* could it be foreseeable that *this* particular impact would lead to *psychiatric* harm. Therefore, if the test for foreseeability applicable to *secondary* victims was applied in this case, the claim would fail.

In the following passage, Lord Lloyd (for the majority) makes clear that the test of foreseeability for 'secondary' victims is a special test which has no place in the case of primary victims.

Lord Lloyd of Berwick, *Page v Smith* [1996] AC 155, at 188–9

My noble and learned friend, Lord Keith of Kinkel, has drawn attention to an observation of Lord Wright in *Bourhill v. Young* [1943] A.C. 92, 110, that in nervous shock cases the circumstances of the accident or event must be viewed ex post facto. There are similar observations by Lord Wilberforce and Lord Bridge in *McLoughlin v. O'Brian* [1983] 1 A.C. 410, 420 and 432. This makes sense, as Lord Keith points out, where the plaintiff is a secondary victim. For if you do not know the outcome of the accident or event, it is impossible to say whether the defendant should have foreseen injury by shock. It is necessary to take account of what happened in order to apply the test of reasonable foreseeability at all. But it makes no sense in the case of a primary victim. Liability for physical injury depends on what was reasonably foreseeable by the defendant before the event. It could not be right that a negligent defendant should escape liability for psychiatric injury just because, though serious physical injury was foreseeable, it did not in fact transpire. Such a result in the case of a primary victim is neither necessary, logical nor just. To introduce hindsight into the trial of an ordinary running-down action would do the law no service.

In fact, both Lord Browne-Wilkinson, and Lord Lloyd thought that in the case of a car accident such as this, both physical and psychiatric harm *were* foreseeable, judging this in the 'practical' way. Judged at the time of the careless driving, the defendant could have foreseen *either* physical harm, *or* psychiatric damage. But Lord Lloyd went on to explain that foreseeability of psychiatric injury was not essential in such a case, provided that *some* personal injury (of whatever kind) was foreseeable.

Lord Lloyd, at 190

. . . The test in every case ought to be whether the defendant can reasonably foresee that his conduct will expose the plaintiff to risk of personal injury. If so, then he comes under a duty of care to that plaintiff. If a working definition of "personal injury" is needed, it can be found in section 38(1) of the Limitation Act 1980: " 'Personal injuries' includes any disease and any impairment of a person's physical or mental condition . . . " There are numerous other statutory definitions to the same effect. In the case of a secondary victim, the question will usually turn on whether the foreseeable injury is psychiatric, for the reasons already explained. In the case of a primary victim the question will almost always turn on whether the foreseeable injury is physical. But it is the same test in both cases, with different applications. There is no justification for regarding physical and psychiatric injury as different "kinds" of injury. **Once it is established that the defendant is under a duty of care to avoid causing personal injury to the plaintiff, it matters not whether the injury in fact sustained is physical, psychiatric or both.** . . .

Lord Lloyd argues here that secondary victim cases are logically different from primary victim cases. In the case of a primary victim (of the sort represented by the plaintiff in this case), personal injury is foreseeable and a duty of care is easily established. That being the case, the *kind* of 'personal injury' suffered is irrelevant. In a secondary victim case, there is no likelihood of physical impact involving the claimant. Thus, the *only* way that damage can foreseeably be done is through the psychiatric route, and foreseeability of injury by this route must be established.

Page v Smith was severely criticized by Lord Goff in the course of his dissenting judgment in *White v Chief Constable of South Yorkshire Police* [1998] 3 WLR 1509 (extracted below), though it was defended by Lord Griffiths in the same case as a sensible development. In Lord Goff's view, the special meaning of foreseeability has historically been applied to primary victims as much as to secondary victims and ought to have applied in *Page v Smith* also. The case has also been subject to academic criticism. Such criticism generally focuses not on the generous approach to foreseeability in *Page v Smith*, but on its apparently restrictive approach to the definition of a *primary victim*. It is suggested however that Lord Lloyd did not intend to *limit* the category of primary victims to those who are endangered. This interpretation of his words was later adopted in *White v Chief Constable of South Yorkshire Police*. But it is equally likely that Lord Lloyd concentrated on primary victims who were physically endangered simply because that was the kind of primary victim case before him. His words on the matter are extracted below. Lord Lloyd referred to the three previous cases of psychiatric damage decided by the House of Lords[5] and continued:

Lord Lloyd of Berwick, *Page v Smith* [1995] 2 WLR 644

In all these cases the plaintiff was the secondary victim of the defendant's negligence. He or she was in the position of a spectator or bystander. In the present case, by contrast, the plaintiff was a participant. He was himself directly involved in the accident, and well within the range of foreseeable physical injury. He was the primary victim. This is thus the first occasion on which your Lordships have had to decide whether, in such a case, the foreseeability of physical injury is enough to enable the plaintiff to recover damages for nervous shock.

The factual distinction between primary and secondary victims of an accident is obvious and of long-standing. It was recognised by Lord Russell of Killowen in *Bourhill v. Young* [1943] A.C. 92, when he pointed out that Mrs. Bourhill was not physically involved in the collision. In *Alcock's* case [1992] 1 A.C. 310 Lord Keith of Kinkel said, at p. 396, that in the type of case which was then before the House, injury by psychiatric illness "is a secondary sort of injury brought about by the infliction of physical injury, or the risk of physical injury, upon another person." In the same case, Lord Oliver of Aylmerton said, at p. 407, of cases in which damages are claimed for nervous shock:

> "Broadly they divide into two categories, that is to say, those cases in which the injured plaintiff was involved, either mediately, or immediately, as a participant, and those in which the plaintiff was no more than the passive and unwilling witness of injury caused to others."

Later in the same speech, at pp. 410–411, he referred to those who are involved in an accident as the primary victims, and to those who are not directly involved, but who suffer from what they see or hear, as the secondary victims. This is, in my opinion, the most convenient and appropriate terminology.

Although Lord Lloyd clearly said that a party who is within the zone of physical danger is a primary victim, he did not say that *only* such a party is a primary victim. On the contrary, he referred to Lord Oliver's broader category of claimants who are 'involved as participants in events'.

Considerable difficulty surrounds the question of when a party who is *not* physically endangered will count as a primary victim. We will specify some categories of victim who are not physically endangered, but who are recognized to be 'primary' victims, immediately below. More recently, the House of Lords has restricted the categories of primary victim in cases where there *is* physical impact or endangerment of somebody. Most of the primary victim cases below involve no endangerment at all.

The following recent decision of the Court of Appeal (currently under appeal to the House of Lords) is within the 'endangerment' category. The reasoning in this decision is difficult to reconcile with *Page v Smith*.

Grieves v FT Everard [2006] EWCA Civ 27

We outlined the facts of this case in Chapter 4. The claimants had all developed 'pleural plaques' as a result of occupational exposure to asbestos dust, but these plaques were not

---

[5] *Bourhill v Young*; *McLoughlin v O'Brian*; and *Alcock v Chief Constable of South Yorkshire Police*.

considered by a majority of the Court of Appeal to amount to 'material physical injury' (Smith LJ dissented on this point). One of the claimants had also developed an anxiety neurosis concerning the prospect of future disease, and this would be capable of giving rise to liability if it could be established that a duty was owed. The Court of Appeal decided that such a duty of care was *not* owed.

Lord Phillips of Worth Matravers CJ

[88]   Lord Lloyd's formulation of principle in *Page v Smith* has not been without its critics, not least Lord Goff of Chievely in his dissent in *Frost v Chief Constable of South Yorkshire Police* [1992] AC 455. The decision is none the less binding on this court. The issue is whether Lord Lloyd's test of liability can be applied to the facts of this case. Lord Lloyd's test was applied in the context of a road traffic accident in which the Plaintiff was a participant and which, for that reason, foreseeably exposed him to the risk of physical injury. The report of *Norfolk v Western Railway* suggests that the American Supreme Court has adopted a similar approach. At para146 Ginsburg J referred to the 'zone-of-danger' test:

> 'That test confines recovery for stand-alone emotional distress claims to Plaintiffs who: (1) 'sustain a physical impact as a result of a defendant's negligent conduct'; or (2) 'are placed in immediate risk of physical harm by that conduct' that is, those who escaped instant physical harm, but were 'within the zone of danger of physical impact'.'

[89]   Following *Metro North Commuter Rail Co. v Buckley* 521 US 424 138 L. Ed. 2d 560 (which involved exposure to asbestos but no physical manifestation of disease) the Supreme Court held that the zone-of-danger test could not properly be extended so as to render a defendant who negligently exposed a plaintiff to the risk of asbestos-induced cancer liable for emotional distress caused by the fear of developing cancer.

[90]   By similar reasoning we do not consider that the test in *Page v Smith* can properly be extended so as to render a defendant who negligently exposes a claimant to the risk of contracting a disease liable for free-standing psychiatric injury caused by the fear of contracting the disease. In so holding we are mindful of the view expressed by Lord Steyn in *Frost v Chief Constable of South Yorkshire*, para 500:

> '(T)he law on the recovery of compensation for pure psychiatric harm is a patchwork quilt of distinctions which are difficult to justify . . . In my view the only sensible general strategy for the courts is to say thus far and no further. The only prudent course is to treat the pragmatic categories as reflected in [case law] as settled for the time being, but by and large to leave any expansion or development in this corner of the law to Parliament. In reality there are no refined analytical tools which will enable the courts to draw lines by way of compromise solution in a way that is coherent and morally defensible. It must be left to Parliament to undertake the task of radical law reform.'

[91]   For these reasons we reject Mr Allan's submission that Mr Grieves is entitled to recover damages for his psychiatric illness under the principle in *Page v Smith*.

It is not at all clear which factor is decisive here. Lord Phillips relies upon a decision of the US Supreme Court which held that *emotional distress* caused by the fear of developing cancer was not recoverable. *Grieves* is not the same as that case, because it concerns a *distinct psychiatric condition*, and not mere anxiety or distress. Equally, it is hard to see how a claimant who was exposed to asbestos dust, and is thus susceptible to future disease, is not 'within the zone of danger', unless 'danger' here is restricted to the sort of injury brought about by sudden impact.

There is no explicit reason in the case law to do this. The reference to Lord Steyn's judgment in *White v Chief Constable of South Yorkshire* appeals to the general policy concerns adopted by the House of Lords in that case, where Lord Steyn (in the passage quoted in the above extract) instructed us not to try too hard to achieve a coherent pattern of law in this area. But *White v Chief Constable* was not directly in point in this case.

In all likelihood, Lord Phillips felt that creation of liability in this context—where a particularly susceptible individual suffers mental harm through fear of contracting a disease, and where a person of reasonable fortitude would not—would be to open the floodgates.[6]

The claimant also advanced an alternative argument, based on his status as an employee. This separate argument is considered later.

'Stress at Work' Cases

Cases in this category do not typically involve the threat of physical impact. Damage is done 'by the psychiatric route', generally speaking without threat of injury of any other kind.[7] It is irrelevant whether the resulting harm is 'wholly' psychiatric or has physical effects too. The claimant is not a 'secondary' victim but could be described as the primary beneficiary of the distinct duty to avoid psychiatric harm. An example is the duty of an employer towards an employee, to take reasonable care not to cause injury through stress at work. The possibility of a negligence action in such cases was recognized only relatively recently, in the case extracted below, but the reasoning in that case has been applied and developed subsequently. Indeed, it can be said that since *Walker*, the entire shape of tort liability for psychiatric harm has altered. The previous focus on secondary victims has shifted, and it is much clearer that it is not the *type of harm* that is the main problem here, so much as the 'secondary' status of some of the victims. The relationship between these cases, and 'endangerment' cases, has emerged as a problem.

Walker v Northumberland County Council [1995] 1 All ER 737

The plaintiff was employed by the defendant as an area social services officer. He managed four teams of social services fieldworkers in an area with a high proportion of child care problems. In 1986 the plaintiff suffered a nervous breakdown and had three months away from work. Before his return, the plaintiff's superior agreed that assistance would be available to lessen the burden of his work. In the event, he had very limited assistance. Six months later he suffered a second breakdown and had to leave work permanently. Colman J held that an employer owed a duty to take reasonable steps to avoid exposing an employee to a health-endangering workload. The duty had not been breached at the time of the first breakdown, since this was unforeseeable in the light of information available to the employer. But it *had* been breached at the time of the second breakdown.

[6] Revealingly, Lord Phillips stated in a lecture delivered during the hearing of these cases that he did not think much of *Page v Smith*: ' . . . I regard the test laid down by the House of Lords in *Page v Smith* as unattractive. If a claimant has not in fact sustained such injury, I do not see why he should be entitled to recover for psychiatric injury which he has sustained because of a special susceptibility, although a person of reasonable fortitude would not have been affected'. Lord Phillips, 'Liability for Psychiatric Injury', Personal Bar Association Annual Lecture, 23 November 2004, at 30. This is precisely the element of *Page v Smith* not applied in *Grieves*.

[7] Though note the variation in *White v Chief Constable*, below.

Colman J

There has been little judicial authority on the extent to which an employer owes to his employees a duty not to cause them psychiatric damage by the volume or character of the work which the employees are required to perform. It is clear law that an employer has a duty to provide his employee with a reasonably safe system of work and to take reasonable steps to protect him from risks which are reasonably foreseeable. Whereas the law on the extent of this duty has developed almost exclusively in cases involving physical injury to the employer as distinct from injury to his mental health, there is no logical reason why risk of psychiatric damage should be excluded from the scope of an employer's duty of care or from the co-extensive implied term in the contract of employment. That said, there can be no doubt that the circumstances in which claims based on such damage are likely to arise will often give rise to extremely difficult evidential problems of foreseeability and causation. This is particularly so in the environment of the professions, where the plaintiff may be ambitious and dedicated, determined to succeed in his career in which he knows the work to be demanding, and may have a measure of discretion as to how and when and for how long he works, but where the character or volume of the work given to him eventually drives him to breaking point. Given that the professional work is intrinsically demanding and stressful, at what point is the employer's duty to take protective steps engaged? What assumption is he entitled to make about the employee's resilience, mental toughness and stability of character, given that people of clinically normal personality may have a widely differing ability to absorb stress attributable to their work?

Colman J predicted that issues of foreseeability and causation would be particularly significant in the development of employers' liability, and this has proved to be correct. In *Hatton v Sutherland* [2002] EWCA Civ 76, the Court of Appeal accepted that a duty of care was owed in respect of psychiatric harm caused by stress at work, and set out guidance on the issues relating to breach of the duty. On the facts, there had been no breach of duty. One of the claimants appealed, and in *Barber v Somerset County Council* [2004] UKHL 13, the House of Lords upheld the appeal. The House of Lords unanimously approved the guidelines offered by the Court of Appeal though disagreeing with the conclusion reached in the particular case in hand. The following guidelines (extracted from the Court of Appeal) therefore carry significant authority.

Hale LJ, *Hatton v Sutherland* [2002] EWCA Civ 76; [2002] 2 All ER 1

[43] From the above discussion, the following practical propositions emerge.

(1) There are no special control mechanisms applying to claims for psychiatric (or physical) illness or injury arising from the stress of doing the work the employee is required to do . . . . The ordinary principles of employer's liability apply . . . .

(2) The threshold question is whether this kind of harm to this particular employee was reasonably foreseeable: this has two components (a) an injury to health (as distinct from occupational stress) which (b) is attributable to stress at work (as distinct from other factors).

(3) Foreseeability depends upon what the employer knows (or ought reasonably to know) about the individual employee. Because of the nature of mental disorder, it is harder to foresee than physical injury, but may be easier to foresee in a known individual than in the population at large. An employer is usually entitled to assume that the employee can withstand the normal pressures of the job unless he knows of some particular problem or vulnerability.

(4) The test is the same whatever the employment: there are no occupations which should be regarded as intrinsically dangerous to mental health.

(5) Factors likely to be relevant in answering the threshold question include: (a) The nature and extent of the work done by the employee. Is the workload much more than is normal for the particular job? Is the work particularly intellectually or emotionally demanding for this employee? Are demands being made of this employee unreasonable when compared with the demands made of others in the same or comparable jobs? Or are there signs that others doing this job are suffering harmful levels of stress? Is there an abnormal level of sickness or absenteeism in the same job or the same department? (b) Signs from the employee of impending harm to health. Has he a particular problem or vulnerability? Has he already suffered from illness attributable to stress at work? Have there recently been frequent or prolonged absences which are uncharacteristic of him? Is there reason to think that these are attributable to stress at work, for example because of complaints or warnings from him or others?

(6) The employer is generally entitled to take what he is told by his employee at face value, unless he has good reason to think to the contrary. He does not generally have to make searching inquiries of the employee or seek permission to make further inquiries of his medical advisers.

(7) To trigger a duty to take steps, the indications of impending harm to health arising from stress at work must be plain enough for any reasonable employer to realise that he should do something about it.

(8) The employer is only in breach of duty if he has failed to take the steps which are reasonable in the circumstances, bearing in mind the magnitude of the risk of harm occurring, the gravity of the harm which may occur, the costs and practicability of preventing it, and the justifications for running the risk.

(9) The size and scope of the employer's operation, its resources and the demands it faces are relevant in deciding what is reasonable; these include the interests of other employees and the need to treat them fairly, for example, in any redistribution of duties.

(10) An employer can only reasonably be expected to take steps which are likely to do some good: the court is likely to need expert evidence on this.

(11) An employer who offers a confidential advice service, with referral to appropriate counselling or treatment services, is unlikely to be found in breach of duty.

(12) If the only reasonable and effective step would have been to dismiss or demote the employee, the employer will not be in breach of duty in allowing a willing employee to continue in the job.

(13) In all cases, therefore, it is necessary to identify the steps which the employer both could and should have taken before finding him in breach of his duty of care.

(14) The claimant must show that that breach of duty has caused or materially contributed to the harm suffered. It is not enough to show that occupational stress has caused the harm.

(15) Where the harm suffered has more than one cause, the employer should only pay for that proportion of the harm suffered which is attributable to his wrongdoing, unless the harm is truly indivisible. It is for the defendant to raise the question of apportionment.

(16) The assessment of damages will take account of any pre-existing disorder or vulnerability and of the chance that the claimant would have succumbed to a stress-related disorder in any event. . . .

In the relatively short space of time since *Walker*, claims for employment-related psychiatric illness have become common. Recent litigation by former members of the armed forces against the Ministry of Defence provides an example. It was made clear in these cases that there was no duty to maintain a safe system of work for service personnel in the course of combat, and it was also held that there was no *general* failure in the relevant systems for the prevention, detection, and treatment of stress and trauma: *Multiple Claimants v Ministry of Defence* [2003] EWHC 1134. The majority of claims against the Ministry of Defence in respect of post traumatic stress disorder were therefore struck out. However, there were three exceptions. In one of these cases, there was a failure of diagnosis by an army consultant psychiatrist (*X v Ministry of Defence* [2005] EWHC 1645). In two others, it was found that earlier referral and treatment would probably have avoided the lasting damage suffered (*New v Ministry of Defence* [2005] EWHC 1647; *West v Ministry of Defence* [2005] EWHC 1646). In these three cases, where the breaches of duty did not relate to 'combat' but to subsequent diagnosis and management of the claimants' condition, damages were awarded.

Grieves v Everard: The Employment Relationship Argument

We have already considered one argument put for the claimant in *Grieves v Everard* in respect of his anxiety neurosis brought on my fear of developing disease in the future. This argument, turning on an application of *Page v Smith*, was rejected by the Court of Appeal for reasons that were not particularly clear. The alternative argument for the claimant was that the anxiety neurosis was a foreseeable result of the employer's breach of duty to an employee, consistent with *Walker* and *Hatton*. This claim too was rejected. Here the reasoning was clearer. The crucial factor was lack of foreseeability. It was not foreseeable that a person of reasonable fortitude would have suffered the anxiety neurosis; and there was no reason to think (at the time of exposure) that the claimant was *not* a person of reasonable fortitude. The case was not similar to *Walker* itself, where there was knowledge of the employee's susceptibility. It failed the foreseeability criterion in *Walker*.

Lord Phillips, *Grieves v Everard* [2006] EWCA Civ 27

[92] We turn to the alternative route by which recovery can be made for free-standing psychiatric injury. It is well established that an employee can recover for psychiatric injury caused as a result of being exposed to stress at work provided that certain requirements are satisfied. Those requirements were set out by Hale LJ in *Barber v Somerset CC* . . . in a passage that was approved when the case reached the House of Lords. Hale LJ's starting point was that an employer was usually entitled to assume that his employee was up to the usual pressures of the job. The threshold question was thus whether it was reasonably foreseeable that the particular employee was liable to suffer psychiatric injury as a result of those pressures. A duty to take steps to reduce pressure would only arise if a reasonable employer should have foreseen that he was exposing his employee to the risk of psychiatric injury and this normally involved knowledge that the employee had a particular vulnerability.

[93] In *Melville v Home Office* [2005] EWCA Civ 6; [2005] ICR 782 this court held that, where an employer had knowledge that particular stresses carried with them the risk of psychiatric injury to employees, failure to implement recommended precautions against such injury could attract liability without any need to demonstrate knowledge that an employee was particularly vulnerable.

[94]   How, if at all, do these principles apply to a case such as that of Mr Grieves? We are here dealing, not with stress at work causing psychiatric injury in the course of employment, but exposure to noxious substances at work causing psychiatric injury as a result of anxiety after employment has ceased. On principle, were the evidence to establish that it was foreseeable that men of reasonable fortitude, if exposed to asbestos dust, might suffer psychiatric injury as a consequence of anxiety about their future health, then it should follow that employers would owe a duty of care not to expose employees to that risk. As we have said, however, there is no evidence in this case that would enable us to find that such a risk was foreseeable.

[95]   We were referred to two authorities which are relevant in the present context. In The Creutzfeldt-Jacob Disease Litigation Group B Plaintiffs v Medical Research Council [2000] Lloyds Law Rep (Medical) 161 Morland J had to rule on preliminary issues in a group action. The Claimants had been negligently injected as children with Hartree HGH, a human growth hormone that exposed them to the risk of contracting CJD. The relevant issue was whether this rendered the Defendants liable for psychiatric illness caused by the shock of learning of the risk to which they had been exposed. Morland J held that the Defendants should reasonably have foreseen that they were exposing the Claimants to the risk of sustaining psychiatric injury in this way and that they were liable for so doing. He held at p 168:

> 'I can see no logical reason why foreseeability of or responsibility for shock and psychiatric injury should be limited to an area of time contemporaneous or almost contemporaneous to the negligent physical event ie the injection of Hartree HGH. If the psychiatric injury was reasonably foreseeable it should be untrammelled by spatial physical or temporal limits (see per Lord Scarman in McLoughlin at p 414A).'

Morland J's conclusion is in line with that which we have reached above.

[96]   The question remains of whether a claimant should be entitled to recover damages for psychiatric injury caused by anxiety at the risk of sustaining a disease where a person of reasonable fortitude would not have reacted in this way. *Fletcher v The Commissioners of Public Works in Ireland* [2003] 1 IR 465 is a decision of the Irish Supreme Court which is directly in point. The Plaintiff was negligently exposed by the Defendants to asbestos dust. This led to anxiety, which developed into 'reactive anxiety neurosis', which the court treated as a recognisable psychiatric illness. The trial judge found that it was reasonably foreseeable that a person of 'normal fortitude' would suffer from the kind of anxiety and develop the psychiatric condition experienced by the Plaintiff. He awarded the Plaintiff substantial damages.

[97]   This decision was reversed by the Supreme Court, essentially on grounds of policy.

Lord Phillips examined the reasons given by the Irish Supreme Court in *Fletcher* and continued:

[100]   We have some difficulty in reconciling the Chief Justice's finding [in *Fletcher*] that it was reasonably foreseeable that the Plaintiff would suffer psychiatric injury as a result of fear of disease with his finding that a person of ordinary fortitude would not have done so. He made reference to the 'eggshell skull' principle, but that is a principle that enables a claimant to recover damages for an injury the extent of which was not foreseeable. Despite this difficulty, we concur with the result reached in Fletcher. It would be possible to postulate that an employer who negligently exposes an employee to the risk of sustaining a disease should be liable for psychiatric injury resulting from anxiety at the risk of such disease, even if this is not a reaction to be foreseen in an employee of ordinary fortitude, but so to do would be to extend the law in a manner not supported by established principle. We have not been persuaded that it would be right to make such an extension.

Beyond employment cases: assumptions of responsibility and contractual relationships

There are other cases where the claimant will be regarded as a primary victim in the absence of physical danger, beyond the employment cases. In *Leach v Chief Constable of Gloucestershire Constabulary* [1999] 1 WLR 1421, the police asked the plaintiff, a volunteer worker on a youth homelessness project, to act as 'appropriate adult' during interviews of a suspect, West. This was in accordance with the Codes of Practice under section 66 of the Police and Criminal Evidence Act 1984, requiring such a person to be present if the suspect is mentally disordered. West proved to be a serial killer and the details of his murders were exceptionally harrowing. The plaintiff claimed that she was not warned of the circumstances of the case, was offered no counselling until after West committed suicide in custody, and was told (falsely) that she would not be required to give evidence in court. She brought an action against the police for damages, claiming that she had suffered post traumatic stress disorder, psychological injury, and a stroke. A first instance judge held that no duty was owed. The Court of Appeal allowed her appeal in part. Although no duty should be recognized which would interfere with the conduct of police interviews, it was nevertheless possible that a duty to provide counselling may be owed, and there also might be a duty in respect of any false assurances that might have been given.

In the course of his judgment, Brooke LJ emphasized that there is a wide range of cases where a duty of care is now recognized in respect of psychiatric illness, and that many of these are cases where there is no 'physical' imperilment at all. He stressed that some such cases are decided on the basis of an 'assumption of responsibility' (see further Section 2 below). In respect of the present claims, so far as they related to the *conduct of the interviews*, there was no such assumption of responsibility.

Brooke LJ

Most of the cases in the books are concerned with situations in which a plaintiff suffers psychiatric illness as a result of his own imperilment—as in *Page v. Smith*—or reasonable fear of danger to himself, or as a result of the physical injury on imperilment of a third party (or parties) which has been caused by the defendant. . . .

There is, however, a less familiar line of cases in which, as in the present case, a defendant has neither imperilled nor caused physical injury to anyone. One example is *Walker v. Northumberland County Council*. There was, of course, no difficulty in indentifying the existence of such a duty in the context of an employer-employee relationship.

Another example is *Attia v. British Gas Plc.*, where a plaintiff suffered reasonably foreseeable psychiatric illness as a result of the defendant causing damage to her property: she had to witness her house burning down as a result of the defendants' negligence. This court declined to strike the claim out, and allowed it to go to trial on the facts.

In addition to these two types of case which can be readily categorised, the Law Commission has identified a miscellaneous group of cases in which recovery may be available for a negligently inflicted psychiatric illness (assuming that the standard elements of the tort of negligence can be made out): see its report, Liability for Psychiatric Illness (1998) (Law Com. No. 249), p. 29, para. 2.51. These include a case where a patient suffers a psychiatric illness because of negligent treatment by his/her psychiatrist (cf. *X (Minors)) v. Bedfordshire County Council* [1995] 2 A.C. 633); where a prisoner foreseeably suffers a psychiatric illness as a result of ill-treatment by prison officers (cf. *Reg. v. Deputy Governor of Parkhurst Prison, Ex parte Hague* [1992] 1 AC 58, 165–166, *per* Lord Bridge of Harwich) and where recipients of distressing news suffer reasonably foreseeable psychiatric illness as a result of the news being broken in an insensitive manner; *A.B. v. Tameside & Glossop Health Authority* [1997] 8 Med.L.R. 91 and *Allin v. City & Hackney Health Authority* [1996] 7 Med.L.R. 167. These are useful illustrations, but there is not yet any English case of the types described in which it has not been comparatively easy to establish that the requisite duty of care exists, whether from a psychiatrist's duty to his patient, the prison service's assumption of responsibility for the care of prisoners, or, in the two medical cases I have mentioned, from the defendant health authorities' acceptance that they owed a relevant duty of care to their patient or former patients . . . .

A case which appears to break new ground, but which was not mentioned by the Law Commission, is *Swinney v. Chief Constable of Northumbria Police Force* [1997] Q.B. 464. The plaintiffs, who were wife and husband, claimed that they were suffering from psychiatric illnesses because they had been threatened with violence and arson after some confidential information furnished by the first plaintiff to the police had been stolen from a police vehicle broken into by criminals. This court did not pay any particular attention to the fact that the claims were for damages for psychiatric illness. It allowed the action to proceed to trial on the facts because it was arguable that the police had assumed responsibility towards the first plaintiff and that there were no policy grounds on which the claim should be barred from proceeding. In evaluating all the public policy considerations that might apply, Peter Gibson L.J. said, at p. 486A, that it seemed to him plain that the position of a police informer required special consideration from the viewpoint of public policy; see also Hirst L.J., at p. 484A-C, and Ward L.J., at p. 487A-C.

Swinney's case illustrates vividly the way in which, after *Page v. Smith*, the courts in future are not going to have their way blocked by some supposed difference in kind between physical injury and psychiatric injury which may ipso facto bar cases of the latter type. . . .

There is indeed a wide range of cases in which there is recognized to be a duty not to cause psychiatric damage to the claimant, contradicting any general perception that such damage by its very nature constitutes a 'problem'. In addition to the cases mentioned by Brooke LJ in the valuable summary above, we may add the recognized duty of a school to protect its pupils against bullying (*Bradford-Smart v West Sussex County Council* [2002] EWCA Civ 7); the duty of an employer not to expose employees to bullying by fellow employees (*Waters v Commissioner of Police for the Metropolis* [2000] 1 WLR 1607); the duty of a doctor toward a patient (*Re Organ Retention Litigation* [2005] QB 506); and the duty of a solicitor to conduct a client's defence with due care (*McLoughlin v Jones* [2002] 1 QB 1312, psychiatric injury after a period of imprisonment).

Hale LJ, *McLoughlin v Jones*

56   It is quite clear that the claimant in this case should also be regarded as a primary victim. Indeed the judge said so: "In my view it is clear on any common sense view that the claimant in this case would be described as a 'primary' victim and that the particular rules developed for secondary victims have no application to him." The one consequence of that which is also quite clear is that the question of what might be foreseen in a person of "ordinary phlegm" does not arise. The question of foreseeability must be considered in relation to this particular claimant, and what the defendants knew or ought to have known about him.

As such, the 'customary phlegm' requirement does not apply to primary victims where the duty arises from a contractual relationship other than one of employment. But as we have just seen, the need for foreseeability in *employment* cases has been taken to be strong. There is some inconsistency then between different classes of primary victim case.

Damage to Claimant's Property?

In the extract above, Brooke LJ mentions the case of *Attia v British Gas* [1988] QB 304. In that case, which was decided before *Alcock* and *Page v Smith*, the Court of Appeal decided not to strike out a claim in respect of psychiatric damage caused by witnessing a fire which extensively damaged the plaintiff's home. The defendants (who had contracted to install central heating at the property) had admitted negligence in the starting of the fire, and had settled a claim for damage to the house and its contents. Is *Attia v British Gas* simply an anomalous case? In *Attia*, the Court of Appeal thought that *psychiatric illness* might be considered foreseeable, in light of all the circumstances. In very few cases will psychiatric illness be a foreseeable consequence of property damage, particularly if the 'reasonable fortitude' test is also applied. However, *Attia* is probably now best understood as a case where there was a pre-existing contractual relationship, like that in *McLoughlin v Jones*. On this interpretation, it would not lay down any general rule in respect of property damage.

Despite this rationalization, it is hard to justify the outcome in *Attia*, compared to secondary victim cases. The law requires a claimant who sees their brother or sister crushed to death to prove the closeness of their ties of affection in addition to showing general foreseeability (*Alcock v Chief Constable of South Yorkshire Police*, below); but applies no particular control devices to a case of property damage within a contractual relationship.

1.4 SECONDARY VICTIMS

A secondary victim is one whose psychiatric injury flowed from the injury to, or death or endangerment of, another party. In some of the earliest case law to recognize a duty in respect of psychiatric harm, it was proposed that only if the plaintiff herself is injured or endangered can there be recovery (*Victorian Railways Commissioners v Coultas* (1888) 13 App Cas 222; *Dulieu v White*, above; *Bell v Northern Railway of Ireland* (1890) 26 LR Ir 428).[8] In later cases, it was accepted that some of those who were not endangered could recover for psychiatric harm, but only if their injury is the effect of 'shock' suffered in a relevant way. In *Hambrook v Stokes* [1925] 1 KB 141, a mother saw a lorry careering down a hill and round a bend, where she knew her three children to be. There was a collision, which was out of sight, and the plaintiff feared that her children were involved. The Court of Appeal held that in these circumstances, the mother was owed a duty so far as she suffered psychiatric injury as a consequence of what she saw and perceived directly. Fear for her children, rather than fear for herself, would suffice.

We will turn directly to the more modern cases concerned with secondary victims.

McLoughlin v O'Brian [1983] 1 AC 410

The plaintiff's husband and three of her children were involved in a serious road accident caused by the negligence of the first defendant. The plaintiff was informed of the accident around two hours after the event and was driven to the hospital where her family had been

---

[8] As we explained in Chapter 2.5 above, the action in *Wilkinson v Downton* [1897] 2 QB 57 (which recognizes liability for *deliberately* inflicted psychiatric harm) was probably devised in order to evade the limitations of *Coultas*.

taken. There she learned that her youngest daughter had been killed. In the midst of chaotic and harrowing scenes, she saw her husband and other children who were still being treated. She alleged that she had suffered severe shock resulting in psychiatric illness including depression and personality change. At first instance, her claim for psychiatric injury was dismissed on the basis that the injury was unforeseeable. The Court of Appeal accepted that her injury was foreseeable, but ruled that even so no duty was owed to a plaintiff who was not present at the scene of the accident and had not seen its consequences until two hours later.

The House of Lords allowed the plaintiff's appeal. The judgments raise the important question of whether a duty of care may be denied on policy grounds, in cases where the injury is reasonably foreseeable. Different answers to this question will be found in the judgments extracted. But there is agreement that compensation of secondary victims without the addition of control devices may lead to over-extensive liability.

Lord Wilberforce, at 420

Foreseeability, which involves a hypothetical person, looking with hindsight at an event which has occurred, is a formula adopted by English law, not merely for defining, but also for limiting, the persons to whom a duty may be owed, and the consequences for which an actor may be held responsible. It is not merely an issue of fact to be left to be found as such. When it is said to result in a duty of care being owed to a person or a class, the statement that there is a "duty of care" denotes a conclusion into the forming of which considerations of policy have entered. That foreseeability does not of itself, and automatically, lead to a duty of care is, I think, clear.

At 420–3

. . . there remains, in my opinion, just because "shock" in its nature is capable of affecting so wide a range of people, a real need for the law to place some limitation upon the extent of admissible claims. It is necessary to consider three elements inherent in any claim: the class of persons whose claims should be recognised; the proximity of such persons to the accident; and the means by which the shock is caused. As regards the class of persons, the possible range is between the closest of family ties—of parent and child, or husband and wife—and the ordinary bystander. Existing law recognises the claims of the first: it denies that of the second, either on the basis that such persons must be assumed to be possessed of fortitude sufficient to enable them to endure the calamities of modern life, or that defendants cannot be expected to compensate the world at large. In my opinion, these positions are justifiable, and since the present case falls within the first class, it is strictly unnecessary to say more. I think, however, that it should follow that other cases involving less close relationships must be very carefully scrutinised. I cannot say that they should never be admitted. The closer the tie (not merely in relationship, but in care) the greater the claim for consideration. The claim, in any case, has to be judged in the light of the other factors, such as proximity to the scene in time and place, and the nature of the accident.

As regards proximity to the accident, it is obvious that this must be close in both time and space. It is, after all, the fact and consequence of the defendant's negligence that must be proved to have caused the "nervous shock." Experience has shown that to insist on direct and immediate sight or hearing would be impractical and unjust and that under what may be called the "aftermath" doctrine one who, from close proximity, comes very soon upon the scene should not be excluded. In my opinion, the result in *Benson v. Lee* [1972] V.R. 879 was correct and indeed inescapable. It was based, soundly, upon "direct perception of some of the events which go to make up the accident as an entire event, and this includes . . . the immediate aftermath . . . " (p. 880.)

. . .

Lastly, as regards communication, there is no case in which the law has compensated shock brought about by communication by a third party. . . . The shock must come through sight or hearing of the event or of its immediate aftermath. Whether some equivalent of sight or hearing, e.g. through simultaneous television, would suffice may have to be considered.

My Lords, I believe that these indications, imperfectly sketched, and certainly to be applied with common sense to individual situations in their entirety, represent either the existing law, or the existing law with only such circumstantial extension as the common law process may legitimately make. They do not introduce a new principle. Nor do I see any reason why the law should retreat behind the lines already drawn. I find on this appeal that the appellant's case falls within the boundaries of the law so drawn. I would allow her appeal.

Lord Bridge, at 441–3

In approaching the question whether the law should, as a matter of policy, define the criterion of liability in negligence for causing psychiatric illness by reference to some test other than that of reasonable foreseeability it is well to remember that we are concerned only with the question of liability of a defendant who is, ex hypothesi, guilty of fault in causing the death, injury or danger which has in turn triggered the psychiatric illness. A policy which is to be relied on to narrow the scope of the negligent tortfeasor's duty must be justified by cogent and readily intelligible considerations, and must be capable of defining the appropriate limits of liability by reference to factors which are not purely arbitrary. A number of policy considerations which have been suggested as satisfying these requirements appear to me, with respect, to be wholly insufficient. I can see no grounds whatever for suggesting that to make the defendant liable for reasonably foreseeable psychiatric illness caused by his negligence would be to impose a crushing burden on him out of proportion to his moral responsibility. However liberally the criterion of reasonable foreseeability is interpreted, both the number of successful claims in this field and the quantum of damages they will attract are likely to be moderate. . . .

To attempt to draw a line at the furthest point which any of the decided cases happen to have reached, and to say that it is for the legislature, not the courts, to extend the limits of liability any further, would be, to my mind, an unwarranted abdication of the court's function of developing and adapting principles of the common law to changing conditions, in a particular corner of the common law which exemplifies, par excellence, the important and indeed necessary part which that function has to play. In the end I believe that the policy question depends on weighing against each other two conflicting considerations. On the one hand, if the criterion of liability is to be reasonable foreseeability simpliciter, this must, precisely because questions of causation in psychiatric medicine give rise to difficulty and uncertainty, introduce an element of uncertainty into the law and open the way to a number of arguable claims which a more precisely fixed criterion of liability would exclude. I accept that the element of uncertainty is an important factor. I believe that the "floodgates" argument, however, is, as it always has been, greatly exaggerated. On the other hand, it seems to me inescapable that any attempt to define the limit of liability by requiring, in addition to reasonable foreseeability, that the plaintiff claiming damages for psychiatric illness should have witnessed the relevant accident, should have been present at or near the place where it happened, should have come upon its aftermath and thus have had some direct perception of it, as opposed to merely learning of it after the event, should be related in some particular degree to the accident victim—to draw a line by reference to any of these criteria must impose a largely arbitrary limit of liability. . . .

My Lords, I have no doubt that this is an area of the law of negligence where we should resist the temptation to try yet once more to freeze the law in a rigid posture which would deny justice to some who, in the application of the classic principles of negligence derived from *Donoghue v. Stevenson* [1932] A.C. 562, ought to succeed, in the interests of certainty, where the very subject matter is uncertain and continuously developing, or in the interests of saving defendants and their insurers from the burden of having sometimes to resist doubtful claims. I find myself in complete agreement with Tobriner J. in *Dillon v. Legg*, 29 A.L.R. 3d 1316, 1326 that the defendant's duty must depend on reasonable foreseeability and

> "must necessarily be adjudicated only upon a case-by-case basis. We cannot now predetermine defendant's obligation in every situation by a fixed category; no immutable rule can establish the extent of that obligation for every circumstance of the future."

In terms of its *ratio*, this judgment moves the line of recovery only slightly, so that it incorporates an extended understanding of the 'immediate aftermath'. More broadly, the speeches of Lords Wilberforce and Bridge contain the essential elements of the 'control devices' which were, later, authoritatively stated in *Alcock v Chief Constable of South Yorkshire Police* (extracted below). For a claimant who has no physical involvement in an accident to recover damages for psychiatric injury, it is clear that they must show **closeness** of more than one form: closeness to the victim in terms of relationship, and physical closeness in time and place, are essential elements. Also important is the 'means by which the shock is caused'. Although the judgments do not altogether rule out recovery for shock caused in some way other than through direct and unaided perception of the event, Lord Wilberforce states that any sufficient alternative would need to be 'equivalent to' such direct perception—for example, through watching simultaneous television broadcasts. Lord Bridge was willing to countenance a relaxation in this requirement in appropriate circumstances.

Beyond these common elements, there appears to be a major distinction in approach between the judgments of Lord Wilberforce, and Lord Bridge. Lord Wilberforce gives greater emphasis to policy considerations, and he recognizes that 'foreseeability' in the psychiatric damage cases is a 'limiting' device (though he gives the false impression that this is the same test that is applied throughout the tort of negligence). Lord Wilberforce also regards the requirements of 'closeness' in relationship and in time and space, and of directness of perception, as clearly set by the existing authorities. Lord Bridge on the other hand appears to suggest that the relevant questions are all questions of 'foreseeability', and he argues that the limiting rules should be supported by reasoned justifications. Lord Bridge maintained that this area of law could be developed cogently through incremental evolution. This latter approach has now been abandoned by the House of Lords, in *White v Chief Constable of South Yorkshire Police* (extracted below).

Alcock v Chief Constable of South Yorkshire [1992] 1 AC 310

This case, like *White*, arose from the disaster at the Hillsborough Football Stadium on 15 April 1989. The events themselves are outlined in the extract from Lord Keith's judgment, below. The *Alcock* claims were brought by relatives of some of the supporters who were killed, injured, or endangered through admitted negligence in the policing of the crowd. The claim is for psychiatric harm to the relatives themselves. This case remains the leading authority on the criteria of recovery by 'secondary victims'.

Lord Keith of Kinkel, at 392

My Lords, the litigation with which these appeals are concerned arose out of the disaster at Hillsborough Stadium, Sheffield, which occurred on 15 April 1989. On that day a football match was arranged to be played at the stadium between the Liverpool and the Nottingham Forest football clubs. It was a semi-final of the F.A. Cup. The South Yorkshire police force, which was responsible for crowd control at the match, allowed an excessively large number of intending spectators to enter the ground at the Leppings Lane end, an area reserved for Liverpool supporters. They crammed into pens 3 and 4, below the West Stand, and in the resulting crush 95 people were killed and over 400 physically injured. Scenes from the ground were broadcast live on television from time to time during the course of the disaster, and recordings were broadcast later. The Chief Constable of South Yorkshire has admitted liability in negligence in respect of the deaths and physical injuries. Sixteen separate actions were brought against him by persons none of whom was present in the area where the disaster occurred, although four of them were elsewhere in the ground. All of them were connected in various ways with persons who were in that area, being related to such persons or, in one case, being a fiancée. In most cases the person with whom the plaintiff was concerned was killed, in other cases that person was injured, and in one case turned out to be uninjured. All the plaintiffs claimed damages for nervous shock resulting in psychiatric illness which they alleged was caused by the experiences inflicted on them by the disaster.

Lord Ackner, at 402–3

The three elements

Because "shock" in its nature is capable of affecting such a wide range of persons, Lord Wilberforce in *McLoughlin v. O'Brian* [1983] 1 A.C. 410, 422, concluded that there was a real need for the law to place some limitation upon the extent of admissible claims and in this context he considered that there were three elements inherent in any claim. It is common ground that such elements do exist and are required to be considered in connection with all these claims. . . .

The three elements are (1) the class of persons whose claims should be recognised; (2) the proximity of such persons to the accident—in time and space; (3) the means by which the shock has been caused.

I will deal with those three elements seriatim.

(1) The class of persons whose claim should be recognised

When dealing with the possible range of the class of persons who might sue, Lord Wilberforce in *McLoughlin v. O'Brian* [1983] 1 A.C. 410 contrasted the closest of family ties—parent and child and husband and wife—with that of the ordinary bystander. He said that while existing law recognises the claims of the first, it denied that of the second, either on the basis that such persons must be assumed to be possessed with fortitude sufficient to enable them to endure the calamities of modern life, or that defendants cannot be expected to compensate the world at large. He considered that these positions were justified, that other cases involving less close relationships must be very carefully considered, adding, at p. 422:

> "The closer the tie (not merely in relationship, but in care) the greater the claim for consideration. The claim, in any case, has to be judged in the light of the other factors, such as proximity to the scene in time and place, and the nature of the accident."

I respectfully share the difficulty expressed by Atkin L.J. in *Hambrook v. Stokes Brothers* [1925] 1 K.B. 141, 158–159—how do you explain why the duty is confined to the case of parent or guardian and child and does not extend to other relations of life also involving intimate associations; and why does it not eventually extend to bystanders? As regards the latter category, while it may be very difficult to envisage a case of a stranger, who is not actively and foreseeably involved in a disaster or its aftermath, other than in the role of rescuer, suffering shock-induced psychiatric injury by the mere observation of apprehended or actual injury of a third person in circumstances that could be considered reasonably foreseeable, I see no reason in principle why he should not, if in the circumstances, a reasonably strong-nerved person would have been so shocked. In the course of argument your Lordships were given, by way of an example, that of a petrol tanker careering out of control into a school in session and bursting into flames. I would not be prepared to rule out a potential claim by a passer-by so shocked by the scene as to suffer psychiatric illness.

As regards claims by those in the close family relationships referred to by Lord Wilberforce, the justification for admitting such claims is the presumption, which I would accept as being rebuttable, that the love and affection normally associated with persons in those relationships is such that a defendant ought reasonably to contemplate that they may be so closely and directly affected by his conduct as to suffer shock resulting in psychiatric illness. While as a generalisation more remote relatives and, a fortiori, friends, can reasonably be expected not to suffer illness from the shock, there can well be relatives and friends whose relationship is so close and intimate that their love and affection for the victim is comparable to that of the normal parent, spouse or child of the victim and should for the purpose of this cause of action be so treated.

(At 404–6)

(2) The proximity of the plaintiff to the accident

It is accepted that the proximity to the accident must be close both in time and space. Direct and immediate sight or hearing of the accident is not required. It is reasonably foreseeable that injury by shock can be caused to a plaintiff, not only through the sight or hearing of the event, but of its immediate aftermath.

Only two of the plaintiffs before us were at the ground. However, it is clear from *McLoughlin v. O'Brian* [1983] 1 A.C. 410 that there may be liability where subsequent identification can be regarded as part of the "immediate aftermath" of the accident. Mr. Alcock identified his brother-in-law in a bad condition in the mortuary at about midnight, that is some eight hours after the accident. This was the earliest of the identification cases. Even if this identification could be described as part of the "aftermath," it could not in my judgment be described as part of the *immediate* aftermath. *McLoughlin's* case was described by Lord Wilberforce as being upon the margin of what the process of logical progression from case to case would allow. Mrs. McLoughlin had arrived at the hospital within an hour or so after the accident. Accordingly in the post-accident identification cases before your Lordships there was not sufficient proximity in time and space to the accident.

(3) The means by which the shock is caused

Lord Wilberforce concluded that the shock must come through sight or hearing of the event or its immediate aftermath but specifically left for later consideration whether some equivalent of sight or hearing, e.g. through simultaneous television, would suffice: see p. 423. Of course it is common ground that it was clearly foreseeable by the defendant that the scenes at

Hillsborough would be broadcast live and that amongst those who would be watching would be parents and spouses and other relatives and friends of those in the pens behind the goal at the Leppings Lane end. However he would also know of the code of ethics which the television authorities televising this event could be expected to follow, namely that they would not show pictures of suffering by recognisable individuals. Had they done so, Mr. Hytner accepted that this would have been a "novus actus" breaking the chain of causation between the defendant's alleged breach of duty and the psychiatric illness. As the defendant was reasonably entitled to expect to be the case, there were no such pictures. Although the television pictures certainly gave rise to feelings of the deepest anxiety and distress, in the circumstances of this case the simultaneous television broadcasts of what occurred cannot be equated with the "sight or hearing of the event or its immediate aftermath." Accordingly shocks sustained by reason of these broadcasts cannot found a claim. I agree, however, with Nolan L.J. that simultaneous broadcasts of a disaster cannot in all cases be ruled out as providing the equivalent of the actual sight or hearing of the event or its immediate aftermath. Nolan L.J. gave, ante, pp. 386G-387A, an example of a situation where it was reasonable to anticipate that the television cameras, whilst filming and transmitting pictures of a special event of children travelling in a balloon, in which there was media interest, particularly amongst the parents, showed the balloon suddenly bursting into flames. Many other such situations could be imagined where the impact of the simultaneous television pictures would be as great, if not greater, than the actual sight of the accident.

Conclusion

Only one of the plaintiffs, who succeeded before Hidden J., namely Brian Harrison, was at the ground. His relatives who died were his two brothers. The quality of brotherly love is well known to differ widely—from Cain and Abel to David and Jonathan. I assume that Mr. Harrison's relationship with his brothers was not an abnormal one. His claim was not presented upon the basis that there was such a close and intimate relationship between them, as gave rise to that very special bond of affection which would make his shock-induced psychiatric illness reasonably foreseeable by the defendant. Accordingly, the judge did not carry out the requisite close scrutiny of their relationship. Thus there was no evidence to establish the necessary proximity which would make his claim reasonably foreseeable and, subject to the other factors, to which I have referred, a valid one. The other plaintiff who was present at the ground, Robert Alcock, lost a brother-in-law. He was not, in my judgment, reasonably foreseeable as a potential sufferer from shock-induced psychiatric illness, in default of very special facts and none was established. Accordingly their claims must fail, as must those of the other plaintiffs who only learned of the disaster by watching simultaneous television. I, too, would therefore dismiss these appeals.

Lord Oliver of Aylmerton added some very important comments regarding the distinction between 'primary' and 'secondary' victims; and the nature of 'proximity'.

Lord Oliver, at 407–8

It is customary to classify cases in which damages are claimed for injury occasioned in this way under a single generic label as cases of "liability for nervous shock." . . . Broadly . . . [the cases] divide into two categories, that is to say, those cases in which the injured plaintiff was involved, either mediately or immediately, as a participant, and those in which the plaintiff was no more than the passive and unwilling witness of injury caused to others. . . .

Lord Oliver considered case law including *Dulieu v White* (above) and *Schneider v Eisovitch* [1960] 2 QB 430, where the plaintiff had been directly involved in the same accident in which her husband had died. These were 'primary victim' cases.

(At 408)

Into the same category, as it seems to me, fall the so called "rescue cases." It is well established that the defendant owes a duty of care not only to those who are directly threatened or injured by his careless acts but also to those who, as a result, are induced to go to their rescue and suffer injury in so doing. The fact that the injury suffered is psychiatric and is caused by the impact on the mind of becoming involved in personal danger or in scenes of horror and destruction makes no difference.

"Danger invites rescue. The cry of distress is the summons to relief . . . the act, whether impulsive or deliberate, is the child of the occasion:" *Wagner v. International Railway Co.* (1921) 232 N.Y. 176, 180–181, *per* Cardozo J.

So in *Chadwick v. British Railways Board* [1967] 1 W.L.R. 912, the plaintiff recovered damages for the psychiatric illness caused to her deceased husband through the traumatic effects of his gallantry and self-sacrifice in rescuing and comforting victims of the Lewisham railway disaster.

These are all cases where the plaintiff has, to a greater or lesser degree, been personally involved in the incident out of which the action arises, either through the direct threat of bodily injury to himself or in coming to the aid of others injured or threatened. Into the same category, I believe, fall those cases such as *Dooley v. Cammell Laird & Co. Ltd.* [1951] 1 Lloyd's Rep. 271, *Galt v. British Railways Board* (1983) 133 N.L.J. 870, and *Wigg v. British Railways Board*, The Times, 4 February 1986, where the negligent act of the defendant has put the plaintiff in the position of being, or of thinking that he is about to be or has been, the involuntary cause of another's death or injury and the illness complained of stems from the shock to the plaintiff of the consciousness of this supposed fact. The fact that the defendant's negligent conduct has foreseeably put the plaintiff in the position of being an unwilling participant in the event establishes of itself a sufficiently proximate relationship between them and the principal question is whether, in the circumstances, injury of that type to that plaintiff was or was not reasonably foreseeable.

In those cases in which, as in the instant appeals, the injury complained of is attributable to the grief and distress of witnessing the misfortune of another person in an event by which the plaintiff is not personally threatened or in which he is not directly involved as an actor, the analysis becomes more complex.

(At 410–11)

The failure of the law in general to compensate for injuries sustained by persons unconnected with the event precipitated by a defendant's negligence must necessarily import the lack of any legal duty owed by the defendant to such persons. That cannot, I think, be attributable to some arbitrary but unenunciated rule of "policy" which draws a line as the outer boundary of the area of duty. Nor can it rationally be made to rest upon such injury being without the area of reasonable foreseeability. It must, as it seems to me, be attributable simply to the fact that such persons are not, in contemplation of law, in a relationship of sufficient proximity to or directness with the tortfeasor as to give rise to a duty of care, though no doubt "policy," if that is the right word, or perhaps more properly, the impracticability or unreasonableness of entertaining claims to the ultimate limits of the consequences of human activity, necessarily plays a part in the court's perception of what is sufficiently proximate.

... in the end, it has to be accepted that the concept of "proximity" is an artificial one which depends more upon the court's perception of what is the reasonable area for the imposition of liability than upon any logical process of analogical deduction.

The 'Alcock Criteria'

To be successful, a 'secondary victim' must satisfy each of the following criteria.

Category of relationship

The plaintiff must be in a close and loving relationship with the primary victim. In certain cases (spouse, parent, or child . . .), the law will presume such a close and loving relationship, though the defendant may rebut this presumption by bringing evidence that the relationship was not close and loving. In other cases, no close ties of affection are presumed, and as such the plaintiff must prove that they existed. This applies even to siblings.

Physical proximity

The plaintiff must be close to the accident in time and space. Although the 'immediate aftermath' will suffice, identification of a body some eight hours later was held in this case not to be close enough.

Immediate perception and 'shock'

The injury must have been caused by a 'shocking event' and there must either be direct sight or hearing of the event, or something equivalent to this. In *Alcock*, some of the plaintiffs saw the events unfold on television. However, it was held that because the broadcasts did not show the suffering of individuals, they were not sufficient to give rise to the sort of 'shock' that would be equivalent to witnessing an event. It was again left open whether broadcasts could ever be equivalent to direct perception, but it was pointed out that a broadcast which showed individual suffering would be in breach of the Broadcasting Code of Ethics and might well amount to a *novus actus interveniens* (see Chapter 3.6, Remoteness).

It was left open whether there might be circumstances so horrific that even a bystander without close relationship to the primary victims (but fulfilling the other requirements) might be able to recover. We will consider where we stand with this potential exception to the first requirement, below.

Arbitrary or Principled?

There are substantial differences in approach between the judgments extracted, despite their agreement on the outcome of the case. Lord Ackner continued to seek sound reasons of principle for the limitations placed on recovery by 'non-participating' plaintiffs. Specifically, he explains the need for a close and loving relationship (the first criterion above) in terms of foreseeability. If there is a particularly close and loving relationship, he explains, then the defendant ought to foresee that psychiatric harm to that plaintiff is likely to follow. But this is a long way from the usual, 'practical' form of foreseeability. The defendant would never be aware of the precise relationship between the primary victim, and any friends or relatives who may be within sight and hearing of events. Indeed the defendant would not be likely to know who was present, let alone the details of their relationships (see Hedley, 'Morbid Musings of the Reasonable Chief Constable' [1992] CLJ, 16). The truth is, foreseeability here is itself a 'control device', as we have recognized throughout this chapter, and as was recognized in *Page v Smith*. Lord Oliver on the other hand appealed not to foreseeability but to 'proximity'. Although he thought that proximity did not operate as a precise test, he suggested that it captured the real issues of policy that arose—where, in other words, to draw the line.

Bystanders

This category provides a particular challenge for a 'foreseeability' approach. Even the restrictive form of foreseeability would allow that, in an extreme case, a mere bystander may be able to recover. Some incidents are so shocking that even a person of reasonable fortitude having no relationship with the immediate victims would foreseeably suffer harm if they witnessed the incident closely and directly. If on the other hand the true justification for the control devices lies in avoiding claims by remote parties, then the courts might be reluctant to recognize a duty to bystanders even in the case of an extremely shocking event.

In *McFarlane v EE Caledonia* [1994] 2 All ER 1, the Court of Appeal tended to the latter course. The Court could not reconcile the existence of control devices in *Alcock* (above), with the possibility that a mere bystander may exceptionally be owed a duty on the grounds of foreseeability. The Court of Appeal preferred not to undermine the control devices, and refused to recognize a duty of care towards a mere bystander.   *foreseeable party.*

The plaintiff was at sea on board a vessel within sight of a major disaster in which flames engulfed the Piper Alpha oil rig, in which 164 men were killed. This was an unusually 'horrific' event and so the Court of Appeal decision would appear to amount to a rejection of the dicta in *Alcock* concerning recovery of damages by bystanders.

Stuart-Smith LJ

[In *Alcock v Chief Constable of South Yorkshire Police*] Lord Keith at p 397E said:

> . . . The case of a bystander unconnected with the victims of an accident is difficult. Psychiatric injury to him would not ordinarily, in my view, be within the range of reasonable foreseeability, but could not perhaps be entirely excluded from it if the circumstances of a catastrophe occurring very close to him were particularly horrific.

Mr Wilkinson submits that it is hardly possible to imagine anything more horrific than the holocaust on Piper Alpha, especially to the plaintiff who knew that some of his mates were on board.

I share Lord Keith's difficulty. The whole basis of the decision in Alcock's case is that where the shock is caused by fear of injury to others as opposed to fear of injury to the participant, the test of proximity is not simply reasonable foreseeability. There must be a sufficiently close tie of love and affection between the plaintiff and the victim. To extend the duty to those who have no such connection, is to base the test purely on foreseeability.

It seems to me that there are great practical problems as well. Reactions to horrific events are entirely subjective; who is to say that it is more horrific to see a petrol tanker advancing out of control on a school, when perhaps unknown to the plaintiff none of the children are in the building but are somewhere safe, than to see a child or group of children run over on a pedestrian crossing? There must be few scenes more harrowing than seeing women and children trapped at the window of a blazing building, yet many people gather to witness these calamities.

In my judgment both as a matter of principle and policy the Court should not extend the duty to those who are mere bystanders or witnesses of horrific events unless there is a sufficient degree of proximity, which requires both nearness in time and place and a close relationship of love and affection between plaintiff and victim.

In a comprehensive rejection of the plaintiff's claims, the Court of Appeal also found that he was not in danger; was not reasonably in fear for his own safety (even though at one stage a fireball was seen heading straight at the ship); and could not be counted as a rescuer because although the vessel went to offer assistance, he personally played no useful role. He was also not a person of reasonable fortitude, although after *Page v Smith* this would not be relevant if he was physically endangered. In *Hegarty v EE Caledonia* [1997] 2 Lloyd's Rep 259, another plaintiff who had been on the same support vessel at the same incident also failed to recover damages. This plaintiff was considered to be of reasonable fortitude, but it was judged that he had not been in physical danger and it was concluded that his fear for his own safety could not therefore have been 'reasonable'. We can take it that 'reasonable fear' is interpreted narrowly, since it was not satisfied by a claimant who turned and ran from a fireball which landed just short of the bow of the vessel he was on.

To return to our assessment of the *Alcock* criteria, despite Lord Ackner's attempts to provide a principled basis for them, the end result does not pass the most basic test, of offering satisfactory reasons why the disappointed party should have lost. For a brother to be required to provide *evidence* of close ties of love and affection is unseemly. To have Cain and Abel cited in evidence against presuming such close ties will have added insult to the injury. Jane Stapleton has justly described the law as stated in the *Alcock* case in the following terms:

J. Stapleton, 'In Restraint of Tort' in P. Birks (ed.), *The Frontiers of Liability*, vol 2 (Oxford: OUP, 1994), 95

That at present claims can turn on the requirement of 'close ties of love and affection' is guaranteed to produce outrage. Is it not a disreputable sight to see brothers of Hillsborough victims turned away because they had *no more* than brotherly love towards the victim? In future cases will it not be a grotesque sight to see relatives scrabbling to prove their especial love for the deceased in order to win money damages and for the defendant to have to attack that argument?

Employees and Rescuers Who Witness Injury to Others: Primary or Secondary Victims?

White v Chief Constable of South Yorkshire Police [1999] 2 AC 455 (on appeal from *Frost v Chief Constable of South Yorkshire Police* [1998] QB 254)

This case also arose from the Hillsborough football stadium disaster. A number of police officers brought claims for psychiatric injury suffered as a result of involvement in the event and its aftermath. Liability was admitted in respect of those officers who were most actively involved in the immediate area of the ground where the deaths and injuries occurred. Five plaintiffs were chosen as representative of the roles played by the other plaintiffs. Four were on duty at the stadium; the fifth was responsible for stripping bodies and completing casualty forms in hospital. Waller J dismissed the claims, although he accepted that the Chief Constable owed a duty to his officers analogous to an employer's duty to employees (see *Walker v Northumberland*, above). The Court of Appeal allowed appeals by the four officers who had been on duty at the stadium, on the ground that the Chief Constable's duty of care to a police officer in relation to psychiatric injury suffered in the course of employment arose irrespective of whether the employee would otherwise have been classified as a primary or a secondary victim. Likewise, a tortfeasor owed a rescuer a duty of care irrespective of whether the rescuer was physically endangered.

In the House of Lords, the defendant's appeal was allowed. The House of Lords ruled (by a majority on each point):

1. That the employer's duty to employees did not extend to avoiding psychiatric harm where the employee would (without the contract of employment) be a secondary victim. The '*Alcock* criteria' applied. They were of course unable to show close ties of love and affection with the victims, and therefore failed to satisfy the criteria.

2. That a rescuer who had not been exposed to the risk of physical injury was not a 'primary victim' and also had to satisfy the *Alcock* criteria.

Lord Hoffmann, at 505–7

. . . Should the employment relationship be a reason for allowing an employee to recover damages for psychiatric injury in circumstances in which he would otherwise be a secondary victim and not satisfy the *Alcock* control mechanisms? I think, my Lords, that the question vividly illustrates the dangers inherent in applying the traditional incrementalism of the common law to this part of the law of torts. If one starts from the employer's liability in respect of physical injury, it seems an easy step, even rather forward-looking, to extend liability on the same grounds to psychiatric injury. It makes the law seem more attuned to advanced medical thinking by eliminating (or not introducing) a distinction which rests upon uneasy empirical foundations. It is important, however, to have regard, not only to how the proposed extension of liability can be aligned with cases in which liability exists, but also to the situatiohs in which damages are not recoverable. If one then steps back and looks at the rules of liability for psychiatric injury as a whole, in their relationship with each other, the smoothing of the fabric at one point has produced an ugly ruck at another. In their application to other secondary victims, the *Alcock* control mechanisms stand obstinately in the way of rationalisation and the effect is to produce striking anomalies. Why should the policemen, simply by virtue of the employment analogy and irrespective of what they actually did, be treated different from first aid workers or ambulance men?

. . . In principle . . . , I do not think it would be fair to give police officers the right to a larger claim merely because the disaster was caused by the negligence of other policemen. In the circumstances in which the injuries were caused, I do not think that this is a relevant distinction and if it were to be given effect, the law would not be treating like cases alike.

(At 508)

The second way in which the plaintiffs put their case is that they were not "bystanders or spectators" but participants in the sense that they actually did things to help. They submit that there is an analogy between their position and that of a "rescuer," who, on the basis of the decision of Waller J. in *Chadwick v. British Railways Board* [1967] 1 W.L.R. 912, is said to be treated as a primary victim, exempt from the control mechanisms.

In *Chadwick's* case, the plaintiff suffered psychiatric injury as a result of his experiences in assisting the victims of a railway accident. He spent 12 hours crawling in the wreckage, helping people to extricate themselves and giving pain killing injections to the injured. Waller J. said, at p. 921, that it was foreseeable that "somebody might try to rescue passengers and suffer injury in the process." The defendants therefore owed a duty of care to the plaintiff. He went on to say that it did not matter that the injury suffered was psychiatric rather than physical but in any event "shock was foreseeable and . . . rescue was foreseeable." Thus the judge's reasoning is based purely upon the foreseeability of psychiatric injury in the same way as in other cases of that time.

(At 509–11)

There does not seem to me to be any logical reason why the normal treatment of rescuers on the issues of foreseeability and causation should lead to the conclusion that, for the purpose of liability for psychiatric injury, they should be given special treatment as primary victims when they were not within the range of foreseeable physical injury and their psychiatric injury was caused by witnessing or participating in the aftermath of accidents which caused death or injury to others. It would of course be possible to create such a rule by an ex post facto rationalisation of *Chadwick v. British Railways Board* [1967] 1 W.L.R. 912. In both *McLoughlin v. O'Brian* [1983] 1 A.C. 410 and in *Alcock v. Chief Constable of South Yorkshire* [1992] 1 A.C. 310, members of the House referred to *Chadwick's* case [1967] 1 W.L.R. 912 with approval. But I do not think that too much should be read into these remarks. In neither case was it argued that the plaintiffs were entitled to succeed as rescuers and anything said about the duty to rescuers was therefore necessarily obiter. If one is looking for an ex post facto rationalisation of *Chadwick's* case, I think that the most satisfactory is that offered in the Court of Appeal in *McLoughlin v. O'Brian* [1981] Q.B. 599, 622 by my noble and learned friend, Lord Griffiths, who had been the successful counsel for Mr. Chadwick. He said:

> "Mr. Chadwick might have been injured by a wrecked carriage collapsing on him as he worked among the injured. A duty of care is owed to a rescuer in such circumstances . . . "

If Mr. Chadwick was, as Lord Griffiths said, within the range of foreseeable physical injury, then the case is no more than an illustration of the principle applied by the House in *Page v. Smith*, namely that such a person can recover even if the injury he actually suffers is not physical but psychiatric. And in addition (unlike *Page v. Smith*) Waller J. made a finding that psychiatric injury was also foreseeable.

Should then your Lordships take the incremental step of extending liability for psychiatric injury to "rescuers" (a class which would now require definition) who give assistance at or after some disaster without coming within the range of foreseeable physical injury? It may be said that this would encourage people to offer assistance. The category of secondary victims would be confined to "spectators and bystanders" who take no part in dealing with the incident or its aftermath. On the authorities, as it seems to me, your Lordships are free to take such a step.

In my opinion there are two reasons why your Lordships should not do so. The less important reason is the definitional problem to which I have alluded. The concept of a rescuer as someone who puts himself in danger of physical injury is easy to understand. But once this notion is extended to include others who give assistance, the line between them and bystanders becomes difficult to draw with any precision. For example, one of the plaintiffs in the *Alcock* case [1992], a Mr. O'Dell, went to look for his nephew. "He searched among the bodies . . . and assisted those who staggered out from the terraces:" p. 354. He did not contend that his case was different from those of the other relatives and it was also dismissed. Should he have put himself forward as a rescuer?

But the more important reason for not extending the law is that in my opinion the result would be quite unacceptable. I have used this word on a number of occasions and the time has come to explain what I mean. I do not mean that the burden of claims would be too great for the insurance market or the public funds, the two main sources for the payment of damages in tort. The Law Commission may have had this in mind when they said that removal of all the control mechanism would lead to an "unacceptable" increase in claims, since they described it as a "floodgates" argument. These are questions on which it is difficult to offer any concrete evidence and I am simply not in a position to form a view one way or the other. I am therefore willing to accept that, viewed against the total sums paid as damages for personal injury, the increase resulting from an extension of liability to helpers would be modest. But I think that such an extension would be unacceptable to the ordinary person because (though he might not put it this way) it would offend against his notions of distributive justice. He would think it unfair between one class of claimants and another, at best not treating like cases alike and, at worst, favouring the less deserving against the more deserving. He would think it wrong that policemen, even as part of a general class of persons who rendered assistance, should have the right to compensation for psychiatric injury out of public funds while the bereaved relatives are sent away with nothing.

. . . It may be said that the common law should not pay attention to these feelings about the relative merits of different classes of claimants. It should stick to principle and not concern itself with distributive justice. An extension of liability to rescuers and helpers would be a modest incremental development in the common law tradition and, as between these plaintiffs and these defendants, produce a just result. My Lords, I disagree. It seems to me that in this area of the law, the search for principle was called off in *Alcock v. Chief Constable of South Yorkshire Police* [1992] 1 A.C. 310. No one can pretend that the existing law, which your Lordships have to accept, is founded upon principle. I agree with Jane Stapleton's remark that "once the law has taken a wrong turning or otherwise fallen into an unsatisfactory internal state in relation to a particular cause of action, incrementalism cannot provide the answer:" see *The Frontiers of Liability*, vol. 2, p. 87.

Consequently your Lordships are now engaged, not in the bold development of principle, but in a practical attempt, under adverse conditions, to preserve the general perception of the law as system of rules which is fair between one citizen and another.

I should say in passing that I do not suggest that someone should be unable to recover for injury caused by negligence, in circumstances in which he would normally be entitled to sue, merely because his occupation required him to run the risk of such injury. Such a rule, called "the fireman's rule" obtains in some of the United States but was rejected by your Lordships' House in *Ogwo v. Taylor* [1988] A.C. 431. This would be too great an affront to the idealised model of the law of torts as a system of corrective justice between equals. But the question here is rather different. It is not whether a policeman should be disqualified in circumstances in which he would ordinarily have a right of action, but whether there should be liability to rescuers and helpers as a class. And in considering whether liability for psychiatric injury should be extended to such a class, I think it is legitimate to take into account the fact that, in the nature of things, many of its members will be from occupations in which they are trained and required to run such risks and which provide for appropriate benefits if they should suffer such injuries.

Lord Hoffmann's judgment contains some unusually open statements concerning the arbitrary nature of the law on psychiatric harm and indeed on the distributive failings of the law of tort in general. If (he argues) we recognize that very few of those in need of compensation are able to establish claims in tort, it becomes clear that abolishing some or even all recovery for psychiatric injury would 'add little to the existing stock of anomaly' to be found in the law of tort (at 504). Lord Hoffmann said, loud and clear, that there was no longer scope for incremental development in this area, as a result of *Alcock*. Lord Steyn said the same thing:

Lord Steyn, at 500

The only sensible strategy for the courts is to say thus far and no further . . . In reality there are no refined analytical tools which will enable the courts to draw lines by way of compromise solution in a way that is coherent and morally defensible.

These comments amount to an abandonment of the traditional common law method, and of incremental development under *Caparo*, in respect of this category of case.

Rescuers after White

According to Lord Hoffmann, the majority in this case merely declined to *extend* the boundaries of liability to rescuers who were not themselves primary victims, because they were not physically endangered. The definition of a primary victim as one who is physically endangered was said to be drawn from *Page v Smith*. But as Lord Goff pointed out in his dissent, and as we said clearly above, it is most unlikely that Lord Lloyd in *Page v Smith* was seeking to set out an *exclusive* test for primary victims.

The interpretation of the majority amounted, in Lord Goff's view, to the introduction of a new control device. It was not to be derived from *Page v Smith*.

Lord Goff (dissenting, at 486)

A new control mechanism?

As I have already recorded, it was submitted by Mr. Collender on behalf of the appellants, relying on certain passages in the opinion of Lord Lloyd in *Page v. Smith* [1996] A.C. 155, 184A–B, 187E–F, that it was a prerequisite of the right of recovery by primary victims in respect of psychiatric injury suffered by them that they should have been within the range of foreseeable physical injury. I have already expressed the opinion that no such conclusion can be drawn from Lord Lloyd's opinion in *Page v. Smith*. I understand however that, even if my view on that point is accepted as correct, some of your Lordships nevertheless consider that a new control mechanism to the same effect should now be introduced and imposed by this House as a matter of policy.

I am compelled to say that I am unable to accept this suggestion because in my opinion (1) the proposal is contrary to well established authority; (2) the proposed control mechanism would erect an artificial barrier against recovery in respect of foreseeable psychiatric injury and as such is undesirable; and (3) the underlying concern is misconceived.

Lord Goff considered reasons (1) and (2) in the light of the case law before continuing:

> . . . (3) The underlying concern is misconceived
>
> I sense that the underlying concern, which has prompted a desire to introduce this new control mechanism, is that it is thought that, without it, the policemen who are plaintiffs in the present case would be "better off" than the relatives in the *Alcock* case who failed in their claims, and that such a result would be undesirable. To this, there are at least three answers. First, the control mechanisms which excluded recovery by the relatives in the *Alcock* case would, in my opinion, have been equally applicable to the policemen in the present case if on the facts they had (like the relatives) been no more than witnesses of the consequences of the tragedy. Second, the question whether any of the relatives might be able to recover because he fell within the broad category of rescuer is still undecided; and, strangely, the control mechanism now proposed to exclude the claims of the policemen in the present case would likewise exclude the claims of relatives if advanced on the basis that they were rescuers. Third, however, it is in any event misleading to think in terms of one class of plaintiffs being "better off" than another. Tort liability is concerned not only with compensating plaintiffs, but with awarding such compensation against a defendant who is responsible in law for the plaintiff's injury. It may well be that one plaintiff will succeed on the basis that he can establish such responsibility, whereas another plaintiff who has suffered the same injury will not succeed because he is unable to do so. In such a case, the first plaintiff will be "better off" than the second, but it does not follow that the result is unjust or that an artificial barrier should be erected to prevent those in the position of the first plaintiff from succeeding in their claims. The true requirement is that the claim of each plaintiff should be judged by reference to the same legal principles.
>
> For all these reasons I am unable to accept the need for, or indeed the desirability of, the new control mechanism now proposed.

Lord Griffiths too offered some reasons why those disappointed by the *Alcock* decision ought to be able to accept a different answer in respect of the police officer's claims.

> **Lord Griffiths,** at 465
>
> After a careful analysis of the evidence, Rose L.J. identified three of the police officers as rescuers. I would myself dismiss the appeals in respect of those officers, namely White, Bairstow and Bevis. I would add that I do not share the view that the public would find it in some way offensive that those who suffered disabling psychiatric illness as a result of their efforts to rescue the victims should receive compensation, but that those who suffered the grief of bereavement should not. Bereavement and grief are a part of the common condition of mankind which we will all endure at some time in our lives. It can be an appalling experience but it is different in kind from psychiatric illness and the law has never recognised it as a head of damage. We are human and we must accept as a part of the price of our humanity the suffering of bereavement for which no sum of money can provide solace or comfort. I think better of my fellow men than to believe that they would, although bereaved, look like dogs in the manger upon those who went to the rescue at Hillsborough.

It is naive to think that relatives of those caught up in the tragedy would be persuaded by these reasons. But there is a strong argument that that is not really to the point. The law's job is to provide pertinent reasons, not to ensure that these reasons are universally accepted by the public. Whether the courts' approach to the duty of care since *Caparo* has allowed the giving of pertinent reasons to thrive is the main theme of this chapter. In later sections of this chapter, the general conclusion is that decisions in most 'problem' areas are becoming more convincing. That is not the case with *White*. Existing doctrinal confusion was described as beyond remedy; and then extended to rescuers.

Unwilling participants other than rescuers

In the extract above, Lord Hoffmann expressly left open the possibility that claims may be brought by other unwilling participants, particularly those who reasonably believe that they are responsible for death or serious injury to others. This category of case was described by Lord Oliver in *Alcock* in terms of harm to a 'participant'. He treated such participants as primary victims. Lord Oliver's comments were based partly on previous cases such as *Dooley v Cammell Laird & Co Ltd* [1951] 1 Lloyd's Rep 271 (a crane operator whose crane, due to a fault, dropped its load towards fellow workers was owed a duty of care in respect of psychiatric damage).

In *Hunter v British Coal Corporation* [1999] QB 140, the Court of Appeal took a restrictive view of the 'direct participant' category. Brooke LJ pointed out that Lord Oliver's formulation of involuntary participants would extend the law beyond the point marked by *Dooley* and cases of its kind. In *Dooley*, the plaintiff had been close to the accident in time and space and had witnessed it with his own unaided senses. Lord Oliver made no reference to the applicability of these factors and perhaps intended them not to apply to 'participants'.

In *Hunter*, the plaintiff was a driver in a coal mine. Through no fault of his own, but due to a breach of duty on the part of his employers, he drove into a hydrant which was protruding into a narrow roadway in the mine, and which began to leak. He went in search of a hose to divert the water and avoid a flood. While he was gone, the hydrant exploded through pressure of water and his fellow workman was killed. The plaintiff was 20–30 yards away and heard but did not see the explosion. He then heard that his workmate had been killed. He suffered irrational feelings of guilt and reactive depression. His claim was dismissed by a majority of the Court of Appeal, who held that there must be proximity of time and space for the defendant to succeed in his claim as a primary victim. Perhaps harshly, it was judged that the plaintiff's depression was an abnormal reaction to receiving the news of his workmate's death, which was not caused by direct perception and was not a foreseeable consequence of the defendant's breach. Although this case was decided shortly before the House of Lords' judgment in *White v Chief Constable of South Yorkshire Police*, it was neither approved nor disapproved in that case.

A much more open but very imprecise approach was adopted by the House of Lords in *W v Essex County Council* [2001] 2 AC 592. Here, the House of Lords declined to strike out a claim by parents who had accepted a foster child into their home. Explicit assurances that the child was not an abuser proved to be incorrect. A month after the placement the parents discovered that the child had sexually abused their children. The parents alleged that as a result of the abuse they had suffered psychiatric illness. Lord Slynn said that since this area of the law, and particularly the distinction between primary and secondary victims, was still developing, their case was not clearly hopeless and should be allowed to proceed to trial.

Lord Slynn of Hadley, at 601

I do not consider that any of the cases to which your Lordships have been referred conclusively shows that, if the psychiatric injury suffered by the parents flows from a feeling that they brought the abuser and the abused together or that they have a feeling of responsibility that they did not detect earlier what was happening, they are prevented from being primary victims.

Lord Slynn did not state whether 'direct perception' would be required for participants. However, in what appears to be an alternative suggestion that the parents could argue their case as *secondary* victims, Lord Slynn continued:

> Whilst I accept that there has to be some temporal and spatial limitation on the persons who can claim to be secondary victims, very much for the reasons given by Lord Steyn in the *Frost* case, it seems to me that the concept of "the immediate aftermath" of the incident has to be assessed in the particular factual situation. I am not persuaded that in a situation like the present the parents must come across the abuser or the abused "immediately" after the sexual incident has terminated. All the incidents here happened in the period of four weeks before the parents learned of them. It might well be that if the matter were investigated in depth a judge would think that the temporal and spatial limitations were not satisfied. On the other hand he might find that the flexibility to which Lord Scarman referred indicated that they were.

Horrifying Events and the Aftermath—Incremental Development Returns?

It is clear from the authorities, including especially *McLoughlin v O'Brian* and *Alcock v Chief Constable of South Yorkshire Police*, that no duty will be owed to a claimant whose psychiatric injury flows from bereavement and grief *per se*. There must be perception of a 'shocking event'. This requirement as we have said is related to a felt need to limit the number of potential claims, and it leads to some very hard distinctions. In *Sion v Hampstead Health Authority* [1994] 5 Med LR 170, a father sat at his son's bedside for 14 days after he had been involved in a motorcycle accident, watching him deteriorate and die. His claim was struck out and his appeal dismissed by the Court of Appeal, as there had been only a gradual accumulation of assaults on his nervous system, and no single shocking event. By contrast in *Tredget v Bexley Health Authority* [1994] 5 Med LR 178, a baby was born in a severely asphyxiated condition because of the defendant's negligence and died two days later. His parents were owed a duty of care because the actual birth was chaotic and horrifying, that 'event' playing a significant part in the pathological grief reaction of the parents.

The fine lines that need to be drawn in order to satisfy the requirement of a 'shocking event' in tragic circumstances are difficult to defend. In two recent cases, the Court of Appeal has shown a willingness to develop the law in respect of this criterion. In the first, the Court of Appeal held that a duty of care was owed in respect of psychiatric harm to a mother whose 10-month-old son suffered an epileptic seizure and died 36 hours later. These events could have been avoided through proper diagnosis and treatment of his condition at an early stage. The claimant was with her son throughout the period but due partly to misleading assurances from medical staff she only gradually became aware of the seriousness of his condition. The Court of Appeal found that a process covering 36 hours could constitute one shocking event.

Ward LJ, *North Glamorgan NHS Trust v Ceri Ann Walters* [2002] EWCA Civ 1792

> **34** In my judgment the law as presently formulated does permit a realistic view to be taken from case to case of what constitutes the necessary 'event'. . . . .It is a matter of judgment from case to case depending on the facts and circumstances of each case. In my judgment on the facts of this case there was an inexorable progression from the moment when the fit occurred as a result of the failure of the hospital properly to diagnose and then to treat the

baby, the fit causing the brain damage which shortly thereafter made termination of this child's life inevitable and the dreadful climax when the child died in her arms. It is a seamless tale with an obvious beginning and an equally obvious end. It was played out over a period of 36 hours, which for her at the time and as subsequently recollected was undoubtedly one drawn-out experience.

35 Mr Miller submits that the court cannot take account of what the mother was told about her son's condition from time to time. I do not agree. The distinction in the authorities is between the case where the claim is founded upon 'merely being informed of, or reading, or hearing about the accident' and directly perceiving by sight or sound the relevant event. Information given as the events unfold before one's eyes is part of the circumstances of the case to which the court is entitled to have regard.

The decision was presented as turning on the facts of the case, and involving no new judgment of legal policy. However, Clarke LJ said that although it was 'too late' (as Lord Hoffmann put it) to go back on the *Alcock* criteria, this does not mean 'that those criteria have to be applied too rigidly or mechanistically'.

Clarke LJ

50 This is a developing area of the common law. I note that Lord Ackner introduced his five propositions with the phrase 'whatever may be the future development of the law' and in his proposition (5) he said that 'shock' has *yet* (my emphasis) to include psychiatric illness caused by the accumulation over a period of time of more gradual assaults on the nervous system.

51 For my part, although I agree with Ward LJ that the decision of the judge does not involve the taking of an incremental step advancing the frontiers of liability, if it did, I for my part would take that step on the facts of this case.

Clearly Clarke LJ thought that the majority of the House of Lords had been too swift to announce that this area could not be improved by incremental development and that the only answer was to declare (as Lord Steyn put it in *White*) 'Thus Far and No Further'. His approach in this case has been described by Lord Phillips, in the lecture cited above, as 'not taking any notice of Lord Steyn'.[9]

In *Galli-Atkinson v Seghal* [2003] EWCA Civ 697, the claimant's 16-year-old daughter was struck by a car and killed while she was walking to a ballet class. Having left the house to look for her daughter, the claimant came across the scene of the accident, where a police officer told her that her daughter was dead. She then went to the mortuary where she cradled her daughter's body. There was no dispute that the claimant suffered a psychiatric illness as a result of the death, but was this as a result of 'direct perception of a shocking event'?

At first instance, the Recorder held that the visit to the mortuary was for the purposes of identification and was quite separate from the relevant 'event'. A duty was ruled out on the basis that a similar visit to the mortuary did not amount to perception of the event or its aftermath in *Alcock* (above). The claimant succeeded on appeal. The Court of Appeal cited the case of *Ceri Ann Walters* as authority for the proposition that an event may be made up of several distinct components. The court found that, on the medical evidence, the visit to the accident

---

[9] Lord Phillips, 'Liability for Psychiatric Injury', Personal Injury Bar Association Annual Lecture, at 22.

scene and to the mortuary in those conditions had 'amplified' the effects of the bereavement, and as a matter of law these could be treated as part of the relevant 'event'. Again, although this is a decision turning on interpretation of facts, there seems to have been a more sympathetic reading of the facts than can be found in the *Alcock* case itself. Is it likely that the visit to the mortuary in *Alcock* had no substantial influence in 'amplifying the effect' of the bereavement in the claimant's mind?

Conclusions

Where secondary victims are concerned, the law has always imposed certain restrictions. It has proved difficult to provide a proper justification which would allow the courts to distinguish between successful and unsuccessful cases. Justifications have ranged from foreseeability, through floodgates, to proximity. We have pointed out that foreseeability itself is applied in a particular form in respect of psychiatric injury and that this in turn relates to a felt need to restrict the range of claimants. In *White*, the various control devices set out in the case of *Alcock v Chief Constable of South Yorkshire Police* were first declared to be arbitrary, and then extended to categories (employees and rescuers) who had not previously been covered, in order to avoid apparent inconsistency between classes of claimant.

Meanwhile however, duty techniques such as 'voluntary assumption of responsibility' in combination with the test for *breach* of duty have been applied by the Court of Appeal in order to distinguish between recoverable and unrecoverable psychiatric damage in a wide range of cases where there was no endangered party at all. This might suggest that there is nothing intrinsically problematic about psychiatric damage. Rather, there is a problem where the person suffering the eventual illness is not the immediate victim of a physical impact, nor close to the event. Although the shadow of *White* still hangs over the law, with its conclusion that incremental change is now impossible, the Court of Appeal has generally *not* called off the search for principle. Even so, it is widely accepted that the law on secondary victims needs legislative change, to free the law from some of the more unattractive control factors.

In Australia, development has moved the other way. Courts have removed control devices, and state legislatures have to some extent set about restoring them. In *Annetts v Australian Stations Pty Ltd* (2002) 211 CLR 317, the High Court of Australia recognized that a duty was owed to parents whose 16-year-old son was left to die in the outback through the negligence of the defendants. The parents were informed of his disappearance by telephone. It was not felt that the plaintiffs should have to prove that they had 'witnessed' the death. Psychiatric harm to the parents was foreseeable, and the tests of direct perception and sudden shock were disposed of.[10] But in a number of states (including New South Wales) restrictive legislation has now been introduced requiring the plaintiff to witness the injury directly.

Legislative Change?

In conclusion to its *Report on Liability for Psychiatric Illness* (Law Commission No 249 (1998)), the Law Commission proposed legislation in this area. Although the Law Commission's proposals have to some extent been overtaken by events, it is useful to study the key proposals.

---

[10] P. Handford, 'Psychiatric Injury: the New Era' (2003) 11 *Tort L Rev* 13.

(Draft) Negligence (Psychiatric Illness) Bill 1998

New duties of care

1.—(1) Subsection (2) imposes a duty of care for the purposes of the tort of negligence . . . .

(2) A person (the defendant) owes a duty to take reasonable care to avoid causing another person (the plaintiff) to suffer a recognisable psychiatric illness as a result of the death, injury or imperilment of a third person (the immediate victim) if it is reasonably foreseeable that the defendant's act or omission might cause the plaintiff to suffer such an illness.

(3) The defendant must be taken not to have owed the duty unless—

    (a) his act or omission caused the death, injury or imperilment of the immediate victim, and

    (b) the plaintiff and the immediate victim had a close tie of love and affection immediately before the act or omission occurred or immediately before the onset of the plaintiff's illness (or both).

    . . .

[Clause 2 sets out a duty of care where the defendant is the immediate victim. At present such a duty is ruled out on policy grounds.]

2.—(1) Subsections (2) to (5) have effect to determine whether for the purposes of section 1 the plaintiff and the immediate victim had a close tie of love and affection at a particular time.

(2) If at the time concerned the plaintiff fell within any of the categories listed in subsection (4) he and the immediate victim must be conclusively taken to have had a close tie of love and affection at that time.

(3) Otherwise it is for the plaintiff to show that he and the immediate victim had a close tie of love and affection at the time concerned.

(4) The categories are—

    (a) the immediate victim's spouse;

    (b) either parent of the immediate victim;

    (c) any child of the immediate victim;

    (d) any brother or sister of the immediate victim;

    (e) the immediate victim's cohabitant. . . .

    . . .

5—(2) It is not a condition of the claim's success that it should be caused by a shock.

(3) The court may allow the claim even if the illness results from the defendant causing his own death, injury or imperilment.

The Law Commission's proposals would abolish some of the existing control devices and make adjustments to the requirement for close ties of love and affection.

In the proposed new duty of care (Clause 1), there is no requirement that the damage should be shock-induced, and no requirement that the claimant should have directly witnessed an event or been in close physical proximity to it. These changes would mark a considerable relaxation of the controls applied. The prospect of 'indeterminate claims' is met by retaining a requirement that there be close ties of love and affection between claimant and immediate victim, and by retaining a foreseeability requirement. There is no definition of the *kind* of foreseeability required, except that it must be foreseeability of psychiatric harm. It is not clear whether foreseeability will be judged in the light of the accident in question, or in the more usual way from the point of view of the defendant without hindsight. It seems likely that the former, 'specific' form of foreseeability traditionally applied to psychiatric damage cases is intended. This 'control device' would therefore continue to apply.

More modest changes are proposed for the 'relationship' criterion. In particular, Clause 3 expands the list of relationships in which close ties of love and affection are assumed, to include siblings and cohabitants. The latter category is further defined and includes same-sex relationships. Claimants who fall into the listed categories would be *conclusively* taken to have a close enough tie of love and affection, avoiding the prospect of intrusive evidence being gathered by defendants who are eager to avoid liability.

In summary, in abolishing the other control devices, but retaining closeness of relationship, the Law Commission has accepted the possibility of indeterminacy in claimants as a valid policy concern, but has not accepted the argument that illness *flowing from bereavement* needs to be excluded from compensation, where the family relationship is sufficiently close.

In Clause 2, the Law Commission sets out a new duty where the defendant foreseeably causes injury to another by harming or endangering himself. This was ruled out as a matter of public policy in the case of *Greatorex v Greatorex* [2000] 1 WLR 1970 (a first instance decision), partly because it would inhibit the defendant's freedom of action, and partly because it may cause family strife where claimants and defendants are related.

The Law Commission did not include any provisions relating to employees or rescuers, believing that there was no particular reason to interfere with the then developing common law on these issues. This has proved to be incorrect. In Clause 4, the Law Commission only proposed to abolish the common law duty so far as it depended on close ties of love and affection to the immediate victim. It was not thought at the time of drafting the Bill (before the House of Lords' decision in *White*) that this requirement had any application to rescuers or employees. Similarly, it never applied (by definition) to mere bystanders, so that the Bill would not resolve the question of whether they can seek compensation. If legislation is ever to be enacted in this field, then the situation of rescuers and employees who witness harm to others would have to be considered again in the light of *White v Chief Constable of South Yorkshire Police*. Preferably, such legislation would also resolve the question of bystanders (see *McFarlane v EE Caledonia*, above). But the larger question is whether any broadening of liability is likely to be taken forward, given the political climate currently surrounding tort liability.

FURTHER READING

Case, P., 'Secondary Iatrogenic Harm: Claims for Psychiatric Damage Following a Death Caused by Medical Error' (2004) 67 MLR 561.

Handford, P., 'Psychiatric Injury: The New Era' (2003) 11 *Tort L Rev* 13.

Handford, P., 'Psychiatric Injury in Breach of a Relationship' (2007) 27 LS 26–50.

Hedley, S., 'Morbid Musings of the Reasonable Chief Constable' [1992] CLJ 16.

Hilson, C., 'Liability for Psychiatric Injury: Primary and Secondary Victims Revisited' (2002) 18 PN 167–76.

Jones, M., 'Liability for Psychiatric Illness—More Principle, Less Subtlety?' [1995] 4 Web JCLI.

Mullaney N.J., and Handford P.R., *Tort Liability for Psychiatric Damage* (2nd edn, Lawbook Co, 2005).

Stapleton, J., 'In Restraint of Tort', in P. Birks (ed.), *The Frontiers of Liability*, vol 2 (Oxford: OUP, 1994).

Steele, J., 'Scepticism and the Law of Negligence' [1993] 52 CLJ 437.

Teff, H., 'Liability for Negligently Inflicted Psychiatric Harm: Justifications and Boundaries' [1998] 57 CLJ 91.

Teff, H., 'Liability for Psychiatric Illness: Advancing Cautiously' (1998) 61 MLR 849.

Trindade, F., 'Nervous Shock and Negligent Conduct' (1996) 112 LQR 22.

2. PURE ECONOMIC LOSSES

This section relates to the recovery of 'pure economic losses'. Economic losses suffered by the claimant will be regarded as 'pure' if they do not flow from any personal injury to the claimant nor from any physical damage to his or her property. The boundaries between 'pure' economic loss, and loss which is 'consequential' upon physical damage to the claimant's property, were investigated by the Court of Appeal in *Spartan Steel v Martin* [1973] QB 27, which we extract in section 2.1 below.

Like psychiatric injury, pure economic loss is often described as a problematic form of damage. The problems in question may, however, be rather different. Although 'floodgates' arguments are sometimes encountered in this area (for example in cases of 'relational' economic loss, category A below), there are other reasons why *a duty to take care not to cause foreseeable economic loss to the claimant* is not always appropriate. Here is one judicial statement of the distinctions between these two different 'problem areas':

Hale LJ, *McLoughlin v Jones* [2002] QB 1312

58 Psychiatric injury is different in kind from economic loss. The law has traditionally regarded both with some scepticism. It has restricted the scope of any duty to avoid causing purely economic loss: this is obviously right. The object of a great deal of economic activity is to succeed while others fail. Much economic loss is intentionally, let alone negligently, caused. Only, therefore, where unlawful means are used or the defendant has assumed some responsibility towards another to avoid such loss should there be liability. The considerations in relation to psychiatric injury are rather different: hardly anyone sets out to cause such injury to competitors or anyone else (if they do, the tort of intentionally inflicting harm under the principle in *Wilkinson v Downton* [1897] 2 QB 57 is committed). The law's scepticism has rather to do with the infinite scope of adverse psychiatric reactions and the other difficulties identified by Lord Steyn in the *Frost* case. . . .

Hale LJ reminds us here of the limited scope of liability in 'the economic torts' (considered in Chapter 2). It is not always appropriate to impose liability for *deliberate* infliction of economic loss, in the absence of unlawful means and intention to harm. By definition, it cannot always be appropriate to impose a duty of care to avoid causing economic loss through negligence. This is very different from the argument that 'over-extensive' liability may follow, which Hale LJ perceives to be the main concern in cases of psychiatric harm. Rather, it is an argument that cases of economic loss do not always require a remedy.

Even so, it would be wrong to suggest that the issues arising are entirely concerned with the nature of the injury. Cases involving economic loss frequently share certain particular features. The damage is often caused 'indirectly'; the relationship between claimant and defendant is sometimes remote; and the number of potential parties is sometimes large. In these respects, economic loss claims do indeed bear comparison with claims by 'secondary victims' considered in Section 1 above. Courts also have regard to a broader legal policy context including the availability of other protection for the claimant and the possibility for conflict with the law of contract.[11] The current trend is for factors of this sort to be explicitly considered in determining whether a duty to take care is owed.

It is important to note that such concerns are not *only* relevant to cases of pure economic loss. The House of Lords has made clear that if similar considerations are relevant to a case involving *physical damage to property*, then a restricted approach to the duty of care may be taken in that case also: *Marc Rich v Bishop Rock Marine (The Nicholas H)* [1996] AC 211.[12] Equally, approaches forged in cases of economic loss may also be employed in a relevant case of *psychiatric* harm: *McLoughlin v Jones* [2002] QB 1312. We will see in the next section that in *Phelps v Hillingdon* [2001] 2 AC 619, the same approach (seeking an 'assumption of responsibility') was applied by the House of Lords to a case of educational malpractice, irrespective of whether the loss was personal injury, or economic loss (Section 6.3, below). It must be appreciated that the reasoning within this category is sensitive to different circumstances; and (at the same time) that similar reasoning may also be useful in certain cases which do *not* concern economic loss.

Categories of Economic Loss Case

In Chapter 3.3, we outlined the *Caparo* approach to establishing a duty of care in negligence. The hallmarks of the *Caparo* approach included the reinstatement of 'proximity' as a separate criterion which would *restrict* the operation of foreseeability; and the adoption of an 'incremental' technique in which courts will turn to established categories of case rather than to broad universal principles in order to reach their decisions. In a major article published soon after the decision in *Caparo*, Jane Stapleton criticized the new approach as likely to further entrench an approach based on 'pockets' of liability.

---

[11] Peter Benson, 'The Basis for Excluding Economic Loss in Tort Law', in D. Owen (ed.), *Philosophical Foundations of Tort Law* (OUP, 1997), offers a holistic explanation of the shape of recovery (and non-recovery) of pure economic losses, through analysis of the contractual context of many such losses and the relationship with concepts of ownership.

[12] In *The Nicholas H*, the contractual allocation of risks between claimant cargo owner, and the ship owner (who was not a party to the tort action) would be disturbed if the defendant ship surveyors were liable for damage to the cargo. This was a reason for finding that there was no duty of care under *Caparo*: it would not be 'fair, just and reasonable' to impose such a duty.

Jane Stapleton, 'Duty of Care and Economic Loss: A Wider Agenda'
(1991) 107 LQR 249, at 284

The central flaw in the House of Lords' approach to economic loss is the assumption—most explicit in *Caparo*—that difficult issues of duty should be analysed within and by analogy to pockets of 'relevant' case law. With respect, this can become a process akin to the tail wagging the dog, because the selection of the 'relevant' pocket can, at the outset, preclude consideration of factors or 'policies' which would provide a more coherent overall approach.

Stapleton's key point was that by dividing the case law into categories, artificial barriers would be set up and too much attention would be paid to irrelevant considerations (such as whether the damage was caused by an act or a statement), distracting attention from the more important policy issues that ought to drive decision-making in this area. Some of these, she argued, could be seen as relevant to all categories of economic loss.

With hindsight, it is obvious that Stapleton was correct to argue that the apparent distinction between 'losses caused by words' and 'losses caused by acts' is not a reliable way to divide the case law. This distinction was never easy to justify, since words as we will explain appeared to give rise to liability more easily than acts, where an exclusionary rule was (sometimes) thought to apply.

Now, it is clear that the leading authority of *Hedley Byrne v Heller* extends beyond losses caused by statements. Certainly, it extends to professional services more broadly. This is in itself a good enough reason for abandoning the acts/words distinction. But it would also be beneficial to go further, and to recognize that there is no *general* exclusionary rule applying to economic losses caused by acts, nor to economic losses generally. (For support of this view see further B. Feldthusen, 'Pure Economic Loss in the High Court of Australia: Reinventing the Square Wheel?' (2000) 8 *Tort L Rev*, 33.) Rather than a *general* exclusionary rule, in English law there are two specific areas where exclusionary rules apply. Even here, the exclusionary rules are not applied *because* the loss is purely economic, but for more specific reasons. These are categories A and B below.

The following categories are used to explain the law in this section.

A. Economic loss caused by **damage to property of another party**. This sort of loss can also be referred to as **'relational' economic loss**. It is not recoverable in English law, with one exception (*The Greystoke Castle*, below). One reason against liability is the prospect of actions by an indeterminate number of claimants (*Spartan Steel*). If physical harm is done to the property (or person) of one party, this may have a 'ripple effect' on the *financial* interests of many others. But this reason for the exclusionary rule is not always valid. Supplementary reasons include reluctance to interfere with contractual allocations of risk, and desire to encourage other means of protecting the claimant's interests (*Spartan Steel*; *The Aliakmon*). This general rule against liability has no application in Australia, and Canada recognizes a number of exceptions to it. Is the no-liability rule in this area arbitrary, or justified?

B. Economic loss caused by **acquiring a product that turns out to be defective**. This sort of loss is also not recoverable in English law. In *Murphy v Brentwood*, it was explained that such cases are simply not covered by *Donoghue v Stevenson*. Cases of this kind involve no injury to the person or to property other than the defective product itself. To recognize a duty here would make significant inroads into the rules of contract, because these cases involve a 'bad bargain' rather than harm to separate property. This approach is most controversial when it is

[margin note:] Nov recoverable.

applied to realty (specifically buildings) rather than to chattels, and in these cases, *Murphy v Brentwood* has been rejected in a number of common law jurisdictions. *Murphy* cannot be said to state a truly *arbitrary* rule (it is clear why it sets the boundaries where they are set), but is it overly restrictive given the policy context?

C. Economic loss caused by **reliance on negligent statements**. This kind of case was the subject of the key decision in *Hedley Byrne v Heller*. *Hedley Byrne* set out specific criteria for recognizing a duty of care where the claimant has relied upon a statement made by the defendant. There is much debate surrounding the exact criteria set out in *Hedley Byrne* and concerning its rationale and limits. But criteria drawn from *Hedley Byrne* are extensively in use in the English case law, even if they no longer capture the same concepts that were intended in that case. The relationship between the *Hedley Byrne* criteria, and the 'three-stage test' under *Caparo v Dickman*, continues to cause problems.

D. **'Extended'** *Hedley Byrne* **liability**. *Hedley Byrne* liability has been recognized as extending beyond its particular context, in which statements were delivered by one party directly to another party. First, *Hedley Byrne* liability has been extended to cases that involve more than one party, including some where the claimant does not rely on the statement at all. Second, liability on the basis of *Hedley Byrne* has been found outside the area of negligent statements, including cases of professional services more generally. In fact, these cases form the historical background to *Hedley Byrne*, and if anything it was the application in that case to mere statements (outside an existing relationship) that constituted the 'extension'. There seems to have been further movement at the margins of this category, suggesting that the existing boundaries are provisional. The problem here is certainly not rigidity of categories, but the elusive nature of the relevant criteria. Chief among these criteria is the idea of an 'assumption of responsibility'. The relationship between this criterion, and the broader idea of 'proximity', is as hard to define as the meaning of the terms themselves.

The English solution has generally been to maintain the specific exclusionary rules in categories A and B against challenge. These exclusionary rules are based on policy reasons as we will explain. In the remaining cases, there is an attempt to develop some general principles to explain the division between recoverable and unrecoverable losses. To date, the protection of the policy-based exclusions in categories A and B has been more successful than the development of convincing general principles in categories C and D.

Are 'categories' appropriate?

It will be obvious that we are taking a 'categorized' approach to the case law on economic loss. The virtues of categorization are hotly contested. Feldthusen (above), writing from a Canadian perspective, has suggested that a categorized approach is likely to shorten the length of judgments and enhance certainty. Feldthusen's proposed list of categories is longer and more complete than the one adopted in this section, which reflects the development of English law.[13] Categorization has been particularly criticized by certain Australian writers (P. Cane, 'The Blight of Economic Loss: Is There Life After *Perre v Apand*? (2000) 8 TLJ 1; J. Stapleton, 'Comparative Economic Loss: Lessons From Case-Law-Focused "Middle Theory" ' 50 UCLA L Rev 531), who would prefer the courts to develop more satisfying criteria based on identifiable and generalized policy goals. For our more modest purposes,

---

[13] See P. Giliker, 'Revisiting Pure Economic Loss: Lessons to be Learnt From the Supreme Court of Canada?' (2005) LS 49, arguing that English law could learn from a more complete categorizing approach.

which is explanation of the English case law, a degree of categorization will certainly be helpful. No grand claims are being made for our categories, and there is room for overlap and for conflict between them. In such cases, the courts will tend to be influenced by a diversity of factors and especially by the relative strength of any policy reasons.[14]

We now turn to the case law, organized in accordance with the four categories A–D above.

2.1 RELATIONAL ECONOMIC LOSS (CATEGORY A)

In cases of 'relational' economic loss, A causes damage to the property of B, causing C to lose money. C may lose money for a number of different reasons when the property of B is damaged, as will be illustrated by the case law. One such reason is that there may be a *contractual* link between C, and the damaged property.

Cattle v The Stockton Waterworks Co (1875) LR 10 QB 453

The plaintiff was engaged by K (a landowner) to carry out work on K's land. Due to a leak in the defendants' pipes, the work had to be delayed, causing the plaintiff to lose money under the terms of the contract. Blackburn, Mellor, and Lush JJ held that the plaintiff could not maintain an action against the defendant water company in these circumstances, even if K could have done so. (Any such action might have been in negligence, or under the rule in *Rylands v Fletcher* (1868) LR 3 H 330: see Chapter 11 below.) Even at this early stage, the reason offered is one of proximity; but behind proximity lies a reluctance to open the floodgates to an indeterminate number of claims. Because of these considerations, there would be no recovery even in a case, such as this one, where there would not be excessive liability on the facts. This case still encapsulates the English approach to relational economic loss.

Blackburn J, at 457–8

In the present case the objection is technical and against the merits, and we should be glad to avoid giving it effect. But if we did so, we should establish an authority for saying that, in such a case as that of *Fletcher v. Rylands* . . . the defendant would be liable, not only to an action by the owner of the drowned mine, and by such of his workmen as had their tools or clothes destroyed, but also to an action by every workman and person employed in the mine, who in consequence of its stoppage made less wages than he would otherwise have done. And many similar cases to which this would apply might be suggested. It may be said that it is just that all such persons should have compensation for such a loss, and that, if the law does not give them redress, it is imperfect. Perhaps it may be so. But, as was pointed out by Coleridge, J., in *Lumley v. Gye* [22 LJ QB 479], Courts of justice should not "allow themselves, in the pursuit of perfectly complete remedies for all wrongful acts, to transgress the bounds, which our law, in a wise consciousness as I conceive of its limited powers, has imposed on itself, of redressing only the proximate and direct consequences of wrongful acts." In this we quite agree. No authority in favour of the plaintiff's right to sue was cited, and, as far as our knowledge goes, there was none that could have been cited.

---

[14] For example, the case of *Junior Books v Veitchi* [1983] 1 AC 520, which has rarely if ever been followed, could be explained as a case under category C or D—special relationship and reliance. Instead, it is regarded as incorrect because of the strength of the general rule against recovery in category B cases.

Relational economic loss clearly illustrates the fear of a potential 'ripple effect' if liability is imposed. The effect of damage to one party may be multiplied as others suffer economic losses, giving rise to 'indeterminate liability'.

A good example is *Weller v Foot and Mouth Disease Research Institute* [1966] 1 QB 569. The plaintiffs (who were cattle auctioneers) claimed that the defendant research institute had imported an African virus and allowed it to escape, causing the disease to spread to cattle and giving rise to financial harm to the plaintiffs since cattle markets had to be closed. Widgery J held that no duty was owed to the auctioneers. The then recent authority of *Hedley Byrne* (Section 2.3 below) made no difference to the general rule on relational economic loss. (We should note that the auctioneers in this case did not even have a contractual interest in the cattle whose health was foreseeably affected by the virus. Theirs was a very general economic interest in the property that was subject to physical harm.) This case illustrates that courts were addressing policy issues in terms of 'categories' of case long before *Caparo v Dickman*, since *Cattle* was seen as more relevant to this case than *Hedley Byrne*.

Spartan Steel & Alloys v Martin & Co [1973] QB 27

Through negligence in digging up a road, the defendant contractors inadvertently severed a power supply. The plaintiffs' factory was engaged in smelting. Loss of power supply for a period of 14 hours or more caused a number of forms of damage to the plaintiff which are set out in Lord Denning's judgment.

Lord Denning MR, at 34

At the time when the power was shut off, there was an arc furnace in which metal was being melted in order to be converted into ingots. Electric power was needed throughout in order to maintain the temperature and melt the metal. When the power failed, there was a danger that the metal might solidify in the furnace and do damage to the lining of the furnace. So the plaintiffs used oxygen to melt the material and poured it from a tap out of the furnace. But this meant that the melted material was of much less value. The physical damage was assessed at £368.

In addition, if that particular melt had been properly completed, the plaintiffs would have made a profit on it of £400.

Furthermore, during those 14 hours, when the power was cut off, the plaintiffs would have been able to put four more melts through the furnace: and, by being unable to do so, they lost a profit of £1,767.

Lord Denning considered the case law on relational economic loss and continued:

(At 37–9)

. . . I turn to the relationship in the present case. It is of common occurrence. The parties concerned are: the electricity board who are under a statutory duty to maintain supplies of electricity in their district; the inhabitants of the district, including this factory, who are entitled by statute to a continuous supply of electricity for their use; and the contractors who dig up the road. Similar relationships occur with other statutory bodies, such as gas and water undertakings. The cable may be damaged by the negligence of the statutory undertaker, or by the negligence of the contractor, or by accident without any negligence by anyone: and the power may have to be cut off whilst the cable is repaired. Or the power may be cut off owing to a short-circuit in the power house: and so forth. If the cutting off of the supply causes economic loss to the consumers, should it as matter of policy be recoverable? And against whom?

Lord Denning offered a number of reasons why pure economic loss should not, as a matter of policy, be recoverable in such a situation, including the following:

> The second consideration is the nature of the hazard, namely, the cutting of the supply of elec-tricity. This is a hazard which we all run. It may be due to a short circuit, to a flash of lightning, to a tree falling on the wires, to an accidental cutting of the cable, or even to the negligence of someone or other. And when it does happen, it affects a multitude of persons: not as a rule by way of physical damage to them or their property, but by putting them to inconvenience, and sometimes to economic loss. The supply is usually restored in a few hours, so the economic loss is not very large. Such a hazard is regarded by most people as a thing they must put up with—without seeking compensation from anyone. Some there are who instal a stand-by sys-tem. Others seek refuge by taking out an insurance policy against breakdown in the supply. But most people are content to take the risk on themselves. . . .

[margin note:] + strong reason

> The third consideration is this: if claims for economic loss were permitted for this particular hazard, there would be no end of claims. Some might be genuine, but many might be inflated, or even false. . . . Rather than expose claimants to such temptation and defendants to such hard labour—on comparatively small claims—it is better to disallow economic loss altogether, at any rate when it stands alone, independent of any physical damage.

[margin note:] ② floodgates. general exclusion.

> The fourth consideration is that, in such a hazard as this, the risk of economic loss should be suffered by the whole community who suffer the losses—usually many but comparatively small losses—rather than on the one pair of shoulders, that is, on the contractor on whom the total of them, all added together, might be very heavy. . . .

[margin note:] ③ risk spreading.

> These considerations lead me to the conclusion that the plaintiffs should recover for the phys-ical damage to the one melt (£368), and the loss of profit on that melt consequent thereon (£400): but not for the loss of profit on the four melts (£1,767), because that was economic loss independent of the physical damage. I would, therefore, allow the appeal and reduce the damages to £768.

[margin note:] held.

In this case, it was found that even where a plaintiff is clearly owed a duty in respect of phys-ical damage to property, any 'pure' economic losses suffered in addition to physical damage are unrecoverable as either too remote, or outside the scope of the duty of care. These 'pure' economic losses are not consequent on damage to the plaintiff's property, but on damage to some other property (in this case, the cable) in which the plaintiff has no proprietary interest. Thus, these losses are an example of 'relational' economic loss. It will be seen that in this case, there were also *recoverable* economic losses, which were judged not to be 'purely' economic, but to be **consequential upon** the damage to the metal in the melt. Into this category fell the lost profits on the *damaged* metal.

It is clear that Lord Denning considered it best that *relational* economic losses should be covered by a general exclusionary rule. On the particular facts of *Spartan Steel*, one of the more persuasive of the reasons he offers is his fourth: it is better that a series of small losses should be spread across the community, rather than being concentrated on the shoulders of one party. But this reason does not apply to all cases of relational economic loss. It would not apply to *Cattle*, for example. Neither would it apply to *The Aliakmon* (below). Therefore, we should also note his second reason. Losing one's power supply is a fairly normal occurrence and most people take steps to deal with the risk that it will happen. They might do so through insurance, or through having an emergency generator. This is arguably the strongest reason in support of the category A exclusionary rule, because in order to encourage people (at least in a commercial setting) to take precautions before the event, it is best to have a clear rule: see further the discussion of the Canadian case law, below.

In *Candlewood v Mitsui (The Mineral Transporter)* [1986] AC 1, the Privy Council confirmed that the general exclusionary rule for relational losses survived the new approach to the duty of care set out in *Anns v Merton* [1978] AC 728 (discussed in Chapter 3.3 above). The Privy Council argued that the well-understood policy reasons behind the exclusionary rule were sufficient reason for its retention under the second limb of the *Anns* test, amounting to policy concerns that would justify negativing the duty of care.[15]

A long-standing exception to the rule is the case of *Morrison Steamship v Greystoke Castle* [1947] AC 265. A ship was damaged in a collision and had to put into port, discharging and reloading her cargo. The cargo owners became liable to the shipowners for 'general average contribution'. This refers to a means of pooling risk among cargo owners, by which they would have to pay a percentage of the costs of loading and reloading. It was held by the House of Lords that the cargo owners could claim against the defendant, whose negligence was partly to blame for the collision, even though their own property was not damaged. The House of Lords did not indicate that *Cattle v Stockton Waterworks* was in any way relevant to this case, citing only maritime authorities. In the course of their judgments, the House of Lords expressed the view that the plaintiff cargo owners were engaged in a 'common adventure' (Lord Roche) or 'joint adventure' (Lord Porter) with the shipowners. This idea has not been developed into a broader exception in English law, where it is regarded as confined to this special area of maritime law and the particular collusion of interests between the 'ship' and the 'cargo' (for further discussion see *The Nicholas H* [1996] AC 211, at 226–7, per Lord Lloyd of Berwick). But the idea of 'joint venture' has been used as the basis of a duty of care for relational economic loss in Canada (*Norsk Pacific*, below).

Leigh and Sillivan v Aliakmon Shipping Co Ltd [1986] AC 785 ('*The Aliakmon*')

In this case, the House of Lords refused to recognize a *limited* exception to the rule against recovery for relational economic loss. There was no prospect of indeterminate liability, and the case demonstrates a robust defence of the exclusionary rule in respect of relational economic loss.

Goods were damaged during shipment, through the negligence of charterers. Due to an unusual series of negotiations, the final contractual arrangements were not of a standard type. The end result was that the *risk of damage* had already passed to the plaintiffs on shipment, but *property* in the goods did not pass to the plaintiff until the goods were discharged and warehoused. The plaintiffs did not acquire any rights of suit in respect of damage done during shipment, their interest in the goods at that time being merely contractual. The sellers meanwhile had suffered no loss, so that they could not bring an action on their own account.

---

[15] *Candlewood v Mitsui* was an appeal from the Supreme Court of New South Wales. The exclusionary rule stated by the Privy Council has however been rejected in Australia: see the discussion of *Perre v Apand*, below.

This was an instance of property damage in respect of which neither buyer nor seller could bring an action, much to the benefit of the negligent party. On the other hand, the plaintiff buyers could argue that they were *prospectively* the legal owners of the damaged goods, a feature of their case that a sympathetic court might use to distinguish them from the unsuccessful plaintiffs in previous cases such as *Cattle v Stockton Waterworks*.

In the Court of Appeal, Robert Goff LJ suggested that this could be treated as a case of 'transferred loss'. Such cases, he argued, were in a special category to which the policy arguments against recovering relational losses did not apply. The concept is explained in the following extract.

Robert Goff LJ [1985] QB 350, at 399 (CA)

In my judgment, there is no good reason in principle or in policy, why the c. and f. buyer should not have . . . a direct cause of action. . . . I am particularly influenced by the fact that the loss in question is of a character which will ordinarily fall on the goods owner who will have a good claim against the shipowner, but in a case such as the present the loss may, in practical terms, fall on the buyer. It seems to me that the policy reasons pointing towards a direct right of action by the buyer against the shipowner in a case of this kind outweigh the policy reasons which generally preclude recovery for purely economic loss. There is here no question of any wide or indeterminate liability being imposed on wrongdoers; on the contrary, the shipowner is simply held liable to the buyer in damages for loss for which he would ordinarily be liable to the goods owner. There is a recognisable principle underlying the imposition of liability, which can be called the principle of transferred loss. Furthermore, that principle can be formulated. For the purposes of the present case, I would formulate it in the following deliberately narrow terms, while recognising that it may require modification in the light of experience. Where A owes a duty of care in tort not to cause physical damage to B's property, and commits a breach of that duty in circumstances in which the loss of or physical damage to the property will ordinarily fall on B but (as is reasonably foreseeable by A) such loss or damage, by reason of a contractual relationship between B and C, falls upon C, then C will be entitled, subject to the terms of any contract restricting A's liability to B, to bring an action in tort against A in respect of such loss or damage to the extent that it falls on him, C.

This suggested innovation was not accepted by other members of the Court of Appeal, and it was also rejected on appeal by the House of Lords. Lord Brandon said that he would, even if he felt there to be a pressing need for such a remedy, be too 'faint-hearted' to introduce it given that it was clearly, in his view, against the established authorities. He also emphasized the importance of certainty, which was protected by the existence of the general rule. But he clearly felt that there was no need for such an innovation:

Lord Brandon [1986] AC 785, at 818–19

. . . English law does, in all normal cases, provide a fair and adequate remedy for loss of or damage to goods the subject matter of a c.i.f. or c. and f. contract, and the buyers in this case could easily, if properly advised at the time when they agreed to the variation of the original c. and f. contract, have secured to themselves the benefit of such a remedy.

The exception proposed by Robert Goff LJ could not be said to create any excessive liability to defendants, since it would apply only to cases where the same loss which was foreseeably caused by damage to goods is transferred through the contractual structure, from the property owner, to a third party. Lord Brandon's reluctance to allow such a claim stems from a wish to protect the general rule for reasons unconnected with the specific parties.[16]

In more recent years, the House of Lords has been far from 'faint hearted' in this context (see category D below). In the House of Lords, Lord Goff later used a very similar argument to his proposed 'transferred loss' idea, in a case where intended beneficiaries sued a solicitor for depriving them of legacies under a will: *White v Jones* [1995] 2 AC 207. Clearly, *White v Jones* was not a case of 'relational' economic loss because there was no property damage, but given that the case did not involve reliance by the beneficiaries upon the solicitor and was not even a statements case, neither did it fit easily within the *Hedley Byrne* category of recoverable economic losses. Here, there is a jangling inconsistency between different categories of case law, though whether blame should fall on the exclusionary rule in *The Aliakmon*, or on the creative interpretation of the law in *White v Jones*, is a matter for debate. Alternatively, the problem in these cases may be said to lie with rigidity in the rules of contract law.

Some assistance in assessing the exclusionary rule can be gained from looking to other common law jurisdictions and their treatment of 'relational' economic loss. Of particular interest is the approach taken in Canada.

Canadian National Railway Co v Norsk Pacific Steamship Co (1992) 91 DLR (4th) 289 (Supreme Court of Canada)

The defendants damaged a railway bridge over the Fraser river. The bridge was owned by Public Works Canada and the plaintiff railway company was its principal user, accounting for 85–86 per cent of the traffic. The plaintiff suffered economic loss in rerouting its traffic while the bridge was being repaired, and brought the present action against the defendants to recover that loss. By a majority, the Supreme Court held in the plaintiff's favour.

We first extract the judgment of McLachlin J, for the majority. (Stevenson J delivered a separate and different judgment for the plaintiffs. L'Heureux–Dubé and Cory JJ agreed with McLachlin J.)

McLachlin J

49   In summary, it is my view that the authorities suggest that pure economic loss is prima facie recoverable where, in addition to negligence and foreseeable loss, there is sufficient proximity between the negligent act and the loss. Proximity is the controlling concept which avoids the spectre of unlimited liability. Proximity may be established by a variety of factors, depending on the nature of the case. To date, sufficient proximity has been found in the case of negligent misstatements where there is an undertaking and correlative reliance (*Hedley Byrne*); where there is a duty to warn (*Rivtow*); and where a statute imposes a responsibility on a municipality toward the owners and occupiers of land (*Kamloops*). But the categories are not closed. As more cases are decided, we can expect further definition on what factors give rise to liability for pure economic loss in particular categories of cases. In determining whether liability should be extended to a new situation, courts will have regard to the factors traditionally relevant to proximity, such as the relationship between the parties, physical propinquity, assumed or imposed obligations and close causal connection. And they will insist on sufficient

---

[16] Subsequently, the position has been reversed by legislation, giving a remedy to the buyers: s 2(1) Carriage of Goods by Sea Act 1992.

special factors to avoid the imposition of indeterminate and unreasonable liability. The result will be a principled, yet flexible, approach to tort liability for pure economic loss. It will allow recovery where recovery is justified, while excluding indeterminate and inappropriate liability, and it will permit the coherent development of the law in accordance with the approach initiated in England by *Hedley Byrne* and followed in Canada in *Rivtow, Kamloops* and *Hofstrand*.

(At 375–6)

(4) Application to this case

65 The plaintiff, CN, suffered economic loss as a result of being deprived of its contractual right to use the bridge damaged by the defendants' negligence. Applying the *Kamloops* approach, its right to recover depends on: (1) whether it can establish sufficient proximity or "closeness," and (2) whether extension of recovery to this type of loss is desirable from a practical point of view.

66 The first question is whether the evidence in this case establishes the proximity necessary to found liability. The case does not fall within any of the categories where proximity and liability have been hitherto found to exist. So we must consider the matter afresh. . . .

68 In addition to focusing upon the relationship between the appellant Norsk and CN—a significant indicator of proximity in and of itself—the trial judge based his conclusion that there was sufficient proximity on a number of factors related to CN's connection with the property damaged, the bridge, including the fact that CN's property was in close proximity to the bridge, that CN's property could not be enjoyed without the link of the bridge, which was an integral part of its railway system, and that CN supplied materials, inspection and consulting services for the bridge, was its preponderant user, and was recognized in the periodic negotiations surrounding the closing of the bridge.

69 MacGuigan J.A. summarized the trial judge's findings on proximity as follows, at p. 167 [F.C.]:

> In effect, the Trial Judge found that the CNR was so closely assimilated to the position of PWC that it was very much within the reasonable ambit of risk of the appellants at the time of the accident. That, it seems to me, is sufficient proximity: In Deane J.'s language, it is both physical and circumstantial closeness.

70 Such a characterization brings the situation into the "joint" or "common venture" category under which recovery for purely economic loss has heretofore been recognized in maritime law cases from the United Kingdom (*Greystoke Castle*) and the United States (*Amoco Transport*). The reasoning, as I apprehend it, is that where the plaintiff's operations are so closely allied to the opera tions of the party suffering physical damage and to its property (which—as damaged—causes the plaintiff's loss) that it can be considered a joint venturer with the owner of the property, the plaintiff can recover its economic loss even though the plaintiff has suffered no physical damage to its own property. To deny recovery in such circumstances would be to deny it to a person who for practical purposes is in the same position as if he or she owned the property physically damaged.

71 The second question is whether extension of recovery to this type of loss is desirable from a practical point of view. Recovery serves the purpose of permitting a plaintiff whose position for practical purposes, vis-à-vis the tortfeasor, is indistinguishable from that of the owner of the damaged property to recover what the actual owner could have recovered. This is fair and avoids an anomalous result. Nor does the recovery of economic loss in this case open the

floodgates to unlimited liability. The category is a limited one. It has been applied in England and the United States without apparent difficulty. It does not embrace casual users of the property or those secondarily and incidentally affected by the damage done to the property. Potential tortfeasors can gauge in advance the scope of their liability. Businesses are not precluded from self-insurance or from contracting for indemnity, nor are they "penalized" for not so doing. Finally, frivolous claims are not encouraged.

72 I conclude that here, as in *Kamloops*, the necessary duty and proximity are established; that valid purposes are served by permitting recovery; and that recovery will not open the floodgates to unlimited liability. In such circumstances, recovery should be permitted.

In a very full dissenting judgment, La Forest J objected that McLachlin J had not given appropriate emphasis to the specific exclusionary rule relating to relational economic loss. Instead, she had considered and rejected a *general* rule against recoverability of economic loss, and explained the *general* approach to identifying recoverable cases, in terms of proximity. There is, he argued, no such general rule.

La Forest J defined the case from the outset as raising the question of whether the exclusionary rule on *relational* economic loss was justified, and whether there were sound reasons to depart from it in this kind of case. The dominant consideration in a commercial setting such as this, he argued, was that the rules should 'place some incentive on both parties to act in an economically rational manner' (at 336). He made the following remarks in his conclusions:

At 355

. . . In making arrangements for allocating risks in essentially maritime matters, those engaged in navigating and shipping should, so far as possible, be governed by a uniform rule, so that they can plan their affairs ahead of time, whether by contract or insurance against possible contingencies.

In my view, to justify recovery in cases of this nature, the plaintiff would, at the very least, have to respond effectively not only to the concern about indeterminacy but also show that no adequate means of protection was available. . . .

La Forest J stated that the rule should be departed from only on compelling grounds and that this was not even a borderline case. It was not truly a joint venture, and was certainly not a case of transferred loss. The plaintiff was well aware of the risk of bridges being damaged, and ought to have taken steps to protect itself against losses in case this should occur. Finally, this sort of case did not raise issues of 'social justice', and practicality was the most important concern.

On the face of it, most of the disagreements between La Forest and McLachlin JJ relate to the substance of the policy considerations. But there is also a difference in the structure of their reasoning. With the majority approaching this case through a general analysis in terms of proximity, had the Supreme Court rejected the rule against liability for relational economic losses in particular?

If so, then the rejection was short-lived. In the case of *Bow Valley Husky v Saint John Shipbuilding Ltd* [1997] 3 SCR 1210, McLachlin J managed to 'meld' her own approach with that of La Forest J in a judgment with which the latter agreed. This judgment resembled La Forest's approach in that it stated the *specific* exclusionary rule relating to relational economic loss at the outset. It then outlined three very limited exceptions to that rule, and stated that any further exceptions should be justified on policy grounds. On the facts of that case, there was no joint venture, and no compelling reason for departing from the exclusionary rule:

McLachlin J, *Bow Valley Husky v Saint John Shipbuilding* [1997] 3 SCR 1210

48 Despite [our] difference in approach [in *Norsk Pacific*], La Forest J. and I agreed on several important propositions: (1) relational economic loss is recoverable only in special circumstances where the appropriate conditions are met; (2) these circumstances can be defined by reference to categories, which will make the law generally predictable; (3) the categories are not closed. La Forest J. identified the categories of recovery of relational economic loss defined to date as: (1) cases where the claimant has a possessory or proprietary interest in the damaged property; (2) general average cases; and (3) cases where the relationship between the claimant and property owner constitutes a joint venture.

49 The case at bar does not fall into any of the above three categories. The plaintiffs here had no possessory or proprietary interest in the rig and the case is not one of general averaging. While related contractually, the Court of Appeal correctly held that the plaintiff and the property owner cannot, on any view of the term, be viewed as joint venturers.

50 However, that is not the end of the matter. The categories of recoverable contractual relational economic loss in tort are not closed. Where a case does not fall within a recognized category the court may go on to consider whether the situation is one where the right to recover contractual relational economic loss should nevertheless be recognized. This is in accordance with *Norsk, per* La Forest J., at p. 1134:

> Thus I do not say that the right to recovery in all cases of contractual relational economic loss depends exclusively on the terms of the contract. Rather, I note that such is the tenor of the exclusionary rule and that *departures from that rule should be justified on defensible policy grounds.* [Emphasis added.]

More particularly, La Forest J. suggested that the general rule against recovery for policy-based reasons might be relaxed where the deterrent effect of potential liability to the property owner is low, or, despite a degree of indeterminate liability, where the claimant's opportunity to allocate the risk by contract is slight, either because of the type of transaction or an inequality of bargaining power. I agreed with La Forest J. that policy considerations relating to increased costs of processing claims and contractual allocation of the risk are important (p. 1164). I concluded that the test for recovery "should be flexible enough to meet the complexities of commercial reality and to permit the recognition of new situations in which liability ought, in justice, to lie as such situations arise" (p. 1166). It thus appears that new categories of recoverable contractual relational economic loss may be recognized where justified by policy considerations and required by justice. At the same time, courts should not assiduously seek new categories; what is required is a clear rule predicting when recovery is available.

With *Bow Valley Husky*, it is clear that Canadian law recognizes a policy-based rule against recovery of relational economic loss in particular. Although Canadian law is more receptive to exceptions to this rule than English law has been, it is clear from the new 'melded' approach above that the intention is to recognize only clear *categories* of exception, rejecting an excessively 'case by case' approach as unworkable.

In Australia, relational economic loss was accepted as capable of giving rise to a duty of care in the case of *Caltex Oil v The Dredge 'Willemstad'* (1976) 136 CLR 529. There, the defendant had damaged a pipeline carrying oil, and was held to owe a duty of care to the plaintiff who depended upon the supply of oil through the pipeline. *Caltex Oil* was rejected by the Privy Council in *Candlewood v Mitsui* (above), but it is clearly *Caltex* and not *Candlewood v Mitsui* that is taken to represent Australian law on relational economic loss.

In *Perre v Apand* (1999) 198 CLR 180, the High Court set out a diversity of approaches to the case in hand but it was common ground that many factors will be relevant to establishing a duty of care where economic loss is concerned. Particularly relevant factors would be knowledge on the part of the defendant; the existence of an ascertainable class of plaintiffs; and 'vulnerability' to loss. The idea of 'vulnerability' focuses upon other reasonable avenues of protection that may be open to the plaintiff. Also relevant would be the likely impact of any finding of liability. The relevant factors appear to be intended for application to *all* cases of economic loss, and not specifically to cases of relational economic loss. In *Perre v Apand*, the High Court also reaffirmed its earlier rejection of 'proximity' as providing a test for the existence of a duty of care (*Hill v Van Erp* (1999) 188 CLR 159; S. Yeo, 'Rethinking Proximity: A Paper Tiger?' (1997) *Tort L Rev* 174–80; see later a definitive statement in *Sullivan v Moody* (2001) 207 CLR 562, 578–9).

As such, the High Court of Australia has now rejected *Anns v Merton*, *Caparo v Dickman*, proximity, and any exclusionary rule, as the basis for approaching cases of liability for economic loss, and replaced all these with a 'multi-factoral' approach. However, it was accepted by the High Court in *Perre v Apand* that 'incremental' (gradual) development is therefore essential in order to provide some guidance on likely future outcomes. It seems inevitable that categorization will be an *effect* of the multi-factoral approach. In the meantime, courts will need to 'hug the coast' of established principle, 'avoiding the open sea of system or science' (McHugh J at para 93, referring to Lord Wright, 'The Study of Law' (1938) 54 LQR 185, 186) in order to develop the law on a case by case basis.

Whichever jurisdiction might be judged to have the better approach, the following general remarks on the difference between Australian, Canadian, and English approaches to *relational* economic loss provide us with a helpful summary of cases in this category:

B. Feldthusen, 'Pure Economic Loss in the High Court of Australia: Reinventing the Square Wheel?' (2000) *Tort L Rev* 33, 46

Experience in other jurisdictions suggests that some form of an exclusionary rule for relational loss works best to address relevant policy concerns and to guide prospective litigants before an accident occurs. . . . Such a rule applies only to relational losses and need have no bearing on other types of economic loss cases. The form of the rule can be strict, as in England. Or it might be thought worthwhile to commit judicial resources to developing rational exceptions that themselves can be recognised prior to the accident, as in Canada. What experience has taught courts elsewhere is that attempts to develop less restrictive general rules for relational loss may 'work' in a given case, but invariably prove unsatisfactory in others. Nor do they tend to be any less arbitrary, or any more just, than the exclusionary rule that they attempt to replace. This, I predict, will prove true of the principles that govern recoverability in *Perre v Apand*—knowledge, ascertainable class and vulnerability.

We can defend the exclusion of liability for relational losses, as requiring few judicial resources and giving rise to no less workable rules than the exclusionary rule with predictable exceptions (the Canadian approach). We will have a much harder time explaining the rest of the English approach to economic losses, below.

2.2 ECONOMIC LOSSES CAUSED BY ACQUIRING DEFECTIVE PRODUCTS OR PREMISES (CATEGORY B)

In *Anns v Merton LBC*, as we saw in Chapter 3.3 above, the House of Lords held that a local authority may owe a duty of care in negligence in exercise of its powers of inspection under the Public Health Act 1936. The judgment was dominated by the interplay between statutory powers and common law duties (as to which, see the discussion in the next section of this chapter). Relatively little attention was paid to the definition of the *loss* suffered by the disappointed purchasers. Lord Wilberforce clearly thought that the loss was not purely economic:

Lord Wilberforce, *Anns v Merton LBC* [1978] AC 728, at 759

. . . The damages recoverable include all those which foreseeably arise from the breach of the duty of care which, as regards the council, I have held to be a duty to take reasonable care to secure compliance with the byelaws. Subject always to adequate proof of causation, these damages may include damages for personal injury and damage to property. In my opinion they may also include damage to the dwelling house itself; for the whole purpose of the byelaws in requiring foundations to be of a certain standard is to prevent damage arising from weakness of the foundations which is certain to endanger the health or safety of occupants.

To allow recovery for such damage to the house follows, in my opinion, from normal principle. If classification is required, the relevant damage is in my opinion material, physical damage, and what is recoverable is the amount of expenditure necessary to restore the dwelling to a condition in which it is no longer a danger to the health or safety of persons occupying and possibly (depending on the circumstances) expenses arising from necessary displacement.

As a matter of 'classification', Lord Wilberforce was mistaken. The damage suffered was economic loss. No separate 'damage' had been done to property of the plaintiffs, other than the building itself, by the defendants' alleged breach of duty. Eleven years later in the case next extracted, the House of Lords seized upon this error. But did this case set the law on another wrong turning by exaggerating the importance of the type of loss?

D and F Estates v Church Commissioners [1989] AC 177 ~~HL~~

The defendants were employed in the construction of a block of flats. The plaster-work was carried out by sub-contractors who were not parties to the action. The plaintiffs were lessees of a flat in the block. In the fullness of time, it was discovered that some of the plaster was loose. Some of it fell down. The plaintiffs brought an action in negligence claiming the cost of stripping and replacing the plaster, and a number of other items including loss of rent, cleaning of carpets, and damage to possessions in the flat. The judge at first instance held that the plaster had been incorrectly applied and that the defendants were in breach of duty. An appeal by the defendants was successful, and the House of Lords dismissed a further appeal by the plaintiffs. The damage amounted to irrecoverable economic loss falling outside the ambit of ~~no duty.~~ *Donoghue v Stevenson*.

What were the reasons for suggesting that this kind of economic loss can give rise to no liability in tort? The logic in *D and F Estates* (and also in *Murphy v Brentwood*, below) is that a builder is like the manufacturer of any other product. The builder may owe duties in contract or in tort. Contract duties are generally owed only to those who are parties to the contract (see our discussion of *Donoghue v Stevenson*, Chapter 3.3 above). (This latter point, concerning contract, must now be qualified by some fundamental recent developments in respect of privity, which are discussed briefly in respect of category D cases, below.) First and subsequent purchasers who wished to benefit from contractual terms should negotiate to secure such protection. Tort duties on the other hand may be owed to ultimate consumers of a product even though these consumers do not contract with the manufacturer, as we saw in respect of *Donoghue* itself.

According to the House of Lords in *D and F Estates*, and later in *Murphy*, tort duties under *Donogue v Stevenson* are only owed in respect of *damage done* by the item that is manufactured by the defendant. To go further than this, and to hold that the defendant is liable for repair costs or loss of investment in the property itself, would be (as Lord Bridge put it) 'to impose upon [the contractor] for the benefit of those with whom he had no contractual relationship the obligation of one who warranted the quality of the plaster as regards materials, workmanship and fitness for purpose' (at 207). A warranty, it is argued, will be available *free of charge*, and *for the benefit of non-contracting parties*, if a duty of care in tort is recognized in respect of losses of this nature. This justification for denying the duty of care is specific to losses arising from defects in quality. Although the cases concerning defective premises have been controversial, the same analysis has been applied to defective products, where recovery in tort is limited to damage done to separate property or to the person.[17]

Where did this leave *Anns*?

D and F Estates was not the appropriate case in which to depart from *Anns*. It did not involve the foundations of a building, but only faulty plastering. There was no question of damage to the structure itself. Did the decision in *D and F Estates* nevertheless make the later departure in *Murphy v Brentwood* inevitable?

Lord Bridge attempted to point out a way in which *Anns* itself could be salvaged. This was the 'complex structure theory'. Lord Bridge's comments were offered as a means of bringing *Anns v Merton* within the ambit of *Donoghue v Stevenson* liability, by suggesting that in the case of a complex structure (or even chattel) such as a house, a defect in one part of the property could be seen as causing damage to a 'separate' piece of property. The larger structure would then be treated as a separate item. For example, a defect in foundations could conceivably, on this approach, be said to cause damage to other property if it leads to cracks in walls and floors. But this could not be extended to the defective plaster. This 'theory' (which was really only a suggestion) was considered and rejected by the House of Lords in *Murphy*. *Anns* was beyond salvation by these means. However, the rejection of this theory came with qualifications, leaving some uncertainty in the law.

Murphy v Brentwood DC [1991] 1 AC 398

Two houses, constructed on landfill, required a concrete raft foundation. The plans for the raft were submitted to Brentwood District Council for approval, pursuant to its duty under section 64 of the Public Health Act 1936. Having no suitably qualified staff of its own, Brentwood District Council referred the plans to qualified structural engineers. Their report was favourable, and the plans were duly passed. As it turned out, there were errors in the design of

---

[17] See for example *Muirhead v Industrial Tank Specialities* [1985] 3 All ER 705.

the foundations which were not spotted by the engineers consulted by the Council, and as a result the foundations as constructed were faulty.

The foundations cracked and there was damage to the walls and pipes of the house. The plaintiff could not raise the entire repair costs (£45,000) from his insurer. Instead he sold the house for £35,000 less than its market value if sound. (Incidentally, he recovered from his insurer the sum of £35,000 in respect of a claim for subsidence damage.) A first instance judge awarded the plaintiff £38,777 in respect of diminution in the value of the house, and expenses incurred as a result of damage to it. The Court of Appeal dismissed an appeal by the Council.

On appeal to the House of Lords, a specially constituted panel of seven judges invoked the practice statement of 26 July 1966 (*Practice Statement (Judicial Precedent)* [1966] 1 WLR 1234), and departed from its previous decision in *Anns v Merton*. This technique is equivalent to overruling the earlier decision (see J. W. Harris, 'And *Murphy* Makes It Eight—Overruling Comes to Negligence' (1991) 11 OJLS 416–30).

Lord Keith of Kinkel, at 466–7

In my opinion it must now be recognised that, although the damage in *Anns* was characterised as physical damage by Lord Wilberforce, it was purely economic loss. In *Council of the Shire of Sutherland v. Heyman*, 157 C.L.R. 424 where, as observed above, the High Court of Australia declined to follow *Anns* when dealing with a claim against a local authority in respect of a defectively constructed house, Deane J. said, at pp. 503–505:

> "Nor is the respondents' claim in the present case for ordinary physical damage to themselves or their property. Their claim, as now crystallized, is not in respect of damage to the fabric of the house or to other property caused by collapse or subsidence of the house as a result of the inadequate foundations. It is for the loss or damage represented by the actual inadequacy of the foundations, that is to say, it is for the cost of remedying a structural defect in their property which already existed at the time when they acquired it. . . . "

Lord Keith quoted at greater length from *Sutherland Shire Council*, and continued (at 468):

It being recognised that the nature of the loss held to be recoverable in *Anns* was pure economic loss, the next point for examination is whether the avoidance of loss of that nature fell within the scope of any duty of care owed to the plaintiffs by the local authority. On the basis of the law as it stood at the time of the decision the answer to that question must be in the negative. The right to recover for pure economic loss, not flowing from physical injury, did not then extend beyond the situation where the loss had been sustained through reliance on negligent mis-statements, as in *Hedley Byrne*. There is room for the view that an exception is to be found in *Morrison Steamship Co. Ltd. v. Greystoke Castle (Cargo Owners)* [1947] A.C. 265. That case, which was decided by a narrow majority, may, however, be regarded as turning on specialties of maritime law concerned in the relationship of joint adventurers at sea. Further, though the purposes of the Act of 1936 as regards securing compliance with building byelaws covered the avoidance of injury to the safety or health of inhabitants of houses and of members of the public generally, these purposes did not cover the avoidance of pure economic loss to owners of buildings: see *Governors of the Peabody Donation Fund v. Sir Lindsay Parkinson & Co. Ltd.* [1985] A.C. 210, 241. Upon analysis, the nature of the duty held by *Anns* to be incumbent upon the local authority went very much further than a duty to take reasonable care to prevent injury to safety or health. The duty held to exist may be formulated as one to take reasonable care to avoid putting a future inhabitant owner of a house in a position in which he is threatened, by reason of a defect in the house, with avoidable physical injury to person or health and is obliged, in order to continue to occupy the house without suffering such injury, to expend money for the purpose of rectifying the defect.

The existence of a duty of that nature should not, in my opinion, be affirmed without a careful examination of the implications of such affirmation. To start with, if such a duty is incumbent upon the local authority, a similar duty must necessarily be incumbent also upon the builder of the house. If the builder of the house is to be so subject, there can be no grounds in logic or in principle for not extending liability upon like grounds to the manufacturer of a chattel. That would open up an exceedingly wide field of claims, involving the introduction of something in the nature of a transmissible warranty of quality. The purchaser of an article who discovered that it suffered from a dangerous defect before that defect had caused any damage would be entitled to recover from the manufacturer the cost of rectifying the defect, and presumably, if the article was not capable of economic repair, the amount of loss sustained through discarding it. Then it would be open to question whether there should not also be a right to recovery where the defect renders the article not dangerous but merely useless. The economic loss in either case would be the same. There would also be a problem where the defect causes the destruction of the article itself, without causing any personal injury or damage to other property. A similar problem could arise, if the *Anns* principle is to be treated as confined to real property, where a building collapses when unoccupied.

(At 471)

In my opinion it is clear that *Anns* did not proceed upon any basis of established principle, but introduced a new species of liability governed by a principle indeterminate in character but having the potentiality of covering a wide range of situations, involving chattels as well as real property, in which it had never hitherto been thought that the law of negligence had any proper place.

Lord Bridge of Harwich, at 476–9

The complex structure theory

In my speech in *D. & F. Estates* [1989] A.C. 177, 206G–207H I mooted the possibility that in complex structures or complex chattels one part of a structure or chattel might, when it caused damage to another part of the same structure or chattel, be regarded in the law of tort as having caused damage to "other property" for the purpose of the application of *Donoghue v. Stevenson* principles. I expressed no opinion as to the validity of this theory, but put it forward for consideration as a possible ground on which the facts considered in *Anns* [1978] A.C. 728 might be distinguishable from the facts which had to be considered in *D. & F. Estates* itself. I shall call this for convenience "the complex structure theory" . . .

. . . The reality is that the structural elements in any building form a single indivisible unit of which the different parts are essentially interdependent. To the extent that there is any defect in one part of the structure it must to a greater or lesser degree necessarily affect all other parts of the structure. Therefore any defect in the structure is a defect in the quality of the whole and it is quite artificial, in order to impose a legal liability which the law would not otherwise impose, to treat a defect in an integral structure, so far as it weakens the structure, as a dangerous defect liable to cause damage to "other property."

A critical distinction must be drawn here between some part of a complex structure which is said to be a "danger" only because it does not perform its proper function in sustaining the other parts and some distinct item incorporated in the structure which positively malfunctions so as to inflict positive damage on the structure in which it is incorporated. Thus, if a defective central heating boiler explodes and damages a house or a defective electrical installation malfunctions and sets the house on fire, I see no reason to doubt that the owner of the house, if he can prove that the damage was due to the negligence of the boiler manufacturer in the one case or the electrical contractor on the other, can recover damages in tort on *Donoghue v. Stevenson* [1932] A.C. 562 principles. But the position in law is entirely different where, by reason of the inadequacy of the foundations of the building to support the weight of the superstructure, differential settlement and consequent cracking occurs. Here, once the first cracks appear, the structure as a whole is seen to be defective and the nature of the defect is known. Even if, contrary to my view, the initial damage could be regarded as damage to other property caused by a latent defect, once the defect is known the situation of the building owner is analogous to that of the car owner who discovers that the car has faulty brakes. He may have a house which, until repairs are effected, is unfit for habitation, but, subject to the reservation I have expressed with respect to ruinous buildings at or near the boundary of the owner's property, the building no longer represents a source of danger and as it deteriorates will only damage itself.

For these reasons the complex structure theory offers no escape from the conclusion that damage to a house itself which is attributable to a defect in the structure of the house is not recoverable in tort on *Donoghue v. Stevenson* principles, but represents purely economic loss which is only recoverable in contract or in tort by reason of some special relationship of proximity which imposes on the tortfeasor a duty of care to protect against economic loss.

Lord Oliver of Aylmerton, at 485–7

The fact is that the categorisation of the damage in *Anns* as "material, physical damage," whilst, at first sight, lending to the decision some colour of consistency with the principle of *Donoghue v. Stevenson* [1932] A.C. 562, has served to obscure not only the true nature of the claim but, as a result, the nature and scope of the duty upon the breach of which the plaintiffs in that case were compelled to rely.

It does not, of course, at all follow as a matter of necessity from the mere fact that the only damage suffered by a plaintiff in an action for the tort of negligence is pecuniary or "economic" that his claim is bound to fail. It is true that, in an uninterrupted line of cases since 1875, it has consistently been held that a third party cannot successfully sue in tort for the interference with his economic expectations or advantage resulting from injury to the person or property of another person with whom he has or is likely to have a contractual relationship: see *Cattle v. Stockton Waterworks Co.* (1875) L.R. 10 Q.B. 453; *Simpson & Co. v. Thomson* (1877) 3 App.Cas. 279; *Société Anonyme de Remorquage à Hèlice v. Bennetts* [1911] 1 K.B. 243. That principle was applied more recently by Widgery J. in *Weller & Co. v. Foot and Mouth Disease Research Institute* [1966] 1 Q.B. 569 and received its most recent reiteration in the decision of this House in *Leigh and Sullavan Ltd. v. Aliakmon Shipping Co. Ltd.* [1986] A.C. 785. But it is far from clear from these decisions that the reason for the plaintiff's failure was simply that the only loss sustained was "economic." Rather they seem to have been based either upon the remoteness of the damage as a matter of direct causation or, more probably, upon the "floodgates" argument of the impossibility of containing liability within any acceptable bounds if the law were to permit such claims to succeed. The decision of this House in *Morrison Steamship Co. Ltd. v. Greystoke Castle (Cargo Owners)* [1947] A.C. 265 demonstrates that the mere fact that the primary damage suffered by a plaintiff is pecuniary is no necessary bar to an action in negligence given the proper circumstances—in that case, what was said to be the "joint venture" interest of shipowners and the owners of cargo carried on board—and if the matter remained in doubt that doubt was conclusively resolved by the decision of this House in *Hedley Byrne & Co. Ltd. v. Heller & Partners Ltd.* [1964] A.C. 465 where Lord Devlin, at p. 517, convincingly demonstrated the illogicality of a distinction between financial loss caused directly and financial loss resulting from physical injury to personal property.

The critical question, as was pointed out in the analysis of Brennan J. in his judgment in *Council of the Shire of Sutherland v. Heyman*, 157 C.L.R. 424, is not the nature of the damage in itself, whether physical or pecuniary, but whether the scope of the duty of care in the circumstances of the case is such as to embrace damage of the kind which the plaintiff claims to have sustained: see *Caparo Industries Plc. v. Dickman* [1990] 2 A.C. 605. The essential question which has to be asked in every case, given that damage which is the essential ingredient of the action has occurred, is whether the relationship between the plaintiff and the defendant is such—or, to use the favoured expression, whether it is of sufficient "proximity"—that it imposes upon the latter a duty to take care to avoid or prevent that loss which has in fact been sustained. That the requisite degree of proximity may be established in circumstances in which the plaintiff's injury results from his reliance upon a statement or advice upon which he was entitled to rely and upon which it was contemplated that he would be likely to rely is clear from *Hedley Byrne* and subsequent cases, but *Anns* [1978] A.C. 728 was not such a case and neither is the instant case. It is not, however, necessarily to be assumed that the reliance cases form the only possible category of cases in which a duty to take reasonable care to avoid or prevent pecuniary loss can arise. *Morrison Steamship Co. Ltd. v. Greystoke Castle (Cargo Owners)*, for instance, clearly was not a reliance case. Nor indeed was *Ross v. Caunters* [1980] Ch. 297 so far as the disappointed beneficiary was concerned. . . .

Lord Oliver referred to the decision in *Spartan Steel v Martin* and the attempt to draw the line between recoverable and unrecoverable losses, and continued:

I frankly doubt whether, in searching for such limits, the categorisation of the damage as "material," "physical," "pecuniary" or "economic" provides a particularly useful contribution. Where it does, I think, serve a useful purpose is in identifying those cases in which it is necessary to search for and find something more than the mere reasonable foreseeability of damage which has occurred as providing the degree of "proximity" necessary to support the action. In his classical exposition in *Donoghue v. Stevenson* [1932] A.C. 562, 580–581, Lord Atkin was expressing himself in the context of the infliction of direct physical injury resulting from a carelessly created latent defect in a manufactured product. In his analysis of the duty in those circumstances he clearly equated "proximity" with the reasonable foresight of damage. In the straightforward case of the direct infliction of physical injury by the act of the plaintiff there is, indeed, no need to look beyond the foreseeability by the defendant of the result in order to establish that he is in a "proximate" relationship with the plaintiff. But, as was pointed out by Lord Diplock in *Dorset Yacht Co. Ltd. v. Home Office* [1970] A.C. 1004, 1060, Lord Atkin's test, though a useful guide to characteristics which will be found to exist in conduct and relationships giving rise to a legal duty of care, is manifestly false if misused as a universal; and Lord Reid, in the course of his speech in the same case, recognised that the statement of principle enshrined in that test necessarily required qualification in cases where the only loss caused by the defendant's conduct was economic. The infliction of physical injury to the person or property of another universally requires to be justified. The causing of economic loss does not. If it is to be categorised as wrongful it is necessary to find some factor beyond the mere occurrence of the loss and the fact that its occurrence could be foreseen. Thus the categorisation of damage as economic serves at least the useful purpose of indicating that something more is required and it is one of the unfortunate features of *Anns* that it resulted initially in this essential distinction being lost sight of.

Commentary and Appraisal

Murphy was described by Richard O'Dair as 'a deeply disappointing decision both in relation to the substantive law on defective premises and in its implications for the judicial process' ((1991) 54 MLR 561, 570). We will need to be clear about what *Murphy* decided, and why it has been widely rejected in other common law jurisdictions.

On the whole, the judgments in *Murphy* do not set out (and certainly do not seek to justify) a *general* exclusionary rule for recovery of economic losses. Lord Keith's judgment comes the closest in stating that, at the time of the decision in *Anns*, liability for pure economic losses did not extend beyond the ambit of *Hedley Byrne* liability (category C). Even so, Lord Keith went on to state a *specific* justification for the exclusion of liability in 'defective product' cases, such as this one. Lord Oliver referred to several different categories of economic loss case and explained that the *Hedley Byrne* category was not necessarily the only one in which such losses might be recoverable. Indeed, he pointed out that the only clear exclusionary rule related to 'relational economic loss' (which we have already considered), and doubted whether definition of the loss as 'pecuniary' or 'economic' was of particularly great assistance, except in identifying those cases where 'something more' is required, over and above mere foreseeability. As we noted in the introduction to this section, cases of pure economic loss are by no means the only cases in which 'something more' is required.

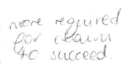

more required for claim to succeed.

Complex Structures and the Separate Damage Requirement

Their Lordships were united in dismissing the complex structure theory as a means of saving *Anns*. It was not possible in this case to treat the foundations as a separate structure from the house. On the other hand, their Lordships thought that in cases where some entirely independent component went wrong, it might be possible to bring the case within the ambit of *Donoghue v Stevenson*. There were variations in the approach to when this might be the case. Lord Bridge distinguished between foundations (an integral part of the larger structure), and a central heating boiler (a 'distinct item'). Lord Keith argued that components could not realistically be seen as separate property if the entire house was provided by a single contractor. Lord Jauncey (at 497) also clearly stated that certain 'integral' components could be treated as 'separate property' only if they were installed by a separate contractor. He seems to have thought however that these 'integral components' could be distinguished from the examples of the central heating boiler or electrical installations, which he described as 'ancillary equipment'. This illustrates that the potential exists for quite complex argument about the application of *Murphy*.[18]

On the other hand in *Bellefield Computers v Turner* [2000] BLR 97, it proved that the *Murphy* approach was too clear to be evaded despite reservations on the part of the Court of Appeal. A fire broke out in the claimants' premises, damaging the premises themselves and some of their contents. On the assumed facts, the builders had not complied with building

---

[18] In *Jacobs v Morton* 1994 72 BLR 92, a concrete raft was added to foundations as part of repair work. In all the circumstances, the raft (added later, by a different contractor) was separate property. If it was defective, a duty may be owed in respect of damage to the house as a whole.

regulations in respect of a fire wall which would, if properly constructed, have prevented the fire from spreading. There was no claim for damage to the wall itself. The Court of Appeal concluded reluctantly that any claim for damage to the building itself was ruled out by the decision in *Murphy v Brentwood*, although the court clearly thought it artificial to describe the loss as 'purely economic' where there had in fact been fire damage to the premises. It was concluded that *Murphy* left no room for manoeuvre in a case, such as this, where the 'fire wall' was provided at the same time, and by the same contractors, as the rest of the building. Schiemann LJ described the conclusion as 'odd' and perceived it as arising from a policy decision, to impose control devices over the liability to subsequent purchasers of a building. The legally 'correct' definition of the loss was found on the facts to be counter-intuitive, and as justified by policy rather than logic. Nevertheless, the *Murphy* approach was regarded as allowing for no variation in such a case.

Latency of Defect

It is clear from their Lordships' judgments in *Murphy* that even in the case of defects that cause actual damage to a separate structure or indeed to the person, there will be liability only if the damage is caused by a defect that remains 'latent'. Once the defect becomes known, then the defect 'no longer poses a danger'. (Lord Bridge conceded that a danger may remain if the property is close to the boundary of a neighbour's land, and suggested that the occupier may perhaps be able to recover for the costs of avoiding such dangers.) This was sound enough reasoning in respect of defective plaster (*D and F Estates*) but is an over-simplification when applied to more structural defects. A defect will 'no longer pose a danger' *only* if the owner or occupier of the premises is reasonably able to do something to prevent the danger. This may depend upon financing costly repairs, or it may mean moving house or premises (itself a costly undertaking). The truth is that knowledge of the defect does not *per se* remove the danger associated with it. Rather, the law chooses to treat defects that are 'patent' as the responsibility of the occupier, together with associated costs. This is not an exercise in logic.

Targett v Torfaen BC (1992) HLR 164 illustrates this. The claimant suffered physical injury when a handrail gave way on a staircase. The defendant council was landlord of the premises of which the claimant was a tenant. The council had also designed and built the premises. Because the claimant was aware of the defect in the handrail, it was suggested for the defendants that the claim was ruled out under *Murphy v Brentwood* as it was caused by a 'patent defect'. This would mean that *Murphy* had, by implication, overruled the decision in *Rimmer v Liverpool City Council* [1985] QB 1 (defining the duty owed by a landlord who had designed or built the premises: see Chapter 12.2 below). Russell LJ argued that *Murphy* was simply irrelevant to such a case, since a weekly tenant is 'in a very different position from an owner of a house defectively constructed who discovers the defect thereby rendering it no longer a latent defect'. Sir Donald Nicholls V-C expressed himself more broadly. While acknowledging the reasoning in *Murphy* by which knowledge of a defect renders that defect no longer dangerous, he added that:

Sir Donald Nicholls V-C

. . . knowledge of the existence of a danger does not always enable a person to avoid the danger. In simple cases it does. In other cases, especially where buildings are concerned, it would be absurdly unrealistic to suggest that a person can always take steps to avoid a danger once he knows of its existence, and that if he does not do so he is the author of his own misfortune. Here, as elsewhere, the law seeks to be realistic.

Taken seriously, this approach would make the latent/patent distinction a matter not only of knowledge but also of the availability of reasonable steps to avoid danger. This could have implications not only for tenants but for the owners of defective premises also. There has not, however, been a reopening of this issue subsequent to *Targett*.[19]

The Wider Picture: The Role of Policy

In *Murphy v Brentwood*, their Lordships unanimously rejected the idea that policy and justice required a remedy at common law. Relatively little space was devoted to the policy arguments, and the judgments were chiefly presented as confirming a definitional error into which *Anns* had fallen. The majority of commentators have thought that this was a misleading presentation of their Lordships' decision in *Murphy*.

Sir Robin Cooke (1991) 107 LQR 46, at 57

... the majority speeches in *Donoghue v Stevenson* were patently not meant to close the categories of liability in negligence, so the decision in that great case could certainly not be said to require the decisions now reached in *D and F Estates*, *Murphy*, and *Thomas Bates*. Analytically it was open to the House of Lords in those recent cases to decline to take further the ideas which won the day in *Donoghue v Stevenson*. But, analytically, it was just as open to the House as constituted in the *Anns* and *Dorset Yacht* cases to take the more expansive approach. (I avoid the word "liberal" in this context as being emotive.) The choice was a policy one.

The truth of this cannot now be denied. In *Invercargill City Council v Hamlin* [1996] AC 624, an appeal from the Court of Appeal of New Zealand,[20] it was found by the Privy Council to be appropriate for New Zealand law to continue to develop in a direction influenced both by *Anns* and by the prior New Zealand decision in *Bowen v Paramount Builders* [1977] 1 NZLR 394, even though this was inconsistent with *Murphy*. The New Zealand approach was partly determined by the New Zealand courts' reading of social conditions in that jurisdiction and therefore involved no error of law, even though it could justly be said that the decisions in *Dutton v Bognor Regis UDC* [1972] 1 QB 373 and *Anns v Merton* amounted to a 'wrong turning' for *English* law.

Invercargill CC v Hamlin [1996] 1 AC 624

Lord Lloyd of Berwick (giving the judgment of the Board), at 642–3

In truth, the explanation for divergent views in different common law jurisdictions (or within different jurisdictions of the United States of America) is not far to seek. The decision whether to hold a local authority liable for the negligence of a building inspector is bound to be based at least in part on policy considerations. . . .

---

[19] Though in *Nitrigin Eireann Teoranta v Inco Alloys Ltd* [1992] 1 WLR 498, May J was reluctant to categorize a defect as 'patent' even though there had been awareness of cracks in the product (a factory pipe): he reasoned that since the plaintiff had taken reasonable steps to investigate the cause of the cracks, the true defect remained 'latent' and a claim was not ruled out by *Murphy*.

[20] At the time of the *Invercargill* litigation, the Judicial Board of the Privy Council was the final appellate authority for New Zealand. This is no longer the case since the creation of a New Zealand Supreme Court.

> In a succession of cases in New Zealand over the last 20 years it has been decided that community standards and expectations demand the imposition of a duty of care on local authorities and builders alike to ensure compliance with local byelaws. New Zealand judges are in a much better position to decide on such matters than the Board. Whether circumstances are in fact so very different in England and New Zealand may not matter greatly. What matters is the perception. Both Richardson and McKay JJ. [1994] 3 N.Z.L.R. 513, 528, 546 in their judgments in the court below stress that to change New Zealand law so as to make it comply with *Murphy's* case [1991] 1 A.C. 398 would have "significant community implications" and would require a "major attitudinal shift." It would be rash for the Board to ignore those views.

Lord Lloyd went on to discuss the absence, in New Zealand, of a statute similar to the Defective Premises Act 1972, as one important difference between the two jurisdictions.

Murphy v Brentwood: Relevant Policy Factors

What then were the policy arguments which influenced the House of Lords in *Murphy*? First, their Lordships noted that *Anns* had instigated an entirely novel form of liability (or rather, it had confirmed a novel form of liability introduced when the Court of Appeal decided *Dutton v Bognor Regis* [1972] 1 QB 373 six years previously). The introduction of novel forms of liability was best left to Parliament.

Second, in respect of local authorities in particular, it was noted that the majority of English cases on defective premises were fought between insurance companies—*Murphy* itself included. It was not obvious that drawing on the insurance policies of local authorities (thereby tending to increase their insurance premiums) was preferable to leaving the job to first party insurance (by which the homeowner takes out insurance to cover defects in their home). This is, in part, an argument that the consumer is already adequately protected by alternative means, which is one of the main policy reasons isolated by Jane Stapleton in her influential article 'Duty of Care and Economic Loss' (1991) 107 LQR 249. It is also similar to the Australian focus on 'vulnerability': *Perre v Apand*, above. This point can be amplified into an argument that purchasers *can* in some circumstances seek alternative protection, in which case they are not to be regarded as vulnerable. The first purchaser of a property, for example, may be able to negotiate contractual terms which could include a 'transmissible' warranty— that is to say, a warranty that may operate for the benefit of subsequent purchasers. The advantage to the first purchaser is that this may increase the market value of their premises, or simply assist future sales. In *Woolcock Street Investments Pty Ltd v CDG Pty Ltd* [2004] HCA 16, the High Court of Australia relied on the possibility of such a 'transmissible warranty' as one reason why a subsequent purchaser of property may *not* be regarded as 'vulnerable' in the relevant sense.[21] An alternative route is for the purchaser to seek independent appraisal of the state of the premises, and it is recognized that a surveyor offering such an appraisal may owe duties to take care both in contract and, in an appropriate case, in tort (*Smith v Eric Bush*, below). It should be noted however that some defects may remain genuinely hidden from a competent surveyor.

The third policy reason is that there is a consumer protection statute in this area which was ignored by the House of Lords in *Anns*. The Defective Premises Act 1972 would not have provided a remedy to either plaintiff in *Murphy* or *Anns*, because the local authorities in those

---

[21] Although the case concerned commercial, rather than domestic, property, the High Court was careful to explain that this was not the decisive factor.

cases would not be covered in the wording of section 1: 'a person taking on work for or in connection with the provision of a dwelling'. The point is rather that the common law should not provide *more* extensive liabilities than the legislature had adopted after lengthy consideration by the Law Commission. The Defective Premises Act 1972 does apply to the benefit of subsequent purchasers, and its protection cannot be excluded or limited via contract. On the other hand, it only applies to 'dwellings', and (crucially) an action can only be brought within six years of completion of the work (s 1(5)).

In summary, although purchasers of defective premises are not owed a tort duty in respect of mere defects, they are not left without any means of protection. They may be able to obtain financial compensation in the following ways.

1. Through first party insurance, as in the case of *Murphy v Brentwood* itself.

2. Through obtaining advice at the time of purchase. If the advice should prove to be negligent, there may be an action in contract or in tort: *Smith v Eric Bush* [1990] 1 AC 831. The relationship between this case, and *Murphy v Brentwood*, is considered below.

3. In the case of dwellings, a builder, architect, or other party involved in the 'provision' of the dwelling may be liable under the Defective Premises Act 1972. This, however, is subject to a limitation period of six years from the time that the work is completed. By contrast, the six-year limitation period in negligence begins to run at the time that the damage occurs, which may be significantly later. In cases of latent damage, a special three-year time period may begin to run later than this, at the time when the claimant could have discovered the damage (s 14A Limitation Act 1980). There is an overriding limitation period for such cases of fifteen years from the time of the negligence (s 14B Limitation Act 1980): see further Chapter 7 below.

4. If the builder of the premises is a member of the National House Building Council, purchasers (including subsequent purchasers) of the building will benefit from the terms of the NHBC's 'Buildmark' warranty. This is a voluntary guarantee and insurance scheme operated by the NHBC and which offers significant protection to purchasers of property in respect of which the scheme operates. Further details are available on the NHBC website: <www.nhbc.co.uk/NHBCpublications>.

Effectively, both section 1 of the DPA 1972 and the NHBC scheme provide 'transmissible warranties' in respect of properties to which they apply, during the period for which they are effective.

The Surveyor's Liability: Reconcilable Contradiction?

Among the alternative forms of liability just listed, the only one that operates through the common law is the potential liability of valuers and surveyors who negligently advise on the state of premises.

Where a surveyor is instructed directly by the purchaser of premises, it is clear that the surveyor will owe a duty to take reasonable care in the inspection and report, both in contract and in tort. There is no real controversy surrounding this duty even though the most likely form of damage to flow from breach of such a duty is economic. This 'simple case' scenario illustrates that one of the most widespread criticisms of the law in this area is misplaced. Why, it is asked, should a surveyor be liable for failing to spot a defect, when a builder is not liable to a subsequent purchaser for the defective act of building in the first place, unless some separate damage is done? The answer lies in the directness of the relationship between the parties, whether this is expressed in terms of assumption of responsibility, of direct and specific reliance, or in some other way. The surveyor offers targeted advice to a particular client and in respect of a specific transaction. The acts–statements distinction has nothing much to offer our analysis of this situation.

The real controversy in the leading case of *Smith v Eric Bush* [1990] 1 AC 831 is that a duty of care was imposed despite the indirect contractual structure which existed in that particular case. The surveyor did not contract directly with the plaintiff purchasers, but only with the building society which was providing the plaintiffs with their mortgage. The valuation and report contained a proviso stating that only the building society should rely upon the report. On the other hand, it was clear that the purchaser would ultimately pay for the report since the purchaser was charged by the building society for the surveyors' fees. Equally, it was found by the House of Lords that it was to be expected that a purchaser would be provided with a copy of the valuation and report (which they had paid for), *and* that they would rely upon that valuation and report without seeking further advice. It was found to be unreasonable under the Unfair Contract Terms Act 1977 for the surveyor to attempt to exclude liability to the purchaser. Though not without controversy, this interpretation of the relationship is quite realistic, since it reflects the way in which most domestic purchases of realty are arranged. In circumstances of this sort, the surveyor is reasonably to be treated as the purchaser's 'independent investigator' and there are good reasons why a duty ought to be owed in tort.

Summary of Categories A and B

In categories A and B, we have found that English law is at least substantially clear and predictable, even if not generous to claimants. Furthermore, we have found that some reasonably clear policy reasons are available which would explain the existence of rules against recovery for economic losses of these types. In each case, it is not particularly the nature of the loss as 'purely economic', but other identifiable considerations, which explained the rule against recovery. In the case of relational economic loss, the general reason is the 'ripple effect'; but *The Aliakmon* confirms that the no-liability rule will be maintained even where the ripple effect does not exist. In this commercial context, the House of Lords considered that alternative protection could have been obtained by the plaintiff, via contractual negotiation. In the case of economic losses caused by defectiveness in a product or premises, the policy reasons are concerned with the maintenance of contractual rules and avoidance of new legal categories whose recognition may lead to awkward problems of definition. There is, again, an argument that claimants have alternative protection available to them. In neither category A nor category B is the non-availability of recovery for pure economic losses said to follow logically from the nature of the loss.

Our difficulties lie in reconciling these areas of no-liability, with the recognized and emerging categories of recoverable economic loss instigated by *Hedley Byrne v Heller* [1964] AC 465.

2.3 ECONOMIC LOSS CAUSED BY RELIANCE ON NEGLIGENT STATEMENTS (CATEGORY C)

The Decision in *Hedley Byrne* and its Legacy

According to McHugh J of the High Court of Australia, 'Since the decision in *Hedley Byrne & Co Ltd v Heller & Partners Ltd*, confusion bordering on chaos has reigned in the law of negligence' (*Woolcock Street Investments v CDG Pty Ltd* [2004] HCA 16, para 45). There is some truth in this. *Hedley Byrne* is a difficult case to interpret even in its own terms, but to establish its relationship with other categories of economic loss is an even harder task. This is important because English judges have to a large extent adopted and adapted language employed in *Hedley Byrne* in order to identify cases of recoverable economic loss in other contexts. It is possible that many of the problems in this area have been caused by over-emphasis on words and phrases—or 'verbal formulae'—whose meaning will not become any clearer with sustained attention.

Hedley Byrne v Heller & Partners [1964] AC 465

The appellants were advertising agents, who planned to place orders for a company and who therefore asked their bankers to enquire into the financial stability of the company. Their bankers approached the company's bankers, the respondents, with inquiries. The respondents gave favourable responses to the inquiries, but stipulated that these statements were made 'without responsibility'. No fee was charged. The appellants relied upon the favourable references in placing orders, and suffered a loss. They brought an action against the company's bankers, in respect of alleged negligence.

The majority of the House of Lords concluded that in principle, a negligent (but honest) misrepresentation may give rise to a cause of action even in the absence of a contract or fiduciary relationship. However, since in this case there was an express disclaimer of responsibility, no such duty would be implied. Lords Morris and Hodson doubted whether, in circumstances such as these, there could be any duty to take care, even in the absence of the disclaimer. Arguably, they thought, the only duty would be to give an honest answer.

The majority of the discussion in *Hedley Byrne* related to the special status of statements, as opposed to acts. The fact that the loss was 'purely economic' seems to have been treated as of little importance. Perhaps this is because in this particular context, no form of loss other than economic loss was involved or could have been anticipated. As such, the *economic* losses are in no sense 'secondary' or 'remote' consequences of any carelessness.

Here we extract only three of the judgments. Further judgments were delivered by Lords Hodson and Pearce. The three judgments extracted have continued to influence the law on recovery of economic losses. But the most influential of the three is the judgment of Lord Devlin.

Lord Reid, at 482–4

The appellants' first argument was based on *Donoghue v. Stevenson*. That is a very important decision, but I do not think that it has any direct bearing on this case. That decision may encourage us to develop existing lines of authority, but it cannot entitle us to disregard them. Apart altogether from authority, I would think that the law must treat negligent words differently from negligent acts. The law ought so far as possible to reflect the standards of the reasonable man, and that is what *Donoghue v. Stevenson* sets out to do. The most obvious difference between negligent words and negligent acts is this. Quite careful people often express definite opinions on social or informal occasions even when they see that others are likely to be influenced by them; and they often do that without taking that care which they would take if asked for their opinion professionally or in a business connection. The appellant agrees that there can be no duty of care on such occasions. . . . But it is at least unusual casually to put into circulation negligently made articles which are dangerous. A man might give a friend a negligently-prepared bottle of homemade wine and his friend's guests might drink it with dire results. But it is by no means clear that those guests would have no action against the negligent manufacturer.

Another obvious difference is that a negligently made article will only cause one accident, and so it is not very difficult to find the necessary degree of proximity or neighbourhood between the negligent manufacturer and the person injured. But words can be broadcast with or without the consent or the foresight of the speaker or writer. It would be one thing to say that the speaker owes a duty to a limited class, but it would be going very far to say that he owes a duty to every ultimate "consumer" who acts on those words to his detriment. . . .

So it seems to me that there is good sense behind our present law that in general an innocent but negligent misrepresentation gives no cause of action. There must be something more than the mere misstatement. I therefore turn to the authorities to see what more is required. The most natural requirement would be that expressly or by implication from the circumstances the speaker or writer has undertaken some responsibility, and that appears to me not to conflict with any authority which is binding on this House. Where there is a contract there is no difficulty as regards the contracting parties: the question is whether there is a warranty. The refusal of English law to recognise any jus quaesitum tertii causes some difficulties, but they are not relevant, here. Then there are cases where a person does not merely make a statement but performs a gratuitous service. I do not intend to examine the cases about that, but at least they show that in some cases that person owes a duty of care apart from any contract, and to that extent they pave the way to holding that there can be a duty of care in making a statement of fact or opinion which is independent of contract.

Much of the difficulty in this field has been caused by *Derry v. Peek* ((1889) 14 App. Cas. 337). The action was brought against the directors of a company in respect of false statements in a prospectus. It was an action of deceit based on fraud and nothing else. But it was held that the directors had believed that their statements were true although they had no reasonable grounds for their belief. The Court of Appeal held that this amounted to fraud in law, but naturally enough this House held that there can be no fraud without dishonesty and that credulity is not dishonesty. The question was never really considered whether the facts had imposed on the directors a duty to exercise care. It must be implied that on the facts of that case there was no such duty. But that was immediately remedied by the Directors' Liability Act, 1890, which provided that a director is liable for untrue statements in a prospectus unless he proves that he had reasonable ground to believe and did believe that they were true.

It must now be taken that *Derry v. Peek* did not establish any universal rule that in the absence of contract an innocent but negligent misrepresentation cannot give rise to an action. It is true Lord Bramwell said (p.347): "To found an action for damages there must be a contract and breach, or fraud." And for the next 20 years it was generally assumed that *Derry v. Peek* decided that. But it was shown in this House in *Nocton v. Lord Ashburton* ([1914] A.C. 932) that that is much too widely stated. We cannot, therefore, now accept as accurate the numerous statements to that effect in cases between 1889 and 1914, and we must now determine the extent of the exceptions to that rule.

In *Nocton v. Lord Ashburton* a solicitor was sued for fraud. Fraud was not proved but he was held liable for negligence. Viscount Haldane L.C. dealt with *Derry v. Peek* (14 App.Cas. 337) and pointed out that while the relationship of the parties in that case was not enough, the case did not decide "that where a different sort of relationship ought to be inferred from the circumstances the case is to be concluded by asking whether an action for deceit will lie . . . There are other obligations besides that of honesty the breach of which may give a right to damages. These obligations depend on principles which the judges have worked out in the fashion that is characteristic of a system where much of the law has always been judge-made and unwritten." It hardly needed *Donoghue v. Stevenson* to show that that process can still operate. Then Lord Haldane quoted a passage from the speech of Lord Herschell in *Derry v. Peek* where he excluded from the principle of that case "those cases where a person within whose special province it lay to know a particular fact has given an erroneous answer to an inquiry made with regard to it by a person desirous of ascertaining the fact for the purpose of determining his course."

(At 485–6)

Lord Haldane gave a further statement of his view in *Robinson v. National Bank of Scotland Ltd.* 1916 S.C.(H.L.) 154, 157. . . . Having said that in that case there was no duty excepting the duty of common honesty, he went on to say: "In saying that I wish emphatically to repeat what I said in advising this House in the case of *Nocton v. Lord Ashburton*, that it is great mistake to suppose that, because the principle in *Derry v. Peek* clearly covers all cases of the class to which I have referred, therefore the freedom of action of the courts in recognising special duties arising out of other kinds of relationship which they find established by the evidence is in any way affected. I think, as I said in *Nocton's* case, that an exaggerated view was taken by a good many people of the scope of the decision in *Derry v. Peek*. The whole of the doctrine as to fiduciary relationships, as to the duty of care arising from implied as well as express contracts, as to the duty of care arising from other special relationships which the courts may find to exist in particular cases, still remains, and I should be very sorry if any word fell from me which should suggest that the courts are in any way hampered in recognising that the duty of care may be established when such cases really occur." This passage makes it clear that Lord Haldane did not think that a duty to take care must be limited to cases of fiduciary relationship in the narrow sense of relationships which had been recognised by the Court of Chancery as being of a fiduciary character. He speaks of other special relationships, and I can see no logical stopping place short of all those relationships where it is plain that the party seeking information or advice was trusting the other to exercise such a degree of care as the circumstances required, where it was reasonable for him to do that, and where the other gave the information or advice when he knew or ought to have known that the inquirer was relying on him. I say "ought to have known" because in questions of negligence we now apply the objective standard of what the reasonable man would have done.

A reasonable man, knowing that he was being trusted or that his skill and judgment were being relied on, would, I think, have three courses open to him. He could keep silent or decline to give the information or advice sought: or he could give an answer with a clear qualification that he accepted no responsibility for it or that it was given without that reflection or inquiry which a careful answer would require: or he could simply answer without any such qualification. If he chooses to adopt the last course he must, I think, be held to have accepted some responsibility for his answer being given carefully, or to have accepted a relationship with the inquirer which requires him to exercise such care as the circumstances require.

Lord Reid concluded his judgment, however, in the following terms:

At 493

I am . . . of opinion that it is clear that the respondents never undertook any duty to exercise care in giving their replies. The appellants cannot succeed unless there was such a duty and therefore this appeal must fail.

Lord Morris of Borth-y-Gest, at 502–3

My Lords, I consider that it follows and that it should now be regarded as settled that if someone possessed of a special skill undertakes, quite irrespective of contract, to apply that skill for the assistance of another person who relies upon such skill, a duty of care will arise. The fact that the service is to be given by means of or by the instrumentality of words can make no difference. Furthermore, if in a sphere in which a person is so placed that others could reasonably rely upon his judgment or his skill or upon his ability to make careful inquiry, a person takes it upon himself to give information or advice to, or allows his information or advice to be passed on to, another person who, as he knows or should know, will place reliance upon it, then a duty of care will arise.

(At 504)

. . . There was in the present case no contemplation of receiving anything like a formal and detailed report such as might be given by some concern charged with the duty (probably for reward) of making all proper and relevant inquiries concerning the nature, scope and extent of a company's activities and of obtaining and marshalling all available evidence as to its credit, efficiency, standing and business reputation. There is much to be said, therefore, for the view that if a banker gives a reference in the form of a brief expression of opinion in regard to credit-worthiness he does not accept, and there is not expected from him, any higher duty than that of giving an honest answer. I need not, however, seek to deal further with this aspect of the matter, which perhaps cannot be covered by any statement of general application, because, in my judgment, the bank in the present case, by the words which they employed, effectively disclaimed any assumption of a duty of care. They stated that they only responded to the inquiry on the basis that their reply was without responsibility. If the inquirers chose to receive and act upon the reply they cannot disregard the definite terms upon which it was given. They cannot accept a reply given with a stipulation and then reject the stipulation. Furthermore, within accepted principles (as illustrated in *Rutter v. Palmer* [1922] 2 KB 87) the words employed were apt to exclude any liability for negligence.

Lord Devlin, at 524–5

What Lord Atkin called [in *Donoghue v Stevenson*] a "general conception of relations giving rise to a duty of care" is now often referred to as the principle of proximity. You must take reasonable care to avoid acts or omissions which you can reasonably foresee would be likely to injure your neighbour. In the eyes of the law your neighbour is a person who is so closely and directly affected by your act that you ought reasonably to have him in contemplation as being so affected when you are directing your mind to the acts or omissions which are called in question.

The specific proposition arising out of this conception is that "a manufacturer of products, which he sells in such a form as to show that he intends them to reach the ultimate consumer in the form in which they left him with no reasonable possibility of intermediate examination, and with the knowledge that the absence of reasonable care in the preparation or putting up of the products will result in an injury to the consumer's life or property, owes a duty to the consumer to take that reasonable care."

Now, it is not, in my opinion, a sensible application of what Lord Atkin was saying for a Judge to be invited on the facts of any particular case to say whether or not there was "proximity" between the plaintiff and the defendant. That would be a misuse of a general conception and it is not the way in which English law develops. What Lord Atkin did was to use his general conception to open up a category of cases giving rise to a special duty. It was already clear that the law recognised the existence of such a duty in the category of articles that were dangerous in themselves.

What *Donoghue v. Stevenson* did may be described either as the widening of an old category or as the creation of a new and similar one. The general conception can be used to produce other categories in the same way. An existing category grows as instances of its application multiply until the time comes when the cell divides.

Lord Thankerton and Lord Macmillan approached the problem fundamentally in the same way, though they left any general conception on which they were acting to be implied. They inquired directly—Lord Thankerton and Lord Macmillan—whether the relationship between the plaintiff and the defendant was such as to give rise to a duty to take care. It is significant, whether it is a coincidence or not, that the term "special relationship" used by Lord Thankerton is also the one used by Lord Haldane in *Nocton v. Lord Ashburton*. The field is very different but the object of the search is the same.

In my opinion, the appellants in their argument tried to press *Donoghue v. Stevenson* too hard. They asked whether the principle of proximity should not apply as well to words as to deeds. I think it should, but as it is only a general conception it does not get them very far. . . .

(At 529–31)

I have had the advantage of reading all the opinions prepared by your Lordships and of studying the terms which your Lordships have framed by way of definition of the sort of relationship which gives rise to a responsibility towards those who act upon information or advice and so creates a duty of care towards them. I do not understand any of your Lordships to hold that it is a responsibility imposed by law upon certain types of persons or in certain sorts of situations. It is a responsibility that is voluntarily accepted or undertaken, either generally where a general relationship, such as that of solicitor and client or banker and customer, is created, or specifically in relation to a particular transaction. In the present case the appellants were not, as in *Woods v. Martins Bank Ltd.* ([1959] 1 Q.B. 55) the customers or potential customers of the bank. Responsibility can attach only to the single act, that is, the giving of the reference, and only if the doing of that act implied a voluntary undertaking to assume responsibility. This is a point of great importance because it is, as I understand it, the foundation for the ground on which in the end the House dismisses the appeal. I do not think it possible to formulate with exactitude all the conditions under which the law will in a specific case imply a voluntary undertaking any more than it is possible to formulate those in which the law will imply a contract. But in so far as your Lordships describe the circumstances in which an implication will ordinarily be drawn, I am prepared to adopt any one of your Lordships' statements as showing the general rule: and I pay the same respect to the statement by Denning L.J. in his dissenting judgment in *Candler v. Crane, Christmas & Co* about the circumstances in which he says a duty to use care in making a statement exists.

I do not go further than this for two reasons. The first is that I have found in the speech of Lord Shaw in *Nocton v. Lord Ashburton* and in the idea of a relationship that is equivalent to contract all that is necessary to cover the situation that arises in this case. Mr. Gardiner does not claim to succeed unless he can establish that the reference was intended by the respondents to be communicated by the National Provincial Bank to some unnamed customer of theirs, whose identity was immaterial to the respondents, for that customer's use. All that was lacking was formal consideration. The case is well within the authorities I have already cited and of which *Wilkinson v. Coverdale* (1 Esp. 75) is the most apposite example.

I shall therefore content myself with the proposition that wherever there is a relationship equivalent to contract, there is a duty of care. Such a relationship may be either general or particular. Examples of a general relationship are those of solicitor and client and of banker and customer. For the former *Nocton v. Lord Ashburton* has long stood as the authority and for the latter there is the decision of Salmon J. in *Woods v. Martins Bank Ltd* ([1959] 1 Q.B. 55) which I respectfully approve. There may well be others yet to be established. Where there is a general relationship of this sort, it is unnecessary to do more than prove its existence and the duty follows. Where, as in the present case, what is relied on is a particular relationship created ad hoc, it will be necessary to examine the particular facts to see whether there is an express or implied undertaking of responsibility.

I regard this proposition as an application of the general conception of proximity. Cases may arise in the future in which a new and wider proposition, quite independent of any notion of contract, will be needed. There may, for example, be cases in which a statement is not supplied for the use of any particular person. any more than in *Donoghue v. Stevenson* the ginger beer was supplied for consumption by any particular person; and it will then be necessary to return to the general conception of proximity and to see whether there can be evolved from it, as was done in *Donoghue v. Stevenson*, a specific proposition to fit the case. When that has to be done, the speeches of your Lordships today as well as the judgment of Denning L.J. to which I have referred—and also, I may add, the proposition in the American Restatement of the Law of Torts, Vol. III, p. 122, para. 552, and the cases which exemplify it— will afford good guidance as to what ought to be said. I prefer to see what shape such cases take before committing myself to any formulation, for I bear in mind Lord Atkin's warning, which I have quoted, against placing unnecessary restrictions on the adaptability of English law. I have, I hope, made it clear that I take quite literally the dictum of Lord Macmillan, so often quoted from the same case, that "the categories of negligence are never closed." English law is wide enough to embrace any new category or proposition that exemplifies the principle of proximity.

Commentary

Although there was clearly a difference of view between Lords Reid and Morris on the important question of whether there would, in the absence of the disclaimer, be a duty to take care in this case, the greater difference in method is between these two judgments, and that of Lord Devlin. Lords Reid and Morris attempted to set out in quite general terms the circumstances in which there will be a duty to take care in respect of statements. In the extract above, Lord Reid seeks to identify the components of a 'special relationship' that will be sufficient to establish that the duty of care arises. This he says will be established if it is plain that the recipient of a statement is trusting the defendant to take care; if it is reasonable to trust the statement-maker in this way; and if the information or advice was given where the statement-maker ought to have known that the inquirer was relying on him. Lord Morris on the other hand adds the requirement of 'special skill'. The reason why Lord Morris doubted whether this was a case where a duty of care should arise, even in the absence of the disclaimer, is that there was no reasonable expectation that the defendant would go to any great lengths to ensure that their opinion was soundly based. As such, one could say that this was not a statement on which it was reasonable to rely; alternatively, that there is no greater duty in this case than one of honesty.

Both Lord Reid and Lord Morris proceeded by setting out the requirement of proximity as it applies to acts of manufacture and the like, then examining the reasons why statements may need to be treated with more caution. It is clear that they considered themselves to be stating *additional* criteria applicable to statements. They certainly did not think that they were establishing that statements gave rise to special responsibility for economic losses that would be unavailable if the defendant's negligence consisted of an act.

Lord Devlin and the 'Voluntary Undertaking of Responsibility'

Lord Devlin, by contrast with Lords Reid and Morris, did not seek to establish *general* rules for application to all future cases of negligent misstatement. In disposing of this particular case, he emphasized the closeness to contract of the relationship between the parties. The only difference between this case and a formal contract, he argued, is that in this case there is no consideration since no fee was payable for the bankers' statement. In such circumstances, he argued, it is clear that there would have been an 'undertaking of responsibility' on the part of the defendant, if it had not been for the disclaimer of responsibility. He stressed that a *voluntary* undertaking of responsibility in the making of the statement was also required by each of the other judges, despite the broader statements highlighted above; and that this was evidenced by the fact that all of the other judges gave decisive weight to the disclaimer of responsibility, which was thought to exclude the possibility that any duty of care might arise.

Lord Devlin made clear that he thought the 'voluntary undertaking of responsibility' was an application of the broader conception of 'proximity'. In the passages extracted above, he made plain that there is no sense in asking courts simply to 'decide whether there is proximity' in a given case. Proximity is only a *general conception*, whose meaning will vary from one category of case law to another. Lord Devlin proposes that the particular facet of 'proximity' which is decisive in this particular case is 'nearness to contract'.

Although Lord Devlin argues that nearness to contract is a sufficient idea to dispose of this case, he concedes that there will be future cases in which this idea is not applicable. Unlike Lords Reid and Morris, he prefers not to predict the likely criteria that will need to be met in order to determine whether there is indeed proximity in such a case. As such, it is a mistake to suggest that Lord Devlin thought that 'nearness to contract' was *essential* for a duty to take care in the giving of statements. He merely said that it sufficed. He suggested that the criteria set out by the other judges in *Hedley Byrne* itself will be helpful in future cases, but he considered it unwise to attempt a broad general statement in advance of seeing the particular circumstances that might arise. Apart from the other judgments in *Hedley Byrne*, he also commended as likely to provide helpful guidance the *dissenting* judgment of Denning LJ in *Candler v Crane Christmas* [1951] 2 KB 164. (The majority decision in that case was overruled by the House of Lords in *Hedley Byrne*.)

Denning LJ would have recognized that a duty was owed by accountants where they were instructed to draw up accounts specifically for the purpose of inducing the plaintiff to invest money in a company. The majority of the Court of Appeal held that there could be no such duty in the absence of a contractual or fiduciary relationship between the parties.

The following passage was approved by Lord Devlin in *Hedley Byrne*:

Denning LJ, *Candler v Crane Christmas*, at 181

. . . there are some cases—of which the present is one—where the accountants know all the time, even before they present their accounts, that their employer requires the accounts to show to a third person so as to induce him to act on them, and then they themselves, or their employers, present the accounts to him for the purpose. In such cases I am of opinion that the accountants owe a duty of care to the third person.

The test of proximity in these cases is: Did the accountants know that the accounts were required for submission to the plaintiff and use by him?

According to Lord Devlin, future cases which are not 'close to contract', will need to be settled by considering the hallmarks of a sufficient relationship of 'proximity' in the specific context of statements.

Lord Devlin's endorsement of the approach of Denning LJ in *Candler* is important, because that approach is consistent with the decision of a later House of Lords in the case of *Caparo v Dickman*. It has often been said that the approach in *Caparo* is in conflict with the approach in *Hedley Byrne*. Indeed this perceived conflict has led to considerable tension in recent case law. Since the expression 'assumption of responsibility'—adapted from Lord Devlin's words in *Hedley Byrne*—has come increasingly into vogue (Section 2.4 below), it is possible that part of the perceived conflict between *Hedley Byrne* and *Caparo* results from reading Lord Devlin as laying down *criteria* (which, in fact, he sought to avoid), rather than simply *explaining* which elements of the case had led him to conclude that there was sufficient proximity between the parties. The latter makes his approach entirely compatible with the 'case by case' approach heralded by *Caparo v Dickman*. Indeed, Lord Devlin's judgment was quoted at length, and with approval, by Lord Oliver in *Caparo*. Lord Devlin's reading of proximity in the passage extracted may have inspired Lord Oliver's idea that proximity is no more than a 'general conception'.

Shortly before *Caparo*, doubt was cast on the continued relevance of 'assumption of responsibility' by the next case.

Smith v Eric S Bush; Harris v Wyre Forest District Council [1990] 1 AC 831

We have already outlined the facts of *Smith v Bush*, and the importance of the decision in respect of defective premises, when considering category B cases of economic loss, above. Here we are more concerned with what this case said about the *approach* to be taken where economic losses have been caused by negligent statements.

Lord Templeman considered that the relationship between the parties fitted Lord Devlin's criterion of being 'akin to contract' (a conclusion expressly doubted by Lord Jauncey):

Lord Templeman, at 846

In the present appeals, the relationship between the valuer and the purchaser is "akin to contract." The valuer knows that the consideration which he receives derives from the purchaser and is passed on by the mortgagee, and the valuer also knows that the valuation will determine whether or not the purchaser buys the house.

He also considered that, even though there was a disclaimer in the valuation report, the valuer could still be said to have assumed responsibility to the purchaser.

At 847

. . . in my opinion the valuer assumes responsibility to both mortgagee and purchaser by agreeing to carry out a valuation for mortgage purposes knowing that the valuation fee has been paid by the purchaser and knowing that the valuation will probably be relied upon by the purchaser in order to decide whether or not to enter into a contract to purchase the house. The valuer can escape the responsibility to exercise reasonable skill and care by an express exclusion clause, provided the exclusion clause does not fall foul of the Unfair Contract Terms Act 1977.

Since the decision in *Hedley Byrne*, the law on exclusion of liability had been altered by the Unfair Contract Terms Act 1977. An attempted exclusion of liability would be effective only if it was judged to be 'reasonable'. In the case of *Smith v Bush*, the valuation had included a specific disclaimer of responsibility to any party other than the mortgagee building society which had commissioned the valuation (though at the purchaser's expense). Lord Templeman treated the disclaimer as relevant only to the question of whether liability had been validly excluded, *not* to the question of whether responsibility had been 'assumed' in the first place. In his view, the exclusion of liability was not, in these circumstances, reasonable:

At 854

The public are exhorted to purchase their homes and cannot find houses to rent. A typical London suburban house, constructed in the 1930s for less than £1,000 is now bought for more than £150,000 with money largely borrowed at high rates of interest and repayable over a period of a quarter of a century. In these circumstances it is not fair and reasonable for building societies and valuers to agree together to impose on purchasers the risk of loss arising as a result of incompetence or carelessness on the part of valuers . . . different considerations may apply where homes are not concerned.

Lord Griffiths by contrast cast doubt on the usefulness of the 'voluntary assumption of responsibility' idea. Understandably, he thought that he could not hold that there was a duty of care on the basis of a 'voluntary assumption' when the defendants had done all in their power to *disclaim* responsibility. Unlike Lord Templeman, who approached the disclaimer in terms of an attempted 'exclusion of liability', he treated the disclaimer as important to the very question of whether a duty of care could be said to arise. A judgment in favour of the plaintiff in this case could only be compatible with *Hedley Byrne* if the criterion of 'assumption of responsibility' was very considerably watered down.

At 862

Mr Ashworth . . . submitted, on the authority of *Hedley Byrne & Co. Ltd. v. Heller & Partners Ltd.* [1964] A.C. 465 that it was essential to found liability for a negligent misstatement that there had been "a voluntary assumption of responsibility" on the part of the person giving the advice. I do not accept this submission and I do not think that voluntary assumption of responsibility is a helpful or realistic test for liability. It is true that reference is made in a number of the speeches in *Hedley Byrne* to the assumption of responsibility as a test of liability but it must be remembered that those speeches were made in the context of a case in which the central issue was whether a duty of care could arise when there had been an express disclaimer of responsibility for the accuracy of the advice. Obviously, if an adviser expressly assumes responsibility for his advice, a duty of care will arise, but such is extremely unlikely in the ordinary course of events. The House of Lords approved a duty of care being imposed on the facts in *Cann v. Willson* (1888) 39 Ch.D. 39 and in *Candler v. Crane, Christmas & Co.* [1951] 2 K.B. 164. But if the surveyor in *Cann v. Willson* or the accountant in *Candler v. Crane, Christmas & Co.* had actually been asked if he was voluntarily assuming responsibility for his advice to the mortgagee or the purchaser of the shares, I have little doubt he would have replied, "Certainly not. My responsibility is limited to the person who employs me." The phrase "assumption of responsibility" can only have any real meaning if it is understood as referring to the circumstances in which the law will deem the maker of the statement to have assumed responsibility to the person who acts upon the advice.

Later in his judgment, Lord Griffiths set out an alternative formulation by which to judge whether a duty of care should be recognized as arising in such a case, avoiding the terminology of 'assumption of responsibility'.

At 864–5

I have already given my view that the voluntary assumption of responsibility is unlikely to be a helpful or realistic test in most cases. I therefore return to the question in what circumstances should the law deem those who give advice to have assumed responsibility to the person who acts upon the advice or, in other words, in what circumstances should a duty of care be owed by the adviser to those who act upon his advice? I would answer—only if it is foreseeable that if the advice is negligent the recipient is likely to suffer damage, that there is a sufficiently proximate relationship between the parties and that it is just and reasonable to impose the liability. In the case of a surveyor valuing a small house for a building society or local authority, the application of these three criteria leads to the conclusion that he owes a duty of care to the purchaser. If the valuation is negligent and is relied upon damage in the form of economic loss to the purchaser is obviously foreseeable. The necessary proximity arises from the surveyor's knowledge that the overwhelming probability is that the purchaser will rely upon his valuation, the evidence was that surveyors knew that approximately 90 per cent. of purchasers did so, and the fact that the surveyor only obtains the work because the purchaser is willing to pay his fee. It is just and reasonable that the duty should be imposed for the advice is given in a professional as opposed to a social context and liability for breach of the duty will be limited both as to its extent and amount. The extent of the liability is limited to the purchaser of the house— I would not extend it to subsequent purchasers. The amount of the liability cannot be very great because it relates to a modest house. There is no question here of creating a liability of indeterminate amount to an indeterminate class. I would certainly wish to stress that in cases where the advice has not been given for the specific purpose of the recipient acting upon it, it should only be in cases when the adviser knows that there is a high degree of probability that some other identifiable person will act upon the advice that a duty of care should be imposed. It would impose an intolerable burden upon those who give advice in a professional or commercial context if they were to owe a duty not only to those to whom they give the advice but to any other person who might choose to act upon it.

As we saw above, the search for a 'voluntary assumption of responsibility' was intended by Lord Devlin to be a way to judge whether proximity was present in a case like *Hedley Byrne*.

Doubting the relevance of 'voluntary assumption' on the facts of *Smith v Bush*, Lord Griffiths suggests an alternative approach which appears to take us straight back to that general conception—proximity—together with foreseeability and the question of what is 'fair, just and reasonable'. Together, these became the components of the 'three-stage test' in *Caparo v Dickman* (Chapter 3.3). However, it should be noted that the reasons why Lord Griffiths ultimately thought that the relationship in this case was 'proximate' are compatible with Lord Devlin's analysis of *Candler v Crane Christmas*. The surveyors knew at all times for whose benefit, and for what purpose, they were producing the valuation. This was perhaps a case in which an alternative approach to justifying the duty of care was simply more appropriate. Lord Griffiths' attempt to make the assumption of responsibility fit the facts amounted to a complete distortion of the concept, and has caused considerable subsequent confusion (see the discussion in category D below).

Caparo Industries plc v Dickman plc [1990] 2 AC 605

The facts of this case were outlined in Chapter 3.3 above, where we also noted the general approach to the duty of care which it set out.

Once again, the idea of 'voluntary assumption of responsibility' was not found particularly helpful by the House of Lords, who concentrated instead on various features of the case which showed that there was, on the facts, insufficient proximity between the parties. In particular, the defendant auditors had produced only general audited accounts, and had not envisaged that they would be relied upon by the claimants in making decisions concerning a takeover of the company. The purpose of the accounts was not to advise in respect of such transactions. Even though the claimants were existing shareholders of the company, they could not reasonably rely on published annual accounts in making such decisions. The Court of Appeal, whose decision was reversed by the House of Lords, had held that a duty of care was owed *to existing shareholders* (including the plaintiffs) in respect of the accuracy of the accounts. The House of Lords added that this was not specific enough. One must also take into account the *purpose* for which it is reasonable to rely upon the accounts, and the purpose for which the defendants know that the statement will be relied upon. The only duty of accuracy owed to shareholders related to the governance of the company.

In commenting on the cases in which a duty of care is recognized to arise (at least potentially) in respect of statements (*Cann v Wilson, Candler v Crane Christmas, Hedley Byrne v Heller, Smith v Eric Bush*), Lord Bridge said:

At 620–1

The salient feature of all these cases is that the defendant giving advice or information was fully aware of the nature of the transaction which the plaintiff had in contemplation, knew that the advice or information would be communicated to him directly or indirectly and knew that it was very likely that the plaintiff would rely on that advice or information in deciding whether or not to engage in the transaction in contemplation. In these circumstances the defendant could clearly be expected, subject always to the effect of any disclaimer of responsibility, specifically to anticipate that the plaintiff would rely on the advice or information given by the defendant for the very purpose for which he did in the event rely on it. So also the plaintiff, subject again to the effect of any disclaimer, would in that situation reasonably suppose that he was entitled to rely on the advice or information communicated to him for the very purpose for which he required it. The situation is entirely different where a statement is put into more or less general circulation and may foreseeably be relied on by strangers to the maker of the statement for any one of a variety of different purposes which the maker of the statement has no specific reason to anticipate. To hold the maker of the statement to be under a duty of care in respect of the accuracy of the statement to all and sundry for any purpose for which they may choose to rely on it is not only to subject him, in the classic words of Cardozo C.J. to "liability in an indeterminate amount for an indeterminate time to an indeterminate class:" see *Ultramares Corporation v. Touche* (1931) 174 N.E. 441, 444; it is also to confer on the world at large a quite unwarranted entitlement to appropriate for their own purposes the benefit of the expert knowledge or professional expertise attributed to the maker of the statement. Hence, looking only at the circumstances of these decided cases where a duty of care in respect of negligent statements has been held to exist, I should expect to find that the "limit or control mechanism . . . imposed upon the liability of a wrongdoer towards those who have suffered economic damage in consequence of his negligence" rested in the necessity to prove, in this category of the tort of negligence, as an essential ingredient of the "proximity" between the plaintiff and the defendant, that the defendant knew that his statement would be communicated to the plaintiff, either as an individual or as a member of an identifiable class, specifically in connection with a particular transaction or transactions of a particular kind (e.g. in a prospectus inviting investment) and that the plaintiff would be very likely to rely on it for the purpose of deciding whether or not to enter upon that transaction or upon a transaction of that kind.

I find this expectation fully supported by the dissenting judgment of Denning L.J. in *Candler v. Crane, Christmas & Co.* [1951] 2 K.B. 164, 179, 180–181, 182–184 . . .

We should note that according to the logic of Lord Bridge's approach (at 620–1), there will be cases in which auditors do owe a duty of care to particular claimants in the preparation of accounts, provided it is clear at the time of preparing the accounts that they may be relied upon for the particular purpose and by the claimant. This was accepted in *Morgan Crucible v Hill Samuel Bank Ltd* [1991] 1 All ER 148, where the directors and financial advisors of a company had made representations about that company's accounts after a takeover bid had been made by the plaintiffs. The Court of Appeal thought it arguable that *Caparo* could be distinguished, since the representations were made after the bid emerged, and with the intention that they should be relied upon. Similarly, in *Law Society v KPMG Peat Marwick* [2000] 4 All ER 540, the Court of Appeal held that the criteria set out in *Caparo* were fulfilled. Here the defendants prepared the accounts of a firm of solicitors, which subsequently proved to have defrauded its clients. This led to claims against the Law Society's compensation fund. The accountants knew that the purpose of the accounts was to enable the Law Society to ensure that there were no irregularities, and that they would be both communicated to the Law Society and relied upon. Therefore, a duty was owed to the Law Society.

After *Caparo*, 'assumption of responsibility' appeared to have been fatally weakened as a justification for the duty of care in cases of economic loss. Certainly, it was clear that the duty of care is to be understood as 'imposed by law' rather than voluntarily assumed, and the strongest interpretation of the concept, as applied by Lord Devlin in *Hedley Byrne*, was therefore not available. But the term was surprisingly resuscitated in the cases next considered.

2.4 'EXTENDED' *HEDLEY BYRNE* LIABILITY (CATEGORY D)

The following cases show that *Hedley Byrne* principles are no longer restricted to cases of negligent statement (in they ever were). Indeed, criteria derived from *Hedley Byrne* are increasingly applied outside the area of pure economic loss.

In three House of Lords decisions delivered between July 1994 and February 1995, Lord Goff almost single-handedly propelled the concept of 'assumption of responsibility' back to a prominent place. The second of the cases in this sequence of three, *Henderson v Merrett* [1995] 2 AC 145, was described by Lord Mustill in his dissenting opinion in *White v Jones* [1995] 2 AC 207 as having 'brought back to prominence' both *Hedley Byrne* itself and *Nocton v Lord Ashburton*, and as the case that 'gave them new life as a growing point for the tort of negligence'. It will be seen that Lord Mustill, in this comment, emphasizes the importance of *Hedley Byrne* in very general terms. He does not describe it as important only in respect of the recovery of economic losses, nor solely in respect of statements. This has proved to be prophetic.[22] These cases also 'extended' the liability in *Hedley Byrne* to circumstances outside the reliance by one party (the claimant) on a statement given directly to him or her by the defendant.

Spring v Guardian Assurance [1995] 2 AC 296

The plaintiff had been a company representative for the first defendants. He later sought a position with a different company. Under the rules of the relevant regulatory body ('Lautro'), the prospective employer was under a duty to obtain a reference, and the first defendants were under a duty to supply a reference. The reference was unfavourable, and the plaintiff was not appointed. At first instance, the judge held that the reference was negligently prepared, and that this amounted to a breach of a duty of care owed by the first defendant to the plaintiff.

Part of the special controversy of this case lies in the fact that the same facts might give rise to an action in defamation, since it is natural to define the harm caused by a negligent reference in terms of damage to reputation (Chapter 13 below). If approached as a defamation case, it is clear that the reference would be protected by the defence of 'qualified privilege'. This defence exists in order to protect free expression on a privileged occasion (*Horrocks v Lowe* [1975] AC 135). Assuming the statement to be made on a privileged occasion, a defendant will lose the protection of qualified privilege only if the statement is made with 'malice'. Although malice is not always easy to define, it is clear that mere lack of care is insufficient. To recognize a duty of care in negligence would appear to circumvent this important public policy defence.

The judgments in the House of Lords varied in approach. Lord Keith, who dissented, thought it significant that the plaintiff had not relied upon the statement. In his view, this took the case outside the ambit of *Hedley Byrne*. He was also concerned not to circumvent the existing limitations on the action in defamation through recognizing a duty of care. For the majority, Lord Woolf approached the question of whether a duty of care was owed through a direct application of the three *Caparo* criteria of **foreseeability**; **proximity**; and what was '**fair, just, and reasonable**'. He conceded that this was not determinative since *Caparo* also required that a court consider whether the case was sufficiently analogous to existing categories where a duty is owed. Since *Hedley Byrne* concerned an allegedly negligent *positive* reference, Lord Woolf reasoned that it was not too large a step to recognize a duty in respect of a negligent *negative* reference. Of course, one significant difference not noted by Lord Woolf is that the person who suffers loss as a result of the *negative* reference is not the person to whom the statement was directed, nor the person who relied upon it. As we have already noted, Lord Keith thought that this took the case outside the ambit of *Hedley Byrne* liability. But Lord Woolf applied looser criteria, drawn directly from *Caparo*.

---

22 See the discussion of cases such as *Phelps v Hillingdon* [2001] 2 AC 619 in Section 6.3 below.

Applying the *Caparo* criteria, Lord Woolf concluded that loss to the plaintiff was clearly a foreseeable result of an adverse reference. Lord Woolf dealt very briefly with the 'proximity' criterion, saying (at 342) that '[t]he relationship between the plaintiff and the defendants could hardly have been closer'. This tends to prove Lord Devlin's point when he said, in *Hedley Byrne*, that 'proximity' is not the sort of criterion that judges can sensibly be invited to apply directly. The public policy considerations that surrounded the qualified privilege defence were dealt with by Lord Woolf under the third of the *Caparo* criteria. He weighed up the public interest (protected by qualified privilege) in 'full and frank' expression in this context, with the competing public interest (as he saw it) that references should not be based upon negligent investigation. He concluded that public policy did not preclude the recognition of a duty to take care in the giving of references.

Alone among the majority, Lord Goff reached his decision through a specific application of principles drawn from *Hedley Byrne v Heller*, rather than through interpretation of the *Caparo* three-stage test. As he made clear, counsel had not considered this line to be worth arguing. He proposed that the basis of *Hedley Byrne* liability was indeed an assumption of responsibility, coupled with reliance on that assumption. In this case, he thought that there was reliance in the general sense that the 'employee' (whose exact employment status was not relevant) relied upon an 'employer' to take due care in the protection of his interests. This amounts to general reliance on the defendant 'to take due care', but *not* reliance upon the truth of the statement.

Arguably, Lord Goff thereby misapplied the idea of reliance to be found in *Hedley Byrne*, which clearly did concern reliance upon the truth of a statement. But alternatively, he might be said to have merely resurrected the broader basis of *Hedley Byrne* liability in relationships of responsibility and reliance, such as professional services between a solicitor and a client, rather than in the giving of statements more narrowly. As such, although the careless act in *Spring* is the making of a statement, Lord Goff's judgment opened the door for *Hedley Byrne* to be released from its perceived restriction to statements. For example, discussing a relationship in which a *Hedley Byrne* 'assumption of responsibility' is recognised to apply—the relationship between solicitor and client—Lord Goff explained:

At 319

I can see no reason why a solicitor should not be under a duty to his client to exercise due care and skill when making statements to third parties, so that if he fails in that duty and his client suffers damage in consequence, he may be liable to his client in damages.

In general terms, Lord Goff approached *Hedley Byrne* in the following way:

Lord Goff, at 318

. . . All the members of the appellate Committee in [*Hedley Byrne*] spoke in terms of the principle resting upon an assumption of responsibility by the defendant towards the plaintiff, coupled with reliance by the plaintiff on the exercise by the defendant of due care and skill. . . . Accordingly, where the plaintiff entrusts the defendant with the conduct of his affairs, in general or in particular, the defendant may be held to have assumed responsibility to the plaintiff, and the plaintiff to have relied on the defendant to exercise due skill and care, in respect of such conduct.

The main mystery here is in the meaning that Lord Goff attached to the key criterion of 'assumption of responsibility'. Since Lord Goff has dropped the word 'voluntary', and since he speaks of the defendant as being '*held* to have assumed responsibility to the plaintiff', we can take it that his test is objective, and does not reflect an intention on the part of the defendant to assume potential liability. If so, then arguably this formulation has lost its foundation as expressed by Lord Devlin. The latter, it will be recalled, suggested that the relevant duty is not 'imposed by law', but is voluntarily undertaken by the defendant. Instead, there is a reference to the plaintiff 'entrusting the defendant with his affairs'. But the criterion is not wholly empty. In this particular case, Lord Goff's formulation appears to place emphasis on relationships of trust and reliance, an element which was expressly developed by Lord Browne-Wilkinson in the subsequent cases of *Henderson v Merrett*, and *White v Jones*.

An important subsidiary mystery lies in the relationship between the duty under *Hedley Byrne*, and the policy issue in respect of qualified privilege which was outlined above. Lord Goff stated that the policy issues were irrelevant where there was a sufficient relationship under *Hedley Byrne*, but he did not explain why this was so:

At 324

Since, for the reasons I have given, it is my opinion that in cases such as the present the duty of care arises by reason of an assumption of responsibility by the employer to the employee in respect of the relevant reference, I can see no good reason why the duty to exercise due skill and care which rests upon the employer should be negatived because, if the plaintiff were instead to bring an action for damage to his reputation, he would be met by the defence of qualified privilege which could only be defeated by proof of malice. It is not to be forgotten that the *Hedley Byrne* duty arises where there is a relationship which is, broadly speaking, either contractual or equivalent to contract. In these circumstances, I cannot see that principles of the law of defamation are of any relevance.

In the next case extracted, Lord Goff clearly proposed that the presence of an 'assumption of responsibility' made it unnecessary to consider policy factors in accordance with the third stage of the *Caparo* test. This conclusion requires the idea of 'assumption of responsibility' to have some real meaning, even if it falls short of the strongest, 'voluntary' meaning which was present in *Hedley Byrne* itself. It seems to be proposed that it *compels* a finding of responsibility, if established to be present.

Henderson v Merrett [1995] 2 AC 145   HL

The facts of *Henderson* were complex, but the solution favoured by the House of Lords was reasonably simple. The case arose out of losses suffered by investors (referred to as 'Names') in the Lloyds Insurance market in London during the 1980s. The plaintiffs brought these actions against underwriting and managing agents for negligent conduct of their affairs which, they argued, exposed them to unreasonable risk of losses. The role of the various agents is explained in the following extract from the judgment of Lord Goff:

Every person who wishes to become a Name at Lloyd's and who is not himself or herself an underwriting agent must appoint an underwriting agent to act on his or her behalf, pursuant to an underwriting agency agreement. Underwriting agents may act in one of three different capacities. (1) They may be members' agents, who (broadly speaking) advise Names on their choice of syndicates, place Names on the syndicates chosen by them, and give general advice to them. (2) They may be managing agents, who underwrite contracts of insurance at Lloyd's on behalf of the Names who are members of the syndicates under their management, and who reinsure contracts of insurance and pay claims. (3) They may be combined agents, who perform both the role of members' agents, and the role of managing agents in respect of the syndicates under their management.

The agency agreements were contractual. In some cases, there was a direct contract between the Names and the managing agents. In these cases, the plaintiffs were referred to as 'direct Names'. In other cases, the Names entered into a contract with the underwriting agent, who entered into a 'sub-Agency' agreement with the managing agent. In these cases, the plaintiffs were referred to as 'indirect Names'. The plaintiffs argued that the defendant managing agents were liable in tort to both the 'direct' and 'indirect' Names. The reason for pursuing actions in tort as well as in contract is partly that in some instances as we have seen there was no contract between the Name and the managing agent; and partly because in the case of the direct Names the plaintiffs could claim the benefit of a more generous 'limitation period' in tort. As we noted in respect of defective premises, the limitation period in negligence begins to run only when some damage has been caused, since this is when the 'cause of action' accrues. In contract, the relevant period runs from the breach.

Giving the leading judgment in a unanimous House of Lords, Lord Goff decided that the *direct Names* could choose to sue the managing agents either in contract, or in tort. Furthermore, the *indirect Names* could sue the managing agents in tort despite the existence of a contractual chain. Building on his own judgment in *Spring v Guardian Assurance*, Lord Goff again emphasized the concept of assumption of responsibility drawn from *Hedley Byrne*; noted that *Hedley Byrne* was founded on earlier case law in which there was concurrent liability in contract and in tort which was not solely for negligent statements but extended to professional services more generally; and defended the idea that there was a role for tort law even in circumstances where the parties had entered into contractual arrangements. Such arrangements did not exclude the possibility of a tort action. However, he also emphasized that the action in tort would be subject to limitations derived from the terms of the relevant contracts.

Lord Goff, at 180–1

We can see that [the decision in *Hedley Byrne*] rests upon a relationship between the parties, which may be general or specific to the particular transaction, and which may or may not be contractual in nature. All of their Lordships spoke in terms of one party having assumed or undertaken a responsibility towards the other . . . though *Hedley Byrne* was concerned with the provision of information and advice, the example given by Lord Devlin of the relationship between solicitor and client, and his and Lord Morris's statements of principle, show that the principle extends beyond the provision of information and advice to include the performance of other services. It follows, of course, that although, in the case of the provision of information and advice, reliance upon it by the other party will be necessary to establish a cause of action (because otherwise the negligence will have no causative effect), nevertheless there may be other circumstances in which there will be the necessary reliance to give rise to the application of the principle. In particular, as cases concerned with solicitor and client demonstrate, where the plaintiff entrusts the defendant with the conduct of his affairs, in general or in particular, he may be held to have relied on the defendant to exercise due skill and care in such conduct.

In subsequent cases concerned with liability under the *Hedley Byrne* principle in respect of negligent misstatements, the question has frequently arisen whether the plaintiff falls within the category of persons to whom the maker of the statement owes a duty of care. In seeking to contain that category of persons within reasonable bounds, there has been some tendency on the part of the courts to criticise the concept of "assumption of responsibility" as being "unlikely to be a helpful or realistic test in most cases" (see *Smith v. Eric S. Bush* [1990] 1 A.C. 831, 864–865, *per* Lord Griffiths; and see also *Caparo Industries Plc. v. Dickman* [1990] 2 A.C. 605, 628, *per* Lord Roskill). However, at least in cases such as the present, in which the same problem does not arise, there seems to be no reason why recourse should not be had to the concept, which appears after all to have been adopted, in one form or another, by all of their Lordships in *Hedley Byrne* [1964] A.C. 465 (see, e.g., Lord Reid, at pp. 483, 486 and 487; Lord Morris (with whom Lord Hodson agreed), at p. 494; Lord Devlin, at pp. 529 and 531; and Lord Pearce at p. 538). Furthermore, especially in a context concerned with a liability which may arise under a contract or in a situation "equivalent to contract," it must be expected that an objective test will be applied when asking the question whether, in a particular case, responsibility should be held to have been assumed by the defendant to the plaintiff: see *Caparo Industries Plc. v. Dickman* [1990] 2 A.C. 605, 637, *per* Lord Oliver of Aylmerton. In addition, the concept provides its own explanation why there is no problem in cases of this kind about liability for pure economic loss; for if a person assumes responsibility to another in respect of certain services, there is no reason why he should not be liable in damages for that other in respect of economic loss which flows from the negligent performance of those services. It follows that, once the case is identified as falling within the *Hedley Byrne* principle, there should be no need to embark upon any further enquiry whether it is "fair, just and reasonable" to impose liability for economic loss—a point which is, I consider, of some importance in the present case.

In respect of the question of 'concurrency' (liability in both contract and tort on the same facts), Lord Goff examined the case of *Hedley Byrne* and considered whether the principle of 'assumption of responsibility' should be thought to apply only in the *absence* of a contract. Like Oliver J in the earlier case of *Midland Bank Trust Co v Hett, Stubbs and Kemp* [1979] Ch 384, Lord Goff considered that the *Hedley Byrne* principle of 'assumption of responsibility' could give rise to a claim in tort in contractual situations. He also considered that, if his reading of *Hedley Byrne* was incorrect in this respect, it was time to develop tort liability based on assumptions of responsibility to cases where there is indeed a contractual relationship between the parties (at 192). The practical result of this was that a plaintiff who had available remedies in both contract and tort could 'choose that remedy which appears to him to be the most advantageous' (at 194).

Lord Browne-Wilkinson, in the only other full judgment offered, was in substantial agreement with Lord Goff. In particular, he agreed that the central concept was that of 'assumption of responsibility'. But he placed considerable emphasis on 'fiduciary duties' (which are, broadly speaking, relationships of trust and dependence) as forming the historical basis for the action in *Hedley Byrne v Heller*.

At 205

[The] derivation from fiduciary duties of care of the principle of liability in negligence where a defendant has by his action assumed responsibility is illuminating in a number of ways. First, it demonstrates that the alternative claim put forward by the Names based on breach of fiduciary duty, although understandable, was misconceived. The liability of a fiduciary for the negligent transaction of his duties is not a separate head of liability but the paradigm of the general duty to act with care imposed by law on those who take it upon themselves to act for or advise others. Although the historical development of the rules of law and equity have, in the past, caused different labels to be stuck on different manifestations of the duty, in truth the duty of care imposed on bailees, carriers, trustees, directors, agents and others is the same duty: it arises from the circumstances in which the defendants were acting, not from their status or description. It is the fact that they have all assumed responsibility for the property or affairs of others which renders them liable for the careless performance of what they have undertaken to do, not the description of the trade or position which they hold. In my judgment, the duties which the managing agents have assumed to undertake in managing the insurance business of the Names brings them clearly into the category of those who are liable, whether fiduciaries or not, for any lack of care in the conduct of that management.

White v Jones [1995] 2 AC 207

In terms of its treatment of the legal principles, *White v Jones* is perhaps the most controversial of this sequence of three cases. On the other hand, the solution adopted was intended to be confined to the facts of this and other cases relating to negligence in respect of wills. (In fact, the decision has been applied in the different but analogous situation of advice in respect of pension rights, where the defendant advisor is aware that the client intends to make provision for his or her dependents: *Gorham v British Telecommunications plc* [2000] 1 WLR 2129, Court of Appeal.)

In *White v Jones*, a testator executed a new will after a family quarrel, disinheriting his two daughters, the plaintiffs. After a reconciliation, he contacted his solicitors with instructions to draw up a new will, restoring the legacies to the plaintiffs. Little progress was made, and the testator died before the new will was completed. In the earlier case of *Ross v Caunters* [1980] Ch 297, a solicitor was held to owe a duty of care to intended beneficiaries in respect of the proper execution of a will. In that earlier case, it was held that a duty was owed through application of the principle in *Donoghue v Stevenson*. In *White v Jones*, the House of Lords accepted that the simple approach in *Ross v Caunters* could not be maintained in view of the many conceptual problems involved in the case. However, it was also noted that no significant dissatisfaction had ever been expressed with the practical impact of that decision.

Lord Goff frankly acknowledged that there was no true assumption of responsibility on the part of the defendant, towards the plaintiffs. In his judgment, this case concerned a wrong which required a remedy, and the best way of providing this remedy was to 'deem' that the assumption of responsibility which existed between the defendant solicitor and his client also *extended to* the intended beneficiaries who were the plaintiffs in the case. Although this was not truly a case of 'transferred loss' (see our discussion of *The Aliakmon*, above), it was analogous to such a case. The reasons why it was not such a case are set out in the extract below. Part of the controversy was whether this case would have been more appropriately resolved through a contractual remedy.

Lord Goff, at 265–9

. . . Here there is a lacuna in the law, in the sense that practical justice requires that the disappointed beneficiary should have a remedy against the testator's solicitor in circumstances in which neither the testator nor his estate has in law suffered a loss. Professor Lorenz (*Essays in Memory of Professor F. H. Lawson*, p. 90) has said that "this is a situation which comes very close to the cases of 'transferred loss,' the only difference being that the damage due to the solicitor's negligence could never have been caused to the testator or to his executor." In the case of the testator, he suffers no loss because (in contrast to a gift by an inter vivos settlor) a gift under a will cannot take effect until after the testator's death, and it follows that there can be no depletion of the testator's assets in his lifetime if the relevant asset is, through the solicitors' negligence, directed to a person other than the intended beneficiary. The situation is therefore not one in which events have subsequently occurred which have resulted in the loss falling on another. It is one in which the relevant loss could never fall on the testator to whom the solicitor owed a duty, but only on another; and the loss which is suffered by that other, i.e. an expectation loss, is of a character which in any event could never have been suffered by the testator. Strictly speaking, therefore, this is not a case of transferred loss.

Even so, the analogy is very close. In practical terms, part or all of the testator's estate has been lost because it has been dispatched to a destination unintended by the testator. Moreover, had a gift been similarly misdirected during the testator's lifetime, he would either have been able to recover it from the recipient or, if not, he could have recovered the full amount from the negligent solicitor as damages. In a case such as the present, no such remedies are available to the testator or his estate. The will cannot normally be rectified: the testator has of course no remedy: and his estate has suffered no loss, because it has been distributed under the terms of a valid will. In these circumstances, there can be no injustice if the intended beneficiary has a remedy against the solicitor for the full amount which he should have received under the will, this being no greater than the damage for which the solicitor could have been liable to the donor if the loss had occurred in his lifetime.

A contractual approach

It may be suggested that, in cases such as the present, the simplest course would be to solve the problem by making available to the disappointed beneficiary, by some means or another, the benefit of the contractual rights (such as they are) of the testator or his estate against the negligent solicitor, as is for example done under the German principle of Vertrag mit Schutzwirkung fur Dritte. Indeed that course has been urged upon us by Professor Markesinis, 103 L.Q.R. 354, 396–397, echoing a view expressed by Professor Fleming in (1986) 4 O.J.L.S. 235, 241. Attractive though this solution is, there is unfortunately a serious difficulty in its way. The doctrine of consideration still forms part of our law of contract, as does the doctrine of privity of contract which is considered to exclude the recognition of a jus quaesitum tertio. To proceed as Professor Markesinis has suggested may be acceptable in German law, but in this country could be open to criticism as an illegitimate circumvention of these long established doctrines; and this criticism could be reinforced by reference to the fact that, in the case of carriage of goods by sea, a contractual solution to a particular problem of transferred loss, and to other cognate problems, was provided only by recourse to Parliament. Furthermore, I myself do not consider that the present case provides a suitable occasion for reconsideration of doctrines so fundamental as these.

Lord Goff considered potential contractual routes to a remedy in this case, none of which would suffice to fill the 'lacuna':

The tortious solution

I therefore return to the law of tort for a solution to the problem. For the reasons I have already given, an ordinary action in tortious negligence on the lines proposed by Sir Robert Megarry V.-C. in *Ross v. Caunters* [1980] Ch. 297 must, with the greatest respect, be regarded as inappropriate, because it does not meet any of the conceptual problems which have been raised.

Furthermore, for the reasons I have previously given, the *Hedley Byrne* [1964] A.C. 465 principle cannot, in the absence of special circumstances, give rise on ordinary principles to an assumption of responsibility by the testator's solicitor towards an intended beneficiary. Even so it seems to me that it is open to your Lordships' House, as in the *Lenesta Sludge* case [1994] 1 A.C. 85, to fashion a remedy to fill a lacuna in the law and so prevent the injustice which would otherwise occur on the facts of cases such as the present. In the *Lenesta Sludge* case [1994] 1 A.C. 85, as I have said, the House made available a remedy as a matter of law to solve the problem of transferred loss in the case before them. The present case is, if anything, a fortiori, since the nature of the transaction was such that, if the solicitors were negligent and their negligence did not come to light until after the death of the testator, there would be no remedy for the ensuing loss unless the intended beneficiary could claim. In my opinion, therefore, your Lordships' House should in cases such as these extend to the intended beneficiary a remedy under the *Hedley Byrne* principle by holding that the assumption of responsibility by the solicitor towards his client should be held in law to extend to the intended beneficiary who (as the solicitor can reasonably foresee) may, as a result of the solicitor's negligence, be deprived of his intended legacy in circumstances in which neither the testator nor his estate will have a remedy against the solicitor. Such liability will not of course arise in cases in which the defect in the will comes to light before the death of the testator, and the testator either leaves the will as it is or otherwise continues to exclude the previously intended beneficiary from the relevant benefit. I only wish to add that, with the benefit of experience during the 15 years in which *Ross v. Caunters* has been regularly applied, we can say with some confidence that a direct remedy by the intended beneficiary against the solicitor appears to create no problems in practice. That is therefore the solution which I would recommend to your Lordships.

As I see it, not only does this conclusion produce practical justice as far as all parties are concerned, but it also has the following beneficial consequences.

(1) There is no unacceptable circumvention of established principles of the law of contract.

(2) No problem arises by reason of the loss being of a purely economic character.

(3) Such assumption of responsibility will of course be subject to any term of the contract between the solicitor and the testator which may exclude or restrict the solicitor's liability to the testator under the principle in *Hedley Byrne*. It is true that such a term would be most unlikely to exist in practice; but as a matter of principle it is right that this largely theoretical question should be addressed.

(4) Since the *Hedley Byrne* principle is founded upon an assumption of responsibility, the solicitor may be liable for negligent omissions as well as negligent acts of commission: see the *Midland Bank Trust Co.* case [1979] Ch. 384, 416, *per* Oliver J. and *Henderson v. Merrett Syndicates Ltd.* [1995] 2 A.C. 145, 182, *per* Lord Goff of Chieveley. This conclusion provides justification for the decision of the Court of Appeal to reverse the decision of Turner J. in the present case, although this point was not in fact raised below or before your Lordships.

(5) I do not consider that damages for loss of an expectation are excluded in cases of negligence arising under the principle in the *Hedley Byrne* case [1964] A.C. 465, simply because the cause of action is classified as tortious. Such damages may in principle be recoverable in cases of contractual negligence; and I cannot see that, for present purposes, any relevant distinction can be drawn between the two forms of action. In particular, an expectation loss may well occur in cases where a professional man, such as a solicitor, has assumed responsibility for the affairs of another; and I for my part can see no reason in principle why the professional man should not, in an appropriate case, be liable for such loss under the *Hedley Byrne* principle.

In the result, all the conceptual problems, including those which so troubled Lush and Murphy JJ. in *Seale v. Perry* [1982] V.R. 193, can be seen to fade innocuously away. Let me emphasise that I can see no injustice in imposing liability upon a negligent solicitor in a case such as the present where, in the absence of a remedy in this form, neither the testator's estate nor the disappointed beneficiary will have a claim for the loss caused by his negligence. This is the injustice which, in my opinion, the judges of this country should address by recognising that cases such as these call for an appropriate remedy, and that the common law is not so sterile as to be incapable of supplying that remedy when it is required.

Lord Goff pointed out that the route to a contractual remedy is blocked by the doctrine of privity. English law did not recognize a right on behalf a stranger to a contract to sue on the terms of the contract. He considered some important cases which qualified the doctrine of privity, including *The Albazero* [1977] AC 774 and *Linden Gardens v Lenesta Sludge* [1994] 1 AC 85. However, these cases were inapplicable for two reasons. First, the cases did not give a remedy directly to the third party, but only allowed a *contracting* party to sue for damages that they had suffered. The cases did not allow the third party (who had suffered the loss) to *compel* the contracting party to sue. Here, the executors, as representatives of the contracting party (the testator), may have been unwilling to commit resources to bringing an action on behalf of the disappointed beneficiaries, to the possible detriment of the estate. Second, the previous case law only allowed actions in contract on behalf of third parties where the loss suffered by the third parties was *the same loss* that the contracting party would have suffered, had that loss not been 'transferred' in one way or another. In *Linden Gardens*, for example, there had been an assignment of contractual rights. In *White v Jones*, as Lord Goff pointed out, the loss of *[not contract]* expectation on the part of the beneficiaries was not the sort of loss that the testator could ever have suffered.

Subsequently, there has been significant legislative qualification of the doctrine of privity of contract. The Contracts (Rights of Third Parties) Act 1999 provides that:

1.—(1) . . . a person who is not a party to a contract (a 'third party') may in his own right enforce a term of the contract if—

(a) the contract expressly provides that he may, or

(b) . . . the term purports to confer a benefit on him *[White v Jones type of case]*

The Law Commission, in its Report *Privity of Contract: Contracts for the Benefit of Third Parties* (Law Com No 242, 1996), stressed that this reform was intended to be 'a relatively conservative and moderate measure' (para 5.10), which should not prevent the courts from instigating more radical change if they thought it appropriate. The Law Commission (referring to Kit Barker's analysis in 'Are We Up To Expectations? Solicitors, Beneficiaries and the Tort/Contract Divide' (1994) 14 OJLS 137, 142) explained that:

7.25 It is our view . . . that the negligent will-drafting situation ought to lie, and does lie, just outside our proposed reform. It is an example of the rare case where the third party, albeit expressly designated "as a beneficiary" in the contract, has no presumed right of enforcement. Indeed it is arguable that, by merely adjusting the wording of the second limb to include promises that are "of benefit to" expressly designated third parties, rather than those that "confer benefits on" third parties, we would have brought the negligent will-drafting situation within our reform. But we believe that these words draw the crucial distinction between the situation where it is natural to presume that the contracting parties intended to confer legal rights on the third party and the situation where that presumption is forced and artificial.

As such, the Law Commission would support the extension of tort law to fit a case such as this.

As we have seen, Lord Goff's solution was intended to be contained in its scope. It was an attempt to resolve what he considered to be an obvious injustice, and the extension of the assumption of responsibility was overtly fictional. Lord Browne-Wilkinson, on the other hand, decided the case not on the basis of a fiction, but by an extended understanding of the concept of 'voluntary assumption of responsibility' itself. Again, he argued that the duty of care in *Hedley Byrne* cases is but one example of a fiduciary duty. In the case of fiduciary duties, he argued, it was not necessary to show that the plaintiff had consciously relied upon the defendant. In fact, it was not necessary to show that the plaintiff had any knowledge of the defendant's role in respect of his or her interests at all. Rather, it is sufficient for the fiduciary to know that the 'economic welfare' of the plaintiff depends upon his exercise of due care. The difference between Lord Goff's understanding of 'assumption of responsibility' (rooted in 'closeness to contract'), and Lord Browne-Wilkinson's understanding (based in 'fiduciary relationships') becomes clear. On the latter interpretation, the plaintiffs here are owed a fiduciary duty, since this can arise without any knowledge on their part. There is a true 'assumption of responsibility'. On Lord Goff's analysis, the assumption was merely 'deemed' to extend to the plaintiffs, in order to deal with a particular, perceived injustice.

Lord Browne-Wilkinson, at 275–6

The solicitor who accepts instructions to draw a will knows that the future economic welfare of the intended beneficiary is dependent upon his careful execution of the task. It is true that the intended beneficiary (being ignorant of the instructions) may not rely on the particular solicitor's actions. But, as I have sought to demonstrate, in the case of a duty of care flowing from a fiduciary relationship liability is not dependent upon actual reliance by the plaintiff on the defendant's actions but on the fact that, as the fiduciary is well aware, the plaintiff's economic well-being is dependent upon the proper discharge by the fiduciary of his duty. Second, the solicitor by accepting the instructions has entered upon, and therefore assumed responsibility for, the task of procuring the execution of a skilfully drawn will knowing that the beneficiary is wholly dependent upon his carefully carrying out his function. That assumption of responsibility for the task is a feature of both the two categories of special relationship so far identified in the authorities. It is not to the point that the solicitor only entered on the task pursuant to a contract with the third party (i.e. the testator). There are therefore present many of the features which in the other categories of special relationship have been treated as sufficient to create a special relationship to which the law attaches a duty of care. In my judgment the analogy is close.

Moreover there are more general factors which indicate that it is fair just and reasonable to impose liability on the solicitor. Save in the case of those rash testators who make their own wills, the proper transmission of property from one generation to the next is dependent upon the due discharge by solicitors of their duties. Although in any particular case it may not be possible to demonstrate that the intended beneficiary relied upon the solicitor, society as a whole does rely on solicitors to carry out their will making functions carefully. To my mind it would be unacceptable if, because of some technical rules of law, the wishes and expectations of testators and beneficiaries generally could be defeated by the negligent actions of solicitors without there being any redress. It is only just that the intended beneficiary should be able to recover the benefits which he would otherwise have received.

The three cases extracted above remove boundaries. They seek to articulate principles which cross the boundaries between acts and statements, acts and omissions, and even contract and tort. Importantly, one of the boundaries that is broken down is the boundary between economic and other forms of loss. The nature of the loss as purely 'economic' has indeed received relatively little emphasis in these more recent cases. Whether or not there is a 'statement' is barely mentioned. And as we have already said, beyond these cases the verbal formula 'assumption of responsibility' has been increasingly used in a wide range of different situations, including cases of psychiatric harm and educational failure. On the other hand, the meaning of that term is elusive. Could the case law in categories C and D be explained without it?

The authors of the following article argue that the case law under *Hedley Byrne* could indeed be explained without reference to this terminology. Writing shortly after *White v Jones*, they suggest that the basis of liability under *Hedley Byrne* was in fiduciary duties along the lines proposed by Lord Browne-Wilkinson in *White*. Not all of the case law (including *White*) fits into the idea that the claimant has 'entrusted the defendant with his affairs'. Therefore, a broader formulation is preferred:

N. J. McBride and A. Hughes, '*Hedley Byrne* in the House of Lords: An Interpretation' (1995) 15 LS 376, 384

The defendant has accepted power over the plaintiff knowing that he is expected to use reasonable care and skill in exercising that power. He has failed to do so and the plaintiff has suffered loss as a result.

This, the authors argue, could encompass 'statements' cases such as *Smith v Bush* (and those other cases that satisfy the criteria in *Caparo*) since the giving of the statement amounts to accepting power over the plaintiff. The advantage of this formulation is that it shows how a defendant can be said to have accepted *something* of significance, without having accepted legal liability in the fullest sense.[23]

2.5 SUBSEQUENT DEVELOPMENTS IN CATEGORIES C AND D: THE ROLE OF 'VOLUNTARY ASSUMPTION OF RESPONSIBILITY' CONSIDERED

Since *White v Jones*, the House of Lords has had two major opportunities to reconsider the proper approach to cases of economic loss outside categories A and B.[24] The Court of Appeal, meanwhile, has struggled to divine from the existing case law what approach ought to be taken

---

[23] McBride and Hughes also suggest that *Hedley Byrne* is wholly separate from negligence liability derived from *Donoghue v Stevenson*. This would however be inconsistent with Lord Devlin's discussion of 'proximity' in *Hedley Byrne* itself.

[24] We do not here include *Phelps v Hillingdon* or *McFarlane v Tayside* (and its follow up *Rees v Darlington*). These cases said little about assumption of responsibility and the former is now interpreted as a case of personal injury. These cases are discussed in subsequent sections of this chapter.

to such cases. We will suggest that the most recent decision of the House of Lords has offered some important clarification.

Williams v Natural Life Health Foods [1998] 1 WLR 830

This case was of an exceptional kind and the conclusions related closely to the facts in hand.

The second defendant M, an individual, formed a limited company (the first defendant). He was the managing director and principal shareholder in the company. The plaintiffs negotiated a franchise with the company, dealing directly with M. The franchise was much less successful than expected, and the plaintiffs traded at a loss before eventually going out of business. They argued that they had been negligently advised. When the company was wound up, the plaintiffs joined M as a party to the action. Ordinarily, the director of a limited company has no personal liability in respect of the company's debts. The plaintiffs argued that M had *assumed personal responsibility* to them, so that he owed a duty in tort. The judgment should be understood as directed to this rather special argument, which had to be sufficiently strong to overcome the protection offered to those involved in running a company by the principle of limited liability. As Lord Steyn put it:

> **Lord Steyn,** at p. 835
>
> What matters is not that the liability of the shareholders is limited but that a company is a separate entity, distinct from its directors, servants or other agents. The trader who incorporates a company to which he transfers his business creates a legal person on whose behalf he may afterwards act as director.

Giving the sole judgment in the case, Lord Steyn made clear that the guiding principles to be applied were to be drawn from the judgments of Lord Goff (rather than of Lord Browne-Wilkinson) in the cases of *Henderson v Merrett* and *White v Jones*. As such, there must not only be an assumption of responsibility on the part of the defendant (in the case of M, an assumption of 'personal' responsibility), but the plaintiffs must have *reasonably relied upon* that assumption. *White v Jones* itself did not fit this description particularly well since there was no reliance, and *Smith v Bush* also did not fit it well for the reasons we explored above. Lord Steyn explained both cases on the basis that, '[c]oherence must sometimes yield to practical justice' (at 837). Academic criticisms of the principle of assumption of responsibility, he argued, were overstated so far as they were based on these two exceptional cases. In this particular case:

> **Lord Steyn,** at 835
>
> . . . it is important to make clear that a director of a contracting company may only be made liable where it is established by evidence that he assumed personal liability and that there was the necessary reliance. There is nothing fictional about this species of liability in tort.

Because the plaintiffs' case depended on showing not just an assumption of responsibility by the company (now wound up), but an assumption of *personal* responsibility on the part of M, it was necessary to show evidence of specific words or conduct which crossed an important line. For example, in the case of *Fairline Shipping Corporation v Adamson* [1975] QB 180, a company director was held personally liable in tort, because he had created the 'clear impression' that he was personally answerable for services. He had not, for example, used company notepaper when writing to the plaintiffs, nor issued an invoice in the name of the company. On the other side of the line was the New Zealand case of *Trevor Ivory Limited v Anderson* [1992] 2 NZLR 517, in which there was (in the words of McGechan J), 'no singular feature which would justify belief that Mr Ivory was accepting a personal commitment, as opposed to the known company obligation'. Applying these principles to the case in hand:

Lord Steyn, at 838

In the present case there were no personal dealings between Mr Mistlin and the plaintiffs. There were no exchanges or conduct which crossed the line which could have conveyed to the plaintiffs that Mr Mistlin was willing to assume personal responsibility to the plaintiffs . . . I am also satisfied that there was not even evidence that the plaintiffs believed that Mr Mistlin was undertaking personal responsibility to them. Certainly, there was nothing in the circumstances to show that the plaintiffs could reasonably have looked to Mr Mistlin for indemnification of any loss.

If this seems a very strong test for assumption of responsibility, this can be explained by the particular need to show an assumption of *personal* responsibility sufficient to by-pass the corporate structure within which the parties were working.

Application of the Principles in the Court of Appeal

Recent cases in the Court of Appeal have shown a confused response to the developments above. Three wrong directions have been taken by the Court of Appeal. In theory, all should be discontinued after the decision of the House of Lords in *Customs and Excise Commissioners v Barclays Bank* (below).

First, the Court of Appeal has in recent cases treated the 'assumption of responsibility', and the *Caparo* three stage approach, as alternative tests. To be on the safe side, it has attempted to apply both tests, and has argued that these tests 'should' lead to the same result. In fact there is no reason to assume, as the Court of Appeal has done in these cases, that the two tests will lead to the same answer, and the House of Lords' decision in *CEC v Barclays Bank* illustrates this.

Second, the Court of Appeal has doubted whether 'assumption of responsibility' has any distinct meaning. In *Merrett v Babb* [2001] EWCA Civ 214; [2001] QB 1174 the Court of Appeal held that an individual surveyor owed a duty of care to the claimants when he prepared a negligent valuation of a domestic property. May LJ implied that the notion of 'assumption of responsibility' has been so weakened through evolution in the case law that it no longer provides a distinct test, but 'merges with' *Caparo*. Rather lamely, we are told that the question in each case is 'whether the law recognises that there is a duty of care' (para [41]). The main evidence for this is in the following brief remarks of Lord Slynn in the case of *Phelps v Hillingdon* [2000] 3 WLR 776, 791:

[assumption of responsibility] means simply that the law recognises that there is a duty of care. It is not so much that responsibility is assumed as that it is recognised or imposed by law.

The remarks in *Phelps* are pitched at a very general level and could be said to have done no more than to stress the objectivity of the assumption of responsibility. We have already said that the objectivity of the test does not mean that it has no distinct meaning *at all. Henderson,* as we have said, is authority against that proposition, Lord Goff continuing to maintain that assumption of responsibility could be understood in terms of 'closeness to contract', while Lord Browne-Wilkinson maintained that the concept could be understood as a species of 'fiduciary' duty. *Barclays Bank* is further evidence that assumption of responsibility has some meaning, as we will see.

Third, in *Bank of Credit and Commerce International (Overseas) Ltd v Price Waterhouse* [1998] BCC 617, Sir Brian Neill suggested that there are not two, but three tests for the duty of care, each of which ought to be applied in turn. These are the threefold test under *Caparo*; the assumption of responsibility; and the 'incremental test'. It should be clearly said that the incremental test has always been a part of the *Caparo* approach, and is not a separate test. Proximity, in particular, should not be approached under *Caparo* without reference to analogous cases.

In *Barclays Bank*, the House of Lords clearly did not approach 'incremental development' as a separate test. Lord Bingham expressly said that incrementalism did not stand alone. There needs to be incremental development *of* something (the applicable idea of proximity, for example). More fundamentally, the other tests ('voluntary assumption' and the three-stage test from *Caparo*) are not 'rival' tests in any sense. They are appropriate to different cases, and they need not give the same result. At most, there are two alternative tests, not three rival methods. In fact, if 'assumption of responsibility' is treated as an aspect of proximity, there is only one test though it calls for different techniques in different circumstances.

Customs and Excise Commissioners v Barclays Bank [2004] 1 WLR 2027 (Colman J); [2005] 1 WLR 2082 (CA); [2006] 3 WLR 1 (HL)

We will explore all three levels of decision in this case, from first instance to House of Lords. Despite first appearances, this case sheds light on the role of voluntary assumption of responsibility, and on the appropriate general method in deciding economic loss cases outside the exclusionary rules in categories A and B.

The Customs and Excise Commissioners obtained 'freezing orders', and served them on the defendant bank. The purpose of these orders was to prevent two companies from removing funds from their bank accounts, so that the claimants could recover outstanding VAT from those accounts. The defendant bank, which held the relevant accounts, failed to take action to prevent funds from being moved out of the accounts. It was alleged that this failure was negligent. The Customs and Excise Commissioners could not recover the full sums owing. They sought to recover the shortfall (amounting to several million pounds) from the defendant bank on the basis that it had breached a duty of care owed to them, to abide by the orders. On a preliminary issue, Colman J held that no duty of care was owed by the bank ([2004] 1 WLR 2027). His decision was reversed by the Court of Appeal.

The first instance judgment of Colman J was particularly cogent. In respect of the 'assumption of responsibility', he made clear that this was not *always* a prerequisite of the duty of care in cases of economic loss. Colman J accepted that the assumption of responsibility was based on an 'objective' test, not on voluntary acceptance of legal responsibility in the fullest sense. But he was clear that the 'assumption of responsibility' is not an entirely empty phrase.

Colman J [2004] EWHC 122 (Comm)

51 In my judgment, [the] authorities do not support the proposition that in every case where there has been negligent provision of a service which is said to have caused the claimant pure economic loss there has to be a relationship akin to contract before a duty of care can be

imposed. If, objectively analysed, the relationship is too oblique or indirect to bear that analogy there can be an assumption of responsibility only in the artificial sense that a responsibility is imposed as a matter of law. However, when one comes to the void at which Lord Oliver arrived in *Caparo Industries plc v Dickman* [1990] 2 AC 605, 637G, the methodology appropriate to a relationship akin to contract has to be replaced and in those circumstances it is the threefold test which provides a broad analytical guideline towards the existence of a duty of care. However, there may be novel factual situations where it is appropriate to supplement application of the threefold test by reference to other comparable situations in which the courts have imposed or, as the case may be, declined to impose a duty of care. This supplementation has been explained by Phillips LJ in *Reeman v Department of Transport* [1997] 2 Lloyd's Rep 648, 677:

> "When confronted with a novel situation the court does not . . . consider these matters [foreseeability, proximity and fairness] in isolation. It does so by comparison with established categories of negligence to see whether the facts amount to no more than a small extension of a situation already covered by authority, or whether a finding of the existence of a duty of care would effect a significant extension to the law of negligence. Only in exceptional cases will the court accept that the interests of justice justify such an extension of the law."

Colman J argued that if there is a relationship 'akin to contract' in the sense explained in *Henderson v Merrett*, there is no reason to consider the three-stage test under *Caparo v Dickman*. If however there is no relationship akin to contract (if the relationship is 'too oblique'), then in terms of *Hedley Byrne* we arrive at a 'void'. This is the void that the *Caparo* three-stage test was designed to fill. The three-stage test cannot however be applied without reference to analogous cases, otherwise proximity in particular has no clear meaning.

In this case, there was no relationship akin to contract. Colman J saw this as a case where the relationship between the parties was akin to that between adversaries in civil litigation.[25] The bank had not *chosen* to enter any relationship at all with the claimants, but had been served with an order, carrying potential legal implications should they fail to act. In *Connolly-Martin v Davis* [1999] PNLR 826; *Welsh v CC of Merseyside Police* [1993] 1 All ER 692; and *Elguzouli-Daf v Commissioner of Police for the Metropolis* [1995] QB 335, it had been said that parties to litigation could only owe one another duties to take care if there was some special feature of conduct to suggest an assumption of responsibility. Colman J regarded this as requiring an assumption of responsibility in the strong sense exemplified by *Williams* (above). In this sort of case, there needs to be specific conduct which amounts to an assumption of responsibility and which crosses the line between one party, and another. Without this, there could not be said to be 'proximity'; and Colman J also doubted whether the imposition of the duty could be 'fair, just and reasonable'.

It is suggested that this element of Colman J's reasoning is particularly useful. It amounts to an argument that an assumption of responsibility may *either* be deduced from the general nature of the relationship (as in *Henderson v Merrett*), or—if the general nature of the relationship is not compatible with such a deduction—it may be deduced from specific words, conduct or circumstances which (applying *Williams*) override the general features of the relationship. This is consistent with the subsequent decision of the House of Lords.

The only special element of the defendants' conduct which could be said to show that they had assumed responsibility was the writing of a letter, acknowledging the freezing order. This, however, was received by the claimants only after the funds had been released. So even if this

---

25 The House of Lords did not go quite so far, but did decide that the relationship was 'adverse'.

letter could amount to conduct which established that responsibility was assumed, it was too late. The House of Lords for its part declined to attach any importance at all to the letter:

Lord Bingham (HL)

3. ... Had the letters reached the Commissioners before release of the funds, the judge would have attached significance to them. ... But in my respectful opinion they were of no significance. The Bank was bound to comply with the order of the court irrespective of any confirmation on its part. The letters did not affect the factual or the legal position. Their purpose was to pave the way to reimbursement of the costs of compliance incurred by the Bank.

In support of Colman J's conclusion that no duty is owed, there were strongly involuntary elements in the relationship between the parties. Recalling McBride and Hughes' formulation, quoted above, had the defendants 'accepted power over' the claimants? Certainly not. They had done nothing other than accept deposits from clients that might, in the future, attract freezing orders. It is a very long stretch to get this relationship into any meaningful interpretation of *Hedley Byrne*.

In the Court of Appeal, Longmore LJ proposed that the various different tests for the duty of care 'should' arrive at the same answer if they are applied in turn. Longmore LJ primarily decided this case in accordance with the three-fold test derived from *Caparo v Dickman*. On the way to concluding that this test was satisfied, his analysis was not always convincing. For example, he defined the relationship between the parties as 'proximate' because it was not in any sense 'remote' (para [30]). This does not take adequate account of the special position of a bank which receives a freezing order. It will be recalled that Colman J dealt with this special position by requiring a *Williams*-style, specific assumption of responsibility. Longmore LJ was also very brief in his comments on the very important issue of 'the incremental approach', which (following dicta in *BCCI v Price Waterhouse*) he erroneously treated as a separate or 'third' approach:

(3) The incremental approach

36 For much the same reasons, the third approach to duty of care, viz, the incremental approach, yields a similar result. It was evidently contemplated in *Z Ltd v A-Z* that the banks could and would exercise reasonable care to preserve a defendant's assets and not allow them to be dissipated. It is but a short step to hold that they should be liable to a claimant who suffers loss if such reasonable care is not exercised. Moreover, the sort of liability envisaged is not so very different from the kind of liabilities to which banks are well accustomed, e g, liability to their own customer if money is paid away in error.

We should note that *Z Ltd v A-Z* [1982] QB 558 was not a case in which a duty of care was established nor even pleaded. It was a case in which banks sought a declaration of the likely legal effects of the newly introduced freezing orders. The short treatment of 'incremental' development is particularly surprising given that this was a case without close analogy, which was neither a case of negligent misstatement nor of negligent services *offered to the claimant*, or *to anyone who wished to benefit the claimant* (see our discussion of *White v Jones*).

Having held, in these brief terms, that the three stage test was satisfied, Longmore LJ was faced with deciding what to do about the 'assumption of responsibility'. There was, in this case, no specific conduct suggesting an assumption of responsibility, but Longmore LJ had already said that the various tests 'should' yield the same result. Therefore, he suggested that an assumption of responsibility could be 'deemed', applying the weakest possible approach in *Phelps* (para [48]).

If this was the correct approach to 'voluntary assumption of responsibility', then it would obviously be desirable for the term to be discontinued as an element of the duty of care inquiry. But we have already suggested that trying to make this concept fit every case of economic loss is unnecessary and unhelpful.

Barclays Bank in the House of Lords [2006] UKHL 28; [2006] 3 WLR 1

The House of Lords restored Colman J's decision that no duty of care was owed.

There were five separate and subtly different judgments in the *Barclays Bank* case (though no dissents). What follows may be seen as a guide to reading the full report; and an outline of the most important conclusions.

1. The first stage in deciding a novel case of economic loss is to ask whether there is a voluntary assumption of responsibility.

2. If an assumption of responsibility is established, this may be sufficient.

In other words, there may be no need to consider policy issues.

Lord Bingham

4 . . . there are cases in which one party can accurately be said to have assumed responsibility for what is said or done to another, the paradigm situation being a relationship having all the indicia of contract save consideration. *Hedley Byrne* would, but for the express disclaimer, have been such a case. *White v Jones* and *Henderson v Merrett Syndicates Ltd*, although the relationship was more remote, can be seen as analogous. Thus, like Colman J (whose methodology was commended by Paul Mitchell and Charles Mitchell, "Negligence Liability for Pure Economic Loss" (2005) 121 LQR 194, 199), I think it is correct to regard an assumption of responsibility as a sufficient but not a necessary condition of liability, a first test which, if answered positively, may obviate the need for further inquiry. If answered negatively, further consideration is called for.

This is consistent with the approach of Colman J.

3. At least two of the judges seem to have treated assumption of responsibility as an aspect of proximity.

Lord Hoffmann was particularly clear on this point.

Lord Hoffmann

35 . . . In . . . cases in which the loss has been caused by the claimant's reliance on information provided by the defendant, it is critical to decide **whether the defendant (rather than someone else) assumed responsibility** for the accuracy of the information to the claimant (rather than to someone else) or for its use by the claimant for one purpose (rather than another). The answer does not depend upon what the defendant intended but, as in the case of contractual liability, upon what would reasonably be inferred from his conduct against the background of all the circumstances of the case. The purpose of the inquiry is to establish

whether there was, in relation to the loss in question, the necessary relationship (or "proximity") between the parties and, as Lord Goff of Chieveley pointed out in *Henderson v Merrett Syndicates Ltd* at 181, the existence of that relationship and the foreseeability of economic loss will make it unnecessary to undertake any further inquiry into whether it would be fair, just and reasonable to impose liability. In truth, the case is one in which, but for the alleged absence of the necessary relationship, there would be no dispute that a duty to take care existed and the relationship is what makes it fair, just and reasonable to impose the duty.

It is suggested that Lord Walker also treated assumption of responsibility as an aspect of proximity, although his reasoning was less explicit (para [74]).

We have already argued that this is the right approach. But if 'assumption of responsibility' is an aspect of proximity, then it forms part of the three-stage test. And if this is the case, how can an assumption of responsibility be 'sufficient', without regard to policy concerns? Proximity supplies only one of the three necessary elements of the three-stage test. In the extract above, Lord Hoffmann hints that where there is an assumption of responsibility, it is the *nature of the relationship* which *makes* the duty fair, just, and reasonable. The proposed 'sufficiency' of assumption of responsibility is important, particularly given the use of the concept *beyond* the area of economic loss. It may need future consideration.

4. No assumption of responsibility could be established.

In this case, there was an *adverse* relationship between the parties. A degree of voluntariness is essential to any 'assumption of responsibility', even if the test for its existence is objective. Here, the defendants did not choose their relationship with the claimant. On the contrary they were exposed, through the freezing order, to the risk of proceedings for contempt of court. On any established test, there was no assumption of responsibility.

Lord Bingham

14   I do not think that the notion of assumption of responsibility, even on an objective approach, can aptly be applied to the situation which arose between the commissioners and the bank on notification to it of the orders. Of course it was bound by law to comply. But it had no choice. It did not assume any responsibility towards the commissioners as the giver of references in *Hedley Byrne* (but for the disclaimer) and *Spring*, the valuers in *Smith v Eric S Bush*, the solicitors in *White v Jones* and the agents in *Henderson v Merrett Syndicates Ltd* may plausibly be said to have done towards the recipient or subject of the references, the purchasers, the beneficiaries and the Lloyd's Names. Save for the notification of the orders (and treating as irrelevant the letters written by the bank: see para 3 above) nothing crossed the line between the commissioners and the bank: see *Williams v Natural Life Health Foods Ltd* [1998] 1 WLR 830, 835. Nor do I think that the commissioners can be said in any meaningful sense to have relied on the bank. The commissioners, having obtained their orders and notified them to the bank, were no doubt confident that the bank would act promptly and effectively to comply. But reliance in the law is usually taken to mean that if A had not relied on B he would have acted differently. Here the commissioners could not have acted differently, since they had availed themselves of the only remedy which the law provided. Mr Sales suggested, although only as a fall-back argument, that the relationship between the commissioners and the bank was, in Lord Shaw's words (in *Nocton v Lord Ashburton* [1914] AC 932, 972) adopted by Lord Devlin in *Hedley Byrne* [1964] AC 465, 529, "equivalent to contract". But the essence of any contract is voluntariness, and the bank's position was wholly involuntary.

This conclusion seems incontrovertible. But it also shows that the House of Lords regards the assumption of responsibility as having *some* meaning. No matter how elastic, it could not stretch to cover this case.

5. If there is no assumption of responsibility (as here), this is not the end of the matter.

The three-stage test from *Caparo* may still lead to the conclusion that a duty is owed. On our preferred account, if there is no assumption of responsibility, the three-stage test is still to be applied. In such a case, proximity must be present but (in the absence of an assumption of responsibility) will not be sufficient. It is suggested that this explains the otherwise obscure reference to proximity in the following paragraph:

Lord Bingham

15   It is common ground that the foreseeability element of the threefold test is satisfied here. The bank obviously appreciated that, since risk of dissipation has to be shown to obtain a freezing injunction, the commissioners were liable to suffer loss if the injunction were not given effect. It was not contended otherwise. The concept of proximity in the context of pure economic loss is notoriously elusive. But it seems to me that the parties were proximate only in the sense that one served a court order on the other and that other appreciated the risk of loss to the first party if it was not obeyed. I think it is the third, policy, ingredient of the threefold test which must be determinative.

nor satisfied earlier.

Lord Bingham says there is 'proximity' here, but only in a form that does not provide a particularly compelling reason for finding that the defendants owed a duty of care. This is why the policy ingredient would be decisive.

Again, this approach (accepting that the three stage test may be satisfied where there is *no* assumption of responsibility) shows that it is wrong to assume that both tests must arrive at the same result, or that there must always be an assumption of responsibility in a successful economic loss case. *Smith v Bush* can finally be reconciled with the other case law under *Hedley Byrne*. *Smith v Bush* is simply a case where there was no assumption of responsibility; but the three requirements of foreseeability, proximity and 'policy' were satisfied in the claimants' favour. *Barclays Bank* however is *not* such a case, because the policy arguments were determined against the claimant.

6. Policy issues were decisive against a duty of care in this case.

A common theme of the judgments in the House of Lords is that in the absence of an assumption of responsibility, and given that there was foreseeability and arguable proximity, policy issues would be key to the outcome. On analysis of the policy issues, it was not 'fair, just and reasonable' to recognize a duty of care on the present facts. Lord Walker found the issues to be more finely balanced than the others, but noted that if freezing orders give rise to duties of care for banks, then other actors who are subject to such orders may also find themselves owing duties of care to the tax authorities. For him, this was the decisive consideration against a duty of care. Lord Bingham usefully encapsulated his own approach to the policy issues as follows:

Lord Bingham

23   Lastly, it seems to me in the final analysis unjust and unreasonable that the bank should, on being notified of an order which it had no opportunity to resist, become exposed to a liability which was in this case for a few million pounds only, but might in another case be for very

much more. For this exposure it had not been in any way rewarded, its only protection being the commissioners' undertaking to make good (if ordered to do so) any loss which the order might cause it, protection scarcely consistent with a duty of care owed to the commissioners but in any event valueless in a situation such as this.

These considerations are broadly present in the other judgments too.

It was also astutely pointed out (for example by Lord Rodger) that the Commissioners did not *rely on the defendants* to comply with the order. The Commissioners relied on the courts to enforce the order, not on the defendants to comply with it.

Lord Rodger's point about reliance brings us to another distinctive feature of this case.

7. Lord Hoffmann's short-cut: no common law duty of care could be said to arise *out of the freezing order itself.*

Lord Hoffmann drew a parallel between this case, and the cases of *Stovin v Wise* [1996] AC 923 and *Gorringe v Calderdale* [2004] 1 WLR 1057 (extracted in Section 6.3 below). The *only* reason for saying that the defendant bank owed a duty to the claimant, other than fore-seeability, is that it had been served with a freezing order. But the order was enforceable through an action for contempt of court, should the bank or its employees 'flout' the order with the required degree of intention. There was no valid way of getting from this order, with its criminal sanctions, to the proposition that a duty was owed *to take care* to comply with the order. Quite the reverse.

Lord Hoffmann

39   There is, in my opinion, a compelling analogy with the general principle that, for the reasons which I discussed in *Stovin v Wise* [1996] AC 923, 943–944, the law of negligence does not impose liability for mere omissions. It is true that the complaint is that the bank did something: it paid away the money. But the payment is alleged to be the breach of the duty and not the conduct which generated the duty. The duty was generated ab extra, by service of the order. The question of whether the order can have generated a duty of care is comparable with the question of whether a statutory duty can generate a common law duty of care. The answer is that it cannot: see *Gorringe v Calderdale Metropolitan Borough Council* [2004] 1 WLR 1057. The statute either creates a statutory duty or it does not. (That is not to say, as I have already mentioned, that conduct undertaken pursuant to a statutory duty cannot generate a duty of care in the same way as the same conduct undertaken voluntarily.) But you cannot derive a common law duty of care directly from a statutory duty. Likewise, as it seems to me, you cannot derive one from an order of court. The order carries its own remedies and its reach does not extend any further.

Summary: *CEC v Barclays Bank*

Their Lordships were unanimous that there was no voluntary assumption of responsibility where the defendant was served with an order compelling it to safeguard certain funds. As such, all agreed that 'voluntary assumption of responsibility' has some meaning. Some referred to the assumption of responsibility as a particularly important form of proximity. But all were agreed that absence of such an assumption was not the end of the matter. The three stage test was still to be applied, and policy would be determinative in this case.

Lord Hoffmann found a short-cut on the policy issues, reasoning that an order of this sort *cannot* be the basis for a duty to take care in negligence.

Although Lord Mance observed that there is no 'common denominator' to the various tests for a duty of care in economic loss cases, *Barclays Bank* has improved understanding of the relationship between the various tests. This is made clearer by identifying the approach of the Court of Appeal, and its rejection in the House of Lords.[26] Apart from the important contribution of this case to the general method to be applied in respect of economic losses, it will become part of the growing jigsaw of economic loss cases decided at the highest level. If nothing else, it is clear that being the involuntary subject of a court order backed by penal sanctions does not give rise to a duty of care.

General Conclusions on Economic Loss

The restrictions on recovery for economic losses are not arbitrary in the sense we identified in the last section. In categories A and B, the reasons for restricting liability are based in policy. In the case of the remaining categories, there has been an attempt to articulate guiding 'principles'. Here however it has been found that the possible range of cases is too diverse to state applicable principles in any simple way. Outside categories A and B, English law has committed itself to a certain amount of chaos associated with open categories and variable concepts. The end result could certainly be described as unpredictable and hard to interpret. One commentator has suggested that the guiding principles are mere 'veils' for hidden or partly revealed policy concerns (Kit Barker, 'Unreliable Assumptions in the Modern Law of Negligence' (1993) 109 LQR 461). Perhaps, with *Barclays Bank*, the policy concerns are becoming more express. Certainly there is little coyness about policy reasoning in this case, nor in many other key cases dealing with the duty of care in the past few years (Section 6.4 below will make this more apparent). The difficulty is in getting beyond a highly specific case-by-case analysis.

In the light of *Barclays Bank*, we can attempt the following position statement:

1. There is no general exclusionary rule applying to economic loss. Rather, there are two specific exclusionary rules, applying to categories A and B.

2. Outside the scope of the exclusionary rules, additional criteria will apply, in addition to foreseeability or 'neighbourhood'. On the other hand, these criteria also apply to other 'novel' cases in negligence. There are many examples in other sections of this chapter.

3. The 'voluntary assumption of responsibility' is not a mere label. If it is present, then it may suffice without separate consideration of policy issues.

4. Though perhaps sufficient, the assumption of responsibility is not always necessary.[27] If there is no voluntary assumption of responsibility, the three-stage test may

---

[26] The more recent Court of Appeal decision in *West Bromwich Albion FC v Medhat El-Safty* [2006] EWCA Civ 1299 gives little clue whether that court's approach will now change. A football club brought actions in contract and tort against a surgeon in respect of treatment of one of its players. Of course the surgeon owed a duty to the patient, but did he owe a duty to the football club who invested in the player? The court simply held that there was no duty of care on any of the relevant approaches. According to Rix LJ, 'the duty of medical care to the patient was not accompanied by a duty of care not to cause financial loss to a third party' (at [62]).

[27] It may be necessary in a case with strong countervailing policy considerations; in these circumstances, it may be a means of overcoming those policy considerations in a particular case: see our discussion of 'immunities' in Section 3 below.

nevertheless be satisfied. But in such cases, policy considerations will be especially important. The 'fair, just, and reasonable' criterion can be frankly and openly reassessed in terms of 'policy': Lord Bingham, *CEC v Barclays Bank*, at [4].

FURTHER READING

Barker, K., 'Unreliable Assumptions in the Modern Law of Negligence' (1993) 109 LQR 461.

Barker, K., 'Are We Up To Expectations? Solicitors, Beneficiaries, and the Tort/Contract Divide' (1994) 14 OJLS 137.

Barker, K., 'Wielding Occam's Razor: Pruning Strategies for Economic Loss' (2006) 26 OJLS 289.

Benson, P., 'The Basis for Excluding Economic Loss in Tort Law', in Owen, D. (ed.), *Philosophical Foundations of Tort Law* (Oxford: Clarendon Press, 1995).

Burrows, A., 'Solving the Problem of Concurrent Liability' (1995) CLP 103.

Cane, P., *Tort Law and Economic Interests* (2nd edn, Oxford: Clarendon Press, 1995).

Cane, P., 'The Blight of Economic Loss: Is There Life After *Perre v Apand*?' (2000) 8 TLJ 246.

Cooke, R., 'An Impossible Distinction' (1991) 107 LQR 46.

Duncan Wallace, I., '*Anns* Beyond Repair' (1991) 107 LQR 228.

Feldthusen, B., *Economic Negligence: The Recovery of Pure Economic Loss* (Toronto: Carswell, 2000).

Feldthusen, B., 'Pure Economic Loss in the High Court of Australia: Reinventing the Square Wheel?' (2000) 8 *Tort L Rev* 33.

Giliker, P., 'Revisiting Pure Economic Loss: Lessons to be Learnt From the Supreme Court of Canada?' (2005) LS 49.

McBride, N.J., and Hughes, A., '*Hedley Byrne* in the House of Lords: An Intepretation' (1995) 15 LS 376.

Mitchell, P., and Mitchell, C., 'Negligence Liability for Pure Economic Loss' (2005) 121 LQR 194.

O'Dair, R., '*Murphy v Brentwood*: A House With Firm Foundations?' (1991) MLR 561.

Spencer, J.R., 'Defective Premises Act 1972—Defective Law and Defective Law Reform' [1974] 33 CLJ 307.

Stapleton, J, 'Duty of Care and Economic Loss: A Wider Agenda' (1991) 107 LQR 249.

Stapleton, J., 'Comparative Economic Loss: Lessons From Case-Law-Focused Middle Theory' (2002) 50 UCLA L Rev 531.

Stapleton, J., 'The Golden Thread at the Heart of Tort Law: Protection of the Vulnerable' (2003) 24 Aust Bar Rev 135.

Whittaker, S., 'The application of the "broad principle" of *Hedley Byrne* as between parties to a contract' (1997) 17 LS 169.

Witting, C., 'Distinguishing Between Property Damage and Economic Loss: A Personality Thesis' (2001) 21 LS 481.

Witting, C., 'Duty of Care: An Analytical Approach' (2005) 25 OJLS 33.

Yeo, S., 'Rethinking Proximity: A Paper Tiger?' (1997) *Tort L Rev* 174–80.

3. NEGLIGENCE ACTIONS AGAINST PUBLIC AUTHORITIES

3.1 THE GENERAL ISSUES

Ordinary Rules of Tort Law Apply

In principle, the nature of the potential defendant—whether that defendant is a public authority or private party, corporation, or individual—makes no difference to the availability of an action in the tort of negligence. Historically, the Crown (though not other public authorities) was accorded a general immunity against liability at common law. This immunity was removed by the Crown Proceedings Act 1947, although as we will see the statute preserved an immunity in respect of the armed forces.[28] Far from being generally protected from actions in tort, public authorities and their individual officers are vulnerable to a few *additional* tort actions,[29] and are especially exposed to an award of exemplary damages,[30] as well as the usual actions in negligence, nuisance, trespass, and so on.[31] Outside tort law, damages may also be sought against a public authority under the Human Rights Act 1998.[32]

On the other hand, the *Caparo* test for determining whether a duty of care arises is sensitive to all manner of circumstances. In particular, the third stage of *Caparo* requires consideration of whether it would be 'fair, just and reasonable' to impose a duty of care. Certain aspects of the work undertaken by local authorities may well influence the court's verdict on whether a duty of care is to be regarded as fair, just and reasonable. The statutory context of local authorities' work will be one such factor. Another, clearly, is that damages and costs paid by local authorities will cut into welfare and amenity budgets. Equally important is that local authorities could often be said to play a 'peripheral' role in the causation of harm. Commonly, they are accused of 'not conferring a benefit',[33] and their alleged negligence frequently consists of an omission. It is not just the third stage of *Caparo*, but also the 'proximity' criterion, which may influence the court to deny that a duty of care is owed.

3.2 THE VARIETY OF POWERS AND DUTIES

In approaching this area of law, it is important to keep in mind that the following powers and duties are quite distinct. The interplay of these powers and duties gives the area much of its complexity.

---

[28] Crown Proceedings Act 1947, s 10. This immunity was prospectively repealed in 1987. See Immunities, Section 4 below.

[29] Actions for misfeasance in a public office, and malicious prosecution, are discussed in Chapter 2.

[30] One of three possible circumstances in which exemplary damages may currently be available is where servants of the government have acted in a particularly high-handed fashion: *Rookes v Barnard* [1964] AC 1129. See Chapter 8.

[31] See C. Harlow, *State Liability* (OUP, 2004), Chapter 1, relating this to Dicey's constitutional theory.

[32] Sections 7 and 8, introduced in Chapter 1.

[33] Such as appropriate schooling (*Phelps v Hillingdon* [2001] 2 AC 619), safer roads and junctions (*Stovin v Wise* [1996] AC 923), or flood control (*East Suffolk v Kent* [1941] 1 AC 74).

The Duty of Care at Common Law

The duty of care arises at common law. The general rule is that *any* party may owe such a duty to another if the applicable criteria (in *Donoghue v Stevenson* and *Caparo v Dickman*) are fulfilled.

Statutory Duties

Legislation often imposes duties. From the point of view of the law of tort, there are two broad types of statutory duty:

(a) Duties which are clear, precise, designed to benefit a particular group including the claimant, and intended to be actionable at common law. Such duties are actionable through the distinct tort of breach of statutory duty (Chapter 16). A leading example is the duty in *Groves v Wimborne* [1898] 2 QB 402: factory legislation required that certain machinery be fenced. This was for the benefit of workers. When a worker lost his forearm because machinery was unfenced, he was able to claim in tort.

(b) The more usual type of statutory duty is one which is *not* actionable at common law. A very *general* statutory duty, or one not designed to benefit a particular group of people including the claimant, or one that Parliament did not intend to be actionable, will not be enforceable through the action for breach of statutory duty. Many duties where there is a criminal or other sanction set out in the statute will fall into this category, though this is not conclusive.[34] An example of a duty not actionable at common law arises in *O'Rourke v Camden* [1998] AC 188. The duty to offer accommodation to those who are homeless was not narrow and defined and was not for the benefit of a prescribed class of people. It was a social welfare duty. A person who was not housed when he presented himself as homeless could not seek damages in tort, and must instead seek judicial review.

Statutory powers

Unlike a duty, a power confers permission: it specifies that the recipient of the power *may* do something, not that they *must*. Formally, statutory powers allow the recipient to decide what to do, and whether to do it. They generally confer discretion. However, powers do bring with them certain duties, and the exercise (or non-exercise) of discretion is not beyond the reach of public law. Public law provides remedies if discretion is *improperly exercised*, or if there is *an improper failure to exercise a power*. Generally speaking, *damages* are not readily available in an action at public law.[35]

The Role of These Powers and Duties in a Negligence Action

Duties of Care at Common Law

A claim in the tort of negligence cannot succeed unless a duty of care at common law is owed to the claimant. A public body, like anyone else, will be liable in negligence only if the *Caparo* criteria are satisfied, and a duty of care is held to exist.

---

[34] See *Groves v Wimborne* itself: Chapter 16.

[35] The Law Commission has initiated discussion on whether they should be more readily available: Law Commission, *Monetary Remedies in Public Law: A Discussion Paper* (2004). For criticism see R. Bagshaw, 'Monetary Remedies in Public Law: Misdiagnosis and Misdescription' (2006) 26 LS 4–25.

Statutory Duties

We noted above that the action for breach of statutory duty will be available only if the duty in question is a type (a) statutory duty. The criteria are restrictive, and the majority of statutory duties are not actionable in this way.[36]

Supposing there is a statutory duty which is *not* actionable at common law, our next question is whether the existence of the statutory duty in any sense *excludes* the existence of a duty to take care at common law. The clear answer to this is that it does not. However, the *Caparo* criteria will still need to be fulfilled.

Statutory Powers

One of the most difficult of all questions in this area concerns the role of statutory powers: can there be a duty of care at common law in respect of a *negligent exercise*, or *negligent failure to exercise*, a statutory power?

The key to answering this is to remember that the common law duty can *only* arise through applying *Caparo v Dickman*. Statutory power, and common law duty, are separate and distinct. As such:

1. A statutory power does not in itself *give rise to* a duty at common law; but

2. The existence of a power does not *exclude* a duty at common law. Statute does not generally *authorise* careless exercise of powers (though it may confer an explicit immunity from liability).[37]

3.3 LEADING CASES FROM *GEDDIS* TO *X V BEDFORDSHIRE*

Geddis v Proprietor of the Bann Reservoir (1878) 3 App Cas 430 (HL) (on Appeal from the Exchequer Chamber in Ireland)

The defendants were incorporated by Act of Parliament for the purpose of securing a regular supply of water to mills on the banks of the River Bann. The relevant statute conferred power to collect several small streams into a reservoir, and to send down waters through a smaller stream, the Muddock. The defendants did not properly regulate the flow of water or scour the stream; and they were liable for the flooding of the plaintiffs' land which resulted.

Although it predates the unified tort of negligence under *Donoghue v Stevenson*, *Geddis* shows that activities undertaken in the exercise of a statutory power are not beyond the reach of private law, *if* those powers are carelessly exercised. The most influential judicial statement in *Geddis* is the remark of Lord Blackburn which is italicized below. It is important to read this highlighted passage within its context.

Lord Blackburn, *Geddis v Proprietors of the Bann Reservoir*, at 455–6

It is agreed on all sides that the Act requires the promoters, the Defendants, to pour into the channel of the River *Muddock* as much water as, on the average, used formerly to go. . . . And they have a permissive power, for the benefit of the millowners on the *Bann*, to send down

---

[36] Discussed in Chapter 16.
[37] These propositions are most clearly expressed by Lord Steyn in *Stovin v Wise* (extracted below).

more water, both greater in quantity and in a different way from what would have gone in the ordinary natural state of things down the *Muddock* if the Act had not been passed. Now, certainly the result has been that the channel of the *Muddock* as it exists at present is not able to carry off the water they have put into it, and if they have no power to cleanse the channel of the *Muddock*, or to alter it, which was the view taken by the majority of the learned Judges of the Court of Exchequer Chamber below, then they are not liable to damages for doing that which the Act of Parliament authorizes, namely, pouring part of the water of the reservoir into the *Muddock* that it may go to the Bann. *For I take it, without citing cases, that it is now thoroughly well established that no action will lie for doing that which the legislature has authorized, if it be done without negligence, although it does occasion damage to anyone; but an action does lie for doing that which the legislature has authorized, if it be done negligently. And I think that if by a reasonable exercise of the powers, either given by statute to the pro-moters, or which they have at common law, the damage could be prevented it is, within this rule, "negligence" not to make such reasonable exercise of their powers.* I do not think that it will be found that any of the cases (I do not cite them) are in conflict with that view of the law.

Now, upon that view of the law, if in this case the learned Judges in the Exchequer Chamber are right in holding that the Defendants have no power to interfere with the channel of the *Muddock* at all, of course no action will lie against them. But if on the other hand Baron *Fitzgerald* and Chief Baron *Palles* are right in the view which they took, that they have power to do so, I think that the conclusion becomes irresistible that they ought to adopt a reasonable exercise of that power by cleansing, scouring, widening, and deepening, the natural channel of the *Muddock*, so as to make it capable of receiving the waters which they pour down it, and that not to do so before they poured down the water, was a neglect to make a reasonable use of the powers given to them by the statute.

(Emphasis added.)

Lord Blackburn's reference to 'negligence' is not a reference to the *tort* of negligence. Rather, it is a reference to the limited scope of 'statutory authority' as a defence. This defence does not assist a defendant who has acted *without due care*. (Statutory authority is analysed as a defence to private nuisance, in Chapter 10, and to the action in *Rylands v Fletcher*, in Chapter 11.)

The last paragraph extracted seems to suggests that there is greater scope for liability where there is a power to do something, than where there is not. This may seem puzzling. A power after all confers a choice over what to do. How can the existence of a *choice* be the basis for liability? The point being made by Lord Blackburn here is that the defendants could not be made liable for *failing* to do something (adjust the nature of the River Muddock) if they were not *entitled* to do it. In this context then, the crucial question was whether the defendants had a power to do that which they (negligently) failed to do. It is important to note that this is not a case of a *pure* omission (like *Gorringe v Calderdale*, below). It is a case where the *activities* of the defendants caused the flooding, because they failed to take steps, which they were author-ized to take, to ameliorate the effects of their own actions.

The following case is different from *Geddis* in this respect. It emphasizes that there is generally **no duty to confer a benefit** simply because a statute confers a power to do so.

East Suffolk Rivers Catchment Board v Kent [1941] 1 AC 74

Owing to a very high tide, a sea wall was breached, and the respondent's farmland was flooded. The appellants, in the exercise of their statutory powers under the Land Drainage Act 1930, entered the respondents' land and began repair work. They carried out the work so inefficiently that the respondents' land remained flooded for 178 days. It appears that the work could have been done, if it had been done with reasonable skill, within 14 days. The respondents claimed damages for the excess time during which their land remained flooded.

A majority of the House of Lords held that the appellants were not liable. They were under no obligation to repair the wall, nor to complete the work after they had begun it. Further, their lack of reasonable skill *had not caused the damage suffered*, which was the result of natural forces. This conclusion was disapproved in *Anns v Merton*, but has returned to haunt the law, particularly in respect of duties owed by 'emergency services' (below).

This case was decided a few years *after* the decision in *Donoghue v Stevenson*, which first recognized a unified tort of negligence. So its legal context is very different from the context of *Geddis*. Lord Atkin, the key figure in the recognition of the unified tort of negligence in *Donoghue*, dissented in *East Suffolk*. Only Lord Atkin adequately recognized the independence of the duty of care in negligence from the statutory powers and duties; and indeed only Lord Atkin mentioned *Donoghue v Stevenson* at all in explaining the potential source of a duty to take care in this case. Viscount Simon, in the majority, did refer to the tort of negligence as connoting 'the complex notion of duty, breach and damage'. However, he mentioned this only to argue that no damage had been caused by the defendant's lack of skill.

Of the majority judgments, Lord Romer's is the most often cited. He distinguished *Geddis*—and particularly the words of Lord Blackburn quoted above—on the basis that *Geddis* was a case where the damage was *caused by* the acts of the defendants. In this case, the defendants had merely permitted the damage to continue.

Lord Romer, at 102

[*Geddis* and *Shepphard v Glossop Corporation* [1921] 3 KB 132[38]] seem to lay down a principle which in my opinion is a thoroughly sound one. It is this: Where a statutory authority is entrusted with a mere power it cannot be made liable for any damage sustained by a member of the public by reason of a failure to exercise that power. If in the exercise of their discretion they embark upon an execution of the power, the only duty they owe to any member of the public is not thereby to add to the damages that he would have suffered had they done nothing. So long as they exercise their discretion honestly, it is for them to determine the method by which and the time within which and the time during which the power shall be exercised; and they cannot be made liable, except to the extent that I have just mentioned, for any damage that would have been avoided had they exercised their discretion in a more reasonable way.

Lord Atkin (dissenting) approached the matter in a very different way. He began by stating the sources of duty in such cases. Amidst the chaos that has followed, the following passages from Lord Atkin's judgment stand out for their clarity of approach:

Lord Atkin (dissenting), at 88–9

My Lords, two material points emerged on the argument of this appeal: (1) Was there a duty owed to the plaintiffs and, if so, what was its nature? (2) If there was a duty owed to the plaintiffs to conduct the work with reasonable dispatch, was there any damage caused to the plaintiffs by the breach of the duty?

---

[38] In this case, decided before *Donoghue v Stevenson* by a Court of Appeal including Lord Atkin (then Atkin LJ) a corporation which had a *statutory power to provide lighting* was held to owe no *duty* to provide lighting that would be enforceable by an individual in a claim for damages.

On the first point I cannot help thinking that the argument did not sufficiently distinguish between two kinds of duties: (1) A statutory duty to do or abstain from doing something. (2) A common law duty to conduct yourself with reasonable care so as not to injure persons liable to be affected by your conduct.

(1) The duty imposed by statute is primarily a duty owed to the State. Occasionally penalties are imposed by the statute for breach; and, speaking generally, in the absence of special sanctions imposed by the statute the breach of duty amounts to a common law misdemeanour. The duty is not necessarily a duty owed to a private citizen. The duty may, however, be imposed for the protection of particular citizens or class of citizens, in which case a person of the protected class can sue for injury to him due to the breach. The cases as to breach of the Factory or Coal Mines Act are instances. As a rule the statutory duty involves the notion of taking care not to injure and in such cases actions for breach of statutory duty come within the category of negligence: see *Lochgelly Iron and Coal Co. v. M'Mullan.*

(2) But apart from the existence of a public duty to the public, every person whether discharging a public duty or not is under a common law obligation to some persons in some circumstances to conduct himself with reasonable care so as not to injure those persons likely to be affected by his want of care. This duty exists whether a person is performing a public duty, or merely exercising a power which he possesses either under statutory authority or in pursuance of his ordinary rights as a citizen. To whom the obligation is owed is, as I see it, the principal question in the present case.

The second kind of duty referred to by Lord Atkin in the passage above is, of course, the duty of care in negligence.

At 90–1

I treat it . . . as established that a public authority whether doing an act which it is its duty to do, or doing an act which it is merely empowered to do, must in doing the act do it without negligence, or as it is put in some of the cases must not do it carelessly or improperly. . . .

I thus come to the crucial point in this case to whom is such a duty owed, or who can complain of the failure to use reasonable dispatch. Now it must be conceded that instances will occur of the performance of powers where it might be difficult for a member of the public generally to complain of unreasonable delay. For instance delay in the work of relaying the surface of a highway may not be actionable at the suit of members of the public who are put to expense and inconvenience by having to make a detour. Even in this case I think something might be said for a householder or shopkeeper on the route under repair who is for an unreasonably long time deprived of access to his premises for himself and his customers. *But we have to deal here with relations between the plaintiffs and the Board which I suggest are much closer than the general relations of members of the public to a public authority. The Board were engaging themselves in repairing the plaintiffs' wall with the object of preventing the further flooding of the land of the plaintiffs and, I think, also one other occupier, and they were operating upon the plaintiffs' land.* Subject to what I have to say upon the causation of damage which I wish for the present purpose to assume, they would know that the longer the work was delayed the longer would the waters ebb and flow over the land with the possibility of damage therefrom. I consider that these relations give rise to a duty owed to the plaintiffs to use reasonable care, including dispatch in doing the work. [Emphasis added.]

The italicized passage in this extract approaches the matter through the concept of *proximity*, which was an aspect of 'neighbourhood' as it was explained in *Donoghue v Stevenson*. Now, we recognize a more complex set of criteria for establishing a duty of care, in accordance with *Caparo v Dickman*. But Lord Atkin's method remains sound: the duty, if it arises, arises through the proximity of the parties, subject to questions of fairness, justice, and reasonableness, and it arises at common law. It is irrelevant that the statute conferred a mere power.

Lord Atkin *also* went on to conclude that the breach of duty might indeed have caused the damage in this case, and that this question should be addressed at trial (at 93).

Anns v Merton [1977] 2 WLR 1024

This is our third visit to this case. We have already seen that *Anns* has been overruled as to its ratio, because it incorrectly stated the form of damage suffered by the plaintiff;[39] and that the expansive two-stage test for a duty of care adopted in *Anns* has been superseded by the more cautious (but equally open-textured) *Caparo* test. Here we consider a different aspect of Lord Wilberforce's judgment, concerning the statutory context of the defendant's act (or failure to act). This aspect of his judgment fared rather better than the rest, but this final element of *Anns* has now been demolished by *Gorringe v Calderdale* [2004] 1 WLR 1057. We must still consider *Anns*, because it provides a vital link between *East Suffolk* and *Geddis*, and the law as it stands now.

Anns: The Issues

We outlined the facts of *Anns* in Chapter 3.

Even leaving aside the 'type of damage', one would have thought the obstacles to the claim were formidable. In particular:

(a) The statute conferred a power not a duty;

(b) On one hypothesis, the local authority had merely failed to inspect;

(c) Applying the majority approach in *East Suffolk*, this is a case of mere failure to avoid harm. The harm was not caused by natural forces of course, but it was caused by a builder, and the local authority had merely failed to notice and prevent the defect.

Despite these features, the House of Lords held that a claim in negligence was arguable, *whether there had been an inspection or not*.

Lord Wilberforce, *Anns v Merton*, at 1035–6

. . . It is said that there is an absolute distinction in the law between statutory duty and statutory power—the former giving rise to possible liability, the latter not, or at least not doing so unless the exercise of the power involves some positive act creating some fresh or additional damage.

My Lords, I do not believe that any such absolute rule exists: or perhaps, more accurately, that such rules as exist in relation to powers and duties existing under particular statutes, provide sufficient definition of the rights of individuals affected by their exercise, or indeed

---

[39] *Murphy v Brentwood*, Section 2 above.

their non-exercise, unless they take account of the possibility that, parallel with public law duties there may coexist those duties which persons—private or public—are under at common law to avoid causing damage to others in sufficient proximity to them. This is, I think, the key to understanding of the main authority relied upon by the appellants—*East Suffolk Rivers Catchment Board v. Kent* [1941] AC 74.

(At 1037–8)

. . . the law, as stated in some of the speeches in *East Suffolk Rivers Catchment Board v. Kent* [1941] AC 74, but not in those of Lord Atkin or Lord Thankerton, requires at the present time to be understood and applied with the recognition that, quite apart from such consequences as may flow from an examination of the duties laid down by the particular statute, there may be room, once one is outside the area of legitimate discretion or policy, for a duty of care at common law. It is irrelevant to the existence of this duty of care whether what is created by the statute is a duty or a power: the duty of care may exist in either case. The difference between the two lies in this, that, in the case of a power, liability cannot exist unless the act complained of lies outside the ambit of the power. In *Dorset Yacht Co. Ltd. v. Home Office* [1970] AC 1004 the officers may (on the assumed facts) have acted outside any discretion delegated to them and having disregarded their instructions as to the precautions which they should take to prevent the trainees from escaping: (see *per* Lord Diplock, at p. 1069). So in the present case, the allegations made are consistent with the council or its inspector having acted outside any delegated discretion either as to the making of an inspection, or as to the manner in which an inspection was made. Whether they did so must be determined at the trial. In the event of a positive determination, and only so, can a duty of care arise. . . .

Apart from anything else, Lord Wilberforce's approach is difficult to apply in practice. The first step, where there is a statutory power, is to show that the act or omission complained of 'lay outside the ambit of the power'. If it is within the ambit of the power, there is no room for the negligence action. The difficulty is that whether the act or omission is within the ambit of a power is a question of public law. Under the *Anns* approach, we therefore have to deal with public law concepts, in a private law action.

Lord Wilberforce seems to have used these public law concepts in order to explain how a *duty* can be derived from a *power* (see the first extract above, from p. 1035). But this is not true to the dissenting judgment of Lord Atkin in *East Suffolk* (which Lord Wilberforce was trying to apply). There, Lord Atkin emphasized the *independence* of the duty of care in negligence, from statutory powers and duties. He determined whether a duty of care arose at common law by applying the neighbourhood test. The duty of care, if it arises at all, arises in its own right, out of foreseeability, proximity, and so on: in short, it arises out of the neighbour principle (now qualified by *Caparo*). This question about statutory powers has returned to exercise the House of Lords on a number of occasions. In the next case extracted, the House of Lords made a serious attempt to resolve the issue. In *some* respects, the solution proved short-lived. But this case still provides an authoritative source of policy arguments, and is the source of much of the current law on child abuse and education claims in negligence.

X v Bedfordshire County Council; M v Newham LBC & Others [1995] 2 AC 633

This decision of the House of Lords dealt with five appeals, all involving claims in negligence and some involving claims for breach of statutory duty. The first two appeals concerned (respectively) an allegation that a local authority had failed to take children into care despite evidence of neglect and abuse by their parents (*X v Bedfordshire* itself), and that a local authority had carelessly taken a child away from her mother on a mistaken suspicion that the mother's partner was abusing the child (*M v Newham*). These are referred to as the 'child abuse cases'. In the remaining three appeals (*E v Dorset*; *Christmas v Hampshire*; and *Keating v Bromley*), local authorities had failed to diagnose learning difficulties on the part of the claimants, or failed to make adequate provision for schooling. These are referred to as the 'education cases'. For convenience and brevity, we will refer to all five appeals—unless an issue arises in respect of some but not all of them—by the name *X v Bedfordshire*. We will sometimes distinguish between the 'abuse cases' and the 'education cases'.

The authority of *X v Bedfordshire* is now qualified in two ways:

(a) The conclusions drawn in the abuse cases would be different today.[40]

(b) Recent case law has simplified the approach to 'discretion' and policy adopted in this case.

General: three types of claim

Lord Browne-Wilkinson broke down the claims in the five cases into three types. Not all types of claim were present in every case; but in most cases, they were.

1. Claims for breach of statutory duty. The relevant statutes in the abuse cases were the Children and Young Persons Act 1969; the Child Care Act 1980; and the Children Act 1989 (*Bedfordshire* only). In the education cases, the relevant statutes were the Education Acts 1944 and 1981.

   In no case was a claim for breach of statutory duty successful. Applying the tests explained in Chapter 16 below (and briefly outlined above), the statutory duties were not of the appropriate sort. They were social welfare duties for the benefit of the public as a whole, and they were not actionable by individuals at common law. (We consider this aspect of *X v Bedfordshire* in Chapter 16.)

2. Claims for negligent breach of a direct duty of care on the part of the defendant local authority, in the exercise of their statutory functions. With one exception, these claims failed too, and were struck out. In general, the duties argued for would be inconsistent with the purposes of the statute.

3. Claims that the local authority was vicariously liable for the breach of a duty of care by an individual employee. Here there was a difference in fortunes between the two types of case.

   (a) Applying the criteria in *Caparo v Dickman*, the abuse cases were struck out. It would not be fair, just, and reasonable to impose a duty of care on the professional social workers and psychologists who made judgments as to the child's welfare. This conclusion is now unsupportable following *D v East Berkshire*.

   (b) Applying the same criteria, the education cases had a chance of success, and would not be struck out. This is because the relationship between professional and child in these cases was arguably similar to a 'normal professional relationship' carrying no potential conflict of interest. In the case of a headmaster, there was also a voluntary assumption of responsibility towards a pupil at the school (applying *Henderson v Merrett*, Section 6.3 above). Later education cases have succeeded on their merits.

---

[40] *D v East Berkshire Health Authority* [2005] 2 AC 373.

It should be noted that Lord Browne-Wilkinson rightly rejected a fourth argument, that there could be an action for 'negligent breach of a statutory duty', distinct from the claim in the tort of negligence *and* from the action at private law for breach of statutory duty. No such action exists (at 732). This is consistent with our analysis so far, and with Lord Atkin's judgment in *East Suffolk*. It is not contradicted by Lord Blackburn's remarks in *Geddis*, provided these are read in context, as we did above.

Lord Browne-Wilkinson, *X v Bedfordshire,* at 737–9

(b) Justiciability and the policy/operational dichotomy

. . . I understand the applicable principles to be as follows. Where Parliament has conferred a statutory discretion on a public authority, it is for that authority, not for the courts, to exercise the discretion: nothing which the authority does within the ambit of the discretion can be actionable at common law. If the decision complained of falls outside the statutory discretion, it *can* (but not necessarily will) give rise to common law liability. However, if the factors relevant to the exercise of the discretion include matters of policy, the court cannot adjudicate on such policy matters and therefore cannot reach the conclusion that the decision was outside the ambit of the statutory discretion. Therefore a common law duty of care in relation to the taking of decisions involving policy matters cannot exist.

3. If justiciable, the ordinary principles of negligence apply

If the plaintiff's complaint alleges carelessness, not in the taking of a discretionary decision to do some act, but in the practical manner in which that act has been performed (e.g. the running of a school) the question whether or not there is a common law duty of care falls to be decided by applying the usual principles i.e. those laid down in *Caparo Industries Plc. v. Dickman* [1990] 2 A.C. 605, 617–618. Was the damage to the plaintiff reasonably foreseeable? Was the relationship between the plaintiff and the defendant sufficiently proximate? Is it just and reasonable to impose a duty of care? See *Rowling v. Takaro Properties Ltd.* [1988] A.C. 473; *Hill v. Chief Constable of West Yorkshire* [1989] A.C. 53.

However the question whether there is such a common law duty and if so its ambit, must be profoundly influenced by the statutory framework within which the acts complained of were done. The position is directly analogous to that in which a tortious duty of care owed by A to C can arise out of the performance by A of a contract between A and B. In *Henderson v. Merrett Syndicates Ltd.* [1995] 2 A.C. 145 your Lordships held that A (the managing agent) who had contracted with B (the members' agent) to render certain services for C (the Names) came under a duty of care to C in the performance of those services. It is clear that any tortious duty of care owed to C in those circumstances could not be inconsistent with the duty owed in contract by A to B. Similarly, in my judgment a common law duty of care cannot be imposed on a statutory duty if the observance of such common law duty of care would be inconsistent with, or have a tendency to discourage, the due performance by the local authority of its statutory duties.

The first stage in the account above is supposedly derived from *Anns* (with reference to intervening cases such as *Rowling v Takaro* [1988] AC 473). Elsewhere, when discussing *Dorset Yacht v Home Office* [1970] AC 1004, Lord Browne-Wilkinson argued that it 'was neither helpful nor necessary to introduce public law concepts as to the validity of a decision into the question of liability at common law for negligence' (at 736). This is often quoted to illustrate that Lord Browne-Wilkinson anticipated the later move away from public law questions in respect of the negligence action. But in fact, he seems to have thought that one type of public law question—relating to *unreasonableness*—was relevant to the action in negligence.

He appeared to *agree* that a negligence action can only be brought in respect of an action taken pursuant to a statutory discretion if the action 'is so unreasonable that it falls outside a statutory discretion' (at 736–7, referring to Lord Diplock in *Dorset Yacht*). Generally speaking, 'unreasonableness' at *public* law has been considered to require a much more demanding test than lack of reasonable care in *negligence*. In *public law*, the test for unreasonableness has proceeded on the basis that it is not for the court to make the decision afresh. The court asks only whether any reasonable person in the position of the defendant *could* have come to the decision reached. The duty of care in negligence on the other hand, asks what the 'reasonable person' would have done in the circumstances. Importantly, this must be qualified where the *Bolam* test applies.[41]

Further, Lord Browne-Wilkinson did not simply replicate the *Anns* approach. In fact, his approach is rather *more* restrictive than the approach in *Anns*. Lord Wilberforce in *Anns* suggested that the area of policy was not entirely beyond the reach of the tort of negligence. In the longer extract above, Lord Browne-Wilkinson says in effect that policy decisions are beyond the reach of negligence. Where such decisions are concerned, the court should not even try to decide whether the decision is protected by a discretion, or not. We need not enter this debate too deeply however, because the approach in subsequent cases has been much simpler.

Lord Browne-Wilkinson turned next to an application of the *Caparo* criteria. Here, he explained that the statutory context will 'profoundly influence' the decision whether there is or is not a duty of care at common law. That context is taken into account when assessing 'fairness, justice and reasonableness' under the third stage of *Caparo*.

Here we outline Lord Browne-Wilkinson's reasoning in respect of the two different classes of claims.

The abuse cases

The following reasoning explains the rejection of the **direct duty of care** in the abuse cases.

Lord Browne-Wilkinson, at 749

I turn then to consider whether, in accordance with the ordinary principles laid down in the *Caparo* case [1990] 2 A.C. 605, the local authority in the *Bedfordshire* case owed a direct duty of care to the plaintiffs. The local authority accepts that they could foresee damage to the plaintiffs if they carried out their statutory duties negligently and that the relationship between the authority and the plaintiffs is sufficiently proximate. The third requirement laid down in *Caparo* is that it must be just and reasonable to impose a common law duty of care in all the circumstances. It was submitted that this third requirement is only applicable in cases where the plaintiffs' claim is for pure economic loss and that it does not apply where, as in the child abuse cases, the claim is for physical damage. I reject this submission: although *Caparo* and many other of the more recent cases were decisions where only pure economic loss was

---

41 The effect of the *Bolam* test, as we saw in Chapter 3.1, is that professionals are judged by the standards of a 'responsible body of opinion' in the relevant field of expertise. It has been argued that the negligence standard and the public law standard of reasonableness may have more in common than the basic contrast in the text will suggest. See in particular Tom Hickman, 'The Reasonableness Principle: Reassessing its Place in the Public Sphere' (2004) 63 CLJ 166–98.

claimed, the same basic principles apply to claims for physical damage and were applied in, for example, *Hill v. Chief Constable of West Yorkshire* [1989] A.C. 53.

Is it, then, just and reasonable to superimpose a common law duty of care on the local authority in relation to the performance of its statutory duties to protect children? In my judgment it is not. Sir Thomas Bingham M.R. took the view, with which I agree, that the public policy consideration which has first claim on the loyalty of the law is that wrongs should be remedied and that very potent counter considerations are required to override that policy ante, p. 663C–D. However, in my judgment there are such considerations in this case.

First, in my judgment a common law duty of care would cut across the whole statutory system set up for the protection of children at risk. As a result of the ministerial directions contained in "Working Together" the protection of such children is not the exclusive territory of the local authority's social services. The system is inter-disciplinary, involving the participation of the police, educational bodies, doctors and others. At all stages the system involves joint discussions, joint recommendations and joint decisions. The key organisation is the Child Protection Conference, a multi-disciplinary body which decides whether to place the child on the Child Protection Register. . . . To impose such liability on all the participant bodies would lead to almost impossible problems of disentangling as between the respective bodies the liability, both primary and by way of contribution, of each for reaching a decision found to be negligent.

Second, the task of the local authority and its servants in dealing with children at risk is extraordinarily delicate. Legislation requires the local authority to have regard not only to the physical wellbeing of the child but also to the advantages of not disrupting the child's family environment: see, for example, section 17 of the Act of 1989. In one of the child abuse cases, the local authority is blamed for removing the child precipitately: in the other, for failing to remove the children from their mother. As the Report of the Inquiry into Child Abuse in Cleveland 1987 (Cm. 412) said, at p. 244:

> "It is a delicate and difficult line to tread between taking action too soon and not taking it soon enough. Social services whilst putting the needs of the child first must respect the rights of the parents; they also must work if possible with the parents for the benefit of the children. These parents themselves are often in need of help. Inevitably a degree of conflict develops between those objectives."

Next, if a liability in damages were to be imposed, it might well be that local authorities would adopt a more cautious and defensive approach to their duties. For example, as the Cleveland Report makes clear, on occasions the speedy decision to remove the child is sometimes vital. If the authority is to be made liable in damages for a negligent decision to remove a child (such negligence lying in the failure properly first to investigate the allegations) there would be a substantial temptation to postpone making such a decision until further inquiries have been made in the hope of getting more concrete facts. Not only would the child in fact being abused be prejudiced by such delay: the increased workload inherent in making such investigations would reduce the time available to deal with other cases and other children.

The relationship between the social worker and the child's parents is frequently one of conflict, the parent wishing to retain care of the child, the social worker having to consider whether to remove it. This is fertile ground in which to breed ill feeling and litigation, often hopeless, the cost of which both in terms of money and human resources will be diverted from the performance of the social service for which they were provided. The spectre of vexatious and costly litigation is often urged as a reason for not imposing a legal duty. But the circumstances surrounding cases of child abuse make the risk a very high one which cannot be ignored.

If there were no other remedy for maladministration of the statutory system for the protection of children, it would provide substantial argument for imposing a duty of care. But the statutory complaints procedures contained in section 76 of the Act of 1980 and the much fuller procedures now available under the Act of 1989 provide a means to have grievances investigated, though not to recover compensation. Further, it was submitted (and not controverted) that the local authorities Ombudsman would have power to investigate cases such as these.

Finally, your Lordships' decision in the *Caparo* case [1990] 2 A.C. 605 lays down that, in deciding whether to develop novel categories of negligence the court should proceed incrementally and by analogy with decided categories. We were not referred to any category of case in which a duty of care has been held to exist which is in any way analogous to the present cases. Here, for the first time, the plaintiffs are seeking to erect a common law duty of care in relation to the administration of a statutory social welfare scheme. Such a scheme is designed to protect weaker members of society (children) from harm done to them by others. The scheme involves the administrators in exercising discretions and powers which could not exist in the private sector and which in many cases bring them into conflict with those who, under the general law, are responsible for the child's welfare. To my mind, the nearest analogies are the cases where a common law duty of care has been sought to be imposed upon the police (in seeking to protect vulnerable members of society from wrongs done to them by others) or statutory regulators of financial dealings who are seeking to protect investors from dishonesty. In neither of those cases has it been thought appropriate to superimpose on the statutory regime a common law duty of care giving rise to a claim in damages for failure to protect the weak against the wrongdoer: see *Hill v. Chief Constable of West Yorkshire* [1989] A.C. 53 and *Yuen Kun Yeu v. Attorney-General of Hong Kong* [1988] A.C. 175.

The policy arguments in the above passage remain influential, although the European Court of Human Rights in *Z v UK* (below) clearly disagreed with the argument that alternative remedies were adequate.

Lord Browne-Wilkinson also rejected claims that the local authority should be *vicariously* liable, where individual social workers and other professionals had breached a duty of care. The following remarks relate to the rejection of the vicarious liability claims in the abuse cases. Vicarious liability is explored in Chapter 9. Here, such liability depended on showing that an *employee* owed (and breached) a duty of care.

At 752–3

The claim based on vicarious liability is attractive and simple. The normal duty of a doctor to exercise reasonable skill and care is well established as a common law duty of care. In my judgment, the same duty applies to any other person possessed of special skills, such as a social worker. It is said, rightly, that in general such professional duty of care is owed irrespective of contract and can arise even where the professional assumes to act for the plaintiff pursuant to a contract with a third party: *Henderson v. Merrett Syndicates Ltd.* [1995] 2 A.C. 145; *White v. Jones* [1995] 2 A.C. 207. Therefore, it is said, it is nothing to the point that the social workers and psychiatrist only came into contact with the plaintiffs pursuant to contracts or arrangements made between the professionals and the local authority for the purpose of the discharge by the local authority of its statutory duties. Once brought into contact with the plaintiffs, the professionals owed a duty properly to exercise their professional skills in dealing with their "patients," the plaintiffs. This duty involved the exercise of professional skills in investigating the circumstances of the plaintiffs and (in the *Newham* case) conducting the interview with the child. Moreover, since the professionals could foresee that negligent advice would damage the plaintiffs, they are liable to the plaintiffs for tendering such advice to the local authority.

Like the majority in the Court of Appeal, I cannot accept these arguments. The social workers and the psychiatrists were retained by the local authority to advise the local authority, not the plaintiffs. The subject matter of the advice and activities of the professionals is the child. Moreover the tendering of any advice will in many cases involve interviewing and, in the case of doctors, examining the child. But the fact that the carrying out of the retainer involves contact with and relationship with the child cannot alter the extent of the duty owed by the professionals under the retainer from the local authority. The Court of Appeal drew a correct analogy with the doctor instructed by an insurance company to examine an applicant for life insurance. The doctor does not, by examining the applicant, come under any general duty of medical care to the applicant. He is under a duty not to damage the applicant in the course of the examination: but beyond that his duties are owed to the insurance company and not to the applicant.

The position is not the same as in the case of the purchaser of property who is owed a duty of care by a surveyor instructed by the building society which is going to advance the money: see *Smith v. Eric S. Bush* [1990] 1 A.C. 831. In such a case the surveyor is only liable to the purchaser in negligence because he is aware that the purchaser will regulate his (the purchaser's) conduct by completing the purchase in reliance on the survey report. In the child abuse cases, even if the advice tendered by the professionals to the local authority comes to the knowledge of the child or his parents, they will not regulate their conduct in reliance on the report. The effect of the report will be reflected in the way in which the local authority acts.

Nor is the position the same as in *Henderson v. Merrett Syndicates Ltd.* where, pursuant to a contract with the members' agents, the managing agents undertook the management of the insurance business of the indirect Names. The managing agents were held to be under a tortious duty of care to the indirect Names, notwithstanding that the managing agents were operating under the terms of a contract with a third party. But the duty of care to the Names in that case arose from, and fell within the ambit of, the terms of the retainer contained in the contract between the managing agents and the members' agents. The Names were not seeking to impose on the managing agents any obligation beyond that which the retainer itself required to be performed. So also in *White v. Jones* [1995] 2 A.C. 207.

In my judgment in the present cases, the social workers and the psychiatrist did not, by accepting the instructions of the local authority, assume any general professional duty of care to the plaintiff children. The professionals were employed or retained to advise the local authority in relation to the well being of the plaintiffs but not to advise or treat the plaintiffs.

The child is merely the 'subject of the report' prepared. The only *duty* is owed to the local authority, as employer. This part of the reasoning has not withstood the more explicit recognition that private law must respect the human rights enshrined in the European Convention on Human Rights, following enactment of the Human Rights Act 1998. See our discussion of *D v East Berkshire*, below.

The education cases

Although the claims for direct duties were also found untenable in the education cases generally, in the *Dorset* case there was thought to be one potential route to establishing such a duty. The duty would arise by analogy with *Hedley Byrne v Heller* and *Henderson v Merrett*, irrespective of the kind of damage (economic loss or not) that followed (at 762–3).[42]

The other critical difference between the abuse cases, and the education cases, was that the **vicarious liability** claims in respect of education were not doomed to fail. The following extract relates specifically to the *Dorset* case, but it is indicative of the general approach.

Lord Browne-Wilkinson, at 763

Common law duty of care—vicarious

The claim is that the educational psychologists and other members of the staff of the defendant authority owed a duty to use reasonable professional skill and care in the assessment and determination of the plaintiff's educational needs. It is further alleged that the plaintiff's parents relied on the advice of such professionals. The defendant authority is vicariously liable for any breach of such duties by their employees.

Again, I can see no ground for striking out this claim at least in relation to the educational psychologists. Psychologists hold themselves out as having special skills and they are, in my judgment, like any other professional bound both to possess such skills and to exercise them carefully. Of course, the test in *Bolam v. Friern Hospital Management Committee* [1957] 1 W.L.R. 582 will apply to them, i.e. they are only bound to exercise the ordinary skill of a competent psychologist and if they can show that they acted in accordance with the accepted views of some reputable psychologist at the relevant time they will have discharged the duty of care, even if other psychologists would have adopted a different view. In the context of advice on the treatment of dyslexia, a subject on which views have changed over the years, this may be an important factor. But that said, I can see no ground on which, at this stage, the existence of a professional duty of care can be ruled out. The position of other members of the defendant's staff is not as clear, but I would not at this stage strike out the claims relating to them.

The position of the psychologists in the education cases is quite different from that of the doctor and social worker in the child abuse cases. There is no potential conflict of duty between the professional's duties to the plaintiff and his duty to the educational authority. Nor is there any obvious conflict between the professional being under a duty of care to the plaintiff and the discharge by the authority of its statutory duties. If, at trial, it emerges that there are such conflicts, then the trial judge may have to limit or exclude any duty of care owed by the professional to the plaintiff. But at this stage no obvious conflict has been demonstrated.

Finally, the defendant authority submitted that the damage claimed, being the cost of providing alternative fee paying education for the plaintiff, is not recoverable. In my view it is not appropriate to decide this point at the striking out stage: the matter will be better resolved at trial when the true facts are known.

My conclusion therefore in the *Dorset* case is that the defendant authority is under no liability at common law for the negligent exercise of the statutory discretions conferred on them by the Education Acts 1944 to 1981, but could be liable, both directly and vicariously, for negligence in the operation of the psychology service and negligent advice given by its officers.

---

[42] The type of damage suffered in the education cases was not settled in *X v Bedfordshire*. Lord Browne-Wilkinson reasoned that the type of damage was not crucial to determining whether there was a duty of care. Since these were novel claims, the *Caparo* test would apply in any event, even if the claims were for personal injury. This was correct. See further the discussion of *Phelps v Hillingdon*, below.

In respect of the *Hampshire* case, an additional factor was that the claimant was a child at a school run by the defendant local authority, and claimed partly in respect of breaches of duty on the part of the headmaster. Lord Browne-Wilkinson pointed out that the relationship between headmaster and pupil was closely analogous to the relationships giving rise to a duty of care in cases of economic loss. Arguably, there was a **voluntary assumption of responsibility** towards the child.

The House of Lords therefore permitted the education cases to proceed to trial on the basis that not only a local education authority *but also its individual teachers* potentially owe a duty of care to their pupils. This has been as controversial as the opposite result in the abuse case (that social workers owed *no* arguable duty of care to children whose well-being they were assessing).[43] In respect of the successful education cases, Lord Browne-Wilkinson placed considerable emphasis on questions of *breach* as devices for filtering undeserving claims. This raises an important question which is common to both education, and abuse cases. Could a more demanding test for **breach of duty** do some of the work currently done by the duty of care? Arguably, such an approach could more successfully distinguish the most meritorious claims, by penalising only the most outrageous forms of professional malpractice.

3.4 CHILD ABUSE AND CHILD WELFARE CASES AFTER *X V BEDFORDSHIRE*

The Influence of *Osman v UK*

In *Osman v UK* [2000] EHRR 245, the European Court of Human Rights concluded that English law conferred an 'immunity' on the police in respect of certain actions in negligence. This immunity was contrary to Article 6 of the European Convention on Human Rights, which states that anyone is entitled to a hearing by a tribunal in respect of their civil rights. This aspect of *Osman v UK* has since been recognized as mistaken by the European Court of Human Rights itself, in *Z v UK* (2002) 34 EHRR 3. We explore these cases more fully in our section on 'Immunities'. But before *Z v UK*, *Osman* had a real (though not precisely quantifiable) influence on negligence cases. Courts undoubtedly showed a new reluctance to strike out actions on policy grounds. More recently, the Human Rights Act 1998 and introduction of domestic law remedies for violations of Convention rights exert a new influence. The substantive Convention rights, and the right to compensation, are now of most central concern, rather than the right of access to a court under Article 6.

Barrett v Enfield [2001] 2 AC 550

The first significant test of *X v Bedfordshire* after the decision in *Osman v UK* arose from distinctly different facts. *Barrett v Enfield* was not a case of suspected child abuse, nor did it concern a decision about *whether* to take a child into care. Rather, the claimant brought an action in negligence in respect of the conduct of his care. The claim was for personal injuries.

The House of Lords declined to strike out the claim, concluding that the case should be heard on its merits.

There are three important points to make about *Barrett*.

---

[43] For support of the extension of negligence liability into a school setting, see D. Fairgrieve, 'Pushing Back the Boundaries of Local Authority Liability: Negligence Enters the Classroom' (2002) PL 288.

1. Less enthusiasm for striking out

Lord Browne-Wilkinson, in this case, was critical of the decision in *Osman v UK*, but also thought that if this case was struck out, a claim would be initiated before the European Court of Human Rights for a violation of Article 6.

Lord Browne-Wilkinson, at 560

In view of the decision in the *Osman* case it is now difficult to foretell what would be the result in the present case if we were to uphold the striking out order. It seems to me that it is at least probable that the matter would then be taken to Strasbourg. That court, applying its decision in the *Osman* case if it considers it to be correct, would say that we had deprived the plaintiff of his right to have the balance struck between the hardship suffered by him and the damage to be done to the public interest in the present case if an order were to be made against the defendant council. In the present very unsatisfactory state of affairs, and bearing in mind that under the Human Rights Act 1998 article 6 will shortly become part of English law, in such cases as these it is difficult to say that it is a clear and obvious case calling for striking out; see also *Markesinis & Deakin, Tort Law*, 4th ed (1999), pp 145 et seq.

On the other hand, elsewhere in his judgment Lord Browne-Wilkinson called for caution in striking out on entirely different grounds, namely that it is difficult to judge the policy issues unless one has a full grasp of the facts (at 557–8). The other judges in *Barrett* also called for caution in striking out, without relying on *Osman v UK*.

2. Less broad brush policy reasoning and more confidence in the negligence action

This second point is related to the first. The policy arguments which proved fatal to the child abuse claims in *X v Bedfordshire* were not thought to apply with the same force to the claims in this case. The potential conflicts identified in *X v Bedfordshire* would not necessarily apply here, and there was much less confidence in the availability of other suitable remedies.

Lord Slynn of Hadley, *Barrett v Enfield* [2001] 2 AC 550, at 568

Whilst not casting doubt on the validity of these factors [outlined in *X v Bedfordshire*] in the context of the investigations, or the steps which it was said should have been taken, in those cases of child abuse and neglect of educational needs, it does not seem to me that they necessarily have the same force separately or cumulatively in the present case. Thus, although once a child is in care, there may well be co-operation between different social welfare bodies, the responsibility is that of the local authority and its social and other professional staff. The decision to remove the child from its home is already taken and the authority has statutory powers in relation to the child which do not necessarily involve the exercise of the kind of discretion involved in taking a child from its family into care. . . .

Nor do I think that the remedies accepted to be available in the *Bedfordshire* case [1995] 2 AC 633 are likely to be as efficacious as the recognition by the court that a duty of care is or may be owed at common law. I agree with Sir Thomas Bingham MR in his dissenting judgment in the Court of Appeal in the *Bedfordshire* case, at p 662g: "I cannot accept, as a general proposition, that the imposition of a duty of care makes no contribution to the maintenance of high standards."

Lord Slynn's reference to the dissenting judgment of Lord Bingham MR in *X v Bedfordshire* (in the Court of Appeal) is particularly important. It suggests greater confidence that tort law may have a positive role in responding to malpractice in the social welfare sphere, as elsewhere. This also tends to suggest that the different approach signalled by *Barrett* is not entirely a defensive response to the decision in *Osman v UK*. As we will see below, Lord Bingham's stance on these issues has been consistent, and the position he took in the Court of Appeal in *X v Bedfordshire* has now been accepted. We will especially note his more recent dissenting opinion, this time in the House of Lords, in *D v East Berkshire*, below.

3. A simpler approach to 'justiciability'

As we have seen, the approach adopted in *Anns v Merton* threatened to make negligence cases turn on an interpretation of public law concepts. In *X v Bedfordshire*, Lord Browne-Wilkinson expressed the view that it was best to keep public law concepts away from the negligence enquiry, but he nevertheless appeared to say that both policy, and discretion, were protected spheres. In *Barrett*, both Lord Slynn and Lord Hutton advocated a more straightforward approach which would keep questions of public law out of negligence cases. At the same time, their approach would permit broader enquiry into local authority decision-making.

Lord Slynn, at 571

Where a statutory power is given to a local authority and damage is caused by what it does pursuant to that power, the ultimate question is whether the particular issue is justiciable or whether the court should accept that it has no role to play. The two tests (discretion and policy/operational) to which I have referred are guides in deciding that question. The greater the element of policy involved, the wider the area of discretion accorded, the more likely it is that the matter is not justiciable so that no action in negligence can be brought. . . . A claim of negligence in the taking of a decision to exercise a statutory discretion is likely to be barred, unless it is wholly unreasonable so as not to be a real exercise of the discretion, or if it involves the making of a policy decision involving the balancing of different public interests; acts done pursuant to the lawful exercise of the discretion can, however, in my view be subject to a duty of care, even if some element of discretion is involved. Thus, accepting that a decision to take a child into care pursuant to a statutory power is not justiciable, it does not in my view follow that, having taken a child into care, an authority cannot be liable for what it or its employees do in relation to the child without it being shown that they have acted in excess of power. It may amount to an excess of power, but that is not in my opinion the test to be adopted: the test is whether the conditions in the *Caparo* case [1990] 2 AC 605 have been satisfied.

Lord Hutton reviewed the existing case law at length, but stated his *conclusion* on this point relatively simply:

Lord Hutton, at 583

. . . these judgments lead me to the provisional view that the fact that the decision which is challenged was made within the ambit of a statutory discretion and is capable of being described as a policy decision is not in itself a reason why it should be held that no claim for negligence can be brought in respect of it. As I read it this is what is said by the Privy Council in its judgment in *Rowling v Takaro Properties Ltd* [1988] AC 473, 501G. It is only where the decision involves the weighing of competing public interests or is dictated by considerations which the courts are not fitted to assess that the courts will hold that the issue is non-justiciable on the ground that the decision was made in the exercise of a statutory discretion.

The combined effect of Lord Slynn and Lord Hutton's judgments in respect of policy, discretion and the duty of care in negligence have been explained as follows:

D. Fairgrieve and P. Craig, 'Barrett, Negligence and Discretionary Powers' (1999) PL 626–50, at 633

A public law hurdle will therefore only be of relevance where the allegation of negligence raised by the plaintiff is felt to raise matters which are not justiciable. Where this was not so then the courts would consider any issue regarding the way in which discretion was exercised within the ordinary framework of the negligence action. Assuming that the courts decide that a duty of care is owed, this will then mean that the way in which the discretion was exercised will, as Lord Hutton stated, be of relevance in deciding whether there was a breach of the duty of care.

The absence of any 'blanket immunity' in such cases was also emphasized by the Court of Appeal in *S v Gloucestershire CC* [2001] 2 WLR 909, for example.

Although the questions addressed here are in some respects very technical, they are of great political importance. Exploring the various policy factors debated in both *X v Bedfordshire* and *Barrett v Enfield*, Fairgrieve and Craig also explain the broader concerns:

Fairgrieve and Craig, at 636–7

Underlying many of these policy factors are complex questions striking at the heart of the role of the State. Is it desirable for financially stretched public authorities to pay compensation to publicly funded complainants for poor services? Is potential liability likely to improve services in the long-term or to be counter-productive? Should causally peripheral public bodies with perceived deep pockets underwrite losses caused by primary wrongdoers? Should the overriding concern of the law be that 'wrongs should be remedied'? Members of the judiciary hold very different views on this, and the debate is not restricted to the legal world. Barrett undoubtedly represents a shift in favour of compensation-seekers.

Barrett v Enfield began the trend in favour of 'compensation-seekers', but in the abuse cases, this trend has since advanced further.

Z v UK and After

Part of the necessary background to the more recent cases is the decision of the European Court of Human Rights in *Z v UK* [2001] 2 FLR 612. The plaintiffs in *X v Bedfordshire* itself (their claims in negligence having been struck out) brought an action against the UK alleging violations of Articles 6 (right of access to a court), 3 (freedom from inhuman and degrading treatment), 8 (respect for private and family life), and 13 (right to compensation in the event of a violation of one of the substantive rights). The Court admitted that its interpretation in *Osman v UK* had been in error. There had been no violation of Article 6. However, there *had* been violations of Articles 3 and 13 in this case. The absence of protection for the interests of the children in this case, *and also* the lack of a remedy in the form of compensation, had violated their Convention rights.

Given the finding that Article 6 had not been violated, there was no necessity that the law of tort should provide a remedy in such a case. The Human Rights Act 1998 as we have seen provides a remedy against public authorities who do not act consistently with Convention rights, under section 8. This is an alternative to the law of tort. But, rightly or wrongly, the trend has been for courts to prefer to adjust *the law of tort* to provide remedies, rather than to award damages for an action under section 7. This is further encouraged by the fact that the court must, by section 2(1) of the Human Rights Act 1998, have regard to the 'Strasbourg jurisprudence' when interpreting the applicable law. In *D v East Berkshire*, it was further pointed out that an action against the local authority for damages under section 8 would not be available where the actions in question occurred before October 2000, when the Human Rights Act 1998 came into force; and that in cases of child abuse it was quite typical for actions to be brought many years after the event.[44] It was preferable for tort law to adapt to allow a remedy.

The provisions of the Human Rights Act 1998 are extracted in Chapter 1.

Whether adaptation of tort law to provide remedies is or is not *generally* to be preferred is a matter that can be debated. In technical terms, the impact of the Human Rights Act on tort claims in relation to child abuse has been:

(a) To encourage courts to identify *specific* policy factors, rather than overly general ones;

(b) To encourage consideration of the interests of the individual whose interests are affected by decision-making, and to think critically about the claim that pressures on decision-makers will be conflicting; and

(c) To encourage consideration of other elements of the tort of negligence besides the duty of care, and specifically the question of *breach of duty*.

D v East Berkshire Community Health NHS Trust and Another [2004] 2 WLR 58 (CA)

In these cases, actions were brought by parents and in one case a child for psychiatric injury suffered as a result of mistaken, and allegedly negligent allegations of child abuse by the parents against the children. The parents' claims were dismissed; but the child's appeal was allowed.

Note: the House of Lords subsequently heard an appeal from this decision; but that appeal related only to the unsuccessful claims brought by parents: see paras [86]–[87] below. The historic decision of the Court of Appeal in this case *not to follow the decision of the House of Lords in X v Bedfordshire* where the child's claim was concerned was not criticized by the House of Lords.

The chief basis on which the Court of Appeal felt it could depart from a recent decision of the House of Lords was that its reasoning was no longer supportable following the Human Rights Act 1998.

Lord Phillips MR (giving the judgment of the Court)

[79] Section 2(1) of the Human Rights Act 1998 requires the court to have regard to the jurisprudence of the Strasbourg court where relevant to proceedings under the Act. Thus any English court, when dealing with a claim under the 1998 Act in relation to action or inaction

---

[44] See further the discussion in Chapter 7 below.

after October 2000 on the part of a local authority in relation to suspected child abuse, must take into account the decisions to which we have just referred. Where a claim alleges breach of art 3, in circumstances such as those in Z v UK and E v UK, the court is likely to have to consider whether the local authority knew, or should have known, that positive action was called for. This will necessarily involve consideration of the conduct of the individuals involved. A claim of this nature will, so it seems to us, necessarily be a claim by a child rather than a parent.

[80]   Where a claim alleges breach of art 8, on the ground that a child has been removed from a parent without justification, this will also require examination of the conduct of the individuals involved to see whether, on the particular facts, the action was 'necessary in a democratic society'.

[81]   Thus litigation involving factual inquiries of the nature considered above is now a potential consequence of the conduct of those involved in taking decisions in child abuse cases. In these circumstances the reasons of policy that led the House of Lords to hold that no duty of care towards a child arises, in so far as those reasons have not already been discredited by the subsequent decisions of the House of Lords, will largely cease to apply. Substantial damages will be available on proof of individual shortcomings, which will be relevant alike to a claim based on breach of s 6 of the 1998 Act and a claim based on breach of a common law duty of care.

[82]   Can there, in these circumstances, be any justification for preserving a rule that no duty of care is owed in negligence because it is not fair, just and reasonable to impose such a duty? It is true that a claim under the 1998 Act will only lie against public authorities and not against the individuals employed by them. But the reality is that claims in negligence are brought primarily to establish liability on the part of the local authorities and individuals are unlikely to be personally at risk. In so far as the risk of legal proceedings will inhibit individuals from boldly taking what they believe to be the right course of action in the delicate situation of a case where child abuse is suspected, we think that this factor will henceforth be present, whether the anticipated litigation is founded on the 1998 Act or on the common law duty of care.

[83]   In so far as the position of a child is concerned, we have reached the firm conclusion that the decision in Bedfordshire cannot survive the 1998 Act. Where child abuse is suspected the interests of the child are paramount: see s 1 of the Children Act 1989. Given the obligation of the local authority to respect a child's convention rights, the recognition of a duty of care to the child on the part of those involved should not have a significantly adverse effect on the manner in which they perform their duties. In the context of suspected child abuse, breach of a duty of care in negligence will frequently also amount to a violation of arts 3 or 8. The difference, of course, is that those asserting that wrongful acts or omissions occurred before October 2000 will have no claim under the 1998 Act. This cannot, however, constitute a valid reason of policy for preserving a limitation of the common law duty of care which is not otherwise justified. On the contrary, the absence of an alternative remedy for children who were victims of abuse before October 2000 militates in favour of the recognition of a common law duty of care once the public policy reasons against this have lost their force.

[84]   It follows that it will no longer be legitimate to rule that, as a matter of law, no common law duty of care is owed to a child in relation to the investigation of suspected child abuse and the initiation and pursuit of care proceedings. It is possible that there will be factual situations where it is not fair, just or reasonable to impose a duty of care, but each case will fall to be determined on its individual facts.

[85]   In reaching this decision we do not suggest that the common law duty of care will replicate the duty not to violate arts 3 and 8. Liability for breach of the latter duty and entitlement
to compensation can arise in circumstances where the tort of negligence is not made out. The
area of factual inquiry where breaches of the two duties are alleged are, however likely to be
the same.

It will be noticed that Lord Phillips thought *both*:

(a) that the policy reasons deployed to deny the abuse claims in *X v Bedfordshire* were
untenable in the light of subsequent decisions by the House of Lords; *and*

(b) that those same policy arguments were untenable given the requirement on the court
under the Human Rights Act 1998 to have regard to the Strasbourg jurisprudence and
(as a public body under section 6) to act compatibly with the Convention rights.

The first aspect of this (that the policy arguments in *X v Bedfordshire* were now untenable as a
matter of common law) is effectively a vindication of the dissent of Lord Bingham MR in the
Court of Appeal in *X v Bedfordshire*. As such, the new dissent of Lord Bingham in the House
of Lords in *D v East Berkshire*, where he alone would have allowed a claim on the part of *parents* to proceed to trial, takes on particular importance. So far as the decision that duties may
be owed to a child in this case might cause some tension between duties owed by individual
social workers to the authority and to individual children, Lord Phillips emphasized that this
tension would be present in any event thanks to the clear impact of sections 6, 7, and 8 of the
Human Rights Act 1998, in the light of the decisions in *Z v UK* and *E v UK*.[45]

Rejecting the parents' claims

Lord Phillips MR

[86]   The position in relation to the parent is very different. Where the issue is whether a child
should be removed from the parents, the best interests of the child may lead to the answer
Yes or No. The Strasbourg cases demonstrate that failure to remove a child from the parents
can as readily give rise to a valid claim by the child as a decision to remove the child. The same
is not true of the parents' position. It will always be in the parents' interests that the child
should not be removed. Thus the child's interests are in potential conflict with the interests of
the parents. In view of this, we consider that there are cogent reasons of public policy for concluding that, where child care decisions are being taken, no common law duty of care should
be owed to the parents. Our reasoning in reaching this conclusion is supported by that of the
Privy Council in B v A–G of New Zealand [2003] 4 All ER 833.

[87]   For the above reasons, where consideration is being given to whether the suspicion of
child abuse justifies taking proceedings to remove a child from the parents, while a duty of
care can be owed to the child, no common law duty of care is owed to the parents.

---

[45] In *E v UK* (2002) 36 EHRR 519, four children complained that their local authority in Scotland had been
in breach of its statutory duties in failing to protect them from sexual abuse by their step-father. They did not
bring a claim in domestic law because they were advised that such a claim would be doomed to fail. The Court
found that there had been violations of rights under Articles 3 and 13.

D v East Berkshire Health Authority [2005] UKHL 23; [2005] 2 AC 373

The question on appeal before the House of Lords concerned the rejected claims on behalf of the parents. The decision of the Court of Appeal to depart from *X v Bedfordshire* was not criticized by their Lordships. One of the most senior members of the House of Lords, Lord Bingham (dissenting) would have gone further than the Court of Appeal, allowing the claims of the parents to proceed to trial. But the majority held that no duty was owed to the parents, and the actions must be struck out.

Lord Bingham of Cornhill (dissenting)

3 The courts below have concluded that . . . no duty of care can be owed by the doctor or the social worker to the parent, that accordingly no claim may lie and that these claims brought by the parents must be dismissed with no evidence called and no detailed examination of the facts. . . . I understand that a majority of my noble and learned friends agree with this conclusion, for which there is considerable authority in the United Kingdom and abroad. But the law in this area has evolved very markedly over the last decade. What appeared to be hard-edged rules precluding the possibility of any claim by parent or child have been eroded or restricted. And a series of decisions of the European Court of Human Rights has shown that application of an exclusionary rule in this sensitive area may lead to serious breaches of Convention rights for which domestic law affords no remedy and for which, at any rate arguably, the law of tort should afford a remedy if facts of sufficient gravity are shown.

. . .

Discussing the case of *Attorney General of New Zealand v Prince* [1998] 1 NZLR 262, the Privy Council decision of *B v AG New Zealand* [2003] 4 All ER 833, Lord Bingham pointed out some significant factual *and legal* distinctions between the present cases, and the situation in New Zealand. In the present cases, where the parents had sought medical advice from their accusers and proximity therefore was particularly strong (para [83]), it was not appropriate to strike out the claims.

Lord Bingham (dissenting)

[48] . . . In *Attorney General v Prince* . . . claims in negligence were made by the natural mother of a child who had been adopted, and also by the child (now adult), complaining of the process followed in the adoption and also of failure to investigate a complaint made about his treatment when the child was still a child. The Court of Appeal of New Zealand struck out the first of these claims as incompatible with the adoption regime laid down by statute in New Zealand, but it also, by a majority, allowed both the claims under the second head to proceed to trial. This case was considered by the Privy Council in B v Attorney General of New Zealand. . . . The claim in that case was made by a father and his two daughters, and was based on the allegedly negligent investigation of a complaint that the father had sexually abused the daughters. At first instance the judge (following *X v Bedfordshire County Council*; *M v Newham London Borough Council*) had struck out the proceedings on the ground that no duty was owed to father or daughters and so the claims were bound to fail. The Court of Appeal of New Zealand had upheld this decision. The Privy Council allowed the appeal by the daughters but dismissed that of the father, holding that a duty was owed to them but not to him.

. . . But there are factual differences between that case and the present cases. The parent had not himself initiated the request for medical advice. There had, it seems, been sexual abuse. The father had not been exonerated from suspicion. No emphasis appears to have been laid on the duty to make disclosure to and cooperate with parents. And there was no discussion of any rights deriving from the New Zealand Bill of Rights Act 1990, since it contains no provision equivalent to article 8 of the European Convention. Since it was the Human Rights Act which led the Court of Appeal in the present case (para 83) to regard *X v Bedfordshire County Council.* , as effectively overruled in relation to claims by children, this is a significant distinction. After the New Zealand Court of Appeal's decision in Prince but before its decision in B, a High Court master in Christchurch refused to strike out a claim in negligence by a father against a psychotherapist who had erroneously concluded that he had sexually abused his daughter, holding that a duty of care might, depending on the evidence, be established and that the matter should be resolved at trial: *N v D* [1999] NZFLR 560.

[49]   It would seem clear that the appellants' claim would not be summarily dismissed in France, where recovery depends on showing gross fault: see Markesinis, Auby, Coester-Waltjen and Deakin, *Tortious Liability of Statutory Bodies* (1999), pp 15–20; Fairgrieve, "Child Welfare and State Liability in France", in *Child Abuse Tort Claims against Public Bodies: A Comparative Law View*, ed Fairgrieve and Green (2004), pp 179–197, Fairgrieve, "Beyond Illegality: Liability for Fault in English and French Law", in *State Liability in Tort* (2003), chap 4. Nor would they be summarily dismissed in Germany where, it is said, some of the policy considerations which influenced the House in *X v Bedfordshire County Council* were considered by those who framed § 839 of the BGB and were rejected many years ago: see Tortious Liability of Statutory Bodies, 58–71; Martina K nnecke, "National Report on Germany", in Fairgrieve and Green, pp 199–207. Yet in neither of those countries have the courts been flooded with claims. If, as some respected academic authorities suggested, *Barrett v Enfield London Borough Council* . . . shifted the emphasis of the English courts from consideration of duty to considerationof breach (see Craig and Fairgrieve, "Barrett, Negligence and Discretionary Powers" [1999] PL 626, Fairgrieve, *State Liability in Tort* (2003), p 84, para 2.1.2.7), I would for my part regard that shift as welcome, since the concept of duty has proved itself a somewhat blunt instrument for dividing claims which ought reasonably to lead to recovery from claims which ought not. But I should make it plain that if breach rather than duty were to be the touchstone of recovery, no breach could be proved without showing a very clear departure from ordinary standards of skill and care. It should be no easier to succeed here than in France or Germany.

[50]   . . . the question does arise whether the law of tort should evolve, analogically and incrementally, so as to fashion appropriate remedies to contemporary problems or whether it should remain essentially static, making only such changes as are forced upon it, leaving difficult and, in human terms, very important problems to be swept up by the Convention. I prefer evolution.

The majority of the House of Lords took a more traditional approach. Lords Nicholls, Brown, and Rodger delivered judgments explaining why the claims by the parents should be struck out. Lord Steyn agreed with all three of these.

Lord Nicholls of Birkenhead

[85]   In my view the Court of Appeal reached the right conclusion on the issue arising in the present cases. Ultimately the factor which persuades me that, at common law, interference with family life does not justify according a suspected parent a higher level of protection than

other suspected perpetrators is the factor conveniently labelled "conflict of interest". A doctor is obliged to act in the best interests of his patient. In these cases the child is his patient. The doctor is charged with the protection of the child, not with the protection of the parent. The best interests of a child and his parent normally march hand-in-hand. But when considering whether something does not feel "quite right", a doctor must be able to act single-mindedly in the interests of the child. He ought not to have at the back of his mind an awareness that if his doubts about intentional injury or sexual abuse prove unfounded he may be exposed to claims by a distressed parent.

. . .

[88]   The claimants sought to meet this "conflict of interest" point by noting that the suggested duty owed to parents has the same content as the duty owed to the child: to exercise due skill and care in investigating the possibility of abuse. This response is not adequate. The time when the presence or absence of a conflict of interest matters is when the doctor is carrying out his investigation. At that time the doctor does not know whether there has been abuse by the parent. But he knows that when he is considering this possibility the interests of parent and child are diametrically opposed. The interests of the child are that the doctor should report any suspicions he may have and that he should carry out further investigation in consultation with other child care professionals. The interests of the parent do not favour either of these steps. This difference of interest in the outcome is an unsatisfactory basis for imposing a duty of care on a doctor in favour of a parent.

. . .

[92]   A wider approach has also been canvassed. The suggestion has been made that, in effect, the common law should jettison the concept of duty of care as a universal prerequisite to liability in negligence. Instead the standard of care should be "modulated" to accommodate the complexities arising in fields such as social workers dealing with children at risk of abuse: *Tort Liability of Public Authorities in Comparative Perspective*, ed Fairgrieve, Andenas and Bell (2002), p 485. The contours of liability should be traced in other ways.

[93   For some years it has been all too evident that identifying the parameters of an expanding law of negligence is proving difficult, especially in fields involving the discharge of statutory functions by public authorities. So this radical suggestion is not without attraction. This approach would be analogous to that adopted when considering breaches of human rights under the European Convention. Sometimes in human rights cases the identity of the defendant, whether the state in claims under the Convention or a public authority in claims under the Human Rights Act 1998, makes it appropriate for an international or domestic court to look backwards over everything which happened. In deciding whether overall the end result was acceptable the court makes a value judgment based on more flexible notions than the common law standard of reasonableness and does so freed from the legal rigidity of a duty of care.

[94]   This approach, as I say, is not without attraction. It is peculiarly appropriate in the field of human rights. But I have reservations about attempts to transplant this approach wholesale into the domestic law of negligence in cases where, as here, no claim is made for breach of a Convention right. Apart from anything else, such an attempt would be likely to lead to a lengthy and unnecessary period of uncertainty in an important area of the law. It would lead to uncertainty because there are types of cases where a person's acts or omissions do not render him liable in negligence for another's loss even though this loss may be foreseeable. . . . Abandonment of the concept of a duty of care in English law, unless replaced by a control

mechanism which recognises this limitation, is unlikely to clarify the law. That control mechanism has yet to be identified. And introducing this protracted period of uncertainty is unnecessary, because claims may now be brought directly against public authorities in respect of breaches of Convention rights.

Did Lord Bingham's dissent (extracted above) amount to an argument for abandonment of the duty of care as a control mechanism? It is suggested that it did not. Lord Bingham argued that the absence of a duty should not be too readily assumed in the absence of knowledge of the relevant facts. Policy reasons should not be applied in too broad and general a fashion. The existence of a duty of care involved a sensitive enquiry but it should be dealt with in the light of the particular facts of the case. Lord Bingham further argued that in circumstances where a duty of care was owed—applying the normal *Caparo* test—public authorities and their employees should be protected by demanding that a high level of fault should be shown, before the breach could be actionable.

This form of 'evolution' (as Lord Bingham put it) would be adventurous indeed for the English tort of negligence, building in a form of 'proportionality' which is familiar in European law (and in the jurisprudence of the European Convention on Human Rights), but not in the English law of tort. The approach of the majority uses generic policy arguments to block claims by parents even in the case of the most outrageous accusations, in order to protect those who make genuinely difficult decisions. Lord Nicholls' comparison with those who are accused of other serious crimes has substance, although it could also be argued that the parents accused in these cases did not enjoy the same procedural rights which are engaged in the usual criminal process. It might also be argued that if a social worker or other professional is already aware that a fundamentally flawed decision to take a child from his or her parents may give rise to liability, the potential 'conflict' in the professional's mind is already present: is this point adequately dealt with in para [88]?

The issues raised by this case cannot be adequately debated in this sort of general work. In respect of the evolving law on parents' as well as children's rights, and for some criticism of the dominance of 'the paramountcy principle' (putting the interests of the child at the forefront), though not in this particular context, see S. Choudhry and H. Fenwick, 'Taking the Rights of Parents and Children Seriously: Confronting the Welfare Principle under the Human Rights Act' (2005) 25 OJLS 453–92.

In many instances, the award of damages to the child might be thought sufficient vindication of damage to the parents' interests. But this is not always the case.

D v Bury Metropolitan Borough Council [2006] EWCA Civ 1; [2006] 1 WLR 917

A five-month-old baby suffered rib fractures while in the care of his parents. The council instituted care proceedings, but did not carry out a risk assessment as recommended by a court, which also made an interim care order. The child was separated from his parents and placed in foster care. Eventually a national children's charity carried out a risk assessment (which should have been done by the council), and the evidence suggested that the child suffered from brittle bone disease. The fractures were not non-accidental, and the child should be returned to his parents.

The Court of Appeal held that the parents were not owed a duty of care in this case. The existence of the interim care order was not a special consideration which would justify a different outcome from the one in *D v East Berkshire*. There was no 'assumption of responsibility' to the parents. In respect of the child, it was 'impossible' to identify what harm had been suffered by such a young child on separation from its parents for four months, and anyway such harm would be transient. Therefore, there was no injury sounding in damages. The parents (to whom injury is evident) are owed no duty of care even in respect of basic procedural safeguards, such as risk assessments.

Does the local authority's decision need protecting on the basis of 'conflict of interest' in such a case?

3.5 EDUCATION CASES AFTER *X V BEDFORDSHIRE*

It will be recalled that in *X v Bedfordshire*, Lord Browne-Wilkinson did not strike out all of the 'education claims'. He said that the individual professionals involved may owe duties of care to the children and, if these were breached, the local authorities could be vicariously liable. Equally, there was one claim based on breach of a direct duty of care which was not struck out. This was a claim based on the proposition that the local authority was offering a 'psychology service' to the public, and that it therefore owed duties of care to members of the public who made use of the service, along the lines of the duty of care for professional services recognized in *Henderson v Merrett*.

In *Barrett v Enfield* (at 557–8), Lord Browne-Wilkinson suggested (rather unusually) that he had been wrong not to strike out the single surviving 'direct duty' claim in *X v Bedfordshire*. This, he thought, had exposed local education authorities to a proliferation of claims. It also illustrated the dangers of striking out, because it showed that appeal courts who are asked to determine questions on a striking out action are in danger of making too many assumptions about the nature of the facts.[46] His mistake was, he now thought, to assume that the 'psychology service' was offered to the public in the same way as any other professional service. In fact, he now understood that the point of the psychology service was not to inform the individuals who were referred to it, but to advise schools and education authorities on the appropriate provision for those individuals. This, he argued, was quite different, and he now thought that recognition of a duty of care would be inappropriate in such circumstances. This point fell to be decided by the House of Lords in the next case, not on assumed facts but in an action on its merits.[47] *Phelps v Hillingdon* is significant for many reasons, but one of the reasons is that the plaintiff succeeded not just in taking her claim to trial, but also in winning damages.

Phelps v Hillingdon [2001] 2 AC 619

In the first of four appeals heard together by the House of Lords, the claimant was referred by her school, at the age of 12, to the defendant local education authority's school psychology service. An educational psychologist employed by the authority reported no specific weaknesses on the part of the claimant. Shortly before leaving school, the claimant was diagnosed as dyslexic. She brought an action against the local authority, and was awarded damages. The Court of Appeal allowed an appeal by the local authority.

---

[46] This is a strange argument to deploy in order to argue that he *should have* struck out this particular direct claim in *X v Bedfordshire*, since it suggests rather that more caution in striking out is appropriate.

[47] *Phelps v Hillingdon* itself was not a striking out action. But the House of Lords heard that appeal together with three other appeals, which were striking out actions.

The House of Lords reinstated the order of the first instance judge. The individual educational psychologist owed a duty to the claimant, which had been breached, causing recoverable damage. The local authority was vicariously liable.[48] Lord Slynn (who gave the leading speech) added that although a *direct duty* could be owed in only limited circumstances.

The following extract relates to the *vicarious liability claim*.

Lord Slynn, *Phelps v Hillingdon*

. . . it does not seem to me that it can be said that Parliament intended that there should be a remedy by way of damages for breach of statutory duty in respect of the matters complained of here.

The common law

It does not follow that the local authority can never be liable in common law negligence for damage resulting from acts done in the course of the performance of a statutory duty by the authority or by its servants or agents. This House decided in *Barrett v Enfield London BC* . . . that the fact that acts which are claimed to be negligent are carried out within the ambit of a statutory discretion is not in itself a reason why it should be held that no claim for negligence can be brought in respect of them. It is only where what is done has involved the weighing of competing public interests or has been dictated by considerations on which Parliament could not have intended that the courts would substitute their views for the views of ministers or officials that the courts will hold that the issue is non-justiciable on the ground that the decision was made in the exercise of a statutory discretion. In Pamela's case there is no such ground for holding that her claim is non-justiciable and therefore the question to be determined is whether the damage relied on is foreseeable and proximate and whether it is just and reasonable to recognise a duty of care (*Caparo Industries plc v Dickman*). If a duty of care would exist where advice was given other than pursuant to the exercise of statutory powers, such duty of care is not excluded because the advice is given pursuant to the exercise of statutory powers. This is particularly important where other remedies laid down by the statute (eg an appeals review procedure) do not in themselves provide sufficient redress for loss which has already been caused.

Where, as in Pamela's case, a person is employed by a local education authority to carry out professional services as part of the fulfilment of the authority's statutory duty, it has to be asked whether there is any overriding reason in principle why (a) that person should not owe a duty of care (the first question) and (b) why, if the duty of care is broken by that person, the authority as employer or principal should not be vicariously liable (the second question).

I accept that, as was said in *X (minors) v Bedfordshire CC*, there may be cases where to recognise such a vicarious liability on the part of the authority may so interfere with the performance of the local education authority's duties that it would be wrong to recognise any liability on the part of the authority. It must, however, be for the local authority to establish that: it is not to be presumed and I anticipate that the circumstances where it could be established would be exceptional.

As to the first question, it is long and well-established, now elementary, that persons exercising a particular skill or profession may owe a duty of care in the performance to people who it

[48] The other appeals were all determined in favour of the claimants, and their claims were allowed to proceed to trial. They principally concerned failure to provide for recognized special needs (and failure to recognize specific special needs).

can be foreseen will be injured if due skill and care are not exercised, and if injury or damage can be shown to have been caused by the lack of care. Such duty does not depend on the existence of any contractual relationship between the person causing and the person suffering the damage. A doctor, an accountant and an engineer are plainly such a person. So in my view is an educational psychologist or psychiatrist or a teacher including a teacher in a specialised area, such as a teacher concerned with children having special educational needs. So may be an education officer performing the functions of a local education authority in regard to children with special educational needs. . . .

I fully agree with what was said by Lord Browne-Wilkinson in *X (minors) v Bedfordshire CC* . . . at 766 that a head teacher owes 'a duty of care to exercise the reasonable skills of a headmaster in relation to such [sc a child's] educational needs' and a special advisory teacher brought in to advise on the educational needs of a specific pupil, particularly if he knows that his advice will be communicated to the pupil's parents, 'owes a duty to the child to exercise the skill and care of a reasonable advisory teacher'. A similar duty on specific facts may arise for others engaged in the educational process, eg an educational psychologist being part of the local authority's team to provide the necessary services. The fact that the educational psychologist owes a duty to the authority to exercise skill and care in the performance of his contract of employment does not mean that no duty of care can be or is owed to the child. Nor does the fact that the educational psychologist is called in pursuance of the performance of the local authority's statutory duties mean that no duty of care is owed by him, if in exercising his profession he would otherwise have a duty of care.

That, however, is only the beginning of the enquiry. It must still be shown that the educational psychologist is acting in relation to a particular child in a situation where the law recognises a duty of care. A casual remark, an isolated act may occur in a situation where there is no sufficient nexus between the two persons for a duty of care to exist. But where an educational psychologist is specifically called in to advise in relation to the assessment and future provision for a specific child, and it is clear that the parents acting for the child and the teachers will follow that advice, prima facie a duty of care arises. It is sometimes said that there has to be an assumption of responsibility by the person concerned. That phrase can be misleading in that it can suggest that the professional person must knowingly and deliberately accept responsibility. It is, however, clear that the test is an objective one (*Henderson v Merrett Syndicates Ltd* . . .). The phrase means simply that the law recognises that there is a duty of care. It is not so much that responsibility is assumed as that it is recognised or imposed by the law.

The question is thus whether in the particular circumstances the necessary nexus has been shown.

The result of a failure by an educational psychologist to take care may be that the child suffers emotional or psychological harm, perhaps even physical harm. There can be no doubt that if foreseeability and causation are established, psychological injury may constitute damage for the purpose of the common law. But so in my view can a failure to diagnose a congenital condition and to take appropriate action as a result of which failure a child's level of achievement is reduced, which leads to loss of employment and wages. Questions as to causation and as to the quantum of damage, particularly if actions are brought long after the event, may be very difficult, but there is no reason in principle to rule out such claims.

As to the second question, if a breach of the duty of care to the child by such an employee is established, prima facie a local or education authority is vicariously liable for the negligence of its employee. If the educational psychologist does have a duty of care on the facts is it to be held that it is not just and reasonable that the local education authority should be vicariously liable if there is a breach of that duty? Are there reasons of public policy why the courts should not recognise such a liability? I am very conscious of the need to be cautious in recognising such a duty of care where so much is discretionary in these as in other areas of social policy. As has been said, it is obviously important that those engaged in the provision of educational services under the statutes should not be hampered by the imposition of such a vicarious liability. I do not, however, see that to recognise the existence of the duties necessarily leads or is likely to lead to that result. The recognition of the duty of care does not of itself impose unreasonably high standards. The courts have long recognised that there is no negligence if a doctor 'exercises the ordinary skill of an ordinary competent man exercising that particular art'. . . .

In this extract, Lord Slynn repeats the simpler approach to policy and discretion that was adopted in *Barrett v Enfield*: so long as the issue is suitable for adjudication (it is 'justiciable'), the court will apply the *Caparo* test. The statutory context will of course be *relevant* to an application of this test. But the existence of statutory powers (or of statutory duties which are themselves unenforceable at private law), is in no sense a 'defence' to a negligence action; nor does it justify immunity from the duty of care.

Lord Slynn also refers to the important protection that is offered to individual officers and education authorities by the applicable *standard* of care. His final remarks are a reference to the *Bolam* test, which judges professional defendants by the standards of their fellow professionals.

In *Carty v Croydon* [2005] 1 WLR 2312, the Court of Appeal echoed this simpler approach to issues of policy and discretion, and appeared to suggest that in fact, issues of duty and breach are interrelated. A duty of care was recognized there in a case where an individual education officer had prepared a statement of special needs in respect of the claimant; but the duty was not breached on the facts, and the claim was dismissed.

What is the damage?

It is not entirely clear whether Lord Slynn regarded the claim as principally for personal injury in the form of psychological harm, or for economic losses flowing from the failure to diagnose. Indeed he does not seem to have differentiated particularly between these forms of damage. One reason why he did not so differentiate is that he thought the *Caparo* criteria would apply in the same way in either event. But the relevant damage may be important for certain purposes, not least for determining the relevant *limitation period*. This identification of 'damage' was raised in one of the other appeals decided together with *Phelps* by the House of Lords: *Anderton v Clwyd*. It had been argued by the Court of Appeal in this case that even if dyslexia could be treated as 'impairment of a person's physical and mental condition' (the definition of 'personal injuries' adopted in section 35(5) of the Supreme Court Act 1981)[49], that impairment had not been *caused by* the defendants. The defendants had not caused the dyslexia, but had failed to benefit the claimant by offering the best educational options. This argument was rejected by the House of Lords:

Lord Slynn, at 664

. . . Having regard to the purpose of the provision it would in any event, in my view, be wrong to adopt an overly legalistic view of what are 'personal injuries to a person'. For the reasons given in my decision in the *Phelps* case, psychological damage and a failure to diagnose a

---

[49] Now Senior Courts Act 1981. The same wording is used in Limitation Act 1980, s 38.

congenital condition and to take appropriate action as a result of which a child's level of achievement is reduced (which leads to loss of employment and wages) may constitute damage for the purpose of a claim. . . . Garland J was right . . . that a failure to mitigate the adverse consequences of a congenital defect is capable of being 'personal injuries to a person' within the meaning of the rules.

Although the reasoning on this point is less than clear, it was adopted by a later House of Lords in *Adams v Bracknell Forest BC* [2005] 1 AC 76. In this case, which was concerned with the important practical question of *when the limitation period begins to run* in a case of failure to diagnose dyslexia, the House of Lords concluded that it was sensible to treat the damage in a case of this sort *as* personal injury. However, this was not an appropriate case in which to exercise the discretion which is available to a court in certain personal injury cases to, in effect, override the applicable time limit. This refusal to exercise the discretion may indicate that courts consider local authorities to be over-exposed to potential claims of this sort. *Adams v Bracknell* is a reminder that the test for duty of care is not the only mechanism for controlling claims.

Limitation periods in general, and *Adams v Bracknell* in particular, are further discussed in Chapter 7.

3.6 PURE OMISSIONS

Shortly after the decision in *X v Bedfordshire*, the House of Lords decided the case of *Stovin v Wise* [1996] AC 923. This decision has seemed puzzling and hard to place. The more recent decision in *Gorringe v Calderdale* helps to explain the ambit of *Stovin*, and even to reconcile it with more recent, and more liberal developments. The key is that *Stovin v Wise* and *Gorringe v Calderdale* are cases of pure omission, or of *doing nothing at all*. They state that the existence of a statutory power, or of a very general and unenforceable statutory duty, cannot be the sole basis for holding that there is a duty to take positive action.

Stovin v Wise [1996] AC 923

The plaintiff was riding his motorcycle, when the defendant pulled out at a junction and collided with him. The plaintiff was seriously injured. When the plaintiff commenced an action against the defendant, the defendant (or rather, the defendant's insurer) joined the local authority as co-defendant, arguing that the junction was known to be dangerous because visibility was impaired by the existence of a bank on adjoining land. Accidents had occurred there on at least three previous occasions. The council had looked into the matter, and agreed a surveyor's recommendation that the bank be removed if the landowner agreed. A letter was written to the landowner, but there was no reply and no action was taken to follow it up. The trial judge held that the council, as highway authority, had not breached any statutory duties, but it was in breach of a common law duty of care. He judged the council to be 30 per cent to blame for the damage. The Court of Appeal dismissed an appeal by the council.

The House of Lords held that the local authority owed no duty (either in public law or in negligence) to take positive steps to remove the bank. On the way to this conclusion, their reasoning was complex and in many respects confusing. It is particularly hard to reconcile their reasoning with later developments in cases such as *Barrett*. The issues have subsequently been better explained in *Gorringe v Calderdale* (below). Here, we explain the problems and the underlying policy concerns. Then, we will consider the explanation in *Gorringe* and some doubts that remain.

Lord Hoffmann delivered the leading judgment for the majority. He pointed out (at 943) that this was a case of an *omission to act*. Equally, in this case the *only* reason why the local authority might be thought to be under a duty to act at all was that it had certain powers and duties conferred or imposed upon it by statute. Indeed, the dissenting judgment of Lord Nicholls (with whom, notably, Lord Slynn agreed)[50] argued that a duty to act was *justified by the existence of a power*.

Lord Nicholls (dissenting), at 931

Omissions and proximity

The council was more than a bystander. The council had a statutory power to remove this source of danger, although it was not under a statutory duty to do so. Before 1978 the accepted law was that the council could be under no common law liability for failing to act. A simple failure to exercise a statutory power did not give rise to a common law claim for damages: see *East Suffolk Rivers Catchment Board v. Kent*. The decision in *Anns v. Merton London Borough Council* . . . liberated the law from this unacceptable yoke. This was the great contribution the Anns case made to the development of the common law.

. . .

The true *ratio* of *Stovin* is its rejection of the proposition above. *The existence of a statutory power does not itself give rise to a common law duty to act.* The 'great contribution of *Anns*' is therefore rejected by the majority in *Stovin* and, subsequently, by *Gorringe*.

Lord Hoffmann clearly considered that the local authority while not a 'mere bystander' was nevertheless a 'peripheral party'—a party who has failed to benefit others. He emphasized that *positive reasons*, beyond foreseeability of harm, must be shown to justify the imposition of a duty of care. This applies to both acts, and omissions.

Lord Hoffmann, at 949

. . . The trend of authorities has been to discourage the assumption that anyone who suffers loss is prima facie entitled to compensation from a person (preferably insured or a public authority) whose act or omission can be said to have caused it. The default position is that he is not.

This approach is (to adopt the language of Fairgrieve and Craig in their comment on *Barrett*, above), very much against the 'compensation-seekers'. But on this occasion it is against compensation-seekers in the particular context of *failure to confer a benefit*.

Despite the conclusion in *Stovin* that the existence of a statutory power does not *in itself* give rise to a duty to act, the possibility was conceded that in some circumstances—primarily in cases of general or specific *reliance*—a positive duty to act may exist.[51] This is very important. The duty in such cases arises from proximity and reliance, subject to policy considerations. It does not arise from the statutory power.

[50] This is notable because of Lord Slynn's important role in *Barrett* and *Phelps*.
[51] An example of general reliance appears to exist in New Zealand in respect of local authority supervision of the safety of buildings: Lord Hoffmann referred with approval to *Invercargill v Hamlin* (above). *Specific* reliance exists where the particular claimant relies on conduct of the defendant in particular circumstances.

Certain other features of Lord Hoffmann's majority judgment in *Stovin* sowed some confusion, and they come together in the following passage.

Lord Hoffmann, at 952–3

In the case of a mere statutory power, . . . the legislature has chosen to confer a discretion rather than create a duty. Of course there may be cases in which Parliament has chosen to confer a power because the subject matter did not permit a duty to be stated with sufficient precision. It may nevertheless have contemplated that in circumstances in which it would be irrational not to exercise the power, a person who suffered loss because it had not been exercised, or not properly exercised, would be entitled to compensation. I therefore do not say that a statutory "may" can never give rise to a common law duty of care. I prefer to leave open the question of whether the *Anns* case was wrong to create any exception to Lord Romer's statement of principle in the *East Suffolk* case and I shall go on to consider the circumstances (such as "general reliance") in which it has been suggested that such a duty might arise. But the fact that Parliament has conferred a discretion must be some indication that the policy of the act conferring the power was not to create a right to compensation. The need to have regard to the policy of the statute therefore means that exceptions will be rare.

In summary, therefore, I think that the minimum preconditions for basing a duty of care upon the existence of a statutory power, if it can be done at all, are, first, that it would in the circumstances have been irrational not to have exercised the power, so that there was in effect a public law duty to act, and secondly, that there are exceptional grounds for holding that the policy of the statute requires compensation to be paid to persons who suffer loss because the power was not exercised.

The difficulties are that Lord Hoffmann appears to accept Lord Romer's general statement in *East Suffolk v Kent* (disapproved in *Anns*, and also not consistent with later cases such as *Barrett* and *Phelps*); he appears to argue that any common law duty in this context would grow out of the statutory powers, whereas we have said that they are independent of such powers; and he makes a public law concept (irrationality) the first stage of establishing any such negligence duty. This too was later thoroughly rejected in *Barrett* and *Phelps*.

In the next case, the *outcome* in *Stovin v Wise* was confirmed as correct, despite the developments in *Barrett* and *Phelps*. There was some important clarification of the reasoning.

Gorringe v Calderdale [2004] 1 WLR 1057

The claimant was driving too fast towards the brow of a hill. Having got to the top, she caught sight of a bus coming up the other side. It was not in her lane but she panicked, crashed, and was injured. She brought an action against the local authority on the basis that it should have repainted the word 'slow' on the road towards the top of the hill.

Here, the local authority was under a relevant statutory *duty*, but this was expressed in such broad and general terms that it could not form the basis of an action at private law. As such, this duty was treated in the same way as the statutory *power* in *Stovin v Wise*. Lord Hoffmann explained:

(a) That the approach in *Stovin v Wise* was limited to cases of pure omission ('doing nothing at all') in which the *only* basis for suggesting there is a duty to act is the existence of a statutory power (or, now, public law duty); and

(b) That there probably would be no exceptional cases meeting his criteria of actionability after all. As such, there was no need to discuss the concept of 'irrationality' at public law in *Stovin v Wise*. It was probably a mistake to have made any remarks on this subject.

Lord Hoffmann

31 . . . The majority [in *Stovin*] rejected the argument that the existence of the statutory power to make improvements to the highway could in itself give rise to a common law duty to take reasonable care to exercise the power or even not to be irrational in failing to do so. It went no further than to leave open the possibility that there might somewhere be a statutory power or public duty which generated a common law duty and indulged in some speculation (which may have been ill-advised) about what that duty might be.

32 Speaking for myself, I find it difficult to imagine a case in which a common law duty can be founded simply upon the failure (however irrational) to provide some benefit which a public authority has power (or a public law duty) to provide. For example, the majority reasoning in *Stovin v Wise* was applied in *Capital & Counties plc v Hampshire County Council* [1997] QB 1004 to fire authorities, which have a general public law duty to make provision for efficient fire-fighting services: see section 1 of the Fire Services Act 1947. The Court of Appeal held, in my view correctly, that this did not create a common law duty.

Emphasizing that the outcomes in these cases do not conflict directly with other developments (in cases such as *Barrett* and *Phelps*), he added:

38 My Lords, I must make it clear that this appeal is concerned only with an attempt to impose upon a local authority a common law duty to act based solely on the existence of a broad public law duty. We are not concerned with cases in which public authorities have actually done acts or entered into relationships or undertaken responsibilities which give rise to a common law duty of care. In such cases the fact that the public authority acted pursuant to a statutory power or public duty does not necessarily negative the existence of a duty. A hospital trust provides medical treatment pursuant to the public law duty in the 1977 Act, but the existence of its common law duty is based simply upon its acceptance of a professional relationship with the patient no different from that which would be accepted by a doctor in private practice. The duty rests upon a solid, orthodox common law foundation and the question is not whether it is created by the statute but whether the terms of the statute (for example, in requiring a particular thing to be done or conferring a discretion) are sufficient to exclude it. The law in this respect has been well established since *Geddis v Proprietors of Bann Reservoir* (1878) 3 App Cas 430.

Lord Steyn agreed in the result, but added some distinct comments. These underline the independence of common law duties from statutory powers and duties. These comments are particularly helpful in explaining the limited ambit of *Stovin* and *Gorringe*, and placing them in the context of more positive developments in other cases.

Lord Steyn, *Gorringe v Calderdale* [2004] 1 WLR 1057

2 There are . . . a few remarks that I would wish to make about negligence and statutory duties and powers. This is a subject of great complexity and very much an evolving area of the law. No single decision is capable of providing a comprehensive analysis. It is a subject on which an intense focus on the particular facts and on the particular statutory background, seen in the context of the contours of our social welfare state, is necessary. On the one hand the courts must not contribute to the creation of a society bent on litigation, which is premised on the illusion that for every misfortune there is a remedy. On the other hand, there are cases where the courts must recognise on principled grounds the compelling demands of corrective justice or what has been called "the rule of public policy which has first claim on the loyalty of the law: that wrongs should be remedied": *M (A Minor) v Newham London Borough Council* and *X (Minors) v Bedfordshire County Council* [1995] 2 AC 633, 663, per Sir Thomas Bingham MR. Sometimes cases may not obviously fall in one category or the other. Truly difficult cases arise.

3   In recent years four House of Lords decisions have been milestones in the evolution of this branch of the law and have helped to clarify the correct approach, without answering all the questions: *X (Minors) v Bedfordshire County Council, Stovin v Wise, Barett v Enfield London Borough Council* and *Phelps v Hillingdon London Borough Council*. There are two comments on these decisions which I would make. First, except on a very careful study of these decisions, there is a principled distinction which is not always in the forefront of discussions. It is this: in a case founded on breach of statutory duty the central question is whether from the provisions and structure of the statute an intention can be gathered *to create* a private law remedy? In contradistinction in a case framed in negligence, against the background of a statutory duty or power, a basic question is whether the statute *excludes* a private law remedy? An assimilation of the two inquiries will sometimes produce wrong results.

4   The second point relates to observations of Lord Hoffmann in his landmark majority judgment in *Stovin v Wise*, to which Lord Hoffmann has made reference in his opinion. . . .

"In summary, therefore, I think that the minimum preconditions for basing a duty of care upon the existence of a statutory power, if it can be done at all, are, first, that it would in the circumstances have been irrational not to have exercised the power, so that there was in effect a public law duty to act, and secondly, that there are exceptional grounds for holding that the policy of the statute requires compensation to be paid to persons who suffer loss because the power was not exercised."

Since *Stovin v Wise* these observations have been qualified in *Barrett's* and *Phelps's* cases. I say that not because of the context of the actual decisions in those cases-in *Barrett's* case a council's duty to a child in care and in *Phelps's* case a duty of care in the educational field. Rather it is demonstrated by the legal analysis which prevailed in those decisions.

5   These qualifications of *Stovin v Wise* have been widely welcomed by academic lawyers. A notably careful and balanced analysis is that of Professor Paul Craig, *Administrative Law*, 5th ed (2003), pp 888–904. He stated, at p 898:

"There are many instances where a public body exercises discretion, but where the choices thus made are suited to judicial resolution. The mere presence of some species of discretion does not entail the conclusion that the matter is thereby non-justiciable. In the United States, it was once argued that the very existence of discretion rendered the decision immune from negligence. As one court scathingly said of such an argument, there can be discretion even in the hammering of a nail. Discretionary judgments made by public bodies, which the courts feel able to assess, should not therefore preclude the existence of negligence liability. This does not mean that the presence of such discretion will be irrelevant to the determination of liability. It will be of relevance in deciding whether there has been a breach of the duty of care. It is for this reason that the decisions in *Barrett* and *Phelps* are to be welcomed. Their Lordships recognised that justiciable discretionary choices would be taken into account in deciding whether the defendant had acted in breach of the duty of care. There may also be cases where some allegations of negligence are thought to be non-justiciable, while others may be felt suited to judicial resolution in accordance with the normal rules on breach."

Although the *result* in *Stovin v Wise* has been endorsed by the House of Lords in *Gorringe*, its narrow ambit has been clarified. Besides the specific conclusion that the local authority owed no duty to take positive steps to remove the hazard in *Stovin*, or to provide a warning in *Gorringe*, the cases hold that existence of a power or public law duty does not give rise to a duty to act at private law; and that there was no reason (for example, of general or specific reliance) to recognize a duty in such cases. This is important enough, but it means the cases should have no application in circumstances where positive steps are taken, such as *East Suffolk* itself. The difficulty is that *East Suffolk* seems to have been applied in certain 'emergency cases', and one of these was referred to by Lord Hoffmann with approval in *Gorringe* (above). Approval of this case seems to mean that Lord Hoffmann endorses the spirit of *East Suffolk*, since the case takes non-liability beyond the limits within which *Stovin* and *Gorringe* should strictly be confined. The case says that there is no duty on the fire service to answer a call *or to put out fires if they attend*; their liability is limited to *additional* damage that they cause.

Capital and Counties plc v Hampshire County Council [1997] 1 QB 1004

A number of appeals were heard together. All concerned claims against local councils in respect of alleged negligence on the part of the fire service. In *Capital and Counties* itself, judgment was entered for the plaintiffs. The fire service had attended a fire, turned off the automatic sprinkler system, and failed to extinguish the fire properly. The Court of Appeal held that a duty of care was owed in such a case. In the other appeals, the Court of Appeal held that no duty of care was owed. In *John Munroe v London Fire and Civil Defence Authority*, the fire service had arrived at a fire and left without properly extinguishing it. The fire restarted some time later. In *Church of Jesus Christ and Latter Day Saints v West Yorkshire Fire and Civil Defence Authority*, the plaintiffs' chapel was destroyed by fire. Fifteen fire engines arrived quickly, but could not fight the fire for lack of water. The surrounding fire hydrants were not operational and water had to be gathered from further afield. It was alleged that there was negligence (and breach of statutory duty) in failing to maintain the hydrants and in failing to locate an alternative nearby source.

It will be seen that none of these cases concerned an omission to answer an emergency call, or even a failure to turn up. All arose from attendance at the scene of a fire.

The Court of Appeal held that a fire service attending a fire was not in a sufficient relationship of proximity with the owner of the premises to come under a duty of care. Their duties were owed to the public at large, even if they were in attendance. This conclusion was supported by the authority of *Alexandrou v Oxford* [1993] 4 All ER 328, in which it was held that no duty was owed by police officers to the owner or occupier of premises which they attended in response to a burglar alarm, on the basis of lack of proximity.

The puzzle therefore is why there *was* liability in the single case, where the fire brigade had not only attended and fought the fire, but had also turned off the sprinkler system which was the plaintiffs' own defence against the spread of fire. This involved discussion of *East Suffolk v Kent*:

Stuart-Smith LJ, *Capital and Counties Bank v Hampshire County Council*, at 1034

We think that the true analogy between the *Hampshire* case and the *East Suffolk* case would be this. Suppose that after the main sea wall had been breached the plaintiff had constructed a temporary wall which contained the flood water to a relatively small area, and that the defendants then came upon the land to repair the main wall and negligently destroyed the plaintiff's temporary wall so that the area of the flooding increased before the repairs were completed. In such circumstances the defendants would at least prima facie be liable for the extra damage unless they could show—and the burden would be upon them—that the damage would have occurred in any event, even if they had never come upon the scene. If they were unable to discharge that burden, then they would be liable. Similarly, in the present case the judge's inability to make such a finding in their favour must in our view render the defendants liable.

This passage explores the burden of proving causation (or lack of it) between the acts of the defendant (turning off the sprinklers) and the additional damage suffered. It does not explain why, given the *lack* of proximity in the majority of the cases, there was thought to be sufficient proximity in the *Hampshire* case. The following remarks appear to supply the answer:

Stuart-Smith LJ, at 1036–7

It has been held that a property owner owes a duty of care to firemen not by his negligence to start a fire or create special hazards to fire-fighting operations: *Ogwo v. Taylor* [1988] A.C. 431. That being so, it was submitted that there ought to be a reciprocal duty on the part of the fire brigade to the property owner, the argument being that if there is proximity in one direction it ought to be in both. But the reason why a duty is owed to rescuers is because the law recognises that if A by his negligence puts the person or property of B at risk, it is reasonably foreseeable that some courageous and public-spirited person, C, will come to the assistance of B. C is the secondary victim of A's negligence and the duty is owed to C as well as B. A has created the danger which causes injury to both B and C. But simply by attending the fire and conducting fire-fighting operations the fire brigade do not, save in exceptional circumstances such as the *Hampshire* case, create or increase the danger.

The distinction drawn between the other appeals, and the *Hampshire* case, appears to rest on an argument that there is *proximity* only where the defendant has created new damage. This cannot be generally correct. For example, the duties owed by doctors and the National Health Service would be considerably narrowed in scope if they related only to duties not to *add to* the damage that would be suffered if they did nothing. In *Gorringe*, Lord Hoffmann explained the duties owed by hospital trusts in terms of their 'acceptance of a professional relationship'. The duty to act to prevent harm, like the duty not to cause harm by acting carelessly, depends on all the circumstances of the relationship between the parties. This is also what Lord Atkin proposed in his dissenting judgment in *East Suffolk*.

Notably, the Court of Appeal rejected the argument that the fire service owed no duty of care on 'public policy grounds'. They treated public policy as entirely separate from proximity.

Stuart-Smith LJ, at 1039

In the *East Suffolk* case, it is clear that the board would have been liable if through their negligence they had added to the damage the plaintiff would otherwise have suffered. The dividing line between liability and non-liability is thus defined and there is no need to pray in aid any concept of public policy. We agree with Mr. Sumption that the courts should not grant immunity from suit to fire brigades simply because the judge may have what he describes as a visceral dislike for allowing possibly worthless claims to be made against public authorities, whose activities involve the laudable operation of rescuing the person or property of others in conditions often of great danger. Such claims may indeed be motivated by what is sometimes perceived to be the current attitude to litigation: "If you have suffered loss and can see a solvent target, sue it." None the less, if a defendant is to be immune from suit such immunity must be based upon principle.

(At 1044)

. . . If we had found a sufficient relationship of proximity in the *London Fire Brigade* and *West Yorkshire* cases, we do not think that we would have found the arguments for excluding a duty of care on the ground that it would not be just, fair and reasonable convincing. The analogy with the police exercising their functions of investigating and suppressing crime is not close. The floodgates argument is not persuasive; nor is that based on insurance. Many of the other arguments are equally applicable to other public services, for example, the National Health Service. We do not think that the principles which underlie those decisions where immunity has been granted can be sufficiently identified in the case of fire brigades.

Kent v Griffiths [2000] 2 WLR 1158

An ambulance had not turned up in time. No convincing reason had ever been given and the ambulance crew had falsified the records. The result of their delay was very severe injury to the claimant, who was suffering an asthmatic attack.[52] If Stuart-Smith LJ in *Capital and Counties* had correctly stated a *general* principle, then this claim must fail:

Stuart-Smith LJ, *Captial and Counties Bank v Hampshire County Council,* at 1030

In our judgment the fire brigade are not under a common law duty to answer the call for help, and are not under a duty to take care to do so. If, therefore, they fail to turn up, or fail to turn up in time, because they have carelessly misunderstood the message, got lost on the way or run into a tree, they are not liable.

The Court of Appeal held in this case however that the judgments in respect of proximity in *Alexandrou* and *Capital and Counties Bank* were not of general application. They depended on all the circumstances of the case. There may be different considerations in relation to different emergency services, and in relation to different circumstances. In the circumstances of this particular case, a duty of care was owed.

Lord Woolf, giving the judgment of the court, attempted to argue that the case came within the 'irrationality' exception in *Stovin v Wise*: it would be irrational not to accede to the request for an ambulance.[53] As we have seen this exception probably does not exist after all (*Gorringe*). On the other hand, the exception is only necessary if an attempt is being made to *derive a common law duty to act from a statutory power*. Here, there is not a pure omission (the ambulance

[52] Could this have been a case of specific reliance? Her GP was in attendance and could have driven to the hospital, perhaps. But the case was not approached in these terms.

[53] Lord Woolf also tried to evade the impact of *Stovin v Wise* in *Larner v Solihull MBC* [2001] RTR 469 (duty owed in respect of warning of dangerous junction). In *Gorringe*, his efforts were disapproved, as amounting to an application of the minority judgments in *Stovin*. *Larner* was overruled.

set off, but did not arrive in time); and the duty of care, if it was to arise at all, would have to arise out of the relationship between the parties. The most doubtful element in the judgment is that it seeks to distinguish between the ambulance service on the one hand, and the fire service on the other. Having made this distinction, Lord Woolf reasoned from first principles in applying the *Caparo* test to this case.

42   The starting point is the fact that even when a statute only establishes a power for a body to act in a particular manner the body can be liable for negligence if there is also a common law duty created on the particular facts of the case. . . .

. . .

45   Here what was being provided was a health service. In the case of health services under the 1977 Act the conventional situation is that there is a duty of care. Why should the position of the ambulance staff be different from that of doctors or nurses? In addition the arguments based on public policy are much weaker in the case of the ambulance service than they are in the case of the police or the fire service. The police and fire services' primary obligation is to the public at large. In protecting a particular victim of crime, the police are performing their more general role of maintaining public order and reducing crime. In the case of fire the fire service will normally be concerned not only to protect a particular property where a fire breaks out but also to prevent fire spreading. In the case of both services, there is therefore a concern to protect the public generally. The emergency services that can be summoned by a 999 call do, in the majority of situations, broadly carry out a similar function. But in reality they can be very different. The ambulance service is part of the health service. Its care function includes transporting patients to and from hospital when the use of an ambulance for this purpose is desirable. It is therefore appropriate to regard the LAS as providing services of the category provided by hospitals and not as providing services equivalent to those rendered by the police or the fire service. Situations could arise where there is a conflict between the interests of a particular individual and the public at large. But, in the case of the ambulance service in this particular case, the only member of the public who could be adversely affected was the claimant. It was the claimant alone for whom the ambulance had been called.

. . .

47   An important feature of this case is that there is no question of an ambulance not being available or of a conflict in priorities. Again I recognise that where what is being attacked is the allocation of resources, whether in the provision of sufficient ambulances or sufficient drivers or attendants, different considerations could apply. There then could be issues which are not suited for resolution by the courts. However, once there are available, both in the form of an ambulance and in the form of manpower, the resources to provide an ambulance on which there are no alternative demands, the ambulance service would be acting perversely "in circumstances such as the present", if it did not make those resources available. Having decided to provide an ambulance an explanation is required to justify a failure to attend within reasonable time.

Lord Woolf's approach in this respect seems consistent with more recent decisions such as *Barrett* and *Phelps* and it should not be regarded as inconsistent with *Gorringe*, which said only that a positive duty to act for the purposes of a negligence action cannot be said to arise (if it arises at all) *simply* because there is a statutory power to act. As we have said, confusion is created by Lord Hoffmann's approval of *Capital and Counties*. *Capital and Counties* describes an area of 'no duty' going well beyond pure omissions. Unfortunately, the result of these cases is that it currently appears that the ambulance service owes duties in respect of emergency calls where the fire service does not.

In conclusion, Lord Woolf also echoed the idea in *Barrett* that the test for *breach of duty* will itself restrict the number of successful claims.

51   The reaction of the judge to the facts of this case accords with the likely reaction of any well-informed member of the public. In such a situation it would be regrettable indeed if there were not to be a right to compensation. It is clearly a factor which influenced May LJ in another case involving the police, *Costello v Chief Constable of Northumbria* [1999] ICR 752, where the chief constable was liable for the negligence of a senior police officer who exposed another police officer to unnecessary risk of injury. May LJ said, at p 767: "I am sure that Astill J was correct to say that the public would be greatly disturbed if the law held that there was no duty of care in this case."

52   I would say exactly the same of the facts in this case. As in *Costello's* case, they are out of the ordinary. I would hope that it is unusual in the extreme for an ambulance to be delayed as this ambulance was delayed without the crew being able to put forward any explanation.

FURTHER READING

Bagshaw, R., 'Monetary Remedies in Public Law—Misdiagnosis and Misprescription' (2006) 26 LS 4.

Bailey, S., 'Public Authority Liability in Negligence: the Continued Search for Coherence' (2006) 26 LS 155.

Bowman, M.J., and Bailey, S., 'Negligence in Public Law—A Positive Obligation to Rescue' [1994] PL 277.

Carnwath, R., 'Welfare Services—Liabilities in Tort After the Human Rights Act' [2001] PL 210.

Carnwath, R., 'Postcript' [2001] PL 475.

Craig, P., 'Compensation and Public Law' (1980) 96 LQR 413.

Craig, P., and Fairgrieve, D., '*Barrett*, Negligence and Discretionary Powers' [1999] PL 626.

Fairgrieve, D., 'The Human Rights Act 1998, Damages, and Tort Law' [2001] PL 695.

Fairgrieve, D., 'Pushing Back the Boundaries of Public Authority Liability: Tort Law Enters the Classroom' [2002] PL 288.

Fairgrieve, D., *State Liability in Tort: A Comparative Study* (Oxford: OUP, 2003).

Harlow, C., *State Liability—Tort Law and Beyond* (Oxford: Clarendon Press, 2004).

Hickman, T., 'The Reasonableness Principle: Reassessing Its Place in the Public Sphere' [2004] CLJ 166.

Howarth, D., 'Public Authority Non-Liability: Spinning Out of Control?' [2004] CLJ 546.

Weir, J.A., 'Governmental Liability' [1989] PL 40.

Wright, J., 'Local Authorities, The Duty of Care and the ECHR' (1998) 18 OJLS 1.

4. IMMUNITIES

European Convention on Human Rights

Article 6   Right to a fair trial

1   In the determination of his civil rights and obligations or of any criminal charge against him, everyone is entitled to a fair and public hearing within a reasonable time by an independent and impartial tribunal established by law. . . .

Hill v Chief Constable of South Yorkshire Police [1989] 1 AC 53

The plaintiff's daughter was the final victim of a serial killer, Peter Sutcliffe, who had been preying on young single women in the area. The plaintiff argued that the police owed a duty to her daughter to conduct their investigation into the murders with reasonable care, that they had breached this duty, and that this had led to the death of her daughter.[54] The House of Lords agreed with the first instance judge and with the Court of Appeal that no duty of care was owed, and the action was struck out.

It is important to notice how the relevant question for appeal was set out.

Lord Keith, *Hill v Chief Constable*, at 59

The question of law which is opened up by the case is whether the individual members of a police force, in the course of carrying out their functions of controlling and keeping down the incidence of crime, owe a duty of care to individual members of the public who may suffer injury to person or property through the activities of criminals, such as to result in liability in damages, on the ground of negligence, to anyone who suffers such injury by reason of breach of that duty.

There is no question that a police officer, like anyone else, may be liable in tort to a person who is injured as a direct result of his acts or omissions. So he may be liable in damages for assault, unlawful arrest, wrongful imprisonment and malicious prosecution, and also for negligence. Instances where liability for negligence has been established are *Knightley v. Johns* [1982] 1 W.L.R. 349 and *Rigby v. Chief Constable of Northamptonshire* [1985] 1 W.L.R. 1242. Further, a police officer may be guilty of a criminal offence if he wilfully fails to perform a duty which he is bound to perform by common law or by statute: see *Reg. v. Dytham* [1979] Q.B. 722, where a constable was convicted of wilful neglect of duty because, being present at the scene of a violent assault resulting in the death of the victim, he had taken no steps to intervene.

Later in his judgment, after reviewing the applicable authorities including *Anns v Merton* and *Dorset Yacht v Home Office*, Lord Keith outlined two separate reasons why no duty of care could be established in this case. Either reason would be sufficient in its own right.

The first reason relates to lack of proximity between the parties. The second reason relates to *policy concerns. Hill* was decided by applying the two stage test for the existence of a duty of care, under *Anns v Merton*. These reasons correspond with the two stages of *Anns*.

---

[54] The claim was brought on behalf of the estate of the deceased daughter, and the relevant duty was alleged to be owed to her: see Chapter 8.3 for an outline of the relevant causes of action in the event of death.

Lord Keith, at 62–3

The *Dorset Yacht* case was concerned with the special characteristics or ingredients beyond reasonable foreseeability of likely harm which may result in civil liability for failure to control another man to prevent his doing harm to a third. The present case falls broadly into the same category. It is plain that vital characteristics which were present in the *Dorset Yacht* case and which led to the imposition of liability are here lacking. Sutcliffe was never in the custody of the police force. Miss Hill was one of a vast number of the female general public who might be at risk from his activities but was at no special distinctive risk in relation to them, unlike the owners of yachts moored off Brownsea Island in relation to the foreseeable conduct of the Borstal boys. It appears from the passage quoted from the speech of Lord Diplock in the *Dorset Yacht* case that in his view no liability would rest upon a prison authority, which carelessly allowed the escape of an habitual criminal, for damage which he subsequently caused, not in the course of attempting to make good his getaway to persons at special risk, but in further pursuance of his general criminal career to the person or property of members of the general public. The same rule must apply as regards failure to recapture the criminal before he had time to resume his career. In the case of an escaped criminal his identity and description are known. In the instant case the identity of the wanted criminal was at the material time unknown and it is not averred that any full or clear description of him was ever available. The alleged negligence of the police consists in a failure to discover his identity. But if there is no general duty of care owed to individual members of the public by the responsible authorities to prevent the escape of a known criminal or to recapture him, there cannot reasonably be imposed upon any police force a duty of care similarly owed to identify and apprehend an unknown one. Miss Hill cannot for this purpose be regarded as a person at special risk simply because she was young and female. Where the class of potential victims of a particular habitual criminal is a large one the precise size of it cannot in principle affect the issue. All householders are potential victims of an habitual burglar, and all females those of an habitual rapist. The conclusion must be that although there existed reasonable foreseeability of likely harm to such as Miss Hill if Sutcliffe were not identified and apprehended, there is absent from the case any such ingredient or characteristic as led to the liability of the Home Office in the *Dorset Yacht* case. Nor is there present any additional characteristic such as might make up the deficiency. The circumstances of the case are therefore not capable of establishing a duty of care owed towards Miss Hill by the West Yorkshire Police.

That is sufficient for the disposal of the appeal. But in my opinion there is another reason why an action for damages in negligence should not lie against the police in circumstances such as those of the present case, and that is public policy. In *Yuen Kun Yeu v. Attorney-General of Hong Kong* [1988] A.C. 175, 193, I expressed the view that the category of cases where the second stage of Lord Wilberforce's two stage test in *Anns v. Merton London Borough Council* [1978] A.C. 728, 751–752 might fall to be applied was a limited one, one example of that category being *Rondel v. Worsley* [1969] 1 A.C. 191. Application of that second stage is, however, capable of constituting a separate and independent ground for holding that the existence of liability in negligence should not be entertained. Potential existence of such liability may in many instances be in the general public interest, as tending towards the observance of a higher standard of care in the carrying on of various different types of activity. I do not, however, consider that this can be said of police activities. The general sense of public duty which motivates police forces is unlikely to be appreciably reinforced by the imposition of such liability so far as concerns their function in the investigation and suppression of crime. From time to time they make mistakes in the exercise of that function, but it is not to be doubted that they apply their best endeavours to the performance of it. In some instances the imposition of liability may lead to the exercise of a function being carried on in a detrimentally defensive frame of mind. The possibility of this happening in relation to the investigative operations of the police cannot be excluded. Further it would be reasonable to expect that if potential liability were to be imposed it would be not uncommon for actions to be raised against police forces on the ground that they had failed to catch some criminal as soon as they might have done, with the result that he went on to commit further crimes. While some such actions might involve allegations of a simple and straightforward type of failure—for example that a police officer negligently tripped and fell while pursuing a burglar—others would be likely to enter deeply into the general nature of a police investigation, as indeed the present action would seek to do. The manner of conduct of such an investigation must necessarily involve a variety of decisions to be made on matters of policy and discretion, for example as to which particular line of inquiry is most advantageously to be pursued and what is the most advantageous way to deploy the available resources. Many such decisions would not be regarded by the courts as appropriate to be called in question, yet elaborate investigation of the facts might be necessary to ascertain whether or not this was so. A great deal of police time, trouble and expense might be expected to have to be put into the preparation of the defence to the action and the attendance of witnesses at the trial. The result would be a significant diversion of police manpower and attention from their most important function, that of the suppression of crime. Closed investigations would require to be reopened and retraversed, not with the object of bringing any criminal to justice but to ascertain whether or not they had been competently conducted. I therefore consider that Glidewell L.J., in his judgment in the Court of Appeal [1988] Q.B. 60, 76 in the present case, was right to take the view that the police were immune from an action of this kind on grounds similar to those which in *Rondel v. Worsley* [1969] 1 A.C. 191 were held to render a barrister immune from actions for negligence in his conduct of proceedings in court.

At the end of this catalogue of policy reasons, Lord Keith refers to the police as 'immune' from such an action. This was perhaps not the best terminology to use to summarize the preceding discussion. But the effect was reinforced by comparison with the barristers' immunity recognized in *Rondel v Worsley* [1969] 1 AC 191. The origins of this immunity are summarized in the following passage (drawn from a case in which the immunity was abolished).

Lord Hoffmann, *Arthur JS Hall v Simons* [2002] 1 AC 615, at 685–6

The old rule for barristers survived until 1967. The way in which it was usually explained was that barristers, unlike solicitors, had no contract with their clients. They could not sue for their fees. And in the absence of a contract there could be no liability. But that reason was undermined when the House of Lords decided in *Hedley Byrne & Co Ltd v Heller & Partners Ltd* [1964] AC 465 that, even without a contract, a person who negligently performed professional or other duties which he had undertaken could be sued in tort. So the whole question was re-examined by the House in *Rondel v Worsley* [1969] 1 AC 191. What emerged was a different rule of immunity, in some respects wider and in others narrower, not based upon any technicalities but upon what the House perceived as the public interest in the administration of justice.

The new rule was narrower because, although their Lordships were not unanimous about its precise limits, they agreed that it should in general terms be confined to acts concerned with the conduct of litigation. None of them thought that it could apply to non-contentious work. Barristers had previously been immune from liability for anything. On the other hand, the new rule was wider in that it also applied to solicitors.

Most of the speeches in *Rondel v Worsley* [1969] 1 AC 191 were devoted to explaining why the new immunity was necessary. The old cases had not relied solely upon the technicalities of contract. The rule was also said to be an expression of public policy. But Lord Reid said, at p 227B–C, that public policy was "not immutable" and that because "doubts appear to have arisen in many quarters whether that rule is justifiable in present day conditions in this country" it was proper to "re-examine the whole matter".

The House of Lords decided that it was time to abolish advocates' immunity. The policy considerations had changed, as had the tort of negligence and the organization of the legal profession.[55]

Lord Hoffmann, at 704

. . . I do not say that *Rondel v Worsley* was wrongly decided at the time. The world was different then. But, as Lord Reid said then, public policy is not immutable and your Lordships must consider the arguments afresh.

Having decided that policy arguments now weighed *against* the immunity, the House of Lords did not consider whether the immunity would be in violation of Article 6 of the European Convention on Human Rights. But it is probable that the barristers' immunity was considered to be under threat, given the European Court of Human Rights' decision in *Osman v UK*. In order to understand *Osman v UK*, it is necessary to examine the way that *Hill* was interpreted by the Court of Appeal in *Osman v Ferguson*, which led to the action against the UK.

Osman v Ferguson [1993] 4 All ER 344 (CA)

A schoolteacher (P) became obsessed with a 15-year-old pupil (O). Because of his conduct (including criminal damage, painting graffiti about O, and changing his name to Osman), he was dismissed from his job. He continued to harass O and his family. The police were aware of these events, and P had told police that he might 'do something criminally insane'. After further acts of aggression, of which the police were aware, P eventually followed O home, and shot him (causing serious injury) and his father (who was killed). P was convicted of manslaughter. O and his mother (for her husband's estate) brought an action in negligence against the police, for failing to arrest and charge P on the basis of what was known, therefore failing to prevent the shooting.

The Court of Appeal accepted that this case was different from *Hill*, in that it was arguable that there was *proximity* and indeed *a special relationship* between the parties. McCowan J distinguished the case of *Alexandrou v Oxford* [1993] 4 All ER 328, where there was insufficient proximity, and no duty of care.

---

[55] The policy arguments for and against advocates' immunity were debated at length. The House of Lords was unanimous in rejecting the immunity in relation to civil matters; in relation to criminal matters the decision to discontinue the immunity was reached by a narrow majority.

McCowan J

Returning to the facts of the present case and again on the assumption that they are proved, it seems to me that it can well be said on behalf of the plaintiffs that the second plaintiff and his family were exposed to a risk from PagetLewis over and above that of the public at large. In my judgment the plaintiffs have therefore an arguable case that as between the second plaintiff and his family, on the one hand, and the investigating officers, on the other, there existed a very close degree of proximity amounting to a special relationship. . . .

The claim was struck out, however, because the policy arguments set out in *Hill* were thought to determine this case. The difficulty is that the judgments in *Hill* seem to have been interpreted as though they laid down a binding rule, that no action against the police could succeed in respect of 'investigation and suppression of crime'. The *Caparo* criteria were not considered afresh in relation to the facts of the case in hand. Rather, the conclusion in one case was seen as binding in another.

. . . Mr Hendy submitted that the present was a case depending on the decision of one or more difficult points of law and that we should therefore refuse to entertain the claim to strike out. I cannot agree. I consider this a plain and obvious case falling squarely within a House of Lords decision. I would therefore allow the appeal.

It is understandable that the European Court of Human Rights interpreted this *particular* case as disclosing an 'immunity'—not least because that word was used in *Hill* itself, and a parallel was drawn with the true immunity, now discontinued, afforded to barristers in the conduct of a case.[56]

Osman v UK [1999] 1 FLR 193

(134)   . . . The applicants maintained that although they had established all the constituent elements of the duty of care, the Court of Appeal was constrained by precedent to apply the doctrine of police immunity developed by the House of Lords in the Hill case (see para (90) above) to strike out their statement of claim. In their view the doctrine of police immunity was not one of the essential elements of the duty of care as was claimed by the Government, but a separate and distinct ground for defeating a negligence action in order to ensure, inter alia, that police manpower was not diverted from their ordinary functions or to avoid overly cautious or defensive policing.

(135)   The Commission agreed with the applicants that Art 6(1) was applicable. It considered that the applicants' claim against the police was arguably based on an existing right in domestic law, namely the general tort of negligence. The House of Lords in the Hill case modified that right for reasons of public policy in order to provide an immunity for the police from civil suit for their acts and omissions in the context of the investigation and suppression of crime. In the instant case, that immunity acted as a bar to the applicants' civil action by preventing them from having an adjudication by a court on the merits of their case against the police.

---

56 *Hill* was also described in terms of an 'immunity'—held not to extend to the fire service—in *Capital and Counties v Hampshire*, above.

(139) . . . the Court considers that the applicants must be taken to have had a right, derived from the law of negligence, to seek an adjudication on the admissibility and merits of an arguable claim that they were in a relationship of proximity to the police, that the harm caused was foreseeable and that in the circumstances it was fair, just and reasonable not to apply the exclusionary rule outlined in the Hill case. In the view of the Court the assertion of that right by the applicants is in itself sufficient to ensure the applicability of Art 6(1) of the Convention.

(140) For the above reasons, the Court concludes that Art 6(1) is applicable. It remains to be determined whether the restriction which was imposed on the exercise of the applicants' right under that provision was lawful.

It will be noticed that the denial of the opportunity for adjudication was sufficient to *engage* Article 6(1). It did not mean in itself that Article 6 had been violated. This is because the general policy objective of *Hill* was legitimate. In finding that there was a violation of Article 6, the court had regard to the *proportionality* of the protection accorded to this policy objective, bearing in mind the gravity of the harm foreseeably suffered by the plaintiff,[57] *and* the way in which the immunity was interpreted in *Osman* itself:

Osman v UK [1999] 1 FLR 193

(149) The reasons which led the House of Lords in the *Hill* case to lay down an exclusionary rule to protect the police from negligence actions in the context at issue are based on the view that the interests of the community as a whole are best served by a police service whose efficiency and effectiveness in the battle against crime are not jeopardised by the constant risk of exposure to tortious liability for policy and operational decisions.

(150) Although the aim of such a rule may be accepted as legitimate in terms of the Convention, as being directed to the maintenance of the effectiveness of the police service and hence to the prevention of disorder or crime, the Court must nevertheless, in turning to the issue of proportionality, have particular regard to its scope and especially its application in the case at issue. While the Government have contended that the exclusionary rule of liability is not of an absolute nature (see para (144) above) and that its application may yield to other public policy considerations, it would appear to the Court that in the instant case the Court of Appeal proceeded on the basis that the rule provided a watertight defence to the police and that it was impossible to prise open an immunity which the police enjoy from civil suit in respect of their acts and omissions in the investigation and suppression of crime.

(151) The Court would observe that the application of the rule in this manner without further inquiry into the existence of competing public interest considerations only serves to confer a blanket immunity on the police for their acts and omissions during the investigation and suppression of crime and amounts to an unjustifiable restriction on an applicant's right to have a determination on the merits of his or her claim against the police in deserving cases.

---

[57] The relationship between Article 2 and Article 6 is interesting in this regard. There was no violation of Article 2, because there was no precise moment at which the police *should* clearly have acted. They could not be criticized, for example, for applying the presumption of innocence. But the gravity of the harm suffered (death and serious injury) was relevant to the way that the policy objectives behind the 'immunity' in tort law were fulfilled.

Osman v UK has been criticized for its interpretation of the role of policy in the tort of negligence.[58] It is indeed incorrect to say that 'policy' is an additional factor, in addition to the *Caparo* criteria. Lord Hoffmann, writing extra-judicially, was particularly trenchant. His broader remarks have some continuing force despite the discrediting of *Osman* itself:

Rt Hon Lord Hoffmann, 'Human Rights and the House of Lords'
(1999) 62 MLR 159, at 164, 165–6

I am bound to say that this decision [*Osman v UK*] fills me with apprehension. Under the cover of an Article which says that everyone is entitled to have his civil rights and obligations determined by a tribunal, the European Court of Human Rights is taking upon itself to decide what the content of those civil rights should be. In so doing, it is challenging the autonomy of the courts and indeed the Parliament[59] of the United Kingdom to deal with what are essentially social welfare questions involving budgetary limits and efficient public administration. . . .

Of course it is true that the Strasbourg court acknowledges the fact that often there is no right answer by allowing what it calls a 'margin of appreciation' to the legislature or courts of a member State. Within limits, they are allowed to differ. And, as I have said, I accept that there is an irreducible minimum of human rights which must be universally true. But most of the jurisprudence which comes out of Strasbourg is not about the irreducible minimum. . . . The *Osman* case, dealing with the substantive civil law right to financial compensation for not receiving the benefit of a social service, is as far as one can imagine from basic human rights. . . .

Notice that here Lord Hoffmann argues that the right to compensation for not receiving the benefit of a social service (protection from crime) is a matter *not* of human rights, but of 'social welfare', involving budgetary constraints.

On the other hand, certain criticisms of *Osman v Ferguson* itself are well made. The Court of Appeal in that decision did indeed seem to interpret the immunity in *Hill* as if it were a general rule to be applied in all cases of 'investigation and suppression of crime', without regard to the precise facts of the case. Subsequent cases such as *Barrett v Enfield* (and *Brooks v Commissioner of the Metropolis*, below) have adopted a much more nuanced approach to the policy issues and courts will not so readily translate—let alone 'apply'—policy arguments developed in one case, in order to dispose of a quite different case.

Z v UK [2001] 2 FLR 612

The losing plaintiffs in *X v Bedfordshire* commenced proceedings against the UK, alleging violations of Articles 3, 8, 6, and 13 of the Convention. Importantly, the European Court of Human Rights accepted that it had been mistaken in the earlier case of *Osman v UK* as to the role of policy in the tort of negligence. The Court concluded that no 'immunity' was applied in *X v Bedfordshire* itself. There was therefore no violation of Article 6. This conclusion was assisted by consideration of *Barrett v Enfield* and other later cases. In the rush to note that *Osman* has been discredited, it is easy to overlook that this has happened partly because courts

---

58 See C. Gearty, 'Unravelling *Osman*' (2001) 64 MLR 159.
59 Note that subsequently, in *Roche v UK* (below), the European Court of Human Rights has accepted (albeit only by a majority) that a *statutory* immunity from civil action does not violate Article 6.

have more recently been careful not to be seen to apply 'blanket' policy reasoning; and to treat 'policy' as part and parcel of the general *Caparo* test.

In the following passage, the Court considers the policy reasoning in *X v Bedfordshire*.

European Court of Human Rights, *Z v UK*

1.   Nor is the Court persuaded by the suggestion that, irrespective of the position in domestic law, the decision disclosed an immunity in fact or practical effect due to its allegedly sweeping or blanket nature. That decision concerned only one aspect of the exercise of local authorities' powers and duties and cannot be regarded as an arbitrary removal of the courts' jurisdiction to determine a whole range of civil claims (see Fayed v. the United Kingdom judgment of 21 September 1994, Series A no. 294, pp. 49–50, § 65). As it has recalled above in paragraph 87 it is a principle of Convention case-law that Article 6 does not in itself guarantee any particular content for civil rights and obligations in national law, although other Articles such as those protecting the right to respect for family life (Article 8) and the right to property (Article 1 of Protocol No. 1) may do so. It is not enough to bring Article 6 § 1 into play that the non-existence of a cause of action under domestic law may be described as having the same effect as an immunity, in the sense of not enabling the applicant to sue for a given category of harm.

2.   Furthermore, it cannot be said that the House of Lords came to its conclusion without a careful balancing of the policy reasons for and against the imposition of liability on the local authority in the circumstances of the applicants' case. Lord Browne-Wilkinson in his leading judgment in the House of Lords acknowledged that the public policy principle that wrongs should be remedied required very potent counter considerations to be overridden (see paragraph 46 above). He weighed that principle against the other public policy concerns in reaching the conclusion that it was not fair, just or reasonable to impose a duty of care on the local authority in the applicants' case. It may be noted that in subsequent cases the domestic courts have further defined this area of law concerning the liability of local authorities in child care matters, holding that a duty of care may arise in other factual situations, where, for example, a child has suffered harm once in local authority care or a foster family has suffered harm as a result of the placement in their home by the local authority of an adolescent with a history of abusing younger children (see *W and Others v. Essex County Council* and *Barrett v. Enfield LBC . . .*).

3.   The applicants, and the Commission in its report, relied on the Osman case (cited above) as indicating that the exclusion of liability in negligence, in that case concerning the acts or omissions of the police in the investigation and prevention of crime, acted as a restriction on access to court. The Court considers that its reasoning in the Osman judgment was based on an understanding of the law of negligence (see, in particular, paragraphs 138 and 139 of the Osman judgment) which has to be reviewed in the light of the clarifications subsequently made by the domestic courts and notably the House of Lords. The Court is satisfied that the law of negligence as developed in the domestic courts since the case of *Caparo*, and as recently analysed in the case of *Barrett v. Enfield LBC*, includes the fair, just and reasonable criterion as an intrinsic element of the duty of care and that the ruling of law concerning that element in this case does not disclose the operation of an immunity. In the present case, the Court is led to the conclusion that the inability of the applicants to sue the local authority flowed not from an immunity but from the applicable principles governing the substantive right of action in domestic law. There was no restriction on access to court of the kind contemplated in the Ashingdane judgment. . . .

The Court held that there were violations of Articles 3 and 13 in this case. We have already explored the impact of this in domestic law, via the Human Rights Act 1998, when we considered *D v East Berkshire* (above).

The following two very important House of Lords cases have raised separate issues about 'immunities'.

Brooks v Commissioner of Police for the Metropolis [2005] 1 WLR 1495

In this case the House of Lords considered whether *Hill v Chief Constable* can be followed, without falling foul of Article 6. The essential facts and background to the case are encapsulated in the first paragraph of Lord Bingham's judgment.[60] In paragraph two, Lord Bingham also sets out the three specific duties argued for by the claimant.

Lord Bingham, *Brooks v Commissioner of Police of the Metropolis*
[2005] UKHL 24; [2005] 1 WLR 1495

1 My Lords, Duwayne Brooks, the respondent, was present when his friend Stephen Lawrence was abused and murdered in the most notorious racist killing which our country has ever known. He also was abused and attacked. However well this crime had been investigated by the police and however sensitively he had himself been treated by the police, the respondent would inevitably have been deeply traumatised by his experience on the night of the murder and in the days and weeks which followed. But unfortunately, as established by the public inquiry into the killing (The Stephen Lawrence Inquiry: Report of an Inquiry by Sir William Macpherson of Cluny (1999)) (Cm 4262–I), the investigation was very badly conducted and the respondent himself was not treated as he should have been. He issued proceedings against the Metropolitan Police Commissioner and a number of other parties, all but one of whom were police officers.

2 ... the only issue before the House is whether, assuming the facts pleaded by the respondent to be true, the Commissioner and the officers for whom he is responsible arguably owed the respondent a common law duty sounding in damages to (1) take reasonable steps to assess whether the respondent was a victim of crime and then to accord him reasonably appropriate protection, support, assistance and treatment if he was so assessed; (2) take reasonable steps to afford the respondent the protection, assistance and support commonly afforded to a key eye-witness to a serious crime of violence; (3) afford reasonable weight to the account that the respondent gave and to act upon it accordingly.

Lord Steyn

27 Since the decision in *Hill's* case there have been developments which affect the reasoning of that decision in part. In *Hill's* case the House relied on the barrister's immunity enunciated in *Rondel v Worsley* [1969] 1 AC 191. That immunity no longer exists: *Arthur J S Hall & Co v Simons* [2002] 1 AC 615. More fundamentally since the decision of the European Court of Human Rights in *Z v United Kingdom* (2001) 34 EHRR 97, 138, para 100, it would be best for the principle in *Hill's* case to be reformulated in terms of the absence of a duty of care rather than a blanket immunity.

---

60 A longer exploration of the mistreatment of the claimant by investigating officers is to be found in the judgment of Lord Steyn.

28   With hindsight not every observation in *Hill's* case [1989] AC 53 can now be supported. Lord Keith of Kinkel observed, at p 63, that

> "From time to time [the police] make mistakes in the exercise of that function, but it is not to be doubted that they apply their best endeavours to the performance of it".

Nowadays, a more sceptical approach to the carrying out of all public functions is necessary.

29   Counsel for the Commissioner concedes that cases of assumption of responsibility under the extended *Hedley Byrne* doctrine (*Hedley Byrne & Co Ltd v Heller & Partner Ltd* [1964] AC 465) fall outside the principle in *Hill's* case. In such cases there is no need to embark on an inquiry whether it is "fair, just and reasonable" to impose liability for economic loss: *Williams v Natural Life Health Foods Ltd* [1998] 1 WLR 830.

30   But the core principle of *Hill's* case has remained unchallenged in our domestic jurisprudence and in European jurisprudence for many years. If a case such as the Yorkshire Ripper case, which was before the House in *Hill's* case, arose for decision today I have no doubt that it would be decided in the same way. It is, of course, desirable that police officers should treat victims and witnesses properly and with respect: compare the Police (Conduct) Regulations 2004 (SI 2004/645). But to convert that ethical value into general legal duties of care on the police towards victims and witnesses would be going too far. The prime function of the police is the preservation of the Queen's peace. The police must concentrate on preventing the commission of crime; protecting life and property; and apprehending criminals and preserving evidence: see section 29 of the Police Act 1996, read with Schedule 4 as substituted by section 83 of the Police Reform Act 2002; section 17 of the Police (Scotland) Act 1967; *Halsbury's Laws of England*, 4th ed reissue (1999), vol 36(1), para 524; *The Laws of Scotland, Stair Memorial Encyclopaedia*, vol 16, (1995), para 1784; *Moylan, Scotland Yard and the Metropolitan Police*, (1929), p 34. A retreat from the principle in *Hill's* case would have detrimental effects for law enforcement. Whilst focusing on investigating crime, and the arrest of suspects, police officers would in practice be required to ensure that in every contact with a potential witness or a potential victim time and resources were deployed to avoid the risk of causing harm or offence. Such legal duties would tend to inhibit a robust approach in assessing a person as a possible suspect, witness or victim. By placing general duties of care on the police to victims and witnesses the police's ability to perform their public functions in the interests of the community, fearlessly and with despatch, would be impeded. It would, as was recognised in *Hill's case*, be bound to lead to an unduly defensive approach in combating crime.

31   It is true, of course, that the application of the principle in *Hill's* case will sometimes leave citizens, who are entitled to feel aggrieved by negligent conduct of the police, without a private law remedy for psychiatric harm. But domestic legal policy, and the Human Rights Act 1998, sometimes compel this result. In *Brown v Scott* [2003] 1 AC 681, Lord Bingham of Cornhill observed, at p 703:

> "The Convention is concerned with rights and freedoms which are of real importance in a modern democracy governed by the rule of law. It does not, as is sometimes mistakenly thought, offer relief from 'The heart-ache and the thousand natural shocks that flesh is heir to.' "

. . .

32   While not challenging the decision of the House of Lords in *Hill's* case counsel submitted that it can be distinguished. The only suggested distinction ultimately pursued was that in *Hill's* case the police negligence was the indirect cause of the murder of the daughter whereas in the present case the police directly caused the harm to Mr Brooks. That hardly does justice to the essential reasoning in *Hill's* case. In any event, *Calveley v Chief Constable of the*

Merseyside Police [1989] AC 1228, *Elguzouli-Daf v comr of Police of the Metropolis* [1995] QB 335, and *Kumar v Comr of Police of the Metropolis* 31 January 1995 were cases of alleged positive and direct negligence by the police. The distinction is unmeritorious.

XIV The three critical questions

33 That brings me to the three critical alleged duties of care before the House. It is realistic and fair to pose the question whether the three surviving duties of care can arguably be said to be untouched by the core principle in *Hill's* case. In my view the three alleged duties are undoubtedly inextricably bound up with the police function of investigating crime which is covered by the principle in *Hill's* case. For example, the second duty of care is to "take reasonable steps to afford [Mr Brooks] the protection, assistance and support commonly afforded to a key eye-witness to a serious crime of violence". It is quite impossible to separate this alleged duty from the police function of investigating crime. The same is, however, true of the other two pleaded duties. If the core principle in *Hill's* case stands, as it must, these pleaded duties of care cannot survive.

34 It is unnecessary in this case to try to imagine cases of outrageous negligence by the police, unprotected by specific torts, which could fall beyond the reach of the principle in *Hill's* case. It would be unwise to try to predict accurately what unusual cases could conceivably arise. I certainly do not say that they could not arise. But such exceptional cases on the margins of the principle in *Hill's* case will have to be considered and determined if and when they occur.

35 Making full allowance for the fact that this is a strike-out application, and that the law regarding the liability of the police in tort is not set in stone, I am satisfied that the three duties of care put forward in this case are conclusively ruled out by the principle in *Hill's* case, as restated, and must be struck out.

On a cynical day, one might say that the only difference between this approach, and *Hill* itself, is the emphasis on the possibility of 'extreme cases' (indicating that this is not a case of 'blanket' policy thinking), and the change in language from 'immunity', to 'no duty'. But Lord Steyn also makes the fundamentally important point that it is not always appropriate for individuals' claims in tort to succeed, without regard to the impact on broader interests. The Human Rights Act 1998, like the European Convention on Human Rights itself, in no way requires that individual interests should always prevail over community interests. This interpretation of the Convention rights is further illustrated in Chapter 13, Defamation.

Matthews v Ministry of Defence [2003] 1 AC 1163 (HL)

In this case the House of Lords considered the validity, in respect of the Convention, of a true immunity, conferred by statute. It concluded that such an immunity, being substantive rather than procedural, did not violate Article 6.

There was some doubt whether this stance would be accepted by the European Court of Human Rights. But in *Roche v UK* (2005), the Court considered the same statutory immunity against actions in tort, and held that Article 6 is violated only when a *procedural* immunity is created.

Matthews concerned section 10 of the Crown Proceedings Act 1947. Prior to 1947, the Crown enjoyed immunity against all actions in tort. It was liable neither directly, nor vicariously. This general immunity was swept away in 1947 and section 2 provided that—subject to other provisions of the Act—the Crown would be subject to the same liabilities in tort as other persons. This included vicarious liability for the torts of servants and agents.

Section 10 of the Crown Proceedings Act enacted exceptions to this. It did not create any new immunities; but specified an exception to the new liability on the part of the Crown created by the Act. The relevant subsection was as follows

---

Crown Proceedings Act 1947, *Provisions Relating to the Armed Forces*

10—(1) Nothing done or omitted to be done by a member of the armed forces of the Crown while on duty as such shall subject either him or the Crown to liability in tort for causing the death of another person, or for causing personal injury to another person, in so far as the death or personal injury is due to anything suffered by that other person while he is a member of the armed forces of the Crown if—

   (a) at the time when that thing is suffered by that other person, he is either on duty as a member of the armed forces of the Crown or is, though not on duty as such, on any land, premises, ship, aircraft or vehicle for the time being used for the purposes of the armed forces of the Crown; and

   (b) the Minister of Pensions certifies that his suffering that thing has been or will be treated as attributable to service for the purposes of entitlement to an award under the Royal Warrant, Order in Council or Order of His Majesty relating to the disablement or death of members of the force of which he is a member:

Provided that this subsection shall not exempt a member of the said forces from liability in tort in any case in which the court is satisfied that the act or omission was not connected with the execution of his duties as a member of those forces.

. . .

Section 10 was prospectively repealed by the Crown Proceedings (Armed Forces) Act 1987 (the relevant acts in *Matthews* took place prior to this). However:

1. By section 2 of the Crown Proceedings (Armed Forces) Act 1987, section 10 may be revived by order of the Secretary of State if it is necessary or expedient to do so, either because of imminent national danger or great emergency; or 'for the purposes of any warlike operations' in any part of the world; and

2. The armed forces continue to enjoy 'combat immunity' at common law. This predates the Crown Proceedings Act 1947, and is narrower than the statutory immunity, since it applies only to injuries sustained or actions performed in the course of active combat: *Mulcahy v Ministry of Defence* [1996] QB 732 (CA) (no duty of care owed in respect of personal injuries sustained in a war zone during active service).

In *Matthews* itself, the claimant served in the Royal Navy between 1955 and 1968. He was diagnosed as suffering from asbestos-related disease. He claimed damages in negligence or breach of statutory duty in exposure to the asbestos dust during his service. The ministry denied liability on the basis of section 10, and a certificate was issued by the Secretary of State under section 10(1)(b). Injury in service will lead to an enhanced pension entitlement.

The claimant argued that section 10 was incompatible with the right to a fair trial in Article 6.1 European Convention on Human Rights, as set out in Schedule 1 of the Human Rights Act 1998. The House of Lords rejected this argument. Section 10 did not impose a *procedural* bar against recovery. Rather, section 10 imposed a limitation as a matter of substantive law. The claimant had no civil right to which Article 6.1 could apply.

The House of Lords, and most particularly Lord Walker, devoted considerable attention to the jurisprudence of the European Court of Human Rights on the applicability of Article 6. In *Roche v UK* (2005), this attention to the Court's decisions was one of the crucial factors in the Court *accepting* the judgment of the House of Lords, that section 10 constituted a substantive, not a procedural bar. Although *Roche v UK* was a case brought by a different applicant, the Article 6 claim in this case turned on the same provision of the Crown Proceedings Act 1947.

Roche v UK (2005)

A certain tension was noted in the case law relating to Article 6. In *Fayed v UK* (1994) 18 EHRR 393, the Court had stated that there might be circumstances in which even substantive limitations on the civil rights of individuals might be contrary to Article 6. Although *Z v UK* (extracted above) clearly seemed to conclude that a substantive restriction would not violate Article 6, the relevant passage in *Fayed v UK* was repeated verbatim a few months later in *Fogarty v UK* (2001) 34 EHRR 302. Therefore, it was of some importance that the Court in *Roche* accepted that a substantive restriction would not violate Article 6—even if the dividing line between substance and procedure was sometimes hard to draw.

European Court of Human Rights, *Roche v UK* (2005) The Times, 27 October

4.   The right of access to court guaranteed by Article 6 at issue in the present case was established in the above-cited *Golder* judgment (at §§ 28–36). In that case, the Court found the right of access to court to be an inherent aspect of the safeguards enshrined in Article 6, referring to the principles of the rule of law and the avoidance of arbitrary power which underlay much of the Convention. Thus, Article 6 § 1 secures to everyone the right to have a claim relating to his civil rights and obligations brought before a court (see, more recently, the above-cited judgment in *Z and Others v. the United Kingdom*, at § 91).

5.   Article 6 § 1 does not, however, guarantee any particular content for those (civil) "rights" in the substantive law of the Contracting States: the Court may not create through the interpretation of Article 6 § 1 a substantive right which has no legal basis in the State concerned (the above-cited *Fayed v. the United Kingdom* judgment, at § 65). Its guarantees extend only to rights which can be said, at least on arguable grounds, to be recognised under domestic law (*James and Others v. the United Kingdom*, judgment of 21 February 1986, Series A no. 98, *Z and Others*, at § 81 and the authorities cited therein together with *McElhinney v. Ireland* [GC], no. 31253/96, § 23, ECHR 2001-XI (extracts)).

6.   The applicant maintained that there was a certain tension between this afore-mentioned principle, on the one hand, and, on the other, the established autonomous meaning accorded by the Court to the notion of "civil rights and obligations". Connected to this, he questioned the distinction between a restriction which delimits the substantive content properly speaking of the relevant civil right (to which the guarantees of Article 6 § 1 do not apply . . . and a restriction which amounts to a procedural bar preventing the bringing of potential claims to court, to which Article 6 could have some application (*Tinnelly & Sons Ltd and Others and McElduff and Others v. the United Kingdom*, § 62, *Al-Adsani v. the United Kingdom* [GC], no. 35763/97, §§ 48–49, ECHR 2001-XI, *Fogarty v. the United Kingdom*, § 26 and *McElhinney v. Ireland*, § 25)). The applicant argued that it was not necessary to maintain that distinction . . . : any restriction should be subjected to a proportionality test because the important point was to protect the courts from the assumption of arbitrary power and control on the part of the executive.

7.   The Court cannot agree with these submissions of the applicant. It does not find any inconsistency between the autonomous notion of "civil" . . . and the requirement that domestic law recognises, at least on arguable grounds, the existence of a "right" . . . . In addition, the Commission decisions in *Ketterick*, *Pinder* and *Dyer* must be read in the light, *inter alia*, of the judgment in the case of *Z and Others* (cited above) and, in particular, in the light of the Court's affirmation therein as to the necessity to maintain that procedural/substantive distinction: fine as it may be in a particular case, this distinction remains determinative of the applicability and, as appropriate, the scope of the guarantees of Article 6 of the Convention. In both these respects, the Court would reiterate the fundamental principle that Article 6 does not itself guarantee any particular content of substantive law of the Contracting Parties (see, amongst other authorities, *Z and Others v. the United Kingdom*, cited above, § 87).

No implication to the contrary can be drawn, in the Court's view, from paragraph 67 of the *Fayed* judgment. . . .

8.   In assessing therefore whether there is a civil "right" and in determining the substantive or procedural characterisation to be given to the impugned restriction, the starting point must be the provisions of the relevant domestic law and their interpretation by the domestic courts (*Masson and Van Zon v. the Netherlands*, judgment of 28 September 1995, Series A no. 327–A, § 49). Where, moreover, the superior national courts have analysed in a comprehensive and convincing manner the precise nature of the impugned restriction, on the basis of the relevant Convention case-law and principles drawn therefrom, this Court would need strong reasons to differ from the conclusion reached by those courts by substituting its own views for those of the national courts on a question of interpretation of domestic law (*Z and Others*, at § 101) and by finding, contrary to their view, that there was arguably a right recognised by domestic law.

Roche v UK is important reinforcement of the view that Article 6 does not compel any particular content for domestic rights. On the other hand as we have already seen, if violation of Convention rights goes unremedied through tort law or any other compensation mechanism, then there may be a violation not only of those substantive rights, but also of Article 13 (the right to compensation). In *Roche* itself, there had been a violation of Article 8.

FURTHER READING

Gearty, C., 'Osman Unravels' (2002) 65 MLR 87.

Hickman, T., 'Negligence and A.6, The Great Escape?' [2002] CLJ 14.

---

5.   FAILED STERILIZATIONS

In the cases explored here, the claimants decided they did not want any children (or any more children). They underwent sterilization procedures, but these procedures were negligently performed, or the claimants were negligently advised that they had succeeded and they need not use contraception. The female claimants conceived. Could they recover damages from the negligent parties in respect of the pregnancy, the birth, and (most controversially) the upbringing of the children?

For the most part, the general story in the last section was of growing confidence in the norms of tort law. Rightly or wrongly, there was a trend towards expansion in 'duty situations', but also a more nuanced approach to *rejection* of the duty of care where appropriate.[61] In the section before that, we even suggested (contrary to the received view of English law) that more rational decision-making is emerging in economic loss cases. The present section deals with a more confined issue which has troubled the courts in a number of jurisdictions, including the House of Lords twice within a short period of time. Here, as with secondary victim cases in relation to psychiatric harm, it is much harder to suggest that the *Caparo* approach has been useful in answering the questions that arise.

Judges have found it genuinely difficult to decide these cases on the basis of existimg criteria. That being so, the question is whether it is wise to express their conclusions in terms of those criteria at all; or whether it is better to say frankly that the decisions have been reached in some other way instead. The former approach (applying existing concepts in such a way that they seem meaningless) was broadly adopted by Lord Slynn in the first case extracted below, holding that no duty was owed in respect of the costs of raising a healthy child. The second approach (stepping outside the usual terminology) was adopted by Lord Steyn, who came to the same conclusion. Both approaches have been criticized. The opposite conclusion has been reached in Australia, where costs of raising a child have been awarded. This gives us a valuable opportunity to compare not only the merits of the decisions, but also the reasoning applied.

McFarlane v Tayside [2000] 2 AC 59

The pursuers,[62] a married couple, already had four children. They did not want a fifth, and decided that the husband would undergo a vasectomy. The pursuers were told that the husband's sperm count was negative and that they could dispense with contraceptive measures. It was claimed that this advice, rather than the operation itself, was negligent. The pursuers acted on the advice, but the wife became pregnant and delivered a healthy child. The pursuers claimed damages associated with the pregnancy and birth, and also claimed the costs of rearing an unwanted (though now of course much loved) but healthy child.

On appeal, the majority of the House of Lords held that the mother would, if negligence was established, be entitled to damages in respect of the pain, suffering, and inconvenience of pregnancy and childbirth, and for the immediate medical and other expenses, and loss of earnings, associated with the birth. However, it was decided (unanimously) that the costs of raising the child were not recoverable.

Lord Slynn of Hadley, at 76

The doctor undertakes a duty of care in regard to the prevention of pregnancy: it does not follow that the duty includes also avoiding the costs of rearing the child if born and accepted into the family. Whereas I have no doubt that there should be compensation for the physical effects of the pregnancy and birth, including of course solatium for consequential suffering by the mother immediately following the birth, I consider that it is not fair, just or reasonable to

---

61 Note *Brooks v Commissioner of Police for the Metropolis* [2005] 1 WLR 1495 compared to *Hill v Chief Constable of South Yorkshire Police* [1989] 1 AC 53; *Gorringe v Calderdale* [2004] 1 WLR 1057 (per Lord Steyn) compared to *Stovin v Wise* [1996] AC 923. In each pair of cases the two decisions were the same in respect of their outcome; in each pair the reasoning in the later case is more open to competing concerns than in the earlier case.

62 This was a Scottish case on appeal from the Inner House of the Court of Session.

impose on the doctor or his employer liability for the consequential responsibilities, imposed on or accepted by the parents to bring up a child. The doctor does not assume responsibility for those economic losses. If a client wants to be able to recover such costs he or she must do so by an appropriate contract.

Unfortunately, in trying to explain his decision in terms of 'assumption of responsibility', Lord Slynn purports to apply a 'test' without any indication of its likely meaning. Like Lord Slynn's other reference to 'assumption of responsibility'—in *Phelps v Hillingdon*—this approach tempts us to conclude that the expression has no meaning at all. Elsewhere in his judgment, Lord Slynn pointed to the sheer scale of the potential damages and the difficulty of placing any limits on what was a reasonable cost in this context. This may have been a decisive factor in his mind (see also Lord Bingham's reference, in the extract from *Rees v Darlington* below, to the prospect of middle class families 'plundering the NHS' for the costs of raising a healthy child).

Lord Slynn, at 74

The question remains whether as a matter of legal principle the damages should include, for a child by then loved, loving and fully integrated into the family the cost of shoes at 14 and a dress at 17 and everything that can reasonably be described as necessary for the upbringing of the child until the end of school, university, independence, maturity?

By contrast with Lord Slynn, who applied an existing 'label' in order to justify his decision, Lord Steyn decided that the ordinary principles of tort law, which he captured in terms of 'corrective justice', did not adequately dispose of the case. While he *could* explain that a duty in this case was not 'fair, just, and reasonable' under *Caparo*, he preferred to be more honest. His reasons, he thought, were best explained as *distributive*. On this occasion, there was a reason of distributive justice for rejecting the claims. People generally would consider it unfair that parents who are fortunate to enjoy the benefit of a loved and healthy child (albeit one they had already decided not to have) should be handsomely compensated for the upkeep of that child. Expressing this, he thought, was better than resorting to a 'formalistic proposition' derived from the terms of an existing legal test.

Lord Steyn, at 82–3

My Lords, to explain decisions denying a remedy for the cost of bringing up an unwanted child by saying that there is no loss, no foreseeable loss, no causative link or no ground for reasonable restitution is to resort to unrealistic and formalistic propositions which mask the real reasons for the decisions. And judges ought to strive to give the real reasons for their decision. It is my firm conviction that where courts of law have denied a remedy for the cost of bringing up an unwanted child the real reasons have been grounds of distributive justice. That is of course, a moral theory. It may be objected that the House must act like a court of law and not like a court of morals. That would only be partly right. The court must apply positive law. But judges' sense of the moral answer to a question, or the justice of the case, has been one of the great shaping forces of the common law. What may count in a situation of difficulty and uncertainty is not the subjective view of the judge but what he reasonably believes that the ordinary citizen would regard as right. Two recent illustrations of the relevance of the moral dimension in the development of the law illustrate the point. In *Smith New Court Securities Ltd. V. scrimgeour Vickers (Asset Management) Ltd.* [1997] A.C. 254 the House differentiated between the measure of damages for fraudulent and negligent misrepresentation. Pointing out that tort law and moral-ity are inextricably interwoven I said (with the agreement of Lord Keith of Kinkel and Lord Jauncey of Tullichettle) that as between the fraudster and the innocent party moral consider-ations militate in favour of requiring the fraudster to bear the risk of misfortunes directly caused by the fraud: p. 280B–C. In *Frost v. Chief Constable of South Yorkshire Police* [1999] 2 A.C. 455 the police officers claimed compensation for psychiatric loss they sustained as a result of the Hillsborough disaster. By a majority the House ruled against the claim. The principal theme of the judgments of the majority was based on considerations of distributive justice. In separate judgments Lord Hoffmann and I reasoned that it would be morally unacceptable if the law denied a remedy to bereaved relatives as happened in *Alcock v. Chief Constable of South Yorkshire Police* [1992] 1 A.C. 310 but granted it to police officers who were on duty. Lord Hoffmann expressly invoked considerations of distributive justice: [1999] 2 A.C. 455, 503–504. Lord Browne-Wilkinson and I expressed agreement with this reasoning. In my judgment I observed, at p. 498D: "The claim of the police officers on our sympathy, and the justice of the case, is great but not as great as that of others to whom the law denies redress." That is the language of distributive justice. The truth is that tort law is a mosaic in which the principles of corrective justice and distributive justice are interwoven. And in situations of uncertainty and difficulty a choice sometimes has to be made between the two approaches.

In my view it is legitimate in the present case to take into account considerations of distribu-tive justice. That does not mean that I would decide the case on grounds of public policy. On the contrary, I would avoid those quicksands. Relying on principles of distributive justice I am persuaded that our tort law does not permit parents of a healthy unwanted child to claim the costs of bringing up the child from a health authority or a doctor. If it were necessary to do so, I would say that the claim does not satisfy the requirement of being fair, just and reasonable.

Lord Steyn's hypothetical opinion poll on the London underground[63] is criticized by Laura Hoyano (in an article which seems to have influenced the High Court of Australia in *Cattanach v Melchior*, below).

Laura Hoyano, 'Misconceptions about wrongful conception' (2002) 65 MLR, 883, at 904

. . . Distributive justice has become just another label, without pretending to intellectual rigour. The transmogrification of the man on the Clapham omnibus is not limited to a change of pub-lic transport, as he is no longer just a convenient measure for the standard of care expected of non-experts, but also the gatekeeper for negligence law itself. . . . Appeals to commuters on the London underground to decide duty of care issues allow the courts to avoid confronting the sharp edges of competence, cheapest cost avoidance of the risk, insurability against loss, other modes of loss-spreading—and whether carving out *ad hoc* exceptions to well-established legal principles is a matter for parliamentary rather than judicial action. . . .

. . . A principled approach can enhance the flexibility which gives the common law its vitality, if the courts directly confront policy factors, both intrinsic and extrinsic to the relationship of the particular parties. . . .

---

[63] Lord Steyn's reference to the passenger on the London underground is an updated and now suitably gen-der neutral version of the 'man on the Clapham omnibus', who has traditionally set the standard for judgments as to reasonableness, but not necessarily morality.

The 'wrongful conception' cases demonstrate that distributive justice can be just as unruly a
horse as public policy for the courts to ride. The London Underground is not the BBC's *Moral
Maze*. Since we are apparently stuck on the Circle Line, however, we can only hope that the
House of Lords, having now granted leave to appeal in *Rees*, will clarify what they really meant
in *McFarlane*.

Laura Hoyano's point is in some respects reinforced by Lord Steyn's reference to *White v Chief
Constable*,[64] above, in which the House of Lords set considerable store –perhaps too much
store, we suggested there—by the expected public response to the judgment. This is the sort
of response which was resisted by Kirby J in particular in *Cattanach v Melchior* (below)—
although the Australian public's response to that decision suggests that Lord Steyn's
hypothetical poll may have been reliable.

Later, in *Rees v Darlington*, Lord Steyn conceded that reading the judgments in *McFarlane*
is a 'gruesome task'. The most that was said to meet Laura Hoyano's wish at the end of the
extract above (to explain what the grounds of the decision actually were) is forthcoming in the
following short passage. Lord Steyn contends that all the different judgments were based not
on 'public policy' in the full sense, but on *legal policy*:

Lord Steyn, *Rees v Darlington*, at 322

29 . . . The House [in *McFarlane*] did not rest its decision on public policy in a conventional
sense: Lord Slynn of Hadley, at p 76D; my judgment, at p 83D–E; Lord Hope of Craighead, at
p 95A; Lord Clyde, at p 100A–C; and Lord Millett, at p 108A–C. Instead the Law Lords relied on
legal policy. In considering this question the House was bound, in the circumstances of the
case, to consider what in their view the ordinary citizen would regard as morally acceptable.
Invoking the moral theory of distributive justice, and the requirements of being just, fair and
reasonable, culled from case law, are in context simply routes to establishing the legal policy.

Lord Steyn's use of the hypothetical commuter in this instance has been defended by Peter
Cane, who agrees that where settled principles do not appropriately determine a case, it would
be wrong either to decide regardless of issues of morality and distributive justice; or to hide
the real reasons behind some distorted version of established principles: see P. Cane, 'Taking
Disgreement Seriously: Courts, Legislatures and the Reform of Tort Law' (2005) 25 OJLS 393.

To return to *McFarlane*, Lord Hope thought that the parents of the child derived benefits
from the presence of that child within the family, as well as costs. Since those benefits were
'incalculable', they could not be set against the costs. Yet the benefits could not be left out of
account, or too much compensation would be paid. Therefore, the economic losses were not
recoverable. Lord Clyde, controversially, argued that the amount of damages recoverable as a
consequence of a wrong ought to be limited to those that are 'reasonable', and indeed proportionate: 'The restitution which the law requires is a reasonable restitution' (at 105).

Lord Millett on the other hand expressly rejected the argument that the potential liability
was disproportionate to the wrong in this case (at 109). He conceded that the parents of a
healthy child could decide for themselves that the burden of a healthy child outweighed the
benefits (clearly, since otherwise parents would simply continue to have as many children as
possible). But society, and the law, could not treat a healthy child as a loss. (Lord Millett would

---

[64] Lord Steyn refers to this case as *Frost v Chief Constable*. We extracted the case in Section 2 of this chapter.

also not have allowed any damages in respect of the pregnancy or birth. Yet surely *these* cannot be described as a 'blessing', mixed or otherwise?)[65] Lord Millett would however have awarded the parents jointly a sum of (around) £5,000, to reflect a different loss: deprivation of the right to limit the size of their family (at 114).

The House of Lords did not express a view on the correct position where either the mother (or presumably father), or the child, or conceivably both (or all three), is not healthy, and where this too increases the burden and the costs of upbringing. Such issues were raised in subsequent cases.

In *Parkinson v St James and Seacroft University NHS Trust* [2002] QB 266, the mother was healthy but the child was disabled. The court decided that the additional costs of rearing the child associated with its disability could be the subject of damages. Unfortunately, the status of *Parkinson* is wholly unclear since *Rees v Darlington* (below). It would appear that the three dissenting judges in *Rees* approved it,[66] and three of the four majority judges disapproved it.[67]

Rees v Darlington Memorial Hospital NHS Trust [2004] 1 AC 309

The claimant suffered from severe visual impairment. Because of this, she particularly did not want the burden of raising a child. She underwent a sterilization operation which was negligently performed at a hospital managed by the defendants. She gave birth to a healthy child, whose father wanted no part in its upbringing.

The House of Lords decided that no duty was owed in respect of the upbringing of a healthy baby, notwithstanding the particular burden this would place upon someone in the position of the claimant. The additional costs of upbringing relating to the mother's visual disability were equally not recoverable. However, the majority decided that a wrong had been committed towards the mother, and that she should be awarded a 'conventional sum' of £15,000 as a measure of recognition of that wrong. She had been denied 'the opportunity to live her life in the way that she wished and planned'.

Lord Bingham, at 316–17

The policy considerations underpinning the judgments of the House were, as I read them, an unwillingness to regard a child (even if unwanted) as a financial liability and nothing else, a recognition that the rewards which parenthood (even if involuntary) may or may not bring cannot be quantified and a sense that to award potentially very large sums of damages to the parents of a normal and healthy child against a National Health Service always in need of funds to meet pressing demands would rightly offend the community's sense of how public resources should be allocated. Kirby J was surely right to suggest in *Cattanach v Melchior* [2003] HCA 38, para 178, that:

"Concern to protect the viability of the National Health Service at a time of multiple demands upon it might indeed help to explain the invocation in the House of Lords in *McFarlane* of the notion of 'distributive justice'."

[65] Lord Millett's treatment of the claim in respect of pain and suffering is broadly explored by C. Witting, 'Physical Damage in Negligence' [2002] CLJ 189–208.

[66] Importantly perhaps, two of these three (Lords Steyn and Hope) were in the majority in *McFarlane*, suggesting that the decision of the Court of Appeal in *Parkinson* is consistent with *McFarlane* (and reinforcing the suspicion that *Rees v Darlington* is not).

[67] Lord Scott particularly pointed out that the disability of the child in *Parkinson* was in no way related to the negligence of the defendant.

It is indeed hard to think that, if the House had adopted the first solution discussed above, its decision would have long survived the first award to well-to-do parents of the estimated cost of providing private education, presents, clothing and foreign holidays for an unwanted child (even if at no more expensive a level than the parents had provided for earlier, wanted, children) against a National Health Service found to be responsible, by its negligence, for the birth of the child. In favouring the third solution, holding the damages claimed to be irrecoverable, the House allied itself with the great majority of state courts in the United States and relied on arguments now strongly supported by the dissenting judgments of Gleeson CJ, Hayne and Heydon JJ in *Melchior*.

7   I am of the clear opinion, for reasons more fully given by my noble and learned friends, that it would be wholly contrary to the practice of the House to disturb its unanimous decision in *McFarlane* given as recently as four years ago, even if a differently constituted committee were to conclude that a different solution should have been adopted. It would reflect no credit on the administration of the law if a line of English authority were to be disapproved in 1999 and reinstated in 2003 with no reason for the change beyond a change in the balance of judicial opinion. I am not in any event persuaded that the arguments which the House rejected in 1999 should now be accepted, or that the policy considerations which (as I think) drove the decision have lost their potency. Subject to one gloss, therefore, which I regard as important, I would affirm and adhere to the decision in *McFarlane*.

8   My concern is this. Even accepting that an unwanted child cannot be regarded as a financial liability and nothing else and that any attempt to weigh the costs of bringing up a child against the intangible rewards of parenthood is unacceptably speculative, the fact remains that the parent of a child born following a negligently performed vasectomy or sterilisation, or negligent advice on the effect of such a procedure, is the victim of a legal wrong. The members of the House who gave judgment in *McFarlane* recognised this by holding, in each case, that some award should be made to Mrs McFarlane (although Lord Millett based this on a ground which differed from that of the other members and he would have made a joint award to Mr and Mrs McFarlane). I can accept and support a rule of legal policy which precludes recovery of the full cost of bringing up a child in the situation postulated, but I question the fairness of a rule which denies the victim of a legal wrong any recompense at all beyond an award immediately related to the unwanted pregnancy and birth. The spectre of well-to-do parents plundering the National Health Service should not blind one to other realities: that of the single mother with young children, struggling to make ends meet and counting the days until her children are of an age to enable her to work more hours and so enable the family to live a less straitened existence; the mother whose burning ambition is to put domestic chores so far as possible behind her and embark on a new career or resume an old one. Examples can be multiplied. To speak of losing the freedom to limit the size of one's family is to mask the real loss suffered in a situation of this kind. This is that a parent, particularly (even today) the mother, has been denied, through the negligence of another, the opportunity to live her life in the way that she wished and planned. I do not think that an award immediately relating to the unwanted pregnancy and birth gives adequate recognition of or does justice to that loss. I would accordingly support the suggestion favoured by Lord Millett in *McFarlane*, at p 114, that in all cases such as these there be a conventional award to mark the injury and loss, although I would favour a greater figure than the £5,000 he suggested (I have in mind a conventional figure of £15,000) and I would add this to the award for the pregnancy and birth. This solution is in my opinion consistent with the ruling and rationale of *McFarlane*. The conventional award would not be, and would not be intended to be, compensatory. It would not be the product of calculation. But it would not be a nominal, let alone a derisory, award. It would afford some measure of recognition of the wrong done. And it would afford a more ample measure of justice than the pure *McFarlane* rule.

The minority judges noted that this conventional award was more than a 'gloss'. It was inconsistent with *McFarlane* itself, where such an award had been proposed by Lord Millett alone.

Lord Steyn

45 No United Kingdom authority is cited for the proposition that judges have the power to create a remedy of awarding a conventional sum in cases such as the present. There is none. It is also noteworthy that in none of the decisions from many foreign jurisdictions, with varying results, is there any support for such a solution. This underlines the heterodox nature of the solution adopted.

46 Like Lord Hope I regard the idea of a conventional award in the present case as contrary to principle. It is a novel procedure for judges to create such a remedy. There are limits to permissible creativity for judges. In my view the majority have strayed into forbidden territory. It is also a backdoor evasion of the legal policy enunciated in *McFarlane*. If such a rule is to be created it must be done by Parliament. The fact is, however, that it would be a hugely controversial legislative measure. It may well be that the Law Commissions and Parliament ought in any event, to consider the impact of the creation of a power to make a conventional award in the cases under consideration for the coherence of the tort system.

47 I cannot support the proposal for creating such a new rule.

Given his unconventional reasoning in *McFarlane*, is it surprising to see Lord Steyn, in particular, criticizing judicial creativity? There are two reasons why the dissenting judges may make some claim to consistency.

First, there was no 'conventional award' in *McFarlane*, and yet it could be said that in that case too the parents had been denied their right to live as they wanted, through the negligence of the defendant. It was not solely because of the claimant's disability, in *Rees*, that the defendants' negligence interfered with her autonomy, although this made the impact greater. The decision of the healthy mother of four children to avoid another pregnancy is equally a decision as to how to lead her life. As such, Lord Bingham here does to some extent undermine his own argument that it is too soon to depart from *McFarlane*.

Second, the idea of a 'conventional award' in recognition of a wrong assumes that a wrong can be specified. Since the majority *also* held that no duty of care was owed in respect of the cost of upbringing, it would appear that there was no recognized legal wrong to which this award could relate. The award requires creation of a new wrong, not just a controversial new remedy for an existing wrong (breach of a duty of care). Duties of care are owed to individuals in respect of particular damage. The majority did not go so far as to spell out what *duty* was being recognized. Was it a duty to take care not to interfere with the claimant's ability to plan her life? This would be novel indeed.[68]

In *Cattanach v Melchior* [2003] HCA 38, the High Court of Australia decided a factually similar case. The plaintiff had undergone a sterilization operation which was negligently performed. She claimed damages for the costs of rearing a healthy child. A majority of the High Court of Australia held that damages could be recovered in such a case. As Peter Cane has pointed out,[69] Kirby J is regarded as the least 'legalistic' and the most 'policy-oriented' of the Australian High Court judges (and is a supporter of the *Caparo* test which he considers to

---

[68] See *Chester v Afshar* (Chapters 2 and 4); and D. Nolan, 'New Forms of Damage in Negligence' (2007) 70 MLR 59–88.
[69] P. Cane, 'The Doctor, the Stork and the Court: A Modern Morality Play' (2004) 120 LQR 23.

provide a useful way of structuring policy discussion).[70] Even so, he decided with the majority not to follow *McFarlane v Tayside*, which is seen as representing a departure from ordinary legal principles. (*Cattanach v Melchior* was decided before *Rees v Darlington* which as we have seen represented an even larger departure from normal tort principles.)

Cattanach could be seen as a rather narrow decision since much was already conceded between the parties. In particular, it was conceded that a duty of care was owed, which was the very issue on which the pursuers lost in the case of *McFarlane v Tayside*. As such, it would have been a larger departure from ordinary tort principles to determine that the consequential losses were unrecoverable, if the existence (and breach) of the duty was assumed. But Peter Cane convincingly argues that there is much more to the decision than this. The decision was widely criticized in the Australian media and this was partly because it seemed to fly in the face of legislative reform of tort law in Australia. These reforms have been aimed at controlling both liability and quantum of damage.[71] Peter Cane argues that the High Court was deliberately reasserting the independence of tort law in this case.

Peter Cane, 'The Doctor, the Stork and the Court: A Modern Morality Play' (2004) 120 LQR 23–6

. . . it is tempting to interpret both the outcome and the majority reasoning in *Cattanach v Melchior* as an attempt by the court to re-assert its role as a forum of legal principle, above the political fray, immune to the siren call of "community values" and contestable moral opinions. Kirby J. captured the mood in a particularly vivid way (at [137]). Referring to the Ipp Review and its legislative aftermath, he argued that Parliaments cannot be trusted to set limits to tort liability. Their interventions, he said, "can be arbitrary and dogmatic"; and they "sometimes respond to the 'echo chamber inhabited by journalists and public moralists'" (quoting Sedley L.J. in *Vellino v Chief Constable of the Greater Manchester Police* [2002] 1 W.L.R. 218 at [60]).[72] "Judges, on the other hand", express and refine the common law "in ways that are logically reasoned and shown to be a consistent development of past decisional law". The understated comment of the leader writer of Melbourne's Age newspaper ("Babies, bungles and compensation" July 18, 2003) offers a different perspective: "The Australian Medical Association . . . has described the ruling as a 'horror story'. This is an overreaction, but the case does illustrate [that] . . . [n]ot all issues are best dealt with in a courtroom, and this may well be one of them".

Lord Reid was famous (amongst other things) for having called the view, that judges do not make law, a "fairy tale". The same might be said of the view of the majority in *Cattanach* that "legal principle" can tell us whether Dr Cattanach should have been held responsible for the cost of rearing Jordan Melchior.

Quite possibly, the stress suffered by the established techniques when some members of the House of Lords sought to apply (or disapply) them in *McFarlane v Tayside* tells us little about the inherent shortcomings of those techniques, although it does tell us that there are limits to the fact situations in which they are useful. It is also instructive to note that there was a significant public reaction to the outcome in *Cattanach v Melchior*. Perhaps Lord Steyn was not so

[70] As we have noted before, the *Caparo* test is generally rejected in Australia.
[71] *Review of the Law of Negligence*, Commonwealth of Australia, 2003, chaired by Ipp JA.
[72] *Vellino* is extracted in Chapter 5.

wrong to consult (at least hypothetically) the commuter on the London underground. There is evidence that the person on the Bourke Street tram or the Bondi bus might have agreed with the proposition he derived from that imaginary poll.[73]

FURTHER READING

Cane, P., 'Taking Disagreement Seriously: Courts, Legislatures and the Reform of Tort Law' (2005) 25 OJLS 393.

Hoyano, L., 'Misconceptions About Wrongful Conception' (2002) 65 MLR 883.

Priaulx, N, 'Joy to the World: A (Healthy) Child is Born! Reconceptualizing "Harm" in Wrongful Conception' (2004) 13 S & LS 5.

Stewart, A., 'Damages for the Birth of a Child' (1995) 40 JLSS 298.

---

6. GENERAL ASSESSMENT: THE DUTY OF CARE TODAY

When we introduced the duty concept in Chapter 3, we ended with a challenge. Are questions of duty currently being resolved in a properly reasoned manner? A first stage in answering this question is to ask whether the outcomes of cases are *predictable*. It has to be admitted that often, they are not. On the other hand, this may indicate only that the issues arising in negligence are both complex and debateable. Perhaps predictability is too much to hope for. A second aspect of the question is whether decisions can be understood in rational terms once they have been reached. As to this, there have been serious doubts in many cases. It has been difficult to reconcile the reasoning in different cases, which have appeared to proceed on directly contradictory approaches. Certain areas continue to show anomalies. A particular example is the law of psychiatric harm, where the decision in *White v Chief Constable* is a significant obstacle to achieving a rational and consistent approach.

But this kind of criticism can be overstated—or at least over-generalized. In some instances, the *Caparo* criteria have offered quite a successful means of focusing attention on the most relevant issues. Indeed in two of the most notoriously difficult areas of application for the tort of negligence—economic loss and public authority liability—it can be argued that courts have applied *Caparo* criteria with increasing success in recent years, and edged their way towards a more consistent method of deciding such cases. On the other hand, it must be conceded that these decisions will only have the appearance of consistency with one another if they are addressed at quite a detailed level.

The *Caparo* approach is also politically expedient in certain respects. As we explained in Chapter 3, *Caparo* requires *positive reasons* for a duty of care to be imposed in a novel situation. As such, *Caparo* can deal with (and even in some respects has allowed the courts to anticipate) the emergent concern with 'compensation culture': the idea that responsibility for harm (even if it is carelessly caused, or carelessly not prevented) should not be too easily

---

[73] Persons on the 'Bourke Street tram' and on the 'Bondi bus' have been referred to as cousins of the man on the Clapham omnibus in Melbourne and Sydney respectively.

passed to others. If tort is becoming more open to public criticism, then the *Caparo* test provides tools for adjusting the balance between claimants, defendants, and broader interests.

Another expedient feature of *Caparo* is that it is more Convention-compliant than *Anns*. This is also connected with the need, under *Caparo*, to show positive reasons for placing the duty to avoid harm (or not to cause it) with the defendant. It is far easier to present a finding of 'no duty' as a matter of substantive law, and not of 'procedure', under the *Caparo* approach. If this appears to be a matter of window dressing (and it is true that the presentation of decisions seems to be an important factor in swaying the European Court of Human Rights),[74] this presentation also reflects reality. The question whether a duty is owed *is* a matter of substantive law, whether or not 'policy' is involved in the argument.

[74] See the discussion of *Roche v UK*, Section 6.4 above.

PART IV

GENERAL MATTERS

7

LIMITATION AND CONTRIBUTION

CENTRAL ISSUES

i) There comes a time where any civil claim is 'statute-barred', unless the court has a statutory discretion which it chooses to exercise. It is simply too late for the claim to be pursued. Statutory rules of 'limitation' govern the time-barring of claims, and are justified by reasons of both practicality and fairness. The current rules of limitation are mainly to be found in the Limitation Act 1980.

ii) A liable party may seek a 'contribution' to damages from other parties who could be sued in respect of the same damage. In principle, contribution proceedings are not the business of the tort claimant and rules of contribution generally play no role in the claim itself. The rules of contribution are set out in the Civil Liability (Contribution) Act 1978.

1. LIMITATION OF ACTIONS

Specific issues relating to limitation periods are discussed in connection with trespass to the person (Chapter 2), defective premises (Chapter 6), and vicarious liability (Chapter 9). The present section outlines the general purpose and contents of the present law on limitation of actions.

1.1 WHAT ARE LIMITATION RULES AND WHY DO WE HAVE THEM?

What are Limitation Rules?

'Limitation' is generally referred to as a 'defence' to an action. It is for the defendant to establish that the relevant period has expired and that the action is 'time-barred'. However, strictly speaking the claim itself is not extinguished by the expiry of the relevant period (with the exception of the action in conversion).[1] Instead, the *remedy* becomes unavailable.

Ronex Properties v John Laing [1983] QB 398

The defendants applied to have the claim against them struck out as disclosing no cause of action, because the applicable time period for bringing the action had expired. The Court of Appeal refused to strike out on this ground (although it would have considered striking out on different grounds, if evidence and argument had been presented).

Donaldson LJ

Authority apart, I would have thought that it was absurd to contend that a writ or third party notice could be struck out as disclosing no cause of action, merely because the defendant may have a defence under the Limitation Acts. . . . it is trite law that the English Limitation Acts bar the remedy and not the right; and, furthermore, that they do not even have this effect unless and until pleaded. . . .

Why have Limitation Rules?

The need for some rules of limitation is not seriously in doubt.[2] Rather, it is the complexity of the current rules, and the existence of potential anomalies in their application, which give rise to most criticism.

The following extract sets out the general reasons why limitation rules are thought to be needed.

A. McGee and G. P. Scanlan, 'Judicial Attitudes to Limitation' (2005) 24 CJQ 460–80

. . . despite the present unsatisfactory state of the law of limitation, the rationale behind a coherent and practical law of limitation is both clear and simple. Potential defendants should not have to live with the risk of legal action indefinitely if for any reason a potential claimant does not pursue his remedy, furthermore, old or stale claims are difficult to try when memories are clouded, and where evidence has probably been lost.[3] Parties should be certain that, in conducting their business and professional affairs, or indeed their everyday activities, they are able to predict when they can regard a potential action in which they could be defendants as stale and expired.[4] The expiration of stale claims is also in the interests of the state, since the state has a legitimate interest in the quality of the justice it achieves for its citizens.[5]

[3] This aspect of a rational law of limitation may be defined as the evidentiary principle.
[4] This aspect of a rational law of limitation may be defined as the certainty principle.
[5] This aspect of a rational law of limitation may be defined as the interests of the state principle.

[1] By Limitation Act 1980, s 3, *title to goods is extinguished* if a claim in conversion is not brought within the relevant limitation period.
[2] Exceptionally, Keith Patten argues against such rules in cases of personal injury in 'Limitation Periods in Personal Injury Claims—Justice Obstructed' (2006) CJQ 349–66. P.J. Davies, 'Limitations on the Law of Limitation' (1982) 98 LQR 249 argues that all fixed periods should be abolished, to be replaced by an entirely discretionary system.

Prompt litigation increases the chances of a measured and just result. It also ensures that public money is not wasted in hearing claims which cannot be dealt with properly. The interests of claimants are also served by a rational law of limitation. The Committee on Limitation of Actions in Cases of Personal Injury in its Report recognised the value of limitation periods in prompting claimants to act swiftly in pursuit of their rights. The authors noted that: "We apprehend that the law is designed to encourage plaintiffs [claimants] not to go to sleep on their rights, but to institute proceedings as soon as it is reasonably practicable for them to do so."[6]

1.2 THE GENERAL POSITION UNDER THE LIMITATION ACT 1980

The present rules on limitation are largely set out in the Limitation Act 1980. The following section states the general approach in cases of tort. It is important to note that there are some large and very important exceptions to this general rule.

Limitation Act 1980

2   Time limit for actions founded on tort

An action founded on tort shall not be brought after the expiration of six years from the date on which the cause of action accrued.

Before we turn to the exceptions, we should clarify what is meant by the date on which the cause of action accrued.

Generally speaking, a cause of action in tort accrues when the relevant invasion of a protected right or interest (which may or may not be the result of wrongful conduct) has occurred. This is when the tort is actionable. It is not necessarily the date of the defendant's tortious act or omission. In the case of torts of damage (including negligence), the cause of action accrues when the relevant *damage* occurs. These torts are *actionable* when there is damage which is not 'insignificant' (*Cartledge v Jopling*, below). That is also when the limitation period starts to run.

As a result, in cases where there are potential claims in *both* tort *and* contract, the tort action is often more long-lived than the action in contract. An action in contract starts to run when the contract is breached, and expires six years later.[7] Time will not begin to run in respect of a claim in the tort of negligence until the damage is done. For an example where this led the claimants to choose to sue in tort—and where the House of Lords allowed them to make this choice—see *Henderson v Merrett* [1995] 2 AC 145 (Chapter 6.2).

Identifying the time *when damage occurred* is not as straightforward as it might sound. We will consider two areas where the interpretation of section 2 and its statutory predecessors has led to potential injustice, so that further legislation has been required. The first and most important relates to personal injury; the second relates to other instances of negligence specifically.

---

[6]   This aspect of a rational law of limitation may be defined as the interests of the claimant principle.
[7]   Limitation Act 1980, s 5.

1.3 PERSONAL INJURY CASES

Cartledge v Jopling [1963] 758

The applicable limitation periods were set out in section 2(1) of the Limitation Act 1939. That provision was expressed in similar terms to the present section 2 (above), but was subject to fewer exceptions and qualifications.[8] This case shows the pressing need for the reforms that are now encapsulated in sections 11, 14, and 33 of the Limitation Act 1980.

The plaintiffs were steel dressers working in a factory. Through exposure to dust, they contracted a lung disease, pneumoconiosis. This is a 'progressive' disease. The workmen commenced actions in negligence and breach of statutory duty, on 1 October 1956. It was established that there had been no breaches of duty after (at the latest) September 1950. Thus, the claim would be out of time unless the cause of action 'accrued' later than the breaches themselves.

Available evidence suggested the plaintiffs had suffered substantial injury without becoming aware of it. They argued that, as a matter of principle, their action could not become time-barred *before they had any relevant knowledge* of the injury suffered. The House of Lords felt compelled to reject their argument. As a matter of statutory interpretation, unless discovery of the injury was prevented by fraud or mistake within section 26 of the Limitation Act 1939, time would begin to run when the injury occurred, and not when the injured party was able to discover it. The House was under no illusions as to the injustice of this, and strongly supported the need for legislative reform.

Lord Reid, at 771–3

. . . It is now too late for the courts to question or modify the rule that a cause of action accrues as soon as a wrongful act has caused personal injury beyond what can be regarded as negligible, even when that injury is unknown to and cannot be discovered by the sufferer, and that further injury arising from the same act at a later date does not give rise to a further cause of action. It appears to me to be unreasonable and unjustifiable in principle that a cause of action should be held to accrue before it is possible to discover any injury and, therefore, before it is possible to raise any action. If this were a matter governed by the common law I would hold that a cause of action ought not to be held to accrue until either the injured person has discovered the injury or it would be possible for him to discover it if he took such steps as were reasonable in the circumstances. The common law ought never to produce a wholly unreasonable result, nor ought existing authorities to be read so literally as to produce such a result in circumstances never contemplated when they were decided.

But the present question depends on statute, the Limitation Act, 1939, and section 26 of that Act appears to me to make it impossible to reach the result which I have indicated. That section makes special provisions where fraud or mistake is involved: it provides that time shall not begin to run until the fraud has been or could with reasonable diligence have been discovered. Fraud here has been given a wide interpretation, but obviously it could not be extended to cover this case. The necessary implication from that section is that, where fraud or mistake is not involved, time begins to run whether or not the damage could be discovered. So the mischief in the present case can only be prevented by further legislation.

---

[8] There were exceptions for cases of disability (for example, where the plaintiff was a minor), fraud, and mistake.

Legislation promptly remedied this unjust result, initially through the Limitation Act 1963. The current position is to be found in sections 11, 14, and 33 of the **Limitation Act 1980**.

11 Special time limit for actions in respect of personal injuries

(1) This section applies to any action for damages for negligence, nuisance or breach of duty (whether the duty exists by virtue of a contract or of provision made by or under a statute or independently of any contract or any such provision) where the damages claimed by the plaintiff for the negligence, nuisance or breach of duty consist of or include damages in respect of personal injuries to the plaintiff or any other person.

[(1A) This section does not apply to any action brought for damages under section 3 of the Protection from Harassment Act 1997.]

(2) None of the time limits given in the preceding provisions of this Act shall apply to an action to which this section applies.

(3) An action to which this section applies shall not be brought after the expiration of the period applicable in accordance with subsection (4) or (5) below.

(4) Except where subsection (5) below applies, the period applicable is three years from—

    (a) the date on which the cause of action accrued; or

    (b) the date of knowledge (if later) of the person injured.

(5) If the person injured dies before the expiration of the period mentioned in subsection (4) above, the period applicable as respects the cause of action surviving for the benefit of his estate by virtue of section 1 of the Law Reform (Miscellaneous Provisions) Act 1934 shall be three years from—

    (a) the date of death; or

    (b) the date of the personal representative's knowledge;

whichever is the later.

Compared with the general statement about civil claims in section 2, section 11 sets out a *shorter* time period of three years for most actions in personal injury. However, this is capable of running from a later date, namely *the date of knowledge of the injured party* (or, if that party has died, from the date of knowledge of their personal representative).

Clearly, the section relates only to claims in respect of personal injury. By section 38 of the Limitation Act 1980:

"personal injuries" includes any disease and any impairment of a person's physical or mental condition . . .

In terms of limitation periods, there is no distinction between *physical* or *mental* injuries: see further *Adams v Bracknell* [2005] AC 76, below.

But to what range of *torts* does section 11 apply? The statutory wording (set out above) refers to 'negligence, nuisance or breach of duty'. In Chapter 2, we noted the interpretation of this section in *Stubbings v Webb* [1993] AC 498, in which the House of Lords held, controversially, that actions in *trespass to the person* involve no 'breach of duty', and therefore come outside the reach of section 11, even if they involve personal injury.[9] The impact of this is to create serious anomalies. It may be possible to sue a party in negligence who has failed to prevent a battery, when the only possible action against the perpetrator (assuming they did not *breach a duty of care*) has expired.

'What is the Date of Knowledge'?

14   Definition of date of knowledge for purposes of sections 11 and 12[10]

(1) . . . In sections 11 and 12 of this Act references to a person's date of knowledge are references to the date on which he first had knowledge of the following facts—

   (a) that the injury in question was significant; and

   (b) that the injury was attributable in whole or in part to the act or omission which is alleged to constitute negligence, nuisance or breach of duty; and

   (c) the identity of the defendant; and

   (d) if it is alleged that the act or omission was that of a person other than the defendant, the identity of that person and the additional facts supporting the bringing of an action against the defendant;

and knowledge that any acts or omissions did or did not, as a matter of law, involve negligence, nuisance or breach of duty is irrelevant.

   . . .

(2) For the purposes of this section an injury is significant if the person whose date of knowledge is in question would reasonably have considered it sufficiently serious to justify his instituting proceedings for damages against a defendant who did not dispute liability and was able to satisfy a judgment.

(3) For the purposes of this section a person's knowledge includes knowledge which he might reasonably have been expected to acquire—

   (a) from facts observable or ascertainable by him; or

   (b) from facts ascertainable by him with the help of medical or other appropriate expert advice which it is reasonable for him to seek;

but a person shall not be fixed under this subsection with knowledge of a fact ascertainable only with the help of expert advice so long as he has taken all reasonable steps to obtain (and, where appropriate, to act on) that advice.

Since 'date of knowledge' is central to the reforms that followed *Cartledge v Jopling*, this section is of fundamental importance. In terms of interpretation, the most problematic aspect of it is subsection (3), which refers to knowledge which the claimant 'might reasonably have been

---

[9] Trespass to the person does not *necessarily* involve personal injury, since trespass is actionable *per se*.

[10] S 12 relates to claims under the Fatal Accidents Act 1976. These are claims for bereavement and loss of dependency by the dependents of a deceased victim of tort: see further Chapter 8.

expected to acquire'. Clearly, this necessitates a judgment as to 'reasonableness'. But should reasonableness be assessed **objectively** (solely by reference to *the reasonable person*), or **subjectively** (taking into account characteristics of the particular claimant)?

Adams v Bracknell Forest BC [2005] 1 AC 76

The claimant, an adult, argued that the defendant education authority had negligently failed to diagnose his dyslexia as a child, and that his untreated condition had led to psychological ill-effects. The House of Lords determined, following *Phelps v Hillingdon* [2005] 1 AC 76, that the claim was one for *personal injuries*, so that it came within the scope of sections 11, 14, and 33.

Under section 11, the claim would be time-barred unless the claimant could show that the 'date of knowledge' (defined, as we have said, by section 14) was substantially delayed. He argued that he could not have been reasonably expected to realize that the problems he experienced in adulthood were related to his undiagnosed dyslexia. This was accepted. However, he further argued that he had no grounds for acting sooner in order to *seek expert advice* in respect of his problems, which would have revealed the connection. Eventually, he spilt out his life story during a chance encounter with an educational psychologist whom he met at a salsa party, and she persuaded him to consult a solicitor. Resolution of the limitation question therefore turned on interpretation of section 14(3)(b) above, setting out the circumstances under which a claimant may reasonably be expected to seek expert advice.

Lord Hoffmann argued that the test for reasonableness in section 14(3) is generally 'objective'. He accepted that the test should reflect the likely characteristics *of a person who had suffered the injury in question*. But even allowing for this, Lord Hoffmann was not persuaded that a reasonable person suffering from undiagnosed dyslexia and its mental effects could fail, over many years, to disclose to his medical adviser the essential facts which would lead to relevant advice under s 14(3)(b) above. In effect, there is an 'obligation of curiosity' upon the injured party.[11]

Lord Hoffmann

47 It is true that the plaintiff must be assumed to be a person who has suffered the injury in question and not some other person. But . . . I do not see how his particular character or intelligence can be relevant. In my opinion, section 14(3) requires one to assume that a person who is aware that he has suffered a personal injury, serious enough to be something about which he would go and see a solicitor if he knew he had a claim, will be sufficiently curious about the causes of the injury to seek whatever expert advice is appropriate.

Constructive knowledge in this case

48 The judge held that Mr Adams acted reasonably in making no inquiry into the reasons for his literacy problems. I do not think that he based this finding upon matters of character or intelligence which were peculiar to Mr Adams. If the judge had been relying upon his personal characteristics, he might have been hard put to explain why someone who was willing to

---

11 This is the expression used by Patten (2006) CJQ 349.

confide in a lady he met at a dancing party was unable to confide in his doctor. But the judge appears to have thought that extreme reticence about his problems was the standard behaviour which ought to be expected from anyone suffering from untreated dyslexia and that the conversation with Ms Harding was an aberration.

49 In principle, I think that the judge was right in applying the standard of reasonable behaviour to a person assumed to be suffering from untreated dyslexia. If the injury itself would reasonably inhibit him from seeking advice, then that is a factor which must be taken into account. My difficulty is with the basis for the finding that such a person could not reasonably be expected to reveal the source of his difficulties to his medical adviser. In the absence of some special inhibiting factor, I should have thought that Mr Adams could reasonably have been expected to seek expert advice years ago. The congeries of symptoms which he described to Dr Gardner, which he said had been making his life miserable for years, which he knew to be rooted in his inability to read and write and about which he had sought medical advice, would have made it almost irrational not to disclose what he felt to be the root cause. If he had done so, he would no doubt have been referred to someone with expertise in dyslexia and would have discovered that it was something which might have been treated earlier.

The time limit having been passed, this left the question of discretion under section 33. But first, we should note the effect of *Adams* on a case of alleged sexual abuse in childhood.

In *KR v Bryn Alyn* [2003] 1 QB 1441, the Court of Appeal adopted a broadly subjective approach to section 14(2) of the Limitation Act 1980.[12] The Court had to decide whether it would reasonably have occurred to the claimant, given his life history, to bring a civil action for damages within three years of his majority. The Court emphasized that each case had to be considered individually taking account of all the circumstances.

The Court of Appeal has more recently departed from that subjective approach: *Catholic Care (Diocese of Leeds) v Kevin Young* [2006] EWCA Civ 1534. Although *Adams* turned on interpretation of section 14(3), and this case (like *Bryn Alyn*) turned on section 14(2), the Court of Appeal held that the meaning of 'reasonableness' must be the same in the two subsections. The personal characteristics of the claimant would not be relevant; but features of the claimant stemming from *the injury itself* would be relevant.

Dyson LJ, *Catholic Care (Diocese of Leeds) v Kevin Young*

46 The *Adams* approach to reasonableness indicates that if a person who has suffered from a particular type of injury would reasonably be inhibited *by the injury itself* from instituting proceedings, then that is a factor that should be taken into account in deciding whether he or she would reasonably have considered it sufficiently serious to justify proceedings. The standard that has to be applied is that of the reasonable behaviour of a victim of child abuse who has suffered the degree of injury suffered by the claimant in question and of which he has knowledge.

---

[12] Unlike *Stubbings v Webb*, which was a claim in trespass to the person to which ss 11, 14, and 33 were held not to apply, this case involved a claim in negligence.

Discretion to Exclude the Time Limit

33 Discretionary exclusion of time limit for actions in respect of personal injuries or death

(1) If it appears to the court that it would be equitable to allow an action to proceed having regard to the degree to which—

(a) the provisions of section 11 [or 11A] or 12 of this Act prejudice the plaintiff or any person whom he represents; and

(b) any decision of the court under this subsection would prejudice the defendant or any person whom he represents;

the court may direct that those provisions shall not apply to the action, or shall not apply to any specified cause of action to which the action relates.

. . .

(3) In acting under this section the court shall have regard to all the circumstances of the case and in particular to—

(a) the length of, and the reasons for, the delay on the part of the plaintiff;

(b) the extent to which, having regard to the delay, the evidence adduced or likely to be adduced by the plaintiff or the defendant is or is likely to be less cogent than if the action had been brought within the time allowed by section 11, [by section 11A] or (as the case may be) by section 12;

(c) the conduct of the defendant after the cause of action arose, including the extent (if any) to which he responded to requests reasonably made by the plaintiff for information or inspection for the purpose of ascertaining facts which were or might be relevant to the plaintiff's cause of action against the defendant;

(d) the duration of any disability of the plaintiff arising after the date of the accrual of the cause of action;

(e) the extent to which the plaintiff acted promptly and reasonably once he knew whether or not the act or omission of the defendant, to which the injury was attributable, might be capable at that time of giving rise to an action for damages;

(f) the steps, if any, taken by the plaintiff to obtain medical, legal or other expert advice and the nature of any such advice he may have received.

. . .

In *Adams v Bracknell* (above), the House of Lords cited with approval the following statement in respect of the application of section 33. Applying this approach, *Adams* was not a suitable case in which to override the time limit.

Sir Murray Stuart-Smith, *Robinson v St Helens Metropolitan Borough Council*
[2003] PIQR 128, at 139–40

32.   The Limitation Acts are designed to protect defendants from the injustice of having to fight stale claims especially when any witnesses the defendants might have been able to rely on are not available or have no recollection and there are no documents to assist the court in deciding what was done or not done and why. These cases are very time consuming to prepare and try and they inevitably divert resources from the education authority to defending the claim rather than teach. Under section 33 the onus is on the claimant to establish that it would be equitable to allow the claim to proceed having regard to the balance of prejudice.

33.   The question of proportionality is now important in the exercise of any discretion, none more so than under section 33. Courts should be slow to exercise their discretion in favour of a claimant in the absence of cogent medical evidence showing a serious effect on the claimant's health or enjoyment of life and employability. The likely amount of an award is an important factor to consider, especially if, as is usual in these cases, they are likely to take a considerable time to try. A claim that the claimant's dyslexia was not diagnosed or treated many years before at school, brought long after the expiry of the limitation period, extended as it is until after the claimant's majority, will inevitably place the defendants in great difficulty in contesting it, especially in the absence of relevant witnesses and documents. The contesting of such a claim would be both expensive and likely to divert precious resources. Courts should be slow in such cases to find that the balance of prejudice is in favour of the claimant.

The end result is that having recognized that failure to diagnose dyslexia may be in breach of a duty of care and that the damage suffered is actionable as 'personal injury', the courts are protecting education authorities from some of the potential effects of this liability, through interpretation of relevant rules of limitation. We have noted the impact of *Adams* in cases of childhood sexual abuse, with our earlier reference to *Catholic Care v Kevin Young*. In that case, the Court of Appeal also mentioned that section 33 imposes a 'heavy burden on a claimant' ([at [71]) to convince the court that the time limit should be overridden. On the facts of the case, the Court was not convinced that a fair trial was possible; as such, this claim, like the claim in *Adams*, was out of time.

Cases still governed by *Cartledge v Jopling*

The interpretation in *Cartledge v Jopling*, as we have seen, no longer applies to most personal injury claims, since legislation provides that the relevant limitation period begins with the claimant's date of knowledge. On the other hand, section 11 (and therefore sections 14 and 33) does not apply to actions brought in trespass to the person (*Stubbings v Webb*, Chapter 2). These statutory provisions also do not apply to claims which **were already time-barred** before the first 'date of knowledge' provision took effect, in 1963. For these claims, the approach in *Cartledge v Jopling* still applies.

   This is illustrated by the case of *McDonnell v Congregation of Christian Brothers Trustees and Others* [2003] UKHL 63; [2004] 1 AC 1101. The claimant alleged that he had suffered severe ill treatment while attending schools run by the first and second defendants. He left school in 1951 aged 15. The limitation periods applicable at this time were set out in the Limitation Act 1939, providing for a non-extendable period of six years which would start to run when the plaintiff reached the age of 21. The claim therefore *expired* on 6 January 1963, in accordance with this provision.

On 31 July 1963 (just over six months later), section 1 of the Limitation Act 1963 came into force. This section was clearly intended to remove the injustice reflected in *Cartledge v Jopling*, and it provided for a new limitation period running, in an appropriate case, *from the date of knowledge*.[13] As we have seen, later Limitation Acts have retained the 'date of knowledge' approach to be seen in the 1963 legislation.

The claimant in *McDonnell* was ready to argue that he did not have the relevant 'knowledge' for the limitation period to start to run, until well into his adulthood. He was also prepared to argue that his claim was not barred by *Stubbings v Webb*. These points were never addressed however. The claim failed because it had *already* expired six months before 31 July 1963, when the relevant provision of the Limitation Act 1963 came into force. The House of Lords applied the reasoning in *Arnold v CEGB* [1988] AC 228,[14] and concluded that where a claim had once become statute-barred, it was not *revived* by later legislation. The claim was out of time.

It has been suggested that the outcome in *McDonnell* should be seen as 'axiomatic', since legislation should not be taken to remove a defence to which the defendant is already entitled.[15] On the other hand, this outcome does to some extent frustrate the purpose of the legislature in passing the Limitation Act 1963 and subsequent legislation, which was to remove the injustice of *Cartledge v Jopling*. The House of Lords in *McDonnell* decided that it was not possible to glean a *specific* Parliamentary intention to allow revival of expired claims either from the wording of the statute, or from the Parliamentary debates of the 1963 legislation. Our point is a looser one: there is still a group of claimants whose entitlement to bring an action for personal injuries will have expired before they might reasonably have become aware of the injury, or of its link with acts or omissions of the defendant. This group will however be confined to those whose claims *had become time-barred* before 31 July 1963.

1.4 OTHER CASES IN NEGLIGENCE

As we have seen, the effects of *Cartledge* were removed for most cases of personal injury by the Limitation Act 1963 and subsequent legislation. But the *Cartledge* approach was still applicable outside the realms of personal injury.

Pirelli General Cable Works v Oscar Faber & Partners [1983] 2 AC 1

A factory chimney was constructed in 1969 and the defendants provided advice as to the appropriate lining for it. The lining turned out to be unsuitable. Evidence suggested that the chimney cracked no later than 1970. The cracks were not discovered however until 1977. This was outside the general limitation period of six years from the 'damage' (if the damage was, indeed, the cracking in the chimney). The plaintiff could not, with reasonable diligence, have discovered the defect, but the House of Lords held that the general six-year limitation period must be applied. Parliament had chosen, in 1963, to alter the effect of *Cartledge v Jopling* but

[13] Like Limitation Act 1980, s 11, this section applied to personal injury cases involving 'negligence, nuisance, or breach of duty'.

[14] The action in *Arnold* was time-barred for the different reason that Limitation Act 1939, s 21 provided a special (and anomalous) one-year period in which to bring an action against a local authority. This period too expired before commencement of the Limitation Act 1963.

[15] A. McGee and G. Scanlan, 'Judicial Attitudes to Limitation' (2005) CJQ 460–80.

had done so only for a range of **personal injury** cases; by implication, there was no intention to alter the effect of *Cartledge* where other types of damage were concerned.

By the Latent Damage Act 1986, two new sections (14A and 14B) were inserted into the Limitation Act 1980 in order to reverse the effect of *Pirelli*. Section 14A provided a 'date of knowledge' alternative to the usual starting date for **claims in negligence** which did not come within section 11. This section is identical to section 14 in the way that it defines 'knowledge'. However, claims to which these sections apply are subject to a long-stop of **fifteen years** from the date of breach (s 14B).

Nowadays, these sections are unlikely to be needed for a case like *Pirelli*. The claim in *Pirelli* was regarded as a claim for 'damage' to the factory chimney, in the form of cracking. Such a claim was actionable on the authority of *Anns v Merton* [1978] AC 728. As we saw in Chapter 6, *Anns v Merton* has been overruled by *Murphy v Brentwood* [1991] 1 AC 398, and the House of Lords has defined the relevant loss as *pure economic loss flowing from the acquisition of a defective product*. It is not to be seen as 'damage to property' at all. In *Murphy* itself, a claim for this sort of economic loss was held to be not actionable.

Therefore, the sort of claim for which sections 14A and B were principally designed may not now be actionable. On the other hand, *some* such cases may come within the *Hedley Byrne* category of recoverable **economic** losses. This category is centrally concerned with negligent advice and services. Let us assume that a case such as *Pirelli* may, exceptionally, be treated as involving a close relationship of proximity and reliance, and/or an assumption of responsibility, so that it comes within *Hedley Byrne*.[16] Now, however, the *injury* suffered is defined as economic loss (repair costs), rather than physical damage (cracking to the chimneys). Even if (as seems unlikely) such a claim is actionable, section 14A is not likely to be needed. This is because no economic loss (whether in the form of repair costs, or loss of market value) will be experienced until the damage *is* discovered.[17] Until that point, no repair costs can be incurred; and the market value is unaffected because the defect is unknown. Once the harm is defined as 'economic', there is no longer a problem of latent damage.

Sections 14A and 14B are not, however, wholly without application, because they are not limited to cases of 'latent damage'. They extend to any claim in negligence, other than a claim for personal injuries, where the claimant's date of knowledge is (reasonably) delayed. For example, it may be that the claimant is aware of the *damage* (it is not 'latent'), but *is unaware that the damage is the result of the defendant's tort.*

In *Coban v Allen* (1997) 8 Med LR 316, the plaintiff was an 'overstayer' (illegally present in the UK). He was cheated out of his share in a property which he and his business partner ran as a fish and chip shop. His share in the property was transferred, without his consent and without payment, to his business partner, who forced him to flee by threatening to reveal his illegal status. Until he received a letter telling him he was entitled to remain in the UK indefinitely, the plaintiff was too scared to seek legal advice in case his illegal status was revealed. He brought an action in negligence against the firm of solicitors who had arranged the transfer of his property, but the action was held to be time-barred. His failure to seek legal advice at an

---

[16] This is not currently very likely, given general disapproval of the decision in *Junior Books v Veitchi*: see Chapter 6 above.

[17] In *Invercargill v Hamlin* [1996] AC 624, this very point was made by the Privy Council in respect of New Zealand law.

earlier stage—explained as it was by fear of being detected as an overstayer—could not be 'reasonable' within the terms of section 14A.

1.5 THE LAW COMMISSION'S PROPOSALS

The Law Commission has proposed a simpler and more uniform scheme. In its *Consultation Paper on Limitation of Actions* (1998) (Law Commission Consultation Paper No 151), the Commission stated its provisional view that there should be a standard three-year time limit which would run from the 'date of discoverability'. 'Discoverability' would be assessed by reference to a more subjective standard than the one currently applied under section 14:

> what ought the plaintiff, in his circumstances and with his abilities, to have known had he acted reasonably?

The intelligence and level of education of claimants, therefore, would be relevant to the judgment of 'date of knowledge'. There would be no discretion to override limitation periods, and a 'long-stop' deadline, like the one in section 14B of the Limitation Act 1980, would be applicable to all claims.

As a result of its consultation exercise, the Law Commission modified its proposals and set out its recommendations in its *Report on Limitation of Actions* (2001) (Law Com No 270). It retained the accent on subjectivity in assessment of the date of knowledge. However, the Commission abandoned the proposed long-stop provision in cases of personal injury, and now proposed that a statutory discretion to override the limitation periods should be retained, though only in personal injury actions. Where personal injury actions are concerned, the revised proposals are therefore more strongly weighted in favour of claimants, and less likely to promote certainty, than the original proposals which formed the basis of consultation. Even so, the Law Commission's proposals would have the merit of removing the distinction between personal injuries caused by negligence, nuisance, or breach of duty, and those caused by trespass to the person, which currently afflicts the law.

It is worth noting the following provision of the NHS Redress Act 2006:

> **7** (1) A scheme must make provision for the period during which a liability is the subject of proceedings under the scheme to be disregarded for the purposes of calculating whether any relevant limitation period has expired.

The usual limitation period will be suspended for the period of a claim under the Act.

FURTHER READING

Davies, P.J., 'Limitations on the Law of Limitation' (1982) 98 LQR 249.

James, R., 'The Law Commission Report on the Limitation of Actions' (2003) 22 CJQ 41.

Law Commission, *Limitation of Actions*, Consultation Paper 151 (HMSO, 1998).

Law Commission, *Limitation of Actions*, Report No 270 (HC 23, HMSO, 2001).

McGee, A. and Scanlan, G.P., 'Constructive Knowledge Within the Limitation Act' (2003) CJQ 248–64.

Mosher, J., 'Challenging Limitation Periods: Civil Claims by Adult Survivors of Incest' (1994) 44 UTLJ 169.

Patten, K., 'Limitation Periods in Personal Injury Claims—Justice Obstructed' (2006) CJQ 349.

2. CONTRIBUTION BETWEEN LIABLE PARTIES

If more than one party is potentially liable for 'the same damage', then the claimant need not bring actions against each such party but may choose to proceed against any one, and recover in full. 'Contribution proceedings' may then be pursued by the liable party, in order to recover a portion of the damages payable.

'Contribution' between liable parties is clearly not in any sense a 'defence' to an action by the claimant since it is generally irrelevant to the tort claim. As such, it is an entirely separate issue from the defence of 'contributory negligence' (which we discussed in Chapter 5). It requires *apportionment* of damages on the basis of relative responsibility; while contributory negligence requires a reduction in damages to reflect fault (in a broad sense) on both sides.

In a case of indivisible damage, the claimant may recover in full against any wrongdoer who has 'caused' that damage. The liable party may then seek contribution. It is not for the *claimant* to seek out every person contributing to the harm.[18] As such, the risk that any particular liable party will turn out to be insolvent (and/or uninsured) remains with liable parties (and with their insurers), rather than with claimants.

2.1 THE STARTING POINT: WHEN A LIABLE PARTY MAY SEEK CONTRIBUTION

Civil Liability (Contribution) Act 1978

1 Entitlement to Contribution

(1) Subject to the following provisions of this section, any person liable in respect of any damage suffered by another person may recover contribution from any other person liable in respect of the same damage (whether jointly with him or otherwise).

---

[18] As we saw in Chapter 4, *Barker v Corus* [2006] UKHL 20 created an important exception to this principle, placing the very significant risk of insolvency upon claimants in a narrow range of cases. *Barker v Corus* has now been reversed in respect of mesothelioma by Compensation Act 2006, s 3. S 3(3) sketches some guidelines in respect of contribution in relation to such claims.

For the application of this statute, neither party needs to be liable *in tort*. For example, one or both parties might be liable in contract, for breach of a statutory duty to which the provisions of the statute extend, or for breach of trust. Certainly, if both *are* liable in tort, they need not be liable in the *same* tort, nor for the same amount. The important thing is that they should both be liable 'for the same damage'.

The above provision applies not only where there is judgment against the defendant, but also where the defendant has *settled* a claim:

Section 1

(4) A person who has made or agreed to make any payment in bona fide settlement or compromise of any claim made against him in respect of any damage (including a payment into court which has been accepted) shall be entitled to recover contribution in accordance with this section without regard to whether or not he himself is or ever was liable in respect of the damage, provided, however, that he would have been liable assuming that the factual basis of the claim against him could be established.

As a result of this section, a party seeking contribution after settling a claim need not 'prove' the case against him or herself, but needs to show that the claim was settled in good faith, for a sound reason of law.

2.2 'THE SAME DAMAGE'

Section 1(1) of the Civil Liability (Contribution) Act 1978 specifies that a liable party can seek contribution from anyone who is liable 'in respect of the same damage'. Contribution proceedings are *not* available where different parties are liable in respect of *different* damage. We need to remind ourselves of the basic principles governing recovery of damages from joint, concurrent, and consecutive tortfeasors, in order to identify clearly when tortfeasors will be considered to have contributed to 'the same damage'. The first step in understanding the contribution legislation therefore requires a grasp of some essential principles of causation.

One type of case to which the contribution legislation applies is the case of **joint liability**. Here, there is only one wrongful act, although several parties may be responsible for it. One form of joint liability is 'vicarious liability' (explored in Chapter 9). Where an employee commits a tort in the course of employment, the employer is held to be 'vicariously liable' in respect of that tort. There is no need to show any breach of duty or other wrongful conduct on the part of the employer at all. Here, there is only one tort (the employee's), but two parties are potentially liable in respect of it. Another, slightly different example of joint liability is the case where two (or more) parties set out **with a common design** and act to cause harm. It is the collective action in concert which leads to damage; and as such both parties commit the *same* wrong, between them. The claimant can choose to proceed against either wrongdoer. The party found liable may seek contribution from the other.

Section 1(1) is explicitly not confined to 'joint liability'. It applies in *any* case where two or more wrongdoers contribute to the same damage, even if they do so through separate actions amounting to separate torts (or other wrongs). If two or more separate wrongs are committed by parties acting without any 'common design', each party will be liable in full (and the contribution legislation will apply) if *and only if* each wrong contributes to damage which is considered to be **indivisible**. This is referred to as a case of **concurrent torts**.

'Indivisible Damage'

In cases where the wrong is not 'joint' (which is to say, where there are separate contributing torts), we therefore need to consider the meaning of 'indivisible damage'. The leading statement on this subject is to be found in the judgment of Devlin LJ in *Dingle v Associated Newspapers* [1961] 2 QB 162, 188–9. This was a case in defamation. A libel was published by several different newspapers and the question was whether one of those newspapers was liable in full for the effect of the libel. The following statement of 'elementary principles' applicable to cases of *personal injury* was set out by Devlin LJ in order to assist consideration of the best approach in a case of damage to *reputation*.

Devlin LJ, *Dingle v Associated Newspapers and Others* [1961] 2 QB 162, at 188–9

. . . Where injury has been done to the plaintiff and the injury is indivisible, **any tortfeasor whose act has been a proximate cause of the injury must compensate for the whole of it.** As between the plaintiff and the defendant it is immaterial that there are others whose acts also have been a cause of the injury and it does not matter whether those others have or have not a good defence. These factors would be relevant in a claim between tortfeasors for contribution, but the plaintiff is not concerned with that; he can obtain judgment for total compensation from anyone whose act has been a cause of his injury. If there are more than one of such persons, it is immaterial to the plaintiff whether they are joint tortfeasors or not. **If four men, acting severally and not in concert, strike the plaintiff one after another and as a result of his injuries he suffers shock and is detained in hospital and loses a month's wages, each wrongdoer is liable to compensate for the whole loss of earnings.** If there were four distinct physical injuries, each man would be liable only for the consequences peculiar to the injury he inflicted, but in the example I have given the loss of earnings is one injury caused in part by all four defendants. It is essential for this purpose that the loss should be one and indivisible; whether it is so or not is a matter of fact and not a matter of law. If, for example, a ship is damaged in two separate collisions by two wrongdoers and consequently is in dry dock for a month for repairs and claims for loss of earnings, it is usually possible to say how many days' detention is attributable to the damage done by each collision and divide the loss of earnings accordingly.

These are elementary principles and readily recognisable as such in the law of damage for physical injury. . . .

Devlin LJ went on to conclude that the same principle must apply in a case of libel, where the injury to reputation is indivisible.

The same principle must apply to general damage for loss of reputation. If a man reads four newspapers at breakfast and reads substantially the same libel in each, liability does not depend on which paper he opens first. Perhaps one newspaper influences him more than another, but unless he can say he disregarded one altogether, then each is a substantial cause of the damage done to the plaintiff in his eyes. . . .

Returning to Devlin LJ's general statement in respect of personal injury, we should note the following points:

1. The principle that each tortfeasor is potentially liable for the full damage depends, as Devlin LJ expressed it, on showing that each tortfeasor has caused the harm in question ('a tortfeasor whose act has been a proximate cause of the injury . . .'). This means that each tort must satisfy the tests for causation that we set out in Chapter 3 and further explored in Chapter 4. In principle, each tort must be a 'but for cause' of the damage. In fact, we have seen that this test is sometimes set aside in cases of concurrent torts. This will be done, for example, in cases where the 'but for' test would lead to the absurd result that no one of a number of torts is considered to have caused the damage, because no one of them independently passes the 'but for' test. The need to *prove* that the 'but for' test is satisfied is also sometimes modified for the very different reason that such proof is impossible (*McGhee v National Coal Board*; *Fairchild v Glenhaven*). We will not explore those issues further here, but simply remind ourselves that these are exceptions to the general rule that each tort must be shown to have 'caused' the harm.

2. If the various torts of different tortfeasors lead to more than one *injury*—or, to put it another way, if the harm is treated as *divisible*—each tortfeasor is liable *only* for the injury that is caused by his or her tort. There is then no scope for contribution proceedings between tortfeasors, because the other parties will not be held to have caused 'the same damage'. The liability of each tortfeasor does not extend to damage to which others have also contributed. The risk of insolvency and the burden of proving each tort lie upon the claimant.

3. In the case where four men in turn hit the claimant and he suffers a single consequential injury (for example in the form of psychiatric harm leading to loss of earnings), then the damage will be treated as indivisible and any of the four may be liable for the whole damage. It is important to notice that it is not the physical harm that, in the example given by Devlin LJ, is said to be indivisible, but the psychiatric consequences of the four incidents. If there are four separate physical injuries, then clearly the damage is divisible. Each assailant will be liable only for the part of the damage that he or she causes; there is no scope for *contribution*. The following case shows that what appears to be a single injury may also be judged to be 'divisible'. A disease or injury which is *made worse by* each tort may be treated as divisible; each tortfeasor is liable only for the *additional harm* that they cause.

Thompson v Smiths Shiprepairers [1984] QB 405

The plaintiffs suffered hearing impairment through exposure to excessive noise in ship-repair and shipbuilding yards. Mustill J awarded damages which reflected not the full impairment of hearing suffered, but only the part of that impairment of hearing which could be said to flow from a *breach of duty*.

The plaintiffs' hearing loss in these cases had been progressive. Mustill J held that at the beginning of the process of impairment, there was no breach of duty because it was not generally recognized that the levels of noise were harmful. Only later, when the possibility of harm was recognized, was the exposure in breach of duty. Although the end result—hearing loss to a particular level—appeared to be a single *injury*, it was not 'indivisible'.

Mustill J relied upon expert evidence in order to calculate the *amount* of impairment likely to have been caused during the period of breach, in order to determine the appropriate level of compensation. The damages only compensated for a part of the loss suffered, reflecting the fact that at the time of breach, the claimant's hearing was already impaired.[19]

Mustill J

This condition is not the direct product of a group of acts, not necessarily simultaneous, but all converging to bring about one occurrence of damage. Rather, it is the culmination of a progression, the individual stages of which were each brought about by the separate acts of the persons sued, or (as the case may be) the separate non-faulty and faulty acts of the only defendant. In my judgment, the principle stated by Devlin L.J. does not apply to this kind of case. Moreover, even if it could be regarded as apposite where the successive deteriorations and their respective causes cannot on the evidence be distinguished, it does not in my opinion demand the conclusion that where the court knows that the initial stage of the damage was caused by A (and not B) and that the latter stage was caused by B (and not A), it is obliged in law to proceed (contrary to the true facts) on the assumption that the faults of each had caused the whole damage. So also in the case where it is known that when the faulty acts of the employer began, the plaintiffs' hearing had already suffered damage.

Rahman v Arearose [2001] QB 351

The plaintiff was assaulted at work while employed by the first defendants, and sustained damage to his eye. He then underwent an operation at the second defendant's hospital. This operation was negligently performed, and led to the loss of the eye. Apart from this physical impairment, the plaintiff suffered a number of consequential psychological difficulties, attributed by experts variously to the initial assault, and to the loss of the eye. Here we consider the *psychological* harm. (As to the eye, see Chapter 3 above.)

The Court of Appeal concluded that this case differed from Devlin LJ's example of four separate assaults causing one sort of psychological harm. Here, the psychological impairment took several different forms (post-traumatic stress disorder; phobia; personality change; depressive disorder of psychotic intensity), and these various forms *could* be attributed, according to the experts, to one or other of the torts committed—even if this could be done only with some lack of certainty. Hence, this was *not* a case of joint or concurrent torts contributing to 'the same damage'.

Laws LJ

23 . . . on the evidence the respective torts committed by the defendants **were the causes of distinct aspects of the claimant's overall psychiatric condition**, and it is positively established that neither caused the whole of it. So much is demonstrated by the document which sets out the conclusions of the three experts. It is true that this agreed evidence does not

---

[19] It is rather hard to reconcile this case with the decision of the House of Lords in *Bonnington Castings v Wardlaw* [1956] AC 613, considered in Chapter 4 above. It could be that *Bonnington*—like *McGhee*—is appropriate only in cases where proof is 'impossible'. We will not reopen that discussion here, where we are attempting only to identify the meaning of 'the same damage'. But this factor did lead the claimants in *Thompson* to argue that their own claim *was impossible to prove*, so as to come within *Bonnington*.

purport to distribute causative responsibility for the various aspects of the claimant's psychopathology between the defendants with any such degree of precision as would allow for an exact quantification by the trial court; no doubt any attempt to do so would be highly artificial. **But the lack of it cannot drive the case into the regime of the 1978 Act to which, in principle, it does not belong**. This view of the matter is by no means displaced by consideration of the oral testimony of the doctors, to which Mr Livesey invited our attention. The fact-finding court's duty is to arrive at a just conclusion on the evidence as to the respective damage caused by each defendant, even if it can only do it on a broad-brush basis which then has to be translated into percentages.

This is a very different case from *Thompson* because different 'aspects' of the psychiatric harm were identified by the experts as continuing to affect the plaintiff. Examining the plaintiff in *Rahman*, medical experts identified a number of different continuing harms. In *Thompson*, the plaintiff was suffering from one harm, impaired hearing. But different levels of impairment were attributed, in the main action and without the need for contribution proceedings, to different periods. In either of these ways, it may be concluded that the different tortfeasors have not contributed to 'the same damage'.

Whether the expert reports *should* have been accepted in *Rahman* is different matter:

Tony Weir, 'The Maddening Effect of Consecutive Torts' [2001] CLJ 237, 238

That left the . . . question of what damage each was liable for. Here the Court accepted an absurd report confected jointly by the experts for the three parties, who tentatively divided up the victim's present condition in terms of the two causes. They should not have been asked to do this, and their answer should have been ignored, for there is no scientific basis for any such attribution of causality; the claimant is not half-mad because of what the first defendant did and half-mad because of what the second defendant did, he is as mad as he is because of what both of them did. His mania is aetiologically indiscerptible, as when grief and shock combine to wreck the life of a parent who witnesses the death of her children. Suppose that the claimant was so maddened that he committed suicide: would his death be divided up by those responsible for triggering the injuries?

Note also our discussion of *Holtby v Brigham and Cowan* [2000] 3 All ER 423, in Chapter 4.

'Damage' not 'Damages'

In *Royal Brompton NHS Trust v Hammond* [2002] 1 WLR 1397, Lord Bingham emphasized that 'the same damage' in section 1(1) (above) does not mean 'the same *damages*'. 'Damage' is equivalent to 'loss' or 'harm', not to amount payable. As such, it is not necessary that the two (or more) liable parties would, if successfully sued, be liable for identical amounts. For example, one party may have acted in such a way that they are susceptible to a claim for aggravated or punitive damages, while the other is not. Or, the parties may be liable on the basis of different causes of action, in which different rules on the extent of recoverable damage apply. These differences may be relevant to the apportionment stage (to which we now turn); but they will not affect the prior question of whether the parties are potentially liable in respect of the same damage.

2.3 APPORTIONMENT

Civil Liability (Contribution) Act 1978

2   Assessment of contribution

2.—(1) . . . in any proceedings for contribution under section 1 above the amount of the contribution recoverable from any person shall be such as may be found by the court to be just and equitable having regard to the extent of that person's responsibility for the damage in question.

(2) . . . the court shall have power in any such proceedings to exempt any person from liability to make contribution, or to direct that the contribution to be recovered from any person shall amount to a complete indemnity.

Section 7(3) of the Act expressly preserves contractual indemnities and exclusions of contribution, and section 2(3)(a) effectively gives priority to contractual and statutory allocations of responsibility. Subject to these caveats, the guiding principle is that apportionment between liable parties should be on the basis of what is 'just and equitable', having regard to 'responsibility for the damage'.

We saw in Chapter 5 that very similar language is used in the Law Reform (Contributory Negligence) Act 1945, which sets out the approach to be taken where damages fall to be reduced for contributory negligence. However, there are significant differences in the way that these two provisions operate.

It is clearly stated in section 2(2) of the Civil Liability (Contribution) Act 1978 that in respect of contribution between liable parties, the court may determine that either party is either *fully exempt from making any contribution*, or *must indemnify the other party completely*. In respect of the Law Reform (Contributory Negligence) Act 1945, by contrast, there cannot be '100 per cent contributory negligence'. The relevant section of that Act provides:

Law Reform (Contributory Negligence) Act 1945

1. (1) Where any person suffers harm as the result partly of his own fault and partly of the fault of another person or persons, a claim in respect of that damage **shall not be defeated by reason of the fault of the person suffering the damage** . . .

A finding of 100 per cent contributory negligence would be inconsistent with this provision. Further, this subsection limits the application of the legislation to cases where the harm is the 'result' of fault on both sides. By contrast, the Civil Liability (Contribution) Act 1978 applies wherever both parties are *liable for* the damage. This need not involve fault in any sense. As such, the two regimes are not identical in the scope of their application.

It is well established that the idea of 'responsibility for damage' incorporates issues of causation, and of relative culpability. However, in respect of contribution under the 1978 Act, 'responsibility' (incorporating causation and culpability) is only a matter to which courts must 'have regard'. *The guiding aim is not to reflect relative responsibility, but to achieve a 'just and equitable' distribution.*

The Role of Culpability

Culpability may be a particularly significant consideration where one party has acted with wrongful intent, or committed a criminal offence, while the other has merely been careless or even acted with no degree of culpability at all. Clearly, these may be circumstances in which the court might lean towards a conclusion that the more 'culpable' party should take a greater share of liability, or indemnify the innocent liable party in full.

Special considerations apply however where one of the defendants is liable 'vicariously' for the torts of another (typically an employee, or a partner under section 10 of the Partnership Act 1890).[20] In these circumstances, the employer is liable independently of any fault on his or her own part; and the employer does not need to have done anything to 'cause' the harm. Should the 'responsibility' of a vicariously liable employer be judged at zero whenever the other potentially liable parties are wrongdoers in their own right? The House of Lords has decided that this is *not* the right approach. The 'responsibility' of a vicariously liable party is judged not in terms of their own innocence, but in terms of the tort of the employee (or partner) in question. The employer 'stands in the shoes' of the party for whose torts they are liable.

Dubai Aluminium v Salaam [2003] 2 AC 366

A, a partner in a solicitors firm, knowingly assisted in a dishonest scheme. The co-partners of A, who were personally innocent of any wrongdoing, were found to be 'vicariously' liable for the losses caused. They sought contribution against S and T, who were also parties to the dishonest scheme. S and T had acted wrongfully and dishonestly and had personally benefited from the scheme. The House of Lords concluded that the innocence of A's co-partners could not in itself justify a total indemnity from S and T, as the judge (Rix J) had thought. (We will see below that such a total indemnity was in fact regarded as justified, but on different grounds which add an extra dimension to the idea of what is 'just and equitable'.)

Lord Nicholls, *Dubai Aluminium v Salaam*

44   When directing that the Amhurst firm should recover from Mr Al Tajir and Mr Salaam contribution amounting to a complete indemnity, the combination of two matters in particular weighed with the judge . . . . The first was that the partners in the Amhurst firm, as distinct from Mr Amhurst himself, were personally innocent of any wrongdoing. This personal innocence of dishonesty was to be contrasted with the dishonesty of Mr Salaam and Mr Al Tajir. Rix J considered it would be unjust if a defendant who was vicariously liable for his employee's fraud could not have his innocence of dishonesty count in his favour . . . . In the Court of Appeal [2001] 1 QB 113 Evans LJ disagreed: see p 136.

45   I prefer the conclusion of Evans LJ. On the approach of Rix J an employer is in a better position, vis-à-vis co-defendants, than the employee for whose wrong the employer is vicariously liable. A co-defendant is worse placed to resist a contribution claim from an employer than he is from the wrongdoing employee.

---

[20] The nature of the liability under this section is debatable; we will simply call it 'vicarious liability' in common with Lords Nicholls and Millett in the following case. For debate see C. Mitchell, 'Partners in Wrongdoing' (2003) 119 LQR 364.

46 This cannot be right. It would mean that a co-defendant's liability to make a contribution payment differs, according to whether contribution is being sought by the employer or the employee. An employer could obtain contribution from a co-defendant in circumstances where the wrongdoing employee himself could not. If an employee was one of two wrong-doers equally to blame, his "innocent" employer could look to the other, blameworthy wrong-doer for a contribution even though the employee could not. Or take a more extreme case, where an employee is four-fifths responsible for an accident and a co-defendant one-fifth. If the employer's blamelessness could be taken into account in contribution proceedings, the co-defendant could find himself saddled with responsibility for more than a one-fifth share of the damages. The personally "innocent" employer, vicariously responsible for the acts of the employee who bears most of the responsibility for the accident, could recover contribution amounting to an indemnity from the individual wrongdoer whose blameworthiness, as between the two individual wrongdoers, is assessed at only one-fifth.

47 Examples such as these point irresistibly to the conclusion that vicarious liability involves the notion that, vis-à-vis third parties, the employer, although personally blameless, stands in the shoes of the wrongdoer employee. This is so, both for the purposes of liability to the claimant and for the purposes of contribution proceedings. In both cases the employer's liability is vicarious, that is, substitutional, not personal. The employer is liable for the fault of another. This approach accords with everyday practice. No contrary authority was cited to your Lordships' House on this point.

48 Rix J was minded to treat cases of dishonesty differently from cases of negligence. I can see no basis for drawing such a distinction. . . .

49 Accordingly, in my view the personal innocence of the partners in the Amhurst firm was not a relevant matter to be taken into account by the judge when deciding the contribution proceedings. The Amhurst firm, vicariously liable for Mr Amhurst's assumed dishonest wrong-doing, stands in his shoes for all relevant purposes. The judge therefore fell into error when taking the personal innocence of Mr Amhurst's partners into account. . . .

Factors not Causative of the Damage

As we have already noted, the House of Lords in *Dubai Aluminium* accepted a *different* reason for ordering S and T to indemnify the innocent partners completely. This reason was not based on 'responsibility' (to which, according to section 2(1), the court must 'have regard'). It was based on the fact that S and T still held undisgorged profits of their wrongdoing, whereas the co-partners did not. This factor justified a total indemnity, despite being irrelevant to 'responsibility' for the damage. The guiding aim is to distribute liability in a manner that is 'just and equitable'; 'responsibility' (incorporating both culpability and causation) is one factor to which the court must 'have regard', but is not the *only* factor.

Lord Nicholls, *Dubai Aluminium v Salaam*

Contribution and proceeds of wrongdoing

50 The other major factor which weighed with the judge when deciding to direct that the Amhurst firm should be entitled to an indemnity was that Mr Salaam and Mr Al Tajir had still not disgorged their full receipts from the fraud. The judge considered it would not be just and equitable to require one party to contribute in a way which would leave another party in possession of his spoils: see [1999] 1 Lloyd's Rep 415, 475.

51 Mr Salaam and Mr Al Tajir submitted that this approach is impermissible. Under section 2(1) of the Contribution Act the court is required to assess the amount of contribution recoverable from a person which is just and equitable "having regard to the extent of that person's responsibility for the damage". "Responsibility" includes both blameworthiness and causative potency. However elastically interpreted, "responsibility" does not embrace receipts.

52 I cannot accept this submission. It is based on a misconception of the essential nature of contribution proceedings. The object of contribution proceedings under the Contribution Act is to ensure that each party responsible for the damage makes an appropriate contribution to the cost of compensating the plaintiff, regardless of where that cost has fallen in the first instance. The burden of liability is being redistributed. But, of necessity, the extent to which it is just and equitable to redistribute this financial burden cannot be decided without seeing where the burden already lies. The court needs to have regard to the known or likely financial consequences of orders already made and to the likely financial consequences of any contribution order the court may make. For example, if one of three defendants equally responsible is insolvent, the court will have regard to this fact when directing contribution between the two solvent defendants. The court will do so, even though insolvency has nothing to do with responsibility. An instance of this everyday situation can be found in *Fisher v C H T Ltd (No 2)* [1966] 2 QB 475, 481, per Lord Denning MR.

53 In the present case a just and equitable distribution of the financial burden requires the court to take into account the net contributions each party made to the cost of compensating Dubai Aluminium. Regard should be had to the amounts payable by each party under the compromises and to the amounts of Dubai Aluminium's money each still has in hand. As Mr Sumption submitted, a contribution order will not properly reflect the parties' relative responsibilities if, for instance, two parties are equally responsible and are ordered to contribute equally, but the proceeds have all ended up in the hands of one of them so that he is left with a large undisgorged balance whereas the other is out of pocket.

54 Rix J considered this was obvious. So did Ferris J, in *K v P* [1993] Ch 140, 149. I agree with them.

In *Re-source America v Platt Site Services* [2004] EWCA Civ 665, the Court of Appeal took into account some rather different factors which affected the judgment of culpability but which were not 'causative of' the harm. Even the manner in which a defendant runs its defence—and any unreasonable attempt to deny responsibility or evade detection—was regarded as a relevant factor in determining contribution. This is not the same as the position in contributory negligence, where it is settled that only fault that *contributes to* the harm is relevant.

2.4 TIME LIMIT FOR CONTRIBUTION CLAIMS

Contribution proceedings attract their own limitation period, set by section 10 of the Limitation Act 1980 at two years.

FURTHER READING

Dugdale, T., 'Civil Liability (Contribution) Act 1978' (1979) 42 MLR 182.

McCaul, C., 'Holtby and the End Game' (2006) JPIL 6–11.

Mitchell, C., *The Law of Contribution and Reimbursement* (Oxford: OUP, 2003).

Tettenborn, A., 'Contribution between Wrongdoers' (2005) 155 NLJ 1722.

8

DAMAGES, COMPENSATION, AND RESPONSIBILITY

CENTRAL ISSUES

i) This chapter is concerned not with rules of liability, but with remedies. We begin by outlining the heads of loss for which damages in tort may be awarded. The heads of damage illustrate the general goal of tort compensation, which is to restore claimants to their pre-tort position. We will see that there are some serious conceptual difficulties involved with this. We will also outline the potential for non-compensatory awards.

ii) Also considered in this chapter are recent developments in respect of the assessment and delivery of damages, the funding of litigation, and the relationship between tort damages and welfare support. Despite their apparent technicality, these developments raise important issues about the nature of tort law, and its broader economic role.

iii) This brings us to an underlying disagreement about how the performance of tort law should be evaluated. At its most basic level, the disagreement concerns whether tort should be judged in functional terms (what are its effects? What are its costs? Who pays for tort damages and the costs of litigation, and do they represent good value?), or in terms of responsibility (for which injuries should wrongdoers pay? What are the limits to this responsibility?). The disagreement has taken a new turn with current political debate over 'compensation culture', with which we end this chapter.

1. A GENERAL ISSUE: INSURANCE

Whatever the correct way of approaching tort law (in functional or ethical terms), the truth is that most awards for personal injury are paid by insurers or employers (and often by insurers of employers). Damages are generally not paid by individual wrongdoers or tortfeasors. To recognize this is not to imply that claimants should always be compensated, or that awards should be as high as possible. Far from it. Since, one way or another, insurance premiums affect all of us, the level and cost of personal injury damages is a topic of broad concern.

On the other hand, the fact that compensation is generally paid by someone other than the tortfeasor does not *necessarily* mean that tort has *no* deterrent effect, nor that *all* the costs of the tort system will be fully 'socialized' or spread through premiums. Unfortunately, although there is some empirical research on these questions,[1] it is not completely conclusive. To an extent, commentators tend to assume that the costs of insurance are entirely spread among the public, or mostly rest with the class of potential tortfeasors, depending on the point of view from which they begin their analysis.[2]

Seen in this light, the statutory provisions and cases extracted in this chapter do not present an entirely coherent picture. No doubt this is partly because legislation will often represent a compromise between different interests.[3] Judicial decision-making too is influenced by social policy, and in this area above all judges can be seen to take account of the likely economic impact of their decisions.[4] It is not (fortunately) that individual judges will devise social policy on the spur of the moment. But judges will examine the likely effects of their decisions in the light of legislative policy. The costs of the tort system (both in terms of damages and litigation costs) are at times clearly perceived by the courts as a *social* cost, which is not borne simply by tortfeasors and those paying compensation awards.

2. COMPENSATORY DAMAGES

Note: remedies not addressed in this section.
Compensatory damages are not the only remedy available in tort.

- Some monetary awards are not compensatory. We address these later in the chapter. There is controversy over whether or not to call them 'damages'.

- Some remedies are available which do *not* take the form of a monetary award. Injunctions are sometimes available to protect the claimant's interests. Injunctive remedies are discussed in relevant substantive chapters particularly Chapter 10 (Nuisance) and Chapters 13 (Defamation) and 14 (Privacy). There is a limited remedy of 'abatement' (self-help) which is discussed in connection with Nuisance (Chapter 10).

Assessment of damages in cases of trespass to property and conversion raise particular issues which are most easily dealt with in Chapter 17.

2.1 THE BASIC APPROACH: *RESTITUTIO IN INTEGRUM*

The guiding principle for an award of compensatory damages is that the award should repair in full the damage done by the tort. The goal is '*restitutio in integrum*', or 100 per cent compensation.

This guiding principle is common to all torts. Where actions in respect of *personal injuries* are concerned, there is a fundamental problem with this principle. That is, it is simply impossible to 'make good' the whole loss suffered. There are always problems of calculation

---

[1] See especially D. Dewees and M. Trebilcock, *Exploring the Domain of Accident Law* (OUP, 1996).

[2] See for example P. S. Atiyah, *The Damages Lottery* (Hart Publishing, 1997), arguing that the costs of insurance are a social cost and that a fairer distribution of accident costs would be achieved through insuring ourselves (first party), rather than through liability insurance, which supports tort law. By contrast Jane Stapleton, 'Tort, Insurance and Ideology' (1995) 58 MLR 820 argues that such a shift would 'enrich' tortfeasors as a class, to the detriment of potential victims. For discussion see Jenny Steele, *Risks and Legal Theory* (Hart Publishing, 2004), Chapter 3; R. Lewis, 'Insurance and the Tort System' (2005) 25 LS 85–116.

[3] The Association of British Insurers (ABI), for example, is a powerful lobbying group: see R. Lewis, 'Insurance and the Tort System', ibid.

[4] Examples in this chapter include *Wells v Wells* (Lord Steyn); *Hodgson v Trapp* (Lord Bridge); and *Rogers v Merthyr Tydfil* (Smith LJ).

concerned with remedying any loss. But the problems with non-pecuniary losses in personal injury cases are of a different order. Where these losses are concerned, full compensation is strictly not possible, since damages cannot achieve equality between the circumstances of the claimant before and after the injury.

More generally, in respect of all heads of compensatory damages, it is important to remember that *only* losses that are caused by the tort will be compensated. Rules of causation and remoteness must be applied. In negligence actions at least, only damage which is 'within the scope of the duty' will be compensated (*South Australia Asset Management Company v York Montague Ltd* [1997] AC 191). Any other damage is treated as not attributable to the tort of the defendant.

Also of general importance is the impact of contributory negligence (Chapter 5) in reducing damages. If a reduction for contributory negligence is found to be appropriate, then the reduction will operate in respect of pecuniary and non-pecuniary awards, and in respect of compensatory and non-compensatory aspects of the award, whether delivered in a lump sum, or through periodical payments. In the case of a serious injury, this clearly affects the adequacy of compensation, particularly where future income and expenses are concerned.

2.2 PECUNIARY LOSSES IN PERSONAL INJURY CLAIMS: INTRODUCTION

In personal injury claims, 'pecuniary' losses fall under two general heads:

- lost earnings; and
- expenses.

Both sorts of pecuniary loss may be divided into two further categories:

- lost earnings and expenses *before* trial; and
- future loss of earnings and expenses.

Most of the problematic issues examined in this chapter relate to future losses.

2.3 LOST EARNINGS AND EXPENSES BEFORE TRIAL

The claimant should be compensated in full for any wages or other earnings lost as a result of the tort whilst awaiting trial, as well as for any expenses reasonably incurred. These may include travel expenses to and from hospital, as well as care costs incurred. Although there is a general principle that only reasonable expenses may be recovered (and that a claimant must 'mitigate his or her loss', by acting reasonably), the claimant is nevertheless not obliged to make use of free care and treatment through the National Health Service. The cost of *private care* may be recovered:

Law Reform (Personal Injuries) Act 1948

2 Measure of damages

(4) In an action for damages for personal injuries (including any such action arising out of a contract), there shall be disregarded, in determining the reasonableness of any expenses, the possibility of avoiding those expenses or part of them by taking advantage of facilities available under the National Health Service Act, 1977, or the National Health Service (Scotland) Act, 1978, or of any corresponding facilities in Northern Ireland.

More complexity is added by the question of deductions. Deductions operate to reduce the award to the claimant, to take account of benefits not received. We will explain the operation of deductions when we have outlined the way in which the whole award is calculated (below).

2.4 FUTURE LOST EARNINGS

Calculation of future losses poses far more difficulty. 'Calculation', in fact, may not be the right description. The exercise has an *appearance* of precision because some mathematical and actuarial techniques are applied.

In the case of a serious long-term injury, lost earnings will typically represent one of the largest elements in the claim. Calculation of future lost earnings is necessarily imprecise. There are two large areas of uncertainty:

1. Uncertainty over what *will* happen to the claimant, in the light of the injury. How long will the claimant live? What work, if any, will the claimant be able to secure? Will the condition improve, or deteriorate?

2. Uncertainty over what *would have* happened to the claimant, had it not been for the injury. Would the claimant have secured promotion? Have worked to pensionable age? Or left the job market early (whether through ill-health or for other reasons) in any event?

While some forms of delayed, staged, or periodic payments could deal with the first sort of uncertainty, no amount of delay in determining or delivering damages will deal with the second sort of uncertainty, because it concerns hypotheticals.

Multiplier and Multiplicand

The first step in 'calculating' an award for future lost earnings is to identify two figures, referred to as the multiplier and the multiplicand. These are multiplied, and certain additions and deductions are then applied. Broadly the same technique is used in assessing future expenses (including care costs), but the figures adopted will be different.

The multiplicand

The multiplicand (or figure 'to be multiplied') represents the claimant's net annual loss, taking into account earnings at the time of the accident, and likely promotion prospects lost as a result of the accident. If the claimant is not totally incapacitated or unable to work, this figure should take account of residual earning capacity. The figure used is not gross but net: there are deductions for income tax, social security contributions, and other expenditure which would have been incurred as a condition of earnings. Particularly where a young person with identifiable prospects is injured, there may be 'staged' increases in the multiplicand to reflect promotion prospects.

The following case is a useful illustration of the approach to younger claimants, and shows the kind of 'informed guesswork' that operates, as well as indicating some policy issues.

An Illustration: *Dixon v John Were* [2004] EWHC 2273 (QB)

The claimant was seriously injured in a road traffic accident at the age of 20, when he was a university student.[5] He suffered brain damage and a consequent personality disorder which

---

[5] His damages were reduced by 27.5% to reflect his contributory negligence. The driver (defendant) and all of the passengers (two of whom were killed in the accident) had been drinking heavily.

made him unemployable. Given his previous 'attractive personality and very considerable charm', together with 'his background, the fact of his degree and, to some extent, his contacts' (and even though his predicted grade on graduation was a lower second), it was considered likely that he would have secured a good job at above average national earnings for a professional male.[6] Having decided this, the multiplicand was then increased in line with the percentage chance of promotions, in a staged increase. There was also allowance in the multiplicand for additional 'benefits' such as a company car and private health insurance, which it was found would most probably have been acquired as part of the employment 'package'. However, the judge rejected an argument that the multiplicand should be further increased to reflect the percentage chance of even higher earnings. Such a possibility was merely speculative, in his case. Had there been a stronger possibility of such a promotion, a 'percentage increase' might have been allowed, on the authority of *Herring v MOD* (below).

The multiplier

The court must make an informed estimate of the number of years for which the claimant has lost earnings. This figure represents the 'multiplier' (though it will also be varied to deal with matters such as investment return, as explained below). A first step in arriving at a multiplier is to identify the number of years between the accident, and the relevant retirement age for the type of employment the claimant would have had but for the accident. However, the court will reduce this figure to reflect the chance that the claimant would not have worked until retirement age, even without the accident. The claimant may have left employment, changed employment, died before retirement, or been incapacitated for some other reason.

Two sorts of reasons why the multiplier might be reduced ought to be distinguished. First, there may be particular evidence relating to the claimant which suggests that their earning life would, even without the accident, have been shortened. For example, they may demonstrably have no desire to work, or they may have a predisposition to develop a particular disease or disability at some stage in the future. It is clear that a court should take account of any such evidence in making deductions from the multiplier.

Second, courts might also take into account the general possibility, not connected to particular features of the claimant, that a working life will be shortened. In judicial language, these general factors are referred to as the vicissitudes of life. Historically, it is accepted that some reduction in the multiplier should be applied on account of life's contingencies or 'vicissitudes'. But how much?

The answer to this last question has been transformed through reference to the Ogden tables.

The Ogden tables and their influence

The 'Actuarial tables with explanatory notes for use in personal injury and fatal accident cases' ('Ogden Tables') were prepared by an inter-professional working party chaired by Sir Michael Ogden QC and their first edition was published in 1984. The tables draw on data, compiled for

---

6 Gross J at para [29]. This illustrates an important point. The court must consider what the claimant *has lost*, even if this means that two equally deserving claimants of the same age and with the same injuries will receive very different awards. Their life prospects without the accident will be reflected in the award and in a sense, social injustice (as well as pure luck) are maintained. This is because tort damages aim to be primarily corrective, and do not aim to be distributive, even if the effect of tort law is on some level to distribute the risks of accidents.

the purposes of insurers, predicting the capital sum required to produce a given income stream for the life of a claimant. The tables themselves take into account only one type of risk, namely the risk of mortality. However, additional commentary offers guidance on relevant adjustments to the multiplier for other factors, particularly employment type. Initially, judges appeared reluctant to adopt multipliers by reference to the tables, preferring to trust to their own experience and to specific evidence related to the individual claimant, rather than to the actuarial experience represented in the tables.

The tables now have a much more central role. In the important case of *Wells v Wells* [1999] AC 345, Lord Lloyd criticized the habit of deducting too many years from the multiplier, and argued for greater use of the tables.

Lord Lloyd, *Wells v Wells*, at 379

I do not suggest that the judge should now be a slave to the tables. There may well be special factors in particular cases. But the tables should now be regarded as the starting-point, rather than a check. A judge should be slow to depart from the relevant actuarial multiplier on impressionistic grounds, or by reference to "a spread of multipliers in comparable cases" especially when the multipliers were fixed before actuarial tables were widely used. . . .

Further reinforcement is to be found in the following case, which sets out important guidance on reducing the multiplier in lost earnings calculations.

Herring v Ministry of Defence [2003] EWCA Civ 528; [2004] 1 All ER 44

The claimant suffered serious spinal injuries in a parachuting accident, caused through the fault of the defendants. At the time of the accident he enjoyed an exceptional ('SAS standard') level of fitness and planned a career in the police force. As a result of the accident, he could not walk more than 500 metres unaided, with the use of a stick. His potential employment prospects were limited.

The judge found that the claimant would in all likelihood, but for the injury, have made a successful career in the police force. Had he failed to do so, he would have found equivalent employment. He drew from the Ogden tables a 'normal' multiplier of 15.54, but reduced it to 11.70 to reflect 'uncertainties' associated with his future hypothetical employment. In particular, he asked:

35 . . . would he have remained in the police throughout his career? He might have become disenchanted, or been injured, or found it incompatible with family life. There are inevitably more uncertainties than with a claimant who is already established in a career and has a "track record".

The Court of Appeal held that the deduction made was too large, and that the judge had wrongly interpreted the role of the tables.

Potter LJ

[27] . . . was the 25% discount applied by the judge to the future earnings loss figure too great as Mr Huckle submits? I consider that it was. By way of preliminary, I would observe that, whereas the judge's starting point was, rightly, to select the appropriate multiplier from the Ogden Tables for loss of earnings, that multiplier takes no account of risks other than mortality. Section B (pp 11–13 (paras 30–44)) of the explanatory notes to the Ogden Tables presents a helpful discussion and guide in relation to the further discount likely to be appropriate for other contingencies/ vicissitudes. It makes the point that these contingencies are principally illness and periods of unemployment, but that specific factors in individual cases may necessitate larger reductions. Tables of percentage figures are then set out, based on research conducted for the Institute of Actuaries, under the heading 'The basic deduction for contingencies other than mortality' (p 12 (para 36)). Table A shows 'Loss of Earnings to Pension Age 65 (Males)' and Table B to 'Pension Age 60 (Males)' (p 12 (para 38)). The deductions set out are notably low compared with the level of discount traditionally applied over the years.

[28] The 'Medium' column in Tables A and B shows the level of discount appropriate to be made if it is anticipated that economic activity is likely to correspond to that in the 1970s and 1980s ignoring periods of high and low unemployment. A discount of 2% is shown under Table B for a man aged 35 at date of trial. In the case of the claimant the pension age of 55 merits a smaller discount. Under the heading 'Variations by occupation' (p 13 (paras 40–42)) the point is made that the risks of illness, injury and disability are less for persons in clerical or similar jobs and greater for those in manual jobs such as construction, mining, quarrying and shipbuilding. However, what matters is the type and nature of the work undertaken by the person in question rather than the industry as such. It is suggested that in more risky occupations the figures given in the tables should be reduced by a maximum of the order of 1% at age 25, 2% at age 40 and 5% at age 55. Taking the tables as a guide, and treating the police as a 'more risky' occupation, the appropriate discount for this claimant would thus be in the order of 3%.

[29] It is perhaps no surprise that the figures based on general research reveal low appropriate discounts when averaged across the board. The observations of Windeyer J in Bresatz v Przibilla (1962) 108 CLR 541 have for long been quoted but perhaps insufficiently recognised so far as deductions for contingencies are concerned. In this connection he stated (at 543–544):

. . .

'I know of no reason for assuming that everyone who is injured and rendered for a period unable to work would probably in any event have been for a quarter of that period out of work, or away from work and unpaid. No statistics were presented to justify this assumption. Moreover, the generalization, that there must be a "scaling down" for contingencies, seems mistaken. All "contingencies" are not adverse: all "vicissitudes" are not harmful. A particular plaintiff might have had prospects or chances of advancement and increasingly remunerative employment. Why count the possible buffets and ignore the rewards of fortune? Each case depends upon its own facts.'

[31] I would only add in respect of the last passage quoted that statistics, or at any rate guidance based upon research, are now available in the notes to the Ogden Tables which demonstrate that so far as the level of any 'arbitrary' or generally applied level of discount is concerned, a figure of 25% is a gross departure from that appropriate simply in respect of future illness and unemployment. In order to justify a substantially higher discount by reason of additional future contingencies, there should in my view be tangible reasons relating to the personality or likely future circumstances of the claimant going beyond the purely speculative.

The result of greater reliance on the tables will be that smaller deductions from the multiplier are made on account of the general 'vicissitudes of life'. As explained at the end of the passage above, use of the tables should not affect the treatment of *specific* issues concerning particular claimants' expected earnings.

Rate of Return and the Multiplier

If damages are awarded as a single lump sum payment (as they always are at common law),[7] it is assumed the lump sum will be invested, and earn interest. The lump sum should be reduced to take account of the fact that it will yield a return in this way. On the other hand, claimants who are dependent on damages—and particularly those with long-term serious injuries who have no opportunity of making up their losses—should not be expected to invest their lump sums in such a way that they are exposed to significant risk. So courts will reduce the multiplier in order to reflect the fact that the sum will earn interest. But what rate of interest should be assumed?

Historically, the courts assumed a high rate of return on investment and discounted the multiplier by 4–5 per cent: see *Mallett v McMonagle* [1970] AC 166, and *Cookson v Knowles* [1979] AC 556. In *Wells v Wells* [1999] 1 AC 345, the House of Lords took a different and much more protective approach to claimants. Claimants could be assumed to invest their lump sums in index-linked government stock (ILGS), which offers a 'risk-free environment' and (naturally) a much lower rate of return than investment in equities. The House of Lords followed the recommendations of the Law Commission, and of Sir Michael Ogden.[8]

Sir Michael Ogden, *The Ogden Tables* (1st edn, 1984), p 8

Investment policy, however prudent, involves risks and it is not difficult to draw up a list of blue chip equities or reliable unit trusts which have performed poorly and, in some cases, disastrously. Index-linked government stocks eliminate the risks. Whereas, in the past, a plaintiff has had to speculate in the form of prudent investment by buying equities, or a 'basket' of equities and gilts or a selection of unit trusts, he need speculate no longer if he buys index-linked government stock. If the loss is, say, £5,000 per annum, he can be awarded damages which, if invested in such stocks, will provide him with almost exactly that sum in real terms.

Lord Lloyd, *Wells v Wells*, at 373–4

Conclusion

My conclusion is that the judges in these three cases were right to assume for the purpose of their calculations that the plaintiffs would invest their damages in I.L.G.S. for the following reasons.

(1) Investment in I.L.G.S. is the most accurate way of calculating the present value of the loss which the plaintiffs will actually suffer in real terms.
(2) Although this will result in a heavier burden on these defendants, and, if the principle is applied across the board, on the insurance industry in general, I can see nothing unjust. It is

---

[7] For new possibilities created by statute, see Section 4 of this chapter.
[8] Cited by Lord Lloyd at 369.

true that insurance premiums may have been fixed on the basis of the 4 to 5 per cent. discount rate indicated in *Cookson v. Knowles* [1979] A.C. 556 and the earlier authorities. But this was only because there was then no better way of allowing for future inflation. The objective was always the same. No doubt insurance premiums will have to increase in order to take account of the new lower rate of discount. Whether this is something which the country can afford is not a subject on which your Lordships were addressed. So we are not in a position to form any view as to the wider consequences.

(3) The search for a prudent investment will always depend on the circumstances of the particular investor. Some are able to take a measure of risk, others are not. For a plaintiff who is not in a position to take risks, and who wishes to protect himself against inflation in the short term of up to 10 years, it is clearly prudent to invest in I.L.G.S. It cannot therefore be assumed that he will invest in equities and gilts. Still less is it his duty to invest in equities and gilts in order to mitigate his loss.

(4) Logically the same applies to a plaintiff investing for the long term. In any event it is desirable to have a single rate applying across the board, in order to facilitate settlements and to save the expense of expert evidence at the trial. I take this view even though it is open to the Lord Chancellor under section 1(3) of the Act of 1996 to prescribe different rates of return for different classes of case. Mr. Leighton Williams conceded that it is not desirable in practice to distinguish between different classes of plaintiff when assessing the multiplier.

(5) How the plaintiff, or the majority of plaintiffs, in fact invest their money is irrelevant. The research carried out by the Law Commission suggests that the majority of plaintiffs do not in fact invest in equities and gilts but rather in a building society or a bank deposit.

(6) There was no agreement between the parties as to how much greater, if at all, the return on equities is likely to be in the short or long term. But it is at least clear that an investment in I.L.G.S. will save up to 1 per cent. per annum by obviating the need for continuing investment advice.

. . .

The end result was to recommend that a lower discount, of 3 per cent, would now be applied to the multiplier to account for investment of the capital sum. Lord Steyn explained the wider importance of this technical issue:

Lord Steyn, *Wells v Wells* [1999] AC 345, at 382

The importance of the issue is shown by a comparison of the awards of the three trial judges, who relied on index-linked government securities to fix the discount rate, and the figures substituted by the Court of Appeal, who used the conventional rate. . . . the use of a 3 per cent. discount rate instead of 4.5 per cent. would increase the awards by very roughly the following sums: Margaret Wells (a 58-year-old nurse), £108,000; Page (a 28-year-old steelworker), £186,000; Thomas (aged six years), £300,000. These figures show the impact of the reduction of the discount rate in cases where damages are calculated over many years. But, since a judicial decision ought to take into account general as well as particular consequences, it is important to realise that the proposed modification of the discount rate would lead to an enormous general increase in the size of awards for future losses. Nobody has ventured a prediction of the likely cost. The sums involved would undoubtedly be huge. The implications of a modification of the conventional rate for the insurance industry would be considerable. Inevitably, it would be reflected in increased premiums. The one certain thing is that if the right decision is to make the suggested modification of the discount rate the public would by and large have to pay for the increase in awards.

Here, Lord Steyn specifically makes the point that awards in tort are ultimately paid for by the public at large.

Subsequent developments in the discount rate

In our earlier extract from *Wells*, Lord Lloyd referred to section 1 of the Damages Act 1996.

Damages Act 1996

1 Assumed rate of return on investment of damages

(1) In determining the return to be expected from the investment of a sum awarded as damages for future pecuniary loss in an action for personal injury the court shall, subject to and in accordance with rules of court made for the purposes of this section, take into account such rate of return (if any) as may from time to time be prescribed by an order made by the Lord Chancellor.

(2) Subsection (1) above shall not however prevent the court taking a different rate of return into account if any party to the proceedings shows that it is more appropriate in the case in question.

(3) An order under subsection (1) above may prescribe different rates of return for different classes of case.

In June 2001, the Lord Chancellor exercised his power under this section and specified a discount rate: Damages (Personal Injury) Order 2001 (SI 2001/2301). He largely accepted the approach of the House of Lords in *Wells v Wells* and indeed, in light of changed economic circumstances, adopted a *lower* discount, of 2.5 per cent. Subsequently, attempts to use section 1(2) above to argue that a lower discount should apply in particular circumstances have been brushed aside by the Court of Appeal as inconsistent with the Lord Chancellor's approach.

In *Warriner v Warriner* [2003] 3 All ER 447 (whose precise facts we do not need to set out), Dyson LJ explained the narrow approach to section 1(2):

33. We are told that this is the first time that this court has had to consider the 1996 Act, and that guidance is needed as to the meaning of 'more appropriate in the case in question' in section 1(2). The phrase 'more appropriate', if considered in isolation, is open-textured. It prompts the question: by what criteria is the court to judge whether a different rate of return is more appropriate in the case in question? But the phrase must be interpreted in its proper context

which is that the Lord Chancellor has prescribed a rate pursuant to section 1(1) and has given very detailed reasons explaining what factors he took into account in arriving at the rate that he has prescribed. I would hold that in deciding whether a different rate is more appropriate in the case in question, the court must have regard to those reasons. If the case in question falls into a category that the Lord Chancellor did not take into account and/or there are special features of the case which (a) are material to the choice of rate of return and (b) are shown from an examination of the Lord Chancellor's reasons not to have been taken into account, then a different rate of return may be 'more appropriate'.

Subsequently, in *Cooke v United Bristol Healthcare Trust* [2004] 1 WLR 251, Laws LJ drew attention to the Lord Chancellor's explanation for adopting a *general* discount rate, for use across very different cases:

The Lord Chancellor[9]

Setting a single rate to cover all cases, whilst highly desirable for the reasons given above, has the effect that the discount rate has to cover a wide variety of different cases, and claimants with widely differing personal and financial characteristics. Moreover, as has become clear from the consultation exercise (including responses by expert financial analysts to questions which I posed them), the real rate of return on investments of any character (including investments in Index-Linked Government Securities) involves making assumptions for the future about a wide variety of factors affecting the economy as a whole, including for example the likely rate of inflation. In these circumstances, it is inevitable that any approach to setting the discount rate must be fairly broad-brush. Put shortly, there can be no single 'right' answer as to what rate should be set. Since it is in the context of larger awards, intended to cover longer periods, that there is the greatest risk of serious discrepancies between the level of compensation and the actual losses incurred if the discount rate set is not appropriate, I have had this type of award particularly in mind when considering the level at which the discount rate should be set . . .

. . . I consider that it is likely that real claimants with a large award of compensation, who sought investment advice and instructed their advisers as to the particular investment objectives which they needed to fulfil (as they could reasonably be expected to do) would not be advised to invest solely or even primarily in Index-Linked Government Securities, but rather in a mixed portfolio, in which any investment risk would be managed so as to be very low. This view is supported by the experience of the Court of Protection as to the independent financial advice they receive. It is also supported by the responses of the expert financial analysts whom I have consulted. No one responding to the consultation identified a single case in which the claimant had invested solely in Index-Linked Government Securities and doubts were expressed as to whether there was any such case. This suggests that setting the discount rate at 2.5% would not place an intolerable burden on claimants to take on excessive, i e moderate or above, risk in the equity markets, and would be a rate more likely to accord with real expectations of returns, particularly at the higher end of awards.

---

[9] Quoted by Laws LJ in *Cooke* at 260–1.

Laws LJ concluded that the Lord Chancellor had built in an element of *additional* security for claimants, precisely in order to reflect the fact that he was applying a 'broad brush'.

In *Cooke* itself, it was argued for the claimants that the costs of care are inclined to rise at a faster rate than inflation, and that the discount method adopted in *Wells v Wells* would therefore leave injured claimants under-compensated. The claimants wished to bring expert evidence of the likely costs of care over time, and sought a lower discount to the multiplier than the 2.5 per cent adopted by the Lord Chancellor. The Court of Appeal rejected the claimants' applications to bring expert evidence to this effect, and said (rather dramatically) that they amounted to an 'illegitimate assault' on the Lord Chancellor's discount rate (para [30]). Laws LJ conceded that through application of a general discount rate, the 100 per cent compensation principle would only be achieved in a 'rough and ready way', but thought that this was the premiss of the Lord Chancellor's decision to set a standard discount as low as he did.

Leaving aside *Cooke*, we will note that the combined result of adoption of the Ogden tables (disapproving large discounts for vicissitudes), and reduction in the discount rate, is to feed an upward trend in personal injuries awards. This trend is enhanced by developments in respect of non-pecuniary losses (particularly *Heil v Rankin*), explored below. On the other hand, these factors are relevant specifically to the *most* serious injuries, since these are the cases where future pecuniary losses are in issue.

Disadvantage in the Job Market

The above method of assessing lost earnings does not deal comfortably with certain less predictable factors. In particular, a claimant with a long-term injury may be in gainful employment at the date of the trial, but what if they lose that employment at some time in the future? Will their impairment (assuming it to be long-term) lead them to struggle to find further work at a similar rate of pay? It is usual to make a modest addition to damages, called a *Smith v Manchester* award,[10] to reflect the claimant's future 'disadvantage in the job market'. In *Herring v MOD*, for example, the '*Smith v Manchester*' award was assessed at £5,000. This highly speculative exercise is not allowed to disturb the multiplier and multiplicand.

Loss of Pension Rights: Balance of Probabilities or Probabilistic Causation?

'100 per cent compensation' requires an award for *loss of pension rights* in appropriate circumstances. But how will the court decide whether the claimant would have remained in relevant employment long enough to have achieved those rights, if the tort had not occurred? This question raises a fundamental issue, related to prediction of future hypothetical events. Should loss of pension rights be addressed simply *on the balance of probabilities*? If so, the value of a full pension will be awarded if the claimant showed they would probably have stayed in employment for long enough. Or, should the court assess the *degree of likelihood of attaining such rights*, and assess damages accordingly? This would lead to partial compensation, proportionate to the assessed chances. This question of method is of broad application and might affect very many claims, not just those relating to pensions.

---

[10] By reference to *Smith v Manchester Corporation* (1974) 17 KIR 1 (Court of Appeal).

Brown v Ministry of Defence [2006] EWCA Civ 546 (CA)

Eight weeks into her service with the army, at the age of 24, the claimant B suffered a serious fracture of her ankle. She could no longer pursue her dream of an army career, and retrained as a physiotherapist. The defendants admitted liability, but challenged the substantial damages claimed. The sums claimed included compensation for loss of pension rights (£148,856.31) calculated on the assumption that B would have remained in the army for the required period of 22 years; and compensation for disadvantage in the labour market (£107,028). The sum for lost pension rights was very considerable because, had B remained in the army for 22 years, she would have become entitled to the pension at age 46, rather than at the age of 60 which would be the rule in most employment. The judge accepted B's argument that she would 'probably' have remained in the army for the required period, applying a 'balance of probabilities' test—informed by her personal commitment to such a career—as he thought was compatible with the approach in *Herring v Ministry of Defence* (extracted above).

The Court of Appeal found that the approach of the first instance judge was wrong, and that he had misunderstood the impact of *Herring v Ministry of Defence*. He had also over-looked a principle, referred to by the House of Lords in both *Mallet v McMonagle* [1970] AC 166, 176 and *Davies v Taylor* [1974] AC 297, that in respect of hypothetical future events (as opposed to past events), it was appropriate to make decisions to reflect the *probability* of those events occurring, and to assess damages accordingly. He should therefore have made a *proportionate* award.

Davies v Taylor was a dependency claim.

Lord Reid, *Davies v Taylor* [1974] AC 207, at 212–13

The peculiarity in the present case is that the appellant had left her husband some five weeks before his death and there was no immediate prospect of her returning to him. He wanted her to come back but she was unwilling to come. But she says that there was a prospect or chance or probability that she might have returned to him later and it is only in that event that she would have benefited from his survival. To my mind the issue and the sole issue is whether that chance or probability was substantial. If it was it must be evaluated. If it was a mere possibility it must be ignored . . . .

When the question is whether a certain thing is or is not true—whether a certain event did or did not happen—then the court must decide one way or the other. There is no question of chance or probability. Either it did or it did not happen. But the standard of civil proof is a balance of probabilities. If the evidence shows a balance in favour of it having happened then it is proved that it did in fact happen.

But here we are not and could not be seeking a decision either that the wife would or that she would not have returned to her husband. You can prove that a past event happened, but you cannot prove that a future event will happen and I do not think that the law is so foolish as to suppose that you can. All that you can do is to evaluate the chance. Sometimes it is virtually 100 per cent.: sometimes virtually nil. But often it is somewhere in between. And if it is some-where in between I do not see much difference between a probability of 51 per cent. and a probability of 49 per cent.

Lord Reid's approach was cited as a clear point of reference—an instance where the law does rightly apply a 'proportionate' approach—in *Gregg v Scott* [2005] 2 AC 176 (Chapter 4). *Gregg v Scott*, as we have seen, rejected a 'proportionate' approach to recovery of damages for lost chance of a cure where there was a negligent failure to diagnose cancer. *Davies v Taylor*, like *Brown*, is not a case like *Gregg v Scott*, since it involves the question of hypothetical future actions of individuals.

In *Brown*, the Court of Appeal applied Lord Reid's approach to future hypothetical events, and awarded a proportion of the lost pension rights. The decision of the Court of Appeal aims to make sense of some apparently conflicting decisions in which the prospects of future earnings have sometimes been based on *balance of probability*, and sometimes on *degrees of probability*, with a consequent effect on damages awarded.

Moore-Bick LJ, *Brown v Ministry of Defence*

22.   In this court [in *Herring v Ministry of Defence*] Potter LJ . . . held that when assessing the claimant's loss of future earnings the judge was wrong to make reduction for the chances of his not being accepted into the police force or of leaving before he reached the age of 55. He pointed out that in order to assess loss of future earnings it is necessary in most cases to adopt what he called a 'career model' for the claimant in question which fairly reflects his earning capability. In many cases that will be the job in which the claimant is currently employed since it can usually be inferred that he would have continued in the same or similar employment. The chances of promotion can then be taken into account by adjusting the multiplicand at appropriate points along the multiplier. In a case where the claimant has yet to enter employment, it is necessary to adopt a career model by reference to his abilities and reasonable aspirations. That may not be an easy task, but provided the career model that is selected does fairly reflect the claimant's earning capability, the chances of his actually obtaining the particular form of employment used as the model or of his leaving it before the normal retirement age will usually be irrelevant, since it can be assumed that, if he does so, he will take up some alternative employment at a broadly comparable rate of pay. The chances of a career change need only be separately assessed if it is one that would significantly alter his earning capability one way or another . . . .

24   . . . the decision in *Herring v Ministry of Defence* is not in any sense inconsistent with the principle in *Davies v Taylor* which continues to be of general application. Nor is there any inconsistency between the decisions in *Doyle v Wallace*,[11] *Langford v Hebran*[12] and *Herring v Ministry of Defence*, each of which simply provides an example of the application of the same principles to different factual situations. In each case the court was seeking to assess by the most appropriate means having regard to the particular circumstances of the case the chances that the claimant would have enjoyed a particular level of economic benefits had his or her working career not been interrupted or prevented by the injury in question. The most appropriate way of making that assessment may vary from case to case, but the underlying principles remain the same. Provided a fair career model is chosen as the basis for the assessment of loss of future earnings and pension entitlement, the prospects of enhanced or reduced earnings resulting from the ordinary chances of life can be allowed for by adjustments to the multiplier and multiplicand as appropriate. It is only when the court has to consider the possibility of an unusual chain of events that would have a significant effect on earnings or

[11]   [1998] PIQR Q146.   [12]   [2001] EWCA Civ 528.

pension rights that it is necessary to assess the chances of such events occurring and to assess their financial consequences. Thus in *Doyle v Wallace* the court had to assess the chances of the claimant's having a well-paid career as a drama teacher and in *Langford v Hebran* it was necessary to assess the claimant's chances of becoming a highly successful professional sportsman. In each case the development in question would have had a significant effect on the claimant's earning capability. In each case the development in question would have had a significant effect on the claimant's earning capability. These decisions were both cited with approval in *Gregg v Scott* [2005] AC 176 as examples of the application of the principle in *Davies v Taylor*.

Lost Life Expectancy

Where the effect of a tort is to shorten the claimant's life expectancy, some difficult issues arise. In this section, we are concerned with *pecuniary* losses. Therefore, we leave aside for the time being questions relating to the award of *non-pecuniary* damages where life expectancy is shortened.

Where a claimant is likely to die earlier because of their injuries, the relevant multiplier for the cost of *expenses* will be lower, since costs will not be incurred beyond the time of their death. But what of the multiplier for *lost earnings*? Should the injured party be able to claim for lost earnings in the years they *would have been earning* but for the tort, which now fall after the expected date of their death? The answer to this depends on the *purpose* of an award for lost earnings. If the purpose of this award is income replacement for the benefit of the claimant, then income that would have been earned during the 'lost years' should not be recoverable, even if it was 'caused by' the tort. The claimant will not now 'need' that income. This, however, would mean that the tort is allowed to reduce the *estate* of the injured party. There will be less money flowing into the estate for the benefit of those inheriting it after his or death. Is it the claimant, or the claimant's estate, that should be returned to the pre-tort position?

Pickett v British Rail Engineering Ltd [1980] AC 136

At the age of 51, the plaintiff contracted mesothelioma through his employer's breach of duty. His expectation of life was reduced to one year. He would otherwise have expected to work to age 65. Thus, compensation for earnings which would have been made during the 'lost years' was the major component of the damages claimed. Future expenses and lost earnings during the remaining year of life were relatively small, although there was an award of general damages (for non-pecuniary losses) of £7,000.

The House of Lords held that the claimant could recover for earnings that would have been made during the lost years. However, an amount must be deducted from this sum to represent the claimant's own living expenses during those years. Leaving aside the interpretation of earlier case law, Lord Scarman encapsulated the difficulties that remained with this solution:

Lord Scarman, at 169–71

Principle would appear . . . to suggest that a plaintiff ought to be entitled to damages for the loss of earnings he could have reasonably expected to have earned during the "lost years." But it has been submitted by the defendant that such a rule, if it be thought socially desirable, requires to be implemented by legislation. It is argued that a judicial graft would entail objectionable consequences—consequences which legislation alone can obviate. There is force in this submission. The major objections are these. First, the plaintiff may have no dependants. Secondly, even if he has dependants, he may have chosen to make a will depriving them of support from his estate. In either event, there would be a windfall for strangers at the expense of the defendant. Thirdly, the plaintiff may be so young (in *Oliver v. Ashman* [1962] 2 Q.B. 210 he was a boy aged 20 months at the time of the accident) that it is absurd that he should be compensated for future loss of earnings. Fourthly—a point which has weighed with my noble and learned friend, Lord Russell of Killowen—if damages are recoverable for the loss of the prospect of earnings during the lost years, must it not follow that they are also recoverable for loss of other reasonable expectations, e.g. a life interest or an inheritance? Fifthly, what does compensation mean when it is assessed in respect of a period after death? Sixthly, as my noble and learned friend Lord Wilberforce has pointed out, there is a risk of double recovery in some cases, i.e. of both the estate and the dependants recovering damages for the expected earnings of the lost years.

Lord Scarman countered most of these objections but continued:

. . .

There is, it has to be confessed, no completely satisfying answer to the fifth objection. But it does not, I suggest, make it unjust that such damages should be awarded. The plaintiff has lost the earnings and the opportunity, which, while he was living, he valued, of employing them as he would have thought best. Whether a man's ambition be to build up a fortune, to provide for his family, or to spend his money upon good causes or merely a pleasurable existence, loss of the means to do so is a genuine financial loss. The logical and philosophical difficulties of compensating a man for a loss arising after his death emerge only if one treats the loss as a non-pecuniary loss—which to some extent it is. But it is also a pecuniary loss— the money would have been his to deal with as he chose, had he lived. The sixth objection appears to me unavoidable, though further argument and analysis in a case in which the point arose for decision might lead to a judicial solution which was satisfactory. But I suspect that the point will need legislation. However, if one must choose between a law which in some cases will deprive dependants of their dependency through the chances of life and litigation and a law which, in avoiding such a deprival, will entail in some cases both the estate and the dependants recovering damages in respect of the lost years, I find the latter to be the lesser evil.

These damages are justified chiefly on the basis that they maintain the value of the claimant's estate. As such, they raise issues of overlap with the provisions on dependency damages under the Fatal Accidents Act 1976, and with the survival of claims after the death of the injured party under the Law Reform (Miscellaneous Provisions) Act 1934. Indeed this is broadly the sixth point referred to by Lord Scarman, and he was correct to suggest that it would need legislative solution. The risk of double recovery was removed by an amendment to the Law Reform (Miscellaneous Provisions) Act 1934, which now holds that the claim for earnings in 'the lost years' no longer survives the claimant's death. We extract this statute in Section 3 of this chapter.

2.5 EXPENSES

By far the largest component of future expenses generally relates to care costs. In the case of a very serious injury, care costs can considerably outstrip lost earnings. But in less serious cases, which make up the majority of tort claims, no future expenses will be in issue at all. Therefore, the cases considered here concern the most serious injuries.

In the case of long-term injury, calculation of care costs will involve its own multiplier, relating not to working years, but to the *life expectancy* of the claimant. Since a claimant with a lower life expectancy will benefit from a lower 'multiplier' under the expenses head, the result is that the defendant will generally pay less under the heading of pecuniary losses if the accident actually *shortens* the life expectancy of the victim. This shows us a different side of the '100 per cent compensation' principle—if the damages are not 'needed', then they are not awarded.

Voluntary provision of care

Many injured people are cared for by relatives or friends, who make no charge for the care provided. To the extent that these carers incur pecuniary losses, particularly by giving up paid employment, it is clear that the award of damages may contain an amount to compensate for this. However, this amount is part of the claim made by the injured party. The care-giver has no claim against the tortfeasor in his or her own right. Although the House of Lords in *Hunt v Severs* (below) concluded that this amount is to be 'held on trust' by the injured party for the care-giver, the volunteer is still dependent on the injured party to bring the action at all.[13]

In *Donnelly* v *Joyce* [1974] QB 454, the plaintiff was a six-year-old boy, whose mother gave up her part time work in order to care for him. The Court of Appeal held that the plaintiff could claim for the cost of the services provided, as an element of his own claim. Rather awkwardly, the cost of services to him was valued in terms of the mother's lost earnings. This tends to show that the Court of Appeal's decision, though no doubt fair and just, was based on a fiction. This fiction is encapsulated in the following passage:

Megaw LJ, *Donnelly v Joyce* [1974] QB 454, at 461–2

Mr. Hamilton's first proposition is that a plaintiff cannot succeed in a claim in relation to someone else's loss unless the plaintiff is under a legal liability to reimburse that other person. The plaintiff, he says, was not under a legal liability to reimburse his mother. A moral obligation is not enough. Mr. Hamilton's second proposition is that if, contrary to his submission, the existence of a moral, as distinct from a legal, obligation to reimburse the benefactor is sufficient, nevertheless there is no moral obligation on the part of a child of six years of age to repay its parents for money spent by them, as in this case.

We do not agree with the proposition, inherent in Mr. Hamilton's submission, that the plaintiff's claim, in circumstances such as the present, is properly to be regarded as being, to use his phrase, "in relation to someone else's loss," merely because someone else has provided to, or for the benefit of, the plaintiff—the injured person—the money, or the services to be valued

---

[13] See Jonathan Herring, 'Where are the Carers in Health Care Law and Ethics?' (2007) 27 LS 51–73.

as money, to provide for needs of the plaintiff directly caused by the defendant's wrongdoing. The loss is the plaintiff's loss. The question from what source the plaintiff's needs have been met, the question who has paid the money or given the services, the question whether or not the plaintiff is or is not under a legal or moral liability to repay, are, so far as the defendant and his liability are concerned, all irrelevant. The plaintiff's loss, to take this present case, is not the expenditure of money to buy the special boots or to pay for the nursing attention. His loss is the existence of the need for those special boots or for those nursing services, the value of which for purposes of damages—for the purpose of the ascertainment of the amount of his loss—is the proper and reasonable cost of supplying those needs. That, in our judgment, is the key to the problem. So far as the defendant is concerned, the loss is not someone else's loss. It is the plaintiff's loss.

The problem with this was exposed in *Hunt v Severs* [1994] 2 AC 350. Referring to the above passage in *Donnelly v Joyce*, Lord Bridge said:

Lord Bridge, *Hunt v Severs*, at 361

With respect, I do not find this reasoning convincing. I accept that the basis of a plaintiff's claim for damages may consist in his need for services but I cannot accept that the question from what source that need has been met is irrelevant. If an injured plaintiff is treated in hospital as a private patient he is entitled to recover the cost of that treatment. But if he receives free treatment under the National Health Service, his need has been met without cost to him and he cannot claim the cost of the treatment from the tortfeasor. So it cannot, I think, be right to say that in all cases the plaintiff's loss is "for the purpose of damages . . . the proper and reasonable cost of supplying [his] needs."

This passage is correct in its criticism of the reasoning in *Donnelly*. But the conclusion reached in *Hunt v Severs* has been widely criticized, and rightly so.

Hunt v Severs [1994] 2 AC 350

The unusual but by no means unique feature of this case was that the defendant was both the tortfeasor, and the care-giver. Through the defendant's negligence, the plaintiff was very severely injured when riding as a pillion passenger on his motorcycle. The defendant later married the plaintiff and provided her with nursing care. Rejecting as a fiction the idea in *Donnelly v Joyce* that the loss represented by the nursing expenses is really the plaintiff's loss, the House of Lords preferred to say that such sums are paid for the benefit of those providing the gratuitous services, and not for the benefit of the plaintiff at all. Unfortunately, the House of Lords went on to hold that *because* the loss is really that of the carer rather than of the plaintiff, *therefore* there could be no claim for such amounts *where the defendant is also the care-giver*; because this would require the defendant to bear the cost of the care twice—once by offering the services, and then again by paying for them:

Lord Bridge, *Hunt v Severs* [1994] 2 AC 350, at 363

By concentrating on the plaintiff's need and the plaintiff's loss as the basis of an award in respect of voluntary care received by the plaintiff, the reasoning in *Donnelly v. Joyce* diverts attention from the award's central objective of compensating the voluntary carer. Once this is recognised it becomes evident that there can be no ground in public policy or otherwise for requiring the tortfeasor to pay to the plaintiff, in respect of the services which he himself has rendered, a sum of money which the plaintiff must then repay to him. If the present case had been brought in Scotland and the claim in respect of the tortfeasor's services made in reliance on section 8 of the Administration of Justice Act 1982, it would have been immediately obvious that such a claim was not sustainable.

The case for the plaintiff was argued in the Court of Appeal without reference to the circumstance that the defendant's liability was covered by insurance. But before your Lordships Mr. McGregor, recognising the difficulty of formulating any principle of public policy which could justify recovery against the tortfeasor who has to pay out of his own pocket, advanced the bold proposition that such a policy could be founded on the liability of insurers to meet the claim. Exploration of the implications of this proposition in argument revealed the many difficulties which it encounters. But I do not think it necessary to examine these in detail. The short answer, in my judgment, to Mr. McGregor's contention is that its acceptance would represent a novel and radical departure in the law of a kind which only the legislature may properly effect. At common law the circumstance that a defendant is contractually indemnified by a third party against a particular legal liability can have no relevance whatever to the measure of that liability.

This reasoning is very selective about which consequences of an award of damages may be considered. The very point of the claim for care offered by the defendant was that he could then be reimbursed by his liability insurer. To hold that it would be *unfair* to such a defendant to require him to pay 'twice' is wholly inappropriate.

Lord Bridge's point in the final paragraph is, essentially, that courts should not distinguish between individual cases depending on whether the *particular* defendant is or is not insured. The existence of an insurance policy should not be a decisive factor. But this misses the point that claims of this sort simply would not be brought unless liability insurance was in place. What benefit could there otherwise be in bringing the claim?[14]

The Law Commission in its Consultation Paper on *Damages for Personal Injury: Medical, Nursing and Other Expenses* (Consultation Paper No 144, 1996) took the view that legislation should reverse the effect of *Hunt v Severs*, but at the same time accepted the House of Lords' decision to ignore the insurance position of the defendant:

3.65 . . . Although the existence of insurance was a vital part of the factual picture, and indeed litigation would scarcely have made sense if the defendant had not been insured against such liability, we do not consider that the existence of insurance should be permitted to affect liability. We believe that the question of the defendant's liability must necessarily precede the one of the defendant's insurer's liability.

---

[14] See L. Hoyano, 'The Dutiful Tortfeasor in the House of Lords' [1995] *Tort L Rev* 63.

This argument might have been acceptable (though not especially persuasive), had the House of Lords in *Hunt v Severs* not made an exception to general principle precisely in order to avoid unfairness to the defendant. Decisions as to 'fairness' in particular should surely not be made without reference to the consequences of the decision for the parties concerned.

Local authority care

Earlier in this chapter, we explained that claimants need not use NHS medical services, but are entitled to choose private medical care, and to claim an amount in respect of this care from the defendant: Law Reform (Personal Injuries Act) 1948, s 2. No equivalent provision exists in respect of care provided by a local authority. Given that local authorities are in many cases under a statutory obligation to provide such care, or indeed to provide direct financial assistance, the question arises of whether the claimant is obliged to depend upon this care, and whether he or she may claim for the costs of future *private* provision.

The Court of Appeal has recently held that the answer depends on whether the private care costs claimed are 'reasonable', and that this in turn depends upon the facts of each individual case. An alternative is to take into account the care which will be provided by the local authority pursuant to its statutory duties, but to award a 'top up' amount, if it is felt that this is reasonably needed to meet the claimant's needs: *Sowden v Lodge; Crookdale v Drury* [2005] 1 WLR 2129. Longmore LJ explained that if claimants generally were permitted to claim for private care for the rest of their lives, claims would tend to be 'astronomically high' (at para [90]).

2.6 DEDUCTIONS

The principle of 100 per cent compensation cuts both ways. The common law does not allow recovery, under the head of compensatory damages, of more than has been lost. Therefore, deductions from the damages award will be made to reflect benefits received. However, certain benefits are not deducted in this way. These are payments from first party insurance policies where premiums were paid by the claimant; and 'benevolent' payments from third parties.

In principle, any deductions to reflect benefits received will be made *only* on a 'like for like' basis. If there is a benefit in the nature of *income*, then it will be deducted only from the amount awarded for *loss of earnings*. As such, in a case where there is no pecuniary loss and the award is entirely made up of damages for non-pecuniary losses, then there will be no deduction on account of financial benefits. No 'double recovery' arises in such a case.

Deductions in Respect of 'Lost Earnings'

Some examples of the principle against double recovery in respect of lost earnings are as follows:

- In *Hussain v New Taplow Mills* (1988) AC 514, a deduction from lost earnings was made in respect of *statutory sick pay*.
- In general, a contributory pension will *not* be set off against the award of damages for lost earnings (*Parry v Cleaver* [1969] 1 All ER 555), *even if* the defendant (generally an employer) also contributed to the pension (*Smoker v London Fire and Defence Civil Authority* [1991] 2 AC 502). However, a disablement pension will be set off against the

part of the award which compensates for loss of pension, rather than earnings (*Longden v British Coal Corporation* [1997] 3 WLR 1336).

- By section 5 of the Administration of Justice Act 1982, a claimant who is maintained at public expense will be susceptible to a deduction from damages *if and to the extent that this leads to reduced living expenses*. For example, they may no longer have to pay rent, or 'board and lodgings'.

The 'Thrift or Gift' Exceptions

Two established exceptions to the rule that benefits should be deducted from relevant heads of damage relate to:

(a) insurance ('thrift') and

(b) benevolence ('gift').

The general thinking is that it is not appropriate for the defendant to gain the benefit of the claimant's thrift and prudence, or of the good motives of third parties.

The Insurance Exception

Lord Reid, *Parry v Cleaver* [1970] AC 1 14   *C's damages will not be reduced due to his insurance payouts*

As regards moneys coming to the plaintiff under a contract of insurance, I think that the real and substantial reason for disregarding them is that the plaintiff has bought them and that it would be unjust and unreasonable to hold that the money which he prudently spent on premiums and the benefit from it should enure to the benefit of the tortfeasor.

The Benevolence Exception

Lord Reid, *Parry v Cleaver*, at 14

It would be revolting to the ordinary man's sense of justice, and therefore contrary to public policy, that the sufferer should have his damages reduced so that he would gain nothing from the benevolence of his friends or relations or of the public at large.

This thinking has not been broadened and indeed the reasoning in recent cases could be extended to challenge the exceptions themselves.

Hodgson v Trapp [1989] AC 807

The plaintiff sustained injuries in a road traffic accident for which the defendants admitted liability. As a result, she was wholly and permanently dependent on the care of others. The defendants argued that her award should be reduced to take account of statutory care and mobility allowances received. These social security benefits relate to elements of the claimant's *care*.

The plaintiff argued that the allowances should be disregarded, since social welfare benefits of this nature were akin to 'benevolent' payments made out of altruistic motives. The House of Lords rejected the 'benevolence' interpretation, and held that the allowances were deductible.

Note: the effect of Hodgson v Trapp *has been modified by the Social Security (Recovery of Benefits) Act 1997. Now, relevant benefits listed in the Act are deducted for a maximum of five years, and the amount deducted is repaid to the state by the party paying compensation. See Section 6 of this chapter.* Hodgson v Trapp *is still an important authority because common law continues to govern any benefits not listed within the statutory provisions.*

In the following short extract, Lord Bridge elaborates on the general reasons for deductions of this nature. The deductions are of course compatible with the 100 per cent principle, but importantly, he also calls attention to the broader economic context of tort damages.

Lord Bridge, at 823

In the end the issue in these cases is not so much one of statutory construction as of public policy. If we have regard to the realities, awards of damages for personal injuries are met from the insurance premiums payable by motorists, employers, occupiers of property, professional men and others. Statutory benefits payable to those in need by reason of impecuniosity or disability are met by the taxpayer. In this context to ask whether the taxpayer, as the "benevolent donor," intends to benefit "the wrongdoer" as represented by the insurer who meets the claim at the expense of the appropriate class of policy holders, seems to me entirely artificial. There could hardly be a clearer case than that of the attendance allowance payable under section 35 of the Act of 1975[15] where the statutory benefit and the special damages claimed for cost of care are designed to meet the identical expenses. To allow double recovery in such a case at the expense of both taxpayers and insurers seems to me incapable of justification on any rational ground. It could only add to the enormous disparity, to which the advocates of a "no-fault" system of compensation constantly draw attention, between the position of those who are able to establish a third party's fault as the cause of their injury and the position of those who are not.

Lord Bridge's comments here are thought-provoking. In particular:

(a) By extension to the general justification of the 'thrift' exception, why should the defendant in this sort of case be entitled to pay less simply because the state has stepped in with some support? Lord Bridge's answer is that most of us pay or contribute to insurance premiums, so that ultimately, it is the ordinary person who would have to pay twice if there was no deduction from damages in these cases—once through insurance, and once through tax.

(b) Since (as Lord Bridge observes) most damages are paid by insurance companies, is it still appropriate to make awards which are recognized to exceed 100 per cent compensation,[16] in order to avoid benefiting tortfeasors? Those tortfeasors are not very likely to have to pay damages themselves. In certain other areas, there is a deliberate policy of

---

[15] Social Security Act 1975.
[16] Because the claimant has not in fact 'lost' all the sums repaid as a consequence of the tort.

minimizing the cost of compensation, even if this is not of benefit to the claimant, or to the Exchequer.[17]

Like *Hodgson v Trapp*, the more recent case of *Gaca v Pirelli* [2004] 1 WLR 2683 also declined to extend the recognized thrift or gift exceptions. The Court of Appeal held that payments which essentially amounted to part of the employment package offered to the claimant, and which were made through insurance *funded by the tortfeasor*, did not fall within the 'gift' or 'benevolence' exception. Nor did they fall within the insurance exception. The claimant had not paid the premiums himself, so that it was the *tortfeasor's* thrift and prudence, not the claimant's, which enabled the insurance payments to be made.

2.7 NON-PECUNIARY LOSSES IN PERSONAL INJURY CASES

'Non-pecuniary losses' suffered in a personal injury case may be divided into two main categories:

(a) pain and suffering

(b) loss of amenity.

In practice, a single award for 'general damages' will be made covering both of these forms of loss, without itemisation between them. Both come close to being purely 'conventional' sums, within a range set out in guidelines from the Judicial Studies Board. In *principle*, the two forms of non-pecuniary loss are rather different. Pain and suffering is supposedly assessed subjectively (how much has the claimant suffered?); 'loss of amenity' is partly objective, so that the award is made *for the fact of loss*, rather than for the experience of loss. The true test of this comes in cases where the claimant is so severely injured that she or he has no awareness of their loss, still less of the award of damages which is supposed to 'make it good'.

West v Shephard [1964] AC 326

The plaintiff sustained very severe injuries in a road traffic accident caused through the negligence of an employee of the defendant. She may or may not have been able to appreciate the condition she was in. Given that she suffered severe mental impairment and was unable to understand very much if anything that was said to her, she would have no awareness of the award of damages itself. In the face of a strong dissent by Lord Reid, the House of Lords held that substantial damages might be awarded for loss of amenity to a plaintiff who is unable to appreciate the award—and, indeed, even to a plaintiff who is unconscious.

The result in *West v Shephard* was confirmed by the House of Lords in *Lim Poh Choo* v *Camden and Islington Area Health Authority* [1980] AC 174. The claimant here suffered a cardiac arrest when undergoing minor surgery and was left with very severe injuries. She was barely sentient and then only intermittently so. The House of Lords upheld an award of £20,000 for pain, suffering, and loss of amenity, as part of a much larger award including substantial sums for lost earnings and future care costs.

---

[17] Legislation now allows a court to impose an award in the form of periodical payments. The key advantage of these to insurers is that the payments are tax free in the hands of the claimant, so that the defendant need not reimburse the claimant for tax due.

Some of the fiercer arguments concerning tort law are conducted over non-pecuniary losses, and the decision in *West v Shephard* serves to fuel these arguments. While the '100 per cent principle' clearly requires the court to attempt to quantify pain, suffering, and loss of amenity, it has been argued that these heads of damages are entirely wasteful in a case like *West v Shephard*, and not necessarily justified even in a more typical case. While general damages will usually amount to a small proportion of the damages awarded to a seriously injured claimant, in a small claim general damages may even be the major component of the award. Are tort damages being appropriately targeted?

In its Report on *Damages for Non-Pecuniary Loss* (Report No 257, 1999), the Law Commission proposed that the level of awards for loss of amenity and pain and suffering should be increased considerably. Awards of £3,000 should be increased by 50–100 per cent, and smaller claims over £2,000 should be subject to a tapered increase. Their thinking on this was heavily based on certain empirical studies, and on responses to the Commission's Consultation Paper. One of the empirical studies was commissioned by the Law Commission itself and carried out by the Office of National Statistics. It sought public opinion on whether damages awards for pain, suffering, and loss of amenity should be increased, and sought to improve the validity of the responses by spelling out to respondents the likely consequence for insurance premiums.

In *Heil v Rankin* [2001] QB 272, the Court of Appeal considered the Law Commission Report, but declined to follow its recommendations. The Court did take the important step of recommending a significant increase in the damages to be awarded for pain, suffering and loss of amenity,[18] but did so only for the more serious cases, defined as awards of over £10,000. These increases should be tapered to a maximum of one third for 'the most catastrophic' injuries. To the relief of the insurance industry, there would be no increase at all for awards of less than £10,000, which make up the majority of tort claims. The Court of Appeal evidently considered the award of general damages to have a serious role to play in compensation awards. But it doubted the frame of reference employed in the Law Commission Report and pointed out, for example, that the research did not explicitly build in the impact on NHS funding. This of course is more indirect than the immediate impact on insurance premiums, and it is of interest that the Court of Appeal mentioned this element of the broader picture.

Heil v Rankin (as well as the Law Commission Report which preceded it) has offered an opportunity for some deeper criticism of the role of non-pecuniary damages.

Richard Lewis, 'Increasing the Price of Pain' (2001) 64 MLR 100, at 107

. . . let us consider questions which people might have been asked if a wider perspective on tort had been taken. These questions explicitly deal with relative priorities for expenditure. The likely responses to these questions are no less predictable than those asking whether victims should get more money, bit they carry very different implications for the future of damages for non-pecuniary loss. The first question begins by explaining that more than two-thirds of accident victims who are so seriously injured that they are unable to work for more than six months are unable to claim any damages at all and, instead, must rely on social security benefits. The remaining third are able to claim not only for their full financial loss but also for their pain and suffering. The question then to ask is: 'When allocating further resources to

---

[18] It should be pointed out that this was an *additional* increase above the level of the Retail Price Index.

accident victims, should more money be spent on those already able to claim damages by giving them more for their pain and suffering?'

Similarly, a second question, although taking a narrower focus, could still attack the priority now given to PSLA.[19] It asks people to place in order of importance the losses which they might choose to insure themselves against if they were to take out a policy against being involved in an accident causing personal injury. Which would they regard as the most important loss to insure against: an interruption in earnings; the cost of medical and other care; or PSLA? . . . . It is clear that those who are knowledgeable about the risks of accident or illness, and seek policies to protect themselves against such eventualities, do not wish to pay much higher premiums for a type of loss for which money cannot easily provide a substitute. If it were left to market forces there would be no cover for PSLA. . . .

The second of the 'alternative questions' proposed by Lewis recalls a hypothetical scenario used by P. S. Atiyah in his essay, 'Personal Injuries in the Twenty First Century: Thinking the Unthinkable' in Birks (ed.), *Wrongs and Remedies in the Twenty-First Century* (OUP, 1996).[20] Atiyah proposed that, if an insurance salesman were to try to sell the tort system door to door, he would have very few takers for the 'policy' it offers, given its costs. Its coverage is far too patchy, leaving the majority of accident victims uncompensated chiefly because of its dependence on showing fault, and providing very expensive benefits only to a lucky few. Atiyah's argument is that it is wrong to force people to pay for a level of 'insurance cover' that they would not buy if left to their own devices—*particularly* if that cover is so full of holes that there is only a 33 per cent chance of recovering under the policy. On this view, the costs of tort law are accepted by the general public only because they are hidden. If we contracted into tort law and were able to select available benefits, we would not choose to pay for non-pecuniary awards.

3. DEATH AND DAMAGES: WHERE THE INJURED PARTY DIES

At common law, causes of action were treated as personal. Where death was concerned, this had two important consequences. First, the death of either party extinguished a civil claim. Second, death could not give rise to a right of action for the benefit of others. In both respects, the position has been reformed by statute.

In this section, we consider the relevant issues in three stages:

1. In what circumstances does a civil claim survive the death of the victim of the tort? The answer to this question is governed by the Law Reform (Miscellaneous Provisions) Act 1934.

2. In what circumstances does causing death create a right of action? And who benefits from such an action? The answers to these questions are governed by the Fatal Accidents Act 1976.

---

[19] Pain, suffering, and loss of amenity.
[20] Discussed in J. Steele, *Risks and Legal Theory* (Hart Publishing, 2004), Chapter 2.

3. How do the two statutes mentioned above interact? Human rights issues have been said to arise in cases which fall between the two statutes, and where there is no civil claim in respect of wrongful death.

3.1 CLAIMS SURVIVING DEATH

Law Reform (Miscellaneous Provisions) Act 1934

1 Effect of death on certain causes of action[21]

(1) Subject to the provisions of this section, on the death of any person after the commencement of this Act all causes of action subsisting against or vested in him shall survive against, or, as the case may be, for the benefit of, his estate. Provided that this subsection shall not apply to causes of action for defamation . . .

[(1A) The right of a person to claim under section 1A of the Fatal Accidents Act 1976 (bereavement) shall not survive for the benefit of his estate on his death.]

(2) Where a cause of action survives as aforesaid for the benefit of the estate of a deceased person, the damages recoverable for the benefit of the estate of that person:—

    [(a) shall not include—

        (i) any exemplary damages;

        (ii) any damages for loss of income in respect of any period after that person's death;]

    (b) . . .

    (c) where the death of that person has been caused by the act or omission which gives rise to the cause of action, shall be calculated without reference to any loss or gain to his estate consequent on his death, except that a sum in respect of funeral expenses may be included.

(4) Where damage has been suffered by reason of any act or omission in respect of which a cause of action would have subsisted against any person if that person had not died before or at the same time as the damage was suffered, there shall be deemed, for the purposes of this Act, to have been subsisting against him before his death such cause of action in respect of that act or omission as would have subsisted if he had died after the damage was suffered.

(5) The rights conferred by this Act for the benefit of the estates of deceased persons shall be in addition to and not in derogation of any rights conferred on the dependants of deceased persons by [the Fatal Accidents Act 1976 . . .] and so much of this Act as relates to causes of action against the estates of deceased persons shall apply in relation to causes of action under the said Acts as it applies in relation to other causes of action not expressly excepted from the operation of subsection (1) of this section.

(6) In the event of the insolvency of the estate against which proceedings are maintainable by virtue of this section, any liability in respect of the cause of action in respect of which the proceedings are maintainable shall be deemed to be a debt provable in the administration of the estate . . .

---

[21] Ss 1A and 1(2)(a) were inserted and substituted (respectively) by the Administration of Justice Act 1982.

Section 1(4) is confusing at first sight, but it deals with two important situations. First, not uncommonly—for example in a road traffic accident—the tortfeasor dies as a result of his own tort, 'before or at the same time as' the injury to the claimant. Second, harm to the victim may be delayed, and the tortfeasor may die (possibly for entirely unrelated reasons) before the cause of action accrues. In both situations, section 1(4) ensures that the action arises notwithstanding the death of the tortfeasor, even if it did not accrue before his or her death.

The statute applies to all causes of action in tort except defamation, and is not confined to personal injury. In defamation claims, it remains the case that the death of either party extinguishes the claim.

The effect of this statute is that a claim which has accrued before death will survive for the benefit of the estate of the deceased victim, subject to a few exclusions. Any reduction in damages on account of contributory negligence will also apply to a claim brought by the estate.

Recoverable Damages

There are certain important exclusions from the damages recoverable under the 1934 Act. Exemplary damages (which are 'punitive' rather than compensatory) may not be claimed after the death of either party. Section 1(2)(c) provides that no loss to the *estate* of the deceased may be claimed under the Act, with the exception of a sum for funeral expenses. This is to avoid duplication with the Fatal Accidents Acts, which confer certain rights of action upon dependants in their own right. On the other hand, some losses now (as a matter of legislative policy) fall between the Acts and are not the subject of compensation under either. We will address the interaction of the two statutes below.

In our account of compensatory damages for personal injury, we considered *Pickett v British Engineering Ltd* [1980] AC 136, and the decision that a claimant could recover damages for income that would have been earned in the 'lost years', if his life expectancy was cut short. In *Gammell v Wilson* [1982] AC 27, the House of Lords held that such a claim for income in 'the lost years' survived under the 1934 Act for the benefit of the estate, as it accrues before the claimant's death. The new section 1(2)(a)(ii), inserted by Administration of Justice Act 1982, section 4, reversed the effect of *Gammell v Wilson*, in order to avoid double recovery by dependants via the Fatal Accidents Act 1976 (for loss of dependancy) and the 1934 Act (through the survival of the action).

The Administration of Justice Act 1982 also abolished recovery of damages for 'loss of expectation of life' in its own right. But it provided that general damages for pain and suffering awarded to a claimant may be increased if awareness of reduced life expectancy added to the claimant's suffering.

Administration of Justice Act 1982

1   Abolition of right to damages for loss of expectation of life

(1) In an action under the law of England and Wales or the law of Northern Ireland for damages for personal injuries—

    (a) no damages shall be recoverable in respect of any loss of expectation of life caused to the injured person by the injuries; but

(b) if the injured person's expectation of life has been reduced by the injuries, the court, in assessing damages in respect of pain and suffering caused or likely to be caused to him by awareness that his expectation of life has been so reduced.

(2) The reference in subsection 1(a) above to damages in respect of loss of expectation of life does not include damages in respect of loss of income.

The interaction of this section with the provisions of the 1934 Act is considered in the following case.

Hicks v Chief Constable South Yorkshire Police [1992] 2 All ER 65

Lord Bridge of Harwich

My Lords, the appellants are the parents of two girls, Sarah and Victoria Hicks, who died in the disaster at Hillsborough Football Stadium on 15 April 1989 when they were respectively 19 and 15 years of age. In this action they claim damages under the Law Reform (Miscellaneous Provisions) Act 1934 for the benefit of the estate of each daughter of which they are in each case the administrators. The respondent is the Chief Constable of the South Yorkshire Police who does not contest his liability to persons who suffered damage in the disaster. The basis of the claim advanced here is that at the moment of death Sarah and Victoria each had an accrued cause of action for injuries suffered prior to death which survived for the benefit of their respective estates. The action was tried by Hidden J who held that the plaintiffs had failed to prove that either girl suffered before death any injury for which damages fell to be awarded. His decision was affirmed by the Court of Appeal (Parker, Stocker and Nolan LJJ) (see [1992] 1 All ER 690). Appeal is now brought to your Lordships' House by leave of the Court of Appeal.

. . .

The difficulty which immediately confronts the appellants in this House is that the question what injuries Sarah and Victoria suffered before death was purely one of fact and Hidden J's conclusion on the evidence that the plaintiffs had failed to discharge the onus of proving any such injury sufficient to attract an award of damages was a finding of fact affirmed by the Court of Appeal. The appellants must therefore pursuade your Lordships to reverse those concurrent findings if they are to succeed . . .

The evidence here showed that both girls died from traumatic asphyxia. . . . Medical evidence which the judge accepted was to the effect that in cases of death from traumatic asphyxia caused by crushing the victim would lose consciousness within a matter of seconds from the crushing of the chest which cut off the ability to breathe and would die within five minutes. There was no indication in the post mortem reports on either girl of physical injuries attributable to anything other than the fatal crushing which caused the asphyxia, save, in the case of Sarah, some superficial bruising which, on the evidence, could have occurred either before or after loss of consciousness. Hidden J was not satisfied that any physical injury had been sustained before what he described as the 'swift and sudden [death] as shown by the medical evidence'. Unless the law were to distinguish between death within seconds of injury and unconsciousness within seconds of injury followed by death within minutes, which I do not understand to be suggested, these findings, as Hidden J himself said 'with regret', made it impossible for him to award any damages.

Mr Hytner sought to persuade your Lordships, as he sought to persuade the Court of Appeal, that on the whole of the evidence the judge ought to have found on a balance of probabilities that there was a gradual build-up of pressure on the bodies of the two girls causing increasing breathlessness, discomfort and pain from which they suffered for some 20 minutes before the final crushing injury which produced unconsciousness. This should have led, he submitted, to the conclusion that they sustained injuries which caused considerable pain and suffering while they were still conscious and which should attract a substantial award of damages. The Court of Appeal, in a judgment delivered by Parker LJ with which both Stocker and Nolan LJJ agreed, carefully reviewed the evidence and concluded, in agreement with Hidden J, that it did not establish that any physical injury was caused before the fatal crushing injury. I do not intend myself to embark on a detailed review of the evidence. In the circumstances I think it sufficient to say that, in my opinion, the conclusion of fact reached by Hidden J and the Court of Appeal was fairly open to them and it is impossible to say that they were wrong.

A good deal of argument in the courts below and before your Lordships was addressed to the question whether damages for physical injuries should be increased on account of the terrifying circumstances in which they were inflicted. This may depend on difficult questions of causation. But on the facts found in this case the question does not arise for decision. It is perfectly clear law that fear by itself, of whatever degree, is a normal human emotion for which no damages can be awarded. Those trapped in the crush at Hillsborough who were fortunate enough to escape without injury have no claim in respect of the distress they suffered in what must have been a truly terrifying experience. It follows that fear of impending death felt by the victim of a fatal injury before that injury is inflicted cannot by itself give rise to a cause of action which survives for the benefit of the victim's estate.

The premise of this decision is that fear of death—or knowledge of shortened life expectancy—can only justify an *increase* in damages for pain and suffering (under section 1(1)(b) of the Administration of Justice Act 1982) if there is a claim for pain and suffering in the first place. Fear itself cannot be the basis of a claim for damages. Given the terms of section 1(1)(b), there is little scope to argue with this aspect of the decision. More controversial is the idea that pain endured only for a few seconds, before unconsciousness intervenes, is *not sufficient* to give rise to an action in damages. Given this interpretation, no cause of action on the part of the daughters had accrued before their deaths, so that the only damage recoverable under the Law Reform (Miscellaneous Provisions) Act 1934 was the cost of funeral expenses. Although there is some scope for disagreement with this second stage in the reasoning, it is nevertheless quite logical and is probably designed to avoid closely picking over the circumstances of death, to determine exactly how much the deceased 'suffered'. So why does the decision in *Hicks* seem intuitively unjust?

Arguably, the action brought by the plaintiffs in this case is artificial in any event. Their real complaint perhaps is that the defendant, through negligence, caused the death of their daughters. If so, the action would be better regarded as an action for bereavement, which is not an action that 'survives' the victim's death for the benefit of his or her estate; it is an action on the part of the relatives themselves, arising from the death of a loved one. As such, it is governed by the Fatal Accidents Act 1976 (below). In truth then, it may be the limited size and recoverability of bereavement damages which chiefly causes the sense of injustice arising out of *Hicks*. Bereavement damages are low because they do not truly attempt to compensate for the loss suffered. 'Real' compensation would be simply impossible. At the same time, they are not available at all in respect of certain deaths. Even parents can only claim bereavement damages in respect of a minor child, and the older daughter in this case was, at 19, not a minor. Here we come across the counter-intuitive result that it is often cheaper to kill a person through tortious conduct than to cause them significant injury (particularly so if they have no dependants, as defined below).

The problem of deaths which give rise to no liability has recently emerged as a human rights issue. We return to this issue after consideration of the Fatal Accidents Act 1976, since it involves cases which fall between the two statutes.

3.2 CLAIMS FOR THE DEATH OF ANOTHER

By the Fatal Accidents Act 1976, two distinct actions are defined in respect of the death of another.

- Section 1 defines a cause of action on the part of 'dependants' of the deceased (a category defined in the section), for **loss of dependency**. Loss of dependency is essentially pecuniary in nature.
- Section 1A defines a cause of action for **bereavement**. Bereavement is non-pecuniary in nature, and the damages available are set at a conventional sum of (for the time being) £10,000. Only those people listed in section 1A have the benefit of a claim for bereavement.

The parties with a cause of action for loss of dependency under section 1 will not necessarily have a cause of action for bereavement under section 1A, and vice versa. They are separately defined.

Section 1: Dependency Damages

Fatal Accidents Act 1976

1 Right of action for wrongful act causing death[22]

(1) If death is caused by any wrongful act, neglect or default which is such as would (if death had not ensued) have entitled the person injured to maintain an action and recover damages in respect thereof, the person who would have been liable if death had not ensued shall be liable to an action for damages, notwithstanding the death of the person injured.

(2) Subject to section 1A(2) below, every such action shall be for the benefit of the dependants of the person ("the deceased") whose death has been so caused.

(3) In this Act "dependant" means—

(a) the wife or husband or former wife or husband of the deceased;

[(a)(a) the civil partner or former civil partner of the deceased;][23]

(b) any person who—

(i) was living with the deceased in the same household immediately before the date of the death; and

---

[22] This section was substituted by the Administration of Justice Act 1982, s 3.
[23] This subsection and ss 1(2)(fa) and 1(4A) inserted by the Civil Partnership Act 2004.

    (ii) had been living with the deceased in the same household for at least two years before that date; and

    (iii) was living during the whole of that period as the husband or wife of the deceased;

(c) any parent or other ascendant of the deceased;

(d) any person who was treated by the deceased as his parent;

(e) any child or other descendant of the deceased;

(f) any person (not being a child of the deceased) who, in the case of any marriage to which the deceased was at any time a party, was treated by the deceased as a child of the family in relation to that marriage;

[(fa) any person (not being a child of the deceased) who, in the case of any civil partnership in which the deceased was at any time a civil partner, was treated by the deceased as a child of the family in relation to that civil partnership]

(g) any person who is, or is the issue of, a brother, sister, uncle or aunt of the deceased.

(4) The reference to the former wife or husband of the deceased in subsection (3)(a) above includes a reference to a person whose marriage to the deceased has been annulled or declared void as well as a person whose marriage to the deceased has been dissolved.

[(4A) The reference to the former civil partner of the deceased in subsection (3)(aa) above includes a reference to a person whose civil partnership with the deceased has been annulled as well as a person whose civil partnership with the deceased has been dissolved.]

(5) In deducing any relationship for the purposes of subsection (3) above—

(a) any relationship by affinity shall be treated as a relationship by consanguinity, any relationship of the half blood as a relationship of the whole blood, and the stepchild of any person as his child, and

(b) an illegitimate person shall be treated as the legitimate child of his mother and reputed father.

(6) Any reference in this Act to injury includes any disease and any impairment of a person's physical or mental condition.

Section 1A: Bereavement Damages

1A Bereavement[24]

(1) An action under this Act may consist of or include a claim for damages for bereavement.

(2) A claim for damages for bereavement shall only be for the benefit—

(a) of the wife or husband [or civil partner] of the deceased; and

(b) where the deceased was a minor who was never married [or a civil partner]—

    (i) of his parents, if he was legitimate; and

    (ii) of his mother, if he was illegitimate.

---

[24] Amended by the Civil Partnership Act 2004.

(3) Subject to subject (5) below, the sum to be awarded as damages under this section shall be [£10,000].

(4) Where there is a claim for damages under this section for the benefit of both the parents of the deceased, the sum awarded shall be divided equally between them (subject to any deduction falling to be made in respect of costs not recovered from the defendant).

(5) The Lord Chancellor may by order made by statutory instrument, subject to annulment in pursuance of a resolution of either House of Parliament, amend this section by varying the sum for the time being specified in subsection (3) above.

It will be apparent that an extremely limited range of people is entitled to bereavement damages. If an unmarried adult, without a civil partner, is killed, and has no children, then there is often no person who can claim bereavement damages. Not even the parent of an adult, or a cohabitant unless they have lived with the deceased for over two years, may claim such damages.

It will also be apparent that bereavement damages are rather low. They represent a conventional sum, which may be described as compensatory only in a limited sense.

Issues Arising in Respect of Dependency Damages

Relationship between the section 1 claim, and a claim by the deceased

The action arising under section 1 is an action on the part of dependants in their own right, but by section 1(1) the action will exist only if the deceased, had he or she been injured rather than killed, could have brought an action. A number of issues flow from this.

1. If the claim of the deceased was *time-barred* under the applicable Limitation Act at the time of their death, then the dependants have no action. However, provided the claim is not time-barred at the date of death, the dependants have three years from the death in which to bring a claim (Limitation Act 1980, section 12(2)). In determining whether a claim by the deceased would have been time-barred, it is possible to invoke the statutory discretion under Limitation Act 1980, section 33, provided the cause of action would be one to which that section applies.[25]

2. It is expressly provided by section 5 of the Fatal Accidents Act 1976 that if damages payable to the deceased would in the circumstances have been reduced by reason of contributory negligence, any damages payable under the Act will also fall to be reduced in the same way.

3. Particular problems arise where more than one tortfeasor is potentially liable for the harm suffered, and the deceased person has settled their claim against one of those parties.

Jameson v CEGB [2000] 1 AC 455

A few days before his death from malignant mesothelioma, J agreed to accept a payment of £80,000 from his former employer B, in 'full and final settlement and satisfaction of all the causes of action in respect of which the plaintiff claimed in the statement of claim'.

---

[25] For example, s 33 does not apply to battery, but it does apply to negligence. See Chapter 7.

The full value of the claim was much greater than £80,000. After J's death, his widow commenced proceedings under Fatal Accidents Act 1976, section 1 against another former employer, the defendant in this action.

The two employers, the defendant and B, were 'concurrent tortfeasors'. They had committed separate torts, but were each potentially liable in full for the same indivisible damage to which they were to be treated as having made a material contribution.[26] By section 4 of the Fatal Accidents Act 1976, the plaintiff if she had succeeded in her action would not have had to account for the benefit that she gained, via her husband's estate, from his settlement of the claim against B:

4   Assessment of damages; disregard of benefits

In assessing damages in respect of a person's death in an action under this Act, benefits which have accrued or will or may accrue to any person from his estate or otherwise as a result of his death shall be disregarded.

There was a chance of over-compensation.

Furthermore, because the two employers were potentially liable *in respect of the same damage*, the provisions of the Civil Liability (Contribution) Act 1978 would apply.[27] The defendant, if found liable to the claimant, could claim a contribution from B, who had already settled the claim (admittedly below its full value) against the deceased.[28]

The House of Lords decided that the widow could not satisfy the terms of section 1(1) of the Fatal Accidents Act 1976, requiring that the deceased would have had a claim against the defendant had he not died. He would not have had such a claim, because he had settled his claim in full against B. His hypothetical claim against the defendant was thus precluded. This was *not* however because the terms of the settlement with B in any sense 'bound' the deceased not to pursue another tortfeasor—such as the defendant—in separate proceedings. The agreement made no mention of any other tortfeasor. Rather, it was because the deceased's claim for damages was *treated* as having been satisfied in full, even though the full *value* of the claim had clearly not been received.

Lord Hope, *Jameson v CEGB*, at 473

. . . The causes of action [against concurrent tortfeasors] are indeed separate. And it is clear that an agreement reached between the plaintiff and one concurrent tortfeasor cannot extinguish the plaintiff's claim against the other concurrent tortfeasor if his claim for damages has still not been satisfied. The critical question . . . is whether the claim has in fact been satisfied.

---

[26] See Chapter 7.

[27] S 1(1) of the Civil Liability (Contribution) Act 1978, explained in Chapter 7.

[28] It is not clear what a court would do if a widow succeeded in such an action, so that contribution between the two tortfeasors fell to be decided. As we explained in Chapter 7, the factors which can be considered by a court in making the apportionment are not limited to those which are causative of the harm suffered. In principle, the fact that B had already paid a sum to the deceased could therefore be taken into account; what is less clear is *how* this factor ought to be treated in proceedings between tortfeasors in a case where there is an element of double compensation. Which party should bear the cost of the double compensation element? This problem is not insurmountable, since the court could decide to share the double compensation element (which is after all a creation of statute) equitably between the tortfeasors.

I think that the answer to it will be found by examining the terms of the agreement and comparing it with what has been claimed. The significance of the agreement is to be found in the effect which the parties intended to give to it. The fact that it has been entered into by way of a compromise in order to conclude a settlement forms part of the background. But the extent of the element of compromise will vary from case to case. The scope for litigation may have been reduced by agreement, for example on the question of liability. There may be little room for dispute as to the amount which a judge would award as damages. So one cannot assume that the figure which the parties are willing to accept is simply their assessment of the risks of litigation. The essential point is that the meaning which is to be given to the agreement will determine its effect.

A later House of Lords in *Heaton v Axa Equity and Law* [2002] UKHL 15; [2002] 2 WLR 1081 (which did not concern a claim under the Fatal Accidents Act) emphasized that *Jameson* laid down no *general* rule. It is not the case that a settlement against one tortfeasor necessarily precludes an action against another concurrent tortfeasor. The question in each case will be whether the claim has been satisfied in full by the settlement. In *Jameson*, it was the deceased's 'loss' which was treated as having been extinguished by the terms and intention of the agreement. In *Heaton*, Lord Bingham proposed that the proposition that '[a] sum accepted in settlement of such a claim may also fix the full measure of a claimant's loss' 'may perhaps have been stated a little too absolutely in *Jameson*' (Lord Bingham, *Heaton v Axa*, at para [8]).[29]

In fact, the reasoning in *Jameson* is none too convincing. It does not seem natural to argue that a settlement at a clear undervalue is intended by both parties to 'extinguish the loss', where there is another party against whom to proceed. After *Heaton*, the way is open for courts to interpret settlements in a less 'absolute' fashion.

Suicide

It is clear that an action for dependency damages may be available even if the deceased committed suicide, provided the usual criteria for liability (including remoteness of damage) are satisfied. In the tort of negligence at least, it may be asked whether the death is within the scope of the duty: *Reeves v Commissioner of Police for the Metropolis* [2000] 1 AC 360 (Chapter 3). In *Corr v IBC* [2006] EWCA Civ 331; (2006) 2 All ER 929 however, it sufficed that depression was a foreseeable result of a serious work injury. Where the deceased committed suicide as a result of his depression, dependency damages could be claimed, whether or not the suicide was foreseeable at the time of the negligence. Death was within the 'compensable damage' flowing from the injury.

Who may claim

Those individuals who may claim dependency damages are listed in section 1. Such a claim is generally brought on behalf of dependants by the executor or administrator of the estate, but the dependants may bring an action in their own right if the executor or administrator declines to do so, or fails to do so within six months of the death.

---

[29] Lord Hope, who gave the leading judgment in *Jameson*, agreed with Lord Bingham in *Heaton v Axa*.

Damages payable to dependants

The Act is fairly general in its outline of the damages that will be recoverable:

3 Assessment of damages

(2) In the action such damages, other than damages for bereavement, may be awarded as are proportioned to the injury resulting from the death to the dependants respectively.

. . .

The general principle is that damages should reflect *what each dependant has actually lost through the death of the deceased*. This process is highly fact-sensitive. The simplest approach is to calculate what income has been lost through the death, chiefly in the form of lost income but with deduction for the living expenses and other outlay that the deceased would have incurred, and then to share this between the dependants appropriately. This may involve complex calculation, since the court must arrive at a multiplier and multiplicand in respect of the deceased (what would have happened to the deceased but for the accident?), and must then assess the expectations of the various claimants. Would a spouse or partner, for example, have survived long enough to have the benefit of the deceased' pension? And at what age would a child cease to be maintained by a parent?

Where deductions are concerned, the law is more generous to those claiming dependency damages, than it is to those claiming in respect of injuries to themselves. By section 4 of the Fatal Accidents Act (extracted above in respect of *Jameson*), no account is to be taken of benefits accruing to the dependant as a consequence of the death. The case law on this point does not seem entirely consistent at the level of principle, and (like the assessment of damages) may fall to be explained chiefly on the basis of the precise facts of individual cases.

In *Auty v National Coal Board* (1985) 1 WLR 784 (CA), the claimant received widow's benefits from her husband's pension fund on his death. Subsequently, in an action under the Fatal Accidents Act, she was clearly able to claim in respect of sums her husband would have *earned* but for his death. There would be no deduction from this sum for the widow's benefits received: they came within section 4. However, she could not *also* claim, on the basis of lost dependency, for a widow's pension that she would have received if her husband had lived until retirement age, and then predeceased her. She was entitled to receive widow's benefits only once—*either* on the event of her husband's death in service (as was the case), *or* in the event of his death in retirement. The court reasoned that there was no 'loss of dependency' arising from the death in respect of the widow's benefits, because she had herself received the alternative payment at an earlier stage. There was no 'injury' within section 3.

Auty is hard to reconcile with the more recent case of *Harland and Wolff Plc v McIntyre* [2006] EWCA Civ 287. The claimant's husband died of mesothelioma through exposure to asbestos in breach of duty on the part of the appellants. When he became aware of his fatal cancer, he decided to return home and his employment was therefore terminated on grounds of ill health. At this stage he received a payment from the company's Provident Fund. Had he remained in employment, he would have received a payment from the same fund on his retirement. The Court of Appeal held that his widow could claim for loss of dependency in the form of the lost benefits on retirement, and that she did not have to account for the benefits received by the deceased on termination of employment. These fell to be disregarded, in accordance with section 4. *Auty* was distinguished because it was treated as being concerned with the widow's *own* benefits under the relevant scheme, and not (as here) with benefits paid to the deceased and accruing to the widow through his estate. There is no denying that in *Harland and Wolff*, the widow is allowed to receive substantially the same benefits twice over. But double counting is in some circumstances an inevitable result of section 4. The more difficult issue is how *Auty* can be satisfactorily explained in terms of the relevant statutory provisions.

Section 4 states that the amounts to be disregarded include *not only* benefits accruing through the estate of the deceased, but *also* benefits accruing *'otherwise as a result of [the] death'*. Widow's benefits clearly accrue as a result of the death. Certainly, they are benefits. On the face of it then, they should fall within section 4, and be discounted. The Court of Appeal in *Auty* argued that the widow had suffered no 'injury' within section 3 of the Act, which governs assessment of damages, so that the question of discounting did not arise. But this makes an important assumption about the priority of section 3 over section 4. It is suggested that the wording of section 4 suggests that this section, and not section 3, is intended to take priority: it states that in *assessing damages*, certain benefits *shall be disregarded*.

3.3 INTERACTION OF THE STATUTES—HUMAN RIGHTS AND UNCOMPENSATED DEATHS

The problem of uncompensated deaths, which we noted in respect of *Hicks*, has arisen as a human rights issue in more recent cases.

Bubbins v UK (2005) 41 EHRR 24 (ECHR)

The police were called to investigate a reported burglary at F's flat. F was drunk, and waved an artificial gun at the window. The police officers assumed that he was the reported burglar, that the gun was real, and that he was threatening them. A major operation was instigated and armed police were called. There was perceived to be an immediate threat and F was shot, dying instantly. Because he died instantly, the reasoning in *Hicks* (above) would apply. He would have had no claim before his death in respect of pain and suffering, so there was no action that could survive for his estate under the Law Reform (Miscellaneous Provisions) Act 1934, apart from the claim for funeral expenses. Because he also had no dependants for the purposes of section 1 of the FAA 1976, and there was no party who was qualified to receive bereavement damages under section 1A of that Act,[30] no other damages of any sort would be recoverable in respect of his death, even if the shooting would have amounted to a tort if he had been injured, rather than killed.

A Coroner's inquest was held. This inquest returned a verdict of lawful killing.

The European Court of Human Rights found that there was no violation of Article 2:

Article 2 Right to life

1. Everyone's right to life shall be protected by law. No one shall be deprived of his life intentionally save in the execution of a sentence of a court following his conviction of a crime for which this penalty is provided by law.

[30] The claimant was the brother of the deceased, and brothers do not qualify for bereavement damages under s 1A.

2. Deprivation of life shall not be regarded as inflicted in contravention of this article when it results from the use of force which is no more than absolutely necessary:

    a. in defence of any person from unlawful violence;

    b. in order to effect a lawful arrest or to prevent the escape of a person lawfully detained;

    c. in action lawfully taken for the purpose of quelling a riot or insurrection.

The individual police officer had honestly and reasonably believed that his actions were necessary, and in the light of the perceived risks the response was not disproportionate. The inquest, moreover, was an appropriate means of achieving a full investigation of the death.

Despite finding that Article 2 was not violated, the court awarded compensation in this case for a violation of Article 13. This calls for further explanation (if indeed it can be explained). First though it should be noted that the damages awarded were for non-pecuniary loss, in the amount of €10,000. As such, this decision in no way questions the *adequacy of the sum for bereavement damages* under the Fatal Accidents Act 1976, which is set rather higher than this, at £10,000. Rather, it calls into question the existence of cases where a wrongful death gives rise to no civil claim.

The greatest difficulty lies with the decision that there had been a violation of Article 13. Article 13 is in the following terms:

Article 13　Right to an effective remedy

Everyone whose rights and freedoms as set forth in this Convention are violated shall have an effective remedy before a national authority notwithstanding that the violation has been committed by persons acting in an official capacity.

Bubbins v UK (2005) 41 EHRR 24 (Opinion of the Court)

170. According to the Court's case-law, Article 13 applies only where an individual has an "arguable claim" to be the victim of a violation of a Convention right (see *Boyle and Rice v. the United Kingdom*, judgment of 27 April 1988, Series A no. 131, § 52, *Douglas-Williams v. the United Kingdom* (dec.), no. 56413/00, 8 January 2002). Although it has found that there has been no breach of Article 2 in this case, that does not prevent the applicant's complaint under that Article from being "arguable" for the purposes of Article 13 (see *Kaya*, cited above, § 107). It notes in this connection that although the inquest procedure provided in the circumstances an effective mechanism for subjecting the circumstances surrounding the killing of Michael Fitzgerald to public and searching scrutiny, and thereby satisfied the respondent State's procedural obligations under Article 2, no judicial determination has ever been made on the liability in damages, if any, of the police on account of the manner in which the incident was handled and concluded. It is true that the Coroner's jury returned a verdict of lawful killing at the close of the inquest. However, that finding cannot be taken to be dispositive of the issue of whether or not any civil liability attached to the police, a matter which has to be resolved in a different domestic fact-finding forum and according to different principles of law and in application of a different standard of proof. Moreover, the Court's own finding on the basis of the

materials before it that there has been no substantive breach of the right to life was reached in the light of the relevant principles derived from its case-law in this area, and in particular from the standpoint of the authorities' Convention liability (see paragraphs 134–136 above).

Neil Martin, *'Bubbins v United Kingdom:* Civil Remedies and the Right to Life' (2006) 69 MLR, 242–9

The court is stating that although the Government satisfied the procedural requirements under Art.2, it had an additional obligation under Art.13 to allow the arguable claim arising from the police operation to be tested in a civil action. The civil claim is arguable, in the eyes of the Court, as the operation did not minimise 'to the greatest extent possible any risk to the life of Michael Fitzgerald'. Therefore, it could be said that a domestic court, applying different substantive and procedural rules, might well have found that a domestic case for compensation had been proved. It is this failing to enable a substantive civil action to take place which leads to the violation of Art.13.

The Court required that there should be a civil claim to pursue, in addition to the Coroner's inquest which was properly conducted. But this is problematic, because Article 13 requires the payment of compensation where one of the other Convention rights or freedoms is violated. But the Court had already decided that the Coroner's inquest was sufficient investigation into whether Article 2 was violated, and had itself decided itself that there was no violation of Article 2 in the circumstances of the shooting.

The reasoning of the Court was criticized on this ground in the partial dissent of Judge Zagrebelsky.

Bubbins v UK (Partially Dissenting Opinion of Judge Zagrebelsky)

In paragraph 170 of the judgment, the Court considers that "although it has found that there has been no breach of Article 2 in this case, that does not prevent the applicant's complaint under that Article from being "arguable" for the purposes of Article 13" and quoted its *Kaya v. Turkey* judgment of 19 February 1998 (§107 thereof) in this connection. The *Kaya* case was, however, very different. In *Kaya* the Court considered that it had not been established beyond reasonable doubt that the deceased was indeed unlawfully killed as alleged and found a violation of Article 2 only under its procedural head on account of the failure of the authorities of the respondent State to conduct an effective investigation into the killing. In *Kaya* it was clear that the procedural obligations under Article 2 had not been fulfilled and, for that reason, the Court found also a violation of Article 13.

. . .

The Court in paragraph 171 recalls that "in the case of a breach of Articles 2 and 3 of the Convention, . . . , compensation for non-pecuniary damage flowing from the breach should, in principle, be available as part of the range of redress". We can then consider that a right to compensation arises from the violation of Article 2 and that this right is a Convention right. Consequently, this right should be considered as one referred to by Article 13. But Article 13 is applicable only if this right gives rise to an arguable claim in the precise case. I wonder how one could consider that a claim founded on a violation of the Convention is "arguable" and at the same time consider that there has not been a violation of the Convention. . . .

The interpretation of the majority could be taken to imply that where there is a killing by an agent of the state, there should always be a tort claim available to test out a suspected violation of Article 2—even if a procedurally correct alternative has been provided. Even more problematic is to link this with the applicable tests for liability in tort. Is it assumed that these should be adjusted to reflect the more demanding standard in respect of Article 2, referred to by Neil Martin above (minimizing risks to life *to the greatest extent possible*)? At the very least, if the problem is to be dealt with through reform of tort law, *Bubbins* would appear to require that a wider range of individuals ought to qualify for bereavement damages—though awkwardly, this may only be the case where death is caused by agents of the state.

The Human Rights Act 1998 was not in force at the time of F's death. The status of wrongful death under the Human Rights Act was raised, but not resolved, in a more recent case brought in domestic law, *Cameron v Network Rail Infrastructure Ltd* [2006] EWHC 1133 (QB). The claimants were relatives of a woman killed in the Potter's Bar rail crash on 10 May 2002. Again the claim related to the 'gap' between the Law Reform (Miscellaneous Provisions) Act 1934, and the Fatal Accidents Act 1976. Two of the claimants did not qualify as dependants under the Fatal Accidents Act, nor were they qualified to receive bereavement damages under section 1A. The only damages recoverable under the Law Reform (Miscellaneous Provisions) Act 1934 were in respect of funeral expenses. The claimants argued as follows:

1. They could pursue a claim for damages under the Human Rights Act 1998 on the grounds of breach of Article 2 (extracted above);

2. They could pursue a claim for damages for 'wrongful death' and the court should create a new tort, expressly to fill the gap between the two statutes addressed in this section;

3. They could seek a declaration that section 1A of the Fatal Accidents Act 1976 was incompatible with the claimants', or the deceased's, rights under the ECHR. There was no discussion of *Bubbins v UK* in respect of this argument.[31]

The claimants failed in respect of all these arguments, and their claims were struck out.

1. Railtrack was not, at the time of the accident, a 'public authority' within the meaning of section 6 of the Human Rights Act 1998. Their role at this stage related chiefly to maintenance of tracks and points. Therefore, the claim for damages under the Human Rights Act failed;

2. There was no violation of Article 2. There is a civil remedy for those who suffer pecuniary loss as a result of the death of the deceased, and:

---

[31] The issues are slightly different since *Cameron* did not involve killing by an agent of the state.

42.   . . . It is within the reasonable margin of appreciation of the state to limit those who are entitled to claim compensation to those who are financially dependent on the deceased. Who otherwise should say where the line should be drawn between those who may claim and those who may not?

This seems to have been sufficient to dismiss claims 2 and 3 above.

3. The action under the Human Rights Act 1998 was out of time in any event, since it was brought outside the one-year limitation period laid down by section 7 of the Act. It would not be 'equitable' to extend the available time period.

4. DELIVERY OF COMPENSATORY DAMAGES: LUMP SUM OR PERIODICAL PAYMENTS

At common law, damages are paid solely by means of a single lump sum. The award is final, and should it prove to be insufficient (because the claimant's condition deteriorates, or they live far longer than expected), or excessive (because they recover quickly, or because they die earlier than expected), then it is simply too late to make any adjustment. An important but limited statutory exception to this was created by the Administration of Justice Act 1982, which inserted the following provision into the Supreme Court Act 1981 (now the Senior Courts Act 1981).

Senior Courts Act 1981

32A   Orders for provisional damages for personal injuries

(1) This section applies to an action for damages for personal injuries in which there is proved or admitted to be a chance that at some definite or indefinite time in the future the injured person will, as a result of the act or omission which gave rise to the cause of action, develop some serious disease or suffer some serious deterioration in his physical or mental condition.

(2) Subject to subsection (4) below, as regards any action for damages to which this section applies in which a judgment is given in the High Court, provision may be made by rules of court for enabling the court, in such circumstances as may be prescribed, to award the injured person—

(a) damages assessed on the assumption that the injured person will not develop the disease or suffer the deterioration in his condition; and

(b) further damages at a future date if he develops the disease or suffers the deterioration.

. . .

The Civil Procedure Rules (CPR) 1998 govern the application of the power in this section.[32] Clearly, this section permits variation in respect of *an identified contingency* of a particular type. That is, it must be established or accepted that the claimant may at some time in the

---

[32] Note that by r 25.7, the power is to be exercised *only* if the defendant *is insured, or is a public authority.*

future suffer a serious disease, or experience a significant deterioration in their condition, as a result of the tort. In these circumstances, provisional damages are wholly appropriate. If damages were awarded on the basis of the percentage chance of developing the serious disease or condition, it would be perfectly clear that these damages would turn out to be *either* wholly excessive (the disease or condition does not develop), *or* wholly inadequate (it *does* develop, and only proportionate damages have been awarded).

In this section we consider a major recent change in the law, which extends the ability of the court to make an order for **periodical payments** in place of a lump sum, or in respect of certain elements of the award.

The following provision of the Damages Act 1996 (substituted by section 100 of the Courts Act 2003 and SI 2005/841) took effect in April 2005. It *requires* courts to consider whether to make an order for periodical payments of damages, rather than a lump sum; and it *permits* the court to make such an order, whether or not the parties have agreed that this would be preferable.

Damages Act 1996

2   Periodical payments

(1) A court awarding damages for future pecuniary loss in respect of personal injury—

    (a) may order that the damages are wholly or partly to take the form of periodical payments, and

    (b) shall consider whether to make that order.

Formerly, section 2 allowed a court to make an order for periodical payments *only* with the consent of both the parties.[33]

4.1 THE PERCEIVED ADVANTAGES OF PERIODICAL PAYMENTS

In *Wells v Wells* (extracted above), Lord Steyn strongly criticized the almost universal award of damages through lump sums, and supported the greater use of orders for periodical payments.

Lord Steyn, *Wells v Wells* [1999] 1 AC 345, 384

Leaving to one side the policy arguments for and against the 100 per cent. principle, there is a major structural flaw in the present system. It is the inflexibility of the lump sum system which requires an assessment of damages once and for all of future pecuniary losses. In the case of the great majority of relatively minor injuries the plaintiff will have recovered before his

---

[33] There is a logical problem with imposing periodical payments *even if the parties have agreed to some other arrangement*: that is, the court will not usually have the benefit of any argument for or against the periodical payments solution. This happened for example in *Godbald v Mahmoud* [2005] EWHC 1002 (QB): de Wilde, 'Periodical Payments—A Journey Into the Unknown' (2005) 4 JPIL 320; R. Lewis, 'The Politics and Economics of Tort Law: Judicially Imposed Periodical Payments' (2006) 69 MLR 418.

damages are assessed and the lump sum system works satisfactorily. But the lump sum system causes acute problems in cases of serious injuries with consequences enduring after the assessment of damages. In such cases the judge must often resort to guesswork about the future. Inevitably, judges will strain to ensure that a seriously injured plaintiff is properly cared for whatever the future may have in store for him. It is a wasteful system since the courts are sometimes compelled to award large sums that turn out not to be needed. It is true, of course, that there is statutory provision for periodic payments: see section 2 of the Damages Act 1996. But the court only has this power if both parties agree. Such agreement is never, or virtually never, forthcoming. The present power to order periodic payments is a dead letter. The solution is relatively straightforward. The court ought to be given the power of its own motion to make an award for periodic payments rather than a lump sum in appropriate cases. Such a power is perfectly consistent with the principle of full compensation for pecuniary loss. Except perhaps for the distaste of personal injury lawyers for change to a familiar system, I can think of no substantial argument to the contrary. But the judges cannot make the change. Only Parliament can solve the problem.

Parliament has now made the change suggested in this extract. But was Lord Steyn right? Periodical payments have the following perceived benefits over lump sums.

1. They are less wasteful. This is because they do not (in their present form) require a calculation of the claimant's life expectancy, which may turn out to be incorrect. So those parts of the award which relate to care costs, for example, may be seriously over-estimated in a lump sum award. Periodical payments, on the other hand, will simply cease when the claimant dies, so that there is no wasteful expenditure on costs that will never be incurred.

2. They provide the claimant with security, since there is no need to seek investment advice and manage a capital sum to produce income. The award cannot be frittered away. Clearly, the order will provide security *only* if the payments are made from a reliable source, and courts must consider this when making an order:

Damages Act 1996

2(3) A court may not make an order for periodical payments unless satisfied that the continuity of payment under the order is reasonably secure.

In *YM v Gloucestershire Hospitals NHS Foundation Trust and Others* [2006] EWHC 820 (QB), the defendants were NHS *foundation* trusts. In the case of insolvency, there is a statutory discretion on the part of the Secretary of State to transfer the liabilities of such a trust, but no obligation to do so. In principle, a discretion is not enough to render the source of the payments 'secure'. Therefore, the NHS Litigation Authority agreed to be named as the source of the periodical payments and to be legally responsible for the payments. Forbes J held that this agreement was sufficient to make the payments 'reasonably secure'.

3. Periodical payments are in one important respect cheaper for defendants to provide. The interest on lump sums invested by claimants is subject to tax. In order to achieve 100 per cent compensation, the lump sum award is therefore increased to take account of this future and

continuing tax on interest. Periodical payments are tax-free in the hands of the claimant. Thus, the increase in respect of tax will not apply to periodical payments. This is, in fact, of no benefit to the claimant, and it means lower revenue to the Exchequer. But it results in lower costs to tortfeasors or their insurers.

4. The order for periodical payments must aim to ensure that they are increased over time to ensure that the claimant is not left under-compensated in future years. However, periodical payments are not inherently sensitive to changes in needs or circumstances. By the statutory instrument extracted below, a court may provide at the time of making an order for periodical payments that it may be varied. This, like the order itself, does not require the consent of the parties. However, like the equivalent provision in respect of provisional damages in lump sums (Senior Court Act 1981, section 32A), this will have effect *only* in circumstances where there is some identified contingency relating to the claimant's condition. Unlike that section, the contingency may take the form of *improvement* in the claimant's condition, as well as deterioration. There is scope for the periodical payments to be reduced.

Damages (Variation of Periodical Payments) Order 2005 (SI 2005/841)

2. If there is proved or admitted to be a chance that at some definite or indefinite time in the future the claimant will—

    (a) as a result of the act or omission which gave rise to the cause of action, develop some serious disease or suffer some serious deterioration, or

    (b) enjoy some significant improvement, in his physical or mental condition, where that condition had been adversely affected as a result of that act or omission,

the court may, on the application of a party, with the agreement of all the parties, or of its own initiative, provide in an order for periodical payments that it may be varied.

There are, however, many problems of uncertainty that periodical payments cannot resolve. Obviously, no system for delivering damages could resolve the problem of uncertainty over *hypotheticals*, or what *would have happened to the claimant if he or she had not suffered the accident*. This aspect of the calculation of 'what has been lost' will remain as uncertain under periodical payments as it does under a lump sum award. Certain other potential drawbacks to the periodical payments option have also been identified.[34]

4.2 POTENTIAL PROBLEMS OF PERIODICAL PAYMENTS

1. It is not obvious that the periodical payments will be cheaper overall. Their delivery will be more expensive, even if the total amount payable is less, since a fund will require long-term administration.

---

[34] In particular by Robin de Wilde, 'Periodical Payments—A Journey into the Unknown' (2005) JPIL 320–37.

2. Although the payments are secure, the claimant loses the opportunity to invest a capital sum in such a way as to gain an above inflation rate of return. Although in practice most claimants do not invest their lump sum awards in high return investments, it could be argued that this flexibility is essential in order to protect against higher than inflation rates of increase in certain expenses, because of wage inflation. This will particularly affect the costs of care.

3. Despite the views expressed by Lord Steyn in *Wells v Wells*, there is a general *loss* of flexibility in the hands of the claimant. Although there is provision for foreseen contingencies (in the nature of deterioration and improvement) there is no way of dealing with *unforeseen* circumstances. The claimant with a capital sum can, in principle, draw it down more quickly in certain circumstances. The recipient of periodical payments has no such options.

4. It has also been argued that periodical payments will not be sufficient to cover pecuniary losses in a case where there is a reduction in the award for contributory negligence. The only solution in such a case is to allow general (non-pecuniary) damages, and the award for past losses, to go into the pot.

Robin De Wilde, 'Periodical Payments—A Journey Into the Unknown' (2005) JPIL 320, at 326

. . . a periodical payments order can only be appropriate when there is full liability, unless you are in a position to steal from other damages which are not 'future pecuniary loss' to compensate for the shortfall. The court cannot impose this, but it can be permitted by the court. . . . a periodical payment order may be better for an uncertain 'short losses period' rather than a 'long losses period'.

If this is correct, periodical payments are most useful for claimants who are older at the time of the injury or on-set of disease and may be severely under-compensated through a lump sum which would only work to the 'average' life expectancy. For example, under a lump sum system a person injured at the age of 62 may only be awarded care costs to the age of 67. If they live to the age of 85, then their lump sum will be of little use to them. They are better off with a periodical payment, which will continue as long as it is needed. It is much more doubtful whether periodical payments will meet the problem of a case such as *Wells v Wells*, where the claimant was of working age at the time of the injury and had a normal life expectancy, but would require constant care throughout that time. There is some doubt therefore whether they will fulfil Lord Steyn's ambitions.

4.3 PROTECTING THE VALUE OF PERIODICAL PAYMENTS

Where lump sums are concerned, no increase to the award is applied to allow for inflation. Money is assumed to 'hold its value' over time, and the capital sum is expected to grow in value so as to outstrip inflation. Rather, a *discount* to the multiplier is applied to account for investment opportunity. We noted that this discount is now modest; but that it still creates a potential problem in respect of *expenses*, since no account is taken of the faster than inflation growth in wages, and thus in care costs (*Cooke v Bristol Healthcare Trust*). In the case of periodical payments, no investment by the claimant is possible. This is why such payments must be 'index linked' to protect them from inflation. But the problem of care costs arises again, because index linking to general inflation may leave the recipient of these payments over-exposed. As we have said, unlike the recipient of a lump sum the claimant with a periodical payment does not have any flexibility.

Damages Act 1996

Section 2[35]

(8) An order for periodical payments shall be treated as providing for the amount of payments to vary by reference to the retail prices index (within the meaning of section 833(2) of the Income and Corporation Taxes Act 1988) at such times, and in such a manner, as may be determined by or in accordance with Civil Procedure Rules.

(9) But an order for periodical payments may include provision—

   (a) disapplying subsection (8), or

   (b) modifying the effect of subsection (8).

These provisions were subject to interpretation by the Court of Appeal in the following case.

Tarlochan Singh Flora v Wakom (Heathrow) Ltd [2006] EWCA Civ 1103

The claimant was seriously injured when he fell 35 feet from a ramp at work. Liability was admitted. Only the form of the order for compensation, and the amount of compensation, were in issue.

The defendants argued that a court should *ordinarily* make the order identified in section 2(8) above, and that subsection (9) should only be triggered in exceptional circumstances. This would provide some symmetry between the approach to be taken in protecting the value of periodical payments, and the approach to be taken in protecting the value of lump sums, through adjustments to the multiplier. The claimant argued to the contrary that the statutory language did not suggest a *presumption* that the approach in section 2(8) should be adopted, and that the court was free to substitute another approach whenever it thought this would be more appropriate. In addition, he would be considerably under-compensated if his periodical payments were linked only to the retail price index (RPI). Rather, he should be able to argue at trial that linking to a wage-related index such as the Average Earnings Index (AEI) was a more appropriate mechanism for achieving 100 per cent compensation—and that 100 per cent compensation remained the aim of compensation whether it was delivered through periodical payments, or through a lump sum. The Court of Appeal accepted the claimant's argument, and rejected the analogy with the calculation of lump sums.

---

[35] The following subsections were added by the Courts Act 2003.

Brooke LJ

27 . . . an award of a lump sum is entirely different in character from an award of periodical payments as a mechanism for compensating for such loss. When setting the appropriate discount rate in the context of a lump sum award the House of Lords or the Lord Chancellor had to guess the future and to hope that prudent investment policy would enable a seriously injured claimant to benefit fully from the award for the whole period for which it was designed to provide him/her with appropriate compensation.

28 A periodical payments order is quite different. This risk is taken away from the claimant. The award will provide him or her year by year with appropriate compensation, and the use of an appropriate index will protect him/her from the effects of future inflation. If he or she dies early the defendants will benefit because payments will then cease. It is unnecessary in the context of this statutory scheme to make the kind of guesses that were needed in setting the discount rate. The fact that these two quite different mechanisms now sit side by side in the same Act of Parliament does not in my judgment mean that the problems that infected the operation of the one should be allowed to infect the operation of the other. There is nothing in the statute to indicate that in implementing s 2 of the 1996 Act (as substituted) Parliament intended the courts to depart from what Lord Steyn described in *Wells v Wells* . . . as the '100% principle', namely that a victim of a tort was entitled to be compensated as nearly as possible in full for all pecuniary losses . . .

In response to an argument that courts would as a consequence be besieged by an army of expert witnesses in the nature of accountants, actuaries, and economists (the very problem that a single discount rate was designed to prevent: see *Cooke v Bristol Healthcare Trust*, above), Brooke LJ explained that this would be a temporary phenomenon:

33 . . . if the experience of the past is any useful guide, it is likely that there will be a number of trials at which the expert evidence on each side can be thoroughly tested. A group of appeals will then be brought to this court to enable it to give definitive guidance in the light of the findings of fact made by a number of trial judges. The armies of experts will then be able to strike their tents and return to the offices or academic groves from which they came.

This suggests that the problem of potential under-compensation created by *Cooke* will not be replicated in the case of periodical payments. But the recipient of these payments is, as we have said, more exposed because they do not have the flexibility of a capital sum. For this reason, in *A v B Hospitals NHS Trust* [2006] EWHC 2833 (Admin), Lloyd Jones J awarded a lump sum, rather than periodical payments, to a young claimant in respect of future care costs.

5. A GLIMPSE OF THE BROADER PICTURE: TORT DAMAGES, INSURANCE, AND STATE BENEFITS

5.1 RECOUPMENT PROVISIONS

Earlier, we considered the deduction of the value of certain benefits from the award payable. The idea of these deductions was that the victim should not be compensated twice over, even if this means that the compensating party is therefore 'let off' to some extent. By the Social

Security (Recovery of Benefits) Act 1997, certain social security benefits are no longer simply deducted from the award of damages (with the effect of benefiting the compensating party). Instead, the value of the benefits deducted from the award is repaid by the party paying damages, to the state. As a result of this legislation, no damages may be paid by any party in respect of personal injuries until they have applied to the Secretary of State for a certificate of recoverable benefits.

In principle, this should not affect the award received by the claimant. However, it can affect that award in certain respects. In particular, no account is taken of reduced damages attributable to contributory negligence, and the benefits must be deducted from the award in full as though no such reduction in the award had been applied. In effect, the claimant is paying for his or her *own* benefits, because of their contributory negligence in these circumstances.

On the other hand, claimants are protected in various respects. In particular, no deduction of benefits may be made against the non-pecuniary elements of the award; and recoverable benefits are listed against a relevant head of damage (lost earnings, cost of care, or loss of mobility) against which they are recoverable. They are not recoverable against any other head of damage. Equally, a set period of recovery is now defined. Benefits to which the Social Security (Recovery of Benefits) Act 1997 applies are to be deducted only until payment is made to discharge the claim (whether this is on settlement or on an award of damages by a court), *or* (if earlier) until a period of five years from the time of the relevant accident or injury. At common law, deductions were made in respect of *future* benefits also.

Social Security (Recovery of Benefits) Act 1997

1. Cases in which this Act applies

(1) This Act applies in cases where—

   (a) a person makes a payment (whether on his own behalf or not) to or in respect of any other person in consequence of any accident, injury or disease suffered by the other, and

   (b) any listed benefits have been, or are likely to be, paid to or for the other during the relevant period in respect of the accident, injury or disease. . . .

3. 'The relevant period'

(1) In relation to a person ("the claimant") who has suffered any accident, injury or disease, "the relevant period" has the meaning given by the following subsections.

(2) Subject to subsection (4), if it is a case of accident or injury, the relevant period is the period of five years immediately following the day on which the accident or injury in question occurred.

(3) Subject to subsection (4), if it is a case of disease, the relevant period is the period of five years beginning with the date on which the claimant first claims a listed benefit in consequence of the disease.

(4) If at any time before the end of the period referred to in subsection (2) or (3)—

   (a) a person makes a compensation payment in final discharge of any claim made by or in respect of the claimant and arising out of the accident, injury or disease, or

(b) an agreement is made under which an earlier compensation payment is treated as having been made in final discharge of any such claim,

the relevant period ends at that time.

5.2 NHS CHARGES AND LOCAL AUTHORITY CARE COSTS

Under the Road Traffic (NHS Charges) Act 1999, NHS hospitals were entitled to claim the costs of hospital care from liability insurers who made compensation payments to those injured in road traffic accidents. Provisions of the Health and Social Care (Community Health and Standards) Act 2003 ('the 2003 Act') repeal the Road Traffic (NHS Charges) Act 1999 as of 29 January 2007, and introduce an extended scheme of recovery of costs beyond road traffic cases.

Under the 2003 Act, NHS charges extending both to both hospital treatment, and to the cost of ambulance services, may be claimed from compensating parties. The legislation extends to any personal injury (physical or psychological) where a compensation payment is made, but excludes diseases. Of course, NHS treatment and ambulance services are free at the point of delivery, so this provision does not require any deduction of damages awarded to the claimant. Rather, it creates a new liability on the part of those paying compensation, including insurers. As with the Social Security (Recovery of Benefits) Act 1997, a compensating party must apply to the relevant Secretary of State (or Scottish Minister) for a certificate. Unlike the position with social security benefits, a reduction in the amounts recovered is applied where there is finding of contributory negligence (by section 153), so that the award of damages is unaffected.

Health and Social Care (Community Health and Standards) Act 2003

150   Liability to pay NHS charges

(1) This section applies if—

(a) a person makes a compensation payment to or in respect of any other person (the "injured person") in consequence of any injury, whether physical or psychological, suffered by the injured person, and

(b) the injured person has—

(i) received NHS treatment at a health service hospital as a result of the injury,

(ii) been provided with NHS ambulance services as a result of the injury for the purpose of taking him to a health service hospital for NHS treatment (unless he was dead on arrival at that hospital), or

(iii) received treatment as mentioned in sub-paragraph (i) and been provided with ambulance services as mentioned in sub-paragraph (ii).

(2) The person making the compensation payment is liable to pay the relevant NHS charges—

(a) in respect of—

(i) the treatment, in so far as received at a hospital in England or Wales,

(ii) the ambulance services, in so far as provided to take the injured person to such a hospital, to the Secretary of State,

(b) in respect of—

    (i) the treatment, in so far as received at a hospital in Scotland,

    (ii) the ambulance services, in so far as provided to take the injured person to such a hospital,

to the Scottish Ministers.

(3) "Compensation payment" means a payment, including a payment in money's worth, made—

(a) by or on behalf of a person who is, or is alleged to be, liable to any extent in respect of the injury, or

(b) in pursuance of a compensation scheme for motor accidents,

but does not include a payment mentioned in Schedule 10.

(4) Subsection (1)(a) applies—

(a) to a payment made—

    (i) voluntarily, or in pursuance of a court order or an agreement, or otherwise, and

    (ii) in the United Kingdom or elsewhere, and

(b) if more than one payment is made, to each payment.

. . .

(5) "Injury" does not include any disease.

164   Liability of insurers

(1) If a compensation payment is made in a case where—

(a) a person is liable to any extent in respect of the injury, and

(b) the liability is covered to any extent by a policy of insurance,

the policy is also to be treated as covering any liability of that person under section 150(2).

(2) Liability imposed on the insurer by subsection (1) cannot be excluded or restricted.

. . .

(5) This section applies in relation to policies of insurance issued before (as well as those issued after) the date on which it comes into force.

. . .

If insurance is a distributive mechanism by which society deals with the risk of accidents, is there any point in moving sums of money from insurers, to the NHS, in the proposed manner? Reminding ourselves of the observations of Lord Bridge in *Hodgson v Trapp*, does this policy overlook the fact that tax payers and premium payers are broadly the same people? The Road Traffic (NHS Charges) Act 1999 was precisely targeted at a class of injuries in which compulsory liability insurance is in place; and the broader scheme under the 2003 Act is explicitly targeted at insurers through section 164.

A more obvious version of the same phenomenon—this time moving the burden of costs *from one publicly funded body to another*—would have resulted had the Court of Appeal not decided against the claimant local authority in the next case extracted. Here the tortfeasor was the NHS, and the care was given by a local authority. The impact of a liability merry go round in this case would have been more serious because the transfer of costs would have depended on an action in tort. Litigation is a much more expensive means of shifting costs and liabilities than the administrative process under the 1999 and 2003 Acts.

Islington LBC v UCL (London) Hospital Trust [2005] EWCA Civ 596; [2006] PIQR P29

J was injured through the negligence of the defendant hospital trust. She was provided with care by the claimant local authority, in accordance with its statutory duty. J was not liable to pay for the care (apart from nominal amounts), so no substantial element for care costs could be included in J's claim against the defendants. The local authority argued that it had a claim in its own right against the defendants, for the costs of care. Like the liability under the 2003 Act, this would amount to a new liability on the part of tortfeasors and their insurers.

The Court of Appeal dismissed the local authority's claim, deciding that the defendants owed no duty of care to the local authority in respect of its treatment of J. Clearly, it was foreseeable that the local authority would incur costs if J were seriously injured, so the first element of the *Caparo* test (foreseeability) was satisfied. The court was divided on the question of whether the parties were 'proximate', which is the second stage of the *Caparo* test. Clarke and Ousley LJJ held that there was no proximity, but Buxton LJ thought that there was.[36] This disagreement did not affect the outcome, because all three judges agreed that it would not be fair, just, and reasonable for such a duty to be recognized. The 'fair, just, and reasonableness' test is not confined to issues arising between the parties.

London Borough of Islington v UCL (London) Hospital Trust [2005] EWCA Civ 596

Buxton LJ

Fair Just and Reasonable

33 Viewing the matter as between the present parties, it indeed seems all of fair, just and reasonable that UCH rather than Islington should bear the cost of Mrs J's care. UCH has been negligent, Islington has not. It is not only unreasonable but also unfair that a tortfeasor should escape liability for part of the results of his negligence simply through the double accident of his victim being cared for by a public body rather than privately, and the victim not being able to afford to pay for that care. And, in contrast to many claims for pure economic loss, the tortfeasor is not faced with liability for an uncertain and possibly infinite amount. All that Islington seeks from UCH is the very amount, or something very close to it, that UCH would have had to pay to Mrs J if Mrs J when injured had been sufficiently wealthy to be able to buy care for herself.

34 But 'fair just and reasonable' is not to be read literally, nor is it to be read solely in the context of the relationship between the instant claimant and defendant. It still assumes what might be called the residue of Lord Wilberforce's test, that wider issues of policy may have to intervene.

---

[36] This is because Buxton LJ thought the proximity test shaded into the foreseeability test, while Clarke and Ousley JJ thought it represented a more distinct aspect of 'legal policy', connected to the relationship between the parties. Our interpretation in Chapters 3 and 6 is closer to the approach of Clarke and Ousley JJ.

The general obstacle to the claim was encapsulated by Buxton LJ as follows:

36 . . . the concern in this case is that, in order to correct what seems to be an inequitable distribution of liability between two public authorities, the common law of negligence is being asked to do a job for which it is not qualified. . . .

Ousley LJ as we have noted thought that the local authority was not in a 'proximate' relationship with the tortfeasor in respect of the injury. He was also influenced by an analogy with *voluntary* care-givers (rather than the statutory care-giver in this case).[37] But he agreed with Buxton LJ that policy concerns of a broader nature were also material to this case:

53 . . . Although I can see that recovery for Islington would be fair just and reasonable in ordinary terminology, that test is the point at which the factors of public policy which Buxton LJ identifies, in [36] and following, are brought in. They make a duty of care owed to Islington, so as to enable it to recover the costs which it was required by statute to incur and which it was unable by statute to recover from the recipient of those services, a leap too far.

It is suggested that this case provides a sobering example of the trouble that would be caused if the tort of negligence were to be developed without regard to policy concerns. Some reasons in favour of the decision are outlined in the following extract.

Andrew Tettenborn, 'Free Care: Who Foots the Bill?' (2005) NLJ 1050

. . . it is suggested that the decision of the Court of Appeal was both right and inevitable. As the court pointed out, Parliament had set up a complex statutory scheme determining what services a citizen was entitled to receive from the community, and on what terms (if any) as to payment. It would be inappropriate to cut across that scheme by extending the law of tort to allow the costs of such services to be laid off elsewhere.

Furthermore, given that Part 3 of the Health and Social Care (Community Health and Standards) Act 2003, when in force, would prospectively provide for a limited right of recoupment for NHS hospitals and ambulance services, it would be particularly misconceived for the common law to overlay its provisions by extending a direct right of recovery to cases not covered by it.

The court might have added a further point: that the independent nature of any direct right of action would raise a host of further problems. What if, for example, the victim had been guilty of contributory negligence? However unfairly, it seems the carer, unlike the victim, would have to recover in full: its claim would be free-standing and independent of the victim's own right against the wrongdoer, and there seems no way under the Law Reform (Contributory Negligence) Act 1945 for the victim's negligence to be attributed to it. Yet again, settlement of claims would be very awkward, since it is hard to see how the victim's agreement to settle

---

[37] According to *Hunt v Severs* [1994] 2 AC 350, any claim for care given by a volunteer must be made by the injured party; the care-giver has no action in his or her own right.

could bind the carer as regards its own (independent) claim. In short, the conclusion is unavoidable that if there is to be a direct cause of action, the issues raised are such as can only be dealt with under a statutory scheme.

6. NON-COMPENSATORY DAMAGES

Not all pecuniary awards in tort are compensatory in nature. Here, we address some of those that are not.[38]

6.1 EXEMPLARY DAMAGES

Exemplary (or 'punitive') damages go beyond what it required to make good the claimant's loss. These damages are inherently controversial, and there is considerable doubt whether they play an appropriate part in the law of tort. Generally speaking, the argument against exemplary damages is that they are *punitive*, and that punishment should be left to criminal law, where standards of proof and rules of admissible evidence are different.

What are Exemplary Damages?

An important first step is to distinguish between exemplary damages, and aggravated damages. The distinction is in principle easy to state, although it has often been said that the distinction is not a real one and that one or the other form of damages should be abolished. Exemplary damages have come the closest to extinction; and although the immediate effect of *Kuddus v Chief Constable of Leicestershire* [2002] 2 AC 122 is expansion in their availability, the House of requiring Lords expressed a willingness to restrict or even (in the case of Lord Scott) to abolish exemplary damages without waiting for Parliament to take action.

Aggravated damages are compensatory by nature. The principle behind aggravated damages is that the injury caused to the claimant is made worse by the 'aggravating' behaviour of the defendant. This contributes to mental torment or hurt suffered by the claimant, and this requires compensation (even if it would not give rise to a cause of action in its own right, in a tort requiring damage). Aggravated damages are clearly regarded as an appropriate aspect of defamation awards, for example, if the behaviour of the defendant is particularly aggressive or the defendant unreasonably maintains the truth of defamatory allegations.[39]

Exemplary damages by contrast are not intended to compensate the claimant. They are available if the defendant's behaviour is such as to give rise to the need for something *more than* a compensatory award. Thus they punish, or express strong disapproval of, the defendant's wrongdoing or invasion of the claimant's rights, even if that wrongdoing adds no

---

[38] We should also note the existence of 'conventional awards'. These are compensatory in a limited sense, because they relate to the claimant's loss. But they do not seek to *make good* the claimant's loss. They are less than compensatory.

[39] See for example the discussion of *Sutcliffe v Pressdram* in Chapter 13.

extra element to the injury suffered by the claimant.[40] They have a role in 'vindicating the strength of the law'.[41]

The availability of exemplary damages is limited. Such damages are not available as a tort remedy whenever a court thinks it would be helpful or appropriate to award them. In the leading case of *Rookes v Barnard* [1964] AC 1129, Lord Devlin set out the three categories of case in which exemplary damages are available.

1. Cases involving 'oppressive, arbitrary or unconstitutional actions by servants of the government';
2. Cases where 'the defendant's conduct has been calculated by him to make a profit for himself which may well exceed the payment to the plaintiff';
3. Cases where the award of such damages is expressly authorized by statute.

The general thrust of Lord Devlin's judgment was that exemplary damages were anomalous and should be carefully confined to these three categories of case. On the other hand, he also expressed the view that in the first two categories of case, exemplary damages could serve a valuable purpose.

In *Cassell v Broome* [1972] AC 1207, the House of Lords confirmed that these were the three categories in which exemplary damages are available, and agreed that the categories were not to be extended. Much debate, in *Cassell v Broome* and since, has surrounded the question of whether Lord Devlin intended a further restriction to the availability of exemplary damages, confining them to causes of action in which such damages had been available *before* 1964. This is the so-called 'cause of action condition'. The general consensus is that the House of Lords in *Cassell v Broome* (or at least, some members of the House) thought that Lord Devlin *did* intend to apply this additional restriction. And even if he did not, such a condition was introduced by *Cassell v Broome*.

In reliance on this condition, in *AB v South West Water Services Ltd* [1993] QB 507, the Court of Appeal decided that exemplary damages could not be awarded in respect of a public nuisance, where drinking water supplied to the public was contaminated. Exemplary damages had not been recognized as available in cases of public nuisance prior to 1964.

AB v South West Water was overruled, and the cause of action condition abandoned, in the following case.

Kuddus v Chief Constable of Leicestershire [2002] 2 AC 122

The claimant sought exemplary damages against the defendant in an action for misfeasance in a public office. Exemplary damages had not been awarded before 1964 in this tort, largely because the tort was virtually unrecognized at the time. Lord Nicholls explained that the cause of action condition 'represents in practice an arbitrary and irrational restriction on the availability of exemplary damages' (at [55]). The restriction would no longer be applied. This decision does not mean that the House of Lords wishes to see expansion of exemplary damages. It means rather that the House would prefer to see restrictions on exemplary damages which (unlike the cause of action condition) are consistent and rational.

---

[40] It is this which leads to much of the overlap between aggravated and exemplary damages. Some authors are sceptical that high-handed behaviour which deserves additional sanctions could fail to add to the claimant's injury.

[41] Lord Devlin, *Rookes v Barnard* [1964] AC 1129 at 1226.

In every other respect, *Kuddus* is an extremely inconclusive decision, reflecting the narrowness of the argument put before the House. Since only the cause of action condition was directly in issue before the House of Lords, the other judicial remarks extracted below are clearly speculative and non-binding.

For this reason, the following summary of the position after *Kuddus* may be found useful:

1. There is no 'cause of action condition' in respect of exemplary damages. If criteria for availability are met, it makes no difference which cause of action is argued;

2. Exemplary damages continue to be available in the three categories of case referred to by Lord Devlin, at least for the time being;

3. Some members of the House of Lords might prefer exemplary damages for torts to be abolished at common law (particularly Lord Scott at [111], and possibly Lord Mackay);[42]

4. Some members of the House of Lords would probably prefer to retain exemplary damages, but with variation in the categories (for example Lord Nicholls seems to prefer a general criterion of 'outrageous conduct' and does not see why category 1 should be confined to agents of the state), and perhaps with particular emphasis on protection of civil liberties (Lord Hutton);

5. Most members of the House of Lords would not wait for legislation, and would consider departing from *Rookes v Barnard* in order to abolish exemplary damages for torts altogether, or to change the applicable categories, since statutory change is plainly unforthcoming (only Lord Slynn seemed reluctant to question the older decisions).[43] The House would be receptive to hearing argument on these points, and regretted that such argument was not put before them in this case (Lord Scott at [106]).

Kuddus v Chief Constable of Leicestershire [2002] 2 AC 122

Lord Nicholls

63 The arguments for and against exemplary damages need no rehearsing. They are familiar enough, and they are set out clearly in the Law Commission's report.[44] In the end, and in respectful agreement with the views expressed by Lord Wilberforce in *Broome v Cassell & Co Ltd* [1972] AC 1027, 1114, the feature I find most striking is the extent to which the principle of exemplary damages continues to have vitality. The availability of exemplary damages has played a significant role in buttressing civil liberties, in claims for false imprisonment and wrongful arrest. From time to time cases do arise where awards of compensatory damages are perceived as inadequate to achieve a just result between the parties. The nature of the defendant's conduct calls for a further response from the courts. On occasion conscious wrongdoing by a defendant is so outrageous, his disregard of the plaintiff's rights so contumelious, that something more is needed to show that the law will not tolerate such behaviour. Without an award of exemplary damages, justice will not have been done. Exemplary damages, as a remedy of last resort, fill what otherwise would be a regrettable lacuna.

---

[42] Obviously, such damages would still be available if legislation so provided.

[43] The House of Lords has the power to depart from its previous decisions under the Practice Direction of 1966. The House did not have this power in 1964; but it is doubtful whether any previous decision of the House of Lords required the retention of exemplary damages at that date.

[44] Law Commission, *Aggravated, Exemplary and Restitutionary Damages*, Law Com No 247 (HMSO, 1997).

. . .

65 If exemplary damages are to continue as a remedial tool, as recommended by the Law Commission after extensive consultation, the difficult question which arises concerns the circumstances in which this tool should be available for use. Stated in its broadest form, the relevant principle is tolerably clear: the availability of exemplary damages should be co-extensive with its rationale. As already indicated, the underlying rationale lies in the sense of outrage which a defendant's conduct sometimes evokes, a sense not always assuaged fully by a compensatory award of damages, even when the damages are increased to reflect emotional distress.

66 In *Rookes v Barnard* [1964] AC 1129, 1226, Lord Devlin drew a distinction between oppressive acts by government officials and similar acts by companies or individuals. He considered that exemplary damages should not be available in the case of non-governmental oppression or bullying. Whatever may have been the position 40 years ago, I am respectfully inclined to doubt the soundness of this distinction today. National and international companies can exercise enormous power. So do some individuals. I am not sure it would be right to draw a hard-and-fast line which would always exclude such companies and persons from the reach of exemplary damages. Indeed, the validity of the dividing line drawn by Lord Devlin when formulating his first category is somewhat undermined by his second category, where the defendants are not confined to, and normally would not be, government officials or the like.

67 Nor, I may add, am I wholly persuaded by Lord Devlin's formulation of his second category (wrongful conduct expected to yield a benefit in excess of any compensatory award likely to be made). The law of unjust enrichment has developed apace in recent years. In so far as there may be a need to go further, the key here would seem to be the same as that already discussed: outrageous conduct on the part of the defendant. There is no obvious reason why, if exemplary damages are to be available, the profit motive should suffice but a malicious motive should not.

68 As I have said, difficult questions arise here. In view of the limited scope of the submissions made by the parties on this appeal, this is not the occasion for attempting to state comprehensive conclusions on these matters. For the purposes of the present appeal it is sufficient, first, to express the view that the House should now depart from its decision in *Broome v Cassell & Co Ltd* [1972] AC 1027, in so far as that decision confirmed the continuing existence of what has subsequently been described as the "cause of action" condition and, secondly, to note that the essence of the conduct constituting the court's discretionary jurisdiction to award exemplary damages is conduct which was an outrageous disregard of the plaintiff's rights. Whether the conduct of PC Cavendish satisfies that test in this case is a matter to be resolved at trial.

Lord Hutton

75 As the point has not been argued I express no concluded opinion on the question whether exemplary damages should continue to be awarded in England, but I think that a number of cases decided by the courts in Northern Ireland during the past 30 years of terrorist violence give support to the opinion of Lord Devlin in *Rookes v Barnard* [1964] AC 1129, 1223, 1226 that in certain cases the awarding of exemplary damages serves a valuable purpose in restraining the arbitrary and outrageous use of executive power and in vindicating the strength of the law. Members of the security forces seeking to combat terrorism face constant danger and have to carry out their duties in very stressful conditions. In such circumstances an individual soldier or police officer or prison officer may, on occasion, act in gross breach of discipline and commit an unlawful act which is oppressive or arbitrary and in such cases exemplary damages have been awarded. . . .

79 In my opinion the power to award exemplary damages in such cases serves to uphold and vindicate the rule of law because it makes clear that the courts will not tolerate such conduct. It serves to deter such actions in future as such awards will bring home to officers in command of individual units that discipline must be maintained at all times. In my respectful opinion the view is not fanciful, as my noble and learned friend Lord Scott of Foscote suggests, that such awards have a deterrent effect and such an effect is recognised by Professor Atiyah in the passage from his work on *Vicarious Liability* (1967) cited by Lord Scott of Foscote in his speech. Moreover in some circumstances where one of a group of soldiers or police officers commits some outrageous act in the course of a confused and violent confrontation it may be very difficult to identify the individual wrongdoer so that criminal proceedings may be brought against him to punish and deter such conduct, whereas an award of exemplary damages to mark the court's condemnation of the conduct can be made against the Minister of Defence or the Chief Constable under the principle of vicarious liability even if the individual at fault cannot be identified.

Lord Scott

118 . . . Misfeasance in public office is a cause of action discovered, or rediscovered, relatively recently. But it is only since *Rookes v Barnard* [1964] AC 1129 that exemplary damages have been clearly distinguished from aggravated damages. The task of discovering whether, pre-*Rookes v Barnard*, exemplary damages had been awarded in a misfeasance in public office case has shown itself to be, and was always likely to be, lengthy and inconclusive. The cause of action criterion for an award of exemplary damages as an addition to the requirement that the conduct of the defendant fall within one or other of Lord Devlin's two categories does no credit to the law.

119 On the other hand the exemplary damages principle is itself an anomaly in the civil law and, as Lord Mackay has pointed out, it should not come as a matter of too much surprise that anomalies are to be found in the criteria that determine the availability of an anomalous remedy.

120 Your Lordships are, it seems to me, caught on the horns of a dilemma. On the one hand, the cause of action test is not based on principle and has serious practical difficulties. On the other hand, the removal of the cause of action test would expand the cases in which exemplary damages could be claimed. Claims could be made in cases of negligence and cases of deceit provided only that the conduct complained of fell within one or other of the two Devlin categories (*Rookes v Barnard* [1964] AC 1129, 1226). Claims could probably also be made, subject to the same proviso, in actions based upon breach of statutory duty whether or not the statute had expressly authorised such claims.

121 My Lords, I view the prospect of any increase in the cases in which exemplary damages can be claimed with regret. I have explained already why I regard the remedy as no longer serving any useful function in our jurisprudence. Victims of tortious conduct should receive due compensation for their injuries, not windfalls at public expense.

Many issues arise from the judgments in *Kuddus*, but we will pick out three.

First, no great enthusiasm was displayed in the judgments of Lords Nicholls and Scott for Lord Devlin's second category of case, namely cases where the defendant *seeks to make a profit* at the expense of the claimant. Here, it seems clear that compensatory damages will not be enough to deter the wrongdoing, because the defendant has already taken account of the likely damages in deciding to go ahead and commit the wrong. Both Lord Nicholls, and Lord Scott, hint that there is no longer any need to deal with these cases through exemplary damages, because the law of 'unjust enrichment' (Lord Nicholls) or 'restitution' (Lord Scott) has moved on and remedies will accordingly be available which will deter the wrong. This seems to amount to an argument that a remedy more appropriate to the law of civil obligations has now been fashioned. The overtly 'punitive' nature of exemplary damages can be put aside while keeping the deterrent effect. We turn briefly to these sorts of damages below.

Second, there is a clear disagreement between Lords Hutton and Scott on the important question of *whether exemplary damages can appropriately be awarded against a vicariously liable party*. Although the House of Lords was not called upon to decide this issue, in this case the defendant's liability was 'vicarious': the chief constable had not himself committed a tort, but was potentially liable for misfeasance in a public office on the part of one of his officers.[45]

Third, Lord Nicholls hints at a role for exemplary damages that is not purely punitive, because it relates the outrageous behaviour of the defendant to the violation of the claimant's right or interest, without necessarily showing that there is increased injury or hurt that would lead to an award of 'aggravated' damages: 'awards of compensatory damages are perceived as inadequate *to achieve a just result between the parties*' (at [63]). This is a very difficult area. For example, it could be argued (particularly in a tort actionable without proof of damage), that the claimant's right is not properly vindicated by an award of compensatory damages, taking into account the particularly outrageous violation of it. An extra, non-compensatory element is needed in order to do justice between the parties, and not simply to achieve some additional or broader goal, such as deterrence or vindication of the strength of the law. Many questions could be raised about the various contrasts implied by this, and whether they are real, but we will simply note that such questions may one day need to be addressed.

Exemplary Damages and Vicarious Liability

The present position is that awards of exemplary damages can clearly be made against vicariously liable parties. In the opinion of Lord Scott, expressed in *Kuddus*, this situation has arisen without careful consideration and cannot be justified. According to Lord Scott, the reasons underlying vicarious liability are largely compensatory, and no reason of fairness can be found for attaching a *punitive* award to a party who is not personally responsible for the wrongdoing.[46] Lord Hutton questions this approach, and cites with approval the arguments of Patrick Atiyah in *Vicarious Liability in the Law of Torts*: an award of exemplary damages against vicariously liable parties will encourage superior officers to exert control over the actions of their agents.

---

[45] The operation of vicarious liability, and the underlying arguments of policy and justice for such liability, are investigated in Chapter 9.

[46] In fact, as we will see in Chapter 9, there are several overlapping justifications for vicarious liability and these include reasons of fairness.

Exemplary Damages and Insurance

It is difficult to make sense of the insurance position in respect of exemplary damages. Generally speaking, it is against the policy of the law to allow enforcement of a contract of insurance indemnifying the insured for the consequences of his or her *criminal* acts.[47] But assuming the tortious act is also criminal, what of the vicariously liable party? In *Lancashire County Council v Mutual Municipal Insurance* [1997] QB 897, the plaintiff was liable vicariously for an amount including exemplary damages in respect of wrongful arrest and false imprisonment on the part of police officers. The Court of Appeal held that the defendant insurers were liable to reimburse the plaintiff for these amounts under a policy of liability insurance. Two strands to the reasoning are of concern to us. First, where the wrongdoing is *criminal* in nature, then a *vicariously* liable party may still enforce the insurance contract in respect of exemplary damages. The wrongdoer would not be able to do so.

Simon Brown LJ, *Lancashire County Council v Mutual Municipal Insurance,* at 907

In my judgment there is nothing either in the authorities or in logic to justify extending this principle of public policy so as to deny insurance cover to those whose sole liability is one which arises vicariously, whether as employers or, as here, under an equivalent statutory provision.

Second, where the tortfeasor's wrongdoing does *not* amount to a criminal offence, the Court of Appeal reasoned that both personally responsible parties, *and* vicariously liable parties, should be able to insure against liability for exemplary damages.

Simon Brown LJ, at 909

. . . there appear to me a number of different policy considerations in play, not by any means all pointing in the same direction. They include the following. (a) Whilst it is true that to allow a defendant liable for exemplary damages to be held harmless against them by insurance must undoubtedly reduce the deterrent and punitive effect of the order upon him, it will greatly improve the plaintiff's prospects of recovering the sum awarded. It is, of course, this consideration—the interests of those harmed by the tortfeasor—which has prompted the law in certain circumstances to require compulsory insurance. (b) Even though the defendant's liability be insurable, an exemplary damages award is still likely to have punitive effect. First, there may well be limits of liability and deductibles under the policy. Second, the insured is likely to have to pay higher premiums in future and may well, indeed, have difficulty in obtaining renewal insurance. (c) There is a separate public interest in holding parties to their contracts, particularly where, as here, it is open to the insurers to exclude liability for exemplary damages. If insurers take the premium, they should meet the risk. (d) True, as some of the foreign cases point out, if the damages are held recoverable against insurers the burden falls onto the general public by way of a rise in premiums. If, however, the damages are not

---

[47] Indeed in *Gray v Barr* [1971] 2 QB 554, indemnity was denied to a man liable in damages for killing another, even though he had been acquitted of murder and manslaughter. More generally, see our discussion of *ex turpi causa* in Chapter 5.

thus recoverable, then, certainly in a case like the present, the burden falls not onto an individual tortfeasor but rather onto the local body of ratepayers.

Outside the rule of public policy against indemnity for one's own criminal wrongdoing, there is nothing to stop anyone from insuring against their own liability for exemplary damages. Is this consistent with their *punitive* and *deterrent* nature? The first of the policy grounds mentioned by Simon Brown LJ, in particular, seems to ignore the fact that exemplary damages are, by definition, not compensatory, and are awarded *above and beyond* the amount required to compensate the claimant.

The Quantum of Exemplary Damages

Another awkward feature of exemplary damages is that there is no clear measure by which they may be 'calculated'. Given that actions for false imprisonment and malicious prosecution—which for obvious reasons may often raise claims derived from Lord Devlin's first category—are still in many instances tried by jury, the scope for high awards has been considerable. In *Thompson v Commissioner of Police for the Metropolis* [1998] QB 498, the Court of Appeal moved decisively to limit the amounts awarded in respect of exemplary damages, clarifying that the maximum figure to mark disapproval of 'oppressive or arbitrary conduct' should be £50,000. In one of the two cases heard by the Court of Appeal, exemplary damages of £200,000 had been awarded by a jury. The Court of Appeal reduced this award to £15,000.[48]

These questions of quantum are related to questions of vicarious liability. Although the Court of Appeal in *Thompson* was clearly concerned at the scale of exemplary awards, it did not doubt the validity of exemplary damages against a vicariously liable party. Indeed, the Court of Appeal suggested that *because* the liability was generally that of the chief officer of police, *therefore* it would be inappropriate to take into account the means of the individual wrongdoer (such as a police officer) when making the award:

Lord Woolf MR, *Thompson v Comr of Police of the Metropolis,* at 518–19

In the case of exemplary damages we have taken into account the fact that the action is normally brought against the chief officer of police and the damages are paid out of police funds for what is usually a vicarious liability for the acts of his officers in relation to which he is a joint tortfeasor: see now section 88 of the Police Act 1996. In these circumstances it appears to us wholly inappropriate to take into account the means of the individual officers except where the action is brought against the individual tortfeasor. This would raise a complication in the event of the chief officer seeking an indemnity or contribution as to his liability from a member of his force. It is our view if this situation does arise it should be resolved by the court exercising its power under section 2(1) or (2) of the Civil Liability (Contribution) Act 1978 to order that the exemplary damages should not be reimbursed in full or at all if they are disproportionate to the officer's means. In deciding upon what should be treated as the upper limits for exemplary

---

[48] This case is closely comparable to other Court of Appeal decisions in the same period, which limited damages in defamation actions by offering 'guidance' to juries. We consider these cases in Chapter 13: see in particular *John v MGN* [1997] QB 586, referred to by the Court of Appeal in *Thompson*.

damages we have selected a figure which is sufficiently substantial to make it clear that there has been conduct of a nature which warrants serious civil punishment and indicates the jury's vigorous disapproval of what has occurred but at the same time recognises that the plaintiff is the recipient of a windfall in relation to exemplary damages. As punishment is the primary objective in this class of case it is more difficult to tie the amount of exemplary damages to the award of compensatory damages, including aggravated. However in many cases it could prove a useful check subject to the upper limits we have identified if it is accepted that it will be unusual for the exemplary damages to produce a result of more than three times the basic damages being awarded (as the total of the basic aggravated and exemplary damages) . . .

6.2 GAIN-BASED DAMAGES

Why, in *Kuddus*, did Lords Nicholls and Scott think that exemplary damages might no longer be required to deal with the ordinary case where the defendant calculates that he might profit from his tort? One reason they hinted at is the extension of gain-based damages in the law of obligations. The *development* of 'the law of unjust enrichment' referred to by Lord Nicholls is probably a reference to the increasing availability of gain-based damages for civil wrongs, such as torts and breach of contract.

Here we should note that there is little agreement over appropriate terminology in this field, and not everyone would be happy with the idea of 'gain-based *damages*'. Some would insist that all 'damages' are compensatory. Along these lines, there is a further problem with Lord Nicholls' formulation, since 'unjust enrichment' is generally seen as entirely separate from the law of wrongs (including tort), being concerned with unjust transfers of value which may be made with or without any 'wrong'.

Essentially, 'gain-based' damages are calculated not according to the loss of the claimant, but according to the gain made by the defendant. One form of 'gain-based' award concentrates on stripping defendants of their profits and may be referred to as 'disgorgement damages'. An account of profits (which is clearly available in the action for breach of confidence: see Chapter 14) involves a form of disgorgement. A possibly separate form of gain-based award is referred to as 'restitutionary damages', and this is aimed at reversing 'transfers of value'.[49]

Two major distinctions must be noted between gain-based damages, and exemplary damages. First, gain-based damages are not punitive in nature. On the other hand, accounts of profits generally do seek to *deter*, through attacking the profit motive directly. Second, there is a clear measure of gain-based damages. The measure is not the loss suffered by the claimant as in compensatory damages, nor the amount required to 'punish' the defendant or vindicate the strength of the law, as in exemplary damages. In the case of disgorgement (profit-based) damages it is the profit wrongfully (in the case of tort) made by the defendant. In the case of restitutionary damages it is the amount gained through the transfer of value.

The following extract gives a general statement of the kinds of actions in which gain-based damages are available for a tort. The author explains that 'restitutionary damages' are clearly established in torts protecting property rights (in the case of trespass to land, see particularly *Ministry of Defence v Ashman* [1993] 40 EG 144); and he suggests that they should be more widely available on the basis of *deliberate wrongdoing*.

---

[49] James Edelman, *Gain-Based Damages* (Hart Publishing, 2002) distinguishes between 'disgorgement damages' and 'restitutionary damages', and proposes that both are available for wrongs, including torts.

A. Burrows, *Remedies for Torts and Breach of Contract* (2nd edn, Butterworths, 1994), 305–6

. . . The sort of torts for which restitutionary awards can be given are . . . not restricted to those in which the plaintiff's property or its proceeds have been acquired.

Taking all three types of restitutionary remedy together (award of money had and received, account of profits, restitutionary damages) the torts for which restitution have been awarded have involved interference with the plaintiff's property, whether that property be real or personal or intellectual. The cases therefore reveal a judicial desire firmly to deter even innocent interference with the plaintiff's property; that is, merely to compensate for any loss caused appears to be regarded as insufficient to deter that interference. This seems sensible. Applying Jackman's illuminating theory [(1989) CLJ 302], restitution is justified as a means of deterring harm to the facilitative institution of private property.

A subsidiary feature exhibited in a few of the account of profits cases (eg for passing off, infringement of trademark, breach of confidence) is that the tort must be committed deliberately if restitution is to be awarded. It could be argued that this category should be expanded so that restitution should be awarded to reverse gains made by, eg deliberately inducing a breach of contract or a deliberate libel. . . .

Given the established categories referred to by Burrows, was Lord Nicholls hinting at a more general role for gain-based damages in *intentional* torts? If so, why did he refer to 'unjust enrichment' (which denotes a wrongful transfer *of value*)?

On the whole, Lord Nicholls appears to have recognized that some role could still be played by exemplary damages; and that this would be dependent on showing 'outrageous' conduct. However, he doubted whether either of Lord Devlin's two categories could be justified. He may have thought that the profit motive in itself (as opposed to outrageous conduct in pursuit of profit) was properly dealt with through the measure of gain-based damages. Whether this is right depends partly on how widely such damages are available for torts in general. Perhaps Lord Nicholls would like to expand their availability: see also Chapter 17.

7. THE FUNDING OF LITIGATION

Undergraduate law courses do not traditionally spend much time considering the way that litigation is funded. But the enormous changes that have been made in respect of the funding of civil litigation in recent years have a direct impact on the themes of this chapter. Indeed, these funding methods may be implicated in the phenomenon known as 'compensation culture'—though not necessarily in the way that has been popularly alleged.

7.1 COSTS

The general presumption is that costs of civil litigation will be awarded **in the cause**, which is to say that the losing party will reimburse the costs of the winning party. Solicitors who wish to stay in business will in most instances be unwilling to take a case for claimants who have no prospect of paying their costs in the event of failure.[50] Historically therefore, personal injuries claims have often been funded by trades unions, or state-funded through legal aid. Alternatively, claimants with first party insurance will often be 'funded by' their insurance company—which is to say that it is really the insurer who is seeking indemnification from a potential wrongdoer.[51] In recent years, it has been felt by successive governments that the burden of legal aid is simply too great for the state to continue to fund civil claims.

Lord Bingham, *Callery v Gray* [2002] UKHL 28; [2002] 1 WLR 2000

1   My Lords, for nearly half a century, legal aid provided out of public funds was the main source of funding for those of modest means who sought to make or (less frequently) defend claims in the civil courts and who needed professional help to do so. By this means access to the courts was made available to many who would otherwise, for want of means, have been denied it. But as time passed the defects of the legal aid regime established under the Legal Aid and Advice Act 1949 and later statutes became more and more apparent. While the scheme served the poorest well, it left many with means above a low ceiling in an unsatisfactory position, too well off to qualify for legal aid but too badly off to contemplate incurring the costs of contested litigation. There was no access to the courts for them. Moreover, the effective immunity against adverse costs orders enjoyed by legally-aided claimants was always recognised to place an unfair burden on a privately-funded defendant resisting a legally-aided claim, since he would be liable for both sides' costs if he lost and his own even if he won. Most seriously of all, the cost to the public purse of providing civil legal aid had risen sharply, without however showing an increase in the number of cases funded or evidence that legal aid was directed to cases which most clearly justified the expenditure of public money.

2   Recognition of these defects underpinned the Access to Justice Act 1999 which, building on the Courts and Legal Services Act 1990, introduced a new regime for funding litigation, and in particular personal injury litigation with which alone this opinion is concerned. . . . The 1999 Act and the accompanying regulations had (so far as relevant for present purposes) three aims. One aim was to contain the rising cost of legal aid to public funds and enable existing expenditure to be refocused on causes with the greatest need to be funded at public expense, whether because of their intrinsic importance or because of the difficulty of funding them otherwise than out of public funds or for both those reasons. A second aim was to improve access to the courts for members of the public with meritorious claims. It was appreciated that the risk of incurring substantial liabilities in costs is a powerful disincentive to all but the very rich from becoming involved in litigation, and it was therefore hoped that the new arrangements would enable claimants to protect themselves against liability for paying costs either to those acting for them or (if they chose) to those on the other side. A third aim was to discourage weak claims and enable successful defendants to recover their costs in actions brought against them by indigent claimants. Pursuant to the first of these aims publicly-funded assistance was withdrawn from run-of-the-mill personal injury claimants. The main

---

[50] If a claim *settles* the situation is still more unpredictable, since the terms of the settlement may or may not include full costs.

[51] See for example *Stovin v Wise*, where a motor insurer tried to displace liability to the local authority, rather than to another motor insurer. It would be wrong to suggest that this phenomenon is limited to personal injuries: see also *Murphy v Brentwood*, where a buildings insurer sought to displace liability, also to a local authority.

instruments upon which it was intended that claimants should rely to achieve the second and third of the aims are described by my noble and learned friend: they are conditional fee agreements and insurance cover obtained after the event giving rise to the claim.

. . .

4   If the objects underlying the new procedural regime were not new, those underlying the new funding regime were. Arrangements which had until relatively recently been professionally improper were to become the norm. It was however evident that the success of the new funding regime was threatened by two contingencies which, had they occurred, could have proved fatal. One was that lawyers, in particular solicitors, would decline to act on a conditional fee basis. To counter that risk the maximum permissible uplift, on the first introduction of conditional fees in 1995, had been fixed, despite very strong opposition, at 100% and this high level of permissible uplift was retained. It was no doubt felt, rightly as events have proved, that if solicitors were permitted in some cases to earn, as the reward for success, double the fee otherwise receivable, they would be tempted into the market. The other contingency was that no accessible market would develop in after the event insurance. There was at the outset very little knowledge and experience of whether or how such a market would develop.

The Solution: Its Components

As explained in the extract above, the current solution to the problem of litigation funding is to permit lawyers to charge on a **no win no fee** or **contingency fee basis**—an arrangement that was unlawful at common law. Such arrangements still are unlawful outside the conditions set by relevant legislation, and will be unenforceable in any other circumstances than those set out in the following section.

Courts and Legal Services Act 1990[52]

58   Conditional fee agreements

(1) A conditional fee agreement which satisfies all of the conditions applicable to it by virtue of this section shall not be unenforceable by reason only of its being a conditional fee agreement; but (subject to subsection (5)) any other conditional fee agreement shall be unenforceable.

(2) For the purposes of this section and section 58A—

  (a) a conditional fee agreement is an agreement with a person providing advocacy or litigation services which provides for his fees and expenses, or any part of them, to be payable only in specified circumstances; and

  (b) a conditional fee agreement provides for a success fee if it provides for the amount of any fees to which it applies to be increased, in specified circumstances, above the amount which would be payable if it were not payable only in specified circumstances.

(3) The following conditions are applicable to every conditional fee agreement—

  (a) it must be in writing;

---

[52] This section was substituted by Access to Justice Act 1999 s 27(1).

(b) it must not relate to proceedings which cannot be the subject of an enforceable conditional fee agreement; and

(c) it must comply with such requirements (if any) as may be prescribed by the [Lord Chancellor].

(4) The following further conditions are applicable to a conditional fee agreement which provides for a success fee—

(a) it must relate to proceedings of a description specified by order made by the [Lord Chancellor];

(b) it must state the percentage by which the amount of the fees which would be payable if it were not a conditional fee agreement is to be increased; and

(c) that percentage must not exceed the percentage specified in relation to the description of proceedings to which the agreement relates by order made by the [Lord Chancellor].

As we noted above, the maximum permissible success fee is an uplift of 100 per cent. By section 58A, conditional fee agreements (CFAs) are not enforceable in respect of criminal proceedings (excluding certain 'environmental' crimes under the Environmental Protection Act 1990), and 'family proceedings' (further defined in that section).

But providing for enforceable conditional fee agreements is not sufficient in itself to secure broad access to justice. The present funding regime incorporates two essential additional features.

Fee uplifts

Lawyers accepting work on a contingency fee basis are taking a risk. If they lose the claim, and costs are awarded in the cause, they will be paid nothing. To make this risk worthwhile, the legislation allows fee uplifts on a contingency basis. Thus, the lawyer gains nothing for those claims that are lost; but gains extra fees (above the value of the time spent on the case) for those that are won. A claimant lawyer who assesses risks appropriately should not lose out over time.

Since the maximum permissible 'success fee' (uplift) is set at 100 per cent, fees can in some cases be demanded which are double the value of the work actually undertaken.[53] The burden of this inflated fee was initially placed on claimants, the 'success fee' being reclaimed out of damages. In some instances, this might make the action much less worthwhile, and in a personal injury action might lead to significant under-compensation. By the Access to Justice Act 1999, there has been an extremely significant change in the CFA regime. The burden of the success fee is now placed upon losing defendants.

---

[53] Note however that the reasonableness of the success fee is dependent on the nature of the case: see further *Callery v Gray*, below.

Courts and Legal Services Act 1990

Section 58A[54]

. . .

(6) A costs order made in any proceedings may, subject in the case of court proceedings to rules of court, include provision requiring the payment of any fees payable under a conditional fee agreement which provides for a success fee.

(7) Rules of court may make provision with respect to the assessment of any costs which include fees payable under a conditional fee agreement (including one which provides for a success fee).

Practice Directions accompanying the Civil Procedure Rules explain how the reasonableness of the success fee should be addressed. Such assessment may include reference to the risks associated with undertaking the claim. While there is a general overriding objective that the costs of civil litigation should be 'proportionate', the recoverability of a success fee necessarily means that in some circumstances, costs will be recovered which are *not* 'proportionate' *to the work required in that particular case.*

Behind these provisions is a deliberate strategy, aiming to displace the costs of litigation *from* the state (via legal aid), *to* losing defendants. Recently, this policy goal was bluntly spelt out by Lord Hoffmann in a case concerned not with personal injury but with breach of confidence. This case is further explored in Chapter 13, since it draws out some special implications of the new funding arrangements as they relate to freedom of speech and actions to protect reputation, confidence, and privacy.

Lord Hoffmann, *Campbell v MGN (No 2)* [2005] UKHL 61; [2005] 1 WLR 3394

16 . . . there is no doubt that a deliberate policy of the 1999 Act was to impose the cost of all CFA litigation, successful or unsuccessful, upon unsuccessful defendants as a class. Losing defendants were to be required to contribute to the funds which would enable lawyers to take on other cases which might not be successful but would provide access to justice for people who could not otherwise have afforded to sue. In some kinds of litigation, such as personal injury actions, the funds provided by losing defendants were intended to be in substitution for funds previously provided by the state in the form of legal aid.

Given that the goal is to displace risks from the taxpayer, to losing defendants, it is worth noting that a good proportion of losing defendants will be public authorities, or others (such as NHS Trusts) funded at public expense. Although there has been much debate about risk aversion and the deterrent effect of liability, it is reasonable to consider whether and to what extent the deterrent effect of paying inflated fees is inclined to tip the balance against the provision of certain valuable services by defendants.

---

[54] Inserted by Access to Justice Act 1999, s 27(1).

ATE Insurance

The second additional problem is that, if costs are awarded in the cause, a losing claimant can presume that he or she will be ordered to *pay the winning defendant's costs*. Few claimants in a personal injury action will have the means to do this. Therefore, an essential component of the new funding arrangements is After the Event (ATE) Insurance. This insurance is taken out after the accident or injury, generally at the time of making a claim.[55] In return for a premium, the ATE insurer will pay the defendant's costs if the claim fails. ATE policies are negotiated by claimants' solicitors, rather than by claimants themselves. Initially, ATE premiums were, like success fees, payable by a winning claimant. Through the 1999 changes, ATE premiums too are payable by losing defendants.

Access to Justice Act 1999

29 Recovery of insurance premiums by way of costs

Where in any proceedings a costs order is made in favour of any party who has taken out an insurance policy against the risk of incurring a liability in those proceedings, the costs payable to him may, subject in the case of court proceedings to rules of court, include costs in respect of the premium of the policy.

The implications of this particular change have proved troubling. Whereas the possibility of recoverable success fees aimed to transfer the costs of litigation from the state to losing defendants, the recoverability of ATE premiums from losing defendants means that the claimant now pays neither costs nor insurance premiums, win or lose; while claimants' solicitors are indemnified provided they do not take more unsuccessful than successful claims. The problem with this is the lack of any incentive on claimants and their solicitors to keep costs to a reasonable level; and the lack of any control over costs on the part of defendants. These problems have emerged very strongly in recent case law concerned with recovery of ATE premiums.

Callery v Gray [2002] UKHL 28; [2002] 1 WLR 2000

This was a small-scale road accident case involving minor injuries. There was a very low (even tiny) risk that the claim would be resisted. The claimant entered into a CFA with solicitors, agreeing a fee uplift of 60 per cent despite the straightforward nature of the work. He also paid an ATE insurance premium of £350 to cover the possibility of failure (and therefore of paying costs), even though this possibility was remote. The defendant quickly admitted liability and agreed to pay both damages, and reasonable costs, but then argued that the costs claimed were excessive. The 60 per cent uplift was too high, and there was no need to take out ATE insurance at such an early stage, when there was no reason to think that the claim would be resisted.

A district judge in costs only proceedings ruled that a success fee of 40 per cent (but not 60 per cent) was reasonable, and that the costs of the insurance premium could also be recovered. This decision was upheld on appeal to a judge. The Court of Appeal ([2001] 1 WLR 2112)

---

[55] The appropriate time for taking out this insurance—on making the claim, or on discovering whether it would be resisted—was the subject of discussion in *Callery v Gray*.

agreed that it was reasonable to take out ATE insurance on first consulting a solicitor in respect of a modest claim of this nature, and provided the premium was reasonable this would be recoverable even if there was an early settlement in respect of liability.[56] However, the maximum allowable success fee was 20 per cent. Recoverable costs were reduced accordingly.

The House of Lords declined to interfere with the judgment of the Court of Appeal, noting that that court had 'front-line responsibility for making the new system work fairly and effectively' (Lord Bingham at [5]). However, the House noted certain problems associated with the risk free environment enjoyed by claimants under the new arrangements. Lord Hoffmann described the claim in issue as being 'as certain of success as anything in litigation can be' (at [21]), and noted that the Court of Appeal called it a 'very, very low risk case'. A success fee of 20 per cent, and the early decision to take out ATE insurance, could be justified only by taking a 'global' view (taking into account the policy of the changes), and not by reference to the risks of the claim in question. The difficulties were identified by various members of the House. The following extract is illustrative.

Lord Hoffmann, *Callery v Gray* [2002] 1 WLR 2000

24 The second argument was that by agreeing to a success fee at the first meeting, the client so to speak insures himself against having to pay a higher one later if his case turns out to be more difficult than at first appeared. (This is very similar to the argument for an early ATE insurance, which I shall come to later.) At first sight, therefore, one could say that agreeing an immediate success fee is no more than economically rational behaviour on the part of any client and that the fee should therefore be recoverable as an expense reasonably incurred.

25 The difficulty is that while, in principle, it may be rational to agree a success fee at the earliest moment, it is extremely difficult to say whether the actual "premium" paid by the client was reasonable or not. This is because the client does not pay the "premium", whether the success fee is agreed at an earlier or later stage. The transaction therefore lacks the features of a normal insurance, in which the transaction takes place against the background of an insurance market in which the economically rational client or his broker will choose the cheapest insurance suited to his needs. Since the client will in no event be paying the success fee out of his pocket or his damages, he is not concerned with economic rationality. He has no interest in what the fee is. The only persons who have such an interest are the solicitor on the one hand and the liability insurer who will be called upon to pay it on the other. And their interest centres entirely upon whether the agreed success fee will or will not exceed what the costs judge is willing to allow.

Although the House was willing to accept the Court of Appeal's judgment, Lords Hoffmann and Scott rather doubted whether further time and experience would really assist in the judgment of a 'reasonable' success fee (uplift) for routine cases, because of the absence of any real market in respect of costs and ATE insurance; and because the judgment of 'reasonableness' was now being conducted in 'global' terms, rather than by reference to the issues in the particular case.

---

[56] The reasonableness of the particular premium was confirmed by the Court of Appeal in a second judgment, arrived at with the benefit of further evidence: [2001] 1 WLR 2142.

Lord Hoffmann

35 As my noble and learned friend, Lord Scott of Foscote has observed, the criteria prescribed by the Civil Procedure Rules for determining whether costs are reasonable are framed
entirely by reference to the facts of the particular case. Once one invokes a global approach
designed to produce a reasonable overall return for solicitors, one moves away from the judicial function of the costs judge and into the territory of legislative or administrative decision.

There are signs that the Court of Appeal has begun to share some of the scepticism
expressed by the House of Lords over the fairness of the current funding structure.

Rogers v Merthyr Tydfil County Borough Council [2006] EWCA Civ 1134 (CA)

The claimant (aged 11 at the time of the accident) was injured when he fell on broken glass in
a play area in Merthyr Tydfil. He sued the local authority. The action was initially resisted, but
liability was eventually conceded and damages were assessed at £3,105 plus interest. Costs
were assessed at £16,821.30, clearly much higher than the value of the claim. Included in these
costs was an ATE premium of £5,103 (again, higher than the value of the claim). A 100 per cent
success fee was also upheld: the evidence was that the claimant's legal advisers lost 70 per cent
of 'slipping and tripping' cases that it brought to trial, so the risks were high. The size of the
ATE premium was explained partly by the size of the likelihood of failure, and partly by the
fact that it operated through a 'three-stage' premium. The size of the premium increased at
each stage, if the claim had not settled. A smaller total premium could have been paid at the
start to cover the whole risk; but of course if the advisers habitually adopted that sort of policy for their clients, very low risk claims which did settle immediately (such as the claim in
Callery v Gray, above), would be more costly to insure.

The Court of Appeal upheld the judge's assessment that the staged premium was
reasonable, and could be recovered. The fact that costs were high compared to the value of the
claim did not necessarily mean that those costs were *disproportionate*. Proportionality is
affected by risk of failure, as well as by the size of likely damages. Again, we must approach
matters in a global manner. The Court was influenced by the contention that ATE insurers
priced their products in the light of risk experience, and that the entire funding structure
presently adopted would collapse if ATE insurers were to depart the market. Although this
decision was unanimous, some strong reservations about the present funding structure were
expressed by Smith LJ in an annex to the judgment. Brooke LJ explained that the two other
members of the Court also agreed with her comments, which we now extract.

Smith LJ, *Rogers v Merthyr Tydfil* [2006] EWCA Civ 1134

124 First, the figures . . . show that, of the 5% of slipping and tripping cases which proceed
to trial, about 70% fail. Legal advisers are being insufficiently robust in the advice they give at
the late stage when a decision has to be taken whether to abandon the case or go to trial.

. . .

125 When the government of the day abolished legal aid for most personal injury actions and brought in the provisions of the Access to Justice Act 1999, my understanding was that it was intended that all claimants would have as good a means of access to the courts as a litigant who could afford to fund his claim from his own resources. This was to be achieved through CFAs and ATE. By the use of uplifts on base costs, solicitors would take the rough with the smooth and make about the same level of profit as they would if they were acting for private clients. The other costs of litigation, particularly the risk of paying the defendants' costs, were to be insured by ATE and, in the end, passed to liability insurers and through them to the general premium paying public.

126 However, I do not think it was the intention of Parliament that would-be claimants should be able to litigate weak cases without any risk whatsoever to themselves. But it seems to me that this is what is happening. ATE premiums are set on the basis of a high expected failure rate at trial. Even cases that are assessed at a prospect of success of only 51% receive ATE insurance. Thus the premiums have to be significantly higher than they would be if a more rigorous standard were applied. Often no premium has to be paid upfront. If the case is lost the premium is rarely paid. That practice inevitably increases the premiums even further. If the case is won, the premium is in principle recoverable from the liability nsurer and, as this court has held in the instant case, if it was necessary for the claimant to take out ATE insurance and the solicitor has acted reasonably, the whole premium will be recovered.

127 Two things concern me about this situation. One is that there is very little incentive for solicitors to look for the best value in ATE insurance. One can understand the position of someone like Mr Cater whose primary concern is to protect his client from the kind of problem that he had experienced with his previous provider. He can quite sensibly justify opting for a more expensive product. His client will never have to pay the premium regardless of the outcome. As the judgement of the court acknowledges, there is a pressure on insurers to keep their premiums at a reasonable level in order to avoid challenges such as has occurred in this case. However, the judgement in this case may well have the effect of reducing that pressure.

128 ... At present, the insured claimant can notionally pay the high premium which reflects his poor chances of success, secure in the knowledge that, if he wins, the premium will be recovered and, if he loses, he can walk away unscathed. I find it hard to believe that Parliament intended that claimants should be in so much better a position than a private litigant.

A higher premium reflects a greater risk of failure. A high premium would, in an ordinary market, focus the mind of the purchaser on whether it is worth paying that premium (and thus, whether it is worth taking the risk of failure). But this is no ordinary market, and the high premium has no effect at all on the claimant's decision. Provided legal advisers are willing to accept a 70 per cent failure rate, they will persist with weak claims and the insurance premium will do nothing to stop this. The premium will however add considerably to the costs of public authority defendants who are faced with many unmeritorious claims. Can they really afford not to settle these claims?

How Big is the Problem?

The background to CFAs and the associated funding arrangements is that governments have not wanted to burden a reluctant taxpayer with the cost of civil claims through legal aid. But we need to consider whether the present funding structure is also contributing to the phenomenon which is commonly called 'compensation culture'. In the following extract, Kennedy LJ (writing extra-judicially) argues strongly that it is.

Paul Kennedy, 'Is this the way we want to go?' (2005) JPIL 117–28, 121–2

What if anything went wrong?

So what if anything went wrong round about the turn of the century? Almost everyone seems to agree that things did begin to go wrong, but there is little agreement as to the reasons for the distortion of the employers' liability market place. I have already mentioned rising damages and costs, but what really troubled insurers was the obligation to pay damages in respect of risks of which they had been unaware, such as mesothelioma manifesting itself long after exposure. Until the condition began to manifest itself there was often little, if any, appreciation of the risk, so the employer had never been called upon to pay an appropriate premium. There are other examples of these long tail claims, as they are called, which have emerged during the last decade, and, partly because many of the relevant events took place so long ago, they are very expensive to investigate and difficult to meet. In addition, insurers have had to shoulder two other burdens, neither of which confers any benefit on claimants or their employers.

First, insurers have been required, when they pay damages, to repay in full to the state the benefits received by the claimant during his period of incapacity. That is logical, and I do not seek to challenge it, but it is a big change as there used to be no repayment and the tortfeasor used to be able to set against any claim for loss of earnings one half of the benefits which the claimant had received, so the impact upon employers and their insurers of the change in the law is obvious.

The second additional burden cast upon employers and their insurers is a huge increase in the costs which they are required to pay to a successful claimant. This is largely as a result of the changes introduced by the Access to Justice Act 1999 which opened the way to conditional fees and after the event insurance. It may also to some extent be due to the front-loading of fees which has resulted from the changes known as the Woolf Reforms.

The justification offered for opening the door to conditional fees and after the event insurance was that the burden of legal aid had become unsustainable, and that the changes would render justice more accessible. In relation to employers' liability, I have never been persuaded by that attempt to justify what was done, and everyone now recognises that the changes had some appalling results. I accept that the demands on the legal aid fund had become enormous, and probably unsustainable, but that was largely because of criminal and family litigation. As I have already indicated, demands from employers' liability claims were limited, because of the role of trade unions, and where legal aid was granted it was at least initially well controlled. If, in later years, it became less well controlled then the remedy surely was to restore control, not to eliminate, and the Bar Council under the chairmanship of Lord Brennan Q.C. put forward a scheme which would have made legal aid in personal injury cases largely, if not completely, self-financing. It required successful claimants to contribute a small percentage of their damages to the fund. Why that scheme was not adopted I do not know. Of course I recognise the inability of the old scheme to protect a potential plaintiff of limited means, or an uninsured defendant sued by a legally aided plaintiff, but those were problems which could have been sorted out piecemeal without opening the door to claims management companies and their ambulance chasers. Obviously the advent of contingency fees was bound to increase the costs which an employer or his insurers had to pay to settle a claim, and it seems clear that the increase has far outweighed any advantage to employers and their insurers which arises from their increased ability to recover costs when a claim fails.

Initially, it seems, the problems faced by insurers were not passed on to employers in the form of higher premiums because the insurers operate in their own competitive market place and at least one competitor, Independent Insurance, was charging premiums which were so low that they eventually resulted in insolvency. The bubble then burst. The insurers who remained, and it is worth noting that five multinational companies write 70 per cent of the business, raised their premiums sharply. Some employers operating in higher risk areas found it very difficult indeed to get insurance at a price they could afford, and both in government and in the City people began to get worried. If employers cannot get employers' liability, and for that matter, public liability insurance at a realistic price, they will either eliminate exposure by going out of business with the result that some services will become unobtainable, or they will expose their employees and others by trading illegally uninsured, and if in due course they cannot meet an obligation, that will be yet another burden on the insurers who continue to operate in the field.

The implication is that legal changes including the government's own strategy of reform to litigation contribute to the growing costs of personal injury litigation, and perhaps encourage a perverse and undesirable pattern of liability. In short, defendants find it increasingly risky to resist claims brought by a claimant with the benefit of a CFA and ATE insurance. But a growing consensus holds that sometimes, it is desirable if defendants *do* resist claims. This brings us to the next issue.

8. 'COMPENSATION CULTURE' DEBATE

The idea that a 'compensation culture' is taking root in the UK, and that this culture must be eradicated, has recently gained political currency. It has been taken up with some enthusiasm by the popular press.

8.1 WHAT IS 'COMPENSATION CULTURE'?

'Compensation culture' is a political not a legal term. The following assertion by the Rt Hon Lord Falconer of Thoroton, the Lord Chancellor, is quoted by the House of Commons Constitutional Affairs Committee in its Report on Compensation Culture (3rd Report Session 2005–6) at p 14:

The Lord Chancellor (speaking at a Conference on Risk and Redress: Preventing a Compensation Culture, 17 November 2005)

It is vital compensation claims continue to play their part in improving health and safety. But we must be clear that our continued commitment to legitimate compensation claims is entirely consistent with rejecting a culture which says for every injury there must be someone liable to pay. That culture stultifies reasonable risk taking, it hits organisational efficiency and competitiveness and it prevents worthwhile activity.

This statement captures nicely two aspects of the alleged phenomenon of a 'compensation culture'. These two aspects are:

1. A culture, unhealthy in itself, which says that someone must be liable to pay for every injury.

2. The effect of this culture, which is *to stultify reasonable risk-taking*.

8.2 DOES 'COMPENSATION CULTURE' EXIST?

A number of studies have sought to test the existence of a 'compensation culture'.[57] One potential indicator of such a culture would be an excessive number of claims. It is clear that there has been a rise in personal injury claims in the last 30 years, though even this does not mean that there are now *excessive* claims. These claims might be highly meritorious, and the rise may be due to a laudable improvement in access to justice, for example, or to the success of legislative policy over this period. But more importantly, the empirical results consistently suggest that there has been no rise—in fact a decline—in personal injury claims since 2000, which is the time that the major reforms to litigation funding outlined in the last section began to take effect.[58] Further, personal injury awards continue to represent a relatively low proportion of the UK's Gross Domestic Product, compared with other European countries. It seems we are *not* in the grip of a widespread 'culture of claiming'.

On the other hand, it is generally accepted that the new funding arrangements and the relaxation of advertising rules have between them given rise to an industry of 'claims farming'. This includes not just general advertising but seeking potential business by targeting individuals who may have a claim—inside or outside hospitals for example, or by contract with those who operate recovery vehicles. It is easy to see how this might feed a *sense* that there is a culture of blame, whether there really is or not. The second part of the Compensation Act 2006 sets out a framework for the regulation of claims management companies, and this has been almost universally welcomed.

8.3 RISK AVERSION?

Perhaps bizarrely, the most substantial remaining concern appears to be not that there is an excessive claims culture, but that *those who are responsible for taking beneficial risks in society are prone to act as though there were*. They act too defensively, depriving society of many amenities and opportunities. The real crux of the government's concern here appears to be with the unnecessary avoidance of risk-taking, where risk-taking would be beneficial.[59]

The legislative 'solution' adopted so far is section 1 of the Compensation Act 2006, which we extracted in Chapter 3.

---

[57] See Better Regulation Task Force, *Better Routes to Redress* (May 2004); R. Lewis et al, 'Tort Personal Injury Claims Statistics: Is There a Compensation Culture in the UK?' (2006) 14 TLJ 158–75; K. Williams, 'State of Fear: Britain's Compensation Culture Reviewed' (2005) 25 LS 499.

[58] The Department of Constitutional Affairs suggests a decline of 5% in all personal injury claims in the period 2000–2005.

[59] We have already seen, by reference to the funding of litigation, that the construction of a risk free environment for claimants, together with higher costs as a result of success fees, is making it much more hazardous for defendants to resist claims. The relative importance of this has not been explored by the government, which has no wish to return to extensive civil legal aid.

The following extract is taken from a work examining the impact of liability on outdoor activities including school trips. The perceived reluctance of schools and teachers to offer such activities is often given as an example of 'compensation culture' at work:

Julian Fulbrook, *Outdoor Activities, Negligence and the Law*
(Ashgate, 2005), at 261

No doubt there will continue to be a spirited debate on the right balance between safety consciousness and the demands of spontaneity, between what Lord Scott of Foscote in the House of Lords in the leading case of *Tomlinson v Congleton BC* suggested were the contrasts of 'some risks of accidents arising out of the *joie de vivre* of the very young' and the straitjacket of 'imposing a grey and dull safety regime on everyone'. . . . Lord Hoffmann's strident perspective in a sub-heading in that case, 'FREE WILL' (his capitals), led to those *obiter* remarks being duly translated by the *Sunday Telegraph* as 'Britain's most senior judges have demanded an end to 'the culture of "blame and compensation" in a landmark ruling which decrees that individuals must take responsibility for their own actions'. The *Daily Mail* followed suit with a diatribe against 'ambulance-chasing' law firms stating with enthusiasm in a headline that the law lords in *Tomlinson* 'brand compensation culture as a crippling "evil"', and quoting a representative of the law firm representing the Borough Council saying that 'this decision effectively means that people can enjoy themselves as much as before'. While some might quibble that 'enjoyment' can include breaking your neck, a more reasoned view of that case might see a difficult balance on 'cost-benefit analysis', with the majority in the Court of Appeal tilting in one way and the House of Lords tilting in the opposite direction. The old aphorism that 'hard cases make bad law' suggests that this might be a 'fact sensitive' judgment, rather than a clarion call for the overthrow of tort law.

Given the status of the question of school trips (and their scarcity) in discussion of 'good risk-taking' and deterrence, it is important to note the general conclusion of Fulbrook's study. He suggests that although 'zero risk' obviously cannot be attained, 'there have been very considerable gains made in safety at relatively low cost'—and 'there are still plenty of inexpensive advances yet to be made'. Risk assessment, and health and safety procedures, remain highly cost effective ways of saving life and limb.

FURTHER READING

Atiyah, P., *The Damages Lottery* (Oxford: Hart Publishing, 1997).

Beever, A., 'The Structure of Aggravated and Exemplary Damages' (2003) 23 OJLS 87–110.

Burrows, A., *Remedies for Torts and Breach of Contract* (2nd edn, Oxford: OUP, 1994).

Cane, P., *Atiyah's Accidents, Compensation and the Law* (8th edn, Cambridge: CUP, 2006).

Edelman, J., *Gain-Based Damages* (Oxford: Hart Publishing, 2002).

Harris, D., Campbell, D., and Halson, R., *Remedies in Contract and Tort* (2nd edn, Cambridge: CUP, 2002).

Hoyano, L., 'The Dutiful Tortfeasor in the House of Lords' [1995] *Tort L Rev* 63.

Law Commission, *Aggravated, Exemplary and Restitutionary Damages*, Law Com No 247 (London: HMSO, 1997).

Lewis, R., 'Insurance and the Tort System' (2005) 25 LS 85.

Lewis, R., 'The Politics and Economics of Tort Law: Judicially Imposed Periodical Payments of Damages' (2006) 69 MLR 418.

Morgan, J., 'Tort, Insurance and Incoherence' (2004) 67 MLR 384.

Stapleton, J., 'Tort, Insurance and Ideology' (1995) 58 MLR 820.

Williams, K., 'State of Fear: Britain's Compensation Culture Reviewed' (2005) 25 LS 499.

Worthington, S., 'Reconsidering Disgorgement for Wrongs' (1999) 62 MLR 219.

9

VICARIOUS LIABILITY AND NON-DELEGABLE DUTIES

CENTRAL ISSUES

i) Vicarious liability involves a notable departure from general tort principles. It imposes liability for another's tort, and may be referred to as a form of secondary liability.

ii) Vicarious liability typically operates where the person committing the tort is an **employee or agent** of the defendant. If that person is an 'independent contractor', there will be no vicarious liability. For vicarious liability to bite in an employment case, the tort must be committed **in the course of employment**. This requirement has been redefined by the courts in recent years and is now judged in terms of 'close connection' with the employment. This redefined test has been developed chiefly in cases of deliberate acts of criminal wrongdoing on the part of employees. Here, the strictness of the liability imposed on employers is particularly stark.

iii) There is a division between those who embrace vicarious liability with some enthusiasm; and those who are more sceptical of its justifications. The latter group tend to require a closer connection between the tort, and the employer's own duties or actions, before vicarious liability can operate. But this can compromise the clarity of the doctrine as a form of secondary liability. It leads to some unfortunate blurring of the lines between vicarious liability, and the forms of primary liability to which we turn next.

iv) Under some circumstances, parties are said to be subject to **non-delegable duties**. This means that although *tasks* creating certain risks can appropriately be delegated to others, *duties* in respect of those risks cannot. Analytically, this is very different from vicarious liability because it gives rise to liability for the breach of one's own duty, even if the breach is committed by another. It is a form of primary (or 'personal') liability. But in practice, the effect will be much the same, since the defendant is liable where the fault (if any) was someone else's. Glanville Williams described the idea of 'non-delegable duty' as a 'logical fraud', but Australian

> courts have made extensive use of the 'non-delegable duty' device.
>
> v) There are also some more straightforward ways in which primary liability may be imposed on a person whose
>
> independent contractor has committed a tort. For example, carelessly selecting or (if relevant) failing to supervise a contractor or employee may involve a breach of one's own duty of care.

1. VICARIOUS LIABILITY

Under the principle of vicarious liability, an employer will be liable for the tort of his or her employee, provided that tort is sufficiently connected with the individual's employment. The principle is not confined to negligence but is general: recent case law illustrates that it extends both to intentional torts and to statutory liability. There are also some circumstances outside the employment relationship where vicarious liability applies. An example is liability within a partnership for the torts of a partner.

Historically, attempts were made to explain the doctrine of vicarious liability by suggesting that the tort is really that of the employer.[1] The better view is the simpler one, that the employee commits a tort; but the employer is liable.[2] Such a departure from general principle requires justification.

There are a number of possible justifications for vicarious liability and to some extent we must accept that these are mutually reinforcing. It is important to be clear about the justifications, not least because they tend to overlap. As McLachlin J put it in *Bazley v Curry* [1999] 2 SCR 534 at 551, in this context 'the best route to enduring principle may well lie through policy'.[3] We should make clear though that 'policy' in this context is a very wide term, which is not confined to 'public interest' arguments, but includes considerations of justice and fairness.

1.1 POSSIBLE JUSTIFICATIONS FOR VICARIOUS LIABILITY

Here we divide the possible justifications for vicarious liability into three main categories. Many variations are possible.[4] Writing in 1967, Atiyah discussed nine traditional justifications for vicarious liability and added 'social insurance' as a modern addition, making ten.[5]

---

[1] This idea is discussed by G. Williams, 'Vicarious Liability: Tort of the Master or Tort of the Servant?' (1956) 72 LQR 522.

[2] This was clearly stated by the House of Lords in *Dubai Aluminium v Salaam* [2003] 2 AC 366 and reiterated by Lord Nicholls in *Majrowski v Guy's and St Thomas's NHS Trust* [2006] UKHL 34. On the other hand, we will explain below that some ambiguity even in respect of this very basic point continues to flow from the leading case of *Lister v Hesley Hall* [2002] 1 AC 215.

[3] As Stephen Waddams has pointed out, on the same day and on a similar issue Binnie J said in a judgment of the same court that 'judicial policy must yield to legal principle': *Jacobi v Griffiths* [1999] 2 SCR 570 at 593. McLachlin J dissented. S. Waddams, *Dimensions of Private Law* (CUP, 2003), 192.

[4] These particular three reasons broadly follow the outline in G. Williams and B. Hepple, *Foundations of the Law of Tort* (1976), 112–15.

[5] Atiyah, *Vicarious Liability* (Butterworths, 1967), 15–27. Some of the nine are more addressed to the conduct of the employer, and are perhaps less relevant now that the nature of vicarious liability as liability for the employee's tort has been clarified.

In *Bazley v Curry*, McLachlin J (following the lead of the late John Fleming, *Law of Torts*, 9th edn, pp. 409–10) referred to two key justifications. The Fleming approach was recently endorsed by Lord Nicholls in *Majrowski v Guy's and St Thomas' NHS Trust* [2006] UKHL 34. In fact, the two justifications referred to by Fleming ('fair compensation' and deterrence) are effectively the same as the three below, but justice and compensation are run together. Here we introduce them separately since they may operate either separately, or together.

We should note that the effect of justifications for vicarious liability is cumulative:

Atiyah, *Vicarious Liability in the Law of Tort*, at 15

In a complex modern society the justification for a particular legal principle may frequently have to be sought in many considerations. None of them taken by itself may be a sufficient reason for the principle, but the combined effect of all of them may be overwhelming. Of course this means that in any particular case where some of the factors put forward in justification are present and others are not, some sort of balancing operation needs to be made, but this is itself a familiar part of the legal process.

We will return to this point periodically. Recent case law tends to underline its force.

Justice Arguments

At first sight, it is strange to offer arguments of justice for holding someone liable for the torts of another. But there are some very respectable justice arguments to this effect. In particular, it is said that the defendant should take the *risk* of harm, either because s/he takes the *benefit* of the activity that creates that risk, or because of his or her role in creating the risk.[6] This argument can be described as a theory of enterprise risk, of a moral rather than an economic sort. That is to say, the enterprise should take on the risks it creates and from which it benefits; it is not fair and just that these risks should be passed to others. This justice argument does not depend on saying that there is anything 'wrong' with creating the risk. Further, this approach can be used to justify 'normal' risks inherent in an enterprise, and does not require that the defendant should have 'enhanced' those inherent risks in any way.[7]

An alternative, *economic* variant of 'enterprise risk' is sometimes encountered, for example in the law of nuisance (Chapter 10 above). The idea here is that the costs of an enterprise ought to be 'internalized' in order to stimulate the most *efficient* level of risk taking. If the enterprise is able to place the risks on another, then it will be tempted to take risks which are not socially efficient, because they come at no cost. This economic variant has not been fully addressed in the recent case law on vicarious liability. It is the moral version that has been emphasized.

The moral version of the enterprise risk analysis may need variation where the defendant is carrying out an activity for the benefit of the whole community; or where the defendant has

---

[6] This is essentially the same as the fairness argument for strict liability under *Rylands v Fletcher*, which is debated in Chapter 11 below. The link between *Rylands* liability, and vicarious liability issues is strong since *Rylands* itself was a case of negligence on the part of contractors (rather than employees).

[7] Lord Nicholls has clearly embraced this principle in *Dubai Aluminium v Salaam* [2003] 2 AC 366; *Majrowski v Guy's and St Thomas's Hospital Trust* [2006] UKHL 34.

no choice in the matter because there is a statutory obligation to carry out the risk-creating activity. An alternative analysis is on hand to suit such cases: it would not be fair and just for an individual to take the whole risk which is created by satisfying the community's need for (say) policing, or national defence.[8] The costs and risks of essential public services should be spread around.

This justification seems not to explain why there is *no* vicarious liability for the torts of independent contractors. Liability whenever I 'benefit from' a risk would be very far-reaching since I benefit from many risks. One answer to this is that independent contractors, being independent and working for their own profit, form their own separate 'enterprise': 'it is the contractor who is the *entrepreneur*'.[9] In other words, although enterprise risk *could* justify imposing broad vicarious liability, there is a particular reason why we might choose to draw the line here. Glanville Williams adds in support a practical argument, that liability for contractors would simply be inconvenient. Since the contractor would also remain liable, it would multiply the number of parties against whom an action may be brought and increase expense and uncertainty.

Whether these arguments remain convincing given change in the nature of modern employment relationships is open to debate. Many non-employees are not really 'entrepreneurs'. Rather, they are part of a shifting and informal work force: see the discussion by E. McKendrick, 'Vicarious Liability and Independent Contractors—A Reexamination' (1990) 53 MLR 770. This does not undermine the enterprise risk justification; rather, it shows how important that justification may be in considering the appropriate response to current changes.[10]

Incentive and Deterrence Arguments

The argument from deterrence is that the employer has the *opportunity* to increase standards of safety, for example through better procedures for selecting employees and for their supervision. Therefore, it is best if there is an *incentive* for him or her to do so, through liability for the employee's tort.

It is sometimes said that this argument does not explain why liability is justified in cases where the accident was unavoidable, in that all due care has been applied in selection of employee, maintenance of equipment, and so on. But this criticism is misplaced. Modern theories of regulation suggest that better outcomes will be achieved not by setting fixed standards, but by offering incentives through which the enterprise may *improve* safety standards. The deterrence theory is better expressed as an *incentive* theory: vicarious liability gives employers incentives to find ways to improve safety standards beyond those set by the

---

[8] An argument along these lines will be encountered in Chapter 10 in respect of nuisances that are in the public interest: see in particular *Dennis v MoD* [2003] EWHC 793 (QB).

[9] Y. B. Smith (1923) 23 Col. L Rev 444, 461; quoted by G. Williams, 'Liability for Independent Contractors' (1956) CLJ 180, 196.

[10] For a similar problem caused by complex *corporate* structures (making it more difficult to identify a solvent responsible party), see Hugh Collins, 'Ascription of Legal Responsibility to Groups in Complex Patterns of Economic Integration' (1990) 53 MLR 731–84.

standard of the 'reasonable person':

McLachlin J, *Bazley v Curry*

Beyond the narrow band of employer conduct that attracts direct liability in negligence lies a vast area where imaginative and efficient administration and supervision can reduce the risk that the employer has introduced into the community.

Equally, and for the same reasons, the idea that an employer is in the best position to 'control' risks is not simply a covert reference to employer's 'fault'. Indeed any such reference would be most unhelpful as it would blur the distinction between vicarious and 'primary' liability. Rather, the incentive argument is general and prospective: liability on employers creates incentives to think up good ways of minimizing risks.

Loss Spreading/Deep Pockets Arguments

The third set of justifications for vicarious liability focuses on the need to compensate victims of tortious conduct. Generally, the most promising route for compensation is through the liability of the employer. At its most basic, this is no more than a deep pockets argument: where funds are available, the best solution is to attach liability to the person with the ability to pay. Introducing *insurance* into the equation makes this into a more modern argument: the risk of harm should be managed by the defendant and spread through a risk-bearing community, not placed entirely upon the vulnerable claimant. This justification was described by Atiyah in 1967 as the dominant justification for vicarious liability among North American writers; and Atiyah himself concluded that the loss-spreading argument was broadly sound:

Atiyah, *Vicarious Liability in the Law of Tort*, at 26

. . . it seems that in general the policy of placing the liability for the torts of the servants on their employers is broadly a sound one. It is sound simply because, by and large, it is the most convenient and efficient way of ensuring that persons injured in the course of business enterprises do not go uncompensated. Of course if all workmen insured themselves against third party risks, and if wages and salaries were slightly increased in order to allow workmen to do this, we could get on pretty well without vicarious liability at all. But this would not be so efficient or convenient a way of doing things simply because it would involve an enormous number of insurance policies instead of relatively few, with consequent increase in insurance costs. . . .

In recent case law a 'pure' loss-spreading argument has not been accepted. Rather, loss-spreading has been combined with the first, justice-based form of justification explored above. As we have said, this is the version propounded by John Fleming and endorsed by the Supreme Court of Canada in *Bazley v Curry*. It is almost the reverse of Atiyah's position since he doubted whether vicarious liability was in fact the most *equitable* means of spreading losses, even though he accepted that it was a convenient and efficient one. He doubted its fairness because often, risks are contributed to by many people: there is no single 'risk creator'.[11]

In conclusion, vicarious liability is best justified at the intersection of all three of the reasons above. It is important to be clear about this because typically, English case law does little more than hint at the policy rationales for the doctrine. Judgments contain references to (apparently) different concerns, such as loss spreading and also 'fairness'. We have just seen that these justifications are not necessarily in conflict. In *Viasystems v Thermal Transfer* [2006] 2 WLR 428, Rix LJ used judicial shorthand to encapsulate this when he said that vicarious liability applies where it is 'fair, just, and convenient' for it to do so.

On the other hand, these different concerns will not necessarily all pull in the same direction in every case. Where they pull in different directions (as for example in the claims against non-profit organizations in *Bazley v Curry* and *Jacobi v Griffiths*, considered below), then as Aityah proposed, the most difficult judgments have to be made.

1.2 WHO IS AN EMPLOYEE (AND WHO IS THEIR EMPLOYER)?

Vicarious liability depends in an employment case on showing that the person committing the tort was an 'employee' of the defendant. If this is established, then it will also be necessary to show that the tort was committed 'in the course of employment' (below).

Employee or 'Contractor'?

The question of who counts as an 'employee' is not decided by reference to any single authoritative test. A first question is whether there is a single test of 'employment' which applies for all purposes (employment law, tax, tort liability), or whether employment status can be determined differently for different purposes.[12] Recent case law takes the latter approach and extends it, holding that employment status is determined not even for the purposes of actions in tort but *for the purposes of a particular accident* (see *Viasystems v Thermal Transfer* [2006] 2 WLR 428 and *Hawley v Luminar* [2006] EWCA Civ 18, below).

Even so, the next extract is not drawn from a tort case, but from an action to restrain publication for breach of confidence. Denning LJ explained that the traditional test for employment is one of **control**; that there are nevertheless many cases where the relationship is said to be one of employment despite the absence of control, for example where the employee is skilled;[13] and that an alternative question is how far the individual is 'integrated into' the business of the 'employer'.

Terminological note: A **contract of service** is the sort of contract that is entered into between employer and employee; a **contract for services** is the sort of contract entered into when appointing an independent contractor.

---

[11] Atiyah, *Vicarious Liability in the Law of Tort*, at 26.

[12] McKendrick, 'Vicarious Liability and Independent Contractors—A Reexamination' (above), argued that a more partitioned approach to the employment relationship was one way of addressing the limitations to vicarious liability in modern conditions.

[13] This has been very important in respect of medical staff. In *Cassidy v Ministry of Health* [1951] 2 KB 343, vicarious liability of hospital authorities for their staff was established. Earlier in *Gold v Essex County Council* [1942] 2 KB 293, the Court of Appeal had resorted to the idea of a 'non-delegable duty' in respect of such staff (see Section 2 below); this will not now be necessary.

Denning LJ, *Stephenson, Jordan and Harrison Ltd v Macdonald & Evans*
[1952] 69 RPC 10

[This case] raises the troublesome question: What is the distinction between a contract of service and a contract for services? The test usually applied is whether the employer has the right to control the manner of doing the work. Thus in *Collins v. Herts County Council* [1947] K.B. 598, Hilbery, J., said (at p. 615): "The distinction between a contract for services and a contract of service can be summarised in this way: In the one case the master can order or require what is to be done, while in the other cases, he can not only require what is to be done but how it shall be done". But in *Cassidy v. The Ministry of Health* [1951] 2 K.B. 343, Somervell, L.J., at pp. 352–3, pointed out that that test is not universally correct. There are many contracts of service where the master cannot control the manner in which the work is to be done, as in the case of a captain of a ship. Somervell, L.J., went on to say that "One perhaps cannot get much beyond this 'Was the contract a contract "of service within the meaning which an ordinary person would give under the words'." I respectfully agree. As my Lord has said it is almost impossible to give a precise definition of the distinction. It is often quite easy to recognise a contract of service when you see it, but very difficult to say wherein the difference lies. A ship's master, a chauffeur, and a reporter on the staff of a newspaper are all employed under a contract of service; but a ship's pilot, a taxi-man, and a newspaper contributor are employed under a contract for services. One feature which seems to me to run through the instances is that, under a contract of service, a man is employed as part of the business and his work is done as an integral part of the business: whereas under a contract for services his work, although done for the business, is not integrated into it but is only accessory to it.

The integration test expressed in this passage has not managed to displace the control test altogether. Rather, both tests are referred to in the most recent case law. In *Ready Mixed Concrete v Ministry of Pensions and National Insurance* [1968] 2 QB 497, where the court was required to categorize an individual as an employee or contractor for the purposes of deciding obligation to pay national insurance contributions, MacKenna J argued that the control test was still the dominant test, but was not sufficient. Even if there is sufficient control, it must still be asked whether the terms of the contract as a whole were *consistent with* treating it as a 'contract of service'. For example:

MacKenna J, at 520–1

If a man's activities have the character of a business, and if the question is whether he is carrying on the business for himself or for another, it must be relevant to consider which of the two owns the assets ("the ownership of the tools") and which bears the financial risk ("the chance of profit," "the risk of loss"). He who owns the assets and takes the risk is unlikely to be acting as an agent or a servant.

Borrowed and Transferred Employees, and 'Dual Employment'

What happens when the employee of one enterprise is 'hired' by another enterprise for a particular task (or for a period of time), and commits a tort while so engaged?

The leading case on this issue is *Mersey Docks and Harbour Board v Coggins* [1947] AC 1. The harbour authority (the 'Board') was the general employer of a crane operator. The Board let the crane—with its operator—to a firm of stevedores. The terms of the let provided that the crane operator would be the servant of the stevedores. Through negligent operation of the crane, injury was caused to a third party.

The House of Lords held that in these circumstances, the Board remained the employer of the crane operator. The agreement as to employment between the parties was not conclusive. The crane operator would only be regarded as employed by the stevedores if there was *clear evidence* that the employment *had been transferred* (Lord Macmillan, at 13). On the other hand, many different factors would be relevant in assessing whether employment had been so transferred.

Lord Porter, at 17

Many factors have a bearing on the result. Who is paymaster, who can dismiss, how long the alternative service lasts, what machinery is employed, have all to be kept in mind. The expressions used in any individual case must always be considered in regard to the subject matter under discussion but amongst the many tests suggested I think that the most satisfactory, by which to ascertain who is the employer at any particular time, is to ask who is entitled to tell the employee the way in which he is to do the work upon which he is engaged. If someone other than his general employer is authorized to do this he will, as a rule, be the person liable for the employee's negligence. But it is not enough that the task to be performed should be under his control, he must also control the method of performing it. It is true that in most cases no orders as to how a job should be done are given or required: the man is left to do his own work in his own way. But the ultimate question is not what specific orders, or whether any specific orders, were given but who is entitled to give the orders as to how the work should be done. Where a man driving a mechanical device, such as a crane, is sent to perform a task, it is easier to infer that the general employer continues to control the method of performance since it is his crane and the driver remains responsible to him for its safe keeping. In the present case if the appellants' contention were to prevail, the crane driver would change his employer each time he embarked on the discharge of a fresh ship. Indeed, he might change it from day to day, without any say as to who his master should be and with all the concomitant disadvantages of uncertainty as to who should be responsible for his insurance in respect of health, unemployment and accident. I cannot think that such a conclusion is to be drawn from the facts established. I would dismiss the appeal.

Lord Porter clearly thought that a transfer of employment for one purpose (vicarious liability) would imply a transfer of employment for all purposes (including unemployment insurance).

Less helpfully for those seeking to understand the basis of vicarious liability, Lord Simonds (at 18) suggested that:

The doctrine of the vicarious responsibility of the "superior," whatever its origin, is to-day justified by social necessity, but, if the question is where that responsibility should lie, the answer should surely point to that master in whose act some degree of fault, though remote, may be found. Here the fault, if any, lay with the appellants who, though they were not present to dictate how directions given by another should be carried out, yet had vested in their servant a discretion in the manner of carrying out such directions.

This is part of a recurring problem which we will also see exemplified in the following section. There is a reluctance to accept that vicarious liability is not concerned with *fault* on the part of the employer. We have emphasized above that the justifications for vicarious liability are independent of fault, though they may in some respects turn on justice (and responsibility) of a different sort.

Viasystems v Thermal Transfer [2006] 2 WLR 428 (CA)

The claimants had contracted with the first defendants to install air conditioning. The first defendants (who were liable in contract when the damage occurred) sub-contracted ducting work to the second defendants. The second defendants hired a fitter and his mate from the third defendants, to work under the supervision of an employee of the second defendants. The fitter's mate negligently crawled through a duct, fractured a fire protection sprinkler system, and caused severe flooding to the factory. Which defendant would be considered his employer for the purposes of vicarious liability?

May LJ

16 . . . The inquiry should concentrate on the relevant negligent act and then ask whose responsibility it was to prevent it.

. . .

18 The relevant negligent act was Darren Strang crawling through the duct. This was a foolish mistake on the spur of the moment. I have said that a central question is: who was entitled, *and perhaps in theory obliged*, to give orders as to how the work should or should not be done? Here there is no suggestion, on the facts found by the judge, that either Mr Horsley or Mr Megson had any real opportunity to prevent Darren's momentary foolishness. The judge specifically acquitted Mr Horsley of personal negligence: and we should proceed on the footing that Mr Megson was not personally negligent either. Vicarious liability is liability imposed by a policy of the law upon a party who is not personally at fault. So the core question on the facts of this case is who was entitled, and in theory, if they had had the opportunity, obliged, so to control Darren as to stop him crawling through the duct. In my judgment, the only sensible answer to that question in this case is that both Mr Megson and Mr Horsley were entitled, and in theory obliged, to stop Darren's foolishness. Mr Megson was the fitter in charge of Darren. Mr Horsley was the foreman on the spot. They were both entitled and obliged to control Darren's work, including the act which was his negligence.

According to this approach, the test for employment is the entitlement to control. May LJ adds that there is (perhaps) an implied *obligation* to control. This idea of 'obligation' might give the false impression (firmly rejected by May LJ in the sentences that followed) that the liability of the employer is in any sense dependent on a *failure* to control. The test for employment in respect of a particular act is capacity to control. Capacity to control indicates (even if rather roughly) the party on whom it is fair and useful to impose vicarious liability. But liability itself flows from a breach of duty by the employee.

May LJ concluded that both second and third defendants could be said to have an entitlement (and perhaps an obligation) to control Darren's actions. In principle therefore, they should both be regarded as employers. Before this case, there had long been an assumption that there could not be dual employment in respect of a single act. May LJ explained that this assumption stemmed from certain observations made by Littledale J in the case of *Laugher v Pointer* (1826) 5 B & C 547, and that there was no *binding* authority against dual employment for the purposes of vicarious liability. May LJ also pointed out that *Laugher* was decided at a time when the policy of the law was to avoid liability on the part of multiple parties. Given statutory provisions in the Law Reform (Contributory Negligence) Act 1945 and the Civil Liability (Contribution) Act 1978, this is clearly no longer the case. Since both defendants had sufficient control over the negligent party to be regarded as his employer, both would be vicariously liable. Their contribution under the Civil Liability (Contribution) Act 1978 was determined to be equal, a division regarded as inevitable given that neither employer could be said to be at fault.[14]

While agreeing that dual employment was established in this case, Rix LJ argued that 'control', though important, was not sufficient to act as a sole test for employment. Other 'structural and practical considerations' might also be relevant. In this context, he suggested, one needs to ask:

> 79 . . . whether or not the employee in question is so much part of the work business or organisation of both employers that it is just to make both employers answer for his negligence. What has to be recalled is that the vicarious liability in question is one which involves no fault on the part of the employer. It is a doctrine designed for the sake of the claimant imposing a liability incurred without fault because the employer is treated by law as picking up the burden of an organisational or business relationship which he has undertaken for his own benefit.

Rix LJ therefore emphasized the underlying policy rationale of vicarious liability. Referring to the need to divide liability according to relative 'responsibility' under the Civil Liability (Contribution) Act 1978, he went on to say:

> 84 It has been established that "responsibility" includes both causative potency and blameworthiness. However, in the case of vicarious liability, the employer is liable without personal fault. The fault in question is the employee's. The employer thus stands fully in the shoes of the negligent employee as regards both aspects of responsibility: see *Dubai Aluminium Co Ltd v Salaam* [2003] 2 AC 366, paras 47 and 160.

> 85 Where, therefore, there is dual vicarious liability arising out of the negligence of a single employee, it follows that the responsibility of each employer for the purposes of contribution must be equal. In other words, in the absence of any personal fault on the part of either employer in respect of the same damage, and in the absence of any other negligence by another employee contributing to the same damage, as here in the absence of any negligence by either Mr Megson or Mr Horsley, the essential decision as regards contribution as well as liability occurs at the time when the court determines that there is dual vicarious liability. The realisation that dual vicarious liability means equal responsibility and equal financial liability could and probably should therefore enter into the earlier and determinative decision. The question would be whether in all the circumstances, including the important question of

---

[14] Concerning the role of 'fault' in the contribution legislation, see Chapter 7.

control, vicarious liability should be shared, on the basis that the employee in question, although not formally the employee of the temporary employer, is, at least for relevant purposes, so much a part of the work, business or organisation of both employers as to make it just for there to be dual and shared liability.

The two different approaches in *Viasystems* (control, and integration) were further considered in *Hawley v Luminar* [2006] EWCA Civ 18.

A nightclub door steward, hired to keep order at the defendant's nightclub, punched the claimant and knocked him to the ground. He suffered severe brain damage. The defendant nightclub proprietor did not hire its own door staff directly, but contracted with ASE (now in liquidation),[15] to provide appropriate staff. Was Warren, who delivered the punch, to be regarded as an employee of Luminar (for whose purposes he kept order); of ASE (who contracted directly with him and with Luminar); or of both? The Court of Appeal held that it was Luminar—in whose business he was engaged at the time of the tort—who should be regarded as his sole employer.

Delivering the judgment of the court, Hallett LJ argued first that Luminar did not need to rely on the 'skill and expertise' of ASE in providing qualified door staff. They would be well capable of recruiting such staff themselves, and used the services of ASE 'partly as a device to get round employment laws' (at [74]). This approach has clear resonances with Ewan McKendrick's arguments for a more flexible and issue-specific approach to the definition of an employee.[16]

Second, although ASE had 'undertaken to provide door staff who knew how to behave':

> . . . we find it impossible to accept the further argument that responsibility for controlling this sort of behaviour fell to ASE's staff, their head doorman and the area manager. (at [75])

Rather, 'detailed control' of the door staff was exercised by Luminar's management.

Further, Warren was present at the club, 'decked out' in Luminar uniform and taking instructions from Luminar's management, for two years. To customers and passers by, he would be taken to be an employee of Luminar.

As to dual employment, whether the test applied was control (the approach of May LJ in *Viasystems*), or the wider question of whether Warren was 'embedded in' the business of Luminar (Rix LJ), the answer was the same: 'there has been effectively and substantially a transfer of control and responsibility from ASE to Luminar'.

---

[15] Where the employer is in liquidation a claim may be brought against its insurer pursuant to the Third Parties (Rights Against Insurers) Act 1930. In this case, important issues arose in respect of the liability of ASE's insurers; these issues concerned the meaning of 'accidental injury'. Was the injury inflicted on the claimant an 'accidental injury', covered by the policy? If not, the insurer would not be liable under the Act. The Court of Appeal decided that the injury was 'accidental' for these purposes. It was perhaps not 'accidental' from the point of view of Warren; but it was 'accidental' from the point of view of the assured party, ASE. The tortfeasor and the employer are treated as separate for this purpose (interpretation of the insurance policy), even though the vicariously liable employer 'stands in the shoes of' the employee for other purposes (such as Contribution: Chapter 7, and below).

[16] McKendrick, 'Vicarious Liability and Independent Contractors—A Reexamination', discussed above.

84   On the facts of the present case, the answer to the question "who was entitled and therefore obliged to control Mr Warren's act so as to prevent it?", on the judge's view, is Luminar. ASE had no immediate or effective control over the activities of Mr Warren. . . . If anyone was going to prevent Mr Warren's behaving badly and this particular act, it was Luminar's manager . . . .

85   . . . In our view, Mr Warren was seconded to Luminar's club for so long as Luminar wanted. In such circumstances he had become embedded in Luminar's organisation and, therefore, fits the third situation envisaged by Rix LJ in the concluding words of paragraph 80 of his judgment in the *Viasystems* case. He was no longer recognisable as an employee of ASE. If, therefore, the question to be answered is whether Mr Warren was so much part of the work business or organisation of both employers that it is just to make both answer for his negligence the answer on the facts of this case must be no.

Although this was not a case of dual employment, important issues of contribution nevertheless arose. It seems that Wilkie J, at first instance, considered it possible that ASE had been negligent in the selection of Warren since they did not verify some aspects of his application, and he was not in all respects qualified for the role. This would be *primary* liability, of the type discussed in Section 3 of this chapter. The provision of appropriate staff was one area where Luminar clearly relied on ASE. Yet Wilkie J had assessed the contribution payable by ASE at zero. The Court of Appeal accepted this assessment. Although Luminar was not at fault, nevertheless it 'stood in Warren's shoes' as employer. The actual fault (if any) of ASE was too remote from the incident to be relevant.

89 We remind ourselves, as Wilkie J properly reminded himself, that the lack of fault of a person vicariously liable for the wrongful act of his employee is not relevant for the purposes of determining contribution proceedings between that person and another wrongdoer (see the decision of the House of Lords in *Dubai Aluminium* . . .). Luminar must stand in the shoes of their deemed employee Warren and the judge was obliged to assess the responsibility for the fateful blow as between Warren and ASE his general employer.

90 As Wilkie J observed ASE's failing was in not making proper enquiries at the time they first employed Mr Warren. That was far from the incident itself. . . . During the 2 year period that Mr Warren had worked at the club under Luminar's direction nothing had occurred to alert ASE to any proclivity he may have to unprovoked violence. . . . There was nothing that ASE could have done on that fateful night to control his behaviour and it was his behaviour that night which was the cause of the injuries. As between Mr Warren and ASE the blame lay fairly and squarely at Mr Warren's door.

This amounts to very clear recognition that in a case of vicarious liability, the fault (if any) is that of the tortfeasor, *not* of the employer. The test of 'control' is independent of questions of fault. This matches our discussion of the policy basis of vicarious liability above. 'Opportunity to control' makes a principle of vicarious liability useful because of the incentives that it creates, and to some extent it helps to make it fair because it gives the opportunity to minimize (as well as manage) the risk.

In both of the cases extracted above, the Court of Appeal relied on the House of Lords' decision in *Dubai Aluminium v Salaam* as having clearly stated the nature of vicarious liability: the employer stands in the employee's shoes for the purposes of liability. In the next section, we will see that the clear interpretation in *Dubai Aluminium* is not universally accepted. Indeed there is considerable disagreement over the basic purpose of vicarious liability even within the House of Lords.

1.3 'THE COURSE OF EMPLOYMENT'

An employer will only be liable for the torts of employees that are committed in the course of employment In recent years, courts have developed a new 'close connection' test to deal with this requirement. However, the content of this test is still uncertain, and this displays continuing disagreements about the very basis of vicarious liability.

In deciding whether the tort was committed 'in the course of employment', the traditional starting point has been '*the Salmond test*'.

Sir John Salmond, *Torts* (1st edn, 1907), at 83

A master is not responsible for a wrongful act done by his servant unless it is done in the course of employment. It is deemed to be so done if it is either (a) a wrongful act authorised by the master, or (b) a wrongful and unauthorised *mode* of doing some act authorised by the master.

In *Lister v Hesley Hall* [2002] 1 AC 215, Lord Millett pointed out that Salmond's statement is not beyond criticism. For one thing, the possibility in (a) is not an example of vicarious liability at all: if the tort is authorized, it is the tort of the master and not of the servant, so that there is simply no need for vicarious liability to apply. A second problem is (according to Lord Millett) that the possibility in (b) is not easily applied to a case like *Lister*, where the tortfeasor carries out assaults for his own personal gratification. (This is only a problem of course if there is some reason why vicarious liability in such circumstances is thought desirable.)

In *Lister*, Lords Steyn, Clyde, and Millett all attached importance to a further element of Salmond's exposition (at pp 83–4):

But a master, as opposed to the employer of an independent contractor, is liable even for acts which he has not authorised, provided they are so connected with acts which he has authorised that they may rightly be regarded as modes—although improper modes—of doing them.

They used this to justify a new approach, placing less emphasis on the idea of 'unauthorized modes of performing a duty', and more emphasis on the idea of **'close connection'** with the employment. The difficulty is that in itself, this only amounts to a change in *words*. It does not take us very far. In subsequent case law, the test has been developed further, but not in a consistent way. To understand the origins of the change, we need to consider the decision of the Supreme Court of Canada in *Bazley v Curry*, which has strongly influenced the development of English law.

Bazley v Curry (1999) 2 SCR 534

The defendant Children's Foundation operated residential care facilities for emotionally troubled children. One of the Foundation's employees was a paedophile. He used his position to abuse children, and was ultimately convicted of sexual abuse of children including the respondent.

At first instance, Lowry J attempted to apply the Salmond test. The employees carried out intimate duties such as bathing the children and putting them to bed. He held that abusing a child during these activities could be said to be an unauthorized mode of doing the relevant authorized act. Thus, the Foundation was vicariously liable. The British Columbia Court of Appeal upheld the decision but on different grounds. Understandably, they felt that the Salmond test applied only very awkwardly to such a case. In the Supreme Court, McLachlin J agreed, adding that the decided case law was of little help. There was a need to return to first principles to determine the case.

McLachlin's judgment outlines the most general issues (articulating the *policy concerns* that govern the whole of vicarious liability) and moves to the more specific (given these concerns, what *factors* help to decide the right outcome in a given case?).

> [29] . . . two fundamental concerns underlie the imposition of vicarious liability: (1) provision of a just and practical remedy for the harm; and (2) deterrence of future harm. While different formulations of the policy interests at stake may be made (for example, loss internalization is a hybrid of the two), I believe that these two ideas usefully embrace the main policy considerations that have been advanced.
>
> . . .
>
> [34] The policy grounds supporting the imposition of vicarious liability—fair compensation and deterrence—are related. The policy consideration of deterrence is linked to the policy consideration of fair compensation based on the employer's introduction or enhancement of a risk. The introduction of the enterprise into the community with its attendant risk, in turn, implies the possibility of managing the risk to minimize the costs of the harm that may flow from it.
>
> . . .
>
> [37] . . . the policy purposes are served only where the wrong is so connected with the employment that it can be said that the employer has introduced the risk of the wrong (and is thereby fairly and usefully charged with its management and minimization). The question in each case is whether there is a connection or nexus between the employment enterprise and that wrong which justifies imposition of vicarious liability on the employer for the wrong, in terms of fair allocation of the risk and/or deterrence.

The aim is for vicarious liability to be both 'fair' and 'useful'. The relevant test for when this will be so is closeness of connection. This in turn is explained in terms of 'introduction of risk'—an idea yielded by the policy rationales for vicarious liability, and especially the idea of 'enterprise risk'. However, introduction of risk is not a simple idea. The connection between employment, and risk, must be 'salient', and the employment of the tortfeasor must have made a 'material contribution' to the risk. The question here is whether the employment enhanced the risk *in a material way*, not simply *to a material extent*. The Supreme Court set out some factors which would help future courts to apply this rather artificial test. In particular:

> . . . (3) In determining the sufficiency of the connection between the employer's creation or enhancement of the risk and the wrong complained of, subsidiary factors may be considered. These may vary with the nature of the case. When related to intentional torts, the relevant factors may include, but are not limited to, the following:
>
> (a) the opportunity that the enterprise afforded the employee to abuse his or her power;
> (b) the extent to which the wrongful act may have furthered the employer's aims (and hence be more likely to have been committed by the employee);
> (c) the extent to which the wrongful act was related to friction, confrontation or intimacy inherent in the employer's enterprise;
> (d) the extent of power conferred on the employee in relation to the victim;
> (e) the vulnerability of potential victims to wrongful exercise of the employee's power.

Since, in this case, the wrongful acts were related to intimacy which was inherent in the employer's enterprise, and given the power of the employee over the very vulnerable victim, vicarious liability for the intentional acts of abuse could be justified.

McLachlin J then considered whether there should be an exemption from these general rules where the defendant is a non-profit organization.[17] McLachlin J rejected an argument that it would not be 'fair' to place responsibility on the defendant organization because of its valuable work, which was done for the benefit of the community. Liability may be fair, she said, from the point of view of the vulnerable victim, 'as between him and the institution that enhanced the risk'. This departs from the full enterprise risk justification, and lapses into a comparison between the victim, and the employer who introduced the risk. Second, McLachlin J argued that deterrence (or incentive) arguments were equally valid for non-profit organizations. Third, and finally, she addressed the general loss distribution arguments:

> [53] The third argument, essentially a variation on the first, is that vicarious liability will put many non-profit organizations out of business or make it difficult for them to carry on their good work. . . . In sum, attaching liability to charities like the Foundation will, in the long run, disadvantage society.

McLachlin J rejected this distributive argument, arguing that it smacks of 'crass and unsubstantiated utilitarianism' (at [54]). Yet, 'utilitarian' argument *in combination with fairness* was earlier treated as a persuasive reason for making a blameless defendant liable. This tends to illustrate our earlier point that the justifications are strongest in combination; and it illustrates Atiyah's point that where not all the justfiying factors are present, there will be difficult questions of balance.

In *Jacobi v Griffiths* [1999] 2 SCR 570, a majority of the Supreme Court led by Binnie J (McLachlin J and two other justices dissenting) decided that the balance came down against vicarious liability. Here the defendant Boys' and Girls' Club had employed Griffiths as

---

[17] Non-state non-profit defendants may raise different issues from public authority defendants, particularly if one focuses on *distributive* justifications.

program director. He used his position of authority in the Club to develop a relationship with the two claimants, and sexually assaulted them.

Holding that the assaults were not committed in the course of employment, the majority justices purported to follow the approach in *Bazley v Curry*, requiring a close connection with employment in the sense of material contribution to the risk of assault. And indeed the employee's duties did not require intimate contact with the children in the same way as the defendant's employment in *Bazley*. But the majority justices also seem to have rejected the approach to non-profit defendants outlined by McLachlin J, arguing that such defendants 'lack an efficient mechanism to internalize . . . costs'. In the absence of this justification, they appear to have wanted stronger evidence that the particular terms of employment fostered the risk of abuse in a relevant way.   *No vicarious*

Summary

The approach in *Bazley* is a qualified success. It makes a clean break from any idea that the employer's liability is premised on authorization or any residual element of fault; and it seeks to articulate policy concerns rather than just concentrating on a 'verbal formula' as a test for liability. On the other hand, the idea of 'material contribution to risk' is likely to be contentious, most particularly if there is disagreement over the underlying policy concerns.

The English Case Law

Lister v Hesley Hall [2001] UKHL 22; [2002] 1 AC 215

The claimants had been resident in a boarding house attached to a school owned and managed by the defendants. The warden of the boarding house, who was employed by the defendants, systematically abused children within his care. A claim that there was primary liability on the part of the defendants for their own negligence in the selection or supervision of the warden was rejected at first instance. The first instance judge also rejected a claim that the defendants could be vicariously liable for the acts of abuse committed by the warden, holding that these could not be said to come within the Salmond test for 'course of employment'. The judge nevertheless held that the defendants could be vicariously liable for the warden's *failure to report* his own acts and/or to report the harm suffered by the children, since his duties included these aspects of their welfare. This was, clearly, an artificial argument designed to evade the restrictions of the Salmond test. The Court of Appeal rejected it and held that there was no vicarious liability at all in this case. Both courts were bound by the earlier decision in *Trotman v North Yorkshire County Council* [1999] LGR 584 (CA).

In *Trotman*, the deputy headmaster of a special school sexually assaulted a pupil with whom he shared a bedroom on a foreign holiday. Butler-Sloss LJ applied the Salmond test, and concluded that the assault could not be said to be a mode of carrying out the teachers' duties. Rather, it was 'a negation of the duty of the council to look after children for whom it was responsible' (at 591).

The House of Lords in *Lister* overruled *Trotman v North Yorkshire CC* and held the defendants vicariously liable. Influenced by *Bazley v Curry*, the judgments set vicarious liability in a new direction by rephrasing the test for 'course of employment' in terms of 'close connection'. Although the decision was unanimous, there are important variations between the judgments. Lord Steyn's may be called the leading judgment in that Lord Hutton concurred with his reasoning as did Lord Hobhouse with the addition of some further observations. (As we will see some of these further observations tend to cloud the general picture in respect of vicarious liability.) Lord Millett's judgment has also been influential, but is incompatible with that of Lord Hobhouse. These divisions continue to haunt the case law.

Lord Steyn

16   It is not necessary to embark on a detailed examination of the development of the modern principle of vicarious liability. But it is necessary to face up to the way in which the law of vicarious liability sometimes may embrace intentional wrongdoing by an employee. If one mechanically applies *Salmond's* test, the result might at first glance be thought to be that a bank is not liable to a customer where a bank employee defrauds a customer by giving him only half the foreign exchange which he paid for, the employee pocketing the difference. A preoccupation with conceptualistic reasoning may lead to the absurd conclusion that there can only be vicarious liability if the bank carries on business in defrauding its customers. Ideas divorced from reality have never held much attraction for judges steeped in the tradition that their task is to deliver principled but practical justice. How the courts set the law on a sensible course is a matter to which I now turn.

17   It is easy to accept the idea that where an employee acts for the benefit of his employer, or intends to do so, that is strong evidence that he was acting in the course of his employment. But until the decision of the House of Lords in *Lloyd v Grace, Smith & Co* [1912] AC 716 it was thought that vicarious liability could only be established if such requirements were satisfied. This was an overly restrictive view and hardly in tune with the needs of society. In *Lloyd v Grace, Smith & Co* it was laid to rest by the House of Lords. A firm of solicitors were held liable for the dishonesty of their managing clerk who persuaded a client to transfer property to him and then disposed of it for his own advantage. The decisive factor was that the client had been invited by the firm to deal with their managing clerk. This decision was a breakthrough: it finally established that vicarious liability is not necessarily defeated if the employee acted for his own benefit. On the other hand, an intense focus on the connection between the nature of the employment and the tort of the employee became necessary.

Lord Steyn turned his attention to the case of *Trotman*:

24   It is useful to consider an employer's potential liability for non-sexual assaults. If such assaults arise directly out of circumstances connected with the employment, vicarious liability may arise: see F D Rose, "Liability for an Employee's Assaults" (1977) 40 MLR 420, 432–433. Butler-Sloss LJ considered this analogy. In the critical paragraph of her judgment, which I have already quoted in full, she stated, at p 591:

> "Acts of physical assault may not be so easy to categorise, since they may range, for instance, from a brutal and unprovoked assault by a teacher to forceful attempts to defend another pupil or the teacher himself. But in the field of serious sexual misconduct, I find it difficult to visualise circumstances in which an act of the teacher can be an unauthorised mode of carrying out an authorised act, although I would not wish to close the door on the possibility."

If I correctly understand this passage, it appears to be indicating that there could not be vicarious liability by an employer for a brutal assault or serious sexual misconduct whatever the circumstances. That appears to be a case of saying "The greater the fault of the servant, the less the liability of the master": *Morris v C W Martin & Sons Ltd* [1966] 1 QB 716, 733, per

Diplock LJ. A better approach is to concentrate on the relative closeness of the connection between the nature of the employment and the particular tort.

25   In my view the approach of the Court of Appeal in *Trotman v North Yorkshire County Council* [1999] LGR 584 was wrong. It resulted in the case being treated as one of the employment furnishing a mere opportunity to commit the sexual abuse. The reality was that the county council were responsible for the care of the vulnerable children and employed the deputy headmaster to carry out that duty on its behalf. And the sexual abuse took place while the employee was engaged in duties at the very time and place demanded by his employment. The connection between the employment and the torts was very close. I would over-rule *Trotman v North Yorkshire County Council.*

. . .

VII. The application of the correct test

27   My Lords, I have been greatly assisted by the luminous and illuminating judgments of the Canadian Supreme Court in *Bazley v Curry* 174 DLR (4th) 45 and *Jacobi v Griffiths* 174 DLR (4th) 71. Wherever such problems are considered in future in the common law world these judgments will be the starting point. On the other hand, it is unnecessary to express views on the full range of policy considerations examined in those decisions.

28   Employing the traditional methodology of English law, I am satisfied that in the case of the appeals under consideration the evidence showed that the employers entrusted the care of the children in Axeholme House to the warden. The question is whether the warden's torts were so closely connected with his employment that it would be fair and just to hold the employers vicariously liable. On the facts of the case the answer is yes. After all, the sexual abuse was inextricably interwoven with the carrying out by the warden of his duties in Axeholme House. Matters of degree arise. But the present cases clearly fall on the side of vicarious liability.

Lord Hobhouse

54   What these cases and *Trotman's* case in truth illustrate is a situation where the employer has assumed a relationship to the plaintiff which imposes specific duties in tort upon the employer and the role of the employee (or servant) is that he is the person to whom the employer has entrusted the performance of those duties. These cases are examples of that class where the employer, by reason of assuming a relationship to the plaintiff, owes to the plaintiff duties which are more extensive than those owed by the public at large . . . .

55   The classes of persons or institutions that are in this type of special relationship to another human being include schools, prisons, hospitals and even, in relation to their visitors, occupiers of land. They are liable if they themselves fail to perform the duty which they consequently owe. If they entrust the performance of that duty to an employee and that employee fails to perform the duty, they are still liable. The employee, because he has, through his obligations to his employers, adopted the same relationship towards and come under the same duties to the plaintiff, is also liable to the plaintiff for his own breach of duty. The liability of the employers is a *vicarious* liability because the actual breach of duty is that of the employee. The employee is a tortfeasor. The employers are liable for the employee's tortious act or omission because it is to him that the employers have entrusted the performance of their duty. The employers' liability to the plaintiff is also that of a tortfeasor. I use the word "entrusted" in

preference to the word "delegated" which is commonly, but perhaps less accurately, used. Vicarious liability is sometimes described as a "strict" liability. The use of this term is misleading unless it is used just to explain that there has been no *actual* fault on the part of the employers. The liability of the employers derives from their voluntary assumption of the relationship towards the plaintiff and the duties that arise from that relationship and their choosing to entrust the performance of those duties to their servant. Where these conditions are satisfied, the motive of the employee and the fact that he is doing something expressly forbidden and is serving only his own ends does not negative the vicarious liability for his breach of the "delegated" duty. . . .

60 My Lords, the correct approach to answering the question whether the tortious act of the servant falls within or without the scope of the servant's employment for the purposes of the principle of vicarious liability is to ask what was the duty of the servant towards the plaintiff which was broken by the servant and what was the contractual duty of the servant towards his employer. The second limb of the classic *Salmond* test is a convenient rule of thumb which provides the answer in very many cases but does not represent the fundamental criterion which is the comparison of the duties respectively owed by the servant to the plaintiff and to his employer. Similarly, I do not believe that it is appropriate to follow the lead given by the Supreme Court of Canada in *Bazley v Curry* 174 DLR (4th) 45. The judgments contain a useful and impressive discussion of the social and economic reasons for having a principle of vicarious liability as part of the law of tort which extends to embrace acts of child abuse. But an exposition of the policy reasons for a rule (or even a description) is not the same as defining the criteria for its application. . . .

Lord Millett

65 Vicarious liability is a species of strict liability. It is not premised on any culpable act or omission on the part of the employer; an employer who is not personally at fault is made legally answerable for the fault of his employee. It is best understood as a loss-distribution device: (see Cane's edition of *Atiyah's Accidents, Compensation and the Law*, 6th ed (1999), p 85 and the articles cited by Atiyah in his monograph on *Vicarious Liability in the Law of Torts*, at p 24). The theoretical underpinning of the doctrine is unclear. Glanville Williams wrote ("Vicarious Liability and the Master's Indemnity" (1957) 20 MLR 220, 231):

> "Vicarious liability is the creation of many judges who have had different ideas of its justification or social policy, or no idea at all. Some judges may have extended the rule more widely, or confined it more narrowly than its true rationale would allow; yet the rationale, if we can discover it, will remain valid so far as it extends."

Fleming observed (*The Law of Torts*, 9th ed, p 410) that the doctrine cannot parade as a deduction from legalistic premises. He indicated that it should be frankly recognised as having its basis in a combination of policy considerations, and continued: "Most important of these is the belief that a person who employs others to advance his own economic interest should in fairness be placed under a corresponding liability for losses incurred in the course of the enterprise . . . " *Atiyah, Vicarious Liability in the Law of Torts* wrote to the same effect. He suggested, at p 171: "The master ought to be liable for all those torts which can fairly be regarded as reasonably incidental risks to the type of business he carries on." These passages are not to be read as confining the doctrine to cases where the employer is carrying on business for profit. They are based on the more general idea that a person who employs another for his own ends inevitably creates a risk that the employee will commit a legal wrong. If the employer's objectives cannot be achieved without a serious risk of the employee committing the kind of wrong which he has in fact committed, the employer ought to be liable. The fact that his employment gave the employee the opportunity to commit the wrong is not enough to make the employer liable. He is liable only if the risk is one which experience shows is inherent in the nature of the business.

. . .

82 In the present case the warden's duties provided him with the opportunity to commit indecent assaults on the boys for his own sexual gratification, but that in itself is not enough to make the school liable. The same would be true of the groundsman or the school porter. But there was far more to it than that. The school was responsible for the care and welfare of the boys. It entrusted that responsibility to the warden. He was employed to discharge the school's responsibility to the boys. For this purpose the school entrusted them to his care. He did not merely take advantage of the opportunity which employment at a residential school gave him. He abused the special position in which the school had placed him to enable it to discharge its own responsibilities, with the result that the assaults were committed by the very employee to whom the school had entrusted the care of the boys. It is not necessary to conduct the detailed dissection of the warden's duties of the kind on which the Supreme Court of Canada embarked in *Bazley v Curry* 174 DLR (4th) 45 and *Jacobi v Griffiths* 174 DLR (4th) 71. I would hold the school liable.

83 I would regard this as in accordance not only with ordinary principle deducible from the authorities but with the underlying rationale of vicarious liability. Experience shows that in the case of boarding schools, prisons, nursing homes, old people's homes, geriatric wards, and other residential homes for the young or vulnerable, there is an inherent risk that indecent assaults on the residents will be committed by those placed in authority over them, particularly if they are in close proximity to them and occupying a position of trust.

84 I would hold the school vicariously liable for the warden's intentional assaults, not (as was suggested in argument) for his failure to perform his duty to take care of the boys. That is an artificial approach based on a misreading of *Morris v C W Martin & Sons Ltd*. The cleaners were vicariously liable for their employee's conversion of the fur, not for his negligence in failing to look after it. Similarly in *Photo Production Ltd v Securicor Transport Ltd* the security firm was vicariously liable for the patrolman's arson, not for his negligence. The law is mature enough to hold an employer vicariously liable for deliberate, criminal wrongdoing on the part of an employee without indulging in sophistry of this kind. I would also not base liability on the warden's failure to report his own wrongdoing to his employer, an approach which I regard as both artificial and unrealistic. Even if such a duty did exist, on which I prefer to express no opinion, I am inclined to think that it would be a duty owed exclusively to the employer and not a duty for breach of which the employer could be vicariously liable. The same reasoning would not, of course, necessarily apply to the duty to report the wrongdoing of fellow employees, but it is not necessary to decide this.

The relevant test?

These extracts provide different versions of the 'close connection' test. Lord Steyn was the most directly influenced by *Bazley v Curry* (above). He did not state in very clear terms what the content of the 'close connection' case would be; but he did state that the warden's acts of abuse were 'inextricably interwoven' with his duties. This seems a less demanding test than the majority approach in *Jacobi v Griffiths*, which distinguished *Bazley* as we have seen. On the other hand, in *Lister* the defendants ran the school on a commercial basis and the approach in *Jacobi* may be specific to non-profit organizations.

Lord Hobhouse rejected the approach in *Bazley v Curry* as insufficiently clear. His expression of the relevant test seems to depart in certain important respects from the idea that in vicarious liability, the employee commits a tort but on grounds of justice and practicality, liability is imposed on the employer. Lord Hobhouse says that *the defendant itself* owed a duty to the children to guard their welfare since it had *assumed responsibility to them*. Hence the relationship between defendant (school) and claimant (child) is all-important. This duty the school had 'entrusted to' the warden, taking into account the terms of his employment. Thus, although the *breach of duty* is that of the employee, the *duty breached* is owed by the school: '[T]he employers' liability to the plaintiff is also that of a tortfeasor' (at [55]). This interpretation makes *Lister* a case of liability for the breach of a primary duty owed by the school, through the conduct of the employee to whom that duty had been entrusted. If we want to maintain any clarity in this area of law, this is better not referred to as 'vicarious liability'. It is identical to the idea of 'non-delegable duty' as employed by the High Court of Australia in *NSW v Lepore* [2003] HCA 4 (Section 2 of this chapter).

Conversely, Lord Millett's approach was broader than the one adopted by the Supreme Court of Canada in *Bazley* and did not require close analysis of the precise duties of the employee. Instead he embraced the idea of liability for risks that are reasonably incidental to employment. Lord Millett's approach was further developed by a differently constituted House of Lords in *Dubai Aluminium v Salaam* (2003) 2 AC 366 (below). It is drawn directly from ideas of loss distribution and enterprise risk.

Which tort?

The judgment of Lord Hobhouse may cloud the picture but it focuses attention on an important question. Which tort formed the basis of liability in *Lister v Hesley Hall*? Clearly, the warden's acts amounted to a deliberate assault or 'trespass to the person' (Chapter 2). Lord Millett made clear (para [84] extracted above) that on his approach, where the employer 'stands in the shoes' of the tortfeasor, the employer's vicarious liability is *liability for the assaults*, and not for a negligent failure to take care of the boys. Lord Hobhouse as we have explained regarded the duty in this case as owed by the employer, and it seems that this must be a duty to take proper care of the vulnerable children. On his approach, *Lister* would be a case in negligence, despite the deliberate nature of the acts that breached the duty. Lord Steyn's judgment is quite unclear on this point, although he did expressly reserve judgment (at para [29]) on the question of whether there might be an alternative action for the warden's failure to report his own wrongdoing and its effect on the children. This alternative action would, clearly, be in negligence.

The House of Lords seems not to have considered that the identification of the relevant tort would affect the limitation period which would apply to the action (Chapter 7 above). In cases recently heard by the Court of Appeal, the fundamental importance of this issue (which tort?) has become obvious.

Sexual Assaults: The Limitation Problem

A victim of sexual abuse, particularly if that abuse occurs during childhood, may take many years to understand what has occurred, and to appreciate the actual harm that follows from that assault. Yet in *Stubbings v Webb* [1993] AC 498, some years before *Lister*, the House of Lords held that under the Limitation Act 1980, a claim based on trespass to the person is subject to a *non-extendable* six-year limitation period (see Chapter 2.2).

Under the Limitation Act 1980, actions for contract and tort must generally be initiated within six years *from the date that the action accrues*. For torts requiring damage, the action accrues when the damage is suffered. However, in cases of 'negligence, nuisance, or breach of duty' involving a claim for damages for personal injury, there is a separate limitation period of three years. Although the period is shorter, the provision often works to the benefit of the claimant because the period will run from the *date of the claimant's knowledge*, and this may be much later than the time of the injury.

Section 11 of the Limitation Act 1980 is extracted in Chapter 7.

In *Stubbings v Webb* [1993] AC 498, the House of Lords held that assaults amounting to trespass to the person (including sexual abuse) did not come within the meaning of 'breach of duty' for the purposes of section 11(1) and therefore did not benefit from the extendable limitation period. If Lord Millett was correct to say that the tort for which there was vicarious liability in *Lister* was the intentional assault, then the claim should probably have been time-barred on this basis.[18]

In *KR v Bryn Alyn* [2003] QB 1441, the Court of Appeal held that claims based on deliberate acts of sexual assault were time-barred. Only if there was *systematic failure to take care* on the part of the defendant employees would there be an arguable case in negligence, in which case the extendable time limit under section 11 would be available. Auld LJ specifically adopted Lord Millett's approach to vicarious liability in *Lister*. He thus discounted the possibility, raised by Lord Hobhouse, that the acts of employees could be said to be in breach of the employer's own direct duty of care to the children; and he also discounted the other (rather artificial) possibility raised above, that the school could perhaps be vicariously liable for the warden's failure to report his own intentions and/or the harm suffered by the children in his care.

More recently in *A v Hoare; H v Suffolk County Council; X & Y v London Borough of Wandsworth* [2006] 1 WLR 2320,[19] the Court of Appeal analysed the speeches in *Lister* and suggested that there was nothing in the judgments to indicate that Lord Millett's view—that the vicarious liability in that case was liability for battery on the part of the warden—was shared by the other members of the House of Lords. Indeed, in the view of the Court of Appeal, this could not be the right interpretation, because:

[99] . . . To identify the only wrongs which the warden committed as intentional assaults would be to run straight into the *Stubbings v Webb* limitation problem, of which these experienced judges could not have been unaware.

'Unconstrained by authority', the Court of Appeal would have explored the possibility that there was vicarious liability *for negligence* in *Lister v Hesley Hall*; and/or that there might be liability for the warden's 'failure to report'. But they felt bound by the decision in *Bryn Alyn* to treat Lord Millett's approach in *Lister* as authoritative. Whatever one thinks of Lord Millett's

[18] Lord Millett should have been well aware of this. When in the Court of Appeal, he criticized exactly this effect of *Stubbings v Webb* in *S v W* [1995] 1 FLR 862 (see Chapter 2).

[19] The limitation point arose in a very different way in *A v Hoare* itself. The defendant had been convicted of assault but was impecunious and not worth pursuing until, while on parole, he bought a single lottery ticket and won £7 million.

approach, it causes a significant problem for subsequent abuse cases. This problem is caused primarily by the decision in *Stubbings v Webb* itself, and partly by the failure of the House of Lords in *Lister* to note the problem and consider explicitly whether negligence and intentional torts might overlap on the same facts. The latter issue also divided the High Court of Australia in *NSW v Lepore*.

A v Hoare is currently under appeal before the House of Lords.

Subsequent Developments

Subsequently, the House of Lords has reconsidered vicarious liability on two occasions, and the Privy Council has had to consider a number of cases from the Commonwealth concerning vicarious liability for criminal acts by employees.

In *Dubai Aluminium v Salaam* [2003] 2 AC 366, the House of Lords adopted a passage (at [65]) in Atiyah's *Vicarious Liability* (p 171), which had also been cited by Lord Millett in *Lister v Hesley Hall* [at 107]:

> The master ought to be liable for all those torts which can fairly be regarded as reasonably incidental risks to the type of business he carries on.

In the case of criminal wrongdoing, there is vicarious liability if *the risk of wrongdoing* can *fairly be said* to be *reasonably incidental to* the employer's business. This reflects Lord Millett's judgment in *Lister*, in which risks incidental to employment were of predominant importance. As we noted above, this is broader than the approach in *Bazley v Curry*, which required a detailed analysis of the employee's particular wrongdoing in the light of their specific duties. It is drawn directly from the 'enterprise risk' justification, and is not qualified by the artificial idea of 'material contribution to risk' employed in the Canadian decision.

Lord Nicholls, *Dubai Aluminium v Salaam* [2003] 2 AC 366

21 ... Whether an act or omission was done in the ordinary course of a firm's business cannot be decided simply by considering whether the partner was authorised by his co-partners to do the very act he did. The reason for this lies in the legal policy underlying vicarious liability. The underlying legal policy is based on the recognition that carrying on a business enterprise necessarily involves risks to others. It involves the risk that others will be harmed by wrongful acts committed by the agents through whom the business is carried on. When those risks ripen into loss, it is just that the business should be responsible for compensating the person who has been wronged.

22 This policy reason dictates that liability for agents should not be strictly confined to acts done with the employer's authority. Negligence can be expected to occur from time to time. Everyone makes mistakes at times. Additionally, it is a fact of life, and therefore to be expected by those who carry on businesses, that sometimes their agents may exceed the bounds of their authority or even defy express instructions. It is fair to allocate risk of losses thus arising to the businesses rather than leave those wronged with the sole remedy, of doubtful value, against the individual employee who committed the wrong. To this end, the law has given the concept of "ordinary course of employment" an extended scope.

23 If, then, authority is not the touchstone, what is? . . . Perhaps the best general answer is that the wrongful conduct must be so closely connected with acts the partner or employee was authorised to do that, for the purpose of the liability of the firm or the employer to third parties, the wrongful conduct *may fairly and properly be regarded* as done by the partner while acting in the ordinary course of the firm's business or the employee's employment. Lord Millett said as much in *Lister v Hesley Hall Ltd* [2002] 1 AC 215, 245. So did Lord Steyn, at pp 223–224 and 230. McLachlin J said, in *Bazley v Curry* (1999) 174 DLR (4th) 45, 62:

> "the policy purposes underlying the imposition of vicarious liability on employers are served only where the wrong is so connected with the employment that it *can be said* that the employer has introduced the risk of the wrong (and is thereby fairly and usefully charged with its management and minimisation)." (Emphasis added.)

To the same effect is Professor Atiyah's monograph *Vicarious Liability* (1967), p 171 . . .

24 In these formulations the phrases "may fairly and properly be regarded", "can be said" and "can fairly be regarded" betoken a value judgment by the court. The conclusion is a conclusion of law, based on primary facts, rather than a simple question of fact.

Lord Slynn concurred with Lord Nicholls. **Lord Hutton** concurred with Lords Nicholls and Millett. **Lord Hobhouse** delivered a separate judgment but also professed agreement with the reasons given by Lords Millett and Nicholls.

Not only is Lord Nicholls' approach distinctly 'distributive' in its approach to risk, which it treats as susceptible to forward planning; it also treats criminal and intentional wrongdoing (fraud, violence, sexual assault) as subject to prediction and management in the same way as carelessness. Whether this is a sensible step forward or a heresy depends on one's view of the policy behind vicarious liability. It is broadly compatible with the policy justifications as we have stated them. So we may treat it as a sensible step forward.

In *Dubai Aluminium* itself, vicarious liability extended to a firm of solicitors where a fraud was committed by one individual partner. This was not an employment case since a partner is not an employee, partnership representing a special form of relationship defined in the Partnership Act 1890. Nevertheless, the applicable principles are the same as those applying to employees: the question is whether the fraud was perpetrated 'in the ordinary course of the firm's business'.[20] Lord Millett suggested that if the policy reasons for vicarious liability are satisfied, then it does not matter that the wrong committed is a tort, an equitable wrong, or a breach of statutory duty (at [107]).

Violent Employees: Which Principles Apply?[21]

In *Mattis v Pollock* [2003] 1 WLR 2158, the defendant was a nightclub owner who employed C as a doorman. C was inclined to violence and indeed it was expected that he would act in a threatening manner. On the night in question, C had hit at least two customers with a weapon, but was met with resistance. He went home, armed himself with a knife, and returned to the nightclub. Outside the club, he attacked the claimant with the knife. The attack rendered the

[20] Here the firm of solicitors had settled the claim against them and therefore *sought* a finding of vicarious liability; this would enable them to pursue other participants in the fraud for a contribution (Chapter 7).

[21] For further discussion of these issues see R. Weekes, 'Vicarious Liability for Violent Employees' (2004) 63 CLJ, 53.

claimant paraplegic. The Court of Appeal determined that the nightclub owner was vicariously liable for the assault. The broad governing test was derived from *Dubai Aluminium*.

This decision has been criticized because the stated reasons for the final decision tended to emphasize the *fault* of the owner in employing an unlicensed doorman (in breach of regulations) and then encouraging him to act in an aggressive manner. These factors are certainly relevant to consideration of 'close connection'; but they were stated in such a way that they ran together the questions of *vicarious* and *primary* liability. It will be remembered that the judgment of Lord Millett in *Lister*, from which the *Dubai* formulation is developed, clearly stated that vicarious liability was liability for the tort of the employee, requiring no fault on the part of the employer, and related to the 'incidental' risks of employment rather than requiring any specific encouragement of the tort.[22] The Court of Appeal thought that primary liability would also be established on the facts of this particular case.

Bernard v AG Jamaica [2004] UKPC 47 (Privy Council)

A police constable of the Jamaica Constabulary Force shot the plaintiff in the head at close range when he refused to hand over a telephone. He then followed the plaintiff to hospital where he arrested him and handcuffed him to a bed. The plaintiff brought actions in tort against the individual officer (who could not be traced), and also against the Attorney General as representative of the Crown.[23] The judge found the Attorney General vicariously liable for the torts of the constable, namely assault, false imprisonment, and malicious prosecution, but this finding was reversed by the Court of Appeal of Jamaica. Bingham JA emphasized that this kind of case was becoming too familiar and that the applicable legal principles were leading to injustice. He proposed that the state should institute 'some measure of reform aimed at assisting the many innocent victims of the barbarous conduct of agents of the state'. Clearly, in the language used in *Dubai Aluminium*, this sort of incident was known to be an 'incidental risk' of arming police constables in Jamaica.

Allowing the appeal and holding the Attorney General vicariously liable, Lord Steyn (who gave the judgment of the Court) referred to the creation of risks to others as a 'relevant factor' in deciding whether there should be vicarious liability; and he also quoted from the judgment of Lord Nicholls in *Dubai Aluminium*.

> **19** . . . Throughout the judgments [in *Dubai*] there is an emphasis on the proposition that an employer ought to be liable for a tort which can fairly be regarded as a reasonably incidental risk to the type of business he carried on.

Lord Steyn made no direct criticism of this proposition, but he was clearly concerned that this 'direct' application of enterprise risk ideas might give rise to almost unlimited liability for the torts of employees:

> **23** . . . the Board is firmly of the view that the policy rationale on which vicarious liability is based is not a vague notion of justice between man and man. It has clear limits. This

---

[22] And see the more recent 'door steward' case of *Hawley v Luminar*, extracted above, which relied on the approach in *Dubai Aluminium*.

[23] It is settled in Jamaican law that a police officer is an employee of the Crown.

perspective was well expressed in *Bazley v Curry* . . . where McLachlin J observed (at 62):

> "The policy purposes underlying the imposition of vicarious liability on employers are served only where the wrong is so connected with the employment that it can be said that the employer has introduced the risk of the wrong (and is thereby fairly and usefully charged with its management and minimization). The question is whether there is a connection between the employment enterprise and that wrong that justifies imposition of vicarious liability on the employer for the wrong, in terms of fair allocation of the consequences of the risk and/or deterrence."

The principle of vicarious liability is not infinitely extendable.

Consistently with the *Bazley* approach, Lord Steyn identified specific 'factors' arising from the facts of the case which pointed in this case to vicarious liability. First, by identifying himself as a police officer and demanding that the plaintiff should give him the phone, the constable had acted within his purported authority as a police officer. Second, the subsequent arrest at hospital reinforced this purported use of authority. Finally:

> 27   . . . one must consider the relevance of the risk created by the fact that the police authorities routinely permitted constables . . . to take loaded service revolvers home, and to carry them when off duty . . . the State certainly created risks of the kind to which Bingham JA made reference. It does not follow that the use of a service revolver by an officer would without more make the police authority vicariously liable. That would be going too far. But taking into account the dominant feature of this case, viz that the constable at all material times purported to act as a policeman, the risks created by the police authorities reinforce the conclusion that vicarious liability is established.

The creation of risk was not decisive on its own but was sufficient when taken in conjunction with the purported exercise of authority.

In *Brown v Robinson* [2004] UKPC 56 (another appeal from Jamaica), an official employed (and armed) by a security company to keep order at a football match shot the plaintiff who suffered paraplegia and eventually died of septicaemia. Again the Privy Council held the defendant employer vicariously liable. But the differently constituted Board appeared to reach its decision on different grounds and gave little *positive* indication of the steps in its reasoning. In particular, the Privy Council relegated the creation of risk to the level of a mere 'consideration':

Lord Carswell (delivering the judgment of the Court)

11   . . . The risk which may have been created by such acts on the employer's part as arming his employees is a relevant consideration, as it may form a strong policy reason underlying the legal rule: . . . *Bazley v Curry*. Their Lordships agree, however, with the view expressed by Lord Hobhouse of Woodborough at para 60 of his opinion in *Lister's* case that it does not constitute the criterion for application of the rule defining the ambit of vicarious liability.

Having downplayed the idea of creation of risk in this way, and having agreed with Lord Hobhouse (who said in *Lister* that the *Bazley* criteria did not show the way forward), the Court seemed to give little positive guidance. Their final decision in favour of liability is expressed chiefly on the basis that this was *not* a case of mere revenge or retaliation: 'therefore' (it seemed to follow), it was within the course of employment.

Majrowski v Guy's and St Thomas's NHS Trust [2006] UKHL 34; [2006] 3 WLR 125

The issue arising in this case was whether an employer was vicariously liable for acts of harassment by its employee. The liability in question would arise under the Protection from Harassment Act 1997, which we extracted in Chapter 2. The House of Lords decided (mostly on narrow grounds) that an employer may be vicariously liable under this statute.

Only Lord Nicholls gave serious consideration to the policy basis of vicarious liability. He broadly reiterated the policy justifications expressed in *Dubai Aluminium v Salaam* and considered that these were as valid in respect of breaches of statutory duty as they were in respect of common law torts.

Lord Nicholls, *Majrowski v Guy's and St Thomas's NHS Trust* [2006] UKHL 34

9. Whatever its historical origin, this common law principle of strict liability for another person's wrongs finds its rationale today in a combination of policy factors. They are summarised in Professor Fleming's *Law of Torts*, 9th ed, (1998) pages 409–410. Stated shortly, these factors are that all forms of economic activity carry a risk of harm to others, and fairness requires that those responsible for such activities should be liable to persons suffering loss from wrongs committed in the conduct of the enterprise. This is 'fair' because it means injured persons can look for recompense to a source better placed financially then individual wrongdoing employees. It means also that the financial loss arising from the wrongs can be spread more widely, by liability insurance and higher prices. In addition, and more importantly, imposing strict liability on employers encourages them to maintain standards of 'good practice' by their employees. For these reasons employers are to be held liable for wrongs committed by their employees in the course of their employment.

10. With these policy considerations in mind, it is difficult to see a coherent basis for confining the common law principle of vicarious liability to common law wrongs. The rationale also holds good for a wrong comprising a breach of statutory duty or prohibition which gives rise to civil liability, provided always the statute does not expressly or impliedly indicate otherwise. A precondition of vicarious liability is that the wrong must be committed by an employee in the course of his employment. A wrong is committed in the course of employment only if the conduct is so closely connected with acts the employee is authorised to do that, for the purposes of the liability of the employer to third parties, the wrongful conduct may fairly and properly be regarded as done by the employee while acting in the course of his employment: see *Lister v Hesley Hall* . . . , para 69, per Lord Millett, and *Dubai Aluminium v Salaam* . . . , para 23. If this prerequisite is satisfied the policy reasons underlying the common law principle are as much applicable to equitable wrongs and breaches of statutory obligations as they are to common law torts.

Lord Nicholls went on to argue (at para 16) that, given the general policy justifications for vicarious liability, if a statute does not specify whether vicarious liability should arise where there is a breach of statutory duty by an employee, there should be a presumption that such liability *does* arise.

The other members of the House of Lords agreed with the result (the Trust was vicariously liable for harassment by an employee), but on entirely different gounds. Lord Brown and Baroness Hale thought that policy considerations would weigh *against* vicarious liability under the Act. Baroness Hale referred to the Compensation Bill (now the Compensation

Act 2006) and legislative concern at the growth of a 'compensation culture' (para 69), and was concerned that claims for vicarious liability would be routinely added to 'stress at work' claims which were themselves a growing phenomenon.[24] Lord Brown agreed, and also thought that, were it not for a decisive point of statutory interpretation not noted in the Court of Appeal, he might have agreed with Scott Baker LJ who thought the general purpose of the statute was inconsistent with anything other than personal responsibility. Lord Carswell thought the policy considerations were evenly balanced. Apart from Lord Nicholls, the members of the House of Lords finally decided the case *on the basis of a point of statutory interpretation*, rather than on the basis of general principle.

The decisive issue was explained most fully by Lord Hope. Section 10(1) of the Protection from Harassment Act 1997 (referring to actions for harassment in Scotland), introduces a new section 18B into the Prescription and Limitation (Scotland) Act 1973. The new section 18B(2)(b) provides for an extended limitation period for damages in an action for harassment. Such actions must be brought within a period of three years from the date that the alleged harassment ceased, or (if later), from:

Section 18B(2)(b) Prescription and Limitation (Scotland) Act 1973

. . . the date . . . on which the pursuer . . . became, or on which, in the opinion of the court, it would have been reasonably practicable for him in all the circumstances to have become, aware that the defender was a person responsible for the alleged harassment **or the employer or principal of such a person.**

The emphasized words could not relate to personal responsibility on the part of the employer (for example, if the employer had encouraged the harassment),[25] since the 'employer or principal' in this subsection is contrasted with the 'person responsible'. The words could only relate to vicarious liability. It was this conclusion which determined the outcome of the case: the legislature had intended (indeed, assumed) that vicarious liability would operate in respect of harassment as defined in the Act. It would be ridiculous to suggest that vicarious liability was intended for harassment under the Act in Scotland, but not in England and Wales.

2. NON-DELEGABLE DUTIES

In the case of a 'non-delegable duty', the defendant is under a duty which cannot be passed on by entrusting its performance to others, whether employees or contractors. If the duty is breached, then even if the defendant has taken all due care, liability will attach to the defendant not vicariously, but as tortfeasor. The duty may be breached with or without fault on anyone's part.

---

[24] See our discussion in Chapter 6.1. The claim in *Daniels v Commissioner of Police for the Metropolis* [2006] EWHC 1622, decided a few days before *Majrowski*, tends to prove the point. Here, Mackay J held that there was no 'course of conduct', as required by the Act, where the claim was for harassment by a number of separate employees, each on an isolated occasion, where there was no common purpose on the part of the employees. This was an attempt to find a 'course of conduct' for which liability could be attached to the employer vicariously, where no individual had pursued a relevant course of conduct at all.

[25] Here Lord Hope referred to *Mattis v Pollock*, a case where violence on the part of the employee had been encouraged.

'Non-delegable duty' is clearly a useful idea for those wishing to justify liability outside the reach of vicarious liability. Typically, it will be of most use where there is a tort committed by an independent contractor who is for some reason not worth pursuing, but this is not its only application. As we saw above, in *Lister v Hesley Hall* the approach of Lord Hobhouse appears to have been based on a 'non-delegable duty' owed by the school because of an assumption of responsibility, so that the school was a tortfeasor in its own right even in the absence of fault on its part.

The most well-established non-delegable duties owed in English law are owed by an employer to his or her employees, to provide a safe place and system of work, with competent staff and safe equipment: *Wilsons and Clyde Coal v English* [1938] AC 57; *McDermid v Nash Dredging* [1987] AC 906. According to Williams,[26] these duties owe their origin to a gap in the protection offered by vicarious liability. Under the 'doctrine of common employment' (which no longer forms any part of English law), it was considered that an employee could not be liable for careless injury to an employee of the same master. As such, there could be no vicarious liability for servants' failure to discharge their duties to fellow employees in respect of safety. The idea of a non-delegable duty owed to employees in respect of their safety has outlived the problem that made it a necessary device.

The problem with non-delegable duties is, as Williams pointed out, that there are no clear principles on which to determine which duties are delegable, which non-delegable. Williams traces this problem to a statement of Lord Blackburn in the House of Lords in *Dalton v Angus* (1881) 6 App Cas 740 at 829:

Lord Blackburn

a person causing something to be done, the doing of which casts on him a duty, cannot escape from the responsibility attaching on him of seeing that duty performed by delegating it to a contractor.

Lord Blackburn's statement gives the impression that this is universally true of all duties, but of course this is not the case, or there would be no need for the doctrine of vicarious liability at all:

Glanville Williams, 'Liability for Independent Contractors' (1956) CLJ 180, 181

. . . [Lord Blackburn's] doctrine of the nondelegability of the legal duty cannot have been intended to apply to every duty. He did not, however, say to which duties it did apply. The use made of the dictum in later cases has advanced it to the rank of one of the leading sophistries in the law of tort. Since the judge is left to determine, within the limits of precedent, whether a particular duty is non-delegable or not, the dictum gives him freedom to decide the case as he wishes, while presenting him with a verbal "reason" that conceals his real motivation; and sometimes perhaps it operates as a hypnotic formula inducing the judge to think that he is required to reach a particular conclusion when in fact he is not.

[26] 'Liability for Independent Contractors' (1956) CLJ 180.

Williams' sceptical view of the non-delegable duty device is reinforced by the case of *Honeywill & Stein v Larkin* [1934] 1 KB 191, which stated that a person undertaking an 'extra-hazardous activity' will be subject to a non-delegable duty. In that case, it was held that the act of taking a photograph in a theatre with magnesium powder amounted to such an 'extra hazardous' or dangerous act, so that the person hiring the photographer could be liable where the act was done without due care. Williams argued that this decision was justified neither in terms of principle, since there was nothing so special about this undertaking that would truly set it apart as exceptional, nor in terms of policy. For the most part, cinema owners would be expected to carry insurance policies covering fire, so that the need for liability was not established. In England, *Honeywill v Larkin* has not blossomed into a useful category of case law, although the same judge (Slesser LJ) extended it to the tort of nuisance—where if anything its boundaries are still more uncertain—in the case of *Matania v National Provincial Bank* [1936] 2 All ER 633 (see Chapter 10).

The High Court of Australia has however made extensive use of the non-delegable duty analysis. In *Kondis v State Transport Authority* (1984) 152 CLR 672, the High Court of Australia justified the existence of non-delegable duties *to employees* by reference to the special relationship between the employer (who was subject to the duty), and the employee who it was intended to protect. This has been taken up and developed by the High Court in the cases of *Commonwealth v Introvigne* (1982) 150 CLR 258 (where it explained the liability of a school to a pupil) and *Burnie Port Authority v General Jones* (1994) 179 CLR 520 (where it explained why there was liability in negligence to a neighbouring occupier when a fire was started by a negligent independent contractor). In the latter case, the High Court required a close relationship of 'proximity'. As we have said, in *Lister v Hesley Hall* Lord Hobhouse regarded the school as having 'assumed responsibility' to the claimants who were within its care. 'Assumption of responsibility' is appropriately regarded as a demanding form of the proximity test for a duty of care in negligence. As such, the approach of Lord Hobhouse in *Lister* closely resembles the Australian case law on non-delegable duties.

However, the issue of sexual abuse of children by employees is precisely where the 'non-delegable duty' device appears to have reached its limits in Australia. In *NSW v Lepore* (2003) 195 ALR 412, a majority of the High Court held that a school could not be liable under a non-delegable duty for the *intentional* torts of its employees. The 'non-delegable duty' is a duty specifically to avoid injury through negligence. Contentiously, the majority also suggested that liability for negligence could not arise from deliberate acts of wrongdoing—such acts could not appropriately be referred to in terms of 'negligence' at all. Thus, if there could be any liability on a school or other employer in respect of deliberate sexual assaults by employees, this would need to be either on the basis of lack of care on the part of the employer (for example in the selection or supervision of the employee), or on the basis of vicarious liability. The question of whether vicarious liability was established on the facts was remitted for retrial, with the members of the High Court offering conflicting views.

3. OTHER PRIMARY DUTIES: CARE IN SELECTION AND SUPERVISION

There are certain circumstances in which a duty is clearly owed to exercise care in the selection of contractors. As an example, an occupier may discharge its duty to keep visitors reasonably safe by entrusting work to competent contractors, provided reasonable care is taken to select the contractor: Occupiers' Liability Act 1957, section 2(4)(b), extracted in Chapter 12. The benefit of this provision will also be lost if the occupier does not take reasonable steps (*if any such steps are reasonably required*) to check that the contractor's work is appropriately done. In *Gwilliam v West Herts Hospital NHS Trust* [2003] QB 443, the Court of Appeal decided that this duty was merely 'illustrative' of a general obligation to exercise due care in the selection and (where appropriate) the supervision of contractors. A similar duty will arise where the contractor is *not* engaged in a work of 'construction, maintenance, and repair'. In that case, there was a duty to select competent contractors for the supply and operation of a 'Splat-wall' at a fund-raising event. In *Bottomley v Todmorden Cricket Club* [2003] EWCA Civ 1575, the Court of Appeal said that the same duty to select contractors with care arose at common law, so that it also applied to a case brought in negligence.

The key controversy of *Gwilliam v West Herts Hospital Trust* lies in the content of the primary duty recognised by the majority of the Court of Appeal. The only grounds on which it could be argued that the defendant hospital had *not* taken reasonable care in that case was that they had not ensured that the contractor had a valid policy of public liability insurance. The policy expired shortly before the claimant's injury, so that there was no value in proceeding against the contractor. As such, the claim was in effect that the negligence of the hospital (in not checking the validity of the contractor's insurance) had caused the claimant to be exposed, not to a risk of physical harm, but to a risk of not being compensated should she suffer physical harm. Strictly, this was not the formulation adopted by Lord Woolf CJ, who argued that '[t]he fact of insurance would go to [the contractors'] competence' (para 15). In other words, the requirement to enquire about insurance is merely an aspect of the duty to keep the claimant reasonably *safe* as a visitor to the premises.[27] But the other two members of the Court of Appeal recognized the novelty of the claim. Waller LJ who (with Lord Woolf) thought that such a duty *should* be recognized, went so far as to say that:

> 37 . . . the duty sought to be imposed by the claimant in this case cannot actually be limited to a duty to see that there is public liability insurance; it must in fact be a duty to see that the independent contractor is in a position to meet such a claim.

Waller LJ reasoned that it would be 'fair, just, and reasonable' to impose such a duty. He also thought that such a duty was not ruled out on the basis of decided cases, even though it appears contrary to the decisions in *Reid v Rush and Tomkins* [1990] 1 WLR 212 (where an employer was under no duty to advise an employee on insurance in respect of personal injury when working abroad), and *Van Oppen v Clerk to the Bedford Charity Trustees* [1990] 1 WLR 235 (where a school failed to advise of the need for personal accident insurance for those playing rugby). In both of these Court of Appeal decisions, the absence of insurance (caused, the claimants argued, by carelessness on the part of the defendant) was interpreted as having caused *economic* loss, rather then physical harm, so that stricter rules for recognition of a duty would apply. Waller LJ thought that, even if the loss was regarded as 'economic', a duty should still be recognized because of the 'hazardous' nature of the activities in which the hospital had invited the claimant to take part.

As it happened, both Waller LJ and Lord Woolf thought that the duty thus recognized had not been breached on the facts of the case. The defendant had raised the question of liability

---

[27] This was also the approach of the Court of Appeal in *Bottomley v Todmorden Cricket Club*, and on the facts of that particular case (defendant's employee injured while assisting in a badly organized pyrotechnic display; contractors had no liability insurance at all), the analysis is slightly more convincing. Absence of insurance appears to have been just one of several indicators of lack of competence.

insurance and had even entered into a contract which specified that the hospital would have the benefit of that contractor's public liability insurance. All that the defendant had not done was to check the insurance policy, which would have shown its expiry date.

Sedley LJ on the other hand did not agree that a duty to check the insurance status of a contractor should be recognized so easily, even if he did agree (para 54) that the duty proposed might meet 'important goals of distributive and corrective justice' (he balanced this statement by doubting the fairness of such a duty if it applied to ordinary householders contracting for work to be done). Sedley LJ correctly identified that the duty to check insurance was 'not a small extension of an existing category but a jump across a factual and logical gap', which might also lead to more unpredictable developments (para 59). Obligations to insure, he pointed out, have previously been the creation of statute not of common law, and this was in part because the social and economic impact of such a duty would be hard for a court to evaluate. Referring to the third limb of the *Caparo* test (the 'fair, just, and reasonable' requirement), which Waller LJ applied in support of a new duty, Sedley LJ added:

> 56 . . . The test is, as I understand it, at least as much a restrictive as an expansive test, designed among other things to keep a check on the tendency of contemporary western tort law to creep towards a situation in which anyone can sue anyone for anything.

Such issues, which were also encountered in the judgment of Baroness Hale in *Majrowski* (above), are a counterpoint to the 'enterprise risk' and loss spreading justifications for vicarious liability, and they are never far from the surface when discussing liability arising out of the wrongdoing of others. Sedley LJ's judgment serves as a warning against setting aside the limitations of vicarious liability too readily, simply because one party seems to have been in a position to avoid the loss.

3.1 DUTIES TO SUPERVISE EMPLOYEES

Even where injury is caused through the tortious conduct of an *employee*, there may be scope for liability of the employer in accordance with a primary duty. For example, breach of such a primary duty was recognized by the Court of Appeal in *Mattis v Pollock*, above. In that case such primary liability was simply an alternative to vicarious liability. Breach of a primary duty to select and supervise employees with care may become important, for example, if the injury is not caused 'in the course of employment', so that it is outside the reach of vicarious liability.

An example is provided by *Attorney-General of the British Virgin Islands v Hartwell* [2004] UKPC 12; [2004] 1 WLR 1273. A police officer shot at his girlfriend in a crowded bar and injured the claimant, a tourist. The Privy Council judged that the shooting was not connected with his employment as a police officer: he had left his post on the island of Jost Van Dyke, improperly helped himself to a police revolver, and taken it to the Bath and Turtle in pursuit of a personal vendetta. This was judged to fall outside the course of employment. On the other hand, there was a breach of the employer's primary duty since, in the light of previous incidents, the officer was plainly not a proper person to have access to firearms.

FURTHER READING

Atiyah, P., *Vicarious Liability in the Law of Tort* (London: Butterworths, 1967).

Cane, P., 'Liability for Sexual Abuse' (2000) 116 LQR 21–6.

Giliker, P., 'Rough Justice in an Unjust World' (2002) 65 MLR 269–79.

McBride, N., 'Vicarious Liability in England and Australia' [2003] CLJ 255–60.

McKendrick, E., 'Vicarious Liability and Independent Contractors—A Reexamination' (1990) 53 MLR 770.

Vines, P., 'Schools' Responsibility for Teachers' Sexual Assault: Non-delegable Duty and Vicarious Liability' [2003] MULR 22.

Weekes, R., 'Vicarious Liability for Violent Employees' [2004] 63 CLJ 53–63.

Williams, G., 'Liability for Independent Contractors' [1956] CLJ 180.

Williams, G., 'Vicarious Liability: Tort of the Master or Tort of the Servant?' (1956) 72 LQR 522.

PART V

NUISANCE AND DUTIES RELATING TO LAND

10

NUISANCE

CENTRAL ISSUES

i) There are two forms of action in nuisance, namely **public** and **private** nuisance. Tort lawyers are primarily concerned with private nuisance, which may be defined as an unreasonable interference with use and enjoyment of land or with some right over, or in connection with it. Public nuisance by contrast is a crime and is actionable by the Attorney-General in the public interest. It extends to a far wider range of interests than private nuisance, including especially public health.

ii) The basis of liability in private nuisance is not straightforward. But, despite some confusing dicta in cases where nuisance and negligence overlap, the tort is clearly very different from negligence. The main concern is not the quality of the defendant's conduct unless this is relevant for some particular reason (for example, in the defence of statutory authority). The main concern is the reasonableness and lawfulness of interference with the claimant's interests in land. A nuisance is an unlawful interference with such interests.

iii) Cases of overlap between negligence and nuisance have caused particular difficulty. Some have argued that cases of overlap should be removed from the ambit of nuisance, in the interests of its long-term survival as a separate action. One category of overlap arises where actual damage is caused by a nuisance which has not been created by the defendant, but which has arisen on land occupied by the defendant. Recent House of Lords decisions have minimised the overlap between negligence and nuisance, by removing cases of personal injury from the whole area of nuisance, and by ensuring that only those with an interest in land may bring an action. There is now a restricted range of cases in which negligence and private nuisance arise as alternatives.

iv) The relationship between private and public interests has always been a key concern surrounding nuisance, and it is now even more pertinent. The influence of the Human Rights Act 1998 has of course added a new element to such issues, giving rise to some perhaps surprising developments although the full

> extent of its influence is still a matter of conjecture. There are considerable unresolved questions surrounding the conflict between personal rights and community interests, particularly where remedies are concerned, but also in respect of protected interests.

1. PRIVATE NUISANCE

1.1 MAKING SENSE OF PRIVATE NUISANCE

For a student approaching the tort of private nuisance, the early signs are often not encouraging. Nuisance has been described as presenting an 'impenetrable jungle' of case law (Prosser and Keeton on *Torts*, 5th edn, 1984, quoted by Deakin, Johnston, and Markesinis, *Markesinis and Deakin's Tort Law*, 5th edn, 2003, p 455), and as being both immersed in uncertainty (Fleming, *The Law of Torts*, 9th edn, p 457) and so amorphous as to defy rational explanation (ibid). Its boundaries are said by the Privy Council to be 'uncertain' (*Goldman v Hargrave* [1967] 1 AC 645, 657), and it has been politely described as 'protean' (Lord Wright, *Sedleigh-Denfield v O'Callaghan* [1940] AC 880, 903). It is true that the many nineteenth-century cases on nuisance are prone to contradiction, and there has been no single authoritative case which 'organised' the field or presented a simple statement of liability—nothing, in other words, to compare with *Donoghue v Stevenson*.

But students should not feel too downhearted. For one thing, there are many examples of successful recent cases. Private nuisance is clear enough to be workable in many cases, even if it is not so easy to understand in all its details. Equally, some help is at hand in understanding the contradictory nineteenth century cases. The issue of what economic and political influences helped to shape nineteenth century nuisance law has been subject to academic enquiry: see for example J. P. S. McLaren, 'Nuisance Law and the Industrial Revolution—Some Lessons from Social History' (1983) 3 OJLS 155. Some commentary on the intellectual history of nuisance has also been undertaken by judges. For example, in *Wildtree Hotels v Harrow LBC* [2001] 2 AC 1 Lord Hoffmann has sought to explain some important features of nineteenth-century nuisance cases in economic terms, attributing contradictions in the case law to different economic theories held by judges of influence, most particularly as regards the 'internalization of costs': who should bear the burden when beneficial undertakings such as the construction of the railways cause incidental losses? This gives us an unusual opportunity to observe how current judges approach some mixed questions of economics and justice.

Private nuisance has a longer and richer history than negligence, and this gives rise to certain challenges in interpreting and applying the law. It could be said though that through recent higher court activity, the ambit of nuisance is becoming clearer, though at the price of some restriction in its scope. Most such cases suggest that nuisance is not about to be absorbed by negligence, as has sometimes been predicted. Nuisance as we describe it here (and no such description will be free from controversy) is separate from the tort of negligence, and to a large extent conceptually independent of it.

1.2 THE BASIS OF LIABILITY: PLACING PRIVATE NUISANCE ON THE 'MAP' OF TORT LAW

A Basic Statement of Actionability in Nuisance

'Private nuisance may be described as unlawful interference with a person's use or enjoyment of land, or some right over, or in connection with it.'

The above statement was adopted by Scott LJ in *Read v Lyons* [1945] KB 216 at 236 and approved in a number of other cases. It is cited in *Winfield and Jolowicz on Tort* (16th edn, 2002), p 508. However, it is declared to be a *description* (rather than a definition). With nuisance it is often necessary to turn to previous decisions, rather than to abstract definitions, to settle the detailed questions of whether any particular interference is actionable.

Other writers provide variations on this general description. For example, Deakin, Johnston, and Markesinis (*Markesinis and Deakin's Tort Law*, 5th edn, 2003, p 455) refer to a private nuisance as an 'unreasonable' interference, and add the proviso that the interference must be 'substantial'. R. A. Buckley (*The Law of Nuisance*, 2nd edn, 1996, p 1) begins with a statement approved by Dillon LJ in *Khorasandjian v Bush* [1993] QB 727, and derived from *Clerk and Lindsell on Torts* (then the 16th edn): ' . . . the essence of nuisance is a condition or activity which unduly interferes with the use or enjoyment of land'. Again, this only seeks to describe the 'essence' of nuisance, and is not restrictive as to its range. The explicit reference to 'conditions or activities' implies a useful distinction from the negligence-type focus on what Buckley calls 'momentary carelessness' (Buckley, p 4).

Placing Private Nuisance on the Tort Map

Protected interests and relevant conduct

Remembering the way that we 'mapped' tort law in Chapter 1, the description above shows that nuisance is different from negligence in more than one way. It is different from negligence because the definition of **protected interests** in nuisance is both narrower (relating only to interests in or rights over land), and within that field in some senses broader (including losses that would be regarded as intangible and probably some that would be regarded as purely economic in negligence terms).

In terms of **relevant conduct**, there is no requirement that the conduct of the defendant should be careless, although it is often said that reasonableness of conduct plays a part and we will explore whether and when this is so. In some instances, nuisances can arise from perfectly careful, deliberate behaviour. As Lord Goff clearly put it in a key modern case:

Cambridge Water v Eastern Counties Leather plc [1994] 2 AC 264, at 299

. . . if the user is reasonable, the defendant will not be liable for subsequent harm to his neighbour's enjoyment of land; but if the user is not reasonable, the defendant will be liable, even though he may have used reasonable care and skill to avoid it.

Although 'conduct' need not be unreasonable in the sense of lack of due care or falling short of a standard, it is clear that there must be some element of 'unreasonableness' before the interference can fulfil the definition of a nuisance. In the above statement, Lord Goff describes the applicable idea of reasonableness through the terminology of 'reasonable user' of the land. Unfortunately, the precise *meaning* of 'reasonable user' has remained rather unclear, as has its range of applicability. This can be traced to some large ambiguities in the important case of *St Helen's v Tipping*, which is extracted below.

Lord Goff also suggested that 'liability for nuisance has generally been regarded as strict' (ibid, p 299). In fact, most writers avoid describing it in quite that way. Fleming, for example, categorizes nuisance with 'Miscellaneous' torts, rather than under the category of 'Strict Liability': John G. Fleming, *The Law of Torts*, 9th edn (Law Book Company). Nevertheless, with the support of Lord Goff's statement above, we can say that conduct need not be faulty in all cases of nuisance. In fact, we can go further and suggest that lack of care is only relevant to nuisance actions of particular kinds, and then for particular reasons. Nuisance is, typically, 'stricter than' negligence.

'Continuing' Nuisances

It is also important to notice that nuisances may be, and often are, *continuing*. The core concern is with deliberate activities causing interference, rather than with momentary carelessness causing loss. Dealing with a continuing nuisance requires looking to the future, while negligence cases by contrast invite a retrospective outlook. The key question in cases of continuing nuisance is whether there should be an injunction to stop the unreasonable interference; it is normally thought that only in rare instances would damages be awarded 'in lieu' of the injunction in such a case, although damages may also be sought to compensate for past interference. The overlap between nuisance and negligence is largely confined to cases where the interference amounts to damage of a relevant sort and *has already occurred*. In cases of continuing nuisance where the claimant seeks an *injunction* to prevent the nuisance, there is no question of foreseeability, which is so central to negligence.

Lord Goff, *Cambridge Water*, at 300

. . . we must be on our guard, when considering liability for damages in nuisance, not to draw inapposite conclusions from cases concerned only with a claim for an injunction. This is because, when an injunction is claimed, its purpose is to restrain further action by the defendant which may interfere with the plaintiff's enjoyment of his land, and ex hypothesi the defendant must be aware, if and when an injunction is granted, that such interference may be caused by the act which he is restrained from committing. It follows that these cases provide no guidance on the question whether foreseeability of harm of the relevant type is a prerequisite of the recovery of damages for causing such harm to the plaintiff.

In the case of continuing nuisances, it is especially clear that a state of affairs may amount to a nuisance even if all due care is taken in the course of the activity which gives rise to it. In *Rushmer v Polsue and Alfieri*, Cozens-Hardy LJ imagined a noise nuisance from the operation of a steam-hammer: 'it would be no answer to say that the steam-hammer is of the most modern approved pattern and is reasonably worked' ([1906] 1 Ch 234 at [251]). This comment was expressly approved by Lord Loreburn LC on appeal [1907] AC 121 at 123. And in *Gillingham v Medway (Chatham) Dock Co Ltd* [1993] QB 343, Buckley J explained that the reasonableness of the defendant's manner of operating its docks was not in issue. No matter how carefully the docks were operated, if the interference was found to be unreasonable, then it was capable of being classed as a nuisance.

In summary, nuisance requires that the interference must be judged 'unreasonable', and this incorporates assessment of all the circumstances. However, there is no general requirement that *conduct* should be unreasonable. In particular, lack of due care will not be essential.

1.3 ELEMENTS OF ACTIONABILITY

Interference

Our basic description of nuisance above referred to unreasonable interference with the use and enjoyment of land, or with some right over, or in connection with the use and enjoyment of land. In itself, this does not describe the types of interference which may be involved. In *Hunter v Canary Wharf*, Lord Lloyd said that:

> Private nuisances are of three kinds. They are (1) nuisance by encroachment on a neighbour's land; (2) nuisance by direct physical injury to a neighbour's land; and (3) nuisance by interference with a neighbour's quiet enjoyment of his land.

It has been suggested that the last of Lord Lloyd's three categories, 'quiet enjoyment'— complaints about discomfort or inconvenience typically caused by noise, dust, vibration, or smell—make up the bulk of nuisance cases (Buckley, *The Law of Nuisance*, p 23). As Lord Lloyd suggests, nuisance also incorporates cases of physical encroachment (for example by tree roots), and cases of actual physical damage to land. Acid smuts, for example, may affect one's enjoyment of a property; may damage one's trees; or may even damage one's health. It is well established that the first two of these are actionable as nuisances; but the decision in *Hunter v Canary Wharf* heavily qualifies the way that nuisance will approach the third.

There is also another category of case not mentioned by Lord Lloyd, namely interferences with specific rights over land, such as easements. These too are actionable as nuisances: see for example *Colls v Home and Colonial Stores Ltd* [1904] AC 179, concerning interference with light.[1] In *Midtown v City of London Real Property Co Ltd* [2005] EWHC 33, the claimants established that they had acquired a right to light by prescription pursuant to section 3 of the Prescription Act 1832: a right to light to a building is absolute and indefeasible if it 'shall be naturally enjoyed therewith for a period of twenty years without obstruction' (*Midtown* at [6]). But was the *interference* with this right from construction of a neighbouring building sufficient to amount to a nuisance? Peter Smith J explained the approach to this question:

> [55] . . . the fact that light enjoyment by the relevant windows is diminished as a result of the proposed development, does not itself show that the development constitutes a nuisance. The question to be posed is not what light is taken away, but what light is left, and whether the light is sufficient for normal purposes according to the ordinary notions of mankind having regard to the purposes for which the building was designed and the nature of that design . . .

---

[1] In this case, the interference fell short of a nuisance.

In this particular case, the interference did indeed amount to a nuisance.

In the absence of a positive right (such as the right to light acquired by prescription in *Midtown*), the mere presence of a building on the defendants' land would not generally amount to a nuisance. Ordinarily, there will need to be some sort of 'emanation' from the defendant's land, as explained in the following extract:

Hunter v Canary Wharf [1997] AC 655

Lord Goff, at 684–6

. . . the complaint rests simply upon the presence of the defendants' building on land in the neighbourhood as causing the relevant interference. The gravamen of the plaintiffs' case is that the defendants, by building the Canary Wharf Tower, interfered with the television signals and so caused interference with the reception on the plaintiffs' television sets . . . In this respect the present case is to be distinguished from the *Bridlington Relay* case, in which the problem was caused not just by the presence of a neighbouring building but by electrical interference resulting from the defendant electricity board's activities. As a general rule, a man is entitled to build on his own land, though nowadays this right is inevitably subject to our system of planning controls. Moreover, as a general rule, a man's right to build on his land is not restricted by the fact that the presence of the building may of itself interfere with his neighbour's enjoyment of his land . . . .

. . . in the absence of an easement, more is required than the mere presence of a neighbouring building to give rise to an actionable private nuisance. Indeed, for an action in private nuisance to lie in respect of interference with the plaintiff's enjoyment of his land, it will generally arise from something emanating from the defendant's land. Such an emanation may take many forms—noise, dirt, fumes, a noxious smell, vibrations, and suchlike. Occasionally activities on the defendant's land are in themselves so offensive to neighbours as to constitute an actionable nuisance, as in *Thompson-Schwab v. Costaki* [1956] 1 W.L.R. 335, where the sight of prostitutes and their clients entering and leaving neighbouring premises were held to fall into that category. Such cases must however be relatively rare. In one New Zealand case, *Bank of New Zealand v. Greenwood* [1984] 1 N.Z.L.R. 525, the glass roof of a verandah which deflected the sun's rays so that a dazzling glare was thrown on to neighbouring buildings was held, prima facie, to create a nuisance; but it seems that the effect was not merely to reflect the sunlight but to deflect it at such an angle and in such a manner as to cause the dazzling glare, too bright for the human eye to bear, to shine straight into the neighbouring building . . . such a case can be distinguished from one concerned with the mere presence of a building on neighbouring land. At all events the mere fact that a building on the defendant's land gets in the way and so prevents something from reaching the plaintiff's land is generally speaking not enough for this purpose.

Lord Goff (and Lord Hoffmann) offered inconclusive remarks on the question of whether interference with television reception—which was the subject of the comments above—could ever amount to a nuisance in English law.[2] If it is so capable, it will be on the basis that there is a substantial interference with 'an important incidence of ordinary user of property'. The

---

[2] In the older case of *Bridlington Relay v Yorkshire Electricity Board* [1965] Ch 436, such interference was not recognized as capable of amounting to a nuisance. The House of Lords in *Hunter* accepted that circumstances may have changed since 1965, but did not decide the point since the existence of the building, as we have seen, was not actionable in the absence of an easement.

latter expression was adopted as the relevant test at first instance in the case of *Network Rail Infrastructure v Morris* [2004] EWCA Civ 172, where the defendants' electrical equipment had interfered with the operation of the claimant's sound studio. The Court of Appeal, however, decided the case on the basis that the interference was not *foreseeable*.

Unreasonableness of Interference

In order to be actionable as a nuisance, the relevant interference must also be judged to be 'unreasonable'. 'Unreasonableness' is one of the key concepts in nuisance law. Unfortunately, it is also one of the key puzzles. Some cases discuss the issues in terms of whether the defendant's use of land constitutes a 'reasonable user'. The meaning of *'reasonable user'* is introduced here through two influential nineteenth-century cases.

Bamford v Turnley (Court of Exchequer Chamber, 1862: 3 B & S 66; 31 LJQB 286; 6 LT 721; 9 Jur NS 377; 10 WR 803; 122 ER 27)

The plaintiff complained of interference from smoke and smell arising from the burning of bricks by the defendant. On the basis of *Hole v Barlow* (1858, 6 WR 619; 140 ER 1113), Lord Cockburn CJ directed 'that if the jury thought that the spot was convenient and proper, and the burning of bricks was, under the circumstances, a reasonable use by the defendant of his own land, the defendant would be entitled to a verdict'. It will be seen that this statement incorporated both reasonable user, and the appropriateness of the locality in which the offending activity was carried out. The jury found for the defendant, and the plaintiff appealed to the Court of Exchequer Chamber. By a majority, the Court of Exchequer Chamber allowed the plaintiff's appeal. The main majority judgment dealt narrowly with the correctness of *Hole v Barlow*, which was disapproved as unsupported by prior authority. But it is the separate concurring judgment of Bramwell B that is most often referred to and that continues to inspire most comment. It proposes a potential compromise which has continued to return to the agenda.

Bramwell B

. . . those acts necessary for the common and ordinary use and occupation of land and houses may be done, if conveniently done, without subjecting those who do them to an action. This principle would comprehend all the cases I have mentioned, but would not comprehend the present, where what has been done was not the using of land in a common and ordinary way, but in an exceptional manner—not unnatural or unusual, but not the common and ordinary use of land.

Then can this principle be extended to, or is there any other principle that will comprehend, the present case? I know of none. It is for the defendant to show it. There is an obvious necessity for such a principle as I have mentioned. It is as much for the benefit of one owner as of another, for the very nuisance the one has complained of as the result of his neighbour's ordinary use of his neighbour's land, he himself will create in the ordinary use of his own, and the reciprocal nuisances are of a comparatively trifling character. The convenience of such a rule may be indicated by calling it a rule of give and take, live and let live. But none of the above reasoning is applicable to such a case of nuisance as the present. . . .

But it is said that, temporary or permanent, it is lawful, because it is for the public benefit. In the first place, that law, to my mind, is a bad one which, for the public benefit, inflicts loss on an individual without compensation. But, further, with great respect, I think this consideration misapplied in this and in many other cases. The public consists of all the individuals of it, and a thing is only for the public benefit when it is productive of good to those individuals on the balance of loss and gain to all; so that if all the loss or all the gain were borne and received by one individual, he or the whole would be a gainer. But wherever this is the case, wherever a thing is for the public benefit, properly understood, the loss of all the individuals of the public who lose will bear compensation out of the gains of those who gain. It is for the public benefit there should be railways, but it would not be unless the gain of having the railway was sufficient to compensate the loss occasioned by the use of the land required for its site, and accordingly noone thinks it would be right to take an individual's land, without compensation, to make a railway . . . So in like way in this case: a money value indeed cannot easily be put on the plaintiff's loss, but it is equal to some number of pounds or pence—£10, £50, or what not. Unless the defendant's profits are enough to compensate this, I deny it is for the public benefit he should do what he has done. If they are, he ought to compensate.

The only objection I can see to this reasoning is, that by injunction or abatement of a nuisance a man who would not accept a pecuniary compensation might put a stop to works of great value, and much more than enough to compensate him. This objection, however, is of small practical importance. It may be that the law ought to be amended, and some means provided to legalise such cases, as I believe is the case in some foreign countries giving compensation; but I am clearly of opinion, that though the present law may be defective, it would be made worse, and be unjust and inexpedient, if it permitted such power of inflicting loss and damage on individuals without compensation, as is claimed by the argument for the defendants. . . .

Bramwell B divided the cases of amenity nuisance into two. First were those where the inconvenience arose from the 'common and ordinary' use of land. Here, the law of nuisance applies a principle of 'give and take' in a situation understood as one of general reciprocity. As one facet of this, the locality is important. It is appropriate to ask whether the offending use of land is conducted in a suitable location. Second, there are other cases which would fall outside this principle of 'give and take'. In these cases, the defendant's activities go beyond the 'common and ordinary' use of land, even though they are not in any sense 'unnatural or unusual'. Here, it would be no answer to the claim that the activity in question was for the public benefit. On the contrary, the argument that something was for the public benefit would be *believed* only if the activity was still considered worthwhile after the payment of compensation to those whose interests in land were thereby compromised. Only if it remained worthwhile to the defendant in these circumstances could it be said that the activity was of benefit overall.

This idea is often referred to as the principle of 'internalization of costs': those who undertake costly activities should be forced to take into account the *true* costs of their activity. Bramwell's overtly economic approach continues to inspire interest. Although it appears to be based in welfare economics rather than in fairness or equity, its outcomes have resonances with more recent approaches to compensation for losses imposed upon individuals by activities that are justified in the public interest (see Section 1.7, Remedies, below). Bramwell even suggests, in effect, that a change in the law to allow greater availability of damages in lieu of an injunction would encourage productive activities and enhance economic efficiency. Here, he proposes a constructive compromise which he says would enhance the public interest. It is essentially the same solution proposed by a number of judges and commentators in more recent years (see the judgment of Buckley J in *Dennis v MoD*, extracted in Section 1.7 below; and Tromans, 'Nuisance—Prevention or Payment?' [1982] CLJ 87). On the other hand, it might be suspected that this is an elaborate 'smokescreen' for the protection, on grounds of nothing more than a sense of fairness, of traditional property rights against broadly profitable industrial development (see A. W. B. Simpson, *Leading Cases in the Common Law* (OUP, 1995), Chapter 7, 'Victorian Judges and the Problem of Social Cost', p 175).

St Helen's Smelting Co v Tipping (1865) 11 HL Cas 642, HL(E)

In a case which symbolizes the historic conflict between landed and industrial interests, and which appeared likely to bring to a head the question of public interest or at least local prosperity as against established property rights, the plaintiff brought an action in respect of the damage allegedly being caused to his property by copper smelting works on neighbouring land. He had purchased what is described in the judgment of Lord Westbury LC as an 'estate of great value' in June 1860; the particular smelting works in question had commenced later in the same year. However, he had purchased the estate in an area in which the industrial smelting of copper was a well-established activity, and he almost certainly had full knowledge of the defendant's plans at the time of the purchase: it has been suggested that the negotiated price was affected by the construction of the smelting works (Simpson, *Leading Cases in the Common Law*, p 184).

Having succeeded in this action, Tipping later applied successfully for an injunction to restrain the smelting works: *Tipping v St Helen's Smelting Co* (1865) [LR] 1 Ch App 66. The equitable remedy was granted,[3] notwithstanding that Tipping's predecessor in title had sold the neighbouring land to the defendants with full knowledge of their plan to construct copper smelting works.

The extract that follows is one of the most cited passages in nuisance law, so that its ambiguities are highly significant. Certain key phrases have been highlighted.

Lord Westbury LC, at 650–2

. . . my Lords, in matters of this description it seems to me that it is a very desirable thing to mark the difference between an action brought for a nuisance upon the ground that the alleged nuisance produces material injury to the property, and an action brought for a nuisance on the ground that the thing alleged to be a nuisance is productive of sensible personal discomfort. With regard to the latter, namely, the personal inconvenience and interference with one's enjoyment, one's quiet, one's personal freedom . . ., whether that may or may not be denominated a nuisance, must undoubtedly depend greatly on the circumstances of the place where the thing complained of actually occurs. If a man lives in a town, it is necessary that he should subject himself to the consequences of those operations of trade which may be carried on in his immediate locality, which are actually necessary for trade and commerce, and also for the enjoyment of property, and for the benefit of the inhabitants of the town and of the public at large . . .

But when an occupation is carried on by one person in the neighbourhood of another, and the result of that trade, or occupation, or business, is a material injury to property, then there unquestionably arises a very different consideration. I think, my Lords, that in a case of that description, the submission which is required from persons living in society to that amount of

3 The importance of the 'equitable' nature of the injunctive remedy is that it is available at the discretion of the court, and not as of right: see Section 1.7 on Remedies, below.

discomfort which may be necessary for the legitimate and free exercise of the trade of their neighbours, would not apply to circumstances the immediate result of which is sensible injury to the value of the property . . .

[. . . the only ground on which Your Lordships are asked to set aside the verdict is that] . . . the whole neighbourhood where these copper smelting works were carried on, is a neighbourhood more or less devoted to manufacturing processes of a similar kind, and therefore it is said, that inasmuch as the this copper smelting is carried on in what the Appellant contends is a fit place, it may be carried on with impunity, although the result may be the utter destruction, or the very considerable diminution, of the value of the plaintiff's property. . . . The word 'suitable' unquestionably cannot carry with it this consequence, that a trade may be carried on in a particular locality, the consequence of which trade may be injury and destruction to the neighbouring property . . .

The House of Lords was asked to set aside the judgment of the courts below on the important, but narrow ground that the neighbourhood was one devoted to manufacturing processes. This has become known as an issue concerning the **'locality'** or **'character of the neighbourhood'**. The *St Helen's* case seems to lay down that the 'character of the neighbourhood' is relevant only to certain cases of nuisance, namely those which relate to 'amenity' nuisance, or (mere) interference with 'comfort and convenience'. The difficulty is that Lord Westbury was not consistent in identifying the features of this case which made the locality principle inapplicable. The interference is variously described in the extract above as causing 'material injury to the property'; 'sensible injury to the value of the property', and 'considerable diminution of the value of the property'. The first of these seems to suggest physical damage; the others do not.

Even so, the case is usually understood as dividing cases of material *physical* damage to property (which was present in this case in the form of damage to trees), from cases falling short of that:

Veale J, *Halsey v Esso Petroleum* [1961] 1 WLR 683, at 691–2

So far as the present case is concerned, liability for nuisance by harmful deposits could be established by proving damage by the deposits to the property in question, provided of course that the injury was not merely trivial. Negligence is not an ingredient of the cause of action, and the character of the neighbourhood is not a matter to be taken into consideration. On the other hand, nuisance by smell or noise is something to which no absolute standard can be applied. It is always a question of degree whether the interference with comfort or convenience is sufficiently serious to constitute a nuisance. The character of the neighbourhood is very relevant and all the relevant circumstances have to be taken into account. What might be a nuisance in one area is by no means necessarily so in another. In an urban area, everyone must put up with a certain amount of discomfort and annoyance from the activities of neighbours, and the law must strike a fair and reasonable balance between the right of the plaintiff on the one hand to the undisturbed enjoyment of his property, and the right of the defendant on the other hand to use his property for his own lawful enjoyment.

However, even if this was the distinction intended by Lord Westbury (and as we have seen his language was by no means clear), then no particular reason was given for dividing material physical damage from other interferences in this way. Many amenity nuisances are capable of persisting in the long term, and permanent and severe interference with personal comfort, or even with quiet enjoyment, is easily capable of affecting the market value of property. Perhaps this is a point more readily appreciated in the context of the modern domestic housing market, than in the context of competing productive economic uses of land. The status of Tipping's estate was itself ambiguous: it was a working farm; but it also provided a gentleman's residence.

Whatever the true interpretation of the *St Helen's* case, it represents a compromise solution. It places the dividing line in a different position from that proposed by Bramwell B in *Bamford v Turnley*, and unfortunately (since it is the leading authority in this field) it lacks reasoned justifications for doing so.

In the earlier case, Bramwell B wanted the principle of 'give and take' (which would encompass the locality rule) to be confined to cases where land was used in a 'common and ordinary' way. Beyond this, the convenience of the location and the reasonableness of the activity could not, in his view, justify an interference which would otherwise amount to a nuisance. *Bamford v Turnley* itself was a case of nuisance through interference with comfort and enjoyment, but the locality rule did not apply. So some amenity nuisances, on his approach, were *outside* the rule of 'give and take'.

In the *St Helen's* case, it was suggested that in cases of 'material injury to property', there was no place for the locality rule to operate, since no location could be regarded as 'convenient' for an activity having such effects. This much is narrowly compatible with the decision in *Bamford v Turnley*. But in placing the line here, Lord Westbury appears to have meant that *all* cases falling short of 'material injury to property', *are* subject to the locality rule, notwithstanding the nature of the activity as going quite beyond what was common and ordinary. This means that the ambiguous meaning of 'material injury to property' is exceedingly important.

Although Lord Westbury's comments are particularly directed at the locality principle, it is typically assumed that the 'reasonable user' test as a whole is applicable only to amenity nuisances; and then to all such nuisances. An example of this understanding is the following statement of Lord Hoffmann in *Wildtree Hotels v Harrow LBC* [2001] 2 AC 1, concerning claims for damage caused by noise, dust, or vibration:

> Being things 'productive of material physical discomfort' within the meaning of Lord Westbury's dichotomy in *St Helen's Smelting v Tipping* . . ., the claim is subject to the principle that a reasonable use of land, with due regard to the interests of the neighbours, is not actionable (at 12).

In the context of building works, Lord Hoffmann went on to explain that '[a]ctionability at common law therefore depends upon showing that the works were conducted without reasonable consideration for the neighbours' (at 13). Building works—in their nature typically both necessary and temporary—are thus subject to questions of 'reasonable consideration'.

An important gloss on the idea of 'reasonable user' is provided by the recent case of *Eileen Anthony & Others v The Coal Authority* [2005] EWHC 1654 QB. This shows that user may begin by being reasonable; but then *become* unreasonable, giving rise to a **duty to abate**. In this case, the defendants had collected coal spoil on their premises without appreciating the risk of spontaneous combustion. The risk was unforeseeable at the time of collecting the spoil. At some point, with changing knowledge, the chance of combustion became 'foreseeable'. In the event, a fire started spontaneously, and burnt for four years before being extinguished.

It caused extensive (and long-lasting) interference with use and enjoyment of neighbouring land. Pitchford J held that the user of land became unreasonable when the risk of combustion became foreseeable. A duty to 'abate' the nuisance (which is to say, to take reasonable steps to avoid the fire starting) then arose.

Summary: unreasonableness and reasonable user

Our general statement of private nuisance referred to 'unreasonable interference'. The idea of 'reasonable user' introduces slightly different terminology, focusing on the defendant's use of the land, rather than the effect on the claimant. Because of the accepted interpretation of *St Helen's v Tipping*, 'reasonable user' is applicable, as things stand, to those nuisances falling short of 'material physical damage'.

Reasonable user is not by any means the same as reasonable conduct, since some activities in some places are destined to be judged unreasonable no matter how carefully they are carried out. On the other hand, the idea of 'give and take' means that some activities are protected unless they are carried on without due regard for one's neighbours. We noted the example of reasonable building works. In such cases, there will be attention to methods employed, times of operation, precautions taken, and so on. These are similar to negligence questions surrounding breach of duty, but they are aspects of a different enquiry.

This illustrates a general point about the nature of 'reasonableness' in nuisance. We noted at the start of this section that the crucial question is whether the interference is to be judged unreasonable, *not* whether the defendant's activity is carried out with due care. Nevertheless, there have been cases where the nature of the defendant's activities has been influential, and occasionally decisive, in the balancing exercise. And there are other cases where the nature of the claimant's interests has been a crucial element. The next section considers some 'special' issues in the broader reasonableness enquiry.

Unreasonableness: Special Considerations

Sensitivity

In the case of 'amenity' type nuisances, in which there is interference with personal comfort or convenience, private nuisance will not protect unduly sensitive claimants. Private nuisance protects only *ordinary* use and enjoyment of land. This principle was clearly expressed by Knight-Bruce V-C in *Walter v Selfe* (1851) 4 De G & Sm 315 at 322 as cited, for example, in *Vanderpant v Mayfair Hotel Co Ltd* [1930] 1 Ch 138:

Luxmoore J, at 165

[I]t is necessary to determine whether the act complained of is an inconvenience materially interfering with the ordinary physical comfort of human existence, not merely according to elegant or dainty modes and habits of living, but according to plain and sober and simple notions obtaining among English people: see *Walter v. Selfe* and the remarks of Knight Bruce V.-C.

But what of cases of actual physical damage? In *Robinson v Kilvert* (1889) 41 Ch D 88, the idea that nuisance would not protect those making particularly sensitive use of property applied in a case of actual physical damage. Hot, dry air in a cellar caused damage to paper stored by the plaintiff, the defendant's tenant, on the floor above. Ordinary paper would not have been damaged. The action in nuisance failed. The defendant could not, by choosing a particularly sensitive use of the premises, prevent the defendant from making use of the cellar in a reason-able way, nor convert that use into a nuisance. Cotton LJ put it in the following way (at 94):

> If a person does what in itself is noxious, or which interferes with the ordinary use and enjoyment of a neighbour's property, it is a nuisance. But no case has been cited where the doing something not in itself noxious has been held a nuisance, unless it interferes with the ordinary enjoyment of life, or the ordinary use of property for the purposes of residence or business. It would, in my opinion, be wrong to say that the doing something not in itself noxious is a nuisance because it does harm to some particular trade in the adjoining property, although it would not prejudicially affect any ordinary trade carried on there, and does not inter-fere with the ordinary enjoyment of life. Here it is shewn that ordinary paper would not be damaged by what the Defendants are doing, but only a particular kind of paper, and it is not shewn that there is heat such as to incommode the workpeople on the Plaintiff's premises. I am of opinion, therefore, that the Plaintiff is not entitled to relief on the ground that what the Defendants are doing is a nuisance.

Even so, it should be remembered that in cases of physical damage, the remoteness rules applicable in nuisance are similar to those in negligence. In particular, if the claimant's sensitivity affects only the *extent* of damage suffered, then the defendant must compensate to the full extent of the loss. The Canadian case of *McKinnon Industries v Walker* [1951] 3 DLR 577 illustrates this well. Emissions from the defendant's factory foreseeably damaged the plaintiff's plants. These happened to be valuable orchids, thus increasing the sum payable in damages. The plaintiff's sensitivity had not caused the defendant's activities to constitute a nuisance, but had merely increased the size of the losses suffered.

In *Network Rail Infrastructure v Morris* [2004] EWCA Civ 172, the claimant argued that he should be able to recover damages in nuisance in respect of electromagnetic interference caused by Railtrack's signalling system, to electric guitar music played in his recording studio. The Court of Appeal observed that application of the approach in *Robinson v Kilvert* in such a case would be difficult, since use of sensitive equipment is now widespread. Lord Phillips thought that the balance to be struck would be a matter of reasonableness (which, as we have already said, is the traditional underlying test, of which *Robinson v Kilvert* is only an example). He also noted (at para 19) that foreseeability is now recognized to be a vital ingredient in the tort of nuisance. Foreseeability was not established on the facts of the case.

Although Lord Phillips noted that the tort of private nuisance has 'moved on' since cases such as *Robinson v Kilvert*, Buxton LJ was much more explicit, arguing that:

> **35** . . . it is difficult to see any further life in some particular rules of the law of nuisance, such as for instance the idea of "abnormal sensitiveness" drawn from *Robinson v Kilvert* . . . . That rule was developed at a time when liability in nuisance . . . was thought to be strict.

He went on to argue that the 'general view of the law of nuisance' had been changed by the judgment of Lord Cooke in *Delaware Mansions v Westminster City Council* [2002] 1 AC 321 (a case of encroaching tree roots), and that questions of reasonableness would now be considered in terms of 'foreseeability'.

It is suggested, against the approach of Buxton LJ, that key recent decisions such as *Cambridge Water* and *Hunter v Canary Wharf* do not mitigate the strictness of nuisance liability. *Delaware Mansions* concerned the duty of an occupier (there the Highway Authority) to compensate a neighbour for reasonable repair costs when a nuisance (in the form of *physical damage*) was created by trees on the defendant's land. In this sort of case, in accordance with cases such as *Goldman v Hargrave* and *Leakey v National Trust* (below), it has long been recognized that foreseeability, and the definition of *reasonable steps to abate a nuisance*, are relevant. This is not a proper basis on which to suggest that more typical forms of nuisance are to be approached in terms closer to negligence. Certainly, there is little justification for treating *Delaware Mansions* as marking a major reorientation in the law of nuisance, akin to *Donoghue v Stevenson* in the tort of negligence (Buxton LJ at [35]).

Malice

Turning from claimant's use, to defendant's use, bad motive on the part of the defendant will sometimes tip the balance decisively in the claimant's favour. In *Christie v Davey* [1893] 1 Ch 316, the defendant deliberately created a noise nuisance, solely in retaliation against his neighbours, the plaintiffs. The plaintiffs provided music lessons from the semi-detached house which shared a party wall with the defendant's house. Since there was no legitimate reason for the noise interference from the defendants, in contrast with the innocent (if perhaps raucous) activities of the plaintiffs, the defendant would be restrained from continuing.

North J, *Christie v Davey*, at 326–7

If what has taken place had occurred between two sets of persons both perfectly innocent, I should have taken an entirely different view of the case. But I am persuaded that what was done by the Defendant was done only for the purpose of annoyance, and in my opinion it was not a legitimate use of the Defendant's house to use it for the purpose of vexing and annoying his neighbours . . . This being so, I am bound to give the Plaintiffs the relief which they ask.

Christie v Davey was followed in *Hollywood Silver Fox Farm v Emmett* [1936] 2 KB 468. Here the plaintiff kept silver foxes. The defendant arranged for guns to be fired near to his boundary with the plaintiff's land, and as near to the vixens' pens as possible, solely in order to prevent successful breeding of the animals. Macnaghten J awarded damages, and an injunction to prevent such behaviour during the foxes' breeding season. In doing so, he had to contend with the case below, which has inspired much comment and more confusion over the years.

Bradford Corporation v Pickles [1895] AC 587

Between the two authorities of *Christie v Davey* (1893) and *Hollywood Silver Fox Farm* (1936), an opposite result was obtained in the very different case of *Bradford Corporation v Pickles*. The plaintiffs in this case supplied water to the city of Bradford. Some of it derived from a spring known as Many Wells, situated on land owned by the Corporation. Pickles owned land above Many Wells. His land acted as a sort of natural reservoir for subterranean water which flowed in undefined channels. The water flowed naturally from Pickles' land, to Many Wells. It was common ground that neither party had any legal interest over the water itself, because of its nature as percolating in undefined channels. In 1892, Pickles began work on his land which would divert water from its natural route, and would eventually diminish the supply of water to Many Wells. The Corporation claimed that these works were done 'maliciously', to deprive them of water, and sought an injunction.

In refusing the injunction, the House of Lords regarded the matter as resolved by the decision in *Chasemore v Richards* (1859 7 HLC 349): there is no ownership in underground water percolating in undefined channels.[4] Rather, a property owner such as Pickles has the right to divert or appropriate such water from beneath his own land. A neighbouring owner has no right to prevent this. In trying to avoid the impact of *Chasemore v Richards*, the Corporation relied on two matters. First, there was a point of statutory interpretation which will not affect us. But second, they claimed that Pickles' motive was 'malicious', and that he had therefore acted in excess of his rights. The members of the House were not persuaded by Pickles' own explanation of his acts (that he was seeking to work minerals under his land), and they seem to have concluded that he was seeking to extract an inflated price for his land. As it happens, they were not persuaded that this motive could be described as 'malicious'. But more importantly, they did not consider that motive, malicious or not, was in any sense relevant to the case.

Lord Halsbury LC, at 594–5

The only remaining point is the question of fact alleged by the plaintiffs, that the acts done by the defendant are done, not with any view which deals with the use of his own land or the percolating water through it, but is done, in the language of the pleader, "maliciously." I am not certain that I can understand or give any intelligible construction to the word so used. Upon the supposition on which I am now arguing, it comes to an allegation that the defendant did maliciously something that he had a right to do. If this question were to have been tried in old times as an injury to the right in an action on the case, the plaintiffs would have had to allege, and to prove, if traversed, that they were entitled to the flow of the water, which, as I have already said, was an allegation they would have failed to establish.

This is not a case in which the state of mind of the person doing the act can affect the right to do it. If it was a lawful act, however ill the motive might be, he had a right to do it. If it was an unlawful act, however good his motive might be, he would have no right to do it. Motives and intentions in such a question as is now before your Lordships seem to me to be absolutely irrelevant . . .

So, here, if the owner of the adjoining land is in a situation in which an act of his, lawfully done on his own land, may divert the water which would otherwise go into the possession of this trading company, I see no reason why he should not insist on their purchasing his interest from which this trading company desires to make profit.

Lord Macnaghten, at 601

He [Pickles] prefers his own interests to the public good. He may be churlish, selfish, and grasping. His conduct may seem shocking to a moral philosopher. But where is the malice? Mr. Pickles has no spite against the people of Bradford. He bears no ill-will to the corporation. They are welcome to the water, and to his land too, if they will pay the price for it. So much perhaps might be said in defence or in palliation of Mr. Pickles' conduct. But the real answer to the claim of the corporation is that in such a case motives are immaterial. It is the act, not the motive for the act, that must be regarded. If the act, apart from motive, gives rise merely to damage without legal injury, the motive, however reprehensible it may be, will not supply that element.

---

[4] *Chasemore v Richards* is discussed by Joshua Getzler, *A History of Water Rights at Common Law* (OUP, 2004), pp 302–25.

'Nuisance' was mentioned only once in the judgment of the House of Lords, and then as providing an analogy (Lord Watson, at 508). This lends support to the view of Macnaghten J in the *Hollywood Silver Fox Farm* case, that *Bradford v Pickles* has no application to a case of noise nuisance. Macnaghten J further pointed out (at 476) that in *Allen v Flood* [1898] AC 1, 101, decided soon after *Bradford v Pickles*, Lord Watson had explained that 'No proprietor has an absolute right to create noises upon his land, because any right which the law gives him is qualified by the condition that it must not be exercised to the nuisance of his neighbours or of the public.' One interpretation then is that some of the rights enjoyed by property owners are qualified by the need not to create a nuisance, whereas others are not. One must be careful how much noise one makes, but need not be careful about how much percolating underground water one extracts.

A more satisfactory way of dividing noise nuisances from the activities of a landowner such as Pickles, is to suggest that to deprive one's neighbours of water flowing in undefined channels, rather than (for example) to subject them to insufferable amounts of noise, is not capable of amounting to a nuisance at all. This time we do not focus exclusively on the defendant, but pay attention also to the claimant. There is no right (absolute or qualified) to receive percolating ground water, whereas there is a right of quiet enjoyment of one's property. The latter right is, of course, only a relative one, dependent on showing that any interference is unreasonable in the relevant sense. In the same way, there is a right to receive one's groundwater in an uncontaminated form, but this right is qualified by the need to show that any interference with it is a nuisance, or within the rule in *Rylands v Fletcher* (*Ballard v Tomlinson* (1885) 29 Ch D 115, as interpreted by the House of Lords, and not the Court of Appeal, in *Cambridge Water v Eastern Counties Leather plc* [1994] 2 AC 264). On this interpretation, it is because of the absence of any right to receive groundwater that there is no space for the tort of nuisance to operate, if the only damage suffered is the absence of the resource itself.

It is true that the House of Lords focused on the motive of Pickles in particular, rather than on the nature of the damage suffered by the plaintiff, perhaps because this was the only ground on which the plaintiffs could seek to distinguish *Chasemore v Richards* (1859) 7 HL Cas 349. But the remarks quoted above are consistent with the present interpretation. See for example Lord Halsbury's statement about what would have been needed to be proved in an action upon the case: 'If this question were to have been tried in old times as an injury to the right in an action on the case, the plaintiffs would have had to allege, and to prove . . . that they were entitled to the flow of water, which, as I have already said, they would have failed to establish'. The interpretation is further supported by his comments at 592:

> [I]t is necessary for the plaintiffs to establish that they have a right to the flow of water, and that the defendant has no right to do what he is doing.

As Lord Macnaghten put it in the extract above, Pickles' acts gave rise to 'damage without legal injury', and this remains true whatever the motive. If so, Macnaghten J was correct to distinguish *Bradford v Pickles* in the *Hollywood Silver Fox Farm* case, for it has no application to cases of noise nuisance.

Rights

Bradford v Pickles has continued to cause trouble in the much more recent cases of *Langbrook Properties v Surrey CC* [1969] 3 All ER 1424; [1970] 1 WLR 161, and *Stephens v Anglian Water*

Authority [1987] 3 All ER 379; [1987] 1 WLR 1381. It is suggested that these cases take *Bradford v Pickles* too far.

In both *Langbrook Properties*, and *Stephens v Anglian Water*, it was concluded that, if even *malicious* action was protected by the existence of a right to abstract, then there could be no grounds for an action based on *negligence* in the process of abstraction. But this concentrates too much on the quality of the defendant's conduct, and not sufficiently on the nature of the complaint made by the plaintiff in these cases. In neither case was the underground water sought by the plaintiffs as a resource in its own right; rather, the abstraction of the water had caused settlement and damage to their property.

In the *Langbrook Properties* case, Plowman J held that, where the defendants had extracted percolating groundwater which had caused settlement of the plaintiffs' land, there was no room for the law of nuisance or negligence to operate, even if (as alleged) more caution on the part of the defendants could have allowed the pumping to be carried out without damage to the plaintiffs. In *Stephens v Anglian Water*, only negligence was pleaded. This time the Court of Appeal took it as settled that there was no room for an action in negligence, on the basis that a landowner is entitled to exercise his right to abstract subterranean water flowing in undefined channels 'regardless of the consequences, whether physical or pecuniary, to his neighbours' (Slade LJ, at 384). The decisions in both cases relied on *Bradford v Pickles*.

It was suggested above that the emphasis on the 'lawfulness' of Pickles' actions was produced partly by consideration of the *absence* of any right on the part of the plaintiff to receive the water. In other words, his actions were lawful partly because they did not interfere with any such right. In *Bradford v Pickles* itself, there was no recognized right in connection with land to be protected by a nuisance action. The House of Lords simply decided that malice made no difference to the application of *Chasemore v Richards*, a case which determined that Pickles' exercise of his rights was 'lawful'. But the exercise of a right is lawful only so long as it does not create a tort, and this is implicit in the words chosen by Lord Halsbury. The element of physical damage in these cases should, arguably, have taken them outside the authority of *Bradford v Pickles*.

1.4 CONNECTION WITH THE NUISANCE—WHO MAY BE SUED?

What is the necessary relationship between the defendant and the nuisance? The simplest cases are those where the occupier of land on which a nuisance originates is also the creator of the nuisance. Equally, the case law has treated as without difficulty those cases where the nuisance is created by the servant or agent of the occupier (independent contractors are considered separately below). But what of other cases where the occupier does not create the nuisance? Can the occupier of land on which a nuisance arises be sued? A substantial body of case law surrounds this question. It raises issues of personal responsibility, and brings into question the nature of the overlap between nuisance, and the tort of negligence.

Occupiers Who do not Create the Nuisance

Some occupiers clearly benefit from states of affairs which were created by someone else (typically a previous occupier). In the terms used in *Sedleigh-Denfield v O'Callaghan* [1940] AC 880 (extracted below), such nuisances may be 'adopted' by the occupier. As defined by that case, all that is required for 'adoption' is that the occupier should make some use of whatever constitutes the nuisance. This will be sufficient even if the nuisance was initially created through the act of a trespasser, as in *Sedleigh-Denfield* itself. But falling short of this, there are many other states of affairs which arise on land and where the occupier, though he may not expressly adopt the nuisance, is the party in a position to do something to prevent the nuisance from arising or continuing. Although these may arise through the actions of third parties, they may equally arise through natural processes affecting the land. Should there be an action against such an occupier?

If there is such an action, then there will be a *positive duty to act* in order to prevent damage to another. Such positive duties are rare in tort law, and especially in negligence. Successive decisions have determined that there is scope for positive duties as regards nuisances arising on land, even where the occupier is not the originator. The content of these duties requires that the occupier should take 'reasonable steps' to abate the nuisance. This sounds very much like negligence, and the language of negligence has been applied (see *Goldman v Hargrave*, below). But what should we make of this? It is true that in a case of nuisance, we do not usually ask whether there is a 'duty', nor concentrate on the nature of the steps taken or not taken by the defendant, as is done in the cases extracted below. On the other hand, these cases are not typical of negligence analysis either. They recognize *positive* duties to take action; and the standard applied is *subjective*, whereas the typical negligence standard is of course *objective*. Despite the terms used in *Goldman v Hargrave*, the more recent cases are clearly treated as cases of nuisance.

Sedleigh-Denfield v O'Callaghan [1940] AC 880

Sedleigh-Denfield v O'Callaghan is the root authority for many of the more recent cases on the positive duties of an occupier. In this case, a pipe was laid on the defendants' land without their knowledge or consent, by a trespasser.[5] The occupiers subsequently became aware of the existence of the pipe, which had the function of draining their fields. A grating was placed on the pipe, but because of its position it did not adequately prevent the pipe from becoming blocked. During a heavy rainstorm, the pipe became blocked and the water overflowed onto the plaintiff's neighbouring land. The House of Lords held that the defendants had sufficient connection with the nuisance to be treated as both adopting it, and continuing it. These terms are explained in the extract from the judgment of Viscount Maugham below. Either ground was sufficient for the defendants to be held liable in nuisance.

Viscount Maugham, at 894–5

The statement that an occupier of land is liable for the continuance of a nuisance created by others, e.g., by trespassers, if he continues or adopts it—which seems to be agreed—throws little light on the matter, unless the words "continues or adopts" are defined. In my opinion an occupier of land "continues" a nuisance if with knowledge or presumed knowledge of its existence he fails to take any reasonable means to bring it to an end though with ample time to do so. He "adopts" it if he makes any use of the erection, building, bank or artificial contrivance which constitutes the nuisance. In these sentences I am not attempting exclusive definitions. . . .

My Lords, in the present case I am of opinion that the respondents both continued and adopted the nuisance. After the lapse of nearly three years they must be taken to have

---

[5] This was a rather unusual trespasser: Middlesex County Council laid the culvert for the benefit of another neighbouring occupier.

suffered the nuisance to continue; for they neglected to take the very simple step of placing a grid in the proper place which would have removed the danger to their neighbour's land. They adopted the nuisance for they continued during all that time to use the artificial contrivance of the conduit for the purpose of getting rid of water from their property without taking the proper means for rendering it safe.

Lord Atkin, at 896–7

... For the purpose of ascertaining whether as here the plaintiff can establish a private nuisance I think that nuisance is sufficiently defined as a wrongful interference with another's enjoyment of his land or premises by the use of land or premises either occupied or in some cases owned by oneself. The occupier or owner is not an insurer; there must be something more than the mere harm done to the neighbour's property to make the party responsible. Deliberate act or negligence is not an essential ingredient but some degree of personal responsibility is required, which is connoted in my definition by the word "use." This conception is implicit in all the decisions which impose liability only where the defendant has "caused or continued" the nuisance. We may eliminate in this case "caused." What is the meaning of "continued"? In the context in which it is used "continued" must indicate mere passive continuance. If a man uses on premises something which he found there, and which itself causes a nuisance by noise, vibration, smell or fumes, he is himself in continuing to bring into existence the noise, vibration, etc., causing a nuisance. Continuing in this sense and causing are the same thing. It seems to me clear that if a man permits an offensive thing on his premises to continue to offend, that is, if he knows that it is operating offensively, is able to prevent it, and omits to prevent it, he is permitting the nuisance to continue; in other words he is continuing it.

A useful definition of adopting and continuing is spelt out in Viscount Maugham's judgment. However, given our interest in the similarities and differences between nuisance and negligence, it is also instructive to note the observations of Lord Atkin, coming as they did within a few years of his judgment in *Donoghue v Stevenson*. In particular, Lord Atkin specifies here that the action in nuisance does not require any degree of negligence, but that it does require some degree of 'personal responsibility'. In other words, in addition to the question of whether the interference amounts to a 'nuisance' (is it an unreasonable interference?), there is the further and separate question of whether there is a sufficient link between the occupier of land, and the nuisance, to justify liability on the part of the occupier. As Lord Atkin says, if the occupier *creates* the nuisance then there is of course an adequate link. In the particular case of *Sedleigh-Denfield*, knowledge of the nuisance (or, as Viscount Maugham put it, 'presumed knowledge') together with the opportunity to take steps to abate the nuisance amounted to sufficient connection.

Since a 'very simple step' would have sufficed to abate the nuisance in *Sedleigh-Denfield* itself, the case did not test the question of what the *content* of the positive duty might be. Questions about the content of the duty were considered in the case of *Goldman v Hargrave*.

Goldman v Hargrave [1967] 1 AC 645

The decision of the Privy Council in *Goldman v Hargrave* does not use the kind of language that is typical of nuisance cases. Indeed in specifying that there must be breach of a 'duty of care' Lord Wilberforce appears to imply that this is a case of negligence properly so called.

However, it is suggested that the references to 'negligence' in this case should be read as referring above all to the quality of the actions of the defendant. We should be careful how we read Lord Wilberforce's remark that this is a case 'where liability, if it exists, rests upon negligence and nothing else'. Lord Wilberforce expressly pointed out (at 656) that the Privy Council would decide the case without answering the 'disputable question' of categorization. Despite the language used, it was not expressly suggested that we should approach this as a case in the *tort* of negligence.

Goldman v Hargrave was a decision on appeal from the High Court of Australia. A giant redgum tree on the defendant's property was struck by lightning and caught fire. The blaze was impossible to deal with while the tree was standing, so it was cut down, and the defendant cleared a space around the tree. From the following day, the defendant did nothing to extinguish the fire, preferring to let it burn itself out. It was found that the defendant could have extinguished the fire by spraying it with water either immediately after the tree was felled, or on the following day. A change in the weather caused the fire to flare up and spread to the plaintiff's land, after which it could not be stopped. The Court of Western Australia found that there was no action available either in nuisance, or in *Rylands v Fletcher*. On appeal, the High Court of Australia held that the appellant was under a duty to use reasonable care once the tree was felled in order to stop the fire from causing damage to his neighbours. The appeal raised the question of whether the principle in *Sedleigh-Denfield* would apply to nuisances arising naturally. But it also raised questions about the *content* of the positive duty.

Lord Wilberforce (giving the judgment of the Board), at 656–7

The result of the evidence, in their Lordships' opinion, is that the appellant both up to February 26 and thereafter was endeavouring to extinguish the fire; that initially he acted with prudence, but that there came a point, about the evening of February 26 or the morning of February 27, when, the prudent and reasonable course being to put the fire out by water, he chose to adopt the method of burning it out. That method was, according to the finding of the trial judge, unreasonable, or negligent in the circumstances: it brought a fresh risk into operation, namely, the risk of a revival of the fire, under the influence of changing wind and weather, if not carefully watched, and it was from this negligence that the damage arose. That a risk of this character was foreseeable by someone in the appellant's position was not really disputed: in fact danger arising from weather conditions is given official recognition in the Bush Fires Act, 1954–1958, which provides for their classification according to the degree of danger arising from them.

This conclusion has an important bearing upon the nature of the legal issue which has to be decided. It makes clear that the case is not one where a person has brought a source of danger onto his land, nor one where an occupier has so used his property as to cause a danger to his neighbour. It is one where an occupier, faced with a hazard accidentally arising on his land, fails to act with reasonable prudence so as to remove the hazard. The issue is therefore whether in such a case the occupier is guilty of legal negligence, which involves the issue whether he is under a duty of care, and, if so, what is the scope of that duty. Their Lordships propose to deal with these issues as stated, without attempting to answer the disputable question whether if responsibility is established it should be brought under the heading of nuisance or placed in a separate category. As this Board has recently explained in *Overseas Tankship (U.K.) Ltd. v. Miller Steamship Co. Pty. Ltd. (The Wagon Mound No. 2)* ([1966] 3 WLR 498), the tort of nuisance, uncertain in its boundary, may comprise a wide variety of situations, in some of which negligence plays no part, in others of which it is decisive. The present case is one where liability, if it exists, rests upon negligence and nothing else; whether it falls within or overlaps the boundaries of nuisance is a question of classification which need not here be resolved.

What then is the scope of an occupier's duty, with regard to his neighbours, as to hazards arising on his land? With the possible exception of hazard of fire, to which their Lordships will shortly revert, it is only in comparatively recent times that the law has recognised an occupier's duty as one of a more positive character than merely to abstain from creating, or adding to, a source of danger or annoyance. It was for long satisfied with the conception of separate or autonomous proprietors, each of which was entitled to exploit his territory in a "natural" manner and none of whom was obliged to restrain or direct the operations of nature in the interest of avoiding harm to his neighbours. . . .

Lord Wilberforce reviewed the older case law including *Giles v Walker* (1890) 24 QBD 656, and rejected a suggested distinction between the present case (natural hazard) and the case of *Sedleigh-Denfield v O'Callaghan* (nuisance created by a third party). He concluded (at 661) that:

On principle . . . , their Lordships find in the opinions of the House of Lords in *Sedleigh-Denfield v O'Callaghan* . . . support for the existence of a general duty upon occupiers in relation to hazards occurring on their land, whether natural or man-made.

Later, he considered the *content* of the occupier's duty to neighbours (at 663):

So far it has been possible to consider the existence of a duty, in general terms. But the matter cannot be left there without some definition of the scope of his duty. How far does it go? What is the standard of the effort required? What is the position as regards expenditure? It is not enough to say merely that these must be "reasonable," since what is reasonable to one man may be very unreasonable, and indeed ruinous, to another: the law must take account of the fact that the occupier on whom the duty is cast has, ex hypothesi, had this hazard thrust upon him through no seeking or fault of his own. His interest, and his resources, whether physical or material, may be of a very modest character either in relation to the magnitude of the hazard, or as compared with those of his threatened neighbour. A rule which required of him in such unsought circumstances in his neighbour's interest a physical effort of which he is not capable, or an excessive expenditure of money, would be unenforceable or unjust. One may say in general terms that the existence of a duty must be based upon knowledge of the hazard, ability to foresee the consequences of not checking or removing it, and the ability to abate it. And in many cases, as, for example, in Scrutton L.J.'s hypothetical case of stamping out a fire, or the present case, where the hazard could have been removed with little effort and no expenditure, no problem arises. But other cases may not be so simple. In such situations the standard ought to be to require of the occupier what it is reasonable to expect of him in his individual circumstances. Thus, less must be expected of the infirm than of the able-bodied: the owner of a small property where a hazard arises which threatens a neighbour with substantial interests should not have to do so much as one with larger interests of his own at stake and greater resources to protect them: if the small owner does what he can and promptly calls on his neighbour to provide additional resources, he may be held to have done his duty: he should not be liable unless it is clearly proved that he could, and reasonably in his individual circumstance should, have done more. This approach to a difficult matter is in fact that which the courts in their more recent decisions have taken. It is in accordance with the actual decision in the *Job Edwards* case ([1924] 1 K.B. 341), where to remove the hazard would have cost the occupier some £1,000—on this basis the decision itself seems obviously right. It is in accordance with *Pontardawe Rural District Council v. Moore-Gwyn* ([1929] 1 Ch. 656; 45 T.L.R. 276), where to maintain the rocks in a state of safety would have cost the occupier some£300. And if some of the situations such as those in *Giles v. Walker* (24 QBD 656) (thistledown) and *Sparks v. Osborne* (7 CLR 51) (prickly pears) were to recur today, it is probable that they would not be decided without a balanced consideration of what could be expected of the particular occupier as compared with the consequences of inaction. That *Giles v. Walker* might now be decided differently was indeed suggested by Lord Goddard C.J., giving the judgment of the English Court of Appeal in *Davey v. Harrow Corporation* ([1958] 1 QB 60). In the present case it has not been argued that the action necessary to put the fire out on February 26–27 was not well within the capacity and resources of the appellant. Their Lordships therefore reach the conclusion that the respondents' claim for damages, on the basis of negligence, was fully made out.

Leakey & Others v National Trust [1980] QB 485

The plaintiffs' two houses had been built at the foot of a large mound of earth, 'The Burrow Mump', which was owned and occupied by the defendants. Due to natural weathering and the particular steepness of the relevant banks of the Mump, soil and debris had fallen on the houses over a number of years. After a hot summer and a wet autumn in 1976, the plaintiffs drew the defendants' attention to a large crack in the soil above their houses. Some time later, there was a fall of soil and tree roots onto the plaintiffs' property, and the plaintiffs brought an action in nuisance seeking orders for the abatement of the nuisance and damages.

The Court of Appeal reaffirmed the proposition in *Goldman v Hargrave* that the occupier of land owes positive duties to a neighbour in respect of a nuisance arising on his land through the operation of natural forces, and confirmed that this proposition formed part of English law. It also reaffirmed that the duty as outlined in *Goldman v Hargrave* was subjective, so that the steps which ought reasonably to be taken would vary depending on the resources of the defendant. Such questions, according to Megaw LJ, could be addressed in a broad and general way, and would not require long enquiry into the exact resources available to the parties.

Megaw LJ dealt briefly with the question of the cause of action:

Megaw LJ, at 514–15

. . . The plaintiffs' claim is expressed in the pleadings to be founded in nuisance. There is no express reference to negligence in the statement of claim. But there is an allegation of a breach of duty, and the duty asserted is, in effect, a duty to take reasonable care to prevent part of the defendants' land from falling on to the plaintiffs' property. I should, for myself, regard that as being properly described as a claim in nuisance. But even if that were, technically, wrong, I do not think that the point could or should avail the defendants in this case. If it were to do so, it would be a regrettable modern instance of the forms of action successfully clanking their spectral chains; for there would be no conceivable prejudice to the defendants in this case that the word "negligence" had not been expressly set out in the statement of claim. The suggestion that if it had been so pleaded the defendants could have raised a defence of volenti non fit injuria, which they could not raise as against a claim pleaded in nuisance, is, in my judgment, misconceived. As counsel for the plaintiffs submitted, while it is no defence to a claim in nuisance that the plaintiff has "come to the nuisance," it would have been a properly pleadable defence to this statement of claim that the plaintiffs, knowing of the danger to their property, by word or deed, had showed their willingness to accept that danger.

Megaw LJ also suggested that the case of *Sedleigh-Denfield v O'Callaghan* marked a turning point in the law, and that:

> That change in the law, in its essence and in its timing, corresponds with, and may be viewed as being a part of, the change in the law of tort which achieved its decisive victory in *Donoghue v. Stevenson* [1932] A.C. 562: though it was not until eight years later, in the House of Lords decision in *Sedleigh-Denfield v. O'Callaghan* [1940] A.C. 880, that the change as affecting the area with which we are concerned was expressed or recognised in a decision binding on all English courts: and, even then, the full, logical effect of the decision in altering what had hitherto been thought to be the law was not immediately recognised. But *Goldman v. Hargrave* has now demonstrated what that effect was in English law.

The 'change' with which Megaw LJ is concerned is the recognition of positive duties to act consequent on the occupation of property, and requiring reasonable steps to be taken to prevent harm to one's neighbours. And yet, positive duties to act are no less controversial in the tort of negligence, than they have been in nuisance. Megaw LJ may or may not be correct to say that the developments in *Sedleigh-Denfield* and *Goldman v Hargrave* were encouraged by the development of the tort of negligence, but it cannot be assumed that an analysis of those cases in terms of negligence alone would necessarily have led to the decisions as they were reached. The result may be reached either via the tort of nuisance, or via the tort of negligence, but adaptations are needed whichever route is taken.

Writing in 1989, Conor Gearty suggested that cases such as *Sedleigh-Denfield*, which concerned indirectly-caused physical damage to property, were historically more appropriately categorized as aspects of the newly emerging tort of negligence, rather than of nuisance, and that their treatment as nuisance cases 'has done serious damage to nuisance by introducing an emphasis on the conduct of the defendant which is foreign to the action and subversive of its doctrines' (C. Gearty, 'The Place of Private Nuisance in a Modern Law of Torts' (1989) 48 CLJ 214–42, p 218). Nuisance had therefore 'lost all sense of that for which it stands' (p. 216). Emphasizing that nuisance is potentially an 'environmental tort' which has nevertheless been underused, he therefore proposed a 'strategic surrender' of such cases of physical damage to the tort of negligence:

C. Gearty (1989) 48 CLJ 48 214

With its independence assured, and freed from negligence's debilitating concern with the yardstick of the reasonable defendant, there is no reason why nuisance (and hence environmental protection) should not thrive once again.

In recent cases such as *Cambridge Water* and *Hunter v Canary Wharf*, the House of Lords has reemphasized the independence of nuisance from negligence. Arguably, there is now more confidence in the general irrelevance of the defendant's conduct to the majority of nuisance actions, and nuisance exists more securely as an independent action. As such, there may be less 'strategic' need to evacuate the cases of overlap studied here from the tort of nuisance, and it is suggested that the continuation of the *Sedleigh-Denfield* line of cases is now too well established as an aspect of nuisance to make such a move desirable. Given Gearty's emphasis on the potential environmental protection function of the tort of nuisance, it is worth noting that the clear demarcation of certain claims as beyond the reach of the tort of nuisance, and their confirmation as exclusively the preserve of negligence, has arguably weakened the ability of nuisance to fulfil an environmental protection function, at least so far as environmental protection is understood to encompass protection of the well-being of individuals (*Hunter v Canary Wharf*, extracted with commentary below).

The developments in *Leakey* were tested again before the Court of Appeal in a coastal erosion case, *Holbeck Hall Hotel Ltd v Scarborough BC* [2000] QB 836.

The defendant owned the undercliff between the grounds of the plaintiffs' hotel, and the sea. There had been two landslips on the defendants' land below the hotel in the 1980s, and investigations had been conducted accordingly, leading to some remedial works. In 1993, a major landslip caused loss of support to the hotel and grounds and the hotel itself had to be demolished. This case raised questions about the content and extent of the 'measured duty of care' which had not arisen in any significant form in the previous case law.

The Court of Appeal determined that *Sedleigh-Denfield* and *Leakey* applied to a case of loss of support, and considered whether the defendants 'ought to have known' of the danger to the plaintiffs' land, and thus whether a measured duty of care arose. Further, if such a duty did arise, what was the extent of that duty?

In determining whether the 'measured duty of care' arose, Stuart-Smith LJ drew a distinction between *patent* dangers and defects (which can easily be observed), and *latent* dangers and defects. In respect of latent defects, no duty arose to conduct investigations. The emphasis was on 'knowledge' and (through the idea of 'presumed knowledge') on what 'should have been seen'.

Stuart-Smith LJ, *Holbeck Hall Hotel v Scarborough BC*

42. The duty arises when the defect is known and the hazard or danger to the claimants' land is reasonably foreseeable, that is to say it is a danger which a reasonable man with knowledge of the defect should have foreseen as likely to eventuate in the reasonably near future. It is the existence of the defect coupled with the danger that constitutes the nuisance; it is knowledge or presumed knowledge of the nuisance that involves liability for continuing it when it could reasonably be abated. . . . if the defect is latent, the landowner or occupier is not to be held liable simply because, if he had made further investigation, he would have discovered it. . . .

On these particular facts,

43 . . . it is in my view clear that Scarborough did not foresee a danger of anything like the magnitude that eventuated. It was common ground that the G.E.N. report gave no clue of such an eventuality; and it seems clear that they could not have appreciated the risk without further investigation by experts.

Stuart-Smith LJ then drew a distinction between the measured duty of care, and 'most cases where physical injury either to the person or the property of the claimant is reasonably foreseeable' (para 44). In the normal run of such cases, he pointed out, there will be liability for all damage of the type that was foreseeable, notwithstanding the extent.[6] The measured duty of care, on his analysis, operates in a way which is contrary to this usual remoteness rule, for it places limits on the *extent* of damage for which the defendant is potentially liable. It does this because of the special subjective nature of the duty. Stuart Smith LJ particularly highlighted one sentence from the judgment of Lord Wilberforce in *Goldman v Hargrave* quoted above, namely that: '*One may say in general terms that the existence of a duty must be based upon knowledge of the hazard, ability to foresee the consequences of not checking or removing it, and the ability to abate it*' (Lord Wilberforce at 663, quoted by Stuart-Smith LJ at para 46). In conclusion:

49. . . . I do not think justice requires that a defendant should be held liable for damage which, albeit of the same type, was vastly more extensive than that which was foreseen or could have been foreseen without extensive further geological investigation; and this is particularly so where the defect existed just as much on the plaintiffs' land as on their own. In considering the scope of the measured duty of care, the courts are still in relatively uncharted waters. But I can find nothing in the two cases where it has been considered, namely *Goldman's* case [1967] 1 A.C. 645 and *Leakey's* case [1980] Q.B. 485 to prevent the court reaching a just result.

In *Delaware Mansions v Westminster City Council* [2002] 1 AC 321, the House of Lords applied *Goldman v Hargrave* and *Sedleigh-Denfield v O'Callaghan* to a case of encroaching tree roots. Where there was a continuing nuisance of which the defendant knew or ought to have known, a neighbouring occupier who had been forced to undertake remedial work could recover the reasonable costs of that work from the defendant on whose land the nuisance (encroaching tree roots) had originated. This would include the cost of abating damage some of which had occurred before the claimant took possession of the land.

Marcic v Thames Water Utilities Ltd [2004] 2 AC 42, reversing Court of Appeal ([2002] EWCA Civ 64; [2002] 2 WLR 932)

Here the Court of Appeal made surprising use of the *Leakey* line of cases in order to hold a sewerage undertaker liable in nuisance for external flooding by foul water suffered by the plaintiff's property. (They would also have awarded a remedy under the Human Rights Act 1998, had the remedy in nuisance not been sufficient.) The decision was surprising because it was contrary to previous case law determining the liability of sewerage undertakers; and because of the way in which the Court interpreted the burden of proving 'fairness' for the purposes of the measured duty of care. The Court proposed that the burden of proving that the duty was discharged (which in this instance would be the case if their system of priorities was 'fair') lay on the defendants. Ordinarily, it is of course for the claimant to show that a duty has been breached. Indeed, the Court of Appeal suggested that the taking of 'reasonable steps' to alleviate a nuisance was a *defence* to an action in nuisance. It is clear from the cases reviewed above that the subjective content of the measured duty of care is relevant to whether duties

---

6 This is the consequence of *The Wagon Mound*: see Chapter 3.

arise and are breached, rather than to whether defences are made out in order to rebut some form of presumed liability.

Still more surprising was the content of the 'measured duty' in this case. The flooding of Mr Marcic's property could be alleviated only by acquiring land and building more sewers. In holding that the positive duty under *Leakey* could compel a defendant to take such steps, the Court of Appeal discovered a far more onerous positive duty than has previously been associated with the 'measured duty of care'. The estimated cost of £1,000 million to alleviate the flooding problems of all those in the same position as the plaintiff ([2002] EWCA Civ 64, para 38) is a significant investment even for a trading company of the size of the defendants.[7]

The House of Lords reversed the Court of Appeal's decision. Their Lordships argued that the *Leakey* line of cases did nothing to alter the position in respect of sewerage undertakers stated by Denning LJ in *Pride of Derby and Derbyshire Angling Association v British Celanese Ltd* [1953] Ch 149, which was itself based on consideration of the *Sedleigh-Denfield* case:

Denning LJ, at 190, quoted by Lord Hoffmann, *Marcic v Thames Water Utilities* para [55]

. . . they [the plaintiffs] have a perfectly good cause of action for nuisance, if they can show that the defendants created or continued the cause of the trouble; and it must be remembered that a person may "continue" a nuisance by adopting it, or in some circumstances by omitting to remedy it: see *Sedleigh-Denfield v. O'Callaghan.*

This liability for nuisance has been applied in the past to sewage and drainage cases in this way: when a local authority take over or construct a sewage and drainage system which is adequate at the time to dispose of the sewage and surface water for their district, but which subsequently becomes inadequate owing to increased building which they cannot control, and for which they have no responsibility, they are not guilty of the ensuing nuisance. They obviously do not create it, nor do they continue it merely by doing nothing to enlarge or improve the system. The only remedy of the injured party is to complain to the Minister.

The House of Lords added that there were good reasons for the common law not to interfere further than this with the activities of sewerage undertakers through the law of nuisance, in particular that the issues had been allocated by statute to an independent regulator with elaborate powers of enforcement.[8] The existence of the statutory scheme was said to exclude the operation of the tort of nuisance, although we may assume from the approval of Denning LJ's statement in the *Pride of Derby* case that the common law is only excluded so far as it relates to cases where the sewerage undertaker has taken over sewers built by another, and where the sewers have become inadequate due to increased demand. This was the situation in *Marcic* itself.

Lord Nicholls, *Marcic v Thames Water Utilities*

34 In my view the cause of action in nuisance asserted by Mr Marcic is inconsistent with the statutory scheme. Mr Marcic's claim is expressed in various ways but in practical terms it always comes down to this: Thames Water ought to build more sewers. This is the only way

---

[7] Annual profits were estimated at £344 million. Having said that, it appears that by the time the case reached the House of Lords, there had been a change in priorities, and the required work had been carried out.

[8] Water Industry Act 1991.

Thames Water can prevent sewer flooding of Mr Marcic's property. This is the only way because it is not suggested that Thames Water failed to operate its existing sewage system properly by not cleaning or maintaining it. Nor can Thames Water control the volume of water entering the sewers under Old Church Lane. Every new house built has an absolute right to connect. Thames Water is obliged to accept these connections: section 106 of the 1991 Act. A sewerage undertaker is unable to prevent connections being made to the existing system, and the ingress of water through these connections, even if this risks overloading the existing sewers. But, so Mr Marcic's claim runs, although Thames Water was operating its existing system properly, and although Thames Water had no control over the volume of water entering the system, it was within Thames Water's power to build more sewers, as the company now has done, to cope with the increased volume of water entering the system. Mr Marcic, it is said, has a cause of action at law in respect of Thames Water's failure to construct more sewers before it eventually did in June 2003.

35 The difficulty I have with this line of argument is that it ignores the statutory limitations on the enforcement of sewerage undertakers' drainage obligations. Since sewerage undertakers have no control over the volume of water entering their sewerage systems it would be surprising if Parliament intended that whenever sewer flooding occurs, every householder whose property has been affected can sue the appointed sewerage undertaker for an order that the company build more sewers or pay damages. On the contrary, it is abundantly clear that one important purpose of the enforcement scheme in the 1991 Act is that individual householders should not be able to launch proceedings in respect of failure to build sufficient sewers. When flooding occurs the first enforcement step under the statute is that the director, as the regulator of the industry, will consider whether to make an enforcement order. He will look at the position of an individual householder but in the context of the wider considerations spelled out in the statute. Individual householders may bring proceedings in respect of inadequate drainage only when the undertaker has failed to comply with an enforcement order made by the Secretary of State or the director. The existence of a parallel common law right, whereby individual householders who suffer sewer flooding may themselves bring court proceedings when no enforcement order has been made, would set at nought the statutory scheme. It would effectively supplant the regulatory role the director was intended to discharge when questions of sewer flooding arise.

36 For this reason I consider there is no room in this case for a common law cause of action in nuisance as submitted by Mr Marcic and held by the Court of Appeal.

Lord Hoffmann

61 Why should sewers be different? If the *Sedleigh-Denfield* case [1940] AC 880 lays down a general principle that an owner of land has a duty to take reasonable steps to prevent a nuisance arising from a known source of hazard, even though he did not himself create it, why should that not require him to construct new sewers if the court thinks it would have been reasonable to do so?

62 The difference in my opinion is that the Sedleigh-Denfield, Goldman and Leakey cases were dealing with disputes between neighbouring land owners simply in their capacity as individual land owners. In such cases it is fair and efficient to impose reciprocal duties upon each landowner to take whatever steps are reasonable to prevent his land becoming a source of injury to his neighbour. Even then, the question of what measures should reasonably have been taken may not be uncomplicated. As Lord Wilberforce said in Goldman's case [1967]

1 AC 645, 663, the court must (unusually) have regard to the individual circumstances of the defendant. In Leakey's case [1980] QB 485, 526 Megaw LJ recoiled from the prospect of a detailed examination of the defendant's financial resources and said it should be done on a broad basis.

63 Nevertheless, whatever the difficulties, the court in such cases is performing its usual function of deciding what is reasonable as between the two parties to the action. But the exercise becomes very different when one is dealing with the capital expenditure of a statutory undertaking providing public utilities on a large scale. The matter is no longer confined to the parties to the action. If one customer is given a certain level of services, everyone in the same circumstances should receive the same level of services. So the effect of a decision about what it would be reasonable to expect a sewerage undertaker to do for the plaintiff is extrapolated across the country. This in turn raises questions of public interest. Capital expenditure on new sewers has to be financed; interest must be paid on borrowings and privatised undertakers must earn a reasonable return. This expenditure can be met only by charges paid by consumers. Is it in the public interest that they should have to pay more? And does expenditure on the particular improvements with which the plaintiff is concerned represent the best order of priorities?

64 These are decisions which courts are not equipped to make in ordinary litigation. It is therefore not surprising that for more than a century the question of whether more or better sewers should be constructed has been entrusted by Parliament to administrators rather than judges. . . .

Lord Hoffmann described the approach to 'fairness' adopted by the first instance judge, Sir Richard Havery QC, and drew attention to the fact that the judge could not decide whether the system of priorities adopted was 'fair' on the basis of the evidence before him. Lord Hoffmann continued:

69 As a result, the judge had to resort to deciding the matter upon the burden of proof: he said that the burden was upon Thames Water to satisfy him that it had done what was reasonable and that it had not done so. The judge said this in the context of whether Thames Water was in breach of its duty under section 6 of the Human Rights Act 1998, having previously decided that there was no cause of action in nuisance. But the Court of Appeal treated it, at p 995, para 87, as a finding that Thames Water had not taken reasonable steps to abate the nuisance emanating from its sewers: "Thames failed to persuade the judge that their system of priorities was a fair one."

70 My Lords, I think that this remark, together with the judge's frank admission that the fairness of the priorities adopted by Thames Water was not justiciable, provides the most powerful argument for rejecting the existence of a common law duty to build new sewers. The 1991 Act makes it even clearer than the earlier legislation that Parliament did not intend the fairness of priorities to be decided by a judge. It intended the decision to rest with the director, subject only to judicial review. It would subvert the scheme of the 1991 Act if the courts were to impose upon the sewerage undertakers, on a case by case basis, a system of priorities which is different from that which the director considers appropriate.

There will be more to say concerning the House of Lords' handling of the Human Rights Act claim in this case, in Section 2 below. However, for the moment it is worth considering whether the House of Lords was too sceptical about the ability of a court to consider the fairness of the situation as it affected the plaintiff. For all that the Court of Appeal required a very significant investment by the defendants, that investment had somehow become possible by the time of the action in the House of Lords, and the remedial action had been carried out. Furthermore, the Director had stated in the process of consultation that the *Marcic* case had concentrated *his* mind on the need for 'robust and rational prioritisation schemes' (Lord Nicholls, para [28]), so that it contributed to the formulation of a new and perhaps more defensible approach. Lord Nicholls further admitted in his judgment that '[i]n Mr Marcic's case, matters plainly went awry' (para [43]). Without recourse to the courts, whether through the nuisance claim or the Human Rights Act claim, would 'fairness' have received such an emphasis in the new priorities adopted?

Connection with 'Creator' of the Nuisance

The *Sedleigh-Denfield* case, above, concerned the position where the creator of the nuisance is a complete stranger to the occupier—in that case, a trespasser. In such a case, it was essential to determine whether there was any link with the nuisance through the concepts of adoption or 'continuation'. But there are many other instances where the nuisance is created by someone other than the occupier, who is nevertheless not a stranger. The case of servants and agents is clear: the occupier will ordinarily be liable for the nuisances they create. However, other categories give rise to more difficulty.

Independent contractors

The general rule, in nuisance as in negligence, appears to be that there is no liability for torts committed by one's independent contractors provided these are not negligently selected. If the occupier expressly *authorizes* a nuisance, then it may be assumed that the occupier should be treated as the creator or originator of the nuisance. It is suggested that this is the best explanation of the following much-cited passage from the judgment of Cockburn CJ in *Bower v Peate* (1876) 1 QBD 321, at 326–7:

> The answer to the defendant's contention may, however, as it appears to us, be placed on a broader ground, namely, that a man who orders a work to be executed, from which, in the natural course of things, injurious consequences to his neighbour must be expected to arise, unless means are adopted by which such consequences may be prevented, is bound to see to the doing of that which is necessary to prevent the mischief, and cannot relieve himself of his responsibility by employing some one else—whether it be the contractor employed to do the work from which the danger arises or some independent person—to do what is necessary to prevent the act he has ordered to be done from becoming wrongful. There is an obvious difference between committing work to a contractor to be executed from which, if properly done, no injurious consequences can arise, and handing over to him work to be done from which mischievous consequences will arise unless preventive measures are adopted. While it may be just to hold the party authorizing the work in the former case exempt from liability for injury, resulting from negligence which he had no reason to anticipate, there is, on the other hand, good ground for holding him liable for injury caused by an act certain to be attended with

injurious consequences if such consequences are not in fact prevented, no matter through whose default the omission to take the necessary measures for such prevention may arise.

In other cases, it has been suggested that the rule in nuisance is no different from that in negligence. In *Matania v National Provincial Bank Ltd* [1936] 2 All ER 633, Slesser LJ (who also delivered the only judgment in the leading negligence case of *Honeywill & Stein v Larkin Bros* [1934] 1 KB 191: Chapter 9) explained that the rules in negligence and nuisance were the same, and that there was liability for the acts of independent contractors only in circumstances where the works contracted were 'hazardous'. However, we should note the meaning of 'hazardous' works given here:

Slesser LJ, *Matania v National Provincial Bank Ltd*

Here, of course, we are not concerned with danger such as might found an action for negligence. We are here concerned with annoyance such as may found an action for nuisance, but the principles in my opinion are the same as regards the liability of a person who employs an independent contractor, that is to say, that if the act done is one which in its very nature involves a special danger of nuisance being complained of, then it is one which falls within the exception for which the employer of the contractor will be responsible if there is a failure to take the necessary precautions that the nuisance shall not arise. Now, what are the facts of the present case? They are these. It is really not in dispute that as regards the place where this work was to be done this noise and this dust were inevitable. That is the evidence of both the plaintiff and the defendants, and it is the conclusion of the learned judge. The only question which I see is whether in that state where the production of noise and dust is inevitable, sufficient precautions were taken to prevent that noise and dust affecting Mr Matania. In every case, whether it be a case of ordinary employment of a contractor or whether it be a case of a hazardous operation, the problem must arise whether a precaution would or would not prevent the result of an operation. To say that a precaution will prevent the result of an operation does not by itself take the case outside the rule that a person may be responsible, where the act is a hazardous one, for the acts of his contractor. Where the act is hazardous, to presume that every hazardous act would result in the danger or the nuisance would be to say that the act was inevitable in its consequences, regardless of any question of precaution or not, but that is not the right way of looking at it. In the case to which I referred, the case of Honeywill & Stein Ltd v Larkin Bros Ltd it was not inevitable that the fire, which was brought into the theatre, would necessarily under proper precautions set the theatre on fire, but it was a hazardous operation to bring the fire into the theatre. So it was hazardous as regards the possible nuisance to Mr Matania to bring the noise and dust immediately below his apartment. What is said is with sufficient and proper precaution the result of that hazardous operation could have been avoided without detriment to him. The case of Honeywill & Stein Ltd follows, as I have said, the case of Dalton v Angus which in its turn had approved the earlier case of Bower v Peate. I do not think it necessary myself to consider these cases, because I think the principle has been sufficiently stated so recently in this court that it is enough to say that I am of opinion that this was a hazardous operation within the meaning of the exceptions stated in Honeywill & Stein Ltd v Larkin Bros Ltd, that the principle which is there dealing with a case of negligence applies equally to the tort of nuisance, and that, therefore, this being a case of this kind, I think that the Elevenist Syndicate are responsible for the fact that neither they nor the contractors, Messrs Adamson, took those reasonable precautions which could have been taken to prevent this injury to the plaintiff.

Although this passage suggests that there is no special rule for nuisance,[9] it proceeds by applying the idea of 'hazardous' activities to acts that are especially likely to cause a nuisance in the form of annoyance. Arguably, this does alter the impact of the principle in *Honeywill v Stein*, by placing non-delegable duties on occupiers in respect of a broader range of risks.[10] 'Hazardous' in this context means very likely to be tortious, rather than highly likely to cause significant damage.

Tenants

Baxter v Camden LBC (No 2) [2001] 1 AC 1

Here, the council had divided a house into three dwellings, and the plaintiffs were tenants of the middle floor. The tenant complained to the council that she suffered serious interference in her enjoyment of the flat as a result of the normal day to day noise generated by her neighbours. Although this noise was not unusual, its effect was made worse by the poor sound insulation installed during conversion of the premises. She brought proceedings both on the basis of breach of the covenant of quiet enjoyment in her tenancy, and for nuisance. Her claim for breach of covenant was dismissed because the problem that arose was a result of the state of the premises at the time they were let. The claim in nuisance was also dismissed:

Lord Hoffmann, *Baxter v Camden LBC (No 2)*, at 15–16

I turn next to the law of private nuisance. I can deal with this quite shortly because it seems to me that the appellants face an insuperable difficulty. Nuisance involves doing something on adjoining or nearby land which constitutes an unreasonable interference with the utility of the plaintiff's land. The primary defendant is the person who causes the nuisance by doing the acts in question. As Sir John Pennycuick V-C said in *Smith v Scott* [1973] Ch 314, 321:

> "It is established beyond question that the person to be sued in nuisance is the occupier of the property from which the nuisance emanates. In general, a landlord is not liable for nuisance committed by his tenant, but to this rule there is, so far as now in point, one recognised exception, namely, that the landlord is liable if he has authorised his tenant to commit the nuisance."

What is the nuisance of which the appellants complain? The sounds emanating from their neighbours' flats. But they do not allege the making of these sounds to be a nuisance committed by the other tenants. . . .

. . .

If the neighbours are not committing a nuisance, the councils cannot be liable for authorising them to commit one. And there is no other basis for holding the landlords liable. They are not themselves doing anything which interferes with the appellants' use of their flats. Once again, it all comes down to a complaint about the inherent defects in the construction of the building. The appellants say that the ordinary use of the flats by their neighbours would not have caused them inconvenience if they had been differently built. But that, as I have said more than once, is a matter of which a tenant cannot complain.

---

[9] To like effect see *Alcock v Wraith & Others* (1991) 59 BLR 16.
[10] The idea of a 'non-delegable duty' is explained in Chapter 9.

As explained here, the lessor is liable for nuisances created by a tenant only if he or she has authorized that nuisance. If the tenant does not create a nuisance, then the landlord does not authorize a nuisance, and so cannot be liable. As Lord Millett put it, at p. 22:

> The logic of the proposition is obvious. A landlord cannot be liable to an action for authorising his tenant to do something that would not be actionable if he did it himself.

In determining whether there is a nuisance, the 'reasonableness' test applies to the activities *of the tenant*, and the tenants were doing nothing out of the ordinary. Therefore, the appellant failed in her argument that the council authorized use of the premises in circumstances where that use would inevitably constitute a nuisance. Authorizing a nuisance, rather than creating it by bad design of the premises let, therefore appears to be the only basis on which a landlord will be liable for noise nuisance resulting from the activities of tenants. In fact, the result does not seem to be entirely compelled by logic, as Lord Millett here suggests. The House of Lords adopts quite a narrow formulation, particularly when compared with the decision of the Court of Appeal in *Lippiatt*, concerning the congregation of people likely to commit a nuisance upon one's land (below).

In the slightly earlier case of *Hussain v Lancaster City Council* [2000] QB 1, the Court of Appeal also emphasized that the landlord's liability for nuisances caused by the tenant are limited. In this case, the acts of the tenants certainly constituted a nuisance. They carried out a series of acts including racial harassment of neighbours and acts of vandalism against their properties. The council, as landlords, were subject to actions in negligence and nuisance for failing to control the acts of the tenants. Both claims failed. In respect of the action in nuisance, Hirst LJ concluded that the acts of the tenants 'did not involve the tenants' use of the tenants' land and therefore fell outside the scope of the tort' (at 23). This seems to be a reference to the fact that they left their own homes in order to carry out their actions, although this reasoning will be hard to reconcile with the law on licensees (below). Giving what appeared to be a separate sufficient reason for the decision, Hirst LJ added that according to *Smith v Scott* [1973] Ch 314, a similar case involving nuisances created (on that occasion foreseeably) by council tenants, the only grounds for holding a landlord liable for the nuisances of his or tenant is that the landlord authorized the nuisance.

Licensees

On the face of it, owners of land appear to have been more readily held liable in nuisance where mere licensees on the land, without a tenancy, have created nuisances affecting neighbours. One such case is *Page Motors Ltd v Epsom and Ewell* (1981) 80 LGR 337 (Court of Appeal), where a local authority had allowed travellers to take up residence on their land for a number of years as a temporary solution to an ongoing problem of finding appropriate sites for them. The local authority was held liable for nuisances created by these temporary residents whom they had allowed to congregate on the land.

In *Lippiatt v S. Gloucestershire CC* [2000] QB 51, travellers had congregated on the defendant council's land, on one edge of a road. The plaintiffs were tenant farmers of land situated on either side of the road. They complained that the travellers frequently trespassed on their land and carried out various acts amounting to a nuisance, including obstruction, fouling with rubbish and excrement, theft, and actual damage. The first instance judge, Judge Weeks QC, had struck out the statement of claim on the basis that it could not succeed following the newly decided *Hussain* case: the nuisance, he concluded, had not arisen from the licensees' use of the council's land. The Court of Appeal ruled however that the action should not be struck out. The Court therefore had to suggest that this case was at least arguably distinguishable from the *Hussain* case.

Evans LJ, at 61

In my judgment, the facts alleged in *Hussain's* case [2000] Q.B. 1 were materially different from those in the present case. The disturbance complained of in *Hussain's* case was a public nuisance for which the individual perpetrators could be held liable, and they were identified as individuals who lived in council property; but their conduct was not in any sense linked to, nor did it emanate from, the homes where they lived. Here, the allegation is that the travellers were allowed to congregate on the council's land and that they used it as a base for the unlawful activities of which the plaintiffs, as neighbours, complain. It is at least arguable that this can give rise to liability in nuisance, and so the claim should not be struck out; and it seems to me that upon proof of the alleged facts, and subject to any defences, e.g. the statutory responsibilities of the council, such liability could be established.

The view taken in *Hussain's* case was that the alleged nuisance was "originally perpetrated by the culprits:" . . . . It may be that the correct analysis, where it is alleged that the owner/occupier of the land is liable for the activities of his licensees, is that he is liable, if at all, for a nuisance which he himself has created by allowing the troublemakers to occupy his land and to use it as a base for causing unlawful disturbance to his neighbours. . . . If that is correct, then strictly the question whether the owner/occupier has "adopted" a nuisance created by the travellers may not arise. For that reason I express no other view than that, on the facts alleged in the present case, the council's objection that the claim in nuisance cannot succeed, as a matter of law, must be rejected and the appeal should be allowed.

Evans LJ seems to suggest in the extract above that the nuisance is not that of the tenants or licensees in carrying out the acts, but that of the council in allowing the licensees to congregate. The question of whether the council authorized or adopted the nuisance therefore need not arise. But if this is what justifies the potential liability in *Lippiatt*, why could the same argument not be used against the council in *Hussain*—that they ought to have taken steps to have evicted the tenants? Perhaps the answer is that the eviction of tenants with a right to occupation, by a housing authority with obligations to provide housing, is a more complex operation which involves many different agencies. Some reasons of this sort were discussed in *Hussain* as militating against the success of an action in negligence, but they were not discussed in respect of the action in nuisance. However, it is possible that the same underlying policy reasons explain the different thinking to date on licensees (where allowing the people to gather may itself amount to a nuisance), and tenants, in an action for nuisance. The same distinction also seems implicit in Sir Christopher Staughton's short judgment in *Lippiatt*: he proposed that the offenders were either licensees or trespassers, and 'could be moved on'. If the dividing line is indeed based in policy of this kind, then it may be susceptible to change in future cases, as the nature of the relationship between landlord and either licensee or tenant is subject to closer scrutiny.

1.5 WHO MAY SUE?

The question of who may sue in private nuisance goes to the very heart of the tort, for it is related to the question of which interests it protects. In the case of *Hunter v Canary Wharf*, the House of Lords has affirmed that nuisance is to be regarded as a tort against property, and not a tort against the person. This has closed off the possibility of certain developments in the tort of nuisance which many had regarded as appropriate for more modern conditions. Perhaps the argument against such development is that the tort of private nuisance as a whole is not easily susceptible to being modernized.

Hunter v Canary Wharf [1997] AC 655

The plaintiffs lived in London's Docklands area, which was designated by the Secretary of State as an urban development area and enterprise zone. The consequence of this was that the normal planning process was suspended. It amounted in effect to a general grant of planning permission. Some of the plaintiffs were property owners or leaseholders; others were mere occupiers. The latter group included children. In the first of two actions, the plaintiffs claimed for damages in negligence and nuisance in respect of interference with television reception following the construction of the 'Canary Wharf' tower (250 metres high and over 50 metres square). In the second action, the plaintiffs claimed damages for negligence and nuisance in respect of deposits of dust on their properties and homes caused by the construction of a link road. At first instance, the judge ruled that interference with television reception could amount to a nuisance, but that to claim in private nuisance it was necessary to have a right to exclusive possession of property. The Court of Appeal unanimously reversed these two rulings. The appeal to the House of Lords concerned two points relating to private nuisance. First, could interference with television signals amount to a private nuisance? On this aspect of the case, see the extract in Section 1.3 above. Second, were all of the plaintiffs entitled to sue in nuisance? We will concentrate here on this crucial second point.

Lord Goff, at 687

Right to sue in private nuisance

. . . In the two cases now under appeal before your Lordships' House, one of which relates to interference with television signals and the other to the generation of dust from the construc-tion of a road, the plaintiffs consist in each case of a substantial group of local people. Moreover they are not restricted to householders who have the exclusive right to possess the places where they live, whether as freeholders or tenants, or even as licensees. They include people with whom householders share their homes, for example as wives or husbands or partners, or as children or other relatives. All of these people are claiming damages in private nuisance, by reason of interference with their television viewing or by reason of excessive dust.

Lord Goff considered a number of authorities including *Foster v Warblington Urban District Council* [1906] 1 KB 648. In this case, an oyster fisherman who occupied and worked an oyster bed to which he could prove no title had been entitled to sue in nuisance. He continued (at 689):

Subject to this exception, however [*Foster v Warblington*], it has for many years been regarded as settled law that a person who has no right in the land cannot sue in private nuisance. For this proposition, it is usual to cite the decision of the Court of Appeal in *Malone v. Laskey* [1907] 2 K.B. 141. In that case, the manager of a company resided in a house as a licensee of the company which employed him. The plaintiff was the manager's wife who lived with her husband in the house. She was injured when a bracket fell from a wall in the house. She claimed damages from the defendants in nuisance and negligence, her claim in nuisance being founded upon an allegation, accepted by the jury, that the fall of the bracket had been caused by vibrations from an engine operating on the defendants' adjoining premises. The Court of Appeal held that she was unable to succeed in her claim in nuisance. Sir Gorell Barnes P. said, at p. 151:

> "Many cases were cited in the course of the argument in which it had been held that actions for nuisance could be maintained where a person's rights of property had been affected by the nuisance, but no authority was cited, nor in my opinion can any principle of law be formulated, to the effect that a person who has no interest in property, no right of occupation in the proper sense of the term, can maintain an action for a nuisance arising from the vibration caused by the working of an engine in an adjoining house. On that point, therefore, I think that the plaintiff fails, and that she has no cause of action in respect of the alleged nuisance."

. . .

I should add that an alternative claim by the plaintiff in negligence also failed, though that claim would have succeeded today: see *A.C. Billings & Sons Ltd. v. Riden* [1958] A.C. 240.

The decision in *Malone v. Laskey* on nuisance has since been followed in many cases, of which notable examples are *Cunard v. Antifyre Ltd.* [1933] 1 K.B. 551 and *Oldham v. Lawson (No. 1)* [1976] V.R. 654. Recently, however, the Court of Appeal departed from this line of authority in *Khorasandjian v. Bush* [1993] Q.B. 727, a case which I must examine with some care.

The plaintiff, a young girl who at the time of the appeal was 18, had formed a friendship with the defendant, then a man of 28. After a time the friendship broke down and the plaintiff decided that she would have no more to do with the defendant, but the defendant found this impossible to accept. There followed a catalogue of complaints against the defendant, including assaults, threats of violence, and pestering the plaintiff at her parents' home where she lived. As a result of the defendant's threats and abusive behaviour he spent some time in prison. An injunction was granted restraining the defendant from various forms of activity directed at the plaintiff, and this included an order restraining him from "harassing, pestering or communicating with" the plaintiff. The question before the Court of Appeal was whether the judge had jurisdiction to grant such an injunction, in relation to telephone calls made to the plaintiff at her parents' home. The home was the property of the plaintiff's mother, and it was recognised that her mother could complain of persistent and unwanted telephone calls made to her; but it was submitted that the plaintiff, as a mere licensee in her mother's house, could not invoke the tort of private nuisance to complain of unwanted and harassing telephone calls made to her in her mother's home. The majority of the Court of Appeal (Peter Gibson J. dissenting) rejected this submission, relying on the decision of the Appellate Division of the Alberta Supreme Court in *Motherwell v. Motherwell* (1976) 73 D.L.R. (3d) 62. In that case, the Appellate Division not only recognised that the legal owner of property could obtain an injunction, on the ground of private nuisance, to restrain persistent harassment by unwanted telephone calls to his home, but also that the same remedy was open to his wife who had no interest in the property. In the Court of Appeal Peter Gibson J. dissented on the ground that it was wrong in principle that a mere licensee or someone without any interest in, or right to occupy, the relevant land should be able to sue in private nuisance.

It is necessary therefore to consider the basis of the decision in *Motherwell v. Motherwell* that a wife, who has no interest in the matrimonial home where she lives, is nevertheless able to sue in private nuisance in respect of interference with her enjoyment of that home. The case was concerned with a claim for an injunction against the defendant, who was the daughter of one of the plaintiffs, the other two plaintiffs being her brother and sister-in-law. The main ground of the complaint against the defendant was that, as a result of a paranoid condition from which she suffered which produced in her the conviction that her sister-in-law and her father's housekeeper were inflaming her brother and her father against her, she persistently made a very large number of telephone calls to her brother's and her father's homes, in which she abused her sister-in-law and the housekeeper. The Appellate Division of the Alberta Supreme Court, in a judgment delivered by Clement J.A., held that not only could her father and brother, as householders, obtain an injunction against the defendant to restrain this activity as a private nuisance, but so also could her sister-in-law although she had no interest in her husband's property. Clement J.A. said, at p. 78:

> "Here we have a wife harassed in the matrimonial home. She has a status, a right to live there with her husband and children. I find it absurd to say that her occupancy of the matrimonial home is insufficient to found an action in nuisance. In my opinion she is entitled to the same relief as is her husband, the brother."

This conclusion was very largely based on the decision of the Court of Appeal in *Foster v. Warblington Urban District Council* [1906] 1 K.B. 648, which Clement J.A. understood to establish a distinction between "one who is 'merely present' " and "occupancy of a substantial nature," and that in the latter case the occupier was entitled to sue in private nuisance. However *Foster v. Warblington Urban District Council* does not in my opinion provide authority for the proposition that a person in the position of a mere licensee, such as a wife or husband in her or his spouse's house, is entitled to sue in that action. This misunderstanding must, I fear, undermine the authority of *Motherwell v. Motherwell* on this point; and in so far as the decision of the Court of Appeal in *Khorasandjian v. Bush* is founded upon *Motherwell v. Motherwell* it is likewise undermined.

But I must go further. If a plaintiff, such as the daughter of the householder in *Khorasandjian v. Bush*, is harassed by abusive telephone calls, the gravamen of the complaint lies in the harassment which is just as much an abuse, or indeed an invasion of her privacy, whether she is pestered in this way in her mother's or her husband's house, or she is staying with a friend, or is at her place of work, or even in her car with a mobile phone. In truth, what the Court of Appeal appears to have been doing was to exploit the law of private nuisance in order to create by the back door a tort of harassment which was only partially effective in that it was artificially limited to harassment which takes place in her home. I myself do not consider that this is a satisfactory manner in which to develop the law, especially when, as in the case in question, the step so taken was inconsistent with another decision of the Court of Appeal, viz. *Malone v. Laskey* [1907] 2 K.B. 141, by which the court was bound. In any event, a tort of harassment has now received statutory recognition: see the Protection from Harassment Act 1997. We are therefore no longer troubled with the question whether the common law should be developed to provide such a remedy. For these reasons, I do not consider that any assistance can be derived from *Khorasandjian v. Bush* by the plaintiffs in the present appeals.

It follows that, on the authorities as they stand, an action in private nuisance will only lie at the suit of a person who has a right to the land affected. Ordinarily, such a person can only sue if he has the right to exclusive possession of the land, such as a freeholder or tenant in possession, or even a licensee with exclusive possession. Exceptionally however, as *Foster v. Warblington Urban District Council* shows, this category may include a person in actual possession who has no right to be there; and in any event a reversioner can sue in so far his reversionary interest is affected. But a mere licensee on the land has no right to sue.

The question therefore arises whether your Lordships should be persuaded to depart from established principle, and recognise such a right in others who are no more than mere licensees on the land. At the heart of this question lies a more fundamental question, which relates to the scope of the law of private nuisance. Here I wish to draw attention to the fact that although, in the past, damages for personal injury have been recovered at least in actions of public nuisance, there is now developing a school of thought that the appropriate remedy for such claims as these should lie in our now fully developed law of negligence, and that personal injury claims should be altogether excluded from the domain of nuisance. The most forthright proponent of this approach has been Professor Newark, in his article "The Boundaries of Nuisance," 65 L.Q.R. 480 from which I have already quoted. Furthermore, it is now being suggested that claims in respect of physical damage to the land should also be excluded from private nuisance: see, e.g., the article by Mr. Conor Gearty on "The Place of Private Nuisance in a Modern Law of Torts" [1989] C.L.J. 214. In any event, it is right for present purposes to regard the typical cases of private nuisance as being those concerned with interference with the enjoyment of land and, as such, generally actionable only by a person with a right in the land. Characteristic examples of cases of this kind are those concerned with noise, vibrations, noxious smells and the like. The two appeals with which your Lordships are here concerned arise from actions of this character.

. . .

Moreover, any such departure from the established law on this subject, such as that adopted by the Court of Appeal in the present case, faces the problem of defining the category of persons who would have the right to sue. The Court of Appeal adopted the not easily identifiable category of those who have a "substantial link" with the land, regarding a person who occupied the premises "as a home" as having a sufficient link for this purpose. But who is to be included in this category? It was plainly intended to include husbands and wives, or partners, and their children, and even other relatives living with them. But is the category also to include the lodger upstairs, or the au pair girl or resident nurse caring for an invalid who makes her home in the house while she works there? If the latter, it seems strange that the category should not extend to include places where people work as well as places where they live, where nuisances such as noise can be just as unpleasant or distracting. In any event, the extension of the tort in this way would transform it from a tort to land into a tort to the person, in which damages could be recovered in respect of something less serious than personal injury and the criteria for liability were founded not upon negligence but upon striking a balance between the interests of neighbours in the use of their land. This is, in my opinion, not an acceptable way in which to develop the law.

. . . .

Lord Hoffmann, at 704–8

. . . the concept of nuisance as a tort against land has recently been questioned by the decision of the Court of Appeal in *Khorasandjian v. Bush* [1993] Q.B. 727. . . . Dillon L.J. brushed *Malone v. Laskey* [1907] 2 K.B. 141 aside. He said, at p. 734:

> "To my mind, it is ridiculous if in this present age the law is that the making of deliberately harassing and pestering telephone calls to a person is only actionable in the civil courts if the recipient of the calls happens to have the freehold or a leasehold proprietary interest in the premises in which he or she has received the calls."

This reasoning, which is echoed in some academic writing and the Canadian case of *Motherwell v. Motherwell*, 73 D.L.R. (3d) 62 which the Court of Appeal followed, is based upon a fundamental mistake about the remedy which the tort of nuisance provides. It arises, I think, out of a misapplication of an important distinction drawn by Lord Westbury L.C. in *St. Helen's Smelting Co. v. Tipping* (1865).

Lord Hoffmann quoted from Lord Westbury's judgment in *St Helen's Tipping* and continued:

St. Helen's Smelting Co. v. Tipping was a landmark case. It drew the line beyond which rural and landed England did not have to accept external costs imposed upon it by industrial pollution. But there has been, I think, some inclination to treat it as having divided nuisance into two torts, one of causing "material injury to the property," such as flooding or depositing poisonous substances on crops, and the other of causing "sensible personal discomfort" such as excessive noise or smells. In cases in the first category, there has never been any doubt that the remedy, whether by way of injunction or damages, is for causing damage to the land. It is plain that in such a case only a person with an interest in the land can sue. But there has been a tendency to regard cases in the second category as actions in respect of the discomfort or even personal injury which the plaintiff has suffered or is likely to suffer. On this view, the plaintiff's interest in the land becomes no more than a qualifying condition or springboard which entitles him to sue for injury to himself.

If this were the case, the need for the plaintiff to have an interest in land would indeed be hard to justify. The passage I have quoted from Dillon L.J. (*Khorasandjian v. Bush* [1993] Q.B. 727, 734) is an eloquent statement of the reasons. But the premise is quite mistaken. In the case of nuisances "productive of sensible personal discomfort," the action is not for causing discomfort to the person but, as in the case of the first category, for causing injury to the land. True it is that the land has not suffered "sensible" injury, but its utility has been diminished by the existence of the nuisance. It is for an unlawful threat to the utility of his land that the possessor or occupier is entitled to an injunction and it is for the diminution in such utility that he is entitled to compensation.

I cannot therefore agree with Stephenson L.J. in *Bone v. Seale* [1975] 1 W.L.R. 797, 803–804 when he said that damages in an action for nuisance caused by smells from a pig farm should be fixed by analogy with damages for loss of amenity in an action for personal injury. In that case it was said that "efforts to prove diminution in the value of the property as a result of this persistent smell over the years failed." I take this to mean that it had not been shown that the property would sell for less. But diminution in capital value is not the only measure of loss. It seems to me that the value of the right to occupy a house which smells of pigs must be less than the value of the occupation of an equivalent house which does not. In the case of a transitory nuisance, the capital value of the property will seldom be reduced. But the owner or occupier is entitled to compensation for the diminution in the amenity value of the property during the period for which the nuisance persisted. To some extent this involves placing a value upon intangibles. But estates agents do this all the time. The law of damages is sufficiently flexible to be able to do justice in such a case: compare *Ruxley Electronics and Construction Ltd. v. Forsyth* [1996] A.C. 344.

There may of course be cases in which, in addition to damages for injury to his land, the owner or occupier is able to recover damages for consequential loss. He will, for example, be entitled to loss of profits which are the result of inability to use the land for the purposes of his business. Or if the land is flooded, he may also be able to recover damages for chattels or livestock lost as a result. But inconvenience, annoyance or even illness suffered by persons on land as a result of smells or dust are not damage consequential upon the injury to the land. It is rather the other way about: the injury to the amenity of the land consists in the fact that the persons upon it are liable to suffer inconvenience, annoyance or illness.

It follows that damages for nuisance recoverable by the possessor or occupier may be affected by the size, commodiousness and value of his property but cannot be increased merely because more people are in occupation and therefore suffer greater collective discomfort. If more than one person has an interest in the property, the damages will have to be divided among them. If there are joint owners, they will be jointly entitled to the damages. If there is a reversioner and the nuisance has caused damage of a permanent character which affects the reversion, he will be entitled to damages according to his interest. But the damages cannot be increased by the fact that the interests in the land are divided; still less according to the number of persons residing on the premises.

. . .

Once it is understood that nuisances "productive of sensible personal discomfort" (*St. Helen's Smelting Co. v. Tipping*, 11 H.L.Cas. 642, 650) do not constitute a separate tort of causing discomfort to people but are merely part of a single tort of causing injury to land, the rule that the plaintiff must have an interest in the land falls into place as logical and, indeed, inevitable.

Is there any reason of policy why the rule should be abandoned? Once nuisance has escaped the bounds of being a tort against land, there seems no logic in compromise limitations, such as that proposed by the Court of Appeal in this case, requiring the plaintiff to have been residing on land as his or her home. This was recognised by the Court of Appeal in *Khorasandjian v. Bush* [1993] Q.B. 727 where the injunction applied whether the plaintiff was at home or not. There is a good deal in this case and other writings about the need for the law to adapt to modern social conditions. But the development of the common law should be rational and coherent. It should not distort its principles and create anomalies merely as an expedient to fill a gap.

The perceived gap in *Khorasandjian v. Bush* was the absence of a tort of intentional harassment causing distress without actual bodily or psychiatric illness. This limitation is thought to arise out of cases like *Wilkinson v. Downton* [1897] 2 Q.B. 57 and *Janvier v. Sweeney* [1919] 2 K.B. 316. The law of harassment has now been put on a statutory basis (see the Protection from Harassment Act 1997) and it is unnecessary to consider how the common law might have developed. But as at present advised, I see no reason why a tort of intention should be subject to the rule which excludes compensation for mere distress, inconvenience or discomfort in actions based on negligence: see *Hicks v. Chief Constable of the South Yorkshire*

Police [1992] 2 All E.R. 65. The policy considerations are quite different. I do not therefore say that *Khorasandjian v. Bush* was wrongly decided. But it must be seen as a case on intentional harassment, not nuisance.

So far as the claim is for personal injury, it seems to me that the only appropriate cause of action is negligence. It would be anomalous if the rules for recovery of damages under this head were different according as to whether, for example, the plaintiff was at home or at work. It is true, as I have said, that the law of negligence gives no remedy for discomfort or distress which does not result in bodily or psychiatric illness. But this is a matter of general policy and I can see no logic in making an exception for cases in which the discomfort or distress was suffered at home rather than somewhere else.

Lord Cooke of Thornden (dissenting on the issue of who can sue in nuisance), at 711–12

My Lords, having had the privilege of reading in draft the opinions of the other four members of your Lordships' Committee in these cases, I begin my own contribution by respectfully acknowledging that they achieve a major advance in the symmetry of the law of nuisance. Being less persuaded that they strengthen the utility or the justice of this branch of the common law, I am constrained to offer an approach which, although derived from concepts to be found in those opinions, would lead to principles different in some respects. Naturally I am diffident about disagreeing in any respect with the majority of your Lordships, but such assistance as I may be able to give in your deliberations could not consist in mere conformity and deference; and, if the common law of England is to be directed into the restricted path which in this instance the majority prefer, there may be some advantage in bringing out that the choice is in the end a policy one between competing principles . . .

At 713–14

Malone v. Laskey, a case of personal injury from a falling bracket rather than an interference with amenities, is not directly in point, but it is to be noted that the wife of the subtenant's manager, who had been permitted by the subtenant to live in the premises with her husband, was dismissed by Sir Gorell Barnes P., at p. 151, as a person who had "no right of occupation in the proper sense of the term" and by Fletcher Moulton L.J. as being "merely present." My Lords, whatever the acceptability of those descriptions 90 years ago, I can only agree with the Appellate Division of the Alberta Supreme Court in *Motherwell v. Motherwell*, at p. 77, that they are "rather light treatment of a wife, at least in today's society where she is no longer considered subservient to her husband." Current statutes give effect to current perceptions by according spouses a special status in respect of the matrimonial home, as by enabling the court to make orders regarding occupation (see in England the Family Law Act 1996, sections 30 and 31).

The status of children living at home is different and perhaps more problematical but, on consideration, I am persuaded by the majority of the Court of Appeal in *Khorasandjian v. Bush* [1993] Q.B. 727 and the weight of North American jurisprudence to the view that they, too, should be entitled to relief for substantial and unlawful interference with the amenities of their home. Internationally the distinct interests of children are increasingly recognised. The United Nations Convention on the Rights of the Child, ratified by the United Kingdom in 1991 and the most widely ratified human rights treaty in history, acknowledges children as fully-fledged beneficiaries of human rights. Article 16 declares, inter alia, that no child shall be subjected to unlawful interference with his or her home and that the child has the right to the protection of law against such interference. International standards such as this may be taken into account in shaping the common law.

The point just mentioned can be taken further. Article 16 of the Convention on the Rights of the Child adopts some of the language of article 12 of the Universal Declaration of Human Rights and article 8 of the European Convention for the Protection of Human Rights and Fundamental Freedoms (1953) (Cmd. 8969). These provisions are aimed, in part, at protecting the home and are construed to give protection against nuisances . . . . The protection is regarded as going beyond possession or property rights: see *Harris, O'Boyle and Warbrick, Law of the European Convention on Human Rights* (1995), p. 319. Again I think that this is a legitimate consideration in support of treating residence as an acceptable basis of standing at common law in the present class of case.

At 717–18

The preponderance of academic opinion seems also to be against confining the right to sue in nuisance for interference with amenities to plaintiffs with proprietary interests in land. Professor John G. Fleming's condemnation of a "senseless discrimination"—see now his 8th ed., p. 426—has already been mentioned. His view is that the wife and family residing with a tenant should be protected by the law of nuisance against forms of discomfort and also personal injuries, "by recognising that they have a 'right of occupation' just like the official tenant." *Clerk & Lindsell on Torts*, 17th ed., pp. 910–911, para. 18–39, is to the same effect, as is *Linden, Canadian Tort Law*, 5th ed. (1993), pp. 521–522; while *Winfield & Jolowicz on Tort*, 14th ed. (1994), pp. 419–420 and *Markesinis & Deakin, Tort Law*, 3rd ed. (1994), pp. 434–435 would extend the right to long-term lodgers. *Salmond & Heuston on the Law of Torts*, 21st ed. (1996), p. 63, n. 96 and the New Zealand work *Todd, The Law of Torts in New Zealand*, 2nd ed. (1997), p. 537 suggest that the status of spouses under modern legislation should at least be enough; and the preface to the same edition of *Salmond & Heuston* goes further, by welcoming the decision in *Khorasandjian v. Bush* [1993] Q.B. 727 as relieving plaintiffs in private nuisance cases of the need to show that they enjoyed a legal interest in the land affected.

My Lords, there is a maxim communis error facit jus. I have collected the foregoing references not to invoke it, however, but to suggest respectfully that on this hitherto unsettled issue the general trend of leading scholarly opinion need not be condemned as erroneous. Although hitherto the law of England on the point has not been settled by your Lordships' House, it is agreed on all hands that some link with the land is necessary for standing to sue in private nuisance. The precise nature of that link remains to be defined, partly because of the ambiguity of "occupy" and its derivatives. In ordinary usage the verb can certainly include "reside in," which is indeed the first meaning given in the *Concise Oxford Dictionary*.

In logic more than one answer can be given. Logically it is possible to say that the right to sue for interference with the amenities of a home should be confined to those with proprietary interests and licensees with exclusive possession. No less logically the right can be accorded to all who live in the home. Which test should be adopted, that is to say which should be the governing principle, is a question of the policy of the law. It is a question not capable of being answered by analysis alone. All that analysis can do is expose the alternatives. Decisions such as *Malone v. Laskey* [1907] 2 K.B. 141 do not attempt that kind of analysis, and in refraining from recognising that value judgments are involved they compare less than favourably with the approach of the present-day Court of Appeal in *Khorasandjian* and this case. The reason why I prefer the alternative advocated with unwonted vigour of expression by the doyen of living tort writers is that it gives better effect to widespread conceptions concerning the home and family.

Of course in this field as in most others there will be borderline cases and anomalies wherever the lines are drawn. Thus there are, for instance, the lodger and, as some of your Lordships note, the au pair girl (although she may not figure among the present plaintiffs). It would seem weak, though, to refrain from laying down a just rule for spouses and children on the ground that it is not easy to know where to draw the lines regarding other persons. . . . Occupation of the property as a home is, to me, an acceptable criterion, consistent with the traditional concern for the sanctity of family life and the Englishman's home—which need not in this context include his workplace. As already mentioned, it is consistent also with international standards.

Commentary

The key judgments in *Hunter v Canary Wharf* have been extracted at some length because of their central importance to the development of the tort of private nuisance, and because of the importance of the variations between them. The majority of the House of Lords resoundingly affirmed that private nuisance was a tort against land and not against the person. The argument that nuisance might be 'modernized' by developing it to protect certain personal interests was rejected. The House of Lords preferred such personal rights to be protected by other means which may be more appropriately designed for the task.

The interpretation of nuisance as exclusively a tort against land resolved the question of who could sue in nuisance; but it also had far-reaching implications for the way that damages are assessed in cases of amenity nuisance (see Lord Hoffmann above), and indeed for the range of injuries for which damages are recoverable in a nuisance action. In particular, it is clear that nuisance will not provide damages for personal injury *per se*. There is a difference of view over whether this effects a change in the law affecting nuisance, but it has already had a knock-on effect concerning the action in *Rylands v Fletcher* (see the discussion of *Transco v Stockport* in the next chapter).

Although the majority judgments extracted above are generally notable for their logic and coherence, they are not altogether above criticism. In particular, as regards Lord Goff's refusal to treat the home as a special case, it may be objected that there are substantial grounds for doing exactly this: see Article 8 of the European Convention on Human Rights and Fundamental Freedoms, itself increasingly important in nuisance law since enactment of the Human Rights Act 1998. Seen in this light, their Lordships' concerns over how one should interpret the interests of the 'au pair girl' for these purposes would simply come down to a question about what counts as a home. This may not be an easy question to answer, but it surely does not require rejection of the whole concept of the home as having special status. Perhaps presciently, Lord Cooke made a broader point about the status both of the home and of children in international human rights instruments in the course of his dissenting judgment.

It is suggested that Lord Cooke is right to say that it is policy, rather than logic, that compels the majority view in *Hunter*. The question is not only the historical one of what nuisance has in the past been able to protect, but the more forward-thinking question of whether nuisance is really adequate to the task of protecting an expanded range of interests. We may accept or reject the policy behind the decision even if we do not accept that the logic is inescapable. In rejecting the idea of a 'substantial link' with the land as giving sufficient standing to sue, Lord

Goff suggested that such a change (as he saw it) in the tort of nuisance 'would transform it from a tort to land to a tort to the person, in which damages could be recovered in respect of something less serious than personal injury and the criteria for liability were founded not upon negligence but upon striking a balance between the interests of neighbours in land'. The question remains: is there justification for giving these interests extra protection in tort law, because of their status as events in the home?

Lord Hoffmann's judgment goes furthest in its drive to divorce nuisance from the sorts of personal interest typically protected through the tort of negligence. He explains that cases of nuisance causing personal discomfort do not constitute a 'separate tort' of causing discomfort to people but are still concerned only with the protection of interests in land. From here, he concludes that damages will not be increased 'merely' because more people are on the land, and therefore more people suffer personal discomfort. On the other hand, the 'size, commodiousness, and value' of the property will have an impact on the damages awarded, because the damage to the amenity of the land is valued at a greater sum. This thinking was applied in the case of *Dennis v MoD*, which could be seen as a sort of latter-day *St Helen's v Tipping*. We consider *Dennis* later. Lord Hoffmann's approach suggests that it is quite right to award much more substantial damages for noise nuisance to a family or even a single person occupying an exceptionally valuable estate (as in *Dennis*), than to a similar or larger family living in an ordinary dwelling. The 'loss of amenity in the property' will be valued at a much higher sum.

In the Docklands litigation, *Hunter v Canary Wharf* was the decisive blow to the claimants as a whole. Although some claimants did possess interests of the kind that may be protected by private nuisance, the low amenity value of their interests in land ensured that there would be little benefit in pursuing the actions. This was succinctly expressed by the European Commission on Human Rights in *Khatun v UK* (1998) 26 EHRR CD212, an action brought by disappointed Docklands plainiffs:

> This decision meant that legal aid would be discharged on cost benefit grounds. The predicted value of the collective claim was so low that any pursuit of such claim in the UK courts would be futile.

In *Khatun*, the European Commission on Human Rights dismissed the application, finding no arguable breach of Article 14 ECHR (discrimination on grounds, in this instance, of poverty); of Article 8 ECHR (interference with home, family, or private life); nor of Article 13 (no effective remedy in domestic law).

So far as **personal injury** is concerned, we should be careful how we state the conclusion to be drawn from *Hunter v Canary Wharf*. It is clear that no damages will be awarded in respect of personal injury as such. Private nuisance will not operate as an alternative to negligence in this respect. However, it should be clear enough that an activity whose effects cause personal injury on the property—perhaps from noxious fumes, for example—is capable of amounting to a nuisance because the amenity value of premises is inevitably affected by such a state of affairs. Although injured persons will not have an action in their own right as a consequence of being injured, there will presumably be grounds for an action in nuisance either for an injunction, or for damages in respect of the loss of amenity value, just as there would be for other interference with comfort and enjoyment. Indeed, invasions which threaten actual personal injury should logically be subject to increased damages as there is serious loss of amenity. (See further L. Crabb, 'The Property Torts' (2003) 11 *Tort L Rev* 104–18.)

1.6 DEFENCES

Prescription

In principle, the right to commit a nuisance may be obtained by prescription. However, it is necessary that the interference should amount to a nuisance throughout the whole prescriptive period. In *Sturges v Bridgman* (1879) 11 Ch D 852, the plaintiff began a conflicting use of the land some time during the period that was claimed to give rise to the right by prescription. As there was no nuisance prior to this, then the time period began to run only when the plaintiff initiated his use of the land.

Coming to the Nuisance?

It is well established in the case law that the defendant cannot argue, by way of defence, that the claimant 'came to the nuisance'. Being there first is not a sufficient reason to allow a defendant to create an interference with the claimant's enjoyment of land. Allowing such a defence would entitle a defendant to 'tie up' the potential uses of neighbouring land. *Sturges v Bridgman* (above) is itself a leading authority for this proposition.

Contributory negligence and *volenti non fit injuria*[11]

The wording of the Law Reform (Contributory Negligence) Act 1945 is certainly sufficiently broad to apply to nuisance. However, in the light of the principle that 'coming to the nuisance' is no defence, the applicability of this defence is likely to be limited and it is hard to envisage a case of contributory negligence unless it came very close to failure to mitigate. Similarly, the defence of *volenti non fit injuria* is theoretically applicable to nuisance but there would perhaps be a need for some active steps on the part of the claimant, encouraging the creation of the nuisance. It is especially hard to imagine a case of *continuing* nuisance in which the defence of *volenti* is made out. Even in *Gillingham v Medway (Chatham) Dock Co Ltd* ([1993] QB 343, extracted below), where a local authority had granted planning permission, the authority was not prevented from changing its mind about the desirability of the defendant's activity. The case was decided on other grounds. This was, however, a case of public nuisance brought for the protection of the rights of local residents, and not ostensibly to protect the plaintiff's own interests.

Statutory Authority

Direct authorization by statute is an important defence to an action in private nuisance. A starting point in determining the limits to this defence is the statement of Lord Blackburn in *Geddis v Proprietors of the Bann Reservoir* (1878) 3 App Cas 430, 455–6: 'no action will lie for doing that which the legislature has authorised, if it be done without negligence'. Certainly, negligence in the conduct of an authorised activity is likely to take it out of the scope of the defence. However, it has been doubted whether Lord Blackburn's statement is fully appropriate if applied to nuisance, and it has been suggested that in this tort, the proper test is whether the authorized activity could 'realistically' be carried out without creating a nuisance

---

[11] For details of these two defences, see Chapter 5.

(Buckley, *The Law of Nuisance*, 2nd edn, at pp 103–4). The emphasis is on whether a finding of liability would effectively deprive the statutory authorization of its content.

An alternative formulation is the statement of Viscount Dunedin in *Manchester Corporation v Farnworth* [1930] AC 171, at 183: where the 'making or doing' of any thing has been expressly or impliedly authorized by statute, there can be no action in nuisance 'if the nuisance is the inevitable result of the making or doing so authorised'. This suggests that the defence of statutory authority protects only those nuisances which are an 'inevitable' result of the activity authorized. Buckley, in his reference to what can 'realistically' be done, softens this a little, perhaps implying that the authorization should not be read so closely as to deny it of practical utility.

In the leading case of *Allen v Gulf Oil* [1981] AC 1013, the statement of Viscount Dunedin above was quoted with approval.

Lord Wilberforce, *Allen v Gulf Oil* [1981] AC 1013

. . . The respondent alleges a nuisance, by smell, noise, vibration, etc. The facts regarding these matters are for her to prove. It is then for the appellants to show, if they can, that it was impossible to construct and operate a refinery upon the site, conforming with Parliament's intention, without creating the nuisance alleged, or at least a nuisance. Involved in this issue would be the point discussed by Cumming-Bruce L.J. in the Court of Appeal, that the establishment of an oil refinery, etc. was bound to involve some alteration of the environment and so of the standard of amenity and comfort which neighbouring occupiers might expect. To the extent that the environment has been changed from that of a peaceful unpolluted countryside to an industrial complex (as to which different standards apply—*Sturges v. Bridgman* (1879) 11 Ch.D. 852) Parliament must be taken to have authorised it. So far, I venture to think, the matter is not open to doubt. But in my opinion the statutory authority extends beyond merely authorising a change in the environment and an alteration of standard. It confers immunity against proceedings for any nuisance which can be shown (the burden of so showing being upon the appellants) to be the inevitable result of erecting a refinery upon the site—not, I repeat, the existing refinery, but any refinery—however carefully and with however great a regard for the interest of adjoining occupiers it is sited, constructed and operated. To the extent and only to the extent that the actual nuisance (if any) caused by the actual refinery and its operation exceeds that for which immunity is conferred, the plaintiff has a remedy.

From this statement, we can see that the defendant will not succeed with this defence if the claimant can show *either* that the works in question could have been differently sited within the terms of the statute, and thus the nuisance could have been avoided (as in *Metropolitan Asylum District v Hill*, 6 App Cas 193); *or* if the works were not 'carefully' constructed and operated, and due care could have avoided the nuisance. In *Allen v Gulf Oil* itself, the statute was specific about the siting of the refinery; *and* no lack of due care was apparent in its construction and operation. Thus the nuisance was an inevitable consequence of the authorized activities, and the defence succeeded.

Allen v Gulf Oil also raised the question of 'implied' authorization. It was held that the defendants could rely on the defence of statutory authorization even though the statute in question, the Gulf Oil Refining Act 1965, expressly authorized only the acquisition of the specific land and the construction of a refinery upon it. It did not expressly authorize the *operation* of the refinery. As Lord Diplock put it (at 1014):

> Parliament can hardly be supposed to have intended the refinery to be nothing more than a visual adornment to the landscape in an area of natural beauty. Clearly the intention of Parliament was that the refinery was to be operated as such; and it is perhaps relevant to observe that in *Metropolitan Asylum District v. Hill*, 6 App.Cas. 193, all three members of this House who took part in the decision would apparently have reached the conclusion that the nuisance caused by the small-pox hospital could not have been the subject of an action, if the hospital had been built upon a site which the board had been granted power by Act of Parliament to acquire compulsorily for that specific purpose.

Emphasis here is upon the 'intention of Parliament', but it should be noted that the defence of statutory authorization is also underscored by a particular approach to public and private interests. In those cases where a nuisance has been 'authorized' by statute, it is assumed that public and private interests have been weighed by Parliament, and the public interest has been allowed to prevail. The idea that public interest outweighs private interests in these circumstances was made explicit by Lord Roskill in *Allen v Gulf Oil Ltd*, at 1023:

> My Lords, for a period of over 150 years the principles upon which statutes such as the Act of 1965 have to be construed, have been considered and authoritatively determined by your Lordships' House. Where Parliament by express words or necessary implication authorises the construction or use of an undertaking, that authorisation is necessarily accompanied by immunity from any action based on nuisance. The underlying philosophy plainly is that the greater public interest arising from the construction and use of undertakings such as railways, must take precedence over the private rights of owners and occupiers of neighbouring lands not to have their common law rights infringed by what would otherwise be actionable nuisance. In short, the lesser private right must yield to the greater public interest.

Relationship between statutory authorization and planning permission

Planning permission is not granted by Parliament but, generally, by local planning authorities. Planning authorities will generally consider the benefits of a proposed development in accordance with statutory procedures and if they grant permission will generally have taken into account the needs of the local area. There will be appropriate procedures, an element of participation, and an element of local representative democracy where the decision-maker is the local authority.

Planning permission is not a defence in the same way as statutory authority. Local planning authorities do not have authority to override private rights. However, the impact of planning permission is complex and it appears that in some instances such permission may determine the outcome of the case.

Gillingham v Medway (Chatham) Dock Co Ltd [1993] QB 343

Following the closure of the naval docks at Chatham, Gillingham Borough Council granted planning permission (in 1983) for the operation of a commercial dockyard in part of the old port. There was concern with employment and profitability. It seems to have been understood that this would probably need to operate as a 24-hour port in order to be profitable. The Dock became commercially successful, and began to operate on a 24-hour basis. In 1988, the same council initiated proceedings in public nuisance in respect of noise affecting local residents at night. As Buckley J put it, the defendant council had 'changed its priorities' (at 363). The case was decided on the basis that the principles of public nuisance in such a case were the same as those in private nuisance, at least so far as the points below were concerned (see *AG v PYA Quarries*, below).

Buckley J, at 358–60

Public nuisance and planning permission

. . . The dock company obtained planning permission to operate the dock as a commercial port, which cannot sensibly be done other than on a 24-hour basis. In any event, the plaintiff, as I have found, knew that 24-hour operation was anticipated and no condition curtailing such use was attached to the permission . . .

. . . .

I have not been referred to any case which has directly considered the interplay between planning permission and the law of nuisance. Many cases, of course, have considered statutory authority as a defence to nuisance. . . . Lord Templeman in the *Tate & Lyle* case said, at p. 538:

> "The defence of statutory authority to an action for nuisance was summarised in the speech of my noble and learned friend, Lord Wilberforce, in *Allen v. Gulf Oil Refining Ltd.* [1981] A.C. 1001, 1011 as follows: 'It is now well settled that where Parliament by express direction or by necessary implication has authorised the construction and use of an undertaking or works, that carries with it an authority to do what is authorised with immunity from any action based on nuisance. The right of action is taken away; . . . To this there is made the qualification, or condition, that the statutory powers are exercised without 'negligence'—that word here being used in a special sense so as to require the undertaker, as a condition of obtaining immunity from action, to carry out the work and conduct of the operation with all reasonable regard and care for the interests of other persons; . . . ' "

Doubtless one of the reasons for this approach is that Parliament is presumed to have considered the interests of those who will be affected by the undertaking or works and decided that benefits from them should outweigh any necessary adverse side effects. I believe that principle should be utilised in respect of planning permission. Parliament has set up a statutory framework and delegated the task of balancing the interests of the community against those of individuals and of holding the scales between individuals, to the local planning authority. There is the right to object to any proposed grant, provision for appeals and inquiries, and ultimately the minister decides. There is the added safeguard of judicial review. If a planning authority grants permission for a particular construction or use in its area it is almost certain that some local inhabitants will be prejudiced in the quiet enjoyment of their properties. Can they defeat the scheme simply by bringing an action in nuisance? If not, why not? It has been said, no doubt correctly, that planning permission is not a licence to commit nuisance and that a planning authority has no jurisdiction to authorise nuisance. However, a planning authority can, through its development plans and decisions, alter the character of a neighbourhood. That may have the effect of rendering innocent activities which prior to the change would have been an actionable nuisance: *Allen v. Gulf Oil Refining Ltd.* [1980] Q.B. 156, 174, *per* Cumming-Bruce L.J., referred to in the speech of Lord Wilberforce [1981] A.C. 1001, 1013–1014.

The point arises in this case. Prior to January 1984 Medway and Bridge Roads had been relatively quiet residential roads. True, they led to the old Naval Dockyard but that did not generate many heavy goods vehicles and probably none at night. For obvious reasons sites for naval bases were not chosen for their land communications. It seems to me that I must judge the present claim in nuisance by reference to the present character of the neighbourhood pursuant to the planning permission for use of the dockyard as a commercial port. Thus, these roads are now in the neighbourhood of and lead immediately to a commercial port which operates 24 hours per day. In those circumstances I hold that the undoubted disturbance to the residents is not actionable. . . .

At 361

In short, where planning consent is given for a development or change of use, the question of nuisance will thereafter fall to be decided by reference to a neighbourhood with that development or use and not as it was previously.

Wheeler v Saunders Ltd [1996] Ch 19

This case concerned nuisance by smell emanating from two pig houses situated close to the plaintiff's property. Planning permission had been obtained for construction of the houses. The members of the Court of Appeal were unanimous in holding that the defendants could not rely on the planning permission either as a defence, or as changing the character of the neighbourhood, in this particular case. Their confidence in the correctness of the *Gillingham* case (above) was more variable, and Staughton LJ in particular was reluctant to lay down any general principles.

Staughton LJ, at 30

I accept what was said by Cumming-Bruce L.J. [in *Allen v Gulf Oil*, above]: first, that a planning authority has in general no jurisdiction to authorise a nuisance; and, secondly, if it can do so at all, that is only by the exercise of its power to permit a change in the character of a neighbourhood. To the extent that those two propositions feature in the judgment of Buckley J., I agree with his decision, but I would not for the present go any further than that.

It would in my opinion be a misuse of language to describe what has happened in the present case as a change in the character of a neighbourhood. It is a change of use of a very small piece of land, a little over 350 square metres according to the dimensions on the plan, for the benefit of the applicant and to the detriment of the objectors in the quiet enjoyment of their house. It is not a strategic planning decision affected by considerations of public interest. Unless one is prepared to accept that any planning decision authorises any nuisance which must inevitably come from it, the argument that the nuisance was authorised by planning permission in this case must fail. I am not prepared to accept that premise. It may be—I express no concluded opinion—that some planning decisions will authorise some nuisances. But that is as far as I am prepared to go. There is no immunity from liability for nuisance in the present case.

Because of the reluctance of the Court of Appeal to state clear general principles, *Wheeler v Saunders* does not replace *Gillingham* as the leading case on the impact of planning permission. It does however underline that at most (which is to say if *Gillingham* is correctly decided), planning permission will be decisive in only a limited range of cases. The negative aspect of Buckley J's approach in *Gillingham*, stating that the grant of planning permission does not 'license' a nuisance, is given clear support in the case extracted above, but his positive decision that the permission may 'change the character of the neighbourhood' is not clearly stated to be correct.

In *Hunter v Canary Wharf*, Lord Hoffmann further considered the impact of a developed system of planning law, specifically on the plaintiffs' action for interference with TV reception. Like Lord Goff, whose judgment on this point was extracted in Section 1.3 above, he concluded that the existing case law excluded an action based simply on the presence of a large building on the defendant's land, in the absence of an easement. But he also considered the impact of planning law.

Lord Hoffmann [1997] AC 655, at 710–11

Once again we must consider whether modern conditions require these well established principles to be modified. The common law freedom of an owner to build upon his land has been drastically curtailed by the Town and Country Planning Act 1947 and its successors. It is now in normal cases necessary to obtain planning permission. The power of the planning authority to grant or refuse permission, subject to such conditions as it thinks fit, provides a mechanism for control of the unrestricted right to build which can be used for the protection of people living in the vicinity of a development. In a case such as this, where the development is likely to have an impact upon many people over a large area, the planning system is, I think, a far more appropriate form of control, from the point of view of both the developer and the public, than enlarging the right to bring actions for nuisance at common law. It enables the issues to be debated before an expert forum at a planning inquiry and gives the developer the advantage of certainty as to what he is entitled to build.

In saying this, I am not suggesting that a grant of planning permission should be a defence to anything which is an actionable nuisance under the existing law. It would, I think, be wrong to allow the private rights of third parties to be taken away by a permission granted by the planning authority to the developer. The Court of Appeal rejected such an argument in this case and the point has not been pursued in your Lordships' House. But when your Lordships are invited to develop the common law by creating a new right of action against an owner who erects a building upon his land, it is relevant to take into account the existence of other methods by which the interests of the locality can be protected.

In this case, as I mentioned at the beginning of this speech, the normal protection offered to the community by the Act of 1971 was largely removed. Parliament authorised this to be done on the ground that the national interest required the rapid regeneration of the Docklands urban development area. The plaintiffs may well feel that their personal convenience was temporarily sacrificed to the national interest. But this is not a good enough reason for changing the principles of the law of nuisance which apply throughout the country.

On the one hand, therefore, we have a rule of common law which, absent easements, entitles an owner of land to build what he likes upon his land. It has stood for many centuries. If an exception were to be created for large buildings which interfere with television reception, the developers would be exposed to legal action by an indeterminate number of plaintiffs, each claiming compensation in a relatively modest amount. Defending such actions, whatever their merits or demerits, would hardly be cost-effective. The compensation and legal fees would form an unpredictable additional cost of the building. On the other hand, the plaintiffs will ordinarily have been able to make their complaints at the planning stage of the development and, if necessary, secure whatever conditions were necessary to provide them with an alternative source of television signals. The interference in such a case is not likely to last very long because there is no technical difficulty about the solution. In my view the case for a change in the law is not made out.

Public Interest?

The role of the public interest has been mentioned several times. It will be apparent that public interest is by no means irrelevant to a nuisance action, and the correct means of balancing public against private interests is of particular concern in considering the defences of statutory authorization and the status of planning permission. However, most commentators conclude that public interest in the activities of the defendant is not *in itself* a defence to an action in nuisance. In *Dennis v MoD* (further extracted below in respect of remedies), Buckley J reviewed the authorities in the following terms:

Dennis v Ministry of Defence [2003] EWHC 793 (QB)

[30]   This case raises an important and problematic point of principle in the law of nuisance. Namely, whether and in what circumstances a sufficient public interest can amount to a defence to a claim in nuisance. In several cases the point has arisen in a less dramatic form than here. For example, the local cricket club case: Miller v Jackson [1977] QB 966, [1977] 3 All ER 338 and Kennaway v Thompson [1981] QB 88, [1980] 3 All ER 329 in which the Court of Appeal affirmed the principle in Shelfer v City of London Electric Lighting Company [1894] 1 Ch 287, namely, the fact that the wrong doer is in some sense a public benefactor has never been considered a sufficient reason to refuse an injunction. (See Lindley LJ. At 315/6). Clerk and Lindsell concludes that public interest is "not in itself a defence, but a factor in assessing reasonableness of user". 18th Edition para 19.72. Fleming The Law of Torts 9th Edition at 471 points out that some weight is accorded to the utility of the defendant's conduct, but suggests that the argument "must not be pushed too far." He cites Bohlen Studies 429:

"If the public be interested let the public as such bear the costs."

He points out this can be achieved by holding the defendant liable and leaving him to include the cost in charges to the public, or by statutory authority with provision for compensation. The former suggestion, of course, would only apply to a service provider capable of raising charges.

Buckley J clearly considered the meagre case law not to determine the answer to his simple question of whether the public interest could amount to a defence. Indeed, the case of *Miller v Jackson* [1977] QB 966 appears to be unique in stating clearly that the public interest—in preserving the playing of cricket on village greens—outweighed the private interests of neighbours such that they could have no action in nuisance. Later in his judgment, Buckley J considered the different ways in which he might give effect to public interest in his decision:

[44]   What is the effect of a public interest in an activity continuing, where that activity would otherwise constitute a nuisance? It seems to me that it would be unsatisfactory to attempt a general answer. It will depend on all the circumstances, not least the strength of the public interest in question. If public interest can be a relevant consideration, one solution would be that the particular public interest should be put in the scales at the stage when the court is seeking to balance the competing interests of the parties. As the cases indicate, very often the

private interest will prevail. The alternative approach would be to exclude any public interest from consideration of whether a nuisance should be found and consider it as relevant only to remedy.

[45]   Where there is a real public interest in a particular use of land, I can see no objection in principle to taking that public interest into account, in one way or another, in deciding what is best to be done. Indeed, in effect that happens at present where use is authorised by statute. A recent example is *Marcic v Thames Water Utilities Ltd* . . . . Manifestly a nuisance existed in Marcic. Plainly there is a public interest in the continuing operation of sewers and statute recognises that. The common law contribution is to ensure that the operator exercises reasonable care in pursuing its undertaking. The result is that, if due care is exercised, the nuisance continues. The public interest prevails, provided no more damage is done than is reasonably necessary. See also *Allen v Gulf Oil Refining Ltd* . . . . The difference in the instant case is that it is left to the common law to provide the answer, no statutory framework is present to assist. However, the public interest in question here, albeit very different, may be considered just as important, if not more so. It could also be thought that the MOD's position, charged as it is with the defence of the realm, should be no less protected than commercial or other undertakings authorised directly by statute.

Here, Buckley J considered whether he should give effect to the public interest by holding that it afforded a defence in itself, or by varying the remedy that could be awarded. He preferred to take the latter course. There was a nuisance; but damages should be awarded in lieu of an injunction. This was a controversial course to take, but in view of the absence of authority concerning the status of public interest, there was no 'uncontroversial' path available to resolve this case. Because of the solution adopted, it is extracted further in respect of 'Remedies', below.

1.7   REMEDIES

Broadly speaking, there are three remedies for nuisance. These are abatement, injunction, and damages.

Abatement

Abatement is a form of self-help. It justifies the claimant in entering onto land from which a nuisance emanates, in order to prevent its continuation. The following statement from the case of *Burton v Winters* [1993] 1 WLR 1077 gives an indication of the types of case in which abatement will be appropriate:

Lloyd LJ, at 1081

[T]he courts have confined the remedy by way of self-redress to simple cases such as an overhanging branch, or an encroaching root, which would not justify the expense of legal proceedings, and urgent cases which require an immediate remedy.

Abatement is regarded by the courts with some caution. This is not surprising, given the possible adverse consequences of self-help especially in the context of neighbour disputes.

Indeed in *Burton v Winters* itself, the plaintiff had been committed to prison for two years for breaching the terms of an injunction which prevented her from damaging the defendants' garage. She had earlier been denied a mandatory injunction requiring the demolition of the garage, even though the court had granted a declaration that it encroached upon her land. The Court of Appeal denied her claim that abatement was an appropriate remedy in such a case.

Injunctions

In cases of continuing nuisance, the majority of claimants will seek an injunction. As already indicated, the availability of injunctive relief (or indeed of damages in respect of future interference) is one of the factors marking a distinction between negligence and nuisance. An injunction is an equitable remedy and as such is not available as of right. Rather, it is within the discretion of the court whether to award an injunction, and on what terms. This gives considerable flexibility. Rather than prohibiting the defendant's activities, the court may for example set limits to the times during which the activity may continue, or even order that certain technical alterations are made to ameliorate the nuisance. Mandatory injunctions (which require the defendant to take positive steps) are however rarely used, and their terms must be very clearly expressed.

Damages for Past Injury and Interference

Some cases of nuisance do not have any continuing element, but are actions in respect of damage or interference that has already been suffered. Furthermore, even in cases of continuing nuisance there will typically be some element of past interference. In these cases, claimants may be awarded damages to compensate for injury in the usual way. However, it should be noted that the comments of Lord Hoffmann in *Hunter v Canary Wharf* (above) regarding the nature of the interests protected by the tort of nuisance may have invalidated some of the existing case law on the assessment of damages. In particular, he disapproved of the approach of Stephenson LJ in *Bone v Seale* [1975] 1 WLR 797, which suggested that the court should draw analogies with personal injury awards in negligence when compensating for a nuisance by smell. The sums awarded in cases of amenity nuisance must, according to Lord Hoffmann's approach, reflect instead the diminution of amenity value (though this may be temporary) in the property affected.

Damages in Lieu of Injunction

Since the Chancery Amendment Act of 1858 ('Lord Cairns' Act'), courts have had the power to award damages for future interference in lieu of an injunction. However, the power to do this has been restrictively interpreted by the courts themselves. Courts have mostly regarded themselves as bound by the criteria set out by A. L. Smith LJ in the case of *Shelfer v City of London Electric Lighting Co* [1895] 1 Ch 287, at 322–3:

> In my opinion, it may be stated as a good working rule that—
>> (1) If the injury is small,
>> (2) And is one which is capable of being estimated in money,
>> (3) And is one which can adequately be compensated by a small money payment,

(4) And the case is one in which it would be oppressive to the defendant to grant an injunction:—

then damages in substitution for an injunction may be given.

These conditions focus on the interests of the claimant, rather than on extraneous grounds such as the social utility of the defendant's activities. A. L. Smith LJ also suggested that particular conduct on the part of the defendant (amounting to 'reckless disregard for the plaintiff's rights') might militate against the award of damages *in lieu*, even if all four of the conditions above were satisfied.

There are well known older cases in which the presumption in favour of an injunction as opposed to damages, and indifference to issues of public interest, appears to have had striking effects. In *Manchester Corporation v Farnworth* [1930] AC 171, the House of Lords said it would disregard the effect of an injunction on Manchester's electricity supply. On the other hand, the demanding nature of the *Shelfer* criteria (bearing in mind that *all* of them should be satisfied) could incline a court against the award of any relief at all, given that the injunction, as an equitable remedy, is not available 'as of right'.

This point is clearly made by Millett LJ in the following extract. The case was concerned not with nuisance but with the award of damages in lieu of an injunction where there had been breach of a restrictive covenant. The issues relating to injunctions are equally applicable, and the passage quoted was relied upon by Peter Smith J in the nuisance case of *Midtown v City of London Real Property Co Ltd* [2005] EWHC 33.

Millett LJ, *Jaggard v Sawyer* [1995] 1 WLR 269

At 286

It has always been recognised that the practical consequence of withholding injunctive relief is to authorise the continuance of an unlawful state of affairs. If, for example, the defendant threatens to build in such a way that the plaintiff's light will be obstructed and he is not restrained, then the plaintiff will inevitably be deprived of his legal right. This was the very basis upon which before 1858 the Court of Chancery had made the remedy of injunction available in such cases. After the passing of Lord Cairns's Act many of the judges warned that the jurisdiction to award damages instead of an injunction should not be exercised as a matter of course so as to legalise the commission of a tort by any defendant who was willing and able to pay compensation.

. . .

At 287–8

Nevertheless references to the "expropriation" of the plaintiff's property are somewhat overdone, not because that is not the practical effect of withholding an injunction, but because the grant of an injunction, like all equitable remedies, is discretionary. Many proprietary rights cannot be protected at all by the common law. The owner must submit to unlawful interference with his rights and be content with damages. If he wants to be protected he must seek equitable relief, and he has no absolute right to that. In many cases, it is true, an injunction will be granted almost as of course; but this is not always the case, and it will never be granted if this would cause injustice to the defendant. Citation of passages in the cases warning of the danger of "expropriating" the plaintiff needs to be balanced by reference to statements like that of Lord Westbury L.C. in *Isenberg v. East India House Estate Co. Ltd.*(1863) 3 De G. J. & S. 263, 273 where he held that it was the duty of the court not

> "by granting a mandatory injunction, to deliver over the defendants to the plaintiff bound hand and foot, in order to be made subject to any extortionate demand that he may by possibility make, but to substitute for such mandatory injunction an inquiry before itself, in order to ascertain the measure of damage that has been actually sustained."

It follows from this that if the effect of granting an injunction *as between the parties* would be disproportionate, then an injunction may be declined. The *Shelfer* criteria, Millett LJ explained, were not to be strictly construed, but were illustrative of the general approach to be taken. In *Midtown* (above), Peter Smith J held that it would be disproportionate and oppressive to prevent the defendant's building works in order to protect a right to light in offices where the claimants' interests were purely commercial. It is too easy, otherwise, for claimants to use legal rights in order to demand extortionate payments from their neighbours.

These cases are not directly concerned with *public* interest. As noted above, the strongest statement to the effect that the public interest must prevail over the private interest was to be found in the case of *Miller v Jackson* [1977] QB 966, and most particularly in the judgment of Lord Denning, in which the Court of Appeal refused to grant an injunction to prevent the playing of cricket despite the threat of damage and physical injury to the plaintiff and his property. However, the correctness of this case has been questioned, most particularly in the case of *Kennaway v Thompson* [1981] QB 88, a case which itself illustrates the potential flexibility of the injunctive remedy.

As early as 1862 and the case of *Bamford v Turnley*, it was proposed that more flexibility as to remedy might enhance the ability of courts to bring about socially productive outcomes to actions in nuisance (see the comments of Bramwell B, extracted in Section 1.3 above), and in particular to achieve a more productive compromise between private rights and public interests. Greater flexibility has been championed by a number of academic commentators.[12] Such flexibility, it has been argued, would avoid the need to make a stark choice between either public or private interests. This approach resembles a principle of equity which underlies certain aspects of state liability in French law (see Fairgrieve, *State Liability in Tort* (OUP, 2003), 146–50).

The following case raised the matter of public interest in a very direct manner. Given that the *Shelfer* criteria were not fulfilled, and given that there was a substantial noise nuisance, was Buckley J bound to award an injunction? As we have seen in Section 1.6, this case involved no less a public interest than the defence of the realm.

Dennis v Ministry of Defence [2003] EWHC 793 (QB)

The claimants were owners of Walcott Hall Estate, an exceptional property with extensive grounds of 1,387 acres. The Hall itself was built in 1678. The Estate is a close neighbour of RAF Wittering, and the action concerned sustained and extreme noise nuisance from Harrier

---

[12] See for example Fleming, *The Law of Torts*, 9th edn, 1998, 471–2.

Jump Jets. Such was the intensity of the noise endured, Buckley J had little difficulty in determining that it amounted to a nuisance. The remaining questions were, first, whether public interest could amount to a defence in nuisance. Here, the case law was as we have noted unhelpful and contradictory. However, Buckley J concluded that, on balance, public interest did not constitute a defence and could not operate to deny that such a level of noise amounted to a nuisance. Second, what remedy could be awarded, and could this reflect the nature of the public interest in the case? In the extract below, Buckley J considers this to be an alternative to the idea that public interest may be a defence. He further considered the separate possibility of an action for damages under the Human Rights Act 1998, but it is clear that his conclusions on damages were themselves influenced by human rights considerations.

Buckley J, *Dennis v MoD*

[46]   The problem with putting the public interest into the scales when deciding whether a nuisance exists, is simply that if the answer is no, not because the claimant is being over sensitive, but because his private rights must be subjugated to the public interest, it might well be unjust that he should suffer the damage for the benefit of all. If it is to be held that there is no nuisance, there can be no remedy at common law. As this case illustrates, the greater the public interest, the greater may be the interference. If public interest is considered at the remedy stage and since the court has a discretion, the nuisance may continue but the public, in one way or another, pays for its own benefit. The court in Marcic[13] was not called upon to make that decision. It was applying the law to an undertaking being pursued with statutory authority and simply holding that the undertaking should be carried on with all due care. However, the comments in paras 111 et seq suggest that it might have favoured the second option, or at least an option that gives effect to public interest but at the public expense, particularly if the common law is to develop consistently with European decisions involving human rights. Allowing a human rights claim but denying a remedy in nuisance would, of course, be another solution, but it would be one that reflected adversely on the flexibility of the common law. I fear neither Lord Loreburn nor Lord Halsbury would have approved of such an outcome.[14]

[47]   The principles or policy underlying these considerations are that public interest should be considered and that selected individuals should not bear the cost of the public benefit. I am in favour of giving effect to those principles. I believe it is necessary to do so if the common law in this area is to be consistent with the developing jurisprudence on human rights.

[48]   I therefore hold that a nuisance is established but that the public interest clearly demands that RAF Wittering should continue to train pilots. Mr Wood did raise the possibility of granting the declaration sought, but suspending it to give the MOD time to find an alternative site or, as I understood him, to provide evidence that none existed or none that could be conveniently utilised. I have already commented on the evidence before me and find it sufficient to reach the conclusion that I should not grant a declaration. In reaching that conclusion I have had in mind, in particular, the nature of the public interest, the defence of the realm, the enormous inconvenience and cost of uprooting RAF Wittering and RAF Cottesmore to another location and that, even assuming one might be found away from population, it would probably not be as

---

[13] This is a reference to the Court of Appeal judgment in *Marcic* [2002] EWCA 64.
[14] *Rushmer v Polsue & Alfieri* [1907] AC 121, 123.

convenient generally as Wittering/Cottesmore. On the other side, I have considered, particularly, the property rights of Mr Dennis; the fact that he has lived at Walcot Hall since childhood and hopes that one day one of his children will continue to maintain the Estate; and the very considerable noise interference with his enjoyment of it. I have also noted that diminution in the market value of the Estate may be compensated financially and that there has been considerable delay in bringing these proceedings.

[49]   I do not believe that the conclusion at which I have arrived is prohibited by authority. The facts of this case are extreme and not analogous to others to which I was referred. I am conscious that there is no authority directly in point which supports my solution. However, save where it may be considered more appropriate to leave the matter to legislation, the common law should develop in line with European decisions on human rights, which I consider later. . . .

Human Rights

[63]   Following the implications of S v France as identified in Marcic and, with respect, with which I agree, I would hold that a fair balance would not be struck in the absence of compensation. I would thus award damages under s 8 [Human Rights Act 1998] in respect of arts 8 and 1. I would hold, as I believe is implicit in the decision in S v France, that the public interest is greater than the individual private interests of Mr and Mrs Dennis but it is not proportionate to pursue or give effect to the public interest without compensation for Mr and Mrs Dennis. I do not accept Mr Elvin's submissions to the effect that the Claimants are not called upon to bear an individual burden. The facts are that the MOD has operated its schemes for purchase of property or grants for double-glazing in the locality generally, but Walcot Hall could not be included. But in any event the local inhabitants constitute a very small proportion of the tax paying community at large. The same imbalance would apply even if one considered all RAF airfields. I have no evidence on this, but it must be the case. In my view, common fairness demands that where the interests of a minority, let alone an individual, are seriously interfered with because of an overriding public interest, the minority should be compensated. To its credit the MOD appears to accept that principle since it operates the voluntary schemes to which I have referred.

Buckley J refers here to the Court of Appeal judgment in *Marcic*, which as we have seen was reversed by the House of Lords. In that case, the Court of Appeal took an unusual approach to the question of flexibility in remedy, and the possibility of awarding damages in lieu of injunctions to claimants where there was a strong public interest on the side of the defendant. Not only were the remarks *obiter*, but they were included in a section entitled 'unanswered questions'. Here the Court of Appeal deliberately sought to prevent its decision in favour of the claimant from being construed narrowly.

Marcic v Thames Water Utilities Ltd [2002] EWCA Civ 64; [2002] 2 WLR 932 (Court of Appeal, reversed on appeal to House of Lords [2003] UKHL 66; [2003] 3 WLR 1603)

Lord Phillips of Worth Matravers MR (giving the judgment of the Court)

[113]   Where a nuisance results because an existing system becomes surcharged as a consequence of increased user, it does not seem to us just that the liability of the undertaker should depend upon whether in all the circumstances there are steps which the undertaker should reasonably have taken to abate the nuisance. If a single house is at risk of flooding by

sewerage discharge once every five years, this may not justify the investment that would be needed to remove that risk. It does not follow, however, that it is just that the householder should receive no compensation for the damage done. The flooding is a consequence of the benefit that is provided to those making use of the system. It seems to us at least arguable that to strike a fair balance between the individual and the general community, those who pay to make use of a sewerage system should be charged sufficient to cover the cost of paying compensation to the minority who suffer damage as a consequence of the operation of the system.

[114] This result would be achieved if the principle in *Rylands v Fletcher* LR 3 HL 330 were to be applied to sewage, although, as we have indicated above, it is questionable whether this could be achieved without a degree of modification of legal principle. Such modification may, however, be necessary if our common law is to march in step with the requirements of the Convention.

[115] When considering Mr Marcic's claim under the Human Rights Act, the judge proceeded on the premise that this required a fair balance to be struck between the competing interests of Mr Marcic and Thames's other customers. In this context he was prepared to contemplate that the system of priorities used by Thames might be "entirely fair", notwithstanding that this would result in nothing being done to remedy Mr Marcic's flooding in the foreseeable future. We doubt whether such a situation would be compatible with Mr Marcic's rights under article 8. The decision of the European Commission of Human Rights in *S v France* (1990) 65 DR 250 suggests to the contrary.

[116] In that case the claimant complained that her rights under article 8 and article 1 of the First Protocol were interfered with as a result of the nuisance caused to her home by a nearby power station. The commission held that, although noise and other types of nuisance might be the unavoidable consequence of measures not directed against the claimant, they none the less interfered with her human rights, but that payment to her of compensation had had the result that the interference did not go beyond what was necessary in a democratic society. The commission observed, at p 263:

> "It is not in dispute that the nuclear power station was lawfully built and brought into service by Electricité de France. Nor can there be any doubt that the construction of a nuclear power station serves the interest of the economic well-being of the country. In order to determine whether the interference in this case can be regarded as 'necessary in a democratic society', it must first be decided whether it was proportionate in relation to the legitimate interest the works were intended to serve. When a state is authorised to restrict rights or freedoms guaranteed by the Convention, the proportionality rule may well require it to ensure that these restrictions do not oblige the person concerned to bear an unreasonable burden."

[117] This suggests that where an authority carries on an undertaking in the interest of the community as a whole it may have to pay compensation to individuals whose rights are infringed by that undertaking in order to achieve a fair balance between the interests of the individual and the community.

[118] We have referred to these matters, which have not been explored in the present action, lest sewerage undertakers assume from our judgment that their liability to pay compensation for damage done by discharge from an overcharged sewer is dependent upon whether or not there are measures which they should reasonably have taken to prevent the discharge. That does not necessarily follow from our judgment.

The decision of Buckley J is significant as the first attempt to use ideas of this sort in order to dispose of a case. Candidly, he suggests that his solution is 'not ruled out by' the authorities. He does not propose that the previous case law actually compels or justifies such a solution. Our review of the role of public interest (above) suggests that there are no reliable precedents for the judge's important conclusion in paragraph [48], 'that a nuisance is established but that RAF Wittering should continue to train pilots'. However, this position was carefully reached, and there are two factors mentioned by the judge which would justify this unconventional approach. First, the legal landscape has been changed by the enactment of the Human Rights Act 1998. Second, the public interest issue was inescapable. It demanded a solution.

For the most part, Buckley J's solution was based upon analysis from first principles, although he did of course derive support from the persuasive comments of the Court of Appeal in the *Marcic* case. How acceptable is the solution? A query may be raised concerning the level of damages awarded in nuisance. Tort damages are, relative to other forms of compensation, generous. Does this militate against the idea that the public interest prevails, at the expense of compensating those individuals who suffer loss? How damaging would it be to the public interest itself to be subject to a number of successful tort actions?

In the *Dennis* case, damages were assessed at the substantial figure of £950,000. No doubt the figure awarded reflected the fact that the claimant's estate was 'exceptional'. Applying the approach in *Hunter v Canary Wharf*, we can assume that not very many claimants would succeed in obtaining judgment for such a figure, even if they lived in equally close proximity and were subject to the same levels of noise. Families living in 'less commodious' properties would, if the noise insulation scheme did not benefit them sufficiently, obtain far lower sums from nuisance actions.

This does beg the further question of whether such a result is truly compatible with an approach based on protection of human rights. Article 8 of the European Convention on Human Rights (below) protects an individual's 'private and family life, his home and his correspondence'. If this is the source of this recent development in the tort of nuisance, is it appropriate that different valuations should be placed upon such rights, depending on the value of one's home? Perhaps matters are clearer in respect of Article 1 of the First Protocol to the Convention. As will be seen below, this protects the right to peaceful enjoyment of possessions. It may be inevitable that damages in respect of the rights in Article 1 should be assessed relative to the value of possessions enjoyed by any given individual.

2. NUISANCE AND THE HUMAN RIGHTS ACT 1998

2.1 THE CONVENTION RIGHTS AND THEIR STATUS

Perhaps surprisingly, private nuisance was one of the first torts to test the impact of the Human Rights Act 1998. The impact of that Act was discussed in a general sense in Chapter 1, where the statute was extracted. Here, we remind ourselves of the key provisions.

By section 6 of the Human Rights Act 1998, it is unlawful for a public authority—which is defined to include a court—to act incompatibly with a Convention right. It has been generally concluded that this will not mean that new causes of action will arise at common law, but it may mean that existing actions (like private nuisance) may be interpreted differently in light of the Convention rights (see Chapter 1, and further discussion in Chapter 14).

By sections 7 and 8 of the Human Rights Act 1998, actions may be brought against a public authority, seeking damages for unlawful acts (in violation of a Convention right). This is not an action in tort, but the existence of remedies under section 8 may influence the development of tort actions (see particularly Chapter 6.3 above).

In Chapter 1, we did not extract the Convention rights that are scheduled to the Human Rights Act. Here, we reproduce the two Articles of the Convention that are most relevant to actions in private nuisance.

Human Rights Act 1998 (1998, c.42)

Schedule 1   The Articles

Part I   The Convention

Rights and Freedoms

Article 8

Right to respect for private and family life

1 Everyone has the right to respect for his private and family life, his home and his correspondence.

2 There shall be no interference by a public authority with the exercise of this right except such as is in accordance with the law and is necessary in a democratic society in the interests of national security, public safety or the economic well-being of the country, for the prevention of disorder or crime, for the protection of health or morals, or for the protection of the rights and freedoms of others.

. . . .

Part II   The First Protocol

Article 1

Protection of property

Every natural or legal person is entitled to the peaceful enjoyment of his possessions. No one shall be deprived of his possessions except in the public interest and subject to the conditions provided for by law and by the general principles of international law.

The preceding provisions shall not, however, in any way impair the right of a State to enforce such laws as it deems necessary to control the use of property in accordance with the general interest or to secure the payment of taxes or other contributions or penalties.

. . .

2.2 APPLICATIONS

The Interests Protected by Nuisance

In Section 1.5 above, we extracted the House of Lords' decision in *Hunter v Canary Wharf.* That case reaffirmed that nuisance is a tort against land and not against the person, and declined to support any 'modernization' of the tort so as to protect those occupying property as a home. Their Lordships considered that such a move would lead to incoherence in the law, and would also be unnecessary. We noted the dissent of Lord Cooke, which was supported in part by the existence of international human rights documents affirming rights specific to the home. With the enactment of the Human Rights Act 1998, will the restrictions to the tort of nuisance stated by *Hunter v Canary Wharf* begin to create difficulties? It is suggested that they may.

In *McKenna & Others v British Aluminium* [2002] Env LR 30, Neuberger J declined to strike out actions in nuisance and in *Rylands v Fletcher* which were brought on behalf of children with no proprietary interests in their home. The general nature of their complaints concerned pollution and annoyance from neighbouring industrial activities. (There were additional actions on behalf of adults with proprietary interests, and there were also actions in negligence brought on behalf of all of the claimants, and the striking out action did not apply to these.)

Neuberger J concluded that, in the absence of the Human Rights Act 1998, the actions both in nuisance and (by analogy) in *Rylands v Fletcher*, would clearly have failed and would have been struck out. This would have been the effect of the decision in *Hunter v Canary Wharf*, extended to *Rylands v Fletcher* on the authority of *Cambridge Water v Eastern Counties Leather plc*. The relationship between nuisance, and the action in *Rylands v Fletcher*, is considered in the next chapter. For now, we are interested in the way that Neuberger J addressed the impact of the Human Rights Act 1998 on what was a clear, recent, and binding authority of the House of Lords.

Neuberger J clearly considered that the common law as stated in *Hunter* might be inconsistent with the rights stated in Article 8.1 of the Convention. And he also considered it to be a matter of great uncertainty what steps would or should be taken (if any) to give effect to the relevant Convention right.

Neuberger J, at 16–17

But assuming, which I should and do for today's purposes, that it is the duty of the court to extend the common law to enable the relevant claimants to have a claim in the present case (provided, of course, that the factual basis for their claim is made out) then how the court decides to achieve that is a matter for great speculation. We are in the early days of the Human Rights Act 1998 and [o]f its application to the common law. Accordingly, as the cases where that topic has been touched on tend to show, we are very much in an area where any expression of a view must be tentative.

If the courts decide that the common law should be extended to cover the relevant claimants, whether it should be extended to cover them by reference to the law of nuisance, the law of strict liability, the law of negligence or (and I quote from the pleading) 'a common law tort analogous to nuisance' appears to me to be a matter of speculation and uncertainty.

This merely assumes that the common law ought to be changed in order to cover the particular claimants. However, in the next extract Neuberger J suggests some compelling reasons why the judgment in *Hunter v Canary Wharf* may be thought not to give effect to the Convention rights of claimants such as those in the *McKenna* case.

Neuberger J, at 17–18

There is obviously a powerful case for saying that effect has not been properly given to Article 8.1 if a person with no interest in the home, but who has lived in the home for some time and had his enjoyment of the home interfered with, is at the mercy of the person who owns the home, as the only person who can bring proceedings. I think it also questionable that it would be Article 8 compliant if, in such a case, damages are limited, as Lord Lloyd of Berwick indicated [in *Hunter v Canary Wharf*, 698H–699A]. If the law is as he stated, then in practice an infant or other person with no interest in the home, has no claim in his own right to those damages. In any event those damages would be calculated so as, in many people's eyes, not to satisfactorily reflect the damage he has suffered in his home.

In *Hunter v Canary Wharf*, a clear and unambiguous decision of the House of Lords reaffirmed that nuisance was a tort against land. That decision clearly declined to treat occupation of the 'home' as capable of being given special status within the tort of nuisance. Yet Neuberger J points out some cogent reasons why the interests of mere occupiers of the home are insufficiently protected, in terms of Article 8, by this state of affairs. The options are either to amend the tort of nuisance, which seems unlikely in the short term given the strength of the *Hunter* authority, or to concede that the tort of nuisance is incapable of protecting the rights stated in Article 8. If the latter course is taken, then how will domestic courts give effect to those rights? An option, as hinted in the first extract from Neuberger J, above, is that there might be a separate cause of action 'analogous' to nuisance. But the creation of new causes of action creates particular problems of interpretation and may well be outside the scope of what courts are empowered to do under the terms of the Human Rights Act 1998. Beale and Pittam, for example, rely on remarks of the Lord Chancellor during debates on the Human Rights Bill to emphasize that the courts 'may not act as legislators and grant new remedies for Convention rights unless the common law itself enables them to develop new rights or remedies' (Beale and Pittam, 'The Impact of the Human Rights Act 1998 on English Tort and Contract Law', in Friedmann and Barak-Erez, *Human Rights in Private Law* (Hart, 2001) at p 136).[15] Ecapsulating the issue, Neuberger J quoted from the Court of Appeal's judgment in *Douglas v Hello! Ltd* [2001] 2 WLR 992:

Keene LJ, *Douglas v Hello! Ltd*

166 Since the coming into force of the Human Rights Act 1998, the courts as a public authority cannot act in a way which is incompatible with a Convention right: (Section 6(1)). That arguably includes their activity in interpreting and developing the common law, even where no public authority is a party to litigation. Whether this extends to creating a new cause of action between private persons and bodies is more controversial, since to do so would appear to contravene the restrictions on proceedings contained in section 7(1) of the Act and on remedies in section 8(1). But it is unnecessary to determine that issue in these proceedings.

Yet the alternative, if it is considered that common law does not give effect to the Article 8 rights of claimants such as those in *McKenna*, appears to be a concession that those rights are not sufficiently met by common law. This might seem an unacceptable conclusion.

In fact, there is a further alternative, and we will see it exemplified by *Marcic v Thames Water*, below. In areas of potential conflict between tort law and Convention rights, domestic courts may instead decide that the interests of claimants have in fact been adequately 'considered' by some other applicable process, which has appropriately balanced those rights against other interests. Thus, they may argue that there is no failure to secure the Convention rights.

---

[15] This issue has been particularly pertinent in respect of the protection of privacy: Chapter 14 below.

In the case of actions in nuisance, particular questions surround the relevance of the planning process, for example. Does this process give adequate scope for consideration of the rights of individuals? In *Hunter v Canary Wharf* itself, the normal planning process had been suspended, as Docklands was an enterprise zone and an area of 'fast track' development. If the case were to be decided today, should this alter the way that the claims were treated? Lord Hoffmann said this:

> The plaintiffs may well feel that their personal convenience was temporarily sacrificed to the national interest. But this is not a good enough reason for changing the principles of the tort of nuisance that apply throughout the country.

After the Human Rights Act, this statement no longer seems unassailable. But there is an argument that the question of human rights protection should focus on reform of the planning regime, rather than on the law of nuisance.

Questions of planning were important in *Khatun v UK* (1998) 26 EHRR CD12. Here, the European Commission of Human Rights rejected as inadmissible the claims of 181 applicants, arising from the same interferences as were concerned in *Hunter v Canary Wharf*. In particular, the Commission said that it could not rule that a fair balance had not been struck between the competing interests of the individuals, and of the community as a whole. This was partly because the regeneration of Docklands was carried out in pursuit of a legitimate and important aim. Not every case in which regeneration is claimed to give rise to interference with Article 8 rights will necessarily be safe from a claim based on interference with Convention rights. The Commission noted that neither personal injury nor depreciation in the value of property was complained of in these particular cases; that the period of interference was limited to three-and-a-half years; and that there was no attempt on the applicants' part to prevent the alleged nuisance whilst it was happening. The case was very different from *McKenna v British Aluminium* [2002] Env LR 30.

Sooner or later, it seems likely that a case will arise where there is no alternative but to consider the relationship between Article 8, and the question of who can sue in nuisance.

Changes in the Relationship between Private Right and Public Interest?

We have had to consider the relationship between private and public interests at a number of points in this chapter. The enactment of the Human Rights Act 1998 may be expected to change the nature of this relationship in subtle ways.

The Human Rights Act has already led to some tentative developments in the award of damages in nuisance. The authority of *S v France* ((1990) D&R 250) was used by Buckley J in *Dennis v MoD* (extracted above) in order to effect a compromise where strong public interest justified continuing a nuisance, but on condition of paying damages to the claimant. The very relevance of public interest was, in terms of the domestic case law, doubtful.

We saw above that the compromise solution reached was based in part on obiter dicta of the Court of Appeal in *Marcic*. Were these dicta deprived of all credibility by the House of Lords' reversal of their decision? At a general level, there is certainly a conflict between the two courts' approach to the issue of Convention rights, and to the Convention jurisprudence. The Court of Appeal was of the view that new developments in the common law of nuisance might be *compelled* by the Human Rights Act, and by the need to enforce Convention rights, and they referred in this respect to the decision of the European Commission of Human Rights in

S v France. The House of Lords by contrast emphasized the margin of appreciation available to domestic legislatures which, in a case involving the status of a statutory scheme, was considered decisive.

It can be agreed that the Court of Appeal set too much store by *S v France.* In that case, the European Commission of Human Rights accepted as appropriate a decision by the French authorities to allow construction of a nuclear power station, but with the payment of compensation to S, who lived in the vicinity. Thus there was approval of a particular practice of French law. But as one commentator has succinctly put it:

Chris Miller, 'Environmental Rights in a Welfare State? A Comment on De Merieux' (2003) 23 OJLS 111–25, at 121

The fact that the Commission once viewed with approbation the payment of compensation to a French citizen, aggrieved at the arrival of a nuclear power plant, seems thin grounds for binding all statutory undertakers to one particular conception of distributive justice.

Nevertheless, the route taken in *Dennis v MoD*—with some reliance on the Court of Appeal in *Marcic*—is one potential way of giving effect to individual rights while also taking into account the public interest. Even if not compelled by the Human Rights Act, such exercises in flexibility are encouraged by it, and by the attention to a broader European case law which comes with it. So far, we have seen that lower courts and the Court of Appeal are willing to seek flexible approaches to the action in nuisance in the light of the need to give effect to Convention rights. The House of Lords' judgment in *Marcic* suggests there will be resistance to such changes in the highest court.

Marcic v Thames Water Utilities Ltd [2003] UKHL 66; [2004] 2 AC 42—Human Rights Act Elements

Extracts in Section 1.4 above dealt with the claim in nuisance and specifically with the liability of sewerage undertakers in the light of the *Leakey* line of cases. In addition, since the defendant could be treated as a 'public authority' for the purposes of section 6 of the Act, there was scope for a separate claim for damages under section 8 of the Act. This claim had succeeded before the first instance judge, Sir Richard Havery QC. The Court of Appeal did not disagree with his analysis, although the damages they awarded for nuisance afforded just satisfaction for the infringement and they therefore commented only briefly on this aspect of the case. The House of Lords rejected the claim for damages under the Human Rights Act for infringement of Convention rights, just as they had rejected the claim in nuisance. The extracts below deal with the Human Rights Act claim. As with the claim in nuisance, the statutory context was treated as decisive.

Lord Nicholls

The claim under the Human Rights Act 1998

37   I turn to Mr Marcic's claim under the Human Rights Act 1998. His claim is that as a public authority within the meaning of section 6 of the Human Rights Act 1998 Thames Water has acted unlawfully. Thames Water has conducted itself in a way which is incompatible with

Mr Marcic's Convention rights under article 8 of the Convention and article 1 of the First Protocol to the Convention. His submission was to the following effect. The flooding of Mr Marcic's property falls within the first paragraph of article 8 and also within article 1 of the First Protocol. That was common ground between the parties. Direct and serious interference of this nature with a person's home is prima facie a violation of a person's right to respect for his private and family life (article 8) and of his entitlement to the peaceful enjoyment of his possessions (article 1 of the First Protocol). The burden of justifying this interference rests on Thames Water. At the trial of the preliminary issues Thames Water failed to discharge this burden. The trial judge found that the system of priorities used by Thames Water in deciding whether to carry out flood alleviation works might be entirely fair. The judge also said that on the limited evidence before him it was not possible to decide this issue, or to decide whether for all its apparent faults the system fell within the wide margin of discretion open to Thames Water and the director: [2002] QB 929, 964, para 102.

38 To my mind the fatal weakness in this submission is the same as that afflicting Mr Marcic's claim in nuisance: it does not take sufficient account of the statutory scheme under which Thames Water is operating the offending sewers. The need to adopt some system of priorities for building more sewers is self-evident. So is the need for the system to be fair. A fair system of priorities necessarily involves balancing many intangible factors. Whether the system adopted by a sewerage undertaker is fair is a matter inherently more suited for decision by the industry regulator than by a court. And the statutory scheme so provides. Moreover, the statutory scheme provides a remedy where a system of priorities is not fair. An unfair system of priorities means that a sewerage undertaker is not properly discharging its statutory drainage obligation so far as those who are being treated unfairly are concerned. The statute provides what should happen in these circumstances. The director is charged with deciding whether to make an enforcement order in respect of a sewerage undertaker's failure to drain property properly. Parliament entrusted this decision to the director, not the courts.

39 What happens in practice accords with this statutory scheme. When people affected by sewer flooding complain to the director he considers whether he should require the sewerage undertaker to take remedial action. Before doing so he considers, among other matters, the severity and history of the problem in the context of that undertaker's sewer flooding relief programme, as allowed for in its current price limits. In many cases the company agrees to take action, but sometimes he accepts that a solution is not possible in the short term.

40 So the claim based on the Human Rights Act 1998 raises a broader issue: is the statutory scheme as a whole, of which this enforcement procedure is part, Convention-compliant? Stated more specifically and at the risk of over-simplification, is the statutory scheme unreasonable in its impact on Mr Marcic and other householders whose properties are periodically subjected to sewer flooding?

41 The recent decision of the European Court of Human Rights, sitting as a Grand Chamber, in *Hatton v United Kingdom* (Application No 36022/97) The Times, 10 July 2003 confirms how courts should approach questions such as these. In *Hatton's* case the applicants lived near Heathrow airport. They claimed that the Government's policy on night flights at Heathrow violated their rights under article 8. The court emphasised "the fundamentally subsidiary nature" of the Convention. National authorities have "direct democratic legitimation" and are in principle better placed than an international court to evaluate local needs and conditions. In matters of general policy, on which opinions within a democratic society may reasonably differ widely, "the role of the domestic policy maker should be given special weight": see paragraph 97. A fair balance must be struck between the interests of the individual and of the community as a whole.

42   In the present case the interests Parliament had to balance included, on the one hand, the interests of customers of a company whose properties are prone to sewer flooding and, on the other hand, all the other customers of the company whose properties are drained through the company's sewers. The interests of the first group conflict with the interests of the company's customers as a whole in that only a minority of customers suffer sewer flooding but the company's customers as a whole meet the cost of building more sewers. As already noted, the balance struck by the statutory scheme is to impose a general drainage obligation on a sewerage undertaker but to entrust enforcement of this obligation to an independent regulator who has regard to all the different interests involved. Decisions of the director are of course subject to an appropriately penetrating degree of judicial review by the courts. 43 In principle this scheme seems to me to strike a reasonable balance. Parliament acted well within its bounds as policy maker. In Mr Marcic's case matters plainly went awry. It cannot be acceptable that in 2001, several years after Thames Water knew of Mr Marcic's serious problems, there was still no prospect of the necessary work being carried out for the foreseeable future. At times Thames Water handled Mr Marcic's complaint in a tardy and insensitive fashion. But the malfunctioning of the statutory scheme on this occasion does not cast doubt on its overall fairness as a scheme. A complaint by an individual about his particular case can, and should, be pursued with the director pursuant to the statutory scheme, with the long stop availability of judicial review. That remedial avenue was not taken in this case.

44   I must add that one aspect of the statutory scheme as presently administered does cause concern. This is the uncertain position regarding payment of compensation to those who suffer flooding while waiting for flood alleviation works to be carried out. . . .

45   It seems to me that, in principle, if it is not practicable for reasons of expense to carry out remedial works for the time being, those who enjoy the benefit of effective drainage should bear the cost of paying some compensation to those whose properties are situated lower down in the catchment area and who, in consequence, have to endure intolerable sewer flooding, whether internal or external. As the Court of Appeal noted, the flooding is the consequence of the benefit provided to those making use of the system: [2002] QB 929, 1001, para 113. The minority who suffer damage and disturbance as a consequence of the inadequacy of the sewerage system ought not to be required to bear an unreasonable burden. This is a matter the director and others should reconsider in the light of the facts in the present case.

46   For these reasons I consider the claim under the Human Rights Act 1998 is ill-founded. The scheme set up by the 1991 Act is Convention-compliant. The scheme provides a remedy for persons in Mr Marcic's unhappy position, but Mr Marcic chose not to avail himself of this remedy.

47   Accordingly this appeal should be allowed. Save as to costs, the order of the Court of Appeal should be set aside and the order of the trial judge varied so as to answer all the preliminary issues in the negative. As to costs, the House gave leave to Thames Water to appeal on terms that the existing costs orders in the courts below remain undisturbed and that Thames Water pay Mr Marcic's costs in the House in any event.

Lord Hoffmann

71   That leaves only the question of whether the remedies provided under the 1991 Act do not adequately safeguard Mr Marcic's Convention rights to the privacy of his home and the protection of his property. The judge, who found for Mr Marcic on this ground, did not have the

benefit of the decision of the Grand Chamber of the European Court of Human Rights in *Hatton v United Kingdom* (Application No 36022/97) The Times, 10 July 2003. That decision makes it clear that the Convention does not accord absolute protection to property or even to residential premises. It requires a fair balance to be struck between the interests of persons whose homes and property are affected and the interests of other people, such as customers and the general public. National institutions, and particularly the national legislature, are accorded a broad discretion in choosing the solution appropriate to their own society or creating the machinery for doing so. There is no reason why Parliament should not entrust such decisions to an independent regulator such as the director. He is a public authority within the meaning of the 1998 Act and has a duty to act in accordance with Convention rights. If (which there is no reason to suppose) he has exceeded the broad margin of discretion allowed by the Convention, Mr Marcic will have a remedy under section 6 of the 1998 Act. But that question is not before your Lordships. His case is that he has a Convention right to have the decision as to whether new sewers should be constructed made by a court in a private action for nuisance rather than by the director in the exercise of his powers under the 1991 Act. In my opinion there is no such right.

Commentary

When considering compatability with Convention rights, the House of Lords declined to consider the acts of the defendants as sewerage undertakers, but focused instead on the sufficiency of the statutory scheme as a whole. Although it was considered by Lord Nicholls that in this case 'matters plainly went awry', the existence of a statutory scheme for complaints and enforcement under the Water Industry Act 1991 in effect shielded the Water Company itself from action under the Human Rights Act 1998. Furthermore, the statutory scheme was considered to be Convention-compliant despite concerns, again expressed by Lord Nicholls at para 44, surrounding the availability of compensation to those suffering external flooding. It was also emphasized that the appropriate route for challenging the operation of the scheme was by judicial review as against the director, *not* in common law (or under the Human Rights Act) directly against the sewerage undertaker.

The members of the House of Lords placed considerable emphasis upon the then very recent decision of the Grand Chamber of the Court of Human Rights in *Hatton v UK* ((2003) 37 EHRR 28). This, they argued, showed that in arriving at a fair balance between the interests of people whose homes and property are affected by an activity, and the interests of other people (and the public) in the activity in question, national institutions have a broad discretion in choosing the appropriate machinery and the appropriate solution to achieve this balance.

The precise use made of *Hatton* is not beyond dispute. It is true that the Grand Chamber decided that the national authority should be left a choice in the means by which it achieved a balance between different interests. Nevertheless, the Grand Chamber did still address the *substantive* question of whether or not the solutions in question had achieved a fair balance. It did not confine itself to the procedural question of whether appropriate machinery exists for determining what the appropriate balance might be.

123 . . . While the State is required to give due consideration to the particular interests the respect for which it is obliged to secure by virtue of Art.8, it must in principle be left a choice between different ways and means of meeting this obligation. The Court's supervisory function being of a subsidiary nature, it is limited to reviewing whether or not the particular solution adopted can be regarded as striking a fair balance.

Furthermore, the *Hatton* case was not a situation in which priorities needed to be set for the use of resources, so that some needs would go entirely unmet. Rather, it was a case of serious disagreement over what *level* of protection against noise from night flying was acceptable. It was thus the *substance* of the regime adopted, in terms of how it measured noise disturbance and what criteria were set for its control, that was challenged:

Hatton v UK (2003) 37 EHRR 28

125 . . . [The Court] notes the dispute between the parties as to whether aircraft movements or quota counts should be employed as the appropriate yardstick for measuring night noise. However, it finds no indication that the authorities' decision to introduce a regime based on the quota count system was as such incompatible with Art.8

In considering whether an appropriate balance had been struck, the Court also stated that it was relevant to consider the impact upon the applicants' interests. For example:

127 . . . The Court also notes that the applicants do not contest the substance of the Government's claim that house prices in the areas in which they live have not been adversely affected by the increase in night noise. The Court considers it reasonable, in determining the impact of a general policy on individuals in a particular area, to take into account the individuals' ability to leave the area.

It was relevant that the applicants' interests were not entirely disregarded, and it was also relevant that they may not be so adversely affected as first appeared, if they were able to move out of the area. None of this is quite the same as saying that a fair mechanism for deciding priorites will suffice, or that it is sufficient to entrust the decision to a regulator. The truth is that the House of Lords preferred that the issues concerning Article 8 be considered in a public law context, if necessary through judicial review, and not through an action in the tort of nuisance.

There is also a question over the proper role of the 'margin of appreciation' in a *national* (as opposed to an international) court. Hart and Wheeler, for example, suggest in their analysis of *Hatton v UK* that a national court should be less deferential when asked to rule on similar issues: 'Night Flights and Environmental Human Rights' (2004) 16 JEL 132–9, at 138.

3. PUBLIC NUISANCE

3.1 GENERAL STATEMENT—VARIETIES OF PUBLIC NUISANCE

Public nuisance is a crime at common law. Although it no doubt provides a very useful tool for the prosecutor, it has been doubted whether it is an appropriate element in modern criminal law. Historically, it has been broad, impressionistic, and even more indistinct in its boundaries than the tort of private nuisance.

Prior to *Rimmington and Goldstein*, the most authoritative definition of the **crime** of public nuisance was as follows:

Archbold's Criminal Pleading and Practice, 2005, para 31.40

A person is guilty of a public nuisance (also known as common nuisance), who (a) does an act not warranted by law, or (b) omits to discharge a legal duty, if the effect of the act or omission is to endanger the life, health, property, morals or comfort of the public, or to obstruct the public in the exercise or enjoyment of rights common to all her Majesty's subjects.

So broad is the potential scope of this definition, J. R. Spencer in his much-cited study of public nuisance ('Public Nuisance—A Critical Examination' [1989] CLJ 55) wondered whether there was really much need for any other criminal law at all. He concluded however that a trimmed-down version of public nuisance would have a valuable gap-filling role for use against behaviour which seriously threatens public health or the environment, but which fails to fit with the definition of more specific crimes.

In *R v Rimmington and Goldstein* [2005] UKHL 63; [2006] 1 AC 459, two appellants challenged their convictions of offences of public nuisance, arguing (amongst other things) that the offence was so loosely defined that it violated Article 7 ECHR:

Article 7   No punishment without law

1. No one shall be held guilty of any criminal offence on account of any act or omission which did not constitute a criminal offence under national or international law at the time when it was committed. Nor shall a heavier penalty be imposed than the one that was applicable at the time the criminal offence was committed.

The House of Lords determined that the crime of public nuisance was tolerably clear, provided the reference to 'public morals' was removed from the standard definition. Thus the ambit of the offence has been reduced. Equally, the House proposed that a common law offence should only very rarely be used where statutory offences were applicable to the same conduct.[16]

Lord Bingham of Cornhill, *R v Rimmington and Goldstein* [2006] 1 AC 459

30   There is in my opinion considerable force in the appellants' second contention under this head. Where Parliament has defined the ingredients of an offence, perhaps stipulating what shall and shall not be a defence, and has prescribed a mode of trial and a maximum penalty, it must ordinarily be proper that conduct falling within that definition should be prosecuted for the statutory offence and not for a common law offence which may or may not provide the

---

[16] The defendants also escaped conviction because there was not a sufficient 'public' dimension to their acts, or in other words no 'common injury'. One had sent offensive racist literature through the post to prominent people; the other had posted salt to a friend in New York as a practical joke, and this had caused an anthrax alert when it spilt out of the envelope at a sorting office.

same defences and for which the potential penalty is unlimited. . . . I would not go to the length of holding that conduct may never be lawfully prosecuted as a generally-expressed common law crime where it falls within the terms of a specific statutory provision, but good practice and respect for the primacy of statute do in my judgment require that conduct falling within the terms of a specific statutory provision should be prosecuted under that provision unless there is good reason for doing otherwise.

31   It follows from the conclusions already expressed in paras 29 to 30 above that the cir cumstances in which, in future, there can properly be resort to the common law crime of public nuisance will be relatively rare. It may very well be, as suggested by J R Spencer in his article cited in para 6 above, at p 83, that "There is surely a strong case for abolishing the crime of public nuisance". But as the courts have no power to create new offences (see para 33 below), so they have no power to abolish existing offences. That is a task for Parliament, following careful consideration (perhaps undertaken, in the first instance, by the Law Commission) whether there are aspects of the public interest which the crime of public nuisance has a continuing role to protect. It is not in my view open to the House in resolving these appeals to conclude that the common law crime of causing a public nuisance no longer exists.

The end result of *Rimmington and Goldstein* is that the crime of public nuisance is more closely defined, and less flexible.

For tort lawyers, the issues that arise from public nuisance are narrower and somewhat more controllable, even if they are the product of historical accident and therefore do not conform to tidy categorization (F. Newark, 'The Boundaries of Nuisance' (1949) 65 LQR 480). From the tort lawyer's point of view, it is probably easiest to divide public nuisances into two types, which are important to tort law for different reasons. The first category consists of a relatively minor subset consisting of those public nuisances which could be said to be made up of a series of private nuisances. Where a sufficiently substantial number of people suffer relevant interferences, then the interferences will amount to a 'public' nuisance. As a matter of procedure, the Attorney-General may then bring a civil action for an injunction. This type of 'public' nuisance, which is public because of the numbers of people involved, was summed up in *AG v PYA Quarries* [1957] 2 QB 169, 187:

Romer LJ

Some public nuisances (for example, the pollution of rivers) can often be established without the necessity of calling a number of individual complainants as witnesses. In general, how-ever, a public nuisance is proved by the cumulative effect which it is shown to have had on the people living within its sphere of influence. In other words, a normal and legitimate way of proving a public nuisance is to prove a sufficiently large collection of private nuisances.

In such a case, the action is brought by the Attorney-General, but the case is one of 'amalgamated' private nuisances. We have already seen that some cases brought in public nuisance therefore provide important authority concerning the principles of private nuisance. An example is *Gillingham v Medway Chatham Dock Co* [1993] QB 343, extracted above, which also exemplifies that local authorities may bring such actions pursuant to section 222 of the Local Government Act 1972.

AG v PYA Quarries is also a leading authority on the question of what constitutes a sufficient 'class' of people for the purposes of an action in public nuisance, a question of importance to all cases of public nuisance.

Romer LJ, at 184

It is clear . . . that any nuisance is "public" which materially affects the reasonable comfort and convenience of life of a class of Her Majesty's subjects. The sphere of the nuisance may be described generally as "the neighbourhood"; but the question whether the local community within that sphere comprises a sufficient number of persons to constitute a class of the public is a question of fact in every case. It is not necessary, in my judgment, to prove that every member of the class has been injuriously affected; it is sufficient to show that a representative cross-section of the class has been so affected for an injunction to issue.

Denning LJ, at 191

So here I decline to answer the question how many people are necessary to make up her Majesty's subjects generally. I prefer to look to the reason of the thing and to say that a public nuisance is a nuisance which is so widespread in its range or so indiscriminate in its effect that it would not be reasonable to expect one person to take proceedings on his own responsibility to put a stop to it, but that it should be taken on the responsibility of the community at large.

Cases of 'amalgamated private nuisance', and therefore of overlap between private and public nuisance, are however the exception and not the rule. The second (and more typical) sort of public nuisance concerns interference with the 'comfort and convenience' of a class of Her Majesty's subjects. Public nuisance is thus broader in its coverage than private nuisance, for it encompasses damage to a far wider range of interests. A particular subset of such cases involves obstructions to or endangerment on the highway. Again, public nuisances of this type are actionable by the Attorney-General in civil proceedings (in addition to criminal proceedings), where injunctions may be awarded. Historically such 'relator' actions were often brought by the Attorney-General on behalf of specific individuals.

J. T. R. Spencer [1989] CLJ 55, 68

On the face of it the idea of the Attorney-General bringing civil proceedings on behalf of a private citizen in order to suppress a criminal offence seems a doubly curious notion. The Attorney-General is the legal representative of the King, not of the private citizen, and if he did wish to do the citizen a good turn by suppressing a criminal offence we would have expected him to prosecute and not to go to the civil courts.

According to Spencer, these actions soon supplanted criminal prosecutions as the favoured method of restraining threats to public health or obstructions to the highway. He offers some practical reasons why this may have been the case:

> No doubt the main reason that this occurred is that in most of these cases the plaintiff or pros-
> ecutor wanted to put an end to an unsatisfactory state of affairs rather than to punish the
> author, and an injunction did this better than a prosecution . . . There were subsidiary reasons,
> however, and one of these was the increasing part played by corporations in spreading pollu-
> tion; first as manufacturers, and then as builders of sewers.
>
> A corporation was difficult to prosecute, but quite easy to sue.' (p 70)

Secondly though, a public nuisance which affects the comfort or convenience of a sufficient class may also be actionable by an individual seeking damages. Such cases are clearly of direct concern to tort lawyers. In order to recover compensation in an action for private nuisance, the individual will need to show that he or she has suffered 'special damage'.

3.2 INDIVIDUALS SUFFERING 'SPECIAL DAMAGE'

Special damage must be 'particular, direct, and substantial' (*Benjamin v Storr* (1873–74) LR 9 CP 400, Brett J; Buckley, *The Law of Nuisance*, 2nd edn, pp 74–5). A very broad range of damage is actionable, including purely financial losses. In *Tate and Lyle v GLC* [1983] 2 AC 509, the defendants caused siltation of the River Thames and an obstruction to the public right of navigation. There was no damage to any property owned by the defendants, but they were put to particular expense in dredging the river around their jetties in order to continue their business. While such a claim would surely fail in negligence, the costs incurred were sufficient to represent a special damage for the purposes of public nuisance.

Strictly speaking, 'particular' damage should be damage which is distinct in type from that suffered by other members of the public. Mere inconvenience for example, if it is suffered by the public generally, will not be sufficient to give rise to a claim for special damage. On the other hand, proven pecuniary loss will normally bring the claimant within the head of special damage, as illustrated not only by *Tate and Lyle v GLC*, but also by the later siltation case of *Jan d Nul v NV Royale Belge* [2000] 2 Lloyd's Rep 700 (a claim for lost profits).

3.3 STRUCTURES ADJOINING OR OVERHANGING THE HIGHWAY

A number of authorities concern dangerous structures adjoining or overhanging the highway. These authorities appear to conflict concerning the relevant standard of liability. In *Tarry v Ashton* [1876] 1 QBD 314, the defendant was considered to be under a 'non-delegable duty of care' to repair a lamp overhanging the highway, and was therefore liable to the plaintiff for personal injuries suffered even though she had recently paid reputable contractors to repair the lamp. Perhaps the defendant could reasonably be expected to have been aware of the continuing hazard presented by the lamp. If so, then the later case of *Wringe v Cohen* [1940] 1 KB 229 went further, in that there was liability for artificial structures adjoining the highway whether the defendant could reasonably have known of their condition, or not. By contrast, in *Noble v Harrison* [1926] 2 KB 332, a landowner was found to be not liable when a branch from one of his trees damaged the plaintiff's vehicle, on the basis that the defect in the tree was not reasonably discoverable. On the face of it, a different standard of liability will apply depending on whether the damage is caused by an artificial structure (*Wringe v Cohen*), or by a natural feature (*Noble v Harrison*). This scarcely seems defensible, and it has been proposed (Buckley, *The Law of Nuisance*, 2nd edn, p 84) that the interpretation in *Wringe v Cohen* does not represent the law. To accept this would also bring the law concerning structures overhanging the highway into line with the law of nuisance more generally concerning hazards which are not originated by the occupier. It was the view of A. L. Goodhart, writing in 1930, that the following broad and simple conclusion could be drawn in respect of both public and private nuisance:

A. L. Goodhart, 'Liability for Things Naturally on the Land' (1930) 4 CLJ 13, 30

The correct principle seems to be that an occupier of land is liable for a nuisance of which he knows, or ought to know, whether that nuisance is caused by himself, his predecessor in title, a third person or by nature. Whether a natural condition is or is not a nuisance is, of course, a question of fact. Is the injury caused by the natural condition more than a reasonable neighbour can be asked to bear under the rule of 'live and let live'? In other words, the ordinary rules of nuisance apply in the case of natural conditions. As we must all bear with our neighbour's piano-playing so we must also submit to his thistle down. This does not mean that we have no remedy if he introduces a large orchestra, or if he allows his tree, even of natural growth, to remain in a dangerous condition along the highway.

This statement was endorsed as correct so far as public nuisance is concerned by Kennedy LJ in the recent public nuisance case of *Wandsworth LBC v Railtrack plc* [2001] EWCA Civ 1236; [2002] 2 WLR 512, para [9].

4. THE ENVIRONMENTAL TORT?

On a number of occasions, we have mentioned the potential 'environmental protection' function of both public and private nuisance; and we have also explored cases (such as *Marcic* and *Hatton*) which involve, even if tangentially, the question of environmental rights. Because of the subject matter of the nuisance action—polluted water, noise, smells, acid smuts, damaged trees, and so on—actions in nuisance are generally recognized to have played some part in the battle against pollution, particularly before the emergence of that range of measures which can be loosely referred to as 'environmental law'. Even so, the action in nuisance suffers from a number of limitations which have meant that the tort actions covered here and in the subsequent chapter will never be a central plank in environmental protection. Some of these are practical, concerning means of enforcement and the essentially reactive nature of an action in common law. Others are a question of more fundamental principle.

Private nuisance is concerned with protection of rights over land. Environmental law is usually thought to concern a more general public interest in protection of the environment. The question therefore is simple—how can the protection of certain selected private interests be an effective means of securing environmental protection? To the extent that the interests of property owners overlap with environmental interests, this could be described as coincidental. Nevertheless, such overlap undoubtedly exists in numerous cases of pollution, for example. Many aspects of this overlap are considered by contributors to Lowry and Edmunds, *Environmental Protection and the Common Law* (2002). We will see below that some commentators would go further than this, and argue that property rights have much more than a coincidental relationship with environmental protection.

Public nuisance raises a rather different issue, since it is undoubtedly concerned with public health. Public health is a precursor of environmental law and in many respects overlaps with it, but it is still a relatively limited concern when compared with environmental protection in its broadest and most developed modern guise. For example, in the case of statutory nuisances under the Environmental Protection Act 1990 (sections 79–82), the historical link to public health is considered to give rise to certain limitations in the environmental protection function of the statutory nuisance provisions.

As noted above, there continues to be lively disagreement about the degree to which the action in private nuisance, in particular, can play a part in environmental protection. Some commentators argue that the protection of property rights by affected individuals is an effective means of attaining environmental protection (see for example Brubaker, *Property Rights in the Defence of Nature*). This challenges the prevailing orthodoxy, that environmental law must entail the deterrence of private pollution through public law means. Other commentators argue that nuisance is potentially an effective means of attaining an *efficient* level of environmental protection, which is argued to be the only appropriate measure. (The latter argument is derived in part from Ronald Coase's classic essay, 'The Problem of Social Cost' (1960) 3 JLE 1.) And there is also a contrary and subtle argument that philosophically speaking, environmental protection is misunderstood if it is cast primarily as a welfare-based public interest issue. Rather, environmental law should be understood precisely through a modified concept of property rights which recognizes the intrinsic rather than the purely instrumental value of natural resources (Coyle and Morrow, *Philosophical Foundations of Environmental Law*).

The problem is that the law of nuisance as it stands does not entirely fit either of the last two conceptual arguments in favour of its use in environmental protection. As regards Coyle and Morrow's argument, we have seen that the primary focus of contemporary nuisance law is on 'use and enjoyment' of land, rather than on intrinsic value. And as regards the argument that nuisance may provide a distinct and independent property-based system for achieving optimum environmental protection, we have seen that the case law on nuisance is pervasively influenced by questions of public interest, by ideas of welfare quite independent of the satisfaction of individual preferences, and of course by deference to legislative intent. To borrow the words of David Campbell, 'Of Coase and Corn: A (Sort Of) Defence of Private Nuisance' (2000) 63 MLR 197–215, nuisance does not in its current form provide any sort of 'bright-line' method of attaining environmental protection, independent of perceived judgments of public interest for resolving environmental issues. (Campbell suggests that nuisance ought to be reformed in order to do just this. In effect, he suggests that judgments as to public interest should be removed from the ambit of nuisance so that through the claims of those with property rights it may better perform its role of enhancing welfare, including environmental protection. This is of course a deeply controversial proposition.)

The limitations to the common law actions are mostly practical rather than principled:

J. Steele, 'Private Law and the Environment, Nuisance in Context' (1995) 15 LS 236–59, 239

Common law suffers from severe structural obstacles to fulfilling any central role in environmental protection. In particular, it is essentially reactive, providing compensation for past damage, or injunctions to prevent present damage from continuing; its enforcement processes are unpredictable, depending on litigants to come forward with both the will and the means to proceed; and it is also an expensive process for all concerned.

The expensive and unpredictable process of common law litigation, dependent on open-textured notions such as 'reasonableness' and on the resolve, resources, and qualifying property rights of affected parties, is not in itself the most effective way to achieve fundamental environmental improvements. Even in the apparent heyday of the nuisance actions, the nineteenth century, our focus on decided cases such as *St Helen's v Tipping* is misleading, for that case is an isolated instance of a sufficiently determined litigant: see further J. P. S. McLaren, 'Nuisance Law and the Industrial Revolution—Some Lessons From Social History' (1983) 3 OJLS 155; J. P. S. McLaren, 'The Common Law Nuisance Actions and the Environmental Battle—Well-Tempered Swords or Broken Reeds?' (1972) 10 Osgoode Hall LJ 505; A. W. B. Simpson, 'Victorian Judges and the Problem of Social Cost', in *Leading Cases in the Common Law* (1995).

It was noted above that whether protection of property rights is likely to assist in environmental protection is in any event a controversial question. Environmental law is typically understood to place restrictions on the rights of property owners. Now however, changes are under way in the relationship between nuisance and environmental law, thanks to the development of case law on environmental questions derived from the European Convention on Human Rights. This evolving case law, together with the impact of the Human Rights Act 1998 discussed in Section 2 of this chapter, could ultimately transform nuisance law. There is certainly an area in which environmental law, and nuisance law, are capable of a new overlap.

FURTHER READING

Ashworth, A., 'Public Nuisance: Elements of Offence' (2006) Crim LR 153.

Buckley, R.A., *The Law of Nuisance* (2nd edn, London: Butterworths, 1991).

Campbell, D., 'Of Coase and Corn: a (Sort of) Defence of Private Nuisance' (2000) 63 MLR 197.

Coase, R., 'The Problem of Social Cost' (1960) 3 JLE 1.

Crabb, L., 'The Property Torts' (2003) 11 *Tort L Rev* 104–18.

DeMerieux, M., 'Deriving Environmental Rights from the European Convention on Human Rights and Fundamental Freedoms' (2001) 3 OJLS 521.

Fairgrieve, D., *State Liability in Tort: A Comparative Law Study* (Oxford: OUP, 2003).

Gearty, C., 'The Place of Private Nuisance in a Modern Law of Tort' (1989) 48 CLJ 214–42.

Getzler, J., *A History of Water Rights at Common Law* (Oxford: OUP, 2004)

Goodhart, A.L., 'Liability for Things Naturally on the Land' (1930) 4 CLJ 13.

Hart, D., and Wheeler, M., 'Night Flights and Strasbourg's Retreat from Environmental Human Rights' (2004) 16 JEL 100–39.

Hunt, M., 'The Effect on the Law of Obligations', in Markesinis (ed.), *The Impact of the Human Rights Bill on English Law* (Oxford: Hart Publishing, 1998).

Hunt, M., 'The Horizontal Effect of the Human Rights Act' [1998] PL 423.

Jolowicz, J.A., 'Damages in Equity—A Study of Lord Cairns' Act' [1975] CLJ 224.

Lowry, J., and Edmunds, R., *Environmental Protection and the Common Law* (Oxford: Hart Publishing, 2000).

McLaren, J.P.S., 'Nuisance Law and the Industrial Revolution—Some Lessons from Social History' (1983) 3 OJLS 155.

McLaren, J.P.S., 'The Common Law Nuisance Actions and the Environmental Battle—Well-Tempered Swords or Broken Reeds?' (1972) 10 Osgoode Hall LJ 505.

Miller, C., 'Environmental Rights in a Welfare State? A Comment on DeMerieux' (2003) 23 OJLS 111–25.

Newark, F.H., 'The Boundaries of Nuisance' (1949) 65 LQR 480.

Ogus, A.I., and Richardson, G.M., 'Economics and the Environment—A Study of Private Nuisance' [1977] CLJ 248.

Pontin, B., 'Tort Law and Victorian Government Growth: The Historiographical Significance of Tort in the Shadow of Chemical Pollution and Factory Safety Regulation' (1998) 18 OJLS 661–80.

Simpson, A.W.B., 'Victorian Judges and the Problem of Social Cost', in *Leading Cases in the Common Law* (Oxford: OUP, 1995).

Spencer, J., 'Public Nuisance—A Critical Examination' [1989] CLJ 55.

Steele, J., 'Private Law and the Environment: Nuisance in Context' (1995) 15 LS 236.

Taggart, M., *Private Property and the Abuse of Rights in Victorian England* (Oxford: OUP, 2002).

11

RYLANDS V FLETCHER AND STRICT LIABILITY

CENTRAL ISSUES

i) The 'rule in *Rylands v Fletcher*' appears to determine that there is liability for damage done by the escape of dangerous things accumulated on one's land, regardless of fault. The rule applies only if those things were accumulated for one's own purposes, and were not accumulated in the course of a 'natural' use of land. The strictness of the rule is mitigated by a number of defences and criteria, some of which appear incompatible with the underlying logic of the rule itself.

ii) The zone of application of *Rylands v Fletcher* has been in decline pretty much since its inception. The probable reason is unease, even in the nineteenth century, with the idea of liability in the absence of any personal fault. Yet the existence of strict liability for dangerous activities (including 'accumulations') is far from being outdated. Despite the apparent conflict in principle between negligence and strict liability, in practice the greater problem is not so much conflict, but overlap. Arguably, the tort of negligence can adapt to impose liability in situations

far removed from cases of individual fault, including the situations covered by *Rylands v Fletcher*. This was the view of the Australian High Court, in *Burnie Port Authority v General Jones Pty Ltd*. The view that *Rylands v Fletcher* merely introduces incoherence into an area which negligence has the flexibility to handle was also put forward as long ago as 1916—well before the English decision of *Donoghue v Stevenson*—by Dean Thayer of the Harvard Law School ('Liability Without Fault' (1916) 29 *Harv L Rev* 801–15). His forward-thinking account was influential in the development of the Australian High Court's solution.

iii) In England and Wales, a less purposive approach has dominated. Through historical analysis of its origins, *Rylands* has been interpreted as an aspect of nuisance relating to isolated escapes. On the face of it, this interpretation should make the rule more independent of fault-based thinking, but in practice the main impact has been that extra limits are imposed on the operation of the rule, for example in respect of the kinds of damage that are recoverable.

iv) The growth both of strict liability statutes, and of negligence liability divorced from fault, underline that areas of strict liability are entirely acceptable to contemporary thinking. But the growth of these alternative methods of imposing strict liability have left the rule itself exposed as arbitrary, limited, and in this sense archaic. Studying the lingering decline of *Rylands v Fletcher* is a good way of approaching the subtle relationship between negligence, and strict liability; and also allows us to question the underlying purposes of strict liability in tort (see also Chapters 9 and 15).

1. INTRODUCTION

In England and Wales, the 'rule in *Rylands v Fletcher*' is now treated as a branch of the tort of private nuisance. In Australia, the rule has been largely absorbed into negligence, which now provides an alternative route to liability without personal fault where some hazardous activities are concerned. In the United States, a specific and limited principle of strict liability has evolved in respect of 'dangerous' activities. This has clearly developed from the rule in *Rylands v Fletcher* but it is not confined by the limits associated with nuisance, particularly in respect of the types of damage that are recoverable. In Scotland, the rule does not apply: *RHM Bakeries (Scotland) Ltd v Strathclyde Regional Council* 1985 SLT 214, 217)). *Rylands* is unlike most cases of nuisance because it deals with 'isolated escapes' (more akin to the typical one-off event covered by the majority of negligence cases), and furthermore it deals with cases of actual damage, rather than general 'interference'. As such it provides a direct alternative to negligence in some circumstances.

This chapter falls into three parts. The first part considers the case of *Rylands v Fletcher* itself and the origins of the rule. The second identifies the elements of the rule so far as this can be done despite the confused case law. The third part turns to the categorization and boundaries of the rule today. Here we will extract the major English cases of *Cambridge Water Company v Eastern Counties Leather plc*, and *Transco v Stockport MBC*, which treat *Rylands* as an aspect of nuisance; and (by contrast) the Australian High Court's decision in *Burnie Port Authority v General Jones Pty Ltd*, which deals with a very similar problem through the tort of negligence.

2. ORIGINS OF THE RULE: *RYLANDS & ANOTHER V FLETCHER*

Rylands & Another v Fletcher (Court of Exchequer Chamber LR 1 Ex 265 (1866); House of Lords LR 3 HL 330 (1868))

The plaintiffs were tenants of land on which they worked a mine. Their workings extended (under licence) through underground shafts to an area beneath neighbouring land. The defendants were neighbouring mill owners. They arranged for the construction of a reservoir in connection with the operation of their mill. There were old shafts under the reservoir, and these shafts connected with the plaintiffs' mine shafts.

Because of the old shafts beneath the ground, the reservoir was not strong enough to bear the pressure of water when filled. As a consequence, it burst downwards and the water flooded the plaintiffs' mineshafts. The action proceeded on the basis that there had been no negligence on the part of the defendants themselves. It would appear that they had employed a competent engineer and competent contractors. However, it was also stated that reasonable and proper care had not been used by those individuals employed in the planning and construction of the reservoir. The majority of the Court of Exchequer held that the failure of due care on the part of those employed to construct the reservoir did not, in the absence of any notice to the defendants, affect the defendants with any liability. The plaintiffs appealed to the Court of Exchequer Chamber.

Court of Exchequer Chamber

Blackburn J (reading the judgment of the Court)

The plaintiff, though free from all blame on his part, must bear the loss, unless he can establish that it was the consequence of some default for which the defendants are reponsible. The question of law therefore arises, what is the obligation which the law casts on a person who, like the defendants, lawfully brings on his land something which, though harmless whilst it remains there, will naturally do mischief if it escape out of his land. It is agreed on all hands that he must take care to keep in that which he has brought on the land and keeps there, in order that it may not escape and damage his neighbours, but the question arises whether the duty which the law casts upon him, under such circumstances, is an absolute duty to keep it in at his peril, or is, as the majority of the Court of Exchequer have thought, merely a duty to take all reasonable and prudent precautions, in order to keep it in, but no more. If the first be the law, the person who has brought on his land and kept there something dangerous, and failed to keep it in, is responsible for all the natural consequences of its escape. If the second be the limit of his duty, he would not be answerable except on proof of negligence, and consequently would not be answerable for escape arising from any latent defect which ordinary prudence and skill could not detect.

Supposing the second to be the correct view of the law, a further question arises subsidiary to the first, viz., whether the defendants are not so far identified with the contractors whom they employed, as to be responsible for the consequences of their want of care and skill in making the reservoir in fact insufficient with reference to the old shafts, of the existence of which they were aware, though they had not ascertained where the shafts went to.

We think that the true rule of law is, that the person who for his own purposes brings on his lands and collects and keeps there anything likely to do mischief if it escapes, must keep it in at his peril, and, if he does not do so, is primâ facie answerable for all the damage which is the natural consequence of its escape. He can excuse himself by shewing that the escape was owing to the plaintiff's default; or perhaps that the escape was the consequence of vis major, or the act of God; but as nothing of this sort exists here, it is unnecessary to inquire what excuse would be sufficient. The general rule, as above stated, seems on principle just. The person whose grass or corn is eaten down by the escaping cattle of his neighbour, or whose mine is flooded by the water from his neighbour's reservoir, or whose cellar is invaded by the filth of his neighbour's privy, or whose habitation is made unhealthy by the fumes and noisome vapours of his neighbour's alkali works, is damnified without any fault of his own; and it seems but reasonable and just that the neighbour, who has brought something on his own property which was not naturally there, harmless to others so long as it is confined to his own property, but which he knows to be mischievous if it gets on his neighbour's, should be obliged to make good the damage which ensues if he does not succeed in confining it to his own property. But for his act in bringing it there no mischief could have accrued, and it seems but just that he should at his peril keep it there so that no mischief may accrue, or answer for the natural and anticipated consequences. And upon authority, this we think is established to be the law whether the things so brought be beasts, or water, or filth, or stenches.

The case that has most commonly occurred, and which is most frequently to be found in the books, is as to the obligation of the owner of cattle which he has brought on his land, to prevent their escaping and doing mischief. The law as to them seems to be perfectly settled from early times; the owner must keep them in at his peril, or he will be answerable for the natural consequences of their escape; that is with regard to tame beasts, for the grass they eat and trample upon, though not for any injury to the person of others, for our ancestors have settled that it is not the general nature of horses to kick, or bulls to gore; but if the owner knows that the beast has a vicious propensity to attack man, he will be answerable for that too.

Blackburn J continued his analysis of the law relating to escaping cattle and continued (at 282):

As has been already said, there does not appear to be any difference in principle, between the extent of the duty cast on him who brings cattle on his land to keep them in, and the extent of the duty imposed on him who brings on his land, water, filth, or stenches, or any other thing which will, if it escape, naturally do damage, to prevent their escaping and injuring his neighbour, and the case of *Tenant v. Goldwin* (1 Salk. 21, 360; 2 Ld. Raym 1089; 6 Mod. 311), is an express authority that the duty is the same, and is, to keep them in at his peril.

Commentary

The rule as stated by Blackburn J does not require that any negligence should be established on anyone's part. Rather, his rule of liability requires the following elements:

(a) a person brings something on his or her land and collects and keeps it there;

(b) this is done for his or her own purposes;

(c) the thing in question is likely to do mischief if it escapes;

(d) the damage done is a natural consequence of the escape.

Blackburn J expressly differentiated this 'true rule of law', from the alternative possibility that liability in the case might have rested upon proof of negligence. As Blackburn J explained, if liability did rest upon negligence, then a subsidiary question would arise, namely 'whether the defendants are not so far identified with the contractors whom they employed, as to be responsible for their lack of care or skill'.

In effect, this alternative is the route adopted by the High Court of Australia in *Burnie Port Authority v General Jones Pty Ltd* (1992–94 179 CLR 520), recognizing a 'non-delegable duty' on the part of the occupier to ensure that dangerous works are conducted with reasonable care. The main difference between these two approaches appears to be simple. On the Australian analysis, negligence on the part of the contractors needs to be established; in *Rylands v Fletcher*, there need be no negligence at all.[1]

The High Court of Australia doubted whether this difference is really so great in practical terms, arguing that negligence would be found on pretty much all those sets of facts where *Rylands* would be available. As we will see below, this depends on a particular interpretation of the tort of negligence as it applies between neighbouring occupiers. The High Court recognized both that there is a special relationship between neighbouring occupiers giving rise to positive duties relating to dangerous activities; and that varying degrees of care would be demanded within the tort of negligence, depending on the degree of danger involved in a particular use of land.

The apparent contradiction between negligence liability, and the rule in *Rylands v Fletcher*, requires a little more attention. The manner in which the rule was stated by Blackburn J seems designed to appeal to a simple sense of fairness: the thing that escapes is accumulated for D's own purposes; therefore D, and not C, must take the consequences should that thing escape. Negligence liability, as stated in *Donoghue v Stevenson*, also had simple intuitive appeal. So how can both make sense in terms of intuitive fairness?

The answer lies in the idea of 'keeping things in at one's peril'. We do not primarily regard the damage as the result of an isolated event, namely the escape. Rather, we see it as the result of a risk that is created by an activity on one's land. As already mentioned, this is critically different from most nuisance cases, where the interference is a result—sometimes an inevitable result—of the conflict between two uses of land. *The rule in Rylands v Fletcher differs from both negligence and nuisance in suggesting that the risks in question may legitimately be run.* It does not suggest that the accumulation of a dangerous thing per se amounts to an actionable nuisance. However, the risks associated with an accumulation may not be placed altogether upon an innocent claimant. Rather, the risks are run 'at the peril of' the person who accumulates a dangerous thing for their own purposes. In a sense then, the defendant 'insures' the neighbouring occupier against risk.

We will see later that this idea of 'insuring' against harm was diluted from the start, in particular through the development of broad defences relating to the manner of the escape itself (which should really have been irrelevant in most circumstances). But we should also notice that the apparent contrast with negligence may not be real given the ability of negligence to adapt to different circumstances. In particular, the degree of care that would be undertaken by a prudent person in the exercise of a dangerous calling may bring the negligence duty very close to the duty in *Rylands v Fletcher*, at least in its diluted form. The following extract expresses the issue very clearly.

E.R. Thayer, 'Liability Without Fault' (1916) 29 *Harv L Rev* 801–15, 805–6

How powerful a weapon the modern law of negligence places in the hands of the injured person, and how little its full scope has been realized until recently, is well shown by the law of carrier and passenger. The futility of degrees of care in general has long been recognized; but in the case of public service companies the habit of talking as if the carrier owed some

---

[1] It appears though that the contractors were negligent in *Rylands* itself.

special degree of care other than that of the ordinary prudent man has persisted and is common today. Clear-headed judges, however, have pointed out that the distinction is illusory. The ordinary prudent man would never take human beings into his keeping in conditions where they trusted utterly in him, and where life and limb was the stake, without qualifying himself in advance in all practicable ways for so dangerous a business and without using all available precautions in carrying it on. In such a business the highest care is thus nothing more than ordinary care under the circumstances; and it may be conjectured that in the case of carrier and passenger there is little difference, as a practical matter, between the results reached by the law of negligence and the doctrine of *Rylands v Fletcher*. Few cases are likely to arise in which a railroad company would escape today, except where the accident was caused by the unforeseeable intervention of some natural force or human being. Yet those are the very things which excuse him also under *Rylands v Fletcher*.

This stringent liability of the carrier is not due to his public calling, but to the nature of the agencies he uses, the helplessness of the passengers, and the peril to life and limb. . . . . And in these respects the parallel between the carrier and the defendant in a case like *Rylands v Fletcher* is close. In each case the defendant has chosen to create a condition dangerous to others unless kept in control. In each the plaintiff has no means of protecting himself and is left helpless and forced to look to the plaintiff for protection. In the one case as in the other the argument is overwhelming that ordinary prudence requires the defendant not only to take every precaution to inform himself of the dangers of his enterprise before undertaking it, and to guard against such dangers in construction, but also to use unremitting diligence in maintenance and inspection. And so great are the resources of modern science that an accident occurring without the intervention of a new unforeseeable agency will make a hard case for the defendant. There may, of course, be facts which will entitle him to prevail, but they are most unlikely. It will be a strange case where the accident was due to conditions existing when the defendant did the responsible act, or where new forces operated which should have been foreseen, and yet the defendant was free from blame in failing to guard against them. A proper study of the plaintiff's case with expert assistance will be likely to disclose the elements of liability under the modern law of negligence in the vast majority of cases where, assuming the rule in *Rylands v Fletcher*, the defendant would not be excused in view of *Nicholls v Marsland* and *Box v Jubb*.

The idea of 'keeping things in at one's peril', softened by a range of defences, could be comprehended from the vantage point of the tort of negligence, according to Thayer's analysis.

The House of Lords, 1868 3 LR HL

The judgment of Blackburn J was approved by the House of Lords. Of the two judges named in the Report, Lord Cairns added some comments about non-natural user. The non-natural user criterion has subsequently been taken to be an additional requirement for the application of the rule. (The absence of a named third judge in the report simply adds to the mystery of *Rylands v Fletcher*, since it seems to underline the fact that the case was seen by its authors as relatively inconspicuous and unproblematic.)[2]

---

[2] For an investigation see R. Heuston, 'Who Was the Third Judge in *Rylands v Fletcher*? (1970) 86 LQR 160–5.

Lord Cairns LC, at 383

My Lords, the principles on which this case must be determined appear to me to be extremely simple. The Defendants, treating them as the owners or occupiers of the close on which the reservoir was constructed, might lawfully have used that close for any purpose for which it might in the ordinary course of the enjoyment of land be used; and if, in what I may term the natural user of that land, there had been any accumulation of water, either on the surface or underground, and if, by the operation of the laws of nature, that accumulation of water had passed off into the close occupied by the Plaintiff, the Plaintiff could not have complained that that result had taken place. If he had desired to guard himself against it, it would have lain upon him to have done so, by leaving, or by interposing, some barrier between his close and the close of the Defendants in order to have prevented that operation of the laws of nature.

As an illustration of that principle, I may refer to a case which was cited in the argument before your Lordships, the case of *Smith v. Kenrick* in the Court of Common Pleas (7 C. B. 515).

On the other hand if the Defendants, not stopping at the natural use of their close, had desired to use it for any purpose which I may term a non-natural use, for the purpose of introducing into the close that which in its natural condition was not in or upon it, for the purpose of introducing water either above or below ground in quantities and in a manner not the result of any work or operation on or under the land,—and if in consequence of their doing so, or in consequence of any imperfection in the mode of their doing so, the water came to escape and to pass off into the close of the Plaintiff, then it appears to me that that which the Defendants were doing they were doing at their own peril; and, if in the course of their doing it, the evil arose to which I have referred, the evil, namely, of the escape of the water and its passing away to the close of the Plaintiff and injuring the Plaintiff, then for the consequence of that, in my opinion, the Defendants would be liable. As the case of *Smith v. Kenrick* is an illustration of the first principle to which I have referred, so also the second principle to which I have referred is well illustrated by another case in the same Court, the case of *Baird v. Williamson* (15 C. B. (N. S.) 317), which was also cited in the argument at the Bar.

My Lords, these simple principles, if they are well founded, as it appears to me they are, really dispose of this case.

The same result is arrived at on the principles referred to by Mr. Justice *Blackburn* in his judgment, in the Court of Exchequer Chamber, where he states the opinion of that Court as to the law in these words: "We think that the true rule of law is, that the person who, for his own purposes, brings on his land and collects and keeps there anything likely to do mischief if it escapes, must keep it in at his peril; and if he does not do so, is *prima facie* answerable for all the damage which is the natural consequence of its escape. He can excuse himself by shewing that the escape was owing to the Plaintiff's default; or, perhaps, that the escape was the consequence of *vis major*, or the act of God; but as nothing of this sort exists here, it is unnecessary to inquire what excuse would be sufficient. The general rule, as above stated, seems on principle just. The person whose grass or corn is eaten down by the escaping cattle of his neighbour, or whose mine is flooded by the water from his neighbour's reservoir, or whose cellar is invaded by the filth of his neighbour's privy, or whose habitation is made unhealthy by the fumes and noisome vapours of his neighbour's alkali works, is damnified without any fault of his own; and it seems but reasonable and just that the neighbour who has brought something on his own property (which was not naturally there), harmless to others so long as it is confined to his own property, but which he knows will be mischievous if it gets on his neighbour's, should be obliged to make good the damage which ensues if he does not succeed in confining it to his own property. But for his act in bringing it there no mischief could have accrued, and it seems but just that he should at his peril keep it there, so that no mischief may accrue, or answer for the natural and anticipated consequence. And upon authority this we think is established to be the law, whether the things so brought be beasts, or water, or filth, or stenches."

My Lords, in that opinion, I must say I entirely concur. Therefore, I have to move your Lordships that the judgment of the Court of Exchequer Chamber be affirmed, and that the present appeal be dismissed with costs.

Lord Cranworth

. . . I come without hesitation to the conclusion that the judgment of the Exchequer Chamber was right. The Plaintiff had a right to work his coal through the lands of Mr. *Whitehead*, and up to the old workings. If water naturally rising in the Defendants' land (we may treat the land as the land of the Defendants for the purpose of this case) had by percolation found its way down to the Plaintiff's mine through the old workings, and so had impeded his operations, that would not have afforded him any ground of complaint. Even if all the old workings had been made by the Plaintiff, he would have done no more than he was entitled to do; for, according to the principle acted on in *Smith v. Kenrick*, the person working the mine, under the close in which the reservoir was made, had a right to win and carry away all the coal without leaving any wall or barrier against *Whitehead's* land. But that is not the real state of the case. The Defendants, in order to effect an object of their own, brought on to their land, or on to land which for this purpose may be treated as being theirs, a large accumulated mass of water, and stored it up in a reservoir. The consequence of this was damage to the Plaintiff, and for that damage, however skilfully and carefully the accumulation was made, the Defendants, according to the principles and authorities to which I have adverted, were certainly responsible.

Commentary

Lord Cranworth reiterated clearly that negligence or lack of care was not required for the application of the principle of liability, despite the apparent negligence of the contractors in the case itself. But it was the judgment of Lord Cairns that added the criterion of *non-natural user*. As Lord Cairns put it, the defendants would have been entitled to use the land for any purpose 'for which it might in the ordinary course of the enjoyment of land be used', and the plaintiffs would have been unable to seek redress for any damage that might flow from that 'ordinary' use in the absence of negligence. But if the defendants made a *non-natural* use of the land (as here), then the defendants were to be treated as doing so 'at their own peril'.

Unfortunately, it will be apparent that Lord Cairns' judgment here contains more than one formulation of this additional criterion of liability, since it refers first to the 'ordinary' use of the land, and second to a distinction between 'natural' and 'non-natural' use. More unfortunately, in discussion of 'non-natural' use he makes some reference to 'that which in its natural condition was not in or upon it'—a reference to that which is or is not naturally there. In the article extracted below, Professor Newark traces different meanings of 'non-natural' as used in the judgment of Lord Cairns, and outlines a major change in the more recent case law beginning with *Rickards v Lothian* in 1913.

F. Newark, 'Non-Natural User and Rylands v Fletcher' (1961) 24 MLR 557–71, 570–1

Lord Cairns had dealt with three distinct conceptions, and he kept them distinct, but it was his fault to introduce the word "natural" into each. The first is a reference to an escape "by the laws of nature." Here he meant no more than that the dangerous agent moved on to the plaintiff's close in consequence of a natural force, *e.g.*, gravity, and was not propelled thither by act of the defendant. The second is a reference to "the user of land in the ordinary course of enjoyment" which he equates with "natural user." But his very next words show that he was referring to *a user of land which caused the dangerous agent to escape*, as in the *Smith v Kenrick* type of case. And thirdly he refers to "non-natural use" which is artificially introducing the dangerous agent on to the land.

Shortly, what has happened by the time of *Rickards v Lothian* in 1913 is that "ordinary" which had been used as a synonym for "natural" in Lord Cairns' second conception (*viz.*, the user which caused the dangerous agent to escape) had been transferred to the third conception which relates to the introduction of the dangerous agent on the land, so that whereas Lord Cairns asserted that bringing the dangerous agent on to the land was necessarily "non-natural use" we are now led to believe that it is only "non-natural" if it is "not ordinary." And the result as applied in the modern cases is, we believe, one which would have surprised Lord Cairns and astounded Blackburn J.

Now however the non-natural user criterion has become the main mechanism for setting some appropriate limits to the rule, and it does so quite independently of the idea of natural in the sense of 'natural condition'. Its content may now (belatedly) be in the process of developing in a manner uncluttered by confusion over the origins, purpose, and nature of the rule. But because of other limitations to the rule (particularly in the form of defences, but also through the close association with other forms of nuisance) this development is probably too late to convert *Rylands v Fletcher* into a workable rule of strict liability.

We will revisit non-natural user on page 689 below. On page 697, we will explore its most recent interpretation in *Transco v Stockport MBC*. For now, we will simply note that one of Lord Cairns' formulations of the rule—the reference to 'ordinary use'—is similar to the expression used by Bramwell B in *Bamford v Turnley* 1862 122 ER 27, where he summarized a range of cases that was subject to the principle of 'give and take' in the tort of private nuisance. Lord Bramwell's judgment in *Bamford v Turnley* was extracted in Chapter 10. Bramwell B was the single dissenting judge in *Fletcher v Rylands* in the Court of Exchequer, who would have awarded damages to the plaintiff Fletcher, and who was supported on appeal both by the Court of Exchequer Chamber and by the House of Lords. In a footnote to the article extracted above ('Non-Natural User and *Rylands v Fletcher*', at n. 53), Newark suggests that the similarity between natural user in *Rylands*, and ordinary user in *Bamford v Turnley*, is merely superficial. No comparison could have been intended because (he argues) it would surely otherwise have been mentioned. But as we will see the version of the 'non-natural user' criterion which has been accepted, with variations, since *Rickards v Lothian* in 1913 is precisely an ordinary user test. The most recent interpretations of the non-natural user criterion, to be found in Lord Goff's judgment in *Cambridge Water*, and in the judgments of both Lord Bingham and Lord Hoffmann in *Transco v Stockport MBC* (below), turn on 'ordinary' user and certainly bear comparison with Bramwell B's analysis in *Bamford v Turnley*.

3. ELEMENTS OF ACTIONABILITY

A general principle of strict liability for hazardous activities has never developed in English law. Ironically perhaps, it is in the United States that a general principle of strict liability for ultra-hazardous acts has been adopted, despite the 'initially cool reception' given to *Rylands v Fletcher* itself (Fleming, *The Law of Torts*, 9th edn, p 370; Rest. (Torts) 2d §519). The components of the rule as stated by Blackburn J have been read as strict requirements. In addition, a number of other limitations to the rule have become apparent. As we have seen, these include the requirement (added by Lord Cairns, but reinterpreted over the years) that the defendant's user of the land should be 'non-natural'; but also include a range of defences not mentioned in *Rylands v Fletcher* itself.

Courts have struggled to reconcile the action in *Rylands*, with negligence liability, and this makes it hard to give a wholly consistent account of the case law. This struggle began straight away with cases such as *Jones v Festiniog Railway* ((1868) LR 3 QB) and *Nicholls v Marsland* ((1868) 2 Ex D 1), both of which are discussed below.

Accumulation of Something Likely to do Mischief

The defendant must have 'accumulated' something on his or her land; and that thing must be something that, in the words of Blackburn J, is 'likely to do mischief if it escapes'. The thing may be brought onto the land by the defendant. Alternatively, it may come onto the land by a natural process, provided that some action of the defendant has caused it to gather or accumulate. For example, the defendant may have constructed a reservoir that will fill with rain water, or may have dammed a stream to create a lake. Clearly though, an entirely natural accumulation will not fulfil the requirements of *Rylands v Fletcher*. Thus, *Rylands v Fletcher* itself distinguished the earlier case of *Smith v Kendrick* (1849 7 CB 515), in which the accumulation of water was entirely natural. It should be noted however that a case like *Smith v Kendrick* will now be interpreted in terms of a 'measured duty of care' in nuisance within the terms of *Leakey v National Trust* [1980] QB 485 (Chapter 10 above). The more recent growth of positive duties in tort associated with particular situations (in this case occupation of land) deprives the strict liability rule of significance within those boundaries.

In *Giles v Walker* (1890) 24 QBD 656, a defendant had neglected to mow thistles which had seeded naturally upon his land, thus causing damage to his neighbour when thistledown was blown onto the neighbour's land. The very brief judgment in *Giles v Walker* did not mention *Rylands v Fletcher*, but its implication was that the rule does not apply to natural accumulations. So far as reported, this is the leading judgment in full:

Lord Coleridge CJ

I never heard of such an action as this. There can be no duty as between adjoining occupiers to cut the thistles, which are the natural growth of the soil. The appeal must be allowed.

Giles v Walker was overruled in *Leakey*, in consequence of the recognition of a positive duty to take reasonable steps to protect one's neighbour. The degree to which positive duties have overtaken the rule in *Rylands v Fletcher* is a question to which we return below.

The additional idea that the things accumulated are 'likely to do mischief' if they escape draws attention to the likely consequences should such an escape occur. Thus an element of foreseeability has been present in *Rylands v Fletcher* from the start, even if it was not expressed in these terms. Because of more recent controversies, we should note that it is foreseeability of danger, not foreseeability of escape specifically, which is implicit in Blackburn J's statement.

Escape

Rylands liability requires an escape. This is one of the most artificial elements of the rule, and the retention of this requirement illustrates clearly that the rule has not developed into a general principle of strict liability.

Viscount Simon, *Read v Lyons* [1947] AC 156, 168

"Escape," for the purpose of applying the proposition in *Rylands v. Fletcher*, means escape from a place where the defendant has occupation of or control over land to a place which is outside his occupation or control. Blackburn J. several times refers to the defendant's duty as being the duty of "keeping a thing in" at the defendant's peril and by "keeping in" he does not mean preventing an explosive substance from exploding but preventing a thing which may inflict mischief from escaping from the area which the defendant occupies or controls.

An event which occurs entirely within the confines of the defendant's land will therefore not satisfy the criterion. As a result, there was no 'escape' for the purposes of the rule when there was an explosion in a munitions factory, no dangerous thing thus escaping from the defendant's premises. This decisive aspect of *Read v Lyons* was described by Fleming as having in itself ended the possibility of a general rule based on *Rylands v Fletcher*:

J. Fleming, *The Law of Torts* (9th edn, NSW: Law Book Company, 1998)

The most damaging aspect of the decision in *Read v Lyons* was that it prematurely stunted the development of a general theory of strict liability for ultra-hazardous activities.

It should be noted that the House of Lords in *Rickards v Lothian* also suggested (obiter) that if they were forced to decide the point, they might hold that the manufacture of munitions was a 'natural' use of land, at least in wartime. This interpretation has been superseded by the cases of *Cambridge Water* (in passing) and *Transco v Stockport* (where non-natural user was the key issue). On the other hand, Lord Macmillan's view that neither private nuisance, nor *Rylands v Fletcher*, would provide a remedy for personal injuries, has now been reiterated by the House of Lords in *Transco v Stockport*.

Who can Sue and for What Damage?

When Lord Macmillan said, in *Read v Lyons* (above) that the rule would not allow recovery for personal injuries, his comments were against the run of authority. They were based on an analysis of the origins of the action in nuisance, and not on the later case law. Later, in *Hale v Jennings* [1938] 1 All ER 579, the Court of Appeal said that the rule applied where personal injuries were caused by a fairground 'Chair-o-Plane' becoming detached and striking the plaintiff. There was no discussion of the personal injury point. Rather, the Court was concerned with the question of whether the Chair-o-Plane was dangerous in itself, or whether the defendant should be exonerated because of the 'fooling about' of one of its customers. In *Perry v Kendricks* [1956] 1 WLR 85, Parker LJ thought that on the balance of authority, it was not open to the Court of Appeal to exclude personal injury from the ambit of the rule. In particular, the Court of Appeal would be bound by its earlier decision in *Musgrove v Pandelis* [1919] 2 KB 43. But *Musgrove v Pandelis* was a case of property damage, and not of injury to the person. The Court of Appeal had there considered the important distinction between physical damage (in that case, to chattels), and damage to proprietary interests, and decided that *Rylands* liability was not confined to the latter.

Now however, the incorporation of *Rylands v Fletcher* into nuisance, coupled with the decision in *Hunter v Canary Wharf* ([1997] AC 655, Chapter 10), determines clearly that personal injuries will not be compensated under the rule.[3] The same developments also suggest that only those in occupation of land will be able to claim in *Rylands*, but there is much less clarity concerning the nature of the occupation that will suffice. In *Shiffman v Order of St John* [1936] 1 All ER 557, Atkinson J remarked that damages *might* be recoverable under the rule when children were injured by the fall of a flag pole erected by the defendants.[4] Dealing with the occupancy issue, he stated that: 'if it fell it was certain to fall on land of which [the defendants] were not in occupation and on which the public had a right to be'. This kind of 'licence' to be present he thought would be sufficient. More significantly perhaps, in *Charing Cross Electricity Supply Company v Hydraulic Power Company* [1914] 3 KB 772, the Court of Appeal clearly stated that the rule in *Rylands v Fletcher* applied even where the plaintiff suffered injury on a site occupied under licence, and not under any right of property in the soil. The damage suffered there was damage to a pipe (a chattel) laid under (not on) the highway. Notably, the Court of Appeal in the *Charing Cross* case clearly considered liability under *Rylands v Fletcher* to be a species of nuisance, since they assumed that it came within the terms of a clause of the relevant act which saved actions in respect of nuisances arising from the defendants' exercise of their powers (London Hydraulic Power Act 1884 section 17).

Defences

Vis major/act of God; act of a stranger

These defences relate to the means by which the escape occurs. Any defence based on the idea that the defendant was not 'to blame' for the way in which an escape occurred will undercut the impact of the rule, which is calculated to place the risk of an escape—and the burden of keeping the thing safe—upon the person who accumulates it.

If these defences are broadly applied, this will further illustrate that *Rylands* has not been wholeheartedly applied by the courts. An early example is the case of *Nicholls v Marsland* (1868) 2 Ex D 1, in which 'exceptionally heavy rain' was held to take the escape beyond the reach of the rule in *Rylands v Fletcher*. A modern court could choose to differ from its nineteenth-century counterpart on the basis that the occurrence of 'exceptional' conditions is now rather more predictable than once was the case, and is thus more foreseeable. And it is

---

[3] This was clearly stated by the House of Lords in *Transco v Stockport*.

[4] These hypothetical remarks were no part of the *ratio* of the case, which was not decided on the basis of *Rylands v Fletcher* although it is sometimes assumed that it was (see for example *Transco v Stockport*, at [35]).

arguable that the breadth of these defences has in any event been overstated. Lord Hoffmann, in *Transco v Stockport MBC* (para [32]), cites *Carstairs v Taylor* (1871) LR 6 Ex 217 as evidence that 'act of God' is interpreted broadly. Here, a rat gnawed through a gutter box, causing a flood. There was no liability on the part of the occupier. However, Lord Hobhouse correctly pointed out in response to Lord Hoffmann (*Transco*, para [59]) that apart from Kelly CB, the other judges in that case distinguised *Rylands v Fletcher*, so that it is not strong authority on the content of the defence of act of God. Bramwell B, for example, distinguished *Rylands* on the basis that in *Carstairs v Taylor*, the accumulation (of rainwater in guttering) was made as much for the benefit of the plaintiff as of the defendant. Thus it was not made by the defendant 'for his own purposes'.

Further, in the case of 'act of a stranger', Lord Hoffmann suggests that it is sufficient to show that the escape had been caused by a vandal, for example, and is not attributable to the defendant (*Rickards v Lothian* [1913] AC 263). However, the discussion in *Shiffman v Order of St John* (above) suggests that a *foreseeable* act of vandalism would not trigger the defence. And in *Perry v Kendricks* (where the defence was decisive), the court did indeed emphasize the *unforeseeable* nature of the intervention. Some acts of vandalism being quite foreseeable, and the kind of thing that should be guarded against, this interpretation would place some positive duties upon the defendant to 'keep the thing in', even if it falls short of imposing a duty to insure against damage. In *Hale v Jennings* [1938] 1 All ER 579, it was emphasized that the dangerous thing (a fairground 'Chair-o-Plane') was likely to produce the very danger that occurred, where a customer loosened the Chair through his 'folly'. The fact that this third party had caused the 'escape' through his own fault did not absolve the defendants from liability under *Rylands v Fletcher*, since it was within the foreseeable risk associated with the operation of the equipment:

Scott LJ, *Hale v Jennings*

The behaviour of [the customer] in causing the chair to become detached, was in my view just the kind of behaviour which ought to have been anticipated as being a likely act with a percentage of users of the apparatus. People go there in a spirit of fun. Many of them are ignorant, and many of them are wholly unaware of the dangers incidental to playing with the chairs in that sort of way, and they cause a danger that they do not in the least realise. That kind of accident does not come within the exceptions to the rule at all. The apparatus is dangerous within the meaning of the rule because it is intended to be used by that sort of person; and is likely to produce this very danger.

The fact remains that under a serious rule of strict liability a defendant could not expect to enjoy broad defences concerning operation of nature and acts of third parties. We can see this exemplified by the strict liability rule for abnormally dangerous activities in the US Restatement of Torts (2nd). The general principle of liability for 'abnormally dangerous activities' is stated in paragraph 519 as follows:

519 General Principle

1. One who carries on an abnormally dangerous activity is subject to liability for harm to the person, land or chattels of another resulting from the activity, although he has exercised the utmost care to prevent the harm.

2. This strict liability is limited to the type of harm, the possibility of which makes the activity abnormally dangerous.

The criterion of an 'abnormally dangerous activity' is subject to further comment in paragraph 520. It is in paragraph 522 that we find a contrasting approach to the English defences discussed here. A defendant will not escape liability because the immediate cause of the injury is 'unexpectable':

(a) innocent, negligent or reckless conduct of a third person, or

(b) action of an animal, or

(c) operation of a force of nature

The rationale offered for the general approach in paragraph 522 is as follows:

> The reason for imposing strict liability upon those who carry on abnormally dangerous activities is that they have for their own purposes created a risk that is not a usual incident of the ordinary life of the community. If the risk ripens into injury, it is immaterial that the harm occurs through the unexpectable action of a human being, an animal or a force of nature. This is true irrespective of whether the action of the human being which makes the abnormally dangerous activity harmful is innocent, negligent, or even reckless.

The 'abnormal' nature of the risk is regarded as a central element of the rationale for the strict liability. This is almost certainly different from the 'non-natural user' requirement in English law, though it bears some comparison. But the central purpose of the rule being clear, it is possible at least to address issues concerning the ambit of particular defences, without beginning to invoke inappropriate arguments derived from an analysis in terms of 'fault'. The clear statement of a rationale in the restatement, and its following through into the details of the liability set out, indicates how beneficial it might have been to establish the rationale for the rule in *Rylands v Fletcher*, and the contents of the 'non-natural user' test, more clearly. English courts have never been sufficiently confident in the purpose of the rule, to apply it wholeheartedly.

Statutory authority

Significant issues also arise in respect of the defence of statutory authority. We considered this defence in the chapter above, concerning nuisance. But the issues are subtly different in respect of *Rylands v Fletcher*. The normal case of private nuisance concerns ongoing activities. In some cases, inevitable interferences arise from those activities. Since those interferences are an inevitable aspect of the authorized activity, a finding of nuisance would contradict the statute. The defence of statutory authority in private nuisance is therefore close to being a logical necessity, although its application to specific circumstances is of course a matter of debate. But in the context of liability under *Rylands v Fletcher*, the escape itself is generally accidental and not an 'inevitable' aspect of the authorization. Authorization for an accumulation clearly authorizes the *risk* of an escape, but this does not compel the view that there should be no liability when an escape actually occurs.

In *Transco* as we shall see below, Lord Hoffmann has suggested that statutory authority removes liability for escapes in the absence of negligence. In support of this interpretation, Lord Hoffmann quotes from the advice given by Blackburn J himself to the House of Lords in *Hammersmith and City Railway Co v Brand* 1869 [LR] 4 HL, and refers also to Lord Blackburn's statement in *Geddis v Proprietors of the Bann Reservoir* 1878 3 App Cas 430: '. . . no action will lie for doing that which the legislature has authorized, if it be done without negligence, although it does occasion damage to anyone; but an action does lie for doing that which the legislature has authorized, if it be done negligently'.

Neither of these cases concerned the rule in *Rylands v Fletcher* directly. Nevertheless, the statements are very general. Should we take it that they were meant to encompass liability under *Rylands*? It appears that Blackburn J himself *did* consider that the defence applies to *Rylands v Fletcher* in the manner stated in *Brand* and *Geddis*. In *Jones v Festiniog Railway* (1868 [LR] 3 QB), Blackburn and Lush JJ applied the newly-formulated rule in *Rylands v Fletcher* to a case of damage caused by sparks emitted from locomotives. In order to hold that there was liability in *Rylands* despite statutory authorization for the operation of the railroad, they clearly thought they first had to hold that as a matter of statutory interpretation, authorization for the running of a railroad did not include authorization for the running of locomotives specifically. These were not essential to the purpose of the enterprise so authorized. Although the plaintiffs in that case were successful, the judges clearly thought that if the accumulation was expressly permitted, then this would be enough to oust the strict liability rule.

This state of affairs seriously restricts the practical ambit of *Rylands v Fletcher*. It also further illustrates that the courts have never really accepted that the rule in *Rylands v Fletcher* exists with the purpose of internalizing risks.

Sellers LJ, *Dunne v NW Gas Board* [1964] 2 QB 806, 834

It is not easy to contemplate a case where the inevitable result of doing what a statute required would result in damage except directly to property interfered with, but it could be contemplated, as here, that the result might do so. Gas, water and electricity all are capable of doing damage, and a strict or absolute liability for any damage done by them would make the undertakers of these services insurers.

Sellers LJ clearly thought that this possibility amounted to a conclusive argument *against* the application of the rule. But there is an argument that the undertakers of public services *should be* the insurers of damage done by their activities. Obviously, there may be arguments either way as to whether this is desirable or not. But the evident surprise of the Court of Appeal that such a thing might be suggested illustrates a general lack of clarity about the purpose of the rule. It is not simply that there is disagreement over the purpose of the rule; it is more that the history of the rule is marred by an absence of concern with questions of purpose and rationale.

Remoteness

Foreseeability of some kind is inherent in the rule as initially stated. The decision in *Cambridge Water* (below) employed an historical analysis to interpret *Rylands* as an aspect of the law of nuisance, and thus determined that the normal rules on remoteness of damage, as expressed in *The Wagon Mound*, apply also to *Rylands v Fletcher*. Not only must the accumulated thing be liable to do mischief if it escapes, but the eventual damage must in a relevant sense be foreseeable. On the rather peculiar facts of *Cambridge Water* itself, the absence of foreseeability in respect of the claimants' damage was plain; but that damage was unforeseeable in a number of different ways.

Non-natural User

In the most recent cases, the idea of 'non-natural user', derived from the judgment of Lord Cairns, has received more direct and sustained consideration. We noted above that in his article 'Non-natural User and *Rylands v Fletcher*', Newark argued that Lord Cairns had used the expression in a number of different ways, but that its essence as he used it lay in the contrast between 'natural' and 'artificial' uses of the land. That meaning has now been confined to history, being described by Lord Goff as being 'redolent of a different age' (*Cambridge Water v Eastern Counties Leather plc*). It is in *Rickards v Lothian* [1913] AC 263, and specifically in the following statement, that the origins of the modern approach to non-natural user are now recognized to lie:

Lord Moulton, *Rickards v Lothian,* at 280

It is not every use to which land is put that brings into play that principle. It must be some special use bringing with it increased danger to others, and must not merely be the ordinary use of the land or such a use as is proper for the general benefit of the community.

Lord Moulton's idea that the use should not be merely 'ordinary' is the basis for the reasoning in recent case law, where Lord Bingham has suggested that the terminology of 'ordinary user' is preferable to that of 'natural user' (*Transco v Stockport*, below, para 11). But there has been general rejection of the other element in Lord Moulton's statement, that use 'for the general benefit of the community' should be sufficient to make out the defence.

The newer interpretations of non-natural user, based on Lord Moulton's statement, are further considered below.

4. CATEGORIZATION AND BOUNDARIES

The English Approach: A Species of Nuisance

After much conflicting and inconclusive case law, in the last few years two House of Lords decisions have considered and retained the rule: *Cambridge Water v Eastern Counties Leather plc* [1994] 2 AC 264, and *Transco v Stockport MBC* [2003] UKHL 61; [2004] 2 AC 1. These cases have considered the categorization of the rule, and have clarified the contents of the applicable tests of foreseeability and of natural user, respectively. When we have considered these English cases, we will turn to the decision of the Australian High Court in *Burnie Port Authority v General Jones*, which absorbed *Rylands* into negligence liability for hazardous activities in Australia.

Cambridge Water v Eastern Counties Leather plc: foreseeability and non-natural user

The defendants were leather manufacturers operating from a site on an industrial village in Sawston, near Cambridge. In the course of their business, they used a chlorinated solvent, perchloroethene ('PCE'). Quantities of PCE were stored in drums on their premises.

The plaintiffs owned a borehole at Sawston Mill, from which they extracted water. This water was supplied to domestic users. The borehole was 1.3 miles from the defendants' premises. At the time that the plaintiffs bought Sawston Mill, the presence of PCE in a public water supply was not a matter for concern. Subsequently, pursuant to a European Council Directive (80/778/EEC), the Department of the Environment set a standard for the presence of PCE among other compounds in water intended for domestic use. The water from Sawston Mill was subsequently tested, and it was found that the concentrations of PCE in the water were many times higher than the permitted levels. In 1983, the plaintiffs ceased extracting water from Sawston Mill. They initiated a complex investigation, which traced the PCE levels in the water to the defendants' operations.

Lord Goff discussed the applicability and interpretation of the remoteness criterion in nuisance and continued:

Cambridge Water Co v Eastern Counties Leather plc [1994] 2 AC 264

Lord Goff of Chieveley

Foreseeability of damage under the rule in Rylands v. Fletcher

I start with the judgment of Blackburn J. in *Fletcher v. Rylands* (1866) L.R. 1 Ex. 265 itself.

Lord Goff quoted from the passage of Blackburn J's judgment extracted above and continued:

In that passage, Blackburn J. spoke of "anything *likely* to do mischief if it escapes;" and later he spoke of something "which he *knows* to be mischievous if it gets on his neighbour's [property]," and the liability to "answer for the natural *and anticipated* consequences." Furthermore, time and again he spoke of the strict liability imposed upon the defendant as being that he must keep the thing in at his peril; and, when referring to liability in actions for damage occasioned by animals, he referred, at p. 282, to the established principle that "it is quite immaterial whether the escape is by negligence or not." The general tenor of his statement of principle is therefore that knowledge, or at least foreseeability of the risk, is a pre-requisite of the recovery of damages under the principle; but that the principle is one of strict liability in the sense that the defendant may be held liable notwithstanding that he has exercised all due care to prevent the escape from occurring.

There are however early authorities in which foreseeability of damage does not appear to have been regarded as necessary: see, e.g., *Humphries v. Cousins* (1877) 2 C.P.D. 239. Moreover, it was submitted by Mr. Ashworth for C.W.C. that the requirement of foreseeability of damage was negatived in two particular cases, the decision of the Court of Appeal in *West v. Bristol Tramways Co.* [1908] 2 K.B. 14 and the decision of this House in *Rainham Chemical Works Ltd. v. Belvedere Fish Guano Co. Ltd.* [1921] 2 A.C. 465.

He considered these two cases and continued:

I feel bound to say that these two cases provide a very fragile base for any firm conclusion that foreseeability of damage has been authoritatively rejected as a prerequisite of the recovery of damages under the rule in *Rylands v. Fletcher*. Certainly, the point was not considered by this House in the *Rainham Chemical* case. In my opinion, the matter is open for consideration by your Lordships in the present case . . . .

The point is one on which academic opinion appears to be divided . . . . However, quite apart from the indications to be derived from the judgment of Blackburn J. in *Fletcher v. Rylands*, L.R. 1 Ex. 265 itself, to which I have already referred, the historical connection with the law of nuisance must now be regarded as pointing towards the conclusion that foreseeability of damage is a prerequisite of the recovery of damages under the rule. I have already referred to the fact that Blackburn J. himself did not regard his statement of principle as having broken new ground; furthermore, Professor Newark has convincingly shown that the rule in *Rylands v. Fletcher* was essentially concerned with an extension of the law of nuisance to cases of isolated escape. Accordingly since, following the observations of Lord Reid when delivering the advice of the Privy Council in *The Wagon Mound (No. 2)* [1967] 1 A.C. 617, 640, the recovery of damages in private nuisance depends on foreseeability by the defendant of the relevant type of damage, it would appear logical to extend the same requirement to liability under the rule in *Rylands v. Fletcher*.

Even so, the question cannot be considered solely as a matter of history. It can be argued that the rule in *Rylands v. Fletcher* should not be regarded simply as an extension of the law of nuisance, but should rather be treated as a developing principle of strict liability from which can be derived a general rule of strict liability for damage caused by ultra-hazardous operations, on the basis of which persons conducting such operations may properly be held strictly liable for the extraordinary risk to others involved in such operations. As is pointed out in *Fleming on the Law of Torts*, pp. 327–328, this would lead to the practical result that the cost of damage resulting from such operations would have to be absorbed as part of the overheads of the relevant business rather than be borne (where there is no negligence) by the injured person or his insurers, or even by the community at large. Such a development appears to have been taking place in the United States, as can be seen from section 519 of the *Restatement of the Law (Second) Torts* 2d, vol. 3, pp. 34–36. The extent to which it has done so is not altogether clear; and I infer from section 519, and the Comment on that paragraph, that the abnormally dangerous activities there referred to are such that their ability to cause harm would be obvious to any reasonable person who carried them on.

I have to say, however, that there are serious obstacles in the way of the development of the rule in *Rylands v. Fletcher* in this way. First of all, if it was so to develop, it should logically apply to liability to all persons suffering injury by reason of the ultra-hazardous operations; but the decision of this House in *Read v. J. Lyons & Co. Ltd.* [1947] A.C 156, which establishes that there can be no liability under the rule except in circumstances where the injury has been caused by an escape from land under the control of the defendant, has effectively precluded any such development. . . . there is much to be said for the view that the courts should not be proceeding down the path of developing such a general theory. In this connection, I refer in particular to the Report of the Law Commission on Civil Liability for Dangerous Things and Activities (1970) (Law Com. No. 32). In paragraphs 14–16 of the Report, the Law Commission expressed serious misgivings about the adoption of any test for the application of strict liability involving a general concept of "especially dangerous" or "ultra-hazardous" activity, having regard to the uncertainties and practical difficulties of its application. If the Law Commission is unwilling to consider statutory reform on this basis, it must follow that judges should if anything be even more reluctant to proceed down that path.

Like the judge in the present case, I incline to the opinion that, as a general rule, it is more appropriate for strict liability in respect of operations of high risk to be imposed by Parliament, than by the courts. If such liability is imposed by statute, the relevant activities can be identified, and those concerned can know where they stand. Furthermore, statute can where appropriate lay down precise criteria establishing the incidence and scope of such liability.

It is of particular relevance that the present case is concerned with environmental pollution. The protection and preservation of the environment is now perceived as being of crucial importance to the future of mankind; and public bodies, both national and international, are taking significant steps towards the establishment of legislation which will promote the protection of the environment, and make the polluter pay for damage to the environment for which he is responsible—as can be seen from the W.H.O., E.E.C. and national regulations to which I have previously referred. But it does not follow from these developments that a common law principle, such as the rule in *Rylands v. Fletcher*, should be developed or rendered more strict to provide for liability in respect of such pollution. On the contrary, given that so much well-informed and carefully structured legislation is now being put in place for this purpose, there is less need for the courts to develop a common law principle to achieve the same end, and indeed it may well be undesirable that they should do so.

Having regard to these considerations, and in particular to the step which this House has already taken in *Read v. J. Lyons & Co. Ltd.* [1947] A.C. 156 to contain the scope of liability under the rule in *Rylands v. Fletcher*, it appears to me to be appropriate now to take the view that foreseeability of damage of the relevant type should be regarded as a prerequisite of liability in damages under the rule. Such a conclusion can, as I have already stated, be derived from Blackburn J.'s original statement of the law; and I can see no good reason why this prerequisite should not be recognised under the rule, as it has been in the case of private nuisance. . . . It would moreover lead to a more coherent body of common law principles if the rule were to be regarded essentially as an extension of the law of nuisance to cases of isolated escapes from land, even though the rule as established is not limited to escapes which are in fact isolated. I wish to point out, however, that in truth the escape of the P.C.E. from E.C.L.'s land, in the form of trace elements carried in percolating water, has not been an isolated escape, but a continuing escape resulting from a state of affairs which has come into existence at the base of the chalk aquifer underneath E.C.L.'s premises. Classically, this would have been regarded as a case of nuisance; and it would seem strange if, by characterising the case as one falling under the rule in *Rylands v. Fletcher*, the liability should thereby be rendered more strict in the circumstances of the present case.

The facts of the present case

Turning to the facts of the present case, it is plain that, at the time when the P.C.E. was brought onto E.C.L.'s land, and indeed when it was used in the tanning process there, nobody at E.C.L. could reasonably have foreseen the resultant damage which occurred at C.W.C.'s borehole at Sawston.

. . .

Natural use of land

I turn to the question whether the use by E.C.L. of its land in the present case constituted a natural use, with the result that E.C.L. cannot be held liable under the rule in *Rylands v. Fletcher*. In view of my conclusion on the issue of foreseeability, I can deal with this point shortly.

The judge held that it was a natural use. He said:

> "In my judgment, in considering whether the storage of organochlorines as an adjunct to a manufacturing process is a non-natural use of land, I must consider whether that storage created special risks for adjacent occupiers and whether the activity was for the general benefit of the community. It seems to me inevitable that I must consider the magnitude of the storage and the geographical area in which it takes place in answering the question. Sawston is properly described as an industrial village, and the creation of employment is clearly for the benefit of that community. I do not believe that I can enter upon an assessment of the point on a scale of desirability that the manufacture of wash leathers comes, and I content myself with holding that this storage in this place is a natural use of land."

It is a commonplace that this particular exception to liability under the rule has developed and changed over the years. It seems clear that, in *Fletcher v. Rylands*, L.R. 1 Ex. 265 itself, Blackburn J.'s statement of the law was limited to things which are brought by the defendant onto his land, and so did not apply to things that were naturally upon the land. Furthermore, it is doubtful whether in the House of Lords in the same case Lord Cairns, to whom we owe the expression "non-natural use" of the land, was intending to expand the concept of natural use beyond that envisaged by Blackburn J. Even so, the law has long since departed from any such simple idea, redolent of a different age; and, at least since the advice of the Privy Council delivered by Lord Moulton in *Rickards v. Lothian* [1913] A.C. 263, 280, natural use has been extended to embrace the ordinary use of land. . . . .

Rickards v. Lothian itself was concerned with a use of a domestic kind, viz. the overflow of water from a basin whose runaway had become blocked. But over the years the concept of natural use, in the sense of ordinary use, has been extended to embrace a wide variety of uses, including not only domestic uses but also recreational uses and even some industrial uses.

It is obvious that the expression "ordinary use of the land" in Lord Moulton's statement of the law is one which is lacking in precision. There are some writers who welcome the flexibility which has thus been introduced into this branch of the law, on the ground that it enables judges to mould and adapt the principle of strict liability to the changing needs of society; whereas others regret the perceived absence of principle in so vague a concept, and fear that the whole idea of strict liability may as a result be undermined. A particular doubt is introduced by Lord Moulton's alternative criterion—"or such a use as is proper for the general benefit of the community." If these words are understood to refer to a local community, they can be given some content as intended to refer to such matters as, for example, the provision of services; indeed the same idea can, without too much difficulty, be extended to, for example, the provision of services to industrial premises, as in a business park or an industrial estate. But if the words are extended to embrace the wider interests of the local community or the general benefit of the community at large, it is difficult to see how the exception can be kept within reasonable bounds. A notable extension was considered in your Lordships' House in *Read v. J. Lyons & Co. Ltd.* [1947] A.C. 156, 169–170, *per* Viscount Simon, and p. 174, *per* Lord Macmillan, where it was suggested that, in time of war, the manufacture of explosives might be held to constitute a natural use of land, apparently on the basis that, in a country in which the greater part of the population was involved in the war effort, many otherwise exceptional uses might become "ordinary" for the duration of the war. It is however unnecessary to consider so wide an extension as that in a case such as the present. Even so, we can see the introduction of another extension in the present case, when the judge invoked the creation of employment as clearly for the benefit of the local community, viz. "the industrial village" at Sawston. I myself, however, do not feel able to accept that the creation of employment as such, even in a small industrial complex, is sufficient of itself to establish a particular use as constituting a natural or ordinary use of land.

Fortunately, I do not think it is necessary for the purposes of the present case to attempt any redefinition of the concept of natural or ordinary use. This is because I am satisfied that the storage of chemicals in substantial quantities, and their use in the manner employed at E.C.L.'s premises, cannot fall within the exception. For the purpose of testing the point, let it be assumed that E.C.L. was well aware of the possibility that P.C.E., if it escaped, could indeed cause damage, for example by contaminating any water with which it became mixed so as to render that water undrinkable by human beings. I cannot think that it would be right in such circumstances to exempt E.C.L. from liability under the rule in *Rylands v. Fletcher* on the ground that the use was natural or ordinary. The mere fact that the use is common in the tanning industry cannot, in my opinion, be enough to bring the use within the exception, nor the fact that Sawston contains a small industrial community which is worthy of encouragement or support. Indeed I feel bound to say that the storage of substantial quantities of chemicals on industrial premises should be regarded as an almost classic case of non-natural use; and I find it very difficult to think that it should be thought objectionable to impose strict liability for damage caused in the event of their escape. It may well be that, now that it is recognised that foreseeability of harm of the relevant type is a prerequisite of liability in damages under the rule, the courts may feel less pressure to extend the concept of natural use to circumstances such as those in the present case; and in due course it may become easier to control this exception, and to ensure that it has a more recognisable basis of principle. For these reasons, I would not hold that E.C.L. should be exempt from liability on the basis of the exception of natural use.

Comment

Foreseeability

The decisive finding of the House of Lords in this case was that reasonable foreseeability is an essential element of liability in *Rylands v Fletcher*, just as it is in nuisance. There were several stages in the reasoning that led to this conclusion.

First, Blackburn J's own statement of the rule incorporated the idea that the substance accumulated is 'likely' to do damage if it escapes. Although there is some case law which does not require that there should be foreseeability, this case law is limited and offers a 'fragile basis' for an argument against a foreseeability requirement. Second, *Rylands v Fletcher* is accepted to be a branch of nuisance, relating to isolated escapes. Therefore, the development of a remoteness rule for nuisance in the form of reasonable foreseeability, as explained in *The Wagon Mound (No 2)*, could not have been intended to by-pass *Rylands v Fletcher*. Here Lord Goff leans heavily on Professor Newark's classic article, 'The Boundaries of Nuisance' (1949) 65 LQR 480, as revealing the true historical basis of *Rylands v Fletcher*. This element of the reasoning in *Cambridge Water* has been extremely important, for example in the *Transco* decision.

Third, Lord Goff rejected an invitation to develop the principle in *Rylands* beyond its narrow confines and to see it as part of a developing principle of strict liability for ultra-hazardous operations, in which case he might be free to dispense with the 'reasonable foreseeability' criterion. His rejection of this invitation was supported by three separate reasons:

(a) If there is to be a principle of strict liability for ultra-hazardous activities, why would this be limited to cases of escape, as *Rylands v Fletcher* has been? Here of course it may be objected that *Read v Lyons* (1947) AC 156 could be overruled, if it was thought that a broadened principle would be desirable. But the difficulty remains that there is no clear principled basis to the rule which would set alternative limits to it.

(b) The Law Commission considered a general principle of strict liability for dangerous activities in 1970, and rejected the idea of statutory development (*Report of the Law Commission on Civil Liability for Dangerous Things and Activities*, Law Com No 32 (1970)). Therefore the common law should be still more wary.

(c) The case is one of environmental pollution, and it is wise for the common law not to become too involved in this specialized and evolving area.

On the face of it, this third reason may be the weakest. Judges sometimes underestimate the extent to which Parliament works around rules of common law and takes a lead from the principles which are embedded in that law. On the other hand, Lord Goff's words of caution are not without justification. In particular, the evolution of environmental law involves considerable change having an impact on a wide variety of interests. Statutory liabilities generally take effect *prospectively*, and those whose interests are affected may be given fair warning of change to come.

When it came to addressing the facts of the case however, Lord Goff's conclusions on foreseeability were brief. The result is that it is not entirely clear which type of foreseeability he had in mind, since it is not clear which particular element of the facts made the damage in a relevant sense unforeseeable:

> it is plain that, at the time when the PCE was brought onto ECL's land, and indeed when it was used in the tanning process there, nobody at ECL could reasonably have foreseen the result-ant damage which occurred at CWC's borehole at Sawston.

In this brief statement, Lord Goff refers to 'foreseeability of damage'. He does not explicitly require that the escape should be foreseeable. Should we conclude that the escape need not be foreseeable? Not necessarily. Damage may be unforeseeable *because* the escape is unforeseeable. Capturing this ambiguity, two different potential meanings of foreseeability in the context of this case are identified in the following extract.

David Wilkinson, '*Cambridge Water Company v Eastern Counties Leather plc: Diluting Liability for Continuing Escapes*' (1994) 57 MLR 799–811, at 803–4

. . . Consider the following options.

- Strict liability means that liability is limited to foreseeable damage and, in determining what damage is foreseeable, the escape itself is not to be assumed. On this view, a defendant would be liable for only that damage caused by the escape which a reasonable bystander would have anticipated. The foreseeability of the escape itself is an integral part of foreseeability of damage. If no escape is foreseeable then, as a matter of logic, no damage of any kind is foreseeable. We may refer to this view as 'full foreseeability.'

- Strict liability means that liability is limited to foreseeable damage and, in determining what damage was foreseeable, the escape is to be assumed (whether or not it was foreseeable). On this view, a defendant would be liable for all damage caused by the escape that a reasonable bystander, upon being informed of the escape, would have anticipated. The foreseeability of the escape is irrelevant to the foreseeability of damage. We may refer to this as 'semi-foreseeability' . . .

- Strict liability means that foreseeability is irrelevant to liability. On this view, a defendant would be liable for all damage caused by the escape, whether or not foreseeable. This view is no longer tenable in the light of the present case.

It seems likely that Lord Goff had in mind the reasons given by the first instance judge, Kennedy J, for saying that the damage was unforeseeable for the purposes of an action in either nuisance or negligence. The appeal to the House of Lords concerned the question of whether absence of foreseeability *also* ruled out an action in *Rylands v Fletcher*. The reasons given by Kennedy J were summarized by Lord Goff (at 292) in his judgment as follows. The reasons are multiple, reflecting the facts of this particular case:

Lord Goff [1994] 2 AC 264, at 292

However, as the judge found, a reasonable supervisor at ECL would not have foreseen, in or before 1976, that such repeated spillages of small quantities of solvent would lead to any environmental hazard or damage—ie that the solvent would reach the aquifer or that, having done so, detectable quantities would be found down-catchment. *Even if he had foreseen that solvent might enter the aquifer, he would not have foreseen that such quantities would produce any sensible effect upon water taken down-catchment, or would otherwise be material or deserve the description of pollution* . . . The only harm that could have been foreseen from a spillage was that somebody might have been overcome by fumes from a spillage of a significant quantity'.

(Emphasis added.)

If we do, as Wilkinson proposes, 'presume the escape', it was therefore not reasonably foreseeable in this case that the type of damage in question would be done. This 'additional' aspect of unforeseeability mentioned by Kennedy J and repeated by Lord Goff, italicized in the extract above, could be referred to as 'semi-foreseeability' in Wilkinson's sense. Therefore, *both* forms of unforeseeability were present in *Cambridge Water*, and it is not possible to be entirely clear which one was decisive. 'Semi-foreseeability' would be more consistent with the general purpose of the rule in *Rylands v Fletcher*, than would full foreseeability.

The House of Lords in the later case of *Transco v Stockport MBC* gave a far clearer account of the foreseeability criterion and even appeared to treat the issue as clearly settled. Their interpretation does not require foreseeability of escape. Lord Bingham said that the foreseeability criterion will be satisfied 'however unforeseeable the escape', provided that the defendant ought to have recognized the risk of damage (at [10]); and Lord Hoffmann said (at [33]) that under *Rylands v Fletcher*, 'the defendant will be liable even if he could not reasonably have foreseen that there would be an escape'. As explained above, this interpretation is the most appropriate to the strict liability rule.

Non-natural user

Lord Goff added some comments on non-natural user, though they did not form part of the decision.

Lord Goff generally accepted that the principle of 'natural' user can be equated with 'ordinary' user. He was also clear that being 'for the general benefit of the community' is not sufficient to create an 'ordinary' user of land, and in this respect he disagreed with the first instance judge. Even though the defendant's activities were generally beneficial in providing local employment, this could not be a reason for defining their use as a 'natural' one. But he thought that there was some room for ambiguity in the space between these two clear cases, since some uses which are for the benefit of a *local* community will be thought to amount to a natural user: 'If these words [referring to the 'benefit of the community'] are understood to refer to a local community, they can be given some content . . .'. Here, Lord Goff seems to have been thinking of accumulations which are of general or reciprocal benefit to all. Potential claimants may gain directly from the accumulation, or may have made similar accumulations of their own, as in the provision of domestic water supplies.

In any case, Lord Goff made very clear that the storage of chemicals in drums, no matter how appropriate that storage might be in the precise location stored, was not in his opinion capable of amounting to a 'natural user'. Neither appropriateness of the location, nor general public interest (for example, in providing local employment), were relevant tests to apply for the purposes of this criterion. We will take up the development of non-natural user in our discussion of *Transco v Stockport*.

Transco plc v Stockport Metropolitan Borough Council [2003] UKHL 61; [2004] 2 AC 1

The House of Lords was invited by counsel to follow the Australian lead, and to declare *Rylands v Fletcher* to have been absorbed by negligence. It declined to do so. Although this seems to preserve the relative strictness of the rule for some categories of case, it arguably leaves strict liability in a rather more patchy state in England and Wales than in Australia, where non-delegable duties in negligence appear to be more readily found. The 'non-natural user' criterion was unanimously thought not to be satisfied where the use in question was provision of a domestic water supply to a block of flats. Additional reasons for rejecting the claim were offered by Lord Bingham (there was no accumulation of a 'dangerous' thing) and Lord Scott (there was no relevant escape). Lord Hoffmann's judgment merits separate consideration because it grapples with the boundaries of the strict liability rule, through the non-natural user criterion, not only through analysis of the (confused and contradictory) case law, but also in policy terms.

The facts of the case are briefly summarized in the extract from Lord Bingham's judgment.

Lord Bingham of Cornhill

2 . . . The salient facts appear to me to be these. As a multi-storey block of flats built by a local authority and let to local residents, Hollow End Towers was typical of very many such blocks throughout the country. It had been built by the respondent council. The block was supplied

with water for the domestic use of those living there, as statute has long required. Water was carried to the block by the statutory undertaker, from whose main the pipe central to these proceedings led to tanks in the basement of the block for onward distribution of the water to the various flats. The capacity of this pipe was much greater than the capacity of a pipe supplying a single dwelling, being designed to meet the needs of 66 dwellings. But it was a normal pipe in such a situation and the water it carried was at mains pressure. Without negligence on the part of the council or its servants or agents, the pipe failed at a point within the block with the inevitable result that water escaped. Since, again without negligence, the failure of the pipe remained undetected for a prolonged period, the quantity of water which escaped was very considerable. The lie and the nature of the council's land in the area was such that the large quantity of water which had escaped from the pipe flowed some distance from the block and percolated into an embankment which supported the appellant Transco's 16-inch high-pressure gas main, causing the embankment to collapse and leaving this gas main exposed and unsupported. There was an immediate and serious risk that the gas main might crack, with potentially devastating consequences. Transco took prompt and effective remedial measures and now seeks to recover from the council the agreed cost of taking them.

. . .

The future development of *Rylands v Fletcher*

4 In the course of his excellent argument for the council, Mr Mark Turner canvassed various ways in which the rule in *Rylands v Fletcher* might be applied and developed in future, without however judging it necessary to press the House to accept any one of them. The boldest of these courses was to follow the trail blazed by a majority of the High Court of Australia in *Burnie Port Authority v General Jones Pty Ltd* (1994) 120 ALR 42 by treating the rule in *Rylands v Fletcher* as absorbed by the principles of ordinary negligence. . . .

6 I would be willing to suppress an instinctive resistance to treating a nuisance-based tort as if it were governed by the law of negligence if I were persuaded that it would serve the interests of justice to discard the rule in *Rylands v Fletcher* and treat the cases in which it might have been relied on as governed by the ordinary rules of negligence. But I hesitate to adopt that solution for four main reasons. First, there is in my opinion a category of case, however small it may be, in which it seems just to impose liability even in the absence of fault. In the context of then recent catastrophes *Rylands v Fletcher* itself was understandably seen as such a case. With memories of the tragedy at Aberfan still green, the same view might now be taken of *Attorney General v Cory Bros & Co Ltd* [1921] 1 AC 521 even if the claimants had failed to prove negligence, as on the facts they were able to do. I would regard *Rainham Chemical Works Ltd v Belvedere Fish Guano Co Ltd* [1921] 2 AC 465, and *Cambridge Water Co v Eastern Counties Leather plc* [1994] 2 AC 264 (had there been foreseeability of damage), as similarly falling within that category. Second, it must be remembered that common law rules do not exist in a vacuum, least of all rules which have stood for over a century during which there has been detailed statutory regulation of matters to which they might potentially relate. With reference to water, section 209 of the Water Industry Act 1991 imposes strict liability (subject to certain exemptions) on water undertakers and Schedule 2 to the Reservoirs Act 1975 appears to assume that on facts such as those of *Rylands v Fletcher* strict liability would attach. If the law were changed so as to require proof of negligence by those previously thought to be entitled to recover under the rule in *Rylands v Fletcher* without proving negligence, the effect might be (one does not know) to falsify the assumption on which Parliament has legislated, by significantly modifying rights which Parliament may have assumed would continue to exist.

Third, although in *Cambridge Water* [1994] 2 AC 264, 283–285, the possibility was ventilated that the House might depart from *Rylands v Fletcher* in its entirety, it is plain that this suggestion was not accepted. Instead, the House looked forward to a more principled and better controlled application of the existing rule: see, for example, p 309. While this is not a conclusive bar to acceptance of the detailed argument presented to the House on this occasion, "stop-go" is in general as bad an approach to legal development as to economic management. Fourth, while replacement of strict *Rylands v Fletcher* liability by a fault-based rule would tend to assimilate the law of England and Wales with that of Scotland, it would tend to increase the disparity between it and the laws of France and Germany. Having reviewed comparable provisions of French and German law, van Gerven, Lever and Larouche (*Cases, Materials and Text on National, Supranational and International Tort Law* (2000), p 205) observe: "Even if the contours of the respective regimes may differ, all systems studied here therefore afford a form of strict liability protection in disputes between neighbouring landowners." The authors indeed suggest (p 205) that the English rule as laid down in *Rylands v Fletcher* is "the most developed of these regimes".

7   Should, then, the rule be generously applied and the scope of strict liability extended? There are certainly respected commentators who favour such a course and regret judicial restrictions on the operation of the rule: see *Fleming, The Law of Torts*, 9th ed (1998), p 377; *Markesinis & Deakin, Tort Law*, 5th ed (2003), p 544. But there is to my mind a compelling objection to such a course, articulated by Lord Goff of Chieveley in *Cambridge Water* [1994] 2 AC 264, 305:

> "Like the judge in the present case, I incline to the opinion that, as a general rule, it is more appropriate for strict liability in respect of operations of high risk to be imposed by Parliament, than by the courts. If such liability is imposed by statute, the relevant activities can be identified, and those concerned can know where they stand. Furthermore, statute can where appropriate lay down precise criteria establishing the incidence and scope of such liability."

. . .

8   There remains a third option, which I would myself favour: to retain the rule, while insisting upon its essential nature and purpose; and to restate it so as to achieve as much certainty and clarity as is attainable, recognising that new factual situations are bound to arise posing difficult questions on the boundary of the rule, wherever that is drawn.

9   The rule in *Rylands v Fletcher* is a sub-species of nuisance, which is itself a tort based on the interference by one occupier of land with the right in or enjoyment of land by another occupier of land as such. From this simple proposition two consequences at once flow. First, as very clearly decided by the House in *Read v J Lyons & Co Ltd* [1947] AC 156, no claim in nuisance or under the rule can arise if the events complained of take place wholly on the land of a single occupier. There must, in other words, be an escape from one tenement to another. Second, the claim cannot include a claim for death or personal injury, since such a claim does not relate to any right in or enjoyment of land. This proposition has not been authoritatively affirmed by any decision at the highest level. It was left open by Parker LJ in *Perry v Kendricks Transport Ltd* [1956] 1 WLR 85, 92, and is inconsistent with decisions such as *Shiffman v Order of the Hospital of St John of Jerusalem* [1936] 1 All ER 557 and *Miles v Forest Rock Granite Co (Leicestershire) Ltd* (1918) 34 TLR 500. It is however clear from Lord Macmillan's opinion in *Read* [1947] AC 156, 170–171 that he regarded a personal injury claim as outside the scope of the rule, and his approach is in my opinion strongly fortified by the decisions of the House in *Cambridge Water* [1994] 2 AC 264 and *Hunter v Canary Wharf Ltd* [1997] AC 655, in each of which nuisance was identified as a tort directed, and directed only, to the protection of interests in land.

10 It has from the beginning been a necessary condition of liability under the rule in *Rylands v Fletcher* that the thing which the defendant has brought on his land should be "something which . . . will naturally do mischief if it escape out of his land" (LR 1 Ex 265, 279 per Blackburn J), "something dangerous . . . ", "anything likely to do mischief if it escapes", "something . . . harmless to others so long as it is confined to his own property, but which he knows to be mischievous if it gets on his neighbour's" (p 280), "anything which, if it should escape, may cause damage to his neighbour" (LR 3 HL 330, 340, per Lord Cranworth). The practical problem is of course to decide whether in any given case the thing which has escaped satisfies this mischief or danger test, a problem exacerbated by the fact that many things not ordinarily regarded as sources of mischief or danger may none the less be capable of proving to be such if they escape. . . . Bearing in mind the historical origin of the rule, and also that its effect is to impose liability in the absence of negligence for an isolated occurrence, I do not think the mischief or danger test should be at all easily satisfied. It must be shown that the defendant has done something which he recognised, or judged by the standards appropriate at the relevant place and time, he ought reasonably to have recognised, as giving rise to an exceptionally high risk of danger or mischief if there should be an escape, however unlikely an escape may have been thought to be.

11 . . . I think it clear that ordinary user is a preferable test to natural user, making it clear that the rule in *Rylands v Fletcher* is engaged only where the defendant's use is shown to be extraordinary and unusual. This is not a test to be inflexibly applied: a use may be extraordinary and unusual at one time or in one place but not so at another time or in another place (although I would question whether, even in wartime, the manufacture of explosives could ever be regarded as an ordinary user of land, as contemplated by Viscount Simon, Lord Macmillan, Lord Porter and Lord Uthwatt in *Read v J Lyons & Co Ltd* [1947] AC 156, 169–170, 174, 176–177, 186–187). I also doubt whether a test of reasonable user is helpful, since a user may well be quite out of the ordinary but not unreasonable, as was that of *Rylands*, *Rainham Chemical Works* or the tannery in *Cambridge Water*. Again, as it seems to me, the question is whether the defendant has done something which he recognises, or ought to recognise, as being quite out of the ordinary in the place and at the time when he does it. In answering that question, I respectfully think that little help is gained (and unnecessary confusion perhaps caused) by considering whether the use is proper for the general benefit of the community. In *Rickards v Lothian* itself, the claim arose because the outflow from a wash-basin on the top floor of premises was maliciously blocked and the tap left running, with the result that damage was caused to stock on a floor below: not surprisingly, the provision of a domestic water supply to the premises was held to be a wholly ordinary use of the land. An occupier of land who can show that another occupier of land has brought or kept on his land an exceptionally dangerous or mischievous thing in extraordinary or unusual circumstances is in my opinion entitled to recover compensation from that occupier for any damage caused to his property interest by the escape of that thing, subject to defences of Act of God or of a stranger, without the need to prove negligence.

The present appeal

. . .

13 It is of course true that water in quantity is almost always capable of causing damage if it escapes. But the piping of a water supply from the mains to the storage tanks in the block was a routine function which would not have struck anyone as raising any special hazard. In truth, the council did not accumulate any water, it merely arranged a supply adequate to meet the residents' needs. The situation cannot stand comparison with the making by Mr Rylands of a substantial reservoir. Nor can the use by the council of its land be seen as in any way extraordinary or unusual. It was entirely normal and routine. Despite the attractive argument of Mr Ian Leeming for Transco, I am satisfied that the conditions to be met before strict liability could be imposed on the council were far from being met on the facts here.

Lord Hoffmann

. . .

The social background to the rule

28   Although the judgment of Blackburn J [in *Fletcher v Rylands*] is constructed in the traditional common law style of deducing principle from precedent, without reference to questions of social policy, Professor Brian Simpson has demonstrated in his article "Legal Liability for Bursting Reservoirs: The Historical Context of *Rylands v Fletcher*" (1984) 13 J Leg Stud 209 that the background to the case was public anxiety about the safety of reservoirs, caused in particular by the bursting of the Bradfield Reservoir near Sheffield on 12 March 1864, with the loss of about 250 lives. The judicial response was to impose strict liability upon the proprietors of reservoirs. But, since the common law deals in principles rather than ad hoc solutions, the rule had to be more widely formulated.

29   It is tempting to see, beneath the surface of the rule, a policy of requiring the costs of a commercial enterprise to be internalised; to require the entrepreneur to provide, by insurance or otherwise, for the risks to others which his enterprise creates. That was certainly the opinion of Bramwell B, who was in favour of liability when the case was before the Court of Exchequer: (1865) 3 H & C 774. He had a clear and consistent view on the matter: see *Bamford v Turnley* (1862) 3 B & S 62, 84–85 and *Hammersmith and City Railway Co v Brand* (1867) LR 2 QB 223, 230–231. But others thought differently. They considered that the public interest in promoting economic development made it unreasonable to hold an entrepreneur liable when he had not been negligent . . . . On the whole, it was the latter view—no liability without fault—which gained the ascendancy. With hindsight, *Rylands v Fletcher* can be seen as an isolated victory for the internalisers. The following century saw a steady refusal to treat it as laying down any broad principle of liability. I shall briefly trace the various restrictions imposed on its scope.

Restrictions on the rule

Lord Hoffmann here considered restrictions on the rule in the form of defences, remoteness, escape, and the absence of recovery for personal injury (all of which we dealt with above), and turned to non-natural user as the final restriction:

(f) Non-natural user

36   The principle in *Rylands v Fletcher* was widely expressed; the essence was the escape of something which the defendant had brought upon his land. Not surprisingly, attempts were immediately made to apply the rule in all kinds of situations far removed from the specific social problem of bursting reservoirs which had produced it. Leaks caused by a rat gnawing a hole in a wooden gutter-box (*Carstairs v Taylor* LR 6 Ex 217) were not at all what Blackburn J and Lord Cairns had had in mind. In some cases the attempt to invoke the rule was repelled by relying on Blackburn J's statement that the defendant must have brought whatever escaped onto his land "for his own purposes". This excluded claims by tenants that they had been damaged by escapes of water from plumbing installed for the benefit of the premises as whole. Another technique was to imply the claimant's consent to the existence of the accumulation. But the most generalized restriction was formulated by Lord Moulton in *Rickards v Lothian* [1913] AC 263, 280 . . . .

37 The context in which Lord Moulton made this statement was a claim under *Rylands v Fletcher* for damage caused by damage to stock in a shop caused by an overflow of water from a wash-basin in a lavatory on a floor above. To exclude domestic use is understandable if one thinks of the rule as a principle for the allocation of costs; there is no enterprise of which the risk can be regarded as a cost which should be internalised. That would at least provide a fairly rational distinction. But the rather vague reference to "the ordinary use of the land" and in particular the reference to a use "proper for the general benefit of the community" has resulted in the rule being applied to some commercial enterprises but not others, the distinctions being sometimes very hard to explain.

38 In the *Cambridge Water Co* case [1994] 2 AC 264, 308–309 Lord Goff of Chieveley noted these difficulties but expressed the hope that it would be possible to give the distinction "a more recognisable basis of principle". The facts of that case, involving the storage of substantial quantities of chemicals on industrial premises, were in his opinion "an almost classic case of non-natural use". He thought that the restriction of liability to the foreseeable consequences of the escape would reduce the inclination of the courts to find other ways of limiting strict liability, such as extension of the concept of natural use.

Where stands the rule today?

39 I pause at this point to summarise the very limited circumstances to which the rule has been confined. First, it is a remedy for damage to land or interests in land. As there can be few properties in the country, commercial or domestic, which are not insured against damage by flood and the like, this means that disputes over the application of the rule will tend to be between property insurers and liability insurers. Secondly, it does not apply to works or enterprises authorised by statute. That means that it will usually have no application to really high risk activities. As Professor Simpson points out (1984) 13 J Leg Stud 225 the Bradfield Reservoir was built under statutory powers. In the absence of negligence, the occupiers whose lands had been inundated would have had no remedy. Thirdly, it is not particularly strict because it excludes liability when the escape is for the most common reasons, namely vandalism or unusual natural events. Fourthly, the cases in which there is an escape which is not attributable to an unusual natural event or the act of a third party will, by the same token, usually give rise to an inference of negligence. Fifthly, there is a broad and ill-defined exception for "natural" uses of land. It is perhaps not surprising that counsel could not find a reported case since the second world war in which anyone had succeeded in a claim under the rule. It is hard to escape the conclusion that the intellectual effort devoted to the rule by judges and writers over many years has brought forth a mouse.

Is it worth keeping?

40 In *Burnie Port Authority v General Jones Pty Ltd* (1994) 179 CLR 520 a majority of the High Court of Australia lost patience with the pretensions and uncertainties of the rule and decided that it had been "absorbed" into the law of negligence. Your Lordships have been invited by the respondents to kill off the rule in England in similar fashion. It is said, first, that in its present attenuated form it serves little practical purpose; secondly, that its application is unacceptably vague ("an essentially unprincipled and ad hoc subjective determination" said the High Court (at p 540) in the *Burnie* case) and thirdly, that strict liability on social grounds is better left to statutory intervention.

41 There is considerable force in each of these points. It is hard to find any rational principle which explains the rule and its exceptions. . . . And the proposition that strict liability is best left to statute receives support from the speech of Lord Goff of Chieveley in the *Cambridge Water* case . . .

42 An example of statutory strict liability close to home is section 209 of the Water Industry Act 1991:

> "(1) Where an escape of water, however caused, from a pipe vested in a water undertaker causes loss or damage, the undertaker shall be liable, except as otherwise provided in this section, for the loss or damage . . . "

> "(3) A water undertaker shall not incur any liability under subsection (1) above in respect of any loss or damage for which the undertaker would not be liable apart from that subsection and which is sustained . . . (b) by any public gas supplier within the meaning of Part I of the Gas Act 1986 . . . "

This provision is designed to avoid all argument over which insurers should bear the loss. Liability is far stricter than under the rule in *Rylands v Fletcher*. There is no exception for acts of third parties or natural events. The undertaker is liable for an escape "however caused" and must insure accordingly. On the other hand, certain potential claimants like public gas suppliers (now called public gas transporters) must insure themselves. The irony of the present case is that if the leak had been from a high pressure water main, belonging to the North West Water Authority, a much more plausible high-risk activity, there could have been no dispute. Section 209(3)(b) would have excluded a statutory claim and the authority's statutory powers would have excluded the rule in *Rylands v Fletcher*.

43 But despite the strength of these arguments, I do not think it would be consistent with the judicial function of your Lordships' House to abolish the rule. It has been part of English law for nearly 150 years and despite a searching examination by Lord Goff of Chieveley in the *Cambridge Water* case [1994] 2 AC 264, 308, there was no suggestion in his speech that it could or should be abolished. I think that would be too radical a step to take.

44 It remains, however, if not to rationalise the law of England, at least to introduce greater certainty into the concept of natural user which is in issue in this case. In order to do so, I think it must be frankly acknowledged that little assistance can be obtained from the kinds of user which Lord Cairns must be assumed to have regarded as "non-natural" in *Rylands v Fletcher* itself. . . . So nothing can be made of the anomaly that one of the illustrations of the rule given by Blackburn J is cattle trespass. Whatever Blackburn J and Lord Cairns may have meant by "natural", the law was set on a different course by the opinion of Lord Moulton in *Rickards v Lothian* [1913] AC 263 and the question of what is a natural use of land or, (the converse) a use creating an increased risk, must be judged by contemporary standards.

45 Two features of contemporary society seem to me to be relevant. First, the extension of statutory regulation to a number of activities, such as discharge of water (section 209 of the Water Industry Act 1991) pollution by the escape of waste (section 73(6) of the Environmental Protection Act 1990) and radioactive matter (section 7 of the Nuclear Installations Act 1965). It may have to be considered whether these and similar provisions create an exhaustive code of liability for a particular form of escape which excludes the rule in *Rylands v Fletcher*.

46 Secondly, so far as the rule does have a residuary role to play, it must be borne in mind that it is concerned only with damage to property and that insurance against various forms of damage to property is extremely common. A useful guide in deciding whether the risk has been created by a "non-natural" user of land is therefore to ask whether the damage which eventuated was something against which the occupier could reasonably be expected to have insured himself. Property insurance is relatively cheap and accessible; in my opinion people should be encouraged to insure their own property rather than seek to transfer the risk to others by means of litigation, with the heavy transactional costs which that involves. The present substantial litigation over £100,000 should be a warning to anyone seeking to rely on an esoteric cause of action to shift a commonplace insured risk.

47 In the present case, I am willing to assume that if the risk arose from a "non-natural user" of the council's land, all the other elements of the tort were satisfied. . . .

48 The damage which eventuated was subsidence beneath a gas main: a form of risk against which no rational owner of a gas main would fail to insure. The casualty was caused by the escape of water from the council's land. But the source was a perfectly normal item of plumbing. The pipe was, it is true, considerably larger than the ordinary domestic size. But it was smaller than a water main. It was installed to serve the occupiers of the council's high rise flats; not strictly speaking a commercial purpose, but not a private one either.

49 In my opinion the Court of Appeal was right to say that it was not a "non-natural" user of land. I am influenced by two matters. First, there is no evidence that it created a greater risk than is normally associated with domestic or commercial plumbing. . . . I agree with my noble and learned friend, Lord Bingham of Cornhill, that the criterion of exceptional risk must be taken seriously and creates a high threshold for a claimant to surmount. Secondly, I think that the risk of damage to property caused by leaking water is one against which most people can and do commonly insure. This is, as I have said, particularly true of Transco, which can be expected to have insured against any form of damage to its pipe. It would be a very strange result if Transco were entitled to recover against the council when it would not have been entitled to recover against the water authority for similar damage emanating from its high-pressure main.

Lord Hobhouse of Woodborough

52 I consider that the rule is, when properly understood, still part of English law and does comprise a useful and soundly based component of the law of tort as an aspect of the law of private nuisance. It derives from the use of land and covers the division of risk as between the owner of the land in question and other landowners. It is not concerned with liability for personal injuries which is covered by other parts of the law of torts (*Read v J Lyons & Co Ltd* [1947] AC 156) and which does not rise for discussion in this case . . .

54 The salient features of the rule are easily identified: the self interest of the landowner, his conduct in bringing or keeping on his land something dangerous which involves a risk of damaging his neighbours' property, the avoidance of such damage by ensuring that the danger is confined to his own property and liability to his neighbours if he fails to do so, subject to a principle of remoteness. The subsequent complications and misunderstandings have arisen, not from the original rule and its rationale, but from additional criteria, often inappropriately expressed, introduced in later cases.

The principle

55   The principle which the rule reflects is also easily apparent. It is that the law of private nuisance recognises that the risk must be born by the person responsible for creating it and failing to control it. It reflects a social and economic utility. The user of one piece of land is always liable to affect the users or owners of other pieces of land. An escape of water originating on the former, or an explosion, may devastate not only the land on which it originates but also adjoining and more distant properties. The damage caused may be very serious indeed both in physical and financial terms. There may be a serious risk that if the user of the land, the use of which creates the risk, does not take active and adequate steps to prevent escape, an escape may occur. The situation is entirely under his control: other landowners have no control. In such a situation, two types of solution might be adopted. One would be to restrict the liberty of the user of the land, the source of the risk, to make such use of his land as he chooses. The other is to impose a strict liability on the landowner for the consequences of his exercising that liberty. The rule adopts the second type of solution . . . . It is a coherent principle which accords with justice and with the existing legal theory at the time.

56   This approach was entirely in keeping with the economic and political culture of the 19th century, laissez faire and an understanding of the concept of risk. During the 20th century and particularly during the second half, the culture has changed. Government has increasingly intervened to limit the freedom of a landowner to use his land as he chooses, e g through the planning laws, and has regulated or forbidden certain dangerous or anti-social uses of land such as the manufacture or storage of explosives or the emission of noxious effluents. Thus the present state of the law is that some of the situations where the rule in *Rylands v Fletcher* applies are now also addressed by the first type of solution. But this does not deprive the rule of its utility. . . . As Lord Goff pointed out in *Cambridge Water* [1994] 2 AC 264, the occasions where *Rylands v Fletcher* may have to be invoked by a claimant may be reducing but that is not to say that it has ceased to be a valid part of English law. The only way it could be rendered obsolete is by a compulsory strict public liability insurance scheme for all persons using their land for dangerous purposes. However this would simply be to re-enact *Rylands v Fletcher* in another guise.

57   *Rylands v Fletcher* was unremarkable in the mid 19th century since there was then nothing peculiar about strict liability. There were many other fields in which strict liability existed, for example conversion. For those following a "common" calling, such as common carriers or common inn-keepers, liability was also strict. Although the origins were already present in the 19th century in the defence of "inevitable accident" in trespass cases, it was only later that the generalised criterion of negligence was developed, culminating in *Donoghue v Stevenson* [1932] AC 562. That is a fault—i e, breach of a duty of care—not a risk concept. But, where the situation arises as between landowners and arises from the dangerous use of his land by one of them, the risk concept remains relevant. He who creates the relevant risk and has, to the exclusion of the other, the control of how he uses his land, should bear the risk. It would be unjust to deny the other a risk based remedy and introduce a requirement of proving fault.

Lord Scott and **Lord Walker** delivered concurring judgments, Lord Scott adding that there had been no relevant escape (from land under the occupation and control of the defendant, to other land).

Comments

Although there were no dissenting judgments, the members of the House of Lords varied widely in their emphasis and in their reasons for retaining the rule in *Rylands v Fletcher*. Lord Bingham clarified the content of the rule, suggesting that the mischief or danger test should be hard to satisfy, and that it is preferable to refer to 'ordinary' rather than to 'natural' user. On the other hand, he made it clear that 'ordinary' is not a synonym for 'reasonable'; that a perfectly reasonable use of land may well be judged 'non-natural'; and that public utility will (additionally) be no defence. Although Lord Bingham thought that the conditions of the rule should be hard to fulfil, he also thought that there are circumstances in which it is still justified. Specifically, he mentioned the facts of *Cambridge Water*, had there been foreseeability of damage, as well as the older cases of *AG v Cory Brothers* [1921] 1 AC 521, and *Rainham Chemical Works v Belvedere Fish Guano Ltd* [1921] 2 AC 465. In these cases, he suggested that strict liability is 'just'. While he considered that any *extension* of the principle in *Rylands* would be better left to legislation, he made the point that to abrogate the existing rule may well be to 'falsify' the assumption on which various statutory strict liabilities had been enacted, and that this step should therefore be avoided. It is clear from Lord Bingham's judgment that personal injury damages will not be available in *Rylands v Fletcher*. He also thought there had been no relevantly hazardous accumulation of a 'dangerous' thing on these specific facts.

Lord Hobhouse appeared to be the most enthusiastic of their Lordships about the retention of strict liability under *Rylands v Fletcher*. He defended the justice and coherence of the rule in *Rylands*, arguing that the many confusions concerning its extent are created by later cases, and are not aspects of the original rule. However, this does not deal with the question of why there should be rather arbitrary limitations (especially the requirement of an escape) inherent in a rule that is supposedly based on defensible principles. Lord Hobhouse implies that strict liability was a more familiar and widely-accepted principle of liability at the time of the decision in *Rylands v Fletcher* than it is today. His historical account here differs, at least in its emphasis, from that of A. W. B. Simpson, who has suggested that fault was already on the ascendant at the time that *Rylands* was decided, and who has proposed that the decision was primarily a reaction to the problem of bursting reservoirs.

A. W. B. Simpson, 'Bursting Reservoirs and Victorian Tort Law: *Rylands and Horrocks v Fletcher*', in Simpson, *Leading Cases in the Common Law* (Oxford: OUP, 1996), 195–226 at 197–8

Writers on the common law have long regarded *Rylands v Fletcher* as an anomalous decision. Back in the nineteenth century Pollock criticised it in his treatise on the law of torts; Holmes had considerable difficulty fitting it into his general theory of tort law. A commonly held view used to be that the original common law proceeded on the basis that a man acted at his peril, but this harsh doctrine was progressively relaxed in the nineteenth century with the reception of the principle of liability only for negligent conduct. The law was thus moralized, and *Rylands v Fletcher* can only be explained as an atavistic decision, a throwback or a survival of more primitive times. This picture of legal development would today not be accepted by serious legal historians, but the alternative story still leaves much to be explained. It goes like this. Before the nineteenth century, questions of fault, contributory fault, assumption of risk, standards of appropriate behaviour, causation, and so forth, certainly arose in litigation. But there was virtually no law about them. They were treated as jury questions, to be handled in the main by lay common sense. The trial judge might well give the jury some guidance, but what he said was not subject to review and did not feature in law reports or legal treatises. What happened in the nineteenth century was the creation of law on issues where there had been none before. But on this view *Rylands v Fletcher* still appears puzzling, for it was decided at the end of a period in which the negligence principle had been steadily gaining ground through the extension of the tort of negligence.

The numerous judges who were involved in the case must have been aware that, if tort law was to incorporate two different principles of liability, there was a need to explain the relationship between them. Only two of them attempted to do so. One was Bramwell B., who favoured strict liability in his dissenting opinion in the Court of Exchequer, and the other was Blackburn J . . . Bramwell B dealt with the problem very briefly, but thought that in collision cases the negligence principle had to apply as a matter of logic, and this because of a problem over causation . . . Blackburn J, the judge most closely associated with the so-called rule in *Rylands v Fletcher*, offered a much more radical theory. It was that the *primary* principle of tort law was that of strict liability. The negligence principle applied only as an exception in situations in which people had, by implication, agreed that it should—the theory of assumption of risk . . . .

Blackburn's theory was not very convincing, but his contention that strict liability was the norm was stated in an opinion agreed by Willes, Keating, Mellor, Montague Smith, and Lush JJ . . . It seems as if Willes J and his colleagues were persuaded in *Rylands v Fletcher* that strict liability was the basic common law rule, and fault liability the exception. This, viewed at least from a modern perspective, seems to reverse the natural order of things, and certainly nothing of the sort had ever been said in the nineteenth century before this.

The way in which the rule in *Rylands v Fletcher* was restrictively interpreted in early cases such as *Carstairs v Taylor* (1871) LR 6 Ex 217, *Nicholls v Marsland* (1868) 2 Ex D 1, and even *Jones v Festiniog Railway* (1868) [LR] 3 QB, suggest that many nineteenth century courts did not find the idea of strict liability in this particular context as natural and comfortable as Lord Hobhouse implies. If they had, then a more robust rule, and a clearer rationale, would surely have developed in the years immediately following the decision in *Rylands v Fletcher* itself.

Lord Hoffmann's interpretation

The most contentious of the judgments in *Transco* is that of Lord Hoffmann. His general interpretation of the rule, or what is left of it, is almost as negative as the majority judgment in *Burnie Port Authority v General Jones Pty* (1994) 179 CLR 520 (extracted below), but for different reasons. Like the High Court of Australia, Lord Hoffmann contends that the rule in *Rylands* is now of very limited application. However, he concludes that this is the case not because of the ability of negligence to apply on the same facts, but because the most exceptional or dangerous uses of land are now dealt with via statute. In many cases, the relevant 'accumulation' will today be permitted by statute, giving rise to a defence of statutory authority. In Lord Hoffmann's analysis, the recognition of this defence is one of the key reasons why claims under *Rylands v Fletcher* are now so rarely successful. In other cases, there will be a statutory regime of *liability* in force, which will displace the common law rule, and frequently exceed it. Examples include the Nuclear Installations Act 1965, the Water Industry Act 1991, section 209, and the Water Resources Act 1991, section 208. In these instances, the relevant liability is strict, and excludes defences such as 'act of God' or of a third party. In the particular case before the House, Lord Hoffmann points out (at [42]) that the claimant gas company would have been barred, by statute, from claiming if the leak had been from water mains belonging to a water authority (Water Industry Act 1991, section 209(3)(b)). This provision governs the distribution between two public utilities of a particular sort of risk, and also precludes expensive transaction costs involved in litigation between these utilities at the expense of users. By extension, Lord Hoffmann considered that this was a reason why litigation was also inappropriate between the gas supplier, and the local authority. The gas company would be imprudent not to seek insurance against the possibility of damage caused by flooding. A first party insurance solution was regarded as preferable by Lord Hoffmann, primarily because of the lower transaction costs.

But Lord Hoffmann's preoccupation with distributive questions went further than this. Importantly, he suggested that the ambit of the rule in *Rylands v Fletcher*, and particularly the non-natural user criterion, should itself now be understood in terms of insurability. If an occupier of land can reasonably be expected to insure against the kind of danger posed by the defendant's use of land, then that use should on his analysis be seen as a 'natural user'. It appears to be only those risks that are *not* readily insurable by those exposed to them that will count as 'non-natural' (or extraordinary) uses.

This approach identifies a reason of policy which might both justify the retention of the rule, and at the same time be used to keep it within ascertainable limits, without heavy reliance on artificial concepts such as 'escape'. We should notice that this solution is in an important respect more restricted in its scope than the Australian approach, which recognised a strict form of liability between neighbours, via the tort of negligence. In the Australian approach outlined below, the activity carried on by the defendant occupier must be shown to be hazardous. However, many hazardous activities, which might fit the definition in *Burnie Port Authority*, are also insurable. The Australian approach places the burden of insurable losses on the defendant so long as they arise from a relevantly hazardous activity, and of course provided a relevant standard of care has been breached. Lord Hoffmann would place the burden of insuring against such losses on the claimant, provided the risk is readily insurable.

The question of whether a user is non-natural therefore becomes one of who should pay for insurance to cover the risk that the activity creates. On Lord Hoffmann's approach, the far lower transaction costs associated with insuring against one's own losses, when compared with the costs of litigation, suggest that first party insurance is to be preferred where this is possible (see our discussion of *The Damages Lottery*, in Chapter 8 above). It can readily be seen why this might be appropriate as between two public utilities, or between a public utility and a local authority, as in *Transco* itself. But is it generally a sound means of distinguishing natural from non-natural user, and therefore for establishing and rationalizing the boundary between strict liability and negligence? Here we should note again that ever since its inception, *Rylands* has been a rule in search of a robust rationale.

It is suggested that more empirical information would be required before reaching a conclusion on this. For example, we might ask what is the most *efficient* allocation of the burden of insurance, drawing attention to the importance of risk-rating. How can insurers establish the appropriate *cost* of insurance, if they deal only with those who are *exposed to* risk? In most such situations, the risk-creator has the fullest information about the risk. This may be adapted to a point about coverage. Will a potential claimant have sufficient knowledge to ensure that they *seek* insurance? This point about ignorance is not far removed from the Australian analysis in terms of 'dependence'.

More simply, the issue of insurability also raises an issue of fairness, which was mentioned by Lord Hobhouse in the extract above. Who ought to bear the *cost* of insurance? In the circumstances of *Rylands v Fletcher* liability, many claimants and defendants will be linked only by physical neighbourhood, and not (for example) by contractual or quasi-contractual relationships such as employment or consumer–producer relationships; nor will they have an immediate correspondence in interests. Here, there is no direct way in which the cost of insurance (if imposed primarily on defendants) will be passed to the group of potential claimants; nor will it be shared directly with prospective claimants in renewed premiums, as in motor insurance. It makes sense in this context to discuss the *fairness* of the burden of insurance, and on whom it should fall. However, this analysis does not fit so well where the defendant is a public utility or public authority, and this underlines the significance of Lord Hoffmann's observations concerning the vital importance of statutory intervention into most cases of dangerous accumulation.

At a much more general level, Lord Hoffmann's approach is important because it gives reasons based in distributive concerns, for limiting the ambit of the strict liability rule. It therefore directly counters any suggestion that the principle of strict liability ought to be developed further into a general principle relating to dangerous activities, and it gives some distributive reasons why 'internalization' through liability may not be the appropriate way forward. Thus, even if we move our discussion to distributive questions Lord Hoffmann's approach suggests that the 'internalizers' should not be allowed to have things all their own way. In this, he continues an academic discussion that he initiated in the case of *Wildtree Hotels*, concerning a particular and long-lived economic interpretation of private nuisance. It is in one respect a more radical approach than the one adopted by the Australian High Court (below), since it questions whether strict liability can be justified even in situations where it might appear 'fair'. It further illustrates the strength of overt *policy* reasoning in recent English tort law.

Australian High Court: Non-Delegable Duties in Negligence

The High Court of Australia decided the following case very soon after the House of Lords' decision in *Cambridge Water v Eastern Counties Leather plc*. While the House of Lords as we have seen decided to treat *Rylands* liability as an aspect of the tort of nuisance, emphasizing its historical origins, the High Court of Australia decided that *Rylands*-type cases should generally be dealt with by the tort of negligence. The High Court's conclusion that there was liability *in negligence* on the facts of *Burnie Port Authority* illustrates both that the tort of negligence is not always permeated by a concern with personal 'fault'; and that the idea of fault is so adaptable that it may sometimes impose stringent duties on individuals, dependent on the activity being carried out. Whose duty was it to take care, and what degree of care was required? Since the duty was non-delegable, it amounted to a positive duty to take action. On the other hand, the content of the duty relates to 'taking care': it takes the *form* of a duty to *ensure that care is taken*. The High Court recognized that the *standard* of care would be variable, depending on the hazardous nature of the activity.

Burnie Port Authority had retained an independent contractor to carry out building work. This work involved welding in close proximity to cartons of Isolite, a highly flammable substance. Through the contractors' negligence, a fire started which spread to premises occupied by the plaintiff, ruining a quantity of the plaintiffs' frozen vegetables. This case recalls the facts of *Rylands v Fletcher* itself, where there had been negligence on the part of the contractors employed to construct the reservoir.

Burnie Port Authority v General Jones Pty Limited (1994) 179 CLR 520; 120 ALR 42,
High Court of Australia

Mason CJ, Deane, Dawson, Toohey, and Gaudron JJ

At 549–52

Inevitably, the past adjustments and qualifications of the rule in Rylands v Fletcher to reflect aspects of the law of ordinary negligence have greatly reduced the likelihood that Rylands v Fletcher liability will exist in a case where liability would not exist under the principles of negligence. Thus, the editors of the last five editions of Winfield and Jolowicz on Tort have expressed the view that, putting to one side the factual situations in which a plaintiff will succeed equally well either under the rule or in nuisance, "[w]e have virtually reached the position where a defendant will not be considered liable when he would not be liable according to the ordinary principles of negligence". A similar view has been expressed by other distinguished academic writers. Nonetheless, there remains the perception of an underlying antithesis between the rule in Rylands v Fletcher and the principles of negligence. Liability under the rule is still theoretically seen as "strict liability" in the sense that it can arise without personal fault whereas liability in negligence is fault liability, that is to say, liability flowing from breach of a duty owed by the defendant to the plaintiff. The judicial transformation of Blackburn J.'s requirement of "not naturally there" into a test of "special" and "not ordinary" use and the expanded defences to a Rylands v Fletcher claim have, as has been seen, deprived that perception of underlying antithesis of some of its theoretical validity and most of its practical significance. However, as Professor Thayer indicated in a posthumous article published in the Harvard Law Review in 1916 ('Liability without Fault', *Harvard Law Review*, vol. 29, p. 801), the final answer to any argument based on that perceived theoretical contrast lies in ordinary negligence's concepts of a "non-delegable" duty and a variable standard of care.

The "non-delegable" duty

As was pointed out in the majority judgment in Cook v Cook ((1986) 162 CLR, at p. 382), "[t]he more detailed definition of the objective standard of care [under the ordinary law of negligence] for the purposes of a particular category of case must necessarily depend upon the identification of the relationship of proximity which is the touchstone and control of the relevant category." It has long been recognized that there are certain categories of case in which a duty to take reasonable care to avoid a foreseeable risk of injury to another will not be discharged merely by the employment of a qualified and ostensibly competent independent contractor. In those categories of case, the nature of the relationship of proximity gives rise to a duty of care of a special and "more stringent" kind, namely a "duty to ensure that reasonable care is taken" (See Kondis v State Transport Authority (1984), 154 CLR 672, at p. 686). Put differently, the requirement of reasonable care in those categories of case extends to seeing that care is taken. One of the classic statements of the scope of such a duty of care remains that of Lord Blackburn in Hughes v Percival ((1883) 8 App. Cas. 443, at p. 446):

> "that duty went as far as to require [the defendant] to see that reasonable skill and care were exercised in those operations . . . If such a duty was cast upon the defendant he could not get rid of responsibility by delegating the performance of it to a third person. He was at liberty to employ such a third person to fulfil the duty which the law cast on himself . . . but the defendant still remained subject to that duty, and liable for the consequences if it was not fulfilled."

In Kondis v State Transport Authority ((1984) 154 CLR, at pp. 679–687 . . .), in a judgment with which Deane J. and Dawson J. agreed, Mason J. identified some of the principal categories of case in which the duty to take reasonable care under the ordinary law of negligence is non-delegable in that sense: adjoining owners of land in relation to work threatening support or common walls; master and servant in relation to a safe system of work; hospital and patient; school authority and pupil; and (arguably), occupier and invitee. In most, though conceivably not all, of such categories of case, the common "element in the relationship between the parties which generates [the] special responsibility or duty to see that care is taken" is that "the person on whom [the duty] is imposed has undertaken the care, supervision or control of the person or property of another or is so placed in relation to that person or his property as to assume a particular responsibility for his or its safety, in circumstances where the person affected might reasonably expect that due care will be exercised"(*Kondis v State Transport Authority* at p. 687; see also *Stevens v Brodribb Sawmilling Co. Pty Ltd.* (1986) 160 CLR, at pp.31, 44–46). It will be convenient to refer to that common element as "the central element of control". Viewed from the perspective of the person to whom the duty is owed, the relationship of proximity giving rise to the non-delegable duty of care in such cases is marked by special dependence or vulnerability on the part of that person *(The Commonwealth v Introvigne* (1982) 150 CLR 258, at p.271, per Mason J.).

The relationship of proximity which exists, for the purposes of ordinary negligence, between a plaintiff and a defendant in circumstances which would prima facie attract the rule in Rylands v Fletcher is characterized by such a central element of control and by such special dependence and vulnerability. One party to that relationship is a person who is in control of premises and who has taken advantage of that control to introduce thereon or to retain therein a dangerous substance or to undertake thereon a dangerous activity or to allow another person to do one of those things. The other party to that relationship is a person, outside the premises and without control over what occurs therein, whose person or property is thereby exposed to a foreseeable risk of danger . . . . In such a case, the person outside the premises is obviously in a position of special vulnerability and dependence. He or she is specially vulnerable to danger if reasonable precautions are not taken in relation to what is done on the premises. He or she is specially dependent upon the person in control of the premises to ensure that such reasonable precautions are in fact taken. Commonly, he or she will have neither the right nor the opportunity to exercise control over, or even to have foreknowledge of, what is done or allowed by the other party within the premises. Conversely, the person who introduces (or allows another to introduce) the dangerous substance or undertakes (or allows another to undertake) the dangerous activity on premises which he or she controls is "so placed in relation to [the other] person or his property as to assume a particular responsibility for his or its safety".

Conclusion

Once it is appreciated that the special relationship of proximity which exists in circumstances which would attract the rule in Rylands v Fletcher gives rise to a non-delegable duty of care and that the dangerousness of the substance or activity involved in such circumstances will heighten the degree of care which is reasonable, it becomes apparent, subject to one qualification, that the stage has been reached where it is highly unlikely that liability will not exist under the principles of ordinary negligence in any case where liability would exist under the rule in Rylands v Fletcher. . . .

At 556

The qualification mentioned in the preceding paragraph is that there may remain cases in which it is preferable to see a defendant's liability in a Rylands v Fletcher situation as lying in nuisance (or even trespass) and not in negligence . . . . It follows that the main consideration favouring preservation of the rule in Rylands v Fletcher, namely, that the rule imposes liability in cases where it would not otherwise exist, lacks practical substance. In these circumstances, and subject only to the above-mentioned possible qualification in relation to liability in nuisance, the rule in Rylands v Fletcher, with all its difficulties, uncertainties, qualifications and exceptions, should now be seen, for the purposes of the common law of this country, as absorbed by the principles of ordinary negligence. Under those principles, a person who takes advantage of his or her control of premises to introduce a dangerous substance, to carry on a dangerous activity, or to allow another to do one of those things, owes a duty of reasonable care to avoid a reasonably foreseeable risk of injury or damage to the person or property of another. In a case where the person or property of the other person is lawfully in a place outside the premises that duty of care both varies in degree according to the magnitude of the risk involved and extends to ensuring that such care is taken.

The present case

. . . Fortunately, our conclusion that the rule in Rylands v Fletcher has been absorbed by the principles of ordinary negligence makes it unnecessary to attempt to derive from the decided cases some basis in principle for answering the question whether the welding activities in the circumstances of the present case were or were not a "non-natural" or "special" use of the Authority's premises. The critical question for the purposes of applying the principles of ordinary negligence to the circumstances of the present case is whether the Authority took advantage of its occupation and control of the premises to allow its independent contractor to introduce or retain a dangerous substance or to engage in a dangerous activity on the premises. The starting point for answering that question must be a consideration of what relevantly constitutes a dangerous substance or activity . . .

At 559

. . . the overall work which the independent contractor was engaged to carry out on the premises was a dangerous activity in that it involved a real and foreseeable risk of a serious conflagration unless special precautions were taken to avoid the risk of serious fire. It was obvious that, in the event of any serious fire on the premises, General's frozen vegetables would almost certainly be damaged or destroyed. In these circumstances, the Authority, as occupier of those parts of the premises into which it required and allowed the Isolite to be introduced and the welding work to be carried out, owed to General a duty of care which was non-delegable in the sense we have explained, that is to say, which extended to ensuring that its independent contractor took reasonable care to prevent the Isolite being set alight as a result of the welding activities. It is now common ground that W. & S. did not take such reasonable care.

It follows that the Authority was liable to General pursuant to the ordinary principles of negligence for the damage which General sustained.

Brennan J and McHugh J delivered separate judgments, concluding that the rule in *Rylands v Fletcher* was still a part of the law of Australia.

Comment

The solution adopted by the High Court of Australia was to 'absorb' *Rylands* to negligence, by recognising a non-delegable duty of care in circumstances such as these. The idea of a non-delegable duty has certain advantages over the rule in *Rylands v Fletcher*. It can be explained in principled terms, through the ideas of dangerousness, proximity, and dependence, rather than through apparently arbitrary 'rules' relating to (for example) accumulation, and escape. And it is clearly not limited to protection of interests in land. However, this solution depends on accepting some controversial ideas about the position now reached in the tort of negligence, particularly in recognizing non-delegable duties in a broadened range of circumstances.[5]

A crucial aspect of the majority judgment in *Burnie Port Authority* is its description of the occupier as being in a position of 'control', while the occupier of neighbouring premises is in a 'position of special vulnerability and dependence', so that the relationship is cast in terms of a 'special relationship of proximity'. There is currently no reason to think that English courts would reason along the same lines. We have already seen (in Chapter 6.2) that at the time of *Burnie Port Authority*, the High Court of Australia was willing to take a freer view of 'proximity' in the duty of care than its English counterpart. In fact, as we also noted there, the High Court has more recently *disapproved* the central role previously attributed to proximity.[6] Yet without this specific proposition, would there be any force in the assertion that *Rylands* liability is unnecessary, since negligence will be an appropriate action in the same circumstances? On this point, the High Court relied upon a rationalization of positive duties offered by Mason J in the case of *Kondis v State Transport Authority* (1984) 152 CLR 672. But it also broadened it. *Kondis* was a case concerning the non-delegable duty of an employer towards an employee, in circumstances where an independent contractor had been negligent. Mason J's analysis was aimed at providing reasons which might support the established proposition that the employer is under a non-delegable duty to provide a safe system of work to employees. These justifying reasons turned on the employer's position of control, and the employee's special position of dependence or vulnerability. Mason J explained that the employment relationship was one of a series of relationships which were recognized as giving rise to positive duties. A further example, as can be seen from the extract above, was provided by occupiers and their invitees. In the UK, no such rationalization has been attempted, and it is doubtful whether the *Kondis* interpretation would be easily accepted. Even if it was accepted, it is still more doubtful whether it could be relied upon in order to allow recognition of a 'special relationship', based on control and dependence, between neighbours where one is carrying out a hazardous operation.

Through its use of positive duties to ensure that care is taken, the *Burnie* case accepts that there is nothing outdated about a rule whose effect is to impose liability in the absence of personal fault. Indeed, it suggests that the negligence principle has adapted over the years to the point that those conducting particular activities have a duty to ensure that a high level of

---

[5] Note that it is also quite possible that the majority of the High Court would revert to nuisance law if faced with facts closely analogous to *Cambridge Water*. But how would they decide such a nuisance case without reference to the specific requirements of an action in *Rylands v Fletcher*, now that they have concluded that the action is too ambiguous to be applied?

[6] See our discussion of economic loss cases in Chapter 6.2.

care is taken to protect certain others against the risk of harm. But it also suggests, in effect, that it is too late for *Rylands v Fletcher* to be developed in such a way as to provide a coherent rule of strict liability. Whether it is right to say that negligence can adapt to provide sufficient coverage of all those areas where stricter standards of liability at common law are justified is more contentious. It depends on recognizing that standards of care are highly flexible according to the danger posed by one's activities. It also depends on recognizing occupation of neighbouring land as giving rise to one of a group of relationships involving special, positive duties of care. Nevertheless, as clearly predicted by Thayer in the 1916 article extracted earlier in this chapter, it certainly provides more adaptable tools than the revised rule in *Rylands v Fletcher*, which as noted above has been confined to protection of a narrow range of interests associated with nuisance.

FURTHER READING

Bagshaw, R., '*Rylands* Confined' (2004) 120 LQR 388–92.

Heuston, R.V.F., and Buckley, R.A., 'The Return of *Rylands v Fletcher*' (1994) 110 LQR 506–9.

Newark, F.H., 'The Boundaries of Nuisance' (1949) 65 LQR 480.

Newark, F.H., 'Non-Natural User and *Rylands v Fletcher*' (1961) 24 MLR 557–71.

Law Commission, *Civil Liability for Dangerous Things and Activities* Report No 32 (London: HMSO, 1970).

Molloy, R.J., '*Fletcher v Rylands*—A Reexamination of Juristic Origins' (1942) 9 U *Chi L Rev* 266.

Nolan, D., 'The Distinctiveness of *Rylands v Fletcher*' (2005) 121 LQR 421.

Simpson, A.W. Brian, 'Bursting Reservoirs and Victorian Tort Law: *Rylands and Horrocks v Fletcher*', in Simpson, *Leading Cases in the Common Law* (Oxford: OUP, 1995); previously published in a slightly different version as 'Legal Liability for Bursting Reservoirs: The Historical Context of *Rylands v Fletcher*' (1984) 13 JLS 209.

Stallybrass, W.T.S., 'Dangerous Things and Non-Natural User of Land' [1929] CLJ 376.

Thayer, E.R., 'Liability Without Fault' (1916) 29 Harv L Rev 801–15.

Wilkinson D., *Cambridge Water Company v Eastern Counties Leather plc*: Diluting Liability for Continuing Escapes' (1994) 57 MLR 781–99.

12

LIABILITY FOR DANGEROUS PREMISES

CENTRAL ISSUES

i) This chapter concerns damage which arises out of dangers encountered on premises. The duties we consider here are different from the duties in private and public nuisance (Chapter 10) and under the rule in *Rylands v Fletcher* (Chapter 11), in that they are owed to parties who are present on the premises, and not to neighbouring occupiers or (for example) users of the highway.

ii) In Section 1, we consider the duties owed by occupiers toward visitors and non-visitors entering their land, in respect of dangers encountered on the premises. Historically, different duties were owed at common law, depending on the classification of the person who brought the claim. The relevant duties and liabilities have now been codified and in some respects simplified by two pieces of legislation. The first, the Occupiers' Liability Act 1957 ('the 1957 Act') applies to 'visitors'. Visitors are (very broadly speaking) parties who have a right or a permission to be present: see further page 721 below. The second, the Occupiers' Liability Act 1984 ('the 1984 Act'), applies to

most other entrants onto the premises, including trespassers.

iii) In their content, the duties under the 1957 and 1984 Acts are similar to negligence duties. Indeed the occupier's duties to visitors and licensees were among the examples of duties to take care mentioned by Lord Atkin in *Donoghue v Stevenson* (Chapter 3 above). On the other hand, it is unusually clear in the case of the occupier's liabilities that some positive duties (for example, to repair fences or to provide appropriate warnings) are intended. The precise extent of the duty imposed on occupiers involves significant questions of responsibility and fairness, but also engages questions of insurability and deterrence.

iv) Section 2 concerns the potential liabilities of certain non-occupiers where injury or damage arises from hazards created on premises. We consider the liability of builders and others who have created such hazards. Where the damage and latency requirements in *Murphy v Brentwood* [1991] 1 AC 398 are satisfied, there is no longer any immunity attaching to those who have created such hazards before disposing of premises (section 3 of the Defective Premises Act 1972). As is indicated by *Rimmer v Liverpool City Council* [1985] QB 1 and *Targett v Torfaen* [1992] HLR 194, there may also be liability on the part of those who design or build premises in respect of harm done by certain *patent* defects, particularly if the claimant is a weekly tenant who cannot be expected to rectify the defect themselves.

v) Section 2 continues by addressing the non-contractual liability of landlords for injury caused by defects in the premises let. Although there is an important statutory duty in Defective Premises Act 1972, s 4(1), the protection of this duty is limited where the relevant harm arises not from a state of 'disrepair' but from design faults in the premises.

1. OCCUPIERS' LIABILITY UNDER STATUTE

1.1 PRELIMINARIES

When are the Occupiers' Liability Acts Engaged?

Does the injury or damage occur on premises occupied by the defendant?

In order to decide whether a particular set of facts gives rise to an 'Occupiers' Liability' claim, the first question is whether this is a case where personal injury or property damage is suffered *while the claimant or the claimant's property is on premises occupied by the defendant*.[1] If the only injury or damage done is suffered *outside* those premises, then the case is not one of occupiers' liability. On such facts, there may of course be an action in negligence; in nuisance if there is an unreasonable interference with the claimant's interests in land (Chapter 10); or in *Rylands v Fletcher* if damage is done by escape of a dangerous thing (Chapter 11).

Does the damage arise from the state of the premises?

If the injury or damage is suffered on the premises as above, we must ask whether the injury or damage arises from a danger associated with the state of the premises?

The duties set out in the Occupiers' Liability Acts have been understood as 'occupancy duties' (concerned solely with the state of the premises), to be contrasted with 'activity duties' (concerned with conduct or activities carried out on the premises). Despite the broad wording of both Occupiers' Liability Acts (1957 Act, s 1(1); 1984 Act, s 1(1)(b), 'dangers due to the state of the premises or to things done or omitted to be done on them'), the Court of Appeal has held in *Fairchild v Glenhaven Funeral Services Ltd* [2002] 1 WLR 1052, paras [113]–[131][2]; and in *Bottomley v Todmorden Cricket Club* [2003] EWCA Civ 1575, para [31]; that only dangers associated with the state of the premises are within the scope of the Acts.

---

[1] The 1957 Act covers both personal injury and property damage; property damage is excluded from the operation of the 1984 Act.

[2] Although there was an appeal to the House of Lords in *Fairchild* [2002] UKHL 22; [2003] 1 Ac 32 that appeal did not concern the occupiers' liability issue.

The same distinction was observed by the Court of Appeal in the case of a trespasser (in that particular instance, a burglar) in *Revill v Newbery* [1996] QB 567. Since that case involved an activity (shooting a shotgun through the closed door of a shed) rather than a state or condition of the premises, it was dealt with as a case in negligence. However, the provisions of the 1984 Act were still treated as relevant to the court's understanding of the negligence duty.

But beyond the distinction between occupancy and activity duties, when can it be said that the danger arises from the state of the premises, and not (in particular) from the willing activities of the *claimant*? This wider question has become increasingly important.

The Wider Issues: Whose Responsibility to Guard against the Risks?

It is true that some fairly technical questions arise in interpreting the statutory liabilities. But the underlying question of whose obligation it is to take precautions in respect of dangers is of great social importance. For many years, the obvious need in this area was for a greater awareness of the duties of occupiers, particularly in respect of children. Under *Addie v Dumbreck* [1929] AC 358, the only duty owed to a trespasser (even a child) was the duty not deliberately or recklessly to *cause* harm. In that case, a four-year-old child was killed when he fell through the unprotected cover of a mill wheel. Despite knowledge on the part of the defendants that young children trespassed on their premises, no duty was owed in respect of this glaring hazard. The 1984 Act was a response to the House of Lords' later inconclusive efforts to set out the contents of a more humane duty towards trespassers in another case involving a child: *British Railways Board v Herrington* [1972] AC 877. Although the members of the House were agreed that a duty was owed to the child in that case, there was considerable variation in the formulation of the duty itself and of the circumstances in which it arose. The Law Commission proposed clarifying legislation which became the 1984 Act: Law Com No 75, Cmnd 6428, 1976.

In more recent years, the chief concern has changed. There is perceived to be a risk of over-protection and (therefore) of over-deterrence. In a number of recent cases, the House of Lords and (less consistently) the Court of Appeal have emphasized that not all hazards are the responsibility of occupiers. Rather, there has been a greater emphasis on the obligations of individuals—particularly adults—in respect of obvious risks affecting their own safety. The House of Lords has expressly rejected the idea that occupiers of land, including especially those whose land provides important public amenity, should be compelled to over-prioritize safety in the face of obvious hazards. Safety is of course important, but as Lord Scott of Foscote has put it, this 'is no reason for imposing a grey and dull safety regime on everyone' (*Tomlinson v Congleton BC* [2003] UKHL 47, at para [94]). The common thread of these cases is in rejection of the idea that competent adults must be, in effect, prevented from running risks that they can easily appreciate for themselves.

In terms both of freedom of action and of public amenity, the potential benefits of the clear approach taken in cases such as *Tomlinson v Congleton* (also *Ratcliffe v McConnell* [1999] 1 WLR 670, *Darby v National Trust* [2001] EWCA Civ 189, and—more controversially since there was a hidden hazard—*Donoghue v Folkestone* [2003] QB 1008) is illustrated by the case of *R (Hampstead Heath Winter Swimming Club and Another) v Corporation of London and Another* [2005] EWHC 713; [2005] 1 WLR 2930. Relying on the clear line taken in these civil cases, Stanley Burnton J allowed a claim for judicial review, on the application of keen swimmers who wished to be able to take the obvious risks of swimming when there were no lifeguards present.[3] The Corporation of London had taken the decision to forbid swimming in the early morning on the basis that lifeguards could not be afforded at all hours, and that it might be subject not to a civil action (which it was accepted was clearly ruled out by the above cases), but to prosecution under the Health and Safety at Work Act 1974 ('the 1974 Act'), if harm befell the swimmers. In respect of the *criminal* liability in section 3 of the 1974 Act, no prosecution would succeed, because:

Stanley Burnton J

64   . . . As the decision of the House of Lords in *Tomlinson's* case and the judgment of Lord Phillips MR in *Donoghue's* case [2003] QB 1008 show, the risks incurred by adult swimmers who choose to swim in the Mixed Pond, if it has no hidden dangers (and it is not suggested that it has) are not attributable to the condition of the pond, but to the decision of the swimmers to swim in it.

1.2 WHO IS AN OCCUPIER?

Under both statutes, the duties are owed by an 'occupier'. There is no statutory definition of 'occupier', and the meaning of the term is to be deduced from case law (1957 Act, s 2(1)).

'Occupation' is a matter not of ownership but of effective control. There may be more than one occupier of premises, as the next case illustrates.

Wheat v Lacon [1966] AC 552

The defendant brewers were the owners of a public house. The running of the business was entrusted to a manager, employed under a service agreement. The manager and his wife lived on the first floor of the premises.

The plaintiff and her husband were staying on the first floor as paying guests of the manager's wife. The plaintiff's husband suffered a fatal fall while on his way downstairs to buy drinks from the bar. It was found that the accident was caused by a handrail which was too short, in combination with absence of proper lighting on the stairs. Were the defendant brewers liable as 'occupiers'?

The House of Lords found that the defendants were 'occupiers' of the first floor of the premises, and owed the common duty of care under the 1957 Act. However, they had not breached this duty. The defendant brewers, and their manager, could both be occupiers of the premises simultaneously. Although they might be in occupation of different parts of the premises, in this case *both* parties were occupiers of the first floor. The relevant duties owed under the Act would depend upon the 'circumstances' of the occupation:

Lord Denning, at 580–1

In the light of these cases, I ask myself whether the brewery company had a sufficient degree of control over the premises to put them under a duty to a visitor. Obviously they had complete control over the ground floor and were "occupiers" of it. But I think that they had also

---

[3] Vividly illustrating that the amenities necessary to avoid a 'grey and dull' existence are a matter of subjective variation, the swimmers wished to be free to swim in the Ponds on Hampstead Heath, London, before 7.15 am in winter.

sufficient control over the private portion. They had not let it out to Mr. Richardson by a demise. They had only granted him a licence to occupy it, having a right themselves to do repairs. That left them with a residuary degree of control which was equivalent to that retained by the Chelsea Corporation in *Greene's* case [1954] 2 Q.B. 127. They were in my opinion "an occupier" within the Act of 1957. Mr. Richardson, who had a licence to occupy, had also a considerable degree of control. So had Mrs. Richardson, who catered for summer guests. All three of them were, in my opinion, "occupiers" of the private portion of the "Golfer's Arms." There is no difficulty in having more than one occupier at one and the same time, each of whom is under a duty of care to visitors. . . .

What did the common duty of care demand of each of these occupiers towards their visitors? Each was under a duty to take such care as "in all the circumstances of the case" is reasonable to see that the visitor will be reasonably safe. So far as the brewery company are concerned, the circumstances demanded that on the ground floor they should, by their servants, take care not only of the structure of the building, but also the furniture, the state of the floors and lighting, and so forth, at all hours of day or night when the premises were open. But in regard to the private portion, the circumstances did not demand so much of the brewery company. They ought to see that the structure was reasonably safe, including the handrail, and that the system of lighting was efficient. But I doubt whether they were bound to see that the lights were properly switched on or the rugs laid safely on the floor. The brewery company were entitled to leave those day-to-day matters to Mr. and Mrs. Richardson. They, too, were occupiers. The circumstances of the case demanded that Mr. and Mrs. Richardson should take care of those matters in the private portion of the house. And of other matters, too.

. . . So far as the handrail was concerned, the evidence was overwhelming that no one had any reason before this accident to suppose that it was in the least dangerous. So far as the light was concerned, the proper inference was that it was removed by some stranger shortly before Mr Wheat went down the staircase. Neither the brewery company nor Mr and Mrs Richardson could be blamed for the act of a stranger.

Premises that are empty are not necessarily 'unoccupied' for these purposes. In *Harris v Birkenhead Corporation* [1976] 1 All ER 341, the local authority made a compulsory purchase order and served notices on the tenant and owner of a house requiring them to surrender occupation of the premises. The local authority was treated as 'occupier' of the premises from the time that they were vacated, even though they had taken no further positive steps and had no physical 'presence' on the property. It was through their lawful actions that the property had become vacant, and they therefore exercised control over the premises.

Contractors who are engaged in carrying out work on premises may attain sufficient control over the site to be treated as 'occupiers'. This may lead to a situation of dual occupation: see Lord Goff, *Ferguson v Welsh* [1987] 1 WLR 1553, below.

1.3 THE DUTY OWED TO 'VISITORS' UNDER THE OCCUPIERS' LIABILITY ACT 1957

Occupiers' Liability Act 1957

Preliminary

1.—(1) The rules enacted by the two next following sections shall have effect, in place of the rules of the common law, to regulate the duty which an occupier of premises owes to his visitors in respect of dangers due to the state of the premises or to things done or omitted to be done on them.

(2) The rules so enacted shall regulate the nature of the duty imposed by law in consequence of a person's occupation or control of premises and of any invitation or permission he gives (or is to be treated as giving) to another to enter or use the premises, but they shall not alter the rules of the common law as to the persons on whom a duty is so imposed or to whom it is owed; and accordingly for the purpose of the rules so enacted the persons who are to be treated as an occupier and as his visitors are the same (subject to subsection (4) of this section) as the persons who would at common law be treated as an occupier and as his invitees or licensees.

(3) The rules so enacted in relation to an occupier of premises and his visitors shall also apply, in like manner and to the like extent as the principles applicable at common law to an occupier of premises and his invitees or licensees would apply, to regulate—

    (a) the obligations of a person occupying or having control over any fixed or moveable structure, including any vessel, vehicle or aircraft; and

    (b) the obligations of a person occupying or having control over any premises or structure in respect of damage to property, including the property of persons who are not themselves his visitors.

(4) A person entering any premises in exercise of rights conferred by virtue of—

    (a) section 2(1) of the Countryside and Rights of Way Act 2000, or

    (b) an access agreement or order under the National Parks and Access to the Countryside Act 1949,

is not, for the purposes of this Act, a visitor of the occupier of the premises.

Extent of occupier's ordinary duty

2.— (1) An occupier of premises owes the same duty, the "common duty of care", to all his visitors, except in so far as he is free to and does extend, restrict, modify or exclude his duty to any visitor or visitors by agreement or otherwise.

(2) The common duty of care is a duty to take such care as in all the circumstances of the case is reasonable to see that the visitor will be reasonably safe in using the premises for the purposes for which he is invited or permitted by the occupier to be there.

(3) The circumstances relevant for the present purpose include the degree of care, and of want of care, which would ordinarily be looked for in such a visitor, so that (for example) in

proper cases—

    (a) an occupier must be prepared for children to be less careful than adults; and

    (b) an occupier may expect that a person, in the exercise of his calling, will appreciate and guard against any special risks ordinarily incident to it, so far as the occupier leaves him free to do so.

(4) In determining whether the occupier of premises has discharged the common duty of care to a visitor, regard is to be had to all the circumstances, so that (for example)—

    (a) where damage is caused to a visitor by a danger of which he had been warned by the occupier, the warning is not to be treated without more as absolving the occupier from liability, unless in all the circumstances it was enough to enable the visitor to be reasonably safe; and

    (b) where damage is caused to a visitor by a danger due to the faulty execution of any work of construction, maintenance or repair by an independent contractor employed by the occupier, the occupier is not to be treated without more as answerable for the danger if in all the circumstances he had acted reasonably in entrusting the work to an independent contractor and had taken such steps (if any) as he reasonably ought in order to satisfy himself that the contractor was competent and that the work had been properly done.

(5) The common duty of care does not impose on an occupier any obligation to a visitor in respect of risks willingly accepted as his by the visitor (the question whether a risk was so accepted to be decided on the same principles as in other cases in which one person owes a duty of care to another).

(6) For the purposes of this section, persons who enter premises for any purpose in the exercise of a right conferred by law are to be treated as permitted by the occupier to be there for that purpose, whether they in fact have his permission or not.

. . . .

Implied Term in Contracts

5.— (1) Where persons enter or use, or bring or send goods to, any premises in exercise of a right conferred by contract with a person occupying or having control of the premises, the duty he owes them in respect of dangers due to the state of the premises or to things done or omitted to be done on them, in so far as the duty depends on a term to be implied in the contract by reason of its conferring that right, shall be the common duty of care.

. . .

To Whom is the Duty Owed?

The 1957 Act replaces the various duties owed by occupiers at common law with a single statutory duty, the **common duty of care** (s 2(1)). The duty is owed to all those who would have been classed either as invitees, or as licensees, at common law.

Lord Denning, *Roles v Nathan* [1963] 1 WLR 1117, at 1122

[The 1957 Act] has been very beneficial. It has rid us of those two unpleasant characters, the invitee and the licensee, who haunted the courts for years, and it has replaced them by the attractive character of the visitor, who has so far given no trouble at all.

An **invitee** was a person who has been invited onto the premises. A **licensee** was someone who merely had permission to enter the premises. This permission did not need to be express. Whether an individual had an 'implied' licence to be present was a question of fact.

In addition to those counting as invitees or licensees, section 1(6) adds to the category of 'visitors' all those who enter premises **in the exercise of a right conferred by law**. Section 5 provides that where a person enters premises **under the terms of a contract**, a term will (if necessary) be implied into the contract that the common duty of care is owed.

There have been some uncertainties in the relevant classification of visitors to whom the common duty of care is owed, and we now consider some of these uncertainties.

Implied licences

When is it to be *implied* that a party has permission to enter onto the premises? This has become much less of an issue since the introduction of clear duties to non-visitors under the 1984 Act. However before the decision in *Herrington* (above), when very few duties were owed to trespassers, courts were perhaps over-eager to think of reasons why permission to enter could be implied. Children became the main beneficiaries of implied licences (though see *Lowery v Walker* [1911] AC 10 for a case where adults were treated as implied licensees, since the occupier had done nothing over a period of many years to deter people from walking across his land). In *Cook v Midland Great Western Railway Co of Ireland* [1909] AC 229, the House of Lords was prepared to accept that children who entered onto the defendant's land without permission and played on a railway turntable might be treated as doing so with the 'leave and licence' of the defendants, given their knowledge that children often came onto the land, and given that the turntable was likely to be very attractive to children. This case was later described by Devlin J as the 'classic case' of an *allurement to children* (*Phipps v Rochester* [1955] 1 QB 450, 462). As we will see in Section 1.4 below, it is in respect of children that a duty to provide protection to non-visitors is now most likely to be established under the 1984 Act. As such, implied licences are not regularly discussed in recent case law.

Purpose of the visit

It is important to remember that a person may have permission to enter premises for one reason, yet cease to be classed as a visitor if he or she exceeds the terms of that permission. This was confirmed by the House of Lords in the case of *Tomlinson v Congleton* [2003] UKHL 47; [2004] 1 AC 46, in which the claimant suffered catastrophic injuries through diving in shallow water in a lake where swimming was not permitted. His head had struck the sandy bottom of the lake, and he had broken his neck. The claimant's advisers conceded that he was, at the time of his injury, a trespasser. There was some controversy in the House of Lords over whether that concession was correctly made, partly because the claimant's argument was precisely that more steps should have been taken to *prevent him* from swimming. It was accepted by the majority of judges (with the disagreement of Lord Scott, at para [91]) that he was indeed a trespasser. But it was also accepted that this would not be the decisive factor in this case, which was treated as involving an obvious hazard. Neither visitors nor trespassers need to be warned of obvious hazards (see our discussion of *Staples v West Dorset*, and *Darby v National Trust*, below).

Lord Hoffmann, *Tomlinson v Congleton* [2003] UKHL 47; [2004] 1 AC 46

7 . . . The council . . . said that once he entered the lake to swim, [the claimant] was no longer a "visitor" at all. He became a trespasser, to whom no duty under the 1957 Act is owed. The council cited a famous bon mot of Scrutton LJ in *The Carlgarth* [1927] P 93, 110: "When you invite a person into your house to use the staircase, you do not invite him to slide down the banisters". This quip was used by Lord Atkin in *Hillen v ICI (Alkali) Ltd* [1936] AC 65, 69 to explain why stevedores who were lawfully on a barge for the purpose of discharging it nevertheless became trespassers when they went on to an inadequately supported hatch cover in order to unload some of the cargo. They knew, said Lord Atkin, at pp 69–70, that they ought not to use the covered hatch for this purpose; "for them for such a purpose it was out of bounds; they were trespassers". So the stevedores could not complain that the barge owners should have warned them that the hatch cover was not adequately supported. Similarly, says the council, Mr Tomlinson became a trespasser and took himself outside the 1957 Act when he entered the water to swim.

8 Mr Tomlinson's advisers, having reflected on the matter, decided to concede that he was indeed a trespasser when he went into the water. Although that took him outside the 1957 Act, it did not necessarily mean that the council owed him no duty.

. . .

13 . . . I have . . . come to the conclusion that the concession was rightly made. The duty under the 1984 Act was intended to be a lesser duty, as to both incidence and scope, than the duty to a lawful visitor under the 1957 Act. That was because Parliament recognised that it would often be unduly burdensome to require landowners to take steps to protect the safety of people who came upon their land without invitation or permission. They should not ordinarily be able to force duties upon unwilling hosts. In the application of that principle, I can see no difference between a person who comes upon land without permission and one who, having come with permission, does something which he has not been given permission to do. In both cases, the entrant would be imposing upon the landowner a duty of care which he has not expressly or impliedly accepted. The 1984 Act provides that even in such cases a duty may exist, based simply upon occupation of land and knowledge or foresight that unauthorised persons may come upon the land or authorised persons may use it for unauthorised purposes. But that duty is rarer and different in quality from the duty which arises from express or implied invitation or permission to come upon the land and use it.

14 In addition, I think that the concession is supported by the high authority of Lord Atkin in *Hillen v ICI (Alkali) Ltd* [1936] AC 65. There too, it could be said that the stevedores' complaint was that they should have been warned not to go upon the hatch cover and that logically this duty was owed to them, if at all, when they were lawfully on the barge.

Lord Scott of Foscote (concurring in the result but disagreeing on this point)

91 In the present case it seems to me unreal to regard Mr Tomlinson's injury as having been caused while he was a trespasser. His complaint, rejected by the trial judge but accepted by the majority in the Court of Appeal, was that the council ought to have taken effective steps to

discourage entry by visitors into the waters of the lake. The notices were held to be inadequate discouragement. But, if there was this duty, it was a duty owed to visitors. The people who read the notices, or who could have read them but failed to do so, would have been visitors. These were the people to be discouraged. The alleged duty was a 1957 Act duty.

The categorization of the claimant as a trespasser in *Tomlinson v Congleton*, notwithstanding Lord Scott's disagreement, influenced another appellant to make a similar concession in *Rhind v Astbury Water Park* [2004] EWCA Civ 756. This was a similar case of catastrophic injuries suffered in shallow water, though this time there was a concealed hazard. The appellant accepted on the basis of *Tomlinson v Congleton* that when he had entered the water contrary to express prohibition, he had become a trespasser and any duty owed would be under the 1984 Act. This was eventually decisive, since a 1984 Act duty is only owed if the occupier has knowledge which ought to alert him to the existence of the danger. That was not the case in *Rhind*, where there was a concealed hazard of which the occupier was not aware.

It should also be noted that the duty owed under the 1957 Act is only a duty to keep the visitor safe *for the purposes for which he is invited or permitted by the occupier to be there* (s 2(1)). This will often reinforce the effect of the above cases, since the duty will not extend to prohibited activities unless (for example) the prohibition is not sufficiently clear.

Users of rights of way

Persons who are using a right of way are not owed a duty under the 1957 Act, since they do not come within any of the categories above: *Holden v White* [1982] QB 679 (private rights of way); *Greenhalgh v BRB* [1969] 2 QB 286 (public rights of way). Users of **private** rights of way are expressly included within the provisions of the 1984 Act (below). Users of **public** rights of way, however, seem to enjoy no protection under either statute.

Those who enter premises under the 'right to roam' provisions of the Countryside and Rights of Way Act 2000, or via an access agreement under the National Parks and Access to the Countryside Act 1949, are excluded from the 1957 Act (s 1(4)(a) and (b) respectively). We consider duties owed to non-visitors when we turn to the 1984 Act, below.

The Content of the 'Common Duty of Care' under the 1957 Act

The duty owed by the occupier is to 'take such care as in all the circumstances of the case is reasonable to see that the visitor will be reasonably safe in using the premises . . . ' (s 2(2)).

This is clearly a negligence-type duty, since it turns on acting reasonably. However, it is also clearly a duty to *take steps*, and this is obviously capable of including positive elements in the form of obligations to repair, fence, warn, and so on.

Warnings

The occupier may be able to discharge the common duty of care by issuing an appropriate warning. However, it is important to note that a warning does not discharge the duty *unless* it is sufficient to keep the visitor reasonably safe (s 2(4)(a)). For example, a sign may warn of a dangerous bridge, but does the sign also make clear where a safe crossing point may be found? (*Roles v Nathan* [1963] 1 WLR 1117, at 1124.) It should also be emphasized that the duty is to ensure that *the visitor* is safe, not that the *premises* are safe. Thus, the warning must be sufficient for the particular claimant to be made reasonably safe. In the case of children (unless perhaps there is a reasonable expectation that they will be accompanied), a warning may need to be much clearer. Conversely, in *Roles v Nathan*, the particular visitors in question were specialists and, given this (particularly in the light of section 2(3)(b)), the warning that was given sufficed.

Importantly, recent cases have emphasized that there is no duty to warn adults of dangers that are obvious. In *Staples v West Dorset District Council* [1995] PIQR 439, the plaintiff fell on 'the Cobb' at Lyme Regis. The Cobb is an obviously slippery algae-covered surface (which is frequently drenched with sea water). The Court of Appeal rejected an argument that the claimant should have been warned of the danger:

Kennedy LJ, at 442

. . . if the danger is obvious, the visitor is able to appreciate it, he is not under any kind of pressure and he is free to do what is necessary for his safety, then no warning is required. So, for example, it is unnecessary to warn an adult of sound mind that it is dangerous to go near the edge of an obvious cliff (see *Cotton v Derbyshire Dales District Council* (June 10, 1994 Court of Appeal, unreported).

Darby v National Trust [2001] EWCA Civ 189

The claimant's husband drowned while swimming in a pond on National Trust property. Visitors often swam or paddled in the pond, and little was done to prevent this. There were no warning notices close to the pond, only very inconspicuous terms 'somewhere near the entrance to a car park', incorporating opening hours as well as a number of prohibitions. It was not suggested that the pond posed any particular hazards other than those that are connected with swimming in an open expanse of water. These hazards were regarded as obvious to an adult. It was suggested by the claimant that since there was a risk of Weil's disease associated with swimming in the pond, the defendants ought to have placed warning notices relating to Weil's disease around the pond. The claimant argued that had the defendants done this, her husband would have been deterred from swimming, and would not have drowned. The Court of Appeal concluded that, on an application of *South Australia Asset Management Company v York Montague Ltd* [1997] AC 191 (Chapter 3 above), Mr Darby's death was not within the scope of the duty breached by failing to warn of the only *non-obvious* danger, which was Weil's disease.

May LJ

25   . . . a case which promotes a duty based on the risk of a swimmer catching Weil's disease will not, in my opinion, support a breach of duty based on a risk of drowning. The risks are of an intrinsically different kind and so are any dependent duties. . . . Failures which are not causative do not give rise to a liability in negligence . . .

26   In my judgment the risks to competent swimmers of swimming in this pond from which Mr Darby so unfortunately succumbed were perfectly obvious. There was no relevantly causative special risk of which the National Trust would or should have been aware which was not obvious. One or more notices saying 'Danger No Swimming' would have told Mr Darby no more than he already knew. . . .

This reasoning was applied in the Court of Appeal in *Clare v Perry (Widemouth Manor Hotel)* [2005] EWCA Civ 39. The first instance judge had found that a steep drop ought to have been fenced in case people accidentally fell over the edge. The claimant, who had deliberately jumped off the wall in the dark and without looking, was held by the Court of Appeal not to be owed a duty in respect of the obvious risks of jumping in this way. At least two of the judges (Mance LJ and Keene LJ) thought it appropriate to distinguish between the risk of an accidental fall, and the risk of a deliberate jump. Mance LJ in particular acknowledged some difficulties in this, since the required *precautions* against the two potential causes of injury would be the same. He referred in particular to the House of Lords' judgment in *Jolley v Sutton* [2000] 1 WLR 1082 (extracted in Chapter 3 above). In *Jolley*, a boat fell onto a child who was working underneath it. The very extensive damage caused by this event, which was not regarded as foreseeable in its specifics, was treated as within the foreseeable risk of injury posed by the presence of a decaying boat. Again, the precautions required to guard against the risks of moderate injury, and severe injury, were the same—the boat ought to have been removed. In Chapter 3, we criticized some elements of Lord Hoffmann's judgment in *Jolley v Sutton*. In particular, we pointed out that the emphasis on the fact that the *required precautions* were the same in respect of foreseeable and unforeseeable events was inconsistent with the general case law on remoteness of damage (including *The Wagon Mound* itself). It may be this particular contentious element in *Jolley* which led to the problems of interpretation in *Clare v Perry*. Alternatively, it is possible that the sole difference between *Jolley* on the one hand, and *Clare v Perry* or *Darby* on the other, is that *Jolley* concerned a child (albeit not a small child). The risk of the boat falling was treated as *not obvious to the particular claimant (a child)*, so that it was within the risks *to a child* that the occupier should have guarded against.

'Specialists'

To paraphrase section 2(3)(b), an occupier can expect a specialist (a 'person in the exercise of his calling') to guard against risks ordinarily associated with his job. This is provided the occupier 'leaves him free to do so'. In *Roles v Nathan* [1963] 1 WLR 1117, two chimney sweeps were given appropriate information about a defective boiler. The occupier was not liable for their deaths because, had they heeded the warnings given and acted with due care, they could have made themselves safe. It does not follow from section 2(3)(b) that *no duty at all* is owed in respect of 'ordinary' risks of specialized work. In *Salmon v Seafarer Restaurants* [1983] 1 WLR 1264, a fireman was injured when attending a fire started through the negligence of the occupier's employees. Woolf J (giving judgment for the Court of Appeal) pointed out that 'when [the firefighters] attend they will be at risk even though they exercise all the skill of their calling'. Section 2(3)(b) only provides that the occupier may expect the specialist to exercise a level of care appropriate to his or her calling. If the visitor exercises such skill and care and the risk nevertheless remains, then this subsection gives no reason to deny compensation to the injured party. This case can be clearly contrasted with *Roles v Nathan*, where the evidence was that the sweeps did not act with appropriate regard for their own safety, and did not heed clear warnings.

Children

Section 2(3)(a) states the converse rule, that occupiers must be prepared for children to be *less* careful than adults when it comes to their own safety. Dangers which are perfectly obvious to an adult may not be obvious to a child. Pre-1957 Act case law may be expected to be of some use in the interpretation of this section, but this case law (though plentiful) is inconsistent.

In *Glasgow Corporation v Taylor* [1922] 1 AC 44, the defendants were occupiers of a Botanical Garden to which children (including unaccompanied children) had free access. The plaintiff's son, who was seven years old, went to the garden unaccompanied and died when he ate the berries of a poisonous shrub. Since the child was entitled to be present in the relevant part of the gardens, which was much frequented by children, and since there was ready access to the tree, the House of Lords held on a preliminary issue that there was a good cause for trial. The berries could constitute a hidden danger as against a child. As such, this case indicates that the idea of an 'allurement' or 'trap' for children may have some use where children are present with permission, and is not limited to cases of 'implied licence'.

A continuing puzzle, mentioned but not resolved in *Glasgow Corporation v Taylor*, concerns the degree to which occupiers are obliged to make their premises safe for *unaccompanied* children. Smaller children are of course expected to be less careful than older ones; but by the same token adults are expected to supervise those small children to a greater extent. The degree of parental supervision that is considered appropriate may well be expected to change over time, although it is also not surprising that in the days where (it appears) children as young as four were left to wander public parks alone,[4] the courts refused to impose on occupiers the duties that parents did not (or could not)[5] fulfil.

Devlin J attempted to set out a workable approach to such cases in *Phipps v Rochester Corporation* [1955] 1 QB 450 (a pre-1957 Act case in which he treated a five-year-old child wandering onto an unfenced 'building site' near to his home as an implied licensee). His approach to the content of the duty owed requires an interpretation of where 'prudent people' will allow their children to go unaccompanied:

At 471

[The occupier's] duty is to consider with reasonable care whether there are on his premises, so far as he knows their condition, any dangers that would not be obvious to the persons whom he has permitted to use them; and if there are, to give warning of them or to remove them. If he rightly determines a danger to be obvious, he will not be liable because some individual licensee, albeit without negligence in the special circumstances of his case, fails to perceive it. . . .

I think that it would be an unjustifiable restriction of the principle if one were to say that although the licensor may in determining the extent of his duty have regard to the fact that it is the habit, and also the duty, of prudent people to look after themselves, he may not in that determination have a similar regard to the fact that it is the habit, and also the duty, of prudent people to look after their little children. If he is entitled, in the absence of evidence to the contrary, to assume that parents will not normally allow their little children to go out unaccompanied, he can decide what he should do and consider what warnings are necessary on that basis. He cannot then be made liable for the exceptional child that strays, nor will he be required to prove that any particular parent has been negligent.

---

[4] Apart from *Glasgow Corporaton v Taylor*, see *Hastie v Edinburgh Magistrates* 1907 SC 1102 (four-year-old fell into a lake); *Stevenson v Glasgow Corporation* 1908 SC 1034 (small child falling into a river in a public park). In *Thomas v BRB* [1976] 1 QB 912, Lord Denning did express momentary interest in how a two-year-old came to be wandering alone, but in that case she had wandered from her own garden while her mother was in and out of the house and it was inherent to her claim that the railway line should have been properly fenced off.

[5] Absence of a 'nurse' for the children—mentioned in *Hastie v Edinburgh Magistrates*—is of course some indication that the children were not those of well-off families.

The result of this was that if the child was so young that a degree of supervision by an adult ought to be expected, then the only required warnings are those that would be needed to alert a guardian to the danger. The relevant danger in *Phipps* (a trench in the ground) being obvious to an adult, there was no breach of the occupier's duty. It should be noted that this was not a case where fencing the entire area was regarded as feasible or necessary, and this distinguishes it from cases where children wander onto the railway, for example. It should also be noted that parents and other guardians who *do* accompany their children, should not be expected to exercise total control over those children.

So far as older children are concerned, it was suggested in *Phipps* that 'big' children are more like adults than they are like 'little' children. But in *Jolley v Sutton* [2000] 1 WLR 1082, it was proposed that older children too are more likely to encounter danger—and less able to appreciate it—than an adult. Commenting on the application of 'foreseeability' to children, Lord Hoffmann said of children that 'their ingenuity in finding unexpected ways of doing mischief to themselves and others should never be underestimated'.

Dangers created by independent contractors

According to section 2(4)(b) of the 1957 Act, an occupier is not liable 'without more' for dangers created by independent contractors in the execution 'of any work of construction, maintenance or repair'. In *Ferguson v Welsh* (below) this was interpreted by the House of Lords as extending to demolition work. To benefit from the protection of this provision, the occupier must have acted reasonably in entrusting the work to a contractor and must also have taken reasonable steps *both* to ensure that the contractor was competent, *and* that the work had been 'properly done'. It should be remembered that these are ways in which the occupier may *discharge* the common duty of care, since they amount to reasonable steps to keep the visitor safe. Under what circumstances will an occupier still be liable under the Act for harm done by an independent contractor on the premises? This has become a vexed question.

In *Ferguson v Welsh* [1987] 1 WLR 1553, a district council contracted with a company (S) to carry out demolition work on their premises. The council prohibited sub-contracting of the work without permission. S nevertheless did sub-contract the work to two brothers (W) who adopted unsafe working practices. The plaintiff (F) was offered a job by the W brothers, and while assisting with the demolition was seriously injured. Judgment was given against the W brothers. The appeal to the House of Lords concerned the possible liability of the council as occupier.

The House of Lords determined that the council had not breached its duty under the 1957 Act in this case. However, Lord Keith's interpretation of the potential duties was broad. Lords Brandon and Griffiths concurred with Lord Keith, but Lords Oliver and Goff added some qualifications. As we will see below, more recent cases in the Court of Appeal are hard to reconcile with Lord Keith's expansive view of the duties under the 1957 Act, and are more consistent with the views of Lords Oliver and Goff.

Lord Keith's statements were expansive in a number of ways. First, he thought that the council should be treated as having 'invited' F onto the premises, since it had put S into occupation of the premises and 'put him [S] into a position to invite the W brothers and their employees onto them' (at 1559). This is questionable, since there was a prohibition on sub-contracting without permission. Lord Goff by contrast thought it possible that F might be a visitor in respect of S, but a trespasser in respect of the council, although he was prepared to accept that F was a visitor for the sake of argument.

Second, Lord Keith decided that the injury to F arose out of a danger that fell within the scope of the 1957 Act. This was expressly doubted by Lord Goff, who thought that F's injury 'arose not from the state of the premises but from the manner in which he carried out his work on the premises'. Lord Keith on the other hand said that the 'dangers' covered by the Act are 'not only . . . dangers due to the state of the premises but also known dangers due to things done or omitted to be done on them' (at 1559).

Third, Lord Keith interpreted the occupiers' duties under section 2(4)(b) quite broadly. Considering this provision, Lord Keith said:

At 1560–1

It would not ordinarily be reasonable to expect an occupier of premises having engaged a contractor whom he has reasonable grounds for regarding as competent, to supervise the contractor's activities in order to ensure that he was discharging his duty to his employees to observe a safe system of work. In special circumstances, on the other hand, *where the occupier knows or has reason to suspect that the contractor is using an unsafe system of work*, it might well be reasonable for the occupier *to take steps to see that the system was made safe*.

The crux of the present case therefore, is whether the council knew or had reason to suspect that Mr. Spence, in contravention of the terms of his contract, was bringing in cowboy operators who would proceed to demolish the building in a thoroughly unsafe way. The thrust of the affidavit evidence admitted by the Court of Appeal was that Mr. Spence had long been in the habit of sub-contracting his demolition work to persons who proceeded to execute it by the unsafe method of working from the bottom up. If the evidence went the length of indicating that the council knew or ought to have known that this was Mr. Spence's usual practice, there would be much to be said for the view that they should be liable to Mr. Ferguson. No responsible council should countenance the unsafe working methods of cowboy operators.

[Emphasis added.]

Lord Keith here speculates that *if* an occupier has 'reasonable grounds to suspect' unsafe working practices, they *may* have a duty to *supervise* the contractor's activities. Lord Oliver (at 1562), while agreeing that there was no breach of duty in this case, emphasized that he did not think any such duty of supervision, if it arose, would arise out of the defendant's status as occupier. More would be required than that:

It is possible to envisage circumstances in which an occupier of property engaging the services of an independent contractor to carry out work on his premises may, as a result of his state of knowledge and opportunities of supervision, render himself liable to an employee of the contractor who is injured as a result of the defective system of work adopted by the employer. But I incline to think that his liability in such case would be rather that of joint tortfeasor than of an occupier.

Similarly, Lord Goff (at 1564) thought that Lord Keith's approach threatened to impose too extensive a duty on occupiers:

. . . I do not, with all respect, subscribe to the opinion that the mere fact that an occupier may know or have reason to suspect that the contractor carrying out work on his building may be using an unsafe system of work can of itself be enough to impose upon him a liability under the Occupiers' Liability Act 1957, or indeed in negligence at common law, to an employee of the contractor who is thereby injured, even if the effect of using that unsafe system is to render the premises unsafe and thereby to cause the injury to the employee. I have only to think of the ordinary householder who calls in an electrician; and the electrician sends in a man who, using an unsafe system established by his employer, creates a danger in the premises which results in his suffering injury from burns. I cannot see that, in ordinary circumstances, the householder should be held liable under the Occupiers' Liability Act 1957, or even in negligence, for failing to tell the man how he should be doing his work.

We have already noted that more recently, in *Fairchild v Glenhaven* [2001] EWCA Civ 1881; [2002] 1 WLR 1052, the Court of Appeal has set out a more restricted approach to the coverage of the two Occupiers' Liability Acts. In particular, the Court of Appeal has ruled that the 1957 Act and the 1984 Act are confined to 'occupancy duties', and do not extend to dangers arising out of *activities* carried out on the premises. This is inconsistent with Lord Keith's view that the injury to F in *Ferguson v Welsh* arose out of a danger that was within the scope of the duties under the 1957 Act.

The distinction in *Fairchild* was reaffirmed by the Court of Appeal in *Bottomley v Todmorden Cricket Club* [2003] EWCA Civ 1575, a case which bears comparison with *Ferguson v Welsh*:

Brooke LJ

42   It appears . . . that some confusion lingers over the effect of the decision of this court in *Fairchild v Glenhaven Services Ltd*. Of course, there may be many occasions when an occupier may be legally liable in negligence in respect of the activities which he permits or encourages on his land. This liability stems from his 'activity duty'. He may also be legally liable for the state of his premises, and this liability stems from his 'occupancy duty'. *Fairchild* was a rare case in which it was necessary to make a distinction between the two, and this court held that an employee of a very well-known firm of contractors was owed no occupancy duty by the CEGB in the early 1950s as occupiers of the power station in which the claimant contracted mesothelioma during the contract works.

43   It was unnecessary for the House of Lords in *Ferguson v Welsh* [1987] 1 WLR 1553 to get themselves involved in this arcane debate.

In *Bottomley v Todmorden*, the defendant cricket club had arranged for a two-man stunt team named 'Chaos Encounter' to conduct a pyrotechnic display at an annual fundraising event. The members of Chaos Encounter (who did not appeal a finding of liability against them) had invited the claimant to assist, and he was injured. The Court of Appeal found that this was a case where the occupier was liable because it had failed to exercise reasonable care to select competent and safe 'contractors' (albeit unpaid on this occasion). However, this liability was in negligence, and *not* under the 1957 Act (paras [48]–[49]). Brooke LJ argued that the duty passed the *Caparo* test and that it was 'fair, just, and reasonable'.

In *Bottomley*, it was made clear that the duty to select a competent contractor also exists in the tort of negligence. It was this duty which was breached by the cricket club. Similarly, in *Gwilliam v West Herts Hospital NHS Trust* [2002] EWCA Civ 1041; [2003] QB 443, it was held that the duty also arose within the 1957 Act, but outside the specific area of works of 'construction, maintenance, or repair'. Section 2(4)(b) is merely illustrative of a broader principle.

Liability insurance?

One of the factors addressed in *Bottomley v Todmorden* was that the pyrotechnic display team did not carry public liability insurance. This in itself was not the hallmark of a competent contractor in an inherently dangerous field. In Chapter 9, we discussed *Gwilliam v West Herts Hospital NHS Trust*, and the question of whether there is a duty on the part of an occupier to *enquire into* the insurance status of a contractor who is to carry out dangerous (though not strictly ultra-hazardous) work on the premises. We saw that Waller LJ, in *Gwilliam*, clearly thought there was a free-standing duty to protect visitors from the effects of a contractor being uninsured, and we discussed the controversy surrounding this conclusion. In *Bottomley*, no such free-standing duty was in issue. Rather, it was thought by the Court of Appeal that lack of public insurance cover would be one factor suggesting a lack of competence.

Exclusion of Liability, and Defences

A note about notices

We have already seen that occupiers may provide warnings—sometimes in the form of notices—which if sufficient to keep the visitor safe may discharge the common duty of care. Notices may have more than one function, however. Of course, they may seek to exclude visitors altogether ('Keep Out!'), or they may set out the limits of permission ('No swimming'). In either case, they may be relevant in defining the status of the claimant as visitor or non-visitor (*Tomlinson v Congleton*, above). Some notices, however, go further, and seek to exclude liability for injury or damage done ('the occupier accepts no liability for any injury suffered on the premises', or more simply, 'Enter at your own risk'). It is wise to keep in mind all three of these potential uses of a notice. In terms of their legal implications, they need separate consideration. Here we consider the last variation.

Exclusion of liability

How far is the occupier able to exclude or limit liability for injury or damage under the 1957 Act? Even in the absence of a contract, such notices are governed by the Unfair Contract Terms Act 1977.

Unfair Contract Terms Act 1977

1 Scope of Part I

(1) For the purposes of this Part of this Act, "negligence" means the breach—

  (a) of any obligation, arising from the express or implied terms of a contract, to take reasonable care or exercise reasonable skill in the performance of the contract;

  (b) of any common law duty to take reasonable care or exercise reasonable skill (but not any stricter duty);

  (c) of the common duty of care imposed by the Occupiers' Liability Act 1957 or the Occupiers' Liability Act (Northern Ireland) 1957.

. . .

(3) In the case of both contract and tort, sections 2 to 7 apply (except where the contrary is stated in section 6(4)) only to business liability, that is liability for breach of obligations or duties arising—

    (a) from things done or to be done by a person in the course of a business (whether his own business or another's); or

    (b) from the occupation of premises used for business purposes of the occupier;

and references to liability are to be read accordingly but liability of an occupier of premises for breach of an obligation or duty towards a person obtaining access to the premises for recreational or educational purposes, being liability for loss or damage suffered by reason of the dangerous state of the premises, is not a business liability of the occupier unless granting that person such access for the purposes concerned falls within the business purposes of the occupier.

2 Negligence liability

(1) A person cannot by reference to any contract term or to a notice given to persons generally or to particular persons exclude or restrict his liability for death or personal injury resulting from negligence.

(2) In the case of other loss or damage, a person cannot so exclude or restrict his liability for negligence except in so far as the term or notice satisfies the requirement of reasonableness.

(3) Where a contract term or notice purports to exclude or restrict liability for negligence a person's agreement to or awareness of it is not of itself to be taken as indicating his voluntary acceptance of any risk.

11 The "reasonableness" test

(1) In relation to a contract term, the requirement of reasonableness for the purposes of this Part of this Act . . . is that the term shall have been a fair and reasonable one to be included having regard to the circumstances which were, or ought reasonably to have been, known to or in the contemplation of the parties when the contract was made.

. . .

The Act expressly extends to liability under the 1957 Act (s 1(1)(c)). The provisions of section 2 apply *only* to 'business liability' (s 1 (3)), which are defined by reference to the use of the premises for business purposes (s 1 (3)(b)). If people gain access to the property for educational or recreational purposes, any resulting liability is *not* business liability, *unless* those educational or recreational purposes fall within the business purposes of the occupier.

Business liability

In cases of business liability, the position is clear. It is not possible to exclude or restrict liability for personal injury or death (s 2(1)). In the case of other damage (and property damage is covered by the 1957 Act), any attempt to exclude or restrict liability is subject to the test for reasonableness set out in section 11.

Non-business liability

In other cases, section 2 and (therefore) section 11 of the Unfair Contract Terms Act 1977 (UCTA) do not apply. At common law, before the enactment of UCTA, occupiers were regarded as free to exclude their liability to visitors provided they took reasonable steps to bring the exclusion of liability to the attention of the visitor. Since the occupier was free to grant or withhold permission to enter the premises, he or she should also be free to set the conditions of entry (*Ashdown v Williams* [1957] 1 QB 409). It is assumed that the position remains the same for occupiers whose occupation is not caught by the definition of 'business occupation' (above). In an extended discussion, Jones argues that several qualifications are needed to this general assumption (Jones, *Textbook on Tort*, 8th edn, Chapter 6, pp 308–11). In particular, it is doubtful whether the reasoning in *Ashdown* is applicable to those who enter premises in exercise of a 'right conferred by law' (s 1(6)); it is possible that exclusion clauses should be ineffective against children (unless perhaps it is reasonable to expect them to be supervised by an adult—see above); and there is an argument that the duty owed to non-visitors is unexcludable (see below) so that it should also apply against visitors if all other liability is excluded.

Other defences

Although the 1957 Act does not mention contributory negligence, it is clear that the provisions of the Law Reform (Contributory Negligence Act) 1945 are relevant to liabilities arising under both Occupiers' Liability Acts. As such, the partial defence of contributory negligence is available in actions under these statutes (see Chapter 5 above).

Section 2(5) of the 1957 Act specifically refers to risks which are 'willingly accepted' by the visitor, amounting to a statutory form of the general defence of *volenti non fit injuria* or willing acceptance of risk (Chapter 5 above). It is made clear in section 2(5) that the principles to be applied are the same as those applied at common law. We touch on some controversies with *volenti* in respect of non-visitors, below.

1.4 THE DUTY OWED TO 'NON-VISITORS' UNDER THE 1984 ACT

Occupiers' Liability Act 1984

1 Duty of occupier to persons other than his visitors

(1) The rules enacted by this section shall have effect, in place of the rules of the common law, to determine—

  (a) whether any duty is owed by a person as occupier of premises to persons other than his visitors in respect of any risk of their suffering injury on the premises by reason of any danger due to the state of the premises or to things done or omitted to be done on them; and

  (b) if so, what that duty is.

(2) For the purposes of this section, the persons who are to be treated respectively as an occupier of any premises (which, for those purposes, include any fixed or movable structure) and as his visitors are—

(a) any person who owes in relation to the premises the duty referred to in section 2 of the Occupiers' Liability Act 1957 (the common duty of care), and

(b) those who are his visitors for the purposes of that duty.

(3) An occupier of premises owes a duty to another (not being his visitor) in respect of any such risk as is referred to in subsection (1) above if—

(a) he is aware of the danger or has reasonable grounds to believe that it exists;

(b) he knows or has reasonable grounds to believe that the other is in the vicinity of the danger concerned or that he may come into the vicinity of the danger (in either case, whether the other has lawful authority for being in that vicinity or not); and

(c) the risk is one against which, in all the circumstances of the case, he may reasonably be expected to offer the other some protection.

(4) Where, by virtue of this section, an occupier of premises owes a duty to another in respect of such a risk, the duty is to take such care as is reasonable in all the circumstances of the case to see that he does not suffer injury on the premises by reason of the danger concerned.

(5) Any duty owed by virtue of this section in respect of a risk may, in an appropriate case, be discharged by taking such steps as are reasonable in all the circumstances of the case to give warning of the danger concerned or to discourage persons from incurring the risk.

(6) No duty is owed by virtue of this section to any person in respect of risks willingly accepted as his by that person (the question whether a risk was so accepted to be decided on the same principles as in other cases in which one person owes a duty of care to another).

[(6A) At any time when the right conferred by section 2(1) of the Countryside and Rights of Way Act 2000 is exercisable in relation to land which is access land for the purposes of Part I of that Act, an occupier of the land owes (subject to subsection (6C) below) no duty by virtue of this section to any person in respect of—

(a) a risk resulting from the existence of any natural feature of the landscape, or any river, stream, ditch or pond whether or not a natural feature, or

(b) a risk of that person suffering injury when passing over, under or through any wall, fence or gate, except by proper use of the gate or of a stile.

(6B) For the purposes of subsection (6A) above, any plant, shrub or tree, of whatever origin, is to be regarded as a natural feature of the landscape.

(6C) Subsection (6A) does not prevent an occupier from owing a duty by virtue of this section in respect of any risk where the danger concerned is due to anything done by the occupier—

(a) with the intention of creating that risk, or

(b) being reckless as to whether that risk is created.]

(7) No duty is owed by virtue of this section to persons using the highway, and this section does not affect any duty owed to such persons.

(8) Where a person owes a duty by virtue of this section, he does not, by reason of any breach of the duty, incur any liability in respect of any loss of or damage to property.

(9) In this section—

"highway" means any part of a highway other than a ferry or waterway;

"injury" means anything resulting in death or personal injury, including any disease and any impairment of physical or mental condition; and

"movable structure" includes any vessel, vehicle or aircraft.

[1A   Special considerations relating to access land]

[In determining whether any, and if so what, duty is owed by virtue of section 1 by an occupier of land at any time when the right conferred by section 2(1) of the Countryside and Rights of Way Act 2000 is exercisable in relation to the land, regard is to be had, in particular, to—

(a) the fact that the existence of that right ought not to place an undue burden (whether financial or otherwise) on the occupier,

(b) the importance of maintaining the character of the countryside, including features of historic, traditional or archaeological interest, and

(c) any relevant guidance given under section 20 of that Act.]

To Which Parties is the Duty Owed?

Subject to the exclusion in section 1(7) of persons using the highway, the duty under the 1984 Act is capable of being owed to all those who are not visitors under the 1957 Act. Duties to people who enter in accordance with the 'right to roam' provisions of the Countryside (Rights of Way) Act 2000 are subject to special conditions.

When is the Duty Owed?

It has been said that the duty under the 1984 Act is a 'lesser duty, as to both incidence and scope' (Lord Hoffmann, *Tomlinson v Congleton*, para [13]). Not every non-visitor is owed a duty on every occasion. The criteria relevant to establishing *whether a duty arises* on a specific occasion are set out in section 1(3) of the 1984 Act. These provisions have no direct counterpart in the 1957 Act, since the common duty of care under that Act is always owed to visitors.

According to section 1(3)(a), no duty will arise unless the occupier is aware of the danger *or has reasonable grounds to believe* that it exists. Similarly, according to section 1(3)(b), no duty will be owed to the non-visitor unless the occupier knows *or has reasonable grounds to believe* that the non-visitor is in (or likely to come into) the vicinity of the danger. Having 'reasonable grounds to believe' involves a subjective element: what knowledge did the occupier actually have?

In *Donoghue v Folkestone Properties* [2003] QB 1008, the claimant (a professional diver) chose to dive from a slipway into a harbour after midnight in mid-winter. He struck his head on a grid-pile under the water and broke his neck, becoming tetraplegic. At first instance, the judge held that the defendants knew that substantial numbers of people used the slipway for diving into the harbour and that the gridpiles constituted a danger at certain states of the tide. Since these constituted a concealed danger, this was the sort of risk against which the occupier ought to offer some protection. As such, the defendants had a duty at least to place a warning notice on the slipway, since this would have deterred the claimant from diving. This was not a case, it might be noted, where the claimant had full knowledge of the risk involved.

The Court of Appeal reversed the judge's finding of liability, on the basis that the condition in section 1(3)(b) was not satisfied. Although the occupier was aware that people did use the slipway *at certain times*, they had no relevant knowledge of the likely presence of an individual at the actual time and place of the accident. A duty may thus be owed in the summer, but not in the winter. It should be noticed that although diving into a harbour in midwinter is not ordinarily to be expected, offering protection to winter visitors might not impose any additional burdens. A permanent notice, for example, would deter both summer and winter visitors. Lord Phillips suggested that if the council had displayed a notice during the summer, but taken it down during the winter, they would not have been in breach of a duty (para [56]). He concluded that a council which offered no protection at all could not therefore be in breach during the winter, either.

In *Rhind v Astbury Water Park* [2004] EWHC Civ 756 the position was more straightforward in that the defendant occupier was not in possession of any information which would have indicated the presence of the hidden danger—in this case, a submerged fibreglass container resting on the bottom of a lake. As such, the claim was dismissed on an application of section 1(3)(a). This illustrates the less onerous nature of the 1984 Act duties. In principle there is no obligation to check for hidden dangers in the water if swimming is prohibited. If the claimant had been a visitor, there would have been a duty to take positive steps of just this sort in order to ensure that he was reasonably safe.

There is a further important condition in section 1(3)(c). A duty will be owed only if the risk is one against which the occupier *may reasonably be expected to offer the non-visitor some protection*. It is important to note that this requires an examination of what is reasonable in relation to the *specific* trespasser. In *Ratcliff v McConnell*, the Court of Appeal emphasized that the claimant was an adult and could reasonably be expected to appreciate obvious risks which would be less obvious to a child. The Court of Appeal drew attention to the earlier case of *McGinlay (or Titchener) v BRB* [1983] 1 WLR 1427, a case under the Occupiers' Liability (Scotland) Act 1960. Here, a 15-year-old child had been considered sufficiently mature to appreciate the dangers of slipping through the gaps in a fence and wandering onto a railway line.

Obvious dangers

The 1984 Act duty will not generally be owed in respect of obvious dangers, at least where adults are concerned (*Donoghue v Folkestone*, paras [33]–[35]). If there are reasons to expect the presence of a *child* trespasser, however, then the same danger may give rise to a duty, unless (in the light of *Keown*, below), the child should be mature enough to appreciate the danger.

In *Young v Kent County Council* [2005] EWHC 1342, the presence of children on a school roof was to be expected, even though the roof was clearly out of bounds. The child claimant was present at the school while attending a youth club, and it was known that children had gone onto the roof from time to time. On this occasion, the child was retrieving a football. Insufficient measures were taken to prevent access to the roof:

Morison J

33 . . . the danger of serious injury to a child, albeit a trespasser, was or should have been apparent to the school, and the prevention of accident was cheap. In my view, any school such as this one ought to have carried out a risk assessment of their premises and, if they had done so, they would have come to the conclusion that there was a risk of children getting onto the roof and suffering injury or death, and their failure to fence off the access point was negligent. Having invited children onto their property, they did owe a duty to ensure that the wandering

child, the non-visitor, the trespasser, was not allowed to encounter this danger. In my judgment, the defendants were in breach of their duty under the 1984 Act.

Interestingly, although the risk of harm from going onto the roof was not treated as sufficiently obvious to the 12-year-old claimant to come into the category of risks against which no protection is required, the claimant was still seen as sufficiently careless for his damages to be reduced by 50 per cent on account of contributory negligence. This was largely because of his behaviour while on the roof, where he jumped on a skylight. The school's duty was to take reasonable steps to deter him from going onto the roof at all, which was considered to be a dangerous place to be.

Subsequently in *Keown v Coventry Healthcare Trust* [2006] 1 WLR 953, the Court of Appeal applied both the reasoning and the spirit of *Tomlinson v Congleton* [2004] 1 AC 46 to a case involving injury to an 11-year-old child. The distinction between adults and children is one of 'fact and degree' where their understanding of risk is concerned (para [12]). The claimant had fallen while climbing the outside of a fire escape on the defendant's hospital grounds, but the fire escape was not faulty and the child should have appreciated the risk. Therefore there was no danger due to the state of the premises for the purposes of section 1(1)(a). Longmore LJ distinguished *Young*, arguing that in that case it was the 'brittle skylights' which made the roof dangerous premises in that case. It could not have been that the child did not understand the risk, because he was thought to be contributorily negligent. The thinking in *Keown* seems hard to reconcile with the reasoning in *Jolley v Sutton*, above. The case may represent a hardening in attitude towards risk-taking claimants including 'older' children.

The Content of the Duty

The content of the duty in section 1(4) is stated in very similar terms to the common duty of care under the 1957 Act. The sole difference is that under the 1984 Act, reasonable steps must be taken to ensure that the entrant does not 'suffer injury', while the 1957 Act obliges the occupier to take reasonable steps to ensure that the visitor is 'safe'. The difference reflects the exclusion from the 1984 Act of liability for property damage (s 1(8)).

Warnings/Discouragement

As with the 1957 Act, the duty may in appropriate cases be discharged by a relevant warning (s 1(5)). However, we have already seen that there is no duty to warn a visitor of risks that are obvious (*Staples v West Dorset*, above). Clearly, the same is true of trespassers: *Ratcliff v McConnell*, below, at para [27]; *Tomlinson v Congleton*; *Darby v National Trust*, above.

It should be noted that in the 1984 Act, in addition to warnings, it may also be sufficient to discharge the duty if an occupier has taken reasonable steps to 'discourage persons from incurring the risk'.

Ratcliff v McConnell [1999] 1 WLR 670

The plaintiff, a 19-year-old student, chose to climb the fence of his college swimming pool at night, and execute a running dive into the water. He was very seriously injured. The college had fenced the pool in order to discourage swimming, and employed security guards to patrol the campus. The Court of Appeal held that there was no obligation to warn an adult trespasser of the obvious dangers of diving into a pool. It is well known that pools vary in their depth and configuration and that diving without checking the depth is dangerous. There was no hidden danger, and the existence of a slope between deep end and shallow end did not constitute such a hidden danger or trap (para [37]). There was no need to post more specific notices than those prohibiting swimming. Further, the steps taken by the college to discourage use were sufficient, even though there was some evidence of sporadic night-time use of the pool prior to the claimant's accident. The college did not have to punish offenders to emphasize the rules in order to satisfy their duty under the 1984 Act: such a suggestion 'goes far beyond discouragement' (para [47]). Further, the Court of Appeal thought it clear that in this case the claimant had 'willingly accepted the risk' (para [47]): see below.

Exclusion and Defences

Exclusion of liability

The Unfair Contract Terms Act 1977 (UCTA) has not been amended to refer to the duty owed by occupiers under the 1984 Act. While there was some doubt over whether UCTA extended to the common law duty of humanity under *Herrington*,[6] it is clear that sections 2 and (therefore) 11 UCTA do *not* apply to the duty under the 1984 Act. Are we to conclude from this, as with the exclusion of non-business liability under the 1957 Act, that occupiers are entirely free (in accordance with *Ashdown v Samuel Williams*) to exclude liability? Before the 1984 Act, John Mesher suggested that since the reasoning in *Ashdown* turned on the occupier's ability to lay down criteria governing entry onto the premises, this reasoning cannot be extended to trespassers ([1979] 43 Conv 58, 63). Though he was writing of the *Herrington* duties, the reasoning is just as apposite now that the 1984 Act is in place. Should the duty therefore be regarded as an 'unexcludable minimum'? After all, such duties are owed only where it is 'reasonable in all the circumstances of the case' to offer the entrant some protection. Alternatively, if the 1984 Act can be excluded, is the *Herrington* duty still unexcludable as it is a duty of 'common humanity'?

Volenti/willing acceptance of risk

Section 1(6) of the 1984 Act clearly states that the question of willing acceptance of risk is to be considered on the same principles as in other cases. In Chapter 5, we investigated the limited applicability of the *volenti* defence, at least so far as negligence is concerned. It was emphasized that *knowledge* of the risk is not the same as *willing acceptance* of the risk. However, in the case of occupiers' liability to trespassers under the 1984 Act, courts seem to have thought it sufficient to show that the claimant had full knowledge of and appreciated the risk; and that he or she had decided to enter the premises (or engage in prohibited use of the premises) notwithstanding the existence of that risk. This appears to have been the approach in both *McGinlay (or Titchener) v BRB* [1983] 3 All ER 770 and *Ratcliff v McConnell* (above).

The approach of the House of Lords in *McGinlay v BRB* has been criticized. As Jaffey points out in the article extracted below, the case law on *volenti non fit injuria* is divided as to whether a real agreement to exempt the defendant from liability is required and, if it is, whether such an agreement can realistically be implied when the claimant only encounters the danger *after* the relevant negligence. Jaffey points out that in *McGinlay* the House of Lords appeared to say that such an agreement was required, in a case when realistically, any such agreement was in the realms of fiction.

---

[6] Mesher, 'Occupiers, Trespassers, and the Unfair Contract Terms Act 1977' [1979] 43 Conv 58, argued at p 63 that UCTA did not extend to this duty.

A. J. E. Jaffey, 'Volenti Non Fit Injuria' (1985) 44 CLJ 87, at 90–1

. . . The main ground of the decision was that, having regard to the plaintiff's knowledge of the danger and her knowledge that she should keep a proper lookout for trains, and the other circumstances of the case, the Railways owed her no duty to do more than they had done to maintain the fence. Alternatively, even if the defendants would otherwise have been in breach of their duty to the plaintiff, they were protected by s 2(3) of the [Occupiers' Liability (Scotland) Act], which provides:

> Nothing in the foregoing provisions of this Act shall be held to impose on an occupier any obligation to a person entering on his premises in respect of any risks which that person has willingly accepted as his; ad any question whether a risk was so accepted shall be decided on the same principles as in other cases in which one person owes to another a duty to take care.

Lord Fraser, with whose judgment all the other members of the House of Lords agreed, said that this section 'merely put into words the principle *volenti non fit injuria*' [[1983] 1 WLR 1427, at p. 1434]. The result of such a defence, he said, would be that 'whether the respondents would otherwise have been in breach of their duty to the appellant or not, the appellant had exempted them from any obligation towards her.' He referred to Salmond and Heuston [*The Law of Torts*, 18th edition, 467] for this formulation. To 'exempt' someone from an obligation surely requires some agreement with, or promise to, that person by which he is released or excused from an obligation to which he would otherwise be subject. Indeed, in the passage referred to by Lord Fraser Salmond and Heuston speak of the 'agreement of the plaintiff, express or implied, to exempt the defendant . . . .' It is hard to see however how the plaintiff's entering on the land with full knowledge of the danger can amount to an agreement with, or promise to, the defendant. At what moment were the Railways relieved of their obligations in relation to the safety of the plaintiff? At the moment when she passed through the gap in the fence or a split second before that? We are clearly in the realms of fiction if a person's conduct in voluntarily taking a known risk is treated as an implied agreement with the person who created the danger.

Contributory negligence

This defence is clearly available in principle in actions under the 1984 Act, but there is reduced scope for its applicability given the prerequisites for the existence of a duty. For a case where the defence did operate, see *Young v Kent CC*, above. This case involved a child who was old enough to be regarded as contributorily negligent (he should have realized it was dangerous to jump on a skylight), but young enough to need protection from his own decision to go into a prohibited area (the roof). *Keown v Coventry Healthcare Trust*, however, illustrates the general point. If is there no duty at all, contributory negligence will not arise.

Specific users

Users of public rights of way

We noted above that users of public rights of way are excluded from protection under the 1984 Act. If the right of way is adopted as a highway maintainable at public expense, there is a duty on the relevant highway authority (not the occupier whose land is crossed by the highway) to maintain it (Highways Act 1980, section 41). There would of course remain the possibility that the user of a public right of way will be owed a duty at common law, through the tort of negligence. Section 1(7) expressly preserves any existing duties.

As explained by F. R. Barker and N. D. M. Parry 'Private Property, Public Access and Occupiers' Liability' (1995) 15 LS 335, the difficulty with any such negligence duty is that the occupier of land has traditionally been subject to no *positive* obligations (giving rise to liability for *failures to repair*) in respect of public rights of way: this is the rule in *Gautret v Egerton* (1867) LR 2 CP 371. Barker and Parry explain that this general approach was challenged in the case of *Thomas v British Railways Board* [1976] 1 QB 912, in which a two-year-old child crossed through a gap where a stile had been on a public footpath and wandered onto a railway line. She was still on the footpath when she was struck by a train. In *Thomas*, the Court of Appeal decided that the defendants owed a duty of care which had been breached through failure to replace the missing stile.[7] However, Barker and Parry also concede that there are several problems with attempting to develop a consistent approach based on *Thomas*. One such problem is that in *Thomas*, the Court of Appeal was influenced by the House of Lords' then-recent judgment in *BRB v Herrington* [1972] AC 877, and perhaps reasoned by analogy with the 'duty of common humanity'. As the authors point out, *Herrington* was afflicted by serious ambiguity and this is why it was superseded by legislation. Users of the highway were deliberately and expressly omitted from coverage under the resulting 1984 Act. It might therefore be bizarre to resurrect *Herrington*, with all its uncertainties, to cover an expressly excluded group, although there have been other suggestions that *Herrington* duties may survive, for example if the 1984 Act duty is validly excluded (see below). A further significant problem is that in the case of *McGeown v Northern Ireland Housing Executive* [1995] 1 AC 233, the House of Lords held (while not discussing *Thomas*) that an occupier could not be liable to the user of a public right of way for negligent nonfeasance (including failure to repair), explicitly affirming the rule in *Gautret v Egerton* (1867) LR 2 CP 371. If this means that *Thomas* is wrongly decided, then it means that a two-year-old child wandering through a broken stile or fence on a footpath is owed no duty, while a two-year-old or even 12-year-old child wandering through a broken fence into an area where she is not allowed to be will (if the knowledge conditions are satisfied) be quite likely to be owed a duty (see *Young v Kent CC*, discussed above).

Access land

The Countryside (Rights of Way) Act 2000 (CROW) introduced an important public 'right to roam' on certain land (referred to as 'access land'). Through amendments to the 1957 and 1984 Acts, CROW introduced specific limitations on the duties that may arise in respect of 'access land'. Individuals exercising the 'right to roam' are excluded from the definition of visitor in the 1957 Act (s 1(4)(a)), and new provisions in the 1984 Act add particular conditions governing the question of whether a duty is owed. We should also note section 12(1):

Countryside (Rights of Way) Act 2000

12 (1) The operation of section 2(1) in relation to any access land does not increase the liability, under any enactment not contained in this Act or under any rule of law, of a person interested in the access land or any adjoining land in respect of the state of the land or of things done or omitted to be done on the land.

---

[7] It was found that such a young child, who had left her garden nearby, would not have climbed a stile.

Since the existence of the right to roam and its exercise will on many occasions give occupiers a reason to know that 'non-visitors' are likely to be present on the land for the purposes of section 1(3)(b) OLA 1984, the introduction of that right may well increase the liability of a landowner by broadening the number of occasions on which he owes a duty. Therefore, this provision is capable of giving rise to some conflict between the two statutes and some interesting questions of statutory interpretation. For example, section 12(1) states that the new rights do not increase the liability of the occupier *at all*, whereas the new section 1A(a) of the 1984 Act simply says that regard must be had to whether the duty contended for would 'place an **undue burden** on the occupier'. That is a quite different question.

The general political concerns which led to these amendments to the Occupiers' Liability Acts are encapsulated in the following extract.

M. Stevens-Hoare and R. Higgins, 'Roam Free?' (2004) NLJ 1856

Much of the concern expressed about the introduction of the right to roam focused on the fear that landowners would find themselves facing heavier duties to those who pass over their land. It was suggested that landowners may need to take insurance against the risk that they would be the subject of a successful claim by a walker injured while exercising the right to roam. In response, the government made clear that, as a matter of policy, the burden on landowners should not be increased by the creation of the right to roam . . .

Considering the various restrictions on the duties owed to those entering onto access land, the authors conclude:

The somewhat bizarre effect of [the] express limits on the landowners' liability appears to be that someone exercising the right to roam is owed a more restricted duty of care than a trespasser. A trespasser may be owed a duty in relation to a naturally occurring feature—for instance, where the landowner is aware of the danger created by the feature and the prospect that trespassers will come on to the land. In the same circumstances, a roamer would not be owed any duty of care. Such an effect may be an unintended anomaly created by over-enthusiastic attempts to ensure liabilities are not increased. However, it is more likely the logical rolling out of the quid pro quo that, in exchange for the right to roam, those exercising that right should take the full risk themselves, as a matter of policy.

We may add a few comments to this useful summary.

1. As mentioned above, it is not clear that the amendments to the 1984 Act entirely succeed in avoiding *any* increased liabilities on the part of occupiers, since use of the right to roam may mean that the knowledge condition for presence of non-visitors is more easily satisfied. This leads to the possibility of conflict between the 1984 Act and s 12 CROW.

2. Some of the restrictions on the scope of the duty to those exercising the right to roam are clearly intended not only to protect the interests of the occupier but also to preserve the character of the environment to which the roamers wish to have access (s 1A (b) and perhaps s 1(6A)(a) of the 1984 Act). For example there will be no obligation to 'fence' a natural feature or have it surrounded by warning notices.

3. Despite the restrictions, those exercising the right to roam still appear to be in a better position than users of a public right of way (*McGeown*, above).

1.5 CONCLUSIONS—OCCUPIERS' LIABILITY UNDER STATUTE

In 1979, in the article cited at fn 6 above, John Mesher blamed the problems with exclusion of occupiers' liability on 'the folly of attempting to work within the framework of fault liability for personal injuries' (pp 64–7):

> There is a desire to allow accident victims compensation. At the moment this can only be done by ensuring that there is a defendant who is legally liable and able to pay damages. Hence the difficulties in attempting to define on which defendants it will be fair to impose a non-excludable duty.
>
> Until we can break the pernicious link between compensation and individual liability by moving to some kind of no-fault system it will be impossible to define on a rational basis the class of victims whom we believe to deserve compensation.

By contrast, the recent House of Lords' judgment in *Tomlinson v Congleton* (above) has been warmly applauded as a return to individual responsibility and indeed to the 'individualistic values of the common law' (Jonathan Morgan, 'Tort, Insurance and Incoherence' (2004) 67 MLR 384, 401). But it is suggested that this is too simple a reading of the recent cases denying liability on the part of occupiers for obvious risks. Although these recent cases emphasize the free choice of claimants (and of those others who may wish to make the same sort of choice in the future), they are equally preoccupied with certain 'collective' questions. In particular, there is a concern with public amenity and its continued availability. 'Compensation culture' does not necessarily stem from over-protectiveness. It can also be a creation of an individualistic approach, if 'blame' is considered a sufficient reason for imposition of liability, whatever the consequences.[8] In other words, there may on occasion be *collective* reasons for emphasizing freedom of choice on the part of particular individuals, just as there may be good *distributive* justifications for rejecting particular insurance obligations upon occupiers, if these do not represent fair and workable solutions (see our discussion of Nuisance, in Chapter 10 above, and of the general place of tort law in compensating for torts, in Chapter 8). This is illustrated by some comments of Longmore LJ in a recent case discussed above. In this case, it was decided that there was no danger 'due to the state of the premises'. Here, Longmore LJ considers whether he would have thought there was a duty to guard against such a danger, if it had existed.

---

[8] See the discussion of the Compensation Act, s 1, Chapter 3 above.

Longmore LJ, *Keown v Coventry Healthcare Trust* [2006] 1 WLR 953

17 My tentative (obiter) view is that it would not be reasonable to expect a National Health Service Trust to offer protection from such a risk. . . . I say this for two reasons. First, the resources of a National Health Service Trust are much more sensibly utilised in the treatment and care of patients together with proper remuneration of nurses and doctors rather than catering for the contingency . . . that children will climb where they know they should not go. . . . Secondly, . . . it will not just be a matter of putting a fence round a fire escape or hiring an extra security guard. . . . The trust has now built a perimeter fence around the entire site; there is only one entrance; . . . children are turned away . . . the hospital ground is becoming a bit like a fortress. The amenity which local people had of passing through the grounds . . . and which children had of harmlessly playing in the grounds has now been lost. It is not reasonable to expect that this should happen to avoid the occasional injury, however sad it is when such injury occurs. . . .

In our chapters on negligence liability we found that there was no aspect of that tort that was unaffected by questions such as this. There is an argument that we have entered a new era where questions of individual and collective responsibility find a more complex balance both in the political resolution of such questions,[9] and in the judicial response to such questions at the highest level. The 'incoherence' in the case law referred to by Morgan will not be eased by refusing to consider broader distributional effects. It is suggested that despite the emphasis on 'choices' made by adult claimants, there is no such refusal in the recent occupiers' liability cases, but a broader concern with the distribution of responsibilities and the maintenance of public amenity.

2. LIABILITY OF NON-OCCUPIERS IN RESPECT OF DANGERS ON PREMISES

In Chapter 6.2, in our discussion of 'economic losses', we considered the position where premises are defective, but where the defects in the premises have done no harm to person or property. We noted that the relevant losses were unrecoverable in a negligence action as against the builder, or against a local authority accused of not preventing the defect. This was true even though the defects may be dangerous.

This chapter is concerned with dangerous defects. The liabilities that we discuss are liabilities in respect of *harm suffered* by those using the premises. In the previous section, we considered the liabilities of occupiers. In this section, we briefly consider liability of *non-occupiers* in respect of harm suffered by those using premises.

[9] See the provisions of the Countryside (Rights of Way) Act 2000 for a statute which combines concerns with public access, with responsibility, and with the preservation of amenity.

2.1 BUILDERS AND OTHERS WHO CREATE A DANGEROUS DEFECT

It was accepted in *Murphy v Brentwood* [1991] 1 AC 398 that if a *latent* defect in a building causes harm to property or person, then a builder who carelessly created that latent defect may be liable in the tort of negligence. Likewise, a supervising architect or structural engineer may be liable in the same way if it is through their lack of care that a defect exists. On the other hand, it was expressly reserved in *Murphy* whether a local authority which had approved plans for the structure, or inspected its foundations, would be under a common law duty in respect of such damage. It now seems almost impossible that a local authority which fails to inspect under a statutory power (as in *Anns* itself) could be considered to owe a duty of care in negligence (*Gorringe v Calderdale* [2004] UKHL 15: see Chapters 3, Omissions, and 6, Duty of Care, above).

As we saw in Chapter 6, in *Targett v Torfaen* [1992] HLR 194, a weekly tenant was able to recover damages from the defendant—a local authority which constructed and designed the premises—even though the defect was patent. The tenant had complained about an inadequate handrail on the steps where he fell. Under these circumstances, it would be unrealistic to expect the tenant to take steps to remove the defect. The local authority was held to be liable in respect of the design flaw. The decision in *Targett v Torfaen* confirms that *Rimmer v Liverpool City Council* [1985] QB 1 has survived the decision in *Murphy v Brentwood*, despite its reasoning being based upon *Anns v Merton* and *Batty v Metropolitan Property Realisations Ltd* [1978] QB 554—decisions which were (respectively) departed from and overruled by *Murphy*.

In *Rimmer v Liverpool City Council* [1985] QB 1, a council which had designed and built residential flats was liable to the plaintiff, a tenant, when he slipped and put his hand through a plate glass window, causing serious injury to his hand and arm. He had complained that the glass was too thin and posed a danger to his five-year-old son, but had been told that nothing could be done. It is important to note that the liability in *Rimmer*, as in *Targett*, depended on the role of the local authority in *designing and building* the premises. It did not arise from their status as landlords. Nor was it owed to the plaintiff as a *tenant*. It was a duty of care in negligence towards the plaintiff as a person foreseeably likely to be harmed by the defect in design and construction. The status of the plaintiff as a weekly tenant did however mean that it was unreasonable to expect him to remove the defect himself.

One reason why the Court of Appeal in *Rimmer* considered it necessary to rely upon *Anns* and *Batty* was that at common law, those who created defects in premises obtained an immunity when they disposed of that property either through sale, or letting. That immunity was revoked by *Dutton* and this was confirmed in *Anns* and, subsequently, *Batty*. Although these three cases (*Dutton, Anns,* and *Batty*) are no longer good law, the same effect is achieved in statutory form by section 3 of the Defective Premises Act 1972.

Defective Premises Act 1972

3   Duty of care in respect to work done on premises not abated by disposal of the premises

(1) Where work of construction, repair, maintenance or demolition or any other work is done on or in relation to premises, any duty of care owed, because of the doing of the work, to persons who might reasonably be expected to be affected by defects in the state of the

premises created by the doing of the work shall not be abated by the subsequent disposal of the premises by the person who owes the duty.

. . .

Sale or letting of the premises will no longer confer an immunity. However, it is important to note that this does not in itself impose any duties. In *Rimmer*, the duty in question was the duty not to create dangerous defects through careless design and construction, and this duty was derived from *Donoghue v Stevenson*.

In Chapter 3, we briefly discussed section 1 of the Defective Premises Act 1972, which imposes a duty on all those who are involved with 'the provision of a dwelling' to see that the work is appropriately done, so that the dwelling is 'fit for habitation'. This duty will enable any party who suffers loss (including a subsequent purchaser of the premises) to claim the costs of repair so as to return the property to a condition where it is 'fit for habitation'. As such, patent defects which are prejudicial to health and safety may be remedied through this section. We will say no more about the section 1 duty here, since it is concerned with repair costs, rather than injury.

2.2 LANDLORDS

At common law, liability on the part of those landlords who let premises with a dangerous defect, but do not positively create that defect, are surprisingly limited. In *Cavalier v Pope* [1906] AC 428, the House of Lords refused to award damages to the wife of a tenant who fell through the dangerous floor of a dilapidated house: 'fraud apart, there is no law against letting a tumble-down house; and the tenant's remedy is upon his contract, if any'.[10] Tenants may benefit from contractual remedies if there are relevant provisions in the lease, but these terms must amount to a warranty of fitness for safe habitation—a duty to maintain and repair will not do for these purposes (*Rimmer v Liverpool CC* [1985] QB 1, 10). Equally, a landlord who retains occupation of certain parts of the premises will be subject to duties under the Occupiers' Liability Acts (see *Wheat v Lacon*, Section 1.2 above). The landlord of a block of flats may, for example, retain occupancy of the common parts of the building.

The area of application of *Cavalier v Pope* has been restricted in various ways. Apparently, different principles always applied to furnished lettings: *Wilson v Finch Hatton* (1877) 2 Ex D 336, discussed in *McNerny v London Borough of Lambeth* (1988) 21 HLR 188. In *Greene v Chelsea Borough Council* [1954] QB 127, the Court of Appeal declined to apply *Cavalier v Pope* outside the area of landlord and tenant. In this case, the property had been requisitioned and the plaintiff (who was injured when a ceiling collapsed) was entitled to damages. He was a licensee, not a tenant. In *Dutton v Bognor Regis UDC* [1972] 1 QB 373, Lord Denning MR went so far as to say that *Cavalier v Pope* had been reversed by the enactment of a new statutory duty (at that stage contained in s 4 OLA 1957, now extended and re-enacted in s 4 DPA 1972). This however is not the case. Important thought it is, the duty under section 4 has significant limits.

10 These words derive from *Robbins v Jones* (1863) 15 CBNS 221, 240.

Defective Premises Act 1972

4 Landlord's duty of care in respect of obligation or right to repair premises

(1) Where premises are let under a tenancy which puts on the landlord an obligation to the tenant for the maintenance or repair of the premises, the landlord owes to all persons who might reasonably be expected to be affected by defects in the state of the premises a duty to take such care as is reasonable in all the circumstances to see that they are reasonably safe from personal injury or from damage to their property caused by a relevant defect.

(2) The said duty is owed if the landlord knows (whether as the result of being notified by the tenant or otherwise) or if he ought in all the circumstances to have known of the relevant defect.

(3) In this section 'relevant defect' means a defect in the state of the premises existing at or after the material time and arising from, or continuing because of, an act or omission of the landlord which constituted or would if he had had notice of the defect, have constituted a failure by him to carry out his obligation to the tenant for maintenance and repair of premises . . . .

(4) Where premises are let under a tenancy which expressly or impliedly gives the landlord the right to enter the premises to carry out any description of maintenance or repair of the premises, then, as from the time when he first is, or by notice or otherwise can put himself, in a position to exercise the right and so long as he is or can put himself in that position, he shall be treated for the purposes of subsections (1) to (3) above (but for no other purpose) as if he were under an obligation to the tenant for that description of maintenance or repair of the premises; but the landlord shall not owe the tenant any duty by virtue of this subsection in respect of any defect in the state of the premises arising from, or continuing because of, a failure to carry out an obligation expressly imposed on the tenant by the tenancy.

Section 4 is clearly an important provision which provides a route to compensation for tenants, their families, and others, since it imposes duties owed to all those who may foreseeably be affected by the defect. However, the defect that causes the injury must be shown to come within the repairing obligation of the landlord (s 4(3)). There is some assistance in section 4(4), which provides that landlords with the *right* to enter and repair will be treated as though they were under an obligation to repair. Even so, the relevant defect must still fall within the area of the relevant right to repair.

In *McAuley v Bristol City Council* [1992] QB 134, a tenant tripped and fell on a concrete step in the back garden. The council was under no *obligation* to carry out repairs in the garden; nor did it have an express *right* to do so. The question was whether s 4(4) DPA would operate so that the landlord would be *treated as* having an obligation to repair. The tenant was under an obligation to allow the council to enter the premises at any reasonable time and 'for any purpose'. The Court of Appeal held that this general obligation on the part of the tenant gave rise to an implied right on the part of the landlord to carry out repairs or correct any defects which might expose the tenant or visitors to the risk of injury. Because this implied right to enter and repair was broad enough to include repairs to the step in the garden, section 4(4) would operate so that the tenant had the protection of section 4(1).

In *Sykes v Harry* [2001] EWCA Civ 167, (2001) QB 1014, the plaintiff (a tenant) suffered brain damage as a result of carbon monoxide poisoning from a defective gas fire. The defendant landlord had no knowledge of the specific defects in the fire, but the Court of Appeal held that the duty in section 4(1) had been breached in any event, since the defendant had failed to take such care as was reasonable in all the circumstances. For the purposes of section 4(2), he did not need to have had actual notice of the defect. He *should* have known of the defect precisely because he ought to have had the gas fire serviced regularly, or made enquiries of the tenant since he knew that the tenant would not have the appliance serviced. In this particular case, the first instance judge had assessed contributory negligence on the part of the tenant at 80 per cent, since he would have been able to observe actual defects in the fire and may even have experienced symptoms on other occasions. The Court of Appeal accepted this evaluation.

Despite these successful cases, there are a number of other very significant instances where section 4 has failed to provide a remedy to tenants in respect of defects that are seriously prejudicial to health. The chief reason for this is the dependence of the duty in section 4(1) on the existence and extent of the obligation to repair. According to section 4(3) as we have explained, it is only when damage arises from defects that fall within the obligation to repair that the landlord may be liable under section 4(1). When will a duty to repair arise if it is not explicitly included in the tenancy? Section 11 of the Landlord and Tenant Act 1985 implies a repairing covenant into many tenancies. However, this is a covenant to 'keep in repair the structure and exterior of the dwelling-house'. In *Quick v Taff-Ely Borough Council* [1985] 3 WLR 981 and *McNerny v London Borough of Lambeth* (1988) 21 HLR 188, it was decided that the covenant to repair did not impose an obligation to carry out work in order to prevent the damp and mould which was affecting the plaintiffs' health. These were caused by *design defects* and not by *disrepair* of the structure or appliances. Therefore, section 4(1) was not engaged.

At first sight, the claimants in cases such as these should be assisted by an implied covenant that premises let should be fit for human habitation: section 8(1) of the Landlord and Tenant Act 1985. This covenant would clearly be broad enough to encompass the kinds of defect prejudicial to health found in *McNerny* and *Quick*. However, there is a problem. The covenant is implied only into those tenancies having a rental value below a certain sum. That sum has not been raised since 1957 (*McNerny*), and is far too low to include a typical council let. The rule in *Cavalier v Pope* therefore survives in respect of unfurnished lets in respect of health hazards which are not within existing covenants to repair.

In *Issa v Hackney LBC* [1997] 1 WLR 956, two children whose asthmatic condition had been worsened by living in seriously damp council accommodation failed in an enterprising attempt to gain damages for breach of the council's statutory duty (see Chapter 16). Commenting on the reasons why other routes to compensation would be unsuccessful, Brooke LJ was deeply critical of the present law as outlined in this section:

Brooke LJ, at 964

Successive decisions of this court have shown how this remedy [under s 4(1) DPA] is now a completely dead letter if the deplorable, unhealthy state of the premises, which has rendered them unfit for human habitation, cannot be connected with an express or implied breach of covenant by the landlord.

In the present case . . . the family's flat was severely affected with condensation and associated mould growth, which spread to the bedrooms. In *Quick v. Taff Ely Borough Council* [1986] Q.B. 809, 815 Dillon L.J. said that because of fungus, mould growth and dampness the tenant's council house was virtually unfit for human habitation in the winter when the condensation was at its worst. In *McNerny v. Lambeth London Borough Council* (1988) 21 H.L.R. 188, 190 Dillon L.J. observed that the scale of the dampness which had to be endured in that case led to constant colds and minor ailments being suffered by the plaintiff and her children who had to live in those unhealthy conditions. In *Habinteg Housing Association v. James* (1994) 27 H.L.R. 299 a female tenant endured six years of misery caused by cockroaches, which Peter Gibson L.J. described as a quite appalling infestation for which she was in no way responsible. In none of these cases has the tenant or her family had any civil remedy for the injuries to their health or to their property which they have had to endure through living in unfit conditions.

. . . Unless and until Parliament is willing to revive, in new tenancies at first, the covenant that premises of this type should be fit for human habitation, as the Law Commission has recommended in its 1996 report,[11] people in the position of the present plaintiffs will remain wholly without remedy in the civil courts against their landlords, however grievously their health may have suffered because they are living in damp, unfit conditions.

This situation was challenged in *Ruth Lee v Leeds City Council; Ratcliffe v Sandwell Metropolitan Borough Council* [2002] EWCA Civ 6; (2002) 1 WLR 1488, further cases where damp and mould made council housing virtually uninhabitable. The claimants argued that these conditions, and the lack of any civil remedy, amounted to a violation of their human rights under Article 8 ECHR (see Chapter 10 above). Consistently with other housing cases where Human Rights Act arguments have been attempted, the claimants were unsuccessful.[12] The Court of Appeal reaffirmed the existing interpretation of section 4 DPA 1972. Works required to remedy defects in design were not works of 'repair', and so section 4 was not engaged. In addition, section 3 of the Human Rights Act[13] did not require that the court should now reinterpret the covenant to repair in section 11 of the Landlord and Tenant Act as imposing an obligation to keep premises in good (or habitable) condition. If the position of tenants was to be improved, it would need to be done through legislation.

FURTHER READING

Barker, F.R., and Parry, N.D.M., 'Private property, public access and occupiers' liability' (1995) 15 LS 335.

Buckley, R.A., 'The Occupiers' Liability Act 1984—Has Herrington Survived?' [1984] Conv 413.

Goodhart, A.L., 'The Herrington Case' (1972) 88 LQR 310.

Jaffey, A.J.E., 'Volenti non fit injuria' [1985] CLJ 87.

Jones, M., 'The Occupiers' Liability Act 1984' (1984) 47 MLR 713.

Law Commission (Reports on Occupiers' Liability).

Law Commission, *Landlord and Tenant: Responsibility for State and Condition of Property* (Law Com No 238, London: HMSO, 1996).

[11] Law Commission, *Landlord and Tenant: Responsibility for State and Condition of Property* (Law Com No 238, HMSO, 1996).
[12] *Southwark LBC v Tanner* [2001] 1 AC 1.
[13] 'In so far as it is possible to do so, primary legislation . . . must be read and given effect in a way which is compatible with the Convention rights'.

Mesher, J., 'Occupiers, Trespassers, and the Unfair Contract Terms Act 1977' [1979] 43 Conv 58–60.

Morgan, J., 'Tort, Insurance, and Incoherence' (2004) 67 MLR 384.

North, P.M., *Occupiers' Liability* (London: Butterworths 1971).

Stevens-Hoare, M. and Higgins, R., 'Roam Free?' (2004) NLJ 1846.

PART VI

DEFAMATION AND PRIVACY

13

DEFAMATION

CENTRAL ISSUES

i) Common law has provided powerful protection to reputation through the torts of libel and slander. **Slanders** are generally transitory in form while **libels**, broadly, are more permanent in form. Both of these torts protect a claimant's interest in reputation against defamatory 'statements' (which need not take the form of words). Neither tort requires any particular state of mind on the part of the defendant, except in special circumstances (for example, where the statement is one of opinion, not of fact, in which case lack of honest belief must generally be shown). Libel and slander are therefore torts of strict liability which in special circumstances become dependent on 'malice'.

ii) It has long been recognized that the protection thus afforded to reputation can conflict with freedom of expression. This has been the chief reason for gradual modification in the law of defamation, both at common law and through the Defamation Acts 1952 and

1996. In recent years the relationship between the protected interest in **reputation** and the competing interest in **freedom of expression** has begun to change. The full extent and implications of this change are still to be explored. The most important recent cases, including centrally *Reynolds v Times Newspapers* [2001] 2 AC 127, explain freedom of expression in terms of the public interest in receiving and imparting information in the context of a democratic society. This approach is clearly influenced by the Human Rights Act 1998 and the changed status of rights under the European Convention on Human Rights, particularly the rights in Article 10. Freedom of expression is no longer to be regarded as a residual personal right (if it ever was), but is interpreted as a positive right reinforced by the public interest. The implications of this change may prove to be far-reaching and provide the central themes of this chapter.

1. THE COMPETING INTERESTS—EXPRESSION AND REPUTATION

Libel and slander are not the oldest torts, but they still have a long history—far longer, for example, than negligence. Protection of reputation through civil law was well established by the start of the sixteenth century,[1] and significantly pre-dates the recognition of 'human rights' in any form. Even so, in modern times the law of defamation has openly reflected the tension between freedom of expression, and protection of reputation. This tension affects the manner in which the torts are defined; the defences and remedies available; and (most recently) the funding of litigation. With the development of a 'new legal landscape' after the Human Rights Act 1998,[2] reputation and freedom of expression compete in a new context, and the balance between them is changing. We will therefore begin this chapter by examining the rival interests in expression and reputation and the changing nature of their recognition in law.

1.1 FREEDOM OF EXPRESSION

Why protect expression?

There is more than one possible reason for protecting freedom of expression. As we will see throughout this chapter, the choice of rationale has considerable practical impact on the law of defamation, and the evolution of its principles.

David Feldman, *Civil Liberties and Human Rights in England and Wales*
(2nd edn, Oxford: OUP, 2002), 762–6

THE IMPORTANCE OF FREEDOM OF EXPRESSION

The liberty to express one's self freely is important for a number of reasons, which help to shape the development and application of the law on freedom of expression. First, self-expression is a significant instrument of freedom of conscience, personal identity, and self-fulfilment. From the point of view of civil liberties, this is probably the most important of the justifications which can be offered for free speech. . . . The freedom to choose between values, to have fun through communication, to identify and be identified with particular values or ideas, and to live one's life according to one's choice, is the essence of liberty. Freedom of expression has an important role to play here. . . .

The second justification concerns the contribution of communication to the growth of knowledge and understanding. Freedom of expression enables people to contribute to debates about social and moral values. It is arguable that the best way to find the best or truest theory or model of anything is to permit the widest possible range of ideas to circulate. The interplay of these ideas, challenging each other and allowing the strengths and weaknesses of each to be exposed, is more likely than any alternative strategy to lead to the best possible conclusion. This treats freedom of expression as an instrumental value, advancing other goods (the development of true or good ideas) with a consequential benefit for the individual and society.

---

[1] In fact the first known action in slander is said by Warren and Brandeis to have been recorded in 1356: 'The Right to Privacy' (Chapter 14 below), at 198.

[2] Loveland, 'A New Legal Landscape?' [2000] EHRLR 476–92.

This is the basis on which freedom of expression appealed to John Milton, in *Aeropagitica*, and to the utilitarian mind of John Stuart Mill, who gave the most famous, and most convincing, justification for freedom of speech in *On Liberty*.

Mill argued on utilitarian grounds that there was a distinction in principle between facts and opinion. When dealing with opinions, all should be freely expressed, subject to any restrictions necessary to protect against identifiable harm. . . . Assertions of fact, on the other hand, could by definition be either true or false. There would be good reason to allow free expression of the truth, as this would lead to advances in knowledge and material improvements in society, but this does not justify permitting free expression of falsehoods. However, it is not always possible to say whether an assertion is true or false, and many benefits may flow from allowing statements of fact to be asserted so that they may be tested. . . . on a rule-utilitarian analysis the benefits of a general principle permitting freedom of expression are held to outweigh the disbenefits resulting from particular aspects of the rule. It is therefore preferable to permit freedom to express opinions and facts, even if untrue, rather than to adopt a general rule which permits censorship and coercion in relation to expression. . . .

A third justification for free expression is that it allows the political discourse which is necessary in any country which aspires to democracy. . . . A democratic rationale for freedom of expression makes perfect sense if applied to a society in which the operative model of democracy is one in which the people have the right to participate directly in day-to-day governmental decision making, or to have their views considered in the choice of policies by government. It works less well if the prevailing model is one in which the people merely choose a government, which is then free to get on with the job of governing . . . The representative system, such as we have in the UK, would offer less support to free-expression rights than a participatory system.

In this extract, David Feldman outlines three justifications for freedom of expression.[3] He suggests that from a 'civil liberties' point of view—which in this context is concerned chiefly with personal freedom and autonomy—the first justification is the most important. This justification values freedom of expression for its contribution to personal fulfilment. We will suggest that in defamation law, this has not been the most strongly argued justification for freedom of expression. If it had been, defamation would be seen in terms of the relationship between an individual liberty of the defendant (self-expression) and an equally individual interest of the claimant (reputation). We will see that recent judgments in defamation cases consider freedom of expression in much more 'instrumental' terms than this, appealing more to the *public* interest in freedom of expression and to the goals that it serves. The second and third justifications outlined by Feldman, both of which are concerned with the public interest and which seek to protect freedom of expression for instrumental reasons, are of growing influence. Here is a leading example:

Lord Nicholls, *Reynolds v Times Newspapers* [2001] 2 AC 127, at 200

The high importance of freedom to impart and receive information and ideas has been stated so often and so eloquently that this point calls for no elaboration in this case. At a

---

[3] He continues by identifying two further, less influential justifications: forcing the development of a capacity for tolerance, and fostering artistic and scholarly endeavour.

pragmatic level, freedom to disseminate and receive information on political matters is essential to the proper functioning of the system of parliamentary democracy cherished in this country. This freedom enables those who elect representatives to Parliament to make an informed choice, regarding individuals as well as policies, and those elected to make informed decisions.

Lord Nicholls appears to embrace the argument from democracy, while Feldman (at the end of the extract above) was rather sceptical of its value in a representative democracy such as ours. For Lord Nicholls, political representatives will be inclined to act more appropriately if the public is better informed, and they may even be influenced by public debate. The judgments in *Reynolds* were clearly influenced by Article 10 of the European Convention on Human Rights, and by the Human Rights Act 1998 which was then on the verge of commencement.

Freedom of Expression: The Legal Provisions

European Convention for the Protection of Human Rights and Fundamental Freedoms, 1950 ('the Convention')

Article 10   Freedom of Expression

1. Everyone has the right to freedom of expression. This right shall include freedom to hold opinions and to receive and impart information and ideas without interference by public authority and regardless of frontiers. . . .

2. The exercise of these freedoms, since it carries with it duties and responsibilities, may be subject to such formalities, conditions, restrictions or penalties as are prescribed by law and are necessary in a democratic society, in the interests of national security, territorial integrity or public safety, for the prevention of disorder or crime, for the protection of health or morals, for the protection of the reputation or rights of others, for preventing the disclosure of information received in confidence, or for maintaining the authority and impartiality of the judiciary.

This provision is one of the 'Convention rights' referred to in the Human Rights Act 1998. We have analysed the way in which the 'Convention rights' are treated in the Human Rights Act in Chapters 1 and 10.

Section 6 of the Human Rights Act 1998, extracted in Chapter 1, is of particular importance for the law of defamation. This section states that it is unlawful for a public authority (which is defined to include a court) to act in a way that is incompatible with a Convention right.

As a consequence of section 6, any court must probably ensure that its decisions are compatible with the relevant Convention rights, including those in Article 10. In Chapter 1 we considered whether this introduces 'horizontal effect' into the Human Rights Act, affecting the rights and obligations between citizens, rather than just the rights of citizens against the State. Recent developments in defamation suggest an element of 'indirect' horizontal effect. 'Indirect' horizontal effect influences the interpretation of existing causes of action, rather than the creation of new actions.

The right to freedom of expression protected by the Human Rights Act is specifically the 'Convention right' expressed in Article 10. Therefore, we must examine the terms of Article 10 itself.

Article 10: Essential Features

Certain important features of this Article should be highlighted. First, the right is very broadly expressed and includes expression of information, opinions, and ideas. Second, the Article is not only concerned with *imparting* information, opinions, and ideas, which is probably the most natural meaning of the term 'expression', but also with *receiving* them. Third, states may legitimately restrict the right defined in Article 10(1), as described in Article 10(2). Among the legitimate restrictions are penalties designed to protect *reputation*. However, it is equally important that any such restrictions must be '*prescribed by law*', and that they should be '*necessary in a democratic society*'. The European Court of Human Rights has on more than one occasion found that English defamation law violated Article 10 because it fails to comply with these qualifications to Article 10(2) (*Tolstoy Miloslavsky v UK* (1995) 20 EHRR 442; *Steel and Morris v UK* (2005) 41 EHRR 403).

Referring to the case law of the European Court of Human Rights in interpreting Article 10, Ovey and White argue as follows:

C. Ovey and R. White, *Jacobs and White: The European Convention on Human Rights* (4th edn, Oxford: OUP, 2006), 319–20

The Court takes into account the fact that, in the context of political democracy and respect for human rights mentioned in the Preamble to the Convention, freedom of expression is not only important in itself, but also plays a central role in the protection of other rights under the Convention. Thus the Court consistently gives a higher level of protection to publications and speech which contribute towards social and political debate, criticism and information—in the broadest sense. Artistic and commercial expression, by contrast, receive a lower level of protection.

Freedom of expression gains its particular importance in a 'democratic society' because without it, other human rights and freedoms are unlikely to flourish. On the other hand, Lord Steyn in the *Reynolds* case argued that the European Court of Human Rights proceeds on a 'fact-specific' basis, rather than grading speech on the basis of strict categories.[4] English law also has not identified a specific category of political or 'high grade' speech for special protection. Even so, a difference in treatment between speech which is considered to serve a public interest goal, and other forms of expression, is clearly reflected in recent case law on defamation.

The 'Chilling Effect'

The prospect of an action in defamation may have unhealthy deterrent effects, inhibiting publication not only of falsehoods but also of some worthwhile and important material. This prospect is captured in the idea of a 'chilling effect'. This expression originated in the United States and was imported into English law in *Derbyshire v Times Newspapers* [1993] AC 534, through reference to the Supreme Court's decision in *New York Times v Sullivan* (1964) 376 US 254.[5] It is another way of referring to a 'deterrent'.

---

[4] *Reynolds* at p. 211, citing J. Fleming, 'Libel and Constitutional Free Speech', in P. Cane and J. Stapleton (eds), *Essays for Patrick Atiyah* (OUP, 1991).

[5] More information about *Sullivan* will be found in Section 5.4 of this chapter.

Since *Derbyshire*, reference to the chilling effect has become an established aspect of judicial discussion of defamation. The risk of 'chilling' is exacerbated by certain features of the current law.[6] By definition, the chilling effect is important chiefly from the point of view of 'functional' justifications for freedom of expression: the danger is that the public will remain uninformed of potentially serious issues, and the quality of debate on important matters will be adversely affected.

An influential study into the impact of libel on the British media confirmed that the chilling effect was clearly observable.

E. Barendt L. Lustgarten, K. Norrie, and H. Stephenson, *Libel and the Media: The Chilling Effect* (Oxford: Clarendon Press, 1997), 191–3

. . . whilst the idea of the chilling effect is entirely valid, it requires some reformulation to reflect fully the complexity of the ways in which its pernicious effects are actually brought about.

The most obvious manifestation, which may be called the *direct* chilling effect, occurs when articles, books or programmes are specifically changed in the light of legal considerations. Most often perhaps this takes the form of omission of material the author believes to be true but cannot establish to the extent judged sufficient to avoid an unacceptable risk of legal action and an award of damages. This produces the attitude exemplified by most magazine editors and publishers . . . : 'if in doubt, strike it out'. 'Doubt' here, it should be emphasized, relates to their ability to present a legally sustainable defence, not to the editor's view of the validity of the story. . . . This conscious inhibition, or self-censorship within the organization, remains hidden from the public who are unaware of how their television programme, book, or newspaper is actually produced. . . .

However, there is another, deeper, and subtler way in which libel inhibits media publication. This may be called the *structural* chilling effect. It is not manifest through alteration or cancellation of a specific article, programme or book. Rather it functions in a preventive manner: preventing the creation of certain material. Particular organizations are considered taboo because of the libel risk; certain subjects are treated as off-limits, minefields into which it is too dangerous to stray. Nothing is edited to lessen libel risk because nothing is said in the first place.

By its very nature, the structural chilling effect is far more difficult to quantify, and even to pinpoint, than the direct effect. . . . in this respect, unlike the direct chilling effect, there is no indication that the national press is any less affected. Preventive self-censorship seems just as effective in ensuring that journalists and editors on these newspapers steer well clear of, for example, investigations into deaths in police custody; exploitative employment practices by various large companies operating in the United Kingdom; or bribery and other corrupt practices by British companies bidding for overseas contracts. . . .

A secondary form of structural chilling effect may be discerned, if less clearly. It is best encapsulated by the remark of a journalist on a national broadsheet . . . , who suggested that the libel laws had made the British press more 'polemical'—by which he meant the antithesis of factually-oriented—than it might otherwise be.

---

[6] Examples we will see in this chapter are the burden of proving truth; the scale of possible damages; the uncertainty of the *Reynolds* privilege; the absence of financial support for defendants; and the general costs of litigation including especially the risk of disproportionate costs where the claimant enters into a conditional fee agreement.

The final remark hints that English law's traditionally stronger protection for opinion rather than fact (Fair Comment, below) may have some adverse consequences for the quality of reporting.

1.2 REPUTATION

As we noted above, defamation actions protect reputation. Historically, defamation has been unique in protecting personal reputation,[7] but developments in the tort of malicious falsehood (below) have created some potential overlap.

There is no Convention *right* explicitly protecting reputation. However, we have seen that protection of reputation is a legitimate reason to restrict freedom of expression, so long as the restrictions are necessary and prescribed by law (Article 10(2)). The practical impact of this is that any restriction on freedom of speech—including those restrictions that are intended to protect reputation—must be necessary, proportionate, and clear. On the face of it, there is no equivalent requirement affecting failures to protect *reputation*. This is the reverse of the traditional common law hierarchy of interests:

Peter Cane, *The Anatomy of Tort Law* (Oxford: Hart Publishing, 1997), 134

. . . in traditional English tort law, reputation is more highly prized than (the countervailing interest in) freedom of speech and information, and such protections for the latter as are recognised are embodied in defences to a claim for defamation rather than in the definition of the wrong of defamation.

Peter Cane contends that historically, strong protection has been offered to reputation because it has been treated as analogous to—even a form of—property:

Cane, above, at 73

. . . one of the most curious aspects of the law of defamation is that it imposes liability not for damaging a person's reputation but for making a statement which the court thinks could damage the person's reputation. The plaintiff in a defamation action need present no evidence that his or her reputation was actually damaged. Conceptually, this is probably a result of viewing reputation as a form of property, and defamation as an interference with that property. An important feature of tortious liability for interference with property is that it is actionable without proof of any actual damage to the property.

The impact that defamatory statements may have on an individual is not to be doubted. They can sour personal relationships, cause distress, and have much more tangible effects such as loss of employment prospects. Substantial damages may however be available in defamation where no actual harm is shown. Cane suggests that this is because the *function* of defamation

---

[7] Corporations can sue in defamation in the same way as individuals. On one argument, 'trading reputation' is adequately protected through malicious falsehood, which requires proof of damage. In *Jameel v Wall Street Journal* [2006] UKHL 44, a majority of the House of Lords declined to introduce a 'special damage' requirement for corporations.

is not merely to compensate (nor even to repair) harm, but to protect the interest in reputation *per se* or in its own right. An alternative argument (used by Lord Scott in respect of trading corporations in *Jameel*), is that *causation of harm* is very hard to establish in cases of defamation.

Change in the legal status of reputation

In *Reynolds v Times Newspapers* [2001] 2 AC 127, much emphasis was placed on protection of reputation as a matter of public interest. This allows the interest in reputation to compete on a more even footing with freedom of expression.

Lord Nicholls, *Reynolds v Times Newspapers*, at 201

Reputation is an integral and important part of the dignity of the individual. It also forms the basis of many decisions in a democratic society which are fundamental to its well-being: whom to employ or work for, whom to promote, whom to do business with or to vote for. Once besmirched by an unfounded allegation in a national newspaper, a reputation can be damaged for ever, especially if there is no opportunity to vindicate one's reputation. When this happens, society as well as the individual is the loser. For it should not be supposed that protection of reputation is a matter of importance only to the affected individual and his family. Protection of reputation is conducive to the public good. It is in the public interest that the reputation of public figures should not be debased falsely. In the political field, in order to make an informed choice, the electorate needs to be able to identify the good as well as the bad. Consistently with these considerations, human rights conventions recognise that freedom of expression is not an absolute right. Its exercise may be subject to such restrictions as are prescribed by law and are necessary in a democratic society for the protection of the reputations of others.

The crux of this appeal, therefore, lies in identifying the restrictions which are fairly and reasonably necessary for the protection of reputation.

The implied reference to Convention rights in this passage is clear, and it illustrates that the 'human rights era' is not necessarily—or at least not uniquely—an individualistic era.

2. JUDGE AND JURY

Some of the subtlety of defamation law derives from the continued role played by juries in defamation actions. The different functions of judge and jury need to be separated. In particular, the judge must make certain rulings *as a matter of law*. One matter to be determined as a matter of law is whether the defendant's statement is *capable of* the defamatory meaning proposed by the claimant. Another is whether the statement is *capable of* an alternative, innocent meaning, if the defendant proposes one (see Defamatory Meaning, and Justification, below). These are questions of law, relating to the reasonable interpretation of words or other statements. The *jury* however must decide, on the basis of the judge's directions as to the correct approach, which *one* of the proposed meanings is actually conveyed by the statement.

It is also important to keep in mind that where a defamation case is heard by a judge alone, it will still be necessary for the judge to keep distinct his or her respective functions in *deciding matters of law*, and *determining questions of fact*.

3. LIBEL, SLANDER, AND MALICIOUS FALSEHOOD

3.1 LIBEL AND SLANDER: STATUTE AND COMMON LAW

Libel and slander are separate torts. At common law, a libel is a defamatory statement in permanent or semi-permanent form.[8] The written word may be a libel, while the spoken word is, at common law, capable of amounting to a slander. The practical difference between the two is that libel is actionable *per se* or without proof of damage. Slander, at common law, is actionable only if 'special damage' is shown.

A number of exceptions apply. Some of these specify that certain statements, not easily defined as permanent in form, may amount to libels. Others remove the special damage requirement from certain forms of slander.

Statements that are Potential 'Libels' by Statute

By section 4(1) of the Theatres Act 1968, the publication of defamatory words in the course of a theatrical performance amounts to a libel.

By section 166 of the Broadcasting Act 1990, publication of defamatory words, pictures, gestures, and other 'statements' broadcast on *radio or television* amounts to a libel.

Slanders that are Actionable without Proof of Damage

There are four exceptions to the general rule that slander is actionable only on proof of special damage.

1. Imputation of a criminal offence punishable with imprisonment. This exception is recognized at common law.

2. Imputation of 'unchastity' or adultery, of a woman or girl: Slander of Women Act 1891.

3. Imputation of certain diseases. This is an exception recognized at common law, and the qualifying diseases are not well-defined.

4. By section 2 of the Defamation Act 1952:

In an action for slander in respect of words calculated to disparage the plaintiff in any office, profession, calling, trade or business held or carried on by him at the time of the publication, it shall not be necessary to allege or prove special damage, whether or not the words are spoken of the plaintiff in the way of his office, profession, calling, trade or business.

Malicious Falsehood

We outlined the tort of malicious falsehood in Chapter 2. It is very different from defamation in that it requires the claimant to show **a false statement; made with malice;** and (unless section 3 of the Defamation Act 1952 applies) **special damage.** This may make the action appear considerably less attractive to claimants than the actions in defamation, which universally presume

---

[8] In *Monson v Tussauds* [1894] 1 QB 671, a defamatory waxwork image of the plaintiff (placed close to the famous 'Chamber of Horrors') would be treated as a potential libel.

falsehood and require no malice (unless to displace certain defences). But it is worth bearing in mind, from a policy point of view, that defamation is not the only route to protection of reputation—and, most particularly, trading reputation.

4. ELEMENTS OF A CLAIM IN DEFAMATION

Unless the action is one in which special damage must be shown, the claimant in a defamation action need only prove the following.

The defendant has published a statement with defamatory meaning, referring to the claimant.

We have already seen how broad the category of 'statements' may be. Here, we will break down the claim into its three remaining elements: defamatory meaning, publication, and reference to the claimant. Even if the claimant can show all of these elements, the defendant may nevertheless be able to establish one of the defences described in the next section. If the action is for a slander which is not actionable *per se*, then the claimant will also need to show that special damage was caused by the statement.

4.1 DEFAMATORY MEANING

A Basic 'Definition'

Lord Atkin, *Sim v Stretch* [1936] 2 All ER 1237

Judges and textbook writers alike have found difficulty in defining with precision the word "defamatory." The conventional phrase exposing the plaintiff to hatred, ridicule and contempt is probably too narrow. The question is complicated by having to consider the person or class of persons whose reaction to the publication is the test of the wrongful character of the words used. . . . . I propose in the present case the test: *would the words tend to lower the plaintiff in the estimation of right-thinking members of society generally?* Assuming such to be the test of whether words are defamatory or not there is no dispute as to the relative functions of judge and jury, of law and fact. It is well settled that the judge must decide whether the words are capable of a defamatory meaning. That is a question of law: is there evidence of a tort? If they are capable, then the jury is to decide whether they are in fact defamatory.

(Emphasis added.)

Lord Atkin's encapsulation is still the leading statement of 'defamatory meaning'. It will be noted that no *actual effect* on reputation needs to be shown. On the other hand, there is an objective element to the idea of defamatory meaning because it refers to *right-thinking members of society*. If the only people who would think ill of the claimant as a result of the statement are not 'right-thinking', then in principle there is no defamatory meaning, even if the opinion of such people is important to the claimant. Such a case was *Byrne v Dean* [1937] 1 KB 818. Here the plaintiff was a member of a golf club. Someone informed the police that there were gambling machines on club premises, and they were removed. An anonymous poem was pinned to the wall implying that the mystery informant was the plaintiff.

This, according to the majority of the Court of Appeal, could not be defamatory:

Slesser LJ, at 834

In no case as it seems to me can it be said that merely to say of a man that he has given information which will result in the ending of a criminal act is in itself defamatory where he is doing
no more than reporting to the police that which if known by the police might well end in the
discovery of an illegal act . . .

This 'objective' element has its limits, however. For example in *John v MGN* [1997] QB 586 it
was considered defamatory to allege that the plaintiff was suffering from an eating disorder.
Logically, 'right-thinking people' might be expected to meet such information with sympathy
rather than criticism. In *Lewis v Daily Telegraph* [1964] AC 234, it was emphasized that logic
is not the guide to defamatory meaning. The 'right-thinking' person, we might conclude, is
taken to be *morally upstanding*, but not necessarily entirely rational.

The defamatory meaning

Unfortunately for all those involved in communication, statements are inherently ambiguous
and few, if any, succeed in conveying the same meaning to all those who read, see or hear them.
Even so, defamation requires that ultimately, a 'single meaning' is attached to the statement.
This is where the subtleties begin.

The claimant is required to specify a defamatory meaning which is conveyed as the 'natural
and ordinary' meaning of the statement. It does not need to be shown that this is the meaning
intended by the defendant. As was made clear in *Sim v Stretch* (above), provided the judge
determines that the meaning is *capable of being conveyed by the statement*, the jury will decide
whether the meaning was in fact defamatory. Equally, if the statement has a defamatory meaning, then a defendant who wishes to assert truth must ensure that the 'justification' offered is
sufficient to deal with that defamatory meaning.[9] It is not good enough to show that the words
are true on the face of them, if they are held to carry a different meaning which is defamatory
of the claimant.

'True' and 'False' Innuendo

Generally, with the exception of 'true' innuendo (below), both parties will propose the meaning that they consider to be the 'natural and ordinary' meaning of the words used. This is a
rather misleading phrase. The 'natural and ordinary meaning' can often involve an element of
'reading between the lines'. This is referred to as an 'innuendo'. There are two sorts of innuendo. The 'false' innuendo is a matter of implication from the words themselves, and is an
aspect of their ordinary meaning. The 'true' innuendo is a meaning available only to those
who have knowledge of certain additional facts, outside the statement itself. We will consider
each in turn.

False innuendo

As Lord Devlin explained in *Lewis v Daily Telegraph*, the difference between **literal meaning**
and **false innuendo** is a matter of degree.

---

[9] *Substantial* justification will generally be sufficient, as we will see.

Lewis v Daily Telegraph [1964] AC 234, at 278

A derogatory implication may be so near the surface that it is hardly hidden at all or it may be more difficult to detect. If it is said of a man that he is a fornicator the statement cannot be enlarged by innuendo. If it is said of him that he was seen going into a brothel, the same meaning would probably be conveyed to nine men out of ten. But the lawyer might say that in the latter case a derogatory meaning was not a necessary one because a man might go to a brothel for an innocent purpose. An innuendo pleading that the words were understood to mean that he went there for an immoral purpose would not, therefore, be ridiculous. To be on the safe side, a pleader used an innuendo whenever the defamation was not absolutely explicit. That was very frequent, since scandalmongers are induced by the penalties for defamation to veil their meaning to some extent. Moreover, there were some pleaders who got to think that a statement of claim was somehow made more forceful by an innuendo, however plain the words. So rhetorical innuendoes were pleaded, such as to say of a man that he was a fornicator meant and was understood to mean that he was not fit to associate with his wife and family and was a man who ought to be shunned by all decent persons and so forth. Your Lordships were told, and I have no doubt it is true, that before 1949 it was very rare indeed to find a statement of claim in defamation without an innuendo paragraph.

An example of a 'false innuendo' is *Sim v Stretch* (above). The defendant Sim had sent a telegram to the plaintiff, concerning a house maid named Edith, which was received at the village shop (and was therefore 'published' to a third party). The telegram read:

Edith has resumed her service with us today. Please send her possessions and the money you borrowed also her wages to Old Barton.

Taking exception to this, the plaintiff argued:

By the said words the defendant meant and was understood to mean that the plaintiff was in pecuniary difficulties, that by reason thereof he had been compelled to borrow and had in fact borrowed from the said housemaid, that he had failed to pay the said housemaid her wages and that he was a person to whom no one ought to give any credit.

The House of Lords was doubtful whether the words could carry this meaning, but did not decide this point, since they concluded that even if the meaning was established, such a meaning was not capable of being defamatory. Right-thinking people would think nothing of borrowing from a servant. It was an almost daily occurrence, according to Lord Atkin. The point here is that the pleaded meaning is simply a matter of *implication from* the words used. It is a false innuendo.

If the words used are considered 'incapable' of the meaning alleged by the claimant, then the issue of defamatory meaning will not be left to the jury and the claim will fail. This was the case in *Lewis v Daily Telegraph* [1964] AC 234.

The defendant newspapers had published stories reporting (truthfully) that the City of London Fraud Squad was inquiring into the affairs of a company. Since the literal meaning of the story (existence of an investigation) was true, the plaintiff sought to argue that the articles suggested, by implication, that there was not only suspicion (this too could perhaps be justified), but also guilt.

Lord Devlin, *Lewis v Daily Telegraph* [1964] AC 234, at 285–6

It is not . . . correct to say as a matter of law that a statement of suspicion imputes guilt. It can be said as a matter of practice that it very often does so, because although suspicion of guilt is something different from proof of guilt, it is the broad impression conveyed by the libel that has to be considered and not the meaning of each word under analysis. A man who wants to talk at large about smoke may have to pick his words very carefully if he wants to exclude the suggestion that there is also a fire; but it can be done. One always gets back to the fundamental question: what is the meaning that the words convey to the ordinary man: you cannot make a rule about that. They can convey a meaning of suspicion short of guilt; but loose talk about suspicion can very easily convey the impression that it is a suspicion that is well founded.

In the libel that the House has to consider there is, however, no mention of suspicion at all. What is said is simply that the plaintiff's affairs are being inquired into. That is defamatory, as is admitted, because a man's reputation may in fact be injured by such a statement even though it is quite consistent with innocence. I dare say that it would not be injured if everybody bore in mind, as they ought to, that no man is guilty until he is proved so, but unfortunately they do not. It can be defamatory without it being necessary to suggest that the words contained a hidden allegation that there were good grounds for inquiry. A statement that a woman has been raped can affect her reputation, although logically it means that she is innocent of any impurity: *Yousoupoff v. Metro-Goldwyn-Mayer Pictures Ltd* [(1934) 50 T.L.R. 581, C.A.]. So a statement that a man has been acquitted of a crime with which in fact he was never charged might lower his reputation. Logic is not the test. But a statement that an inquiry is on foot may go further and may positively convey the impression that there are grounds for the inquiry, that is, that there is something to suspect. Just as a bare statement of suspicion may convey the impression that there are grounds for belief in guilt, so a bare statement of the fact of an inquiry may convey the impression that there are grounds for suspicion. I do not say that in this case it does; but I think that the words in their context and in the circumstances of publication are capable of conveying that impression. But can they convey an impression of guilt? Let it be supposed, first, that a statement that there is an inquiry conveys an impression of suspicion; and, secondly, that a statement of suspicion conveys an impression of guilt. It does not follow from these two suppositions that a statement that there is an inquiry conveys an impression of guilt. For that, two fences have to be taken instead of one. While, as I have said, I am prepared to accept that the jury could take the first, I do not think that in a case like the present, where there is only the bare statement that a police inquiry is being made, it could take the second in the same stride. If the ordinary sensible man was capable of thinking that wherever there was a police inquiry there was guilt, it would be almost impossible to give accurate information about anything: but in my opinion he is not. I agree with the view of the Court of Appeal.

Lord Devlin here concedes that a statement of investigation could be defamatory if it was untrue, because there might be a temptation to think there was 'no smoke without fire'. But he then argues that a reasonable reader *could* not, if the statement was true, conclude that there was guilt. 'Logic', certainly, is not the guide.

'True' innuendo

In some cases, the defamatory meaning complained of can be understood *only* if certain additional facts—not mentioned in the statement—are known. If so, this is a case of 'true' innuendo. In such cases, the claimant must make clear the additional facts that are relevant when pleading the defamatory meaning. An example is *Tolley v Fry* [1931] AC 333. The defendants had advertised their 'Fry's Chocolate Creams' with a cartoon representing the plaintiff, a well-known amateur golfer, and a verse which referred to him by name. His likeness was being exploited in order to promote the goods of another, without permission and without reward, and the case is therefore often cited as an early example of 'appropriation of personality'. In this particular case however, the plaintiff was able to claim successfully in libel. The necessary additional fact providing the innuendo was that earning money from golf or from associated activities or sponsorship, including advertising, was inconsistent with his status as an amateur golfer. This case contains both 'false' and 'true' innuendo.

> **Viscount Hailsham,** at 337·
>
> He did not complain of the caricature or the words as being defamatory in themselves; but the innuendo alleged that the "defendants meant, and were understood to mean, that the plaintiff had agreed or permitted his portrait to be exhibited for the purpose of the advertisement of the defendants' chocolate; that he had done so for gain and reward; that he had prostituted his reputation as an amateur golf player for advertising purposes, that he was seeking notoriety and gain by the means aforesaid; and that he had been guilty of conduct unworthy of his status as an amateur golfer."

In *Hough v London Express* [1940] 2 KB 507, it was made clear that in the case of a true innuendo, there is no need to show that any person who knows the relevant facts actually understands the article to be defamatory, or believes the defamatory meaning to be true.

4.2 PUBLICATION

If the defamatory statement is made available to any party other than the subject of the defamation, then it is 'published'. This requirement is met even if it is made available to only one person, such as the person at the village shop who took the telegram in *Sim v Stretch*. *Huth v Huth* [1915] 3 KB 32 explores the limits of 'publication'. Here, there was held to have been no publication where a butler opened a letter addressed to the subject of the alleged libel, because he was not authorized to do so. This amounts to a remoteness rule. More recently, foreseeability has been held to be the test for 'remoteness' in defamation, in respect of the consequences of publication and republication: *Slipper v BBC* [1991] 1 All ER 165. If a newspaper makes previous editions available through an internet archive, then there is the potential for republication on each occasion that the archive is accessed.[10]

Any person who is involved in the dissemination of statements can be said to be 'publishing' those statements and is therefore vulnerable to an action in defamation. There is no need to show that the defendant is the *originator* of the statement, in the sense of being the first to make it. To repeat a rumour, even while disowning it, is capable of amounting to a libel or slander. There may now be some adjustment in the impact of this rule, through development of the qualified privilege defence in *Reynolds v Times Newspapers*, where allegations on a matter of **public interest** are **neutrally reported without adoption**: see *Al-Fagih v HH Saudi Research and Marketing (UK) Ltd* [2001] EWCA Civ 1634, below (Defences).

[10] *Loutchansky v Times Newspapers (Nos 2–5)* [2002] QB 783.

'Secondary' parties (printers, newsagents, and so on) were, at common law, open to defamation actions even where they have not failed to exercise due care. By section 1 of the Defamation Act 1996, a defence has been introduced for those who play a secondary role in publication of defamatory material, provided they take appropriate care. Section 1 is discussed under Defences, below.

4.3 REFERENCE TO THE CLAIMANT

A statement need not mention the claimant by name in order to be understood as referring to him or her. Reference to the claimant can also occur by implication. This implication may, as with meaning, depend on knowledge of special facts, provided *some* people are aware of those facts. Such people may make up a relatively small group. In *Hough v London Express* [1940] 2 KB 507, the plaintiff was the wife of a boxer (Frank Hough). The defendant newspaper published an article describing the words of an entirely different woman, who was described as his wife. The defamatory meaning depended on knowledge that the plaintiff lived with Frank Hough as his wife. This additional fact *not only* supplied the defamatory meaning (that she lived as his wife, but was not), but was also needed in order to establish that the words referred, by implication, to the plaintiff.

Reference to the claimant may be entirely accidental. At common law, this was no defence. Now, sections 1 and 4 of the Defamation Act 1996 provide potential defences for some (but not all) defendants who had no grounds for believing that the statement was defamatory of the claimant. These provisions are further explored under Defences.

Can a statement made about a *group* of people be defamatory of any member of that group? The answer is that it can, and that there really are no special rules of thumb which apply in 'group defamation' cases. The overriding question, as in any case of defamation where a person is not explicitly named, is whether the statement 'pointed to' or would be taken to refer to the individual (*Knupffer v London Express Newspapers* [1944] 1 AC 116; *Riches v Mirror Group Newspapers* [1986] QB 256).

5. DEFENCES

5.1 THE MEANING OF 'MALICE'

The defences of fair comment and qualified privilege are defeated on proof of 'malice', and it has been held that a malice standard is also relevant to section 4 of the Defamation Act 1996. It is therefore useful to have in mind the leading statement of 'malice' in this context, which derives from a case on qualified privilege. There is now some debate whether malice has the same meaning in fair comment, as we will see in due course.

Lord Diplock, *Horrocks v Lowe* [1975] AC 135, at 149–50

. . . in all cases of qualified privilege there is some special reason of public policy why the law accords immunity from suit—the existence of some public or private duty, whether legal or moral, on the part of the maker of the defamatory statement which justifies his communicating it or of some interest of his own which he is entitled to protect by doing so. If he uses the occasion for some other reason he loses the protection of the privilege.

> So, the motive with which the defendant on a privileged occasion made a statement defamatory of the plaintiff becomes crucial. The protection might, however, be illusory if the onus lay on him to prove that he was actuated solely by a sense of the relevant duty or a desire to protect the relevant interest. So he is entitled to be protected by the privilege unless some other dominant and improper motive on his part is proved. "Express malice" is the term of art descriptive of such a motive. Broadly speaking, it means malice in the popular sense of a desire to injure the person who is defamed and this is generally the motive which the plaintiff sets out to prove. But to destroy the privilege the desire to injure must be the dominant motive for the defamatory publication; knowledge that it will have that effect is not enough if the defendant is nevertheless acting in accordance with a sense of duty or in bona fide protection of his own legitimate interests.

> The motive with which a person published defamatory matter can only be inferred from what he did or said or knew. If it be proved that he did not believe that what he published was true this is generally conclusive evidence of express malice, for no sense of duty or desire to protect his own legitimate interests can justify a man in telling deliberate and injurious falsehoods about another, save in the exceptional case where a person may be under a duty to pass on, without endorsing, defamatory reports made by some other person.

According to Lord Diplock, 'malice' is concerned either with knowing publication of falsehood; or (in the alternative) with desire to injure the claimant provided this is the dominant motive for the publication. Either form will do.

5.2 JUSTIFICATION OR TRUTH

The truth of a defamatory statement, if established, is a complete defence no matter how careless, ignorant, or vindictive the defendant.

'Justification' (or truth) is a defence of the first importance. The actions in defamation are designed to penalize falsehood, and true accusations are treated as lowering reputation only to its rightful level. If the truth of the defamatory meaning can be established, then the motive of the defendant in publishing the statement is entirely irrelevant. The defendant need not have known nor cared whether the allegation was true, and (with one exception) may even have acted out of spite toward the claimant.

The one exception arises under section 8 of the Rehabilitation of Offenders Act 1974: where a person has a 'spent' conviction for an offence, and where the alleged defamation is a statement referring to the claimant's guilt in respect of that offence, the defence of justification will be lost if 'malice' is proved.

On the other hand, the very fact that truth is merely a defence, and that falsehood plays no part in the *definition* of a defamatory statement, complicates this simple picture. Because truth is a defence, the burden of establishing it falls on the defendant rather than the claimant.

Justification and Defamatory Meaning

We have already seen that the claimant must set out the defamatory meaning of the words complained of. In doing this, the claimant is able to gain an element of control over litigation. Although the defendant is free to choose which defamatory meaning he or she will seek to 'justify' (show to be true), nevertheless the justification offered must be sufficient to remove the 'sting' of the allegation. That is to say, the *effect* of the statement on the claimant's reputation, *in the light of the defamatory meaning conveyed*, must be justified. 'The justification must be as wide as the charge'.[11]

Some help is at hand for defendants in the form of section 5 of the Defamation Act 1952. This section may appear complex, but the essential point of section 5 is simple:

Lord Denning, *Moore v News of the World Ltd* [1972] 1 QB 441, at 448

. . . a defendant is not to fail simply because he cannot prove every single thing in the statement to be true.

Defamation Act 1952

5 Justification

In an action for libel or slander in respect of words containing two or more distinct charges against the plaintiff, a defence of justification shall not fail by reason only that the truth of every charge is not proved if the words not proved to be true do not materially injure the plaintiff's reputation having regard to the truth of the remaining charges.

As the wording of the section makes clear, it applies where there is more than one defamatory allegation complained of. Before it is applied, the court must decide that the defamatory allegations in question are 'distinct'—that is to say, that they do not have a 'common sting'.

If the allegations *do* have a '**common sting**', the situation is both simpler, and much more beneficial to defendants: they may justify any of the allegations, using evidence drawn from any source including other parts of the same publication. These cases do not require the protection of section 5 and they do not fall within it.

If the allegations are **distinct**, then section 5 comes into play. This section provides that a defendant who can justify only one of the allegations may still argue that the remaining charge is insignificant—that is to say, that it does not materially injure the claimant's reputation once the truth of the justified charge is taken into account. Alternatively, damages may be paid in respect of the remaining charge. Given that one allegation has been justified, these damages (depending of course on the nature of the two allegations) may be relatively moderate.

That is the basic principle, but it is not the end of the matter. As we have said, it is the *claimant* who sets out the defamatory statement complained of, and its meaning. What if the claimant does not complain at all about certain defamatory statements in the publication, yet those statements *can* be justified? Does this put the defendant in a worse position than if a complaint had been made about each allegation, by preventing him or her from setting out relevant evidence?

In short, the answer is yes, and this is illustrated by *Cruise and Kidman v Express Newspapers* [1999] QB 931. The plaintiffs objected to a magazine article, the whole of which was attached to their statement of claim. This statement of claim, however, only complained of certain specific allegations made in the article. The defendants sought to bring evidence which would

---

[11] Since the Court of Appeal's decision in *Lucas-Box v News Group Newspapers Ltd* [1986] 1 WLR 147, defendants have been required to set out precisely what meaning they intend to justify: just as the meaning contended for by the claimant must be *capable of being conveyed* by the statement, so also must the meaning argued (and justified) by the defendant pass the same test.

justify *other* elements of the article, of which no complaint was made. They were not permitted to do so, because the 'sting' of the libel which the defendants sought to justify (relating to the Church of Scientology) was quite different from the sting of the libel complained of (relating to personal issues).

Bookbinder v Tebbit [1989] 1 WLR 640 illustrates the same point in a slightly different way. Here, the plaintiff initially alleged that a specific statement by the defendant—relating to the wasteful over-printing of school stationery with the words 'Support Nuclear-Free Zones'— contained a broader allegation that the plaintiff wasted public funds generally. When the defendant offered to bring substantial evidence to justify the broader charge, the plaintiff quickly applied to narrow his complaint to cover only the more specific charge of wasting money on a single occasion. He was entitled to narrow his pleadings in this way, because the court agreed that the words complained of *could not convey* the broader meaning. The result was that the defendant was forced to withdraw much of the evidence he wished to bring. He could not seek to justify a broad charge which could not be implied from the words used, even though this might have 'drawn the sting' of the libel.

The guiding principles to be applied in a case where there are several defamatory allegations are summarized in *Polly Peck v Trelford* [1986] QB 1000. The points made in the extract will be most easily understood in the light of the concrete examples above:

O'Connor LJ, at 1032

. . . In cases where the plaintiff selects words from a publication, pleads that in their natural and ordinary meaning the words are defamatory of him, and pleads the meanings which he asserts they bear by way of false innuendo, the defendant is entitled to look at the whole publication in order to aver that in their context the words bear a meaning different from that alleged by the plaintiff. The defendant is entitled to plead that in that meaning the words are true and to give particulars of the facts and matters upon which he relies in support of his plea. . . . It is fortuitous that some or all of those facts and matters are culled from parts of the publication of which the plaintiff has not chosen to complain.

Where a publication contains two or more separate and distinct defamatory statements, the plaintiff is entitled to select one for complaint, and the defendant is not entitled to assert the truth of the others by way of justification.

Whether a defamatory statement is separate and distinct from other defamatory statements contained in the publication is a question of fact and degree in each case. The several defamatory allegations in their context may have a common sting, in which event they are not to be regarded as separate and distinct allegations. The defendant is entitled to justify the sting, and once again it is fortuitous that what is in fact similar fact evidence is found in the publication.

5.3 FAIR COMMENT

Comment on a matter of public interest will not give rise to an action in defamation provided the comment could be made by a fair-minded person; is based on true facts indicated in the statement; and is not motivated by 'malice'. 'Comment' in this context means 'opinion'.

Fair comment is a cherished defence and many judicial (and other) statements have supported its existence in a robust and general form. That the need to protect statements of opinion is especially important has been recognized for many years. In *Slim v Daily Telegraph*

[1968] 2 QB 157, Lord Denning captured the protective judicial approach towards statements of opinion as follows:

> . . . the right of fair comment is one of the essential elements which go to make up our free-dom of speech. We must ever retain this right intact. It must not be whittled down by legal refinements.

Unfortunately, it has not been possible to keep the defence entirely clear of legal refinements. Principally, this is because it is necessary to distinguish a comment from a statement of fact; and because there are some limits (whether defined in terms of the speaker's motive or of the likely impact of his or her words) beyond which the defence will not operate.

Why give Special Protection to Comment?

The particularly strong protection offered to comment, as opposed to fact, can be explained through two linked ideas.

> 1. *Free expression of opinions is essential to debate, and free and lively debate is essential to democracy and the emergence of truth.*

There is clearly some judicial support for this approach:

Scott LJ, *Lyon v Daily Telegraph* [1943] KB 746, at 752

The reason why, once a plea of fair comment is established, there is no libel, is that it is in the public interest to have a free discussion of matters of public interest.

Similarly, the following statement was quoted with approval by Lord Nicholls, in *Albert Cheng v Tse Wai Chun Paul* [2000] 4 HKC 1 at 14:[12]

J. G. Fleming, *The Law of Torts* (9th edn, NSW: Law Book Company, 1998), 648

. . . untrammelled discussion of public affairs and of those participating in them is a basic safeguard against irresponsible political power. The unfettered preservation of the right of fair comment is, therefore, one of the foundations supporting our standards of personal liberty.

> 2. *Misguided comment is less dangerous than inaccurate statements of fact.*

The theory adopted by common law appears to be that people in general will not be misled by what is evidently mere comment. There is therefore less *need* to penalize comment than fact: it is less dangerous both to reputation, and to truth, because the reader is 'free' to assess the opinions offered (and will not be unduly influenced by them). This presumes a fairly robust and healthy level of public debate and fits well with the broadly instrumental, 'democratic' justifications for

---

[12] Lord Nicholls was sitting in this case as a member of the Hong Kong Court of Final Appeal.

freedom of speech identified at the start of this chapter. As such, it is no surprise to see this approach reflected in Lord Nicholls' brief remarks on fair comment in *Reynolds*:

Lord Nicholls, *Reynolds v Times Newspapers Ltd* [2001] 2 AC 127, at 201

. . . [r]eaders and viewers may make up their own minds on whether they agree or disagree with defamatory statements which are recognisable as comment and which, expressly or impliedly, indicate in general terms the facts on which they are based.

Applying these two justifications for the defence, one would expect its boundaries to be set by reference to *the impact of the publication upon the reader*, rather than by judging fairness in the light of the defendant's intentions. But there is an element of inconsistency in the case law.

The Ingredients of the Fair Comment Defence

1. The comment must be on a matter of public interest.

'Public interest' has different meanings in different contexts. The classic exposition of 'public interest' in the particular context of 'fair comment' is to be found in the case of *London Artists v Littler*. As a result of the approach taken in this case, most issues except those which can be described as genuinely 'private' will fall within the definition of 'public interest' for the fair comment defence.

Lord Denning, *London Artists v Littler* [1969] 2 QB 375, at 391

. . . was the comment made on a matter of public interest? The judge ruled that it was not, [1968] 1 W.L.R. 607, 623. I cannot agree with him. There is no definition in the books as to what is a matter of public interest. All we are given is a list of examples, coupled with the statement that it is for the judge and not for the jury. I would not myself confine it within narrow limits. Whenever a matter is such as to affect people at large, so that they may be legitimately interested in, or concerned at, what is going on; or what may happen to them or to others; then it is a matter of public interest on which everyone is entitled to make fair comment. A good example is *South Hetton Coal Co. v. North-Eastern News Association* [1894] 1 Q.B. 133. A colliery company owned most of the cottages in the village. It was held that the sanitary condition of those cottages—or rather their insanitary condition—was a matter of public interest. Lord Esher M.R., said at p. 140, that it was "a matter of public interest that the conduct of the employers should be criticised." There the public were legitimately *concerned*. Here the public are legitimately interested. Many people are interested in what happens in the theatre. The stars welcome publicity. They want to be put at the top of the bill. Producers wish it too. They like the house to be full. The comings and goings of performers are noticed everywhere. When three top stars and a satellite all give notice to leave at the same time—thus putting a successful play in peril—it is to my mind a matter of public interest in which everyone, Press and all, are entitled to comment freely.

---

2. The 'comment' must be genuine comment as opposed to imputation of fact.

In judging whether a statement is comment or fact the *form* in which it is expressed is not decisive. An assertion that a work of art is 'rubbish' takes the form of a fact, but clearly expresses an opinion. As with defamatory meaning, the question is how the words complained of would be *understood*.

Whether a statement consists of comment or fact will in many cases depend on the context of the statement. The requirement that facts should be indicated in the statement (see page 774, below) is not a mere technicality, but affects the meaning of the comment itself.

Lord Porter, *Kemsley v Foot* [1952] AC 345, at 356

The question, therefore, in all cases is whether there is a sufficient substratum of fact stated or indicated in the words which are the subject-matter of the action, and I find my view well expressed in the remarks contained in Odgers on Libel and Slander (6th ed., 1929), at p. 166. "Sometimes, however," he says, "it is difficult to distinguish an allegation of fact from an expression of opinion. It often depends on what is stated in the rest of the article. If the defendant accurately states what some public man has really done, and then asserts that 'such conduct is disgraceful,' this is merely the expression of his opinion, his comment on the plaintiff's conduct. So, if without setting it out, he identifies the conduct on which he comments by a clear reference. *In either case, the defendant enables his readers to judge for themselves how far his opinion is well founded;* and, therefore, what would otherwise have been an allegation of fact becomes merely a comment. But if he asserts that the plaintiff has been guilty of disgraceful conduct, and does not state what that conduct was, this is an allegation of fact for which there is no defence but privilege or truth. The same considerations apply where a defendant has drawn from certain facts an inference derogatory to the plaintiff. If he states the bare inference without the facts on which it is based, such inference will be treated as an allegation of fact. But if he sets out the facts correctly, and then gives his inference, stating it as his inference from those facts, such inference will, as a rule, be deemed a comment. . . . " (Emphasis added.)

The idea emphasized in the middle of this paragraph—that readers of the publication are able to judge the validity of the comment for themselves only if they can make out the facts on the basis of which the comment is made—is essential.

Telnikoff v Matusevitch [1992] 2 AC 343 illustrates why this is so. The plaintiff had published an article in a daily newspaper. Offended by the contents of the plaintiff's article, which he considered to carry anti-Semitic implications, the defendant wrote a letter to the newspaper commenting upon it. Since this letter was (as is usual) published in a subsequent issue, not all of those reading the letter would have read the article (and fewer still would recollect all of its details). The plaintiff brought libel proceedings against the defendant, complaining that the letter imputed anti-Semitic views to him. The defendant argued that the letter amounted to fair comment: he was drawing conclusions from the words used by the plaintiff in his article, and *the allegation of anti-Semitism was therefore comment rather than fact*.

The House of Lords accepted that if the letter was looked at alone, without the plaintiff's words for reference, then it would be possible (as a matter of law) to decide that the letter included some statements of fact. The question of whether there were factual assertions in the letter ought then to be left to the jury to resolve, and a new trial would have to be ordered. If at trial the jury thought that the letter did contain assertions of fact, then the defendant would have to *justify* those assertions. This would be far more demanding than showing 'fairness' (defined below), and the defendant would probably fail. On the other hand, if the letter were to be read *alongside* the article, it would clearly amount to comment. There would be no need for a new trial, and the defendant would succeed. The key issue to resolve, therefore, was the *context* in which the letter should be read.

The House of Lords decided that the contents of the letter should be read *alone*, without reference to the earlier article, because this was the way that the letter would generally be read. The effect of this decision is to impose a burden on letter writers and also on newspapers (since they too are publishing the letters) to ensure that the facts on which opinions are based are clarified. As it happens, such a duty fits quite comfortably with our 'public interest' interpretation of freedom of speech, and of the defence of fair comment. It is *the impact on the reader*, and not *the intention of the writer* that is important.

3. *The comment must be based on facts that are true (or protected by privilege); and*

4. *The comment must indicate (if only very generally) the facts on the basis of which the comment is made.*

Together, these two criteria require that the statement must amount to comment on the basis of 'true facts stated'.

Generally, the facts on which the comment is based must be set out in the publication complained of. But if the facts are *generally known to the public*, then the defendant need not set them out explicitly in the publication. Rather, such facts must be sufficiently 'indicated'. This is because readers will still be free to form their own judgment as to the validity of the comment.

Kemsley v Foot [1952] AC 345

The defendant had published an article attacking the conduct of a newspaper, under the title 'Lower than Kemsley'. There was no other reference in the article to Kemsley, who was proprietor of an entirely separate newspaper. Kemsley brought an action in libel on the basis that the article, through its title, attacked his reputation. The House of Lords decided that a sufficient 'substratum of fact' was present in the statement made. The *fact* referred to by implication was that Kemsley was responsible for the press of which he was proprietor. This was well known, and did not have to be spelt out explicitly. The *criticism* was that the Kemsley press was 'low'. This might be fact or comment, but in any case it was not (as the plaintiffs contended) pure comment made without reference to relevant facts. The defence could therefore go before the jury.

Lord Porter, at 354

It is not, as I understand, contended that the words contained in that article are fact and not comment: rather it is alleged that they are comment with no facts to support it. The question for your Lordships' decision is, therefore, whether a plea of fair comment is only permissible where the comment is accompanied by a statement of facts upon which the comment is made and to determine the particularity with which the facts must be stated . . .

At 357

Is there, then, in this case sufficient subject-matter upon which to make comment? In an article which is concerned with what has been described as "the Beaverbrook Press" and which is violently critical of Lord Beaverbrook's newspapers, it is, I think, a reasonable construction of the words "Lower than Kemsley" that the allegation which is made is that the conduct of the Kemsley Press was similar to but not quite so bad as that of the press controlled by Lord Beaverbrook, i.e., it is possibly dishonest, but in any case low. The exact meaning, however, is not, in my opinion, for your Lordships but for the jury. All I desire to say is that there is subject-matter and it is at least arguable that the words directly complained of imply as fact that Lord Kemsley is in control of a number of known newspapers and that the conduct of those news-papers is in question. Had the contention that all the facts justifying the comment must appear in the article been maintainable, the appeal would succeed, but the appellant's representatives did not feel able to and, I think, could not support so wide a contention. The facts, they admitted, might be implied, and the respondents' answer to their contention is: "We have pointed to your press. It is widely read. Your readers will and the public generally can know at what our criticism is directed. It is not bare comment; it is comment on a well-known matter, much better known, indeed, than a newly printed book or a once-performed play."

The next important question is whether the defendant needs to show the *truth* of all facts used as the basis of the comment. Here, the House of Lords in *Kemsley* provided defendants with significant leeway.

Lord Porter, *Kemsley v Foot* [1952] AC 345, at 357–8

In a case where the facts are fully set out in the alleged libel, each fact must be justified and if the defendant fails to justify one, even if it be comparatively unimportant, he fails in his defence.[13] Does the same principle apply where the facts alleged are found not in the alleged libel but in particulars delivered in the course of the action? In my opinion, it does not. Where the facts are set out in the alleged libel, those to whom it is published can read them and may regard them as facts derogatory to the plaintiff; but where, as here, they are contained only in particulars and are not published to the world at large, they are not the subject-matter of the comment but facts alleged to justify that comment.

. . . As I hold, any facts sufficient to justify [the] statement would entitle the defendants to succeed in a plea of fair comment. Twenty facts might be given in the particulars and only one justified, yet if that one fact were sufficient to support the comment so as to make it fair, a fail-ure to prove the other nineteen would not of necessity defeat the defendants' plea.

In *Rupert Lowe v Associated Newspapers* [2006] EWHC 320 (QB), Eady J ruled that the defend-ant should not be allowed to prove facts *of which he had been unaware at the time of making the statement* in order to support a defence of fair comment. This would be permitted in a plea of *justification*, but the purpose of the fair comment defence was, in his view, very different:

At 74

The purpose of the defence of fair comment is to protect honest expressions of opinion upon, or inferences honestly drawn from, specific facts.

There is some room to doubt this conclusion. So far, we have suggested that the *reader's* knowledge—and the impact on the reader's ability to distinguish between fact and comment

---

[13] The modern understanding of justification—and of Defamation Act 1952, s 5—set out earlier in this chapter would require only that the assertions must be *substantially* justified: the defendant will not fail just because he or she cannot prove every single assertion to be true.

and to form an independent view—is the guiding principle. If this is right, then it should be possible to be 'fair' without meaning to be, just as it is possible for a statement to be inadvertently 'true'.

5. *The comment must be one which could have been made by an honest person.*

It is clear that the comment does not need to be *reasonable*. The defence is available even where the comment is 'prejudiced, wrong-headed, and grossly exaggerated'.

We have already outlined the facts of *Telnikoff v Matusevitch* [1992] 2 AC 343, and explained one element of the House of Lords' conclusions. A second point before the House of Lords concerned the test for fairness.

Lord Keith, at 354

Drake J. also refused to leave to the jury the question whether, assuming that paragraphs 6 and 7 were pure comment, they constituted fair comment on a matter of public interest, and the Court of Appeal upheld his decision on this matter also. Both took the view that on an application of the normal objective test of fair comment any reasonable jury would be bound to hold that it was satisfied. Lloyd L.J. correctly stated the test as being whether any man, however prejudiced and obstinate, could honestly hold the view expressed by the defendant in his letter. I agree with Drake J. and the Court of Appeal as to the only reasonable outcome of a proper application of that test, and find it unnecessary to elaborate the matter. It was, however, argued by counsel for the plaintiff before the Court of Appeal and in your Lordships' House that in addition to satisfying the objective test a defendant pleading fair comment must prove affirmatively that the comment represented his own honest opinion, which the present defendant failed to do, since the case was withdrawn from the jury before any evidence had been given by him. Lloyd L.J., after an extensive review of the authorities, concluded that this argument was unsound. These authorities included *Cherneskey v. Armadale Publishers Ltd.* (1978) 90 D.L.R. (3d) 321, in the Supreme Court of Canada. The defendants were the editor and the owner and publisher of a newspaper which had published a letter to the editor in which the writers accused the plaintiff of holding racist views. The writers of the letter did not give evidence, but the defendants in their evidence made it clear that the letter complained of did not represent the honest expression of their own views. The trial judge refused to leave the defence of fair comment to the jury, and the Supreme Court, by a majority of six to three, held that he had acted rightly. Lloyd L.J. expressed himself as preferring the judgment of the minority to that of the majority, and as regarding the former as being fully supported by the English authorities cited in his extensive review. I find myself in respectful agreement with him and feel that to repeat his review would be a work of supererogation. The law is correctly stated in *Gatley on Libel and Slander*, 8th ed. (1981), p. 348, para. 792:

"*Onus of proof of malice: fair comment.* In the same way, the defendant who relies on a plea of fair comment does not have to show that the comment is an honest expression of his views. 'In alleging any unfairness the plaintiff takes on him or herself the onus, also taken by an allegation of malice, to prove that the criticism is unfair either from the language used or from some extraneous circumstance.' "

The House of Lords expressly endorsed the judgment of Lloyd LJ in the Court of Appeal ([1991] 1 QB 102). In the judgment referred to, Lloyd LJ carefully explained the important difference between 'fairness' and 'honesty'. *Fairness* is objective and is for the defendant to establish; *lack of honest belief* is subjective and is relevant only at the malice stage, where it is for the claimant to establish.

Lloyd LJ, at 115

In my view the correct view of the English law is that where the defendant's comment is fair by the objective test, it is presumed to be the honest expression of his view unless the plaintiff pleads and proves express malice.

In *Telnikoff*, the Court of Appeal and House of Lords both had in mind the Supreme Court of Canada's decision in *Chernesky v Armadale* (1978) 90 DLR (3d) 321. The facts of that case were very similar to *Telnikoff* itself, except (importantly) that it was the *newspaper* that was the subject of an action in defamation, as publisher of the letter. Of course, the newspaper was unable to show that it had a positive, honest belief in the opinions expressed by the letter writer. In *Chernesky*, this was fatal to its defence; on the approach in *Telnikoff*, it would not have been. *The objective test aims to ensure that defendants do not have the burden of showing their state of mind.* This would often be an onerous task, and sometimes (for example in the case of the newspaper as secondary publisher) it would be impossible.

More recently, in the case of *Branson v Bower* [2002] QB 737, Eady J reached a very different conclusion, arguing that 'honesty alone' is the touchstone of fair comment. Again this was intended to protect the right to express opinions no matter how obstinate, prejudiced, or exaggerated. He was eager not to 'water down' the protection afforded to defendants by introducing an objective test, and he justified his apparent divergence from the older law (including *Telnikoff*) by reference to the chilling effect and the need to comply with Article 10:

27 It is clear (as illustrated in a number of European cases) that there is a significant inhibition upon freedom of speech if one is required to prove the unprovable. A commentator may be able to prove facts objectively, but it is neither just nor logical to seek to subject opinion to the same test. To impose a test of reasonableness or fairness is to bring in objective criteria which have no place in the context of subjective opinion. "The objective safeguards, coupled with the need to have a genuine belief in what is said, are adequate to keep the ambit of permissible comment within reasonable bounds": per Lord Nicholls in *Cheng v Tse Wai Chun* [2000] 3 HKLRD 418, 430.

28 I have therefore come to the conclusion (I believe consistently both with Lord Nicholls in *Cheng's* case and with the article 10 jurisprudence) that the only two requirements in this context are (1) that a defendant should have expressed the opinions honestly and (2) that he should have done so upon facts accurately stated. This second requirement is the only objective criterion that makes sense, because such facts are capable of proof.

Yet the *objective* test referred to in *Telnikoff* is not (and never was intended to be) a reasonableness test. Rather, the objective test in *Telnikoff* is *more* strongly supportive of defendants' freedom to express opinions than the honesty test, because it refers to the honesty of a *hypothetical* commentator: the comment must be one which *could have been made by an honest person*, however prejudiced he might be. This is merely an application of the long-standing test for fairness adapted by Lord Porter in *Turner v MGM* [1950] 1 All ER 449:

Lord Porter, *Turner v MGM*

To a similar effect were the words of LORD ESHER, M.R. (20 Q.B.D. 281), in Merivale v. Carson which are so often quoted:

" . . . would any fair man, however prejudiced he may be, however exaggerated or obstinate his views, have [written] this criticism . . . ?"

I should adopt them except that I would substitute "honest" for "fair" lest some suggestion of reasonableness instead of honesty should be read in.

That the *hypothetical* honesty test gives greater protection to free speech than a requirement of *actual* honest belief can be illustrated by applying it to the newspaper publishing a letter. The editor has no honest belief in the opinions, which are those of another; however, he may well be able to show that an honest but prejudiced person could have held those views. Equally, the individual letter-writer would benefit from the objective approach because he or she would need to bring no evidence of honesty unless an issue of malice was raised by the claimant—where it would be for the claimant to show *lack* of honesty (below). Eady J, in *Branson v Bower*, appears to have been arguing against a test—of *reasonableness*—that has never been adopted in the case law.

In both *Telnikoff* (particularly in the judgment of Lloyd LJ), and in *Turner v MGM*, it is clear that there is no need to show 'genuine belief' in order to establish fairness. Leaving aside *Branson v Bower* and the Hong Kong case relied upon in the extract from it above (which we next extract), the authorities make clear that subjective issues are relevant only at the next stage, which is malice.

6. Malice

The fair comment defence is not available if the claimant can establish that the defendant acted with 'express malice'.

At the start of this section on defences, we outlined the general test for 'express malice', derived from *Horrocks v Lowe*. *Horrocks v Lowe* itself concerned qualified privilege, but it has generally been presumed that the test would be the same in fair comment. In *Cheng v Tse Wai Chun* [2000] 4 HKC 1,[14] Lord Nicholls proposed that malice may operate quite differently in these two defences. In particular, intent to injure, ill will, or spite, will certainly suffice to lose the protection of qualified privilege, but Lord Nicholls doubted whether this should be the case in fair comment. In particular, 'intent to injure' is not inconsistent with the *purpose* for which the defence of fair comment exists, since many (if not most) contributors to debate have an ulterior motive of some kind. According to Lord Nicholls, malice in such cases should turn instead on 'lack of honest belief'. This idea is sufficiently broad to cover cases where the defendant *knows* that the comment is not true, or *is recklessly indifferent to* the truth or falsity of the comment.

---

[14] This decision is binding in Hong Kong law, but not in English law. An extract is set out here because Lord Nicholls' assessment of the case law is drawn from the English authorities, and is the clearest recent exposition of fair comment. Given that Lord Nicholls was the main architect of the *Reynolds* privilege (below) his interpretation of the parallel defence of fair comment is of considerable importance. *Cheng* has also been referred to in first instance decisions as we have seen: *Branson v Bower*.

Lord Nicholls, *Cheng v Tse Wai Chun* [2000] 4 HKC 1

The purpose and importance of the defence of fair comment are inconsistent with its scope being restricted to comments made for particular reasons or particular purposes, some being regarded as proper, others not. Especially in the social and political fields, those who make public comments usually have some objective of their own in mind, even if it is only to publicise and advance themselves. They often have what may be described as an 'ulterior' object. Frequently their object is apparent, but not always so. They may hope to achieve some result, such as promoting one cause or defeating another, elevating one person or denigrating another. In making their comments they do not act dispassionately, they do not intend merely to convey information. They have other motives.

The presence of these motives, and this is of crucial importance for present purposes, is not a reason for excluding the defence of fair comment. The existence of motives such as these when expressing an opinion does not mean that the defence of fair comment is being misused. It would make no sense, for instance, if a motive relating to the very feature which causes the matter to be one of public interest were regarded as defeating the defence.

On the contrary, this defence is intended to protect and promote comments such as these. Liberty to make such comments, genuinely held, on matters of public interest lies at the heart of the defence of fair comment. That is the very object for which the defence exists. Commentators, of all shades of opinion, are entitled to 'have their own agenda'. Politicians, social reformers, busybodies, those with political or other ambitions and those with none, all can grind their axes. The defence of fair comment envisages that everyone is at liberty to conduct social and political campaigns by expressing his own views, subject always, and I repeat the refrain, to the objective safeguards which mark the limits of the defence.

. . .

Spiteful comments

One particular motive calls for special mention: spite or ill-will. This raises a difficult point. I confess that my first, instinctive reaction was that the defence of fair comment should not be capable of being used to protect a comment made with the intent of injuring another out of spite, even if the person who made the comment genuinely believed in the truth of what he said. Personal spite, after all, is four square within the popular meaning of malice. . . .

On reflection I do not think the law should attempt to ring-fence comments made with the sole or dominant motive of causing injury out of spite or, which may come to much the same, causing injury simply for the sake of doing so. In the first place it seems to me that the postulate on which this problem is based is a little unreal. The postulate poses a problem which is more academic than practical. The postulate is that the comment in question falls within the objective limits of the defence. Thus, the comment is one which is based on fact; it is made in circumstances where those to whom the comment is addressed can form their own view on whether or not the comment was sound; and the comment is one which can be held by an honest person. This postulate supposes, further, that the maker of the comment genuinely believes in the truth of his comment. It must be questionable whether comments, made out of spite and causing injury, are at all likely to satisfy each and every of these requirements. There must be a query over whether, in practice, there is a problem here which calls for attention. . . .

The final paragraph depends on 'honest belief' being part of the test for fairness, so that it need not feature in the test for malice. But as we said above, it was clearly stated in *Telnikoff* that honest belief was not required. This issue must be regarded as unsettled.

5.4 SECTIONS 1 AND 2 TO 4 OF THE DEFAMATION ACT 1996: INNOCENT DEFAMATION AND OFFERS TO MAKE AMENDS

Innocent Defamation

'Innocence' in respect of a defamatory statement was no defence at common law. The Defamation Act 1996 introduces two defences of use to those who are not at fault in the publication of a defamatory statement. The first, in section 1, benefits only those who are not in the position of 'author, editor, or publisher' of a statement, and requires reasonable care to be taken. 'Publisher' for these purposes is a narrower category than the class of people 'publishing' a statement at common law (see *Bunt v Tilley*, below), and is defined in the section itself. This section is intended to assist those with a 'secondary' role in the publication.

Defamation Act 1996

1 Responsibility for publication

(1) In defamation proceedings a person has a defence if he shows that—

   (a) he was not the author, editor or publisher of the statement complained of,

   (b) he took reasonable care in relation to its publication, and

   (c) he did not know, and had no reason to believe, that what he did caused or contributed to the publication of a defamatory statement.

(2) For this purpose "author", "editor" and "publisher" have the following meanings, which are further explained in subsection (3)—

   "author" means the originator of the statement, but does not include a person who did not intend that his statement be published at all;

   "editor" means a person having editorial or equivalent responsibility for the content of the statement or the decision to publish it; and

   "publisher" means a commercial publisher, that is, a person whose business is issuing material to the public, or a section of the public, who issues material containing the statement in the course of that business.

(3) A person shall not be considered the author, editor or publisher of a statement if he is only involved—

   (a) in printing, producing, distributing or selling printed material containing the statement;

   (b) in processing, making copies of, distributing, exhibiting or selling a film or sound recording (as defined in Part I of the Copyright, Designs and Patents Act 1988) containing the statement;

   (c) in processing, making copies of, distributing or selling any electronic medium in or on which thestatement is recorded, or in operating or providing any equipment, system or service by means of which the statement is retrieved, copied, distributed or made available in electronic form;

(d) as the broadcaster of a live programme containing the statement in circumstances in which he has no effective control over the maker of the statement;

(e) as the operator of or provider of access to a communications system by means of which the statement is transmitted, or made available, by a person over whom he has no effective control.

In a case not within paragraphs (a) to (e) the court may have regard to those provisions by way of analogy in deciding whether a person is to be considered the author, editor or publisher of a statement.

. . .

(5) In determining for the purposes of this section whether a person took reasonable care, or had reason to believe that what he did caused or contributed to the publication of a defamatory statement, regard shall be had to—

(a) the extent of his responsibility for the content of the statement or the decision to publish it,

(b) the nature or circumstances of the publication, and

(c) the previous conduct or character of the author, editor or publisher.

Section 1 only benefits those who have no reason to believe that the publication is defamatory and who take reasonable care. Once put on notice that the publication contains defamatory material, the protection of section 1 ceases to operate (s 1(1)(c)).

Godfrey v Demon Internet [2001] QB 201

Demon Internet is an Internet Service Provider ('ISP'), providing subscribers with access to (amongst other things) bulletin boards. The claimant put Demon on notice of a defamatory statement posted on the board, and requested its removal. Demon did not remove the posting. Morland J held that the ISP had 'published' the statement:

. . . every time one of the defendants' customers accesses [the bulletin] and sees that posting defamatory of the plaintiff there is a publication to that customer.

Having been put on notice, Demon could not benefit from the protection of section 1 of the Defamation Act 1996.

Bunt v Tilley [2006] EWHC 407

This case also concerned an ISP, but the case was crucially different from *Godfrey*. First, the defendants appear to have played a much more passive role in publication. As such, they did not satisfy the *threshold* test of having 'published a defamatory statement' which, quite independently of section 1 of the Defamation Act 1996, is a prerequisite of a successful action in defamation. Second, no adequate steps were taken by the claimant to put them on notice of the defamatory contents for the purposes of section 1 of the Defamation Act 1996. And third, the defendants were protected by the Electronic Commerce (EC Directive) Regulations 2002, reg 13. As a result, there was no liability on the part of the internet service providers.

For present purposes, it is particularly important to notice the first of these distinctions. There is no need to bring into play the section 1 defence if the defendant has not passed the threshold test of 'publishing' the defamatory statement as a matter of common law. 'Publication' for these purposes requires some element of knowledge. There is of course no need to know that the statement *is defamatory* (this is the very point of section 1). But the defendant should at least intend a publication:

Eady J, *Bunt v Tilley* [2006] EWHC 407 (QB)

22 I have little doubt . . . that to impose legal responsibility upon anyone under the common law for the publication of words it is essential to demonstrate a degree of awareness or at least an assumption of general responsibility, such as has long been recognised in the context of editorial responsibility. As Lord Morris commented in *McLeod v St. Aubyn* [1899] AC 549, 562:22

> "A printer and publisher intends to publish, and so intending cannot plead as a justification that he did not know the contents. The appellant in this case never intended to publish."

In that case the relevant publication consisted in handing over an unread copy of a newspaper for return the following day. It was held that there was no sufficient degree of awareness or intention to impose legal responsibility for that 'publication'.

Offers to make Amends

Any defendant may respond to an action in defamation by 'offering to make amends'. The appropriate contents of such an offer, and its implications, are explained in sections 2 to 4 of the Defamation Act 1996. 'Amends' for these purposes must include a suitable apology and correction, together with appropriate damages. Damages should be agreed. If an offer to make amends is accepted, but no agreement is reached as to damages, then damages will be assessed by a court on broadly the same basis as in defamation generally. However, the offer to make amends will be taken into account and a suitable discount applied.[15] The only *defence* to flow from these provisions is provided by section 4. By this section, it will be a defence to an action in defamation to show that an offer to make amends has been made, provided the defendant had no grounds for believing that the statement made was defamatory of the claimant.

4 Failure to accept offer to make amends

. . .

(2) The fact that the offer was made is a defence (subject to subsection (3)) to defamation proceedings in respect of the publication in question by that party against the person making the offer.

. . .

(3) There is no such defence if the person by whom the offer was made knew or had reason to believe that the statement complained of—

(a) referred to the aggrieved party or was likely to be understood as referring to him, and

(b) was both false and defamatory of that party;

---

[15] *Nail v News Group Newspapers* [2005] 1 All ER 1040; see further Damages below.

but it shall be presumed unless the contrary is shown that he did not know and had no reason to believe that was the case.

(4) The person who made the offer need not rely on it by way of defence, but if he does he may not rely on any other defence.

On the face of it, section 4(3) is similar to section 1 and appears to be concerned with failure to exercise due care in publication. But in *Milne v Express Newspapers* [2005] 1 WLR 772, the Court of Appeal made clear that this is not the correct interpretation. Rather, by subsection (3) the defence is lost only if there is a state of mind akin to malice under *Horrocks v Lowe*. If the defendant makes a publication *knowing or having reason to believe* that the statement is false and defamatory, then this is equivalent to knowledge of falsity, or recklessness as to truth, as required by malice. The required state of mind for section 4 is therefore quite different from due care under section 1.

5.5 PRIVILEGE

Some statements are recognized to be so important that they ought to be made with full confidence that they are beyond the reach of an action in defamation. In other words, these statements are to be protected *regardless of truth or falsity*, despite their inclusion of factual assertions. Such statements are protected by privilege.

Absolute and Qualified Privilege

There are two levels of privilege in English law. Statements that attract 'absolute privilege' cannot be the subject of proceedings in defamation no matter what the motive of the speaker. Statements that attract 'qualified privilege' can only be the subject of proceedings in defamation if it can be shown that they were made with 'express malice'.

Absolute privilege

In some situations, being able to speak freely is of such public importance (or, in the case of judicial proceedings, defamatory statements are so unavoidable a part of the procedure), that no action in defamation is possible, no matter what the motive of the speaker. Key examples of 'absolute privilege' are statements in Parliament; statements made in the course of judicial proceedings; and fair and accurate reports of judicial proceedings (Defamation Act, s 14).

Qualified privilege

Statutory qualified privilege: section 15 of the Defamation Act 1996 specifies that the reports and other statements mentioned in Schedule 1 to the Act are protected by qualified privilege. The Schedule is lengthy and may be directly consulted by those who are curious to see these listed.

Qualified privilege at common law: the leading statement of qualified privilege at common law, outside the area defined by *Reynolds v Times Newspapers*, is the following:

Lord Atkinson, *Adam v Ward* [1917] AC 309

A privileged occasion is . . . an occasion where the person who makes a communication has an interest or a duty, legal, social, or moral, to make it to the person to whom it is made, and the person to whom it is so made has a corresponding interest or duty to receive it. This reciprocity is essential.

Leaving aside the many variations of common law privilege and concentrating on this short but widely accepted statement of principle, we can see that Lord Atkinson emphasizes *both sides* of a relationship. The *giver of the statement* must be under a duty, which may be legal, social, or moral, to make the statement to the relevant person (and not more widely). The person who receives it must have a corresponding *interest or duty* in receiving it. Lord Atkinson goes so far as to underline that *the reciprocity is essential*. With this in mind, it is clear that the form of privilege recognized in *Reynolds v Times Newspapers* (below) is a striking departure for common law. That was not clearly stated by the House of Lords in that decision itself, which was presented chiefly as an interpretation of the previous common law position. But members of the House have now more openly said (some more openly than others) that the *Reynolds* privilege is a new departure: *Jameel v Wall Street Journal* [2006] UKHL 44. In the latter case, Lord Hoffmann and Baroness Hale have said that it is a misnomer to call the defence a privilege at all; it is really a (restricted) defence of 'public interest'. The House of Lords in *Jameel* displayed some frustration that the privilege was being applied too cautiously by the lower courts. It has sent a reasonably clear signal that those involved in *responsible journalism*—emerging more clearly now as the target of the *Reynolds* privilege—should be given a wide margin of discretion. (It should be noted that 'responsible journalism' does *not* equate with everything that is published in the 'quality press' on weighty political matters. The *Sunday Times* failed by some way to convince the House of Lords that its report was privileged in *Reynolds* itself.)

The *Reynolds* Privilege: *Reynolds v Times Newspapers Ltd* [2001] 2 AC 127

Lord Nicholls set out the facts that gave rise to this case at 191:

The events giving rise to these proceedings took place during a political crisis in Dublin in November 1994. The crisis culminated in the resignation of Mr Reynolds as Taoiseach (prime minister) of Ireland and leader of the Fianna Fáil party. The reasons for Mr Reynolds's resignation were of public significance and interest in the United Kingdom because of his personal identification with the Northern Ireland peace process. Mr Reynolds was one of the chief architects of that process. He announced his resignation in the Dáil (the House of Representatives) of the Irish Parliament on Thursday, 17 November 1994. On the following Sunday, 20 November, the "Sunday Times" published in its British mainland edition an article entitled "Goodbye gombeen man". The article was the lead item in its world news section and occupied most of one page. The article was sub-headed "Why a fib too far proved fatal for the political career of Ireland's peacemaker and Mr Fixit." On the same day the Irish edition of the "Sunday Times" contained a three-page article headed "House of Cards" concerning the fall of the Government. This article differed in a number of respects from the British mainland edition. Mr Reynolds took strong exception to the article in the British mainland edition. In the libel proceedings which followed, Mr Reynolds pleaded that the sting of the article was that he had deliberately and dishonestly misled the Dáil on Tuesday, 15 November 1994 by suppressing vital information. Further, that he had deliberately and dishonestly misled his coalition cabinet colleagues, especially Mr Spring, the Tanaiste (deputy prime minister) and minister for foreign affairs, by withholding this information and had lied to them about when the information had come into his possession.

The material differences between English and Irish editions—and particularly the rather more sensationalist reporting in the English edition—played a part in the newspaper's failure to persuade the House of Lords that it should benefit from a qualified privilege in this case. On the particular approach adopted by the House of Lords in *Reynolds*, the conduct of the newspaper was relevant to the question of whether the publication was or was not potentially covered by privilege.

The Context of *Reynolds*: Political Speech

This case presented an opportunity for English law *to recognize and protect a general category of 'political speech'*. The suggestion advanced by the newspaper was that such a category should be recognized as attracting a special privilege, subject of course to proof of malice. This suggestion was explicitly related to the historic decision of the United States Supreme Court in *Sullivan v New York Times* (1964) 376 US 254. *Sullivan*, and its invocation of the 'chilling effect', had been explicitly relied on some years earlier by the House of Lords when it determined, in *Derbyshire v Times Newspapers* [1993] AC 534, that an elected entity such as a local authority would be unable to sue for defamation (Section 6 below). With the Human Rights Act 1998 on the verge of commencement, the defendants sought to extend this invocation of *Sullivan* to achieve more general protection for political speech.

In *Sullivan*, the US Supreme Court recognized that 'political speech' must be protected against the threat of defamation actions. The case was brought by an elected official who argued that he was accused in an advertisement (by implication, since he was not named in the publication) of violent intimidation of civil rights protesters. The Supreme Court held that in the absence of a relevant state of mind on the part of the defendants, this publication could not be the subject of libel proceedings.

The relevant state of mind which would take the publication outside the protection of the *Sullivan* defence was similar to 'malice' as that expression is used in *Horrocks v Lowe*. It would not be essential (although it would be sufficient) to show actual spite or ill will. Rather, intentional deceit (knowing publication of lies), or reckless disregard for truth, would suffice. Unusually, this state of mind would have to be shown with 'convincing clarity', and not simply on the balance of probabilities.[16] In effect, this amounted to a 'qualified privilege' for political speech, and this is what was contended for by the newspaper's lawyers in *Reynolds*.

Rejecting the newspaper's argument, the House of Lords pointed out that the idea of 'political speech' was inherently difficult to define and that it could lead to overly narrow protection.[17] The privilege that was recognized in *Reynolds* is in one sense broader, in that it can arise in respect of any matter of *public interest*. However, in other respects it is much narrower and more uncertain than the rule argued for by the defendants. The House of Lords did not offer unqualified protection to all public interest publications, subject to malice. Instead, a more modest but still controversial adaptation of the common law was undertaken, developing the duty-interest version of the qualified privilege defence so that it would cover certain publications made to the world at large. A new and very different sort of 'duty-interest' privilege is recognized, in which the relevant interest is explicitly the *public* interest in receiving information irrespective of its truth or falsity.

---

16 Loveland points out that the majority of the Supreme Court will not have trusted the Alabama courts with the 'balance of probabilities' test in such cases: Loveland, *Political Libels* (Hart Publishing, 2000).

17 In the United States, the boundaries of the *Sullivan* privilege have been elastic and it has been interpreted as including actions brought by 'public', not just 'political' figures.

In terms of its starting points in respect of freedom of speech and the role of defamation law, Lord Nicholls' judgment in *Reynolds* shares some important features with the decision of the US Supreme Court in *Sullivan*. Neither judgment was expressly concerned with the interests of potential defendants; both indicated a desire to protect the *democratic* function of free speech. Here the similarities end, and the political and legal contexts of the two decisions are also wholly different. *Sullivan* was a decision imposed on the courts of Alabama by the Supreme Court during a period of intense political tension between civil rights activists and racist white politicians in the Southern states. The Supreme Court in *Sullivan* recognized that there was a balance between freedom of speech, and duties to behave responsibly, but it shifted the balance decisively in favour of free speech. The House of Lords in *Reynolds* by contrast displays an openly sceptical opinion of the press and a protective attitude to the public. The *Reynolds* privilege leaves many important decisions over proper journalistic conduct to the courts and, unlike *Sullivan*, it (effectively) focuses on the *conduct* of the defendant. This was a relatively novel departure for defamation law, which is not typically concerned with negligence-type standards. But it was a particularly unexpected approach to a *privilege*, since as we have said the purpose of privilege is generally to permit *publication with confidence*.

Reynolds v Times Newspapers [2001] 2 AC 127

At 193–5

The defence of honest comment on a matter of public interest . . . does not cover defamatory statements of fact. But there are circumstances, in the famous words of Parke B in *Toogood v Spyring* (1834) 1 CM & R 181, 193, when the "common convenience and welfare of society" call for frank communication on questions of fact. In *Davies v Snead* (1870) LR 5 QB 608, 611, Blackburn J spoke of circumstances where a person is so situated that it, "becomes right in the interests of society" that he should tell certain facts to another. There are occasions when the person to whom a statement is made has a special interest in learning the honestly held views of another person, even if those views are defamatory of someone else and cannot be proved to be true. When the interest is of sufficient importance to outweigh the need to protect reputation, the occasion is regarded as privileged. . . .

Over the years the courts have held that many common form situations are privileged. Classic instances are employment references, and complaints made or information given to the police or appropriate authorities regarding suspected crimes. The courts have always emphasised that the categories established by the authorities are not exhaustive. The list is not closed. The established categories are no more than applications, in particular circumstances, of the underlying principle of public policy. The underlying principle is conventionally stated in words to the effect that there must exist between the maker of the statement and the recipient some duty or interest in the making of the communication. Lord Atkinson's dictum, in *Adam v Ward* [1917] AC 309, 334, is much quoted. . . .

The requirement that both the maker of the statement and the recipient must have an interest or duty draws attention to the need to have regard to the position of both parties when deciding whether an occasion is privileged. But this should not be allowed to obscure the rationale of the underlying public interest on which privilege is founded. The essence of this defence lies in the law's recognition of the need, in the public interest, for a particular recipient to receive frank and uninhibited communication of particular information from a particular source. That is the end the law is concerned to attain. The protection afforded to the maker of the statement is the means by which the law seeks to achieve that end. Thus the court has to assess whether, in the public interest, the publication should be protected in the absence of malice.

In determining whether an occasion is regarded as privileged the court has regard to all the circumstances: see, for example, the explicit statement of Lord Buckmaster LC in *London Association for Protection of Trade v Greenlands Ltd* [1916] 2 AC 15, 23 ("every circumstance associated with the origin and publication of the defamatory matter"). And circumstances must be viewed with today's eyes. The circumstances in which the public interest requires a communication to be protected in the absence of malice depend upon current social conditions. The requirements at the close of the twentieth century may not be the same as those of earlier centuries or earlier decades of this century.

Privilege and publication to the world at large

Frequently a privileged occasion encompasses publication to one person only or to a limited group of people. Publication more widely, to persons who lack the requisite interest in receiving the information, is not privileged. But the common law has recognised there are occasions when the public interest requires that publication to the world at large should be privileged. . . .

Lord Nicholls reviewed various older authorities, most of which appear to have been concerned with the reporting of public proceedings and were by no means as broad as the general duty–interest test that he next expressed:

At 197

In its valuable and forward-looking analysis of the common law the Court of Appeal in the present case highlighted that in deciding whether an occasion is privileged the court considers, among other matters, the nature, status and source of the material published and the circumstances of the publication. In stressing the importance of these particular factors, the court treated them as matters going to a question ("the circumstantial test") separate from, and, additional to, the conventional duty-interest questions: see [1998] 3 WLR 862, 899. With all respect to the Court of Appeal, this formulation of three questions gives rise to conceptual and practical difficulties and is better avoided. There is no separate or additional question. These factors are to be taken into account in determining whether the duty-interest test is satisfied or, as I would prefer to say in a simpler and more direct way, whether the public was entitled to know the particular information. The duty-interest test, or the right to know test, cannot be carried out in isolation from these factors and without regard to them. A claim to privilege stands or falls according to whether the claim passes or fails this test. There is no further requirement.

At 200

A new category of privileged subject matter?

I turn to the defendants' submissions. The newspaper seeks the incremental development of the common law by the creation of a new category of occasion when privilege derives from the subject matter alone: political information. Political information can be broadly defined, borrowing the language used by the High Court of Australia in the *Lange* case, as information, opinion and arguments concerning government and political matters that affect the people of the United Kingdom. Malice apart, publication of political information should be privileged regardless of the status and source of the material and the circumstances of the publication. The newspaper submitted that the contrary view requires the court to assess the public interest value of a publication, taking these matters into account. Such an approach would involve an unpredictable outcome. Moreover, it would put the judge in a position which in a free society ought to be occupied by the editor. Such paternalism would effectively give the court an undesirable and invidious role as a censor or licensing body.

These are powerful arguments, but I do not accept the conclusion for which the newspaper contended. My reasons appear from what is set out below.

At 201–2

This is a difficult problem. No answer is perfect. Every solution has its own advantages and disadvantages. Depending on local conditions, such as legal procedures and the traditions and power of the press, the solution preferred in one country may not be best suited to another country. The defendant newspaper commends reliance upon the ethics of professional journalism. The decision should be left to the editor of the newspaper. Unfortunately, in the United Kingdom this would not generally be thought to provide a sufficient safeguard. In saying this I am not referring to mistaken decisions. From time to time mistakes are bound to occur, even in the best regulated circles. Making every allowance for this, the sad reality is that the overall handling of these matters by the national press, with its own commercial interests to serve, does not always command general confidence.

As highlighted by the Court of Appeal judgment in the present case, the common law solution is for the court to have regard to all the circumstances when deciding whether the publication of particular material was privileged because of its value to the public. Its value to the public depends upon its quality as well as its subject matter. This solution has the merit of elasticity. As observed by the Court of Appeal, this principle can be applied appropriately to the particular circumstances of individual cases in their infinite variety. It can be applied appropriately to all information published by a newspaper, whatever its source or origin.

At 204–5

Conclusion

My conclusion is that the established common law approach to misstatements of fact remains essentially sound. The common law should not develop "political information" as a new "subject matter" category of qualified privilege, whereby the publication of all such information would attract qualified privilege, whatever the circumstances. That would not provide adequate protection for reputation. Moreover, it would be unsound in principle to distinguish political discussion from discussion of other matters of serious public concern. The elasticity of the common law principle enables interference with freedom of speech to be confined to what is necessary in the circumstances of the case. This elasticity enables the court to give appropriate weight, in today's conditions, to the importance of freedom of expression by the media on all matters of public concern.

Depending on the circumstances, the matters to be taken into account include the following. The comments are illustrative only. 1. The seriousness of the allegation. The more serious the charge, the more the public is misinformed and the individual harmed, if the allegation is not true. 2. The nature of the information, and the extent to which the subject matter is a matter of public concern. 3. The source of the information. Some informants have no direct knowledge of the events. Some have their own axes to grind, or are being paid for their stories. 4. The steps taken to verify the information. 5. The status of the information. The allegation may have already been the subject of an investigation which commands respect. 6. The urgency of the matter. News is often a perishable commodity. 7. Whether comment was sought from the plaintiff. He may have information others do not possess or have not disclosed. An approach to the plaintiff will not always be necessary. 8. Whether the article contained the gist of the plaintiff's side of the story. 9. The tone of the article. A newspaper can raise queries or call for an investigation. It need not adopt allegations as statements of fact. 10. The circumstances of the publication, including the timing.

This list is not exhaustive. The weight to be given to these and any other relevant factors will vary from case to case. Any disputes of primary fact will be a matter for the jury, if there is one. The decision on whether, having regard to the admitted or proved facts, the publication was subject to qualified privilege is a matter for the judge. This is the established practice and seems sound. A balancing operation is better carried out by a judge in a reasoned judgment than by a jury. Over time, a valuable corpus of case law will be built up.

There was a partial dissent by Lords Steyn and Hope, who thought that the case should be returned for a new trial at which the issues could be more fully addressed. Lord Steyn did not explicitly dissent on matters of principle, although he has since suggested (extra-judicially) that *Reynolds* may need to be reconsidered. The recent reconsideration of *Reynolds* in *Jameel* has led to an attempt to reinforce its message, rather than its details. Lord Hope claimed in *Jameel* that he had not disagreed with Lord Nicholls on matters of principle at all.

Commentary

It should be remembered that the problem dealt with in *Reynolds* arises from the limitations of the justification defence. Under what circumstances does a newspaper, or other party, have the freedom to report matters whose truth is uncertain, in the confidence that there will be no defamation proceedings? In writing an employment reference, for example, there can be confidence that views expressed honestly and without ill will are immune from an action in defamation (although, following *Spring v Guardian Assurance* [1995] 2 AC 296, not from an action in negligence: Chapter 6). Broadly, the newspaper is entitled to publish unproven allegations where there is a **duty** to do so, and a corresponding public **right to know** the information. The most significant, and most obvious criticism levelled at *Reynolds* is that this test will do little to foster an editor's 'confidence' in publishing any given story.

A number of significant points concerning *Reynolds* can be highlighted.

1. The *Reynolds* privilege is constructed on public interest. 'Public interest' is identified as providing the justification not only for freedom of speech, but also for the law of defamation as a whole, and for the existence of a qualified privilege defence in particular.

2. Lord Nicholls attempts a unified interpretation of the occasions on which the defence of qualified privilege is available. He identifies the existence of a **duty** of disclosure, combined with an **interest** in receiving the information. In these terms, the surprising element of *Reynolds* is that the duty–interest analogy is applied where the publication is to the whole world. Here the relevant interest is the *public's* interest in receiving information, and Lord Nicholls explains that the combination of duty and interest may also be expressed in terms of **the public's right to know**. There must be a public right to know certain information

irrespective of its truth or falsity. This is, evidently, much more demanding than the loose test for public interest in the fair comment defence, for example.

In *Loutchansky v Times Newspapers (Nos 2–5)* [2002] QB 783, the Court of Appeal explained that the issue of qualified privilege will generally be considered *before* the issue of justification, as a preliminary matter. As such, the right to know must be taken to relate to a statement *whose truth or falsehood has not been determined*. The function of the privilege is to allow the publication of important allegations which cannot be conclusively shown to be true, where withholding such information would be detrimental to the public interest.

On the other hand, the Court of Appeal in *Loutchansky* also rejected a very demanding interpretation of the 'duty' that would suffice for the *Reynolds* privilege. The judge at first instance had taken the formulation of the *Reynolds* test rather too seriously, and ruled that there would be a duty sufficient to satisfy the *Reynolds* test only if *failure to reveal the information* would be *grounds for legitimate criticism*. This treated *Reynolds* as quite consistent with the general principle in *Adam v Ward*, and not as a major new departure. According to the Court of Appeal, this was no part of the test, which simply required that the defendants act according to the standards encapsulated in the ten 'factors' set out by Lord Nicholls. These factors, said the Court of Appeal, are not to be applied as strict tests, but indicate the likely ingredients of 'responsible journalism'.

3. Lord Nicholls was well aware that his solution represented a compromise, and that it introduced considerable uncertainty into the law. Further, he explicitly recognized that this uncertainty could enhance the 'chilling effect'. The concepts used, and the list of factors set out in order to indicate how the concepts will apply, are elastic. As such, an editor will not be able to act with total confidence when faced with a breaking story. We have already said that this is the biggest challenge to the value of the *Reynolds* privilege. The point of a privilege is to allow publication with confidence. But a publisher obtains little help in this regard from a privilege which is inherently uncertain in its application. On the other hand, Lord Nicholls also makes the point that the press has a large *commercial* interest in publishing stories which have not necessarily been well researched. The privilege is not intended to protect this commercial interest; and freedom of expression, at least in respect of political matters, is of primarily instrumental value. *The privilege is there for protection of the public interest and not for the profit or convenience of editors.*

Subsequent Case Law

Before the decision of the House of Lords in *Jameel v Wall Street Journal*, subsequent case law indicated that the *Reynolds* privilege had some benefits for defendants, but that the limits of 'responsible journalism' expressed in Lord Nicholls' ten factors were carefully patrolled. In *Al-Fagih v HH Saudi Research and Marketing (UK) Ltd* [2001] EWCA Civ 1634, the *Reynolds* privilege had a significant effect on the impact of the 'repetition rule', which holds that republication of a rumour or allegation is itself defamatory. The defendant had made a clear, balanced, and neutral report of allegations made between two parties on a matter of public interest. In these circumstances, the *Reynolds* privilege offers a defence, because the duty to verify the underlying truth of the allegation (Lord Nicholls' factor 4 in *Reynolds*) is less pressing where the allegation is not adopted. However, newspapers cannot rely on any clear *rule* in this regard: as with the *Reynolds* privilege generally, all depends on the factual context.

In *Al-Fagih*, there was fair and neutral reportage and the public was entitled to receive the information without verification. However, this will not assist a defendant who *adopts* an allegation which is being reported. Such a case was *George Galloway v Daily Telegraph Group* [2006] EWCA Civ 17. The defendant newspaper published information about certain documents found in a building in Baghdad, which according to the newspaper implied that the claimant had taken money for personal gain. The newspaper failed in its attempt to rely on qualified privilege under *Reynolds*. Not only had it 'adopted' the allegations as true (marking a distinction between this case, and *Al-Fagih*), but it had added its own embellishments. According to the Court of Appeal:

> 73. . . . The judge was plainly right to conclude that the newspaper was not neutral but both embraced the allegations with relish and fervour and (as he put it) went on to embellish them.

As we noted in respect of *Loutchansky*, above, the goal of the privilege is to determine whether there was a duty to publish material *regardless of its truth or falsity*. Some allegations which are not protected by privilege (where there is no public interest in receiving the information *regardless of truth*) may nevertheless prove to be justified. This was the situation in *Henry v BBC* [2005] EWHC 2787, in which an NHS manager brought an action against the BBC in respect of allegations of manipulation in waiting list information. The allegations were found not to be protected by privilege because (among other reasons) they were too heavily embellished with editorial comment. But at trial, the BBC was able to establish that the allegations were true: *Henry v BBC* [2006] EWHC 386. This illustrates that where justification is concerned, the inclusion of editorial comment and embellishment (so long as it does not introduce a new libel with a separate sting) is immaterial.

In *Bonnick v Morris* [2003] 1 AC 300, a decision of the Privy Council on appeal from the Court of Appeal of Jamaica, the *Reynolds* privilege was put to use in support of a plea of **justification**. The defendant journalist had written an accurate comment (the plaintiff had been dismissed from his job) which in its context carried a defamatory implication (that he was dismissed for reasons connected with activities discussed in the article). As we saw above, it would usually be necessary to provide justification which went to the 'sting' of the libel. The Privy Council applied the *Reynolds* privilege to the *meaning* of the words, producing almost a 'due care' test in respect of the unintended defamation: would it be obvious to a responsible journalist that the words carried a broader, defamatory implication? Here, the implied meaning would not be obvious to such a journalist, and since the statement was made in the context of an important report on a matter of pressing public interest, the publication would be protected by privilege. Since this sort of issue is likely to arise on many occasions, we should be clear that Lord Nicholls was, again, concerned to ensure that the press should not be tempted to abuse the privilege.

Bonnick v Morris, Lord Nicholls

23 Stated shortly, the *Reynolds* privilege is concerned to provide a proper degree of protection for responsible journalism when reporting matters of public concern. Responsible journalism is the point at which a fair balance is held between freedom of expression on matters of public concern and the reputations of individuals. Maintenance of this standard is in the public interest and in the interests of those whose reputations are involved. It can be regarded as the price journalists pay in return for the privilege. If they are to have the benefit of the privilege journalists must exercise due professional skill and care. . . .

25 This should not be pressed too far. Where questions of defamation may arise ambiguity is best avoided as much as possible. It should not be a screen behind which a journalist is

"willing to wound, and yet afraid to strike". In the normal course a responsible journalist can be expected to perceive the meaning an ordinary, reasonable reader is likely to give to his article. Moreover, even if the words are highly susceptible of another meaning, a responsible journalist will not disregard a defamatory meaning which is obviously one possible meaning of the article in question. Questions of degree arise here. The more obvious the defamatory meaning, and the more serious the defamation, the less weight will a court attach to other possible meanings when considering the conduct to be expected of a responsible journalist in the circumstances.

Summary: the impact of Reynolds

Lower courts patrolled the boundaries of the privilege with a little too much care, according to the House of Lords in *Jameel*. The message conveyed by the majority of judges in this case is that the spirit of *Reynolds* was to enhance the protection of responsible journalism. The ten factors offered by Lord Nicholls were indicative; and the relationship with common law privilege not to be taken too seriously.[18]

In *Jameel v Wall Street Journal* [2006] UKHL 44, the *Wall Street Journal* reported that the Saudi authorities were cooperating with the United States in the investigation of terrorism, and that the accounts of a number of Saudi companies had been frozen in order to pursue this goal. Some of those companies were named in the article, and it was claimed that the articles were thereby defamatory of the claimants. The first instance judge and the Court of Appeal accepted that the subject-matter of the report was of sufficiently weighty public interest to come within the ambit of the *Reynolds* privilege, but concluded that it was not essential to the proper reporting of this story that individuals should be named. As such, the naming of the claimants' company could *not* be covered by the privilege. The House of Lords disagreed, and expressed a variety of strong views on the need to protect responsible journalism.

Lord Bingham and Lord Hope took the most traditional view, still proposing that a reciprocity between 'duty' and 'interest' was essential to the operation of the privilege. Lord Hope however thought the expression 'responsible journalism' was a good summary of the net effect of the ten factors. Lord Scott also thought that the *Reynolds* privilege had involved 'moulding' of previous common law authorities, but he expressed full agreement with Lord Hoffmann. Lord Hoffmann and Baroness Hale were ready to drop the reference to a 'privilege', and admit that *Reynolds* really created a new public interest defence. Lord Hoffmann and Baroness Hale were critical of the way that lower courts were failing to recognize the revolutionary spirit of *Reynolds*.[19]

Baroness Hale, *Jameel v Wall Street Journal* [2006] UKHL 44

146 It should be now be entirely clear that the *Reynolds* defence is a 'different jurisprudential creature' from the law of privilege, although it is a natural development of that law. It springs from the general obligation of the press to communicate important information on matters of general public interest and the general right of the public to receive such information. It is not helpful to analyse the particular case in terms of a specific duty and a specific right to know. That can, as the experience since *Reynolds* has shown, very easily lead to a narrow and rigid approach which defeats its object. In truth, it is a defence of publication in the public interest.

---

[18] Not all of their Lordships were so quick to abandon the link with traditional privilege. Lord Bingham argued that the *Reynolds* privilege is a true emanation of the traditional forms of qualified privilege at common law.

[19] Is this because it was carefully buried under appeal to precedent in *Reynolds* itself?

Lord Hoffmann

46 Although Lord Nicholls uses the word 'privilege' it is clearly not being used in the old sense. It is the material which is privileged, not the occasion on which it is being published. There is no question of the privilege being defeated by proof of malice because the propriety of the conduct of the defendant is built into the conditions under which the material is privileged. . . .

56 In *Reynolds*, Lord Nicholls gave his well-known non-exhaustive list of ten matters which should in suitable cases be taken into account. They are not tests which the publication has to pass. In the hands of a judge hostile to the spirit of *Reynolds*, they can become ten hurdles at any of which the defence may fail. That is how Eady J treated them. The defence, he said, can be sustained only after 'the closest and most rigorous scrutiny' by the application of what he called 'Lord Nicholls' ten tests'. But that, in my opinion, is not what Lord Nicholls meant. . . .

'Malice' in Qualified Privilege

The protection of qualified privilege will be lost if the claimant is able to show malice on the part of the defendant.

An important criticism directed at *Reynolds*, particularly by the New Zealand Court of Appeal in *Lange v Atkinson* (2000) 4 LRC 596, is that it ran together the test for whether the occasion is privileged, and the test for malice.[20] But this appears to have been quite deliberate (it is mentioned with approval by Lord Hoffmann in the extract above, for example). It has become clear that Lord Nicholls' preferred course is to shun the word 'malice' altogether. We have already seen in the context of fair comment that running together the definition of 'fairness' with the subjective issue of malice may be an undesirable development, since it may remove some protection from defendants. Whether a similar development is equally undesirable in the context of privilege depends on one's views as to the balance struck between freedom of speech, and journalistic responsibility, in *Reynolds*.

Cheng v Tse Wai Chun [2004] 4 HKC 1, at 22–3

It is said that this view of the law would have the undesirable consequence that malice would bear different meanings in the defences of fair comment and qualified privilege, and that this would inevitably cause difficulty for juries. I agree that if the term 'malice' were used, there might be a risk of confusion. The answer lies in shunning that word altogether. Juries can be instructed, regarding fair comment, that the defence is defeated by proof that the defendant did not genuinely believe the opinion he expressed. Regarding fair comment, juries can be directed that the defence is defeated by proof that the defendant did not genuinely believe the opinion he expressed. Regarding qualified privilege, juries can be directed that the defence is defeated by proof that the defendant used the occasion for some purpose other than that for which the occasion was privileged.

---

[20] In *Lange v Atkinson* LTL 29/10/99, the Privy Council recommended to the New Zealand Court of Appeal that although the decision as to privilege was for the local courts to reach on the basis of local conditions, they might wish to consider the issue in the light of the *Reynolds* approach. The New Zealand Court of Appeal has duly considered *Reynolds*, but determined not to follow it.

6. PARTIES WHO CANNOT SUE IN DEFAMATION

In *Derbyshire v Times Newspapers* [1993] AC 534, the House of Lords accepted that open criticism of a directly elected body such as a local authority was so important that such a body should not be entitled to bring an action in defamation. The prohibition in *Derbyshire* did not extend to individual politicians. Equally, the local authority retained the right to bring an action in malicious falsehood where, as we have seen, the rules strike a different balance between claimant and defendant, requiring falsehood, actual damage, and inappropriate motive to be established by the claimant.

Lord Keith, at 547–8

There are . . . features of a local authority which may be regarded as distinguishing it from other types of corporation, whether trading or non-trading. The most important of these features is that it is a governmental body. Further, it is a democratically elected body, the electoral process nowadays being conducted almost exclusively on party political lines. It is of the highest public importance that a democratically elected governmental body, or indeed any governmental body, should be open to uninhibited public criticism. The threat of a civil action for defamation must inevitably have an inhibiting effect on freedom of speech. In *City of Chicago v. Tribune Co.* (1923) 139 N.E. 86 the Supreme Court of Illinois held that the city could not maintain an action of damages for libel. Thompson C.J. said, at p. 90:

> "The fundamental right of freedom of speech is involved in this litigation, and not merely the right of liberty of the press. If this action can be maintained against a newspaper it can be maintained against every private citizen who ventures to criticise the ministers who are temporarily conducting the affairs of his government. Where any person by speech or writing seeks to persuade others to violate existing law or to overthrow by force or other unlawful means the existing government, he may be punished . . . but all other utterances or publications against the government must be considered absolutely privileged. While in the early history of the struggle for freedom of speech the restrictions were enforced by criminal prosecutions, it is clear that a civil action is as great, if not a greater, restriction than a criminal prosecution. If the right to criticise the government is a privilege which, with the exceptions above enumerated, cannot be restricted, then all civil as well as criminal actions are forbidden. A despotic or corrupt government can more easily stifle opposition by a series of civil actions than by criminal prosecutions . . . "

. . .

These propositions were endorsed by the Supreme Court of the United States in *New York Times Co. v. Sullivan* (1964) 376 U.S. 254, 277. While these decisions were related most directly to the provisions of the American Constitution concerned with securing freedom of speech, the public interest considerations which underlaid them are no less valid in this country. What has been described as "the chilling effect" induced by the threat of civil actions for libel is very important. Quite often the facts which would justify a defamatory publication are known to be true, but admissible evidence capable of proving those facts is not available. This may prevent the publication of matters which it is very desirable to make public.

It will be noted that Lord Keith here expressed the view that English law had no need for the assistance of the European Convention in protecting freedom of expression.

In *Goldsmith v Bhoyrul* [1998] QB 459, the principle against local authorities suing in defamation was extended to cover *political parties* standing for election. So far, however, this is as far as the restriction has developed. Certainly, an *individual* seeking election may sue for defamation. In *Culnane v Morris and Naidu* [2005] EWHC 2438, an election candidate for the British National Party brought an action in defamation arising from statements in an election leaflet circulated on behalf of the Liberal Democrat candidate. Eady J had to interpret section 10 of the Defamation Act 1952, which provides:

10   Limitation on privilege at elections

A defamatory statement published by or on behalf of a candidate in any election to a local government authority or to Parliament shall not be deemed to be published on a privileged occasion on the ground that it is material to a question in issue in the election . . .

In *Plummer v Charman* [1962] 1 WLR 1469, the Court of Appeal had concluded from this section that the *only* defences available where statements are made in an election campaign were justification, and fair comment—in other words, and despite the title to the section, that *no* privilege could attach to them. Eady J used the authority of the Human Rights Act 1998 to depart from this interpretation (which would otherwise have been binding on him) and to understand the words as providing that no *special or additional* privilege attaches to election material because of its status. As such, the defendant could attempt an argument that the statements made were within the protection of qualified privilege.

7. REMEDIES: DAMAGES AND INJUNCTIVE RELIEF

Superficially at least, libel damages appear very generous, given that the injury suffered by the claimant is typically intangible and in some instances no quantified loss is established at all. Such damage is to some extent 'presumed' on the claimant's behalf.

In the litigation which ultimately led to the judgment of the European Court of Human Rights in *Steel and Morris v UK* [2005] EMLR 15, £24,000 was awarded to McDonalds in respect of leaflets distributed by two individuals in London. No impact on trading profits could be shown and there was no evidence whether anyone had read or believed the allegations in the leaflet. In *Steel and Morris v UK*, this award was held to violate Article 10 on the grounds of disproportion, but the general principle that trading corporations could obtain damages in defamation, even though impact on reputation is *presumed*, was not criticized. Similarly, in *Jameel v Dow Jones* [2005] QB 946, the Court of Appeal considered and rejected an argument that the 'presumption of damage'—the rule that damage is presumed to follow when it is shown that a statement is such that it 'tends to' damage reputation—should be seen as incompatible with Article 10. A majority of the House of Lords agreed (*Jameel v Wall Street Journal*, above). Lord Hoffmann and Baroness Hale would have been willing to remove the presumption of damage from corporations; but the other judges thought the presumption too well established to be removed at common law. Lord Scott in particular also thought it was justified.

There are significant contrasts between defamation damages, and damages in cases of personal injury. As we saw in Chapter 8, awards in respect of non-pecuniary loss in personal injury cases are 'conventional', and all parties are able to ascertain in advance what a 'typical' award for a given injury is likely to be. Defamation awards are not (or have not been until recently) subject to convention in the same way. They are also typically 'at large'—assessed by the jury (if any) and not subject to itemization.

In a series of cases through the 1990s, the Court of Appeal took deliberate action to restrain the level of damages awarded in defamation cases. The tactics of interpretation employed by the Court of Appeal were controversial, but in any event the consequence is that juries are now given considerably more guidance than was previously the case.

In *John v MGN* [1997] QB 587, at the culmination of this process, Sir Thomas Bingham MR explained that before the Court of Appeal took action, the jury had been 'in the position of sheep loosed on an unfenced common, with no shepherd' (at 608). They lacked guidance, and not unexpectedly had no instinctive sense of where to pitch their award. The stages in the Court of Appeal's campaign against this state of affairs were as follows.

1. In *Sutcliffe v Pressdram* [1991] 1 QB 153, the Court of Appeal resolved that the jury had clearly not understood the value of money when it made its award of £600,000 to the wife of a convicted murderer. *Private Eye* magazine had suggested that she benefited from her husband's crimes by selling her story to a newspaper. In future, juries should have more guidance on the real value of the sums awarded. However, the Court of Appeal had no choice but to remit the case for a new trial.

2. By the time of *Rantzen v MGN* [1994] QB 670, the Court of Appeal had acquired a new power under section 8 of the Courts and Legal Services Act 1990 to replace a jury award which was considered to be excessive. It recognized that the jury award of £250,000 might not fit the existing definition of 'excessive', and (referring to *Pepper v Hart*) it was clear that there was no intention to change the definition of this word on the part of the legislature. But the Court of Appeal nevertheless decided—appealing to Article 10 ECHR—that it had a *duty* to interpret section 8 as broadening its powers of intervention in the sense of lowering the threshold of intervention. This case was decided some years before the Human Rights Act 1998 and this interpretation required the Court of Appeal to misapply some observations of Lord Goff in *AG v Guardian (No 2)* [1990] 1 AC 109 where he had said that there was no difference between common law, and Article 10. What he meant by this was that there was no need for change. It is a big step from this to hold that statutory provisions *must* be reinterpreted specifically in order to protect Article 10 rights (or, more strongly still since this is before the Human Rights Act, to protect the UK from litigation on the basis of a violation of Article 10).

Now that there would be awards arrived at by the Court of Appeal, rather than simply by juries, juries should in future have these judicial awards referred to them for attention. However, the corpus of Court of Appeal awards built up slowly, and the Court of Appeal grew impatient.

3. In *John v MGN* [1997] QB 586, the Court of Appeal took two further decisive steps. First, reversing its own conclusion in both *Sutcliffe* and *Rantzen*, the court decided that juries should have the level of non-pecuniary awards in personal injury actions brought to their attention.

Lord Bingham MR, *John v MGN*, at 614

There is also weight in the argument, often heard, that conventional levels of award in personal injury cases are too low, and therefore provide an uncertain guide. But these awards would not be relied on as any exact guide, and of course there can be no precise correlation between loss of a limb, or of sight, or quadriplegia, and damage to reputation. But if these personal injuries respectively command conventional awards of, at most, about £52,000, £90,000 and £125,000 for pain and suffering and loss of amenity (of course excluding claims based on loss of earnings, the cost of care and other specific financial claims), juries may properly be asked to consider whether the injury to his reputation of which the plaintiff complains should fairly justify any greater compensation. The conventional compensatory scales in personal injury cases must be taken to represent fair compensation in such cases unless and until those scales are amended by the courts or by Parliament. It is in our view offensive to public opinion, and rightly so, that a defamation plaintiff should recover damages for injury to reputation greater, perhaps by a significant factor, than if that same plaintiff had been rendered a helpless cripple or an insensate vegetable. The time has in our view come when judges, and counsel, should be free to draw the attention of juries to these comparisons.

Second, counsel for both parties would be invited to suggest an appropriate level of damages. This would not lead to a bidding war, because counsel would learn to be realistic:

Lord Bingham, at 616

The plaintiff will not wish the jury to think that his main object is to make money rather than clear his name. The defendant will not wish to add insult to injury by underrating the seriousness of the libel. So we think the figures suggested by responsible counsel are likely to reflect the upper and lower bounds of a realistic bracket. The jury must of course make up their own mind and must be directed to do so. They will not be bound by the submission of counsel or the indication of the judge. If the jury make an award outside the upper or lower bounds of any bracket indicated and such award is the subject of appeal, real weight must be given to the possibility that their judgment is to be preferred to that of the judge.

There is some indication that 'real weight' will indeed be given to jury decisions where they exceed the suggested band. In *Kiam v MGN* [2002] 3 WLR 1036, the jury had made an award of £105,000, having been advised not to exceed £75,000–£80,000. The Court of Appeal declined to replace the jury's award in this case, since it was not 'out of all proportion to' what could sensibly be awarded.

Whatever the merits of the Court of Appeal's objectives in these cases (and we turn to that question via the next case extract below), in respect of the tactics employed the following critical summary is well placed:

Andrew Halpin, 'Law, Libel and the English Court of Appeal'
(1996) *Tort L Rev* 139, at 142

The Court of Appeal's development of the law in *Rantzen v Mirror Group Newspapers Ltd* and *John v MGN Ltd* is at variance with at least four different doctrines established by precedent in the House of Lords: the doctrine of restraint on judicial law making; the doctrine of the Court being bound by its own previous decisions; the doctrine of statutory interpretation in *Pepper v Hart* [[1993] AC 593]; as well as the substantive doctrine(s) of the law of defamation. . . . In addition, it flies in the face of its own previously established precedents.

Concerning the *substance* of the Court of Appeal's changes to the law, some forceful doubts about the step taken in *John* have recently been set out by Lord Hoffmann in the following appeal from the Jamaican Court of Appeal. This Privy Council decision does not (or at least does not yet) signify a change in English law. Not only was this an appeal on Jamaican law so that it is binding only in Jamaican law, but the comments do not quite amount to formal disapproval of the approach in *John*. Even so, the principles set out by Lord Hoffmann are of general application. As we will explain at the end of the extract, they draw on some traditional arguments as to why defamation damages should not necessarily be compared with personal injury awards, but they place those arguments in a modern social and legal context.

The Gleaner v Abrahams [2004] 1 AC 628

49 Reference to awards in personal injuries cases . . . was advocated as a legitimate comparison by Diplock LJ in *McCarey v Associated Newspapers Ltd (No 2)* [1965] 2 QB 86, 109–110 but rejected by Lord Hailsham of St Marylebone LC in *Broome v Cassell & Co Ltd* [1972] AC 1027, 1070–1071 and by the Court of Appeal in *Rantzen's* case [1994] QB 670, 695. In *John v MGN Ltd* [1997] QB 586, the Court of Appeal reversed itself and since then juries have regularly been told to have regard to awards of general damages (for pain, suffering and loss of amenity) in personal injury actions. These are themselves conventional figures: the current scale was fixed by the Court of Appeal in *Heil v Rankin* [2001] QB 272 and runs to a maximum of £200,000 for the most catastrophic injuries. As a result, Eady J said in *Lillie v Newcastle City Council* [2002] EWHC 1600 (QB) at [1547]–[1551] that there is now a ceiling of £200,000 for compensatory damages in libel cases.

50 Their Lordships express no view on the current practice in England. But the matter is clearly one on which different opinions may be held. The arguments in favour of comparison tend to stress the moral unacceptability of treating damage to reputation as having a higher "value" than catastrophic damage to the person. It is however arguable that the assessment of general damages in both personal injury and libel cases is far more complicated than trying to "value" the damage; an exercise which everyone agrees to be impossible on account of the incommensurability of the subject matter. Other factors enter into the calculation. Personal injury awards are almost always made in actions based on negligence or breach of statutory duty rather than intentional wrongdoing. Furthermore, the damages are almost always paid out of public funds or by insurers under policies which are not very sensitive to the claims records of individual defendants. The cost is therefore borne by the public at large or large sections of the public such as motorists or consumers. The exemplary and deterrent elements in personal injury awards are minimal or non-existent. On the other hand, the total sums of compensation paid for personal injury are very large. They have an effect on the economy which libel damages do not. The amounts of the awards in personal injury actions therefore depend to some extent upon what society can afford to pay victims of accidents over and above compensation for the actual financial loss they have suffered. As Lord Woolf MR said of general damages in personal injury cases in *Heil v Rankin* [2001] QB 272, 297, para 36: "Awards must be proportionate and take into account the consequences of increases in the awards of damages on defendants as a group and society as a whole."

51 Once it is appreciated that the awards are not paid by individual defendants but by society as a whole or large sections of society, there are also considerations of equity between victims of personal injury which influence the level of general damages. Compensation, both for financial loss and general damages, goes only to those who can prove negligence and causation. Those unable to do so are left to social security: no general damages and meagre compensation for loss of earnings. The unfairness might be more readily understandable if the successful tort plaintiffs recovered their damages from the defendants themselves but makes less sense when both social security and negligence damages come out of public funds. So any increase in general damages for personal injury awarded by the courts only widens the gap between those victims who can sue and those who cannot.

. . .

53 Few of these considerations of equity and policy apply to awards in defamation cases. On the other hand, defamation cases have important features not shared by personal injury claims. The damages often serve not only as compensation but also as an effective and necessary deterrent. The deterrent is effective because the damages are paid either by the defendant himself or under a policy of insurance which is likely to be sensitive to the incidence of such claims. Indeed, the effectiveness of the deterrent is the whole basis of Lord Lester's argument that high awards will have a "chilling effect" on future publications. Awards in an adequate amount may also be necessary to deter the media from riding roughshod over the rights of other citizens. In *Kiam's* case Sedley LJ said, at p 304, para 75:

> "in a great many cases proof of a cold-blooded cost-benefit calculation that it was worth publishing a known libel is not there, and the ineffectiveness of a moderate award in deterring future libels is painfully apparent . . . Judges, juries and the public face the conundrum that compensation proportioned to personal injury damages is insufficient to deter, and that deterrent awards make a mockery of the principle of compensation."

. . .

55 In addition, as this case amply illustrates, there are other differences between general damages in personal injury cases and general damages in defamation actions. One is that the damages must be sufficient to demonstrate to the public that the plaintiff's reputation has been vindicated. Particularly if the defendant has not apologised and withdrawn the defamatory allegations, the award must show that they have been publicly proclaimed to have inflicted a serious injury. As Lord Hailsham of St Marylebone LC said in *Broome v Cassell & Co Ltd* [1972] AC 1027, 1071, the plaintiff "must be able to point to a sum awarded by a jury sufficient to convince a bystander of the baselessness of the charge".

56 A second difference is that in an action for personal injury it is usually not difficult for the plaintiff to prove that his injury caused inability to work and consequent financial loss. Loss of earnings is therefore recoverable as special damage and ordinarily, in cases of grievous injury, constitutes by far the greater part of the award. Likewise, the expenses of care, nursing and so forth are recoverable as special damage. They do not constitute a factor in the assessment of general damages. In defamation cases, on the other hand, it is usually difficult to prove a direct causal link between the libel and loss of any particular earnings or any particular expenses. Nevertheless it is clear law that the jury are entitled to take these matters into account in the award of general damages. The strict requirements of proving causation are relaxed in return for moderation in the overall figure awarded. In the present case, in which Mr Abrahams was unable to find any remunerative employment for five years, loss of earnings must have played a significant part in the jury's award.

Lord Hoffmann here underlines a traditionally recognized distinction between the functions of defamation damages, and of damages for personal injury. This distinction was formally noted by the Court of Appeal in *John v MGN*, but was swept aside in pursuit of greater predictability.

Personal injury damages are almost solely compensatory: they seek to make good what has been lost.[21] Defamation damages on the other hand have multiple roles to play. Certainly, they

---

[21] For refinements and qualifications to this statement see Chapter 8.

may seek to **compensate** for hurt feelings and lost opportunities. But they are also aimed at **vindication** of the claimant's good reputation (in other words at repairing the damage suffered), and also at **deterrence**. Equally, they are more frequently inflated by an element of **aggravation**: the injury to the claimant is made worse by the conduct of the defendant after the complaint of defamation is made. For example, in *Sutcliffe v Pressdram*, *Private Eye* responded to the initiation of proceedings by publishing further allegations about the plaintiff. In *John v MGN*, having initially offered a limp apology, the defendants responded aggressively with further allegations. Defamation awards are often increased by an award of **exemplary damages** intended to punish the defendant, most particularly where the defendant *calculated* that he or she could profit from publication of a defamatory statement. This was held to be the case in *John* itself, where the defendant newspaper was treated as having decided that it could achieve higher sales figures through carrying an ill-researched and sensationalist story concerning the plaintiff's alleged eating disorder, irrespective of its truth or falsity.

The deterrence argument mentioned above brings us to a less traditional aspect of Lord Hoffmann's defence of defamation damages. The **economic impact** of defamation damages is, he contends, also different from the impact of personal injury damages. On the one hand, there is no real harm in having high awards, since there is little impact on the economy as a whole: defamation proceedings tend to be 'one-off' affairs between the parties and do not engage a broad sector of the economy.[22] Equally, the award is likely to succeed in having considerable **deterrent effect**, according to Lord Hoffmann. *Either* the defendant will not have insured against this form of liability at all, *or* any relevant insurance contract will provide for penalties in the event of a claim being made.

How does Lord Hoffmann's argument in favour of a separation between libel and personal injury damages stand up to scrutiny, particularly having regard to the new status of Article 10 in English law? It can of course be pointed out by a critic of libel awards that the UK has twice been found to have violated Article 10 on the grounds of disproportionate awards of damages. On the other hand, in neither of these cases (*Tolstoy Miloslavsky v UK*; *Steel and Morris v UK*) was there a media defendant—both awards were made against *individuals*. In the case of *Steel and Morris*, the disproportion in the award was expressly identified as flowing, at least partly, from a comparison with the *defendant's means*. Disproportion is only partly a question of relationship between award and injury suffered. Thus, an award might arguably be 'proportionate' if it is based on the amount needed to *deter* future interference with the reputation of the claimant or of others, particularly where the defendant is in no sense 'impecunious'. Indeed, high awards (particularly those which treat persistence in a defence or course of conduct as grounds for aggravated damages) could be seen as an aspect of a broader goal, to encourage apologies and discourage extended litigation. This is underlined by sections 2 to 4 of the Defamation Act 1996, introducing provisions relating to offers to make amends.

In *Nail v News Group Newspapers* [2005] 1 All ER 1040, an offer to make amends had been accepted but the parties could not agree appropriate damages. The Court of Appeal underlined that the process in those sections was intended to be conciliatory and that the existence of an apology and correction effectively vindicated the claimant's reputation. The deterrence argument also did not apply so strongly in a case where the defendant had apologized. The judge's assessment that damages should be discounted by 50 per cent to reflect the offer to make amends was not unreasonable.

---

[22] This omits the non-economic social harm of the chilling effect; but Lord Hoffmann seems to have considered the 'chilling' of bad journalism to be quite beneficial.

Injunctions

It is quite usual for an award of damages in defamation to be accompanied by a 'final injunction' prohibiting further publication of the defamatory statement. Such an injunction follows a full trial of the merits of the case and is broadly uncontroversial. However, there is a long-standing principle that courts will be much more reluctant to grant injunctions in advance of full trial, which is to say on an 'interim' basis. At common law, interim injunctions have not been granted unless the defendant has *no realistic chance* of succeeding in a defence: *Bonnard v Perryman* [1891] 2 Ch 269. What then is the impact of section 12 of the Human Rights Act 1998 in a defamation action?

Section 12 of the Human Rights Act is extracted in Chapter 1.

If a court is considering whether to restrain publication, section 12(3) requires that the applicant should be 'likely' to succeed in its application at trial, before such restraint can be granted. Even taking into account section 12(4), this would (if applied to defamation) *dilute* the protection afforded to free speech at common law, since *Bonnard v Perryman* requires that the claimant, to obtain such an injunction, needs to show that the defendant has no realistic prospect of success. Clearly, this is much more demanding than the 'likelihood' test.

In *Greene v Associated Newspapers* [2004] EWHC 2322, the Court of Appeal concluded that, despite its general wording, section 12(3) had no application to an action in defamation. A section concerned with protecting 'freedom of expression' could not have been intended to *reduce* the protection afforded to freedom of expression, and it would be absurd to replace the *Bonnard v Perryman* approach with the weaker 'likelihood' test. Prior to *Greene*, the role of section 12 had been considered in respect of actions for *breach of confidence* (*Cream Holdings v Banerjee* [2005] 1 AC 253). Here, section 12(3) introduces the vexed question of balance between rights under Articles 8 (privacy) and 10 (expression). In *Greene*, the Court of Appeal's conclusion in respect of defamation was that *even if* reputation is regarded as protected within the terms of Article 8, defamation actions nevertheless raise distinct issues when it comes to remedies. A reputation can be repaired by an award of damages, while confidentiality is destroyed for good once the information is published. As common law has clearly recognized, there needs to be a very strong reason for prior restraint in an action for defamation.

8. FUNDING DEFAMATION ACTIONS; HUMAN RIGHTS AND POLICY ISSUES

In *Steel and Morris v UK* [2005] EMLR 15, the European Court of Human Rights found the UK to have been in violation of both Articles 6 (access to a court) and 10 (freedom of expression) of the European Convention. Article 6 was violated because no legal aid was available to assist the applicants in defending a defamation action brought by a major corporation. The applicants were forced to conduct protracted litigation in person, against a corporation with significant legal resources at its disposal. Both the Article 6 violation, and the Article 10 violation, were related to a gross 'inequality of arms' in this case. This was produced by a combination of factors. One such factor was that the burden of proof in respect of falsity lay upon the defendants; another was the major imbalance in resources between the parties. Absence of legal aid would not, in itself, necessarily produce a violation of Article 6.[23]

---

[23] See S. Shipman (2006) CJQ 5; E. O'Dell (2006) LQR 395. O'Dell suggests that it would be appropriate (particularly in avoiding the 'inequality of arms' problem), to develop alternative means by which trading corporations may protect their reputation.

Will English law as it now stands comply with the Convention rights in the light of *Steel and Morris*? The Lord Chancellor has an existing discretion under section 6(8) of the Access to Justice Act 1998 to grant legal aid in cases (including defamation) where it is not usually available. One solution then is to exercise this discretion in favour of a weaker party in cases of significant imbalance. But English law has also undergone significant change in respect of the funding of litigation, the preferred model of funding being not legal aid but 'conditional fee agreements' (CFAs). This shifts the burden of paying costs from the public, to unsuccessful defendants. CFAs were extended to defamation actions through the Access to Justice Act 1999. As we noted in Chapter 8, an unsuccessful party to litigation will generally find that the claimant's CFA will lead to a considerable increase in the fees payable, since such fees are of course subject to uplift for the lawyers' risk of earning no fee at all. In *Campbell v MGN*, the uplift was close to 100 per cent, leading to almost a doubling in fees payable. However, the House of Lords concluded that this effect was not itself inconsistent with Article 10. Although costs payable on this basis would on one definition necessarily be 'disproportionate' (they would be much higher than the work itself merited, to account for risk) this would not make them 'disproportionate' within the meaning of Article 10, because they served a legitimate goal (affordable access to justice), and did so in a proportionate fashion.

In a significant digression, the House of Lords expressed deep concern about a different issue, namely the 'blackmailing' possibilities produced where an impecunious claimant obtains a conditional fee agreement. In such a case, the defendant who chooses to proceed with the action (the only alternative being settlement of the claim irrespective of the merits) will do so in the knowledge that his or her own costs will not be repaid even if successful. This must pose a considerable deterrent to reporting, with a potentially greater impact in terms of 'chilling' than the more widely-recognized problem of high damages awards. The reasons why the impact of this is much more important in defamation cases are broadly the same reasons why Lord Hoffmann thought defamation *damages* could excusably be higher: there are fewer repeat players and defendants are rarely backed by insurance.

Campbell v MGN (No 2) [2005] UKHL 61; [2005] 1 WLR 3394

Referring to *Turcu v News Group Newspapers* [2005] EWHC 799 and *King v Telegraph Group* [2005] 1 WLR 2282, Lord Hoffmann summarized the potential effect of CFAs where the claimant is impecunious and chooses not to purchase 'After the Event' (ATE) insurance to cover a successful defendant's costs (see Chapter 8.7 for explanation of these terms):

Lord Hoffmann

[31]   The blackmailing effect of such litigation appears to arise from two factors. First, the use of CFAs by impecunious claimants who do not take out ATE insurance. That, of course, is not a feature of the present case. If MGN are right about Ms Campbell's means, she would have been able to pay their costs if she had lost. The second factor is the conduct of the case by the claimant's solicitors in a way which not only runs up substantial costs but requires the defendants to do so as well. Faced with a free-spending claimant's solicitor and being at risk not only as to liability but also as to twice the claimant's costs, the defendant is faced with an arms race which makes it particularly unfair for the claimant afterwards to justify his conduct of the litigation on the ground that the defendant's own costs were equally high . . . .

. . .

[36]   There are substantial differences between the costs in personal injury litigation which are the subject of the agreement and costs in defamation proceedings. In personal injury litigation

one is for the most part dealing with very large numbers of small claims. The liability insurers are able to pass these costs on to their road user customers. Their own solvency is not threatened. Furthermore, the liability insurers had considerable negotiating strength because they were able to fight what Brooke LJ described as trench warfare, disputing assessments of costs in many cases and thereby holding up the cash flow of the claimants' solicitors. Both sides therefore had good reasons for seeking a compromise.

[37] In defamation cases, on the other hand, the reasons are much weaker. One is dealing with a very small number of claims to payment of relatively large sums of costs, which some publishers may be strong enough to absorb or insure against but which can have serious effects upon their financial position. The publishers do not have the same negotiating strength as the liability insurers because there are few assessments to be contested and disputing them involves considerable additional costs. Of course, one object of extending CFAs to defamation and breach of confidence claims was to enable people of modest means to protect their reputations and privacy from powerful publishers who previously did not have to fear litigation even if their publications were totally unjustified. Henceforward they would be able to vindicate their rights, which are also convention rights, in the way that the rich and powerful have always been able to do. There may well be more of these cases in future. Finding ways of moderating the costs of defamation cases would then be in the best interests of all concerned. But the rich and powerful have also had to pay the price of failure. Finding ways of ensuring that the impecunious claimant can also do this may be more of a challenge. In the end, therefore, it may be that a legislative solution will be needed to comply with art 10.

Since the level of costs awarded in such cases can be similar to the award of damages considered so disproportionate in *Tolstoy v UK*,[24] the combined effect of *Steel and Morris* and *Campbell v MGN* is to put funding, rather than damages, at the top of the reform agenda.

FURTHER READING

Ashby, K., and Glasser, C., 'The Legality of Conditional Fee Uplifts' (2005) 24 CJQ 130, 134.

Barendt, E., *Freedom of Speech* (2nd edn, Oxford: OUP, 2005), Chapters 1–2 and 6.

Collins, M., *The Law of Defamation and the Internet* (2nd edn, Oxford: OUP, 2005).

Dunlop, R., 'Article 10, The Reynolds Test and the Rule in the Duke of Brunswick's Case— The Decision in *Times Newspapers v UK*' (2006) EHRLR 327.

Halpin, A., 'Law, Libel, and the English Court of Appeal' (1996) *Tort L Rev* 139.

Loveland, I., *Political Libels* (Oxford: Hart Publishing, 2000).

Mitchell, P., *The Making of the Modern Law of Defamation* (Oxford: Hart Publishing, 2005).

Steyn, Lord, '2000–2005: Laying the Foundations of Human Rights Law in the United Kingdom' (2005) 4 EHRLR 349.

Trindade, F., 'Malice and the Defence of Fair Comment' (2001) 117 LQR 169.

---

24 In *Campbell*, the defendants were served with a bill for claimant's costs of over £1 million. Damages awarded to the claimant were £3,500.

14

PRIVACY

CENTRAL ISSUES

i) This chapter is concerned with change. It describes the emergence of a new protected interest in privacy. For many years, it was suggested that tort law was able to protect some elements of privacy (though not others), even though no tort expressly did so. It is now clear that in more than one cause of action, protected interests are being expressly redefined, to include privacy in its own right. The stimulus for this development has been the Human Rights Act 1998, and this is of considerable importance to the way in which the law is developing. It means that elements of Convention jurisprudence are absorbed into English case law.

ii) The starting point is that English law recognizes no general tort of invasion of privacy. Despite the changes explored below, this is still the case. Since the Human Rights Act 1998, courts have consistently said that they recognise privacy as an 'underlying value' of English law. Even so, it has been clearly stated that recognition of an underlying value is different from recognition of a legal principle which can be applied in concrete situations (Lord Hoffmann, *Wainwright v Home Office* [2004] 2 AC 406, at [31]). An underlying value is not necessarily a protected interest.

iii) By section 6 of the Human Rights Act 1998, public authorities are required to act compatibly with the specified **Convention rights**. These include the right to respect for '**private and family life**' in Article 8 ECHR. Because courts are themselves defined as public authorities, they must act compatibly with Article 8 as with other Convention rights. In *Campbell v MGN* [2004] 2 AC 457, the House of Lords appears to have decided that section 6 does not allow the creation of new torts for the protection of Convention rights. But it seems to be broadly accepted that existing causes of action will be developed with Convention rights in mind. Oddly, it is through analysis of section 12 of the Human Rights Act (requiring courts to have particular regard to freedom of expression) that the Convention right to privacy has been absorbed into actions between private parties. This has happened because Article 10, as we saw in Chapter 13, is qualified by the rights (including the Convention rights) of others. Therefore, it is qualified by (among other things) the rights in Article 8.

iv) So far, the most obvious substantive effect of these developments has been change in the action for **breach of confidence**. From the traditional action for breach of confidence, an action for *unjustified publication of private information* has emerged. It is not clear whether this is a tort. Breach of confidence has traditionally been seen not as a tort but as an equitable wrong. Interim injunctions to restrain publication are available in many cases, in marked contrast with the position in defamation (Chapter 13), and courts also recognize that 'disgorgement damages' (where defendants are required to repay profits made from the breach of confidence) are often appropriate. Although the substantive requirements of this action have changed, the equitable remedies remain in place.

v) Beyond 'private information', other aspects of privacy continue to receive only patchy protection through established and emerging remedies. It remains to be seen whether the new status of privacy will lead to any broader evolution. Despite the caution expressed in *Wainwright*, there are important changes to be observed beyond the category of 'private information', particularly in actions for harassment, and this suggests the real possibility of further development.

1. IS PRIVACY A PROTECTED INTEREST AT COMMON LAW?

When we considered Defamation, in Chapter 13, we noted that the actions in libel and slander have protected reputation for centuries, and we moved swiftly to the well-recognized potential for conflict between protection of reputation, and the interest in freedom of expression. Protection of privacy, to the extent that tort law attempts it, will also lead to questions of conflict with freedom of expression. But by contrast with defamation, there is a prior difficulty to resolve. This difficulty is that privacy has not been recognized as a protected interest in its own right—at least not in any *general* way—in English tort law.

Privacy, in this respect, is quite different from reputation. Although there is no 'Convention right' requiring states to protect reputation,[1] reputation is strongly protected through tort law. Conversely, although there is a 'Convention right' to privacy, privacy is not (or has not been) a recognized protected interest for the purposes of tort law. Given this converse relationship between Convention rights and interests protected through common law actions, it is easy to see why this area of law has entered a state of flux.

Non-recognition of privacy as a protected interest at common law is not just a matter of words. It is not the case that all aspects of privacy are protected through tort law 'in all but name'. English law has undoubtedly left some claimants without a suitable cause of action where it can be said that their privacy, private space, or 'right to be let alone' has been interfered with. An example often given (although the outcome might be different today)[2] is *Kaye*

---

[1] 'Convention right' is the expression used in the Human Rights Act. Reputation could be interpreted as an aspect of 'private and family life' in Article 8. This suggestion—itself rather strange from the point of view of tort law—was mentioned in Chapter 13 in respect of *Martha Greene v Associated Newspapers* [2004] EWHC 2322. Reputation is also given indirect protection through Article 10(2) (restrictions on the right to freedom of expression).

[2] Because of developments in the action for breach of confidence: see *Campbell v MGN* [2004] 2 AC 457, and other cases, below.

v Robertson [1991] FSR 62. The plaintiff (an actor) was lying unconscious in hospital when journalists broke into his room and took photographs. The defendant's newspaper sought to publish these as part of an 'exclusive interview'. Members of the Court of Appeal made plain that they wished there was a suitable tort through which to restrain publication. In the circumstances, they employed the action in malicious falsehood in order to award an interim injunction.[3] The 'falsehood', clearly, was the claim that the plaintiff had granted an interview; the 'actual damage' required was (less convincingly) that he could not benefit by granting an exclusive interview to any other newspaper.[4] The plaintiff in *Kaye v Robertson* did not try to argue his case in terms of breach of confidence. As we will see below, at the time of the decision it would probably have been thought that this action depended on a relationship of confidentiality.

A few years later, in *Spencer v UK* (1998) 25 EHRR CD 105, the European Commission was persuaded that there was no gap in English law in such cases (publication of unauthorized photographs taken through intrusion into private places). The applicant's privacy rights could have been protected in English law, had they argued their case in terms of breach of confidence. In fact, this argument—that privacy *was* protected in domestic law through the action for breach of confidence—was not very clearly supported by the case law at the time of *Spencer v UK*. The decisive change duly followed in *Douglas v Hello!* [2001] QB 967, which recognized that there may be an action to restrain publication of unauthorized photographs where there is a reasonable expectation of privacy. This case is extracted in Section 4 of this chapter.

But even this does not mean that privacy is now protected at common law in any general way. In *Peck v UK* [2003] EMLR 15, a decision of the European Court of Human Rights, the applicant had been recorded on CCTV in a public street shortly after attempting suicide. The recording was then released to, and pictures from it were broadcast by, a number of news agencies. The European Court of Human Rights held that the claimant's Article 8 right to privacy had been violated. Although the plaintiff was in a public place, namely the street, he could not have anticipated the breadth of publication that ensued. The UK was also in violation of Article 13, which requires a remedy in domestic law where substantive Convention rights have been violated. In *Wainwright v Home Office* [2004] 2 AC 406, Lord Hoffmann denied that *Peck* showed the need for a general 'privacy tort'. Rather, he said that it showed the need for specific *legislative* control of the use of CCTV footage.

Wainwright v Home Office [2004] 2 AC 406 itself shows that not all cases of 'invasion of privacy' are centrally concerned with release of information. The House of Lords declined to develop existing law in order to provide any remedy to individuals who had been subjected to intrusive and inappropriately conducted strip searches on a visit to prison. We will consider whether this too displays a gap in the legal protection of an important interest captured in the idea of 'privacy'. The House of Lords doubted whether it did.

---

[3] The claim that the plaintiff had granted an exclusive interview might also have been defamatory, but as we saw in Chapter 13, interim relief is not readily available in actions in defamation: *Bonnard v Perryman* [1891] 2 Ch 269.

[4] This tends to devalue the plaintiff's complaint since it implies that his right to remain free from interference is of value to him only because he could profit in the future from publicity. Publicity rights and values of privacy overlap in cases such as this, but in principle they are distinct.

2. 'PRIVACY'—ONE RIGHT OR FOUR PROTECTED INTERESTS?

The idea that a general 'right to privacy' can be identified 'immanent in'[5] existing law, and (furthermore) that this right ought to be recognized specifically through creation of a dedicated privacy *tort*, dates to a seminal law review article published in 1890 by Warren and Brandeis, 'The Right to Privacy' (1890) 4 *Harv L Rev* 193. Warren and Brandeis surveyed a range of actions available in English law, and argued that underlying these was a right to 'privacy'. Social conditions required that privacy be recognized and given protection through the law of tort. The authors' chief *concern* (no different from the concern in much recent case law such as *Von Hannover v Germany* [2004] ECHR 294), was with the conduct of the press, and this provided the personal motivation for their article.[6] Their *method* was to suggest that privacy interests should and could be protected in the same way as the familiar interests in physical integrity and personal property. The 'privacy right' is derived from an analogy with *trespass* torts.

S. D. Warren and L. D. Brandeis, 'The Right to Privacy'
(1890) 4 *Harv L Rev* 193, 193–6

That the individual shall have full protection in person and in property is a principle as old as the common law; but it has been found necessary from time to time to define anew the exact nature and extent of such protection. Political, social, and economic changes entail the recognition of new rights, and the common law, in its eternal youth, grows to meet the demands of society. Thus, in very early times, the law gave a remedy only for physical interference with life and property, for trespasses *vi et armis*. . . . Later, there came a recognition of man's spiritual nature, of his feelings and his intellect. Gradually the scope of these legal rights broadened; and now the right to life has come to mean the right to enjoy life,—the right to be let alone; the right to liberty secures the exercise of extensive civil privileges; and the term 'property' has grown to comprise every form of possession—intangible, as well as tangible.

. . . This development of the law was inevitable. The intense intellectual and emotional life, and the heightening of sensations which came with the advance of civilization, made it clear to men that only a part of the pain, pleasure and profit of life lay in physical things. Thoughts, emotions, and sensations demanded legal recognition, and the beautiful capacity for growth which characterizes the common law enabled the judges to afford the requisite protection, without the interposition of the legislature.

Recent inventions and business methods call attention to the next step which must be taken for the protection of the person, and for securing to the individual what Judge Cooley calls the right "to be let alone". [Cooley on Torts, 2d ed., p.29] Instantaneous photographs and newspaper enterprise have invaded the sacred precincts of private and domestic life; and numerous mechanical devices threaten to make good the prediction that "what is whispered in the

---

[5] This means (simply) that the right can be derived from the legal material itself and without having to seek a justification elsewhere.

[6] Warren felt that his wife had been harassed by the press, which was printing too many details of parties at their home. The last straw was intrusive coverage into the wedding of their daughter. Speaking of the Warrens' daughter, and given the extraordinary influence of the Warren and Brandeis article, William Prosser later suggested that hers was the original 'face that launched a thousand law suits' (Prosser, 'Privacy', at 423)

closet shall be proclaimed from the house-tops." ... the question of whether our law will recognize and protect the right to privacy in this and in other respects must soon come before our courts for consideration.

Of the desirability—indeed of the necessity—of some such protection, there can be no doubt. The press is overstepping in every direction the obvious bounds of propriety and of decency. . . . The intensity and complexity of life, attendant upon advancing civilization, have rendered necessary some retreat from the world, and man, under the refining influence of culture, has become more sensitive to publicity, so that solitude and privacy have become more essential to the individual; but modern enterprise and invention have, through invasions upon his privacy, subjected him to mental pain and distress, far greater than could be inflicted by mere bodily injury. . . .

From this extract we can see the method at work in the essay (as well as its polemical style). Remedies for invasion of a right to privacy should emerge as an extension from, and be closely modelled upon, the protection of property (tangible and intangible), of confidence, and of reputation. The reason why it should so emerge is that it is now needed.

In the United States, the arguments of Warren and Brandeis were spectacularly successful (although there is some question whether the exceptions to the right to privacy have swallowed up the rule, at least where *publication* of private information is concerned).[7] After an initial rejection in the New York case of *Roberson v Rochester Folding Box Co* (1902) 171 NY 538, 64 NE 442, Warren and Brandeis' thesis was accepted by the Supreme Court of Georgia in *Pavesich v New England Life Insurance Co* (1905) 122 Ga 190, 50 SE 68 (where the defendant had used the name and image of the plaintiff to advertise their products), and an enforceable right to privacy was recognized. This acceptance rapidly spread to other state jurisdictions. In an equally influential later article, William Prosser explained that in accepting the existence of a right of privacy, the courts had been little concerned to explore what privacy actually *was*.

William Prosser, 'Privacy' (1960) 48 *Cal L Rev* 383, 386–9

In nearly every jurisdiction[8] the first decisions were understandably preoccupied with the question whether the right of privacy existed at all, and gave little or no consideration to what it would amount to if it did. It is only in recent years, and largely through the legal writers, that there has been any attempt to inquire what interests are we protecting, and against what conduct. Today, with something over three hundred cases in the books, the holes in the jigsaw puzzle have been largely filled in, and some rather definite conclusions are possible.

What has emerged from the decisions is no simple matter. It is not one tort, but a complex of four. The law of privacy comprises four distinct kinds of invasion of four different interests of the plaintiff, which are tied together by the common name, but otherwise have almost nothing in common except that each represents an interference with the right of the plaintiff, in the

---

7 G. Phillipson, 'Judicial Reasoning in Breach of Confidence Cases Under the Human Rights Act: Not Taking Privacy Seriously' (2003) EHRLR 53 cites D. Zimmerman, 'Requiem for a Heavyweight: a Farewell to Warren and Brandeis's Privacy Tort' (1983) 68 *Cornell L Rev* 291. Zimmerman suggests that the defence of 'newsworthiness' has effectively destroyed the protection sought by Warren and Brandeis against unwelcome intrusion and publication. A broader line is drawn around press freedom in the United States than in England.

8 Prosser is here referring to *state* jurisdictions within the United States.

phrase coined by Judge Cooley, "to be let alone." Without any attempt to exact definition, these four torts may be described as follows:

1. Intrusion upon the plaintiff's seclusion or solitude, or into his private affairs.
2. Public disclosure of embarrassing private facts about the plaintiff.
3. Publicity which places the plaintiff in a false light in the public eye.
4. Appropriation, for the defendant's advantage, of the plaintiff's name or likeness.

It should be obvious at once that these four types of invasion may be subject, in some respects at least, to different rules; and that when what is said as to any one of them is carried over to another, it may not be at all applicable, and confusion may follow.

Whereas Warren and Brandeis had sought to show that there was a distinctive privacy right underlying a range of case law (which was capable of protection at common law), Prosser set out to divide that case law into a number of categories which, he said, protected slightly *different* interests, even if these protected interests could still (in his view) properly be regarded as aspects of a broader notion of privacy. He did not seek to show *why* these privacy interests are worth protecting, or what the broader idea of privacy (if any) might consist in. He was concerned however about the propensity for the action(s) in privacy to avoid and override important restrictions—such as the defence of truth in defamation actions—which had evolved in the established torts. Such was the influence of Prosser's arguments that they provided the model for revising the outline of privacy torts in the Second US Restatement (Torts).

In England, Prosser's arguments have had a different influence. They have been taken to demonstrate that there is no identifiable core to the right of 'privacy' which would make it capable of protection as a general interest. A clear example is Lord Hoffmann's view in *Wainwright v Home Office* [2004] 2 AC 406:

18 The need in the United States to break down the concept of 'invasion of privacy' into a number of loosely-linked torts must cast doubt upon the value of any high-level generalisation which can perform a useful function in enabling one to deduce the rule to be applied in a concrete case. English law has so far been unwilling, perhaps unable, to formulate such a high level principle. . . .

In 'The Poverty of Principle' (1980) 96 LQR 73, Raymond Wacks turned the tables on the arguments of Warren and Brandeis, suggesting that in some instances the attempt to define a range of existing actions as 'really' to do with privacy has not only been overdone, but has also led to real confusion. He pointed out that in certain decisions of the US Supreme Court,[9] 'privacy' had become synonymous with autonomy itself,[10] a much larger and more fundamental value which surely could not be sensibly used as a protected right or interest for the purposes of tort law, without further definition. The common law simply did not *need* the general idea of privacy.

Wacks suggested abandoning appeal to the 'abstract' idea of privacy, and advocated protection of 'personal information' which he thought was at the core of privacy interests. This sort of thinking (avoiding broad general principles and allowing evolution of existing actions in

---

[9] Particularly regarding sexual freedom and obscene material.

[10] This was only one of seven ways that Wacks suggested privacy had become irretrievably confused with other issues; it may however be the most important.

order to meet current needs) is the most comfortable for common lawyers. However, the present need to give effect to the Convention right to privacy in Article 8 (to which we turn below) changes matters considerably. Arguably, there ought now to be a stronger focus on whether there is a more general, underlying idea of privacy, and if so what it is. Equally, this could be a good time to challenge whether 'control of information' really *is* 'at the core' of privacy.[11] In other words, the Warren and Brandeis/Prosser line of thinking, which circles around development of the law of property and actions such as breach of confidence, could be seen not only as a merely partial solution but even, in terms of its method, as a false start.[12]

In the rest of this chapter, we will observe a central problem in the developing English law. Courts have stated that they will not create new torts in order to give direct effect to Convention rights such as the right to 'private and family life' in Article 8. Even so, existing causes of action are beginning to absorb a new right or interest (in privacy) which is *not* an offshoot of existing ideas of property. English common law is not doing precisely what Warren and Brandeis suggested over 100 years ago, deriving a new idea of property *from existing common law cases* in the light of changing needs. Instead, it is giving effect—in a limited but still very significant sense—to a Convention right.

3. THE ROLE OF HUMAN RIGHTS: ARTICLE 8 ECHR AND THE HUMAN RIGHTS ACT 1998

This section considers the basic tools which have been used in the partial absorption of privacy as a protected interest in common law.

The Human Rights Act 1998 requires that account be taken in English law of specified 'Convention rights'. These include the Article 8 right to 'respect for private and family life'. The requirements of the Human Rights Act are fundamental to this chapter and although we have discussed the Act in earlier chapters, we will further develop that discussion here. First though, we must consider the requirements of Article 8 itself.

3.1 ARTICLE 8, EUROPEAN CONVENTION ON HUMAN RIGHTS AND FUNDAMENTAL FREEDOMS

Article 8 Right to respect for private and family life

1. Everyone has the right to respect for his private and family life, his home and his correspondence.

2. There shall be no interference by a public authority with the exercise of this right except such as is in accordance with the law and is necessary in a democratic society in the interests of national security, public safety or the economic well-being of the country, for the prevention of disorder or crime, for the protection of health or morals, or for the protection of the rights and freedoms of others.

---

[11] For an argument that much broader ideas of privacy need protecting, see Morgan (2003) 62 CLJ 444.

[12] For an exploration of privacy which is not derived from notions of property or equity, see David Feldman, 'Secrecy, Dignity, or Autonomy? Views of Privacy as a Civil Liberty' (1994) 47 CLP 41.

The most authoritative interpretation of the obligations imposed by Article 8 is provided by the following case. Recently, the Court of Appeal has recognized that particular regard must be had to this decision: *Douglas v Hello! (No 3)* [2006] QB 125 at [253]. Though in some respects this case sets a very demanding standard, in other respects (particularly as regards the content of Article 8), the guidance it offers is limited.

Von Hannover v Germany [2004] ECHR 294

In this case, the European Court of Human Rights confirmed that Article 8 imposes *positive* obligations upon States to ensure that rights to privacy are respected. Prior to this decision, there was no definitive statement to this effect,[13] although to a large extent English courts anticipated it through their interpretation of the Human Rights Act (below).

German law has accorded considerable protection to privacy interests, in marked contrast to the UK. It has done so through interpretation of Articles 1 (relating to the dignity of the human being) and 2 (relating to free development of personality) of the Basic Law (*Grundgestetz*). In this case however, the applicant challenged the restrictions on protection of privacy which operate in German law in respect of 'figures of contemporary society'. It is clear that these restrictions aim to protect the competing public interests in expression and information. As such, the applicant was challenging the balance struck by German courts between the protection of individual privacy, and the protection of a public interest in information where the everyday (unexceptional) behaviour of public figures is concerned.

The Applicant's Case

The applicant, Princess Caroline of Monaco, wished to prevent publication of certain photographs. The photographs showed her pursuing a range of 'ordinary' activities. All were taken in places where, to one extent or another, the public had access. The photographs were interpreted by the German courts as being in no sense derogatory (although one showed her tripping and falling at the beach). However, they were taken without permission and on 'unofficial' occasions when she had no wish to be photographed. The German courts ruled that most of the photographs could be published. Princess Caroline was a 'figure of contemporary society *par excellence*' (even though she had no official state functions), and in German law she therefore had to tolerate publication of photographs in which she appeared *in a public place* even if they showed scenes from her daily life. Her interests were outweighed by the need to inform. It was thought however that one of the photographs should not be published as it violated her rights under the Basic Law (as explained above). It showed her at the far end of a restaurant garden, and this counted as a 'secluded place' whereas the interior of a restaurant did not. In the garden, she could have assumed that she was 'not exposed to public view'.

Princess Caroline applied to the European Court of Human Rights, arguing that her rights under Article 8 had been violated. The Court found in her favour. The following extracts show the reason for the decision, and also the general approach to privacy and freedom of expression adopted by the Court.

---

13 See G. Phillipson, 'Transforming Breach of Confidence?: Towards a Common Law Right of Privacy under the Human Rights Act' (2003) 66 MLR 726–58.

The general principles governing the protection of private life and the freedom of expression

56   In the present case the applicant did not complain of an action of the State, but rather of the lack of adequate State protection of her private life and her image.

57   The court reiterates that although the object of Article 8 is essentially that of protecting the individual against arbitrary interference by the public authorities, it does not merely compel the State to abstain from such interference: in addition to this primarily negative undertaking, there may be positive obligations inherent in an effective respect for private or family life. These obligations may involve the adoption of measures designed to secure respect for private life even in the sphere of the relations of individuals between themselves . . .

58   That protection of private life has to be balanced against the freedom of expression guaranteed by Article 10 of the Convention. In that context the Court reiterates that the freedom of expression constitutes one of the essential foundations of a democratic society . . .

In that connection the press plays an essential role in a democratic society. Although it must not overstep certain bounds, in particular in respect of the rights and reputations of others, its duty is nevertheless to impart—in a manner consistent with its obligations and responsibilities—information and ideas on all matters of public interest. . . . Journalistic freedom also covers possible recourse to a degree of exaggeration, or even provocation . . .

59   Although freedom of expression also extends to the publication of photos, this is an area in which the protection of the rights and reputation of others takes on particular importance. The present case does not concern the dissemination of 'ideas', but of images containing very personal or even intimate 'information' about an individual. Furthermore, photos appearing in the tabloid press are often taken in a climate of continual harassment which induces in the person concerned a very strong sense of intrusion into their private life or even of persecution.

60   In the cases in which the Court has had to balance the protection of private life against the freedom of expression it has always stressed the contribution made by photos or articles in the press to a debate of general interest . . . The Court thus found, in one case, that the use of certain terms in respect of an individual's private life was not 'justified by considerations of public concern' and that those terms did not '[bear] on a matter of general importance' . . . and went on to hold that there had not been a violation of Article 10. In another case, however, the Court attached particular importance to the fact that the subject in question was a news item of 'major public concern' and that the published photographs 'did not disclose any details of [the] private life' of the person in question [*Krone-Verlag*] and held that there had been a violation of Article 10. . . .

Application of these general principles by the Court

. . .

63   The Court considers that a fundamental distinction needs to be drawn between reporting facts—even controversial ones—capable of contributing to a debate in a democratic society relating to politicians in the exercise of their functions, for example, and reporting details of the private life of an individual who, moreover, as in this case, does not exercise official functions. While in the former case the press exercises its vital role of 'watchdog' in a democracy by contributing to 'imparting information and ideas on matters of public interest' [*Observer and Guardian v UK*] it does not do so in the latter case.

69   The Court considers that everyone, even if they are known to the general public, must be able to enjoy a 'legitimate expectation' of protection of and respect for their private life . . .

Conclusion

76   As the Court has stated above, it considers that the decisive factor in balancing the protection of private life against freedom of expression should lie in the contribution that the published photos and articles make to a debate of general interest. It is clear in the instant case that they made no such contribution since the applicant exercises no official function and the photos and articles related specifically to details of her private life.

77   Furthermore, the Court considers that the public does not have a legitimate interest in knowing where the applicant is and how she behaves generally in her private life even if she appears in places that cannot always be described as secluded and despite the fact that she is well known to the public.

Even if such a public interest exists, as does a commercial interest of the magazine in publishing these photos and these articles, in the instant case those interests must, in the Court's view, yield to the applicant's right to the effective protection of her private life.

78   Lastly, in the Court's opinion the criteria established by the domestic courts were not sufficient to ensure the effective protection of the applicant's private life and she should, in the circumstances of the case, have had a 'legitimate expectation' of protection of her private life.

Conclusions from *Von Hannover*

As already noted, the biggest contribution of *Von Hannover* to general Convention jurisprudence is its clear recognition of positive obligations on the State to secure privacy in dealings between private parties, and particularly in actions against the press. Domestic legal systems must be able to handle the balancing issue that is explained in *Von Hannover*, where Article 8 rights conflict with Article 10 rights, in such a case.

Some important guidance on this balancing exercise is offered by the Court. In particular, the Court reiterates that the key purpose of the Article 10 right is instrumental: freedom of expression is vital to the flourishing of a democratic society and is a key component in the sort of society that will uphold the other rights and freedoms in the Convention (at [58]). This is compatible with the explanation of Article 10 that we said, in Chapter 13, was adopted in the recent English case law on defamation. In privacy cases, this takes on particular importance because the right of the public to be informed is in potential conflict with the right of an individual to enjoy their privacy. In the *Von Hannover* case, the Court made clear that unless there is a distinct public interest reason for revealing private information (and it seems *particularly* photographs), it will be inappropriate to *allow publication*. Much positive action to secure privacy *will be in restraint of freedom of expression*, and the State is generally obliged *not* to act in such a way as to restrict expression. However, there is no substantial difference in the weight that is accorded to the two rights in privacy, and in freedom of expression. *States cannot evade the need to balance the rights by according priority to freedom of expression; nor by doing nothing.*

The European Court also emphasized an important difference between **the public interest** (in being informed) which often underlies the Article 10 right, and a **public preference** for certain types of reporting, which makes a particular sort of publication commercially successful. The Court clearly does not endorse the views of the German Federal Constitutional Court that 'entertainment in the press is neither negligible nor entirely worthless and therefore falls within the scope of application of fundamental rights'. A report must be demonstrated to serve a particular purpose, if it is to outweigh an individual's right to privacy. In cases such as *A v B* [2005] QB 195 and (more subtly) *Campbell v MGN* [2004] 2 AC 457, English courts have, like their German counterparts, been cautious about restricting the way the press chooses to report stories that the public wishes to read. The *Von Hannover* decision rejects the idea that a free press is good in itself. It requires a specific public interest to be demonstrated in respect of publication. Provided the publication itself is 'low-grade', then it seems that even a relatively anodyne publication (with minor impact on privacy) should be restrained. An alternative reading of the *Von Hannover* case is possible, which would place more emphasis on 'harassment' of the Princess through a course of conduct which deprived her of her private life. But this is hard to sustain given the nature of the conclusions reached and especially the identification of the *contribution made by the photos to public debate* as the 'decisive factor'.

Certain lesser findings of the European Court are also of importance. In particular, the Court emphasized that even a 'public figure' still has an expectation of privacy. This is so not only where the claimant is best described as a 'celebrity' but even when they have some constitutional significance. Privacy is also not to be defined in exclusively spatial terms, limiting protection to areas where the public has no access. The individual claimant does not need to be in a secluded *place*, in order to benefit from the protection of Article 8. Both of these lesser principles are consistent with English law as it has recently developed.[14]

The Court states that its conclusions on release of information are strengthened by consideration of the *manner in which the photographs were acquired*—that is to say, through covert means, without permission, and as part of a campaign amounting to 'harassment'. This element of the Court's reasoning shows how hard it is to distinguish between **intrusion** and **disclosure** cases. It is suggested that this gives extra force to the argument that a more general understanding of the broad Article 8 right is needed. Despite its importance, the case does little to advance the understanding of 'privacy' in any broad sense.[15]

3.2 THE HUMAN RIGHTS ACT 1998

Before the decision of the European Court of Human Rights in *Von Hannover*, English courts had already concluded that they were required to balance the rights in Articles 8 and 10 as a matter of English law, as a consequence of the Human Rights Act 1998 ('HRA'). The *Von Hannover* decision is consistent in some respects with the approach taken by English courts, but inconsistent in other respects. This section considers the relevant provisions of the Human Rights Act. In the next section, we turn to the case law.

---

[14] As to the first see *HRH Prince of Wales v Associated Newspapers* [2006] EWHC 522 (affirmed [2006] EWCA Civ 1776)—the heir to the throne has a reasonable expectation of privacy in his diaries. As to the second, see *Campbell v MGN* (extracted below)—photographs taken in the street may be the subject of an injunction if there is a reasonable expectation of privacy.

[15] See M. A. Sanderson, 'Is Von Hannover v Germany a Step Backwards for the Substantive Analysis of Speech and Privacy Interests?' [2004] EHRLR 631–44. Sanderson argues that the low-grade nature of the publications dominated the decision in *Von Hannover*, so that the Court never analysed the nature of the privacy interest very closely.

Section 6

Section 6 of the Human Rights Act 1998 is extracted in Chapter 1.

We have touched on the general implications of this provision in Chapters 1, 10, and 13. The general issue for tort law is whether the Convention rights will have any effect **in actions between private parties**. It seems plain from sections 7 and 8 (also extracted in Chapter 1) that the Convention rights can be the basis of an action in their own right in 'vertical' cases, which is to say where the individual or other private party brings an action against a public authority. Any impact on actions between private parties is described as **horizontal effect**.

Actions relating to privacy have made a particular contribution to the understanding of horizontal effect. It is clear from these cases that the Human Rights Act does not enable courts to create entirely new causes of action between private parties. The following comments from *Campbell v MGN* are reasonably conclusive on this point.[16]

Campbell v MGN [2004] 2 AC 457

Lord Hoffmann

49 . . . Even now the equivalent of Article 8 has been enacted as part of English law, it is not directly concerned with the protection of privacy against private persons or corporations. It is, by virtue of section 6 of the 1998 Act, a guarantee of privacy only against public authorities. Although the Convention, as an international instrument, may impose upon the United Kingdom an obligation to take some steps (whether by statute or otherwise) to protect rights of privacy against invasion by private individuals, it does not follow that such an obligation would have any counterpart in domestic law.

Baroness Hale

132 . . . The 1998 Act does not create any new cause of action between private persons. But if there is a cause of action applicable, the court as a public authority must act compatibly with both parties' Convention rights. . . .

Section 6 does not entitle courts to *create new torts*; but on the other hand, at least on the approach of Baroness Hale, existing causes of action should be interpreted with regard to the Convention rights. That then is the formal position. In reality, recent changes may go further than this. To some extent, they do so through interpretation of section 12 (below), rather than section 6.

Section 12

Section 12 is concerned with the Convention right to freedom of expression. But it is through consideration of this section that equal weight has been given to other Convention rights, including privacy. The impact of section 12 in this area of private law has been much greater than a surface reading would lead us to expect.

Section 12 of the Human Rights Act 1998 is extracted in Chapter 1.

---

16 See also Lord Steyn, '2000–2005: Laying the Foundations for Human Rights Law' (2005) 4 EHRLR 349.

The section requires that particular regard be had to the Article 10 right *in any case* where a remedy is being considered which may interfere with the Article 10 right. In *Douglas v Hello!*, it was pointed out that because regard must be had to freedom of expression in *any* such case (and not just in cases brought against public authorities), Article 10 must *necessarily* have some horizontal effect. Perhaps surprisingly, this section was also the vehicle through which Article 8 rights were given horizontal effect in that particular case. Having regard to the Article 10 right must involve having regard to the *restrictions* on the right outlined in Article 10(2), since these are an inherent part of the definition of the Convention right to freedom of expression. We extracted Article 10 in Chapter 13 (Defamation). Here is a reminder of the way the restrictions to the right operate.

Article 10.2

The exercise of [freedom of expression], since it carries with it duties and responsibilities, may be subject to such formalities, conditions, restrictions or penalties as are prescribed by law and are necessary in a democratic society, in the interests of national security, territorial integrity or public safety, for the prevention of disorder or crime, for the protection of health or morals, *for the protection of the reputation or rights of others, for preventing the disclosure of information received in confidence,* or for maintaining the authority and impartiality of the judiciary.

(Emphasis added.)

In this way, section 12 gives limited horizontal effect not only to Article 10 rights, but also to all those other rights by which they are expressly qualified: *Douglas v Hello!* [2001] QB 967.

Equality between the rights

On the face of it, section 12(4) gives priority to freedom of expression, since a court must have 'particular regard' to it. Since the section is primarily concerned with remedies, it might be assumed that it works against the availability of injunctions. An injunction was initially sought in *Douglas v Hello!* and importantly, this interpretation (giving priority to freedom of expression) was rejected. The restrictions in Article 10(2) are an inherent part of the definition of the Convention right to freedom of expression. Hence, the right and its restrictions should be given the same 'particular' consideration. This element of the Court of Appeal's approach—**equality between rights**—is consistent with the *Von Hannover* decision as outlined above.[17] Equality between rights is in marked contrast with US law, which gives priority to freedom of expression, a contrast noted by Sedley LJ in *Douglas v Hello!* [2001] QB 967:

135   . . . The European Court of Human Rights has always recognised the high importance of free media of communication in a democracy, but its jurisprudence does not—and could not consistently with the Convention itself—give article 10(1) the presumptive priority which is given, for example, to the First Amendment in the jurisprudence of the United States' courts. Everything will ultimately depend on the proper balance between privacy and publicity in the situation facing the court.

---

[17] As we will see equality between the rights was not so clearly recognized in *A v B plc* [2003] QB 195, for example, but it was endorsed by the House of Lords in *Campbell v MGN* [2004] UKHL; [2004] 2 AC 457.

Section 12(4)(b) also requires a court when considering freedom of expression to have regard to 'any relevant privacy code'. The *Press Complaints Commission Code of Practice* provides:

3. *Privacy* (i) Everyone is entitled to respect for his or her private and family life, home, health and correspondence. A publication will be expected to justify intrusions into any individual's private life without consent. (ii) The use of long lens photography to take pictures of people in private places without their consent is unacceptable. Note—Private places are public or private property where there is a reasonable expectation of privacy.

4. *Harassment* . . . (ii) [Journalists and photographers] must not photograph individuals in private places (as defined in the note to clause 3) without their consent; must not persist in tele-phoning, questioning, pursuing or photographing individuals after having been asked to desist; must not remain on their property after having been asked to leave and should not follow them.

Public interest 1. The public interest includes: (i) Detecting or exposing crime or a serious misdemeanour. (ii) Protecting public health and safety. (iii) Preventing the public from being misled by some statement or action of an individual or organisation . . .

In *Douglas v Hello!* [2001] QB 967, Brooke LJ explained the importance of the section on 'Privacy':

94 It appears to me that the existence of these statutory provisions,[18] coupled with the cur-rent wording of the relevant privacy code, mean that in any case where the court is concerned with issues of freedom of expression in a journalistic, literary or artistic context, it is bound to pay particular regard to any breach of the rules set out in clause 3 of the code, especially where none of the public interest claims set out in the preamble to the code is asserted. A newspa-per which flouts clause 3 of the code is likely in those circumstances to have its claim to an entitlement to freedom of expression trumped by article 10(2) considerations of privacy. . . .

This interpretation promises to give new strength to the Code of Practice, which has generally been regarded as ineffective.

4. THE CASE LAW

4.1 DISCLOSURE OF PRIVATE 'INFORMATION'

The most spectacular developments in protection of privacy have been in the action for breach of confidence. Historically, this action has not been categorized as a tort. Rather, obli-gations of confidence have been recognized in equity, binding the recipient of information as a matter of conscience:

Brooke LJ, Douglas v Hello! [2001] QB 967

65 . . . If information is accepted on the basis that it will be kept secret, the recipient's conscience is bound by that confidence, and it will be unconscionable for him to break his duty of confidence by publishing the information to others . . .

---

[18] This is a reference to the Human Rights Act 1998.

It is still not completely clear whether the action, now that it has developed to protect 'private' information in the absence of any relationship of confidence, is to be called a tort. Lord Nicholls, in *Campbell v MGN*, used the word 'tort' to describe the newly extended action, but gave no explanation for his choice of word. Subsequently, in *Douglas v Hello! (No 3)* [2006] QB 125, the Court of Appeal has said that the action for breach of confidence, even in its adjusted form, is not a tort. In the latter instance, classification as a tort (or not) was of more practical significance because it could affect the appropriate jurisdiction for the litigation, as we will explain. No magic attaches to the word 'tort' perhaps.[19] But students should at least be aware that only some aspects of the large case law on breach of confidence are being covered here. These are the aspects which are needed if we are to reach an understanding of the process by which privacy is emerging as a protected interest.

The Previously Existing Law: What is (or was) 'Breach of Confidence'?

It is true to say that even before the Human Rights Act came into force in October 2000, the action for breach of confidence was in a process of development and had been identified as having the potential to protect some aspects of privacy.[20] This is not surprising since it was one of the actions used by Warren and Brandeis in 1890 to argue that there was a right to privacy 'immanent in' the common law. We can identify three requirements of the action for breach of confidence.

(i) The information in question must have the 'necessary quality of confidentiality'.

(ii) The recipient of the information must be under an obligation of confidence.

(iii) The interest in confidentiality will be balanced against any public interest in disclosure.

The 'necessary quality of confidentiality'

The action certainly protected commercial confidences or 'trade secrets'. In *Attorney-General v Guardian* [1987] 1 WLR 1248, it was found to extend to state secrets (and therefore prevented the defendant newspaper from publishing extracts from the book *Spycatcher*), but in such cases a positive public interest in protecting the confidence needed to be shown. It was important that the protected information must not be already in the public domain; and that it was not merely trivial. 'Confidence' extended to some information of a personal or sexual nature either within marriage (*Argyll v Argyll* [1967] Ch 302), or (more controversially) outside it (*Stephens v Avery* [1988] Ch 449). In the latter case, Sir Nicolas Browne-Wilkinson V-C held that personal information could be subject to a duty of confidence sufficient to give rise to an action to restrain its publication, even though the only relationship between the parties, at the time of disclosure, had been one of friendship.[21]

---

[19] Although it is regarded as sufficiently certain in its meaning to be used in the Private International Law (Miscellaneous Provisions) Act, s 9. Views on this will depend on one's broader opinion of the continued, but very imprecise, distinction between equity and common law.

[20] *Hellewell v Chief Constable of Derbyshire* [1995] 1 WLR 804 per Laws LJ; W. Wilson, 'Privacy, Confidence and Press Freedom: A Study in Judicial Activism' (1990) 53 MLR 43, commenting on *Stephens v Avery* [1988] Ch 449.

[21] The information here was not trivial. It related to a lesbian affair conducted by the plaintiff with a woman who had then, perhaps as a consequence, been murdered by her husband.

The obligation of confidence

It was for a long time considered essential that the information should have been conveyed to its recipient *subject to an obligation of confidence*. This was indeed the foundation of the action. Whereas 'confidentiality' is a quality of information, 'confidence' is a quality of the relationship between confider and the person confided in. This obligation would be binding on the conscience of the recipient and would provide a *prima facie* reason (subject to other considerations such as public interest, below) for protecting the confidence. Such an obligation, once established, could also bind a third party (such as a newspaper) coming into possession of the information with notice of it. The duty might be express (for example a contractual term), or implied from the nature of the relationship within which the information was divulged.

In the more recent case law, it has been clearly stated that this sort of duty is no longer a *requirement* of the action for breach of confidence. The absence of any need for a distinct duty of confidence was described by Lord Hoffmann in *Campbell v MGN* [2004] 2 AC 457 at [48] as 'firmly established'. The question is whether this requirement ended with the Court of Appeal's ground-breaking decision in *Douglas v Hello!*, or before.

The following passage from the House of Lords' decision in *A-G v Guardian (No 2)* [1990] 1 AC 109, 281 has been widely quoted in recent cases. It shows that a **relationship** of confidence was no longer required in all cases even *before* the Human Rights Act. An obligation of confidence could arise where the information had not been deliberately divulged to the recipient at all.

Lord Goff of Chieveley, *Attorney General v Guardian (No 2)* [1990] 1 AC 109, 281

I realise that, in the vast majority of cases, in particular those concerned with trade secrets, the duty of confidence will arise from a transaction or relationship between the parties—often a contract, in which event the duty may arise by reason of either an express or an implied term of that contract. It is in such cases as these that the expressions "confider" and "confidant" are perhaps most aptly employed. But it is well settled that a duty of confidence may arise in equity independently of such cases; and I have expressed the circumstances in which the duty arises in broad terms, not merely to embrace those cases where a third party receives information from a person who is under a duty of confidence in respect of it, knowing that it has been disclosed by that person to him in breach of his duty of confidence, but also to include certain situations, beloved of law teachers—where an obviously confidential document is wafted by an electric fan out of a window into a crowded street, or where an obviously confidential document, such as a private diary, is dropped in a public place, and is then picked up by a passer-by. . . . I have however deliberately avoided the fundamental question whether, contract apart, the duty lies simply "in the notion of an obligation of conscience arising from the circumstances in or through which the information was communicated or obtained" (see *Moorgate Tobacco Ltd v Philip Morris Ltd (No 2)* (1984) 156 CLR 414, 438 . . .)

Much has been made of this passage in recent case law, yet it does not alter the classification of breach of confidence as an action arising **in equity**, out of obligations of confidence that are binding on the conscience of the defendant.[22] The recent developments outlined below undoubtedly take a further decisive step, protecting information *simply because of its private nature*. It may be this further step away from obligations binding in conscience that explains

---

[22] See for example the discussion of breach of confidence in Sarah Worthington, *Equity* (Clarendon Press, 2003), Chapter 5.

Lord Nicholls' decision (otherwise unexplained) to describe the action as a tort in *Campbell v MGN* [2004] 2 AC 457.

Public interest in disclosure

It was certainly realised before the Human Rights Act that public and private interests would have to be balanced when deciding whether to grant injunctions. Equally, it was realised that the 'public interest' in disclosure may engage Article 10 of the Convention. The 'public interest' in disclosure may be based on the need to disclose wrongdoing if that is indicated by the information concerned: 'there is no confidence in iniquity'.[23] Alternatively, there may be some other sort of public interest in disclosure. For example in *W v Egdell* [1990] Ch 359, a doctor who suspected that his patient should not be released on parole because he posed a *danger to public safety* was justified in releasing details from a medical report—ordinarily subject to confidentiality—to relevant parties. In *Attorney-General v Guardian (No 2)* [1990] 1 AC 109, Lord Goff stated the general (pre-Human Rights Act) position like this:

> . . . although the basis of the law's protection of confidence is that there is a public interest that confidences should be preserved and protected by the law, nevertheless that public interest may be outweighed by some other countervailing public interest which favours disclosure. This limitation may apply, as the learned judge pointed out, to all types of confidential information. It is this limiting principle which may require a court to carry out a balancing operation, weighing the public interest in maintaining confidence against a countervailing public interest favouring disclosure.

Like the other elements listed above, the required balancing process has been transformed by the adaptation of the action to deal directly with privacy.

The New Case Law: An Action in Respect of *Private* Information

The new case law stemming from *Douglas v Hello!* protects information *having a necessary quality of privacy*, against publication. There is no longer any need to show that the defendant is *bound in conscience* to keep the information private. Such cases are only very awkwardly described as 'breach of confidence' cases, since no confidence between the parties need be shown. They are to do with protection against (or remedies for) publication *of private information*.

The action to protect private information is now interpreted as having the following *two* requirements, in contrast to the three above:

The claimant must have had a 'reasonable expectation of privacy' in the information (or images) in question

This is the test adopted by the majority of judges in *Campbell v MGN* [2004] 2 AC 457. The test was expressly contrasted (by Baroness Hale and Lord Nicholls) with the test applied in the leading Australian case,[24] which is whether a reasonable person in the position of the claimant would regard it as 'highly offensive' that the material should be disclosed—although confusingly, this test seems to have been applied by Lord Hope. The 'highly offensive' test is derived from the US Restatement, and originates in the article by Prosser extracted above.

[23] *Fraser v Evans* [1969] 1 QB 349; Brooke LJ *Douglas v Hello!* at [65].
[24] *Australian Broadcasting Corporation v Lenah Game Meats Pty Ltd* (2001) 208 CLR 199.

The court must balance the interest in keeping the information private
against the interest in revealing the information

This now clearly involves interpretation of competing Convention rights (and potentially other interests too), in the light of provisions of the Human Rights Act 1998. Article 10(2), as explained above, is the source of this balancing exercise. The right to freedom of expression in Article 10 is inherently qualified by other rights and interests. Further, Article 10 is interpreted chiefly in terms of *public interest* in disclosure. This is essential because in many but not all cases, the person who wishes to publicise the information will be a media defendant, so that their 'personal' interest may be regarded as chiefly commercial. The relationship between commercial and public interests in disclosure is a subject where important differences of principle have emerged (see in particular our discussion of *A v B* and the dissenting judgments in *Campbell v MGN*, below).

Douglas v Hello! [2001] QB 967

A celebrity couple (Michael Douglas and Catherine Zeta-Jones) entered into a contract with OK! Magazine, giving the magazine exclusive rights to publish photographs of the couple's wedding. All employees and guests at the wedding were explicitly instructed that no photography was allowed, except by the official photographer. Somehow, someone at the wedding took photographs and these fell into the hands of OK! Magazine's rival, Hello!, which planned to publish them. Importantly, it was not clear whether these photographs were taken by somebody who had been invited to the wedding; by an employee; or by an intruder. Had they been taken by an intruder, then it could not be said that the photographs in question were taken *in breach of an obligation of confidence*; there would have been no relationship at all. It was this possibility which led the Court of Appeal to consider whether the publication of the photographs could instead be restrained on the basis that they were *private*.

Although the loss suffered by OK! was purely commercial in nature, the couple themselves also lost the opportunity to *control* the published images of this private event, despite their best efforts (see the contractual right of veto referred to in para [140] below), and this could be described in terms of 'privacy'. It should be noted that this was an 'interim' action in which the claimants sought to prevent publication pending the full hearing on the merits. The Court of Appeal discharged the injunctions for reasons we outline below, but the claimants, and OK! magazine whose contractual rights to print the photographs were rendered less valuable, sought damages and these claims were assessed by the Court of Appeal in *Douglas v Hello! (No 3)* [2006] QB 125. In this later decision, the Court of Appeal accepted that the law in this area had moved so rapidly that it could now be seen that an injunction should have been maintained in the present case. This does not alter the far-reaching significance of this case. In fact, it shows how clearly the changes outlined by the Court of Appeal have been recognized in a short space of time.

Of the three judgments, that of Sedley LJ contains the clearest statement that information will now be protected on the basis that it is *private*. His has proved to be the most influential of the judgments.

Sedley LJ

110   . . . The courts have done what they can, using such legal tools as were to hand, to stop the more outrageous invasions of individuals' privacy; but they have felt unable to articulate their measures as a discrete principle of law. Nevertheless, we have reached a point at which it can be said with confidence that the law recognises and will appropriately protect a right of personal privacy.

111   The reasons are twofold. First, equity and the common law are today in a position to respond to an increasingly invasive social environment by affirming that everybody has a right to some private space. Secondly, and in any event, the Human Rights Act 1998 requires the courts of this country to give appropriate effect to the right to respect for private and family life set out in article 8 of the European Convention for the Protection of Human Rights and Fundamental Freedoms. The difficulty with the first proposition resides in the common law's perennial need (for the best of reasons, that of legal certainty) to appear not to be doing any-thing for the first time. The difficulty with the second lies in the word "appropriate". But the two sources of law now run in a single channel because, by virtue of section 2 and section 6 of the Act, the courts of this country must not only take into account jurisprudence of both the Commission and the European Court of Human Rights which points to a positive institutional obligation to respect privacy; they must themselves act compatibly with that and the other Convention rights. This, for reasons I now turn to, arguably gives the final impetus to the recognition of a right of privacy in English law.

112   The reason why it is material to this case is that on the present evidence it is possible that the photographer was an intruder with whom no relationship of trust had been estab-lished. If it was a guest or an employee, the received law of confidence is probably all that the claimants need.

126   What a concept of privacy does . . . is accord recognition to the fact that the law has to pro-tect not only those people whose trust has been abused but those who simply find themselves subjected to an unwanted intrusion into their personal lives. The law no longer needs to con-struct an artificial relationship of confidentiality between intruder and victim: it can recognise pri-vacy itself as a legal principle drawn from the fundamental value of personal autonomy.

The above paragraphs of Sedley LJ's judgment are clearly groundbreaking in that they rec-ognize privacy itself as the basis of a cause of action, independent of the requirement for a relationship of confidence or trust. On his analysis, the Human Rights Act had given the final push to a change that had already been slowly taking shape. Now, since *Wainwright* and *Campbell*, we can clearly see that these particular assertions of Sedley LJ should not be inter-preted too broadly. English law still recognizes no *general* action to protect privacy. But in some actions for breach of confidence (if indeed that title is still adequate), privacy is pro-tected in its own right.

At least equally significant were the more detailed elements of Sedley LJ's judgment, con-sidering the way in which privacy would need to be balanced against freedom of expression when considering remedies. Here he considered the relevant approach to a claim for an injunction to restrain publication. But first, Sedley LJ analysed the provisions of the Human Rights Act. His analysis is a defining moment in that it recognizes horizontality, *and* equity between rights. It does so through interpretation of section 12.

133   Two initial points need to be made about section 12 of the Act. First, by subsection (4) it puts beyond question the direct applicability of at least one article of the Convention as between one private party to litigation and another-in the jargon, its horizontal effect. Whether this is an illustration of the intended mechanism of the entire Act, or whether it is a special case (and if so, why), need not detain us here. The other point, well made by Mr Tugendhat, is that it is "the Convention right" to freedom of expression which both triggers the section (see section 12(1)) and to which particular regard is to be had. That Convention right, when one turns to it, is qualified in favour of the reputation and rights of others and the protection of information received in confidence. In other words, you cannot have particular regard to article 10 without having equally particular regard at the very least to article 8 . . .

The approach in this paragraph was cited with approval by both Lord Hope (in the majority) and Lord Hoffmann (dissenting) in *Campbell v MGN*, below.

Having concluded that Articles 8 and 10 were both given a degree of horizontal effect by section 12 of the Human Rights Act, Sedley LJ went on to consider how the two should be balanced given the nature of the rights themselves, and given the terms of section 12.

136 . . . I accept that section 12 is not to be interpreted and applied in the simplistic manner for which Mr Carr contends.[25] It will be necessary for the court, in applying the test set out in section 12(3), to bear in mind that by virtue of section 12(1)(4) the qualifications set out in article 10(2) are as relevant as the right set out in article 10(1). This means that, for example, the reputations and rights of others—not only but not least their Convention rights—are as material as the defendant's right of free expression. So is the prohibition on the use of one party's Convention rights to injure the Convention rights of others. Any other approach to section 12 would in my judgment violate section 3 of the Act.[26] Correspondingly, as Mr Tugendhat submits, "likely" in section 12(3) cannot be read as requiring simply an evaluation of the relative strengths of the parties' evidence. If at trial, for the reasons I have given, a minor but real risk to life, or a wholly unjustifiable invasion of privacy, is entitled to no less regard, by virtue of article 10(2), than is accorded to the right to publish by article 10(1), the consequent likelihood becomes material under section 12(3). Neither element is a trump card. They will be articulated by the principles of legality and proportionality which, as always, constitute the mechanism by which the court reaches its conclusion on countervailing or qualified rights. It will be remembered that in the jurisprudence of the Convention proportionality is tested by, among other things, the standard of what is necessary in a democratic society. It should also be borne in mind that that the much-quoted remark of Hoffmann LJ in *R v Central Independent Television plc* [1994] Fam 192, 203 that freedom of speech "is a trump card which always wins" came in a passage which expressly qualified the proposition (as Lord Hoffmann has since confirmed, albeit extrajudicially, in his 1996 Goodman Lecture) as lying "outside the established exceptions, or any new ones which Parliament may enact in accordance with its obligations under the Convention". If freedom of expression is to be impeded, in other words, it must be on cogent grounds recognised by law.

The following paragraph gives a useful summary of the entire reasoning process where the privacy action is concerned:

137 Let me summarise. For reasons I have given, Mr Douglas and Ms Zeta-Jones have a powerful prima facie claim to redress for invasion of their privacy as a qualified right recognised

---

[25] This would simply accord priority to freedom of expression.

[26] S 3 provides that 'So far as it is possible to do so, primary legislation and subordinate legislation must be read and given effect in a way that is compatible with the Convention rights'. The only legislation being interpreted in this case was of course the Human Rights Act itself.

and protected by English law. The case being one which affects the Convention right of freedom of expression, section 12 of the Human Rights Act 1998 requires the court to have regard to article 10 (as, in its absence, would section 6). This, however, cannot, consistently with section 3 and article 17, give the article 10(1) right of free expression a presumptive priority over other rights. What it does is require the court to consider article 10(2) along with 10(1), and by doing so to bring into the frame the conflicting right to respect for privacy. This right, contained in article 8 and reflected in English law, is in turn qualified in both contexts by the right of others to free expression. The outcome, which self-evidently has to be the same under both articles, is determined principally by considerations of proportionality.

Having outlined the method by which Article 8 rights may be both recognized as protected in an action to restrain publication, and qualified by the right to freedom of expression, Sedley LJ went on to decide that in this particular case, an interim injunction to restrain publication would **not** be granted.

140   . . . The first two claimants had sold most of the privacy they now seek to protect to the third claimant for a handsome sum. . . . they were careful by their contract to retain a right of veto over publication of "OK!'s" photographs in order to maintain the kind of image which is professionally and no doubt also personally important to them. This element of privacy remained theirs and "Hello!'s" photographs violated it.

142   . . . The retained element of privacy, in the form of editorial control of "OK!'s" pictures, while real, is itself as much a commercial as a personal reservation. While it may be harder to translate into lost money or an account of profits, it can readily be translated into general damages of a significant amount.

. . .

144   In the present case, and not without misgiving, I have concluded that, although the first two claimants are likely to succeed at trial in establishing a breach of their privacy in which "Hello!" may be actionably implicated, the dominant feature of the case is that by far the greater part of that privacy has already been traded and falls to be protected, if at all, as a commodity in the hands of the third claimant. This can be done without the need of an injunction, particularly since there may not be adequate countervailing redress for the defendants if at trial they stave off the claim for interference with contractual relations. The retained element of the first two claimants' privacy is not in my judgment—though I confess it is a close thing—sufficient to tilt the balance of justice and convenience against such liberty as the defendants may establish, at law and under article 10, to publish the illicitly taken photographs.

Sedley LJ considered that the interests of the claimants were predominantly commercial. As such, he mentions an important equitable remedy which goes beyond the kind of compensatory damages with which we have mostly been concerned in this book: the 'account of profits'. This remedy is thought to provide a significant deterrent effect because rather than seeking to compensate the claimant for their losses, it requires the defendant to pay back (or 'disgorge') the profits they have wrongfully acquired in breach of equitable obligation. In principle, it therefore removes the profit motive. Although the boundaries between equity and common law are both fluid and questionable,[27] the account of profits has traditionally been seen as an

---

[27] Sarah Worthington, *Equity*, Chapters 1 and 10.

equitable remedy, particularly appropriate in cases where the balance has come down against the grant of an interim injunction.[28] Apart from its deterrent effect, the remedy will often provide appropriate compensation.

Typically however, *privacy* (as opposed to *commercial confidence*) may not be sufficiently compensated by an account of profits. Although the account of profits is a powerful remedy, in such cases it falls far short, in terms of its value to the claimant, of an injunction. The reason why Sedley LJ thought the balance was a 'close thing' in this case was that there was still, despite the commercial context of the agreements, a small element of retained privacy. This retained element of privacy may have come down to the ability to choose which photographs were released. If so, this was outweighed by the interest in freedom of expression. In *Douglas v Hello! (No 3)* (extracted below) it was said that this retained element of privacy, small though it is, should have been protected through an injunction. Following *Von Hannover v Germany*, it was clear that where *publication* of the photographs was not required on the basis of any public interest argument, there was nothing to put into the balance on the side of Article 10. The small element of retained privacy was therefore sufficient.

The decision in *Venables and Thompson v Newsgroup Newspapers* [2001] Fam 430 followed very shortly after *Douglas v Hello!* The claimants in this action had, whilst children, abducted two-year-old James Bulger and murdered him. It was a particularly notorious crime. On their conviction, injunctions had been put in place, preventing release of any information concerning their whereabouts and their treatment while detained, to expire on the boys' eighteenth birthdays. Shortly after this date, several newspapers sought clarification of any continuing reporting restrictions, and the claimants were given an opportunity to prepare a case. The claimants argued (realistically) that publication of any information which would allow their identities, appearance, and whereabouts to be discovered would put their lives at risk. Dame Elizabeth Butler-Sloss P applied the method in *Douglas v Hello!* to grant injunctions against the whole world, prohibiting release of any information concerning or relating to the whereabouts, appearance, and new identities of the claimants. The law of confidence could extend to protection of information whose release would create the danger of serious injury and death.

This case is far removed from the law of tort, but it also indicates how far the action as interpreted in *Douglas v Hello!* is removed from the idea of an equitable obligation of confidence. There was no relationship between the parties which could conceivably create binding obligations, not least because the injunctions would bind the whole world. Equally, this case shows (as clearly anticipated by Sedley LJ in *Douglas v Hello!*) that not only Article 8, but also all those other rights which qualify Article 10, are given an element of direct horizontal effect as a consequence (intended or not) of section 12. The risk to the claimants' safety and integrity brought into play not Article 8, but Articles 2 and 3 of the Convention (right to life and freedom from persecution).

A v B plc [2003] QB 195

Douglas v Hello! prompted a considerable amount of litigation. In *A v B plc*, the Court of Appeal set out guidelines for the award of interim injunctions in such cases. It is clear that Lord Woolf was concerned to contain the costs of litigation. For example, he suggested that

---

[28] Worthington, *Equity*, pp. 140–3. The availability of profits-based 'disgorgement' damages for tort is discussed by Edelman, *Gain-Based Damages* (Hart Publishing, 2002). The Court of Appeal in *Douglas v Hello! (No 3)* clearly thought the remedy was available and it is unlikely this would depend on categorization as tort or equitable wrong. See N. Witzleb, 'Monetary Remedies for Breach of Confidence in Privacy Cases' (2007) 27 LS (forthcoming).

courts should spend relatively little time considering whether there was a privacy interest which could be protected at all ([11](vii)). But his approach does not necessarily appear true to the 'presumptive equality between rights' set out in *Douglas v Hello!*.

The guidelines offered for lower courts are set out in para [11] of Lord Woolf's judgment. We will select only those of most substantive interest. To the extent that these are incompatible with the judgment in *Von Hannover*, they are unlikely now to remain authoritative.

The claimant in this case, a married professional footballer, sought injunctions against the first defendant (a newspaper), in order to prevent disclosure of sexual relationships he had had with the second defendant and another woman. He also sought an injunction against the second defendant, preventing her from disclosing her 'kiss and tell' story to anyone 'with a view to its publication in the media'. He obtained these injunctions at first instance, but they were discharged by the Court of Appeal.

11 We suggest that if judges direct themselves in accordance with the following paragraphs in many cases they will not need to be burdened by copious reference to other authorities.

. . .

(ii) The fact that the injunction is being sought to protect the privacy of the claimant, and if the injunction is not granted, the claimant may be deprived of the only remedy which is of any value is a relevant consideration. However, this consideration has to be weighed against the defendant's rights of freedom of expression. . . .

. . .

(iv) The fact that if the injunction is granted it will interfere with the freedom of expression of others and in particular the freedom of the press is a matter of particular importance. This well-established common law principle is underlined by section 12(4). Any interference with the press has to be justified because it inevitably has some effect on the ability of the press to perform its role in society. This is the position irrespective of whether a particular publication is desirable in the public interest. The existence of a free press is in itself desirable and so any interference with it has to be justified. . . .

(v) The fact that under section 12(4) the court is required to have particular regard to whether it would be in the public interest for the material to be published does not mean that the court is justified in interfering with the freedom of the press where there is no identifiable special public interest in any particular material being published. Such an approach would turn section 12(4) upside down. Regardless of the quality of the material which it is intended to publish prima facie the court should not interfere with its publication. Any interference with publication must be justified.

. . .

(xii) Where an individual is a public figure he is entitled to have his privacy respected in the appropriate circumstances. A public figure is entitled to a private life. The individual, however, should recognise that because of his public position he must expect and accept that his actions will be more closely scrutinised by the media. Even trivial facts relating to a public figure can be of great interest to readers and other observers of the media. . . . In many of these situations it would be overstating the position to say that there is a public interest in the information being published. It would be more accurate to say that the public have an understandable and so a legitimate interest in being told the information. If this is the situation then it can be appropriately taken into account by a court when deciding on which side of the line a case falls. The courts must not ignore the fact that if newspapers do not publish information which the public are interested in, there will be fewer newspapers published, which will not be in the public interest. The same is true in relation to other parts of the media.

(xiii) In drawing up a balance sheet between the respective interests of the parties courts should not act as censors or arbiters of taste. This is the task of others. If there is not a sufficient case for restraining publication the fact that a more lurid approach will be adopted by the publication than the court would regard as acceptable is not relevant. If the contents of the publication are untrue the law of defamation provides prohibition. Whether the publication will be attractive or unattractive should not affect the result of an application if the information is otherwise not the proper subject of restraint.

Lord Woolf went on to discuss the need, in accordance with section 12(4) of the Human Rights Act, to refer to any 'relevant privacy code', and to the likelihood that where the information in question was acquired through a breach of Press Complaints Commission Code of Practice, the right to privacy would 'trump' the right to freedom of expression. This was not of course the situation in this case, where a participant in the relationship had herself decided to take her story to the newspaper. In the earlier case of *Theakston v MGN* (2002) EMLR 22, Ousley J had similarly refused an injunction to prevent the defendant from publishing details of the claimant's visit to a brothel. The prostitute–client relationship was not inherently *confidential*; neither could all sexual relationships be regarded as private. In both *Theakston*, and *A v B*, a short-lived sexual relationship was treated as less deserving of protection than confidences within marriage, for example.[29] Nevertheless, an injunction was granted in *Theakston* against the printing of photographs which had been covertly taken within the brothel. This was not because the photographs breached the terms of the Press Complaints Commission's Code of Practice. A brothel was not a 'private place' for the purposes of this Code. But there was a *reasonable expectation* that photographs would not be taken inside a brothel without consent. There was a public interest in learning that a children's TV presenter, who to some extent was a 'role model', had been to a brothel; but no public interest in publishing the *photographs* could be shown.

In *A v B*, Lord Woolf explained his general conclusion that the injunction should be discharged:

44 . . . The degree of confidentiality to which A was entitled, notwithstanding that C and D did not wish their relationship with A to be confidential, was very modest.

This was a prelude to the relevant questions of balance. As such, when it came to 'balance', very little went into the balance in A's favour. Lord Woolf's approach in this case will not pass the test of compatibility with the *Von Hannover* decision, for at least two reasons.[30]

First, in para [11(v)], Lord Woolf says that there is no need to show an identifiable public interest in publication, in order to engage Article 10: restraining publication is a restriction of free speech *per se* and requires justification. His approach gives stronger horizontal effect to the *negative* right to freedom of expression (free from interference by the State), than to the positive right to have one's privacy protected (through action on the part of the State). This is directly opposed to the approach taken in *Von Hannover*, which held that the state must act to

[29] We can directly contrast *Stephens v Avery* [1988] Ch 449, where the information was revealed not by a participant, but by a friend who was given the information in confidence and was thus treated as subject to an *equitable obligation of confidence*. But now see *CC v AB* [2006] EWHC 3083 (QB).

[30] For further discussion see Gavin Phillipson, 'Judicial Reasoning in Breach of Confidence Actions Under the Human Rights Act: Not Taking Privacy Seriously?' 2003 EHRLR Supp. 54.

prevent even fairly anodyne photographs from being published, if there was a reasonable expectation of privacy in relation to them, and unless there was a distinct countervailing interest in expression attached to their publication. Although strictly, the House of Lords in *Campbell* unanimously supported *equality between rights*, nevertheless the dissenting judgments of Lords Hoffmann and Nicholls in that case resemble the approach of Lord Woolf to some extent. They show resistance to the idea that fine judgments should be made about the appropriateness of reporting on a case by case basis.

Second, in para 11(xii), Lord Woolf appears to have treated *understandable* interest on the part of the public as equivalent to *legitimate* interest. This seems to mean that voyeurism—at least where celebrities are concerned—weighs in the balance in favour of publication, no matter how lurid the reporting concerned.[31] This too is incompatible with the decision in *Von Hannover*, which requires a specific public interest in disclosure.

Campbell v MGN [2004] UKHL 22; [2004] 2 AC 457

In this case, the House of Lords had its first opportunity to consider the developments charted above. The claimant, Naomi Campbell, was a renowned model, who had publicly stated that she did not take drugs. This was untrue, and it was common ground that this untruth put factual reporting of her drug addiction into the public domain: there is a public interest, engaging Article 10, in correcting untrue information. The defendant newspaper published articles which not only disclosed her drug addiction, but also detailed her self-help treatment through 'Narcotics Anonymous'. The reports gave details of group meetings and showed photographs of her in the street leaving the meetings.

By a majority (Lords Hope and Carswell and Baroness Hale), the House of Lords awarded modest damages. Lords Nicholls and Hoffmann dissented. The reasons for the narrowness of the majority do not relate to the most general questions about privacy and confidence, and the authoritative statements on these topics can be drawn from all five judgments. Significantly, these confirm the steps taken in *Douglas v Hello!* As we have said, all five judges were agreed that certain elements of the reports—the bare fact of addiction for example—were justified in the public interest. The difference of view was whether any of the remaining details were themselves sufficient to warrant an award of damages, or whether they should be regarded as within the area of journalistic discretion. Although Lord Hoffmann was keen to present this as a mere difference in detail, in fact it may indicate some substantial differences in approach to the important balance between Articles 8 and 10.

The issues must be approached in two stages, reflecting the two criteria for the new action that we outlined above. First, did the information have the necessary quality of privacy? Second, if the claimant's interest in privacy was weighed against the public interest in disclosure (protected by Article 10), where did the balance lie? Importantly, all the judges agreed that there was presumptive equality between these rights, *even* in a case between private individuals. Despite the prohibition on new causes of action, the House of Lords has therefore endorsed the horizontal effect of Convention rights *within* causes of action as explained by Sedley LJ in *Douglas v Hello!*. If anything, it was the two dissenting judges who most clearly endorsed the idea that the action for breach of confidence has been transformed and that it now recognizes privacy as a protected interest.

---

[31] The style of reporting was described as a matter of taste not law, and a question for the PCC and the customers of the newspaper concerned, not for the courts.

Lord Nicholls (dissenting)

13   The common law or, more precisely, courts of equity have long afforded protecti
wrongful use of private information by means of the cause of action which became I
breach of confidence. A breach of confidence was restrained as a form of uncon
conduct, akin to a breach of trust. Today this nomenclature is misleading. The breacl. ―.
dence label harks back to the time when the cause of action was based on improper use of
information disclosed by one person to another in confidence. To attract protection the information had to be of a confidential nature. But the gist of the cause of action was that information of this character had been disclosed by one person to another in circumstances
"importing an obligation of confidence" even though no contract of non-disclosure existed:
see the classic exposition by Megarry J in *Coco v A N Clark (Engineers) Ltd* [1969] RPC 41,
47–48. The confidence referred to in the phrase "breach of confidence" was the confidence
arising out of a confidential relationship.

14   This cause of action has now firmly shaken off the limiting constraint of the need for an
initial confidential relationship. In doing so it has changed its nature. In this country this development was recognised clearly in the judgment of Lord Goff of Chieveley in *Attorney General v
Guardian Newspapers Ltd (No 2)* [1990] 1 AC 109, 281. Now the law imposes a "duty of
confidence" whenever a person receives information he knows or ought to know is fairly and
reasonably to be regarded as confidential. Even this formulation is awkward. The continuing
use of the phrase "duty of confidence" and the description of the information as "confidential" is not altogether comfortable. Information about an individual's private life would not, in
ordinary usage, be called "confidential". The more natural description today is that such
information is private. The essence of the tort is better encapsulated now as misuse of private
information.

15   In the case of individuals this tort, however labelled, affords respect for one aspect of an
individual's privacy. That is the value underlying this cause of action. An individual's privacy can
be invaded in ways not involving publication of information. Strip searches are an example. The
extent to which the common law as developed thus far in this country protects other forms of
invasion of privacy is not a matter arising in the present case. It does not arise because,
although pleaded more widely, Miss Campbell's common law claim was throughout presented in court exclusively on the basis of breach of confidence, that is, the wrongful *publication* by the "Mirror" of private *information*.

. . .

Given that the claimant had put her drug addiction into the public domain (by lying), Lord
Nicholls expressly doubted (at [26]) whether further information about her treatment
retained 'the character of private information'. However, he continued:

. . .

28   . . . I would not wish to found my conclusion solely on this point. I prefer to proceed to the
next stage and consider how the tension between privacy and freedom of expression should
be resolved in this case, on the assumption that the information regarding Miss Campbell's
attendance at Narcotics Anonymous meetings retained its private character. At this stage I
consider Miss Campbell's claim must fail. I can state my reason very shortly. On the one hand,
publication of this information in the unusual circumstances of this case represents, at most,

an intrusion into Miss Campbell's private life to a comparatively minor degree. On the other hand, non-publication of this information would have robbed a legitimate and sympathetic newspaper story of attendant detail which added colour and conviction. This information was published in order to demonstrate Miss Campbell's commitment to tackling her drug problem. The balance ought not to be held at a point which would preclude, in this case, a degree of journalistic latitude in respect of information published for this purpose.

Lord Hoffmann also dissented after outlining the traditional action for breach of confidence, Lord Hoffmann turned his attention to more recent changes:

Lord Hoffmann (dissenting)

50   What human rights law has done is to identify private information as something worth protecting as an aspect of human autonomy and dignity. And this recognition has raised inescapably the question of why it should be worth protecting against the state but not against a private person. There may of course be justifications for the publication of private information by private persons which would not be available to the state–I have particularly in mind the position of the media, to which I shall return in a moment–but I can see no logical ground for saying that a person should have less protection against a private individual than he would have against the state for the publication of personal information for which there is no justification. Nor, it appears, have any of the other judges who have considered the matter.

51   The result of these developments has been a shift in the centre of gravity of the action for breach of confidence when it is used as a remedy for the unjustified publication of personal information. It recognises that the incremental changes to which I have referred do not merely extend the duties arising traditionally from a relationship of trust and confidence to a wider range of people. As Sedley LJ observed in a perceptive passage in his judgment in *Douglas v Hello! Ltd* [2001] QB 967, 1001, the new approach takes a different view of the underlying value which the law protects. Instead of the cause of action being based upon the duty of good faith applicable to confidential personal information and trade secrets alike, it focuses upon the protection of human autonomy and dignity—the right to control the dissemination of information about one's private life and the right to the esteem and respect of other people.

55   I shall first consider the relationship between the freedom of the press and the common law right of the individual to protect personal information. Both reflect important civilised values, but, as often happens, neither can be given effect in full measure without restricting the other. How are they to be reconciled in a particular case? There is in my view no question of automatic priority. Nor is there a presumption in favour of one rather than the other. The question is rather the extent to which it is *necessary* to qualify the one right in order to protect the underlying value which is protected by the other. And the extent of the qualification must be proportionate to the need: see Sedley LJ in *Douglas v Hello! Ltd* [2001] QB 967, 1005, para 137.

61   That brings me to what seems to be the only point of principle which arises in this case. Where the main substance of the story is conceded to have been justified, should the newspaper be held liable whenever the judge considers that it was not necessary to have published some of the personal information? Or should the newspaper be allowed some margin of choice in the way it chooses to present the story?

62   In my opinion, it would be inconsistent with the approach which has been taken by the courts in a number of recent landmark cases for a newspaper to be held strictly liable for

exceeding what a judge considers to have been necessary. The practical exigencies of journalism demand that some latitude must be given. Editorial decisions have to be made quickly and with less information than is available to a court which afterwards reviews the matter at leisure. And if any margin is to be allowed, it seems to me strange to hold the "Mirror" liable in damages for a decision which three experienced judges in the Court of Appeal have held to be perfectly justified.

Lord Hope

95   I think that the judge was right to regard the details of Miss Campbell's attendance at Narcotics Anonymous as private information which imported a duty of confidence. He said that information relating to Miss Campbell's therapy for drug addiction giving details that it was by regular attendance at Narcotics Anonymous meetings was easily identifiable as private. With reference to the guidance that the Court of Appeal gave in *A v B plc* [2003] QB 195, 206, para 11(vii), he said that it was obvious that there existed a private interest in this fact that was worthy of protection. The Court of Appeal, on the other hand, seem to have regarded the receipt of therapy from Narcotics Anonymous as less worthy of protection in comparison with treatment for the condition administered by medical practitioners. I would not make that distinction. . . . The private nature of these meetings encourages addicts to attend them in the belief that they can do so anonymously. The assurance of privacy is an essential part of the exercise. The therapy is at risk of being damaged if the duty of confidence which the participants owe to each other is breached by making details of the therapy, such as where, when and how often it is being undertaken, public. I would hold that these details are obviously private.

Lord Hope went on to consider the question of balance between the rights. Notably, there is broader reference to Convention jurisprudence in his judgment than in the dissenting judgments.

114   In the present case it is convenient to begin by looking at the matter from the standpoint of the respondents' assertion of the article 10 right and the court's duty as a public authority under section 6(1) of the Human Rights Act 1998, which section 12(4) reinforces, not to act in a way which is incompatible with that Convention right.

115   The first question is whether the objective of the restriction on the article 10 right—the protection of Miss Campbell's right under article 8 to respect for her private life—is sufficiently important to justify limiting the fundamental right to freedom of expression which the press assert on behalf of the public. It follows from my conclusion that the details of Miss Campbell's treatment were private that I would answer this question in the affirmative. The second question is whether the means chosen to limit the article 10 right are rational, fair and not arbitrary and impair the right as minimally as is reasonably possible. It is not enough to assert that it would be reasonable to exclude these details from the article. A close examination of the factual justification for the restriction on the freedom of expression is needed if the fundamental right enshrined in article 10 is to remain practical and effective. The restrictions which the court imposes on the article 10 right must be rational, fair and not arbitrary, and they must impair the right no more than is necessary.

116   In my opinion the factors that need to be weighed are, on the one hand, the duty that was recognised in *Jersild v Denmark* 19 EHRR 1, para 31 to impart information and ideas of

public interest which the public has a right to receive, and the need that was recognised in *Fressoz and Roire v France* 31 EHRR 28, para 54 for the court to leave it to journalists to decide what material needs to be reproduced to ensure credibility; and, on the other hand, the degree of privacy to which Miss Campbell was entitled under the law of confidence as to the details of her therapy. Account should therefore be taken of the respondents' wish to put forward a story that was credible and to present Miss Campbell in a way that commended her for her efforts to overcome her addiction.

117 But it should also be recognised that the right of the public to receive information about the details of her treatment was of a much lower order than the undoubted right to know that she was misleading the public when she said that she did not take drugs. In *Dudgeon v United Kingdom* (1981) 4 EHRR 149, para 52 the European court said that the more intimate the aspects of private life which are being interfered with, the more serious must be the reasons for doing so before the interference can be legitimate. *Clayton & Tomlinson, The Law of Human Rights* (2000), para 15.162, point out that the court has distinguished three kinds of expression: political expression, artistic expression and commercial expression, and that it consistently attaches great importance to political expression and applies rather less rigorous principles to expression which is artistic and commercial. According to the court's well-established case law, freedom of expression constitutes one of the essential foundations of a democratic society and one of the basic conditions for its progress and the self-fulfilment of each individual: *Tammer v Estonia* (2001) 37 EHRR 857, para 59. But there were no political or democratic values at stake here, nor has any pressing social need been identified: contrast *Goodwin v United Kingdom* (1996) 22 EHRR 123, para 40.

118 As for the other side of the balance, Keene LJ said in *Douglas v Hello! Ltd* [2001] QB 967, 1012, para 168, that any consideration of article 8 rights must reflect the fact that there are different degrees of privacy. In the present context the potential for disclosure of the information to cause harm is an important factor to be taken into account in the assessment of the extent of the restriction that was needed to protect Miss Campbell's right to privacy.

Baroness Hale

156 . . . The editor accepted that even without the photographs, it would have been a front page story. He had his basic information and he had his quotes. There is no shortage of photographs with which to illustrate and brighten up a story about Naomi Campbell. No doubt some of those available are less flattering than others, so that if he had wanted to run a hostile piece he could have done so. The fact that it was a sympathetic story is neither here nor there. The way in which he chose to present the information he was entitled to reveal was entirely a matter for him. The photographs would have been useful in proving the truth of the story had this been challenged, but there was no need to publish them for this purpose. The credibility of the story with the public would stand or fall with the credibility of "Mirror" stories generally.

157 The weight to be attached to these various considerations is a matter of fact and degree. Not every statement about a person's health will carry the badge of confidentiality or risk doing harm to that person's physical or moral integrity. The privacy interest in the fact that a public figure has a cold or a broken leg is unlikely to be strong enough to justify restricting the press's freedom to report it. What harm could it possibly do? Sometimes there will be other justifications for publishing, especially where the information is relevant to the capacity of a public figure to do the job. But that is not this case and in this case there was, as the judge found, a risk that publication would do harm. The risk of harm is what matters at this stage, rather than the proof that actual harm has occurred. People trying to recover from drug addiction need considerable dedication and commitment, along with constant reinforcement from those around them. That is why organisations like Narcotics Anonymous were set up and why they can do so much good. Blundering in when matters are acknowledged to be at a "fragile" stage may do great harm.

Lord Carswell delivered a separate concurring judgment, agreeing with Baroness Hale.

The 'Ultimate Balance'

The *Campbell* approach to balancing the demands of Articles 8 and 10 has been summarized by Lord Steyn in the case of *Re S* [2005] 1 AC 594, in terms of four propositions:

> 17 ...First, neither article has *as such* precedence over the other. Secondly, where the values under the two articles are in conflict, an intense focus on the comparative importance of the specific rights being claimed in the individual case is necessary. Thirdly, the justifications for interfering with or restricting each right must be taken into account. Finally, the proportionality test must be applied to each. For convenience I will call this the ultimate balancing test.

In terms of its presumption of equality and its focus on the specific facts of individual cases, this approach seems to pass the test of compatibility with the *Von Hannover* decision. But is it appropriate? Or is there something to be said for the dissenting view of Lords Nicholls and Hoffmann, that this requires very fine judgments to be made on matters which—in a society that recognizes press freedom—ought to be left to the editors, not to the judges? On one view, the fine balance struck in this case is properly reflected in the very modest damages (£3,500) that were awarded. On the other hand, in Chapter 13 we noted that the real consequence, in terms of costs of the action, was considerably greater. Indeed, thanks partly to the Conditional Fee Agreement entered into by the claimant in respect of the appeal to the House of Lords, the defendants—who so narrowly lost the case on its merits—were served with a bill for the claimant's costs of around £1 million. In *Campbell v MGN (No 2)* [2005] 1 WLR 3394, the House of Lords judged that this did not constitute a 'disproportionate' restriction on freedom of expression, taking into account the intended purpose (allowing access to justice at the expense of losing defendants, rather than of the public generally). Of course, it is not expected that costs of this order would be replicated in future cases since in principle, the applicable law is now relatively settled. Even so, the fine judgment required by the 'ultimate balance', with 'intense focus' on the particular facts, could certainly act as an invitation to litigation. Indeed it could also lead to self-censorship where 'revelatory' journalism is concerned. Whether or not this possibility is a cause for concern depends very much on whether it is thought that anything of value will be put at risk.

Further Refinements: *Douglas v Hello! (No 3)*

In *Douglas v Hello!* as we have seen, the Court of Appeal refused to grant interlocutory injunctions against publication of the photographs. However, there was a strong expectation that damages would be awarded.

In *Douglas v Hello! (No 3)* [2006] QB 125, the case returned to the Court of Appeal. A number of issues arose. Some of them relate to claims not by the couple themselves, but by OK!

magazine. The arguments of OK! magazine, whose contractual interests were affected by the unauthorized publication of photographs by Hello!, are entirely related to commercial interests and some of the issues (particularly as regards the level of *intention* required) have been discussed in Chapter 2. However, the Court of Appeal provided important clarification on a number of issues relating to the privacy claim. Their conclusions show the rapid change in the law affecting this area.

The judgment of the court was delivered by Lord Phillips MR. We will focus on four issues.

The existence of a privacy interest

92 We should make clear at the outset that the only issue on liability was whether the photographs published by Hello! infringed rights of confidence or privacy enjoyed by the Douglases. As the judge recorded, Hello! did not seek to argue that it was in the public interest that they should publish the unauthorised photographs or that their article 10 rights of freedom of expression outweighed any rights of confidence or privacy that the Douglases enjoyed.

93 The judge found, at para 66:

"To the extent that privacy consists of the inclusion only of the invited and the exclusion of all others, the wedding was as private as was possible consistent with it being a socially pleasant event."

He further found that Mr Thorpe took the unauthorised photographs surreptitiously in circumstances where he was well aware that his presence at the wedding was forbidden. Finally the judge found that those responsible for purchasing the unauthorised photographs on behalf of Hello! were aware that the taking of the photographs would have involved at least a trespass or some deceit or misrepresentation on the photographer's part.

. . .

95 Applying the test propounded by the House of Lords in *Campbell v MGN Ltd* [2004] 2 AC 457, photographs of the wedding plainly portrayed aspects of the Douglases' private life and fell within the protection of the law of confidentiality, as extended to cover private or personal information.

What had, at the time of *Douglas v Hello!*, been a complex question of law—was there a privacy interest in the photographs at all?—had now become straightforward. There certainly was such an interest.

Balancing and the award of an injunction

It will be plain from paragraph [92] of Lord Phillips' judgment (above) that following the decision in *Von Hannover*, and provided the required element of privacy is established, it will now be appropriate to weigh an interest in freedom of expression against the privacy interest of the claimant *only if there is a positive public interest reason supporting disclosure*. The general public interest in press freedom or absence of censorship will not be enough (or, to put it another way, there is no such general public interest).[32] Therefore in this case, nothing at all

---

[32] In *Von Hannover*, for example, the European Court of Human Rights rejected the view of the German Federal Constitutional Court that there was a light-weight but potentially useful category of journalism which could be called 'infotainment'.

seems to have gone into the balance on the side of Article 10. This approach is inspired by *Von Hannover* and marks a significant change from the judgment of Sedley LJ in *Douglas v Hello!*, which was dominated by questions of balance. Indeed, without such questions of balance, there would have been no discussion of section 12, and therefore no horizontal effect for the Article 8 privacy right in the first place!

The discharge of the interlocutory injunction

251 We turn to an issue upon which we were not addressed, but which we believe justifies revisiting. It is the decision of this court in November 2000 [2001] QB 967 to lift the interlocutory injunction granted by Hunt J, restraining Hello! from publishing the unauthorised photographs. In our view, in the light of the law as it can now be seen to be, that decision was wrong, and the interlocutory injunction should in fact have been upheld.

252 The reasons given by the three members of this court for concluding that an interlocutory injunction was inappropriate were slightly different. Brooke LJ considered that it was no more than arguable that the Douglases "had a right to privacy which English law would recognise", and that their claim based on privacy was "not a particularly strong one" (paras 60 and 95). Although Sedley LJ thought that the Douglases had "a powerful prima facie claim to redress for invasion of their privacy", he considered that "by far the greater part of that privacy has already been traded and falls to be protected, if at all, as a commodity in the hands of [OK!]": paras 137 and 144. Keene LJ, at para 171, was primarily influenced by the point that the "court in exercising its discretion at this interlocutory stage must still take account of the widespread publicity arranged by the [Douglases] for this occasion".

253 In our view, these analyses, and indeed the decision to discharge the injunction, did not give sufficient weight to . . . the strength of the Douglases' claim for an injunction restraining publication of the unauthorised photographs. Although Sedley LJ took the view that they had a strong case in this connection, it would appear that Brooke and Keene LJJ were more doubtful. The Court of Appeal did not have the benefit of the reasoning in the House of Lords in *Campbell v MGN Ltd* [2004] 2 AC 457 or, even more significantly for present purposes, the reasoning of the European Court of Human Rights in *Von Hannover v Germany* 40 EHRR 1. Had the court had the opportunity to consider those two decisions, we believe that it would have reached the conclusion that the Douglases appeared to have a virtually unanswerable case for contending that publication of the unauthorised photographs would infringe their privacy.

254 Of course, even where a claimant has a very strong case indeed for contending that publication of information would infringe his privacy, there may be good reasons for refusing an interlocutory injunction. In the present case, however, we find it difficult to see how it could be contended that the public interest (as opposed to public curiosity) could be involved over and above the general public interest in a free press. Particularly so, as it was clearly the intention of the Douglases and OK! to publish a large number of (much clearer) photographs of the same event. The fact that the Douglases can be fairly said to have "traded" their privacy to a substantial extent as a result of their contract with OK! does not undermine the point that publication of the unauthorised photographs would infringe their privacy.

Tort or no tort?

Although the photographs were published in the UK, the wedding itself took place in New York. This raised the question of whether English law ought to apply to the dispute, or not.

96 It was not suggested that section 9(1) of the Private International Law (Miscellaneous Provisions) Act 1995 is applicable to this case, but we have none the less considered that question. That section governs the choice of law for determining issues relating to tort. The Douglases' claim in relation to invasion of their privacy might seem most appropriately to fall within the ambit of the law of delict. We have concluded, however, albeit not without hesitation, that the effect of shoehorning this type of claim into the cause of action of breach of confidence means that it does not fall to be treated as a tort under English law: see *Kitechnology BV v Unicor GmbH Plastmaschinen* [1995] FSR 795, para 40 and more generally *Clerk & Lindsell on Torts*, 18th ed (2000), para 27–01, footnotes 2 and 3. Nor has anyone suggested that the facts of this case give rise to a cause of action in tort under the law of New York (see below). Accordingly we have concluded that the parties were correct to have no regard to section 9(1) of the 1995 Act.

A claim in confidence by OK! magazine?

The Court of Appeal also decided that a claim in confidence by OK! magazine, on the basis that the publication breached a duty of confidence owed to them, could not succeed. It was inconsistent with the couple's claim that they had a retained right of privacy in the photos.

136 We have recognised that the Douglases retained a residual right of privacy, or confidentiality, in those details of their wedding which were not portrayed by those of the official photographs which they released. It was in the interests of OK! that the Douglases should protect that right, so that OK! would be in a position to publish, or to authorise the publication of, the only photographs that the public would be able to see of the wedding. On analysis, OK!'s complaint is not that Hello! published images which they had been given the exclusive right to publish, but that Hello! published other images, which no one with knowledge of their confidentiality had any right to publish. The claimants themselves argued that "the unauthorised photographs were taken at different moments to the authorised ones, showed different and informal incidents at the reception, and were naturally much less posed". These photographs invaded the area of privacy which the Douglases had chosen to retain. It was the Douglases, not OK!, who had the right to protect this area of privacy or confidentiality. Clause 10 of the OK! contract expressly provided that any rights not expressly granted to OK! were retained by the Douglases. The claim successfully advanced by the Douglases in this litigation is at odds with OK!'s claim.

The Continuing Influence of *Douglas* and *Campbell*

Despite general agreement that Article 8 does not *create new rights of action*, one effect of *Douglas v Hello!* and its approval in *Campbell v MGN* is that certain areas of law are now entirely recast in terms of these Articles. The House of Lords' judgment in *Re S* [2005] 1 AC 594 is a particularly clear example.

We have already extracted Lord Steyn's authoritative restatement in this case of the balancing process mandated by *Campbell* where different Convention rights have to be weighed against one another. Equally importantly, he explained that the source of the High Court's jurisdiction to restrain publicity in criminal trials was no longer the 'inherent jurisdiction' which had always existed. Instead, this jurisdiction was now to be regarded as founded *directly* upon relevant Convention rights:

23 The House unanimously takes the view that since the 1998 Act came into force in October 2000, the earlier case law about the existence and scope of inherent jurisdiction need not be considered in this case or in similar cases. The foundation of the jurisdiction to restrain publicity in a case such as the present is now derived from Convention rights under the ECHR. This is the simple and direct way to approach such cases.

The 'ultimate balance' is governed by the approach of the House of Lords in *Campbell*. But ultimately, this reorientation in English law has been inspired by Sedley LJ's interpretation of section 12(4) of the Human Rights Act 1998 in *Douglas v Hello!*.[33]

4.2 INTRUSION

Not all invasions of privacy involve *publication*, whether of photographs or of information. While breach of confidence has not previously been recognized as a tort, there are certain other actions which clearly are torts and may serve in the protection of privacy. These include trespass (Chapters 2 and 16), nuisance (Chapter 10), and the action in *Wilkinson v Downton* (Chapter 2).

The judgment of the House of Lords in *Wainwright v Home Office* [2004] 2 AC 406 is a major obstacle to development of a general tort capable of dealing with 'intrusion'. In this case, the claimants had been subjected to a humiliating strip search on a visit to prison. This search was found to have been in contravention of the applicable Prison Rules; however, there was no finding of any particular intent to humiliate the claimants, nor even to breach the rules. The searches were aimed at identifying whether visitors were carrying drugs.

The case was decided after the decision of the Court of Appeal in *Douglas v Hello!*, but before the decision of the House of Lords in *Campbell* and (notably) before the Court of Human Rights' decision in *Von Hannover*. Lord Hoffmann considered the judgment of Sedley LJ in *Douglas v Hello!*, and made very clear that it should not be read in too general a fashion:

30   I do not understand Sedley LJ to have been advocating the creation of a high-level principle of invasion of privacy. His observations are in my opinion no more (although certainly no less) than a plea for the extension and possibly renaming of the old action for breach of confidence. As Buxton LJ pointed out in this case in the Court of Appeal [2002] QB 1334, 1361–1362, paras 96–99, such an extension would go further than any English court has yet gone and would be contrary to some cases (such as *Kaye v Robertson* [1991] FSR 62) in which it positively declined to do so. The question must wait for another day. But Sedley LJ's dictum does not support a principle of privacy so abstract as to include the circumstances of the present case.

31   There seems to me a great difference between identifying privacy as a value which underlies the existence of a rule of law (and may point the direction in which the law should develop) and privacy as a principle of law in itself. The English common law is familiar with the notion of underlying values—principles only in the broadest sense—which direct its development. A famous example is *Derbyshire County Council v Times Newspapers Ltd* [1993] AC 534, in which freedom of speech was the underlying value which supported the decision to lay down the specific rule that a local authority could not sue for libel. But no one has suggested that freedom of speech is in itself a legal principle which is capable of sufficient definition to enable one to deduce specific rules to be applied in concrete cases. That is not the way the common law works.

---

[33] For useful comment on the issues raised by *Re S*, written before the House of Lords' judgment, see H. Fenwick, 'Clashing Rights, the Welfare of the Child and the Human Rights Act' (2004) 67 MLR 889.

32 Nor is there anything in the jurisprudence of the European Court of Human Rights which suggests that the adoption of some high level principle of privacy is necessary to comply with article 8 of the Convention. The European Court is concerned only with whether English law provides an adequate remedy in a specific case in which it considers that there has been an invasion of privacy contrary to article 8(1) and not justifiable under article 8(2). So in *Earl Spencer v United Kingdom* 25 EHRR CD 105 it was satisfied that the action for breach of confidence provided an adequate remedy for the Spencers' complaint and looked no further into the rest of the armoury of remedies available to the victims of other invasions of privacy. Likewise, in *Peck v United Kingdom* (2003) 36 EHRR 719 the court expressed some impatience, at paragraph 103, at being given a tour d'horizon of the remedies provided and to be provided by English law to deal with every imaginable kind of invasion of privacy. It was concerned with whether Mr Peck (who had been filmed in embarrassing circumstances by a CCTV camera) had an adequate remedy when the film was widely published by the media. It came to the conclusion that he did not.

33 Counsel for the Wainwrights relied upon *Peck's* case as demonstrating the need for a general tort of invasion of privacy. But in my opinion it shows no more than the need, in English law, for a system of control of the use of film from CCTV cameras which shows greater sensitivity to the feelings of people who happen to have been caught by the lens. For the reasons so cogently explained by Sir Robert Megarry V-C in *Malone v Metropolitan Police Comr* [1979] Ch 344, this is an area which requires a detailed approach which can be achieved only by legislation rather than the broad brush of common law principle.

34 Furthermore, the coming into force of the Human Rights Act 1998 weakens the argument for saying that a general tort of invasion of privacy is needed to fill gaps in the existing remedies. Sections 6 and 7 of the Act are in themselves substantial gap fillers; if it is indeed the case that a person's rights under article 8 have been infringed by a public authority, he will have a statutory remedy. The creation of a general tort will, as Buxton LJ pointed out in the Court of Appeal [2002] QB 1334, 1360, para 92, pre-empt the controversial question of the extent, if any, to which the Convention requires the state to provide remedies for invasions of privacy by persons who are not public authorities.

35 For these reasons I would reject the invitation to declare that since at the latest 1950 there has been a previously unknown tort of invasion of privacy.

Certain aspects of this judgment now (already) appear quite dated. For example, if Lord Hoffmann was implying in para [30] that he did not agree with Sedley LJ's extension of the law of confidentiality to deal with private information, then he appears to have changed his mind by the time of *Campbell*. And arguably, para [34], refers to an argument over horizontal effect which has now, at least to some extent, been won. However, none of the substantive developments discussed so far have altered the strength of Lord Hoffmann's general point, that a 'high level principle of privacy' is not directly enforceable by means of a general tort. Lord Hoffmann prefers that areas of privacy should be subject to *statutory* change, so that specific rules may be set out.[34]

Having rejected the claimant's argument that English law could recognize an invasion of privacy as tortious, Lord Hoffmann also declined to extend the action in *Wilkinson v Downton* to protect against 'mere anxiety', at least in the absence of very strong evidence of

[34] For the contrary argument, that English law should recognize a general tort of invasion of privacy, see J. Morgan, 'Privacy, Confidence, and Direct Effect: "Hello" Trouble' (2003) 62 CLJ 444–73.

intention. In *Wilkinson v Downton* [1897] 2 QB 57, as we explained in Chapter 2, Wright J held that there was a cause of action where the defendant 'wilfully' caused harm to the plaintiff through a practical joke. *Wilkinson v Downton* was a case of 'intentional' infliction of personal injury, whether physical or psychiatric. It was not a case of compensation for 'anxiety and distress'.

Lord Hoffmann

45 If . . . one is going to draw a principled distinction which justifies abandoning the rule that damages for mere distress are not recoverable, imputed intention will not do. The defendant must actually have acted in a way which he knew to be unjustifiable and either intended to cause harm or at least acted without caring whether he caused harm or not. Lord Woolf CJ, as I read his judgment [2002] QB 1334, 1350, paras 50–51, might have been inclined to accept such a principle. But the facts did not support a claim on this basis. The judge made no finding that the prison officers intended to cause distress or realised that they were acting without justification in asking the Wainwrights to strip. He said, at paragraph 83, that they had acted in good faith and, at paragraph 121, that: "The deviations from the procedure laid down for strip-searches were, in my judgment, not intended to increase the humiliation necessarily involved but merely sloppiness."

. . .

47 In my opinion, therefore, the claimants can build nothing on *Wilkinson v Downton* [1897] 2 QB 57. It does not provide a remedy for distress which does not amount to recognised psychiatric injury and so far as there may be a tort of intention under which such damage is recoverable, the necessary intention was not established. . . .

We have already discussed the implications of this for torts of intention in Chapter 2, and we will therefore make our comments brief. In terms of the traditional categorization of protected interests, the suffering caused by invasion of privacy could very often be categorized as 'mere anxiety or distress'. If the protection of private information could be 'shoe-horned into' the action for breach of confidence—where it is not an entirely comfortable fit—why can the action in *Wilkinson v Downton* not also be adapted to protect against the kind of anxiety caused by invasions of privacy?

The reason may lie in the inherent mechanism which, fortuitously, the action for breach of confidence provides for balancing competing public interests. No such mechanism exists in those torts which are involved broadly with infliction of harm, such as *Wilkinson v Downton*.[35] Even in the tort of private nuisance, which as we have seen (Chapter 10) is familiar with questions of 'balance', *public* interest questions have not easily found a role. Lord Hoffmann draws attention here to the traditional combination of damage, and relevant conduct, which makes up the part of the tort recipe book that includes both *Wilkinson v Downton*, and the tort of negligence (though *not* trespass to the person). Trying to recast 'privacy' in terms of actual damage suffered will tend to give it a lowly status, since the harm suffered frequently is akin to 'anxiety and distress', and this is accorded a lower status than physical injury or psychiatric

---

[35] This is a reason for supporting the suggestion of Moreham (2005) 121 LQR 628, that privacy is best protected by extending the present action for 'breach of confidence' beyond the confines of release of information, to all those cases where there is a 'reasonable expectation of privacy'. This would be modelled on the equitable action for breach of confidence, not on torts of damage such as *Wilkinson*.

harm. Lord Hoffmann suggests that this kind of damage should be actionable only in the presence of strongly intentional conduct.[36]

Lord Hoffmann went on to explain that even if section 8 of the Human Rights Act had been in force at the time of the strip search in question, it should not necessarily be assumed that damages would have been available in this case. Retaining the traditional tort law perspective, he felt that here too, intention might be relevant:

> **51** Article 8 is more difficult. Buxton LJ thought [2002] QB 1334, 1352, para 62, that the Wainwrights would have had a strong case for relief under section 7 if the 1998 Act had been in force. Speaking for myself, I am not so sure. Although article 8 guarantees a right of privacy, I do not think that it treats that right as having been invaded and requiring a remedy in damages, irrespective of whether the defendant acted intentionally, negligently or accidentally. It is one thing to wander carelessly into the wrong hotel bedroom and another to hide in the wardrobe to take photographs. Article 8 may justify a monetary remedy for an intentional invasion of privacy by a public authority, even if no damage is suffered other than distress for which damages are not ordinarily recoverable. It does not follow that a merely negligent act should, contrary to general principle, give rise to a claim for damages for distress because it affects privacy rather than some other interest like bodily safety: compare *Hicks v Chief Constable of South Yorkshire Police* [1992] 2 All ER 65.

In the course of his judgment in *Wainwright*, Lord Hoffmann made the point that certain gaps in the law had been filled by the introduction of a statutory tort under the Protection from Harassment Act 1997. Whereas *Wainwright* starkly illustrates that 'anxiety' is not generally sufficient damage for an action in tort (unless there is strong *intention* perhaps), anxiety clearly can be the subject of damages under the Protection from Harassment Act, provided the conduct comes within the Act. In particular, the Act does not offer damages in respect of an *isolated* invasion of privacy (or as Lord Hoffmann put it a 'single boorish incident'); there must be a 'course of conduct'.

Protection from Harassment Act 1997

The text of this statute is extracted in Chapter 2.6

Although the Protection from Harassment Act does not use the word 'privacy', it clearly offers protection against some forms of 'intrusion'. Further, 'damage' is not a prerequisite of remedies under the Act. In certain recent cases, under the influence of the Human Rights Act, privacy has been identified as the relevant protected interest in certain cases of harassment.

Recent applications of this statute further illustrate the impact of the Human Rights Act in creating direct effect for relevant Convention rights, in this case affecting the interpretation of statute in accordance with section 3 of the Human Rights Act 1998. As a corollary, it has been recognized that the balance between Article 8 rights, and other Convention rights including sometimes freedom of expression,[37] must be considered when applying the statute. Further,

---

[36] For an analysis of protected interests which understands the traditional hierarchy to be 'gendered' (undervaluing those harms typically experienced by women), see J. Conaghan, 'Gendered Harms and the Law of Tort: Remedying (Sexual) Harassment' (1996) 16 OJLS 407.

[37] In *Thomas v News Group Newspapers* [2001] EWCA Civ 1233, the Court of Appeal decided that newspaper publications could in exceptional circumstances satisfy the definition of 'harassment' in the 1997 Act. Where this is the case, compatibility with Article 10 must be considered. In *Thomas* itself the articles in question were found to incite racial hatred, and thus were not protected by Article 10 since such speech is contrary to the underlying values of the Convention. The Court of Appeal did not consider Article 8 in this case.

the justifications for harassing conduct which appear in section 1(3) must be considered in terms of the permitted restrictions on the Article 8 right.

In the extraordinary case of *Howlett v Holding* (2006) EWHC 41 (QB), the defendant was angry that the claimant had opposed his planning application. He flew a light aircraft repeatedly over the claimant's home displaying banners alleging that she was a benefit fraud.[38] This campaign of 'aerial harassment' continued intermittently for four to five years. The claimant now sought an injunction under the Protection from Harassment Act 1997.

Eady J concluded that the defendant's Article 10 rights, and the claimant's Article 8 rights, were obviously engaged. He identified the objectionable element in the course of conduct pursued by the defendant as:

> 5   . . . the impact it has had, and is likely to continue to have, on Mrs Howlett's privacy and psychological well-being.

Because Eady J was able to conclude that this was the 'true nature' of her complaint, he brushed aside the defendant's suggestion that she was turning to the Act in order to avoid the general rule in *Bonnard v Perryman* against injunctive relief in libel claims (discussed in Chapter 13). The defendant had actually admitted that his aim was to make the claimant's life 'a living hell'. In considering the award of an injunction, Eady J derived the appropriate balancing test from *Re S* [2005] 1 AC 593 (above). It was clear that in the circumstances of the case the balance favoured an injunction. Eady J rejected an argument on the part of the defendant that his banners were calling attention to wrongdoing and that they were therefore justified within section 1(3)(a) of the 1997 Act, as being pursued 'for the purpose of preventing or detecting crime'. It is notable that in rebutting this argument, Eady J turned directly to the terms of Article 8, noting that only such interference as was *necessary* was to be permitted. There is no such qualification in section 1(3)(a) itself. As Eady J put it:

> 32   . . . it is not necessary to permit *anyone* to harass his fellow citizens by surveillance. It may well be necessary to leave room for security or law enforcement agencies to have such power in appropriate circumstances, but that is a different matter.

In drawing directly on Article 8, Eady J was influenced by the case of *KD v Chief Constable of Hampshire* [2005] EWHC 2550, in which a police officer had visited a woman on a series of occasions and asked her intimate questions concerning her sexual habits. These were entirely unnecessary for the pursuit of any criminal investigation. The defendant argued that his questions were protected by section 1(3)(a). Tugendhat J considered that:

> 144   . . . in relation to events occurring after the coming into force of the Human Rights Act the courts would be bound to interpret s.1(3)(a) as being subject to the tests of necessity and proportionality.

As such, the questions could not be protected by section 1(3)(a). *KD* was a 'vertical' case in that it was brought by an individual against a public authority. But in *Howlett*, the same interpretive

---

38 The claimant had twice sued the defendant in defamation.

technique was adopted in a case between individual citizens. This is a further illustration that although no general tort of invasion of privacy exists, the recognition of privacy as the true protected interest in a range of existing actions—at least in some cases—will be of more than academic interest. It introduces elements of Convention jurisprudence into existing causes of action, and clearly introduces a qualified form of 'horizontal effect'. It is also clear that the 'ultimate balance' test outlined by Lord Steyn in *Re S* and derived from *Campbell v MGN* and before that *Douglas v Hello!*, is now an established part of English law. Its potential influence is not confined to actions for breach of confidence.

FURTHER READING

Colvin, M., *Developing Key Privacy Rights* (Oxford: Hart Publishing, 2002).

Feldman, D., 'Secrecy, Dignity, or Autonomy? Views of Privacy as a Civil Liberty' (1994) 47 CLP 41.

Feldman, D., 'The Developing Scope of Article 8 of the European Convention on Human Rights' [1997] EHRLR 265–74.

Fenwick, H., and Phillipson, G., 'The Doctrine of Confidence as a Privacy Remedy in the Human Rights Act Era' (2000) 63 MLR 663–93.

Markesinis, B., 'Our Patchy Law of Privacy: Time to do Something About It' (1990) 53 MLR 802.

Markesinis, B. (ed), *Protecting Privacy* (Oxford: Clarendon Press, 1998).

Moreham, N.A., 'Privacy in the Common Law: A Doctrinal and Theoretical Analysis' (2005) 121 LQR 628–56.

Morgan, J., 'Privacy, Confidence, and Direct Effect: "Hello" Trouble' (2003) 62 CLJ 44–73.

Mulheron, R., 'A Potential Framework for Privacy? A Reply to Hello!' (2006) 69 MLR 679–713.

Phillipson, G., 'Judicial Reasoning in Breach of Confidence Cases Under the Human Rights Act: Nor Taking Privacy Seriously?' [2003] EHRLR (Supp) 53–72.

Phillipson, G., 'Transforming Breach of Confidence?: Towards a Common Law Right of Privacy Under the Human Rights Act' (2003) 66 MLR 726–58.

Sanderson, M.A., 'Is *Von Hannover v Germany* a step backwards for the substantive analysis of speech and privacy interests?' [2004] EHRLR 631–44.

Toulson, R. G. and Phipps, C. M., *Confidentiality* (2nd edn, London: Sweet & Maxwell, 2006).

Wacks, R., 'The Poverty of Privacy' (1980) 96 LQR 73.

Warbrick, C., 'The Structure of Article 8' [1998] EHRLR 32–44.

Wilson, W, 'Privacy, Confidence and Press Freedom: A Study in Judicial Activism' (1990) 53 MLR 43.

PART VII

MISCELLANEOUS LIABILITIES

15

PRODUCT LIABILITY

CENTRAL ISSUES

i) Part I of the Consumer Protection Act 1987 introduces a form of strict liability for harm done by defective products. The statute gives effect to an EEC Directive, and it bears the marks of political compromise. The central justification of the Directive is thought to be that it apportions risks associated with products between consumers, and producers. It is one element in a broader European regime of product safety.

ii) The key requirement of liability under the Consumer Protection Act 1987 and under the Directive is that harm must be caused by a 'defect' in the product; and a producer of goods may be exonerated if the state of knowledge at the time did not make it possible for the defect to be discovered. It was argued from the inception of the Directive that these key features would make the statutory liability little different from negligence; but the case law to date suggests that the statutory liability is in some respects easier to establish than liability in negligence.

1. DEFECTIVE PRODUCTS AND THE STANDARD OF LIABILITY

The unified tort of negligence emerged in a case of product liability. In *Donoghue v Stevenson*, the plaintiff claimed that she had consumed part of a bottle of ginger beer; that a decaying snail floated out of the bottle; and that she suffered personal injury in the form of gastroenteritis, and 'shock'. The basis of her claim in tort was that the snail was present through the *negligence* of the manufacturer; and that this negligence led to consequential harm in the form of personal injury.

The key significance of *Donoghue* was that it recognized a general legal relationship that is separate from contract. This legal relationship was marked by proximity or 'neighbourhood' between the defendant (whose alleged negligence created the risk of harm), and the plaintiff (who as ultimate consumer of the product was exposed to that risk). According to Lord Atkin, this relationship gave rise to a duty to take reasonable steps to protect the consumer from harm. The duty owed by the manufacturer to the consumer (provided that consumer is relevantly 'proximate' within the terms of the neighbour principle) is a duty *to take care*; and liability is restricted to *consequential harm*.

The Consumer Protection Act 1987 creates *additional* liability on the part of manufacturers where damage is caused by a defect in a product.[1] Like the action in negligence, liability under this Act only extends to *consequential damage* (in the form of damage to property or personal injury). There is no liability under the Act for damages assessed by reference to the purchase price or value of the product, or for damage done to the product itself. Unlike negligence, damage to what may be broadly called 'commercial' property is not covered under the Act (s 2(3)). It is 'consumer protection' legislation. On the other hand, personal injury is covered by the Act in all contexts.

Liability under the Consumer Protection Act 1987 is defined without reference to fault. The statute was intended to give effect to EEC Directive 85/374/ EEC, on the approximation of the laws, regulations, and administrative provisions of the member states concerning liability for defective products (the 'Directive on Product Liability').[2] The Preamble to this Directive explicitly states that the relevant liability is 'without fault'. Accordingly, there is no need to show lack of care—or other wrongful conduct—on the part of the manufacturer.

But the statute does not create liability for all injuries caused by products. Liability under the Act requires that injury or damage is caused by **a defect in a product**. By section 3(1) of the Act, a 'defect' is defined in terms of the legitimate expectations of 'persons in general'. The key distinction between liability based on fault at common law, and 'strict' liability under the Consumer Protection Act 1987 lies in the difference between **showing negligence**—for example in the design, manufacture or marketing of the product (the position at common law); and **showing defectiveness in the product** (the position under the Consumer Protection Act 1987). It has been argued that this distinction may prove to be very fine or even insignificant; but the (relatively sparse) case law indicates that there is a distinction in effect nonetheless.[3]

Importantly, a controversial defence (**the development risks defence**) was included in both the Directive (where it was said to be at the discretion of member states) and the Consumer Protection Act 1987. The effect of this defence is to further narrow the distinction between common law, and statutory product liability. Broadly speaking, the impact of the defence is that the consumer takes the risk of defects which could not have been discovered at the time of manufacture, because scientific knowledge at the time did not permit the relevant risk to be known.[4] The exact breadth and meaning of this defence is very important to the nature of the liability introduced by the Consumer Protection Act 1987, and we will give it fuller consideration in due course.

---

[1] It is additional because other potential actions against the producer, including the action in negligence, are expressly preserved by s 2(6).

[2] There had already been discussion in the UK concerning strict liability for products, prompted largely by the failure of tort law to compensate the victims of 'Thalidomide'. This was a drug prescribed during the 1960s to pregnant women in order to combat morning sickness, but which led to significant birth defects. In the UK, the issue of strict liability for defective products was for a time treated as part of a wider debate over compensation for disability and disease. As such, the Directive (and the Consumer Protection Act 1987) have been criticized as introducing a mere sectoral solution to the problem of compensation. It is restricted to products, and even then only to defective ones: see J. Stapleton, *Product Liability* (Butterworths, 1994) and J. Stapleton, 'Product Liability Reform—Real or Illusory?' (1986) 6 OJLS 392–422.

[3] See in particular our discussion of *A v National Blood Authority* [2001] 3 All ER 289, below.

[4] Defects which could not be discovered for reasons unconnected with lack of knowledge (for example, because there is no known *method for detection*) are not within the defence.

1.1 FROM NEGLIGENCE TO DEFECTIVENESS: ALLOCATION OF RISKS

The Directive on Product Liability is expressly concerned with the apportionment of risks associated with products. The Directive was the subject of extended political negotiation between member states, and the apportionment of risks it incorporates is in effect a compromise. Broadly, producers take the risks of defectiveness, whether these risks are produced by lack of care or not; while consumers take the risks associated with non-defective products (subject of course to liability in contract and in tort).

The effect of the development risks defence (briefly explained above) is to introduce a major qualification to this basic apportionment. In the case of a defect which in the relevant sense could not have been discovered by the manufacturer (an undiscoverable defect), the risk will not lie on the manufacturer.

The development risks defence has the potential, depending on its interpretation, to undermine the strictness of the product liability regime.[5] Most recently, the EC Commission has justified the defence as protecting socially desirable *innovation*:

Commission of the European Communities, *Third Report on the application of Council Directive 85/374/EEC* (the 'Product Liability Directive') 14 September 2006

The DRC[6] was defined in order to establish a satisfactory compromise between the need to stimulate innovation on the one hand and consumers' legitimate expectations for safer products on the other. The crucial argument of the current debate on the DRC is that removing the clause would stifle innovation.

The findings presented in this report[7] seem to indicate that the often-used argument of the Development Risk Clause being a significant factor in achieving the Directive's balance between the need to preserve incentives to innovation and consumer's interests is well-founded and is based on the following:

- the DRC protects incentives to innovate in reducing the innovation-related risks, by not diverting resources from R & D to insurance policies and by pushing firms to align to state of the art knowledge;

- the DRC is probably one key factor in determining the relative stability of product liability costs in European industry and keeping litigation at a reasonable level;

- in a strict liability regime, companies in high-tech/ high risk sectors would find it very difficult to obtain a reasonable insurance policy which covers their developmental risks.

The combination of these factors lead Fondazione Rosselli to conclude that the costs of letting the producers innovate within a strict liability environment would be extremely high, and would affect consumers in the long term. In effect, both the Lovells and the Rosselli studies conclude that such a defence should be maintained.

---

  5 See the articles extracted and referred to in our analysis of the statutory provisions, below.

  6 The 'Development Risk Clause' (the clause of the Directive that sets out the development risk defence: Directive on Product Liability, Art 7(e)).

  7 The Fondazione Roselli Report (published in 2004), carried out for the European Commission.

From this passage, it follows that companies in 'high tech/high risk sectors' effectively *do not* operate in a 'strict liability regime' under the Directive (see the third bullet point in the extract above). This is the impact of the development risks defence. We give fuller consideration to this state of affairs when we consider Defences, below.

2. THE BROADER CONTEXT: THE LIMITED IMPACT OF THE CONSUMER PROTECTION ACT 1987

Analysis of statutory strict liability for harm done by products is of course very instructive from the point of view of the general law of tort. There are interesting parallels between the statutory liability, and common law liabilities based on negligence and on strict liability. But in some respects, a focus on the terms of the Consumer Protection Act 1987 is misleading. There are two broad reasons for saying this.

2.1 CLOSENESS TO NEGLIGENCE

First, there are relatively few successful product liability claims under the Act which would not also succeed at common law. Indeed, there still appear to be more books and articles written about the statute than there are successful claims under it.[8] Of course, this is partly because of the definition of 'defect' and the inclusion of a number of significant defences, including the important 'development risks defence', which we have already noted and which will be explored in the following section. But there are other significant reasons too, which have received less emphasis.

Causation

Whether an action in respect of harm caused by a product is brought at common law or under statute, and whatever the standard of liability, the claimant must show that the injury suffered was caused by the defect (under statute) or the negligence (at common law). Either way, proving causation will be far from straightforward in many cases where the mechanics of cause and effect are disputed and (particularly) where the major evidence is epidemiological. Among such cases are many pharmaceutical claims.

In an action for product liability at common law or under statute the claimant (or claimants) must show not only that the injury was caused by negligence or a defect; *but also* that the particular product causing the harm was manufactured by the defendant, and not by some other manufacturer. We saw the impact of some such problems—and the ways in which common law moves to some extent to accommodate them—in Chapter 4.

The issue of causation is sometimes linked to problems relating to 'defectiveness'. In *XYZ v Schering* [2002] EWHC 1420, a number of women brought actions against the manufacturers of 'third-generation' combined oral contraceptives. The claimants argued that these products were 'defective' within the terms of the Consumer Protection Act 1987, and that the defects in question had caused them to suffer cardio-vascular injuries such as deep vein thrombosis and pulmonary embolism. The claims failed. Mackay J held that the claimants had not established

---

[8] At least in the UK: the Directive is harmonizing legislation and there is also European case law to draw upon. For a collection of European perspectives see D. Fairgrieve (ed.), *Product Liability in Comparative Perspective* (CUP, 2005).

on the balance of probabilities that the contraceptives had increased their risk of sustaining these injuries, when compared with the risks associated with the previous generation of combined oral contraceptives. Only the *excess* risk associated with the new product would be unknown to the women, who were otherwise treated as making an informed choice to use this method of contraception (combined oral contraceptives). As such, the products were not 'defective': the available evidence could not be said to establish that the risk of injury was enhanced by the defect. The same evidence would have been relevant to proof of causation, had the claims not failed at this initial hurdle.

Funding and Access to Justice

Liability rules will only have an impact if potential claimants have access to justice. On the other hand, in a regime of conditional fees, as we explained in Chapter 8, it is possible for speculative claims to be initiated.

Chris Hodges, 'Approaches to Product Liability in the EU and Member States', in Fairgrieve (ed.), *Product Liability in Comparative Perspective* (Cambridge: CUP, 2005), at 196

Funding and financial risk

This is in many ways the most important area in the practice of product liability. The issue of whether a claimant, or a claimant's lawyer, can afford to litigate a particular claim is of fundamental practical importance. National law and practice governs here, as yet unharmonised by Community measures, and there are many differences in the national rules. The approaches range from the tariff on legal fees in Germany and Austria to an absence of regulation in some other States. . . . The area is highly complex and political. The Commission's Directive on legal aid is preliminary in scope but potentially far-reaching in effect: it requires Member States to provide effective access to justice and representation, whether by funding of lawyers (how much and on what basis is unspecified) or through some form of contingency mechanism. Scotland has long had a contingency system but it is little used. England and Wales largely replaced a legal aid regime with a privatised conditional fee scheme in 1999: significantly, the uplift on standard fees is regulated and capped: this has lowered the incidence of product liability multi-party claims, and there has been debate over whether this denies access to justice or acts as a filter for unjustified cases that waste costs. Member states have noted the conflict of interest issues that can arise with contingency systems: the UK protests that this is not an issue in practice.

The importance of funding is illustrated by the case of *Paul Sayers and Others v SmithKline Beecham plc & Others* [2004] EWHC 1899 (QB) (the 'MMR/MR Vaccine Litigation'). Actions were brought on behalf of a number of claimants, who suffered from autism and whose families blamed that condition on vaccines manufactured by the defendants. It was clear that there would be significant difficulties in proving causation,[9] and the Legal Services Commission withdrew funding from the action. The claimants were therefore exposed to an

---

[9] Numerous studies have been conducted and none have shown a connection between the MMR/MR vaccines and autism.

order of costs against them, should they lose, and their actions were discontinued. This case also illustrates the point made by Hodges (above), that opinion may be divided whether the withdrawal of funding is beneficial (on which view the claim was bound to fail for lack of evidence of causation); or deprived the claimants of an important opportunity of attempting to prove causation on the balance of probabilities.

2.2 REGULATION OF PRODUCT SAFETY

The second general reason why it is misleading to consider 'product liability' in isolation is that the Directive is only one element in a European strategy for increasing product safety. Indeed in 2005, the UK responded to revisions in the EC Directive on General Product Safety with the General Product Safety Regulations 2005, incorporating new powers of recall on the part of regulators, and duties of notification on the part of producers.[10] To the extent that product liability is intended to achieve a measure of deterrence, it therefore overlaps with a developing regulatory regime.

Addressing this topic in the context of the law of tort takes product liability out of its broader context, of enhancing safety. Even so, we can appreciate an underlying theme of consumer safety law: how can we enhance safety and compensate the victims of product defects, without stifling innovation and thereby denying society the benefits of new products, and of economic development? Even simpler products may entail inherent dangers and some such products are wanted nevertheless.[11]

In the next extract, the last two points are brought together.

Chris Hodges, 'Approaches to Product Liability in the Member States' (above) at 201

The level of product liability claims in Europe has consistently remained far lower than that which has been produced in the USA by their procedural rules and constitutional climate, given in particular their different situation in relation to availability of healthcare and insurance. It is widely recognised that the overheated liability system in the USA produces economic results that encourage lawyer-led litigation and in which lawyers can reap very substantial and disproportionate rewards. The impact of reforms to European rules on access to justice, class actions, funding mechanisms and damages should be carefully considered so as to avoid these American problems. Existing variations in national rules on litigation procedure and funding constitute significant barriers to consumers in bringing claims and confusion to all litigants and non-national lawyers in understanding some national systems.

The function of a product liability mechanism is primarily to pay adequate compensation to those to whom claimable harm is caused. . . . A further function is to impose a deterrent on producers to take care that their products are designed, manufactured and labelled so as to minimise the safety risks of use. Deterrence is of limited value as a mechanism of behavioural control since it acts *post facto* whereas the considerable corpus of regulatory controls may be expected to be of greater impact in acting preventatively. . . .

[10] Fairgrieve and Howells, 'General Product Safety—a Revolution Through Reform?' (2006) 69 MLR 59–69; P. Cartwright, 'Enforcement, Risk and Discretion: the Case of Dangerous Consumer Products' (2006) 26 LS 524–43.
[11] See for example *Sam Bogle v McDonald's Restaurants*, below: hot tea and coffee with a removable lid not 'defective'.

3. LIABILITY UNDER THE CONSUMER PROTECTION ACT 1987

The Consumer Protection Act 1987 was enacted to give effect—as the UK was required to do—to the EEC Directive (85/374/EEC) on the approximation of the laws, regulations, and administrative provisions of the member states concerning liability for defective products ('the Product Liability Directive'). Given the breadth and depth of the academic literature surrounding the legislation, it may be startling to note that the first cases applying the Act appear to have been decided some 12 years after the statute came into effect: *Abouzaid v Mothercare* (strap of cosytoes hitting child in the eye: defective); *Richardson v LRC* (2000) 59 BMLR 185 (failed condom: not defective); *A v National Blood Authority* [2001] 3 All ER 289 (blood products infected with hepatitis C virus: defective). By then, the UK legislation had already survived a challenge to the European Court of Justice in *CEC v UK* [1997] 3 CMLR 923. The Commission failed to prove its case, although as we will see this appeared (subject to one significant concession) to be largely a reprieve rather than a vindication of the UK wording.

3.1 THE LIABILITY UNDER THE ACT AND WHO IS LIABLE: SECTION 2

Section 2(1) of the Act states the basic liability introduced by the statute. Section 2(2) states the parties who will be liable in this way.

Consumer Protection Act 1987

2   Liability for defective products

(1) Subject to the following provisions of this Part, where any damage is caused wholly or partly by a defect in a product, every person to whom subsection (2) below applies shall be liable for the damage.

(2) This subsection applies to—

    (a) the producer of the product;

    (b) any person who, by putting his name on the product or using a trade mark or other distinguishing mark in relation to the product, has held himself out to be the producer of the product;

    (c) any person who has imported the product into a member State from a place outside the member States in order, in the course of any business of his, to supply it to another.

(3) Subject as aforesaid, where any damage is caused wholly or partly by a defect in a product, any person who supplied the product (whether to the person who suffered the damage, to the producer of any product in which the product in question is comprised or to any other person) shall be liable for the damage if—

    (a) the person who suffered the damage requests the supplier to identify one or more of the persons (whether still in existence or not) to whom subsection (2) above applies in relation to the product;

(b) that request is made within a reasonable period after the damage occurs and at a time when it is not reasonably practicable for the person making the request to identify all those persons; and

(c) the supplier fails, within a reasonable period after receiving the request, either to comply with the request or to identify the person who supplied the product to him.

. . .

(5) Where two or more persons are liable by virtue of this Part for the same damage, their liability shall be joint and several.

(6) This section shall be without prejudice to any liability arising otherwise than by virtue of this Part.

Primarily, liability is placed on *producers*. However, certain other parties may be liable under particular circumstances. These include 'own-branders' (who are effectively holding themselves out as producers), and parties who import the products from outside the member states. As an alternative, the claim may be made against a supplier who does not identify who the producer is.

We should particularly notice section 2(5): where two or more persons are liable **for the same damage** (a term used in the Civil Liability (Contribution) Act 1978 and whose meaning is explored in Chapter 7.2 above), liability is **joint and several**. The claimant may choose which of the liable parties to bring an action against, and recover in full. However, a party found liable in this way may be able to bring contribution proceedings against any other potentially liable parties.

3.2 WHAT IS A PRODUCT?

1(2)(c) . . . "product" means any goods or electricity and (subject to subsection (3) below) includes a product which is comprised in another product, whether by virtue of being a component part or raw material or otherwise; . . .

By section 2(3) (above), faulty component parts are treated as being separate products, and the party who is potentially liable if those components are defective is the producer (or importer, and so on) of those components, rather than of the product in which they are incorporated. *However*, the manufacturer of a component part will not be liable for damage done *to the larger product in which it is incorporated*: see section 5(2) extracted below, refining the definition of 'damage' recoverable under the Act.

3.3 DAMAGE

5 Damage giving rise to liability

(1) Subject to the following provisions of this section, in this Part "damage" means death or personal injury or any loss of or damage to any property (including land).

(2) A person shall not be liable under section 2 above in respect of any defect in a product for the loss of or any damage to the product itself or for the loss of or any damage to the whole or any part of any product which has been supplied with the product in question comprised in it.

(3) A person shall not be liable under section 2 above for any loss of or damage to any property which, at the time it is lost or damaged, is not—

    (a) of a description of property ordinarily intended for private use, occupation or consumption; and

    (b) intended by the person suffering the loss or damage mainly for his own private use, occupation or consumption.

(4) No damages shall be awarded to any person by virtue of this Part in respect of any loss of or damage to any property if the amount which would fall to be so awarded to that person, apart from this subsection and any liability for interest, does not exceed £275.

(5) In determining for the purposes of this Part who has suffered any loss of or damage to property and when any such loss or damage occurred, the loss or damage shall be regarded as having occurred at the earliest time at which a person with an interest in the property had knowledge of the material facts about the loss or damage.

(6) For the purposes of subsection (5) above the material facts about any loss of or damage to any property are such facts about the loss or damage as would lead a reasonable person with an interest in the property to consider the loss or damage sufficiently serious to justify his instituting proceedings for damages against a defendant who did not dispute liability and was able to satisfy a judgment.

(7) For the purposes of subsection (5) above a person's knowledge includes knowledge which he might reasonably have been expected to acquire—

    (a) from facts observable or ascertainable by him; or

    (b) from facts ascertainable by him with the help of appropriate expert advice which it is reasonable for him to seek;

but a person shall not be taken by virtue of this subsection to have knowledge of a fact ascertainable by him only with the help of expert advice unless he has failed to take all reasonable steps to obtain (and, where appropriate, to act on) that advice.

(8) Subsections (5) to (7) above shall not extend to Scotland.

Clearly, some parts of this section (subsections 5–7) are important in defining the date of damage for the purposes of determining when the limitation period will begin to run: see further Section 3.6 of this Chapter.

The types of 'damage' recoverable under the Act are broadly similar to the types of damage recoverable through the tort of negligence. There must be damage either to the person or to *property other than the product itself*. Defectiveness in the product is not enough in itself; nor is harm to the property that is claimed to be defective.[12] By section 5(2), as already noted, a component part is not treated as having caused damage if it merely damages the product into which it is incorporated. Importantly, by section 5(3) only *consumer* property is protected.

---

[12] For the position in negligence see *Murphy v Brentwood* [1991] 1 AC 398; *Muirhead v Industrial Tank Speciality Ltd* [1986] QB 507.

Damage to property not intended for private or family use (broadly, commercial property) is not recoverable under the Act.

3.4 THE CRUCIAL CONCEPT: DEFECTIVENESS

As we have already discussed, 'defect' is the central criterion for liability under the statute. 'Defectiveness' plays an equivalent role to 'negligence' at common law.

3 Meaning of "defect"

(1) Subject to the following provisions of this section, there is a defect in a product for the purposes of this Part if the safety of the product is not such as persons generally are entitled to expect; and for those purposes "safety", in relation to a product, shall include safety with respect to products comprised in that product and safety in the context of risks of damage to property, as well as in the context of risks of death or personal injury.

(2) In determining for the purposes of subsection (1) above what persons generally are entitled to expect in relation to a product all the circumstances shall be taken into account, including—

(a) the manner in which, and purposes for which, the product has been marketed, its get-up, the use of any mark in relation to the product and any instructions for, or warnings with respect to, doing or refraining from doing anything with or in relation to the product;

(b) what might reasonably be expected to be done with or in relation to the product; and

(c) the time when the product was supplied by its producer to another;

and nothing in this section shall require a defect to be inferred from the fact alone that the safety of a product which is supplied after that time is greater than the safety of the product in question.

By section 3(1), the key question in respect of defectiveness is whether the safety of the product is not such as persons generally are entitled to expect.

It should be noted that in making a judgment as to defectiveness, 'all the circumstances' are to be taken into account (s 3(2)). The listed factors are merely illustrative.

Section 3(1) differs very slightly from the wording of the Directive itself:

Directive on Product Liability

Article 6

1. A product is defective when it does not provide the safety which a person is entitled to expect, taking all circumstances into account . . .

The language in the Directive is ambiguous, since it does not make clear whether the test is what 'a person' who is *consuming* the product is entitled to expect; or what 'a person' who is representative of the general public is entitled to expect. The UK legislation adopts the latter interpretation.

Defectiveness v Negligence

Before the Act came into effect, there was some difference of view among commentators about the difference that the move to a defectiveness test would make. Christopher Newdick argued that 'defect' would be easier to establish than negligence. (He reserved his criticism for the development risks defence (below).)

C. Newdick, 'The Development Risk Defence of the Consumer Protection Act 1987' (1988) 47 CLJ 455–76

The European Directive on Product Liability introduces a new regime of strict product liability to the member states of the Community. Those injured by products may recover by showing that the product is 'defective', *i.e.*, that it 'does not provide the safety that a person is entitled to expect . . . .' The advantage of this approach for the individual is likely to be that liability turns on the existence of a defect alone. Unlike the law of Negligence, no question of foresight of the danger, or of the precautions taken to avoid it, arises for consideration. Strict product liability depends on the condition of the product, not the fault of its maker or supplier.

Jane Stapleton, on the other hand, argued that the concept of 'defectiveness' would itself not operate significantly differently from the 'negligence' standard. She further argued that a special strict liability regime for *products* was in any case anomalous and unjustified.

J. Stapleton, 'Products Liability Reform: Real or Illusory?' (1986) 6 OJLS 392–422, at 420–1

The assumption that stricter liability for products will be provided by the new Directive is unwarranted. On examination, its central concepts such as cost-benefit assessments and the development risk defence are not only inconsistent with the theoretical arguments used to justify the reform but they are also so poorly thought out that it is debatable whether the liability foreshadowed in the Directive will have a significantly wider scope than the current negligence regime.

Even if there are cases in which the new law will provide a remedy where there would have been none under negligence,[13] the reform can be criticised for generating . . . unattractive anomalies in the remedies available to classes of the disabled. Despite trenchant academic criticism the current vogue for *ad hoc* solutions such as products liability reform seems to survive. . . .

Although the volume of case law considering 'defectiveness' is still relatively modest, it has generally become clear that there is scope for a claimant to succeed under the Act, where a claim in negligence would fail. 'Defectiveness' is likely to be easier to prove than negligence in the simpler, more mechanical cases. These are also the cases least likely to attract the development risks defence. Even so, it remains true that (as Stapleton argued) the regime is not a **full** strict liability regime, even for damage done by products. It only applies in cases of 'defect'.

---

[13] Stapleton noted here that the Directive does have some unequivocal advantages for certain plaintiffs—notably in the extended definition of 'producers' in Article 3.

The interpretation of defectiveness is therefore crucial, and if the definition of defect should prove to be capricious or anomalous, the regime that results will be defensible (if at all) only on the basis that it is a 'compromise'.

We therefore turn to the UK case law on the issue of defectiveness.

Iman Abouzaid v Mothercare (UK) Ltd (21 December 2000, CA)

The claimant was helping his mother to attach a 'cosytoes', manufactured by the defendants, to his younger brother's pram. An elastic strap snapped out of his grasp and a metal buckle on the end of the strap struck him in the eye. His vision in that eye was very substantially impaired. The Court of Appeal held that the injury was caused by a defect in the product. No 'development risks' defence could arise because a simple test could have shown that the risk existed at the time the goods were manufactured. The risk was in no sense outside the reach of established knowledge at that time, even if it had not been explicitly recognized.

By contrast, a claim in negligence at common law would fail, largely because the risk of injury was small, and a reasonable manufacturer may well have failed to recognize it.

Pill LJ

27   I have come to the conclusion that, though the case is close to the borderline, the product was defective within the meaning of the Act. The risk is in losing control of an elastic strap at a time when it is stretched and eyes are in the line of recoil. The product was defective because it was supplied with a design which permitted the risk to arise and without giving a warning that the user should not so position himself that the risk arose. Members of the public were entitled to expect more from the appellants. A factor in that expectation is the vulnerability of the eye and the serious consequences which may follow from a blunt injury to the eye. . . .

Section 4(1)(e)

28   The defence under section 4(1)(e) presupposes a finding that a defect is present. The appellants seek to rely, as 'scientific and technical knowledge', not available in 1990, on the absence in the DTI database of any record of a comparable incident at the time of supply. . . . Only with knowledge of accidents might the producer have been expected to discover the defect.

29   In my judgment that argument fails first on the ground that the defect, as defined, was present whether or not previous accidents had occurred. . . . Different considerations apply to negligence at common law where foreseeability of injury, as defined in the authorities, is a necessary ingredient. Secondly I am very doubtful whether, in the present context, a record of accidents, comes within the category of 'scientific and technical knowledge'. The defence contemplates scientific and technical advances which throw additional light, for example, on the propensities of materials and allow defects to be discovered. There are no such advances here. . . .

Common law negligence

31   A decision whether there is a breach of duty in negligence in manufacturing a product which causes injury involves an assessment of the risk of injury it presents, along with other factors. In this context, the absence of previous comparable accidents . . . is a relevant factor. . . .

32 . . . The risk, while identifiable, was not in my judgment such that the manufacturer in 1990 can be held to have been negligent in supplying the product in the form it was. On the present facts, a defect, as defined in section 3 of the Act, was present upon the public expectation test but there was no negligence at common law.

Tesco Stores v Connor Frederick Pollock [2006] EWCA Civ 393

The claimant, aged 13 months, had swallowed dishwasher powder from a plastic bottle bought from Tesco (the first defendant), becoming seriously ill. The powder was Tesco's own brand (see s 2(2)(b)), but the bottle had been manufactured by the second defendant. The case against the defendants was that the bottle was too easily opened. It was supposed to have a 'child resistant' cap, but the claimant managed to open it. Evidence showed that the 'squeeze and turn' cap required considerably less resistance to open than would be required by a cap which met the British Standard for such lids (although in principle, it required more force than a child of 13 months would be *expected* to be able to apply). There was no legal requirement that all dishwasher powder should be sold in containers with caps which met the British Standard. The question was, rather, whether the cap could be opened sufficiently easily for it to be described as 'defective', within the terms of section 3(1) above. Did it provide the level of safety that persons generally would be entitled to expect? The Court of Appeal decided that it did. The product was not defective.

Laws LJ

16 . . . [Counsel for the claimant] at first submitted that the public were entitled to expect that the product in question would function in accordance with whatever safety standard might in the particular case be imposed by any relevant public authority. I apprehend that he appreciated that this was a step too far, since there is not trace of any reference to the British standard on the bottle, packaging or get up of this product. . . . [U]ltimately his argument was that under the statute the public are entitled to expect that the product will function to the full extent of the design standard to which it was manufactured. . . .

17 If Mr Briden is right, it means that every producer of a product whose use causes injury effectively warrants to the general public that the product fulfils its design standards. Now, the producer may have no contract with any member of the public, as here, the appellants did not. Members of the public . . . are unlikely to have the faintest idea to what safety standard the product they are buying has been designed, if it has been designed to any. In my judgment Mr Briden's arguments in truth demand a radical rewriting of the statute. They are an attempt to confer on purchasers and users of everyday products a right to sue the product's producers as if there were a contractual warranty as to the safety standard to which the product had been designed. It is quite impossible to get such a result out of the terms of the 1987 Act.

18 What, on the facts here, were 'persons generally entitled to expect' of the safety features of this cap and bottle? In my judgment they were entitled to expect that the bottle would be more difficult to open than if it had an ordinary screwtop. Anything more specific, as a test of public expectation, runs into the difficulties which I have just described. Here, the bottle was more difficult to open than an ordinary screwtop, though not as difficult to open as it would have been if the British Standard torque measure had been complied with. There was, in my judgment, no breach of the 1987 Act.

Parallels may be drawn between the approach in this case, and the 'compensation culture' debate referred to in Chapter 8. There is emerging—politically at least, but to some extent in judicial language also—a stronger insistence that claimants (or in this case, those with care of small children) should take responsibility for safety.

In this case, there was some scepticism that the young claimant could genuinely have opened the screw top (and therefore some suspicion that the bottle had been left open by an adult), although on balance this matter was settled in favour of the claimant to the satisfaction of the first instance judge. It could be argued that the resistance required to open this cap, being significantly more than a small child would be expected to be able to apply, was sufficient to avoid being held to be 'defective'. But is it really sufficient to say—as Laws LJ did at [18]—that the *only* reasonable expectation of people generally is that a 'child resistant cap' will be 'more difficult to open' than an ordinary screwtop? This is surely expecting too little, since it means (literally) that *any* extra resistance is enough. This is not, it is suggested, what people could legitimately expect of a 'child resistant cap'. On the other hand, the actual resistance of the cap in this particular case could have been held to be within the legitimate expectations of the public. It remained something of a mystery how this particular child had managed to open it.

An earlier case which indicates that consumer **responsibility** is relevant to the fair apportionment of risk is *Sam Bogle and Others v McDonald's Restaurants* [2002] EWHC 490 (QB). Each of the claimants (most of them children) were injured by spillage of hot tea and coffee served at McDonald's restaurants. The claims call to mind a widely-known American case in which a claimant secured substantial damages for scalding injuries sustained when hot coffee sold at a McDonald's 'drive-thru' restaurant spilt onto her lap. In *Bogle v McDonald's* by contrast, the defendants were held not to be liable either in negligence, or under the Consumer Protection Act 1987.

The claim under the Act turned on the heat of the drinks and the design of their container, the lid of which was to be removed for drinking. Later, a differently designed cup was introduced, allowing the coffee to be drunk through a spout. (In this regard note the terms of section 3(2) extracted above: the introduction of a safer product at a later date does not by itself mean that the product which caused the harm was defective. But note also that people may prefer *not* to drink tea and coffee through a spout.)

Field J

81 Persons generally expect tea or coffee to be consumed on the premises to be hot. Many prefer to consume a hot drink from an unlidded cup rather than through a spout in the lid. Persons generally know that if a hot drink is spilled onto someone, a serious scalding injury can result. They accordingly know that care must be taken to avoid such spills, especially if they are with young children. They expect precautions to be taken to guard against this risk but not to the point that they are denied the basic utility of being able to buy hot drinks to be consumed on the premises from a cup with the lid off. Given that the staff were trained to cap the drinks securely and given the capabilities of the cups and lids used, I am satisfied that the safety of the hot drinks served by McDonalds was such as persons generally are entitled to expect.

The reasoning in this extract is more supportable than the reasoning (though not necessarily the outcome) in *Tesco Stores*. It keeps in mind the preference of the public for the very product which is claimed to be defective, notwithstanding its known (indeed obvious) dangers.

A warning has since been added to cups in which tea and coffee are served in McDonald's restaurants; but the risk was effectively treated as obvious enough.

The most sophisticated judicial analysis of 'defectiveness' to date was attempted in *A v National Blood Authority*. Here we consider the issues surrounding 'defectiveness' in this case. In the next section, we consider its implications for the 'development risks defence'.

A and Others v National Blood Authority and Another [2001] 3 All ER 289 (Burton J)

The claimants had all contracted Hepatitis C from blood transfusions. They brought actions against the defendants as suppliers of the relevant blood products. At the time that the transfusions were carried out, the defendants and the medical profession were well aware that there was a risk of infection by Hepatitis C through blood products. This knowledge was not shared with the general public. There was an actual expectation of 'clean blood'. An actual expectation is not however sufficient; section 3(1) refers to the level of safety that people are *entitled* to expect—not the level that they *do* expect. Further, there was no available test that could be used to check individual units of blood for the virus, and therefore the risk of infection was **unavoidable**. Therefore, it was assumed that an action could only be brought under the Consumer Protection Act 1987, and that no action could be brought at common law.[14]

The chief question for the court was whether the blood products, some of which were unavoidably infected by the Hepatitis C virus, were 'defective'. If they were, a subsidiary question was whether the 'development risks defence' could be applied. There was no way of finding the defect. It was held that the infected blood products were defective, and that the development risks defence was not made out. The claimants were successful.

A curious feature of this case was that the judge, Burton J, dispensed with any reference to the Consumer Protection Act 1987 in respect of the primary issues, surrounding defectiveness and the development risks defence. Instead, he referred directly to the corresponding Articles of the Directive (Articles 6 and 7(1)(e) respectively). His reason for this was that the European Court, in *CEC v UK* [1997] 3 CMLR 923, had recently confirmed that the courts of the UK should interpret the Consumer Protection Act 1987 in accordance with the wording of the Directive.

Burton J, *A v National Blood Authority*

21 Although the United Kingdom Government has not amended s4(1)(e) of the CPA so as to bring it in line with the wording of the directive, there is thus binding authority of the Court of Justice that it must be so construed. Hence . . . the major discussions in this case, and all the areas of most live dispute, have concentrated entirely upon the wording of arts 6 and 7(e) of the directive, and not upon the equivalent sections of the CPA, to which I shall make little or no further reference.

---

[14] Could an action have been brought on the basis of a *failure to advise*? The problem with such a claim would lie in causation, if the defendants could argue that the transfusions were emergency treatment and that they would have been accepted even if the risk was known. The test of causation under the Consumer Protection Act 1987 is simpler: did the defect cause the harm?

This approach—bypassing the wording of the CPA itself—has not been adopted in other cases that have analysed the meaning of 'defect', or the development risks defence.

It is hard to capture the dense reasoning in this case, but we can point out some crucial elements in the finding that the blood was 'defective'.

1. Although the medical profession was aware of the unavoidable risk that blood would be infected, the public generally was not aware of this risk. This in itself was not decisive, because Article 6 (like section 3) refers to what people were *entitled* to expect. The public's expectation of 'clean blood' was not unreasonable, even though the medical profession knew it to be unattainable. Members of the public were 'entitled', given the information made publicly available, to expect clean blood. Therefore, although the products made by the defendants were no worse—in terms of the risks of infection—than any blood supplied at the time could have been, they were still 'defective' on the 'expectation' test.

2. Unavoidability of the risk was not relevant to the test for 'defectiveness' ([63]). Although it has been queried how any issue could be excluded from the expression '*all* the circumstances' (which is used in both the Act and the Directive), Burton J pointed out that avoidability was not relevant to the purpose of the Directive—which was to apportion liability for defects to producers, subject to the defences available. Avoidability, then, was not part of the definition of a 'defect'. In support of the judge's interpretation, it can be said that avoidability is in no way similar to the kinds of considerations listed in Article 6 and section 3(2), all of which are likely to affect the safety, in practice, of the product (who is going to use it and when? What instructions are provided?). Avoidability does not go to safety.

3. Burton J held that the infected bags of blood were **non-standard products** (also referred to in the judgment as 'lemons' ([65])). The importance of this in respect of 'defectiveness' was as follows:

The defendants argued that all bags of blood carried the same *risk* of infection. Since there was no test for determining which were the infected bags, they were all to be regarded as equally dangerous. The bags were a standard product. Where a standard product carries an inherent risk, but is still regarded as worthwhile and desirable, the standard product cannot be regarded as defective. This would be true of alcohol for example, or tobacco, whose risks are inherent and cannot realistically be described in terms of 'defects'. Similarly, many drugs have known potential side-effects. All packs of aspirin, for example, carry the same risk of causing internal bleeding, and a pack of aspirin which does turn out to have this effect on a consumer cannot be described as defective. Any pack of aspirin has the potential to do this.

The judge dismissed this argument on two grounds:

(a) The infected bags were not the same as the other bags. The injury was not caused simply by a difference in the reaction of the patient: some of the bags were infected ('non-standard'), the others were not. The infected bags were a non-standard product.

(b) Even in the case of a standard product (such as a normal pack of aspirin), adverse side-effects are only acceptable if they are made known. (We may now add to this that they need not be made known if they are obvious—following subsequent cases such as *Bogle v McDonald's* (above), and applying the spirit of *Tomlinson v Congleton* [2004] 1 AC 46.)

Burton J, *A v National Blood Authority* [2001] 3 All ER 289

[66] . . . I am quite clear that the infected blood products in this case were non-standard products (whether on the basis of being manufacturing or design defects does not appear to me to matter). Where, as here, there is a harmful characteristic in a non-standard product, a decision that it is defective is likely to be straightforward, and I can make my decision accordingly. However, the consequence of my conclusion is that 'avoidability' is also not in the basket of circumstances, even in respect of a harmful characteristic in a standard product. So I shall set out what I consider to be the structure for consideration under art 6. It must be emphasised that safety and intended, or foreseeable, use are the lynchpins: and, leading on from these, what legitimate expectations there are of safety in relation to foreseeable use. . . .

[67] The first step must be to identify the harmful characteristic which caused the injury (art 4). In order to establish that there is a defect in art 6, the next step will be to conclude whether the product is standard or non-standard. This will be done (in the absence of admission by the producer) most easily by comparing the offending product with other products of the same type or series produced by that producer. If the respect in which it differs from the series includes the harmful characteristic, then it is, for the purpose of art 6, non-standard. If it does not differ, or if the respect in which it differs does not include the harmful characteristic, but all the other products, albeit different, share the harmful characteristic, then it is to be treated as a standard product.

Non-standard products

[68] The circumstances specified in art 6 may obviously be relevant-the product may be a second-as well as the circumstances of the supply. But it seems to me that the primary issue in relation to a non-standard product may be whether the public at large accepted the non-standard nature of the product—ie they accept that a proportion of the products is defective (as I have concluded they do not in this case). That, as discussed, is not of course the end of it, because the question is of legitimate expectation, and the court may conclude that the expectation of the public is too high or too low. But manifestly questions such as warnings and presentations will be in the forefront. However, I conclude that the following are not relevant: (i) avoidability of the harmful characteristic—ie impossibility or unavoidability in relation to precautionary measures; (ii) the impracticality, cost or difficulty of taking such measures; and (iii) the benefit to society or utility of the product (except in the context of whether—with full information and proper knowledge—the public does and ought to accept the risk).

Burton J also added some comments relating to *standard* products:

[73] I can accept that resolution of the problem of the defective standard product will be more complex than in the case of a non-standard product. This trial has been in respect of what I am satisfied to be a non-standard product, and I see, after a three-month hearing, no difficulty in eliminating evidence of avoidability from art 6. It may be that, if I am right in my analysis, and if it is followed in other cases, problems may arise in the consideration of a standard product on such basis, but I do not consider any such problems will be insurmountable if safety, use and the identified circumstances are kept in the forefront of consideration. Negligence, fault and the conduct of the producer or designer can be left to the (limited) ambit of art 7(e) . . .

This approach leaves all questions of conduct to the 'development risks defence'. The statutory product liability was clearly interpreted as a strict liability regime, albeit one that is relatively confined in scope. On the other hand, because the court laid such emphasis on the fact that knowledge of the risks concerned was not shared with the public, the burden placed on producers of medical products may not be very difficult to avoid. *Advice* as to risks may be sufficient to avoid the judgment of defectiveness, by altering legitimate expectations of safety.

3.5 DEFENCES

The following defences are of course available *in addition to* the possibility that the product was not defective (Section 3, above). The most important defence as we have said is the 'development risks' defence, in section 4(1)(e).

4 Defences

(1) In any civil proceedings by virtue of this Part against any person ("the person proceeded against") in respect of a defect in a product it shall be a defence for him to show—

    (a) that the defect is attributable to compliance with any requirement imposed by or under any enactment or with any Community obligation; or

    (b) that the person proceeded against did not at any time supply the product to another; or

    (c) that the following conditions are satisfied, that is to say—

        (i) that the only supply of the product to another by the person proceeded against was otherwise than in the course of a business of that person's; and

        (ii) that section 2(2) above does not apply to that person or applies to him by virtue only of things done otherwise than with a view to profit; or

    (d) that the defect did not exist in the product at the relevant time; or

    (e) that the state of scientific and technical knowledge at the relevant time was not such that a producer of products of the same description as the product in question might be expected to have discovered the defect if it had existed in his products while they were under his control; or

    (f) that the defect—

        (i) constituted a defect in a product ("the subsequent product") in which the product in question had been comprised; and

        (ii) was wholly attributable to the design of the subsequent product or to compliance by the producer of the product in question with instructions given by the producer of the subsequent product.

(2) In this section the relevant time in relation to electricity, means the time at which it was generated, being a time before it was transmitted or distributed, and in relation to any other product, means—

    (a) if the person proceeded against is a person to whom subsection (2) of section 2 above applies in relation to the product, the time when he supplied the product to another;

    (b) if that subsection does not apply to that person in relation to the product, the time when the product was last supplied by a person to whom that subsection does apply in relation to the product.

Notice that under section 4(1)(d), the producer will be exonerated if it can establish that the defect was not present at the relevant time (which is, broadly, the time of first supply). This defence was successfully relied upon in *Terence Piper v JRI (Manufacturing) Ltd* [2006] EWCA Civ 1344, where it was held that an artificial hip was probably damaged at the time of surgery, and was not defective when supplied. On the other hand, undue fragility in a product may itself amount to a 'defect'.

Other defences

By section 6(4), the partial defence of contributory negligence (as set out in the Law Reform (Contributory Negligence) Act 1945) is applicable to actions under the Consumer Protection Act. But by section 7, liability under the Act cannot be excluded or restricted by a contract term or notice.

Section 4(1)(e): The Development Risks Defence

As we have seen, the incorporation of the development risks defence has been controversial. Its effect is that a producer of goods only takes the risk of defects that could have been discovered at the relevant time. The risk that defects will be discovered later falls on the consumer. Why is this? The key idea is 'apportionment of risk', and the preamble to the Directive makes this plain:

Directive 85/374/EEC of 25 July 1985, Preamble

Whereas liability without fault on the part of the producer is the sole means of adequately solving the problem, peculiar to our age of increasing technicality, of a fair apportionment of the risks inherent in modern technological production;

. . .

Whereas a fair apportionment of risk between the injured person and the producer implies that the producer should be able to free himself from liability if he furnishes proof that as to the existence of certain exonerating circumstances. . . .

This does not get us very far however, because it simply states that the burden of risk should be apportioned 'fairly'. It is hard to know how to ascertain fairness as between two faultless parties. Such questions, one would have thought, could only be resolved by looking more broadly at the opportunities to manage or minimize unknown risks,[15] and (equally importantly) to the distribution of the *benefits* with which the risks are accompanied. This is the sort of idea which is expressed by Jane Stapleton in terms of 'enterprise liability': the enterprise which benefits from the risks, and has the greatest potential control over those risks, ought to be liable if the risks materialize.[16] The development risks defence, in *any* form, undercuts this goal, as it also undercuts the goal of deterrence.

---

[15] This depends on the idea that although the specific danger is unknown, the general risk that the product will contain dangers is known. But of course as we get further from known dangers, the risks become harder to quantify.

[16] Jane Stapleton, 'Product Liability Reform—Real or Illusory?' (1986) 6 OJLS 392–422.

As we saw in the introductory section to this chapter, the newest justification for the defence turns on encouragement to innovation and the wish not to stifle productive risks. In other words, deterrence *of beneficial risk-creation* is not desired.

Apart from the general controversy surrounding the very existence of the defence, there is also a more particular controversy surrounding the way in which the UK has transposed the Directive in this respect. The UK wording departs from the wording of the Directive, and it appears to most commentators that the defence as expressed in the UK legislation is capable (depending on its application) of exonerating more producers than is envisaged by the Directive. The relevant forms of wording are as follows.

Consumer Protection Act 1987

Section 4(1)(e)

. . . the state of scientific and technical knowledge at the relevant time was not such that a producer of products of the same description as the product in question might be expected to have discovered the defect if it had existed in his products while they were under his control . . .

Directive on Product Liability 1985

Article 7

The producer shall not be liable as a result of this Directive if he proves:

. . .

(e) that the state of scientific and technical knowledge at the time when he put the product into circulation was not such as to enable the existence of the defect to be discovered; . . .

Broadly, there are two criticisms of the UK's particular version of the development risks defence, compared with the version in the Directive.

1. There is claimed to be a substantial difference between what a producer might be *expected* to discover, as in the Act; and what it would be *possible* to discover, given the existing state of knowledge, as in the Directive. It is argued by some that the former sets a standard of reasonable expectation, and is therefore quite similar to negligence.

2. The UK wording seems to suggest that the relevant knowledge (when judging whether it would have been possible to recognize the defect) is knowledge of *producers in the industry*. The wording in the Directive seems to encompass scientific knowledge *wherever* it was being developed.

There has been some support for the UK's interpretation of the development risks defence. For example Christopher Newdick suggested at the time of enactment that the version adopted by the UK simply expressed more clearly what would be the inevitable content of the test.

C. Newdick, 'The Development Risk Defence of the Consumer Protection Act 1987'
(above), at 459–60

There are two reasons for thinking that the government may be right. First, when a court assesses the relevant state of scientific and technical knowledge, it will not require the defendant to prove, conclusively and absolutely, a worldwide absence of knowledge of the defect. It would be impracticable to insist on proof that all the libraries of the world had been scoured and all the unpublished theses in universities, in every language, had been read. More probably, the court will make a judgment on the basis of expert evidence. . . .

Secondly, it is conceivable that the plaintiff could present information which revealed the existence of the defect, but which could not reasonably be expected to have been known to the producer . . .

There is no doubt that the development risk defence in this form sits uneasily in a measure designed to introduce strict product liability. In effect it relieves the producer of liability when he had not been negligent in failing to discover the defect. This apparent contradiction of purpose is the unavoidable result of the inclusion of the defence in the Product Liability Directive.

CEC v UK [1997] 3 CMLR 923

Given the difference in wording between Article 7(e) of the Directive, and section 4(1)(e) of the Consumer Protection Act (extracted above), the European Commission took the view that the UK had not properly transposed the Directive. It therefore began infringement proceedings against the UK.

Before the European Court of Justice, the Commission failed to prove its case. On the narrowest point, the Commission agreed that some aspects of the wording were inconsistent with the Directive; but pointed out that the Commission had failed to refer to any UK case law which showed that section 4(1)(e) would actually be *interpreted* so as to depart from the Directive.[17]

More importantly for the general interpretation of the Directive throughout the member states, the Court of Justice also commented on the defence itself. The Court specified that the relevant state of knowledge for the purposes of Article 7(e) was the objective state of knowledge, not the knowledge to be expected of a producer in the particular industry. However, most controversially, the Court accepted the analysis of Advocate General Tesauro which preceded the judgment, to the effect that the relevant knowledge must be 'accessible'. This seemed to go some way towards accepting that the UK approach represented the *proper* interpretation of the Directive.

The Court's comments on accessibility were relatively brief. Here, we extract Advocate General Tesauro's opinion quite fully. It is not beyond criticism, but it represents the most authoritative statement of the form of liability introduced by the Directive.

---

[17] Necessarily, since there would appear to have been *no* UK case law applying the Act at the relevant time.

Opinion of Mr Advocate General Tesauro

The Advocate General outlined the initial proposals put forward by the Commission, which would not have permitted a producer to 'exonerate' itself where risks were unknown, and continued:

19. In contrast, the Directive as it was adopted by the Council opted for a system of strict liability which was no longer absolute, but limited, in deference to a principle of the fair apportionment of risk between the injured person and the producer, the latter having to bear only quantifiable risks, but not development risks which are, by their nature, unquantifiable. Under the Directive, therefore, in order for the producer to be held liable for defects in the product, the injured party is required to prove the damage, the defect in the product and the causal relationship between defect and damage, but not negligence on the part of the producer.

The producer, however, may exonerate himself from liability by proving that the 'state of the art' at the time when he put the product into circulation was not such as to cause the product to be regarded as defective. This is what Article 7(e) of the Directive provides.

20. It should first be observed that, since that provision refers solely to the 'scientific and technical knowledge' at the time when the product was marketed, it is not concerned with the practices and safety standards in use in the industrial sector in which the producer is operating. In other words, it has no bearing on the exclusion of the manufacturer from liability that no-one in that particular class of manufacturer takes the measures necessary to eliminate the defect or prevent it from arising if such measures are capable of being adopted on the basis of the available knowledge.

Other matters which likewise are to be regarded as falling outside the scope of Article 7(e) are aspects relating to the practicability and expense of measures suitable for eliminating the defect from the product. Neither, from this point of view, can the fact that the producer did not appraise himself of the state of scientific and technical knowledge or does not keep up to date with developments in this area as disclosed in the specialist literature, be posited as having any relevance for the purposes of excluding liability on his part. I consider, in fact, that the producer's conduct should be assessed using the yardstick of the knowledge of an expert in the sector.

21. Some additional considerations need to be explored, however, in order to tie down the concept 'state of knowledge'.

The progress of scientific culture does not develop linearly in so far as new studies and new discoveries may initially be criticized and regarded as unreliable by most of the scientific community, yet subsequently after the passage of time undergo an opposite process of beatification' whereby they are virtually unanimously endorsed. It is therefore quite possible that at the time when a given product is marketed, there will be isolated opinions to the effect that it is defective, whilst most academics do not take that view. The problem at this juncture is to determine whether in such a situation, that is to say, where there is a risk that is not certain and will be agreed to exist by all only ex post, the producer may still rely on the defence provided for in Article 7(e) of the Directive.

In my view, the answer to this question must be in the negative. In other words, the state of scientific knowledge cannot be identified with the views expressed by the majority of learned opinion, but with the most advanced level of research which has been carried out at a given time.

22.   That interpretation, which coincides with that suggested by the Commission at the hearing with the aid of a number of very pertinent examples, is the closest to the ratio legis of the Community rules: the producer has to bear the foreseeable risks, against which he can protect himself by taking either preventive measures by stepping up experimentation and research investment or measures to cover himself by taking out civil liability insurance against any damage caused by defects in the product.

Where in the whole gamut of scientific opinion at a particular time there is also one isolated opinion (which, as the history of science shows, might become with the passage of time opinio communis) as to the potentially defective and/or hazardous nature of the product, the manufacturer is no longer faced with an unforeseeable risk, since, as such, it is outside the scope of the rules imposed by the Directive.

23.   The aspect which I have just been discussing is closely linked with the question of the availability of scientific and technical knowledge in the sense of the accessibility of the sum of knowledge at a given time to interested persons. It is undeniable that the circulation of information is affected by objective factors, such as, for example, its place of origin, the language in which it is given and the circulation of the journals in which it is published.

To be plain, there exist quite major differences in point of the speed in which it gets into circulation and the scale of its dissemination between a study of a researcher in a university in the United States published in an international English-language international journal and, to take an example given by the Commission, similar research carried out by an academic in Manchuria published in a local scientific journal in Chinese, which does not go outside the boundaries of the region.

24.   In such a situation, it would be unrealistic and, I would say, unreasonable to take the view that the study published in Chinese has the same chances as the other of being known to a European product manufacturer. So, I do not consider that in such a case a producer could be held liable on the ground that at the time at which he put the product into circulation the brilliant Asian researcher had discovered the defect in it.

More generally, the 'state of knowledge' must be construed so as to include all data in the information circuit of the scientific community as a whole, bearing in mind, however, on the basis of a reasonableness test the actual opportunities for the information to circulate.

25.   Having thus identified the scope of the Community provision, I consider that I am unable to share the Commission's proposition that there is an irremediable conflict between it and the national provision at issue. Indeed, there is no denying that the wording of section 4(1)(e) of the Act contains an element of potential ambiguity: in so far as it refers to what might be expected of the producer, it could be interpreted more broadly that it should.

Notwithstanding this, I do not consider that the reference to the ability of the producer', despite its general nature, may or even must (necessarily) authorize interpretations contrary to the rationale and the aims of the Directive.

A number of points arising from this opinion deserve to be underlined.

1. The defence does not help a defendant who is able to show simply that the risk was unknown *among producers of the product in question*. The defence only applies where the risk genuinely cannot be discovered in the light of existing knowledge. Existing knowledge for these purposes includes knowledge among those at the forefront of research. Indeed, even one

'isolated opinion' will do (subject to 'accessibility', below). This is partly because it is an objective of the strict liability regime to encourage investment in research and development relating
to risks.[18]

2. The 'development risks defence' *only* assists a defendant in respect of *risks* which cannot
be discovered. It does not apply where the risk is known, but no methodology has been developed for identifying the defect in a particular product, or for removing it. It does not assist a
defendant in respect of risks which cannot be *avoided*, either because no method for doing so
has been discovered, or because that method is too expensive to be applied. This is because the
defence is a narrow exception to the general allocation of risk to producers rather than consumers. It is up to producers to manage, internalize or (so far as possible) avoid risks that
were—in the objective sense— 'known' or 'knowable' at the time of manufacture. The decision as to defect in *A v National Blood Authority* (above) is compatible with this.

3. Most controversially from the point of view of those who support strict liability, the
Advocate General accepted the UK's position that knowledge must be in some sense **accessible** if it is to defeat the defence. This does not mean that the producer *ought to have discovered
it* in the full negligence sense. But the Advocate General does suggest that research published
only in Manchuria, for example, may not be regarded as sufficiently accessible to defeat the
defence against a European producer. The producer is expected to *find* developing knowledge;
but there is a limit to this expectation. Knowledge that is not accessible at all is (in effect) not
there to be found.

Judgment of the European Court of Justice (Wathelet J)

25   Several observations can be made as to the wording of Article 7(e) of the Directive.

26   First, as the Advocate General rightly observes in paragraph 20 of his Opinion, since that
provision refers to scientific and technical knowledge at the time when the producer put the
product into circulation', Article 7(e) is not specifically directed at the practices and safety
standards in use in the industrial sector in which the producer is operating, but, unreservedly,
at the state of scientific and technical knowledge, including the most advanced level of such
knowledge, at the time when the product in question was put into circulation.

27   Second, the clause providing for the defence in question does not contemplate the state
of knowledge of which the producer in question actually or subjectively was or could have
been apprised, but the objective state of scientific and technical knowledge of which the producer is presumed to have been informed.

28   However, it is implicit in the wording of Article 7(e) that the relevant scientific and technical knowledge must have been accessible at the time when the product in question was put
into circulation.

29   It follows that, in order to have a defence under Article 7(e) of the Directive, the producer
of a defective product must prove that the objective state of scientific and technical knowledge, including the most advanced level of such knowledge, at the time when the product in
question was put into circulation was not such as to enable the existence of the defect to be
discovered. Further, in order for the relevant scientific and technical knowledge to be

---

[18] On the other hand it has been argued that this incentive to research can be overdone, so that it begins to
stifle innovation: see Hodges, 'Development Risks: Unanswered Questions', extracted below.

successfully pleaded as against the producer, that knowledge must have been accessible at the time when the product in question was put into circulation. On this last point, Article 7(e) of the Directive, contrary to what the Commission seems to consider, raises difficulties of interpretation which, in the event of litigation, the national courts will have to resolve, having recourse, if necessary, to Article 177 of the EC Treaty.

. . .

32   The Commission takes the view that inasmuch as section 4(1)(e) of the Act refers to what may be expected of a producer of products of the same description as the product in question, its wording clearly conflicts with Article 7(e) of the Directive in that it permits account to be taken of the subjective knowledge of a producer taking reasonable care, having regard to the standard precautions taken in the industrial sector in question.

33   That argument must be rejected in so far as it selectively stresses particular terms used in section 4(1)(e) without demonstrating that the general legal context of the provision at issue fails effectively to secure full application of the Directive. Taking that context into account, the Commission has failed to make out its claim that the result intended by Article 7(e) of the Directive would clearly not be achieved in the domestic legal order.

. . .

37   . . . the Court has consistently held that the scope of national laws, regulations or administrative provisions must be assessed in the light of the interpretation given to them by national courts (see, in particular, Case C-382/92 Commission v United Kingdom 1994 ECR I-2435, paragraph 36). Yet in this case the Commission has not referred in support of its application to any national judicial decision which, in its view, interprets the domestic provision at issue inconsistently with the Directive.

38   Lastly, there is nothing in the material produced to the Court to suggest that the courts in the United Kingdom, if called upon to interpret section 4(1)(e), would not do so in the light of the wording and the purpose of the Directive so as to achieve the result which it has in view and thereby comply with the third paragraph of Article 189 of the Treaty (see, in particular, Case C-91/92 Faccini Dori v Recreb 1994 ECR I-3325, paragraph 26). Moreover, section 1(1) of the Act expressly imposes such an obligation on the national courts.

Not surprisingly, the interpretation of the defence in the decision above has been criticized from very different perspectives.

Chris Hodges, 'Development Risks: Unanswered Questions'
(1998) 61 MLR 560, at 569

At first sight, the test in the defence seems to be whether the defect could have been discovered by any human, using, it is implied, all available powers of logic, data and techniques. Relevant techniques might include the most sophisticated information technology, computing, testing and monitoring in use. Clearly, if this analysis is correct, the standard set by the defence is very high. It would only succeed in very rare circumstances, if ever. It requires all producers to adopt the very highest standard of methodology. Given that many innovations are discovered by small and medium enterprises, is it reasonable to expect all enterprises to adopt the same highest possible standard, irrespective of resources and cost?

These considerations undermine the credibility of this defence. The charge against the wording of the defence in the Directive is, therefore, that it is not capable of being interpreted in practice. It is unworkable on a literal reading and requires interpretation if it is to reflect the policy of protecting innovation . . .

M. Mildred and G. Howells, 'Comment on "Development Risks: Unanswered Questions"' (1998) 61 MLR 570, at 572

The existence of powerful computerised databases will allow the producer to satisfy itself of the nature of published knowledge in the various fields of knowledge before putting a product into circulation. Since they will be available without regard to the industrial sector within which the producer works there is no reason to confine discoverability by accessibility to a particular sector. There is no doubt that this will be a burden to producers but the very title of the Consumer Protection Act 1987 shows that the interests of the producer (which Hodges sets out to defend) are by no means paramount. The producer is, of course, undertaking innovation for competitive and economic advantage just as much as, if not more than, for philanthropic purposes.

Does the motive of the producer make a difference? 'Risky' products may of course be produced by non-profit-making organizations (as in *A v National Blood Authority*) but for the most part it is true that innovation is carried out in pursuit of profit—as indeed products such as hot tea and coffee are made available through the market. Beneficial products are still beneficial no matter what the incentive for producers to make them available, or to develop them. Should profit motive make a difference? If so, does this leave a major gap in justification for strict liability?

A v National Blood Authority: Development Risks Issues

Here we return to the leading UK case, *A v National Blood Authority*, and turn our attention to its treatment of the development risks defence.

For the reasons we explained above, Burton J referred directly to the Directive, rather than to the Act, when interpreting both 'defectiveness', and 'development risks'. His interpretation drew upon the Advocate General's opinion, above. In particular, he explained that the development risks defence does not assist a defendant where the *method for identifying and removing* the defect is unknown, provided the risk of that defect *is* known. Given that the risk of infection with Hepatitis C was clearly recognized, this finding was itself sufficient to dispose of the defence in this case. However, Burton J added a gloss regarding non-standard products (such as the bags of infected blood in this case). That is, non-standard products will very rarely attract the development risks defence. If they do so at all, they will do so only once, until the first non-standard product or 'lemon' is discovered.

Burton J, *A v National Blood Authority*

[75]   The purpose of the directive, from which art 7(e) should obviously not derogate more than is necessary (see Recital 16) is to prevent injury, and facilitate compensation for injury. The defendants submit that this means that art 7(e) must be construed so as to give the opportunity to the producer to do all he can in order to avoid injury: thus concentrating on what can be done in relation to the particular product. The claimants submit that this will rather be achieved by imposing obligation in respect of a known risk irrespective of the chances of finding the defect in the particular product, and I agree.

[76]   The purpose of art 7(e) was plainly not to discourage innovation, and to exclude development risks from the directive, and it succeeds in its objective, subject to the very considerable restrictions that are clarified by European Commission v UK: namely that the risk ceases to be a development risk and becomes a known risk not if and when the producer in question (or, as the CPA inappropriately sought to enact in s 4(1)(e) 'a producer of products of the same description as the product in question') had the requisite knowledge, but if and when such knowledge were accessible anywhere in the world outside Manchuria. Hence it protects the producer in respect of the unknown (inconnu). But the consequence of acceptance of the defendants' submissions would be that protection would also be given in respect of the known.

[77]   The effect is, it seems to me, not, as the BGH[19] has been interpreted as concluding (or perhaps as it did conclude, but if it did then I would respectfully differ) that non-standard products are incapable of coming within art 7(e). Non-standard products may qualify once—ie if the problem which leads to an occasional defective product is (unlike the present case) not known: this may perhaps be more unusual than in relation to a problem with a standard product, but does not seem to me to be an impossible scenario. However, once the problem is known by virtue of accessible information, then the non-standard product can no longer qualify for protection under art 7(e).

The decision in *A v National Blood Authority* has been subjected to some academic criticism (from different perspectives) by C. Hodges, 'Compensating Patients' (2001) 117 LQR 528; and G. Howells and M. Mildred, 'Infected Blood: Defect and Discoverability. A First Exposition of the EC Product Liability Directive' (2002) 65 MLR, 95. Counsel for the claimants and defendants offer some reflections on the case in M. Brooke and I. Forrester, 'The Use of Comparative Law in *A & Ors v National Blood Authority*', in Fairgrieve (ed.), *Product Liability in Comparative Perspective* (CUP, 2005). The chapter includes a postscript by the judge, Sir Michael Burton. The decision is more strongly criticized by J. Stapleton, 'Bugs in Anglo-American Product Liability', in the same collection (at pp. 325–90). In Stapleton's view, the judge tried too hard to give the Directive 'work to do', and to avoid the conclusion that the Directive (and the Consumer Protection Act 1987) were 'not only . . . toothless but pointless'. An alternative reading is that the judgment was thereby true to the objectives of the legislation. On the other hand, the treatment of 'non-standard products' in *A v National Blood Authority* has been met with some considerable doubt and this issue remains to be further explored—if indeed any suitable cases make their way to court.

---

[19]   This is a reference to the 'German bottle case' of 9 May 1995, NJW 1995, 2162 (German Federal Supreme Court, 'BGH'). A mineral water bottle with a hairline crack was defective, and the development risks defence was not made out, even though the producer applied the latest technology in its production process.

3.6 LIMITATION PERIOD

Limitation Act 1980

11A   Actions in respect of defective products

(1) This section shall apply to an action for damages by virtue of any provision of Part I of the Consumer Protection Act 1987.

(2) None of the time limits given in the preceding provisions of this Act shall apply to an action to which this section applies.

(3) An action to which this section applies shall not be brought after the expiration of the period of ten years from the relevant time, within the meaning of section 4 of the said act of 1987; and this subsection shall operate to extinguish a right of action and shall do so whether or not that right of action had accrued, or time under the following provisions of this Act had begun to run, at the end of the said period of ten years.

(4) Subject to subsection (4) below, an action to which this section applies in which the damages claimed by the plaintiff consist of or include damages in respect of personal injuries to the plaintiff or any other person or loss of or damage to any property, shall not be brought after the expiration of the period of three years from whichever is the later of—

   (a) the date on which the cause of action accrued; and

   (b) the date of knowledge of the injured person or, in the case of loss of damage to property, the date of knowledge of the plaintiff or (if earlier) of any person in whom his cause of action was previously vested.

(5) If in a case where the damages claimed by the plaintiff consist of or include damages in respect of personal injuries to the plaintiff or any other person the injured person died before the expiration of the period mentioned in subsection (4) above, that subsection shall have effect as respects the cause of action surviving for the benefit of his estate by virtue of section 1 of the Law Reform (Miscellaneous Provisions) Act 1934 as if for the reference to that period there were substituted a reference to the period of three years from whichever is the later of—

   (a) the date of death; and

   (b) the date of the personal representative's knowledge.

Claims under the Consumer Protection Act 1987 are not within the operation of section 33 of the Limitation Act 1980, which confers a discretion on the court in certain cases of personal injury to allow extension to the limitation period.[20]

Horne-Roberts v SmithKline Beecham [2001] EWCA Civ 2006; [2002] 1 WLR 1662

In this case, the claimant had brought an action for damages under the Consumer Protection Act 1987 in respect of injuries that he argued were caused by a vaccine. The batch number of the vaccine was identified, but was wrongly attributed to another producer. It was in fact produced by SmithKline Beecham. The error came to light in August 2000, the action having

[20] S 33 applies only to claims which are within s 11; and s 11A states that the preceding sections (including therefore s 11) do not apply to claims under the Consumer Protection Act 1987.

been commenced (against the wrong party) in August 1999. The vaccine was administered in June 1990, so that by this time the action was outside the ten-year limitation period set out in section 11A of the Limitation Act 1980 (above).

The Court of Appeal held that the claimant could substitute a different defendant pursuant to section 35 of the Limitation Act 1980, and CPR r 19.5, even when the ten-year period had expired.

Keene LJ, *Horne-Roberts v SKB*

13　The relevant rule of court is now CPR r 19.5, which provides: "(2) The court may substitute a party only if (a) the relevant limitation period was current when the proceedings were started; and (b) the substitution is necessary." Rule 19.5(3) provides: "The substitution of a party is necessary only if the court is satisfied that (a) the new party is to be substituted for a party who was named in the claim form in mistake for the new party"

For the purposes of this rule (and of section 35), claims under the Consumer Protection Act 1987 are to be treated in the same way as claims in contract and tort. But the limitation periods applied to common law actions in contract and tort are *procedural*: generally (and with the exception of the action in conversion) the expiry of the limitation period bars the *remedy*, but does not extinguish the *right*. There was a powerful argument that the variation of defendant in this case should not be permitted, because the Directive on Product Liability itself states that after the ten-year period has expired, the *right to an action* is extinguished. The long-stop provision is not a merely procedural bar.

Article 11

Member states shall provide in their legislation that the rights conferred upon the injured person pursuant to this Directive shall be extinguished upon the expiry of a period of ten years from the date on which the producer put into circulation the actual product which caused the damage, *unless the injured person has in the meantime instituted proceedings against the producer.*

(Emphasis added.)

Section 11A(3) of the Consumer Protection Act 1987 also expressly states that the section operates to *extinguish* the right of action.

The Court of Appeal seems to have thought that in a case where by mistake proceedings had been instituted against the wrong producer, the final proviso of Article 11 (italicized above) would be satisfied: this *is* a case where the injured party had 'instituted proceedings against the producer (albeit the wrong producer).[21] As such, the time limit for claims under the statute set out in section 11A was to be treated *for these purposes* as a normal time limit, and the claim was not extinguished.

---

[21] If this seems to be a stretch to benefit the claimant, it may indicate that courts in personal injuries actions are very used to operating a discretion to permit claims outside the limitation period.

In *O'Byrne v Aventis Pasteur MSD Ltd* (Case C-127/04, 9 February 2006), the European Court of Justice conceded that the issue of substitution of defendants was an issue of *procedural law*, and was therefore a matter for the national court. This appears to preserve the authority of *Horne-Roberts v SKB*.[22]

There is a more general point to be made about the limitation period. In the case of some products—particularly where those products are new and their risks are unfamiliar—it may take many years to recognize that an injury has occurred, or that the injury is related to the product. Section 11A(3) above states that the claim will expire ten years after the 'relevant date' defined in section 4. The relevant date is, broadly, the date of first supply. This is a 'long-stop' provision. Since section 33 of the Limitation Act 1980 does not apply to claims under the Consumer Protection Act 1987, it appears that there is no possibility of bringing a claim outside the ten-year long-stop period, except in the case of a substituted defendant as in *Horne-Roberts v SKB*. This is a further reason why some of the more complex product liability claims may continue to be brought in negligence.

FURTHER READING

Clark, A., *Product Liability* (London: Sweet & Maxwell, 1989).

Fairgrieve, D., (ed.), *Product Liability in Comparative Perspective* (Cambridge: CUP: 2005).

Goldberg, R., *Causation and Risk in the Law of Torts: Scientific Evidence and Medicinal Product Liability* (Oxford: Hart Publishing, 1999).

Hodges, C., 'Development Risks: Unanswered Questions' (1998) 61 MLR 560.

Hodges, C., 'Approaches to Product Liability in the EU and Member States', in D. Fairgrieve (ed.), *Product Liability in Comparative Perspective* (Cambridge: CUP, 2005).

Hodges, C., 'Product Liability: Suppliers, Limitation and Mistake' (2006) 122 LQR 393.

Howells, G., *Comparative Product Liability* (Aldershot: Dartmouth, 1993).

Mildred, M. and Howells, G., 'Comment on "Development Risks: Unanswered Questions"' (1998) 61 MLR 570.

Newdick, C., 'The Development Risk Defence of the Consumer Protection Act 1987' (1988) 47 CLJ 455–76.

Newdick, C., 'The Future of Negligence in Product Liability' (1987) 103 LQR 288–310.

Stapleton, J., 'Product Liability Reform—Real or Illusory?' (1986) 6 OJLS 392–422.

Stapleton, J., *Product Liability* (London: Butterworths, 1994).

Stapleton, J., 'Bugs in Anglo-American Product Liability', in D. Fairgrieve (ed.), *Product Liability in Comparative Perspective* (Cambridge: CUP, 2005) 295–333.

Whittaker, S., *Liability for Products: English Law, French Law, and European Harmonization* (Oxford: OUP, 2005).

---

[22] See however the note by C. Hodges, 'Product Liability: Suppliers, Limitation and Mistake' (2006) 122 *LQR* 393, arguing that *Horne-Roberts* is wrong or the UK has not properly transposed the Directive.

16

BREACH OF STATUTORY DUTY

CENTRAL ISSUES

i) If a statute imposes a duty but does not specify a civil remedy, an action in tort may sometimes be available to remedy harm caused by a breach of the duty. This action in tort will be an action for 'breach of statutory duty'. The duty is defined by statute; but the action is brought at common law.

ii) Historically, the action for breach of statutory duty has been very significant

in the context of industrial safety. Outside that area it has been more restricted in scope, and the trend of recent case law is to adopt an approach which restricts it further. The key issue is the approach to interpretation of legislative intent. Considerable growth in the range and type of legislation has probably contributed to the current restrictions.

1. TORT AND LEGISLATION: THE DISTINCTIVENESS OF THE TORT OF 'BREACH OF STATUTORY DUTY'

Although tort is chiefly a creation of common law, it is deeply affected by legislation. In earlier chapters of this book, we have seen that statutes variously (and among other things) alter the operation of the common law (see for example the Law Reform (Contributory Negligence) Act 1945); create new rights of action dependent on existing tort rules (the Fatal Accidents Act 1976 and its predecessors); allow claimants to proceed against parties other than the tortfeasor (Third Parties (Rights Against Insurers) Act 1930); provide for the time-barring of actions (Limitation Act 1980); and ensure that there is insurance in place to compensate tort victims (Road Traffic Act 1988; Employers' Liability (Compulsory Insurance) Act 1969). Equally, some statutes define self-contained causes of action which can be called 'statutory torts'. Examples which are closely related to existing common law are the Occupiers' Liability Acts 1957 and 1984, and the Consumer Protection Act 1987. There are other examples, which for various reasons are not typically studied as part of the law of tort, including the Nuclear Installations Act 1965, and Water Industry Act 1991.[1] One of the most important statutory

---

[1] For a fuller picture of the contemporary role of statute in tort law, see Stanton, Skidmore, Harris, and Wright, *Statutory Torts* (Sweet & Maxwell, 2003).

civil actions resembling a tort is the action under section 7 of the Human Rights Act 1998, where a public authority breaches (or is likely to breach) its duty to respect a relevant 'Convention right'.

The topic of the present chapter is distinct from all of the examples above. The tort action for breach of statutory duty is a hybrid between statute (defining the duty) and common law (determining whether the breach is actionable).

Lord Wright, *London Passenger Transport Board v Upson* [1949] AC 155, at 168

. . . a claim for damages for breach of a statutory duty intended to protect a person in the position of the particular plaintiff is a specific common law right which is not to be confused in essence with a claim for negligence. The statutory right has its origin in the statute, but the particular remedy of an action for damages is given by the common law in order to make effective, for the benefit of the injured plaintiff, his right to the performance by the defendant of the defendant's statutory duty.

2. THE QUESTION OF INTERPRETATION: DOES THE BREACH GIVE RISE TO LIABILITY AT COMMON LAW?

The general opinion seems to be that this area is thoroughly confused and unpredictable. In fact, we can understand the majority of the case law in terms of two contrasting approaches to Parliamentary intent. There has been a recent drift towards the first and more restrictive of the two approaches, but the second is still applied in most 'health and safety' cases.

2.1 TWO POTENTIAL APPROACHES

Lord Simonds, *Cutler v Wandsworth Stadium Ltd* [1949] AC 398, at 169

The only rule which in all the circumstances is valid is that the answer must depend on a consideration of the whole Act and the circumstances, including the pre-existing law, in which it was enacted.

'What did Parliament intend (or not intend)?' is potentially a very open-ended question. In order to answer it, it is not enough simply to study the statute in its context. We also need to know roughly what we are looking for.

What are We Looking For?

The following two distinct approaches are present in the case law explored in this chapter.[2]

Interpretive approach 1: we are looking for legislative intent to create the cause of action

---

[2] Our coverage is of course selective. For more extensive examination of the action and its development see K. Stanton, *Breach of Statutory Duty in Tort* (2nd edn, Sweet & Maxwell, 1986).

On this approach, the cause of action in tort for breach of statutory duty depends on there being an intention, on the part of the legislature, *to create* such a common law right of action.

If no intention to create the right of action can be identified, no right of action will be held to exist. If this is what we are looking for, then there is a single question of statutory interpretation:

Did Parliament intend there to be a right of action at common law?

There may of course be various factors weighing for or against such an intention.

Interpretive approach 2: we are looking for legislative intent to benefit the claimant

On this approach, the cause of action in tort for breach of statutory duty depends on there being an intention, on the part of the legislature, to *benefit* the claimant or a limited class of people including the claimant.

Here, the right of action arises at common law, in order to give effect to the statutory duty.[3] If this is the correct analysis, there are two questions of statutory interpretation. Both are different from the single question above:

(a) **Did Parliament enact the duty with the intention of benefiting the claimant?; and**

(b) **Is there any reason to think that Parliament intended to exclude the right of action, which is available at common law as a means of enforcing the duty?**

Interpretive question (b) will be triggered if (for example) the statute provides for an alternative means of enforcement, such as a criminal penalty. But in principle, this is only one example of the circumstances in which the court may conclude that Parliament did not intend there to be a right of action.

It should be obvious that *both* these approaches involve interpretation of Parliamentary intention. It is easy to see why they can be and often are understood in terms of the relevant *presumption* that applies. The first approach typically starts with a presumption that there is *no* right of action where a statutory duty is breached, unless there is good reason to think that Parliament intended to create such an action. The second approach involves a presumption that there *is* a right of action, but *only* if (a) is satisfied: the statutory duty seems designed to benefit the claimant or a class including the claimant.

There is now a strong trend towards the first interpretive approach, and this has led to *restriction* in the action for breach of statutory duty.

We start our extracts with a defining case of civil liability for breach of industrial safety legislation. It exemplifies the second approach above, in which the right of action is presumed to arise at common law, *provided* the legislature intended to confer a benefit.

Groves v Wimborne (Lord) [1898] 2 QB 402

The plaintiff was a boy employed in the defendant's Iron Works. By section 5 of the Factory and Workshop Act 1878, certain dangerous machinery had to remain fenced. Relevant machinery was left unfenced, and the plaintiff's arm was caught in the cog-wheels of a steam winch. He was so badly injured that his forearm had to be amputated. There was clearly a breach of section 5. The duty imposed by this section was not subject to reasonable care or to any questions of practicability or efficiency. It was an 'absolute' duty.

The Court of Appeal held that the defendant was liable in damages to the plaintiff. The key difficulty of interpretation arose from the fact that the statute provided sanctions for a breach

---

3 'Benefit' to the claimant may certainly include protection from harm (*Groves v Wimborne*); it may also perhaps include the conferral of rights whose invasion is actionable *per se* (*Cullen v RUC*, Lords Bingham and Steyn, dissenting).

of duty, in the form of fines and penalties. Should these penalties be taken to show that Parliament wished to exclude the action at common law which would otherwise arise from a breach of the statutory duty?

A. L. Smith LJ, *Groves v Wimborne* [1898] 2 QB 402, at 406–7

The Act in question, which followed numerous other Acts in pari materiâ, is not in the nature of a private legislative bargain between employers and workmen, as the learned judge seemed to think, but is a public Act passed in favour of the workers in factories and workshops to compel their employers to do certain things for their protection and benefit. The first question is what duty is imposed by that Act upon the occupiers of factories and workshops with regard to the fencing of machinery. By s. 5 it is enacted that "with respect to the fencing of machinery the following provisions shall have effect." Then by sub-s. 3 of the section, as amended by the Factory and Workshop Act, 1891, s. 6, sub-s. 2, "All dangerous parts of the machinery, and every part of the mill gearing shall either be securely fenced, or be in such position or of such construction as to be equally safe to every person employed in the factory as it would be if it were securely fenced"; and by sub-s. 4, "All fencing shall be constantly maintained in an efficient state while the parts required to be fenced are in motion or use for the purpose of any manufacturing process"; and "a factory in which there is a contravention of this section shall be deemed not to be kept in conformity with this Act." In the present case it is admitted that machinery on the defendant's premises which came within these provisions was not fenced as required by the Act, and that injury was thereby occasioned to the plaintiff, a boy employed on the works. On proof of a breach of this statutory duty imposed on the defendant, and injury resulting to the plaintiff therefrom, primâ facie the plaintiff has a good cause of action. I leave out of the question for a moment the provisions of ss. 81, 82, and 86 of the Act. Could it be doubted that, if s. 5 stood alone, and no fine were provided by the Act for contravention of its provisions, a person injured by a breach of the absolute and unqualified duty imposed by that section would have a cause of action in respect of that breach? Clearly it could not be doubted. That being so, unless it appears from the whole "purview" of the Act, to use the language of Lord Cairns in the case of *Atkinson v. Newcastle Waterworks Co.* (1877) 2 Ex D 441, that it was the intention of the Legislature that the only remedy for breach of the statutory duty should be by proceeding for the fine imposed by s. 82, it follows that, upon proof of a breach of that duty by the employer and injury thereby occasioned to the workman, a cause of action is established. The question therefore is whether the cause of action which primâ facie is given by s. 5 is taken away by any provisions to be found in the remainder of the Act. It is said that the provisions of ss. 81, 82, and 86 have that effect, and that it appears thereby that the purview of the Act is that the only remedy, where a workman has been injured by a breach of the duty imposed by s. 5, shall be by proceeding before a court of summary jurisdiction for a fine under s. 82, which fine is not to exceed £100. In dealing with the question whether this was the intention of the Legislature, it is material, as Kelly C.B. pointed out in giving judgment in the case of *Gorris v. Scott* (1874) LR 9 Ex 125, to consider for whose benefit the Act was passed, whether it was passed in the interests of the public at large or in those of a particular class of persons.

Vaughan Williams LJ, at 415

I am of the same opinion. In the result I entertain no doubt that upon the proper construction of the Factory and Workshop Act, 1878, the Legislature did not intend the remedy or benefit which may be given under s. 82 through the intervention of the Secretary of State to a person

injured through a breach of the provisions of the Act with regard to fencing machinery to be
the only remedy open to a person so injured. . . .

. . . it cannot be doubted that, where a statute provides for the performance by certain persons
of a particular duty, and some one belonging to a class of persons for whose benefit and protection the statute imposes the duty is injured by failure to perform it, primâ facie, and, if there
be nothing to the contrary, an action by the person so injured will lie against the person who
has so failed to perform the duty. I have equally no doubt that, where in a statute of this kind a
remedy is provided in cases of non-performance of the statutory duty, that is a matter to be
taken into consideration for the purpose of determining whether an action will lie for injury
caused by non-performance of that duty, or whether the Legislature intended that there
should be no other remedy than the statutory remedy; but it is by no means conclusive or the
only matter to be taken into consideration for that purpose.

Commentary

In its day, the huge practical significance of *Groves v Wimborne* was that it provided a remedy
to an employee injured at work which could not at that time have been achieved through any
other action in tort. The statutory duty was imposed directly upon the employer and was
absolute in nature. Therefore, even if a fellow employee was directly responsible for removing
the fencing which had at one time been present, the employer could not escape liability by
invoking the 'doctrine of common employment'.[4] *Groves v Wimborne* established an important gap in the protection given to employers by that doctrine, and was compatible with the
general legislative effort to protect the safety of workers at that time. The approach in this case
was subsequently applied in many others.[5]

Today of course there is no doctrine of common employment and vicarious liability is well
established. There is therefore less need for the action for breach of statutory duty. Equally,
most health and safety regulations are now governed by the Health and Safety at Work Act
1974. This Act clearly specifies which breaches are intended to be actionable in a civil claim,
and which are not. Again, the importance of the tort action is reduced. On the other hand, the
authority of *Groves v Wimborne* remains undiminished in respect of duties existing before the
1974 Act was passed, and in respect of other 'safety' cases to which the 1974 Act does not
apply.[6] The advantage of the action for breach of statutory duty over negligence is that the
applicable statutory duty is often specified with precision, and may involve no question of
'reasonable care'. Thus the relevant duties may be both more precise, and stricter, than the
duty to take care in negligence.

On a more technical note, it is clear from the passage above that A. L. Smith LJ thought that
in the absence of provision for a fine or other penalty (see below), there would *clearly* be a right
of action in consequence of the breach of duty. Both he and Vaughan Williams LJ described
this as a '*prima facie*' right where the duty conferred a benefit on the plaintiff, and regarded it
as obvious. Therefore, attention was turned to the question of the fine. Did this show an intention to exclude the 'prima facie' right to an action? Given that the maximum fine was set at

---

[4] This doctrine held that an employee could not bring an action in respect of the tort of a fellow employee
(of the same master). The doctrine no longer exists in any form. See further Chapter 5, in respect of *volenti non
fit injuria* (willing acceptance of risk).

[5] See in particular the decision of the House of Lords in *Butler v Fife Coal Co Ltd* [1912] AC 149.

[6] See *Ziemniak v ETPM Deep Sea Ltd* [2003] EWCA Civ 636—an accident at sea governed by regulations
under the Merchant Shipping Act 1979—below.

£100; that there was no assurance that any part of the fine would go to the plaintiff or his family; and that the fine might in the event be imposed upon an employee (so that the employer would escape liability completely); the Court of Appeal concluded that the existence of the fine did not displace the presumption that there was a common law right of action for breach of the statutory duty, which arose because that duty was for the benefit of the plaintiff. It could not be concluded that Parliament had intended the fine to be the *only* remedy.

Sanctions and other means of enforcement

The Court of Appeal in *Groves v Wimborne* gave due weight to the existence of a *statutory sanction*. The role of sanctions and alternative remedies is often considered with reference to the following judicial comment. (The case from which this comment is derived had nothing to do with the action for breach of statutory duty in tort. It was concerned with the status of a lease under which the statutory manner of paying rent had not been complied with. The question was whether an alternative way of paying the rent was good enough to safeguard the rights of a successor to the lessee.)

Doe d Bishop of Rochester v Bridges [1824–1834] All ER 167 (1831)

. . . Where an Act creates an obligation, and enforces the performance in a specified manner, we take it to be a general rule that performance cannot be enforced in any other manner. If an obligation is created, but no mode of enforcing its performance is ordained, the common law may, in general, find a mode suited to the particular nature of the case.

This statement has been taken to suggest that there cannot be an action for breach of statutory duty if some other means of enforcement of the duty exists. The Court of Appeal in *Groves v Wimborne* quite properly regarded the existence of an alternative means of enforcement as a *factor* to be considered when establishing Parliamentary intent. In *Cutler v Wandsworth Stadium* [1949] AC 398, Lord Simonds referred to the above passage from *Doe v Bridges*. But he also relied upon *Groves* and the subsequent case of *Black v Fife Coal Co Ltd* [1912] AC 149, acknowledging that the existence of a penalty was not *decisive* against an action for breach of statutory duty.

In *Cutler*, Lord Simonds also stated a *positive* presumption flowing from the *absence* of any other means of enforcement:

Lord Simonds, *Cutler v Wandsworth Stadium*, at 170

. . . if a statutory duty is prescribed but no remedy by way of penalty or otherwise for its breach is imposed, it can be assumed that a right of civil action accrues to the person who is damnified by the breach. For, if it were not so, the statute would be but a pious aspiration.

This presumption too may be rebutted in a suitable case.

The importance of statutory interpretation in Groves v Wimborne

On the second interpretive approach outlined above, the *starting* point should be the purpose of the statute. Was the statute intended to benefit the claimant (or a class of people including the claimant)? *Cutler v Wandsworth* itself is a good illustration of this.

Cutler v Wandsworth Stadium [1949] AC 398

The plaintiff was a bookmaker. He brought an action against the occupier of a licensed dog-racing track for failing to provide him with space on the track where he could carry out book-making, in accordance with section 11(2)(b) of the Betting and Lotteries Act 1934. Criminal penalties were specified for failure to comply with this provision. The House of Lords held that no civil action was available on the part of the plaintiff in respect of a breach of this duty.

Lord Simonds, *Cutler v Wandsworth Stadium*, at 409

. . . I have no doubt that the primary intention of the Act was to regulate in certain respects the conduct of race tracks and in particular the conduct of betting operations thereon. If in conse-quence of those regulations being observed some bookmakers will be benefited, this does not mean that the Act was passed for the benefit of bookmakers in the sense in which it was said of a Factory Act that it was passed in favour of the workmen in factories. I agree with Somervell LJ that where an Act regulates the way in which a place of amusement is to be managed, the interests of the public who resort to it may be expected to be the primary con-sideration of the legislature. If from the work of regulation any class of persons derives an advantage, that does not spring from the primary purpose and intention of the Act.

In more recent years, Parliamentary intention has been interpreted in a different way. Here we extract two very significant cases. The approach taken in the second of these, *Ex p. Hague*, is clearly incompatible with the *Groves* case, although the actual outcome could be reconciled with it. The first of the two, extracted next, is more subtle. Is it compatible with *Groves*, or not?

Lonrho v Shell Petroleum (No 2) [1982] AC 173

Lonrho invested considerable sums in the construction and operation of an oil pipeline to take oil from Mozambique to Southern Rhodesia. The pipeline was completed in January 1965. In November 1965 the government of Southern Rhodesia declared unilateral inde-pendence. Measures were put in place prohibiting trade with Southern Rhodesia, including the supply of oil. Lonrho argued that Shell and others had continued to supply oil to Southern Rhodesia although this was prohibited. If so, this would be in breach of the Southern Rhodesia (Petroleum) Order 1965, and a criminal offence. Lonrho further argued that they suffered financial loss through this breach of the Order on the part of Shell, since their actions enabled the regime in Rhodesia to resist international pressure, prolonging the need for sanctions and causing Lonrho to make significant losses. Here, we extract the part of Lord Diplock's judgment which deals with the action for breach of statutory duty.[7]

---

[7] Lord Diplock's was the only full judgment in the case. See also Chapter 2 for discussion of the case in relation to civil conspiracy.

Lord Diplock, *Lonrho v Shell Petroleum (No 2)* [1982] AC 173, at 185–6

The sanctions Order . . . creates a statutory prohibition upon the doing of certain classes of acts and provides the means of enforcing the prohibition by prosecution for a criminal offence which is subject to heavy penalties including imprisonment. So one starts with the presumption laid down originally by Lord Tenterden C.J. in *Doe d. Murray v. Bridges* (1831) 1 B. & Ad. 847, 859, where he spoke of the "general rule" that "where an Act creates an obligation, and enforces the performance in a specified manner . . . that performance cannot be enforced in any other manner"—a statement that has frequently been cited with approval ever since, including on several occasions in speeches in this House. Where the only manner of enforcing performance for which the Act provides is prosecution for the criminal offence of failure to perform the statutory obligation or for contravening the statutory prohibition which the Act creates, there are two classes of exception to this general rule.

The first is where upon the true construction of the Act it is apparent that the obligation or prohibition was imposed for the benefit or protection of a particular class of individuals, as in the case of the Factories Acts and similar legislation As Lord Kinnear put it in *Butler (or Black) v. Fife Coal Co. Ltd.* [1912] A.C. 149, 165, in the case of such a statute:

> "There is no reasonable ground for maintaining that a proceeding by way of penalty is the only remedy allowed by the statute . . . We are to consider the scope and purpose of the statute and in particular for whose benefit it is intended. Now the object of the present statute is plain. It was intended to compel mine owners to make due provision for the safety of the men working in their mines, and the persons for whose benefit all these rules are to be enforced are the persons exposed to danger. But when a duty of this kind is imposed for the benefit of particular persons there arises at common law a correlative right in those persons who may be injured by its contravention.

The second exception is where the statute creates a public right (i.e. a right to be enjoyed by all those of Her Majesty's subjects who wish to avail themselves of it) and a particular member of the public suffers what Brett J. in *Benjamin v. Storr* (1874) L.R. 9 C.P. 400, 407, described as "particular, direct, and substantial" damage "other and different from that which was common to all the rest of the public." Most of the authorities about this second exception deal not with public rights created by statute but with public rights existing at common law, particularly in respect of use of highways. *Boyce v. Paddington Borough Council* [1903] 1 Ch. 109 is one of the comparatively few cases about a right conferred upon the general public by statute. It is in relation to that class of statute only that Buckley J.'s oft-cited statement at p. 114 as to the two cases in which a plaintiff, without joining the Attorney-General, could himself sue in private law for interference with that public right, must be understood. The two cases he said were: " . . . first, where the interference with the public right is such as that some private right of his is at the same time interfered with . . . and, secondly, where no private right is interfered with, but the plaintiff, in respect of his public right, suffers special damage peculiar to himself from the interference with the public right." The first case would not appear to depend upon the existence of a public right in addition to the private one; while to come within the second case at all it has first to be shown that the statute, having regard to its scope and language, does fall within that class of statutes which creates a legal right to be enjoyed by all of Her Majesty's subjects who wish to avail themselves of it. A mere prohibition upon members of the public generally from doing what it would otherwise be lawful for them to do, is not enough.

My Lords, it has been the unanimous opinion of the arbitrators with the concurrence of the umpire, of Parker J., and of each of the three members of the Court of Appeal that the sanctions Orders made pursuant to the Southern Rhodesia Act 1965 fell within neither of these two exceptions. Clearly they were not within the first category of exception. They were not imposed for the *benefit or protection* of a particular class of individuals who were engaged in supplying or delivering crude oil or petroleum products to Southern Rhodesia. They were intended to put an end to such transactions. Equally plainly they did not create any public right to be enjoyed by all those of Her Majesty's subjects who wished to avail themselves of it. On the contrary, what they did was to withdraw a previously existing right of citizens of, and companies incorporated in, the United Kingdom to trade with Southern Rhodesia in crude oil and petroleum products. Their purpose was, perhaps, most aptly stated by Fox L.J.:

> "I cannot think that they were concerned with conferring rights either upon individuals or the public at large. Their purpose was the destruction, by economic pressure, of the U.D.I. regime in Southern Rhodesia; they were instruments of state policy in an international matter."

At first sight, Lord Diplock appears to have adopted a general presumption *against* a civil right of action. But on inspection, this presumption is not general at all, but is *specific* to cases where another means of enforcing the duty (including a criminal penalty) is contained in the statute. The entire discussion in this extract therefore fits into question (b) in the second interpretive approach above.

Even here, where a statutory means of enforcement (a criminal sanction) exists, Lord Diplock went on to explain that there are two ways in which the presumption against a common law action for breach of statutory duty might be rebutted. The first of these exceptions is where the obligation is imposed for the benefit or protection of a particular class of individuals. This would clearly include a case like *Groves*. But if *Groves v Wimborne* is correct, then Lord Diplock has his rules and exceptions the wrong way around. The *general rule* should be that there is an action for breach of a duty, if that duty is intended to benefit the claimant: the possible *exception* is that if there is a statutory penalty, it should be considered whether Parliament intended this to be the only means of enforcement.

Lord Diplock's approach is likely to *broaden* the scope of the action. If 'conferring a benefit' is an exception to the general rule, then how is the intention of Parliament to be further considered? There seems to be no room for an exception to this exception. It is probably Lord Diplock's interpretation which has led to the impression (otherwise plainly untrue) that the presumptions applying in *Groves* do not involve interpretation of the will of Parliament, but give rise to automatic liability (see the argument put for the plaintiff in *Ex p. Hague*, below).

The second of Lord Diplock's exceptional categories is much more difficult to interpret, but it turns on the *creation of legal rights to be enjoyed by all of Her Majesty's subjects*. It is notoriously unclear what Lord Diplock had in mind here, not least because the case he cites (*Benjamin v Storr*) is a case of public nuisance, not of breach of statutory duty.[8] All things considered, we should not struggle unduly with this category, which has not developed since *Lonrho*.[9]

---

[8] It is important to notice that one of Lord Diplock's more puzzling pronouncements—that 'a mere prohibition on members of the public generally . . . is not enough' *relates specifically to this narrow category of case.* Lord Diplock does *not* say here that failure to abide by a prohibition imposed on the general public cannot ever amount to a breach of duty; nor even that it cannot ever give rise to an action for breach of statutory duty. He simply says that such a prohibition will not suffice to create legal rights on the part of the public generally (whatever that might mean).

[9] The authors of the leading work on breach of statutory duty say that 'little is known' about this category, and that 'No action has been successfully based on these words since they were uttered' (Stanton et al, *Statutory Torts*, 2.024, p. 38).

In any event, it is abundantly clear that Lord Diplock did not consider that breach of the Order of 1965 could be interpreted as giving rise to a right of action. The goal of the statute and of the Order was not to benefit companies like Lonrho—nor anyone else. All the Order aimed to do was to contribute to the end of the regime in Southern Rhodesia. This conclusion might have been reached rather more quickly, since this finding as to statutory purpose would mean failure on *either* of the two interpretive approaches we outlined above.

The following case more clearly shows a departure from the approach in *Groves v Wimborne*, though it does not seek to cast doubt upon that case itself.

R v Deputy Governor of Parkhurst, ex p. Hague [1992] 1 AC 58

The plaintiffs, who were lawfully detained in prison, argued that they had been subjected to treatment which was in breach of Prison Rules. In the case of Hague (the first plaintiff), it was alleged that he was segregated from other prisoners in breach of the Rules, and that this breach was subject to an action for breach of statutory duty.[10]

The crucial question is set out in the following passage:

Lord Jauncey

Mr. Sedley for Hague submitted that there had been a breach of the prison rules which sounded in damages. In a carefully reasoned argument to which I hope that I do justice in para-phrasing he argued that a breach of statutory duty unaccompanied by a statutory remedy or penalty affords a right of action to a person injured thereby where the plaintiff belongs to a class which the statutory provision was intended to protect, and the breach has caused the plaintiff damage of a kind against which the provision was intended to protect him. In support of this proposition he relied on *Groves v. Lord Wimborne* [1898] 2 Q.B. 402 and *Cutler v. Wandsworth Stadium Ltd.* [1949] A.C. 398. Where such a situation existed, as it did in the present case, no question of legislative intent arose. . . .

Mr. Laws on the other hand maintained that the first question to be considered was what rights, if any, Parliament intended to confer in passing the statute and that matters such as availability of other remedies merely assisted the resolution of that question and were not in themselves decisive. He also relied on *Groves v. Wimborne* and *Cutler v. Wandsworth Stadium Ltd.* Mr. Laws argued that the Secretary of State had no power under section 47 of the Prison Act 1952 to make rules which conferred private rights on individuals.[11]

These possible approaches, set out by rival counsel, almost precisely reflect the two interpretive approaches we outlined at the start of this section. However there is one crucial difference, which is that the argument put for Hague implies that no reference to Parliamentary intention is required in a case where the statute confers a benefit, and there is no penalty or other means of enforcement specified in the statute. This would make the action for breach of statutory duty *automatic* in such a case. As we have explained, any such implication is at odds with the reasoning in *Groves*.

---

[10] The prisoners also brought actions for false imprisonment (Chapter 2). These actions also failed: the change in conditions of imprisonment could not make their imprisonment unlawful.

[11] Both counsel in this case (Sedley for the plaintiff and Laws for the Deputy Governor) are now Lords Justices of Appeal. In the light of their judgments extracted in other parts of this book, does their professional disagreement as counsel in this case seem to reflect a genuine difference of perspective?

In the event, this ambitious argument backfired. Throughout his judgment, Lord Jauncey took it that *any* reference in the authorities to statutory intention disproved the approach urged by the plaintiffs, and proved the approach urged by the defendants. Every authority consulted referred, of course, to the importance of Parliamentary intention; and Lord Jauncey did not distinguish which *sort* of intention (to create a right of action, or to benefit the claimant) was required.

Lord Jauncey concluded with an approach that is at odds with *Groves v Wimborne*:

At 170

My Lords, I take from these authorities that it must always be a matter for consideration whether the legislature intended that private law rights of action should be conferred upon individuals in respect of breaches of the relevant statutory provision. The fact that a particular provision was intended to protect certain individuals is not of itself sufficient to confer private law rights of action upon them, something more is required to show that the legislature intended such conferment.

The Prison Act 1952 is designed to deal with the administration of prisons and the management and control of prisoners. It covers such wide-ranging matters as central administration, prison officers, confinement and treatment of prisoners, release of prisoners on licence, provision and maintenance of prisons and offences. Its objects are far removed from those of legislation such as the factories and coal mines Acts whose prime concern is to protect the health and safety of persons who work therein. Section 47 empowers the Secretary of State to make rules in relation to many of the matters with which the Act is concerned and is in the following terms, inter alia:

> "(1) The Secretary of State may make rules for the regulation and management of prisons, remand centres, detention centres and Borstal institutions respectively, and for the classification, treatment, employment, discipline and control of persons required to be detained therein."

I find nothing in any of the other sections of the Act to suggest that Parliament intended thereby to confer on prisoners a cause of action sounding in damages in respect of a breach of those provisions. To give the Secretary of State power in section 47 to confer private law rights on prisoners would therefore be to allow him to extend the general scope of the Act by rules.

Lord Jauncey misstates some of the authorities we have explored above when he says that the crucial issue is always whether the legislature intended that private rights of action should be conferred. In both *Groves* and *Lonrho*, and also other decisions quoted by Lord Jauncey such as *Black v Fife*, the question is whether the duty seeks to confer, not a right of action, but *a benefit* (which in the safety legislation takes the form of *protection from harm*) upon the claimant. Lord Jauncey here takes the step from the second interpretive approach we outlined at the start of this section, to the first.

This has proved to be decisive for the action for breach of statutory duty outside the health and safety field. In later decisions, at least outside the health and safety field, it has consistently been said that the crucial question is *whether the legislature intended to confer a right of action*.

As for *Hague* itself, the selection of interpretive approach might have been decisive, if it had been found that the legislature *did* intend to benefit prisoners through the relevant Prison Rule (by setting limits to acceptable treatment). But the purpose of the relevant Prison Rule as the House of Lords interpreted it was not, in any event, to benefit the prisoner:

Lord Bridge, at 160

The purpose of the rule, apart from the case of prisoners who need to be segregated in their own interests, is to give an obviously necessary power to segregate prisoners who are liable for any reason to disturb the orderly conduct of the prison generally. The rule is a purely preventive measure.

In later case law, *Ex p. Hague* has been explained as a case where the relevant Rules were 'regulatory in character'. Therefore, like *Lonrho*, the case could have been disposed of simply by saying that the purpose of the statutory duty was not to benefit the plaintiff.

2.2 FURTHER RESTRICTIONS: 'SOCIAL WELFARE' LEGISLATION AND 'PUBLIC LAW DUTIES'

X v Bedfordshire CC [1995] 2 AC 633

This was a defining case in respect of the duty of care in negligence in the context of statutory *powers* (Chapter 6). It was an equally important case in respect of the action for breach of statutory duty.[12]

The appeals heard together by the House of Lords comprised two cases raising child protection matters; and three cases raising issues of educational malpractice. The applicable child protection legislation involved statutory duties, as well as statutory powers. It was therefore argued that in the child protection cases, there was (in addition to the negligence action) an action for breach of a statutory duty. This, like the negligence claim, was rejected.

Lord Browne-Wilkinson, *X v Bedfordshire CC*, at 731–2

The principles applicable in determining whether such statutory cause of action exists are now well established, although the application of those principles in any particular case remains difficult. The basic proposition is that in the ordinary case a breach of statutory duty does not, by itself, give rise to any private law cause of action. However a private law cause of action will arise if it can be shown, as a matter of construction of the statute, that the statutory duty was imposed for the protection of a limited class of the public and that Parliament intended to confer on members of that class a private right of action for breach of the duty. There is no general rule by reference to which it can be decided whether a statute does create such a right of action but there are a number of indicators. If the statute provides no other remedy for its breach and the Parliamentary intention to protect a limited class is shown, that indicates that there may be a private right of action since otherwise there is no method of securing the protection the statute was intended to confer. If the statute does provide some other means of enforcing the duty that will normally indicate that the statutory right was intended to be

---

[12] When we addressed the negligence claims in *X v Bedfordshire* in Chapter 6, we noted that the authority of the decision in relation to negligence is now doubtful following *Z v UK* (2001) 34 EHRR 97 and *D v East Berkshire* [2005] 2 AC 373. It is just possible that the conclusion on breach of statutory duty—that the duties were not owed to the children—could also be reviewed in the light of these decisions.

enforceable by those means and not by private right of action: *Cutler v. Wandsworth Stadium Ltd.* [1949] A.C. 398; *Lonrho Ltd. v. Shell Petroleum Co. Ltd. (No. 2)* [1982] A.C. 173. However, the mere existence of some other statutory remedy is not necessarily decisive. It is still possible to show that on the true construction of the statute the protected class was intended by Parliament to have a private remedy. Thus the specific duties imposed on employers in relation to factory premises are enforceable by an action for damages, notwithstanding the imposition by the statutes of criminal penalties for any breach: see *Groves v. Wimborne (Lord)* [1898] 2 Q.B. 402.

Although the question is one of statutory construction and therefore each case turns on the provisions in the relevant statute, it is significant that your Lordships were not referred to any case where it had been held that statutory provisions establishing a regulatory system or a scheme of social welfare for the benefit of the public at large had been held to give rise to a private right of action for damages for breach of statutory duty. Although regulatory or welfare legislation affecting a particular area of activity does in fact provide protection to those individuals particularly affected by that activity, the legislation is not to be treated as being passed for the benefit of those individuals but for the benefit of society in general. Thus legislation regulating the conduct of betting or prisons did not give rise to a statutory right of action vested in those adversely affected by the breach of the statutory provisions, i.e. bookmakers and prisoners: see *Cutler's* case [1949] A.C. 398; *Reg. v. Deputy Governor of Parkhurst Prison, Ex parte Hague* [1992] 1 A.C. 58. The cases where a private right of action for breach of statutory duty have been held to arise are all cases in which the statutory duty has been very limited and specific as opposed to general administrative functions imposed on public bodies and involving the exercise of administrative discretions.

Lord Browne-Wilkinson followed the *Ex p. Hague* approach, and thought this consistent with all of the previous case law (including *Groves v Wimborne*). Indeed, he seems to go even further, clearly stating (as Lord Jauncey did not) that there is a presumption *against* a right of action, and that it must be established that Parliament intended such a right to exist, if the action is to succeed. Equally clearly, we can see from the final paragraph above that Lord Browne-Wilkinson thought that the statutory duties arising in a 'scheme of social welfare' are not generally of a type that would give rise to an action in tort. They are too broad and imprecise, and their aim is to benefit the public at large, rather than a specified class of individuals.

Later in his judgment, Lord Browne-Wilkinson applied this general approach to the cases in hand. He seems to have concluded that the particular 'social welfare' scheme involved in these cases *was* designed for the benefit of children at risk; but that this was outweighed by other considerations.

Lord Browne-Wilkinson, *X v Bedfordshire*, at 747–8

It is true that the legislation was introduced primarily for the protection of a limited class, namely children at risk, and that until April 1991 the legislation itself contained only limited machinery for enforcing the statutory duties imposed. But in my view those are the only pointers in favour of imputing to Parliament an intention to create a private law cause of action. When one turns to the actual words used in the primary legislation to create the statutory duties relied upon in my judgment they are inconsistent with any intention to create a private law cause of action.

> Thus, the duty imposed by section 2(2) of the Act of 1969 to bring care proceedings is made conditional upon the subjective judgment of the local authority that there are grounds for so doing. Similarly, the duty to receive a child into care under section 2(1) of the Act of 1980 only arises "where it appears to a local authority" that the parents are prevented from providing properly for the child *and* that its intervention is necessary in the interest of the child. So far as the Act of 1989 is concerned, the duty relied on in section 17 is described as "a general duty" which has two parts: (a) to safeguard the children and (b) "so far as is consistent" with (a) to promote the upbringing of the children by their families. Thus not only is the duty not a specific one but the section itself points out the basic tension which lies at the root of so much child protection work: the decision whether to split the family in order to protect the child. I find it impossible to construe such a statutory provision as demonstrating an intention that even where there is no carelessness by the authority it should be liable in damages if a court subsequently decided with hindsight that the removal, or failure to remove, the child from the family either was or was not "consistent with" the duty to safeguard the child.
>
> All the duties imported by Schedule 2 to the Act of 1989 are to "take reasonable steps" to do certain things. The duty to make inquiries under section 47 is limited to "such inquiries as they consider necessary." Thus all the statutory provisions relied upon in the *Bedfordshire* case are, as one would expect, made dependent upon the subjective judgment of the local authority. To treat such duties as being more than public law duties is impossible.

The right of action is denied, because the duties in question *are not of the right sort*. In particular, they rely upon the exercise of discretion or judgment. Although they are intended to protect children such as the plaintiffs, they are no more than 'public law duties', and their enforcement should be at public law.

The restrictive approach in *X v Bedfordshire* where social welfare legislation is concerned has been adopted by later courts. An example is *O' Rourke v Camden* [1998] AC 188: the duty under section 63(1) of the Housing Act 1985 to provide temporary accommodation to homeless individuals was enforceable only through judicial review. It was in the nature of a public law duty, and the availability of judicial review ensured that the duty would not be reduced to a 'toothless regime' or 'pious aspiration' in the absence of a damages remedy. The existence of the duty also depended on a large amount of judgment.[13] There was no action in tort for breach of the duty.

2.3 OTHER RECENT CASES

Civil Liberties

To what extent have the developments in social welfare cases affected the interpretation of other types of statute?

Cullen v Chief Constable of the Royal Ulster Constabulary [2003] UKHL 39; [2003] 1 WLR 1763

The claimant was arrested on suspicion of an offence of withholding information relating to the murder of a police officer. He later pleaded guilty to an offence. While being questioned,

---

[13] *Thornton v Kirklees MBC* [1979] QB 626, which held that a breach of such a duty was actionable at common law provided the local authority had *actually decided* that it owed a duty to house the plaintiff, was disapproved. Such a distinction would be unfair to local authorities which had taken decisions, as in *Thornton*, in contrast to those which had failed to do so.

his right of access to a solicitor was deferred four times. Such deferrals were permitted by the Northern Ireland (Emergency Provisions) Act 1987, but in contravention of that Act, no reasons for the deferrals were given. The claimant brought an action for damages in respect of the failure to give reasons.

The majority of the House of Lords (Lords Hutton, Millett, and Rodger) held that the claimant had no right of action for breach of statutory duty.

There was a joint dissent by Lords Bingham and Steyn. This dissent distinguished *Ex p. Hague* and *X v Bedfordshire*. The 1987 Act should be taken to *confer a right* on individuals in the position of the claimant; and there were no grounds for displacing the presumption that an action would therefore lie at private law. Here, for reasons of space, we extract only those paragraphs which distinguish *Ex p. Hague* and *X v Bedfordshire*. But this general approach, which starts with the purpose and nature of the legislation and identifies it as conferring a benefit in the nature of a right upon the claimant, is compatible with *Groves v Wimborne* and the second interpretive approach outlined above.

Lords Bingham and Steyn (dissenting), *Cullen v Chief Constable of RUC*

13 It is true, of course, that in *R v Deputy Governor of Parkhurst Prison, Ex p Hague* [1992] 1 AC 58 prisoners were denied a right to claim damages for breach of the Prison Rules on the ground that the rules were not intended to create private rights: the rules were regarded as concerned only with the management, treatment and control of prisoners. Section 58 of PACE, and section 15 of the 1987 Act, are quite differently worded and structured. They are specifically designed to protect individual rights of detained persons. This part of the reasoning of the Court of Appeal cannot be supported.

. . .

15 On a broader basis it is difficult to compare the social welfare legislation in the *X (Minors)* case and the *O'Rourke* case, with no express provision for individual rights, with section 58 of PACE and section 15 of the 1987 Act, which are redolent with the expression of individual rights. Those decisions do, of course, support the proposition that, where the statute is silent, the existence of an alternative remedy, such as judicial review, may be a relevant factor to take into account when considering what is the best interpretation: see, however, *Barrett v Enfield London Borough Council* [2001] 2 AC 550, 589E-H, per Lord Hutton. For Carswell LCJ [1999] NI 237 this was the significance of these decisions. In the present context, however, such arguments are ruled out by a contextual interpretation of section 15. The Royal Commission did not treat judicial review as a sufficient and effective protection for detained persons. In England and Wales cross-examination on an application for judicial review is only permitted in exceptional cases. In any event, it has to be said that the more serious a breach of refusing access to a solicitor under section 15 the more difficult it will be for a detained person to launch judicial review proceedings. There will be cases in which it is not an effective remedy as envisaged by the Royal Commission.

16 Carswell LCJ, at p 257D, regarded the fact that a breach of section 15 was unlikely to result in personal injury, injury to property or economic loss as pointing against a legislative intent to treat a breach of section 15 as giving rise to an action in damages. We cannot accept this proposition. In the context of a breach of a right of access to a solicitor the natural and obvious solution is that the breach is actionable per se, i e, without proof of special damage. That is what the Royal Commission contemplated and what Parliament must have intended. In any event Carswell LCJ rightly accepted and counsel for the Chief Constable conceded that, if a

breach of duty under section 15 is indeed actionable, it would give rise to damages without proof of loss.

It should be noted that protection of this right through an action for damages would *not* have the effect of overburdening the police authorities with claims for compensation. Since the right was actionable *per se*, and no actual loss in the nature of physical injury or economic loss was established, a sum of damages of £500 was proposed by the dissenting judges. Nor would the right of action unsettle a discretion or exercise of judgment: the relevant duty was clear and precise.

The decision of the majority in this case may or may not have been directly influenced by the presumption against actionability expressed in *X v Bedfordshire*. No presumption against the right of action was explicitly invoked, but the majority concluded that the duty was a 'public law' duty, and the appropriate means of enforcing the duty was through an application for judicial review.[14] It is possible that a different conclusion would have been drawn if the claimant had suffered tangible loss or injury.

Lord Rodger of Earlsferry

86 . . . In brief, while the duty of the police under section 15(9)(a) of the Northern Ireland (Emergency Provisions) Act 1987 to tell a detainee, such as the plaintiff, the reason for authorising a delay in complying with his request for access to a solicitor is specific, it is a public law duty. Its principal purpose is to ensure that, in an appropriate case, a detainee can challenge an improper decision under subsection (5) to authorise a delay. The appropriate civil remedy for its breach is by judicial review. Having regard to the guidance given by Lord Bridge of Harwich in *P v Liverpool Daily Post and Echo Newspapers plc* [1991] 2 AC 370, 420A-D, I see no basis for concluding that section 15(9)(a) is intended to give a detainee, such as the appellant, a private law cause of action sounding in damages where, as here, he has suffered no harm as a result of its breach.

Health and Safety

It briefly appeared in the case of *Todd v Adams* [2002] EWCA Civ 509; (2002) 2 All ER (Comm) 97 that restrictions developed in the context of social welfare and regulatory statutes might be imported into health and safety legislation also. In this case, which involved the death of several crew members on a fishing vessel, the Court of Appeal held that no action for breach of statutory duty would lie where there were breaches of regulations made pursuant to section 121(1) of the Merchant Shipping Act 1995. Among the reasons for this decision were the existence of criminal penalties; and the existence of powers to exempt certain vessels from the ambit of any rules. Although many factors were ostensibly weighed, the decisive factor was probably adoption as a starting point of the observations of Lord Browne-Wilkinson in *X v Bedfordshire*.

---

[14] As the dissenting judges pointed out, this may not be a very practicable remedy in the circumstances: 'There are formidable problems in a detainee applying for judicial review when he has been denied access to a solicitor' (para [20]).

Neuberger J

17 . . . [Lord Browne-Wilkinson] identifies two hurdles for the claimants: (a) identification and membership of a class to be benefited, and (b) an intention to confer on that class a right of action.

As we have shown, the intention to *confer a right of action* (the second hurdle referred to) was not part of the approach in the key safety case, *Groves v Wimborne*. This was a clear case of cross-contamination between the social welfare cases, and a health and safety case.

Soon afterwards in *George Ziemniak v ETPM Deep Sea Ltd* [2003] EWCA Civ 636, a differently constituted Court of Appeal expressed well-founded doubts about the decision in *Todd v Adams*. In this case, the claim (which succeeded) was brought by a seaman who was injured during a lifeboat drill on board a merchant vessel. The claim was based upon breaches of regulations (the Life Saving Regulations) made under section 85 (rather than s 121) of the Merchant Shipping Act 1995. The Court of Appeal could not of course depart from *Todd v Adams* which was binding upon it. It noted that an appeal to the House of Lords had been prepared in the case of *Todd v Adams* but that the case had been settled before the appeal was heard. Instead, *Todd v Adams* was distinguished. The judgments in *Ziemniak* explicitly refer to *Groves v Wimborne* (rather than *X v Bedfordshire*) as the key authority where health and safety is concerned.

The following decision was not *explicitly* based upon any particular approach to Parliamentary intention, but deserves to be mentioned because of its significant (and unfortunate) practical consequences. It seems likely that the decision was influenced by the developments in *Ex p. Hague* and *X v Bedfordshire*.

Richardson v Pitt-Stanley [1995] QB 123

The plaintiff was injured in the course of employment. He pursued actions in negligence and breach of statutory duty in respect of his injuries and obtained judgment against the company employing him. Unfortunately, it proved that his employer company was uninsured in respect of his injury, contravening the requirements of the Employers' Liability (Compulsory Insurance) Act 1969. Judgment against his employer was of no practical use; the employer could not pay the damages.

The plaintiff therefore brought an action for damages against the directors of the company personally, for breach of their statutory duty under the Employers' Liability (Compulsory Insurance) Act 1969, s 5. In a surprising piece of reasoning, the Court of Appeal held that no right of action existed, because the relevant legislation was not *solely* designed to benefit those who are injured at work, by ensuring that liability insurance is in place.

Stuart-Smith LJ, *Richardson v Pitt-Stanley* [1995] QB 123

It is accepted in this case by Mr. Haycroft, on behalf of the defendants, that one of the purposes of the Employers' Liability (Compulsory Insurance) Act 1969 is to secure that an injured employee does not obtain a barren judgment against his employer. The deputy judge appears to have thought that this was the primary, if not the sole, social purpose of the Act, and thus it would be frustrated if there was no right of action against a director of a corporate employer who was guilty of an offence under section 5 of the Act.

If this was the sole purpose of the Act there might be more force to the plaintiff's argument, which is based very largely upon it. But, in my judgment, it is not the sole purpose. Insurance is normally taken out for the protection of the insured, so that by paying a relatively small premium he may be protected against a heavy claim or loss. A small, or even medium sized, employer may be faced with disastrous consequences for his business, with adverse consequences for his other employees, if he is faced with a large claim by an injured workman, which will make large inroads into his resources. Although these consequences may not be so catastrophic as they are for a seriously injured employee who cannot enforce his judgment, they are likely to be serious, more widespread and more frequent, since it is only in those cases where the assets of the employer are insufficient to meet the claim that the employee is affected.

This reasoning is suspect because, although the point of insurance generally is to protect the insured, the question before the court was not about the purpose of insurance. It was about the purpose of *a statute which makes such insurance compulsory*. It also seems incorrect to argue that because the employer may be exposed to numerous claims, a worker who is only injured once requires less protection through statute. The exposed employer's losses may be more 'frequent', but this surely does not make them more pressing. The appropriate response was, it is suggested, outlined by Megaw LJ in a dissenting judgment:

Megaw LJ, *Richardson v Pitt-Stanley,* at 135 (dissenting)

The obligation to insure against bodily injury or disease sustained by employees was imposed by Parliament for one purpose, and one purpose only. The purpose was to give protection to a particular class of individuals, the employees, to eliminate, or, at least, reduce, the risk to an injured employee of finding that he was deprived of his lawful compensation because of the financial position of the employer. I am confident that it was no part of the purpose or intention of Parliament in enacting this legislation to confer a benefit or protection on the employer. It might or might not be in the employer's interest, on its own account, to have insurance against this risk. But that would depend on various factors, such as the relationship of the amount of the premium, as compared with its assessment of the risk. The purpose of Parliament's enactment was the protection of the employees.

Hence the statutory requirement of compulsory insurance comes clearly and specifically within Lord Diplock's "first exception." Failure to perform the obligation gives rise to civil liability.

The decision of the majority is in any event very hard to reconcile with *Monk v Warbey* [1935] 1 KB 75. Here, the owner of a car had lent it to a friend, who was not covered by a policy of liability insurance. The friend through his negligence caused injuries to the plaintiff. Because the driver of the car was uninsured and could not meet the claim for damages, the plaintiff brought an action against the car owner, based on his breach of statutory duty:

Road Traffic Act 1930, s 35(1)[15]

. . . it shall not be lawful for any person to use, or to cause or permit any other person to use, a motor vehicle on a road unless there is in force in relation to the user of the vehicle . . . a policy of insurance . . . in respect of third party risks . . .

This claim for breach of statutory duty was successful. The Court of Appeal perceived that the purpose of the Act was to ensure that judgments in relation to personal injury sustained on the roads could be met. As such, the Road Traffic Act is to be treated as relating to health and safety.[16] It is suggested that the Employers' Liability (Compulsory Insurance) Act 1969 should be treated in the same way.

3. THE AMBIT OF THE TORT

Once it is shown that the duty is actionable, there are relatively few difficulties associated with the tort of breach of statutory duty. The duty itself is defined by the statute, and this will determine the relevant liability standard. This may be strict, or it may be dependent on a failure to take reasonable care. The Law Reform (Contributory Negligence) Act 1945 applies to actions for breach of statutory duty, so that damages may be reduced to reflect relative fault on the part of the claimant.

Damage of the Type the Duty was Intended to Prevent

In the much-cited case of *Gorris v Scott* (1874) LR 9 Exch 125, it was emphasized that the only recoverable damage in an action for breach of statutory duty is damage of the sort that the duty was designed to prevent. Here, the defendant shipowner was under a statutory duty to keep cattle penned when in transit on board his ship. The reason for this duty was the avoidance of disease. The claimant's sheep were left unpenned, in breach of the duty, but they did not catch a disease—they were swept overboard. There was no liability, because it was not the purpose of the statute to protect from this sort of danger.

In *Vibixa v Komori UK Ltd* [2006] EWCA Civ 536; [2006] 1 WLR 2472, the Court of Appeal came to the important conclusion that breach of regulations made under the Health and Safety at Work Act 1974 could not give rise to a claim in respect of property or economic harm suffered by an employer. *Consequential* property damage or economic loss suffered by an injured employee would presumably be within the scope of the Act, however. The health and safety legislation aimed to protect against personal injury to workers. Damage to property and

---

[15] The equivalent provision is now s 143 of the Road Traffic Act 1988. It was confirmed in *Norman v Aziz* [2001] Lloyd's Rep IR 52 that the action for breach of statutory duty in such a case survives the creation of the Motor Insurers' Bureau. Any claim against the MIB where injury is caused by an uninsured driver is subject to conditions and may be less beneficial than the claim in tort.

[16] This is reinforced by the decision in *Bretton v Hancock* [2005] EWCA Civ 404; (2005) RTR 22. The statutory duty under s 143 Road Traffic Act 1988 does not exist for the purpose of reimbursing economic losses in the form of liability through contribution (Chapter 7).

economic interests *per se* were not within the statutory purpose. In this case, defective machinery was supplied, causing a fire. Even if the applicable Regulations had been regarded as being made under the Health and Safety at Work Act 1974 (which they were not), the breaches would not found a right of action by the employer.

4. THE EFFECT ON NEGLIGENCE ACTIONS

There is some risk that the restrictive approach to the action for breach of statutory duty might have a knock-on effect in the tort of negligence. The risk arises from certain comments in *Stovin v Wise* and *Gorringe v Calderdale* (both extracted in Chapter 6). In particular:

Lord Hoffmann, *Gorringe v Calderdale MBC* [2004] UKHL 15; [2004] 1 WLR 1057

23 . . . If statute actually imposes a duty, it is well settled that the question of whether it was intended to give rise to a private right of action depends upon the construction of the statute: see *R v Deputy Governor of Parkhurst Prison, ex p. Hague*. . . . If the statute does not create a right of action, it would be, to say the least, very unusual if the mere existence of the statutory duty could generate a common law duty of care.

It is very important to keep these comments within their context. In most (perhaps all) cases of negligence, the duty is said to arise at common law *as a consequence of the relationship between the parties*, as interpreted through the test in *Caparo v Dickman*: there is foreseeability and proximity, and the imposition of a duty is 'fair, just, and reasonable'. The statement in *Gorringe* creates no exceptions to the *Caparo* test where there is a statutory duty unenforceable at common law. Lord Hoffmann simply says that the existence of the duty cannot *form the basis of* a claim in the tort of negligence.[17]

FURTHER READING

Matthews, M.H., 'Negligence and Breach of Statutory Duty' (1984) 4 OJLS 429.

Stanton, K., *Breach of Statutory Duty* (London: Sweet & Maxwell, 1986).

Stanton, K., Skidmore, Harris, and Wright, *Statutory Torts* (London: Sweet & Maxwell, 2003).

Williams, G., 'The Effect of Penal Legislation in the Law of Tort' (1960) 23 MLR 233.

---

[17] See for example *D v East Berkshire* [2005] 2 AC 373, where it was accepted that children (though not their parents) were owed a duty of care in negligence in respect of child welfare decisions, although applicable *statutory* duties were of a 'public law' type, not enforceable through a private law action.

17

TRESPASS TO LAND AND GOODS, AND CONVERSION

CENTRAL ISSUES

i) The torts in this chapter all protect rights to possession, but they do so in different ways. The trespass torts protect against direct interferences with land and goods possessed by the claimant. Conversion on the other hand protects against interferences with goods (but not land) which are actually inconsistent with the claimant's right of possession. In effect, a conversion amounts to a denial of the claimant's right.

ii) Conversion occupies a unique place in English law. It is a tort, but its functions overlap both with property law, and with the law of unjust enrichment. This unique position is reflected in all aspects of the tort but most particularly in the available remedies. These remedies include recovery of the chattel in some cases (though not as of right), and damages based both on value of the goods (if not recovered), and on consequential loss. Though side-lined in the majority of tort courses, conversion is a hard-working tort of broad commercial significance.

1. TRESPASS TO LAND

Trespass to land is constituted by a direct and unjustifiable interference with the possession of land.

The specific interest protected by trespass to land will be more clearly grasped if we compare it with the action in private nuisance (Chapter 10). Both torts protect interests in land in some sense, but there are important distinctions between the interests protected and (therefore) the interferences against which protection is available.

Private nuisance protects against unlawful interference with the **use and enjoyment of land**. It is actionable only by a person with title to the land, in the form of a *right to exclusive possession*. This may be the freeholder, or the leaseholder, or someone who holds a right to exclusive possession through statute. Although injunction is usually the preferred remedy in a case of continuing nuisance, where damages are assessed they are assessed by reference to diminution in the amenity value of the land.[1] Interference must be shown to be 'unreasonable', and this may involve a balancing exercise taking into account the interests of the claimant and the activity of the defendant. Some interferences are not actionable, on the basis of a principle of 'live and let live'.

Trespass to land on the other hand protects against interference with the possession of land itself. It is actionable by anyone with the right to possession, even if this falls short of a right to *exclusive* possession. It is actionable for example by a mere licensee, who would not be able to bring an action in private nuisance. Invasions are actionable without reference to 'reasonableness', and there is no question of permitting minor invasions on a principle of 'live and let live'. This would be incompatible with the rights to possession which are protected by the tort. Although *reasonableness* is no defence, a defendant may escape liability by showing **justification**. As with the other trespass torts examined in Chapter 2, justification may be established in the form of emergency or self-defence, for example.

1.1 NON-DELIBERATE TRESPASS TO LAND

In Chapter 2, we explained that the torts which together constitute trespass to the person are now regarded as 'intentional', even though the form of intention required is not closely related to culpability. It is the *direct physical contact with the person of the claimant* that must be intended, and not any wrongfulness or harm. Equally, in the case of trespass to land, no wrongfulness nor actual harm need be intended. Trespass liability is 'strict'. But does the incursion onto the claimant's land need to be intentional?

League Against Cruel Sports v Scott [1986] QB 240

The claimants owned various parcels of unfenced moorland, over which it did not allow hunting. After several incursions onto their land by the hunt, including incursion by hounds, the claimants brought an action in trespass against the defendants, who were joint masters of the hunt. They claimed not only damages but also a declaration of unlawfulness and an injunction to prevent future trespasses.

The claim was successful. Damages were awarded, together with an injunction.

Park J, *League Against Cruel Sports v Scott* [1986] 1 QB 240

Mr. Blom-Cooper submits that intention, wilfulness, and indeed any concept of fault liability do not constitute an element in the tort of trespass to land. When hounds enter or cross forbidden land the only question is whether such intrusion is voluntary or involuntary. The only defences recognised by law to an action for trespass are inevitable accident and necessity.

. . .

. . . I am, however, unable to spell out from the authorities cited by Mr Blom-Cooper the proposition that he has advanced. I have, therefore, come to the conclusion that, before a master of hounds may be held liable for trespass on land by hounds, it has to be shown that he either intended that the hounds should enter the land, or by negligence he failed to prevent them from doing so.

---

[1] *Hunter v Canary Wharf* [1997] AC 655.

In my judgment the law as I take it to be may be stated thus: where a master of staghounds takes out a pack of hounds and deliberately sets them in pursuit of a stag or hind, knowing that there is a real risk that in the pursuit hounds may enter or cross prohibited land, the master will be liable for trespass if he intended to cause hounds to enter such land, or if by his failure to exercise proper control over them he caused them to enter such land.

. . .

Further, if it is virtually impossible, whatever precautions are taken, to prevent hounds from entering league land, such as Pitleigh for example, yet the master knowing that to be the case, nevertheless persists in hunting in its vicinity, with the result that hounds frequently trespass on the land, then the inference might well be drawn that his indifference to the risk of trespass amounted to an intention that hounds should trespass on the land.

The master's negligence, or the negligence of those servants or agents or followers of the hunt for whose conduct he is responsible, has also to be judged in the light of all the circumstances in which the trespass in question occurred.

It should be re-emphasized that the *unlawfulness* of the trespass need not be intended. The defendant may think the land is his own, or that entry is permitted. 'Mistake' is no defence, even if due care is exercised. The standard of liability is strict. However, trespass to land cannot be committed if the entry onto land itself is *involuntary*. According to the decision above, trespass to land requires the defendant to enter the land either intentionally, or through *carelessness*. Here, the idea of 'involuntary' (as opposed to merely mistaken) entry is quite plausible: the land was unfenced, and some of the incursions were by hounds rather than people.[2] But if the incursion by hounds is impossible to prevent, then 'intention' to enter the land may be inferred from continuing to hunt with hounds at all.

It will be clear from *League Against Cruel Sports v Scott* that *carelessly* entering the claimant's land is sufficient to amount to trespass. We discovered in Chapter 2 that since *Letang v Cooper* [1965] 1 QB 232, trespass to the person has been confined to *intentional* acts. For example, in the tort of battery, only if physical contact is intended is there an action in trespass to the person. Cases of *careless* contact are to be governed only by the principles of the tort of negligence.[3] This reasoning does not seem to be replicated in respect of trespass to land. It is perhaps better that way, since (as we explained in Chapter 2) the reasoning was never very convincing in any event.

Remedies

As with trespass to the person, the claimant may seek an injunction to prevent continuing or future interference; compensatory damages in respect of past interference and any consequential damage caused; and a declaration that the trespass is unlawful.

It has been thought in the past that an injunction to restrain a trespass is generally available as of right, even in circumstances where the invasion of the claimant's rights is minor or temporary, and where the effect of the injunction will be to give undue bargaining power to

---

[2] Another instance of 'involuntary' entry is where the defendant is involved in a traffic accident and is thrown onto the claimant's land.

[3] In *Letang*, the claimant therefore could not take advantage of a longer limitation period which (then) applied to trespass to the person.

the claimant. In *Anchor Brewhouse Developments Ltd v Berkley House Ltd* (1987) 38 BLR 87, Scott J granted an injunction where the jib of a crane on the defendant's land trespassed over the property of the plaintiffs. The crane was involved in construction work. Scott J recognized that the grant of an injunction here would allow the plaintiff to seek extortionate payments for the right to 'use' their space to complete construction works, but considered himself bound to award the injunction.

More recently, in *Jaggard v Sawyer* [1995] 1 WLR 269, the Court of Appeal has taken a different approach. The injunctive remedy, it was pointed out, is an *equitable* remedy which is always within the discretion of the court. Although damages *in lieu* of an injunction may only be awarded where relevant criteria are fulfilled, there is always an option for the court to award no remedy at all. The injunction is not available 'as of right'.

We extracted *Jaggard v Sawyer* in Chapter 10.1 (Nuisance), where we also set out the '*Shelfer* criteria' for award of damages in lieu of an injunction. Here, it is worth additionally noting Millett LJ's comments on the approach in *Anchor Brewhouse*:

Millett LJ, *Jaggard v Sawyer* [1995] 1 WLR 285

In *Anchor Brewhouse Developments Ltd. v. Berkley House (Docklands Developments) Ltd.* . . . Scott J. granted an injunction to restrain a continuing trespass. In the course of his judgment, however, he cast doubt on the power of the court to award damages for future trespasses by means of what he described as a "once and for all payment." This was because, as he put it, the court could not by an award of damages put the defendant in the position of a person entitled to an easement; whether or not an injunction were granted, the defendant's conduct would still constitute a trespass; and a succession of further actions for damages could accordingly still be brought. This reasoning strikes at the very heart of the statutory jurisdiction; it is in marked contrast to the attitude of the many judges who from the very first have recognised that, while the Act[4] does not enable the court to license future wrongs, this may be the practical result of withholding injunctive relief. . . . It is in my view fallacious because it is not the award of damages which has the practical effect of licensing the defendant to commit the wrong, but the refusal of injunctive relief. Thereafter the defendant may have no right to act in the manner complained of, but he cannot be prevented from doing so. The court can in my judgment properly award damages "once and for all" in respect of future wrongs because it awards them in substitution for an injunction and to compensate for those future wrongs which an injunction would have prevented. . . .

The choice is not only between injunction and damages; if damages are not appropriate, there is still a choice between injunction, and nothing.

Gain-Based Damages

If there is consequential loss flowing from the trespass, then this may be the subject of compensation in the usual way. However, there are cases where a non-compensatory award of damages has been made for trespass. In *Penarth Dock v Pounds* [1963] 1 Lloyd's Rep 359, Lord Denning assessed damages against defendants who had trespassed by refusing to remove their

---

[4] Chancery Amendment Act 1858, or 'Lord Cairns's Act', which permitted courts of Chancery to award damages. The Common Law Procedure Act 1854 permitted courts of common law to award injunctions.

pontoon from the plaintiffs' dock. The plaintiffs had not made any loss, and Lord Denning awarded damages 'reversing the gain' that the defendants had made. This benefit though was not in the form of positive profits, but of expenses saved. It represented a rental value of the property. Similarly in *MoD v Ashman* [1993] 40 EG 144, a tenant wrongfully refused to quit when given notice to do so. A majority of the Court of Appeal awarded damages for this trespass to land which were not based on loss to the plaintiffs, but on 'the value of the benefit which the occupier has received'. Hoffmann LJ clearly said that this was a claim for restitution.[5]

2. WRONGFUL INTERFERENCE WITH GOODS: THE TYPES AND THE LEGISLATION

Torts (Wrongful Interference with Goods) Act 1977

1   Definition of "wrongful interference with goods"

In this Act "wrongful interference", or "wrongful interference with goods", means—

    (a) conversion of goods (also called trover),

    (b) trespass to goods,

    (c) negligence so far as it results in damage to goods or to an interest in goods,

    (d) subject to section 2, any other tort so far as it results in damage to goods or to an interest in goods

[and references in this Act (however worded) to proceedings for wrongful interference or to a claim or right to claim for wrongful interference shall include references to proceedings by virtue of Part I of the Consumer Protection Act 1987 [or Part II of the Consumer Protection (Northern Ireland) Order 1987] (product liability) in respect of any damage to goods or to an interest in goods or, as the case may be, to a claim or right to claim by virtue of that Part in respect of any such damage].

The Torts (Wrongful Interference with Goods) Act 1977 made a number of changes to the common law, as well as codifying the law in some respects. Although it abolished the action in detinue,[6] it did not create any new actions nor did it greatly simplify the law.

As can be seen from section 1 above, a range of distinct actions at common law continues to protect interests in goods, and these actions are referred to as instances of 'wrongful interference with goods'. Clearly, 'wrongful interference with goods' is not a tort in its own right, but a term referring to several different torts in appropriate circumstances.

Here, we distinguish between two torts which are *uniquely* concerned with wrongful interference with goods. These are trespass to goods, and conversion.

---

    [5] A. Burrows, *Remedies for Torts and Breach of Contract* (2nd edn, OUP, 1994), 295–7. More recently, in *Horsford v Bird* [2006] UKPC 3, the Privy Council has upheld an award of damages for trespass to land which was not based on stripping the profits of the trespasser, but represented 'the value obtained by a trespasser from the free use of the land': J. Edelman, 'Restitutionary Damages for Torts' (2006) 122 LQR 391, 392.

    [6] By s 2(1), extracted below.

Trespass to goods involves direct and unjustified interference with goods, which are in the possession of the claimant. Examples include poisoning or beating animals, or scratching the paintwork of a vehicle.

A. Hudson, 'Trespass to Goods', in N.E. Palmer and E. McKendrick (eds), *Interests in Goods* (2nd edn, London: Lloyds of London Press, 1998)

Trespass [to goods] bears the marks of its early origins. It is constituted by a direct, immediate and unjustified interference with the possession of the chattels of another.

Conversion by contrast involves actions which are inconsistent with the claimant's right to possession of the goods. We define conversion more fully in the next section.

Trespass to goods, like all forms of trespass, is limited to *direct* interferences.[7] Since many (though not all) cases of trespass to goods involve damage, negligence frequently presents an alternative action, which is not confined to direct interference. Therefore, the practical importance of trespass to goods is quite restricted. It does not have the same practical significance as the action in conversion.

3. AN INSTANCE OF WRONGFUL INTERFERENCE WITH GOODS: CONVERSION

3.1 GENERAL DEFINITION AND DISTINCTIVE FEATURES

A 'conversion' is any deliberate dealing with a chattel in a manner that is seriously inconsistent with the claimant's right to possession.

Distinctive Features

1. Although the defendant's dealing with the chattel must be deliberate, the interference with the claimant's right to possession need not be. Liability is strict, and may catch even an entirely honest defendant (see further Section 3.2 below).

2. Like trespass to land and goods, 'conversion' protects rights to possession. Acts of conversion are inconsistent with the claimant's right to possession, and the action for conversion may be used to vindicate possessory rights.

3. As with any tort, the nature of the protected interest should be reflected in the remedies available. In an appropriate case, a court may in its discretion order the return of a converted chattel to the claimant. But this remedy is not available *as of right* even where the defendant retains possession of the goods. In this and certain other ways, conversion suffers from inconsistency. It is accused of performing too many roles, and none of them wholly satisfactorily. In particular, it has been argued that the process of returning goods

---

[7] For example, Hudson (above) explains that putting poison in an animal's mouth may be trespass to the animal, but putting poison in its *feed* is only trespass to the feed.

to those who have the appropriate interest in them ought to be achieved through the law of property, *not* through the law of obligations.[8]

Andrew Tettenborn, 'Conversion, Tort and Restitution', in N. Palmer and E. McKendrick, *Interests in Goods* (above), at 825

. . . the nub of the problem is that no-one has ever sat down seriously to consider what conversion is *for*. True, it is classified as a tort: but that is only for historical reasons and for lack of anywhere else to file it. In fact it is trying to do not one, but three very different jobs at the same time; it is (1) standing in as a kind of surrogate *vindication*, allowing owners to get back their property or its value from a wrongful possessor (call this the 'recovery function'); (2) acting to compensate owners for losses caused by past misdealings with their property (tort proper); and (3) on occasion reversing unjust enrichment arising from the property or its proceeds which have got into the wrong hands (restitution).

Tettenborn suggests that the three functions of conversion need to be kept distinct, in order to avoid falling into error, and indeed to avoid hardship to 'innocent' converters caught by the strictness of its liability.

The third function specified by Tettenborn in this extract (restitution) requires particular note. It is in the nature of conversion that the defendant often has an opportunity to *use* the chattel in a productive way,[9] and in this sense may be 'unjustly enriched'. The relationship between conversion, and 'unjust enrichment', is extremely awkward, because conversion is (like all torts) a 'wrong', while 'unjust enrichment' need not involve a wrong at all, but seeks to correct transfers which should not have occurred. This issue arises particularly in respect of available 'remedies' (below).[10] Conversion is not only at the boundary of property and tort, but also of tort and 'unjust enrichment'.

3.2 STANDARD OF LIABILITY

Liability in conversion is strict. There need not be any knowledge of inconsistency with the claimant's rights. In fact, there need not be any knowledge of the claimant's rights at all, and conversion may be committed through entirely faultless conduct. Nevertheless, intention *to assert dominion over the goods* is required.

To explain this further, we need to explore the role of 'deliberate dealing', which formed a part of our general definition above.

---

[8] Tony Weir, *Casebook on Tort* (9th edn, Sweet & Maxwell, 2000); Nick Curwen, 'The Remedy in Conversion: Confusing Property and Obligation' (below); Tettenborn, 'Damages in Conversion' (below).

[9] Though not, of course, in the case of a conversion by destroying or losing the chattel: see Section 3.4 below for an outline of relevant behaviour towards a chattel that may amount to conversion.

[10] Not everyone agrees there can be 'remedies' for unjust enrichment. Peter Birks argued that correction of an unjust transfer should not be described as a remedy, but as the vindication of a right.

Lord Nicholls' Analysis of 'Deliberate Dealing' in *Kuwait Airways*

In the course of the House of Lords' most recent analysis of the tort of conversion, Lord Nicholls identified three elements in the general definition of a 'conversion'.

Lord Nicholls, *Kuwait Airways v Iraqi Airways Co (Nos 4 and 5)* [2002] UKHL 19; [2002] 2 AC 883

39 . . . Conversion of goods can occur in so many different circumstances that framing a precise definition of universal application is well nigh impossible. In general, the basic features of the tort are threefold. First, the defendant's conduct was inconsistent with the rights of the owner (or other person entitled to possession). Second, the conduct was deliberate, not accidental. Third, the conduct was so extensive an encroachment on the rights of the owner as to exclude him from use and possession of the goods. The contrast is with lesser acts of interference. If these cause damage they may give rise to claims for trespass or in negligence, but they do not constitute conversion.

Peter Cane has suggested that some trouble is potentially caused by the way that Lord Nicholls expressed the second general feature of conversion: the dealing with the goods must be 'deliberate, not accidental'. It is not the word 'deliberate', but the apparent contrast with 'accidental', which creates the problem.

Lord Nicholls' requirement for deliberate dealing refers to the *quality of the dealing with the defendant's goods*. It is this, not anything else, which must be deliberate rather than accidental. Thus, the taking of someone else's goods by mistake (or 'accidentally'), *may* amount to a conversion. For example, if I take your goods believing them to be mine, I have done so 'by accident'; yet at the same time I 'deliberately' act so as to assert dominion over the goods. This means essentially that I treat them as my own. In such a case, I am particularly likely to treat them as my own, because I think that they *are* my own. This example shows that dealing may be both deliberate and accidental, in different senses.

Therefore, Lord Nicholls did create scope for confusion when he used the word 'accidental' in contrast to 'deliberate'. An accidental taking of the claimant's chattel may still be a conversion, provided I intend to exercise dominion over it.

The opposite sort of case may also exist. This is where the *taking or possession* of the chattel is deliberate, but the defendant does *not* intend to exercise dominion over it. This is not a conversion, though it may well be a trespass. Lord Nicholls also emphasized this point in the *Kuwait Airways* case. He described the lack of intent as relevant to the question whether the owner is excluded from possession at all.

Lord Nicholls, *Kuwait Airways v Iraqi Airways Co (Nos 4 and 5)* [2002] 2 AC 883

14 Whether the owner is excluded from possession may sometimes depend upon whether the wrongdoer exercised dominion over the goods. Then the intention with which acts were done may be material. The ferryman who turned the plaintiff's horses off the Birkenhead to Liverpool ferry was guilty of conversion if he intended to exercise dominion over them, but not otherwise: see *Fouldes v Willoughby*. . . .

In *Fouldes v Willoughby* (1841) 8 M & W 540, referred to by Lord Nicholls, the plaintiff had paid for his two horses to be transported across the River Mersey on the Birkenhead ferry. The defendant ferryman refused to transport them. He removed them from the ferry and turned them loose. This was not a conversion:

Lord Abinger, *Fouldes v Willoughby*

It is a proposition familiar to all lawyers, that a simple asportation of a chattel, without any intention of making any further use of it, although it may be a sufficient foundation for an action of trespass, is not sufficient to establish a conversion. I had thought that the matter had been fully discussed, and this distinction established, by the numerous cases which have occurred on this subject. . . . I think that the learned judge was wrong, in telling the jury that the simple fact of putting these horses on the shore by the defendant, amounted to a conversion of them to his own use. In my opinion, he should have added to his direction, that it was for them to consider what was the intention of the defendant in so doing. If the object, and whether rightly or wrongly entertained is immaterial, simply was to adduce the plaintiff to go on shore himself, and the defendant, in furtherance of that object, did the act in question, it was not exercising over the goods any right inconsistent with, or adverse to, the rights which the plaintiff had in them. . . .

In order to constitute a conversion, it is necessary either that the party taking the goods should intend some use to be made of them, by himself or by those for whom he acts, or that, owing to his act, the goods are destroyed or consumed, to the prejudice of the lawful owner. As an instance of the latter branch of this definition, suppose, in the present case, the defendant had thrown the horses into the water, whereby they were drowned, that would have amounted to an actual conversion; or as in the case cited in the course of argument, of a person throwing a piece of paper into the water for, in these cases, the chattel is changed in quality, or destroyed altogether. But it has never yet been held that the single act of removal of a chattel independently of any claim over it, either in favour of the party himself or anyone else, amounts to a conversion of the chattel. In the present case, therefore, the simple removal of the horses by the defendant for a purpose wholly unconnected with any least denial of the right of the plaintiff to the possession and enjoyment of them, is no conversion . . .

This is an example where there is no conversion because the defendant does not mean by his actions to assert ownership or a right to possession over the horses. This case illustrates the importance of intention to the tort of conversion.[11]

But does this mean, as Lord Nicholls proposes, that the intention of the defendant is relevant to the question of *whether the claimant was deprived of his or her right to possession at all*?

[11] It also illustrates the distinction between conversion, and trespass to goods. If trespass to goods had been pleaded, there would have been a good chance of success. There was a direct and probably unjustified interference with the goods; but no intention on the part of the defendant to treat the goods as his own.

Peter Cane says that Lord Nicholls was *not* correct in this respect:

Peter Cane, 'Causing Conversion' (2002) 118 LQR 544 at 546

An obvious problem with this definition[12] is that it turns independent elements of the Clerk and Lindsell definition into interdependent elements. Under the definition, 'inconsistent dealing' (exercising dominion) is one element of conversion, and depriving the owner of possession is another. The concept of possession relates to a physical state of affairs, and the defendant's state of mind is irrelevant to whether the defendant's conduct has deprived the owner of, or excluded the owner from, possession.

The Clerk and Lindsell definition referred to by both Lord Nicholls and Peter Cane was as follows:

Clerk and Lindsell on Torts, (17th edn, London: Sweet & Maxwell, 1995), 636, para 13-12[13]

. . . conversion is an act of deliberate dealing with a chattel in a manner inconsistent with another's right whereby that other is deprived of the use and possession of it.

Cane's criticism on this point does not, it is suggested, hit home. What conversion protects is the **right to possession** and not simple physical possession, as Cane implies. Otherwise, the action of the ferryman in *Fouldes v Willoughby*—which deprived the claimant of physical possession—would have been a conversion. Dealing is *only* inconsistent with rights to possession if the dealing 'means' that the defendant has dominion over the goods. The 'defendant's state of mind' may be irrelevant, as Cane says, to whether the owner is excluded from *physical* possession. But it is *not* irrelevant to the prior requirement, that the manner of dealing should be (in the words of the Clerk and Lindsell definition) 'inconsistent with another's right'.[14]

This point about intention and the definition of conversion was important to the decision in *Kuwait Airways* itself. The facts of the case also demonstrate that intention can often be construed from actions. For example, someone who repaints a chattel in their own colours, or improves it in some way, is almost certainly asserting 'dominion' over it.

Kuwait Airways Corporation v Iraqi Airways Corporation (Nos 4 and 5) [2002] UKHL 19; [2002] 2 AC 883

In August 1990, Iraq invaded Kuwait, and passed resolutions proclaiming the integration of Kuwait into Iraq. The defendant was ordered by the Iraqi government to fly ten of the claimant's passenger aircraft to Iraq. These were incorporated into the defendant's fleet and used for its own flights. On 11 January 1991, the claimant issued a writ claiming the delivery

---

[12] Peter Cane is referring here to the three-fold general definition of conversion offered by Lord Nicholls, and extracted above.

[13] See now the 19th edition, 2005.

[14] See also Section 3.3 below, on the nature of 'possession' at law.

up of its aircraft with consequential damages for the defendant's unlawful interference with them, alternatively consequential damages in the amount of the value of the aircraft, relying on section 3 of the Torts (Interference with Goods) Act 1977, and common law.

No State recognized the sovereignty of Iraq over the territory of Kuwait. Military action was commenced against Iraq. In the conflict, the subsequent fortunes of the aircraft themselves were mixed. Four of the ten were destroyed by bombing. These planes, stationed at Mosul, are referred to as 'the Mosul four'. The remaining six planes were evacuated to Iran between 15 January and 4 February 1991 (shortly after the writ was issued). These are 'the Iran six'. They were returned by Iran to the claimant in 1992, on payment to Iran of US$20million.

Not surprisingly, the applicable law for this case was a real issue. The writ was issued before the enactment of the Private International Law (Miscellaneous Provisions) Act 1995. That Act would require that the law of the jurisdiction in which the tort was committed would be applied. Therefore, this case would now be approached entirely as a matter of Iraqi law. But before that, common law required that a 'double actionability rule' should be applied. This required that the acts must be tortious according to the law of *both* Iraq *and* England. The House of Lords disregarded the 'repugnant' Iraqi Resolution 369 which purported to extinguish Kuwait as an independent State. Disregarding this Resolution, the acts would amount to 'usurpation' (the relevant wrong under Iraqi law). The remaining questions (in which we are interested here) are whether the acts were *also* tortious under English law (this section); and what damages could be claimed (Section 3.5).

In this case, restoration of the aircraft was not in issue. The Mosul four could not be restored because they had been destroyed. The Iran six had already been reclaimed, but the claimant had paid $20 million to a third party in order to retrieve them.[15]

The main judgment in the case was delivered by Lord Nicholls. Lord Scott dissented in part. The other Lords agreed with Lord Nicholls, though with some additional comments.

We have already extracted some of the crucial elements of Lord Nicholls' judgment so far as they relate to the general requirements of the tort of conversion. In due course (when we consider remedies) we will extract some important comments relating to causation and damages. These were the most difficult issues in the case. The conclusion that the acts of the defendant did in fact amount to a conversion was relatively brief:

Lord Nicholls, *Kuwait Airways v Iraqi Airways (Nos 4 and 5)*

43 Here, on and after 17 September 1990 IAC was in possession and control of the ten aircraft. This possession was adverse to KAC. IAC believed the aircraft were now its property, just as much as the other aircraft in its fleet, and it acted accordingly. It intended to keep the goods as its own. It treated them as its own. It made such use of them as it could in the prevailing circumstances, although this was very limited because of the hostilities. In so conducting itself IAC was asserting rights inconsistent with KAC's rights as owner. This assertion was evidenced in several ways. In particular, in September 1990 the board of IAC passed a resolution to the effect that all aircraft belonging to the (dissolved) KAC should be registered in the name of IAC and that a number of ancillary steps should be taken in relation to the aircraft. In respect of nine aircraft IAC then applied to the Iraqi Directorate of Air Safety for certificates of airworthiness and reregistration in IAC's name. IAC effected insurance cover in respect of five aircraft, and a further four after the issue of the writ. Six of the aircraft were overpainted in

---

[15] Neither Iran nor Iraq could be sued in tort, because of the doctrine of State immunity.

IAC's livery. IAC used one aircraft on internal commercial flights between Baghdad and Basra and for training flights. The two Boeing 767s were flown from Basra to Mosul in mid-November 1990.

44 Mance J concluded that in these circumstances IAC had wrongfully interfered with all ten aircraft. In the Court of Appeal Brooke LJ said, at pp 915C-D, para 74:

> "The board resolution makes it completely clear that as soon as RCC Resolution 369 came into effect IAC resolved to treat these ten aircraft as their own and to exercise dominion over them in denial of KAC's rights, and this continuing usurpation and conversion of KAC's aircraft subsisted right up to the issue of the writ in this action by which KAC demanded the return of all these aircraft."

I agree. IAC's acts would have been tortious if done in this country.

The crucial thing is that IAC was (as Lord Nicholls put it) 'asserting rights inconsistent with KAC's rights as owner', and this was evidenced in various ways. In this case, which did not involve actual taking by the defendant, the *meaning* of the defendant's possession of the aircraft was particularly significant. It was irrelevant that IAC believed itself to *be* the lawful owner of the aircraft, under Iraqi law.

A similar interpretation was expressed by Lord Steyn in a short concurring judgment. His summary on this point serves as valuable reinforcement:

Lord Steyn, *Kuwait Airways v Iraqi Airways (Nos 4 and 5)*

119 Despite elaborate citation of authority, I am satisfied that the essential feature of the tort of conversion, and of usurpation under Iraqi law, is the denial by the defendant of the possessory interest or title of the plaintiff in the goods . . . When a defendant manifests an assertion of rights or dominion over the goods which is inconsistent with the rights of the plaintiff he converts the goods to his own use. I am therefore in agreement with the legal analysis of the Court of Appeal.

In *Kuwait Airways*, the defendant was liable because it 'manifested' an 'assertion of rights or dominion over the goods'.

Summary

Liability for conversion is strict. In some circumstances, an interpretation of the defendant's intentions with regard to the goods is required: did s/he assert dominion over them? But there is *no* need to consider the defendant's intention with regard to the rights of the claimant, as this is irrelevant.

3.3 WHICH GOODS CAN BE 'CONVERTED'?

Only chattels (not land) may be 'converted'. Furthermore, only 'tangible' property (things with physical form that may be 'touched') can be converted. The latter point was recently confirmed by the Court of Appeal in *OBG v Allen* [2005] QB 762.[16] Here, invalidly appointed receivers of a company were not liable in conversion for interfering with the contractual interests of the company (by bringing those contracts to an end and seeking settlements against contracting parties). On the other hand, a *share certificate*, for example, *is* tangible property, as also is a cheque, so that these chattels may be converted. Bearing in mind that consequential losses are recoverable (and potentially disgorgement damages and restitution too), the commercial significance of the tort of conversion is considerable.[17]

3.4 WHAT INTEREST IN THE CHATTELS MUST THE CLAIMANT HAVE?

Sarah Worthington, *Personal Property Law, Text and Materials* (Oxford: Hart Publishing, 2000), at 574

. . . a claimant wishing to sue in conversion must have the right to possession at the time the conversion takes place. If the claimant cannot show this, then the action will fail. However, the claimant does not have to show that he has the ultimate or the best right to possession; all he has to show is that he has a better right than the defendant. It follows that bailees and 'finders' may be able to sue in conversion if the bailed or found property is taken from them by someone with no better right to it than they have.

What is a 'Right in Possession'?

The legal concept of 'possession' is not the same as the lay meaning of 'possession'. Rights to possess a chattel may vary depending on the purpose of possession, and may be relative to the rights of others.

F. H. Lawson and B. Rudden, *The Law of Property* (3rd edn, Oxford: Clarendon Press, 2002), 64–5

Where chattels are concerned, the law's approach reduces costs in the resolution of disputes by protecting possession without requiring the person so protected to prove ownership. It is up to the defendant to justify the taking or detention of the thing. The presumption also imposes a respect for possession, however it was obtained. If someone finds a ring, or a thief steals a bicycle, each is protected against anyone who takes it without consent—except, of course, the person who had prior possession and who lost the ring or had the bicycle stolen and so on.

In more technical language, we may say that there are rights to possess and rights which flow from having acquired possession. For the first phrase English (and American) law tends to use the word 'title': your title to some asset indicates your right to possess it. It is possible for there

---

[16] For comment see Andrew Tettenborn, 'Liability for Interfering with Intangibles: Invalidly-Appointed Receivers, Conversion, and the Economic Torts' (2006) 122 LQR 31–5.
[17] An example of a case of conversion of a cheque is *International Factors Ltd v Rodriguez* [1979] QB 351.

to be two or more titles to a thing, one being stronger than another. If you make a ring from your own hair, there is no doubt whatever that it is yours and that you have a better right to it than anyone else. If you lose it, you can claim it from the finder. But in the absence of any claim by you, the finder is treated as having a title good against everyone. You have a better right to possess the thing than does the finder, but the finder has a better right to possess it than does anyone else.

The Relative Nature of Possessory Rights

Lawson and Rudden make clear that a finder—or even a thief—may acquire rights to possess a chattel, good against everyone except the person who lost the goods.

Parker v British Airways Board [1982] QB 1004

A passenger found a gold bracelet in an executive lounge occupied by the defendant. He handed it to an employee of the defendant and requested that it should be returned to him, if the owner could not be found. It was not claimed, and the defendant sold it for £850.

The passenger successfully sued the defendant in conversion, and recovered £850 as damages.

Donaldson LJ, *Parker v British Airways Board* [1982] QB 1004

Neither the plaintiff nor the defendants lay any claim to the bracelet either as owner of it or as one who derives title from that owner. The plaintiff's claim is founded upon the ancient common law rule that the act of finding a chattel which has been lost and taking control of it gives the finder rights with respect to that chattel. The defendants' claim has a different basis. They cannot and do not claim to have found the bracelet when it was handed to them by the plaintiff. At that stage it was no longer lost and they received and accepted the bracelet from the plaintiff on terms that it would be returned to him if the owner could not be found. They must and do claim on the basis that they had rights in relation to the bracelet immediately before the plaintiff found it and that these rights are superior to the plaintiff's. The defendants' claim is based upon the proposition that at common law an occupier of land has such rights over all lost chattels which are on that land, whether or not the occupier knows of their existence.

The common law right asserted by the plaintiff has been recognised for centuries. In its simplest form it was asserted by the chimney sweep's boy who, in 1722, found a jewel and offered it to a jeweller for sale. The jeweller refused either to pay a price acceptable to the boy or to return it and the boy sued the jeweller for its value: *Armory v. Delamirie* (1722) 1 Stra. 505. Pratt C.J. ruled:

> "That the finder of a jewel, though he does not by such finding acquire an absolute property or ownership, yet he has such a property as will enable him to keep it against all but the rightful owner, and consequently may maintain trover."

In the case the jeweller clearly had no rights in relation to the jewel immediately before the boy found it and any rights which he acquired when he received it from the boy stemmed from the boy himself. The jeweller could only have succeeded if the fact of finding and taking control of the jewel conferred no rights upon the boy. The court would then have been faced with two claimants, neither of which had any legal right, but one had de facto possession. The rule as stated by Pratt C.J. must be right as a general proposition, for otherwise lost property would be subject to a free-for-all in which the physically weakest would go to the wall.

. . . .

Rights and obligations of the finder

1. The finder of a chattel acquires no rights over it unless (a) it has been abandoned or lost and (b) he takes it into his care and control.

2. The finder of a chattel acquires very limited rights over it if he takes it into his care and control with dishonest intent or in the course of trespassing.

3. Subject to the foregoing and to point 4 below, a finder of a chattel, whilst not acquiring any absolute property or ownership in the chattel, acquires a right to keep it against all but the true owner or those in a position to claim through the true owner or one who can assert a prior right to keep the chattel which was subsisting at the time when the finder took the chattel into his care and control.

4. Unless otherwise agreed, any servant or agent who finds a chattel in the course of his employment or agency and not wholly incidentally or collaterally thereto and who takes it into his care and control does so on behalf of his employer or principal who acquires a finder's rights to the exclusion of those of the actual finder.

5. A person having a finder's rights has an obligation to take such measures as in all the circumstances are reasonable to acquaint the true owner of the finding and present whereabouts of the chattel and to care for it meanwhile

Rights and liabilities of an occupier

1. An occupier of land has rights superior to those of a finder over chattels in or attached to that land and an occupier of a building has similar rights in respect of chattels attached to that building, whether in either case the occupier is aware of the presence of the chattel.

2. An occupier of a building has rights superior to those of a finder over chattels upon or in, but not attached to, that building if, but only if, before the chattel is found, he has manifested an intention to exercise control over the building and the things which may be upon it or in it.

3. An occupier who manifests an intention to exercise control over a building and the things which may be upon or in it so as to acquire rights superior to those of a finder is under an obligation to take such measures as in all the circumstances are reasonable to ensure that lost chattels are found and, upon their being found, whether by him or by a third party, to acquaint the true owner of the finding and to care for the chattels meanwhile. . . .

Theft

Despite the proviso expressed by Donaldson LJ in the extract above, that a finder who acts with dishonest intent will acquire only very limited rights over a chattel, claimants who have (on the balance of probabilities) acquired title through *theft* have nevertheless been successful in actions to recover stolen property from the police (provided the police have no statutory powers to retain them): *Costello v Chief Constable of Derbyshire Constabulary* [2001] 1 WLR

1437; *Gough v Chief Constable of West Midlands Police* [2004] EWCA Civ 206. The claimants in these cases would not of course be able to retain the goods if the lawful owner of the goods could be found. In Chapter 5.4, we explained why these actions were not barred by the maxim *ex turpi causa non oritur actio,* or 'illegality'. According to the leading case of *Tinsley v Milligan* [1994] 1 AC 240, this policy bar operates only if the claimant is forced to rely upon evidence of his or her own illegality.

3.5 WHAT AMOUNTS TO A CONVERSION?

Andrew Tettenborn, 'Damages in Conversion—The Exception or The Anomaly?'
(1993) 52 CLJ, at 129–30

Put shortly D commits conversion against P where, without legal justification, he does any of (i) to (vii) below in relation to a thing belonging to P:

  (i) Being in possession of the thing, he fails on demand to return it to P.

  (ii) He takes it, whether from P or from a third party.

  (iii) He receives it from a third party T who has no title to it.

  (iv) He physically transfers it to T, eg by sale or gift, or otherwise acts so as to destroy P's title to it.

  (v) He destroys it.

  (vi) Being a bailee, he wrongfully loses it or allows it to be destroyed.

  (vii) Having obtained it lawfully, he wrongfully keeps or uses it.

The are two further important points on liability in conversion generally. First, it must be borne in mind that liability is prima facie strict, so that in any of the above situations D is liable in damages whether or not he knew the goods he was dealing with were P's or that he was otherwise infringing P's rights. Secondly, it should be remembered that dealings with another's goods may involve D in two or more acts of conversion. In any such case, P can (subject to the law of limitation of actions) rely on any individual conversion that he may choose.

Chains of Conversion

In some cases, there are several acts of conversion in respect of the same chattel. For example, it may be stolen, then sold, and finally destroyed, by different individuals. In this case, the claimant may bring an action against any of the individual converters of the goods. But the claimant may only recover damages (or, of course, the goods themselves if they can be found intact) from one of the potentially liable parties. Obtaining damages extinguishes title to the goods (section 5 of the Torts (Wrongful Interference with Goods) Act 1977, extracted below). It seems that in general, a liable party will be unable to seek contribution against other converting parties. Damages are not generally calculated according to loss.[18] Therefore, the

---

[18] Though see the discussion of *Kuwait Airways* in the next section.

parties would not be potentially liable 'for the same damage', which is the precondition for an action under the Civil Liability (Contribution) Act 1978.[19]

3.6 WHAT ARE THE REMEDIES?

Return of Goods

One would have thought, since conversion protects rights of possession, that the return of goods would, where this is possible, be available as of right. But this is not the case.

Where the defendant is still in possession of the 'converted' goods, the claimant may seek their return. But the limited scope for recovery as a remedy shows that conversion, being merely a tort, provides only a clumsy and limited mechanism for enforcing (or vindicating) proprietary rights.[20]

Historical origins

At common law, recovery of goods *could* sometimes be achieved through the action in detinue. But even detinue carried an alternative in the form of damages. Recovery of goods could not be achieved through the action on the case which began as 'trover', and became conversion.

Nick Curwen, 'The Remedy in Conversion: Confusing Property and Obligation'
(2006) 26 LS 570, 571–2

The failure of the common law to develop an effective action for the recovery of goods has both stunted the growth of a distinct law of property in relation to goods and distorted the principles of the law of tort. The problem goes back to the earliest days of the common law. Detinue was an ancient action brought for the recovery of goods. The remedy was an order that the defendant must return the goods or pay their full value to the claimant. The claim was proprietary in nature, a demand for recovery, but the remedy was personal rather than real because the defendant had the option of paying damages in lieu of restitution.

. . . Trover was an action in trespass on the case for the conversion of goods . . . Brian Simpson[21] . . . relates that in the sixteenth century it was not possible for two types of action to exist on the same set of facts so pleaders had to frame their action so as to avoid any suggestion that detinue was the appropriate action. If detinue lay, that prevented an action in conversion. In the early cases, going back to the late fifteenth century, it was held that if the defendant changed the nature of the goods then that changed the property in them. This development enabled the new action to replace completely detinue but at the expense of perpetrating an obvious fiction.

---

[19] An exception might be a case where there is potential liability for consequential loss; but it seems quite likely that the potentially liable parties in such a case would not be concurrently liable for the *same* consequential losses.

[20] On the other hand, the claimant is freed from the need to *prove ownership*. As Tettenborn points out, the compromise action in conversion may actually work better in some respects than the pure property action that exists in most civilian legal systems: 'Conversion, Tort and Restitution', above, at 826.

[21] A. W. B. Simpson, 'The Introduction of the Action on the Case for Conversion' (1959) 75 LQR 364.

Eventually the rule against overlapping actions disappeared and it was accepted that the claimant did not lose property in the goods until the defendant had satisfied the court order by paying the full value of them to the claimant. But the fiction had done its work and the action remained in essence a tort remediable at common law by compensation. In effect, the claimant was forced to waive their proprietary claim and sue for damages. There was no scope, as in detinue, for ordering restitution in specie or, in the alternative, paying damages.

The extract above explains how the modern tort of conversion emerged. Further confusion was introduced by abolishing detinue, and shifting some of its (already compromised) functions to the tort of conversion. This was achieved by the Torts (Interference With Goods) Act 1977.

Torts (Interference With Goods) Act 1977

2   Abolition of detinue

(1) Detinue is abolished.

(2) An action lies in conversion for loss or destruction of goods which a bailee has allowed to happen in breach of his duty to his bailor (that is to say it lies in a case which is not otherwise conversion, but would have been detinue before detinue was abolished).

3   Form of judgment where goods are detained

(1) In proceedings for wrongful interference against a person who is in possession or in control of the goods relief may be given in accordance with this section, so far as appropriate.

(2) The relief is—

    (a) an order for delivery of the goods, and for payment of any consequential damages, or

    (b) an order for delivery of the goods, but giving the defendant the alternative of paying damages by reference to the value of the goods, together in either alternative with payment of any consequential damages, or

    (c) damages.

(3) Subject to rules of court—

    (a) relief shall be given under only one of paragraphs (a), (b) and (c) of subsection (2),

    (b) relief under paragraph (a) of subjection (2) is at the discretion of the court, and the claimant may choose between the others.

(4) If it is shown to the satisfaction of the court that an order under subsection (2)(a) has not been complied with, the court may—

    (a) revoke the order, or the relevant part of it, and

    (b) make an order for payment of damages by reference to the value of the goods.

(5) Where an order is made under subsection (2)(b) the defendant may satisfy the order by returning the goods at any time before execution of judgment, but without prejudice to liability to pay any consequential damages.

. . .

By section 3(1), the court *may* order delivery up (s 3(1)(a)). If the court does not order delivery up, the claimant may choose between the other remedies; but if (b) is selected, the *defendant* may elect whether to return the goods, or pay their value.

Damages

Damages are available both:

(i) Where the defendant retains the chattel, but an order for recovery is not made; and

(ii) Where the defendant no longer retains the chattel.

In either case, the basic measure has generally been accepted to be *the value of the goods at the date of conversion*; damages in respect of consequential loss will also be available where appropriate. However, the judgment in *Kuwait Airways* may signal a change to come.

In either case, title to the goods is extinguished when the award of damages is satisfied (or payment made in satisfaction of a final settlement): section 5 of the Torts (Wrongful Interference with Goods) Act 1977.

In a case where the defendant retains the goods, and refuses to return them, then this measure of damages (value of the goods) may be appropriate. It also reflects the anomalous position of this sort of action for conversion, which in such a case is performing a function which one would expect to be performed by property law. But it has been argued that a measure of damages that reflects the *value of the goods* rather than the loss caused to the claimant—particularly given that consequential losses are recoverable in any event—is unfair to 'honest converters' who do not retain the goods. It has been argued that beyond the action against converters who *retain* the chattel (section 3), damages assessed by reference to the value of the goods cannot generally be justified. As with other torts, compensatory damages should be assessed by reference to *what the claimant has lost*. On the other hand, the full measure of damages related to the value of the goods might be justified in particular circumstances, for example if the converter is dishonest.[22]

The general measure of damages, and the case for treating dishonest converters differently, were discussed in the case of *Kuwait Airways*. We now turn to the important issues in that case surrounding damages.

Kuwait Airways: Damages Issues

We set out the facts of *Kuwait Airways* above. As we saw, there was no possibility of recovering the aircraft themselves in that case. Some had been destroyed, others had been recovered by the claimant from a third party (Iran) for a large payment.

Various elements of Lord Nicholls' judgment in this case would, taken together, amount to a re-writing of the rules for recovery of damages for conversion. Some of his more adventurous comments—potentially very important—were offered as observations or 'signals to the legal profession',[23] since they concerned possibilities not pleaded by the claimants. In this section, we will identify the key issues.

The Basic Measure of Damages in Conversion

As we said above, the basic measure of damages in conversion is usually based on the value of the converted goods at the date of conversion. After a wide review of the authorities, Lord Nicholls decided that the 'value measure' is intended to reflect the claimant's loss. This is controversial in itself. He then went on to say that sometimes, the claimant's loss is not properly reflected in the value measure; and that when this is the case, the court should not award the value measure. Instead, it should assess damages according to *the loss suffered*.

Lord Nicholls, *Kuwait Airways v Iraqi Airways (Nos 4 and 5)* [2002] 2 AC 883

67 . . . The aim of the law, in respect of the wrongful interference with goods, is to provide a just remedy. Despite its proprietary base, this tort does not stand apart and command awards of damages measured by some special and artificial standard of its own. The fundamental object of an award of damages in respect of this tort, as with all wrongs, is to award just compensation for loss suffered. Normally ("prima facie") the measure of damages is the market value of the goods at the time the defendant expropriated them. This is the general rule, because generally this measure represents the amount of the basic loss suffered by the plaintiff owner. He has been dispossessed of his goods by the defendant. Depending on the circumstances some other measure, yielding a higher or lower amount, may be appropriate. The plaintiff may have suffered additional damage consequential on the loss of his goods. Or the goods may have been returned.

68 This approach accords with the conclusion of the Law Reform Committee in its 18th report (Conversion and Detinue) (1971) (Cmnd 4774) that the general rule as respects the measure of damages for wrongful interference should be that the plaintiff is entitled to recover the loss he has suffered. The committee considered this conclusion was "right in principle", and added, in paragraph 91:

> "In many cases the value of the chattel itself will either represent this loss or form an important element in its calculation; but consideration of the value of the chattel should not be allowed to obscure the principle that what the plaintiff is entitled to recover is his true loss."

This may be sensible, but this element of the Law Reform Committee's recommendations was not explicitly enacted. It seems the House of Lords is willing to consider giving effect to the recommendation itself. On the other hand, its suggestion that the appropriate basic measure of damages in conversion is based on loss suffered—and that the 'value' measure is in effect a loss measure in most cases—has some support. The House of Lords drew particularly on a decision of the High Court of Australia in *Butler v Egg and Egg Pulp Marketing Board* (1966) 114 CLR 185.[24]

Causation

Where the 'Iran six' were concerned, significant questions arose surrounding the operation of causal tests. The defendants had used the planes and treated them as their own. However, even

---

[24] And see J. Edelman, 'Gain-Based Damages and Compensation', in A. Burrows and Lord Rodger (eds), *Mapping the Law* (OUP, 2006) 141, at 154–6.

if the defendants had not put the aircraft to use (or transported them to Iran for safe keeping), the claimants would still not have had possession of the planes. The initial taker was the state of Iraq. Could it then be said that the defendant had not 'caused' the loss of the planes? Lord Nicholls rejected this argument.

80   The existing principle of strict liability as described above is deeply ingrained in the common law. It has survived at least since the days of Lord Mansfield in *Cooper v Chitty* (1756) 1 Burr 20. The hardship it may cause to those who deal innocently with a person in possession of goods has long been recognised. Blackburn J noted this in the leading case of *Fowler v Hollins* (1875) LR 7 HL 757, 764. The hardship arises especially for innocent persons who no longer have the goods. There has been some statutory amelioration of the principle, in the Factors Acts and elsewhere, but in general the principle endures.

81   Consistently with this principle, every person through whose hands goods pass in a series of conversions is himself guilty of conversion and liable to the owner for the loss caused by his misappropriation of the owner's goods. His liability is not diminished by reason, for instance, of his having acquired the goods from a thief as distinct from the owner himself. In such a case, it may be said, looking at the successive conversions overall, the owner is no worse off as a result of the acts of the person who acquired the goods from the thief. Such a person has not "caused" the owner any additional loss.

82   In one sense this is undoubtedly correct. The owner had already lost his goods. But that is really nothing to the point for the purposes of assessing damages for conversion. By definition, each person in a series of conversions wrongfully excludes the owner from possession of his goods. This is the basis on which each is liable to the owner. That is the nature of the tort of conversion. The wrongful acts of a previous possessor do not therefore diminish the plaintiff's claim in respect of the wrongful acts of a later possessor. Nor, for a different reason, is it anything to the point that, absent the defendant's conversion, someone else would wrongfully have converted the goods. The likelihood that, had the defendant not wronged the plaintiff, somebody would have done so is no reason for diminishing the defendant's liability and responsibility for the loss he brought upon the plaintiff.

83   Where, then, does this leave the simple "but for" test in cases of successive conversion? I suggest that, if the test is to be applied at all, the answer lies in keeping in mind, as I have said, that each person in a series of conversions wrongfully excludes the owner from possession of his goods. The exclusionary threshold test is to be applied on this footing. Thus the test calls for consideration of whether the plaintiff would have suffered the loss in question had he retained his goods and not been unlawfully deprived of them by the defendant. The test calls for a comparison between the owner's position had he retained his goods and his position having been deprived of his goods by the defendant. Loss which the owner would have suffered even if he had retained the goods is not loss "caused" by the conversion. The defendant is not liable for such loss.

. . .

85   For these reasons I consider KAC's claims in respect of the Iran Six do not fail at the threshold stage. Had KAC not been unlawfully deprived of its goods by IAC KAC would not have suffered any of the heads of loss it is now claiming. Had KAC retained possession of the Iran Six, the aircraft would not have been evacuated to Iran.

As we can see from the last sentence of this extract (and also from para [83]), the question is not 'would the claimant have been deprived of possession 'but for' the acts of the defendant'; it is rather 'would the claimant have suffered any of these heads of loss, had the claimant retained possession'. The 'but for' test does not apply in the same way to conversion, as it does to any other tort. But to apply it in the usual manner would be inconsistent with the logic of the tort.

Remoteness of Damage

The remaining extracts propose certain distinctions between 'honest' and 'dishonest' convert-ers of goods, in respect of assessment of damages.

A significant issue arose concerning the extent of damages for which the defendants would be liable in respect of the conversion of the Iran six, since the claimants used the temporary unavailability of this part of its fleet (which had not been destroyed) as the occasion for substantial restructuring with new aircraft. As we learned in Chapter 3, rules of 'remoteness of damage' ask which losses are fairly attributable to the tort of the defendant.

100 Expressed in terms of the traditional guideline principles, the choice is between confin-ing liability for consequential loss to damage which is "foreseeable", as distinct from damage flowing "directly and naturally" from the wrongful conduct. In practice, these two tests usu-ally yield the same result. Where they do not, the foreseeability test is likely to be the more restrictive. The prevalent view is that the more restrictive test of foreseeability is applicable to the torts of negligence, nuisance and *Rylands v Fletcher*: see the two *Wagon Mound* cases [1961] AC 388 and [1967] 1 AC 617 and *Cambridge Water Co v Eastern Counties Leather plc* [1994] 2 AC 264. The Court of Appeal recently applied this test to the tort of conversion, appar-ently without any contrary argument, in *Saleslease Ltd v Davis* [1999] 1 WLR 1664, although the members of the court differed in the application of the principle to the facts of the case.

101 In contrast, the less restrictive test is applicable in deceit. The more culpable the defend-ant the wider the area of loss for which he can fairly be held responsible: see the discussion by my noble and learned friend Lord Steyn in *Smith New Court Securities Ltd v Scrimgeour Vickers (Asset Management) Ltd* [1997] AC 254, 279–285.

102 This bifurcation causes difficulty with the tort of conversion. Dishonesty is not an essen-tial ingredient of this wrong. The defendant may be a thief, or he may have acted wholly inno-cently. Both are strictly liable. But it seems to me inappropriate they should be treated alike when determining their liability for consequential loss. Parliament, indeed, has recognised that for some purposes different considerations should apply to persons who steal goods, or knowingly receive stolen goods, and persons who can show they bought the goods in good faith. In respect of the tort of conversion the Limitation Act 1980 prescribes different limitation provisions for these two types of cases: see sections 3 and 4.

103 I have already mentioned that, as the law now stands, the tort of conversion may cause hardship for innocent persons. This suggests that foreseeability, as the more restrictive test, is appropriate for those who act in good faith. Liability remains strict, but liability for conse-quential loss is confined to types of damage which can be expected to arise from the wrong-ful conduct. You deal with goods at the risk of discovering later that, unbeknown to you, you have not acquired a good title. That is the strict common law principle. The risk is that, should you not have acquired title, you will be liable to the owner for the losses he can expect to have suffered as a result of your misappropriation of his goods. That seems the preferable

approach, in the case of a person who can prove he acted in the genuine belief the goods were his. A person in possession of goods knows where and how he acquired them. It is up to him to establish he was innocent of any knowing wrongdoing. This is the approach Parliament has taken in section 4 of the Limitation Act 1980.

104 Persons who knowingly convert another's goods stand differently. Such persons are acting dishonestly. I can see no good reason why the remoteness test of "directly and naturally" applied in cases of deceit should not apply in cases of conversion where the defendant acted dishonestly.

Lord Nicholls here introduces a division in the remoteness test applying to consequential losses in conversion. The 'negligence' measure (foreseeability) applies to innocent conversion. The 'intentional' measure (directness) applies to dishonest conversion. This may have implications for other torts (such as battery, considered in Chapter 2) which may be committed either culpably, or not. If the House of Lords is willing to vary the applicable remoteness test within the tort of conversion depending on the culpability or innocence of the defendant, is the same permissible in a case of trespass to the person?

Gain-based Awards

The claimants in this case had not argued for a gain-based award. But Lord Nicholls gave a clear signal that he might have made such an award, if they had been pleaded. There were two different elements to his discussion of a gain-based award. The first relates to restitution for unjust enrichment; the second to 'user damages' for the tort.

Unjust enrichment

79 . . . Vindication of a plaintiff's proprietary interests requires that, in general, all those who convert his goods should be accountable for *benefits* they receive. They must make restitution to the extent they are unjustly enriched. The goods are his, and he is entitled to reclaim them and any benefits others have derived from them. Liability in this regard should be strict subject to defences available to restitutionary claims such as change of position: see *Lipkin Gorman v Karpnale Ltd* [1991] 2 AC 548. Additionally, those who act dishonestly should be liable to make good any *losses* caused by their wrongful conduct. Whether those who act innocently should also be liable to make good the plaintiff's losses is a different matter. A radical reappraisal of the tort of conversion along these lines was not pursued on these appeals. So I shall say nothing more about it.

As Lord Nicholls says, this suggestion is 'radical'. It is more far-reaching than an adjustment to the measure of damages. It treats the *basis* of the claim in conversion as being unjust enrichment, requiring restitution; with an additional liability (for losses caused) which could potentially be applied to dishonest converters only. This hints at a radical reappraisal of the action in conversion. Loss-based damages would be *additional* to restitution; and they may be available only in cases of dishonest conversion.

'User damages'

Here, Lord Nicholls said that he might have made an award of damages based on the benefit derived by the defendants from 'use' of the aricraft.

The Iran Six: "user damages"

87 I have noted that the fundamental object of an award of damages for conversion is to award just compensation for loss suffered. Sometimes, when the goods or their equivalent are returned, the owner suffers no financial loss. But the wrongdoer may well have benefited from his temporary use of the owner's goods. It would not be right that he should be able to keep this benefit. The court may order him to pay damages assessed by reference to the value of the benefit he derived from his wrongdoing. I considered this principle in *Attorney General v Blake* [2001] 1 AC 268, 278–280. In an appropriate case the court may award damages on this "user principle" in addition to compensation for loss suffered. For instance, if the goods are returned damaged, the court may award damages assessed by reference to the benefit obtained by the wrongdoer as well as the cost of repair.

88 Recognition that damages may be awarded on this principle may assist in making some awards of damages in conversion cases more coherent. For example, I respectfully think this is the preferable basis for the award of damages in *Solloway v McLaughlin* [1938] AC 247 in respect of Solloway's misappropriation of the 14,000 shares deposited with him by McLaughlin. McLaughlin suffered no financial loss from the misappropriation, because equivalent shares were returned to McLaughlin when he closed his account. But Solloway profited by the fall in the value of the shares by selling them when they were deposited with him and repurchasing them at the lower market price obtaining when McLaughlin closed his account.

. . .

90 In the present case no claim for an award of "user damages" has ever been pleaded or formally formulated. Mr Vos sought to advance such a claim before your Lordships' House regarding the Iran Six. I consider it is much too late in these protracted proceedings for KAC now to advance this new claim for the first time.

The damages discussed in this passage might, if they had been awarded, have been described in different ways. It is clear that they are *damages*, since Lord Nicholls uses that term. They are distinct from the award of 'restitution for unjust enrichment' described above. Equally, it is clear that they are a response to the defendant's tort. They are damages for a wrong (a tort), calculated on the basis of benefits to the defendant, not on the basis of financial loss suffered by the claimant (see para [87]: 'the owner suffers no financial loss. But the wrongdoer may well have benefited . . .').

Beyond this, it is rather hard to categorize what is meant by 'user damages'. Perhaps Lord Nicholls is referring to the same sort of 'restitutionary damages' available in the tort of trespass to land (see above), which do indeed quantify the value of having use of the property. If that is the case, the reference to *AG v Blake* in the extract above is not helpful. In that case, Lord Nicholls deliberately avoided describing the award as 'restitutionary'. An award based on 'benefits' in the form of 'profits' (if that is what Lord Nicholls had in mind) might be described as *disgorgement damages*, rather than 'user damages'.

Equally, 'disgorgement' is generally thought to be available only in cases of *dishonest* wrongdoing (not honest wrong-doing). Was this a case of dishonest conversion, or not? IAC well knew the history of ownership of the aircraft, and it knew that the aircraft had been seized through an act of war. This was certainly not a case of 'accidental' conversion. But when discussing the applicable Iraqi law of usurpation, Lord Nicholls made clear that he did *not* think this was a case of 'bad faith', which was relevant to Iraqi law.

Lord Nicholls, *Kuwait Airways*

48 . . . if the property usurped is physically lost or damaged, as happened in the case of the Mosul Four, the owner must show that this loss or damage would not have occurred but for the usurpation (the so-called "but for" test). The burden of proof is on the owner unless the usurper was acting in bad faith. Admittedly that is not the present case. IAC acted in the belief that RCC Resolution 369 gave it a good title. This also was common ground. (In this regard, and to this extent, the existence of this decree will be recognised by an English court. This is not giving effect to Resolution 369. This is doing no more than accept the existence of this decree as the explanation for IAC's state of mind.)

If the test for 'good faith' in usurpation (in Iraqi law) is similar to the idea of 'honesty' which might be applied in the tort of conversion, then there would be no dishonesty on the part of the defendants in this case. IAC honestly believed they had a good claim in law to the aircraft. But if *that* is the case, the 'user damages' discussed by Lord Nicholls should have been *restitutionary* damages, not disgorgement damages. And in that case, the references to *AG v Blake* are not helpful.

It can be seen, at the very least, that the House of Lords is open to discussion of a range of non-compensatory awards for conversion; but the search for the appropriate language to attach to these awards will be challenging. Yet if the appropriate language cannot be devised, it is unlikely that the relevant measure of damages will be clearly identified either.

Exemplary Damages

Exemplary damages were not in issue in *Kuwait Airways*. In *Borders (UK) Ltd v Commr of Police for the Metropolis* [2005] EWCA Civ 197, the Court of Appeal awarded exemplary damages in an action for conversion but, unfortunately, adopted a controversial measure of such damages.

The defendant had converted huge numbers of books by stealing them from the claimants, selling them at a market stall over a number of years. The role of exemplary damages is to 'punish' the defendant, as we explained in Chapter 8.6. Unfortunately, the Court of Appeal accepted the approach of the trial judge, which was to assess *exemplary* damages—which should be assessed according to their punitive goal—according to the profits the defendant was thought to have made from other books. Compensation had not been available for these books, because their theft (amounting to conversion) was not established as a matter of evidence.

As has been clearly pointed out,[25] this manages to confound three different types of damages: it allows **exemplary damages** (a punitive award) to be assessed **on the basis of gains made** (a disgorgement measure), because the goal is to achieve **full compensation** (a compensatory goal) to the claimant. The defendant in this case was considered to be wholly

---

25 By Campbell and Devenney, 'Damages at the Borders of Legal Reasoning' (2006) 65 CLJ 208–25.

undeserving, but even so this reasoning takes several steps too far. Clarity will be very hard to maintain if these different forms of damages are allowed to cross-contaminate in this way.

R. Cunnington, 'The Border Between Compensation, Restitution and Punishment' (2006) 122 LQR, 382, 386

The decision in *Borders* reminds us why nomenclature matters. Compensation, restitution and punishment are distinct functions of the law of damages. The boundaries between those functions should not be blurred because a court cannot determine whether damages should be awarded unless it knows what function those damages are performing. It is to be hoped that, in future, the courts will maintain the clear distinction between compensatory, gain-based and exemplary damages.

FURTHER READING

Cane, P., 'Causing Conversion' (2002) 118 LQR 544.

Cunnington, R., 'The Border Between Compensation, Restitution and Punishment' (2006) 122 LQR 382, 386.

Curwen, N., 'The Remedy in Conversion—Confusing Property and Obligation' (2006) 26 LS 570.

Edelman, J., 'Gain-Based Damages and Compensation', in A. Burrows and Lord Rodger (eds), *Mapping the Law* (Oxford: OUP, 2006) 141.

Hickey, R., 'Stealing Abandoned Goods: Possessory Title and Proceedings for Theft' (2006) 26 LS 584.

Samuel, G., 'Wrongful Interference with Goods' (1982) 31 ICLQ 357

Simpson, A.W.B., 'The Introduction of the Action on the Case for Conversion' (1959) 75 LQR 364.

Tettenborn, A., 'Damages in Conversion—The Exception or the Anomaly?' (1993) 52 CLJ 128–47.

Tettenborn, A., 'Conversion, Tort and Restitution', in N. Palmer and E. McKendrick (eds), *Interests in Goods* (2nd edn, London: Lloyds of London Press, 1998).

INDEX